National
Newspaper Abstracts

Special Edition: The Civil War Years
July 1, 1863–December 31, 1865
Volume 2

Joan M. Dixon

HERITAGE BOOKS
2007

HERITAGE BOOKS
AN IMPRINT OF HERITAGE BOOKS, INC.

Books, CDs, and more—Worldwide

For our listing of thousands of titles see our website
at
www.HeritageBooks.com

Published 2007 by
HERITAGE BOOKS, INC.
Publishing Division
65 East Main Street
Westminster, Maryland 21157-5026

International Standard Book Number: 978-0-7884-4381-X

Civil War-Vol 2
TABLE OF CONTENTS

Dedicated to the Sisters of Notre Dame de Namur
Notre Dame Academy, Washington, D C
Class of 1949
Joan McLaughlin Dixon

iii

PREFACE
Daily National Intelligencer Newspaper Abstracts
July 1, 1863-December 31, 1865
Civil War-Vol 2

Joan M Dixon

The National Intelligencer & Washington Advertiser is hereafter the Daily National Intelligencer. It was the first newspaper printed in Washington, D C; Samuel H Smith, the originator. The same was transferred to Jos Gales, jr on Aug 31, 1810; on Nov 1, 1812, the paper was under the firm of Jos Gales, sr, & Wm W Seaton. The Library of Congress has microfilm of the paper from the first issue of Oct 31, 1800 thru Jan 8, 1870, the final paper. The Evening Star Newspaper of Jan 10, 1870 reports: The Intelligencer is discontinued: the proprietor, Mr Alex Delmar, says that having lost several thousand dollars, & being in poor health, he has resolved to discontinue its publication.

Included in the abstracts are advertisements; appointments by the President; Hse o/Rep petitions; passed Acts; legal notices; marriages; deaths; mscl notices; social events; tax lists; military promotions; court cases; deaths by accident; prisoners; & maritime information-crews. Items or events which might be a clue as to the location, age or relationship of an individual are copied.

No attempt has been made to correct the spelling. Due to the length of some articles, it was necessary to present only the highlights of same. Chancery and Equity records are copied as written.

The index contains all surnames and *tracts of lands/places*. Maritime vessels are found under barge, boat, brig, frig, schn'r, ship, sloop, steamboat, tugboat, yacht or vessel.

ABBREVIATIONS:

AA CO	ANNE ARUNDEL COUNTY
CO	COMPANY/COUNTY
CMDER	COMMANDER
CMDOR	COMMODOR
D C	DISTRICT OF COLUMBIA
ELIZ	ELIZABETH
ELIZA	ELIZA
MONTG CO	MONTGOMERY COUNTY
PG CO	PRINCE GEORGES CO
WASH	WASHINGTON

BOOKS IN THE NATIONAL INTELLIGENCER NEWSPAPER SERIES: 1800-1805/1806-1810/1811-1813/1814-1817/1818-1820/1821-1823/1824-1826/1827-1829/1830-1831/1832-1833/1834-1835/1836-1837/1838-1839/1840/1841/1842/1843/1844/1845/1846/
SPECIAL: CIVIL WAR 2 VOLS, 1861-1865

```
┌─────────────────────────────────────────────┐
│         Daily National Intelligencer          │
│                    1863                        │
│               Civil War Years                  │
└─────────────────────────────────────────────┘
```

Vol II
Jul 1, 1863 thru Dec 31, 1865

WED JUL 1, 1863
Released from the draft on the ground of alienage: [where drafted] Theodore Weber, Seneca Co, Ohio.

Orphans Crt of Wash Co, D C. Case of Wm H Marll, adm of Jos W Marll, dec'd; settlement on Jul 25. -Z C Robbins, rg o/wills

Wm H Kern, ex-provost mrshl of Phil, convicted some time since of obtaining money under false pretense, [securing $50 from a sldr that he had authority to procure for him a discharge,] was sentenced on Sat to 3 months imprisonment.

Wash, D C. Col Williams invites the sldrs of 1812 to be present at the Jul 4th celebration. -S E Douglass, W O Stoddard, A C Richards, cmte

Princeton College has conferred the degree of LL D upon Philip R Fendall, of Wash City.

THU JUL 2, 1863
Died: at Cairo, Ill, Jun 21st, of congestive chills, John Newland, s/o Mr John Clapham, U S N Pyrotechnist, in his 31st yr.

Died: on Jul 1, Emma Lee, only child of Anna E & J W Ryan, in its 5th month.

Supreme Crt of D C. Lancaster Ould & others vs Griffith & others. Ratify sale of part of lot 131, on Dunbarton st, to Daniel Brown, for $3,050; parts of lots 119 & 120, on Montgomery st, to Jas Goddard, for $562.50; other parts of same lots, on Montg st, to Cath A Clappelare, for $277.50; other parts of said lots to Martin Donoghue, on Montg st, for $1,085; part of lot 120, on Beall st, to Reuben Daw, for $230. -R J Meigs, clerk

Cmder Chas Hunter was tried by a navy crt martial & dismissed from svc; charge of violation of Spanish neutrality while commanding the screw steamer *Montgomery*, in capturing & burning the steamer *Blanche*, claimed to be British property, on the coast of Cuba, Oct 7 last. He is a native & resident of R I.

Wash Corp: 1-Ptn of Wm Flenner & others against the opening of a livery stable on I st north: referred to the Cmte on Police. 2-Ptn of Thos Blagden & others, in improving 2nd st east: referred to the Cmte on Police. 3-Ptn of M Maloney, B W Ferguson, & others, in reference to a flag footway on B st north: referred to the Cmte on Improvements. 4-Ptn of Wm R Riley & others, asking for a water main: referred to the Cmte on Drainage, etc. 5-Memorial of D D Foley, praying for the value of certain improvements made along the river front near foot of 7th st: referred to the Cmte on Claims. 6-Cmte on Improvements: was referred the ptn of Jos M Padgett & others for a footwalk: passed. 7-Cmte on Police: reported a bill for relief of A B Stoughton: passed.

1

Mrd: at St Ann's Chr, Annapolis, Md, on Jun 25, by Rev Mr Davenport, J Henry Sellman, U S N, to Sophia, d/o the late Jos N Stockett, of A A Co, Md.

The Army of Gen Rosecrans: 14th Army Corps, [Right Wing,] Maj Gen G H Thomas, commanding; Lt Col Flynt, Ast adj Gen & Chief of Staff; Lt Col McKay, Chief Q M; Lt Col J R Paul, Chief Cmsry of Sub. 20th Army Corps, [Centre] Maj Gen McDowell McCook, commanding. 21st Army Corps, [Left Wing,] Maj Gen Thos Crittenden

FRI JUL 3, 1863

Mrd: at Fordham, on the Hudson river, on Jun 25, by Rev Dr Dickinson, Granville B Smith, of N Y, & Annie, d/o the officiating clergyman.

Honors conferred at Academy of the Visitation, Gtwn, D C; instrumental & vocal: Senior class-Misses Isabel Leyfert, Pa; Blanche Butler, Mass; Julia Turner, Mo. 2nd honors: Misses Nannie Pickrell, D C; Jennie Lenthall, D C; Mary Bridgette, D C; Adah Nokes, D C; Teresa Kengla, D C; Alice Miles, Md.

Orphans Crt of Wash Co, D C. Prsnl estate of Terrence Leonard, late of U S army, dec'd. -Wm R Woodward, adm

Balt: the body of Gen Reynolds, after being embalmed, was taken to the residence of his bro-in-law, Mr Gildersleeve.

The family of Hon John Bell, who are at Nashville, have received intelligence of his dangerous illness at Atlanta, Ga.

SAT JUL 4, 1863

The late Gen John Fulton Reynolds, who fell in the battle of Gettysburg, was born in Lancaster, Pa, in 1820. He was an 1841 grad of West Point.

Gtwn College, D C, Jun 6; degree of A B conferred upon the following grads:

Wm L Hirst, Pa	T M Herran, New Granada
H L McCullough, Pa	Jas A Murphy, N Y
H M Brent, N Y	V F Dominguez, Cuba
Jos A Rice, La	F H Rainy, D C
Wm F Williams, D C	

Fred'k, Jun 28, 1863. This morning a special train arrived here bringing a messenger from the War Dept with an order relieving Gen Hooker of the command of the army & appointing Gen Meade as his successor. It was a surprise to all here.

The venerable Rev Dr Nott, Pres of the Union College, passed his 97th birthday on Jun 25th.

MON JUL 6, 1863

Extra. Glorious News. Lee Defeated. Gen A P Hill & Gen Longstreet wounded & prisoners. Gen Barksdale of Mississippi-his dead body is within our lines. Termination of the great battle which commenced on Wed last, near Gettysburg. Army of the Potomac-we have suffered considerably in killed & wounded. Among the former are Brig Gens Paul & Zook; wounded are Gens Sickles, Barlow, Graham & Warren, slightly. Maj Gen Hancock & Brig Gen Gibbon are wounded.

The wife & little dght of Chas Henry Foster were intercepted last week near Windsor, Berta Co, N C, endeavoring to reach the Union lines, by a company of Ga cavalry, who refused them permission to proceed. On Thu they were compelled to return to their home in Murfreesboro.

Our wounded in large numbers arrived at Balt on Sat & Sun, & were immediately forwarded to Phil. Gen Schimmelpfenning, tho wounded, was not taken, but escaped capture.

Maj Gen Sickles, who was severely wounded in the battle of Thu last at Gettysburg, [his right leg having since been amputated above the knee,] reached this city yesterday, accompanied from the battle field by Maj Tremaine, Capts Moore & Fry, & Dr Simms, & Mr Wm B Cutter. He was conveyed to a private residence on F st on a stretcher, surrounded by a large guard of honor.

TUE JUL 7, 1863
Died: at *Prospect Hill*, Chas Co, Md, on Jun 29, Geo S Watkins, jr, in the 22nd yr of his age.

Died: on Jul 6, Maebelle Gertrude, d/o Robt & Linda Downing, in the 3rd yr of her age. Funeral on Tue, 8th st, between K & L.

Deaths reported to the Navy Dept for the week ending Jul 4, 1863:
Robt Sinson, mstr at arms, injuries, Jun 12, N Y.
Robt Carroll, landsman, wound of scalp, Jun 19, U S steamer *Powhatan*.
Henry B Bohlken, 1st cab boy, debility, Jun 11, U S steamer *Norwich*.
Jas Cole, seaman, inflam of the bowels, Jun 2, do.
Willis Downs, boy, pneumonia, Jun 26, Nav Hosp, N Y.
John Harper, landsman, pyamia, Jun 26, do.
Jas McGrath, landsman, dysentery, Jun 25, do.
Alex S Wiggins, actg mstr, gunshot wound, Feb 9, W Gulf Squad.
And J Savage, boy, fever, Jun 22, Nav Asylum.
Elbridge M Stevens, ord seaman, drowned, May 2, U S steamer *Portsmouth*.

Army of the Potomac, Jul 5. Rebel Gen Pender is wounded; Gens Johnston & Kemper, rebels, are killed. Gen Farnsworth, of our cavalry, is killed. Gen Butterfield's wound is more severe than supposed.

Rebel spy, Wm Richardson, age about 50 yrs, was captured Jul 5 at Oxford, Md, & hung on Jul 6. He admitted to the charge.

Wash, D C. On Jul 4 a negro man, Matthias Butler, while in a groggery on 6th st, was showing a companion an army revolver left in his care, when it went off & the ball passed thru the wrist & heart of Jas Doyle, a white man, sitting in a chair in front of Butler. Doyle was killed instantly & Butler was arrested & held for trial.

Wash, D C. On Sat Mr John Thompson was setting off a Roman candle near his residence on G st, when the candle exploded; shattered his left hand & amputation was performed by Dr Hodges.

Wash, D C. Murder-on Jul 4, Wm Neal, negro, was killed by a bayonet. The wound perforated his heart. Assailant is unknown.

3

WED JUL 8, 1863

Died: on Jun 6, after a long & suffering illness, John S Devlin, eldest s/o the late John S Devlin. Funeral from the residence of his mother, 551 6th st, today.

Orphans Crt of Wash Co, D C. Prsnl estate of Egletine Coke, late of Wash Co, dec'd. -Anna M Cochrane, admx

Prisoners at Richmond were received at the Libby Prison Jun 30th, 47 Federal prisoners, captured in Stafford Co & in Fredericksburg on Jun 15. In the evening 294 arrived from Winchester, including 5 ofcrs, namely: Maj H A White, 13th Pa Cavalry; Capt D Schortz & Lt L Marye, 12th Pa Cavalry; & Lt E L Edmonds & Lt Robt Thompson, 67th Pa Infty. The ofcrs in charge of these prisoners said there were 2,300 more to come.

Wm A Austin, a clerk, has just been held to bail in $15,000 in Boston for robbing his employer, Mr Henry A Peirce, 67 Commercial wharf. He is about 17 yrs of age, his father dead, & his mother, a woman of respectability, resides in Providence. He had been arrested for a series of robberies a year or two since; & was placed on a ship & went to sea. His health not good, he returned & again became a clerk.

Gettysburg, Jul 6. Slaughter among the rebel Gen Ofcrs has been very great. Maj Gen Trimble is a prisoner within our lines with his left foot gone. Brig Gen Kemper is a prisoner & in a dying condition. Gen Armistead, captured on Thu, is dead. Maj Gen Hood was wounded in the arm. Gens Beth, Pender, & Picket are also known to be wounded. Gens Barksdale & Garnett were killed. The enemy are reported to have a trestle bridge just built across the Potomac, above Wmsport.

THU JUL 9, 1863

Died: at his residence, Chapel Hill, Montg Co, Md, on Jul 7, Geo Taylor, in the 74th yr of his age. Funeral at Rock Creek Chr, Thu.

Died: on Jul 8, John A Bennett, s/o Alex'r Bennett, aged 18 yrs. Funeral at the residence, 402 Pa av, today.

Archbishop Kenrick died suddenly on Jul 8th, at his residence in Balt City, Md, age 66 yrs.

Wash Corp: 1-Nominations by the Mayor: for Intendant, Josias Adams; for Physician, S A H McKim
For Com'rs: W G H Newman, John McDevitt, Wm Slater. For Sec to Com'rs, John E Leach. For Resident Student: John K Walsh: referred to the Cmte on the Asylum. 2-Bill for relief of Rachael P Wilson: passed. 3-Nomination of F R Dorsett for Com'r of Improvements: rejected. 4-Ptn of Wm Gunton & others for grading 9th st to Boundary: passed. 5-Ptn of Horatio R Merryman & others: for curbing & paving front of sq 784: passed.

On Wed last Sgt Michl Capars, 3rd S C Regt, who a few nights since escaped from the provost guard-hse, after he had been convicted by crt-martial & sentenced to be hung for the murder of Prince Drayton, servant to Capt F C Ford, post commissary, was arrested in some bushes near Mitchellville. He is not very well resignd to his fate, which he is now convinced is to be death.

A new Post Ofc was est'd at Montrose, Montg Co, Md, & Thos Holmes appt'd postmstr. The ofc is situated directly on the turnpike, between Dorsey's store & Rockville.

Balt, Jul 8. One thousand rebels, captured by Gen Kilpatrick, arrived here today, including Brig Gen Jones, a cavalry ofcr, & 51 other commissioned ofcrs.

FRI JUL 10, 1863
Mrd: on Jul 8, Capt Chas A Eccleston & Miss Mat J Brown, of Montg Co, Md.

Died: on Jul 9, in his 39th yr, Wadsworth Ramsay, Adj Gen of the Militia of D C, eldest s/o Capt Wm Ramsay, U S N. Funeral from the residence of his father on Sat.

Died: on Jul 8, after a short illness, Sallie, only d/o A Jas & Ellen C Falls, aged 5 yrs. Funeral from the residence of her aunt, Mrs Bailey, 406 I st, today.

Died: on Jul 8, at Coney Island, N Y, after a painful illness of 8 weeks, Fannie Norman, infant d/o Thos A & Mary L Stephens, aged 8 months & 19 days. Funeral today.

Brig Gen Gideon R Paul, commanding first brig, 2nd div, First Army Corps, was *not* killed. A buckshot struck the right side of the head above the ear, & passed out the right corner of the left eye. He is doing well, though he may lose the sight of his eye.

SAT JUL 11, 1863
Mrd: on Jul 7, at St Aloysius Chr, Leonardtown, by Rev Fr Enders, Baker A Jamison to Miss Sallie M Gough, both of St Mary's Co, Md.

Died: at Louisville, Ky, on Jun 30, in the 27th yr of her age, Nannie Colston, w/o W Geo Anderson, & d/o Josiah Colston, formerly of Wash City.

Died: on Jul 9, after a lingering illness, John D, y/c/o John K & Sarah A Robinson, aged 3 months. Funeral from their residence, 268 E st, today.

Funeral of Sgt Maj Asa W Blanchard, 19th Regt Ind Vols, who fell in battle at Gettysburg, Jul 1, will take place from the residence of his father, Jas M Blanchard, adjoining St John's Chr, 16th st, Sun.

Supreme Crt of D C, Equity #40. Susan W Harris, by Jos L Woodward vs Arnold Harris. Bill states that some lots in Wash City, were conveyed by deeds, which are exhibited, to Arnold Harris, hsbnd of cmplnt, in trust for her separate us. She is desirous of selling a part of said property, but is unable to do so as her hsbnd & trustee is in the southern part of the U S. -R J Meigs, clerk

Hon Wm Tingle died at his residence in Snow Hill, Md, on Jun 25, age 67 yrs.

Col Jas Husten, 82nd N Y Vols, was killed in the battle of Gettysburg.

MON JUL 13, 1863
Mrd: on Jul 11, by Rev John C Smith, Henry Decamp to Miss Eliz Everitt, all of Wash City.

Died: on Jul 9, Josephine, d/o the late W E Crossfield.

Died: on Jun 26, at Port Hudson, of a gunshot wound while in the discharge of his duties as Ast Topog Eng, Wm Luce, s/o the late Vinal Luce, of Wash.

Died: in Dublin, Ind, on Jul 5, Harriet C, d/o L Lovell & Susan Ingle Lawrence, aged 4 yrs & 4 months.

Died: in Wash City, on Jul 12, Raphael, infant c/o Richd H & Ada Semmes Clarke, aged 10 months. Funeral from their residence, 18th & I sts, Mon.

Orphans Crt of Wash Co, D C. Prsnl estate of David Morran, late of Wash City, dec'd. -Ann Morran, excx

Deaths report to the Navy Dept for the week ending Jul 11, 1863:
Henry Smith, seaman, chronic diarrhoea, Jun 23, Nav Hosp, Memphis.
Geo Lewis, 1st cab boy, chronic diarrhoea, Jun 26, do.
Frederick Jebb, actg Ast Surg, dysentery, Jun 20, Mississippi Squadron.
David Jones, 1st cab boy, dropsy, Jun 20, do.
Henry Clay, contraband, diarrhoea, May 3, do.
Isaac Foster, landsman, gunshot wound, Jun 28, do.
Benj Head, landsman, gunshot wound, May 3, vessel U S S Maratanza.
John M Smith, seaman, gunshot wound, Apr 8, vessel U S S Ceres.
Jacob Haynes, marine, dysentery, Jun 21, vessel U S S Alabama.
Andrew K Snyder, landsman, gunshot wound, Jun 4, vessel U S S Roebuck.
Philip Green, coal heaver, pneumonia, Jun 11, vessel U S S E R Hale.
Geo Kirkby, actg ensign, dysentery, Jun 22, E Gulf Squad.
Amos Burnham, landsman, typhoid fever, Jul 3, Nav Asylum.
Chas Hart, seaman, typhoid fever, Jun 27, vessel Gen Price.
Francis O Blake, actg mstr's mate, drowned, Jun 25, do.
Wm P Beecher, actg ast paymstr, drowned, Jun 26, vessel U S S Ratler.
Jas McCurry, contraband, diarrhoea, Jun 26, vessel U S S Black Hawk.
Edwin Diver, marine, diarrhoea, Jun 26, do.
Chauncey Keyson, 2nd cab boy, consumption, Jun 18, vessel U S S Flag.

Supreme Crt of D C-in Chancery.-1757. The Pres & Dirs of Gtwn College against John H Ferguson. Ratify sale to B F Moxley for $350 of east half of lot 60 in Holmead's add to Gtwn. Moxley transferred same to Helan Baston, who pd $116.66 in cash & has given his 2 notes-each for $116.67 with interest, endorsed by Francis Wheatley & B F Moxley. -R J Meigs, clerk

Funeral of Most Rev Peter Francis Kenrick, Archbishop of Balt, Md, took place at Balt on Sat. He was a native of Dublin, where he was born Dec 3, 1797; educated at Rome; came to the U S in 1821 & settled in Ky.

Wm Wood Worthington, of Woodville, PG Co, Md, was arrested by military guards & brought to Wash City yesterday. He was punishing one of his negroes when he was called on by some sldrs who demanded that he should cease. He asked by what authority they so demanded of him, that if they had the authority of Washington he would comply. As they could not show such authority he would not heed them so they arrested him. [Released & returned to his home.]

Contee Waring, s/o John H Waring, lately sent to Fort Delaware, was arrested near his father's farm in PG Co, Md, charged with attempting to send some trunks across the Potomac to his mother & sisters, who were banished to the South. [Released & returned to his home.]

The death of Col Paul J Revere, Mass 20th, at Westminster, Md, is announced. He was shot thru the lungs at the battle of Gettysburg, & did not long survive his wounds.

TUE JUL 14, 1863
Mrd: at Trinity Chapel, N Y, on Jul 9, by Rev S H Weston, Richd Washington, U S N, to Miss Kate Lee, d/o Col Robt M Lee, of Phil.

Died: at his residence, on Jul 13, in the 62nd yr of his age, Wm Thos Carroll, Clerk of the Supreme Crt of the U S for the past 35 yrs. Funeral from his late residence on Wed.

Died: at Newport, R I, on Jul 10, in the 41st yr of her age, Mrs Evelyn E Colfax, w/o Hon Schuyler Colfax, a Rep in Congress from Indiana.

The late Brig Gen Elon J Farnsworth, who fell in the battle at Gettysburg, was a nephew of Gen John F Farnsworth, Mbr of Congress of this State. He was born in Livingston Co, Mich, in 1835.

Two Catholic clergymen, including Rev Fr Brady, have been drafted in Boston. Among others drafted are Milton Andros, U S D A; Chas F Blake, Prov Mrshl Gen; Wm Mitchell, Armorer of A & H Artl, & 5 persons of the same name of John Smith.

WED JUL 15, 1863
Obit-killed in battle at Gettysburg, on Jul 31, J Tom Green, y/s/o Mr A Green, of Wash City, in the 27th yr of his age. He entered the Confederate army at the beginning of the war & was Capt of Co I, 8th Va Infty, Gen Garnett's brig, Gen Pickett's div, of Gen Longstreet's corps, at the time of his death. He was shot in the breast & died an hour afterwards. He was buried by the Confederates in an unmarked grave & recovery of his body is impossible.

Died: on Jul 14, Mrs Mary E Edwards, w/o John L Edwards, of Wash City. Funeral from the residence of her father-in-law, Jas L Edwards, on F st, Thu.

Died: on Jul 13, Mrs Mary Haslup, w/o the late Wm Haslup,of Howard Co, Md.

Died: on Jul 14, Albert, y/s/o Wm & Eliz Lord, in the 9th yr of his age. Funeral from his father's residence, 5th & G sts, today.

Died: on Jul 13, of dysentery, Lucy, only c/o J W & Alice R Westfall, aged 12 months & 10 days.

Orphans Crt of Wash Co, D C. Prsnl estate of Jos Ingle, late of Wash Co, dec'd. -Moses Kelly, adm

Supreme Crt of D C, Equity #1513. Rachael E Mason against Cynthia B Mason & others, widow & heirs of Jos Mason; distribution of funds will be resumed at my ofc in City Hall, Wash, Jun 6.
-W Redin, auditor

THU JUL 16, 1863
Died: on Jul 14, Henry Percey Morgan, infant child of Edwin C & Evelyn P Morgan, aged 3 months. Funeral from their residence today.

Persons with claims against a balance due from the U S to Jas Cook, Capt of the vessel *Top*, dec'd, are to present same. -Stephen J W Tabor, Auditor, Wash, D C.

Wash, D C. Chas Rosefield, a German aged about 30 yrs, a Col commanding the Cameron Regt, presented an account for subsisting recruits for $14, 760, & verified it in Wash City on Jun 30, 1862. Investigation found it was fraudulent. A warrant was issued & Col Rosefield was arrested & committed to jail on Tue. He alleges that he has been made the dupe of others..

Trustee's sale of farm in Wash Co, on Piscataway rd, near the Insane Asylum, called *Prevention enlarged* & *Giesborough Manor*, with improvements, as surveyed by Thos Jekyll, in Aug 1860.
-Nathaniel M McGregor, trust -Jas C McGuire & Co, aucts

Chancery sale of improved property in Gtwn; decree of Sup Crt for D C, dt'd Jun 4, 1863; John Meem & wife & others, cmplnts, & John Goszler & others were dfndnts. Public auction on the premises, the late residence of the late Geo A Goszler, south side of Bridge st, near Mkt, & opposite the residence of Geo Poe, jr. Improved by a 2 story brick dwlg hse.
-J Carter Marbury, trust; M V Buckey, auct

Mosquito Bars: ready made & put up in five mins by Geo Wilner, 464 9th st, between D & E sts.

FRI JUL 17, 1863
Died: on Jul 11, Mrs Ann Edelen, in the 86th yr of her age, a native of Chas Co, Md, & for 63 yrs a resident of Wash City.

Died: on Jul 16, at his residence in Wash City, at an advanced age, of a protracted illness, John T Sullivan. Obit of Jul 18: age 81 yrs. Funeral from his residence on 7th st, Sun.

Died: at his residence in PG Co, Md, on Jul 12, Geo W Graham, in his 53rd yr.

Adm's notice of the sale of the prnsl est of the late Col John F Carter, of PG Co, Md; at his residence lying in said county: valuable library, hsehld furn etc. -Murray Carter, adm

Orphans Crt of Wash Co, D C. Prsnl estate of Barbara S Young, late of Wash, dec'd.
-Ignatius F Young, exc

Riot in N Y: Tue, the second day. Col H F O'Brien, 11th Regt N Y, was attacked & most brutally beaten to death near his own residence. Fr Clowry, a clergyman of the Catholic Chr, who had witnessed the whole scene, vainly endeavored to prevent the deed of violence, but in vain. He gave the dying man the consolation of the church as he lay. Even then the mob would not permit him to be removed, but threatened with vengeance anyone who should approach the bleeding man.

SAT JUL 18, 1863
Died: on Jul 16, Mrs Eleanor B Tolson, relict of the late John Tolson, aged 73 yrs. Scarce 4 months ago she was called to part with her hsbnd, with whom she had lived long & happily. Funeral from Christ Chr, Navy Yd, today.

Wash Corp: 1-Ptn of Josiah Eggleston asking the return of certain money: referred to the Cmte of Claims. 2-Ptn of Jas Adams & others: referred to the Cmte on Improvements. 3-Bill for relief of Hyacinth Laselle: referred to the Cmte of Claims.

List of captured Genrls:
Lt Gen John C Pemberton
Maj Gen Stevenson, of Ala
Maj Gen Forney, of Ala

Maj Gen Bowen, of Mo
Maj Gen M L Smith, of La

Brig Gens Buford, Lee, Moore, Hebart, Schoepf, Baldwin, [badly wounded] Harris, Vaughn, Taylor, Barton, Cummings, Cockerill.

Maj Wm D Baldwin appt'd Adj Gen of the Militia of D C, with rank of Col, vice Ramsay, dec'd. Capt Wm G Moore appt'd Aid to the commanding ofcr of D C, with rank of Maj, vice Baldwin, promoted. -R C Weightman, Maj Gen

Cavalry fights in Md: Boonsboro Jul 10. Among the casualties on our side the loss of Capt Wm Lindsay, of Co A, 18th Pa, who was shot dead whilst leading the gallant charge into Hagerstown.
Capt Dahlgren, late of Gen Hooker's staff, was severly wounded in the ankle. Capt Snyder was shot in the head, carried into a house & left.

MON JUL 20. 1863
Died: at the Cottage, near Wash, on Jul 10, Wm H Dundas, infant s/o J R C & Eliza D Oldham, of Phil, aged 6 months.

Died: at the Cottage, near Wash City, on Jul 18, Mrs Mary Y Dundas, relict of the late Wm H Dundas, in the 63rd yr of her age. Funeral from her late residence today.

Died: at Nashville, Tenn, on Jul 4, Robt L, only c/o Col Daniel & Julia E McCook, aged 11 months & 25 days.

Died: on Jul 19, Harriet Buckey, infant c/o Geo H B White & Frances V White. Funeral from their residence, 371 9th st, today.

Deaths reported to the Navy Dept for the week ending Jul 18, 1863:
R N Cameron, mstr's mate, remittent fever, Jun 29, Nav Hosp, Memphis.
Wm Buckhart, seaman, typhoid fever, Jun 30, do.
Wm Jordan, 1st cl boy, remittent fever, Jul 5, do.
Warren Hardy, 1st cl boy, smallpox, Jun 27, do.
David Rogers, seaman, delirium tremens, Nav Hosp, N Y.
John McDowell, 1st cab boy, typhoid fever, do.
Wm H Waters, seaman, pneumonia, do.

Orphans Crt of Wash Co, D C. Case of Michael H Conrad & John C Howard, adms of Godrey Conrad, dec'd: settlement on Aug 11. -Z C Robbins, rg o/wills

TUE JUL 21, 1863
Died: on Jul 19, Geo Hercus, a native of Haddington, Scotland, but for the past 46 yrs a resident of D C, aged 71 yrs. Funeral from his late residence, 573 Md av, today.

Jackson, Jul 14. Lt Gen Pemberton & staff arrived here last night. An ofcr with them said they met an escort accompanying the body of Gen Osterhaus to Vicksburg. The Gen was killed by a cannon ball on Jul 12. Gen Johnston sent a flag of truce today to Gen Grant, asking permission to bury the Yankee dead in front of our works. Gen Grant asked permission to send assistance, in order that the dead might be recognized, which was refused. Among their killed & wounded are Col Earl, Lt Col Long, & Capt Hall, 41st Ill; & Lt Abernathy, 3rd Iowa. Among the ofcrs on our side: Maj Lamb, 29th Ga, killed. Lts C C Brader, 19th La; T J Rust, 4th Fla, & A B James, of Cobb btry, wounded.

Gen Fitzhugh Lee is not a prisoner, & is not the ofcr held at Fortress Monroe as a hostage for Capt Sawyer. The prisoner so held is Gen W F Lee, captured some weeks ago on the Peninsula.

Wm H Thompson, a negro, was arrested by Ofcr L D Milstead, & taken to the 5th ward station hse, where he was fined $20.58 by Justice Ferguson. The negro fired on a white man at the corner of 13th & Pa ave. The man was fined for carrying a concealed weapon.

WED JUL 22, 1863
Died: Jul 20, John W Stettinius, M D, aged 36 yrs. Funeral on Wed from his late residence, 8 La av.

Died: on Jul 21, Blanche, infant d/o Thos J & Charlotte M Fisher.

Released from the draft on the ground of alienage: Christian Heinrich Haucke, who was drafted in Ozaukee Co, Wisc.

Brig Gen Paul J Semmes, of Ga, wounded at Gettysburg, is dead.

Wash, D C. Francis Davis, a newsboy, 10 or 12 yrs of age, was run over on Mon, on Pa av, by street car #8 of the passenger railway. Jas *Dingler was arrested & committed to jail for having pushed the boy off the platform where he had been sitting. The boy died on Jul 21. [Jas *Dingley was in no way accountable for the death of Frank Davis. Jul 24th paper.] *2 splgs.

Mrd: at St Matthew's Chr, in Wash City, on Jul 21, by Rev Fr White, John Ward, of her Britannic Maj's civil svc in Bengal, to Carlotta, eldest d/o the Baron F Von Gerolt, Minister Pleni of his Maj the King of Prussia to the U S. The bridesmaids were the young sisters of the lovely bride.

THU JUL 23, 1863
Died: in Wash City, on Jul 22, Lewis C Robinson, in the 32nd yr of his age. Funeral from the residence of his bro-in-law, W E Spalding, on Thu.

Died: on Jul 21, of membrane croup, Ignatius Bertram, aged 4 yrs, y/c/o Richd & Anne Bridget. Funeral from their residence, 360 11th st, today.

Supreme Crt of D C, in Equity #1094. Jas A & John T Lenman, use Wm E Spaulding, against Wm H Winder, Anthony Hyde, Thos R Suter, Wm W Corcoran, Jno B H Smith, Walter D Davidge, & Benj O Tayloe. Statement of trustee's account on Aug 14, City Hall, Wash. -W Redin, auditor

Orphans Crt of Wash Co, D C. Prsnl estate of Geo McNaughton, late of Wash Co, dec'd. -F McNerhany, adm

Supreme Crt of D C, June term, 1863. Solomon Wolf has committed adultery within the city of Washington since his marriage with the said Ellen, the petitioner; proper that a divorce should be granted & Ellen be allowed to resume her former name of Reynolds, & have & hold all her property free & clear of any right thereto on the part of the said Solomon Wolf. Ellen shall have custody of all her chldrn, the issue of said marriage with said Solomon Wolf, -A B Olin, Justice -R S Davis, Solicitor

By direction of the Pres. Retired from active svc, & on the retired list of ofcrs, as of Aug 1, 1863: Maj Gen John E Wool; Brig Gen Wm S Harney; Brev Brig Gen Harvey Brown, Col of the 5th Artl; Col Justin Dimick, 1st Artl; Col Chas S Merchant, 4th Artl; Lt Col Martin Burke, 3rd Artl.

FRI JUL 24, 1863
Mrd: on Jul 21, at the Chr of the Epiphany, Wash, by Rev Dr Hall, pastor, Miss Eleanor Annie Hawkins, d/o the late Dr John Laidler Hawkins, of Chas Co, Md, to Stephen Garnett, late of the U S Army.

Mrd: on Jul 15, at the Chr of the Holy Trinity, Phil, by Rev Phillips Brooks, ast'd by Rt Rev Alonzo Potter, Bishop of Pa, Saml Welsh, jr, & Bettie Conrad, eldest d/o late Cmder Wm S Young, U S Navy.

Capt H W Sawyer, under sentence of death by the rebel authorities of Richmond, is a ctzn of Cape May Co, N J, where his wife & chldrn reside. A true sldr: from a humble position he has risen to the rank of captain, an ofc he most worthily filled with the hard fought action at Beverly Ford, when he was taken prisoner and carried to Richmond. The ltr having reached its destination, has just been published, and will every where be read with sensibility, because of the pathos, and yet the fortitude, which breathes in its every line. Mrs Sawyer immediately started for Washington in company with Capt Whilldin, and from hence proceeded to Fortress Monroe with the proper authority of the Gov't for her conveyance to Richmond in the next flag of truce boat-Provost Marshal's Office. Richmond, Va, Jul 6, 1863 to his wife. *My Dear Wife:* I am under the necessity of informing you that my prospect looks very dark. This morning all the captains now prisoners at the Libby military prison drew lots for two to be executed. It fell to my lot. Myself & Capt Flinn, of the Fifty-first Indiana Infantry, will be executed for two captains executed by Gen Burnside. /The provost general, J H Winder, assures me that the Sec of War of the Southern Confederacy will permit yourself and my dear children to visit me before I am executed. You will be permitted to bring an attendant. Capt Whilldin, or uncle W W Ware, or *Da_, had better come with you. My situation is hard to be borne and I cannot think of dying without seeing you and the children. You will be allowed to return without molestation to your home. /I am resigned to whatever is in store for me, with the consoolation that I die without having committed any crime. I have no trial, no jury, nor am I charged with any crime, but it fell to my lot. You will proceed to Washington. My Government will give you transportation to Fortress Monroe, and you will get here by flag of truce, and return the same way. Bring with you a shirt for me. It will be necessary for you to preserve this letter, to bring evidence at Washington of my condition. My pay is due me from the 1st of March, which you are entitled to. Capt B owes me fifty dollars-money lent him when he went on furlough. You will write to him at once, and he will send it to you. /My dear wife, the fortune of war has put me in this position. If I must die a sacrifice to my country, with God's will I must submit, only let me see you once more, and

I will die as becomes a man and an officer; but for God's sake do not disappoint me. Write to me as soon as you get this, and go to Capt Whilldin: he will advise you what to do. I have done nothing to deserve this penalty. But you must submit to your fate. It will be no disgrace to myself, you, or the children: but you may point with pride and say, " I gave my husband;" my children will have the consolation to say, "I was made an orphan for my country." God will provide for you; never fear. Oh, it is hard to leave you thus! I wish the ball that passed through my head in the last battle would have done its work; but is was not to be so. My mind is somewhat influenced, for it has come so sudden on me. /Write to me as soon as you get this; leave your letter open and I will get it. Direct my name and rank, by way of Fortress Monroe. Farewell, farewell, and hope it is all for the best. I remain yours until death, H W Sawyer, Captain First New Jersey Cavalry. [*The last letter could be "n". Possibly-*Dan*.]

Died: on Jul 23, in his 69th yr, Dr Philip Smith, a native of county Cavan, Ire, but for the last 40 yrs a resident of Wash City. Funeral from his late residence, 612 H st, & from St Aloysius Chr, on Sat.

Died: in Wash City, on Jul 23, at the residence of her uncle, Paulus Thyson, Jenny, 3rd d/o Jos & the late Caroline Brown, of Balt, aged 16 yrs. Interment in Balt.

Orphans Crt-sale of svrl hundred cords of wood, at Vierbuchen's farm, PG Co, Md, belonging to the estate of the late John Vierbuchen, dec'd. -Sophia Vierbuchen, admx

Selling off my Photographic & Optical Establishment, 426 Pa av, Wash, D C. -John Tobias [I am in no connexion with any jewelry establishment]

Capt Dahlgren, who was wounded in a gallant charge at Hagerstown, has suffer amputation of his leg. He is only 21 yrs of age.

Cmder Abner Read, U S Navy, was mortally wounded while in command of the U S steam sloop *Monongahela*, at the batteries above Donaldsonville, on the Mississippi, on Jul 7, & died a few hours afterwards. Capt Thornton A Jenkins, Capt of the fleet, was slightly injured; accident was the bursting of a shell. Cmder Read was a native of Ohio & 42 yrs of age.

Maj McCook has died of wounds received at the fight with Morgan's men, near Buffington Island, Ohio; age 67 yrs & well known in Washington, having been a clerk in the Pension Dept for 2 or 3 yrs when the war began. He had 8 sons, who have all been in the svc except one-Col Geo W McCook, Atty Gen of Ohio, who organized the militia of that State. Maj Gen McCook, who has distinguished himself in the war, was one of the sons of the dec'd. He had lost 3 sons-one at the first Bull Run fight, where he had besides himself 2 sons, & now the brave-hearted father & hsbnd has fallen. May God comfort his wife & mother.

SAT JUL 25, 1863
Died: Jul 24, Henry H McPherson, sr, aged 80 yrs. Funeral from his late residence, 394 E st, today.

Field ofcrs of the rebel army killed at Gettysburg:

Col Mounger, 9th Ga, killed	Col Kennedy, S C, wounded
Col Brown, 59th Ga, wounded	Col E C Edmunds, 38th Va, killed
Maj Gee, Ga, wounded	Col H R Miller, 42nd Miss, killed
Col DeSaussure, S C, killed	Col Carter, 13th Miss, killed

12

Col Holder, 17th Miss, wounded
Col Ellis, Va, reported killed
Col Eppa Bunton, wounded
Col Stuart, Va, wounded
Col L B Williams, Va, killed
Col Jones, 20th Ga, killed
Col Allen, 28th Va, killed
Lt Col McElory, 18th Miss, wounded
Lt Col Feagan, 15th Ala, leg amputated
Col Griner, 61st Va, reported killed
Maj Berkley, Va, wounded
Maj Wilson, 28th Va, killed
Lt Col Elfer, 17th Miss, slightly wounded
Maj Bradley, 13th Miss, wounded

Adj Campbell, 48th Miss, killed
Adj Goodloe, 18th Miss, badly wounded
Col J B Weems, 10th Ga, wounded
Maj John, Ala, wounded
Lt Col Harwick, Ala, wounded
Col Carrington, 18 Va, wounded-now dead
Col Henry Gault, 19th Va, badly wounded
Col W T Patton, Va, wounded, in enemy's hands
Adj Gen Magruder, of Gen Joe Davis' brig, killed

Additional list of wounded field staff ofcrs:
Maj Morris, 7th La
Adj Brooks, 6th La
Maj Brooks, 20th N C
Lt Col Moseley, 43rd Va
Maj Finney, 47th Miss
Maj Cobb, 44th Va
Col Lightfoot, 8th Ala
Maj Culver, 6th Ala
Col Little, 11th Ga
Maj Jones, 9th Ga
Col Himon, 11th N C
Col W J Hoke, 89th N C

Lt Col Ashford, 39th N C
Adj Riddick, 34th N C
Col Barton, Philip's Legion
Maj Dawson, 8th Ga
Col Semmes, 83rd Ga
Maj Gillette, 13th Va Cavalry
Col Withers, 42nd Va
Adj Stewart, 3rd Va
Adj Alexander, 3rd Ga
Surg Fry, 16th N C
Lt Col Gordon, 34th N C
Adj Green, 11th Ga

Released from the draft on the ground of alienage: [where drafted]
John Pinnans, Cuyahoga Co, Ohio   Moses Porter, Mercer Co, Ohio

Fatal blunder at Lawrenceburg, Ind, on Jul 14. Morgan forces returning, & 2 companies of Col Shyrock's Ind Regt were sent out to reconnoitre in different directions. They met & each took the other for the enemy & began firing. Before their mistake was discovered, 7 men were killed & 20 wounded.

Mrs Pomeroy, w/o Sen Pomeroy, of Kansas, died a day or 2 since, on board the steamboat *America*, just before reaching Albany. She was on her way to Geneva, the home of her family, from Washington.

Explosion of a steam boiler at Lowell, Mass, on Mon, killed 5 & injured 7. The bldg was occupied by Wm H Godding as a picker factory & John S Jacques, shuttle mfgr.

Cavalry expedition under Col Toland, 34th Ohio Mounted Infty, & Col Powell, 2nd Va Cavalry, sent by Brig Gen Scamon, from Charleston, Va, to cut the Va & Tenn R R at Wytheville, has been successful. They captured it after a severe fight, & took 120 prisoners, 2 pieces of artl, & 700 stand of arms. Our loss was about 65 killed & wounded, Col Toland & Capt Delany, of Cincinnati were killed, & Col Powell was severely wounded. Our troops were fired on by the ctzns from their hses. The town was totally destroyed. The command reached Fayetteville yesterday, after a hard march.

Both sons of Hon Edw Everett were drafted in Boston. One of them has just returned to this country from England, having recently graduated at Cambridge Univ. Both have their minds to serve in person, instead of procuring substitutes or paying the $300 exemption fee.

It is now said that it was the death of Wm Mulready, the celebrated Irish painter, & not Macready, the tragedian, that was mentioned in the last European news.

MON JUL 27, 1863
Died: on Jul 26, John Y M, s/o Curtis B & Hannah M Graham, aged 6 yrs. Funeral from their residence, 185 K st, today.

Died: on Jul 26, Richd Coolidge, s/o John & Susan M Van Santvoord, aged 8 months. Funeral this afternoon.

Died: in Montg Co, Md, on Jul 23, after a long illness, Miss Georgie R Etchison, aged 17 yrs & 14 days.

Wash City ordinances:
1-Act for relief of Thos W Williams-to build a brick livery stable on his lot, in sq 407, on 8th st.
2-Relief of Rachel P Wilson-refund of $435, same amount deposited on Feb 19, 1863, to the redemption fund. 3-Relief of T C Magruder, refund of $30 for erroneous assessment of taxes.

Frankfort, Jul 26. Hon John J Crittenden died this morning, of debility, aged 77 yrs.

Cincinnati, Jul 26. The funeral of Maj Daniel McCook, Paymstr in the army, took place today.

N Y, Jul 26. The steamer *Arago*, from Charleston bar on the afternoon of Jul 23, has arrived here. Among her passengers are Gens Strong & Seymour, wounded, & Col Jackson & Lt Col Rodman, wounded, & others.
Deaths reported to the Navy Dept for the week ending Jul 25, 1863:
John T Nichols, landsman, dropsy, May 8, vessel U S S *Constellation*.
Frederick Raines, ord seaman, pneumonia, Apr 27, do.
Geo E Jackson, ord seaman, consumption, Jul 8, Hosp Key West.
Abner Read, Lt cmder, gunshot wound, Jul 8, vessel U S S *Montgomery*.
Step S Sherman, Sgt marines, gunshot wound, Jul 9, U S S *Tenn*.
David Brice, landsman, delirium tremens, Jul 15, Nav Hosp, N Y.
Geo Grover, landsman, diarrhoea, do.
Wm Lowry, beneficiary, cardiac disease, Jul 15, Nav Asylum.
Saml Jackson, landsman, consumption, Jul 21, do.
John Williams, landsman, pneumonia, Apr 11, vessel U S S *Onward*.
Levi Johnson, contraband, pneumonia, Jun 29, vessel U S S *Hartford*.
Thon Conroy, seaman, gunshot wound, May 26, vessel U S S *Mohican*.
Phil Pomroy, seaman, pneumonia, Jul 21, Nav Hosp Chelsea.
John Connelly, seaman, gunshot wound, Jun 30, vessel U S S *Sabine*.
Jas Perkins, 2nd Cpl, adynemia, Jun 29, Mississippi Squadron.
Geo Wilson, boatswain's mate, debility, Jun 29, do.
H N Thuner, actg ast paymstr, Jul 2, do.

Jas Smith, seaman, diarrhoea, Jul 6, vessel *Cincassian*.
A H Edson, actg ensign, blank, Jul 8, vessel U S S *Tuscumbia*.
Henry Williams, contraband, Jul 6, do.
H C Medlin, 29th Ill Vols, Jul 6, do.
Wm F Gohlson, 29th Ill Vols, Jul 8, do.
A J Simmons, 29th Ill Vols, Jul 10, do.
Geo Crozier, 2nd cl fireman, diarrhoea, Jun 4, vessel U S S *Clinton*.
Richd B-bby, seaman, gunshot wound, blank, do.
Geo Moier, landsman, remittent fever, Jul 6, Mississippi Squadron.
Jas Preston Contraband, dropsy, Jul 8, do.
John Betfel, seaman, liver cmplnt, Jul 10, do.
Stephen W Sherman, sgt marines, gunshot wound, Jul 10, vessel U S S *Tennessee*.
Nath. Hobbs, actg gunner, epilepsy, Jul 8, do.
Randall G King, landsman, chronic diarrhoea, Jul 14, Nav Hosp, Memphis.
Peter Quartptlacht, qr marines, pyoemia, Jul 15, do.
Jacob Burg, seaman, remittent fever, Jul 19, do.
Thos Kennedy, seaman, chronic diarrhoea, Jul 19, do.

Charleston, Jul 22. Battle of Jul 18th: Col Putnan, Actg Brig Gen, & Col Shaw, commanding the negro regt, were killed. –G T Beauregard, Genr'l

Chambersburg Repository: the property belonging to the Hon Thaddeus Stevens, was the only private property in the valley that was destroyed by order of a rebel ofcr. On Jul 23, a portion of Jenkins' cavalry came upon the works & obtained about 40 horses & 2 mules. Gen Early rode up to the works, the next day with his staff, & avowed his intention to destroy them. On the 3rd day the property was destroyed. The hses occupied by families were not fired. Some $3,000 worth of charcoal was destroyed, 7,000 lbs of bacon was stolen, leaving the families of the laborers without food. Mr Stevens' loss is not less than $50,000.

TUE JUL 28, 1863
Died: on Jul 9, Mary, w/o Leroy H Berryman. Wife, mother, sister & friend.

Died: at Alexandria, Va, on Jul 25, Anna Matilda, w/o Dr C M Hines, U S Army, & d/o the late Wm Devereux, of N Y, in the 29th yr of her age. Funeral from Trinity Chr, Gtwn, this morning.

Crct Crt of U S, sitting at Louisville, Ky. Thos C Shacklett found guilty of treason, sentenced to 10 yrs in the jail of Jeff Co, Ky, fined $10,000, & that your slaves be free.

By the draft in Wash Co, Pa, the Rev Mr Waugh, Prof of Wash College, O S Presby; Rev Mr Johnston, United Presby; & Rev N W Scott, O S Presby, are all called to svc in the army.

WED JUL 29, 1863
Trustees' sale of rl estate in A A Co, Md, near Annapolis; Chas Barber & Cath Barber, cmplnts, & John T Barber of Geo & others dfndnts; rl estate called *Horne Point Farm*, 280 acs; adjoins the farm of Geo Wells. -Nich's Brewer of John, Frank H Stockett, trustees.

Ltr carriers appt'd for Wash City:

Geo B Clark	John E McElwee	C H Wright	Thos F Harkness
Chas J Wright	Alfred C Shaw	D E Brewer	
John H Johnson	E l Frees	Thos F Parker	

Balt, Md, Jul 21, 1863: 8th Army Corps: Headqrtrs Middle Dept. Hon John Lee Chapman, I have the honor to inform you that on Jul 18 last the full wing despatch was addressed to these headqrtrs: "Maj Gen Schenck: Colored troops will be credited to the state the same as any other troops." –Edwin M Santon, Sec of War.

Trusting this may be productive of some action, I have the honor to be your most obedient servant, Don Platt, Lt Col & Chief of Staff.

The estate of the late Thos Carbery is valued between $90,000 & $100,000. -Local Item

Ford's Theatre. The new theatre on 10th st is approaching completion. The entire building has been constructed under the direction of Mr Jas Gifford: iron works from the extensive city foundry of the Messrs Schneiders: gas & water fixtures, chandeliers, & all, furnished by Messrs Jos F Reynolds & Co, 9th st. The water & gas pipes were laid under the direction of the worthy head of the Wash Gas Co, Jos F Brown. The inaugural season of the new house will open during the next month.

THU JUL 30, 1863
U S Mrshl's sale-D C. Lot 38 in sq 403, property of Richd A Hyde, in favor of Smith Harley. -Ward H Lamon, mrshl

The steamship *Mgt & Jessie* arrived in Charleston on Mon. She left Nassau on Fri. Among her passengers was the Hon Pierre Soule.

Wash Corp: 1-Ptn of Benj O Tayloe, asking return of certain money paid to the City Register. 2-Bill for relief of Robt J Rainey: ordered to a 3rd reading. 3-Ptn of W B Mitchell, asking an increase of compensation: referred to the Cmte on Markets. 4-Bill for relief of Curtis & Dearing: referred to the Cmte of Claims.

Cloud's Mill, about 4 miles from Alexandria, Fairfax Co, was totally consumed by fire on Fri night. It had nothing in it at the time. Mr Cloud, the owner of the mill, has lost nearly every thing he possessed since the beginning of the war.

Boston: Jul 29. The 8th Mass Regt arrived home today. They served at Newbern & then in the first corps of the Army of the Potomac shortly after the battle of Gettysburg.

The Navy Dept has contracted with the following parties to build an entirely new type of vessels of war.
Names of the ships from the Dept:
Name/Builders/Where
vessel *Shawnee*/Reaney & Co/Chester, Pa
vessel *Musco_ta*/ F Rowland/Green Point
vessel *Shamokin*/Reaney & Co/Chester, Pa
vessel *Winnipee*/H Loring/South Boston

The rebel Gen Pegram, with between 1,500 & 2,00 men, crossed the Cumberland river a day or two since, & moved north toward Richmond. He was not aware of the capture of Morgan, & contemplated assisting him to escape.

FRI JUL 31, 1863

Confiscation at Alexandria: owners of property in that place, under the confiscation act, previous to judicial proceedings:

Wm G Cazenove	Dr M M Lewis	Meade & Mayre
Dr Orlander Fairfax	Thos Anthony Brewis	Miss E Tebbs
Wm H Fowle	Wm H May	Selden Peach
Lawrence B Taylor	John Crockford	Levi Hurdle
Francis L Smith	Benj H Jenkins	Harrison Kirk
Wm N McVeigh	Dennis R Blacklock	Dr J T Johnson
Jas H McVeigh	Hugh Latham	McVeigh & Witmer
J M & R M Smith	Jas W Nalls	Wm H Smith
Edw Sangster	C M Castleman	J W Vandergrift
Geo Washington	Geo W Davis	
Anthony McLean	Wm S Kemper	

Of the above all are absent, & have been since the commencement of the war, except three.

The slaves of Col John C Waring, of PG Co, Md, who was lately sentenced by crt-martial to confinement during the war, & sent to Fort Delaware, for alleged harboring of Confederate ofcrs, have mostly arrived at the contraband camp, in Wash city: over 60 in number, men, women & chldrn. That they are freed by reason of Col Waring's conviction is not correct, because, as he was not tried by a civil crt, his case does not come under the provision of the act of the last Congress, which frees the slaves of anyone convicted under it. Under what influence these slaves come here can only be surmised.

Died: on Jul 29, at the residence of Jos H Bradley, in Montg Co, Md, Sarah Bradley, infant d/o Chas A & Sarah B Sherman. Funeral at Oak Hill Cemetery on Fri.

Died: of diptheria, on Jul 30, Mary, d/o John & Susan M Van Santvoord, aged 3 yrs. Funeral from 155 F st, Fri.

Died: on Jul 30, at Lincoln Hosp, Wm J McCormick, s/o the late Wm J McCormick, of Wash City.

Died: on Jul 30, after a short illness, Harry O Morrison, infant s/o O H & Emma Morrison, aged 4 months & 6 days. Funeral from the residence, 494 G st, Fri.

Destructive fire in Gtwn, on Water st, at the planing mill owned by J L & Wm H Simms, on Wed night. Loss about 15 to 20 thousand dollars.

Fatal accident on Wed-Augustus Stewart, y/s/o Richd Stewart, was run over by a locomotive. He died during the night; age about 13 yrs. Wash, D C

N Y, Jul 30. Brig Gen Strong died this morning from wounds received at Ft Wagner

Mr Wm Worthington, of PG Co, Md, was brought to Wash City by the military & committed to the Old Capitol prison.

SAT AUG 1, 1863

Mrd: on Jul 28, at St Mary's Chr, Woodville, PG Co, Md, by Rev Dr Marbry, John M Jameson, formerly of Wash, to Miss Mgt J Connick, d/o the late C R Connick, of PG Co, Md.

Died: on Jul 31, Eddie, y/c/o Wm R & Mary A Woodward, aged 21 months.

Died: on Jul 31, Lydia S, infant d/o Ebenezer & the late Indiana H Lord, aged 4 months. Funeral from 201 6th st, today.

Geo W Beall & Alexander E Beall have this day associated themselves in the Grocery Business in the name of Geo W Beall & Bro: corner of Bridge & Congress.

Wash Corp: 1-Act for relief of John H Richardson & Jos M Carson: refund $50 to them.

U S Mrsh's sale-lot 7 sq 512 in Wash City; prop of A E L Keese in favor of John Kulp. -Ward H Lamon, mrshl

MON AUG 3, 1863
Died: in PG Co, Md, on Aug 1, Mgt Faherty, aged 84 yrs, relict of the late Mark Faherty. Funeral from the residence of her son, Wm P Faherty, 502 L st, today.

Died: on Aug 2, Mrs Jane Deakins, born at Newcastle-upon-Tyne, Eng, in 1788, & for the past 69 years a resident of D C. Funeral from the residence of her son-in-law, Jas C McGuire, E st, Tue.

Died: in Wash City, on Aug 2, Eliza, infant d/o Francis & Annie E Lamb, aged 3 months. Funeral today.

Orphans Crt of Wash Co, D C. Regarding-rl estate of the orphans of John Brereton, dec'd. Ratify sale by Mrs Eliza A Drane, guardian, of a portion of the rl estate belonging to the minor heirs of John Brereton, dec'd, of which Edw McManus was purchaser. -Wm F Purcell, Judge -Z C Robbins, rg o/wills

Supreme Crt of D C, in Equity #45. Jos C Chick vs John D Reintzel, John Reintzel, Andrew Reintzel, Columbus Reintzel, Geo Reintzel, & Martha Reintzel. Rg-premises in Gtwn, D C, conveyed by said John D Reintzel & Eliza Reintzel his wife to cmplnt, Mar 21, 1855; defect in said certificate. Martha Reintzel has departed leaving as her only chldrn: John, Columbus, Geo & Martha Reintzel. All reside outside of D C. -R J Meigs, clerk

Balt, Jul 31. About 20 Southern sympathizers, attending the funeral of Capt Wm D Brown, of Balt, Md, who was killed at Gettysburg & was buried at Greenmount Cem on Jul 31, were arrested. It is expected they will soon be released. [Wm D Brown was a shipbuilder. His mother wanted him buried in Balt city in the family lot.]

Deaths reported at the Navy Dept for the week ending Aug 1, 1863.
Wm Martin, seaman, disease of heart, Jun 14, vessel U S S *St Louis*.
Jas Cromwell, landsman, inflam of stomach, Jun 12, do.
W D Parke, 3rd ast engr, albminuria, Jul 11, vessel U S S *Richmond*.
John Williams, 3rd seaman, gunshot wound, Jun 26, do.
Alex'r Baragar, 2nd mstr, chronic dysentery, Jul 23, U S Nav Hosp, N Y.
Wm N Burlingame, landsman, typhoid fever, Jul 15, Mississippi Squadron.
John Carroll, capt forecastle, gunshot, Apr 29, do.
Absalom E Leffler, marine, gunshot, Apr 29, do.
W H Springer, marine, gunshot, Apr 29, do.
Jas Haywood, contraband, gunshot, Apr 29, do.
Richd Gray, landsman, do, do, do.

Gotlieb Springer, marine, do, do, do.
Peter Brady, seaman, intermittent fever, Jun 29, do.
Stephen Tracy, seaman, gunshot, Jun 18, do.
Patrick White, seaman, congestive fever, Jun 24, do.
John Johnson, landsman, typhoid fever, May 27, do.
John H Cole, seaman, intermittent fever, Jun 1, do.
Patrick McMillen, 1st cab boy, remittent fever, Jun 13, do.
Giles T Ransom, 1st ast engr, congestive fever, Aug 5, 1862, do.
Jas Crowell, seaman, traumatic pleuritis, Aug 7, 1862, do.
Jas Hughes, b m, ebrietas, Jun 18, do.
Thos Greenslade, qr gunner, gunshot, Mar 11, do.
Wm Copeland, coal heaver, chronic diarrhoea, Apr 23, do.
Chris Talbot, 1st cab boy, drowned, Mar 16, do.
Robt Murphy, seaman, gunshot, Mar 13, do.
Jos Quigley, seaman, intermittent fever, May 20, do.
Michl Moloy, seaman, drowned, Mar 28, do.
Fred E Davis, mstr's mate, gunshot, Mar 17, do.
Henry Allen, 1st cab boy, hydrothorax, May 5, do.
John B Patterson, landsman, frac of skull, Jul 16, vessel U S S *Pawnee*.

U S Mrshl's sale-east half of lot 7 in sq 553, in Wash City, property of Wm E Carr, in favor of John W Morsell. -Ward H Lamon, mrshl

Local matter-sale of *Pomona*, belonging to the estate of the late Daruis Clagett, inside the District limits, adjoins the land of Francis P Blair-*Silver Spring*. 108 acs bought by John B Clagett, s/o the late owner at $157 per ac; 87 acs to Theodore Mosher at $75 per ac; 100 acs to W R Riely at $31.50 per ac.

TUE AUG 4, 1863
The funeral of the late Hon J J Crittenden took place at Frankfort, Ky, on Wed last. Among the survivors were Maj Gen Thos L, Col Robt H, & Col Eugene W Crittenden, the only surviving sons.

Stanmore School, Sandy Spring, Montg Co, Md, will resume on Oct 1 next. -Francis Miller, Proprietor & Principal

Draft in Wash City was commenced yesterday in the Common Cncl Chamber, City Hall, by the drawing of the names of those liable to military duty. Capt Scheetz, Provost Mrshl superintended. One company of the 153rd Regt N Y Vols, under command of Capt C F Putnam, was in attendance. Francis W Blackford, the com'r, was present & called out the names as they were drawn. Messrs A O Ball, W B Aber, S V Bacorn, J B Winters, & E W Haine_, of Capt Scheetz's ofc, acted as recording clerks. Mr Thos C Burns, a blind man drew the names from the box. 874 white were drawn & 306 colored. Among the "selected" are Capt W R Rutton, of the engrs, now in charge of the Wash Water Works; W A Force & Wm Farre, enrolling ofcrs; Robt Lamon, deputy mrshl; Remus Riggs, bro/o Mr Geo W Riggs, banker; Geo T James, policeman; Ed V House, correspondent of the N Y Times; & Fiedler E Dorsey, of the Globe ofc. Drawing for the 2nd ward followed: of the 2,480 names placed in the box for that ward the number drawn was 741: 494 white & 247 colored. Mr Jehiel Crossfield, the only employee of this ofc residing in ward 2, obtained a prize.

Obit-Colombia Typog Soc on the death of ex-Pres Chas F Lowrey; condolences to the widow & family. -W R McLean, Pres -Wash, D C

Died: on Jul 31, aged 1 yr & 2 days, Roberdeau Wheate, s/o Wm H H & Agnes Virginia Towers. Funeral today at the residence of his grandfather, Wm Towers, 16 K st.

Died: suddenly, John M Snyder, M D, of Gtwn, D C, aged 35 yrs. Funeral from his residence 100 Gay st, Gtwn, D C, on Wed.

Orphans Crt of Wash Co, D C. Prsnl estate of Thos Lumpkin, late of Wash Co, dec'd. -Robt G Lumpkin, exc

WED AUG 5, 1863
Jul 31, 1863: the sad intelligence of the death of Brig Gen Geo C Strong, an ofcr of the Ord Dept recalls the memory & renews the affliction of the double bereavement which the Ord Corps has been called upon to learn & lament. First Reno, & now Strong, both so well known to their corps. -Jas W Ripley, Brig Gen, Chief of Ord

Brig Gen Griffin, who has commanded the 1st Div of the 5th Army Corps for svr'l months past, has resigned for some cause not stated.

Died: in Wash City, on Aug 3, of dropsy, Lytle C, 2nd s/o Geo T & the late Ann E Raub, aged 15 years & 3 days. Funeral from his father's residence, C & 15th sts, on Wed.

Died: at Honesty, Montg Co, Md, on Aug 1, Mrs Eliz Bohrer, consort of the late Jacob Bohrer, in the 82nd yr of her age. Mbr of the Presby Chr.

Mrs Sawyer, w/o Capt Henry W Sawyer, of N J, a prisoner held for retaliatory execution, on arriving at City Point, applied to the Confederate authorities to visit Richmond & interview with her hsbnd before his execution, permission denied. She returned on the same boat. [Aug 15th paper-copy of ltr written by Henry W Sawyer, Capt 1st N J Cavalry, dt'd Libby Prison, Richmond, Va, Aug 2, 1863. Mentions his wife & 2 chldrn old enough to realize his situation.]

Returns of the election in Ky as far as know passed off quietly. In Paris, for Gov'r: Bramlette [Union] has 296 votes; Wickliffe [Dem] 21. For Congress: Clay [Union] 306; Buckner [Dem] 22; Boyle [Union] 1. Maysville: Bramlette 353, Wickliffe 3. For Congress: Wadsworth [Union] 312; Brown 21. Lexington: Bramlette 319, Wickliffe, 355; Clay 583, Buckner 163, Boyle 12. Gtwn: Bramlette 349, Wickliffe 355; Clay 305, Buckner 299, Boyle 13. Nicholasville: Bramlette 152; Wickliffe 2; Congress-Buckner 19, Boyle 16. Cynthiana: Bramlette 135, Wickliffe, 87. Congress: Menzies [Dem] 174, Smith [Union] 100. Covington: Bramlette 1,335, Wickliffe, 59. Congress: Smith 3,331, Menzies 55, Leathers 29.

Hon Wm L Yancey died at his residence, near Montgomery, Ala, on Jul 28th, after 4 weeks illness.

THU AUG 6, 1863
Died: at Bellmont, Montg Co, Md, on Aug 4th, Mrs Eliz H Munro, relict of the late Geo A Munro, of said county. Remains will be interred at Oak Hill Cemetery today.

Died: on Jul 25, at the residence of her son-in-law, Thos A Scott, Mrs Aloysia Graham, in the 85th yr of her age, relict of the late Wm Graham, of Harper's Ferry, Va.

St Louis, Aug 5. The rebel Gen Bowen died of dysentery a few days ago.

St Louis, Aug 5. Maj Febiger, Chief of the Pay Dept of the dist of Miss, received a despatch that the steamer *Ruth*, which left here for Vicksburg on Mon, was burnt a few miles below Cairo, last night. The boat & cargo were entirely consumed, & Maj Greenwall, Paymstr, & 3 clerks were lost.

SAT AUG 8, 1863

Mrd: on Aug 4, at the N Y Av Presby Chr, Wash, by Rev Dr Gurley, Prof Simon Newcomb, U S Navy, to Mary C, d/o the late Dr Chas A Hassler, U S Navy, all of Wash.

Died: on Aug 7, Mgt Bury, w/o the late Capt Jas Bury, in the 82nd yr of her age. Funeral from her son-in-law's, the late Maj Saml Byington, 8 Missouri av, today.

Died: suddenly, on Aug 4, John M Ramsey; native of Perth Scotland.

Capt Amasa Paine, U S Navy, died in Providence, R I, on Jul 27. He entered the navy in 1822 as a Mdshpmn.

Part of the graveyard in *Moravia*, Cayuga Co, N Y, was washed away in a severe rainstorm on Tue last. Sixteen bodies were washed away, & only 8 were recovered. –Albany Argus

The crt-martial of which Maj Gen Hitchcock was president, in the case of Hazell B Cashell, charged with furnishing information to the enemy, returned a verdict of *not guilty*. The War Dept issued an order dissolving the crt & severely censuring its mbrs. –Wash Cor N Y Tribune

Sixty-eight rebel ofcrs-Morgan's men-are confined in the penitentiary at Columbus, Ohio, & will be held there until Col Straight & his ofcrs are released. Col Duke is among the number.

MON AUG 10, 1863

Wash Corp: 1-Ptn of John Hitz & others, asking for a water main in A st south: referred to the Cmte on Drainage. 2-Ptn of Michl Murphy, asking remission of a fine: referred to the Cmte of Claims.

The Montgomery Mail has learned with deep regret that Gen Sterling Price has resigned his commission & retired from the army in Arkansas. Being placed in a subordinate position to Gen Holmes, he was unable to execute his plans for the liberation of Arkansas from the presence of Yankees. The mail said it comes well authenticated. –Whig

Obit-Lucretia M Green, w/o Duff Green, & d/o Benj Edwards, of Ky; at Beech Home, near Dalton, Ga, on Jul 5, in the 72nd yr of her age, & 50th of her mrd life. She was a devoted wife & mother:
lived long in the 5th Ward in Wash City.

Deaths reported at the Navy Dept for the week ending Aug 8, 1863:
Frederick Brown, 2nd cl fireman, chronic diarrhoea, Jul 22, Hosp, Memphis.
Geo Douglas, seaman, rheumatism, Jul 26, U S steamer *Vermont*.
Edw Coxen, landsman, scalds, Jul 24, do.
John Curran, 2nd cl fireman, scalds, Jul 23, do.
Michl Flynn, 3rd ast engr, yellow fever, Jul 19, U S steamer *Rhode Island*.
Robt Brooks, q m, disease of heart, Jul 9, U S steamer *Juniata*.

Robt Murphy, seaman, gunshot wounds, Mar 13, U S steamer *Baron de Kalb*.
John O'Neill, q m, gunshot wounds, Mar 13, do.
Carolina Ford, contraband, typhoid fever, Aug 4, Nav Asylum.
Henry Wilson, seaman, yellow fever, Jul 19, U S steamer *Alabama*.
M J Carson, 3rd ast engr, yellow fever, Jul 24, do.
L J Blanchard, 3rd ast engr, yellow fever, Jul 25, do.
Jas McKenna, marine, yellow fever, Jul 26, do.
J F W Hibbs, marine, yellow fever, Jul 28, do.
Peter Campbell, marine, yellow fever, Jul 29, do.
Wm Upham, landsmand, do, do, do.
Frederick Westcott, boy, yellow fever, Aug 2, do.
Henry C Maxon, actg Chief engr, yellow fever, Aug 3, do.
John Clark, ord seaman, yellow fever, Aug 3, do.
Daniel Driscoll, landsman, yellow fever, do, do.
B F Taylor, 2nd ast engr, yellow fever, Aug 4, do.
Geo W Smar, landsman, consumption, Aug 5, Nav Hosp, Norfolk.
Andrew Young, seaman, gunshot wound, Jul 28, U S steamer *Tennessee*.
John J Hays, paymstr's steward, remittent fever, Jul 21, West Gulf Squad.
Chas Strohuber, seaman, remittent fever, Jul 25, do.
Jas Osborn, seaman, remittent fever, Jul 29, Nav Hosp, Memphis.
Geo Herman, 2nd cl fireman, scurvy, Jul 13, iron clad *Essex*.
Wm Wagner, 2nd cl fireman, chronic diarrhoea, Jul 31, Nav Hosp, Memphis.
Chas Rhodes, seaman, intermittent fever, Aug 1, do.
Jas Kane, seaman, remittent fever, Aug 3, do.

Orphans Crt of Wash Co, D C. Case of Horatio N Easby, John W Easby, & Agnes M Easby, excs of Wm Easby, dec'd. Settlement on Sep 1. -Z C Robbins, rg o/wills

Orphans Crt of Wash Co, D C. 1-Prsnl estate of Thos Clark, late of Wash Co, dec'd. -Philip Clark, exc. 2-Prsnl estate of Mary Y Dundas, late of Wash Co, dec'd. -Will Y Fendall, adm, w a.

Mr John T Tracy arrested in Wash City on Fri last *for treason & conspiracy against the U S Gov't*.

TUE AUG 11, 1863
Died: on Aug 2, of typhoid pneumonia, at his late residence in Scott Co, Ky, Jas K Duke, in the 64th yr of his age.

Died: on Aug 10, after a short illness, Mary Louisa, only d/o Benj & Mary Ann Reiss, aged 1 yr & 15 days. Funeral from their residence, 267 G st, today.

Corp of Washington-A B Stoughton has permission to continue his porch at his dwlg, 421 13th st.

Sale of the estate in PG Co, Md, which Edw W Young is seized & now resides; 525 acs; formerly owned by the late Raphael C Edelin. -Edw W Belt, atty

Col John L Chatfield, 6th Regt of Connecticut Vols, died at Waterbury, Conn, on Aug 9, from wounds received in the assault on Ft Wagner on Jul 18.

Naval Expedition up James River: torpedo explosion: Fortress Monroe, Aug 4. Expedition under the direction of Maj Gen Foster: torpedo exploded under the gunboat *Cmdor Barney*, washing overboard 15 of her men, among whom was Lt Cushing, the Cmder of the *Barney*. Two sailors drowned. Maj Gen Foster was upon this boat when the explosion took place. A new army gunboat *Gen Jesup*, commanded by Lt Col Whipple, accompainied the expedition.

WED AUG 12, 1863
Died: Aug 9, at Alexandria, Va, after a short illness, Thos Randolph Keith, in the 77th yr of his age.

Supreme Crt of D C, in Equity #1558. Wm A Wilson et al vs Wilson, Ballinger, et al. Ratify sale of part of lot 5 & part of lot 6 in sq 171 to Moses Lewis for $800; & part of lot 9 in sq 406 to Johnson & Sutton for $5,551. -R J Meigs, clerk

Supreme Crt of D C. Notice to Henry Hargreaves. Ann Hargreaves filed for divorce on Aug 13, 1863; mrd to said Henry Hargreaves about Aug 9, 1850. Causes of desertion, ill treatment & adultery on part of said Henry. -Meigs, clerk

Destruction of the lighthouse on Smith Island, just outside the mouth of the Chesapeake Bay, on Mon last. The keeper, Wm Webb Stakes & family, as well as the 4 other families, were on the Island. A party of 9 men in a boat informed Stakes they had come to destroy & carry off the moveable property in his charge. The facts were obtained from the lighthouse keeper himself. -Worcester [Md] Shield [Aug 19th paper: Mr Stakes is a native & for a long time a resident of Accomac Co.]

Gen Osterhaus is not dead, as rebel despatches some time ago declared. He was in good health, prepared to do good svc in ridding Mississippi of armed rebels.

THU AUG 13, 1863
Crt Martial-Hazel B Cashell, a ctzn of Md, charged with giving intelligence to the enemy. The Court admonished him to be more on his guard in answering inquiries. Mr Thos Rabbit was with him on his farm in Montg Co, Md, when the incident occurred on Jun 28. Rg-moving of U S cattle.

John Long, a laborer at the Treas extension, was instantly killed yesterday, when a large stone being lowered from the roof, fell & mangled him. –Local

Died: in Wash City, on Aug 12, after a long & painful illness, Mr Thos McCarthy, aged 66 yrs, native of Ireland. Born in the county of Limerick, & for the last 47 years a resident of Wash City. He leaves his wife & 3 chldrn. Funeral from his late residence, 293 3rd st, today.

Died: on Aug 12, after a short illness, Augustine Jullien, in the 51st yr of his age. Funeral from his late residence, 412 13th st, today.

On Tue a sldr belonging to the 15th N Y Engrs, named Scott, endeavored to desert, but was pursued closed by the guard. He hung himself at the Navy Yd: Va ave & 7th st.

A Good Month's work: chronological statement of the successes achieved by the Union forces during Jul: does not include minor skirmishes, nor captures by our blockading squads.

Jul 31-Meade's victory over Lee at Gettysburg: rebel loss in killed, wounded, & prisoners: 35,000.

Jul 4-Capture of Vicksburg by Grant, with 31,000 prisoners & over 200 heavy guns. Gen Prentiss fights the rebels at Helena, Ark, defeats them with a loss of 2,700 killed, wounded & prisoners. Rosecrans compels Bragg to evacuate Tullahoma. Rebel loss in the engagements over 4,000.

Jul 6-Gen Buford whips Stuart & captures 967 prisoners.

Jul 8-Gen Banks captures Port Hudson with 6,000 prisoners. Gen Pleasanton defeats the rebel cavalry near Funkstown, capturing 600 prisoners.

Jul 9-Buford & Kilpatrick engage the enemy near Boonsboro, & defeat them, taking a number of prisoners.

Jul 10-Attack on the approaches to Charleston commenced & the batteries on the lower end of Morris Island captured by our forces.

Jul 13-Yazoo City captured by our gunboats & svr'l hundred prisoners, 6 heavy guns, & a gunboat taken.

Jul 14-Battle of Falling Waters, 1,500 rebels & svr'l guns captured.

Jul 15-Fort Powhatan, on James river, taken by Admiral Lee.

Jul 16-Our forces under Gen Sherman occupy Jackson, Miss, capturing a large amount of stores, driving the rebel Gen Johnston into Central Miss. Gen Blunt obtains a victory over the rebels at Elk Creek, Ark, killing 60 rebels, capturing 100 prisoners & 2 guns.

Jul 17th-On or about that time-expedition sent by Gen Grant to Natchez captures 5,000 head of cattle, 2,000,000 rounds of ammunition, & svr'l pieces of artl.

Jul 18-The guerilla Morgan cornered at Buffington, Ohio, & 1,000 of his men captured.

Jul 19-Col Hatch attacks the rebels at Jackson, Tenn, & captures 2 companies & an artl train.

Jul 20-1,500 of Morgan's men, including Basil Duke, captured at George's Crk.

Jul 22nd-Expedition from Newbern attacks Tarboro, N C, 100 prisoners captured, & an iron clad & 2 gunboats destroyed. Brashear City, La, surrendered to our forces under Col Johnson.

Jul 24-Col Tolland captures Wytheville, with 125 prisoners.

Jul 25-Morgan bagged at Salinville; also, 200 of his men.

Jul 28-Our troops under Col Hatch encountered the rebels at Lexington, Tenn, routing them & capturing a col, 2 lts, 25 pvts, & 2 pieces of artl.

Jul 29-Gen Pegram is engaged by our forces at Paris, Ky, & repulsed with serious loss in killed, wounded & prisoners.

Jul 30-Col Sanders attacks the rebels [2,000 strong] at Winchester, Ky, & routes them with considerable loss.

Jul 31st-Our forces attack the enemy at Lancaster, Ky, kill & wound 20, & take 100 prisoners.

FRI AUG 14, 1863

Died: on Aug 11, at Balt, Md, Lewis H Machen, in his 74th yr. Funeral from the residence of his son, A W Machen, North Chas st, Balt, this morning.

Brutal murder at Compromise Landing, on the Mississippi, on Aug 4, by 18 negro sldrs. Killed were: Maj Benj Beckham, age 80 yrs; his son Frank Beckham, aged 40 yrs, & the part of the family with him at the time, Laura, aged 14; Kate, aged 10, Caroline, aged 7; Richd, aged 2 yrs. Mrs Beckham & a 4 yr old child had gone up to Owensboro, Ky, on a trip. Two other chldrn were at school. -St Louis Rpblcn of Aug 10

Obit-David Hickman died on Jul 18, after a painful illness of 3 mos; born in Hardy Co, Va, on Dec 21, 1792, s/o Adam Hickman, who remv'd from Hardy to Harrison Co In 1795. On formation of Tyler Co, in 1815, Mr Hickman was appt'd clerk of the Crct Crt of that county.

Local Matter. On Wed Mr Chas L Wiggin seating himself in a window of his room, fell on his head, crushing the skull & breaking his neck. His death was instantaneous. He was chief clerk in the q m ofc; his father is postmaster at North Chelsea, Mass. The dec'd had resided at Detroit, Mich, 2 years prior to the outbreak of the rebellion. His body will be interred in Massachusetts.

Local Matter. Timothy Scanlan was accepted as a substitute for David L Perkins, the latter paying him $150. Scanlan was recognized as a sldr in a N Y Regt & committed to the guard hse. Perkins will recover his money.

American's registered at Gun's American Agency, 17 Charlotte st, Bedford Sq, London, for the 2 weeks ending Aug 1:

Mr Jas Dundas, Phil
Mr & Mrs Joshua Lippincott, Phil
Mr J Dundas Lippincott, Phil
Miss Anna Dundas Lippincott, Phil
J J Walsh, Allahabad, India
Mr & Mrs Wm A Francis, N Y
Mrs Hodges & dghts, N Y
Mr W Hodges, N Y
Mr Geo B English, N Y
Mr & Mrs R W Cameron, N Y
Wm M McPherson, St Louis, Mo
G Andrews, St Louis, Mo
T B Lathrop, Wash, D C
Geo Burkhand, N Y
Mrs Todd, Boston
Mrs Geo W Wright, N Y

Mr & Mrs A Carter, N Y
L A Bigelow, Boston
Mr & Mrs Geo A Hearn, N Y
Thos D Lowe, Dayton, Ohio
Geo Haishman, Dayton, Ohio
Aleck Craig & wife, Louisville, Ky
Mrs S H Porter, Phil, Pa
J A Marsh, N Y
Stewart C Marsh, jr, N Y
Harrington J McGrath, N Y
Wm J Tait, Cleveland, Ohio
Wm B Holmes & lady, N Y
A M Gay, Boston, Mass
Henry Stevens, Vt
John F Slater, San Francisco, Calif

Capt Harry McDougal, [says the New Albany Ledger,] who has spent svr'l days at Vicksburg since its surrender, writes that a number of women & chldrn were killed in the city during the bombardment of that town by Gen Grant. He learned the number was 20. Gen Pemberton refused to allow them to leave the city, & he is therefore responsible for their deaths.

SAT AUG 15, 1863

Died: on Aug 13, Mrs Anna Chalmers, eldest d/o the late Dr Tobias Watkins, of Wash City.

Died: on Aug 14, Mary Evans, eldest d/o Emily H & Louis Watkins, & grand-dght of the late Dr T Watkins. Funeral from the family residence, 420 9th st, on Sun.

N Y Aug 14. Cmdor Morris, U S Navy, died today; recently Cmder of the screw sloop *Pensacola*.

Army of the Potomac: Capt Henry Page, Q M of Headqrtrs, was, a day or to ago, the recipient of a magnificent sword, gold & silver mounted, costing about $300, as a testimonial from the employes under him while at Juba Dam, near Aquia crk.

MON AUG 17, 1863

Died: on Aug 14, Geo Humes, of Vansville, PG Co, Md, aged 42 yrs.

First Ward Hdwre Store, 180 Pa av, Wash. -John D Edmond [Ad]

Prize Guns of England, by the eminent English Mkr. John Bennett, 37 Moreton Terr, Pimlico, London, Eng. [Ad]

Desireable farm for sale adjoining Tennallytown, about 2 miles from Gtwn. My country residence. -H W Blunt, 61 La av, Wash.

Brig Gen Thos Welch, commanding the 1st div of the 9th Army Corps, died in Cincinnati on Aug 14th, of congestive fever, acquired during the campaign in Mississippi.

Deaths reported at the Navy Dept for the week ending Aug 15, 1863:
Robt Fero, landsman, Albuminuria, Hosp, N Y.
Daniel Morris, landsman, remittent fever, Jul 23, Richmond.
Sylvanus Cox, actg mstr, gunshot, Aug 6, vessel *Cohassett*.
Pat Connor, beneficiary, debility, Aug 10, Asylum.
John Griffith, capt after-guard, apoplexy, Aug 11, do.
Henry Walk, contraband, drowned, Jul 26, Fortress Monroe.
Granville W Fogg, acts mstr's mate, dysentery, Jul 30, vessel *Mercedita*.
Chas Carbin, sgt of marines, coup de soliel, Aug 11, Washington.
J Johnson, carpenter's mate, scald, Jul 29, vessel *Nahant*.
Wm M Darnes, steward, do, do, do.
Henry McManus, landsman, typhoid fever, Jul 22, Hosp Norfolk.
Jacob Key, mstr at arms, drowned, Jul 28, Penquin.
Chas M Henckler, marine, yellow fever, Aug 7, vessel *Alabama*.
Michael Duggan, 2nd cl fireman, yellow fever, Aug 7, do.
Daniel D Clark, marine, yellow fever, Aug 9, do.
John Haughnout, landsman, yellow fever, Aug 11, do.
Chas H Spahn, boatswain's mate, consumption, Aug 14, Asylum.
Moses Sheldon, ord seaman, consumption, Aug 10, Hosp, Chelsea.

Col Cornyn of the 10th Missouri Cavalry, was recently shot to death by Lt Col Bowen, of same Regt; affray at the camp in Corinth, Miss, or its vicinity. Altercation grew out of proceedings of a crt-martial.

The 173rd Pa Vols was mustered out of svc yesterday, its term of enlistment having expired. For some time past this regt has been doing guard duty at Manassas. The command has never been in action, & numberd 655 men.

TUE AUG 18, 1863

Mrd: on Aug 13, at *Avenel*, the residence of the bride's father, by Rev Jabez Fox, John C Wilson to Selina D, eldest d/o Prof A G Pendleton, U S Navy, all of Montg Co, Md.

Died: on Aug 17, Nicholas Tastet, aged 73 yrs. Funeral from his late residence, 519 10th st, today.

Died: in Balt, Md, on Aug 16, Col Benj L Beall, U S Army, in the 63rd yr of his age; s/o a gallant ofcr of the old Army.

Orphans Crt of Wash Co, D C. 1-Prsnl estate of Patrick Fitzgerald, late of Wash Co, dec'd. -Saml E Douglass, adm 2-Prsnl estate of Raphael H Boarman, late of Chas Co, Md, dec'd. –Chas M Matthews, adm 3-Prsnl estate of Francis Poe, late of Wash City, D C, dec'd. -Toulmin A Poe, exc

Local Items. 1-Actg Mstr Frederick D Stuart, of Wash City, ordered to the command of the gunboat *Fuchsia*. 2-Mr J W Thompson broke his leg on Fri at his farm near Marriottsville, Md.

Medal of Honor awarded on recommendation of the Navy Dept:
Geo Bell, Capt of the after guard, U S frig *Santee*, for cutting out the rebel armed schnr *Royal Yacht* from Galveston Bay, Nov 7, 1861.
Wm Thompson, signal q m, steamer *Mohican*, in the action at Hilton Head, Nov 7, 1861.
John Williams, boatswain's mate, do.
Matthew Arthur, signal q m, steamer *Carondelet*, at the reduction of Fts Henry & Donelson, Feb 6 & 14, 1862, & other actions.
John Mackin, Cpl of marines, steamer *Galena*, in the attack on Ft Darling, at Drury's Bluff, James River, May 15, 1862.
Matthew McClellan, 1st cl fireman; Jos E Vantine, do, John Rush, do, John Hickman, 2nd cl fireman, steamer *Richmond*, in attack on Port Hudson batteries, Mar 14, 1863.
Robt Anderson, q m, in the steamer *Crusader* & steamship *Keokuk*, for svcs during the attack on Charleston.
Peter Howard, boatswain' mate; Andrew Brinn, seaman; P R Vaughn, sgt of marines, steamer *Mississippi*, in the attack on Port Hudson batteries, night of Mar 14, 1863.
Saml Woods, seaman; Henry Thielberg, seaman; Robt B Wood, coxswain; & Robt Jourdan, do, steamer *Minnesota*, but temporarily on board the steamer *Mt Washington*, Nansemond river, Apr 14, 1863.
Thos W Hamilton, q m, steamer *Cincinnati*, in an attack on the Vicksburg batteries, May 27, 1863. Frank Bois, q m, do.
Thos Jenkins, seaman; Martin McHugh, seaman; Thos E Corcoran, landsman; & Henry Dow, boatswain's mate, do.
John Wood, boatswain's mate, steamer *Pittsburgh*, in engagement with the batteries at Grand Gulf, Apr 19, 1863.
Christopher Brennen, seaman, steamer *Mississippi*, but belonging to the vessel *Colorado*, in the capture of Forts St Philip & Jackson & New Orleans, Apr 24 & 25, 1862.
Edw Ringold, coxswain, steamer *Wabash*, in engagements at Pocotaligo, Oct 22, 1862.

Mr Wm C Hardin, of Church Creek, with 56 colored recruits, left here on Mon, in the steamer *Champion*, for Balt; to be sworn into the U S svc. -Cambridge Intell

On Mon last Col J P Creager passed thru Westminster, Md, with some 70 colored vols that he recruited in the neighborhood of Union Bridge & Liberty. -Westminster Sentinel

WED AUG 19, 1863
Died: at New Haven, Conn, on Aug 16, of typhoid fever, Prof Jos S Hubbard, U S Navy; grad at Yale College about 20 years ago; for some time employed as chief astronomer at the High School in Phil; then employed by the Gov't & made his residence in Wash.

Died: at Saratoga Springs, of rapid consumption, on Aug 15, in her 26th yr, Mary H, w/o J Buchanan Henry, of N Y, & d/o Jos H Nicholson, of Annapolis, Md.

Wholesale capture. On Sat morning last 40 Gov't wagons left Wash City & arrived at the estate of Col John H Waring, near Nottingham, PG Co, Md; here the wagons were laden with produce, tobacco, corn, & about 20 svts of Mr Waring. On the same occasion Dr Naylor, three Messrs Perry's, & Henry Clay Orme were arrested. It is reported that Col Waring, who was sent some time since to Fort Delaware, has died within a day or two.

Died: on Aug 18, at her late residence, 455 10th st, Eliz, relict of the late Nathan Orme, in the 85th yr of her age. Funeral tomorrow from St Patrick's Chr; burial in Mt Olivet Cemetery.

N Y, Aug 17. Central America: the steamer *America*, from Greytown, arrived with 330 passengers. Gen Chamorra, one of the revolutionary leaders from Nicaragua, was recently killed in a skirmish near the frontier of Honduras. The war seemed to be about over. It was expected that Gen Martinez would be elected Pres for life.

THU AUG 20, 1863
Orphans Crt of Wash Co, D C. Prsnl estate of Michael Huhn, late of Wash City, dec'd. -Rosina Huhn, admx

Havre De Grace, Md, Aug 19. Capt W L Cannon, 1st Dela Cavalry, s/o Gov Cannon, died on Aug 18 at Belair, Md. Death was produced by fatigue & exposure incidental to his duties.

Albany Argus of Tue: the shoddy mill of Mr Richd Hurst, at Cohoes, was consumed by fire yesterday. In the knitting rm in the 4th story 40 girls were employed, under charge of Peter McHugh. Between 15 to 25 were killed.

FRI AUG 21, 1863
Two prisoners, one named T C Bledsoe, who says he hails from Richmond, & Thos J Thompson, of this city, who were captured off Matthias Point on Sun night crossing the river, had about 100 letters in their possession. Thompson says he was captured a few days before the battle of Gettysburg, near Westminster, Md, by Stuart's cavalry, & taken to Gettysburg, & thence across the Potomac at Wmsport to Richmond, & placed in CastleThunder, & released in a few days thru the interposition of his bro, a resident of Richmond, on the ground of his being a British subject.

Died: on Aug 19, Judge Jos Bryan, of Ala, born in Hancock Co, Ga, in 1800. Funeral at his residence 330 Pa av, Wash, today.

Died: on Aug 18, Mina, d/o Chas W & Martha D Schuermann, aged 7 years & 4 months.

Maj Robt Morris, 6th Pa cavalry, died suddenly at Libby prison on Thu; grandson of Robt Morris of Rev memory; age 26 yrs. Remains were interred in Oakwood Cemetery, & attended to the grave by the captive ofcrs of his Regt.

The execution of Capt Sawyer & Flynn, was to take place on Aug 14; probable their execution was postponed. There is not much danger of its being carried out so long as Gen W H Lee & Capt Winder are held as hostages for them. Richmond papers of Sat.

Cincinnati, Ohio, Aug 29. Hon John A Gurley, mbr of last Congress, & recently appt'd Govn'r of the new Terr of Arizona, died at his residence in this city yesterday. He had been ill for about 10 days.

Fred'k [Md] Examiner of Wed. On Sun last Col J P Creager appeared at the Bethel [colored] chr in this city, & after svcs announced he was there authorized to enlist colored people in the army of the U S, & succeeded in procuring some 25 or 30 names. In the afternoon of the same day, at Asbury Chapel graveyard, [the chr very properly having been denied him by the Rev Mr Carroll,] he enlisted about the same number, including svr'l slaves belonging, as we are informed, to John Loats, of this city, Col Geo R Dennis, John Shearer, Chas Thomas, & others of the neighborhood. Ephraim Creager, of Mt Pleasant dist, whose negro had enlisted, appeared before Justice Wm Mahony, & filed his affidavit charging Col Creager with enticing slaves away from their owners. Col Creager was arrested in the hut of a free negro, John Stanton, & now remains in jail.

N Y, Aug 20. The draft in ward 15 was completed today. Among the drafted are Wm H Fry, of Tribune; John Chaney, of the Leader; Michl B Abraham, Express reporter; John B Halness, Excise Com'r; J Remack, of the Abend Zeitung; Tounsend Harris, late Minister to Japan; John Morrissy, pugilist; aslo svr'l policement & colored persons. While there is no appearance of disturbance, the authorities have not relaxed their vigilance in preparations to suppress disorder.

Yesterday Brig Gen E B Tyler was riding down Fayette st, Balt, & his horse slipped & fell. The Gen's leg was caught under the horse & his knee seriously injured. He will be out a few days.

Gen Thos Welch, Cmder of the 1st div of the 9th Army Corps, died at Cincinnati on Aug 14. He has served with the army for 2 years & was promoted to brig gen on Mar 13, 1863. He was with the 9th Army Corps both in Ky & in Vicksburg, & returned to Cincinnati after the fall of that military position.

SAT AUG 22, 1863
Mrd: on Aug 20, at Wesley Chapel, by Rev B Peyton Brown, Jas F Wollard to Miss Laura E Gittings, all of Wash.

Drowning on Sat last near Schultzville, Luzerne Co, Pa; three dghts & son of Loren Dewey, being the 3 youngest chldrn & the oldest dght, about 21 years of age, together with an orphaned cousin, Miss Brigham, about 21 yr of age, from Vermont, who had come to visit them but a few hours before.

Died: at Broadalbin, Fulton Co, N Y, on Aug 18, after a long & painful illness, Geo W Martin, only s/o Cyrus & Cordelia Martin, aged 15 years & 2 months.

Last week a baby of Mrs Cunningham, the wife of a rebel prisoner at Camp Morton, fell from a window at Indianapolis & was killed. Gen Wilcox immediately sent for the father & hsbnd, & paroled him til the next day noon.

Rebel prisoners on Johnson's Island: among the prominent:
Brig Gen J J Archer, taken at Gettysburg
Brig Gen J R Jones, taken at Smithsburg, Tenn
Capt D P Buckner, nephew of Gen Buckner, on Gen Beale's staff, actg Inspec Gen.
Col M L Wood, 40th Ala Infty, taken at Champion Hills
Capt D H Taylor, grandson of the late Pres Taylor, of Gen Golden's staff, taken at Tripoli, Miss

H C Champlin, M D: Homoeopathist & Surg. Successor to Dr Gaburri. Ofc: 251 F st. Hours: 8 to 11 A M, & 4 to 7 P M.

St Matthew's Academy for Young Ladies: 471 corner of 18th & N Y ave. Exercises will resume on Sep 1. The institution is conducted by the Srs of Charity. Discipline of the school is mild but firm.

MON AUG 24, 1863
Died: on Aug 22, Wm H Werden, in his 23rd yr. Funeral from the family residence, 509 I st, today.

Mrd: on Aug 18, at Vienna, Montg Co, Md, by Rev Robt Prout, Geo G Bradley, of Howard Co, Md, to Laura, d/o the late John Gassaway.

Deaths reported at the Navy Dept for the week ending Aug 22, 1863:
Wm Fisk, actg gunner, pneumonia, Aug 6, N Hosp, Chelsea.
Lawrence Fullam, ord seaman, remittent fever, Aug 12, Phil.
Chas Hudson, seaman, drowned, Jul 26, Mississippi Squadron.
Wm Wesson, ast engr, Jul 7, do.
David A Wilkinson, blank, drowned, Jul 3, do.
Robt Cameron, actg mstr's mate, blank, Jun 29, Hosp, Memphis.
Robt H Hagerman, marine, febris icterocles, Aug 13, Quarantine, N Y.
Geo Cleveland, coal heaver, febris icterocles, Aug 11, do.
Patrick Hart, 2nd cl fireman, febris icterocles, Aug 15, do.
Frederick Bull, 2nd ast engr, remittent fever, Aug 9, vessel *Pocohontas*.
W W Parke, actg Ast Surg, typhoid fever, Aug 3, Mississippi Squadron.
C L Lewis, ord seman, feb remit, Aug 2, do.
Chas Columbus, 1st cl boy, feb interest, Aug 3, do.
John Bolton, seaman, feb remit, Aug 5, do.
John Williams, seaman, feb typhoid, Aug 6, do.
Pat Hogan, landsman, feb remitt, Aug 8, do.
Wm L Hurd, actg ensign, drowned, Jul 31, do.
Joe Tompkins, coal heaver, sudden death, Aug 10, do.
Jas McKuitt, actg mstr's mate, feb interest, Aug 11, do.
Chas Smith, seaman, chronic diarrhoea, Aug 4, do.
Geo Gray, 1st cl boy, feb interest, Aug 8, do.
Jas Collins, seaman, chronic diarrhoea, Aug 11, do.
Herman Barkenstein or Banstantine, 2nd cl fireman, feb remit, Jul 5, do.
Chas S Kendrick, actg mstr commanding, feb remit, Aug 13, do.
Martin Dunn, actg Lt, typhoid fever, Aug 13, do.
Thos Conroy, seaman, gunshot wound, May 30, vessel *Mohican*.

Mr Jos P Davis, of Gtwn, D C, appt'd as clerk in the Dead Ltr Ofc: salary $800 per annum.

Ford's new theatre, 10th st, Wash. Opening on Wed evening; *Naiad Queen*. Bldg designed & erected under the supervision of Mr Jas G Gifford, architect; outer walls & masonry by Mr Geo R Callis; ornamental plastering by Mr Chas Stewart; fresco painting by Messrs Schulter & Lamb, work superintended by the eminent scenic artist, Mr Chas S Getz. Entire bldg constructed in a period of less than 5 months.

Orphans Crt of Wash Co, D C. Prsnl estate of Andrew Minitre, late of Wash Co, dec'd.
-R M Johnson, adm

Maj Prime, of the Engrs Corps, has declined to accept the appointment of Brig Gen of Vols, preferring to retain his position in the Engr Corps. He is regarded as a most valuable ofcr, to whose skill is attributed much of our success at Vicksburg.

TUE AUG 25, 1863

Died: in Gtwn, D C, on Aug 24, Bennet Clements, in his 75th yr. One of the oldest ctzns of the town. Funeral from his late residence, corner of Frederick & 2nd sts, Gtwn, today.

New Orleans-the execution of Francis Scott, guilty of murdering Maj J D Bullen, 28th Maine Div, on Jul 5, at Ft Butler, Donaldsville, was carried out yesterday. Twelve muskets were discharged & the sldr fell, 7 bullets struck him.

Crt Martial convened at hdqrtrs 2nd Brig, 1st Div, 5th Corps,of which Col Jos Hayes, 18th Mass, was president. Found guilty of desertion: John Folancy, alias Grecinto Lerchize; John Reanex, alias Geo Rioneze, G Kuhn, alias G Weik, Chas Walter, alias C Zene; Emile Lai, alias E Duffie; all of the 118th Pa Regt. All sentenced to be shot to death by musketry on Aug 26.

Cmder Geo W Rodgers, whose death before Charleston is reported, was a native of N Y, but a resident & appt'd to the Navy from Connecticut; entered the Navy in 1836.

Attack on Charleston on Mon: vessels composing the fleet, with ofcrs commanding:
Iron-clads:
Iron clad *Ironsides*-Capt S C Rowan; Pilot, Mr Dorey
Iron clad *Passaic*-Lt Cmder, E Simpson, [flag ship] Pilot, Mr Haffords
Iron clad *Catskill*-Cmder, Geo W Rodgers; Pilot, Mr Pe_ton
Iron clad *Montauk*-Cmder, D McN Fairfax; Pilot, Mr Pinckney, [colored]
Iron clad *Nahant*-Cmder, John Downes; Pilot, Mr Sofield
Iron clad *Wechawken*- Cmder E Colhoun; Pilot, Mr Jump
Iron clad *Patapsco*-Lt Cmder O S Badger; Pilot, Mr Be_l, [colored.]
Wooden vessels:
Vessel *Canandaigua*-Capt J F Green
Vessel *Mahaska*-Cmder J B Creighton
Vessel *Cimmarone*-Cmder A K Hughes
Vessel *Ottawa*-Lt Cmder W D Whiting
Vessel *Wissahickon*-Lt Cmder J C Davis
Vessel *Dai Ching*-Lt Cmder J C Chaplin
Vessel *Lodons*-Lt Cmder E Brodhead

WED AUG 26, 1863

Died: on Aug 21, Eliza Ariss, 2nd d/o B F & Eliza A Gallaher, aged 11 months & 13 days.

Orphans Crt of Wash Co, D C. Case of Susanna Borrows & Jas H Dyer, adms of Thos H Borrows, dec'd; settlement on Sept 19. -Z C Robbins, rg o/wills

Mr M Willian departed for Europe in the steamer *America* on Aug 15 to buy his fall & winter goods in Paris. Send orders to M Willian, 7 Cite Trevise, Paris, or leave them at 336 Pa av, Wash.

The greatest capture of men mentioned in modern histroy was made by Bonaparte at the battle of Austerlitz, where he took 20,000 prisoners. Gen Grant took 31,277 at Vicksburg. Napoleon's spoil at Austerlitz was 150 pieces of artl; Grant's at Vicksburg was 339.

Maj Geo L Stearns & Ast Surg John H Cochrane have been ordered to report to Gen Rosecrans' headqrtrs in Tenn, for the purpose of organizing the colored troops in that dept. They are expected to leave Phil today.

THU AUG 27, 1863

Died: on Jul 20th, near Camp Atcheson, Dakotah Terr, in his 35th yr, Geo Edmund Brent, y/s/o the late Robt Y Brent, of Montg Co, Md. [Ltr published in the St Paul Pioneer of the 14th instant: On the 21st the body of Geo E Brent, Capt's Clerk Co D, 1st Regt Minn Mounted Rangers, was brought back to camp, severely wounded by the discharge of his own gun; amongst his last words were *tell my mother*.] He was buried on the 2nd day after on a high knoll overlooking Lake Emily.

Crct Crt of PG Co, Md, where in Rich B B Chew & E C Digges, adms of D C Digges, dec'd; sale of *Green Hill*, 350 acs; adjoins the land of Mrs Mary J Kirkwood, Messrs Robt Clark, Jos Kennedy, & Dr John C Fairfax; with commodious dwlg hse. Trustee is authorized to settle the dower interest of Mrs Norah Digges. Mr Geo A Digges, living on the premises. -Richd B B Chew, trustee, Upper Marlboro, Md. [Property has been in possession of the Digges family since the first settlement of the country. Title is indisputable. Aug 31]

Orphans Crt of Wash Co, D C. Prsnl estate of Wm Johnson, late of the U S Army, dec'd. -Jas O Halloran, adm

The Rev J L Grover, chaplain of the Ohio Penitentary says: there are 68 of Morgan's ofcrs in the prison. They are locked up separately in cells at 7 o'clock in the evening, & unlocked about 7 in the morning. They enjoy the privilege of walking the hall thru the day, which is about 150 ft long & 12 ft wide. At 8 a m & 3 p m they are conducted to the common dining hall & have prison fare. Morgan had no belt filled with gold greenbacks & Confederate notes. His valuables amounted to $23 & a butter nut breastpin. Morgan & his men are all shaved & trimmed in accordance with the rule of the institution.

Loss of the U S brig *Bainbridge*: on her way from N Y to Port Royal on Fri last, when struck by a sudden squall & capsized off Capt Hatteras. Ofcrs:

Thos J Duyer, Act Mstr Commanding	John T Hughes, Slng Mstr
A G Stebbins, Ensign & Exec Ofcr	Edwin E Drake, Ensign
E H Allis, Ast Surg	Francis W Conrelyeu, Paymstr's Clerk
C C Walden, Ast Paymstr	S Horace Smith, Surg's Steward

Elias Smith, jr, Rolph Hotchkiss, Benj N Hamlin, & C P Moore, Mstrs' Mates

Montg Co, Md: a gang of bandits broke into the store of Mr Adler, at Germantown, in this county, & took $700 in cash & goods on hand. The same night, Mr Thos Rawlings, nearby, lost svr'l fine horses, supposed to be carried off by these marauders. In Poolesville on Sat night week, Messrs Jesse T & Darius M Higgins lost from $3,000 to $4,000. Messrs Pletchell & Heffner, lost some $800, & Mr Wm T Walter about $200.

FRI AUG 28, 1863

Mrd: on Aug 27, by Rev John C Smith, Chas T Dorsett to Miss Arabella De Maine, all of Wash City.

Died: on Aug 27, Chester A Colt, formerly of Wilkesbarre, Pa, aged 53 yrs. Funeral from his late residence, 383 12th st, on Sat.

Died: on Aug 18, at her residence in Winchester, Va, Mrs Sarah Jane Conrad, in the 52nd yr of her age. She was the w/o Dr Daniel Conrad, & only d/o the late Alfred H Powell, of Winchester, & sister of Cmdor L M Powell, U S Navy. Mrs Conrad was a mbr of the Episc Chr.

Died: at West Chester, on Aug 25, after a protracted illness, Eliz, w/o A Mehaffy, of Wash, D C.

Local Item. Barney McClusky, 1st Delaware Regt, was knocked down & fatally injured at the R R depot, when hit by the small engine regulating cars on the track, on Wed. The dec'd was a sgl man & hails from Wilmington, Dela.

Wm Harkness has been appt'd a Prof of Math in the U S Navy, vice Prof J S Hubbard, of Connecticut, dec'd. His appointment dates from Aug 24.

Rebel atrocities at Lawrence, Kansas on the 24th inst. The force of the rebels is estimated at 300. Eighteen out of 22 unarmed colored recruits, camped south of the town, were murdered in their tents. Messrs Dr Griswold, Trask, Baker, & Thorp were shot down in the yard of Dr G before the eyes of their families. Judge Carpenter was wounded in his yard, & fell, when his wife & sister threw themselves upon is body, begging for mercy, but to no avail. The fiends dismounted, stuck their pistols between the persons of his protectors & fired. A Miss Stone, d/o the proprietor of the City Htl, had a diamond ring stolen from her finger. Quantril obliged the man to restore it. In revenge for this, the ruffians came back & shot her father before the eyes of his well to hide & the bad air killed him. His son & Patrick Knafe lost their lives in trying to get the father out. The life of Dist Atty Tiggs was saved by the heroism of his wife. The w/o Shrf Brown, 3 successive times, put out the fire kindled to burn the hse. Her hsbnd had hidden under the floor. The books of the County & Dist Clerk were burnt, but those of the Reg of Deeds were in the safe, & supposed to be saved. Jas Eldridge & Jas Perrine gave the rebels all the money in the safe in their store, & were immediately shot down. There were 113 bodies, but the entire massacre will reach 150 killed. Up to this morning 128 bodies have been buried. [Aug 31st paper: also killed-Mr Dix; Mr Hampson shot-wound not considered fatal, his wife tried to interfere, but in vain. One of the first persons out was Col Beitzler. Mr Williamson & myself helped carry off the dead. I cannot describe the horrors. Written for the Bulletin by Mr Kempf, an Attache of the Prov Mrshl's ofc at Lawrence, whose escape from death was miraculous.]

SAT AUG 29, 1863
Election of the following pblc school teachers: [Wash]

S John Thomson	Mrs Emily Myers	Miss Mary E Ramsay
Miss Annie E Evans	Miss E B Billing	Miss Jane G Moss
Mrs M E Rodier	Miss Isabella F Acton	Miss Francis Elvans
Miss A K Lowe	Miss S P Abell	Mrs E W Clark
Miss Fannie E Hoover	Miss Jane Thomas	Miss Lucy E Moore
Miss H H Slater	Miss Mary A Tucker	Miss Kate Sanderson
Miss M J Mills	Miss Martha V Fletcher	Miss Cath Morphy
Miss Letitia B Allen	Miss Alice M McIntosh	Miss Emily E Tucker
Amelia M Kirk	Miss Maggie E Flenner	Miss Lucy B Davis
Emily Robinson	Miss Amanda Baird	Miss Jennie Ramsay
Miss Oceana A Walker	Miss Maria Y Davis	Miss Addie Thompson
Thos M Wilson	Miss Sallie E Rodier	Miss Hellen E Williams
Miss E H Boggs	Mr W W McCathran	Miss Josephine L Bird

Miss Mary A Hill	Miss Emma L Reed	Miss Geneva A Reed
Miss Mary Awkward	Miss Annie E Dawes	Miss Maria F Norris
Miss Eliza J Wheatley	Miss Annie M Adams	Miss Josephine C Lee
Miss Lizzie A Allen	Miss Mary A Lee	Miss Seville Davis
Mrs Alberta Bright	Mrs M E Martin	Miss Alice Adams
Mr John E Thompson	Miss M A Bowen	Miss Hattie Magee
Mrs Mgt A Amidon	Miss Sarah E Eckloff	Miss Annie M Bailey

The Pres had pardoned Mr Wm Duke, charged with divers offences committed by him against the U S & in aid of the rebels in the Commonwealth of Ky.

Died: on Aug 28, Notley Moreland, in his 57th yr. Funeral on Sat from his late residence near Tennalytown. Remains will be conveyed to Rock Crk Chr.

The widow of Adm Foote died in New Haven on Wed: age was 47 yrs. The Adm died 2 months ago.

The late Capt Geo W Rodgers, U S Navy, whose death, in front of Ft Sumter, was announced lately, was a s/o Cmdor Geo W Rodgers, of the war of 1812-15, & nephew of Cmdor John Rodgers, whose fame is associated with the early history of our navy. The mother of Capt Rodgers was Anne, sister of Cmdor O H Perry. Our subject was born in N Y: in his infancy his prnts mv'd to New London, Conn: appt'd Mdshpmn on Apr 30, 1836: he was younger bro of Capt C R P Rodgers: a still younger bro, Alex'r, known as *Sandy Perry*, was a youth when he graduated from West Point & rushed to the front with his command at the battle of Chapultepec, when shot thru his brain a most noble career was ended. Both noble bros were struck in the head.

MON AUG 31, 1863
Died: on Aug 24, at Elmwood, Chas Co, Md, Jas H Blake, aged 65 yrs. Native of D C, & raised in the city; emigrated to N C on arriving at manhood; settled near Charlotte, N C, where he resided for many yrs; returned in 1841 to Wash; remv'd to Chas Co about 2 years since.

Deaths reported to the Navy Dept for the week ending Aug 29, 1863:
Wm O'Connell, landsman, congestive fever, Aug 11, vessel U S S *Gennesee.*
Sam Brown, 1st cl boy, remittent fever, Aug 13, Mississippi Squadron.
Jas E Purnell, do, do, do, do.
Milton Myers, landsman, dysentery, Aug 14, do.
Ed H Peck, fireman, gunshot wound, Aug 1, Mt Vernon.
Jas Garland, seaman, drowned, Jul 4, U S steamer *Saranac.*
Jas McCormack, sgt marines, diarrhoea, Aug 21, vessel U S S *Brooklyn.*
Henry Sweeny, seaman, gunshot wound, Aug 21, Nav Battery, Charleston.
Jas Slawson, ord seaman, gunshot wound, Aug 21, do.
Henry Burrows, seaman, inflam of brain, Aug 24, Nav Hosp, Chelsea.

Seizure of property by the Mrshl of D C: hses of Craven Ashford, formerly a justice of the peace, but now in the South; lots 1 thru 12, of Geo S Houston, formerly in Congress from Alabama, & Gov Letcher, of Va, on Capitol Hill; lot with dwlg on E st, in the name of W H Thomas, now in Confederate army; lot with bldg at Vt av & K st, in the name of H H Lewis, of Va; half of lot near the Canal, in the name of Oscar R Hough, now in Richmond; lots near Balt Depot, etc, of David A Windsor. [See sale below.]

Gen John B Floyd died a few days ago at his residence in Abingdon, Va.

A little s/o Francis B Peabody, of Chicago, came to his death on Mon last when the family was visiting Portland. He was found in his crib with his body pushed thru the bars & was hanging by his head, lifeless.

For sale under the confiscation act: by the Mrshl of the Dist: 1-Two 2 story frame hses of Craven Ashford, formerly a justice of the peace, but now in the south. 2-Lots 1 to 12 inclusive, of Geo S Houston, formerly in Congress from Ala, & Gov Letcher, of Va, on Capitol Hill, now in possession of the Gov't. 3-Lot & 4 story dwlg on E st in the name of W H Thomas, now in the Confederate army; lot at Vt & K st with 2 story frame bldg, in the name of H H Lewis, of Va, formerly a clerk in one of the Depts; half a lot near the Canal in the name of Oscar B Hough, formerly one of the Nat'l Rifles, & now with the provost mrshl's ofc in Richmond. 4-Lot near the Balt Depot, svr'l on S Capt st, near N st, now used as a brick yard, in the name of David A Windsor.

The Persia brings news of the death of Lord Clyde, English General, known by his simple name of Colin Campbell. He was born in Glasgow & entered the English army in 1808.

Wash Corp: 1-Cmte of Claims: asked to be discharged from the further consideration of the bill for the relief of J W Barnaclo: which was ordered. 2-Act to organize a Paid Fire Dept was postponed.

Among the slain in Gen Sibley's expedition against the Indians was John Beemer, a wealthy Englishman, a grad of Oxford, & former ofcr on the staff of Lord Raglan. He had come to England on a buffalo hunt, & took a nominal position on Gen Sibley's staff to gratify his taste of adventure. He was caught in ambuscade, & shot down with iron headed arrows, by the savages. He leaves a splendid yacht & a large library in N Y.

Late information from Vicksburg confirms the death of Confederate Gen Pemberton. He was shot by Texan sldrs.

Gen G R Paul, who was severely wounded at Gettysburg, has arrived in Wash City & is stopping at Mrs Andrews', 335 I st. It is feared that the sight of the Gen will be entirely destroyed by the wound in his eyes.

TUE SEP 1, 1863
Died: on Aug 31, aged 30 years & 6 mos, Francis Marion, 3rd s/o B O & Sarah A Shekell. Funeral from their residence, 366 D st, Wed.

St Louis Democrat says that Gen Pemberton was shot by a Texan ofcr while on his way to Montg, Ala. He was shot & killed at Selma, Ala. [Recent]

In the 19th ward of N Y three bros & a bro-in-law were drafted; another bro is in the naval svc, & another, Col N L Farnham, has given his life to his country. Of the 4 drafted, 2 have served 3 times each with the 7th Regt in the field.

Wash Corp: 1-Act for relief of Curtis & Dearing: to be paid $175 for case fitted up in the cmte room adjoining Cncl Chamber. 2-Relief of Wm Fletcher & others: $1,000 for balance due him in the improvement of 9th st west. 3-Relief of G W G Esslin: sum of $26.88 for repair of alleys in ward 4.

Presentation of a sword, saddle, harness, & horse to Maj Gen John Sedgwick, commanding 6th Army Corps, by ofcrs of the 2nd div of the 2nd Corps, who served under him, was held at Warrenton on Wed last. Also present were Gen Meade, Gen Warren, Gen Hunt, Gen Humphreys, & Gen Webb. Presentation speech was made by Capt Corkmill.

Among the drafted men in Northumberland Co, Pa, are 4 clergymen: Revs Creighton, of Su_bury; Walmpole, of Eleysburg; Riley, of Northumberland, & Spreecher, of Milton.

WED SEP 2, 1863
Died: on Aug 25, at his residence in Calvert Co, Md, after a painful illness of some weeks, Judge Thos H Wilkinson, in his 84th yr.

Died: on Sep 1, J Y Mason Jones, aged 14 yrs, s/o the late Geo H Jones. Funeral from the residence of his mother, 318 N Y av, today.

Died: at *Farmer's Repose*, Loudoun Co, Va, on Aug 21, of putrid sore throat, Johnnie Sprigg, aged 10 yrs, only s/o John C & the late Martha Sprigg, all of Wash City.

Private sale of *NorthWest Branch*, near Colesville, Montg Co, Md, 100 acs; adjoins the property of Elbert Shaw, John T Baker, & Alpheus Middleton. -Josephine Dawes. -Jos Fawcett, agent, Colesville, Montg Co, Md.

Supreme Crt of D C, in Equity #54. Richd Lay, exc of Thos Carbery, vs Jas L Carbery & Jos C Ives & Cora M, his wife. Rg-Jos C Ives & wife conveyed to Jas L Carbery part of sq 106 in Wash City; to secure to the late Thos Carbery $4,340 by his 2 notes; that $3,569.92 is still due; dfndnts have ceased to reside in this district; appt of a new trustee. -R J Meigs, clerk

Orphans Crt of Wash Co, D C. 1-Case of Henry S Davis, adm of Edmund French, dec'd; settlement on Sep 26. -Z C Robins, rg o/wills 2-Prsnl estate of Susan Worthington, late of Wash Co, dec'd.
-Presly W Dorsey, exc 3-Prsnl estate of Sam Hoover, late of Wash Co, dec'd. -Lydia A Hoover, admx

Gonzaga College, F st, between 9th & 10th sts, will resume on Sep 7. -B F Wiget, S J, Dir

Pecularities of the draft: in South Hanover twnshp, Dauphin Co, Pa, the draft struck 3 men out of 27 drawn, named as follows: Christopher B Landis, Christian C Landis, & Christian F Landis. Five pairs of bros were drafted at Pottstown, Pa, out of the 46 drawn. Of the bachelors in town, 3, all of them over 35 years of age, were drawn from the box in succession.

THU SEP 3, 1863
1863 graduating class at the Military Academy at West Point:
John R Meigs, at large, assigned to Corps of Eng

Peter S Michie, Ohio	John R McGuines, Ohio
Jas D Rabb, Ky	Geo W McKee, at lge
Wm J Troining, Ind	Frank H Phipps, Pa
Wm R King, N Y	Jas W Reilly, Pa
W H H Benyaurd, Pa	Josiah H V Field, at lge
Chas W Howell, Ind	Chas F Rockwell, Vt
Aza H Holgate, Ohio	Wm S Beebe, at lge

Thos Ward, at lge
Geo D Ramsey, jr, at lge
Henry C Dodge, N Y
John D Burlte, Pa
Robt Catlin, Wash

Chas H Lester, Conn
Kenelm Robbins, Mass
Jas M Sanne, N J
Jas R Reid, N Y
Jacob H Counselman, Md

Died: on Sep 2, Mrs Julia Crawford Gordon, w/o Chas Gordon. Funeral from her late residence, 265 I st, Fri.

Fire destroyed the soap & tallow establishment of Mr W L Dawson, at the corner of Water & Frederick sts, Gtwn, D C, on Sep 2. Loss about $8,000, insurance amount: $1,500.

The Balt American states that Alfred Spates, Pres of the C & O Canal Co, has been arrested & imprisoned at Ft McHenry. His charges are numerous: most refer to his alleged interviews with Gen Lee & Gen Ewell during the late campaign in Md & Pa. [Sep 21st paper: Mr Spates released on bail-$10,000; Mr Brown-$5,000. They are to report to Gen Morris at the Fort whenever ordered to do so.]

Annual session of St Mary's Academy, Chas Co, Md, will commence first Mon in Sept. Address Mrs Danl Major, at St Mary's, Bryantown, Chas Co, Md.

FRI SEP 4, 1863
Died: on Sep 3, of diptheria, Francis Harper, in the 32nd yr of his age. Funeral from his late residence, 2nd & Lingan sts, Gtwn, this morning. Dec'd was born in county Wexford, Ire, but for the last 15 years a resident of this District.

Miss N S Prout will open a Select School for Girls, on the first Mon in Sept, at 444 D st.

Fred'k [Md] Exam: says on Wed of last week svr'l ctzns attacked a party of 7 guerrillas, suspected of stealing horses, on Catoctin mntn. Skirmish ensued, resulting in the capture of 4 of them, with their horses. Prisoners gave their name as: John C Lee, plumber; Jas Clayton, John Syington, & Geo E Barret, all hailing from Balt. They're in Fred'k City jail to await the action of the grand jury.

The Westminster [Md] Democrat states that 15 or 20 ladies of that town were arrested last week by order of Lt Boarman, military provost mrshl, charged with disloyalty & feeding the Confederates during Gen Lee's late invasion. They were, however, discharged on taking the oath of allegiance.

We understand that Rev E W Syle has resigned the rectorship of Trinity Chr, in Wash City. Resignation to take effect the 10th proximo.

SAT SEP 5, 1863
Obit-Mr Robt C Boggs, aged 70 years & 10 days, died at his residence Cave Spring, in Fayette Co, Ky, on Aug 18. He was born, lived & died on the farm upon which his father settled on the 10th day of Feb, 1784. He never mrd: devoted to a maiden sister, who alone remains of a large family of chldrn.

Died: at Mobile, on Aug 10, Richd L Mackall, late of Gtwn, D C, aged 51 yrs.

Died: on Sep 2, J Marion Sims Gallaher, aged 1 yr & 16 days, 5th d/o Robt H & Harriet E P Gallaher, of N Y, & grand-dght of John S Gallaher, of Wash.

Saratoga, Sep 3. Hon Greene C Bronson died here this evening, sick only a few days.

Leavenworth, Sep 3. From Albuquerque [New Mexico] papers received here, we learn that on Jul 28, Col Kit Carson, with part of the 1st New Mexican Regt, had a fight with the Navajoe Indians beyond Fort Canby. The Indians were defeated, with the loss of 13 killed, 20 wounded, & many prisoners.

Brig Gen St Geo Cooke, U S Army, summoned before the Retiring Brd, has been examined & found fit for active svc. Therefore he has not been retired.

Crt-martial of Capt Howland was concluded today. Accused admitted his guilt: leaving with the money & deserting to Canada. Sentence is not known.

MON SEP 7, 1863

Died: in Wash City, on Sep 5, of typhoid fever, John E Leach, formerly of St Mary's Co, Md, aged 35 yrs. Funeral on Mon at the Chr of St Aloysius.

Died: on Sep 5, aged 9 months & 2 days, Francis Xavier Nelville, infant c/o Francis & Mgt McNerhany.

Deaths reported to the Navy Dept for the week ending Sep 5, 1863:
John Howard, gunners' mate, enlargement of heart, Aug 25, Nav Hosp, N Y.
Wm Reddick, contraband, consumption, Aug 28, Nav Hosp, Norfolk.
Fred Roberts, landsman, chronic diarrhoea, Aug 18, Nav Hosp, Memphis.
John Newbern, seaman, remit fever, Aug 19, do.
Rd Gustin, contraband, diarrhoea, Aug 19, do.
Chs Driscoll, seaman, remit fever, Aug 22, do.
W H Johnson, seaman, remit fever, Aug 23, do.
Pat Hamilton, ord seaman, gunshot, Jul 7, vessel U S S *Monongahela*.
John Burns, 2nd cl boy, drowned, Jul 10, do.
Wm Hutton, marine, hydrothorax, Jun 29, do.
John J Jones, landsman, consumption, Aug 27, vessel U S S *Red Rover*.
Jas Drake, blank, blank, Aug 24, do.
John Bishop, seaman, gunshot, Jul 20, Ft Henry.
Pat Doran, do, do, do, do.
Thos McHenry, actg Ast Surg, remit fever, Aug 18, Key West.
Fred M Nixon, marine, gunshot, Aug 11, vessel Vessel U S S *Miami*
Geo Carathorne, seaman, intermittent fever, Aug 9, do.
Chas Gardener, ord seaman, dysentery, Aug 5, New London.
John Haley, pensioner, debility, Aug 30, Nav Asylum.
Peter J Smith, coal heaver, pneumonia, Aug 2, Kinso.
Alonzo Bennett, ord seaman, pertonitis, Jul 28, vessel U S S *Florida*.
Ezekiel Cooper, landsman, consumption, Sep 2, Nav Asylum.
Hy Cook, seaman, typhoid fever, Aug 15, vessel U S S *Colorado*.
Wm Robertson, Cpl marine, typhoid fever, Aug 16, vessel U S S *Oneida*.
Andrew K Snyder, landsman, gunshot, Jun 4, vessel U S S *Roebuck*.
Jas Falger, actg mstr, gunshot, Apr 15, do.
Andrew Langston, landsman, drowned, Aug 3, do.
Owen Collins, landsman, typhoid fever, Jun 1, vessel U S S *Beauregard*.
John K Flanders, squad printer, typhoid fever, Aug 30, vessel U S S *Philadelphia*.
Jefferson Davis, 2nd cl fireman, aseites, Jul 31, Mississippi Squadron.

J Clark, 1st cl boy, diarrhoea, Aug 24, do.
Robt Keyes, pilot, dysentery, Jul 30, do.
Michl F Hart, seaman, remit fever, Jul 27, do.
January Wardon, 1st cl boy, diarrhoea, Jul 27, do.
Lewis Haskins, do, do, Jun 25, do.
Wm Palxer, coxswain, wounds, Aug 29, vessel U S S *Wabash*.

Orphans Crt of Wash Co, D C. 1-Case of John M Jewell & Jane Boulanger, adms of Jos Boulanger, dec'd; settlement on Sep 27. -Z C Robbins, rg o/wills 2-Prsnl estate of Nicholas Tastet, late of Wash City, dec'd. -Edwin Tastet, adm

Naval Hero: Lt Wm Crowninshield, exc ofcr of the ship *Niphon*, & s/o the late Capt Jacob Crowninshield, of the Navy, was sent on board the British steamer *Hebe*, in Wilmington harbor, on the 18th, with instructions to get her off or set her on fire. Heavy seas & the boat was swamped. Capt Breck, of the *Niphon*, sent another boat, but this was driven on shore & the crew captured. The only remaining boat got nearer, & 4 men & 1 ofcr succeeded getting into her. When Lt Crowninshield saw all the boats were lost, & no chance for him, in a rapid fire from riflemen & a battery of large guns, he set fire to the prize. He wore his father's sword, & the ofcrs of the *Niphon* saw him throw this overboard, so that the rebels should not get it. He was seen jumping into the surf & captured by the rebels. The Capt lost 12 seamen & 3 ofcrs. -N Y Com Adv

TUE SEP 8, 1863

Obit-Wm Tyson died on Sep 6, at *Alnwick*, PG Co, Md; formerly a merchant of Balt, Md, in later years a resident of Wash, but at the time of his death a ctzn of PG Co, Md. At age 81 years death closed a full life. Funeral today.

Navy Dept has received information of the killing, at Natchez, on Aug 23, of Actg Mstr R A Turner, commanding U S steamer *Curlew*, by Maj McKee, provost mrshl of that city. Commission to investigate. [See below.]

Naval ofcr killed by a Provost Mrshl: Navy Dept received the information of the killing at Natchez, on Aug 23, of Actg Mstr R A Turner, commanding U S steamer *Curlew*, by Maj McKee, provost mrshl of that city. A commission to investigate the matter relieved the marshal of all blame.

Capt Bird & Lt Wilson, of Co M, 14th Pa Cavalry, are reported to have been badly wounded in the late fight in Greenbrier Co, Va, & are still missing. Lts Jackson, McNutt, & Shoop are also wounded. Capt Pollock, formerly a lawyer of Pittsburg, is reported missing. Capt Ewing, of Ewing's Btry, & Maj McNally, 2nd Va Regt, were badly wounded. Capt McNally had both legs torn off, & is not expected to recover. Capt Ewing was seriously if not fatally injured in the abdomen. Lt French, Co E, 2nd Va, lost both his arms.

WED SEP 9, 1863

Americans registered at Gun's American Agency, 17 Charlotte st, Bedford sq, London, for the week ending Aug 22, 1863:

E C Litchfield & family, N Y	L A Bigelow, Boston
Edw H House, N Y	G A Edly, St Louis, Mo
Capt W P Downer, N Y	E E Fairfax Williamson, Va
Geo P Bangs, Boston	Saml H Wilcox, Ithaca, N Y
Mortimer Porter & dghts, N Y	E Whitin, Whitinsville, Mass
Rufus Choate, Boston	J R Maltby, Maine

Jas Dennian, Calif
C Sargent, Dorchester, Mass
C A Maltby, Northampton, Mass
Gordon Hall, Northampton, Mass
H C Yates, Syracuse, N Y
S H Moseley, N Y
Chas H Matthews, N Y

C J Bradley, Providence, R I
Wm L Mattson, Hartford, Conn
W S Smith, N Y
Geo B English, N Y
H C White, Hartford, Conn
H C White, jr, Hartford, Conn
Rev J J Kelley, N Y

Died: on Sep 7, Mrs Mary McClelland, widow of the late John McClelland, in the 80th yr of her age. Funeral from her late residence on N Y av between 13 & 14th, today.

Died: near Middleton, Md, on Sep 6, Henrietta C Alexander, w/o Geo W Alexander, of Wash, aged about 30 yrs.

Orphans Crt of Wash Co, D C. 1-Prsnl estate of Wm Johnson, late of the U S Army, dec'd. -Jas O. Halloran, adm. 2-Case of Matthias Snyder, adm of John Snyder, dec'd; settlement on Sep 29. -Z C Robbins, rg o/wills 3-Prsnl estate of Eliz Orme, late of Wash City, dec'd. -Richd H Clark, exc

The first number of the Army & Navy Jrnl appeared Aug 29th. It's proprietor is Capt Church, lately of Gen Casey's staff, & its publisher is D Van Nostrand, 192 Broadway.

Wash Corp: 1-Act for the relief of Michl Murphy: fine imposed by Justice Clayton on Oct 30, 1862, is remitted. Approved, Sep 7, 1863

Mary B Sumner has presented at the ofc of the Comptroller of N Y C a large claim for the loss of prsnl property, furn, clothing, etc, the contents of her boarding hse, at #s 1,188, 1,190, & 1,192 Broadway, which was destroyed by the mob last month. The claim is for $56,553.90.

On the occasion of the August fete Louis Napoleon granted pardons to 1,396 convicts of different categories.

THU SEP 10, 1863

Died: on Sep 8, Caroline Newton, 2nd d/o John P & Caroline S C Boss, in her 6th yr. Funeral from their residence, N Y av between 4th & 5th sts, today.

Mrs David H Burr will resume her classes for young ladies in French & English, at her residence, 364 C st, Wash, D C.

Prof J C Fill has resumed his instruction on the organ, melodon, pianoforte & guitar. Apply at the music establishment of John R Ellis, 306 Pa av, Wash, D C.

Education in English, French & music is offered by Miss E R Nicholls. Apply at the residence of her brother, 27 Indiana av, Wash, D C.

Orphans Crt of Wash Co, D C. Case of Mrs Mgt A Sinon, admx of John Sinon, dec'd; settlement on Oct 3. -Z C Robbins, rg o/wills [w a]

Trustee's sale of rl est, decree of Crct Crt for PG Co, Md; John D Brown, cmplnt, & John Martin & Mary E Martin, his wife, dfndnts. Rg-deed dtd May 12, 1858, & by written authority from the said John D Brown as assignee of Jas M Williams & Henry A Williams, for use of the latter. Public sale of *Sunny Side, Italian Hill,* & part of *Oxen Hill Manor,* 102+ acs, being the same land conveyed by Henry A Williams & Jas M Williams & wife to said John Martin on May 12, 1858. -Fendall Marbury, trustee

Mr Ellis Brown, of Wolf township, Lycoming Co, Pa, has lost 2 sons in the present war. 3 are now serving in the svc, & a 6th was drafted on Sat last.

FRI SEP 11, 1863
Died: on Sep 10, Rose Florence, infant d/o Saml C & Mary E Middleton, aged 17 months & 8 days. Funeral today.

Furniture & Hsekeeping Articles: for sale: Bontz & Griffith, 369 7th st, between I & K sts, Wash. [Ad]

Sale on Wed of confiscated property seized by the Gov't under the confiscation act. Purchasers were:

Capt H B Todd	Wm James	A Lloyd
J H Stewart	Danl E Sowers	Pat Manley
John Van Riswick	Ephraim Wheeler	S E Daly
A R Shepherd	Alf Hall	J B Williamson
C H Lane	Wm Rutherford	Wm A Malone

The Rev J E Cookman, pastor of the Meth Episc Chr at Harburg, N Y, who was lately conscripted, has determined to pack his knapsack & take the field. He is the s/o the late, well known Rev Geo Cookman, who was chaplain to Congress, & who was a passenger in the ill-fated steamer *President.*

SAT SEP 12, 1863
Balt, Md, Sep 11. B H Richardson & his son, Frank A Richardson, & Stephen J Joyce, proprietors & editors of the Balt Rpblcn, were arrested & directed to be sent South for venting their disloyalty by publishing a piece of poetry entitiled *The Southern Cross.*

Battle of Rocky Gap. Huttonsville, Va, Aug 30, 1863. Gen Averill made the following report to Gen Kelley of his recent expedition in Western Va. We drove Gen Jackson out of Pocahontas: fought superior force under command of Maj Gen Sam Jones & Col Patten, at Rocky Gap. Our loss is over 100 ofcrs & men killed & wounded, among whom are Capt Paul & Baron Von Keonig, Aide-de-Camp, killed while leading an assault; & Maj McNally, of the 2nd Va, & Capt Ewing, of the artl, dangerously wounded. One Parrott gun burst the first day, & becoming worthless, was abandoned. We brought in over 30 prisoners, including a Maj & 2 or 3 Lts; also, a large number of cattle, horses, etc. Your Aide-de-Camp, Lt J R Meigs, who accompanied me, is safe. -Wm W Averill, Brig Gen

English & Classical School: corner 20th st & Pa ave: Third annual session will begin Sep 1, 1863. -R W Lowrie, principal

Harper's Monthly Magazine for Sept for sale at Shillington's Bkstore, Odeon Bldg, 4½ st & Pa ave.

Wm B Faxon, Chief clerk of the Navy Dept, has returned to Wash City & resumed his official duties.

The value of the sovereigns stolen from John Curry, & a portion of which was found in a trunk in the hse of detective C V Hogan, amounted to $800. In justice to Mr Hogan the trunk in which the money was found did not belong to him, but to a servant woman in his employ named Ann Moran. Ann, it appears, is the affianced of Wm O'Brien, who was arrested for having one of the sovereigns in his possession. O'Brien is held to answer the charge: Ann has been released.

Chas Cole who was arrested by order of Capt Johnson, on charge of conniving with Chas Simmons, a substitute near the Circle, to escape, has been released, the charge not being substantiated. Cole is a substitute himself, & assigned to a responsible position at the camp. -Star

MON SEP 14, 1863

Died: in Wash City, on Sep 13, Eliz Jane, w/o Anthony Buchly, in the 30th yr of her age. Funeral on Tue from the residence of her hsbnd, 303 Pa av; congregation of Grace Chr, Rev Alfred Holmead, Rector, are invited.

Died: in Wash City, on Sep 13, the infant d/o Geo H & Amanda E King, aged 13 months. Funeral on Tue from their residence, 248 8th st.

PG Co, Md, trustee's sale of the remaining rl estate of which Zachariah B Beall died seized & possessed, 1,239 acs; of these lands, 265 acs have been assigned as the widow's dower, & in this portion the reversion only will be disposed of. -C C Magruder, Edw W Belt, trustees

Orphans Crt of Wash Co, D C. Case of John L Edwards, adm of Sarah C Crawford, dec'd; settlement on Oct 6. -Z C Robbins, rg o/wills

Deaths reported to the Navy Dept for the week ending Sep 12, 1863:
Jno Welsey, 3rd cl boy, acrofula, Aug 24, Nav Hosp, Memphis.
Geo S West, actg ensign, congestion of the lungs, Aug 9, U S steamer *Ratler*.
Wm McKinley, actg ensign, drowned, Aug 14, Mississippi Squadron.
Asa D Thomas, ord seaman, compression of the brain, Sep 5, Rec Ship N Y.
Jas Drake, contraban, pneumonia, Aug 24, Mississippi Squadron
Michl Foy, pensioner, debility, Sep 8, Nav Asylum, Phil.
Phil Birn, seamen's cook, consumption, Apr 27, Mississippi Squadron.
Chs Rommel, fireman, intermittent fever, Aug 11, Valley City.
John Fairbanks, seaman, intermittent fever, Aug 10, do.
Edw Monlack, seaman, remittent fever, Aug 6, vessel *Choctaw*.
Wm Hardicker, landsman, inter fever, Jul 29, do.
Algernon Stout, landsman, diarrhea acute, Jul 13, do.
Thos J Carroll, landsman, inter fever, Jul 21, do.

Judge John C Underwood, of West Va, was captured on Fri by rebel guerrillas near his former residence at Occoquan. He is to be sent to Richmond.

Wash Corp: 1-Cmte of Claims: asked to be discharged from further consideration of the ptn of John H Zile for the remission of a fine. 2-Bill for relief of Wm Boyd: referred to the Cmte on Health.

Detroit, Sep 3: first steamboat to the Saut Ste Marie. Voyage of the steamboat *Henry Clay*, Capt W Norton, visiting Sant Ste Marie in 1827, copied from a diary kept by Gen John A

Granger, of Canandaigua, N Y. Arrived on Jun 18, 1827 at Fort Brady: fort was built 2 years ago: stationed there are 4 companies of the 2nd Regt of Infty, with their ofcrs. Among the cabin passengers: Gov Lewis Cass & his suite, Maj Gen Scott & his aide, Brig Gen Brady, U S A, Col Thos L McKenney, Col DeGarmo Jones, Maj Robt Forsyth, Augustus S Porter, Henry R Schoolcraft, John A Granger, etc.

Americans registered at Gun's American Agency, 17 Charlotte st, Bedford Sq, London, for the week ending Aug 29, 1863

J Gran, N Y	H P Ammidowa, Boston
A Rawlings, N Y	E H House, N Y
Danl Holman, N Y	Capt Downer, N Y
Wm Cornell Jewett, U S	Thos Butler Guan, N Y
Geo N Saunders, Va	Mrs S H Porter, Phil
Col Chas Lamar, Ga	E Rawstorne, R I
Lionel J Noah, N Y	T H Blythe, San Francisco
Geo B Farnam, Chicago	Geo W Martin, Tenn
Geo Buckham, N Y	Hammatt Billings, Boston

TUE SEP 15, 1863
Died: in Wash City, on Sep 13, Willie, aged 3 years & 3 mos, only s/o Jas & Eliza Crown. Funeral from their residence on 14th st, between P & Q, today.

Died: in Cincinnati., on Sep 7, of apoplexy, Wm, eldest s/o the late Thos Adams, of Wash.

Mr Saml Sterritt, of Balt, Md, has been convicted by crt martial of holding treasonable correspondence with the enemy. He was sentenced to Ft Warren during the continuance of the war.

St Matthew's Institute for Boys, 19th st, between G & H sts, classes resume on Sep 1. -Chas J White, D D: 336 H st, near 15th.

WED SEP 16, 1863
Died: on Sep 12, Nellie, infant d/o S M & Maria E Golden, aged 8 months & 20 days.

Application made for duplicate of lost certificate #95, for $200 of Stock of the Corp of Wash, in the name of Iphigenie de Senhaux.

Orphans Crt of Wash Co, D C. 1-Prsnl estate of Mary E C Edwards, late of Wash Co, dec'd. -John L Edwards, exc. 2-Case of John W DeKrafft, adm of Mary E De Krafft, formerly Barney, dec'd; settlement on Oct 10. -Z C Robbins, rg o/wills

Fourth Presby Chr: on Sun last the Rev John C Smith, D D, the Pastor, preached a sermon on the progress of the last 24 yrs. It was founded in 1827, the late Rev J N Danforth being its first Pastor. In 2 or 3 years he was called to another labor, & was succeeded by the Rev Mason Noble, who removed to N Y C in the summer of 1839, & on Sep 10 following Dr Smith, who for svr'l years previously had filled one of the pulpits in Gtwn, was called to the Fourth Chr. On its records were 337 communicants, & of this number 32 have died during the last 24 yrs, & only 46 remain on the roll of the church. 846 communicants have been added to the church, of these 88 have died, making the whole number of deaths in 24 years to be 120. The Pastor has married 452 couples & baptized 607 persons, including infants & adults.

43

John M Stanley, of Washington, *the Indian Painter*, as he is often called, has a new production of a picture representing the Revelation of the Conspiracy of Pontiac by an Indian girl, in 1763.

THU SEP 17, 1863
Died: in Wash City, on Sep 15, Edwin Page Bergman, eldest s/o Lambert & Caroline P Bergman, aged 14 years & 7 months. Funeral from their residence, 404 8th st, this day.

Supreme Crt of D C, in Equity #1242. Mgt Lyons, admx of Eliz Braden, against Oliver E P Hazzard, Agnes A Hazzard, & Saml Chilton. Above named & the trustee are to meet at City Hall, Wash, D C, on Oct 2, for statement of the trustee's account. -W Redin, auditor

Supreme Crt of D C, in Equity. Zadoc W McKnew vs J McLean Hanson, *Spencer M Ball, *Charlotte C Ball, *Caroline E Englebrecht, *Kate Ball, *Chas Ball, *John T Ball, Eli Duvall, jr, & Alice C, his wife. Rg-On Nov 26, 1856, Hanson made a deed conveying lots 11, 12, & 13, in sq 960, Wash City, to Lewellyn Ball, in trust. L Ball died May 16, 1862, without executing said trust. The said lots descended to the dfndnts [minus J McLean Hanson]. Debt has never been pd. *Reside out of D C & cannot be found. -R J Meigs, clerk

Partnership between Herman Richter & Henry F Schonborn, Brewery & Brewing business, is dissolved by mutual consent. The Restaurant at 552 7th st will be continued by Henry F Schonborn; the Brewery will be continued by Herman Richter.

Crct Crt of PG Co, Md-Henry Addison, next friend of Ella Beall vs Ella Beall, Martha E Beall, & others. Public sale of *Largo*, PG Co, Md, 357½ acs, rl estate & residence of the late Zachariah B Beall; adjoins the property of Zachariah Berry, sr, & Washington J Beall. -Hugh Caperton, trustee

FRI SEP 18, 1863
Mrd: at Gtwn, on Sep 17, by Rev Wm A Harris, Rev Geo E Post, M D, of N Y, to Sallie, d/o Robt Read, of Gtwn.

Pvt sale of farm, 225 acs, south extremity of Chas Co, Md, with good dwlg hse. -S B Boarman, at the Bank of Washington.

Ex-Sen Richd Brodhead died at Easton Pa, on Sep 17.

Gtwn College resumed on Sep 11: upwards of a 100 students have entered for the year 1863-64. Fr Early, Pres of the College for the last 6 yrs: Fr Janalik presides over the school of philosophy, & Fr Stonestreet, lately returned from Europe, professes the class of rhetoric. Fr Curley, a scientific scholar is a mbr of the corps of professors.

Navy Dept has received a report of the casualties incurred by the attack on Ft Sumter. Of the vessel *Ironsides* one was taken prisoner: Ensign B H Porter
Of the vessel *Powhatan*, 2 killed, 3 wounded, & 33 missing, including marines
Of the vessel *Housatonic*, 17 missing, including Lt Edwin T Brower & 3rd Ast Engr J M Harmany
Of the vessel *Wissahickon*, 10 missing. Lt Cmder Williams & Actg Ensign E G Dayton, ex-ofcr of this vessel, are also reportd missing.
Of the vessel *Sodona*, 1 wounded & 9 missing
Of the Marine Btln, 1 wounded & 30 missing, including 2nd Lt R L Meade.

Peter J Bellinger, a merchant of Milwaukee, a mbr of the firm of A B Hewitt & Co, of that city, was killed in an affray with svr'l sldrs a few days since, in Juneau Co, Wisc. Mr Bellinger was conversing on political matters in a store with Dr Secor, & sldrs took offence at his remarks. Mr B was seized & beaten to death in the most horrible manner.

Sec of War relieves Herman Haupt from further duty in the War Dept as superintendent of military railroads. He is to turn over the books, papers, & all other property under his control belonging to the U S to Col D C McCallum.

For rent or sale: with possession on Oct 1, a large 4 story dwlg hse, 388, on north side of C st, between 3rd & 4½ sts west. Apply to Jas Towles, property agent, 490 H st north.

North German Lloyd: steam between N Y & Bremen, via Southampton. The Screw Steamers of the North German Lloyd.
1-steamer *Bremen*, Capt C Meyer   3-steamer *Hansa*, Capt H J Von Santem
2-*N Y*, Capt G Wenkee   4-steamer *America*, Capt H Wessels
From N Y to Bremen, London, Havre, & Southampton. First cabin, $105. Second cabin, $62.50 Steerage, $27.50. From Bremen to N Y. First Cabin, $112.50 Second cabin, $75. Steerage, $45.
Passage payable in gold or its equivalent in currenty. Apply to Oelrichs & Co. 68 Broad st, N Y.

Proposals for horses: Cavalry Bureau, Ofc of Chief Q M, Wash-Aug 15, 1863. Address proposals to: C G Sawtelle, Lt Col & C Q M Cavalry Bureau.

SAT SEP 19, 1863
Late homicide, Wash D C. The killing of Lt Jas M Brannin, of Capt Johnson's military detective corps, by policeman Chas W Thompson, on Sep 9. Justice Giberson says this is a case of homicide in self-defence; is sending this case to our next Criml Crt for action of the Grand Jury of Wash Co.

Recent rebel promotions in the army:
Col H W Allen, of La, to Brig Gen, Aug 19
Col C A Battle, of Ala, to Brig Gen, Aug 20
Col W A Quarles, of Tenn, to Brig Gen, Aug 25
Col Goode Bryan, of Ga, & Col W W Kirkland, of N C, to Brig Gens, Aug 29
Col Robt D Johnson, of N C, to Brig Gen, Sep 1
Col M C Butler, of S C, & Col Williams C Wickham, of Va, to Brig Gens of Cavalry, Sep 1.

Died: in Wash City, after a brief illness, Mary Jane, w/o Clifford Evans, in the 29th yr of her age. Funeral on Sun.

Deaths in Winchester, Va, during the past yr: David Barton, lawyer, 2 sons & a son-in-law; Dr Robt T Baldwin, physician; Wm Walters, merchant; John Anderson, sldr of 1812; Jas Bowles, farmer; Powell Conrad, lawyer, s/o Robt Y Conrad; Saml Trenary's wife & dght; a d/o Jos Neale; a d/o Geo Kramer; the wife of Dr Daniel Conrad. Great suffers by the rebellion, subjected, as they have been, to the lawlessness of the sldrs of both armies.

Gen Sam Houston died at his residence in Huntersville, Texas, on Jul 25, age 70 yrs.

MON SEP 21, 1863

Died: on Sep 20, Grace W Clark, aged 5 yrs, 5 months & 18 days, eldest d/o Dr J C R Clark & Julia R Clark. Funeral at 555 13th st, this day.

Deaths reported to the Navy Dept for the week ending Sep 19, 1863:
Chas Clinton, seaman, chronic diarrhoea, Sep 17, Mississippi Squadron.
Jas Lo_ker, landsman, chronic diarrhoea, Aug 31, do.
Jas Smith, seaman, chronic diarrhoea, Sep 5, do.
Dennis Donovan, landsman, peutonitis, Jun 13, U S steamer *Onward*.
Horatio J Richards, seaman, pneumonia, Sep 8, Nav Hosp, N Y.
Chas Webster, q m, scurvy, Sep 10, do.
Jas McMahon, coal heaver, heart disease, Aug 28, U S steamer *Bienville*.
Thos J Jones, landsman, tonsilitis, Aug 27, do.
Jacob Kock, marine, yellow fever, Aug 31, U S steamer *Colorado*.
Wallace E Had, paymstr's clerk, remittent fever, Aug 24, do.
Chas S Winters, marine, yellow fever, Aug 3, do.
Jas H Hartshorn, actg ensign, congestive fever, Aug 18, U S steamer *Katahdin*.
Jas Callahan, ord seaman, bronchitis, Sep 11, Nav Hosp, N Y.
Peter Ball, landsman, typhoid fever, Sep 20, Nav Hosp, Wash.
Wm C Santon, ord seaman, dysentery, Sep 2, U S steamer *San Jacinto*
Andrew Sharp, landsman, heart disease, Sep 10, Nav Hosp, Plymouth, N C.
Robt McCleery, chief engr, exhaustion, Sep 15, Phil.

Supreme Crt of D C, in Chancery, #1745. John Meem, wife, & others, vs Jas Goszler & others. Ratify sale of the residence of the late Geo A Goszler, on Bridge st, Gtwn, to Theodore F Bougher, as trustee for Mrs Mary A Walker, for $1,665. -J Carter Marbury, trustee

Orphans Crt of Wash Co, D C. Prsnl estate of Dr John M Snyder, late of Gtwn, in county aforesaid, dec'd. -Sophia C Snyder, admx

Supreme Crt of D C. Richd W Bryant & others vs Wm P Dement & others. Ratify sale of lot 21 in reservation 11, Wash City, to John H Semmes, for $2,750; & lot 12 in same, to Chas H Lane, for $1,450. -J Carter Marbury, trust

Phil, Jul 15, 1863. Invite to Rear Admr S F Dupont from fellow ctzns of Phil, to dine with them:

Wm M Meredith	Jas L Claghorn	Saml Lewis
Horace Binney, jr	John Welsh	Henry Lewis
Wm H Ashhurst	H P McKean	John C Lewis
J I Clarke Hare	Jos Cabot	Edwin M Lewis
A E Borie	Chas Cabot	Morton McMichael
C L Borie	Chas Gibbons	A J Antelo
Geo Whitney	Chas Gilpin	B H Moore
Geo H Stuart	Ellis Yarnall	Lindley Smith
John Edgar Thompson	Geo D Parish	Andrew Wheeler
J Gillingham Fell	N B Browne	Edw C Clarke
Jos Paterson	Wm S Grant	Arhur G Coffin
Richd S Smith	Geo H Boker	Wm Bucknell
Danl Smith, jr	John C Davis	Wilson C Swan
Geo Trott	John T Lewis	Stephen Colwell
Fred'k Fraley	Geo T Lewis	Wm Hutchinson

A Heaton	W M Tilghman	J F Cabot
G Roberts Smith	Chas Vesin	Saml C Cook
R Ruddle Smith	S A Mercer	Chas Newbold
W R Legee	John Ashhurst	Jos Trimble
Herman J Lombart	Chas E Smith	C A Grove
B Gerhard	Cadwalader Biddle	E C Knight
H C Carey	J W Field	John S Newbold
S M Felton	Jas W Paul	Geo K Ziegler
Thos Robins	Jos C Grubb	Geo A Parker
S J Reeves	Fred'k Brown	Geo H Huddell
John McArthur, jr	Francis G Smith, jr	Thos Webster, jr
Wm Denny	Alfred Stille	Geo B Roberts
M Matsinger	Henry H Smith, M D	E Emerson, M D
John Rice	W W Gerhard	Wm Stearns
J R Fry	H Hoppin	Jos Huddell
H B Fry	Geo Helmuth	F E Felton

[Reply from S F Dupont declining the invitation was dated Louviess, near Wilmington, Dela, Jul 22, 1863.]

An editor warned: Brig Gen John P Slouth, the Military Govn'r at Alexandria, has caused the following letter to be sent to the proprietor of the Alexandria Gaz, Mr Edgar Snowden, jr: "The existence of a paper in Alexandria known to be hostile to the Govn't he represents will be tolerated so long only as there appears nothing in it offensive to the loyal people." – Rollin C Gale, A A G: Alexandria, Sep 16

TUE SEP 22, 1863

Crawford E Smith, of Saline Co, Mo, has been ordered beyond the Federal lines. His property is to be taken possession of by the Provost Mrshl, & his slaves, 125, to be furnished with protection papers in accordance with general order #35, & to remain & be subsisted on his plantation. Dr Smith is the wealthiest man in Saline Co.

Capt Jas E Durham, provost mrshl, & Jasper P Brewster, com'r for the 4th dist of Connecticut, have been dismissed; & the Surgeon of the same Brd of Enrollment, Dr S T Salisbury, has been arrested & ordered for trial before a crt-martial; also, Dr N H Marselas, Surgeon for the first dist of Pa, to be arraigned on similar charges. Ordered for trial before a crt-martial, under the 15th section of the Enrollment Act. The 15th section provides: that any surgeon charged with the duty of such inspection who shall receive from any person any money or valuable thing, or agree to receive same, for making an imperfect inspection or a false or incorrect report, etc, shall be tried by a crt-martial, & on conviction be punished by fine not exceeding $500 or less than $200, & be imprisoned at the discretion of the court, & be cashiered & dismissed from svc.

Julia Holloran & Julia Connell, about 12 or 14 years of age, drowned while bathing in a pond near Boston, Tue. When the bodies were recovered they were found tightly clasped in each other's arms.

The Chief Clerk of the Dept of Agric, Mr Grennell, being on a temporary absence at the North, Mr J R Dodge, of the Dept, is acting as Chief Clerk.

Died: on Sep 20, after a short but painful illness, Jos A Hastings, in his 24th yr. Funeral from the residence of Jos N Fearson on Tue.

Died: on Sep 21, Mrs Beatrix S Browning, w/o Mr Geo B McCartee, of Wash City.

Died: on Sep 20, Albert V Klopfer, eldest s/o Henry A & Rosanna Klopfer, in the 15th yr of his age. Funeral from the residence of F M Detweiler, 643 L st, today.

Orphans Crt of Wash Co, D C. 1-Case of John A Whitall & Chas E Rittenhouse, excs of Lydia N Whitall, dec'd; settlement on Oct 13. -Z C Robbins, rg o/wills 2-Prsnl estate of John S Meehan, late of Wash Co, dec'd. -Rachel T Meehan, excx

WED SEP 23, 1863
Died: on Sep 15, in PG Co, Md, at the residence of her dght, Mrs S M Barnes, Mrs Barbara Sim Suter, in her 84th yr.

Died: on Sep 16, in Cairo, Ill, in the 9th of her age, Alice Lee, d/o Alice Lee & Capt Jas M Pritchett, U S Navy.

Died: at *Mountain View*, Culpeper Co, Va, on Jul 5, after a brief illness, Emily W, w/o Jas B Kirk, of that county, & 3rd d/o Wm Redin, of Gtwn, D C.

Died: on Sep 22, Chas Alexander, infant s/o J Parker & Virginia Milburn, aged 10 months & 20 days. Funeral from the residence of his grandfather, Robt Earl, 336 21st st, near Pa av.

Pvt sale: *Sligo Mills*, 414 acs; *Dobbin Farm*, 447 acs. -Sally Carroll, exc of W T Carroll, dec'd. F & 18th st, Wash, D C.

We have captured Gen Adams, of Texas, & 1,300 men. On Sunday Gen Rosecrans changed the position of his army to points near Chattanooga, with Gen Thomas' command still occupying the front. [Sep 25 paper: Brig Gen John H King, who was reported wounded & a prisoner, is neither. Maj Coolidge, 2nd in command of the same brigade, was certainly killed. Gen Lytle is not killed, but in the hands of the enemy.] [Sep 25 paper: Brig Gen John H King, who was reported wounded & a prisoner, is neither. Maj Coolidge, second in command of the same brigade, was certainly killed.]

Orphans Crt of Wash Co, D C. Prsnl estate of Mrs Maria Wood Van Zandt, of Wash Co, dec'd. -Wm Thomas, adm

Chattanooga, Sep 22, 1863. In the fight of the 19th we had lost about 600 killed & 2,000 wounded, & were the gainers of 3 pieces of artl, & the men were in splendid spirits. Details of the fight included: Gen Thomas, Gen Brannan, Gen Rosecrans, Davis, McCook, Polk, Negley, Sheridan, Van Cleve, Reynolds, Gen Johnston, Gen Garfield, Gens Baird, Palmer, & Stedman. Capt Russell, Gen Granger's adj, was killed before he had been 10 mins in the fight. Col Harker's brig & Gen Wood's div distinguished themselves in the fight. Among the ofcrs killed: Gen Lytle, Col Key, Col King commanding brig, & Col Bartleton, of the 101st Ill. Among the wounded are: [slightly]

Col Craxter, 4th Ky
Col Frankhouse, 98th Ill
Lt Col Mudge, 11th Mich
Col Hunt, 4th Ky
Col Chas Anderson, _ Ohio
Maj Wildman, 18th Ky
Lt Col Tripp, 6th Ill

Col Armstrong, 93rd Ohio
Maj Johnston, 52nd Ill
Lt Col Maxwell, 2nd Ohio
Gen Morton, of Gen Rosecrans staff
Col Bradley, commanding brig in Sheridan's div

Gen John H King is reported wounded & a prisoner

THU SEP 24, 1863

Died: on Sep 23, Walter S Hunter, in the 27th yr of his age. Funeral from the residence of his father, Wm Hunter, 70 Cox's Row, 1st st, Gtwn, on Fri. [Sep 25-Obit: He was the s/o Wm Hunter of the Dept of State, & grandson of Hon Wm Hunter, late minister to Brazel.]

Ad-French Milliner & Dress Mkr, 356½ Pa av, Wash, D C. -Mrs F Borde

Fortress Monroe, Sep 23. Among the rebel losses, killed: Brig Gen Preston Smith, of Tenn; Brig Gen Wolford, of Ga; Brig Gen Waltham, of Mississippi; Brig Gen Helm, & Brig Gen Deshler. Maj Gen Hood was wounded & has since died.

Knoxville, Tenn, Sep 16, 1863. Jas C Lutherell was yesterday appt'd postmstr of Knoxville by Gen Burnside, subject to the approval of the Pres. Col Hartsuff has established his headqrtrs here, & Gen Burnside returned from the Gap on Sat. Col Bird is in command at Athens & telegraphs Gen Hartsuff that the country is full of subsistence.

Harrisburg, on Sep 22. The boiler of Eberly & Lee's saw mill at New Cumberland exploded today, killing J D Kellerman, Saml Icenbergar, John Cromlech, engr J Buckwelter, & Mrs Faekler, & wounding Miss Faekler, a boy, O Prowell, P Justwick, & John F Lee, one of the proprietors. The mill is a wreck.

FRI SEP 25, 1863

Mrd: on Sep 6, by Rev Mr Davis, Wm H Parker to Miss Eliz Miller, all of Wash City.

Mrd: on Sep 24, at the Chr of the Epiphany, by Rev Dr Hall, Capt Louis C Bailey, U S Army, to Emma, y/d/o the late Louis Lindsay, of Va.

Died: in Wash, on Sep 9, Virginia Stewart, formerly of King Geo Co, Va.

Died: on Sep 23, Eugene, 3rd s/o John F & the late Harriet Maria Boyle, in the 16th yr of his age. Funeral from the residence of his father, 25th st, today.

Died: at Charlestown, Jeff Co, Va, on Sep 17, in the 59th yr of his age, Dr Wm Rippey Raum, physician; native of Pa; elder of the Presby Chr.

Yesterday Eugene Boyle, aged 15 yrs, s/o John F Boyle, whilst gunning, was accidentally shot & killed by his younger brother, aged 13 yrs. -Local item

Trials by Crt-Martial, Local. Andrew J Smith, Francis Sullivan & Wm Hill, messengers in the War Dept, & Jas Enright, a clerk in the Paymstr Gen's Ofc, were tried, charged with forging discharge papers & selling them to sldrs. The evidence was very strong & they will be severely dealt with.

Edwin Noyes, Superintendent & Actg Pres of the Maine Central R R, was taken into custody at the Astor Hse, N Y, on Sat, on a charge of embezzlement. Charge made by the directors of the company, who allege that the accused is a defaulter to the extent of $40,000. $26,000 was found upon the person of the fugitive. Noyes fled to Canada first, then thinking that his movements were unknown, disguised himself & came to N Y to take the steamer for Liverpool. Mr Noyes is a lawyer by profession & is represented as a man of more than ordinary abilities.

Obit-Dr Wm Bradley Tyler, ctzn of Fred'k, Md, died suddenly of paralysis at his residence in that city, on Sep 9, in the 76th yr of his age.

Yesterday Andrew J Smith, Francis Sullivan & Wm Hill, messengers in the War Dept, & Jas Enright, a clerk in the Paymstr Gen's Ofc, were tried by crt-martial, charged with forging discharge papers & selling them to sldrs. The case of Capt Ford, charged with extorting money from loyal ladies, [whilst acting as a provost mrshl,] is still in progress, the Capt now producing evidence to substantiate a good character.

Col Wm Weer, whose command was detailed to bush whack in search of Quantrill's guerrillas, wrote on Sep 15 to Brig Gen Ewing, determined to dislodge them. Capt Coleman, of the 9th Kansas, came upon Quantrill's own camp: attacked & killed 2 guerillas. The bushwackers had burned the fine flouring mill at Lone Jack. Col Weer was to start immediately to capture another camp of guerrillas.

SAT SEP 26, 1863
Died: accidentally killed on board the U S steamer *Wyandank*, of the Potomac Flotilla, on Sep 24, Actg Mstr's Mate Alfred Pearce Mathews, aged 20 yrs. Funeral from the residence of his bro-in-law, Chas A Sears, 388 H st, Sun. [Sep 28-Death due to the accidental discharge of a revolver in the hands of the qrtr gunner, Thos Seeger, who was engaged in cleaning it.]

Died: suddenly, on Sep 17, at *Findowry*, Harford Co, Md, Wm Frederick, eldest s/o Brig Gen J G Barnard, aged 18 years & 6 months.

Died: Francis Enoch, y/s/o John F & Jane E Dobbyn, aged 2 yrs, 2 months & 9 days. Funeral today.

On Sep 18, Edw Elliot, Co B, & Chas Eastman, Co I, 14th Conn Regt, were shot at the hdqrtrs of the 3rd Div of the Army of the Potomac for desertion. Elliot was about 21 years of age & a native of Boston; Eastman was about 23 years of age, & from Cornish, Maine. Eastman was baptised on the spot where he met his fate. Elliot died after the shots were fired but Eastman was untouched. The men shot & missed a second time. The Provost Mrshl, in mercy, shot him thru the head & then the heart, with his revolver.

Died: in Wash City, on Sep 24, Wm S Clary, in the 62nd yr of his age, a resident of Wash City for the past 30 yrs. Funeral from his late residence, 438 H st, Sat.

Pblc sale of bldg lot: in the matter of Erasmus J Middleton, guardian of John Albert & Wm Alex'r Anderson, & of Mary E Anderson, guardian of Cecilia Bertha Anderson, minor heirs of Wm Anderson, dec'd. Lot 18 in sq 368, Ninth st, Wash, D C, for sale. -E J Middleton, Mary E Anderson, guardians

Atlanta, Ga, Sep 21, 1863. Engagement between the armies of Gens Bragg & Rosecrans commenced on Sat about 8 miles west of Ringgold, & cont'd Sat & Sun. Our loss is large, about 5,000 killed & wounded. Among the killed: Brig Gen Preston Smith, of Tenn; Brig Gen Woford, of Ga; Brig Gen Walthall, of Miss. The report of the latter's death lacks confirmation. Among the wounded: Maj Gen Preston, of Ky; Maj Gen Cleburn, of Arkansas; Maj Gen Hood, of Texas, who lost a leg; Gen Gregg, wounded in the jaw; Brig Gen Benning wounded in the breast.

Died: on Sep 11, at his late residence in PG Co, Md, after a protracted illness, Benjamin Berry, in the 70th yr of his age.

Wash Corp: 1-Mayor nominates H H Lowrie for Physician to the Poor of the first ward, v J W C Kennon, resigned: referred to the Cmte on Health. 2-Nomination of F S Walsh, jr, as Resident Student of the Asylum, & E C Eckloff for Sec to the Com'rs of the Wash Asylum, in place of Jno E Leach, dec'd: referred to the Cmte on Asylum. 3-Ptn of Ulysses Ward for improvement of a street: referred to the Cmte on Improvements. 4-Ptn of Thos H Robinson, Pres of Columbia Fire Co, for an appropriation for the purchase of hose: referred to the Cmte on Fire Dept. 5-Cmte on Finance: ptn of Thos Cogan for his relief: passed. 6-Ptn of Jas Poole: referred to the Cmte of Claims. 6-Cmte of Claims: ptn of E E Barns, asking remuneration for damage done his night cart: passed. 7-Cmte on Mkts: ptn of W B Mitchell, with a bill increasing the salary of the Ast Clerk of the Centre Mkt: postponed. 8-Bill for relief of John Williams: referred to the Cmte of Claims. 9-Ptn of Jos F Brown, asking permission to extend the fuel vaults in front of hse #483 Tenth st west: referred to the Cmte on Improvements. 10-Chair announced the appointment of Mr Follansbee on the Cmte on Mkts, & Mr Peake on the cmte for the construction of a hse for the use of the Western Hose Co & American Hood & Ladder Co, & for other purposes. 11-Act authorizing Jas W Donelson to improve a certain wharf site: referred to the Cmte on Wharves.

Atlanta, Ga, Sep 22, 1863. Fight yesterday was a most spirited one. Gen Longstreet & Hill attacked the enemy's centre by night. Enemy loss of from 5 to 6 thousand prisoners & 42 pieces of artl. Our loss in general ofcrs is very great. Brig Gen Helm, of Ky, was killed while leading a charge. Maj Gen Hood was mortally wounded. Maj Richmond, of Gen Polk's staff, was killed.

Chickamauga, Sep 20. Gen Preston was killed last night; Gen John C Brown, Gen Hood, Gen Gregg, Gen Danl Adams, & Gen Helm wounded. Gen Deshler killed. The Yankee Gen Little was killed. We have captured about 2,500 prisoners & about 25 or 30 pieces of artl. –Isham G Harris

Wm H Harding, a lawyer of Lee, Mass, had the misfortune a few days since of having his marriage pblshd in the Berkshire Eagle. To this he takes exceptions. The report of my marriage, which I find in your issue of the 27th is not quite correct: First, on Jul 20, 1863, I kept close company with my law books; second, I was never in Lebanon Springs in my life; third, I never, to my knowledge, saw or heard of the Rev E T Hunt; fourth, the young lady mentioned as the bride is the w/o my bro; & fifth, I never was mrd at all, I never came within gun shot of marriage, I never wanted to get mrd; & finally, I never expect to get mrd. With the above exceptions your item is all correct.

MON SEP 28, 1863

Died: Sep 26, Yelverton Peyton Page, of Wash City. Grand Master of the Grand Lodge of the Dist, in his 41st yr. Funeral at First Presby Chr, [Dr Sunderland's Chr,] this afternoon. Wash, D C

Died: at *Glen Allen*, near Gtwn, on Sep 26, Frank, y/s/o Wm W & C S Rapley, aged 13 months.

Died: in Wash City, on Sep 27, Adolphus, y/s/o Lambert & Caroline P Bergman, aged 4 years & 7 months. Funeral from their residence, 404 8th st, Tue.

Died: on Sep 26, Saml Howard Kinsey, in his 19th yr. Funeral from the residence of his father, B S Kinsey, 461 D st, today.

Deaths reported to the Navy Dept for the week ending Sep 26, 1863:
Chas Cooper, ord seaman, drowned, Sep 12, vessel U S S *Connecticut.*
My. Gilman, marine, yellow fever, Sep 2, vessel U S S *Colorado.*
Geo Morris, marine, yellow fever, Sep 4, do.
John O James, hosp nurse, yellow fever, do, do.
Jas H Grimes, landsman, pneumonia, Sep 6, vessel U S S *Wabash.*
Peter Locade, landsman, congestive fever, Aug 31, vessel U S S *Pensacola.*
Jas Brown, seaman, congestive fever, Sep 8, do.
Man'l Cartright, contraband, remit fever, Aug 3, Mississippi Squadron.
McVanible, contraband, remit fever, Aug 3, do.
Jas A Enright, landsman, remit fever, Jun 14, do.
Jas Campbell, landsman, remit fever, Jun 24, do.
Theo F Clarke, 2nd Cpl, cholera morbus, Aug 18, vessel U S S *Monongahela.*
John Sargent, gunner's mate, gunshot wound, Sep 9, vessel U S S *Powhatan.*
Jos S Emerick, landsman, shell wound, Sep 7, do.
Josiah P Hughes, marine, dysentery, Sep 17, do.
John Buck, boy, remit fever, Sep 9, Nav Hosp, Memphis.
John Johnson, seaman, dysentery, Sep 7, do.
Jos Hall, blank, consumption, Sep 12, do.
Dick Jordan, contraband, congestion, Sep 11, do.
Michl Donohue, sgt marines, delirium tremens, Nav Hosp, N Y.
Spencer Mackay, landsman, continued fever, Sep 19, do.
Lenus Patton, 1st cl boy, drowned, Sep 18, vessel U S S *Teazer*
John Brown, landsman, typhoid fever, Sep 19, Nav Hosp, Norfolk.
Rd Thomas, seaman, cholera morbus, Aug 20, vessel U S S *Canandagna*
Clemens Boner, coal heaver, typhus fever, Aug 26, vessel U S S *Kearsage.*
Mark W Emery, ord seaman, typhus fever, Aug 19, do.

Obit-Mr Geo Renick, aged 87 years & 7 days, died at his residence, *Paint Hill,* near Chillicothe, on Sep 15. Born in Hardy Co, Va, on Sep 7, 1776: minority spent in a store in Moorefield, Va. Twice mrd; first in 1802 to Miss Dorothy Harness, of his native county, by whom he had 10 chldrn, 7 of whom survive him: she dying in Dec 1820. He mrd again in 1825 to Mrs Sarah Boss, who survives him, though only a few months his jr in yrs, herself a pioneer of 1798, whose maiden name was Denny, sister of the late Gen Jas Denny. [Long article-recommend copy of same-pertinent details have been copied.]

Orphans Crt of Wash Co, D C. Prsnl estate of Geo Evans, late of Wash City, dec'd.
-Mary A Evans, excx

Rebels captured recently south of the Rapid-Ann; reached Washington on Fri; some captured at Madison Crt-hse & others 7 miles of Gordonsville. Among them are: Col R H Lee, Inspec of 2nd Army Corps of Northern Va; Capt P A Tatum, 2nd N C Cavalry; Lt J B Moore, one of Moseby's gang; Lt M H Norman, 28th N C Regt; H S Bradley, Ast Surg of Cobb's Legion, & W B Shields, Ast Surgeon.

Mstr's Mate Alfred Matthews, of Wash City, was instantly killed, on board the gunboat *Wyandank,* by the accidental discharge of a revolver in the hands of the qrtr gunner, Thos Seeger, who was engaged in cleaning it. [No date-appears as recent news.]

TUE SEP 29, 1863
Mrd: on Sep 27, by Rev S D Finkel, Sebastian Aman & Emma Kolb, all of Wash City.

Farm for sale-adjoining the country seat of Geo W Riggs & opposite the residence of F P Blair; 200 acs. -S S Carroll, excx of Wm Thos Carroll, 18th & F sts, Wash, D C.

The Brannin Homicide-Grand Jury, on Sat, concluded & dismissed the case of U S vs Chas W Thompson. Mr Thompson is again on duty as a mbr of the Met Police force.

C W Boteler & Son: Importers, wholesale & retail dealers in china, glass, crockery ware, etc. 318 Iron Hall, Pa ave, between 9th & 10th sts. -C W Boteler -Jno W Boteler

Emerson Institute: select classical & math school for boys, 14th st, between I & K sts, in the new School Hse recently erected. Chas B Young, A M, Principal, residence: 348 N Y ave, between 9th & 10th sts.

WED SEP 30, 1863
Orphans Crt of Wash Co, D C. 1-Case of Mgt McNamara, excx of Martin McNamara, dec'd; settlement on Oct 17. -Z C Robbins, rg o/wills 2-Prsnl estate of Asbury Dickens, late of Wash Co, dec'd. -Maria Dickens, excx 3-Case of Mrs Eliza M Mosher, excx of Maria Shorter, dec'd; settlement on Oct 17. -Z C Robbins, rg o/wills

Rev Michael Olivetti, pastor of the Catholic Chr at Port Henry, Essex Co, N Y, was murdered on Sep 10, near that place, & his body was found in Lake Champlain, soon after.

Headqrtrs Army & Dist of N C, Newbern, N C, Sep 15, 1863. A Crt of Inquiry, Col T J C Amory, 17th Mass Vols, Pres: convened on Sep 2, upon request of Capt W H Wheeler, Ast Q M Vols, to inquire into cmplnts filed by T H Vanderhoef, Super of Contrabands, & A H Hahn, 3rd N Y Cavalry, have found: evidence presented, that the cmplnts preferred by Mr Vanderhoef & A H Hahn, against Capt Wheeler, are without proper foundation in fact, & have been framed with a malicious intention of injuring a worthy & meritorious ofcr. A complete vindication of Capt Wheeler, are approved. By command of Maj Gen Peck: Benj B Foster, A A G

Local robberies:-Sat night the hse of Bartholomew Dundas, on F st, of $532. Mrs C Nichols was robbed of $380 while on the South side of the avenue, on Sun night, about 12 o'clock.

Maj Gen Sickles is on a visit to Wash, & yesterday had an interview with the Sec of War. He yet walks with crutches, his wound not being sufficiently healed to permit the use of an artificial leg.

It is reported quite currently in military circles that Gen Slocum has resigned.

Phil, Sep 29. Maj Gen McClellan arrived here this evening. He was serenaded at his mother's residence, in Spruce, above 19th st, in the presence of a large crowd of friends & admirers.

Jos Scott & Edw Shandley, detectives, formerly in the employ of Capt Scheetz, were brought before Gen Slough's crt-martial on Mon. They are charged with taking $1,800 from Mr M O Markam, of Atlanta, Ga.

THU OCT 1, 1863

Died: on Sep 30, after a lingering illness, Chas Edw, s/o Chas E & A W Walker, aged 3 yrs. Funeral from the residence of his father, 479 10th st, today.

Supreme Crt of D C. Antonio Buchignani & Mgt Buchignani, cmplnts, vs. Saml Chilton, dfndnt.

Rg-appointment of a new trustee in the place of Saml Chilton, who is no longer a resident of D C. -R J Meigs, clerk

Gen Lytle was killed while gallantly leading his command at the battle of Chickamauga, Sep 20th. -P H Sheridan

Francis J Grund died in Phil on Sep 30, suddenly, of apoplexy. He became excited by the appearance of the crowd before his residence on its way to serenade Gen McClellan & Judge Woodward. He ran in haste to the station-hse, where he fell exhausted & in 10 mins died.

Successful naval raid in the Chesapeake Bay. Enquirer of the 29th says: we are informed by letter, received from one of the participants, that Capt Beall, with young men from this city, who started on an expedition to the Chesapeake Bay some 2 weeks ago, have captured 3 sloops & 4 schnrs. The expedition was commanded by J L Beall, Actg Mstr C S N, with Edw McGuire, Actg Mstr C S N, second in command. One was the schnr *Alliance*, bound from Phil to Port Royal, S C, laden with sutler's stores, her cargo valued at $200,000. About $10,000 worth of the cargo was saved, & the vessel burnt to the water's edge. A considerable amount of property, including a small cargo of cheese, rewarded the party for the pains.

Mrs Willis proposes to receive into her home at Idlewild, Newburgh, 6 little girls between the ages of 9 & 13. She wishes to educate them with her own dghts. She has engaged a competent teacher to assist her. Pupils will be received Nov 2nd. -Mrs Willis, Idlewood, Moodna, Orange Co, N Y

Collision between the street cars & a railroad car on Tue, at First st. The driver, W Croghan, saw the engine approaching, & with great coolness jumped off & jerked the horses around, thereby saving probably the loss of svr'l lives. The conductor, Mr John H Devaugh, was knocked off the back platform, as were others, but none were injured.

Gen Wm Preston, one of the rebel Genr'ls wounded at the Chickamauga battle, was the former U S Minister to Spain.

FRI OCT 2, 1863

U S steam sloop *Wyoming*: Inland Search of Japan, Jul 17, 1863. Engagement with the Japanese at Simonosaki yesterday, I report the following casaulties: killed-Alex Furlong, Marine; Wm Clark, seaman; Geo Watson, landman; & Michl Lynch, coal heaver. Jas Carswell & Wm Thompson, landsmen, very seriously wounded, since dead. Andrew Wallace, capt of after guard, very seriously wounded, since dead. Wounded: Thos Stuvant, landsman; Michl Doyle, Marine; Wilson P Snyder, landsman; Chas J Murphy. Your obedient servant, E R Dealy, Surg, U S Navy

Died: on Sep 30, after a long & painful illness, C Edwin McElfresh, in his 26th yr. Funeral from his parents' residence, N Y av, between 4th & 5th, today.

Died: in Wash City, on Oct 1, Miss Sophia A Clements, in her 23rd yr. Funeral from the residence of her bro-in-law, Jas Daly, Vermont & L sts, Sat.

Died: on Sep 30, near Rockville, Md, Rosa Hagner, infant d/o Isabella & Southey S Parker.

N Y, Oct 1-Maj E B Hunt, of Engr Corps, a bro of ex-Gov Wash Hunt, is in critical condition; injured at the navy yd today while making experiments. Interment at West Point.

SAT OCT 3, 1863

Mr Ketchum's ltrs: from the N Y Jrnl of Commerce. Letter from Morristown, N J, Sep 12, 1863 from F J Porter to Hiram Ketchum, N Y C. Having been with the Army of the Potomac during whe whole of the Peninsular campaign: in the siege of Yorktown, in the capture of Hanover Crt-hse, in the battle of Gaines' Mill, & the battle of Malvera, it become my duty to bear a part somewhat conspicuous. Subj of ltr: reply on articles pblshd in the Commerce on Gen McClellan. Beseiging Yorktown instead of making an assault upon the enemy's lines, etc. Review of the battle of Gaines' Mill: our forces amounted to 32,000 men, under my command. Enemy more than double that. Brave & desperate as the sldrs of the enemy proved themselves, they were over matched by our loyal troops.

Mrd: on Sep 29, at the residence of the bride's father, Maj G F Merriam, U S Army, of Leyden, N Y, to Nina, d/o Thos A Scott, of Wash.

Mrd: on Sep 24, by Rev Mr Morsell, Daniel H Andrews, of N Y, & Miss Sarah E, eldest d/o the late Geo Naylor, of this Dist.

Died: on Oct 1, of paralysis, in her 79th yr, Mrs Ann Duvall, relict of Wm Duvall, of Annapolis, Md. Funeral from her late residence, 70 Indiana av, today.

Died: in Wash City, on Oct 2, John H Goddard, jr, in his 40th yr. Funeral from the residence of his father, Capt J H Goddard, I st, between 6th & 7th, Sun.

Crct Crt of Montg Co, Md, in Equity; John B Clagett, cmplnt, & Smith Thompson & others, dfndnts. Sale of *Locust Grove*, about 60 acs, the farm of the late Darius Clagett, in Montg Co. John England & John T Vinson, trusts.

For sale-my farm *Roseland,* in Eliz City Co, Va, on Hampton Rds; 430 acs. -Jos Segar, Fortress Monroe, Va

Archbishop Purcell left Cincinnati some days ago to visit the Bishop of Mobile, but, not having been permitted to pass the rebel lines, he has returned.

Deacon Jabez Halleck, grandfather of Maj Gen Halleck, died on Sep 17, at Western, N Y, in the 104th yr of his age. He was born at the old homestead on L I, in Mar 1760; remv'd & remained in the valley of the Mohawk in 1801; lived to see the 4th generation. Only one son, Jabez Halleck, of Westerville, survives him.

Orphans Crt of Wash Co, D C. Case of Martha J Troxell, admx of Jos P Troxel, dec'd; settlement on Oct 24. -Z C Robbins, rg o/wills

Criml Crt-D C. Michl Comoford, 13th N Y cavalry, guilty of manslaughter in the death of a comrade, Philip Riley; sentenced to 5 years in the Albany Pen

Jacob Whitehead, [age 60 years old,] of Gateville, N J, died on Thu, from a bite on the hand by a rat last winter, leaving a wound which nothing could be found to cure, & which finally proved fatal.

Gen Slocum's resignation was reported a few days since. The Gen resides in Syracuse, N Y, & the Jrnl Rep, of that city says: "It is understood here that the reason why Maj Gen Slocum has tendered his resignation is an unwillingness to serve under Gen Hooker again. It said that Gen Hooker has been designated to succeed Gen Burnside, & that the 12th Corps [Gen Slocum's] is ordered to join his command in Tenn.

MON OCT 5, 1863

Deaths reported to the Navy Dept for the week ending Oct, 1863:
Chas R Thompson, pensioner, diarrhoea, Sep 25, Nav Asylum.
Jas Mack, contraband, remit fever, Sep 17, Nav Hosp, Memphis.
Will Efferds, landsman, dropsy, Sep 18, do.
Wm McCarty, 3rd ast engr, dysentery, Sep 15, do.
John Benks, 1st cab boy, consumption, Sep 20, do.
Aug. Blanvelt, marine, intermittent fever, Aug 25, Marine Btln.
Peter Hannes, C. Marine, gunshot wound, Sep 19, vessel U S S Vermont.
Warren B Leach, landsman, dysentery, Sep 12, vessel U S S Wabash.
J J Witherbee, actg Ast Surgeon, blank, Aug 30, vessel U S S Currier.
Jas D Manning, ensign, blank, Sep 25, do.
Alfred Matthews, mstr's mate, gunshot wound, Sep 25, vessel U S S Wyandank.
Jas Carswell, landsman, gunshot wound, Jul 18, vessel U S S Wyoming.
Michl Lynch, coal heaver, gunshot wound, Jul 16, do.
Geo Watson, landsman, gunshot wound, Jul 16, do.
Wm Clark, seaman, gunshot wound, Jul 16, do.
Alex'r Furlong, marine, gunshot wound, Jul 16, do.
Jas Edwards, landsman, secoy syphilis, Jul 6, do.
Lawrence Fullam, ord seaman, remit fever, Aug 12, Receiving Ship Philadelphia.
John Rourke, seaman, delirium tremens, Jul 11, do.
Geo W Clarke, boy, typhoid fever, Sep 28, Nav Hosp, N Y.
Frederick H Thompson, a a paymstr, blank, Sep 5, vessel U S S New London.
Jas R Coleman, landsman, meningitis, Sep 29, Nav Hosp, N Y.
D W Ballastone, Ast Surg, blank, Sep 10, Mississippi Squadron.
Thos J Donohue, landsman, gunshot wound, Sept 23, vessel U S S Connecticut.
Chas Williams, qr gunner, gunshot wound, Sep 29, U S Hosp, Norfolk.

Died: at the residence of her father, Col G M Thompson, near Ellicott's Mills, Md, on Sep 30, after a prolonged illness, Mrs Gilbertine L Van Zandt, relict of the late Jos A Van Zandt, of the U S Navy.

Died: Oct 3, at the residence of Rev Smith Pyne, in his 24th yr, Wm Creighton Mead, s/o Rev E N Mead, & grandson of Rev Wm Creighton, of Beechwood, near Tarrytown, N Y.

Chancery #1797-sale of dwlg hse, lot 18 in sq A, in Wash City; as exc of Mrs Eliza Hamilton. -N M McGregor, exc & trust -Jas C McGuire & Co, aucts

Gen Slocum has withdrawn his resignation in the army at the request of the Pres, who gave him satisfactory assurances upon the subject which led to his resignation.

Col J T Wilder, lately in command in the Army of Cumberland, describes the terrible slaughter of Longstreet's men, in the battle of Chickmauga, on Sat, as they were driven back. As the rebels entered the field, in heavy masses fully exposed, the mounted infty, with their 7 shooting rifles, kept up a continuous blast of fire upon them, while Lilly, with his Indiana btry, hurled thru them double shotted canister from his 10 pounder rifles, at less than 300 yrs. The effect was awful. The rebels pushed thru the solid fire to a ditch for shelter. Instantly, Lilly whirled two of his guns & poured right down the whole length of the ditch his horrible double canister. Hardy a man got out of it alive. Wilder, at this Point,said it actually seemed a pity to kill men so. They fell in heaps, but the merciless seven-shooters & canister would not stop, & the flower of Lee's army was crushed into a disorderly mob & driven off. When the firing ceased, one could have walked for 200 yards down the ditch on dead rebels without ever touching the ground. Wilder thinks that no less than 2,000 rebels were killed & wounded in this field. The most disastrous fire of the 2 days.

TUE OCT 6, 1863
Wm Lawrence, of Belfontaine, Ohio, appt'd Judge of the U S Dist Crt of Southern Dist of Fla, in place of Wm Marvin, resigned. The Hon John A Bingham, of Ohio, appt'd to this post some time since, has declined.

Demonstration on Sun in honor of the opening of the St Aloysius new parochial school-hse, corner of 1st & K sts, under the auspices of the Srs of Mercy. Organizations in the procession: Thos H Parsons was Chief mrshl: proceeded to St Mary's Chr, in 5th st, where they received the German Catholic School & associations: thence to Gonzaga College: added were the pupils of St Matthew's Instit; St Dominick's St Patrick's Sunday School, with banners; St Peter's Sunday School, with banners; orphan girls of St Vincent's Asylum, & orphan boys of St Jos' Asylum. Addresses were by Rev A L Hitselbrger & others. Very large attendance of the Catholic community, as well as others. -Sun

Wm Sturgis Hooper, only s/o Hon Saml Hooper, M C, died in Boston on Thu last, aged 30 yrs: grad at Harvard College, class of 1852, was a vol Aide-de-Camp on Gen Banks' staff, & accompanied him to New Orleans, but his failing health was not improved, & he returned home to die.

The Congressmen elect from Calif are Thos B Shannon, Wm Higby, & Cornelius Cole.

Mr John Underwood, of Occoquan, Va, who was recently captured by the guerillas, & subsequently released, has been app'td U S Mrshl for the Eastern Dist of Va, & will reside at Alexandria.

Died: on Oct 4, Thos J, infant s/o H & Susan E Lane, aged 16 months.

Died: on Sep 29, in Loudoun Co, Va, Eleanor, aged 6 yrs, of a putrid throat, child of John C & Susan C Sprigg. [Possibly-all of Wash City-paper creased]

For sale-400 acs, part of Marshall Hall. -Thos Marshall, Piscataway p o, PG Co, Md.

Frank A Hervey-Your mother is distressed to know your whereabouts. You can hear of her by addressing Thos H Ford, 443 9th st, Wash City.

For sale-my farm in Montg Co, Md; 180 acs, with a stone dwlg. -A G Pendleton

Supreme Crt of D C, in Equity. Walter Cadman & Adaline E Cadman, cmplnts, vs Wm B B Cross & Harman Burns, dfndnts. Appointment of new trustee; Cross being a non-resident. -R J Meigs, clerk

WED OCT 7, 1863
Mrd: at St Patrick's Chr, on Oct 5, Mr L G Marini to Miss Marie Garnaux.

Pblc sale, decree of crt. Ptn of Cecilia Lawrence, guardian of Martha Louisa & Ida Virginia Lawrence, minor heirs of Jas Lawrence, dec'd, & of John A Simms, guardian of Geo W Lawrence, minor heir of Isaiah Lawrence, dec'd; lot a in sq 283, with improvements, Wash City. -Cecilia Lawrence, John A Simms, guardians. T M Blount, solicitor for ptnrs.

The Pa campaign: Gen Lee's Official Report. Headqrtrs Army Northern Va: Jul 31, 1863. Brig Gen Pettigrew was mortally wounded in an attack made by a small body of cavalry, which was unfortunately mistaken for our own & permitted to enter our lines. He was brought to Bunker Hill, where he expired a few days afterwards. [Our casualties: Brig Gens Barksdale & Garnett were killed, & Brig Gen Sems mortally wounded. Brig Gens Kemper, Armistead, Seales, G T Anderson, Hampton, J M Jones, & Jenkins, were also wounded. Brig Gen Archer was taken prisoner. Gen Pettigrew, tho wounded at Gettysburg, continued to command until he was mortally wounded near Falling Waters. - R E Lee, General

Hon Erastus Corning, of N Y, has resigned his seat as a Rep in Congress, owing to ill health.

Wood! Sawed & split in any size required. W H Marlow, So side Canal, corner 7th st.

THU OCT 8, 1863
Mrd: on Oct 6, at the Chr of the Epiphany, by Rev Dr Hall, Nathaniel Wilson to Annie E Hutton, all of Wash City.

Mrd: in Balt, Md, on Oct 7, by Rev Dr Fuller, Edgar Speiden, of Wash, to Lucy, d/o the late John Leadbeater, of Alexandria, Va.

Died: on Oct 6, Jeannette Bell, y/c/o Wm P & Eliza L Ferguson, aged 3 years & 8 months.

Died: at Cooperstown, N Y, on Oct 2, Ellen Sophia, w/o Dr Edw Maynard, of Wash, D C.

Wash Corp: 1-Ptn of Geo Small & others, to curb & pave in front of sq 582: referred to the Cmte on Improvements. 2-Cmte on Police: adverse report on the bill for the relief of A R Forrest. 3-Relief of J Thos Thornton was taken up, considered, & passed. 4-Cmte of Claims: adverse on the ptn of Jas Poole for remission of a fine. 5-Bill for relief of G W G Eslin: passed. 6-Ptn of Geo Follansbee & S A Reugh & others, asking the passage of a bill for the erection of a school hse in the 2nd Dist: referred to the Cmte on Pblc Schools.

Burnt property to be paid for by Military order: a short time since the outbldgs on the premises of Wm H Downs & John G Cromwell, enrolling ofcrs in the 5th dist of A A Co, Md, were destroyed by fire, supposed by an incendiary. In Harford Co, when the property of enrolling ofcrs was destroyed by fire, Gen Schenck requires the people residing within 6 miles of the property so destroyed to pay for it.

For sale-*Woodley*, the residence of P A Bowen, near Gtwn, 100 acs; with commodious mansion. -H W Blount, 61 La av, Wash, D C.

FRI OCT 9, 1863
Died: on Oct 8, in his 16th yr, Geo, y/s/o the late Capt E A Capron, U S Army. Funeral from the residence of Chas Vinson, 86 Pa av, today.

Dr Geo Hayward died of apoplexy on Wed, at his residence in Boston, age 73 yrs. He was for many years a Prof in the Med School at Harvard Univ, & at the time of his death held the position of a Fellow of the College, to which he was elected in 1852. He graduated at Cambridge in the class of 1809. -Boston Transcript

Ford's New Theatre-10th st. The orchestral adjunct of the Tenth St Theatre, under the leadership of Prof Wm Withers, jr. New scenery by Mr Chas S Getz. Cast of characters include Miss Maggie Mitchell-the stellar attraction, Mr & Mrs Bishop, Mr Herne, Mr Fred Williams, Mr Chester, Mr Fawcett, Mrs Chapman, Misses Sallie & Mary Melville, & others.

Rochester, N Y, Oct 6. Peter P Murphy, examing surgeon of the board of enrollment at Lockport, has been held to bail in sum of $5,000 for accepting money, & F T Hoyer has been held to bail for same amount for offering money to Murphy to improperly exempt drafted men.

Cincinnati, Oct 7. Maj Wileman, 18th Ky Regt, who was wounded in the battle of Chickamauga, & lately returned home, was taken from his hse in Pendleton Co, Ky, on Mon, by a gang of guerillas, stripped of his clothing, tied to a tree, & shot. Five of the murderers were caught.

Hon G W McLellan, 2nd Ast Postmstr Gen, has so far recovered from a protracted & dangerous illness as to be able to sit up.

Brig Gen Sherman, who lost a leg at the siege of Port Hudson, has nearly recovered. He is still at Newport, & is able to hobble about the streets by the use of crutches.

Optical Establishment: 426 Pa ave. J Tobias calls attention to his large stock of gold, silver, & steel spectacles, & eye glasses, opera, marine, telescopes, & microscopes, & a great variety of opties, all to be sold at N Y prices. Long a resident in this city.

SAT OCT 10, 1863
Sentinel has the following account of the late operations of Mosby near Alexandria, Va: on the 28th ult, the *boarding* hse of Col Danl F Dulany, Aid to Govn'r Pierpont, was ascertained. With a few of his men, among them a s/o Col Dulany, Mosby repaired to the qrtrs of the Aid. He presented himself to the Col & told him he was Mosby. The Col, supposing that he had been taken prisoner, & the sldrs around him were his guard, told the Maj that he was very glad to see him; but when Mosby told him to pack up & come along, he changed his note, & told him he was very sorry to see him.
Recognizing his son, Col Dulany told him there was a pair of old shoes up stairs which he might have. French, the son, presented his feet to his father, showing a pair of cavalry boots captured from a sutler, & remarked that he was the better shod of the two.

Died: on Oct 9, Frank, the y/s/o Francis & Eleanor Mattingly, in his 13th yr. Funeral from their residence, 494 7th st, Sat.

Obit-Mr Geo Sumner, brother of Sen Sumner, of Mass, died on Tue last, in his native city of Boston, after a lingering illness. He was an expert linguist, scholar, & man of the world.

The Confederate steamer *Georgia* is now in Fimon's Bay, which port she reached on Sun: built by Messrs Denny & Co, of Greenock: ofcrs joined her off Ushant Island on Apr 9th after getting her armament on board, hauled down the English & ran up the Confederate flage & put to sea. Apr 25th she captured the ship *Dictator*, of N Y, bound to Shanghai with coals. Burned the *Dictator* & proceeded to the Capt Verde Islands to land her prisoners. May 13th, arrived in Bahia: proceeded down the S A coast: off Cape Frin she captured the vessel *Geo Griswold*, with British cargo on board. The *Georgia* proceeded to the Island of Trinidad; captured the barque *Good Hope*, of Boston, bound to Algon Bay with genr'l cargo. Her Capt had died some days before, & his body preserved in salt. Capt Maury had him brought on board the *Georgia*, read the funeral svcs over him, & committed his body to the deep. The barque *J W Sever* hove in sight & was chased by the *Georgia*. She was from Boston bound to the Amoor river with machinery for the Russian Gov't. Jun 18th the *Georgia* captured the ship *Constitution*, of N Y, loaded with coal for Shanghai, made a prize of her, & took her into the island. Jul 28 the *Georga* captured the ship *City of Bath*, of Bath, from Callao to Antwerp. Cargo being neutral, she was bonded, & the prisoners of the *Constitution* were put on board of her. Jul 16th the *Georgia* captured the ship *Prince of Wales*, of Bath, from Valparaiso, bound to Antwerp with guano. Cargo neutral, the ship was bonded.

Mrs Mary Mitchell was arrested in Wash City on Wed for giving a sldr liquor, the sldr being her hsbnd. She was committed to the Cenral Guardhse. -Star

MON OCT 12, 1863
Deaths reported to the Navy Dept for the week ending Oct 10, 1863:
Jos D Lisle, paymstr, yellow fever, Sep 25, vessel U S S *Pensacola*.
Henry C Russell, 3rd ast engr, pernicious fever, Sep 21, vessel U S S *Hollyhock*.
Fred R Whitlock, paymstr's steward, do, do, do.
Jos Moffat, 3rd ast engr, do, do, do.
Jas McGregor, 3rd ast engr, yellow fever, Sep 24, vessel U S S *Pinola*.
Washington Taylor, contraband, yellow fever, Sep 24, do.
Jas D Manning, actg ensign, gastritis, Sep 29, vessel U S S *Courier*.
Edw Foley, coal heaver, pneumonia, Sep 30, Nav Hosp, N Y.
Jackson Quick, seaman, consumption, Sep 21, do.
John George, coal heaver, remit fever, Sep 28, do.
Jas Porteons, actg mstr's mate, Sep 1, vessel U S S *Niphon*.
Patrick Rodgers, marine, tetanus, Sep 19, vessel U S S *Flag*.
Wm F Hernsworth, 3rd ast engr, remit fever, Aug 24, vessel U S S *Narragansett*.
Frank Lewis, seaman, remit fever, Aug 9, do.
John Tye, boatswin's mate, gunshot wound, Sep 1, vessel U S S *Currituck*.
Eph Hearn, ord seaman, consumption, Aug 20, U S Ft Henry.
Thos Fitzgerald, seaman, consumption, no date, Nav Hosp, N Y.
Hans Hansfield, seaman, dementia & drowned, no date, Nav Hosp, N Y.
Jas R Coleman, landsman, meningitis, no date, do.
Henry Monroe, landsman, pneumonia, do, do.
Jas H Faulkner, landsman, pneumonia, no date, do.
Geo W Clark, 1st cab boy, typhoid fever, do, do.
John Jones, coal heaver, typhoid fever, do, do.
Fred McMullen, marine, delirium tremens, do, do.
Chas W Peck, a surgeon, yellow fever, Sep 4, vessel U S S *Relief*.

Jas Johnson, seaman, enlargement of heart, vessel U S S *Penquin*.
Alfonso S Howes, seaman, smallpox, no date, do.
Alfred R Matthews, mstr's mate, pistol shot, Sep 24, vessel U S S *Wyandank*.

Died: on Oct 11, Richd R Burr, in his 70th yr. Funeral from his late residence, F & 3rd sts, tomorrow.

Died: at Shepherdstown, Va, on Oct 4, Wm Moulder, aged 48 yrs; native of Wash City; ctzn of his adopted State, Va.

Col Percy Windham has asked for a Crt of Inquiry, with a view to ascertain the reasons why he was recently relieved from all military duty.

Business Suits for men: cassimeres or cloths suitable for business. –W M Huster & Co, 38 opposite the Centre Mkt, between 7th & 8th sts, Wash.

Orphans Crt of Wash Co, D C. Prsnl estate of Wm S Clary, late of Wash Co, dec'd. -Jas D Clary, exc

Skirmish near Harper's Ferry on Mon: scouting party belonging to Capt Mean's Cavalry, said to be boys, had a skirmish with Imboden's guerillas. One killed, 3 wounded, & 12 prisoners. On Wed, Capt Somer, with his company of cavalry, entered a fatal ambuscade. At first fire Capt Somers & 10 men were killed, as many more wounded, & nearly all others captured. Capt Somers was a brave & worthy ofcr. Both his Lts were captured.

Memphis: on Oct 4, Gen Sherman's son, 9 years of age, died at the Gayoso Hse.

TUE OCT 13, 1863
Died: on Oct 12, Eugene Fitzgerald, in his 24th yr. Funeral from the residence of his father, 355 F st, today.

Mr Andrew Boyd is preparing a new Directory of Wash & Gtwn, to include businesses of Alexandria; ofc-377 F st, Wash, D C.

Wash Corp: 1-An act for relief of J Thos Thornton: sum of $10.25 to Thornton for amount deposited on a license issued on Sep 15, 1863, which had never been used. 2-Act for relief of John Williams: fine imposed on him for creating a nuisance on K st, between 26th & 27th, is hereby remitted, provided Williams pays the court costs.

A new Literary & Social Club of Wash City has been organized under the name of Metropolitan. It is intended that every branch of Gov't shall represented in it. The Pres is Mr Edw Jordan, Solicitor of the Treas. S York Atlee, Sec. Mgrs of the Met Club, Wash, Oct, 1863.

R J Atkinson	I Smith Homans	Alex W Randall	J F Brown
Geo E Baker	W H Jones	Geo W Riggs	C Knapp
S M Clark	Wm P Dole	Fred P Stanton	Hudson Taylor
H D Cooke	P Philp	John F Starr	
Aug Edwards	L Clephane	J G Stephenson	
J L Graham	Hugh	C M Walker	
G A Henderson	McCulloch	Wm H Whiton	

Rev Louis M Boudrye, chaplain, just returned from Richmond & reports on the inmates of the Libby Prison. He says the fare of Federal prisoners is as scanty as it could be & sustain life. They are without blankets or overcoats, lie upon the hard, dirty floors of warehouses, or the cold ground of *Belle Island*. Deaths are numerous. The record of suffering is still more appalling among citizen prisoners.

The 2nd Dist Col Regt, Col C M Alexander, which has been doing patrol & guard duty in this city, is to leave here this week, having been ordered to report at Fairfax Crt-hse. They will be succeeded by 10 companies of the Invalid Corps.

WED OCT 14, 1863
Died: on Oct 3, Hannah Matilda Walker, aged 52 yrs, 2nd d/o the late Jos Thaw, & widow of the late John Walker, of Wash City

.

Col Jas A Tait, First D C, Prov Mrshl Gen Defences South of Potomac, tried by a crt martial for passing goods & persons into the enemy's country, found not guilty & most honorably acquitted. -Local Item

Danl F Dulaney, the aide to the Yankee Govn'r Pierpont, captured by Maj Mosby, was received at the Castle on Tue: also Chas Sutton & Isaac Wibert, 2 Yankees, captured at the same time. Dulaney is no prisoner of war. There is no war between the traitor Pierpont & the Confederate Gov't. Pierpont & Dulaney are both criminals in the eyes of the Virginia law.

Admiral Milne & his suite, with Lord Lyons & the entire Brig Leg, with Sec of State & Ast, & a s/o the Sec of War, on Sun, visited Mt Vernon, & paid homage to the tomb of Washington. On Mon, with Maj Gen Heintzelman, & a proper military escort, visited the Convalescent Camp, the Contraband Camp, & other places of interest in the Dept of Wash.

The *"Iron Brigade,"* composed of the 19th Indiana, 2nd, 6th, & 7th Wisc, & 24th Mich, is to be sent west, each regt to its own state, to recruit up to the maximum standard before taking the field again.

St Louis, Oct 12. Shelby's & Coffey's raiders left the Pacific R R Sat, moved north & reached Booneville yesterday. The burned no R R property at Tipton as previously reported, but plundered the town of a large amount of money. The citizens of Worfield, Greenfield, & other towns, suffered also.

THU OCT 15, 1863
Charleston Harbor, Oct 10, 1863. On Mon a daring attempt was made to destroy the frig *New Ironsides*, lying near Ft Moultrie, by a torpedo. A small boat with only a portion of the boat above water, with 4 persons, commanded by Lt Glassett, engr Toombs, fireman Scott, & pilot, came up to the vessel without attracting any attention. She struck the Ironsides fairly amid-ship exploding a torpedo, containing 60 pds of rifle powder, at the moment of contact. The rebel steamer was undoubtedly sunk, either by force of explosion or our shot. Lt Glassett swam to a schnr. He & Scott are now prisoners on board the guard ship. Lt Glassett was formerly in our Navy. *Ironsides* was ready for action by Capt Rowan. A musket fired from the rebel steamer dangerously wounded Actg Eng Chas Howard, of the *Ironsides*, who was ofcr of the deck at the time.

Mrd: on Oct 6, by Rev S D Finckel, W C Wineberger to Caroline Berlin, both of Wash City.

Died: on Oct 13, Jessie, only c/o Wm C & Kate Venable Smith, aged 15 months. Funeral from the residence of her uncle, Baker W Johnson, 428 9th st, today.

In the matter of the ptn of Theodore Wheeler, et al, for a division of the estate of Mrs Julia Keep, dec'd; cause will proceed on Oct 26. Order of the Commissioners. Pending in Supreme Crt of D C.

FRI OCT 16, 1863
Mrd: at Gtwn, D C, on Oct 13, by Rev Wm Chapman, Geo Shoemaker, jr, to Mary H Osborn, all of that place.

Died: at her residence, in Wash City, on Sat ult, Harriet Brent, relict of the late Robt Young Brent, of Montg Co, Md.

Died: on Oct 15, Caroline Fenwick, infant d/o John L & Louisa Sterritt Fenwick, aged 3 months. Funeral from the residence of W A Fenwick, 11th & C sts.

Wash Corp: 1-Ptn of D Ragan & others asking improvement of D st: referred to the Cmte on Improvements. 2-Ptn from O C Wight, Chrmn, etc, requesting an increase of the salary of the music teacher in the Pblc Schools: referred to the Cmte on Pblc Schools. 3-Ptn of Wm McCutchen & others, asking for a certain improvement: referred to the Cmte on Improvements. 4-Ptn of Jno T S Croggen & others for grading & gravelling E st: referred to the Cmte on Improvements. 5-Ptn of Jas G Drury & others, asking the remission of a fine: referred to the Cmte of Claims. 6-Ptn of Sarah Otterback & others for permission for E O Sanderson to be allowed to build a frame stable: referred to the Cmte on Police.

Woman's Rights: Mrs Dr Lydia Sayer Hasbrouck, who lives in Wallkill, N Y, won't pay taxes because she can't vote. She was arrested, & with shovel in hand, to work out her taxes, appeared on the road leading to the hse of A G Townley, on Sep 9. She did not work faithfully, remaining idle a considerable portion of the time, talking, leaning on her shovel, & sometimes with one hand tossing pebbles into the wagon, & at other times reading a paper.

SAT OCT 17, 1863
List of Americans registered at Gun's American Agency for the 2 weeks ending Oct 31: 17 Charlotte st, Bedford Sq, London, Eng:

G M Stimson, N J	J W Britan, San Francisco
J S Rogers, N J	T B Caldwell & family, Brooklyn, N Y
Dr J R Riggs, N J	Dr Henry Root, late 58th N Y S Vols
Ed H House, N Y	Geo P Bangs, Boston, Mass
Capt W P Downer, N Y	Wm Wheelwright, Boston, Mass
O T Glenn, Cincinnati	J A Marsh, N Y
Chas Squire, N Y	Stewart C Marsh, jr, N Y
Geo Harvey, N Y	Chas Seymour, Ohio
A J Daniels, N Y	T Harrison, Md
Mrs Saml B_wne, Staten Isl	S M Capron, Hartford, Conn
Miss A Kesly, Staten Isl	B Richmond Keith, Texas
Fletcher Urling Harper, N Y	E C Wheelock, Melbourne
J Henry Harper, N Y	E C Livingstone, New Orleans, La
H A Smythe, N Y	Dr Jenkins, Phil
Rev J M Buckley, Manchester, N H	J W Duane, Chicago, Ill
Jona Goodwin, jr, Hartford, Conn	Dr Clarkson, Chicago, Ill

Dr Littlejohn & wife, Brooklyn, N Y   J L Caspin, Lawrence, Mass
Rev Dr Fairfield, Mich   C L Condit, Brooklyn, N Y
Geo B Keith, Boston, Mass

Died: on Oct 6, at Shepherdstown, Jeff Co, Va, Col Ch Harper, merchant, in his 68th yr.

Sale of *Valley of Owen*, owned by the late Dr Allen Thomas, of Howard Co, Md: 110 acs; with new dwlg. -John R Thomas, Ellicott's Mills, Md

Headqrtrs Army of the Potomac: in the Field, Oct 15, 1863. Gen Meade's army left the vicinity of Culpeper on Sat on its homeward march. Skimishes on Wed with the brigade of Carolinians, commanded by Brig Gen Heth, [Pettigrew's old brig,] who broke & fled & hid behind rocks & bushes along the stream, etc. [Other skirmishes were covered in this article.] Col Mallon, 42nd N Y Regt, commanding the 3rd Brigade of the 2nd div, was shot thu the stomach & died in half an hour. Capt S M Smith, Ast Inspec Gen on Gen Webb's staff, was severely wounded in the shoulder. Capt Francis Wessells, Judge Adv to Gen Webb, wounded in thigh. Orderly Sgt Allman, a brave & true a sldr as ever lived, was killed while bearing the flag of his Genr'ls headqrtrs. Capt Cooper, Inspec Gen of 3rd Brig, was wounded in the thigh. Lt M Caste, of Gen Owen's staff, was killed. Capt Plumb, 125th N Y, killed. Capt Lemon, 125th N Y, wounded. Lt Olsoner, of the same, wounded, as also Lt Lowe, 12th N J, & Capt J Ball, of the 1st Minn. Among the slain rebels & left on the field were Brig Gen Cooke, a s/o Gen Philip St Geo Cooke, of the Union army, & Col Ruffin, of the 1st, & Col Thompson, of the 5th N C cavalry.

Local Matters: the grave yard in the northern limits of the city, near the Old Soldiers' Home, has had over 7,000 interments of the remains of sldrs, of which about 5,000 remain- the other 2,000 having been disinterred by the relatives or friends, who desired to convey them to a resting place among kindred. Many friends of the dec'd persons have come to Washington with a view of removing the remains, & have refrained from doing so after finding them so neatly & satisfactorily put to rest in these grounds. The cemetery is being embellished too, gradually, with artistic beauties.

MON OCT 19,1863

We learn on reliable source that during the cavalry fight on last Mon, near Brandy Station, the Hon John M Botts was arrested or taken prisoner by the rebels, & since taken to Richmond. We suppose he is to be imprisoned & held as a hostage for the return of Shackleford, Bradford, Freeman, & others of Culpeper Co, who were arrested some time ago by Gen Meade as dangerous persons, & confined in the Old Capitol. Mr Botts was arrested at a early stage of the rebellion & held as a prisoner by the Confederates ever since. He was a short time ago released from confinement on parole, & to remain on his farm near Culpeper Crt-hse. -Alexandria Jrnl

In the field, Va, on Oct 14, 1863: the workshop train of the Army of the Potomac, under charge of Capt E J Strang, en route from Brixville, was attacked by a party of guerillas in the vicinity of Bull Run. The men fought bravely but sustained the loss of Mr Sherwood, wagon master in charge of the train, who was killed instantly. This train consisted of 250 wagons, 150 horses, & a 100 mules. The train of Kilpatrick's cavalry division was shelled by the rebels near Brentsville. Capt Meade, who was in charge, succeeded in bringing out his train without loss by way of Wolf Run Shoals.

Deaths reported to the Navy Dept for week ending Oct 17, 1863:
Timothy Sullivan, landsman, interm fever, Sep 25, U S steamer *Memphis*. Nelson McLean, steward, diarrhoea, Sep 22, U S steamer *Black Hawk*.
Chas H Snow, or Laon, sgt steward, yel fever, Sep 22, U S steamer *Fearnot*.
Fred Belden, actg mstr mate, yel fever, Sep 24, do.
Jas H Duffy, 2nd cl fireman, yel fever, Sep 23, U S steamer *Hollyhock*.
E C Gallagher, 2nd cl fireman, do, do, do.
Philip Smith, coal heaver, remit fever, Spe 30, Nav Hosp, Memphis.
Ira Werdell, 1st cl boy, remit fever, Oct 3, do.
Jos Conroy, do, do, do, do.
D H Godfrey, 1st cl fireman, chronic diarrhoea, Oct 4, do.
Henry I Sharp, seaman, diarrhoea, Aug 25, U S steamer *Black Hawk*.
Wm Burr, 1st cl boy, diarrhoea, Aug 25, do.
John Cavendish, seaman, remit fev, Aug 27, U S steamer *Osage*.
Francis D Finnegan, coal heaver, typhoid fev, Sep 24, U S steamer *Albatros*.
Sylvanus W Cox, actg mstr, gunshot wound, Aug 6, U S steamer *Cohassett*.
Henry Curtis, seaman, consumption, no date, Nav Hosp, N Y.
Henry Paul, q m, gastritis, no date, do.
Wm Robinson, boatswain mate, diarrhoea, no date, do.
Jeremiah Johnson, landsman, pneumonia, no date, do.
Wm F Hemsworth, 3rd ast engr, remit fev, Aug 24, vessel U S S *Narragansett*.
Allen F Spear, Lt, yel fev, Sep 18, vessel *Nightingale*.
Jas Mereghere, actg mstr mate, yel fev, no date, vessel *Sarah Bruen*.
Jos Moss, actg ensign, yel fev, no date, vessel *Sea Foam*.
John Lakeman, actg mstr mate, yel fever, no date, do.
Chas Morris, actg mstr mate, blank, Sep 25, steamer *Hollyhock*.
S J Owens, actg ensign, blank, no date, U S S La.
Wilson Jasper, landsman, pneumonia, Sep 2, Mississippi Squadron.
David Lott, fireman, drowned, Sep 14, do.
Geo L Reed, boatswain mate, cong of lungs, Jul 26, do.
Thos Brown, landsman, fever, Mar 25, do.
Jas Driscoll, landsman, drowned, Mar 29, do.
Jos Worthington, contraband, fever, Sep 5, do.
Michl Nicholas, seaman, dysentery, Jan 7, do.
Daniel Young, seaman, dysentery, Jan 14, do.
Thos Hackett, coal heaver, dysentery, Mar 10, do.
Albert C Smith, 2nd ast eng, jaundice, Sep 1, vessel *Saginaw*.
Jas Higgins, 2nd cl fireman, pneumonia, Oct 12, Nav Hosp, Chelsea.

From the S W: Cairo, Oct 16. The expedition under Maj Leed, of the 6th Mo, broke up the camp of the notorious guerrilla Cotter, in Jeff Co. Killed him & took all his men prisoners.

New Orleans, Oct 10. The 19th Army Corps reached the Vermillion river yesterday. There was sharp skirmishing. Lt Col Cowan, of the 3rd Texas Cavalry was wounded.

Died: on Oct 17, Thos Livingston Poiter, in his 45th yr.

TUE OCT 20, 1863
Orphans Crt of Wash Co, D C. Prsnl estate of John E Leach, late of Wash Co, dec'd.
-Jas L Barbour, adm

Supreme Crt of D C. Saml Cole vs Clarissa Thomas, Abby Nugent, & heirs at law of Edw M Thomas, Chas S Wallach. Rg-appointment of a new trustee in the stead of Wallach, now a non-resident of D C. Edw M Thomas died leaving Abby Nugent, his sister, a non-resident of D C, his only heir. -R J Meigs, clerk

War in Tenn: Bridgport, Oct 18. A detachment of the 61st Ohio returned from a scout made to & in the neighborhood of Trenton. They returned with Capt Robt C Kennedy, Inspec Gen of the staff of Gen Wheeler, as prisoner. Capt Kennedy was on his road to Gen Bragg with despatches. These were also captured. The Capt also had with him a flag captured from the 4th East Tenn Union Regt. It was taken by the rebels from said regt at McMinnville. It is now in our possession.

Richmond Examiner says, in regard to the Texas election, that Pendleton Murrah has been elected Govn'r over Gen T T Chambers by about 5,000 votes. F S Stickpole has been elected Lt Govn'r.

WED OCT 21, 1863
Mrd: at Gtwn, D C, on Oct 19, at the residence of the bride's father, by the Rev Wm Chapman, John L Owens to Susanna Frances, 3rd d/o Geo Hill, jr, all of Gtwn.

Mrd: at N Y, on Oct 14, by Rev Thos Farrel, Thos W Spence, of Scotland, to Miss Annie G Powell, of England.

Died: on Oct 20, of diptheria, Martha J Clark, youngest & only child of Dr J C R Clark & Julia R Clark. Funeral at 555 13th st, today.

Col Dan McCook, 52nd Ohio Regt, has destroyed the home of the murderer of his bro, Brig Gen McCook, who was butchered while lying wounded in an ambulance. The hse was near Huntsville, Ala.

Col Thos Ruffin, of N C, Col of the 1st N C rebel cavalry, who was wounded at Bristow's Station on Wed, & was brought into Alexandria, died at Grace Chr hosp on Sun, & was put in the pvt vault of Mr Richd Windsor, in the Methodist Prot burying ground, to be removed after the war to his home in N C. Col Ruffin was a mbr of Congress from N C before the rebellion.

THU OCT 22, 1863
Mrd: on Oct 20, at Grace Chr, Howard Co, Md, by Rev Wm G Jackson, Cmder Foxhall A Parker, U S Navy, to Caroline, d/o Thos Donaldson.

Died: in Wash City, on Oct 20, Jas Stuart, native of county Doure, Ire, in his 53rd yr. Funeral from St Matthew's Chr on Thu, burial at the Cathedral Cemetery, Balt, Md.

Died: on Oct 21, Celestise, eldest d/o the late Capt E A Capron, U S Army. Funeral from the residence of her step father, Chas Vinson, 86 Pa av, Sat.

Resolutions of respect to the memory of Orderly Sgt Eugene Fitzgerald, of the Nat'l Rifles, who departed this life Oct 12, 1863, were adopted at a special meeting of that company on Oct 16.
A man whose relations as husband, father, son, friend, & sldr derived additional lustre from the high moral qualities which ever graced his character.

Mississippi guerilla: ltr intercepted in Boliva Co, Miss, on Sep 19, by command of Lt Col Geo E Currie, of the Mississippi Marine Brig, from Thos B Lenoir, living about 3 miles from Beulah, in Bolivar Co, addressed to his sister in Texas, under date of Sep 4. Passages: women are scouring the country over to find cotton for the Yankees. Our friend, Mrs Manley, is spoken of as being engaged in the trade. A bale of cotton is not considered safe unless placed with a biting dog tied to it. All that I wish for afer the war ends is a good constitution preserved & health cont'd. My dear sister, I don't mind the loss of my property more than the loss of a few head of beef cattle for which I had no immediate use. Pray for me, that I may meet you again when I am held to account for the things of this life. Kiss the little boy, & learn him to hate the Yankee & traitor as bad as I now do.

Twenty-six of Morgan's men escaped from Camp Douglas, Chicago, on Sun, by digging a tunnel from one of their barracks under the fence.

Fatal casualty at the Treas Dept on Tue as workmen were elevating the presses designed to be used in printing the Treas notes from the ground to the attic of the Treas bldg. The tackling gave way & in its descent it struck the scaffolding on which the mstr-rigger, Mr Teasdale, & a man named Corcoran, were knock to the ground. Both badly injured. Jas Stewart & Thos Larkin were knocked from the platform, Stewart falling 30 ft & was instantly killed; Larkin badly but not fatally injured.

FRI OCT 23, 1863
Mrs Cecilia Young Kretschmar is prepared to resume her musical classes.

Died: after a long & painful illness, Chas King, in his 82nd yr. Interment in Balt, Md. [No date-recent]

Tragedy; on Tue last, Lt White went to the plantation of Col J H Sothoron, near Benedict, Chas Co, Md, in St Mary's Co, Md, to enlist slaves. Col Sothoron consented provided the negroes were willing to go. They declined. Sothoron & his son both fired at the Lt, who fell mortally wounded, the Col firing first.

Lost-a dark bay mare, on Oct 21, from the place of E H Brooke, above Chain Bridge & below Ft Sumner. -Mr Brooke's place or the Paymstr Genr'l ofc.

The Crt Martial of Pvt Daniel Murphy, Co F, Scott's 900, U S Vol Cavalry, will convene in Wash City on Oct 20.

Foreign Obit-Dr Whately, Archbishop of Dublin, died on Oct 8, in his 77th yr.

Mrs Frances Trollope has recently died in Florence; born in 1780; resided in Cincinnati from 1829 to 1832, before returning to England; a prolific writer.

Wet nurse wanted: apply to Dr W P Johnston, 406 7th st.

Southern News: Ft Monroe, Oct 22. Dr W P Rucker made his escape from Pittsyvania jail last Sun night & is at large.

Charleston, Oct 20l. Gen D H Hill relieved of his command. Breckinridge takes command of his corps.

Crt Martial to convene in Wash City on Oct 20, 1863, for the trial of Pvt Danl Murphy, Co F, Scott's 900 U S Vol Cavalry, & such other prisoners who may be brought before it. Ofcrs detailed for the court are as follows:

1-Col A J Warner-10 Pa Res Corps
2-Lt Col A H Reynolds-6th Pa Vols
3-Maj R T Elliott-16th Mich Vols
4-Capt H A Wetmore-6th N Y Cavalry
5-Capt B F Sceva-10th N Y Cavalry
6-Capt J Bishop-4th Md Vols
7-Lt & Adj J Daley-12th Ill Cavalry

8-Lt J H Jenkins-2nd N J Vols
9-Lt G C Marvin-168th N Y Vols
10-Lt D R Brown-20th Conn Vols
11-Lt S D Lyon-17th Ind Vols
12-Lt J P Swain-8th N Y Cavalry
13-Lt W H Noyes-5th Conn Vols

Capt Edw Tumbler, 4th Pa Cavalry, Judge Advocate

FRI OCT 24, 1863

Died: in Wash City, on Oct 22, of diptheria, Alfred Gordon, aged 9 yrs, s/o Rev E W Syle. Funeral from Trinity Chr, C & 3rd sts, Sat.

Died: at Langside, Canada West, on Oct 16, Jas Ballantyne, sr, a native of Peebles, Scotland.

Strayed this morning from a yard, pointer dog. Wm B Webb, 516 11th st, D C.

Orphans Crt of Wash Co, D C. Case of John W Clarke & Wm J Rhees, excs of Isaac Clarke, dec'd; settlement on Nov 14. -Z C Robbins, rg o/wills

Wash Corp: Mayor's nominations for Trustees of the Pblc Schools:

Jas O Wilson	M H Miller	F S Walsh	John T Cassell
Wm Wilson	W J Rhees	Ch W Davis	J B Ellis
J S Brown	O C Wight	Robt Ferguson	J E Holmead

Wash Corp: 1-Bill for relief of Wm Riley, assignee of C D Bradley, was referred to the Cmte on Improvements. 2-Bill granting permission to John H Semmes & Wm H Brauner to extend their vaults beyond the curb line: referred to the Cmte on Improvements. 3-Bills referred to the Cmte on Finance: relief of E E Mockabee; relief of Elias Davis; relief of the small-pox hospital.

Election for 3 mbrs of Congress & mbrs of the Leg in W Va took place on Thu. The candidates for Congress are all Union men: Jacob H Blair, John S Burdett, & Wm G Brown, Killian V Whaley, Dr Caldwell, Capt Comstock, & Col Danl Frost. No returns have yet been received.

MON OCT 26, 1863

Deaths reported to the Navy Dept for the week ending Oct 24, 1863:
Jno W Hill, actg ast paymstr, delirum tremens, Sept 28, vessel U S S *Sea Foam*.
Chas H Chapprel, landsman, dysentery, Oct 1, vessel U S S *Wabash*.
Timothy Sullivan, landsman, inter fever, Sep 21, vessel U S S *Memphis*.
Emmarl Pember, ord seaman, yel fever, Oct 2, vessel U S S *Albatros*.
Timothy Trowley, coal heaver, yel fever, Sep 30, do.
Thos Devener, coal heaver, yel fever, Sep 29, do.
Peter Anderson, q m, yel fever, Sep 8, do.
Aug Smith, landsman, diarrhoea, Sep 13, Hosp, New Orleans.
Ed Boyle, coal heaver, pneumonia, Jan 12, Mound City.
Wm Timmons, landsman, typhoid fever, Sep 12, vessel U S S *Lafayette*.
Saml Burns, contraband, diarrhoea, Aug 31, vessel U S S *Red Rover*

J Niel, contraband, anasarca, Oct 7, Nav Hosp, Memphis.

Wm Riley, 2nd cl fireman, chronic diarrhoea, Oct 9, do.

Chas Earnest, 1st clerk, yel fever, Oct 5, vessel U S S *Pensacola.*

Thos Grace, 1st cl fireman, yel fever, Oct 6, do.

S S Hickerson, surg's steward, remit fever, Oct 6, vessel U S S *Estrella.*

John Hover, 2nd cl fireman, remit fever, Oct 6, do.

Cornel P Ryan, paymstr's steward, drowned, Oct 1, do.

John Brannon, alias Pagley, marine, typhoid fever, Oct 17, Navy Yd, Wash.

John Jones, coal heaver, typhoid fever, Oct 3, Nav Hosp, N Y.

Geo Wood, 1st cl fireman, drowned, Oct 3, vessel U S S *Arizona.*

Saml T Silsby, 3rd ast engr, consumption, Oct 17, Nav Hosp, N Y.

Jas Fountain, 3rd ast engr, consumption, Oct 29, Nav Hosp, N Y.

Theodore Johnson, landsman, gunshot wound, Oct 10, vessel U S S *Com Jones.*

S T Strude, actg 3rd ast engr, drowned, Oct 15, vessel U S S *Nansemond.*

Geo Terry, seaman, drowned, Oct 15, do.

Obit- Judge Thos H Wilkinson died at his residence, in Calvert Co, Md, on Aug 25, in his 81st yr. He leaves a widow & 2 chldrn.

Died: on Oct 25, Dr Stephen Bailey, in his 50th yr. Funeral from the Chr of the Epiphany, today.

Died: on Jun 9, at Raroronga, So Seas, after severe suffering, Rev Wm Howe, age 61 yrs.

Died: on Oct 10, at Hamburg, Sussex Co, N J, at the residence of her relative, Thos Lawrence, Martha Ann, y/d/o the late Robt Brooke, of Phil.

Mrd: at the residence of the bride's father, Mr John E Neale, Oct 6, Glorie to Jas W Anderson, formerly of Balt, both of Wash.

Mrd: at the Cathedral, Balt, Md, on Oct 22, by the Rev Vicar Gen, Jas F Mathews, of Chas Co, Md, to Victoria, d/o the late Jas R Brest, of PG Co, Md.

Actg Mstr's Mate Jacob Hahn deserted from the svc, at the Navy Yd, on Oct 6; reward $25.00. -Andrew A Harwood, Commandant, U S Navy Yd, Wash.

Fortress Monroe, Oct 23. The execution of Dr D W Wright, of Norfolk, for the murder of a U S ofcr some time since, took place today at the Fair Grounds. He stated that he had committed the crime without premediation.

The number of Yankee prisoners held in Richmond prisons last night was 12,000. Gen Imboden on the 18th attacked the garrison at Charlestown, in the Shenandoah Valley, capturing 434 prisoners, with their arms, etc. Signed by Robt E Lee.

TUE OCT 27, 1863

Supreme Crt of D C, in Equity #91. Mgt W Handy, Edw G Handy, & others, vs Benj M & Stephan C Wailes, & others, heirs at law of Isaac H Wailes. On Jul 22, 1847, Saml W Handy, of Wash, conveyed to Isaac H Wailes & heirs, ground in sq 226, Wash City, for payment of an annuity of $100 to be paid to Mary G Handy, & if paid, said lot to be released to Saml W Handy & heirs. Isaac H Wailes died Mar 15, 1855; Saml W Handy died on Dec 23, 1856; Mary G Handy died on Sep 6, 1858. Annuity was fully paid. They are entititled to have the rl prop released to them. Some of the heirs are infants & Isaac H Wailes, & the residence of others, is beyond the jurisdiction of this crt. Benj M Wailes & Jacob S Black, 2 of the heirs reside out of D C. -R J Meigs, clerk

.

Judge Savage, of Utica, N Y, died on Oct 19, at age 84 yrs.

Charleston Harbor, Oct 19. Svr'l changes in the Cmders of the iron-clad fleet:

Steam frig *Ironsides*-Capt Rowan	monitor *Nantucket*-Capt J C Beaumont
monitor *Patapsco*-Capt T Stevens	monitor *Passaic*-Capt E Simpson
monitor *Lehigh*-Capt A Bryson	monitor *Catskill*-Lt G Silley
monitor *Weekawken*-Capt Calhoun	monitor *Nahant*-Lt J J Cornwell

The *Nantucket* is in Warsaw Sound. The *Passaic* & *Montauk* are at Port Royal completing repairs. The steamer *Dupont* arrived this morning from Port Royal, having towed the Monitor *Patapsco*, which, with a new smoke-stack & other repairs, looks as good as new again.

WED OCT 28, 1863
Died: in Montg Co, Md, on Oct 25, of diptheria, Lilian Ida, only d/o John E & L Alice Lewis, in her 7th year. Funeral at 573 7th st, today.

Obit-Celestine, eldest d/o the late Capt E A Capron, U S Army, died on Oct 21, of diptheria She was taken from a devoted mother, sisters, & father, in the early blossom of life. She was nutured by her mother in the Episc faith.

Orphans Crt of Wash Co, D C. Prsnl estate of Jane Deakins, late of Wash Co, dec'd. -J C McGuire, adm

Jacob Grimm, celebrated German writer, bro of the late Wm Grimm, died at Berlin, Germany, on Sep 25, after a short illness. He was born on Jan 4, 1785 & therefore reached his 79th year..

Wash Corp: 1-Act for relief of Thos Cogan: sum of $159.61 for the purpose of paying Cogan, assignee for certificate of stock, issued under the act of May 27, to Robt Paine to Wm Fletcher, with interest from Dec 6. 2-Act for relief of E E Barnes, scavenger 5th ward, $197, lose sustained by him in the destruction of his property. That such destruction was caused by his obedience to the directions of the Mayor in the depost of night soil, thereby incurring the displeasure of the sldrs, & to defray the expense thereof a sum sufficient is hereby payable out of the general fund. 3-Act of relief of G W G Eslin: sum of $282.92, to supply a deficiency for repairing D st north.

Fighting on Thu & Fri arose from the enemy crossing the Rappanock at Beverly Ford. The 2nd Pa Cavalry, Lt Col Jas Brinton commanding, encountered 2 regts whom they charged & drove into the river. Maj Taggert led the first charge upon the 10th Va Cavalry, & was shot in the knee cap. He was carried to Warenton where his leg was amputated above the knee by the regt surgeon, Dr Wiedman, & where he died on Sat morning.

THU OCT 29, 1863
Gayoso Hse, Memphis, Tenn, Oct 4-Midnight. Capt C C Smith, Com'g Btln 13th Regulars: My Dear Friend: I cannot sleep tonight till I record an expression of the deep feelings of my heart to you and to the ofcrs and sldrs of the battalion, for their kind behavior to my poor child. I realize that you all feel for my family the attachment of kindred, and I assure you all of full reciprocity. Consistent with a sense of duty to my profession and office, I could not leave my post, and sent for my family to come to me in that fatal climate, and in that

sickly period of the year, and behold the result. The child who bore my name & in whose future I reposed with more confidence than I did in my own plans of life, now floats a mere corpse, seeking a grave in a distant land, with a weeping mother, bro, and sister clustered about him. But for myself I can ask no sympathy. /On, on, I must go till I meet a soldier's fate, or see my country rise superior to all factions, till its flag is adored and respected by ourselves and all the powers of earth. But my poor Willie was, or thought he was, a sergeant of the Thirteenth. I have seen his eye brighten and his heart beat as he beheld the battalion under arms, and asked me if they were not real soldiers. Child as he was, he had the enthusiasm, the pure love of truth, honor and love of country which should animate all soldiers. God only knows why he should die thus young. He is dead, but will not be forgotten till those who knew him in life have followed him to the same mysterious end. /Please convey to the battalion my heartfelt thanks, and assure each and all that if in after years they call on me or mine, and mention that they were of the Thirteenth Regulars when poor Willie was a sergeant, they will have a key to the affection of my family that will open all it has, that we will share with them our last blanket, our last crust. Your friend, W T Sherman, Maj Gen

Died: in Wash City, on Oct 28, of gastric fever, Frank A Goodnough, aged 35 yrs. He will be interred in Pittsburgh, Pa.

Supreme Crt of D C, in Equity #58. Wm G Deale against Wm B Mickum, Sarah B Mickum, & Walter Lenox. Deale, on Jul 1, 1851, borrowed $5,000 from Sarah P Mickum [then Sarah P Ogden], to secure the repayment of which he conveyed to Walter Lenox & heirs part of lot 22 in sq 518; parts of lots 3 & 4 in sq 518; part of lot 6 in sq 518; fully pd with interest. Lenox lives out of D C & cannot have release of said trust deed. -R J Meigs, clerk

FRI OCT 30, 1863
Died: on Oct 29, John Treadway, of typhoid fever, in his 38th yr. Funeral from his late residence on E st, between 11th & 12th sts, today.

Orphans Crt of Wash Co, D C. Prsnl estate of Jos O Hastings, late of Wash Co, dec'd. -M Julia Barrett, admx

Dr Hurley, eminent physician of Nashville, Tenn, having lost his property by his devotion to the Union, has settled in Wash for the practice of his profession.

Supreme Crt of D C. The following persons, holding the ofc of Constable in D C, have not taken the Oath of Allegiance prescribed by the act of Jul 2, 1862, & therefore prohibited from exercising the powers of Constables in D C:

Aquilla R Allen	Robt P Hazzard	Jos B Peerce
Jacob G Fulton	John W Martin	Walter Pomeroy
David Jackson	Jas Burey	Thos Plumsill
Jas H Boss	John H Hilton	Wm Readdy
Wm H Fanning	Wm M Moreland	Geo W Smith
A E L Keese	Wm D Bell	Richd Sedgwick
J M Barneclo	Amos Huntt	Wm E Smith
Henry Grier	Uriah B Mitchell	Jas Thompson
Wm E Martin	Jas Callan	John L Turner
Wm H Barneclo	Horace B House	Jos Williamson
Jas Frazer	Jas S Norwood	John H Wise
Horatio R Maryman	Henry Ebeling	John A Willet
John T Baker	Francis A Jones	Wm R Wall

Jos P Wannell
Jas F Woollard
Geo Wahl
Henry A Wright
Asa Gladman
Jas T Lloyd
Henry S Ward
Wm R Plowman
Jos B Stanley
R H Digges
John T May
John W Reynolds
Hugh Dougherty
Wm Harper
Jos A Fil
John M Lloyd
Jas Baggott
Francis S Edelin
Matthew Collins
Jos Anker
Jas A Cooper
Benj T Watson
Thos Williamson

Wm L Ross
Thos H Robinson
John R Cronin
Augustus F Berry
Wm Young
Jas Ginuaty
John N Gates
Jas H Suit
Francis Ward
Edw C Gardner
Jas Donaldson
Walter B Silence
Saml N Chipley
H C Boudinot
Thos Stackpole
John R Vernon
John W Sibly
Jeff. Robinson
Thos Irwin
Wm Waters
Wm I Craig
Wm H Saunders
Enead Reynolds

Chas W Arnold
A G Haley
Wm D Serrin
John McDermott
Frank Zimmerman
Jacob Ash
Henry Nash
Lewis Hohing
August Gerecke
Jas W Stewart
Chas H Merrill
Thos J Kelly
John A Steele
Geo Donaldson
Julius E Schwabe
Jos S Williams
John S Waugh
Robt L Mastin
Saml I Fearson
Chas L Boarman
Wm G Tanner
Jas Fitzpatrick

Following are the only persons who complied & are authorized to act as Constables in D C:

Pat H Gaughran
Jos H Hilton
David A Harrover
Wm Martin
Geo P Hotchkiss
Richd H Trunnell
Jas M Busher
John Dewdney
Wm H Lusby

Robt F Magee
Francis W Colclazer
Robt B Hughes
John H Stewart
Francis O'Callaghan
Wm Cammack
Jas A McGowan
Chas G Eckloff
Maurice O'Conner

Alfred R Edelin
Geo F Huguely
John H Wise
Jacob F King
Wm A Boss
Geo T Gibbons
Jos F Kelly
-by order of R J Meigs,
clerk

Beautiful lines were written on the death of Celestine Capron, suggested on passing the funeral cortage: inscribed to the mother of the dec'd Col G W Patten, U S Army. [6 stanzas]

Capt Latshaw, the post q m, Lexington, Ky, has been tried by crt-martial, & fined $60,000 & sentenced to 3 years imprisonment for defrauding the Gov't.

SAT OCT 31, 1863

Died: on Oct 29, John R Queen, in his 54th yr. Funeral from his late residence, 604 8th st, today.

Lord Lyndhurst died on Oct 12, in his 92nd yr, of American birth, born in Massachusetts while still a British colony; s/o John Singleton Copley, a painter of note, who is best known by his *Death of Lord Chatham*. His son, born May 21, 1772, sailed for Eng with his mother & sisters May 27, 1775, when he was 3 years old. He mrd in 1819 the widow of a British army ofcr, & leaves 2 dghts. A sister of his, Mrs Gardner Greene, is living in Boston, at a very advanced age. Another sister, also over 90 years of age, resides in England.

Wash Corp: 1-Ptn of B H Seinmetz for digging a drain on N J ave: passed. 2-Ptn of Hugh McCormick: Cmte on Improvements asked to be discharged from further consideration of his ptn.
3-Ptn of A McKinstry & Wm McLean, on curbstones & footway: passed. 4-Act for relief of Thos Byrne: postponed. 5-Ptn of C H H Mills & others for permission to erect a temporary frame bldg: referred to the Cmte on Police. 6-Ptn of P Cullanan, asking an appropriation for a deficiency: referred to the Cmte on Improvements.

Clayton F Becker, of Russelleville, Ky, was admitted to the bar of the Supreme Crt of D C.

MON NOV 2, 1863
Another victim to African exploration; ltr from Dr Livingstone, the African explorer, dt'd Murchison Cataracts, Africa, Apr 25th, announcing the death of Mr Richd Thornton, geologist, of fever. His body was buried near the first cataract. Dr Kirk & Dr Livingstone are to return to England.

Army in La: On the 12th, the advance of Gen Franklin's cavalry captured the rebel Gen Pratt & his nephew, between Carrion Crow bayou & Opelousas. The latter was acting as his Ast Adj Gen. Gen Pratt was born in Hartford, Conn. He is about 50 years of age, 25 of which have been passed in the south. Up to May last he commanded a brig of Louisiana vols, but resigned on account of ill health. When taken prisoner he was engaged in enforcing the conscription act in the state.

Deaths reported to the Navy Dept for the week ending Oct 31, 1863:
Newton Cox, ord seaman, chronic diarrhoea, Oct 12, Nav Hosp, Memphis.
Edw Languish, blank, consumption, Oct 13, do.
Chas Paine, landsman, chronic diarrhoea, Oct 16, do.
L Richmenscheider, landsman, remit fever, Oct 18, do.
Wm M Junken, actg ast paymstr, yel fever, Sep 29, vessel U S S Potomac.
Ad. Brown, ord seaman, yel fev, Sep 10, vessel U S S Pensacola.
Jno Floyd, carp mate, yel fever, Sep 11, vessel U S S Sciota.
Jno Murphy, landsman, dropsy, Oct 23, Nav Hosp.
Wm Snowball, seaman, chronic diarrhoea, Oct 18, vessel U S S Lexington.
Chas W Howard, actg mstr, gunshot wound, Oct 10, vessel U S S New Ironsides.
Louis Johnson, contraband, congestion of brain, Oct 12, vessel U S S Vermont.
Jno Julian, coxswain, sudden, Oct 12, do.
Jno Vandyke, seaman, pneumonia, no date, Nav Hosp Chelsea.
Jas Fountain, 3rd ast engr, consumption, Nav Hosp, N Y.
Thos King, landsman, pneumonia, no date, do.
Geo Fleming, coxswain, viriola, Oct 15, vessel U S S St Mary's.
Andrew J Rich, act ensign, blank, Sep 29, Chelsea, Mass.
D W Hickey, seaman, dysentery, Jun 7, Nav Hosp, Newbern.
Chas Rummel, 2nd cl fireman, intrmttnt fever, Aug 11, Nav Hosp, vessel Plymouth.
Chas Batchelor, landsman, drowned, Sep 20, vessel U S S Valley City.
Jas Fairbanks, seaman, interm fever, Aug 10, do.

Died: at Charlestown, Jeff Co, Va, on Oct 27, of typhoid fever, Miss J C Bird Raum, y/d/o the late Dr Wm Rippey Raum, in her 19th yr.

TUE NOV 3, 1863
Died: at his residence in Alexandria, Va, on Oct 31, Benj Waters, in his 74th yr.

Died: on Oct 31, in Brooklyn, N Y, Capt Edwin D Willards, of the Commissary Dept of the Army of the Potomac.

Orphans Crt of Wash Co, D C. 1-Case of John B Blake, exc of Susan H Strahan, dec'd; settlement on Nov 24th. -Z C Robbins, rg o/wills 2-Prsnl estate of John T Sullivan, late of Wash Co, dec'd. Harriet M Sullivan, John B Blake, excs

Creditors of Wm Luce, of Wash City, dec'd, are to present their claims, at the Navy Yd, Wash. -Andrew A Harwood

Gen John S Darcy, formerly 31 years Pres of N J R R Co, died Nov 1st, at Newark, N J, age about 76 yrs. A physician by profession, practiced until within a few days of his decease. He was a U S Mrshl under the Admin of Gen Jackson & Martin Van Buren.

WED NOV 4, 1863
Orphans Crt of Wash Co, D C. 1-Case of Chas S English, Sarah Frances English, Robt P Dodge, & Walter S Cox, excs of David English, dec'd; settlement on Nov 28. 2-Case of Emily B Thompson, admx w a of Mary Mudd, dec'd; settlement on Nov 28. 3-Case of Geo A Bohrer, exc of Dr Benj S Bohrer, dec'd; settlement on Dec 1. -Z C Robbins, rg o/wills

Jos Detweiler, of York Co, Pa, was arrested last week on charge of attempting to evade the income tax. He divided his property among his chldrn, so that it should not come within the provisions of the law. He has been held to answer.

Died: on Nov 2, T Oscar Dabney, infant s/o Thos S & Virginia *Dahbney, aged 1 yr. Funeral from the residence of his grandmother, Mrs R Sears, 437 H st, today. [*Dahbney-as written.]

War Dept: By directions of the Pres of the U S, Maj Gen B F Butler, U S Vols, is appt'd to the command of the 18th army corps, & the Dept of Va & N C. Maj Gen J G Foster, on being relieved by Maj Gen Butler, will report in person for orders to the Adj Gen of the Army.

THU NOV 5, 1863
Died: on Nov 3, Mrs Maria Gregg. Funeral at the residence of Mr Henry Queen, of Wash Co, today.

Died: on Nov 4, Mary Adair, only c/o Capt G H & Ellen Adair Mendell, aged 10 months. Funeral from the residence of her uncle, B F Pleasants, 272 F st, today.

Farm for sale-*Spring Hill*, adjoining Gtwn College grounds, about 70 acs, with frame dwlg hase. -Dr Chas H Cragin, 124 Dunbarton st, Gtwn, or to J S McKenney, at Patriotic Bank, Wash City.

Col C R Ellet died at Bunker Hill, Ill, on Oct 31: eldest s/o the late Col Chas Ellet, who was killed at the naval battle of Memphis last yr. He was 20 years of age & commanded the Mississippi fleet. He was a nephew of Gen A W Ellet.

Mr J Newton, of Conn, who has devoted many years to the business of teaching the Sword Execise, is about to publish a system of instructions for pupils & teachers.

Southern Items:

Maj Chas Pickett, of the Confederate army, was mrd at Danville, Va, on the 27th ult, to Lizzie H, d/o John H Smith, of Wash, D C.

Col Edmund Kirby, of Richmond, was killed in the battle of Chickamauga.

A duel took place near Augusta, Ga, on the 28th ult, between C A Reed, of Augusta, & R Copeland, of Md. Copeland was killed. Another acc't says he was a native of Fla, & formerly a clerk in one of the Depts at Wash.

Humphrey Marshall has opened a law ofc at Richmond.

Col John H Sothoron, of St Mary's Co, Md, & his son have arrived in Richmond.

J B Lamar, Pres of the Bank of Commerce, at Savanah, Ga, with bank ofcrs in other states, request a meeting of reps of different banks in the Confederate states.

Gen Chas Dimmock, chief of the State Ord Dept & Cmder of the pblc guard at Richmond, died of a paralytic stroke on the 27th ult. He was a grad of West Point, & resigned his commission in the U S army in 1836.

FRI NOV 6, 1863

Died: in Wash City, on Nov 5, Mary Anne Rabbitt, w/o Thos C Rabbitt, aged 59 yrs. Funeral from her late residence, 385 10th st, today.

Trustee's sale of land on West River, A A Co, Md; part of the rl estate of Alexander Franklin, dec'd; lots 4 & 5. Lot 4, 243 acs, assigned to Chas K Cannon, for the term of his life, by decree in partition cause; adjoins the lands of Dr Thos J Franklin, Wm H Hall, & heirs of John C Weems. Lot 5, 181 acs, lying in Swamp Dist of A A Co, adjoins the lands of Frank Brashers & J W Parrott. -A B Hagner, Oliver Miller, trustees, Annapolis, Md

Trustee's sale of land in A A Co, Md, in the case of Johnson vs Hancock; the rl estate of Stephen W Hancock, dec'd, 727 acs, *Rock Crk Farm*; & *Poplar Plains*, 237 acs. Lands adjoin the farms of L Chard, R Chard, Geo Mackubin, & Wm Cole. 211 acs of Rock Creek Farm are subject to the dower-rght of Eliz Hancock, widow. Almost all the bldgs are on dower land. -A Randall, A B Hagner, trustees, Annapolis, Md

Orphans Crt of Wash Co, D C. Case of Stewart Hastings & Mrs Sarah A Hall, excx of Daniel W Hall, dec'd; settlement on Nov 28. -Z C Robbins, rg o/wills

Trustee's sale of land in A A Co, Md, in the case of Hardesty et al vs Gantt et al. Rl estate of Thos P Gantt, dec'd; 339+ acs; adjoins the lands of John Tucker, Essex R Dorsey, Dr Sellman Welch, & Thos K Carey. Mr Wm O Prather, on the premise, will show same. -A B Hagner, trustee, Annapolis, Md

Jas Snowden Pleasants died on Oct 16, near Poolesville, Md. He was in the prime of life, but from a long confinement in the Old Capitol, had contracted disease, which was no doubt the principal cause of his death. -Rockville [Md] Sentinel

The Richmond Exam of Oct 28th announces the arrival in that city of Col John Sothoron & son, of St Mary's Co, Md, the parties who shot & killed Lt White, on Oct 19. They escaped across the Potomac.

Skirmish in East Tenn-Nov 1. On Fri Col Adams, with the 1st & 11th Ky attacked Asby's brig & recaptured the wagons & 300 prisoners. Next day Gen Sanders advanced & drove the enemy 4 miles. They charged this advance, the 8th Mich & 112th Ill, driving them back. Our loss was 4 killed & 45 wounded. Maj Owens was captured & Capt Stanley wounded. Capt Buck & Lt Clark, of 18th Michigan, were wounded.

Ctzns of D C request our fellow ctzns meet with us on Nov 6 at 8 p m, in the Cncl Chamber, City Hall, to join in arrrangements for a Grand Mass Meeting to aid & stimulate enlistments of volunteers in D C, & thereby avoid another draft.

Geo & Thos Parker & Co	Hinton & Teel
Browning & Keating	Geo W Cochran
Edw Hall	Benj De Wolff
Thos Thompson	H S Benson
Jackson Bro & Co	Chas Dawson
Blanchard & Mohun	M H Stevens & Co
Saml Bacon & Co	Rittenhouse, Fant & Co
E H & H L Gregory	W Gunton
Yates & Selby	G M White
Sioussa & Ennis	E Wheeler
A P Hoover	E E White
J B Wilson	Barbour, Semmes & Co
R Cohen	M Taylor & Co
Campbell & Son	A R Potts
H S Johnson	M W Galt & Bro
Chas Stott	Jos W Nairn
S H Bacon	Richd Wallach
John M Young	A B Olin
Murray & Semmes	Andrew Wylie
Thos Young	D K Cartler
Jno H Barth & Co	Chas H Utermehle
Robt M Hart	Jos H Bradley
W H & O H Morrison	S J Bowen
Wm T Duvall	Horatio Beall
Wm E Tucker	John H McCutchen
H Burns	John Brodhead

Union commissioned ofcrs confined in the Richmond prisons now is 964, viz: one Brig Gen, Neal Dow; 14 Cols, 25 Lt Cols 27 Surgs, 53 Ast Surgs, 28 Majs, 246 Capts, 264 1st Lts, 297 2nd Lts & 9 Naval ofcrs. Majority of the ofcrs are from the Western armies, many captured at Chickamauga.

SAT NOV 7, 1863

Died: on Nov 6, at the residence of his father, in Wash City, aged 24 years & nearly 5 mos, Lt Louis M Goldsborough, U S M C, s/o Rear Adm Goldsborough, U S N, & grandson of Wm Wirt. Funeral from the Chr of the Ascension on Sun.

Died:at *Fair Prospect*, Montg Co, Md, on Oct 31, of diptheria, Jas Preston, only s/o Jas M & Louisa V Dawson, aged 5 yrs, 7 months & 12 days.

Supreme Crt of D C, in Chancery, #1797. N M McGregor, vs D A Watterson, et al. Ratify sale by N M McGregor, trust, of lot 18 in sq A, Wash City, to Alexander Hay. -R J Meigs, clerk

Mr Thos R Price, of Balt Co, Md, was arrested on the charge of disloyalty. He subsequently took the oath & was released. -Balt Sun

Adms sale of the library of the late J Louis Kinzer, of Alexandria, Va, on Mon. -Jas C McGuire & Co, aucts

Information received at the Dept of State from Mr Chas S Ogden, the Cnsl of the U S at Quebec, of the issue of an order in Cncl at Quebec, on Oct 29, in which it is declared that, with a view to the encouragement of the Culture of Flax in this Province, a remission of duty will be granted on all Scutching Machines imported into Canada until the close of the present yr. After Jan 1 next, the exemption shall be subject to the duty imposed upon that article by law.

Army of Tenn: attack was made by the rebels on Colliersville on the Memphis & Charleston R R, on Nov 3. The rebel Brig Gen Gary & 13 of his staff are among the prisoners taken. Lt Col Loomis & Maj Herrod, 6th Ill Cavalry, had an altercation when at a supper table, in Germantown, in the evening. Herrod fired 4 shots at Loomis as he left the table, killing him instantly. Col Hatch, 2nd Iowa Regt, was obliged to draw his sword on the sldrs to prevent them from lynching Herrod on the spot. The remains of Loomis were taken to Memphis, & Herrod was conveyed there in irons.

MON NOV 9, 1863
Died: suddenly, at his residence in Wash City, of heart disease, Chas Fisher, past 20 years a clerk in the Treas Dept, & a resident of Wash City for the last 47 yrs. Funeral from his late residence on 13th st, between L & M sts, today.

Died: on Oct 20, at New Orleans, La, of yellow fever, John C Huntly, of Phil, Engr U S Navy, in his 26th yr.

Died: in Wash City, on Nov 8, after a short illness, John Robinson, in his 69th yr. Funeral from the residence of his son-in-law, Mr W E Spalding, Nov 10th.

Supreme Crt of D C, in Equity #26. Jos Smith, cmplnt, against Wm P Johnson & Geo D Fowle, adms of Lauriston B Hardin, Mark B Hardin, Susan L Hardin, & John H Hardin, heirs of said Lauriston, Bernard Hooe, guardian of Mark B Hardin & Phineas L Howitz, dfndnts. Statement of the account, at my residence in Gtwn, on Nov 30th. -W Redin, auditor

Mrd: on Oct 13, at Ascension Chr, in N Y, by Rev John Cotton Smith, Geo C Gardner, of Wash, to Fanny, d/o Geo H Brodhead, of N Y.

Sale of the estate of the late Guy Graham, sq 92, Wash City, with improvements: with good hse. -Wm S Graham

Deaths reported to the Navy Dept for the week ending Nov 7, 1853.
Jas Glenn, fireman, scalded, Sep 8, vessel U S S *Sachem.*
John Munroe, 3rd ast eng, scalded, Sep 9, do.
Jas Taylor, landsman, pneumonia, Sep 29, vessel U S S *Octorora.*
Robt Kenney, ord seaman, pneumonia, Oct 26, Nav Hosp, N Y.
Patrick Murley, landsman, pneumonia, Oct 30, do.
John Barker, gunner's mate, suicide, Oct 28, vessel U S S Grand Gulf.
Jas Travis, fireman, apoplexy, Oct 28, Nav Hosp, Norfolk.
Chas Sheppard, 1st cl boy, smallpox, Oct 28, vessel U S S *Dacotah.*
Wm Smith, 2, q m, smallpox, Oct 23, do.
Levi C Wiley, mstr's mate, yel fever, Sep 13, vessel U S S *Jasmine.*
Henry Clark, 1st cl fireman, yel fever, Aug 30, do.
Jas Hennan, do, do, do, do.

Jas Munan, coal heaver, yel fever, Oct 19, vessel U S S *Estrella*.
Jas Stewart, ord seaman, yel fever, Oct 19, do.
John Jonson, b mate, yel fever, Oct 22, do.
D Heik, 1st cl fireman, yel fever, Oct 22, do.
Geo Williams, capt forecastle, kidney disease, Oct 19, vessel U S S *Arizona*.
Wm Reid, seaman, yel fever, Oct 20, vessel U S S *Sciota*.
Geo Breslyn, seaman, yel fever, Oct 18, vessel U S S *De Soto*.
Cornelius Sullivan, landsman, yel fever, Oct 22, do.
Saml F Train, act actg paymstr, blank, Nov 1, blank.
John Robinson, contraband, chronic diarrhoea, Oct 19, Nav Hosp, Memphis.
Chas Crump, contraband, chronic diarrhoea, Oct 20, do.
Elias Beachman, contraband, chronic diarrhoea, Oct 24, do.
Robt Saunders, seaman, remit fever, Oct 25, do.
L Thompson, landsman, chronic dysentery, Oct 26, co.

Ward H Lamon, U S Mrshl, D C, replies to an invitation from David Wills, Agent for A G
Curtin, Govn'r of Pa, in regard to the dedicating ceremonies of the Nat'l Cemetery at
Gettysburg, Pa, on Nov 19. Lamon accepts the position as Mrshl of the day.

Naval Orders:
Capt John Rodgers, ordered to command the ship *Dictator*.
Cmder Somerville Nicholson, ordered to command the ship *State of Georgia*.
Capt John R Goldsborough is ordered to ord duty at Portsmouth, N H.
Lt Cmder Henry D Todd is detached from the Naval Academy & ordered to the ship
Sangamon.

TUE NOV 10, 1863
Mrd: on Nov 5, at McKendree Parsonage, by Rev John Thrush, Mr Jas L Parsons to Miss
Mary A Brereton, eldest d/o the late John Brereton, all of Wash City.

Orphans Crt of Wash Co, D C. Case of Thos Bayne, exc of Rev Edw A Knight, dec'd;
settlement on Dec 1. -Z C Robbins, rg o/wills

Escape of 2 ofcrs from Richmond: Maj Hinstain & Lt D Von Weltzier. The Maj was
captured in N C last Jul, & with the Lt had been in Libby prison until Oct 25th, when they
escaped by disguising themselves in rebel uniforms.

Daniel Crist, who lived near Middletown, Ind, was killed by the sheriff of the county last
week while resisting arrest. He shot 4 of the sheriff's posse before he was killed.

WED NOV 11, 1863
Died: on Nov 9, Thos Riggles, aged 72 yrs, native of Holbeach Mar_h, Lincolnshire,
England, but for the last 46 years a resident of Wash City. Funeral from his late residence
on 16th st, today.

Died: at Germantown, near Phil, on Nov 4, Jane M Brocchus, w/o Judge Perry E Brocchus,
after a painful & protracted illness. She leaves her hsbnd & chldrn.

Died: in Wash City, on Nov 10, after a brief illness, Rev Jas Richardson, formerly of
Dedham, Mass, in his 49th yr.

Died: in Wash City, on Nov 8, Eliza, infant d/o Chas K & Sally P Sherman, in her 8th mo. Funeral from 571 Pa av, over McPherson's drug store, today.

H S Newcom, late Cmder of the U S steamer *Tioga*, died at Key West recently. He was from R I.

John H Bringler, arrested at Clarksburg, Md, recently, was charged with having been in the rebel svc, & committed to the Old Capitol prison yesterday.

Balt, Md, Nov 10. *The Evening Transcript*, a paper started 2 weeks ago by Wm H Neilson, was today suppressed by order of Gen Schenck.

The Atlantic & Great Western R R completed to Cleveland: Nov 3rd. For the first time a train of cars, made up on the Long Dock, opposite N Y, came thru direct to Cleveland. The train consisted of 10 freight cars of the A & G W & N Y & E Railways, direct from Jersey City, & the elegant private car [48ft x 11ft 3ins] of T W Kennard, the Genr'l Mgt of the A & G W Railway. It was drawn by the A & G W locomotive, #2, Jas McHenry, being named after the contractor for the constructon of the line. The engr was Rich Poor, who is anything but a poor engr, & the conductor of the train was Chas Warren. Party who came on the train: Mr Wm Reynolds, Pres of the N Y & Pa Div of the road; Mr H F Sweetzer, Gen Super; Mr C W Bradley, Super of Telegraph; Mr J H R Rose, Resident Engr; Mr Frank Cummings, Super of Locomotive & Car Dept; Mr C Blakeslee, Pvt Sec of Mr Kennard, with Mr C L Rhodes, Super Cleveland Branch; Mr J Dwight Palmer, Gen Freight Agent, Cleveland Branch; & Mr R M N Taylor, Mgr of the Company's Htl at Meadville. Prominent features of the Atlantic & Great Western line from Cleveland to the Eastern & S W terminus will be photographed by J F Ryder, the well known photographer of this city.

J B Holmes, formerly a civil engr, has been arrested in N Y, charged with killing a police ofcr 10 years ago.

From Ft Monroe, Nov 9. Geo Vandall & Jas Wales, of the 8th Connecticut Regt, were executed this morning at 11 o'clock, near Portsmouth, Va, for desertion.

During the month of Oct the detectives of Capt H A Scheetz, Provost Mrshl, arrested 232 deserters in D C belonging to old regts in the Army of the Potomac.

Francis Meagher reinstated in rank of Brig Gen, with permission to recruit to its complement his old Irish Brigade.

Col Richd H Rush, Ast Prov Mrshl, relieved from charge of the Invalid Corps Bur. Lt Col Cahill, his assistant is left temporarily in charge.

Lt Col Towers, Prov Mrshl of Alexandria, has been relieved by an order from the War Dept, & Capt Gwynn, Med Inspec on Gen Slough's staff, has been appt'd to the ofc.

John H Bringler, arrested at Clarksburg, Md, on the day of the recent election, after taking the oath to vote, charged with having been in the rebel svc, was committed to the Old Capitol yesterday.

Brig Gen Mackall has, at his own request, been relieved of duty in Bragg's dept, & has been ordered to report to Gen Johnston in Mississippi.

Gen N B Forrest is in Atlanta. All mbrs of his staff, except his prsnl staff, have been ordered to the different depts. Gen Armstrong takes command of his division.

THU NOV 12, 1863
Mrd: on Nov 10, by Rev Mr Lynch, Capt Geo Gibson, U S Army, to Fannie Maria Huntt, d/o the late Dr Henry Huntt, of Wash City, & ward of the late Gen Geo Gibson.

Died: at Yucatan, on Aug 15, of yellow fever, Edwin Robinson, formerly of Richmond, Va, & for many years the Pres of the Richmond, Fredericksburg, & Potomac R R Co.

Mrd: in Wash City, at the residence of the bride's father, on Nov 12, by Rt Rev Thos M Clark, Bishop of R I, Hon Wm Sprague, Senator of the U S from R I, to Miss Kate Chase, d/o Hon Salmon P Chase, Sec of the Treas. In the wedding party: her sister, Miss Nettie Chase, her cousin, Miss Alice Skinner, niece of the groom, Miss Ida Nichols; groomsmen were Capt Haven, Maj Baldwin & Capt Ives. [See Nov 13 paper.]

Japan: the Prince of Nagasaki issued an order that Jos Heca, a Japanese, formerly of San Francisco, & the Japanese pilots, who conducted the Wyoming to Simoniski Sound, should be killed.

Dwlg hse at auction: the commodious & desirable residence of the late Thos Carbery, located near the War & Navy Depts.

FRI NOV 13, 1863
Mrd: on Nov 11, by Rev Dr Pinckney, Dr Fred'k G H Bradford, of Maine, to May, d/o W H Gunnell, of Wash City.

$10 reward for stolen or strayed Bay Mare, when lost had a shafter saddle & a work bridle. Return to Gladmon's stable, in Gtwn, or Shreves' stable, on 7th, near I st. –J G Hutchinson

Crt-martial case: Edw Shandley & Jos Scott, 2 detectives under Capt Scheetz, accused of robbing O M Marcom, of Atlanta, Ga, of $1,500 & a diamond pin, are ordered to restore the property to Marcom. The detectives are sentenced to 1 yr imprisonment in the Albany pen. Considering the official position of the parties who committed it, it seems to us rather lenient.

The *New Hampshire Gazette*, claiming to be the oldest newspaper in America, completed its 107th yr on Oct 1.

Mr J Wilkes Booth repeats tonight his personation of Richd III, an effort which, despite the sweeping criticism recently levelled against it by a contemporary of the daily press, meets, we think, no inconsiderable applause.

Mrd: on Nov 12, at the residence of the bride's father, in Wash City, by Rt Rev Thos M Clark, Bishop of R I, the Hon Wm Sprague, Senator of the U S from R I, to Miss Kate Chase, d/o the Hon Salmon P Chase, the Sec of the Treas. She was sustained in the marriage ceremony by her sister, Miss Nettie Chase, her cousin, Miss Alice Skinner, & a niece of the groom, Miss Ida Nichols, who, as bridesmaids were respectively attended by Capt Haven, of Maj Gen McDowell's staff, Maj Baldwin, of the staff of Gen Stahl, & Capt Ives, of the U S Navy, as groomsmen. The Pres of the U S, the Mbrs of the Cabinet, the Diplomatic Corps, eminent Ofcrs of the Army & Navy, with ctzns of Washington & friends, invited from a distance, lent distinction to the scene.

Naval Orders: Cmder Fabius Stanly orderd to duty on the North Atlantic Blockading Squad: Cmder D Lynch, detached from the Beaufort station & ordered to command the ord ship *St Lawrence*; Lt Cmder Walter W Queen, ordered to command the ship *Wyalusing*; Capt Geo H Scott ordered to command the vessel *De Soto*.

SAT NOV 14, 1863

Died: in Wash City, on Nov 13, Mrs Charlotte Poor, relict of the late Moses Poor, at age 82 yrs. Born in Boston, Mass, but for the last 43 years a resident of Wash City, where she has seen grown around her a large family of sons & dghts. Funeral from her late residence, 430 F st, Sun.

Geo W Lane, U S Dist Judge of Ala, died at Louisville, Ky, on Thu, of congestion of the lungs.

Wash Corp: 1-Relief of P Cullinan: referred to the Cmte of Claims. 2-Act authorizing Richd Wimsatt to improve a wharf site, was postponed. Board then adjourned.

MON NOV 16, 1863

Died: on Nov 15, Geo W Garrett, in his 46th yr. Funeral from his late residence, 7th & E sts, tomorrow.

Died: in Fairfax Co, Va, on Nov 11, Mrs Sarah Ball, aged 74 yrs, relict of the late Wm Ball, & mother o/Edw Ball, Sgt-at-Arms of the Representative branch of the Nt'l Legislature. Remains were conveyed to Ohio for interment.

Andrew J Allen, a well-known stationer of Boston, who died a few days since, left an estate worth $100,000 . This, in his will, after leaving to his 5 chldrn & some others annuities, he directs to be sold, & to enure to the city of Boston for the benefit of poor mechanics.

Our prisoners at Richmond: Fortress Monroe, Nov 13, 1863. 1-The steamer *Alma*, with a cargo of salt & liquor, was captured by the U S gunboat *Seneca*, while running the Doboy Sound, Fla, & arrived here today in charge of a prize crew commanded by Lt B W Loring. 2-The rebel Gen W H F Lee, a prisoner here for some months past, was put on a steamer this evening, & understood, to be transferred to Ft Lafayette, N Y harbor. He & Capt Winer are held as hostages for Capts Flynn & Sawyer, 2 of our ofcrs who have been sentenced to be hung by the rebels. 3-The Rev H C Trumbull, Chaplain of the 10th Conn Regt, who was captued on Morris island some 4 months since, came down in the flag of truce boat today, having left Richmond on Wed. The only ration served out to the prisoners was a small wedge of bread, made of corn meal, with a small portion of wheat flour, & weighing less than ½ a lb. This they were expected to subsist on for 24 hours.

Orphans Crt of Wash Co, D C. Case of Benj S Bayly, adm of Ellen Scott, dec'd; settlement on Dec 1. -Z C Robbins, rg o/wills

Deaths reported to the Navy Dept for the week ending Nov 14, 1863:
Martin Crout, landsman, asphyxia, Aug 5, vessel U S S *Com Barney*.
Allan Granby, contraband, asphyxia, Aug 5, do.
Oliver D Root, Ast Surg, yel fever, Oct 30, vessel U S S *Estrella*.
John Frank, ord seaman, yel fever, Oct 24, do.
Geo Wood, landsman, yel fever, Oct 27, do.
Mich'l Welsh, landsman, yel fever, Oct 28, do.

Jas Hicks, 1st cl fireman, yel fever, Oct 20, do.
Thos T Harwick, coal heaver, yel fever, Oct 4, do.
Saml T Strude, actg 3rd ast engr, drowned, Oct 15, vessel U S S *Nansemond.*
Geo Terry, seaman, drowned, Oct 15, do.
Fred'k Furbish, actg ensign, yel fever, Oct 26, vessel U S S *Tennesee.*
Fred'k Knapper, marine, congestion of brain, Sep 19, vessel U S S *Saranac.*
Geo Faulkenberg, 1st cl fireman, yel fever, Oct 24, vessel U S S *Sciota.*
Jas Shietz, 1st ast engr, yel fever, Oct 5, vessel U S S *Hollyhock.*
Henry S Newcomb, cmder, apoplexy, Oct 24, vessel U S S *Tioga.*
Henry Cook, seaman, febris continua, Aug 15, vessel U S S *Colorado.*
Wm Watson, landsman, consumption, Hosp, N Y.
Jas Harden, landsman, consumption, Nov 8, Nav Asylum.
Wm O Geore, contraband, yel fever, Oct 15, vessel U S S *Albatross.*
Michl McConnorgley, seaman, yel fever, Oct 8, do.
John Thompson, capt's mate, yel fever, Oct 17, do.
John Clark, seaman, yel fever, Oct 30, vessel U S S *Kuhn.*
John Moore, landman, bite of a tiger, Oct 28, vessel U S S *Pinola.*
Adolphus Brown, ord seaman, yel fever, Oct 10, vessel U S S *Pensacola.*
Frank T McIntier, actg ast paymstr, yel fever, Oct 13, vessel U S S *De Soto.*
John F Trest, actg mstr, yel fever, Oct 20, Mississippi Squadron.

TUE NOV 17, 1863
Died: on Nov 16, Mrs Eliz O'Neale Jacobs, eldest d/o Jas N Davis, in her 23rd yr. Funeral from the residence of her father, 480 I st, today.

Died: on Nov 16, Helen E, w/o Dr J V D Middleton, U S Army, & d/o David H Burr, of Wash City. Funeral from the Chr of the Epiphany, tomorrow.

Orphans Crt of Wash Co, D C. Prsnl estate of Thos L Potter, late of Wash Co, dec'd.
-A F F Potter, admx

Walla Walla City: Wash Terr, Sep 30, 186. Left Ft Benton on Aug 21 reaching Walla Walla on Sep 19: experienced no difficulty. Stopped at the Coeur d'Alene mission, & was cordially greeted by Fr Gazzoh, a Catholic Priest, in charge of the mission for the last 20 yrs. There are some 5 or 6 lay bros connected with this mission. They raise fine crops of wheat, oats, & vegetables in abundance: built a fine church where regular instruction is given to the Coeur d'Alene Indians. In the mining districts it is estimated about 20,000 persons are here: lies in the new Terr of Idaho. Rev Fr Brouillett, S J, from Vancouver, is here to establish a Catholic seminary & nunnery. He has purchased 40 acs of land from E H Baron, near this city, for said purpose. I have met quite a number of persons from Md, from St Mary's, Chas, & Wash Counties-some from Balt & Annapolis. There is but one company of the Wash Terr Vols, Capt Thompson, now stationed at Ft Walla Walla. Col John Steinberger is the commanding ofcr. [Correspondence of the Balt Sun.]

A T Stewart, of N Y, has purchased the Townsend Place, on Fifth ave, for $250,000, [half of its original cost,] & is going to adorn it with statues, paintings, & other works of art.

WED NOV 18, 1863
Beautiful estate, *Antrim,* for sale at $40,000; in Carroll Co, Md; 445 acs, with dwlg hse, adjoins
Taneytown, Md. -R W Templeman & Co, rl estate brokers, Balt, Md.

Senator Iverson, of Ga, has been appt'd a Brig Gen in the rebel army, & is in command of a division of the state forces, with headqrtrs at Rome or Kingston.

First instance in the Union army of a commissioned ofcr being reduced to the ranks, is the case of 1st Lt Jos J Ennis, 71st Ohio Regt, found guilty of forging an order detailing him to go from La to Cincinnati to arrest deserters. He absented himself 7 months under this forged order. A crt martial sentenced him to serve 3 years or during the war as a pvt in such regt as the Gen commanding the dept might designate, & Gen Burnside selected the 20th Ky Regt, & ordered him to it under guard.

From Memphis on the 12th inst. Burning of the steamer *Sunnyside* on opposite Island #16, 26 miles below New Madrid. 30 passengers in all were either drowned or burned. Among the latter were Mr Boyd & his wife & child, of Memphis; the sister & wife of Maj Boswell; an army surgeon, name unknown; Mrs Van Buren & her dght, Mattie, of Detroit; Mrs Blake, Mr Geo Cox & child; Mrs Croswell & 2 chldrn, Mrs Rose, Mrs Strong, John Powers, fireman, & 4 deck hands, names unknown. The steamer *Glasgow* brought the survivors to Cairo, most of whom lost everything they possessed.

The report that John M Botts had been arrested & sent to Richmond turns out to be incorrect. He was arrested by Stuart, but released on the next day.

The fugitive slave law contines to be duly executed in D C, where the owners in Md think it worth while to follow or seek the fugitives here. An instance occurred on Sat last, when a negro boy, Gusta Bullen, was arrested in the mkt hse, on a writ, as the property of Mr Henry Thorne, of PG Co, Md, & taken before Com'r Cox. Mr Geo E H Day appeared as cnsl for the boy, but Mr Thorn, readily taking the required oath of loyalty & proving by a neighbor, Mr Luther W Kirby, his ownership of the negro, & also producing a letter from Dr J H Byrne, of the army, endorsing his loyalty, the com'r considered the proof sufficient, & remanded the slave to his master. –Corr Sun

Brig Gen Chas K Graham has been relieved, by order of the Sec of War, from his command in the Army of the Potomac, & directed to report to Gen Butler for duty in his dept.

THU NOV 19, 1863
Supreme Crt of D C, in Equity #1797. Nathl M McGregor against Maria M Watterston, D A Watterston, Sarah Holcomb, & others, heir, devisees, & legatees of the late Eliza Hamilton. Statement of trustee's acc't at my residence in Gtwn, on Dec 11. -W Redin, auditor

Wash Corp: 1-Act for relief of Elias Davis: sum of $225.18 be pd to Davis for grading I st north. 2-Act for relief of B W Ferguson: $300 to be pd him for extra svc performed by him as police magistrate from Feb 2, 1863 to Jul 7, 1863, in the 4th ward, & from Aug 25, 1863 to Oct 7, 1863, in the 5th ward. 3-Act for the relief of Wm Riley: $265 to be pd Riley, assignee of C D Bradley.

Died: in Wash City, on Nov 18, Clarence Deslonde Wilson, not yet emerged into manhood. Funeral from the residence of his father, Jos S Wilson, 455 13th st, tomorrow.

The steam carriage yesterday was exhibited in operation in our streets, & ran along with surprising ease over the paved streets, the horses paying no more attention to it than an ordinary wagon. The public will demand the dummy engines as soon as they discover that it is a question between their use & the increase of fare on the city railroads. –Phil Ledger

Admiral Dahlgren has altogether recovered from a nervous disease in his jaw, which confined him below deck for 15 days. He will not need to avail himself of the leave of absence granted him some weeks ago.

Richd Busteed, of N Y C, appt'd U S Dist Judge for the dist of Ala, v Judge Lane, recently dec'd.

FRI NOV 20. 1863
Died: at Lancaster, Pa, on Nov 17, Mrs Eva Heap, w/o G H Heap, of the Navy Dept, & d/o the late Cmdor Porter. Burial in Woodland Cemetery, West Phil, near those of her late father, Cmdor Porter.

Died: on Nov 18, after a short but painful illness, Abraham J Boss, in his 69th yr. Funeral from Fletcher Chapel, N Y av, today.

U S Dist Crt for the Eastern Dist of Va, in session in Alexandria; ordered confiscation of the property of the following:

H W Vandegrift	Elias W Kincheloe	Jas H Reid
W G Cazenove	Dr M M Lewis	S T Stuart
H W Thoma	T A Brewis	Levi Hurdle
French Forrest	Edw Sangster	Geo H Padgett

Address of Hon Edw Everett, delivered at Gettysburg, Nov 19, at the consecration of the cemetery. Prepared for the interment of the remains of those who fell on Jul 1, 2, & 3, in the battles at that place. [7½ columns of coverage may be found in this paper.]

Balt, Nov 19. Shipments to Richmond tomorrow for our starving prisoners from the Balt American Relief Fund: value of $1,100, making the whole amount thus far sent by Mr C C Fulton about $3,400.

The Jrnl of Commerce of yesterday states that the arrest of the Hon J R Giddings, U S Cnsl Gen for Canada, was at the instance of Mr Wm L Redpath, who adopts this method of redressing a personal grievance. No love lost between the two. Redpath was arrested in Montreal Oct 31st.

The 153rd N Y Vols, Col Davis, & the 157th Pa Vols, Maj Thos H Addicks, were yesterday relieved from duty in this city & ordered to hold themselves in readiness to leave this point at any moment. These regts have been doing guard duty in & about the city. They were relieved by the 9th Regt Invalid Corps.

SAT NOV 21, 1863
Wash Corp: 1-Ptn of Robt Bayliss asking the refunding of money deposited by him in the Bank of Wash: referred to the Cmte of Claims. 2-Cmte on Pblc Schools, reported back the nomination of J P Tustin for Trustee of the Pblc Schools in the 1st Dist, & Wm J Murtagh for Trustee in the 4th Dist, recommending they be confirmed: declared unanimously confirmed.

Wash, D C, Nov 20. Mr Wm T Smithson, banker, convicted of holding correspondence with the enemy, in violation of the 57th article of war; to be confined in the penitentiary in Albany, N Y, for 5 yrs.

Procession at the ceremonies at Gettysburg at the consecration of the cemetery. Military portion of the procession was headed by a squad of cavalry, followed by Maj Gen Couch &

Staff. 5th N Y Artl Regt, from Balt, with their fine battery were next in line. Gen Schenck & Staff were also present. Next came the Mrshl-in-Chief, Ward H Lamon, & his numerous staff of Aides, wearing yellow & white scarfs, with tri-colored rosettes on the breast, & black & white shoulder knots. Next came the Pres of the U S, Secs Seward, Usher, & Blair, all finely mounted. Remainder were various civic bodies. Mr B B French gave the signal & the solemn ceremonies began. Prayer by Rev Thos H Stockton, Chaplain of the Hse o/Reps. The Pres evidently felt deeply, & with the venerable statesman & patriot, Hon Edw Everett, who was by his side, made no effort to hide his emotion. The Balt Glee sang a hymn composed by Hon B B French. [Copy of the hymn was in the paper.] The Pres spoke: Four score & seven years ago our fathers brought forth on this continent a new nation, conceived in liberty & dedicated to the proposition that all men are created equal. [Applause.] etc. –Nov 19

Rebel advance upon Knoxville: Nov 17, 1863. Our position was charged & a terrific hand to hand conflict occurred, both sabres & revolvers being used on both sides. Gen Sanders, who commanded the outposts, was critically wounded. Lt Col Smith, 20th Mich, killed at Campbell's Station. Our loss in that fight was between 200 & 300. Gen Shackelford had a brisk fight on Sunday with the rebels on the other side of the Holstein. He kept them in check.

MON NOV 23, 1863

Deaths reported to the Navy Dept for the week ending Nov 21, 1863:
John Heenan, ord seaman, inflam of lungs, no date, vessel U S S *Sonoma*.
Wm H Cotter, landsman, gunshot, Nov 2, vessel U S S *Patapsco*.
John Morris, do, do, do, do.
Geo H Lamette, landsman, hoemoptysis, Oct 31, vessel Vessel U S S Vermont.
Andrew Fagan, marine, consumption, Oct 18, do.
Edmund Neeland, fireman, anassua, Jul 23, hosp, Memphis.
John Carver, seaman, remit fever, Aug 6, do.
Jos Tempkins, coal heaver, sun stroke, Aug 10, do.
Robt Walker, seaman, interm fever, Aug 17, do.
Geo Brown, seaman, remit fever, Aug 18, do.
Daniel Driscoll, seaman, remit fever, Aug 21, do.
Chas Clinton, seaman, chronic diarrhoea, Aug 31, do.
Jas S Collins, 1st cl fireman, chronic diarrhoea, Sep 6, do.
John C Huntley, 3rd ast engr, yel fever, Oct 20, New Orleans.
D Anderson, contraband, consumption, Oct 22, Mississippi Squadron.
Nelson Marvey, 1st cl boy, congestive fever, Oct 12, do.
Richd Martin, 1st cl boy, pthisis pulumbia, Jun 25, do.
Freitz Berwole, surg 38th Ohio, fracture skull, Apr 29, do.
John Bauer, seaman, drowned, May 22, do.
Jas Cleary, qrtr gunner, drowned, Jun 1, do.
Jas Hamilton, contraband, consumption, Jun 30, do.
Chas B Young, pilot, remit fever, Jun 21, do.
Henry N Tanner, actg ast paymstr, cerebritis, Jul 1, do.
Philip Howlet, landsman, congestive fever, Jul 6, do.
Jas Baily, 1st cl boy, drowned, Jul 6, do.
W H Newhall, ord seaman, typhoid fever, Jul 25, do.
Frank Barlow, contraband, dysentery, Jul 17, do.
Patrick Garris, seaman, remit fever, Jul 21, do.
Cicero Fennesen, seaman, interm fever, Jul 21, do.
Levi Sheldon, 1st cl boy, pneumonia, Jul 14, do.

Richard Parker, contraband, remit fever, Aug 22, do.
Henry McCoy, contraband, chronic diarrhoea, Aug 24, do.
John Dillen, boy, typhoid fever, Sep 1, do.
Robt Bruce, 1st cl boy, chronic diarrhoea, Sep 2, do.
Richard Ellis, actg ensign, remit fever, Sep 5, do.
Matthew Monagan, landsman, typhoid fever, Sep 7, do.
Wilber Ward, boy, remit fever, Sep 8, do.
Thos Seymour, landsman, remit fever, Sep 8, do.
Humphrey Termey, landsman, congestive fever, Sep 11, do.
John C Smith, seaman, erysipelas, Sep 13, do.
Geo Maines, 1st cl boy, dysentery, Sep 17, do.
Jas Hirl, landsman, chronic dysentery, Sep 19, do.
Aaron H McKeon, landsman, remit fever, Sep 23, do.
Erwin Parker, landsman, chronic diarrhoea, Sep 27, do.
John Flannigan, coal heaver, remit fever, Sep 27, do.
Manuel Weston, contraband, tetanus, Sep 27, do.
Jas Carey, qrtr gunner, gunshot, Oct 1, do.
Lloyd Robinson, 1st cl boy, diarrhoea, Oct 3, do.
Lewis McDaniel, negro, diarrhoea, Oct 5, do.
Simeon Taylor, contraband, dysentery, Oct 9, do.
Lafayette Dunn, actg mstr's mate, dysentery, Oct 10, do.
John Plunkett, 2nd cl fireman, pneumonia, Oct 12, do.
John Crowell, landsman, remit fever, Oct 22, do.
Albert C Smith, actg 2nd cl ast engr, blank, Sep 1, Pacific Squad.
Saml Ray, actg carp, blank, Sep 4, do.
Chas Barstow, surg's steward, typhoid fever, Oct 28, vessel *Kanawha*.
Geo Schway, landsman, remit fever, Nov 2, hosp, Memphis.
Israel Bowen, fireman, remit fever, Nov 6, do.
Jas Whitaker, contraband, remit fever, Nov 10, do.
David Williams, marine, remit fever, Nov 10, do.
Geo Mallory, 1st cl boy, consumption, Nov 11, do.
Chas A Field, actg gunner, drowned, Nov 7, Mississippi river.
Archibald McGregor, 1st cl fireman, consumption, no date, hosp, N Y.
Thos Tillman, landsman, pneumonia, do, do.

Mrd: on Nov 10, at St Aloysius Chr, by Rev Fr Maguire, Wm N Horstkamp to Miss Marian C Dudley, both of Wash City.

Died: at Columbus, Ohio, on Nov 14, Sophia M, w/o Allen A Hall, U S Minister to Boliva.

Orphans Crt of Wash Co, D C. 1-Case of David A Watterston, exc of Harry Dodson, dec'd; settlement on Dec 15. -Z C Robbins, rg o/wills 2-Prsnl estate of John A Thoele, late of Wash Co, dec'd. -Ferdinand Ehhardt, adm. 3-Prsnl estate of Michael Connington, late of Wash Co, dec'd. -C Cammack, sr, adm

TUE NOV 24, 1863

Died: on Nov 22, Mrs H Ulrich. Funeral from her late residence, 15th & G sts, today.

Died: on Nov 22, after a lingering illness, Mrs Sarah Swain, in her 70th yr.

Died: on Nov 22, Henry W Moore, aged 45 years & 5 months.

Fire destroyed the tobacco warehse & crop of Mr Wm Taylor, on the Potomac, about 5 miles above Point Lookout, Md, on Nov 14: loss about $2,500.

Mrs Gertrude Winder, mother/o Gen Winder, provost mrshl of Richmond, was arrested on Sat last, at the brdg-hse of Mrs Hughes, 77 N Chas st, Balt, Md. One of the charges is her corresponding with persons in the South. No decision.

WED NOV 25, 1863
Supreme Crt of D C, in Equity #109. Peter V Hagner, Frances R Hagner, Alex'r B Hagner, Danl F Hagner, & Alex'r B Hagner & Danl R Hagner, as excs of Frances Hagner, vs **Alex'r Randall, **Jos H Nicholson, & **Eliza Ann, his wife, **Cleland K Nelson & **Mary M, his wife, **Richd H Hagner, Laura S Hagner, *Cora C Hagner, **Kate G Hagner, *Fanny Hagner, *Grattan Hagner, *Chas E Hagner, & *Randall Hagner. Regarding the partition & sale of rl estate of Peter Hagner, dec'd, who died Jul 1850 in Wash City: rl estate consisted of lots in Wash City & land in Michigan. At the time of his death, Peter Hagner left surviving him 8 chldrn, viz: Eliza Ann Nicholson, w/o Jos H Nicholson; John R Hagner, Frances R Hagner, Peter V Hagner, Mary M Hagner, since mrd with Cleland K Nelson, Richd H Hagner, Alex'r B Hagner, & Danl R Hagner; 2 of the chldrn of the testator has previously died, viz: Chas N Hagner, who left a widow, Laura S Hagner, & a child, Cora C Hagner; & Thos H Hagner, who left a widow, Kate G Hagner, & 2 chldrn, Fanny & Grattan Hagner. In Dec 1856, John R Hagner died leaving 2 chldrn, Chas E & Randall Hagner. In May 1863, Frances Hagner died, appointing as excs of her will, Alex'r B Hagner & Danl R Hagner. *Minors; **non-residents of D C along with Fanny & Grattan Hagner. -Geo P Fisher, Justice

Died: in Wash City, very suddenly, on Nov 24, Thaddeus F Clark, formerly of Connecticut, aged 41 yrs. Funeral from his late residence H & First sts, today.

Military arrests in Balt, Md. Mrs Gertrude Winder was released yesterday; Mr Fannie Peet & Mrs Susan P Brooks were arrested on charge of being disloyal & correponding with persons in the South. They took the oath of allegiance & were released. Refused to take the oath: ex-Govn'r Thos G Pratt, Col Jos H Nicholson, Nicholas Green, clerk of A A Co Crct Crt; Jas Revell, State's Atty for A A Co; Robt W Tate; Benj Watkins; Wm Tell Claude; W H McPorlin, G W Duvall, Edwin Boyle, B Longue, Dr S F Owens, Jas E Tate, D Claude Handy, & Thos Franklin. Franklin, due to his age, was permitted to remain in Annapolis under guard.

Mr Jas R Hood, reporter for the Wash press for the past 18 mos, is leaving to re-open the business of the post ofc at Chattanooga, Tenn.

The Atty Genr'l made a decision adverse to the claims of the widow of Aaron Burr for pension money since his death. They mrd in 1833, & divorced in N Y in 1835 for his bad conduct. Burr died in 1836.

On Mon our fellow ctzn, Richd C Washington, was looking at the handsome dwlg hse in course of erection for Dr Hall, on N Y ave, when his foot accidentally slipped from a rafter in the upper story, by which Mr W was precipitated several feet. He was conveyed to his residence & has suffered intensely. He may have received some serious internal injuries.

THU NOV 26, 1863

Mrd: in Wash City, on Nov 12, by Rev B Peyton Brown, Edwin T Steele, of Fairfax Co, Va, to Georgiana Bladen, of Alexandria, Va.

Mrd: in Balt, Md, on Nov 24, by Rev C B Tippett, John A Hancock, of Wash City, to Miss Susie C Harmon, of Balt.

Died: in Wash City, on Nov 24, Harriet L, w/o Geo L Elsworth, & y/d/o the late Capt Wm McLellan, of Portland, Maine. Funeral from the residence of her bro, Hon Geo W McLellan, 596 N J av, today; interment in Portland.

Supreme Crt of D C, in Equity #1465. Rich W Bryan & wife, Ruel K Compton & wife, Geo W Tubman & wife, Chas H Lane & wife, & Mary B Briscoe, vs Jane H Dement, John P Dement, Wm B Dement, & Thos Dement. Parties named & creditors of Richd Dement are to meet on Dec 18, at my ofc in Gtwn; distribution of trust fund among the creditors, widow & heirs of said Richd Dement.
-W Redin, auditor

Supreme Crt of D C, in Equity #1772. John Marbury vs Robt Ould, Henry, Edwin W, Saml A, Francis V, & Walter Robinson, Thos C Cox & Mgt his wife, & Maynadier Mason. Account of the trustees receipts & disbursement at my ofc in Gtwn on Dec 17. -W Redin, auditor

Co-partnership in the practice of law in the city of Nashville, Tenn. -John S Brien & Bailie Peyton. 40 Cherry st.

Orphans Crt of Wash Co, D C. 1-Prsnl estate of Philip Fenwick, late of Wash Co, dec'd. -J Van Riswick, Wm A Fenwick, excs. 2-Prsnl estate of Benj F Larned, late of Wash Co, dec'd. -Maria H Larned, admx. 3-Case of Mgt Bayly & Chas B Bayly, adms of Wm F Bayly, dec'd; settlement on Dec 19. -Z C Robbins, rg o/wills

The body of a dead sldr on the bloody fields of Gettysburg, was identified by a picture of 3 little chldrn found in his hands. His name was Hummerton, & his widow & 3 chldrn live in Portsville, Cattaraugus Co, N Y.

Died: in Wash City, on Nov 25, Leonard Harbaugh, in his 64th yr. Funeral from his late residence, 432 F st, Fri.

Cmdor Wm S Walker, of U S Navy, died in Boston yesterday at age 70 yrs.

SAT NOV 28, 1863

Mrd: on Nov 24, at the residence of the bride's father, Enos Ray, *Kendall Meadows*, Wash Co, D C, by Rev Dr Ryan, C M Keys, of Montg Co, Md, to Miss Martha A Ray.

Mrd: at St Aloysius Chr, Nov 25, by Rev Fr Maguire, Chas M Sioussa & Miss Lizzie, y/d/o Wm T Dove, of Montrose, Montg Co, Md.

Mrd: at the Navy Yd in Wash City, on Nov 26, by Rev Dr Pinkney, Dr Heman P Babcock, U S Navy, to Sally H, y/d/o Cmdor Harwood, U S Navy.

Died: Nov 26, Wm M Cripps, aged 32 yrs. Funeral from the residence of his father, 492 11th st, today.

Died: on Nov 27, Sgt Maj John Robinson, U S M C, aged 47 yrs. Funeral from his late residence on 8th st, near the Marine Barracks, on Sun.

Died: at the Douglas Hosp, in Wash City, on Nov 22, of wound received at Kelly's Ford, Va, Capt Weldon Edwards Davis, of Warrenton, N C, aged 25 yrs, late Cmdr of Co B, 30th Regt of N C troops in the Confederate svc.

Died: in Wash City, on Nov 27, of pneumonia, Francis Alger, sr, of Boston, Mass.

Victory at Chattanooga: Nov 25. The brigade of Gen Carse, with a portion of Gen Lightpew's brig, composed the storming party in the first assault. Gen Carse was wounded quite severely in the thigh. Second assault in which Mathias', Loomis, & Raul's brig were engaged: Gen Mathias was wounded & Col Putnam, 93rd Ohio, was killed. Gen Grant started 2 columns against the weakened centre, driving the main force northward toward Gen Sherman who opened on them. We have taken not less than 5,000 prisoners, & perhaps 10,000. Gen Hooker will probably intercept the enemy near Rossville. Casualties: Lt Col Espy, 68th Ind Regt; Maj McCawley, 10th Iowa; Col Omars, 19th Ill; Lt Col Stuart, 19th Ill; Maj Walker, 10th Mo; Maj Welsh, 56th Ill; Maj Inniss, 5th Iowa, wounded; Maj Irwin, 6th Iowa, killed. Enemy is reported bivouacking near Missionary Ridge. Col Phelps, 38th Ohio, & Maj Glass, 32nd Ind, killed. Gen John E Smith is reported wounded. Col Avery, 102nd N Y, lost a leg, & Maj Elliott is the same as dead.

MON NOV 30, 1863
Mrd: at *Pleasant Prospect*, on Nov 25, by Rev Hatney Stanley, assisted by Rev Mr Chesley, T Blake Brooke, to Florence, eldest s/o the late John Contee, all of PG Co, Md.

N C election: mbrs elect are given in the Richmond Enq of Nov 23rd:

Hon W H N Smith, re-elected	Dr J G Ramsay, re-el
Hon J A Gilmer, new mbr	Dr J T Leach, new mbr
Hon R R Bridgers, re-el	Gen G W Logan, new mbr
S H Christian, re-el	Lt Thos C Fuller, new mbr
B S Gaither, re-el	Capt Josiah Turner, new mbr

Orphans Crt of Wash Co, D C. Prsnl estate of Hannah Ulrich, late of Wash Co, dec'd. -Wm F Mattingly, adm c t a

D W Whitney & W H White, defaulting Gov't contractors, reached Wash City, from the U S Deputy Mrshl at N Y, on Sat, & were committed to the Old Capitol Prison. They will be tried by crt-martial.

Deaths reported to the Navy Dept of week ending Nov 28, 1863:
Wm S Emery, landsman, pneumonia, Aug 28, vessel U S S *Somerset*.
Jno Davis, gunner, consumption, Nov 17, Nav Hosp, N Y.
Chas S Mason, 3rd ast engr, yel fever, Nov 13, vessel U S S *Estrella*.
Frank Myers, landsman, yel fever, Nov 10, vessel U S S *Antona*.
Eudolph Dennis, nurse, yel fever, Nov 6, Nov Hosp, Pensacola.
Jno McMasters, coal heaver, yel fever, Sep 14, vessel U S S *Scioto*.
Jas H McKee, surg's steward, yel fever, Sep 14, vessel U S S *H Beales*.
Jas P Connel, marine, typhoid fever, Oct 11, vessel U S S *Vermont*.
Jno Barry, 2nd cab boy, typhoid fever, Nov 14, do.

Wm R Green, 1st cab coy, spotted fever, Nov 19, Nav Hosp, N Y.
Solomon Shands, contraband, epilepsy, May 27, vessel U S S *Black Hawk.*
Jno Cischafski, landsman, cholera morbus, Jun 30, do.
Mose Brown, contraband, contusion, Jun 7, do.
Thos Rony, seaman, cholera morbus, Jun 30, do.
Adam Smothers, contraband, pneumonia, Sep 30, do.
Tom Dunlap, 1st cab coy, drowned, Oct 9, vessel U S S *New Era.*
Lewis Ellis, seaman, remit fever, Oct 20, vessel U S S *Eastport.*
Jno G Williams, landsman, diptheria, Nov 7, do.
Channey Brafford, seaman, typhoid fever, Nov 1, vessel U S S *Reindeer.*
Ed E Brennard, vol Lt, gunshot wound, Nov 14, vessel U S S *Mound City.*

TUE DEC 1, 1863

Mrd: on Nov 24, by Rev Dr Riley, Wm C McLeod, of N Y C, to Miss Mary Jane Beckwith, of Montg Co, Md. [Corr of Dec 2: Rev D Riley to Rev Dr Riley]

Mrd: on Nov 12, in Allegheny, Pa, by Rev E P Swift, Mr Isaac Beeson, of Mt Braddock, Fayette Co, Pa, to Mrs Eliza L Gibson, of Alleghany.

Died: in Warren, Maine, on Nov 16, Mr Geo R McIntyre, aged 28 yrs. Mr M resided for some time in Wash City.

Died: on Nov 25, in Wash City, of diptheria, Arthur Clifton, first s/o John E & L Alice Lewis, aged 4 yrs.

Died: on Nov 30, Alberta Elmira, d/o Geo T & Joanna Gibbons, aged 10 months. Funeral at their residence, 314 8th st, today.

An order to Cincinnati relieving Maj N H McLean of his command & to report to some volunteer Brig Gen at Ft Vancouver, Wash Terr. McLean is the nephew of the late Justice McLean, U S Supreme Crt: chief to Gen Burnside's Staff in Cincinnati, & genr'l cnslr & indispensable right hand man. He was the Ast Adj Gen of the Dept of the Ohio: in the Peninsula campaign he was Chief of Gen McClellan's Staff in reality. Thoroughly loyal as any man in America. Now, it was the misfortune of this accomplished ofcr to be selected by one Edgar Conklin, of Cincinnati, to assail Maj McLean & demand his removal from ofc.

Rev R J Keeling, of Bel Air, Md, had been invited to the Rectorship of Trinity Parish, & will this week, visit Wash City to confer with the vestry before giving an answer.

WED DEC 2, 1863

Orphans Crt of Wash Co, D C. 1-Case of Wm B Kibbey, exc of John B Kibbey, dec'd; settlement on Dec 26. 2-Case of Joshua A Richie, adm of Sylvanus G Deeth, dec'd; settlement on Dec 26. -Z C Robbins, rg o/wills

Valuable rl est, belonging to the heirs of Geo S Neal, dec'd; sale at pblc auction; part of lots 89 & 90, Gtwn, on so side of Prospect st, with nearly new 2 story frame hse; also east part of lot 131, Gtwn, north side of Dunbarton st, with 2 story frame hse. -John S Paxton, Sarah A Paxton, Leroy Edwards. Guardians of minor heirs of Geo S Neal, dec'd. -Thos Dowling, auct

Wash Corp: 1-Act for relief of E Romain: $40 to be returned to him by the Mayor. 2-Act for relief of P Cullinan: sum of $445.87 to be pd Cullinan for bal due him for grading & gravelling 5th st.

Charleston, Nov 28, 1863. Capt Jacob Valentine & 2 or 3 pvts were severely wounded in Ft Moultrie by the explosion of a Parrott shell. No casualties on James Island.

Col Dick Morgan, a bro of Gen John Morgan, & 6 captains, escaped from the Ohio pen & reached Toronto, Canada. Gen Morgan occupied the cell over Col Morgan's. Gen Morgan was allowed to exchange cells with Dick, who, every thing being prepared, permitted his bro to take his place. Capt T Henry Hines, who is a mason & bricklayer, had charge of the work which resulted in the escape of the prisoners. [They dug with knives thru the floor of the cell to the outside wall.]

Writs issued for the seizure of the following property under the provisions of the confiscation law: Prnsl property of John A Campbell, of Ala, formerly a Justice of the Supr Crt of the U S, consisting of furn in a hse on I st, opposite Franklin Sq. Interest of W B Cross, formerly a well known lawyer of Wash City, now supposed to be in Richmond, in lot 6 in sq 218, with a brick cottage dwlg, on I st, near 15th. The prop of Geo D Fowle, formerly of Alexandria, consisting of subdivisions 15 & 16, of lots 4 & 2, of Davidson's subdiv of sq 222, with handsome 4 story brick dwlg, on H st between 14th & 15th sts; lots 3 to 12 in sq 773, between 3rd & 4th sts east; lots 10 to 14 in sq 814, between B & C sts; lots 1 to 4 & 19 to 28 inclusive, in sq 1,018, between 12th & 13th sts, unimproved. Lots 1 to 5 in sq 737, near the junction of Va & N J aves, in the name of Thos W Greer, late pastor of the Navy Yd Baptist Chr. Lot 2, of subdiv D of Todd's subdiv of sq 352, with improvements, on Md ave, near 11th st [Island] belonging to John L Lancaster, of St Mary's Co, Md, & late clerk in the 6th Aud ofc, now at the south. Lots 1, 29, 30, & part of lot 2 in sq 108, corner of 18th & I sts, with handsome brick hse belonging to Jos C Ives, formerly a Lt in the U S Topog Engrs. The prsnl prop of Dr A Y P Garnett. Lot 3 in sq 317, on I st, between 11th & 12th sts, with handsome 2 story brick dwlg, belonging to Wm L Bailey, of Va, late a clerk in the Adj Genr'ls ofc. Case made returnable on the 3rd Mon in Dec.

THU DEC 3, 1863
Bks for sale, 40,000. Antiquarian bkstore, over Bank of Wash. Alfred Hunter

Orphans Crt of Wash Co, D C. 1-Case of Harmon Burns & Geo W Cochran, excs of Geo Burns dec'd; settlement on Dec 26. -Z C Robbins, rg o/wills 2-Prsnl estate of Yelverton P Page, late of Wash Co, dec'd. -W E Howard, adm, W a. 3-Case of Adelaide J Brown, admx of Wm V H Brown, dec'd; settlement on Dec 26. -Z C Robbins, rg o/wills

On Sep 13 last the Rev Jas J Marks did join in marriage, without consent of her parents, Ann Miller, under age 15 yrs, to Saml McManus, who has since been imprisoned on the charge of murder & desertion from the military svc of the U S. Ann, by her cnsl, N Thompson, has sued for divorce, & Robt M Miller, her father, has by same atty, sued the Rev Mr Marks for 500 pounds.

The Statue of the Goddess of Freedom was raised to it position on the Dome of the Capitol on Dec 2; entire cost from $25,000 to $30,000; modeled in plaster by Crawford, the lamented eminent sculptor, for which model the price of $3,000 was pd. It was cast at the foundry of Clark Mills, of Bladensburg, Md.

Wash Corp: 1-Ptn of Mrs Wm P Dole & others with a bill granting permission to erect a tempo bldg in a pblc reservation to be used for a fair for the benefit of the sick & wounded Union sldrs: passed. 2-Bill for relief of Francis Frontnell: passed as amended. 3-Bill for relief of Michl O'Brien: passed. 4-Cmte of Claims: asked to be discharged from further consideration of the bill for the relief of Wm T Collins: which was ordered.

Dr Flodoardo Howard has returned to Wash City to practice his profession. Ofc & residence, 328 F st.

Col Jas Belger, Chief Q M at Balt, was tried before a crt-martial upon charges of neglect of duty, & fraudulent conduct in hiring transports, & in purchase of supplies, found not guilty. Col B was for nearly a year connected with A C Hall & Coblens in large business transactions, & the amount pd for coal deliveries reached an aggregate of more than $100,000 a yr. Col B pd A C Hall, or Coblens & Hall, 40% & 50% more for the coal to be delivered on board Gov't vessels: rates unaccountably high. Col B was guilty of gross neglect & violation of duty in these transactions, the Sec disapproves of the find of the crt, & declares Col Belger, by order of the Pres, dishonorably dismissed from the U S svc.

Summer resort for sale: *Green Springs*, in Green Spring Valley, 14 miles from Balt City: offered for sale at $250 per ac. Favorite resort contains 81 acs. Previous to the destruction by fire of the hotel, this resort was patronized by the most fashionable families. A dwlg, stabling, tenpin alley, & other hses still remain on the prop. Apply to R W Templeman & Co, Rl Est Brokers, Balt, Md.

Boston, Dec 2. Mrs Jane M Pierce, w/o Ex-Pres Pierce, died this morning at Andover, Mass. She had been in feeble health for some yrs.

FRI DEC 4, 1863
Mrd: on Aug 31, by Rev J G Butler, Mr Wm T Biggs to Hannah M Marden, of PG Co, Md.

Died: on Dec 3, Geo S Noyes, in his 54th yr. Funeral on Fri.

Orphans Crt of Wash Co, D C. Case of Benj A Janvier, adm of Paul Maximillian Engle, dec'd; settlement on Dec 26. -Z C Robbins, rg o/wills

Exec Cmte for the encouragement of Volunteering in D C, beg leave to appeal to the loyal ctzns of Wash for aid in furtherance of the object they have in view.

H C Wilson	John Sessford	Jno H Semmes
S B Noyes	Geo F Gulick	
Alex R Shepherd	R M Coombs	

SAT DEC 5, 1863
Obit-Miss J Eliz Beall, 2nd d/o the late Col Upton Beall, died on Nov 30, at her residence in Rockville, Montg Co, Md, in the 48th yr of her age, after a lingering illness. The triple cord which united 3 sisters has been severed.

Navy Dept: Cmdor A A Harwood has been detached from the command of the Wash Navy yd & granted leave of absence, & Cmdor John B Montgomery, of the Boston yd, ordered to supply his place. Cmdor M was formerly exec ofcr at this yd. -Star

New Flour Hse-Geo T McGlue & Co: 375 & 377 D st, Wash, D C.

Died: at Andover, Mass, on Dec 2, at the residence of Hon John Aiken, Mrs Jane M Pierce, w/o Franklin Pierce, late Pres of the U S, & d/o Rev Dr Appleton, the 2nd Pres of Bowdoin College, aged 57 yrs. During Mr Pierce's official term, Mrs Peirce was prevented by constant illness from mingling in general society or assuming the place in the White Hse which she would have adorned had her strength permitted; but, in private, to those who were permitted the privilage of intercourse with her, she indicated a winning sweetness of temper, an affability & womanly grace as rare as it is pleasant to behold. –Boston Post

Mr Theodore F Boucher died on Oct 26, at Nassau. Tribute by the mbrs of the Young Catholic's Friends Soc of Gtwn, D C, tendered to the bereaved wife & family.

Chattanooga, Dec 3. It is reported by deserters, as well as by ctzns arriving here, that Gen John C Breckinridge had died of the wounds he received in the fight at Ringgold. A s/o Breckinridge & one of his cousins are among the prisoners captured in the recent engagement.

MON DEC 7, 1863
Mrd: on Nov 19, at *Long Meadows*, the residence of Benj Osbourn, A A Co, Md, by Rev Dorsey Jacobs, Wm B Sasscer to Martha E Dixon.

Died: in New Orleans, on Nov 15, Mrs Anna E, w/o Henry N Siebrecht, & formerly a resident of Wash City, in the 41st yr of her age.

The funeral of Miss Laura H Gordon will take place at the residence of her father, C Gordon, 265 I st, today.

Deaths reported to the Navy Dept for the week ending Dec 5, 1863:
Robt Town, 1st cl boy, consumption, Nov 17, Nav Hosp, Memphis.
Louis Caisey, 1st cl boy, remit fever, Nov 18, do.
Edgar H Sherne, coal heaver, chronic diarrhoea, Nov 21, do.
Nelson Black, 1st cl boy, chronic diarrhoea, Nov 23, do.
John R Robinson, sgt Maj, consumption, Nov 27, Marine Barracks, Wash.
Rudolph Dennis, musician, yel fever, Nov 6, blank.
Daniel Davis, seaman, yel fever, Nov 16, vessel U S S *Aroostook.*
Jas Johnson, seaman, wound, Nov 14, vessel U S S *Lackawanna.*
Wm S Walker, cmdor, blank, Nov 24, Boston.
John Stroud, landsman, fever, Nov 25, Nav Hosp, N Y.
John Lockey, marine, consumption, Nov 25, do.
Jas Smith, seaman, dysentery, Nov 17, do.
Eli Washington, blank, blank, blank, vessel U S S, *J P Jackson.*
Geo Kemball, actg mstr, stomach disease, Nov 30, navy yd, Boston.
Chas C Butcher, seaman, remit fever, Oct 8, vessel U S S *Arizona.*
Saml S Wetherell, landsman, remit fever, Oct 18, do.
Chas S Dudley, 3rd ast engr, blank, Nov 26, blank.
Wm I Hotchkiss, actg mstr, gunshot wound, Aug 17, vessel U S S *Gen Putnam.*
Wm Conner, colored, landsman, mania, Nov 5, vessel U S S *Vermont.*

Orphans Crt of Wash Co, D C. 1-Case of Chas M Matthews, adm of Chas A Washington, dec'd; settlement on Dec 29. 2-Case of Jas F Halliday, adm of Ann McMeehan, dec'd; settlement on Dec 29. -Z C Robbins, rg o/wills

Knoxville, Nov 29, 1863. Rebel blow struck this morning, reinforced by the troops of Jones, Jackson, & Williams, Longstreet sought to annihilate the army of the Ohio by one blow. Skirmishing began last night & cont'd until daylight, on our left front, before Fort Saunders, commanded by Gen Ferero, & defended by the 79th N Y, Benjamin's 3rd U S Artl, & Buckley's R I btry, etc. The rebel stormng party, led by the 16th & 17th Ga & 13th Mississippi came to the assault. The ditch was filled with the dead, wounded, & dying. Cost of the assault on Ft Saunders: 1,000 killed, wounded, or prisoners. Col Girare of the 13th Miss, & Lt Col O'Brien, the bro/o Mrs Brownslow, is a prisoner.

Supreme Crt of Ohio: Cincinnati, Dec 5. Govn'r Tod has appt'd Hon Joshua R Swan Supr Judge, vice Judge Gholson, resigned.

Lectures will be delivered in E st Bapt Chr by the following:

Rev Stephen H Tyng, D D, of N Y
Rev Henry Ward Beecher, Brooklyn, N Y
Gen J A Garfield, Ohio
Rev Jacob N Manning, D D, Boston, Mass
Prof R D Hitchcock, D D, N Y
John B Gough, Mass
Rev Richd S Storrs, D D, Brooklyn, N Y
Sgl tkts for the course, $2.50.

Hon B Grats Brown, Mo
Hon Danl S Dickinson, Binghampton, N Y
Rev John Pierpont, Wash, D C
Geo Wm Curtis, N Y

Brd of mgrs:

Lewis Clephane	Z Richards	Chas Roesee
W A Croffut	A G Mall	John Pierpont Pres
C Storrs	N B Devereux	John R Fairbanks, Sec

TUE DEC 8, 1863

Mbrs of the Hse o/Reps:

Conn: Lafayette S Foster, Jas Dixon
Calif: Jas A McDougall, John Conness
Dela: Willard Saulsbury, Jas A Bayard
Ind: Henry Lane, Thos A Hendricks
Ill: Wm A Richardson, Lyman Trumbull
Iowa: Jas W Grimes, Jas Harlan
Ky: Lazarus W Powell, Garrett Davis
Kansas: Saml C Pomeroy, Jas H Lane
Md: Thos H Hicks, Reverdy Johnson
Maine: Wm Pitt Fessenden, Lot M Morrill
Mass: Henry Wilson, Chas Sumner
Mich: Jacob M Howard, Zachariah Chandler
Minnesotta: M S Wilkinson, Alex Ramsay

Mo: Benj Gratz Brown, John B Henderson
N H: John P Hale, Danl Clark
N Y: Ira Harris, Edwin D Morgan
N J: John C Ten Eyck, Wm Wright
Ohio: Benj F Wade, John Sherman
Oregon: Benj F Harding, Jas W Nesmith
Pa: Edgar Cowan, Chas R Buckalew
R I: Henry B Anthony, Wm Sprague
Vt: Jacob Collamer, Solomon Foot
Va: John S Carlile, Lemuel J Bowden
Wisc: Timothy O Howe, Jas R Doolittle
W Va: Waitman T Willey, P G Van Winckle

On Fri Capt Wm Stoddard, a q m at Alexandria, was arrested, by order of the Sec of War, & lodged in the Old Capitol prison. On Sat Capt O B Ferguson, the chief q m at Alexandria, was also arrested & sent to the Old Capitol. Another Capt Stoddard & Capt Casey have been arrested. The charge is frauds upon the Gov't: from half a million to a million dollars. The fraud was principally in large purchases of grain, compounded that the Gov't is cheated out of twenty cents on each bshl.

Orphans Crt of Wash Co, D C. Case of Wm J Donohoo, adm of J B Pittman, dec'd; settlement on Dec 29. -Z C Robbins, rg o/wills

Mrd: on Nov 19, by Rev R S Grier, Frederick Pilling, of Wash, to Mary, 2nd d/o Mr Alexander McAllister, of Taneytown, Carroll Co, Md.

Died: on Dec 6th, at the residence of his mother, Rondout, N Y, Patrick O'Toole, bro of Rev T J O'Toole, late of Wash City. Interment in Mt Olivet Cemetery, Wash, tomorrow.

Died: on Dec 6, of congestion of the brain, Agnes Louisa, in her 5th yr, d/o John W & Louisa Smith. Funeral from the residence of her grandparents, 232 D st, today.

Supreme Crt of D C, Equity #2. Johnston Bros & Co, vs Virginia Benter, [only] heir at law of Wm F Benter, dec'd. Wm F Benter has departed & Virginia Benter is not a resident of D C, & cannot be found. -D K Cartter, Chief Judge

WED DEC 9, 1863
Died: on Dec 8, in the 75th yr of her age, Mrs Jane Hyatt, for 59 years a resident of Wash City. Funeral from her late residence, 339 Pa av, Thu.

R R Accident-on Sat, in Alexandria, Mr & Mrs Kish, of Alexandria, were struck by a locomotive & train when their horse refused to cross the tracks. Mr & Mrs Kish died on Sun. Their dght who was with them is in critical condition. Both Mr & Mrs Kish fell across the track & were run over by the train, cutting off the legs of each. They lingered in great agony until Sun, when death terminated their suffering. –Gazette

Col Wm Whistler died at his residence in Cincinnati on Fri, at a very advanced age. He was the oldest army ofcr in the U S except Gen Scott.

Hon John Wales, formerly U S Senator for Dela, died on Dec 3.

Lawrence J Steele, convicted of obtaining money from the Gov't by means of a forged payroll, was sentenced in Phil on Sat to 3 years & 9 months imprisonment.

A paroled Confederate prisoner named Healy, has been condemned to be shot at New Orleans for violating his parole.

THU DEC 10, 1863
Died: on Dec 7, of typhoid fever, A B Norris, in the 52nd yr of his age.

Orphans Crt of Wash Co, D C. Case of Jas C McGuier, adm of Agricole Favier, dec'd; settlement on Jan 2. -Z C Robbins, rg o/wills

Cuba Cigars for sale at low price. Apply to Jose Picaso, hijo, 448 12th st, between G & H sts.

By command of Gen Augur, all travel over the Long Bridge will be discontinued during Thu, Fri & Sat of this week, for the purpose of repairs.

The Bookstore of Messrs Blanchard & Mohun took fire yesterday from a range in the restaurant below, the flue of which was built too close to the wood-work of the ceiling. Little damage done.

FRI DEC 11, 1863

New Commission & Produce Mkt Hse, La av, between 9th & 10th sts. John Farrell, formerly of N Y.

E Owen & Son, merchant tailors, 212 Pa av, Wash. -E Owen, S W Owen

Bristol, Tenn news of Dec 7, 1863. Our loss at Knoxville is 600 men, principaly of Hood's div. Among them are Col Ruff, of Ga, who was killed, & Col Fisher, of Mississippi, seriously wounded.

A despatch to Gen Hitchcock from Gen Meredith, at Fortress Monroe, states the latter belief that our prisoners on *Belle Isle* are in tents, & also that he has requested Mr Ould to share the clothing & subsistence sent by the Gov't with our ctzn prisoners. He has no doubt that this has been done.

SAT DEC 12, 1863

Jas Armstrong, an old resident of Norfolk, Va, has been sentenced to one month's imprisonment in Ft Norfolk for threatening to shoot negro sldrs.

Supreme Crt of D C, in Equity #1595. Fred'k Sellhausen vs Chas Mades et al. Ratify sale of Lot 10 in sq 785 to Malichi Gateby, for .10 per sq ft; lot 9 in sq 785 to H L Thomas, for .06 per sq ft; lot 12 in sq 785 to Mgt Hart for same; lot 3 in sq 891 to Martin McNamara, at one & a 4th cents per sq ft; lot 8 in said sq to Geo W Mitchell, who has transferred his interest to John Evans. -R J Meigs, clerk

Wash Corp: 1-Act for relief of Wm Boyd: to pay him $18, being the amount of the bill for burying 2 paupers who died of small pox. 2-Bill for relief of Wm Fletcher: passed. 3-John A Rowland has permission to withdraw papers from the file.

MON DEC 14, 1863

Deaths reported to the Navy Dept for the week ending Dec 12, 1863:
Patrick Boyle, coal heaver, endocarditis, Nov 29, Rec ship *Ohio*.
Russell Colby, landsman, chronic diarrhoea, Nov 23, Nav Hosp, Memphis.
Wm Hustin, 2nd cl fireman, consumption, Nov 37, do. [As written]
S E Winthrop, landsman, drowned, Nov 13, vessel U S S *Conestoga*.
Edm Cavender, seaman, consumption, Dec 4, Nav Hosp, Chelsea.
Saml F Ray, carp, remit fever, Oct 4, vessel U S S *Narrgansett*.
Jas Jamison, capt hold, remit fever, Oct 13, do.
John Coleman, boatswain's mate, remit fever, Oct 19, do.
Elias R Woodworth, landsman, drowned, Dec 5, vessel *Sassacus*.
Geo Sweeting, landsman, drowned, Dec 5, do.
Towsand Stites, vol Lt, blank, Nov 29, Phil.
Asa T Hawes, actg mstr's mate, chronic diarrhoea, Nov 26, vessel U S S *Arizona*.
Rodolpho Dennis, nurse, yel fever, Nov 6, Nav Hosp, N Orleans.
Robt Stott, 2nd Ast Surg, gastritis, Nov 24, vessel U S S *Estrella*.
Ely Washington, 3rd cl boy, carditis, Oct 25, vessel *J P Jackson*.
John Hanley, landsman, pneumonia, Aug 9, vessel *Montgomery*.
Hugh Quigley, landsman, typhoid fever, Sept 24, do.
Nunzio Mazzana, musician, consumption, Dec 5, Nav Hosp, N Y.

Orphans Crt of Wash Co, D C. Prsnl estate of David Smith, late of Wash, D C, dec'd. - Mary Smith, her x mark, admx. -Z C Robbins, rg o/wills

Balt, Dec 12. Fort Monroe, Dec 12, 1863: to C C Fulton, Balt, Md. Please give notice that the Confederate authorities decline receiving any more packages or provisions for the Union prisoners, so that parties interested may refrain from forwarding any more goods to this point. –Benj F Butler, Maj Gen Commanding. Rev Mr Torrence, who went to City Point with Dr Clement C Barclay, returned this morning. He had an interview with Capt Hatch, who was sent from Richmond to meet him. He informed that the ofcrs in Libby prison, from the immense supplies which they had received, could set a table from their stores in hand equal to any hotel in the U S.

TUE DEC 15, 1863
Mrd: on Dec 10, by Rev C H Hall, Dr Alfred Edelin, of Md, to Miss Sydney Thruston Bradley, of Wash City.

Mr Abner S Brady, the well known gymnast, & founder of the spacious 7th Regt Gym in N Y, has come to Wash to build & conduct a similar establishment here.

WED DEC 16, 1863
Case of Richd H Clarke, exc of Eliz Chinn, dec'd; settlement on Jan 5. -Z C Robbins, rg o/wills

Wash Corp: 1-Act for relief of Wm Fletcher: sum of $5,005.84 be pd him for a deficiency in the appropriation for grading & gravelling K st north, from Rock Crk to the Circle.

THU DEC 17, 1863
Mrd: at the residence of the bride's father, on Nov 25, by Rev Wm I Garrett, Chas S Bryan to Miss Mildred Y, d/o Wm G Wear, of Otterville, Cooper Co, Mo.

Died: in Balt, Md, on Dec 14, Jessie Sheddon, aged 18 mos, infant d/o J Bayard H & Henrietta Smith.

Maj Gen John Buford died in Wash City, at the residence of Gen Stoneman, after an illness of 4 or 5 weeks, contracted in his duty in the Army of the Potomac, commencing with diarrhea & followed by typhoid fever. He was a native of Ky, 1848 grad of West Point. Mrs Buford is expected from Rock Island, today.

Senate: 1-Ptn from Saml A Duncan & other mbrs of the 4th & 6th U S colored regts, praying for the same pay & allowances as given to white sldrs: referred to the Military Cmte. 2-Cmte on Military Affairs reported back voting the thanks of Congress & a gold medal to Maj Gen Grant, for his distinguished svcs.

From Nashville, Tenn, Dec 15. 1-Gen Palmer resigned his command of the 14th Corps, & had reached Bridgeport on his return home when he received orders to return to Chattanooga, his resignation not having been accepted. 2-Col Mismer reports from Columbia that the rebel deserters & ctzns are flocking to that post in great numbers, asking to be allowed to take the oath under the Pres' proclamation. 3-A few days ago a Capt Perkins, of the 11th Tenn Cavalry, applied to Gen Rosecrans for permision to take the oath of allegiance under the amnesty proclamation-his own eyes have been opened since his capture. 4-The trial of Frank Gurley, the guerilla who killed Gen McCook a yr ago, is now being concluded. He will undoubtedly be hung. 5-Horace Maynard, the Atty Gen of the state, declares, in a pblshd letter, that the usual county elections are to held in Mar next in the state.

The trial of Luther C Saxton, the great *Book Company* swindler, is now progressing in Rochester.

Robberies in the last 48 hours: the store of Mr Thos Powers-over $300 worth of groceries stolen; the rm of Mr Ellison, who boards at Mr John McDowell's on 14th st-robbed of $126; rm 43, at the Met Htl, occupied by Mr Jas H Myers, robbed of a gold watch & chain. Svr'l rms at the Nat'l Htl were robbed: rm occupied by Mr Cisco of a draft for L50 sterling [ab't $240] & $22 in money; rm occupied by Mr C W Colby-robbed of $27 & other valuables; rm occupied by J A Chamberlain-2 gold watches & $70; rm occupied by Dr Smith, relieved of $200. The city is full of thieves from the north. -Star

The 1st Md Cavalry, attached to the Army of the Potomac, handed over to Surgeon Dodson, $690 for the relief of the suffering prisoners in the south. The money will be sent to the Balt Relief Fund.

FRI DEC 18, 1863
Mrd: on Dec 8, in Balt, Md, at the residence of the bride's uncle, Andrew Reid, by Rev Dr Backus, Wm R Riley, of Wash City, to Eliz King, d/o the late Wm Reid, of Norfolk, Va.

Disturbing scene last Sun at the Park st Meth Chr in Cincinnati between Mack R Barnitz, a book pblshr on 4th st, & Mrs Nellie Jacobs, both mbrs of the church. Mr B had preferred serious charges against Mrs J some months ago, & used his influence to have her driven from her position as a teacher of one of the classes. She also was voted out of the church. During the first prayer, gliding along the aisle, Mrs Jacobs, drawing a cowskin which she had concealed in her skirts, gave Mr Barnitz a vehement whack over the head & again about the ears. She was at length removed from the church.

Adj Gen Thomas is said to be lying dangerously ill in the Mississippi Valley.

SAT DEC 19, 1863
Obit-Mr Edw Wayson died at his residence, on 8th st, on Dec 13, in the 98th yr of his age; employee of the Gov't in the Blacksmith Dept of the Wash Navy Yd for 53 yrs. He was a mbr of the Meth Chr for 50 yrs & leaves a large family to mourn him.

Died: in Wash City, on Dec 17, Mrs Louise Brunnert, in her 69th yr. Funeral from Mr B Chambers' residence, 357 11th st, today.

Died: at Catonsville, near Balt, Md, on Dec 16, after a short illness, Martha Magdalen Bowie, w/o Richd C Bowie, & d/o the late Daniel Rapine, of Wash City. Burial in Congressional Cemetery, Wash, D C, today.

Died: on Dec 17, at the residence of Wm Galt, 9th st, Chas H Marriott, of Balt, Md. Funeral from Mr Galt's residence this morning.

Walter Lenox, formerly Mayor of Wash, who has resided in Richmond since the beginning of the war, was arrested on Thu in Balt by the military authorities.

Senate: 1-Bill for relief of L F Cartee: referred to the Cmte on Pblc Lands.

Hse o/Reps: 1-Bill for relief of Wm C Walker & others: referred to the Cmte of Claims.

Wash Corp: 1-Ptn of Lewis Reese & others for the opening of a certain st: referred to the Cmte on Improvements. 2-Ptn of John Baker & others sking the repeal of the pound law: referred to a special cmte. 3-Bill for relief of Jas H Reed: passed. 4-Cmte on Police: reported back on the nomination of Wm Durr for Measurer of Wood & Coal in the 1st Dist: confirmed. 5-Bill for relief of M M White: passed. 6-Bill for relief of Stephen D Castleman: passed. 7-Bill for relief of Thos Morrison: referred to the Cmte of Claims. 8-Bill granting permission to Robt H Graham to tap the water svc-pipe on C st: passed.

Gov Bramlette, of Ky, declined being a candidate for the U S Senate. A sense of duty requires that he should remain at his post until the pblc safety is more clearly defined & peace better assured.

MON DEC 21, 1863
Deaths reported to the Navy Dept for the week ending Dec 19, 1863:
Birgham Brown, seaman, typhoid fever, Dec 11, vessel U S S *Sassacus*.
Wm Russell, landsman, colic, Dec 4, Nav Hosp, N Y.
John N Thompson, landsman, consumption, Dec 11, vessel U S S *Union*.
Alex Eilison, 3rd cl boy, consumption, Nov 21, vessel U S S *Arizona*.
Wm Mitchell, 3rd ast engr, remit fever, Nov 19, do.
John Murphy, 2nd cl fireman, remit fever, Nov 20, do.
Thos Shaw, landsman, remit fever, Nov 12, do.
John H Smith, landsman, remit fever, Nov 12, do.
Ed S Rose, actg mstr's mate, smallpox, Nov 13, vessel U S S *Fredonia*.
Wm Arnold, landsman, diarrhoea, Dec 3, vessel U S S *Chillicothe*.
Geo Cox, landsman, drowned, Nov 30, vessel U S S *Reindeer*.
Jesse Tare, landsman, drowned, Nov 30, do.
Nicholas Coyle, 1st ast engr, dysentery, Sep 24, vessel U S S *Norwich*.
Thos S Kebel, seaman, consumption, Dec 11, Nav Hosp, N Y.
Isaac Webb, 1st cl boy, disease of heart, Nov 20, vessel U S S *Vermont*.
Wm Kennehan, landsman, disease of brain, Nov 22, vessel U S S *Iron Age*.
Henry W Menan, 3rd ast engr, lost, Dec 6, iron clad *Weehawken*.
Same for the following-as above on the *Weehawken*, Dec 6:
Augustus Mitchell, 3rd ast engr
Geo W McGowen, actg 3rd ast engr
Chas Spongberg, actg 3rd act engr
Thos Piper, seaman
Seaman:

Jas Scollen	Wm H Williamson	Robt Nugent
John Buckley	Christian Anderson	Thos Donovan
John Kerrigan	John Rutledge	Wm G Pike
John Carpenter	Ralph Anderson	Geo Leighorn
Jos Crogan	Ed Gayhan	Henry Sumner
Chas F Davis	Ed Mullen	Thos Scothers
John Williams, 2	Jas Lenman	Thos Danlon
Chas H Willson	Thos Hee or Mee	Stephen C Newman

Funeral for the late Maj Gen John Buford took place at the N Y Av Presby Chr, Wash, D C, yesterday; burial in West Point, Dec 24.

Mrd: in Hanover, Pa, on Dec 17, by Rev M J Alleman, Mr David G Ridgely, of Wash City, to Miss Lizzie L Diller, of Hanover, Pa.

Died: at his late residence, in Annapolis, Md, on Dec 9th, Dr Dennis Claude, in his 82nd yr.

Died: at his bro's residence, in PG Co, Md, on Dec 18, Dr Saml McPherson, late of the Auditor's Ofc, P O Dept, in the 55th yr of his age. Burial at Oak Hill Cemetery, Gtwn, today.

Died: on Dec 20, Maggie Jane, y/d/o T V & Martha E Turner, aged 5 months & 28 days. Funeral from 30 Green st, Gtwn, today.

Cmdor Van Brunt, of the U S Navy, died last week at Dedham, Mass.

Rev K I Keeling has accepted the Rectorship of Trinity Parish & to enter upon the duties at beginning of the new yr. We learn that the sermons he preached in Trintiy Chr on the Sabbath, lately, caused quite a demand for pews in the church.

TUE DEC 22, 1863
Died: at the residence of his father, in Gtwn, on Dec 19, Wm Smith, eldest c/o Anthony & Anna Maria Hyde, in his 31st yr. Funeral at St John's Chr, today.

Died: on Dec 21, John N, jr, s/o John S & Sallie A Lovejoy, aged 5 weeks.

Died: in Gtwn, D C, on Dec 21, Francis, s/o Wm T & Henrietta Heron, in the 4th yr of his age. Funeral from their residence, 3rd & Fayette sts, today.

Died: on Dec 21, Maggie J Wells, aged 17 yrs. Funeral from the residence of her uncle, Thos Rich, 307 Pa av, tomorrow.

Died: on Dec 20, Burr Aloysius, infant s/o Emily E & Henry L Johnson, aged 11 months. Funeral at St Matthew's Chr, today.

Orphans Crt of Wash Co, D C. Case of Jane E Boone, now Haslett, & Richd H Clarke, excs of John B Boone, dec'd; settlement on Jan 12. -Z C Robbins, rg o/wills

Actg Mstrs John Y Beall & Edw McGuire, with 15 men, all of the Conf States navy, are now in confinement, in irons, at Ft McHenry, to be tried as pirates.

Sale of confiscated property: the Com'rs of Va have prepared their lists & announce their sale to take place Jan 11th. The first parcel offered will be *Arlington*, the homestead of Gen Lee, comprising 1,100 acs, & most of the remainder are located at Alexandria.

Dec 18. Gen Kelly tonight received a despatch from Gen Sullivan, announcing the capture of Col Carter, 1st Va Cavalry, & a number of other prisoners, by a force of the 22nd Pa Cavalry, sent out on a reconnoissance in Loudoun Co & toward Upperville.

Guardian Soc elected the Hon David K Cartter & Hon Abraham B Olin Trustees to fill vacancies which had occurred in the Board.

WED DEC 23, 1863
Died: on Dec 21, of consumption, Mr John Carr. Funeral on Wed.

Died: on Dec 20, Annie Eliz, d/o Jos S & Sallie E Sessford, aged nearly 3 yrs.

THU DEC 24, 1863

Died: on Dec 23, after an illness of 10 days, Mrs Sarah Weston Seaton, aged 74 yrs, w/o Wm W Seaton. Funeral tomorrow.

Hon Albert G Riddle, an esteemed distinguished mbr of the last & preceding Congress, has recently been appt'd U S Cnsl at Mata_zas.

FRI DEC 25, 1863

Battle of Gettysburg: since copied from a Balt paper a notice of the courageous Misses Callows, 2 young ladies of that city, in connexion with the battle of Gettysburg, where they were attending the Oak Ridge Seminary for young ladies. Since then we have seen a letter from the principal, Miss Carrie Sheades, herself, a superior young lady. During the charge of Buford's Cavalry, the mansion of Mr E Harmon was forcibly occupied by the Federal sharpshooters. On the repulse of the Union cavalry the rebels announced their intention to fire the bldg, since it was used as a fort. The young lady, Miss Amelia E Harmon, [17] the d/o R T Harmon, a subaltern ofcr of a Pa cavalry Regt in Gen Grant's army, protested, explaining that the occupation was forcible & not with their consent. She assured them that her mother, who was not now living, was a southern woman, & she abandoned her burning home with her aunt.

The Great Ladies Relief Fair: meeting held at the residence of the Hon Sayles J Bowen, on Dec 21, 1863, the following ofcrs elected & cmtes appt'd.

Maj B French, Pres
Henry D Cook, V P

Selah Squires, Sec

Mrs L E Chittenden, Treas

Cmte of arrangements:

Richd Wallach	Mrs S J Bowen	Mrs Richd Wallach
Sayles J Bowen	Mrs J W Angus	Mrs H D Cooke
Jas Adams	Mrs B B French	
Job W Angus	Mrs G W McLellan	

Exc Cmte:

J F Brown	Mrs D K Cartter	Wm B Todd
Hon J M Broadhead	Mrs J F Brown	Mrs R Farnham
Hon Geo W McLellan	Mrs J M Blanchard	Mrs W L Nicholson
Mrs Capt Gillis	Mrs W P Dole	Mrs E W Bliss
Mrs R Farnham	Miss B McClellan	Mrs F E Spinner
Mrs E Clarke	Finance Cmte:	

Ladies appt'd to make collections:

Mrs F W Seward	Mrs Admr	Mrs John C Kennedy
Mrs Edw Clark	Goldsborough	Miss Mary Murray
Mrs Com'r Dole	Mrs Lewis Clephane	Mrs Jos Bryan, jr
Mrs Gen Jos P Taylor	Mrs Jas Sykes	Mrs Sec Usher
Mrs Gen M C Meigs	Mrs A T Kieckhoffer	Mrs Senator Sprague
Mrs Gen Wm F Barry	Mrs V Pres Hamin	Mrs Atty Gen Bates
Mrs Gen Halleck	Mrs Edw C Dyer	Mrs Lt Brookfield
Mrs John G Clarke	Mrs Thos J Fisher	Miss Plant
Mrs Geo W Riggs	Mrs Benj F Guy	Mrs Thos U Walter
Miss Geo Mechlin	Mrs J W Angus	Mrs Chas E Evans
Mrs Admiral Lee	Miss Mary P Middleton	Mrs W B Webb
Mrs Com't Henry A	Mrs Green	Mrs Jas Adams
Wise	Mrs Alex R Shepperd	Miss Charlotte Taylor
Mrs Peter Parker	Mrs Geo S Gideon	Miss Carrie Bacon
Mrs Col Freeman	Mrs Thos Berry	Mrs Jos H Bradley

Mrs John Kearon	Miss Mary Barnard	Mrs Robt M Combs
Mrs Franck Taylor	Mrs W L Nicholson	Miss Clarke, d/o Capt R
Mrs Horatio Naier	Mrs Chas McNamee	C
Miss Carrie T Fennelly	Miss Ann Carroll	Mrs John H Semmes
Mrs Edw Clark	Mrs Prof Bache	Mrs Capt Bielaski
Miss Anna Allen	Miss Alida Gardner	Miss Bielaski
Mrs John M Brodhead	Mrs Jos Saxton	Mrs Thos E Lloyd
Mrs Nathan Sargent	Miss Mary Locke	Mrs R B Clark
Mrs Gen Benham	Mrs B B French	Mrs Wm J Murtagh
Mrs Chas P Russell	Mrs Capt Robt Clarke	Mrs John R Elvans
Mrs Ezra L Stevens	Mrs Wm Dixon	Mrs Geo Mattingly
Mrs D W Middleton	Mrs Geo R Wilson	Mrs Mackintosh
Mrs John Hitz	Mrs Jas Nokes	Miss Cumbacker
Mrs L F Poortales	Mrs Col Harris	
Gtwn:		
Mrs Rittenhouse	Miss Kate Barnard	
Mrs Wm H Tenney	Miss Buckey	
At Large:		
Mrs Caleb B Smith, Ind	Mrs Dolphus Skinner, N	
	Y	

Dalton, Geo: Dec 19, 1863. Gen Jos E Johnston is appt'd to the command of the Tenn army, & is expected at Dalton next week. Gen Hindman has arrived & taken command of his old division. Sherman's Corps has fallen back from Knoxville & passed thru Cleveland yesterday.

Died: on Dec 19, Ella, y/c/o Philip & Mary C Mackey, aged 19 months.

MON DEC 28, 1863
Mrd: on Dec 23, by the Rt Rev, Bishop of Montreal, Wm Frederick, Lo_d Abinger, to Helen, 2nd d/o Capt G A Magruder, late of the U S Navy.

Mrd; in Canandagua, N Y, on Dec 24, Maj Benj B Foster, Ast Adj Gen, to Miss Sarah Gibson, d/o Thos M Howell.

Deaths reported to the Navy Dept for the week ending Dec 26, 1863:
Geo T Taylor, 1st cl fireman, scalded, Jun 21, Nav Hosp, New Orleans.
Jas Smith, ord seaman, remit fever, Aug 13, do.
Geo W Branch, landsman, pneumonia, Aug 15, do.
Henry C Hope, 3rd ast engr, typhoid fever, Nov 20, Ft Pike.
John C Cottingham, 2nd cl fireman, yel fever, Nov 30, vessel U S S *Princess Royal.*
Jos Kent, actg mstr's mate, enteritis, Dec 5, vessel U S S *Pensacola.*
Anthony McColton, landsman, smallpox, Dec 7, Memphis.
M J Fitch, q m, chronic diarrhoea, Dec 11, vessel U S S *Kenwood.*
Oscar Pratt, actg mstr, Dec 13, vessel U S S *New National*
Henry Smith, contraband, pneumonia, no date, Nav Hosp, N Y.
Addison White, landsman, pneumonia, no date, do.
Cornelius Russell, marine, apoplexy, Dec 19, do.
Wm Johnson, seaman, peritonitis, Mar 7, vessel U S S *Estrella.*
John Berry, ship's cook, drowned, Feb 23, vessel U S S *Kinsman.*
Patrick McGowan, fireman, drowned, Feb 23, do.
John Kirby, 2nd cl fireman, drowned, Feb 23, do.

Isaac Deer, coal heaver, do, do, do.

Wm Parker, do, do, do, do.

Arthur J Dillon, actg ast paymstr, consumption, Dec 16, St Louis, Mo.

Wm Bowran, marine, apoplexy, Dec 22, Nav Asylum.

John Kelly, 2nd cl fireman, consumption, Dec 22, Nav Hosp, Chelsea.

The steamer *Geo Washington* arrived at N Y on Sat, from New Orleans, bringing rebel prisoners, among whom are: Maj Gen Frank Gardner, formerly comder of Port Hudson, & the following ofcrs:

A D C Alec Dupree	J C Patterson, 23rd Ark
Col J A Jaquess	H L W Johnson, 14 Ark
Lt Col M J Smith	Lt W B Burnett, 12th Ark
Capt Makemp, 9th La cavalry	J W Geer, 10th Ark
Capt J J Slocum, 9th La cavalry	J K Milan, 17th Ark

The remains of Gen Michael Corcoran arrived in N Y C on Fri. Funeral at St Patrick's Chr, then remv'd to City Hall for funeral with full military honors.

Wash Corp: 1-Act for relief of Michl O'Brien: $165.50 to be pd O'Brien for removing & burying dead animals. 2-Act for relief of Wm E Brown, assignee of Geo C Wilson: sum of $332.46 for the laying of flag footways in the 7th ward. 3-Act for relief of Robt Bayllis: $60 be pd to his credit.

Capt Frank C Sands, 11th Ohio Btry, arrived in this city yesterday direct from Little Rock, Ark, & reports that the siutuaion there is favorable to the Union cause. –Cincinnati Gaz

Died: on Dec 25, Mrs Ann Allison Dorsett, in her 66th yr. Funeral from the residence of her hsbnd, F R Dorsett, sr, 206 G st, Mon.

TUE DEC 29, 1863

Mrd: in Wash City, on Dec 28, by Rev W J Purington, Capt John H McCutcheon to Miss Annie E Dawes, of Wash.

Died: on Nov 17, in Austen, Nevada Terr, Chas E E Ould, a native of Wash, D C, aged 34 yrs, [eldest s/o Henry & Eliz Ould]-formerly Under Shrf of Sierra Co, Calif, & late Dpty Shrf of Story Co, Nev Terr. The dec'd was interred by the Masons of Austen, of which fraternity he was a mbr.

D C-Prop to be condemned & seized by order of the Dist Atty Carrington: property of-Judge Campbell, late of the Sup Crt; Gov Letcher, of Va; Geo S Houston, of Ala, & Wm T Smithson.

R R Accident-at Brislow Sta; among the killed were Chas F Robinson, of Phil, formerly a Lt in the 121st Pa Vols; Henry Young, 11th Pa.

Prof Saml Chew, of Md Univ, died at his residence in Balt on Fri last.

WED DEC 30, 1863

Obit-Levin Stanforth died at his late residence in Calvert Co, Md, on Dec 13. He leaves his widow & dght. -Nottingham Lodge of Free & Accepted Masons.

Died: in Wash City, on Dec 28, after a severe illness, Sidney Brainerd, y/s/o Wm & Sidney Johnson, in the 17th yr of his age.

Sale of rl est, Sup Crt of D C, Edw Owen & Ellen Owen, his wife, & others, cmplnts, & Ellen Kelley, widow o/Miles Kelley, & Jas Mulquin are dfndnts; numerous lots in D C. -John F Ennis, Wm J Miller, trustees

Orphans Crt of Wash Co, D C. 1-Prsnl estate of Mrs Mary Farrar, late of Wash Co, dec'd. - Jos F Kelley, exc 2-Case of Alexander E Johnston, adm of Jos V Hitchcock, dec'd; settlement on Jan 23. -Z C Robbins, rg o/wills

Mrs Semmes & her dght, Mrs Milinor, were arrested on the charge of having sent poisoned wine to West's Bldg Hosp to poison the military ofcrs; the wine did contain arsenic. The Grand Jury believed they were unaware of the fact as they sent some of the same wine to their friends. -Balt Sun, 29th

Mrs Mgt Wickliffe, w/o ex-Gov Chas A Wickliffe, died at her residence, near Bardstown, Ky, Dec 18.

THU DEC 31, 1863
Abandoned property on sale for taxes: *Arlington Estate*, lately occupied by Robt E Lee, 1,100 acs, value $31,000, taxes $92.07; *Custis Mill* property, 500 acs, tax $18.90; estates of Dr M M Lewis, Lawrence S Taylor, Orlando Fairfax, & others.

Wash Corp: 1-Act for relief of M M White & others: sum of $18 for burying 2 small pox paupers. 2-Act for relief of P Cullinane: sum of $505.67, for grading & gravelling 14th st. 3-Act for relief of Francis Frommell: permitted to serve with water is brewery on D st from pipe already laid

A large frame store hse, at Alexandria, belonging to C C Smoot, containing $15,000 worth of Gov't hay, with 4 small tenements, corner of So Royal st, was burnt down on Christmas. On Sat, another fire occurred destroying the roof & doing other injury to the bake hse attached to the store & dwlg of John Vincent.

Mutual Benefit Life Ins-J C Lewis, 492 7th st, Wash, D C.
Marble Works-Henry Parry, 22nd st, near 4th ave, N Y.
Nicholas Callan, *Notary Public*, 213 F st, Wash, D C.
H Polkinhorn, *Bk & Job Printer*, 7th st, between D & E sts, D C.
W R Hurley, M D, late of Nashville, Tenn; ofc & residence, Herndon Hse, D C.

FRI JAN 1, 1864

Mrd: on Dec 29, at St Mark's Chr, Phil, by the Rector, Rev Mr Washburne, Walter D Comegys, of Dela, to Anna L, d/o Hon John Bell.

Mr K Brown, a miller, was shot & killed while interfering with some negro sldrs on Fri of last week at
Church Hill, Queen Anne's Co, Md; leaves a wife & number of chldrn. -Kent News

Rev R J Keeling having accepted the Rectorship of Holy Trinity Chr, by the unanimous call of the Vestry, will officiate there on Sun next at 11 a m & 7:30 p m.

Wm S Hamet, of Maine, has received a commisssion as special agent of the P O Dept for the New Eng states, v Good_ow resigned.

Govn'r Cannon, of Dela, announces officially that the enlistment of negro troops has been authorized in that state.

Cmdor Montgomery yesterday relieved Cmdor Harwood of the command of the Wash Navy yd, & at the same time Com'r F A Parker assumed command of the Potomac Flotilla.

SAT JAN 2, 1864

Died: on Dec 31, after a short illness, Dr Benj Hodges, in his 27th yr. Funeral from his late residence, 602 8th st, today.

Died: on Dec 30, of pleurisy, John E Holland, aged 51 yrs. Funeral from his late residence, near the First Toll Gate, on 7th st, Wash Co, D C, today.

Died: on Jan 1, John C Caton, in his 26th yr. Funeral from his parents' residence, 361 5th st, Sun.

Announcement by the Medical Soc of D C, of the death of Dr Hamilton P Howard.

Caleb Barton, one of the oldest & wealthiest residents of Bloomsburg, Pa, was found dead on the R R track on Wed. Supposed he had been killed by a coal train the preceding night.

Sec of War has issued orders which will put a stop at once to the enlistment of negroes here for the New England regts, & the guard at the Balt depot stop all colored men who are apparently endeavoring to go north. Colored recruits gathered at Fortress Monroe for a town in Mass have been discharged.

MON JAN 4, 1864

Died: in Gtwn, D C, on Jan 1, Peter Bohrer, in the 84th yr of his age. One of the oldest residents of the place. Funeral from the residence of Mr R R Shekell, High st, Gtwn, this afternoon.

Within the past 3 months Erastus Corning, of N Y, has purchased over 130,000 acs of land in Michigan. Other purchasers in that state are: the Fairbanks, of St Johnsbury, John W Brooks, & John M Forbes, of Boston, & John W Peckersgill, of N Y.

Deaths reported to the Navy Dept for the week ending Jan 2, 1864:
Edw Diamond, 2nd cl fireman, yel fever, Nov 24, Nav Hosp, New Orleans
John C Horton, landsman, pneumonia, Aug 8, do.
Greenbury Thompson, 1st cl boy, diarrhoea, Dec 15, Nav Hosp, Memphis.
S S Allen, surgeon's steward, diarrhoea, Dec 16, do.
Thos Brown, landsman, consumption, Dec 21, do.
Edw G Wells, yeoman, gunshot wound, no date, vessel U S S *Memphis*.
Harry Bross, q m, heart disease, Mar 12, Houston, Tex.
Danl Morris, carp's mate, old age, Jul 19, Camp Grace, Tex.
Sam Leonard, landsman, erysipelas, Dec 24, Nav Hosp, N Y.
Sam Johnson, landsman, consumption, Dec 25, Nav Hosp, Norfolk.
Jas Cummings, carp's mate, typhoid fever, Dec 8, vessel U S S *Antona*.
Hy Waters, ord seaman, pneumonia, Dec 24, Receiving ship *Ohio*.
Emmanuel Devannes, seaman, pneumonia, Dec 25, vessel U S S *J Belt or Bell*.

Crct Crt of Montg Co, Md-wherein John W Fling & others, cmplnts, & Elias E White & others, dfndnts; sale at the Tavern Stand of the late John White, dec'd; rl estate of which he died possessed: 10 3-8 acs of land; farm of 160 acs with log dwlg hse which adjoins the lands of the late Robt Y Brent, dec'd, & Geo Knowles & others. -John G England, Geo Peter, trustees

Hon Lemuel J Bowden, a senator in Congress from Va, died at his lodgings in Wash City on Sat last of smallpox. Funeral was yesterday.

Archbishop Hughes, Prelate of the R C C, died at N Y on Sat. He was a native of Tyrone Co, Ire & came to this country about 1820.

New Years. The White Hse doors were thrown open to the pblc on Fri last. Mr & Mrs Lincoln stood for 2 hours as the throng passed thru the Green & Blue rooms into the Reception room. Marshal Lamon & Deputy Mrshl Phillips made the presentations to the Pres, who cordially shook hands with each visiter, & Com'r B B French made the presentations to Mrs Lincoln.

TUE JAN 5, 1864

State or Political prisoners confined; list transmitted by the Sec of War to Hon R B Taney, Chief Justice & Judge of U S Crct Crt for Districts of Md & Va.
At Ft McHenry: 1-Eugene Williamson, Balt, Feb 13, 1863, bearing despatches between Confederate states & their agents in Europe. 2-Jas Tilghman & Wm Evergreen, of Queen Anne Co, Md, Feb 14, 1863; burning sloop *Hard Times*.
Confined at Fort Delaware: 1-Geo M E Shearer, Jul 25, 1862; burning bridges on the Balt & Ohio R R, & making maps for rebel use. 2-Jas League, Catonville, Md, Feb 1, 1863: uttering disloyal sentiments & entertaining smugglers. 3-Prelart alias Geo Putnam, Balt, Feb 4, 1863, rebel mail carrier. 4-W H Resin, Chas Co, Md, Jan 4, 1863; rebel mail carrier. 5-Thos

H Fitchell, Northampton Co, Md, Jan 3, 1863; late keeper Chas Light-hse, charged with attempting to run blockade. Charges are at hdqrtrs of 8th Corps. 6-Mary Jane Green, Braxton Co, Va, May 1862: destroying telegraph wire. 7-Mary Jane Prater, Cincinnati, Ohio, Dec 27, 1862: wearing sldrs clothes. Offence committed within [line totally missing] Elliott, Saml Holsburg, Peter Johnson, Wm F Miller, & Saml Halmaker, all of Barbour Co, Va; arrested by order of Gen Pierpont as hostages for Sheriff of Babour Co captured by rebels & taken to Richmond.

At Camp Chase, Ohio: Martain Brittan, Jackson Co, Va, Feb 1, 1863, disloyalty.

Benj Bassill, Upshur Co, Va, Mar 3, 1863, do.

Dallas Gilford & Thos Gilford, sr, Pocahontas Co, Va, Feb 11, 1863, do.

B G Ganier, Randolph Co, Va, Feb 17, 1863, do.

Daniel Hart, Randolph Co, Va, Feb 19, 1863, do.

L B Hart, Randolph Co, Va, Feb 17, 1863, do.

John D Garrott, Logan Co, Va, Dec 4, 1862, do.

Thos Moran, Barbour Co, Va, Dec 17, 1862, do.

Jas W Norman, Calhoun Co, Va, Feb 19, 1863, do.

D L Snodgrass, Marion Co, Va, Aug 6, 1862, do.

David Williams, Harrison Co, Va, Sep 12, 1862, do.

Eli C Williams, Jackson Co, Va, Feb 7, 1863, do.

Eli Emrick, Wood Co, Va, Feb 6, 1863, aiding rebels.

Geo W Mills, Randolph Co, Va, Feb 15, 1863, do.

C N Schoonover, Randolph Co, Va, Feb 17, 1863, do.

Levi Totty, Hampshire Co, Va, Mar 4, 1863, do.

Robt Anderson, Cumberland Co, Va, Feb 1, 1863, do.

Andrew Jones, Cumberland Co, Va, Jan 24, 1863, do.

John A B Leonard & Saml S Floyd, Montg Co, Va, Mar 17, 1863, do.

At Old Capitol Prison:

John A Taber, Balt, Mar 10, 1863, violating blockade.

John Goldsmith, St Mary's Co, Md, Feb 11, 1863, do.

Dearborn Johnson, Saml Johnson, & Isaiah Johnson, Accomac Co, Va, Feb 14, 1863, do.

Thos W Jones, Balt, Md, Mar 10, 1863, do.

Chas H Posey, Chas Co, Md, Mar 10, 1863, do.

John A Scott, Accomac Co, Va, Feb 14, 1863, do.

John J Wilson, PG Co, Md, Mar 2, 1863, do.

Julius G White, no residence given, Feb 4, 1863, do.

John W Taylor, Geo Taylor, & Saml C Taylor, Accomac Co, Va, Mar 13, 1863, attempting to run blockade.

John Tyler, Fred'k, Md, Mar 13, 1863, rebel mail carrier.

Geo Hoyle & Jas W Hilton, Montg Co, Md, Mar 10, 1863, rebel.

Timothy O'Connor, Washington, Feb 9, 1863, refusing to take oath of allegiance.

Bolney Purcell & Stephen R Mount, Loudoun Co, Va, Feb 14, 1863, hostages for Mr Davis, of Snickersville.

John Kelehea, Balt, Md, Feb 28, 1863, British subject.

Jacob, Prussia, Mar 13, 1863, no charge given.

Saml Rich, Prussia, Feb 23, 1863, do.

Geo B Magglisson, Mo, Mar 8, 1863, do. Offence committed within crct.

Daniel Lambert, Montg Co, Md, Feb 26, 1863, from Camp Chase.

John Regan, Ire, Mar 5, 1863, refugee.

W Bourke, alias Brannon, Australia, Mar 14, 1863, do.

Septimus Brown, Alexandria Co, Va, Feb 16, 1863, disloyalty.

J H Barnes, Fairfax Co, Va, Mar 14, 1863, rebel.

Francis Fox, Fairfax Co, Va, Mar 16, 1863, rebel.

Geo H Cook, Fairfax Co, Va, Mar 16, 1863, rabid secesh.
Richard Johnson, Fairfax Co, Va, no date given, do.
John H Mills & N W Mills, Loudoun, Va, Mar 14, 1863, rebels.
Richd Richardson & Albert Wren, Fairfax Co, Va, Mar 16, 1863, rabid secesh.

Winthrop E Hilton, a printer of N Y, has been arrested & sent to Ft Lafayete for furnishing the Rebel Gov't with Confederate notes & bonds.

N Y, Jan 3. Aaron & Geo Wolf, bros, & Messrs Hoffnung, Benjamin, & Encas, have been arrested & confined in Ft Lafayette, being concerned in the blockade running business. Messrs J D Young & J C Budd are in Ft Lafayette as shippers of contraband goods

Maj Gen Burnside arrived in Wash City yesterday. He has not resigned as so many erroneously believed.

Despatch from St Johns, dated Jan 2, says that Linus Seeley, another of the captors of the Chesapeake, was arrested there on Fri & lodged in jail.

Injury to Surg Gen Hammond, from the accident that recently befell him in the west, is greater than was first apprehended. He was going in a hurry out of a door, & struck his head violently against a beam that had escaped his sight. The blow prostrated him insensible. On recovering, his recollection it was thought, he was recovering, but paralysis of the lower limbs soon after set in, & continues upon him. He is able to write to his family here, & hopes soon to be able to be brought to Wash. -Star

WED JAN 6, 1864
Died: on Jan 5, Nannie Chew, w/o Thos C Wheeler, & d/o W B & Mary E Chew. Funeral from the residence of her father, 114 Prospect st, Gtwn, D C, tomorrow.

Mrs Davidson, w/o Lt Hunter Davidson, formerly of the U S Navy, & now of the Confederate svc, was captured a few days ago while crossing the Potomac in a skiff, & has been committed to the Old Capitol prison. She was going to visit friends at Annapolis, Md.

Mrs McDowell, who kept a dry-goods store on 6th st, between G & H, who was so brutally attacked & beaten in the streets last week, has since died from the wounds received on that occassion. Wash, D C

Chas F Mayer, mbr of the Balt bar, died on Sunday, at his residence in Balt City, Md, of neuralgia of the heart. He was about 69 years of age.

Maj Gen Stoneman has, at his own request, been relieved as chief of the Cavalry Bureau in Wash City, & it is stated that Brig Gen Kenner Garrard has been ordered to succeed him. Gen Garrard has been on duty in the Army of the Potomac.

THU JAN 7, 1864
Cigar & Tobacco Business. From this date Mr John W Wetherall, for the past 7 years in my employ, will have an interest in my business. -Geo W Cochran, 398 Pa av, Wash, D C.

Wash Corp: 1-Ptn of A & T Richards & others, for opening a certain st: referred to the Cmte on Improvements. 2-Ptn of John Branan & others for a flag footway in ward 2: passed.

Naval movements: Brooklyn, Jan 5. Yesterday Rear Admr Farragut sailed from the Navy Yard in the flag-ship *Hartford*, to assume command of the East Gulf Squadron.

FRI JAN 8, 1864
Mrd: on Jan 5, at St Patrick's Chr, by Rev Mr McCarthy, Lt Thos W Lay to Miss Annie E Roach, both of Wash.

Wash Corp: 1-Act for relief of Thos Morrison: sum of $15 be refunded to him for amount erroneously paid by him thru mistake for a license obtained. 2-Act for the relief of J A Blan: sum of $55.25 for work & labor rendered by him at the pipe yard.

Dr Stuart Gwynn, of Boston, employed in the Dept of the Treas where the Treas notes are printed, was arrested last night, charged with having abstracted a large amount of said notes. –Rep

Richmond Enquirer of Dec 21st devotes 2 columns to a report of the proceedings in the exam of Mrs Patterson Allan, formerly of Cincinnati, charged with carrying on a treasonable correspondence with persons at the north.

Died: on Jan 6, Mary Alice, d/o the late Wm & Cath McCarthy, aged 19 yrs.

SAT JAN 9, 1864
Mrd: in Balt, Md, on Jan 7, by Rev Mr Cokrey, Thos Green, of Wash, D C, to Nannie Lomax, d/o the late Maj Lomax, U S Army.

Died: on Jan 8, in his 47th yr, Robt Carere Brent, eldest s/o the late Robt Y Brent, of Montg Co, Md. Funeral from 306 Delaware av, tomorrow.

Hon Caleb B Smith, Judge of the U S Dist Crt, & Ex-Sec of the Interior, died at his late residence in Indiana on Wed last. His health had been failing for some weeks past.

Understood that Gen Rufus King, American Minister at Rome, is also to be accredited to the Court of Greece.

Governess wanted: a lady competent to teach 10 or 12 young ladies. She must be a member of the Episc Chr & have the manners & habits of a Southern lady. Address: A M Oxford, Md.

MON JAN 11, 1864
Deaths reported to the Navy Dept for the week ending Jan 9, 1864:
Andrew Wallace, seaman, blank, Sep 26, 1863, vessel U S S *Jamestown*.
Henry S Carmack, landsman, hoemoptysis, Dec 30, 1863, Nav Hosp, Norfolk.
Wm Ryan, landsman, pneumonia, Jan 1, 1864, Nav Hosp, Chelsea.
Jno H Turner, landsman, blank, Jan 2, 1864, Nav Asylum, Phil.
Jas Worrall, seaman, gunshot wound, Oct 17, 1863, Tampa, Fla.
Jos O'Donnell, ord seaman, gunshot wound, Oct 18, 1863, vessel U S S *Adela*.
Jno Roddy, seaman, gunshot wound, Oct 18, 1863, Tampa, Fla.
Adolphus J Johnson, jr, 1st cl boy, contusion, Nov 9, 1863, vessel U S S *Adela*.
Alonzo Wells, 1st cl fireman, cholera morbus, Dec 25, 1863, vessel U S S *Ticonderoga*.
Saml Coling, landsman, blank, Dec 26, 1863, vessel U S S *Saratoga*.
Peter Cain, boatswain's mate, apoplexy, Dec 24, 1863, vessel U S S *Karahdin*.

Died: on Jan 9, Mary Key Wallace, relict of Robt Wallace, & d/o the late Richd Key & Mary Watts of Md. Funeral from her late residence, 471 I st, tomorrow.

Died: Jan 10, Harry C, s/o Jas & Cath Ward, aged 3 months. Funeral from their residence, 8th st, today.

Died: in St Paul, Minn, Dec 30, 1863, Robt Toombs, 2nd s/o Hon Henry M & Matilda W Rice, aged 3 years & 6 months.

On Sat morning last John R Magness, living near Aberdeen, Md, was found within a mile of his home, frozen to death. He had arrived on the evening train from Balt, Md, & started on foot for his home. -Belair [Md] Aegis

Died: in N Y, on Jan 6, Amelia Louisa, d/o the late Cmdor Bigelow, & w/o Lt Cmder J E DeHaven, U S Navy.

Rear Adm Geo W Storer, U S Navy, died on Jan 8 at his residence in Portsmouth, N H, age 74 years & 8 months. He was a nephew of Col Tobias Lear, priv secretary of Geo Washington.

Appointments by the Pres & Senate:
Capt John Rodgers to be Cmdor
Capt Stephen C Rowan to be Cmdor
Andrew Wylie, Justice of the Supreme Crt, D C
T H Clayton, of Ky, Minister at Honduras
Jas H Partridge, Minister at Salvador
A B Dickinson, of N Y, Minister at Nicaragua
A A Hall, of Tenn, Minister at Bolivia
Rufus King, of Wisc, Minister at Rome
Henry Bergy, of N Y, Sec of Leg at St Petersburgh
W M Briggs, of Mass, Sec of Leg at Brazil
Abraham Hanson, of Wisc, Com'r & Cnsl Gen at Liberia
Geo F Stewart, of N Y, Cnsl Gen at Shanghai
Richd Busteed, of N Y, Dist Judge for Ala
H Ballou, of N Y, Cnsl Gen at Havana
Jas D Doty, of Utah, Govn'r of Utah
N Edmonds, of Dakotah, Govn'r of Dakatok
Consuls:
F Chaw, of Maine, at Tampico
J C A Wingate, of N H, at Swatow
F H Ruggles, of N Y, at Jamaica
H J Cuniffe, of New Mexico, at Pasa del Norte
Geo P Hanson, of N Y, at Elsinore
L P Provost, of Maine, at Guayaquil
Aaron Young, of Maine, at Rio Grande, Brazil
A G Brigham, of Mich, at Vortvey, Belgium
C H Simonds, at Santa Martha
Richd E Morse, of Iowa, at Curacoa
A S Hanabergh, of N Y, at Carthagena
C H Upton, of Va, at Geneva
B F Hall, of Colorado, at Naples
B L Hill, of Mich, at San Juan del Sur
C R Follin, at Omoa & Truxillo
C H Lochs, of Pa, at Puerto Cabello
R W Creel, Cnsl at Chihuahua
W H Blake, of Md, at Manzanilla
Jos W Mark, of Ohio, at Amsterdam
W J Trowbridge, of Conn, at Barbadoes
J Cantwell, of Pa, at Dublin
A Rhodes, of Pa, at Jerusalem
L W Tappin, jr, of Mass, at Batabia
A G Riddle, of Ohio, at Matanzas
J W Livingston, of N Y, at La Union

Geo Y Tint, of Maine, at Stockholm
J S Smith, of Pa, at Island of Candia
W W Nevison, of Ohio, at Bayonne

C G Hannah, of N J, at Demerara
Thos Kirkpatrick, of N Y, at Nassau, N P

TUE JAN 12, 1864

Died: on Jan 8, at the Kirkwood Hse, in Wash City, after a short illness, John Rynex, in the 68th yr of his age.

Died: in Gtwn, D C, on Jan 10, Mr Richd T Mathews, aged 47 yrs. Funeral from his late residence, 167 West st, today.

Marshal's sale-Property in Wash City of Wm F Phillips, to satisfy Judicials in favor of Geo Poe, jr. -Ward H Lamon, U S Mrshl D C

Orphans Crt of Wash Co, D C. Prsnl estate of Dr Hamilton P Howard, late of Wash City, dec'd. -Maria E Howard, excx

Senate: 1-Ptn from the Soc of Friends praying military exemption. 2-Resolution introduced tendering the thanks of Congress to Cornelius Vanderbilt, for the presentation by him to the Gov't of the steamer *Vanderbilt*. 3-Mr Carlile announced the death of Hon Lemuel J Bowden, late Senator from Va.

Gen Steele has been superseded in command of the rebel dept in the Indian Territory by Brig Gen Marcy.

The death of Mr Wm Makepeace Thackeray was lately announced. He was a distinguished British novelist & writer: born in Calcutta, India, in 1811, carried to England at age 7 & educated at Cambridge Univ.

Shenandoah Valley: letter dated Harper's Ferry on Jan 8 announces the return to that place of Col Boyd, who with about 800 cavalry, has been on a scouting expedition up the valley. He met a scouting party of the enemy under the notorious guerilla Capt Blackford, on their way towards Winchester. Blackford, found at a hse in the village, was shot dead by one of our men, whom he had fired at & was slightly wounded. A few prisoners were captured.

Frauds at the N Y Navy Yd. Last week an order was received from the Navy Dept at Wash, by Admr Paulding, directing the discharge of Robt W Steele, master carpenter, Isaac H Steele, his bro, clerk, & Wm Robertson & John Kerlin, qrtrmen. Cmte was appt'd on Dec 22 to investigate certain allegations of fraud & corruption against these parties. -Jrnl of Commerce

Gov Thos G Pratt, ex-Govn'r of Md, who was arrested some weeks since by order of Gen Schenck, then commandnt of the Middle Dept, & ordered to be sent south, via Fortress Monroe, arrived in Balt on Sun from Fortress Monroe, & is sojourning at Barnum's Htl.

On Sat last Gen Butler received a telegraph despatch from Pres Lincoln ordering him to release Gov Pratt & permit him to return to his home in Md. -Sun

WED JAN 13, 1864

Died: in N Y C, on Jan 9, of typhoid fever, Wm A, only s/o Dr Wm H & Louisa Van Buren, grandson of Dr Valentine Mott, aged 16 years & 10 months. Funeral was at St Stephens Chr, 28th st, on Mon.

Orphans Crt of Wash Co, D C. Prsnl estate of Chas C Smoot, late of D C, dec'd. -Mary B Smoot

Caleb B Smith, Judge of the U S, died at his ofc in the court room, of hemorrhage, very suddenly; age about 56 yrs, born in Mass. He removed to the West with his parents when a child. [No other details]

Supreme Crt of D C, in Equity #129. Maria L M Peters, excx of Saml Miller, against *Maria B Peters, *Evelyn W Peters, *Saml W M Peters, *Richd Peters, *Thos W Peters, et al. Bill is to procure a decree for the sale of lot 7 in sq 514, Wash City. On May 13, 1854 John M Fries was indebted to Saml Miller for $2,473, bal due on purchase of said lot. Fries conveyed said lot to Francis Peters & heirs. Peters died on May 19, 1861 & legal title descended to his chldrn: Maria B Peters, Evelyn W Peters, Saml W M Peters, Richd Peters, & Thos W Peters. Fries died in 1861 & his interest descended to & is now vested in Ignatius Fries, Geo Fries, Barbara E Fries, Cath F Fries, & Mary J Neff, w/o Wendell Neff, his chldrn & heirs at law. Saml Miller died on Dec 8, 1855, having made his last will & appt'd the cmplnt sole excx thereof. Letters of testamentary on the estate of said Saml Miller were issued to said cmplnt & her hsbnd, Francis Peters, on Dec 17, 1855, by the authority at Phil, Pa, the domicil of said Miller at the time of his death. Francis Peters has since died, & said cmplnt is now sole excx. *Non-residents of D C. -R J Meigs, clerk

Local Matters: the *Arlington* estate was purchased by the Gov't for $26,800. The *Custis Mill* property was sold to M E Flannigan for $4,100, who also bought the hse of Wm H Fowle, for $5,500. The hse of Rev J T Johnson was sold to G S Minor for $4,325. The estate called *Abingdon*, 500 acs, belonging to B W Hunter, was sold to L E Chittenden for $8,000.

Dr Young, of Shultzville, Wash township, who was assistant surgeon to the board of enrollment of this county during the last exam of draftd men, died on Tue night, at his home, from the effects of inhaling too much ether. He had saturated a cloth with ether, laid it on his forehead, to relieve him from a headache, & in that way sent to sleep. It is supposed that during the night the cloth slipped over his nose & mouth, & thus caused the fatal effects of the ether. -Reading [Pa] Gaz

The Mrshl of the Dist seized, under the confiscation act, the interest of Trusten Polk, formerly U S Senator from Missouri, & of Wm T Smithson, lately a banker here, in parts of lots 3 & 4 in sq 488, improved by a 4 story brick dwelling on 6th st west, between E & F sts north.

Mr Robt E Fox, of N Y C, has recently purchased the whole of Fisher's Island, in Long Island Sound, with all its bldgs, stock, & farm fixtures on it for $55,000 cash. It was part of the Winthrop estate, & has been owned by descendents of the illustrious Gov Winthrop until the consummation of this sale. He intends in going largely into the business of stock raising on the island.

Maj Gen Frank Blair, late in command of the 15th Corps of the Army of the Cumberland, has returned to Washington & resumed his seat in the Hse o/Reps.

Michl Algen, of Cambridge, Mass, who was sent to Canada some weeks ago, & furnished with funds to recruit men to fill up the quota of a suburban city, has been convicted in the Queen's Crt, Montreal, of violating the foreign enlistment act, & sentenced to 14 years in the pen.

THU JAN 14, 1864

Mrd: on Jan 12, at McKendree Parsonage, 420 Mass av, by Rev John Thrush, Hollis L Hubbick & Lottie Dorman, all of Wash City.

Died: in Wash City, on Jan 4, in the 18th yr of his age, Geo G Porter, eldest s/o David & the late Mary Jane Porter.

Hse o/Reps: 1-Bill for relief of Lt Wm P Richter, 77th Regt Ohio volunteer infantry: introduced by Mr Morris, of Ohio.

Supreme Crt of D C, in Equity #1595. Fred'k W Sellhausen against Chas Mades & Wilhelmina his wife, Wm H Clementson & Henrietta his wife, Geo C Schadd & Henry R Schadd, exc & heirs of Bonaventura Schadd. Parties to appear at City Hall, Feb 5, Wash, D C. -Wm R Woodward, spec auditor

Supreme Crt of D C, in Equity #112. Eliz A Byington, admx of Saml Byington, dec'd: ptn for sale of rl estate of intestate. Issue to compel the appearance of Geo Byington & C Virginia Byington. Said parties failed to appear on Jan 1, 1864 & must appear by May, 1864. -R J Meigs, clerk

Maj Gen S P Heintzelman has been assigned to the command of the Northern Dept, which will be composed of the states of Mich, Ohio, Ind, & Ill, with his headqrtrs at Columbus, Ohio.

Metropolitan Railroad Co: introduced to the Senate, which was referred to the Cmte on the Dist, to incorporate a company by the above name, with Messrs Alex'r R Shepherd, Richd Wallach, Lewis Clephane, Saml P Brown, Nathl Wilson, Jos L Savage, Wm W Rapley, as corporators. It provides for a system of street railrds, with double tracks for main routes, & proposes first a double track from the north side of the Capitol, up N J ave to D st north, thence by Ind & La aves, Fifth to F to 14th west, to G & 15th, Pa ave, I st to the junction of N H ave & 23rd hence to the Circle. Other minor routes are named, among them one by Massachusetts ave.

The gallant Brig Gen B F Kelley arrived in Wash yesterday from Western Va.

FRI JAN 15, 1864

Mrd: on Jan 13, by Rev John C Smith, Geo B Patch, of Vt, to Miss Lizzie Walker, of Wash.

Mrd: on Jan 14, by Rev Byron Sunderland, Mr Saml T Ellis to Miss Linnie A, d/o Geo B Smith, all of Wash City.

Order of Crct Crt of Chas Co, Md, matter of Geo H Waters, insolvent debtor, sale at *Sandy Point*, the residence of said Waters, 395 acs; another tract called *Milford*, 162 acs. -F Stone, trustee

Supreme Crt of D C, in Equity #31. Esau & A H Pickrell against Johanna Grant & R P Jackson. Cmplnts to prove their account against the late Jas Kennedy, on Jan 19, at my residence, Gtwn. -W Redin, auditor

SAT JAN 16, 1864
Mrd: at Willard's Htl, on Jan 14, by Rev Geo Williamson Smith, Sylvanus C Phinney, of Stoughton, Mass, & Eliz A Bodkin, of Alexandria, Va.

Died: in Wash City, on Jan 14, after a short & painful illness, Ellen, w/o Jas E Bell, & d/o Isaac & Eleanor Trunnell, in the 23rd of her age.

Died: in St Paul, Minn, on Jan 5, of scarlet fever, Mary Welsh, y/c/o Henry M & Matilda W Rice, aged 18 months. This is the 2nd child of which that family has been bereft within one week.

Pres Lincoln recognizes Alonzo Vitt who has been appt'd Vice Cnsl of Italy, at Phil: Jan 13, 1864.

MON JAN 18, 1864
Obit-Wm Sweiland, in his 82nd yr of his age, died on Jan 1, at Plattsburgh, Clinton Co, N Y.

Died: in Phil, on Jan 10, Col Wm McNeir, formerly of Annapolis, Md, & for several years a resident of Wash City.

Testimonial to the late J R Sothoron by the employes of the Qrtrmstr Genrl's Ofc. -Lewis S Wells, chrmn; Geo K Finckel, sec. Wash, D C

Orphans Crt of Wash Co, D C. Prsnl estate of Wm Smith Hyde, late of Gtwn, D C, dec'd. -A Hyde, adm

Died: on Jan 8, at *Ranelagh*, PG Co, Md, Miss Sarah Forrest.

Deaths reported to the Navy Dept for the week ending Jan 16, 1864:
David V Porter, actg mstr's mate, pneumonia, Dec 29, 1863, Mississippi Squadron.
Geo W Storer, rear adm, blank, Jan 8, 1864, Portsmouth, N H.
Ed Williams, 2nd cl boy, typhoid fever, Dec 27, 1863, vessel U S S *Key West*.
Jas Miller, landsman, typhoid fever, Dec 29, 1863, Point Lookout, Md.
John Caunter, blank, remit fever, Dec 22, 1863, Hosp, Memphis.
E Runnels, ord seaman, consumption, Dec 29, 1863, vessel U S S *Niagara*.
Henry Buckley, marine, dysentery, Jan 7, 1861, Nav Asylum, Phil.
Geo Gentrey, landsman, interm fever, Dec 30, 1863, Hosp, Memphis.
Geo Nichols, ord seaman, consumption, do, do.
Michl Scott, marine, pneumonia, Jan 9, Nav Asylum, Phil.
Chas Stone, landsman, jaundice, Jan 7, Nav Hosp, N Y.
John Thomas, landsman, fever, Jan 9, do.
Rt Brown, capt forecastle, gunshot wound, Dec 25, 1863, Stono River, S C.
Jos Phillips, ord seaman, gunshot wound, Dec 25, do.
Lorenzo S Snow, ord seaman, gunshot wound, Dec 25, do.
John Shaughnessy, ord seaman, gunshot wound, Dec 25, 1863, vessel U S S *Peterheff*.
J P Sturgis, actg mstr's mate, disease of kidneys, Jan 2, vessel U S S *Metacomet*.
Rt Mc Whinnie, ord seaman, blank, Jan 6, Nav Hosp, Wash.
Kenneth Beel, ord seaman, acute gastritis, Dec 26, 1863, Nav Hosp, N O.

Mich McCanaghy, landsman, yel fever, Oct 10, 1863, do.
Wm Brown, 2nd ast engr, yel fever, Oct 17, 1863, do.
Wm West, seaman, yel fever, Oct 8, 1863, Nav Hosp, Pensacola.
John Doyle, ord seaman, yel fever, Sep 18, 1863, Santa Rosa Island.
Walter West, ord seaman, yel fever, Sep 23, 1863, Nav Hosp, Pensacola.
John B Washburne, clerk, yel fever, Sep 23, Santa Rosa Island.
Wm Thompson, ord seaman, yel fever, Sep 30, 1863, do.
Francis Perkins, ord seaman, yel fever, Sep 24, 1863, do.
Andrew Green, boatswain's mate, yel fever, Sep 25, do.
Wm Curwin, ord seaman, yel ever, Sep 26, do.
Jas Queen, ord seaman, yel fever, Aug 30, Nav Hosp, Pensacola.
Henry Hammitt, boatswain's mate, yel fever, Oct 16, 1863, do.
A Morningston, seaman, yel fever, Oct 6, 1863, do.
Hugh McGuire, marine, yel fever, Oct 6, 1863, do.
Thos Brown, marine, yel fever, Oct 7, 1863, do.
John Dainey, marine, yel fever, Oct 8, 1863, do.
Geo Manning, marine, yel fever, Oct 11, 1863, do.
Geo E Smith, do, do, do, do.
Thos Walsh, marine, yel fever, Oct 15, 1863, do.
John Donovan, marine, yel fever, Oct 12, 1863, do.
Ephraim Wiley, marine, yel fever, Oct 15, 1863, do.
John C Spofford, marine, yel fever, Oct 16, 1863, do.
Martin Fisher, capenter's mate, yel fever, Oct 24, 1863, do.
Wm S Forman, paymstr's clerk, yel fever, Oct 31, 1863, do.
Pat Donovan, coal heaver, yel fever, Nov 5, 1863, do.
Michl McGinnis, marine, yel fever, Nov 6, 1863, do.
Saml Parker, marine, yel fever, do, do.
Fred Norton, marine, do, do, do.
Michl Harney, marine, yel fever, Nov 16, 1863, do.
C F Brown, surg's steward, dysentery, Sep 28, 1863, do.
Frank Enduly, marine, gunshot wound, Oct 15, B Water River, Fla.
John Thomas, actg mstr's mate, yel fever, Oct 2, 1863, do.
Geo Robinson, landsman, yel fever, Oct 6, 1863, do.
Jas Jackman, seaman, yel fever, Oct 8, 1863, do.
Geo H Benson, actg ensign, yel fever, Oct 9, 1863, do.
Rob McLellan, seaman, yel fever, Oct 15, 1863, do.
Albert C Clark, ord seaman, yel fever, Sep 10, 1863, vessel U S S *Sarah Brown.*
Henry Hampstead, ord seaman, yel fever, Sep 12, 1863, do.
Thos Doyle, landsman, yel fever, Sep 10, vessel U S S *Horace Beales.*
John McManus, landsman, yel fever, Sep 1, 1863, vessel U S S *Orvetta.*
Geo Russell, boy, drowned, Dec 17, 1863, vessel U S S *Geraniem.*
____ Davis, actg mstr's mate, drowned, Dec 17, 1863, vessel U S S *Clover.*
Wm Miller, seaman, drowned, Dec 17, 1863, do.
_ Steele, ord seaman, drowned, Dec 17, 1863, do.
Frank Brown, landsman, drowned, Dec 17, 1863, vessel U S S *Oleander.*
Ben Brown, landsman, drowned, Dec 17, 1863, do.
H P Carr, actg mstr's mate, consumption, Dec 26, 1863, Nav Hosp, Beaufort.
Morris Stepton, 1st cl boy, infl of brain, Jan 12, Nav Hosp, N Y.
Frank Luscombe, seaman, drowned, Jan 5, vessel U S S *Nansemond.*

Died: at Florence, Italy, on Dec 23, Mrs Julia A Stout, widow of the late Lt E C Stout, U S Navy [a gallant ofcr, who lost his life in the svc of his country,] & d/o Cmdor John H Aulick, U S Navy.

Mr H M Warfield, a merchant of Balt, has gone to Richmond to endeavor to effect the exchange of Maj White, a Rpblcn Senator of Pa, for Gen Trimble, of the rebel army. White's absence has given the Democrats the power to prevent the regular organization of the Senate, & embarrass the proceedings of the Leg. It has therefore been an object of importance to secure his release.

TUE JAN 19, 1864
The late Mrs Pierce, w/o Ex-Pres Pierce. Mrs Jane M Pierce was born at Hampton, N H, Mar 12, 1806, d/o Rev Jesse Appleton; mrd Hon Franklin Pierce, then of Hillsboro, in 1834. Her 3 chldrn died before her, the first born-in early infancy, the second in 1843 at age 4 yrs, & the youngest in Jan 1853, a few weeks after Gen Pierce's election to the Presidency. Mrs Pierce died on Dec 2 at Andover, Mass, & on Dec 5th, was laid to her rest by the side of her chldrn at Concord, N H.

Died: at Harper's Ferry, on Jan 16, Mrs Emma Mason Wheaton, w/o Brig Gen Frank Wheaton, d/o the late Brig Gen Richd B Mason, U S Army, & step-dght of Maj Gen D C Buell. Funeral from St Matthew's Chr, today.

Died: on Jan 16, Lilly, y/d/o Jas J & Augusta M Dickins.

Died: on Jan 13, in Brookline, Mass, his native state, Jonathan Seaver, a much esteemed ctzn of Washington, in his 71st yr of age.

Foster, Stephen C, composer of Ethiopian melodies, died in N Y last week. The most popular of his melodies was The Old Folks at Home. Others he has written: Oh Susannah, Old Dog Tray, Nelly Bly, Kentucky Home, Katy Darling, Lilly Dale, Nellie was a Lady; & Hazel Dell.

Died: on Jan 18, Mrs Ellinor Ames, in the 68th yr of her age. Funeral from the residence of her son-in-law, J G Matlock, 513 I st, tomorrow.

WED JAN 20, 1864
Died: on Jan 18, in her 11th yr, Jane Holbrook, d/o Horatio N & Eliz B Easby.

Died: on Jan 17, Matilda Keeffer, in her 64th yr, w/o Abraham Keefer, after a long & painful illness.

Orphans Crt of Wash Co, D C. 1-Case of Geo G King, exc of Chas B King, dec'd; settlement on Feb 16. 2-Case of Moses Kelly, exc of Geo Meade, dec'd; settlement on Feb 16. -Z C Robbins, rg o/wills

Supreme Crt of D C. Riggs & Co, & others, against the admx, widow & heirs of Thos Smith. Parties are to meet at my ofc on Feb 1. -Walter S Cox, spec auditor

Hse o/Reps: 1-Cmte on Military Affairs to inquire into retiring from the service Gen Robt Anderson, of Sumter memory & gallantry, with full pay, & report by bill or otherwise.

For sale: a first class house-store & dwlg, on 7th st, between D & E sts, one of the best stands in the city. -J M Johnson, 383 E st, between 9th & 10th sts.

THU JAN 21, 1864
Mrd: at Ashtabula, Ohio, on Dec 31, by Rev Dr Conklin, the Hon Geo W Julian, of Indiana, to Miss Laura Giddings, y/d/o Hon Joshua R Giddings.

Mrd: on Dec 31, by Rev Mr Davis, Mr Daniel Carroll to Miss Joanna R Bowen, both of Wash City.

Died: on Jan 18, of typhoid fever, John F Clements, late of Chicago, Ill, aged 35 years & 12 days.

Died: in Gtwn, D C, on Jan 20, Mrs Mary A B Cummin. Funeral from the Catholic Chr, today.

Local-Mr John S Anderson, messenger of the banking hse of L Johnson & Co, was robbed of $1,015 on Fri. Geo Payne was arrested by 2 policeman on the spot.

Orphans Crt of Wash Co, D C. Case of Eliza J Bodien, admx of Henry A Bodien, dec'd; settlement on Feb 2. -Z C Robbins, rg o/wills

Fire at Camp Butler, near Springfield, Ill, on Mon, destroyed all the ofcr's qrtrs. Capt Dimon & Lt Bennett, 38th Ill cavalry, were burned to death. Two other Lts were badly burned in their faces & hands.

FRI JAN 22, 1864
Died: on Jan 20, of consumption, Wm Mayne, eldest s/o the late J A M Duncanson, in the 23rd yr of his age. Funeral from the residence of his mother, 478 H st, today.

Died: on Jan 2, at Petersburg, Hardy Co, Va, Dr Jno W Moss, of heart disease; surgeon of the 14th Va Infty; s/o Wm & Gertrude Eliza Moss. He was born Oct 4, 1816, in Fairfax Co, Va.

Destructive fire yesterday in the hse on L st, between 6th & 7th sts, occupied by Mrs Huhn: hse & contents destroyed. Flames extended to 2 frame bldgs owned by Downing Bros, & occupied by John F Parker, policeman, & John Stanford, both of whom lost about half of their furniture. The hse of Peter Ritchter was next burnt, & then 2 hses owned by Mr Himmell, one occupied by himself, & the other by Mr Wm Parker, painter, both of whom lost most of their furn. The flames spread to the 2 hses next adjoining, owned by John Stimell, & occupied by 2 or 3 families. Two hses, owned by the estate of John P Freeman, one occupied by J P Freeman, next caught fire. Value destroyed: $15,000.

We regret to learn that Gen John A McClernand, of this city, has at last felt it due to himself to tender his resignation as a Maj Gen in the vol svc of the U S. He has waited patiently for many months in hope that an investigation into his case would be ordered, but he has waited in vain. Being denied the opportunity either to vindicate himself or to serve his country in the field, he is no doubt unwilling longer to hold a commission while he is practically prevented from discharging the duties which it virtually imposes on him. –Ill State Jrnl

Capt W W White, provost mrshl of the 18ᵗʰ Pa dist, Williamsport, has been dismissed the svc, & arrested & lodged in the Old Capitol prison for alleged frauds in the business of his ofc.

Appointments by the Pres:
Milton B Harrison, to be Coll of Internal Rev of the 9ᵗʰ Collection Dist of Ill.
John Titus to be Chief Justice of Utah.
Elmer S Dandy to be Assoc Justice of Nebraska.
Perry E Brocchus to be Assoc Justice of New Mexico.
John W North to be Assoc Justice of Nevada.
Wm F Turner to be Chief Justice of Arizona.
Powhatan B Locke to be Assoc Justice of Nevada.
Thos J Boynton to be Judge of the Southern Dist of Fla.
Richd Busteed to be Judge of the Dist of Ala.
Jos Remington to be Mrshl of the Northern Dist of Fla.
Edw Dodd to be Mrshl for the Dist of N Y.
Jas Graham, of New Orleans, to be Mrshl for the Eastern Dist of La.
Jos G Easton to be Mrshl for the Eastern Dist of Mo.
John Underwood to be Mrshl for the Eastern Dist of Va.
Edw Banks to be Mrshl of the Consular Crt of the U S at Kanagawha, Japan.
Andrew Wylie to be a Justice of the Supreme Crt for the Dist of Col.
Michl Stock to be Super of Indian Affairs for New Mexico.
Culver P Chamberlin to be Atty for the Northern Dist of Fla.
Fred'k O Rogers to be Atty for the Western Dist of Mich.
Joshua Tevis to be Atty for Ky.
Rufus Waples to be Atty for Eastern Dist of La.
Theodore D Edwards to be Atty for the Terr of Nevada.
Horace H Harrison to be Atty for the Middle Dist of Tenn.
Wm N Grover to be Atty for the Eastern Dist of Mo.
Homer G Plantz to be Atty for the Southern Dist of Fla.

Saml Kirk & Sons-manufacturers of silver-ware: 172 Balt st, Balt, Md, est'd, 1817. [Ad]

SAT JAN 23, 1864
Mrd: Jan 21, by Rev Mr Reese, Mr Saml C Palmer to Miss Mary S Claxton, all of Gtwn,D C.

Died: on Jan 22, Ann Eliz, 2ⁿᵈ d/o Jas T & Cornelia J Clark, aged 9 years & 4 months. Funeral from their residence, 545 13ᵗʰ st, on Sun.

For sale-at Surratt's Tavern, PG Co, Md, the estate, lying in PG Co, Md, of which Edw W Young, is possessed & residing on; 525 acs; 2 contiguous tracts, *Stony Harbor* & *Strife*, which were formerly owned by Raphael C Edelen; with commodious dwlg. -Edw W Bell, atty, Upper Marlborough, Md

Supreme Crt of D C, in Equity #132. A P Hoover against J D Hoover & Lawson P Hoover. Statement of the account of Andrew Hoover, dec'd: meet at my residence in Gtwn, on Feb 15. -W Redin, auditor

Chas A Dana, formerly editor of the N Y Tribune, has been confirmed in Exec session of the Senate as 2ⁿᵈ Ast Sec of War, under the act recently passed & approved for that purpose.

It is stated that Gen Grant has telegraphed to Gen Halleck that Gen Foster, who is suffering from his wound, has asked to be relieved. He requests that either Gen Schofield or Gen McPherson be immediately assigned to that command.

MON JAN 25, 1864

Deaths reported to the Navy Dept for the week ending Jan 23, 1864:
Peter Sullivan, seaman, consumption, Jan 15, Hosp, N Y.
Chas Gray, ofcr's cook, hypertrophia cardes, Nov 29, 1863, Patapsco.
Jas C Bradley, landsman, drowned, Dec 24, 1863, Shuyaw Bay, S C.
Thos Ray, coal heaver, typhoid fever, Dec 21, 1863, Vt.
Tony Smith, landsman, pneumonia, Dec 25, 1863, Vt.
Francis Bunes alias Boyle, landsman, drowned, Jan 7, Nantucket.
Wm Davis, seaman, chronic diarrhoea, Jan 5, Hosp, Memphis.
John Green, contraband, adynamia, Jan 9, do.
Thos Dorian, 2nd cl fireman, febris continua, Jan 11, Hosp, Norfolk.
Wm Moffett, coal heaver, ureamia, Jan 12, do.
J Watson, coal heaver, blank, no date, Hosp, San Francisco.
Westley Burton, 2nd cl boy, rubeala, Jan 8, Mississippi Squadron.
Chub Jenkins, 2nd cl fireman, rubeala, Jan 11, do.
Hamilton McQuirk, seaman, rubeala, Jan 11, do.
John Callister, seaman, gunshot, Jan 11, Folly Inlet, N C.
John Peterson, ord seaman, drowned, Jan 2, Key West.
Michael McDonald, p marine, consumption, Nav 16, Hosp, Key West.
Geo Sisinger, landsman, chronic dysentery, Dec 8, 1863, do.
Thos Williams, landsman, pneumonia, Jan 15, Ohio.
David Ketteridge, pa marine, acute pneumonia, Jan 19, Hosp, N Y.
John Murphy, seaman, rheumatism, Jan 21, Nav Asylum, Phil.
Wm Devereux, seaman, colic, Jan 13, Hartford.
Robt Qiunee, 2nd cl boy, pleurisy, Jan 21, vessel U S S *Ben Morgan*.
Philip Malone, 2nd Cpl, scalded, Jan 20, vessel *Dragon*.
Richd Starr, landsman, scalded, Jan 20, vessel *Dragon*.

Mrd: in Wash City, on Jan 10, by Rev Fr Boyle, John W Richey, of Wash City, to Miss Arabel A V Gardner, d/o the late Wm F Gardner, formerly of Balt, Md.

Died: at the residence of her hsbnd, at *Ellwood*, Muhlenberg Co, Ky, on Oct 15, Mrs Sarah A, w/o Hugh W McNary, in her 58th yr. She was born in 1805, in Richland Dist, S C, & emigrated to Ky in 1826; sister of Mr John Scott, Mrs Dr Jas B Daviss, & Mrs Gov Jas H Adams, of S C.

Obit-Col Wm McNeir died at Phil on Jan 10. He was born in Annapolis, Md, in 1798. In 1822 he established a newspaper called *The Carrolitonian*. He leaves chldrn.

Orphans Crt of Wash Co, D C. Prsnl estate of Jos W Davis, late of Wash, D C, dec'd. -Mary Ann Davis, admx

Orphans Crt of Wash Co, D C. Regarding the rl estate of the minor heirs of Geo S Neil, dec'd. Ratify sale by John S Saxton, Sarah A Paxton & Leroy Edwards, guardians to the minor heirs of Geo S Neil, dec'd; to Saml Queen, Jas H Payne & Mrs Jett, the purchasers. - Wm F Purcell, sole Judge of the Orphan's Crt -Z C Robbins, rg o/wills

Tax Collectors sale the lots & parts of lots in Gtwn, D C, for taxes due:
[Dates vary from 1860 thru 1863] -Chas D Welch, Collector

Adams, John-heir
Abbot, Wm R-heirs
Abbot, Chas
Bausell, Minor
Brown,Wm-heirs
Burll, Henry
Berry, Hezekiah-heirs
Barber, Au'w
Boucher, J W
Bradley, Wm A
Crick, Richd
Cox, R S
Cruit, Richd
Chichester, Mrs Mary
Caton, Michael
Chick, Jos C
Clark, Dr Saml
Clagett, Jas-heirs
Carter, J H
Drill, John
Dorsey, P W
Dashiel, Grayson

Eliason, E W
Eliason, John
Farquahar, Mrs E W
Ferguson, Jas
Fowler, Wm R
Gross, Jas F
Hunt, Ann M-heirs
Hance, Wm S
Hess, John
Hunter, Geo-heirs
Hawkins, Wilson
Hughes, John E
Hazel, Wm C
Hawkins, John S
Johnson, Robt
Ludeke, Jos
Lane, John
Lewis, Wm-heirs
Littleton, Lawson-heirs
Mankins, Wm
Mason, John-heirs
Morton, Wm-heirs

Mackall, Brook
McCann, Mrs Mary
Offutt, Washington
Offutt, E T
O'Donoghue, Mrs Ellen
Offutt, C A
Paine, Chas H
Reaver, H O
Robertson, Miss Ann
Rosenbrush, T
Stone, John
Silence, Walter B
Smallwood, Jos
Thecker, Edw
Tenny, Franklin
White, Mrs R B
Whelan, H
Woodward, Thos
Hayne, David & others
Cropley, Saml & Robt
Barnard-heirs

Mrs Jane E Ward died on Tue, from the accidental inhaling of chloroform while bathing her finger with a painful carbuncle. Mrs Ward was the widow of Capt Ward, late of the U S Vols, N Y, who died from the effects of a gunshot wound received at Bull Run No 2, from the effects of which he died. A large family of orphans survive.

TUE JAN 26, 1864

Died: in St Paul, Minn, on Jan 15, of scarlet fever, Henry M, only surviving s/o Hon H M & Matilda W Rice, aged 7 years & 4 months.

Died: Jan 3, in his 42nd yr, at Cincinnati, L C Valdenar, of Ashland, Ky, & formerly of Montg Co, Md.

Col Alfred Spates, Pres of the Chesapeake & Ohio Canal, who has been confined in Ft Lafayette for some months past, was released on Sat by order of the Sec of War.

Died: at Cambridge, Md, on Jan 23, of pneumonia, Columbus Monroe, of Wash City, aged 63 yrs. Funeral this afternoon from the residence of Mr Seaton, 423 E st.

Wash Corp: 1-Ptn of F W Colclasier & others for an additional police magistrate in the Northern Liberties: referred to the Cmte on Police. 2-Mayor nominates Geo Hepburn for Police Cnstbl v Robt F Magee, resigned. 3-Cmte on Finance reported back on the ptn of Chas Vincent, asking the Corp to purchase his brick vault in Holmead's Buriel Ground: to be laid on the table. 4-Bill for relief of Saml P Jones was taken up & considered. 5-Ptn of B F Beers & E F French & others, for erection of fire plugs: referred to the Cmte on Drainage & Distribution of Water.

W W Treadwell, cashier of the People's Bank of Hudson, Mich, absconded with $6,000 belonging to the Bank.

The Adventure Copper Mine, with all its apurtenances, was sold by auction at Pittsburgh on Tue. It is in Ontonogan Co, Mich-800 acs of land. Purchasers: D T Charles & Thos F Mason, for $110,000.

A Napoleon for Mexico. The Paris Patrie of Dec 28: Prince Napoleon Bonaparte, s/o Prince Canino, has just entered the Foreign Legion, with rank of Capt. His father was the s/o Lucien Bonaparte, & his mother was the d/o Jos Bonaparte. He was born in 1829 & is mrd to a d/o the Roman Prince Ruspoli.

Maj Gen Pleasanton, in command of the Cavalry of the Army of the Potomac, issued on Jan 18, a stringent order against rebel guerillas. Disguised rebel sldrs to be hung.

Wm G Fish, Col of the 1st Conn Cavalry, & for more than a year Military Prov Mrshl of Balt, was arrested on Sun in the camp of his command near the city. Col W S Olcott was here on Sat with orders to convey him to the Old Capitol bldg. Arrest was made by Lt Mulligan, of Gen Lockwood's staff, & he was placed in the Donivan negro jail, having arrived too late for the cars. Col Olcott will take him this morning. Charges: official misconduct, involving fraud & corruption, & he will be tried by crt-martial.

Va constitutional convention: mbrs elect to the convention, which convenes in this city on the 13th prox, so far as heard from: 1-Alex Co-Walter L Penn 2-Alexandria & Fairfax Cos-S Ferguson Beach. 3-Fairfax Co-John Hawxhurst 4-Norfolk City & Co-Dr L W Webb, W W Wing, & LeRoy T Edwards.

WED JAN 27, 1864
Obit-recently, at the residence of his son-in-law, Chas L Bartlett, of Winthrop, Mass, Hiram Plummer, formerly of Haverhill, N H, aged 76 yrs. He was grandfather of Col Bartlett, of Winthrop, Mass. -Boston Post

Died: on Jan 28, Virginia Wilson, in the 14th yr of her age, d/o Esau & Virginia E Pickrell. Funeral from their residence, 58 Second st, Gtwn, D C.

Died: on Jan 26, Rev B Appleby, from inflammation of the bowels. Funeral from St Paul's Luth Chr, H & 11th sts, tomorrow.

Hse o/Reps: 1-Bills introduced & referred: relief of Danl Fuller. 2-Relief of Jacob S Lowrey & Geo A Gray.

Quebec, Jan 25. Ex-Mrshl Kane, of Balt, & 13 other Confederates, mostly escaped ofcrs from Johnson's Isl & Camp Douglas, left here this morning by the Grand Trunk railway for River Du Loup, to take the overland route to Halifax.

John C Underwood appt'd to be Judge of the Dist Crt of the U S for the Eastern Dist of Va.

THU JAN 28, 1864
Died: in Wash City, on Jan 26, at the residence of her bro, Mary Priscilla, w/o Rev Jas H Dulaney, aged 21 years & 8 months.

Died: on Jan 27, John Hitz, Cnsl Gen of Switzerland, aged 67 yrs, native of same, but for 23 years a ctzn of the U S, during 20 years of which he was a resident of Wash City. Funeral from his late residence, 29 south Á st, Fri.

On Tue, Martha Christian, from Alexandria, was knocked-down & run over by a negro hack driver. She was much injured. The hackman was arrested, but proven the affair was purely accidental.

Orphans Crt of Wash Co, D C. Case of John Alexander, adm of Mary B Alexander, dec'd; settlement on Feb 20. -Z C Robbins, rg o/wills

Montreal, Jan 27. Hon Jas B Clay, of Ky, ex-minister at Portugal & ex-mbr of Congress from the Ashland dist, died in this city on Jan 26; interment in Ky.

Senate: 1-Bill introduced for the relief of Geo T Wiggins, of Keokuk, Iowa.

Blockade runners arrested. Patrolman Cline, of the 1st Dist, on Tue, stopped the stage from Port Tobacco & arrested Thos Clayton, Saml Palmer, Jas Thomas, Chris Balgis, & E S Ebbs. They were sent to the Old Capitol by the Prov Mrshl. [The Old Capitol has 757 prisoners. Carroll Prison-287.]

With the charming weather of the past week, Maj Gen Meade has issued permits to many wives & relatives of sldrs now stationed "on the front" to visit their brave relatives, & that the cars thence have been ordered accordingly.

FRI JAN 29, 1864
Died: at St Louis, Mo, on Jan 27, Charlotte E, w/o Chas G Mauro, & d/o Geo M Davis, of Wash City, aged 27 yrs, 2 months & 13 days.

Died: in Brooklyn, N Y, on Jan 22, Mrs Hepasely Silliman, w/o Gold S Silliman, in the 86th yr of her age.

Mr Jas Warder, age 46 yrs, died on Jan 27, after being vaccinated about 10 days ago with impure vaccine matter. He was a well known ctzn of Washington & a coal dealer in the firm of Warder & Stewart. -Local Item

Richmond Enq of the 19th, received at Fortress Monroe, announces the sudden & serious illness of A H Stephens, the rebel V P. He is at his home in Ga.

Mr B G Harris, of the firm of Neale, Harris & Co, commission merchants of Balt, & Rev M M Henkle, pastor of a Meth Episc congregation in the same city, have been arrested on charges of using treasonable language & sent to the south.

SAT JAN 30, 1864
Died: in Wash City, on Jan 29, in the 88th yr of his age, Mr Wm Thompson. Funeral from his late residence, 325 F st, today.

Pres Lincoln recognizes Danl Perez Barreda who has been appt'd Cnsl of Nicaragua at N Y.

J P Crutchett, French Cook, informs his patrons that he continues to attend personally to the preparation of dinners, etc: 477 Sixth st, Wash, D C.

From Fortress Monroe, Jan 28. Dr Ritchie, a rebel gov't contractor, was captured at Brandon in a recent raid on the James River. He was the heaviest contractor in the Confederacy. Maj Burroughs, the guerilla chief, captured some time since in Princess Anne Co, attempted to escape on Jan 26th from the small-pox hospital at Norfolk, & was shot by the guard. He died a 3 o'clock yesterday.

The Pres has nominated Chas R Train, of Mass, to be Ast Adj Gen, with the rank of Capt.

MON FEB 1, 1864
Deaths reported to the Navy Dept for the week ending Jan 30, 1864:
Henry Peterson, landsman, drowned, Aug 29, 1863, Neosho.
Thos T Glasgow, seaman, drowned, Nov 4, Mississippi River.
Robt Hudley, landsman, rubeola, Nov 27, Hastings.
Francis Mealley, seaman, gunshot, Dec 23, Gertrude.
John M Kennedy, landsman, albuminina, hosp, N Y.
Patrick Hynes, landsman, adynamie, Jan 22, do.
Thos Watson, landsman, pneumonia, Jan 21, do.
John Green, carpenter, lung fever, pleurisy, Jan 11, Ohio.
Jas D Carpenter, ast actg engr, consumption, Jan 19, Princeton.
Cook Sea, 3rd cl boy, insanity, Sep 1, hosp, Newbern.
Daniel Lambert, pensioner, rheumatism, Jan 26, Nav Asylum.
David Beaman, 1st cl boy, intermittent fever, Dec 4, Miami.
Francis Jones, negro, variola, Dec 13, Norfolk.
Wm C Keirgham, pilot, variola, Dec 19, do.
Reuben Noble, landsman, diarrhea, Dec 21, hosp, Newbern.
John H Gladding, seaman, typhoid fever, Jan 21, Mystic.
Aloamis S Bennet, marine, eneuresis, Jan 27, Nav Asylum.
Flix Grundy, negro, Nov 17, Mississippi.

Died: Jan 23, at Jonesborough, Ill, in his 30th yr, Capt Chas E Orme, 94th Ill Vols, native of Wash City.

Died: on Jan 31, Jas C, s/o Wm Ballantyne, in his 12th yr. Funeral from the residence of his parents, 322 N Y av, today.

Crt Martial, Louisville, Ky-Capt Saml Black, Capt & Ast Qm of the U S Army, to be dismissed with loss of all pay & allowances, to pay a fine of $10,000, & imprisoned to date from Sep 20, 1863, the day of his arrest, for 2 yrs.

TUE FEB 2, 1864
Mr Fred'k Hambright, of Lancaster, Pa, drowned on Friday while crossing the Eastern Branch to 6th st wharf in a skip. He was employed as a clerk in the Commissary Dept at Giesboro Point for some time previous. His body was recovered. -Wash, D C

Farm for sale: either 100 or 200 acs: only 8 miles from Washington. Apply personally to Wm A Batchelor, or if by ltr address Sligo P O, Montg Co, Md.

C C Spalding, of St Mary's Co, Md, tried by military commission in Wash, on charge of illicit intercourse & trade with the South, has been honorably acquitted.

Wash Corp: 1-Act granting a certain privilege to Stephen D Castleman of using all of that portion of 27th st West & north of L st n, 5 ft from the wing wall of the lime kiln belonging to Wm H Godey.

Crt of Inquiry to investigate the case of Col A A Gibson, 2nd Pa heavy artl, who is charged with refusing to accept a flag presented to his regt by the state of Pa, assigning as a reason that his regt was not fighting for the state of Pa, but for the U S. Crt is composed of Brig Gen De Russey, Pres; Capt Chandler, of Gen Larkins' staff, Recorder; Col Abbott, 1st Conn vols; & Col Weiling, 9th N Y Vols

Four deaf mutes were proceeding to Balt on Sat, walking the rail road tracks. At Scaggs crossing, one of them, Jas Kenney, was knock down by the train & killed. They attended Columbia Institute for the deaf, dumb, & blind at Kendall Green.

WED FEB 3, 1864
Died: in Wash City, on Feb 1, Mrs Sarah Virginia Robinson, relict of the late Sgt Maj John Robinson, U S M C, in the 25th yr of her age. Funeral from her late residence on 8th st, today.

Orphans Crt of Wash Co, D C. 1-Prsnl estate of Christian Anderson, late of U S Navy, dec'd. 2-Prsnl estate of Chas F Davis, late of U S Navy, dec'd. 3-Prsnl estate of John Thervigan, late of U S Navy, dec'd. -Wm L Hodge

Supreme Crt of D C, in Equity #26. Jos Smith et al against Wm P Johnston et al. Ratify sale by T J D Fuller, trustee, of rl estate of L B Hardin, dec'd. -R J Meigs, clerk

Hse o/Reps: Mr McBride presented the credentials of Wm H Wallack, as Delegate from the Nevada Terr; who there upon was qualified & took his seat.

Senate: 1-The Cmte on D C reported adversely on the ptn of A R Davis, of Md, for compensation for certain slaves.

Gen Whipple, of Gen Thomas' staff, asserts that over 7,300 deserters from Bragg's army have come over into our lines since Oct 20th, as shown by the rolls.

Maj Gen Stoneman assigned to the command of the 23rd Army Corps.

THU FEB 4, 1864
Mrd: on Feb 2, at the Chr of the Ascension, by Rev Wm Pinckney, John Peyton Torbert to Lizzie C, d/o Johny Bryant, all of Wash City.

Orphans Crt of Wash Co, D C. 1-Prsnl estate of Jos Gargan, late of U S Navy, dec'd. 2-Prsnl estate of John Rutledge, late of U S Navy, dec'd. 3-Prsnl estate of Wm H Williamson, late of U S Navy, dec'd. 4-Prsnl estate of Geo M Leighton, late of U S Navy, dec'd. -Wm L Hodge

Supreme Crt of D C, in Equity #1675. Henry B Clarke, Sarah E Clarke, Caroline M Talburt, Thos A Talburt, & Mary A Walker, against John H Walter, Sarah I, Thos A, Wm E, Mary V, Florence E, & Wm D Howard, Geo E Clarke, Eugine L & Littleton D Walter, devisees of Alexander Talburt. Parties named & P I Torney, trustee, to appear at my residence in Gtwn on Feb 13. -W Redin, auditor

Wm M Stone, the new Govn'r of Iowa, was once a canal driver between Roscoe & Cleveland, Ohio, at $3.00 a month.

St Louis papers announce the death in that city, on Sunday last, of the Hon Hamilton Rowan Gamble, Govn'r of the State of Missouri. Funeral was Monday. Lt Gov W P Hall will perform the duties of Govn'r.

Senate: 1-Act to provide compensation for the svcs of Geo Morell in adjusting titles to land in Michigan. 2-Cmte on D C: ptn of A R Davis, of Montg Co, Md, praying compensation for slaves alleged to have been freed by the operation of the act emancipating slaves in D C, reported adversely thereon. 3-Ptn of Lucy Gwynne & others, for the incorporation of Providence Hosp, & bill to incorporate same in Wash City: reported the bill with amendments.

Mr John P Sissons, of Syracuse, died suddenly last week from the effects of chloroform. His wife found him lying upon the floor dead & a hankerchief saturated with chloroform nearby.

FRI FEB 5, 1864
Obit-Henry Dielman, elder s/o Dr H Dielman, Prof at Mt St Mary's College, Emmitsburg, Md, died at Alton, Ill, on Dec 25, in his 24th yr. But a few short months have passed since he left parents & home to seed a situation in the West.

Mrd: at Grace Chr, Balt, Md, on Feb 2, by Rev Dr Hall, of Washington, Marianno DeGollado, of Mexico City to Otelia, d/o Col M Jordan, late of Va.

Mrd: on Feb 3, by Rev Geo G Goss, Actg Ensign Henry D Foster, U S Navy, to Jennie B Clarke, d/o Capt Robt Clarke, 1st Dist Vols, all of Wash City.

Mrd: on Jan 28, at the residence of the bride's father, by Rev Mr Coombs, Jas O Withers, of Va, to Emma Gertrude, d/o Thos Foster, formerly of Winchester, Va.

Mrd: at Newport, R I, on Jan 25, by Rev Lewis W P Balch, O Dorsey Robb to Virginia A, d/o Prof A Roget, U S Naval Acad.

Died: at Washington, Pa, on Jan 17, Mr Wm B Rose, aged 68 yrs, a native of Windsor, N C, but had resided for many years at the former; at the time of his death had been for twelve months a clerk in the Patent Ofc in Wash City.

Orphans Crt of Wash Co, D C. 1-Prsnl estate of Wm G Pike, late of U S Navy, dec'd. 2-Prsnl estate of Thos Mec, late of U S Navy, dec'd. 3-Prsnl estate of Thos Donavan, late of U S Navy, dec'd. -Wm L Hodge

Crct Crt of PG Co, Md-sale of prsnl prop of the late Geo Hume, at his residence, near Beltsville, PG Co, Md. -Thos W Burch & John T Burch, adms

Hse o/Reps: 1-Bill for relief of Jacob Weaver was introduced & referred

St Louis, Feb 3. Govn'r Gamble was buried today: many ofcs were closed: flags were at half mast: ceremonies took place in the 2nd Presby Chr with Rev Dr Brown delivering the discourse. The remains were deposited in the Bellefontaine Cemetery.

Senate: 1-Cmte on Naval Affairs: referred the memorial of Edw C Doran: bill to authorize the settlement of the accounts of E C Doran. 2: Cmte on Claims, to whom was referred the ptn of Albert Brown praying for relief, made a report with a bill for his relief. Provides the payment to Albert Brown of Kingston, N H, of $14,000 in full for 100 army wagons manfactured by him under a contract made with Morris S Miller, q m of U S army, dt'd Jul 1, 1861, & duly delivered Aug 13, 1861.

Surprise cordial affair at the parsonage of Wesley Chapel on Tue for Rev B Peyton Brown, Pastor, & his family, welcoming them. Saml Norment addressed the ladies & gentlemen gathered in the parlors & presented him a purse of $225.

SAT FEB 6, 1864
Mrd: on Feb 4, at the residence of the bride's father, by Rev Fr Lynch, Richd Thos Merrick, of Chicago, Ill, to Nannie, d/o Jas C McGuire, of Wash City.

Died: on Feb 5, at his residence, in Montg Co, Md, after a long & painful illness, John L Wilkens, in his 62nd yr. Funeral from his former residence, Mass av & 12th st, Sun.

Died: on Feb 5, at the residence of Warren Murdock, in Brooklyn, N Y, in the 48th yr of his age, Maj Josiah Watson, U S M C.

Died: on Feb 4, of consumption, Alonzo, s/o Jas & Mary Goszler, in his 17th yr. Funeral, today, from the residence of his father, 131 Beall st, Gtwn, D C.

Died: on Feb 5, of heart disease, Solomon Pribram, in his 61st yr. Funeral from his late residence, 409 H st, tomorrow.

Died: in Wash City, on Feb 5, in her 36th yr, Mrs Eliz E Dyer, w/o Edw C Dyer. Funeral on Mon, from the residence, 270 F st; svcs at St Patrick's Chr.

Info from Alexander R McKee, U S Cnsl at Panama, of the death of the following American Ctzns, viz: [to the Dept of State, Official]
Wm Fox, steward on the Americ ship *Salvador*, died on Oct 3, 1863.
Wm Gale, died at the Island of Flamenco, Nov 13, 1863.
John Guinan or Gudnan, died board steamship *Constitution*, at sea, Jul 29 1863.
Jas Russel, died on board steamer *St Louis*, Dec 31, 1863.
John Maywood, jumped overboard from steamer *St Louis*, Dec 30, 1863, & was drowned, residence unknown.
Louis Davis, colored, native of Balt, Md, died in Panama, about Nov 24, 1863.

Orphans Crt of Wash Co, D C. 1-Prsnl estate of John Carpenter, late of U S Navy, dec'd. 2-Prsnl estate of Edw Mullen, late of U S Navy, dec'd. -Wm L Hodge

MON FEB 8, 1864
Mrd: in Wash City, on Feb 4, by Rev Fr McCarthy, John Floor to Miss Ann Lane, both of Ireland.

Died: on Feb 7, Mary E McClelland, w/o Geo McClelland, aged 34 yrs. Funeral from the residence of her hsbnd, 640 L st, today.

Died: at Gtwn College, in the 50th yr of his age, on Feb 7, Rev Jos Aschwanden, for the past 11 years

Pastor of Trinity Chr; native of Switzerland, emigrated to America in 1848, spending his first years in St Louis & Cincinnati. Burial in the College graveyd.

Orphans Crt of Wash Co, D C. Prsnl estate of Wm J Kendrick, late of Wash City, dec'd. -Mgt Kendrick, admx w a

Supreme Crt of D C, in Equity #1814. Jos Libby, assignee of Downing & Co, against Jos F Hodgson, adm of Wm Flaherty, & Mary Ellen, Cath Ann, & Wm Michael Flaherty, his heirs at law. Parties are to meet at my residence in Gtwn, D C, on Feb 19. -W Redin, auditor

Hon Marcus Morton, [50] formerly Govn'r of Mass, died on Sat last at his residence in Taunton.

The Pres has pardoned John H Waring, of PG Co, Md, who was last year sentenced by a crt martial to imprisonment during the war, for harboring certain persons engaged in the rebel service.

Deaths reported to the Navy Dept for the week ending Feb 6, 1864:
Henry P Edgar, seaman, pneumonia, Jan 28, Nav Hosp, Chelsea.
John Sloan, ord seaman, diarrhoea, Aug 1, 1863, Nav Hosp, New Orleans.
John Stephens, seaman, drowned, Nov 3, 1863, Mouth of Rio Grande.
Chs W Warrener, landsman, drowned, Nov 3, 1863, do.
Thos Ford, capt forecastle, wound of head, Jan 10, 1864, Ship Island.
Wm M Young, landsman, angina pectoris, Jan 15, 1864, vessel *Colorado*.
Wm Davis, ord seaman, drowned, Jan 27, 1864, vessel U S S *Minnesota*.
Louis H Rogue, seaman, drowned, Jan 27, 1864, vessel U S S *Itasca*.
Ed Robinson, 1st cl boy, chronic diarrhoea, Jan 21, Nav Hosp, Memphis.
Thos Smith, seaman, apoplexy, Jan 21, vessel U S S *Carolina*.
Rob Williams, contraband, small pox, Dec 22, 1863, Nav Hosp, Memphis.
Walter Williams, cabin steward, consumption, Jan 28, 1864, vessel U S S *Neptune*.
Rob G McLane, landsman, inflam of brain, Feb 3, Nav Hosp, Chelsea.
Christopher Graham, 2nd cl fireman, drowned, Jan 13, Tampa Bay.

TUE FEB 9, 1864
Capt Rollo Gleason, Provost Mrshl of the 3rd Dist of Vt, & Dr J L Chandler, Surgeon of the Brd of Enrollment of the same district, have been suspended from duty awaiting an investigation for enlisting into the U S svc men physically disqualified for military duty. Capt Isaac Plait, Prov Mrshl of the 12th Dist of N Y, & Dr Wm H Pitcher, Surgeon of the Brd of Enrollment of the same dist, have been suspended in like manner & for the same reason.

Boston, Feb 8. The Malden Bank robber, & murderer of the s/o the Pres of the Bank, has been arrested, in the person of Edw W Green, the postmastr of the place, who has confessed his guilt. Green is about 27 years of age & has a wife & one child. He has heretofore borne a good character. [Feb 10 paper: the murdered son was Frank E Converse, the Ast Cashier of the Malden Bank.]

A seaman named Dimadoff, belonging to the Russian steamship *Almay*, now at Annapolis, went ashore on Thu & was killed in a fracas with Wm T League, the keeper of a restaurant. League was arrested. The remains of the dec'd were interred on Sat with due honors according to the ceremonies of the Greek Chr. Ceremony was not only novel, but imposing.

Died: on Feb 8, Horatio G O'Neal, of the Fourth Auditor's ofc, in the 77th yr of his age. Funeral from his late residence, 522 M st, today.

WED FEB 10, 1864

Mrd: at Trinity Chr, on Feb 9, by Rev Wm Pinckney, A H McCormick, U S N, to Isabella, eldest d/o Wm E Howard, of Wash.

Mrd: on Feb 8, at St Dominick's Chr, by Rev Fr Bokee, John A Tafe to Miss Anna Sullivan, both of Wash City.

Died: at Cumberland, Md, on Feb 8, Dorothy, relict of the late Capt Saml Killmon, of Wash City, in her 63rd yr. Funeral from the residence of her son-in-law, R M A Fenwick, H st, between 2nd & 3rd sts, today.

Orphans Crt of Wash Co, D C. 1-Case of Frances Brown, [now Hawkins] admx of Wm A Brown, dec'd; settlement on Mar 5. -Z C Robbins, rg o/wills 2-Prsnl estate of Thos Slother, late of the U S Navy, dec'd. -Wm L Hodge 3-Prsnl estate of Thos Piper, late of the U S Navy, dec'd. -Wm L Hodge

Mrd: on Feb 9, at the Chr of the Ascension, by Rev Dr Pinckney, Dr Geo W Humphreys to Mrs Eliz A Holmead, all of Wash City.

Fair for Providence City Hosp: on Capitol Hill, in care of Srs of Charity. To meet the indebtedness for the new bldgs provided by this institution, the charitable & generous of this community are invited to patronize the sale of desirable articles, which will begin on Feb 28, at Odd Fellows' Hall, 7th st.

THU FEB 11, 1864

Senate: 1-Cmte of Claims was referred the memorial of E F & Saml A Wood, praying for an issue of duplicates of certain Oregon war bonds destroyed on board the steamer *Golden Gate*, submitted a report for the relief of same. 2-Same cmte was referred the ptn of Berendt A Froiseth: asked to be discharged from its further consideration: agreed to. 3-Bill for relief of John H Shepherd & Walter K Caldwwell, of Missouri, was introduced & referred.

New! First issue of the *U S Svc Magazine*-Jan number now ready. Contributors-Admr Davis, U S Navy; Gen J G Barnard, Gen Wm F Barry, U S Army, & Capt E C Boynton, Adj of the Military Acad. Under the editorial care of Henry Coppee, Prof of Eng Lit & History in the Univ of Pa.

Mrd: on Feb 10, at McKendree Parsonage, by Rev John Thrush, Mr Saml S Turner & Miss India Johnson, all of Wash City.

Mrd: at St Barnabas Chr, Balt, Md, on Feb 9, by Rev A P Stryker, Lt Cmder A A Semmes, U S Navy, to Mary M, d/o the late Edwin M Dorsey, of PG Co, Md.

$500 reward-disappeared from his home in Gtwn, on Feb 7, Grosvener Humphreys, age about 18 yrs. His friends fear he has met some casualty. -W B Webb, superintendent of police

Sandusky, Feb 9. Four hundred rebel prisoners, commissioned ofcrs, crossed the Sandusky Bay today in a steamer, & were landed in this city. They will start in the 11 o'clock train for

Balt. The noted guerilla chief, Gen Jeff Thompson, & Capt Breckenridge, s/o the renegade Gen, were among the number. A strong guard from the Hoffman btln will escort them to Balt.

St Mary's Acad, near Bryantown, Chas Co, Md, is for the education of young ladies. For information address Mrs Danl Major, Principal.

Burlington, Iowa, Feb 8. The ofc of the Constitution & Union newspaper, in Fairfield, Iowa, edited by David Sheward, was visited by Co E of the 2nd Iowa Vols today & the types thrown out the windows & the subscription books destroyed.

FRI FEB 12, 1864
Died: on Feb 10, Harriet Patterson, only d/o Eliza C & the late Lt Geo M Bache, U S Navy, age 17 yrs. Funeral from the residence of her mother, 168 F st, today.

Wash Corp: 1-Ptn of John Dunn & John Dilix: referred to the Cmte on Claims. 2-Nomination of Simeon Garrett for Corporation Cnstbl in ward #1 was confirmed. 3-Ptn of A Richards for relief: referred to the Cmte of Claims. 4-Cmte of Claims reported back on the ptn of Jas Rankin for relief: passed.

Special order of the War Dept, 1st Lt Robt B Smith, 11th U S Infty, & Lt E P Bigelow, U S Army, both now under arrest, are ordered to proceed to Ft Monroe, & from that Point explain to the Adj Gen of the army in reference to their neglect of duty & violation of military regulations of the army in mustering boys & men unfitted for the military svc into the 16th N Y Artl. The pay of all regimental ofcrs connected with the 16th N Y Heavy Artl has been stopped until further orders, awaiting an explanation of the matter of improper enlistments into the regt of boys under 18, men over 45, & others physically disqualified for military svc.

By order of Gen Banks, all plantations not in process of cultivation on Feb 1, 1864, unless excepted for special reasons, will be considered abandoned estates, & rented by the Gov't to such persons as will undertake their proper cultivation.

SAT FEB 13, 1864
Died: on Jan 27, at his residence, in Bladensburg, Md, Geo T Crawford, in his 27th yr. He leaves his wife & chldrn, & his mother & sisters.

For rent, on the heights of Wash, at junction of 21st & Boundary sts, the late residence of Cmdor Balch, U S Navy, for one or more yrs. Apply to Chas Vinson, 86 Pa Ave, between 21st & 22nd sts.

Rebel force in Arkansas: Memphis, Feb 12. The Little Rock Democrat gives the following whereabouts of the rebel forces in Arkansas: Price has about 6,000 demoralized troops at Wash; Marmaduke, Brook, & Cabell are in the mntns near Murfreesboro; Shelby's recently routed command is on the lower Sabine; & Cooper, Steele, & McIntosh's Indians are at Warren & North Fork in the Indian Terr. The total force, including guerrillas & camp followers, is about 14,000 men. 2-Capt Majors, of the 1st Nebraska cavalry, recently captured a complete uniform & outfit for Price, sent from St Louis. 3-Report that the 11th Ill has captured svr'l hundred rebels up the Yazoo river, but we have no particulars.

Died: on Feb 8, Horatio G O'Neal, of the Fourth Auditor's ofc, in the 77th yr of his age. Funeral from his late residence, 522 M st, today.

Senate: 1-Cmte on Patents: bill for relief of Phoebe Ann Fisk, wid/o Almons D Fisk, dec'd: postponed for the present.

New Haven-Aaron R Hall, recently with the Connecticut cavalry at Balt, was arrested at Wallingford Feb 12 by Maj Marcy, charged with circulating counterfeit national bills & currency.

MON FEB 15, 1864

Deaths reported to the Navy Dept for the week ending Feb 13, 1864:
Josiah Watson, Maj U S M C, Feb 5, Brooklyn, N Y.
Step Baker, landsman, variola, Feb 2, Nav Hosp, N Y.
Ed Lewis, seaman, consumption, no date, do.
Fred J Morgan, landsman, consumption, no date, do.
Sherman Church, boatswain's mate, dysentery, Jan 12, vessel U S S *Minnesota.*
Conrad Bach, 1st cl boy, pneumonia, Feb 6, Nav Hosp, Chelsea.
Reuben Owens, landsman, chronic dysentery, Feb 6, do.
Cin Anderson, 1st cl boy, typhoid fever, Feb 2, vessel U S S *Benj Morgan.*
Silas Adams, 3rd ast engr, smallpox, Feb 2, Balt, Md.
S J Anderson, actg mstr's mate, consumption, Jan 27, Nav Hosp, Memphis.
Jos Semen, landsman, consumption, Jan 29, do.
Geo Cook, seaman, gunshot wound, Feb 2, Nav Hosp, Portsmouth, Va.
J Williams, landsman, variola, Feb 1, do.
Wright Easton, 1st cl boy, pneumonia, Feb 3, do.
Geo Ferridge, ord seaman, yel fever, Sep 12, 1863, Nav Hosp, Pensacola.
Geo E Lertilla, marine, yel fever, Oct 11, do.
Jas Johnson, seaman, yel fever, oct 9, do.
Q H Martin, surg's steward, yel fever, Oct 3, do.
Wm Ackester, seaman, yel fever, Oct 7, do.
Geo Dereshire, marine, yel fever, Oct 4, do.
Benj Chilver, landsman, yel fever, Oct 5, do.
John Thomas, actg mstr's mate, yel fever, Oct 3, do.
Kingsman Flint, 2nd Lt U S M C, yel fever, Oct 15, do.
Wm Foster, contraband, yel fever, Oct 21, do.
E J Hirst, clerk, yel fever, no date, do.
Ed Hillman, q m, drowned, Feb 9, vessel *U S S Niagara.*
Rd. Lyons, 2nd cl fireman, consumption, Feb 9, Nav Asylum, Phil.
H J Kimball, actg Ast Surg, typhus fever, Feb 6, vessel U S S *Pequot.*

Died: in Gtwn, on Feb 13, Mrs Jane Abbot, wid/o the late John Abbot, aged 89 yrs. Funeral from
the residence of her son, Geo D Abbot, Mon.

Died: on Feb 14, Cecilia Eliz, y/d/o Walter L & Eliz Nicholson, aged 1 yr & 11 months. Funeral from the residence of her father, 284 B st, today.

Orphans Crt of Wash Co, D C: prsnl estate of Sarah Virginia Robinson, late of Wash City, dec'd. Thos Hutchingson, adm 2-Prsnl estate of Henry Cover, late of Gtwn, D C, dec'd. -Mary Cover, adm w a

Senate: 1-Cmte on Pensions, to whom was referred the bill granting a pension to John L Burns, of Gettysburg, Pa, reported it without amendment.

On Fri, as car #45, Mr E B Gilbert, conductor, was passing up Capitol Hill, Mr G driving, having 2 ctzns & sldrs as passengers, they put on the hind brake stopping the car. Mr G expostulated with them. One of them fired a pistol at him, the ball striking him on the right side of the back, near the spine, & making a dangerous wound. Dr Ke_sby was sent for, but he has not been able to extract the ball. The R R Co has offered a reward of $200 for the detection of the would-be assassins. Mr Gilbert is well cared for by the company, & a nurse attends him in a lodging near the depot. -Star

Hse o/Reps: 1-Cmte of Claims: bill for relief of Jacob S Lowrie & Geo A Gray: referred to the Cmte of the Whole. 2-Cmte of Claims: bill for relief of Wm G Brown; F A Holden; Eli Thayer; Hannah Barton; D W Frisby; Darius S Cole; & Hiram Bloss: referred to the Cmte of the Whole.

TUE FEB 16, 1864
Died: at the U S Marine Barracks, in Wash City, on Feb 15, Capt Allan Ramsay, U S M C, in his 26th yr. Funeral at the barracks today.

Died: in Wash City, of pneumonia, on Feb 14, Mrs Ann Rodbird, aged 75 yrs, native of Manchester, Eng, but for the last 45 years a resident of Wash City. Funeral from the residence of her dght, Mrs Jane Campbell, 414 6th st, today.

Died: on Feb 14, Harry L Callan, s/o Nicholas & Christiana V N Callan, in the 18th yr of his age. Funeral from St Matthew's Chr today.

Died: suddenly, on Feb 13, of chronic croup, Wm Edgar, 2nd s/o Ephraim & Lizzie Etchison, in the 3rd yr of his age.

Died: in Balt, Md, on Feb 15, Anne Caroline Smith, the sister of the late Saml Harrison Smith. Funeral from the Chr of the Ascension, in Wash City, on Thu.

Died: at Elk Hill, Goochland Co, Va, on Jan 14, of consumption, Mrs Heningham C Harrison, wid/o the late Randolph Harrison.

Died: at the Episc Mission, Shanghai, China, on Nov 24, 1863, after a painful illness of 7 days, Cath Ella Jones, d/o the late Gen Walter Jones, of Wash City, for 12 years a faithful & active Missionary at Shanghai.

Orphans Crt of Wash Co, D C. Case of Wm B Magruder, exc of Evan Evans, dec'd; settlement on Mar 8. -Z C Robbins, rg o/wills

John Nickinson, an old & esteemed actor, died in Cincinnati on Tue of apoplexy.

Confiscation in Alexandria:-decrees of condemnation of property of: Wm G Cazenove, R H Dulany, [Water Co Stock,] W D Corse, C W Wattles, D G Meade, Edw Sangster, G W Davis, & Wm D Nutt. Cases against J R & S M Smith, Wm Hammersly, & Wm H May were continued. -Local Item

Union meeting at Rockville, Montg Co, Md, Feb 13, 1864, to appoint delegates to attend the Union Convention to be held in Balt, Feb 22nd. B Rush Roberts called to the chair & Jos G White appt'd sec. Dels appt'd: J G England, Washington Bonifant, H F Viers, & U Griffith. R T Bentley, M Moulden, & Wm Brown, alternates.

The d/o W H Bell, of Swanton Falls, Vt, died 2 or 3 days since from the effects of laughing gas, administered by a travelling dentist. She was 17 years of age.

WED FEB 17, 1864
Died: on Feb 16, in the 63rd yr of her age, Mrs Lucy A Laskey, relict of the late Richd Laskey. Funeral from the residence of her sister, Mrs Ann Powers, 548 12th st, today.

Richmond Examiner of Feb 11-list of ofcrs who escaped from Libby Prison: Cols-

J F Boyd, 12 Army Corps	J P Spofford, 97 N Y
W G Ely, 18 Conn	C W Tilden, 16 Maine
H C Hobart, 21 Wisc	T West, 24 Wisc
W P Kendrick, 3rd W Tenn Cavalry	A D Streight, 51 Ind
W E McCreary, 21 Mich	D Miles, 79 Pa
Thos E Bose, 17th Pa	

Majors-

J P Cullins, 29 Ind	A Van Witzel, 74 Pa
G W Fitzsimmons, 13 Ind	J N Walker, 73 Ind
J H Hooper, 15 Mass	J Henry, 5 Ohio
B B McDonald, 100 Ohio	

Richmond Exam of Feb 12-those retaken:

Col J P Spofferd, 97 N Y	Lt W B Pearce, 11 Ky Cavalry
Capt J Yates, 3rd Ohio	Lt A Moore, 4 Ky
Capt G Stair, 104 N Y	P S Edmons, 67 Pa
Capt F Frank, 45 N Y	2nd Lt P H White, 83 Pa
Lt C Hanks, 57 Pa	2nd Lt J M Wasson, 40 Ohio
Lt W N Dailey, 8 Pa	2nd Lt S P Gamble, 63 Pa
Lt A B White, 4 Pa Cavalry	2nd Lt G S Gord, 84 Pa
Lt E Schroder, 74 Pa	2nd Lt S P Brown, 15 U S Cavalry
Lt W S Watson, 21 Wisc	Adj M R Small, 6 Md
Lt F Moran, 73 N Y	Isaac Johnson, engr steamer *Satellite*
Lt C H Morganm 82nd Ill	
Lt H Schwester, 82nd Ill	

Senate: 1-Bill authorizes the Com'r of the Gen Land Ofc to pay to L F Cartee $3,033 for svcs performed in srvys of pblc lands in Oregon in excess of his contract with the surveyor general of Oregon, dt'd Oct 14, 1860: passed. 2-John L Burns, of Gettysburg, Pa, to be placed upon the pension roll at $8 per month for patriotic svcs at the battle of Gettysburg, where he was wounded on Jul 1, 1863. Mr Burns is in the 71st yr of his age; his wife is 65 & in very feeble health. Mr Burns served in the war of 1812 & has voluntered twice in the present war. He supports himself with daily labor & has in a great measure recovered from his wounds. Pension is but an act of justice for gallant & patriotic svcs.

Orphans Crt of Wash Co, D C. 1-Prsnl estate of Eliz Burnside, late of Gtwn, dec'd. -Mary A Harmon, admx 2-Prsnl estate of John Hitz, late of Wash City, dec'd. -John Hitz, exc

Wash Corp: 1-Act for relief of Elias Davis: sum of $110.68 to be pd him for a deficiency in the appropriation for grading & gravelling E st north, from 9th to 10th st west.

THU FEB 18, 1864

Died: in Wash City, on Feb 17, of typhoid pneumonia, Capt Wm J Darden, aged 65 yrs; native of Va, but for the last 20 years a resident of Wash City, & except for a brief period was employed in the Gov't P O Dept. Funeral from his late residence on 9th st, today.

Died: in Wash City, on Feb 17, after a short but painful illness, Jos Blackie, in his 31st yr. Funeral from his late residence, 530 Mass av.

Supreme Crt of D C, in Equity #1141. Matter of the estate of the late Wm Worthington. The accounts of Saml Stott, trustee; & parties interested are to meet at the Court-hse on Feb 25, -W Redin, auditor

Orphans Crt of Wash Co, D C. Case of Sylvester B Boarman, adm of Susannah Boarman, dec'd; settlement on Mar 12. -Z C Robbins, rg o/wills

Obit-Cmdor Wm J McCluney, of U S N, died at his residence in Brooklyn, on Feb 11, in his 69th yr: He entered the navy on Jan 1, 1812 & took his first cruise on the U S sloop-of-war *Wasp* as a Midshipman.

Ofcrs who recently escaped from Libby prison, at Richmond, visited the Balt American:
Maj L P Collins, 77 Ind   Capt Matt Boyd, 73 Ind   Capt Clarke, 79 Ill

Wash Corp: 1-Ptn of Mrs B P Fletcher, asking the return of taxes pd by mistake: referred to the Cmte on Finance. 2-Commuication from Ch S Jones: referred to the Cmte on Health.

Cumberland Gap, Feb 17. Capt J B Watkins, provost mrshl at this post, reports the average number of deserters from Longstreet's army who report to him as 5 per day. They complain of being heartily sick of the war.

Our fellow ctzn, John H Waring, has not yet been released from Fort Delaware. The Pres directed the Sec of War to release him, but Sec Stanton said he would see about it. As yet this functionary has not been carried out the directions of the Pres. -Marlboro Gaz, 17th

FRI FEB 19, 1864

For sale, Snowden's new *Bermingham Manor*, 147+ acs, as in deed from Isaac Simmons & wife to Rachel Tyson, dt'd Mar 21, 1857; land lying partly in A A Co & PG Cos, Md. -Saml Snowden, Fayette st, Balt, Md. Frank H Stockett, Annapolis, Md

Senate: 1-Cmte on Naval Affairs: ptn of Moses Kelly, adm of Maj W W Russell, dec'd, late paymstr in the U S Marine Corps, praying for certain allowances in settlement of Maj Russell's accounts, reported it back, & asked to be discharged from the further consideration of the ptn. They think it is not a matter that comes under their jurisdiction. 2-Cmte on Pblc Lands: bill for relief of the heirs of Noah Wiswall: recommendation that it pass. The claim is a small one, & a very just one. 3-Bill for the relief of Mary A Baker, wid/o Brig Gen Edw D Baker, referred.

Mr E B Gilbert, conductor of the Wash City railway, who was shot by an unknown person on Fri last, died yesterday. The assassin is yet at large. Wash, D C

Fire in Phil, Feb 18, commenced in the cooper shop of John S Curb, in Front st below Lombard, consuming 8 dwlg hses, occupied by poor famlies.

Despatch from the Army of the Potomac says that Mr Theodore Barnard, the Army Correspondent of the Assoc Press, died at headqrtrs yesterday, of penumonia, after nearly 2 weeks sickness. He was a ctzn of Wash, where he leaves a family. He has been employed in the agency ofc in this city, & had been acting correspondent for more than 2 yrs. His death will be deeply regretted by many friends.

SAT FEB 20, 1864
Died: on Feb 18, after a long & painful illness of consumption, Wm Phillips, printer, in his 57th yr. Funeral from his late residence, 436 7th st, today.

Died: on Feb 19, of diptheria & croup, Anthony Howard, s/o Anthony & the late Eliz Jane Buchly, aged 2 yrs, 1 month & 18 days. Funeral from the residence of his father, 303 Pa av, today.

Ft Monroe, Feb 19-escaped ofcrs have arrived here, viz:

Capt D G Caldwell, 123 Ohio	Lt E J Higley, 33 Ohio
Capt R R Adams, 89 Ohio	Lt W A Williams, 123 Ohio
Lt E S Scott, 89 Ohio	Lt Eli Foster, 30 Ind.

Expedition to Fla: N Y, Feb 19. The steamer *Atlantic* brings the following detachments of re-enlisted vets:

118 men of the 52nd Pa, Col Hoyt	125 men of the 89th N Y & 43 men of the
275 men of the 10th Conn, Maj Greely	3rd N Y Artl
407 men of the 24th Mass, Capt Redding	

MON FEB 22, 1864
Mrd: at Balt, Md, on Feb 13, by Rev Edw McColgan, Lt Com A Ward Weaver, U S N, to Ida, d/o Alpheus Hyatt, of Wash City.

Died: on Feb 20, Hon John E Bouligny, of New Orleans, La. Funeral from the residence of Geo Parker, Four-&-a-half & C sts, today.

Died: in Wash City, on Feb 18, at the residence of her step-father, Robt S Wharton, in the 18th yr of her age, Miss Laura V Test, d/o the late Hon John Test, formerly a Rep in Congress from Ind. [Obit in Ntl Intel of Mar 1, 1864.]

Died: on Feb 21, Maggie Eliz, d/o S W K & Annie E Handy, aged 2 years & 7 months. Funeral from their residence, 566 14th st, today.

Deaths reported to the Navy Dept for the week ending Feb 20, 1864:
Michl Whelan, seaman, remit fever, Aug 13, vessel U S S *Curlew*.
Wm Wright, 1st cl boy, remit fever, Oct 2, do.
Overton S Cannon, 1st cl boy, affection of the heart, Oct 18, vessel U S S *Carondelet*.
John Shay, landsman, cerebritis, Feb 4, Nav Hosp, Memphis.
Maurice Fitzgerald, 2nd cook, delerium tremens, Feb 14, do.
Jas McGee, landsman, remit fever, Fev 12, Rec Ship, Phil.
Wm C Aveline, q m, menergetis, Sep 7, vessel U S S *Naumkeag*.
W H Brown, seaman, asphyxia, Nov 17, vessel U S S *Kenwood*.
Thos C Tempest, seaman, pneumonia, Nov 13, vessel U S S *Lafayette*.
Alan Ramsay, Capt, U S M C, smallpox, Feb 15, Washington.
Joel Skepper, landsman, variola, Feb 12, Nav Hosp, N Y.
P Cheeseborough, landsman, consumption, Feb 11, do.

Chas W Tracy, 1st cl boy, pneumonia, Feb 11, do.
Wm H Stackhouse, landsman, inflam of brain, Feb 11, Nav Hosp, Washington.
Wm Davis, pensioner, asthma, Feb 14, Nav Asylum.
Barney Geehen, landsman, consumption, Jan 28, Nav Hosp, N Orleans.
Jas Seede, marine, epilepsy, Jan 25, vessel U S S *Tennessee.*
Lawrence Bellew, ord seaman, inflam of brain, Nov 18, vessel U S S *St Marys.*
John Shea, musician, drowned, Dec 26, do.
Col Wolley, landsman, rubeola, Feb 15, Phil.
Jas Eldridge, 1st cl boy, blank, Dec 19, Cairo, Ill.
Chas W Bott, 1st cl boy, dropsy, Feb 14, vessel U S S *St Lawrence.*
Jas Watts, landsman, consumption, Feb 15, Navy Yd, Washington.
John Little, landsman, pneumonia, Feb 17, Nav Asylum.
Henry Williams, seaman, gastritis, Feb 7, vessel U S S *Metacomet.*
Robt Benton, ofcr's cook, gunshot wound, Jan 3, vessel U S S *Paw Paw.*
John Thomas, seaman, injury from fall, Jan 30, vessel U S S *Tyler.*
Moses Black, landsman, drowned, Feb 15, vessel U S S *Com Jones.*
Thos E Fisher, ofcr's steward, drowned, Feb 15, vessel U S S *Minnesota.*
Townsend Hopkins, actg mstr's mate, gunshot wound, Jan 15, vessel U S S *Choctaw.*
Jas G Spencer, landsman, dysentery, Jan 30, Marine Hosp, Key West.
Chas Tillman, 1st cl boy, consumption, Jan 30, do.

Orphans Crt of Wash Co, D C. Case of Mrs Maria A Johnston, admx of John R Johnston, dec'd; settlement on Mar 15. -Z C Robbins, rg o/wills

Geo A Coffey, U S Dist Atty at Phil, died on Sat of paralysis.

The funeral of Cmder Geo L Selden, of U S N, took place in Balt, Md, last Fri. The dec'd was about 50 years of age, s/o the Cary Selden, of Wash City.

An Irishman named Cornelius Tuell, who lives on Third st, between F & G, murdered his wife on Wed. A son of the murderer, a boy 10 years of age, testified that he saw his father strike his mother with an axe. Father told us [witness & little sister] to go & stay with Mrs Sewell. Mr Tuell buried the body privately alleging that she had died of smallpox. Mr Tuell is about 28 years of age.

TUE FEB 23, 1864
Died: on Feb 22, of consumption, Henry A W Parker, s/o Selby & Sarah A Parker, aged 19 yrs. Funeral from the residence of his mother, 490½ Mass av, today.

Died: in Sacramento, Calif, on Feb 17, Frank W Fuller, formerly a resident of Wash City.

Died: on Feb 21, Henry W Balmain. Funeral from 291 F st, today.

Orphans Crt of Wash Co, D C. Prsnl estate of Eliza Lucas, late of Gtwn, D C, dec'd. -Walter S Cox, exc

Obit-John Edmond Bouligny: born in New Orleans, Feb 5, 1824, died in Wash City, on Feb 20, of consumption.

Died: in Cincinnati, on Feb 17, Wm Key Bond, in his 72nd yr; born in St Mary's Co, Md; came to Ohio in 1812, & settled at Chillicothe, then the capital of the State. He removed to Cincinnati in 1841.

Died: at Booklyn, N Y, on Jan 22, Mrs Hepsa Ely Silliman, w/o Gold S Silliman, in the 86th yr of her age. She leaves a large family.

In Chancery, #1661-Thos E France, et al, against Robt Brockett, et al; report of trustee confirmed unless to the contrary be shown. -R J Meigs, clerk

WED FEB 24, 1864
Died: in Phil, on Feb 20, Mrs Sophie H Phipps, w/o Geo W Phipps, & d/o the late Hon J H Lyman, of Northampton, Mass.

Died: on Feb 22, after a long & painful illness, Mrs Mgt Ann Hutchinson, widow o/the late John Hutchinson, & d/o the late Geo Bean, of Wash City, in her 29th yr. Funeral from her late residence on 3rd st, today.

Col West, commanding the Union forces at Wmsburg, Va, gives the names of ofcrs who escaped from Richmond, & arrived within his lines:

Col Chas W Tilden, 16 Mass Vols	Lt Randolph, 5 U S Artl
Maj Hooper, 15 Mass	Capt Fisher, of the Signal Corps
Capt Chamberlain, 97 N Y	

St Louis, Feb 22-A dght of Rev Dr Elliott, aged 17 yrs, & a dght & son of Thos L Salisbury, of the Home Mutual Ins Co, aged 18 & 14 yrs, were drowned on Sat while skating near this city.

Ex-U S Senator Borland, of Arkansas, died in Texas recently.

Hon Edw W Whelpley, Chief Justice of N J, died at Morristown on Sunday.

THU FEB 25, 1864
Died: on Feb 24, Jacob Gideon, in his 76th yr. Resident of Wash City for 60 yrs. Funeral from his late residence, 468 7th st, Feb 26.

Died: on Feb 22, Horace, infant s/o Thos F & Martha Maguire, aged 15 months & 13 days.

Judge Olin, of the Criminal Crt, on Tue passed sentence upon a number of prisoners amongst whom were Emanuel Pollard, negro, sentenced to death for the murder of Geo Butler, negro. Also, Jeremiah Hendricks, for the murder of Dennis Shanahan. Both to be hung on Apr 1 next. Peter Gooden, negro, convicted of the murder of Geo Banks: a bill of exceptions was filed.

Mr Sam F Briggs, the clerk of Paymstr Malone, arrested on suspicion of $70,000 robbery, has been released, no evidence against him. Maj Malone & his son, age about 21 yrs, are in custody & the affair is being investigated. -Local Item

We take pleasure in stating that Col Waring, PG Co, Md, has been released & will return home.

The Richmond Sentinel of Feb 20 says: all were hung at Kinston, N C, on Feb 16-all for deserting to the enemy & taking up arms on the enemy's side. [Similar coverage below.]

J S Brock	C Hoffman	A J Brittan
Wm Haddock	Stephen Jones	J J Sumerline

137

| W H Doughty | Lewis Freeman | Jos Brooks |
| Lewis Taylor | W D Jones | C R Cuthrell |

Wholesale hanging in N C. The Richmond Sentinel of Feb 20 says: all were hung at Kinstone, N C, on the 16th inst, & 7 were hung on the 13th–all for deserting to the enemy & taking up arms on the enemy's side. They all received the ordinance of baptism, according to their own dictates. [See above coverage.]

J S Brock	A J Britan	Lewis Freeman
Wm Haddock	J J Sumerline	W D Jones
C Hoffman	W H Doughty	Jos Brooks
Stephen Jones	Lewis Taylor	C R Cuthrell

FRI FEB 26, 1864

Mrd: on Feb 24, at New Market, Fred'k Co, Md, by Rev B G W Reed, R B Ferguson, of Wash, to Miss E Virginia Falconer, of the former place.

Died: on Feb 24, Mary, w/o Lemuel J Denham. Funeral from residence of her hsbnd, 430 G st, Sat.

Died: on Feb 24, Mrs Annie H Waters, w/o Geo Waters, in her 49th yr. Funeral from her late residence, 37 Market st, Gtwn, today.

Died: on Feb 5, in Alexandria, Va, in the 74th yr of her age, Mrs Susanna M Kennedy, relict of the late John Kennedy. She was for many years a bookseller in Wash City.

Supreme Crt of D C, in Equity #150. Regarding-decree for sale of lot 30 in sq 367, Wash City for payment of a judgment against J W Nye. Jun 10, 1863, Geo Mattingly obtained a judgment against Nye for $2,450. Nye is owner of said lot & on Jul 2, 1857 a deed was executed by J C Harkness, acting as trustee for Nye, conveying said lot to Walter S Cox, to secure the payment of 3 promissory notes, each dated Jun 25, 1857, payable to Rebecca Pinkney. All notes are fully pd & no release of the lot has been executed. R Pinkney is a non-resident of Wash. -Geo P Fisher, Justice Sup Crt D C. -R J Meigs, clerk

Supreme Crt of D C. Jas Adams et al, vs Asaph K Childs & Susan Childs, his wife, et al. Regarding-appoint a new trustee in place of Griffith Coombe & John P Ingle, dec'd. Dfndnts reside out side of D C. -Geo P Fisher, Justice Sup Crt of D C.

Maj Gen Franz Sigel assigned to the Dept of Western Va. He will at once enter upon his duties.

B B French, Com'r of Pblc Bldgs, heads the list of corporators for a grand Masonic Hall to be extended in this District. The institution is to have a capital of $300,00, in shares of $20 each.

Maj Gen Pleasanton, the distinguished cavalry ofcr, is in town. He was in communication yesterday with the War Dept. It is believed the Gen will be assigned to the position of the Chief of Cavalry Bureau.

SAT FEB 27, 1864

Died: on Feb 25, John T Robinson, the eldest s/o John & Augusta M Robinson, in his 19th yr. Funeral from his father's residence, B & 14th st, today.

Died: on Feb 25, at the residence of his son, in Montg Co, Md, Edw Stubbs, in the 80th yr of his age. Funeral on Sat at *Carroll's Chapel.*

Lot holders of the *Foundry Burial Ground* are to meet in the lecture rm of the church, 14th & G sts, Feb 29. -R T Morsell, sec

From New Orleans & the Gulf. N Y, Feb 26. 1-The steamer *Morning Star* has arrived here from New Orleans on the 20th, via Havana on the 22nd inst. Two Union sldrs, Wells, of 9th Ill Cavalry, & Ferguson, of 6th Ill Cavalry, who were captured at Moscow, Tenn, on Dec 6, had arrived at New Orleans. They escaped from prison at Cahawba, Ala, & walked thru the country at night, eating nothing for 6 days. On reaching East Escambia Bay, Fla, they were taken on board a schnr bound to Pensacola, & thence to New Orleans. 2-The presence of 2 or 3 gunboats in Grand Lake shows that the rebels are again up & doing. Gen Dick Taylor commands the rebel forces.

MON FEB 29, 1864

Deaths reported to the Navy Dept for the week ending Feb 27, 1864:
Jas Caldwell, gunner's mate, cancer, Feb 3, 1864, hosp, New Orleans.
Clifton Gleson, fireman, pericarditi, Feb 12, 1864, hosp, Memphis.
John Smith, seaman, consumption, Feb 13, 1864, do.
Geo Knepfer, marine, adynamia, Feb 16, 1864, hosp, Norfolk, Va.
Mannet Thomas, 3rd cl boy, consumption, Feb 22, 1864, do.
Nap Johnson, 1st cl boy, pneumonia, Jan 1, 1864, vessel U S S *Gen Lyon.*
Morris Mitchell, 1st cl boy, unknown, Jan 10, 1864, do.
Jas O'Leary, [Oliver,] landsman, poisoned, Feb 14, 1864, vessel U S S *Black Hawk.*
Jacob Dubois, colored, seaman, drowned, Feb 11, 1864, vessel U S S *Cameron.*
Geo S Delden, cmder, heart disease, Feb 14, 1864, vessel U S S *Baltimore*
Thos Stephenson, 2nd gunner, hoemoptysis, Sep 19, 1864, vessel U S S *Wyoming.*
Sidney Johnson, contraband, bronchitis, Feb 18, 1864, vessel U S S *Clara Dobson.*
Jos Ross, seaman, fracture, Jan 6, 1864, Hilton Head, S C.
Levi E Bates, marine, erysipelas, Feb 25, *1863, Navy Yd, Wash. *As written.
Oscar D Haggert, coal heaver, debility, Feb 26, 1864, hosp, N Y.
Milton C Cook, landsman, blank, Feb 25, 1864, Rec Ship, Phil.
J S Deuch, actg mstr's mate, typhoid fever, Feb 25, 1864, hosp, N Y.

Balt Annual Conference of the Meth Episc Chr to convene in Wesley Chapel, 5th & F sts, Wash, on Mar 2. Rev Bishop Scott will preside: Rev Wm B Edwards, sec; Rev Henry C Wentwood, Ast Sec of conf. Candidates for admissions as preachers on trial:

Wm Krebs	W T D Clemm	H N Sipes
A S Kank	E D Owen	David Thomas
M L Haley	W F Speake	F S Cassady
T T Wysong	C Parkison	A J Myers
R R Murphy	C A Reid	

Sunday Schools, clerical:

J A McCauley	Jno Thrush	John W Cornelius

Lay:

Richd Donohue	C H Lane	W N Berkley

Members:

M L Hawley	W H Chapman	W F Speake

Tract Cause:

M Goheen	J H M Lemon	W K Boyle

Exec Cmte on Missionary Soc:

W M D Ryan	H C Westwood	F S Cassady

Conf Stewards:

T H W Monroe	J W Start	S V Leech

Necessitous cases:

L F Morgan	C Parkison	B H Smith
B N Brown	W Prettyman	

Church Exensions:

N J B Morgan	E P Phelps	Thos Sewall
John Lanahan	D Thomas	

Preachers' Aid Soc:

Wm Hamilton	Thos Sewall	Jas A McCauley
Wm B Edwards	T A Morgan	

Of the ministers who will be here we may expect to see: Alfred Griffith, now the very oldest preacher of the good old Baltimore Conference. In 1806 his name was entered on the rolls in Balt. Also:

John Beall, 1814	Thos H W Munro, 1827	Jas A McCauley, 1850
Wm Prettyman, 1814	L F Morgan, 1834	Wm M D Ryan, 1839
Wm Hamilton, 1818	Wm H Chapman, 1848	

Thos Sewall & John Lanahan, 1838
Job W Lambeth, Wm Krebs, T T Wysong, 1842

The Wash Dist:

From Wesley Chapel: Rev B Peyton Brown
East Wash: T H W Munro
Fletcher: J N Davis
Asbury & Mount Zion: Job W Lambeth
Gtwn: W H Chapman
Va Dist: Rochville Crct: F S Cassady, W K Boyle
Montg Crct: S V Leech & C H Mytinger

West Gtwn & Tenallytown: J L Gilbert
Ellicott's Mills, Md: W T D Clemm
Patapsco Crct: A S Hank
Howard Crct: W Prettyman
Patuxent Crct: H C McDaniel

Senate: 1-Cmte on P O & Post Rds: bill for relief of A T Spencer & Gordon S Hubbard. 2-Cmte of Claims: adverse report on ptn of Gustavus A Belzur, praying for compensation for losses sustained while in the discharge of his duties as sutler of 75th Regt Pa Vols, in consequence of the capture of his goods by rebels between Wash & the Army of the Potomac. 3-Memorial of John Colhoun, Cmder in the U S Navy, protesting against the action of the late advisory board in withholding from him a recommendation for promotion to which he considers himself entitled. 4-Memorial of Henry French, Cmder in the U S Navy, praying he may be restored to his rightful position in the Navy, which he alleges has been wrongfully & unjustly withheld from him by the board of ofcrs to scrutinize the active list of ofcrs of the Navy. 5-Ptn of Geo W Doty, a Lt in U S Navy, praying for the passage of an act for fair & impartial trial of ofcrs to whom injustice has been done by the board under act of Jul 16, 1862, with accompanying papers. 6-Memorial of R W Meade, Cmder in U S Navy, praying for same. 7-Memorial of Cmder Edmund Lanier, U S Navy, praying for relief from the action of the late advisory board in failing to recommend him for promotion. 8-Ptn of Lt Egbert Thompson, U S Navy, protesting against the action of the late advisory board in failing to recommend him for promotion. 9-Cmte on Pensions: adverse report on ptn of Laura M Newcomb, of Providence, R I, wid/o the late Cmder Henry S Newcomb, U S Navy, praying for a pension; & also an adverse report on ptn of ctzns of Black Hawk, Iowa, praying that a pension may be granted to the wid/o Capt Fred'k S Washburn equal to that of Col, from the time of his death.

Orphans Crt of Wash Co, D C. Prsnl estate of Horatio G O'Neal, late of Wash City, dec'd. -Eliza J O'Neal.

The widow of ex-Pres Harrison died at North Bend yesterday. -Cincinnati, Feb 27

Died: at Lancaster, Ohio, Feb 20th, Mrs Maria Ewing, w/o Hon Thos Ewing, of Ohio.

Died: at Reading, Vt, on Feb 6, Mrs Sarah Rice, aged 95 yrs, 5 months & 14 days; widow of Abiel Rice, a sgt in the Rev army, & has drawn a pension from the Gov't for many years past.

TUE MAR 1, 1864
Died: on Feb 28, at *Alton*, the residence of her father, in Montg Co, Md, Virginia Lee, infant d/o Raymond W & Cath Burche, aged nearly 4 months.

Died: at Kalorama Hospital, near Wash City, on Feb 17, Lt J W Davis, late of Mosby's [rebel] btln, & previous to the rebellion of U S naval svc, in his 27th yr.

Died: on Feb 28, in Wash City, after a lingering pulmonary illness, Royston Betts, aged 50 yrs; native of Va, but for several years past a resident of Wash City, as the Disbursing Clerk of the Agric Dept. Funeral from his late residence, 25 Four & ½ st, today. [Obit-Mar 4: a kind hsbnd, father & friend. Buried at Washington on Mar 1.]

Supreme Crt of D C, in Equity #168. Wm Lyles vs John Douglas, Wm H Smith & others. Sale of land in D C to satisfy judgment in favor of Wm Lyles against John Douglass. In 1856 Douglas purchased from Henry Douglas rl estate in Washington; although Douglas was the real purchaser & pd for same, one of the land records, to be made to Wm H Smith in trust for the sole use of Virginia Douglas, w/o the said John Douglas. Conveyance to Smith was fraudulent. Smith resides out of D C. -R J Meigs, clerk

Orphans Crt of Wash Co, D C. 1-Case of Chas Mades, exc of Bonaventura S Chad, dec'd; settlement on Mar 22. -Z C Robbins, rg o/wills 2-Prsnl estate of Saml F Vinton, late of Wash City, dec'd. -Sarah M Goddard, admx, d b n, w a

WED MAR 2, 1864
Senate: 1-Cmte on Pensions: ptn of Nancy M Gunsally, formerly wid/o Lyman M Richmond, praying for a renewal of pension of half pay, submitted an adverse report. 2-Also from the same cmte, the ptn of Wm Cook, of Decatur Co, Ind, praying for arrears of pension. 3-Same cmte: referred a ptn of ctzns of Ohio, praying that a pension may be granted to Mgt M Stafford, wid/o Reuben Stafford, of Coshocton Co, Ohio, who was killed while assisting the provost mrshl in arresting deserters, submitted a report, with a bill for her relief. 4-Senate passed a joint resolution authorizing the payment of prize money due to Cmder Abner Read, U S Navy, to his widow, Constance Read. The share of prize money due or to become due to him for prizes taken by the U S vessel *New London*, while under his command, in 1861.

Mrd: on Mar 1, by Rev Mr Finckel, Mr Chas G Lorch to Miss Adaline Shubert, all of Wash City.

Orphans Crt of Wash Co, D C. Prsnl estate of Mgt Ann Hutchinson, late of Wash City, dec'd. -Thos Hutchinson, exc

Geo P Kane, formerly Mrshl of Police of Balt, Md, lately arrived in Richmond & has been made a colonel.

Death of a poetess. Adelaide Ann Proctor, the d/o "Harry Cornwall," & author of "Legends & Lyrics. [No date-news item-appears lately.]

Geo P Kane, formerly Mrshl of Police of the city of Balt, lately arrived in Richmond, has been made a colonel.

THU MAR 3, 1864
Orphans Crt of Wash Co, D C. Prsnl estate of Owen Murray, late of Wash City, dec'd. -E M Bartholow, adm, d b n

Prisoner from Richmond. Ft Monroe, Mar 1. Arrived on flag of truce boat today.

Maj Wade, 73rd Ind	Drs Robinson & Baker, Lt Doughty, of
Capt Barton, 10th Mass	Streight's command
Col Dulaney, of Gov Pierpont's staff	Mr Bulkley, of N Y Herald
	7 ctzn prisoners, all from Richmond

For sale-*Willow Brook*, about 814 acs, in Forest of PG Co, Md; with dwlg hse & mill. I desire to give unlimited attention to my profession. -Daniel Clarke, atty. Upper Marlborough, PG Co, Md.

Appointments by the President:
Maj Gen Ulysses S Grant, U S vols, to be Maj Gen, Jul 4, 1863, to fill vacancy.
Maj Gen Geo B Meade, U S vols to be Brig Gen, Jul 2, 1863, vice Sumner, dec'd.
Maj Gen Wm T Sherman, U S vols, to be Brig Gen, Jul 4, 1863, to fill vacancy.
Maj Gen Jas B McPherson, U S vols, to be Brig Gen, Aug 1, 1863, vice Harney, retired.
Maj Gen Geo H Thomas, U S vols, to be Brig Gen, Oct 27, 1863, vice Anderson, retires.
Brig Gen Gouverneur K Warren, U S vols, to be Maj Gen in the vol force now in svc of the U S, May 3, 1863. Brig Gen Alfred Pleasanton, of U S vols, to be Maj Gen in the vol force, Jun 22, 1863.
John Frazier, jr, has been removed from the ofc of provost mrshl of the 1st Dist of Md, & Col Wm J Leonard appt'd in his place.

In the Supreme Crt of D C yesterday a decree of divorce was granted to Caroline M Willard against Jos C Willard.

Mrs Harrison, wid/o Pres Harrison, who died at North Bend, Ohio, on Feb 26, was the d/o John Cleves Symmes, the founder of the Miama settlements. She mrd in 1795 to [then] Capt Harrison, who was in command of Ft Washington, the site of the present city of Cincinnati.

FRI MAR 4, 1864
Died: on Mar 2, of congestion of the lungs, Emily Louisa, y/d/o W W & Helen M Jacob, aged 22 months & 24 days. Funeral from their residence, 525 H st, today.

Died: in Madison, Ga, on Jan 2, Dr Wm S Meire, 34 years of age, leaving a wife & 2 chldrn to mourn their loss.

Municipal election in Alexandria resulted in the choice of Chas A Ware for Mayor, 121 votes; J P L Westcott received 28 votes, & J T Armstrong, 8.

On Wed evening, Roger A Flood, Pres of the Mechanics' Bank of Troy, N Y, returned by train from the Army of the Potomac, where he had been paying bounties to the re-enlisting vets. While walking on the track near the depot in Alexandria, he was struck by a train & died an hour & a half later. He had $80,000 of county funds with him at the time.

Senate: 1-Cmte on Military Affairs: referred the bill for relief of Chas Anderson, assignee of John James, of Texas, reported it without an amendment. 2-Cmte on Claims: ptn of Chas A Pitcher for his relief: resolution was passed. 3-Bill for relief of B C Bailey: to be pd $4,496, being the damages for detention & expenses incurred in the seizure of the ship *Argo* by the flag ofcr of the blockading fleet in May 1861.

SAT MAR 5, 1864

Chancery sale of properrty on High st, Gtwn; in the cause wherein Jos H Shemwell, cmplnt, & Anna E Griffin & another, dfndnts. Improved by a brick hse 2½ stories high. -F W Jones, trust -Thos Dowling, auct, Gtwn, D C

The mgrs of Glenwood Cemetery, Wash, D C, have resolved to raise the price of lots to thirty cents per sq ft. -Jos S Clos, Pres

Guardian sale: Francis Mohun, guardian of Anne Mohun, sale of rl est-parts of lots 4 & 5 in sq 1001, with 2 story brick hse, being the property occupied by Wm H Carico. -F Mohun, guardian -Jas C McGuire & Co, aucts

Wash Corp: 1-Claim of Jas Towles was referred to the Cmte on Finance. 2-Ptn of Geo W Riggs & others, asking that a certain st be graded: referred to the Cmte on Improvements. 3-Ptn of John Clark for the remission of a fine: referred to the Cmte of Claims. 4-Cmte of Claims reported back the bill of the Brd of Cmn Cncl for the relief of Jas Raulsin: read a 3rd time & passed. Same for bill for relief of John Dunn. 5-Cmte of Claims: adverse report on the ptn of John H Diltz, asking that the cmte be discharged: which was so ordered.

MON MAR 7, 1864

Deaths reported to the Navy Dept for the week ending Mar 5, 1864:
Silas Gray, 3rd cl pilot, laryngitis, Feb 6, vessel U S S *Sebago*.
Orven Gator, 1st cl boy, chronic diarrhoea, Feb 16, Nav Hosp, Memphis.
John Cannon, coal heaver, consumption, Feb 19, do.
John Bernard, ship's cook, diarrhoea, Feb 21, do.
Jas Masked, pensioner, remit fever, Feb 27, Nav Asylum.
Addison H Snowman, ord seaman, diarrhoea, Feb 25, Nav Hosp, Portsmouth.
Wm Barry, coal heaver, typhoid fever, Feb 27, Nav Hosp, N Y.
Allen Smith, landsman, blank, Feb 28, do.
Solomon Greshaw, blank, variola, Jan 29, vessel U S S *Ben Morgan*.
John Diggs, blank, variola, Jan 29, do.
Dawson Phoenix, Lt cmder, nervous exhaustion, Feb 20, Phil.
Jerry White, 1st cl boy, congested chill, Feb 29, vessel U S S *St Lawrence*.
John Duffy, 1st cl fireman, remit fever, Jan 16, vessel U S S *Whitehead*.
Wm Rodderman, ord seaman, dysentery, Jan 4, vessel U S S *Hetzel*.

Geo A Smith, 1st cl boy, typhoid fever, Feb 20, Nav Hosp, Pensacola.
Thos Wilson, seaman, typhoid fever, Feb 12, do.

Died: on Mar 5, Alberta Carpenter, the last child of S W K & Annie E Handy, aged 1 yr & 7 months. Funeral today.

$160 reward for runaway slaves, from the farm of the late Geo Humes, in PG Co, Md, who belong to the estate of said Humes: Danl-50; Maria-40; Louis-11; Danl-4; Rebecca-21; Stephen-13; Harriet-5; Matilda-11 months. –Thos W Burch, John T Burch, adms pend lite.

It has been said that Chas A Weed, of Stamford, Conn, bought the estate of Sec Judah P Benjamin, of the Southern Conference, on the Mississippi River, near Baton Rouge, for $140,000.

Hse o/Reps: the clerk read the ltr of the Com'r of Pensions as follows: [dated Pension Ofc, Feb 18, 1864.] Rev pensioners:
Jas Barham, on St Louis, Mo, roll, at $32.33 per annum; born in Southampton Co, Va, May 18, 1761; aged 99 years & 9 months.
John Goodnow, on Boston, Mass, roll, at $36.67 per annum; born in Sudbury, Middlesex Co, Mass, Jan 30, 1762; age 102 years & 1½ months.
Amaziah Goodwin, on Portland, Maine, roll, at $38.33; born in Somersworth, Stafford Co, N H, Feb 16, 1759; age 105 yrs.
Wm Hutchins, on Portland, Maine, roll, at $21.66; born in York, York Co, Maine, [then Massachusetts,] in the yr 1764.
Adam Link, on Cleveland, Ohio, roll, at $30 per annum; born in Wash Co, Pa, age 102 yrs.
Benj Miller, on Albany, N Y, roll, at $24.54 per annum; born in Springfield, Mass, Apr 4, 1764; age 99 years & 10½ months.
Alex'r Maroney, on Albany, N Y, roll, at $8 per mo; born in the yr 1770; enlisted at Lake Geo, N Y; age 94 yrs; enlisted by his father as he was young.
John Pettingill, on Albany, N Y, roll, at $50 per annum; born in Windham, Conn, Nov 30, 1766; age 97 years & 2½ months.
Danl Waldo, on Albany, N Y, roll, at $96 per annum; born in Windham, Conn, Sep 10, 1762; age 101 years & 5¼ months.
Saml Downing, [papers do not show his age,] on Albany, N Y, roll, at $80 per annum, served in 2nd N H Regt.
Lemuel Cook, on Albany, N Y, roll, at $100 per annum; no age or birthplace given in papers.
Jonas Gates/Gales, on the St Johns___, Vt, roll. At $8 per mo; papers mislaid.

TUE MAR 8, 1864
Mrd: on Mar 3, by Rev Mr Drumm, at the residence of the bride's father, near Bristol, Pa, Mary Bovell, d/o J Edw Jones, to Edw J Lewis, of Wash City.

Died: on Mar 6, Mrs Mary C Fitzpatrick, relict of the late John C Fitzpatrick, in her 56th yr. Funeral from her late residence on so B st, Wed.

Died: in Gtwn, D C, on Mar 7, at the residence of her father-in-law, Jacob Ramsburg, Mrs Amanda H Ramsburg, in the 26th yr of her age, w/o Valerius E Ramsburg, & d/o Lewis Payne. Funeral today from the Bridge St Presby Chr.

Orphans Crt of Wash Co, D C. Prsnl estate of Edwin C Morgan, adm of Lewis J Kennedy, dec'd; settlement on Mar 29. -Z C Robbins, rg o/wills

Potomac farm for sale, estate which Richd W Bryan now resides, 350 acs; opposite Mt Vernon; adjoins the lands of Messrs Luke W B Hutchins, Cawood Brawner, & Tubman. -Edw W Belt, atty

Official: Dept of State, Mar 7, 1864. Information from the U S Cnsl at Talcahuano, Chili, of the death, on Nov 28, of M Nicholas, & on Dec 1, 1863, of Geo Diaz, both ctzns of the U S.

Portland, Me, Mar 7. Jacob McLellan, the Union candidate for Mayor, is elected over John B Carroll by a majority of 1,130 votes, viz: McLellan-1,941, Carroll-805.

WED MAR 9, 1863
Died: on Mar 7, John McLeod, in the 30th yr of his age, leaving a bereaved widow. Funeral from his late residence, 522 K st, today. [Mbr of the Topographical Soc.]

Died: at Balt, Md, on Mar 7, Mrs Ann Willson, aged 95 yrs.

Orphans Crt of Wash Co, D C. Case of Sarah Butler & Alex'r Rutherford, excs of Abraham Butler, dec'd; settlement on Apr 2. -Z C Robbins, rg o/wills

Wash, D C. Corporators of the new Union Gas Light Co:

Sayles J Bowen	Robt M Wiltbank	D C Forney
Benj B French	Andrew M Kinny	S P Brown
Wm Elma	Wm H Baldwin	John Green
Wm Bates	Z D Gilman	Gamaliel Guy

Mr Jos L Savage, hardware dealer of Wash City, was arrested in N Y by Gov't ofcrs, & lodged in Ft Lafayette, on charge of defrauding the Gov't. His store on D st, near 10th was taken possession of by military detectives. Alterations in certificates of the navy agency at N Y of the delivery of goods purchased of him for the use of the navy at the Brooklyn navy yd; amounts to a large sum of money.

Senate: Cmte on Pensions: referred ptn of ctzns of Portland, Maine, praying a pension be granted to Jessie Gould, wid/o Danl Gould, who was accidentally shot while assisting in discharging the guns & ammunition from the schnr *Archer*, taken from the Tacony pirates: passed to a 2nd reading.

Hse o/Reps: 1-Bill passed for the benefit of John Dickson, of Ill: to be pd $21,000, to compensate him for damages he sustained by reason of the failure of J W Belger, q m, of U S vols, to receive 100,000 bushels of corn tendered him by said Dickson, under a contract therefor. 2-Mr Brown, of W Va, reported from the Cmte of Claims a joint resolution for the relief of Aaron T Doll: read & committed.

N Y, Mar 8. The Herald's army despatch says that the Richmond Sentinel of the 5th inst states that Col Dahlgren was killed in an encounter with the 9th Va, in King & Queen Co, & that 70 or 80 of his men were captured.

THU MAR 10, 1864
The Richmond Sentinel of Mar 5 contains information of the death of Col Dahlgren; in an encounter with Lt Col Pollard, 9th Va. Some 80 of his men were captured. [See information of Mar 9.]

From Western Va: Cumberland, Md, Mar 6, 1864. Brig Gen G W Cullum, Chief of Staff: A cavalry force, sent under command of Lt Col Root, 15th N Y Cavalry, has just returned from Hardy & Pendleton Counties. They effectually destroyed all the saltpetre works near Franklin, in the latter county.

Gen Crook reports the capture of 40 rebels a few day since by his scouts in the Kanawha. –B F Kelly, Brig Gen

FRI MAR 11, 1864
Mrd: on Mar 10, at the Metropolitan Htl, by Rev P D Gurley, Mr Jos C Willard, of Wash, to Miss Antonia Ford, of Fairfax, Va.

Died: in Gtwn, D C, on Mar 5, Mittie, y/d/o Lewis & Sarah Ann Lewis. Her remains were interred in Oak Hill Cemetery on Sun.

Died: in Wash City, on Mar 9, Sarah Ann Barclay, w/o John M Barclay, & d/o John M Lemon, of Laporte, Ind. Funeral from the residence of her hsbnd, 263 I st, today.

Died: on Mar 10, Miss Sarah Ann Batemen, in her 50th yr. Funeral from 433 F st, today.

Wash Corp: 1-Ptn of Jas Thompson, asking a certain privilege: referred to the Cmte on Police. 2-Ptn of Thos McCanna, asking a remission of a fine: referred to the Cmte on Claims. 3-Cmte on Mkts: bill for relief of Jas Bowen, reported back with amendments: read 3 times & passed. 4-Cmte on Claims: relief of A Aaronson, agreed to.

Senate: 1-Memorial of Geo Griswold & others of the U S, praying indemnification for losses sustained by the spoliations on our commerce by French cruisers prior to Sep, 1800. Referred to the Cmte on Foreign Relations.

Farm for sale in PG Co, Md, near Grimsville; 102 acs. G M Finotti, residing there.

Hon Chas Gilpin appt'd U S Dist Atty for Eastern Dist of Pa, vice Geo Coffey, dec'd.

Wheeling, Mar 10. Maj Gen Sigel arrived here this morning & assumed command of the Dept of West Va, with his headqrtrs at Cumberland, Md.

The residence of Admr Paulding, on Long Island, was recently destroyed by fire. He had been summoned here as a witness in the investigation relative to Admr Wilkes.

SAT MAR 12, 1864
Mrd: on Feb 18, at the Chr of the Epiphany, By Rev Dr Hall, Mr A E Evstaphive, of Buffalo, N Y, to Miss Emmeline L McCormick, of Va, adopted d/o Lt Com Saml Magaw, U S Navy.

Supreme Crt of D C, in Equity #95. Michl Delany & Sophia H Delany, vs Thos J Villard, Richd H Delany, Thos S Delany, & Norah Delany. Decree of the Crct Crt on Dec 19, 1857, Equity #1337. Villard was appt'd trust vice Alex'r Lawrence, dec'd, under the will of John Reitz, late of Wash Co, dec'd. He holds the fund created under the will & has removed from D C. -R J Meigs, clerk

Hse o/Reps: 1-John L Burns, of Pa, to be put upon the pension roll, for patriotic svcs at the battle of Gettysburg where he was wounded on Jul 1, 1863, at which time the pension shall commence.

Confiscatons: the Mrshl of the Dist seized the property of French Forrest, [formerly a Cmdor in the U S Navy,] consisting of a 2 story brick hse on 19th st between Pa ave & I st; & the property of Wm Dougherty, consisting of lot 22 in sq 225, improved by a 3 story brick dwlg, on K st between 12th & 13th sts. The former left the city about the time the rebellion broke out, & the latter was in the south when the war broke out.

The Govn'r of N J has nominated Mercey Beasely, of Trenton, as Chief Justice of the Supreme Crt.

MON MAR 14, 1864
Deaths reported to the Navy Dept for the week ending Mar 12, 1864:
John Lewis, seaman, erysipelas, Feb 26, hosp, Memphis.
Felix Chamberland, 1st cl boy, pneumonia, Feb 28, do.
Jas Supple, landsman, remit fever, Feb 27, do.
Wm Berrill, landsman, drowned, Mar 3, steamer *Scotia.*
Leonard E House, 1st cl boy, remit fever, Feb 18, Nav Hosp, Pensacola.
Geo N Smith, 1st cl boy, typhoid fever, Feb 20, do.
John Bond, landsman, dysentery, Feb 21, vessel U S S *Lacawana.*
Preston Burns, boy, dropsy, Feb 22, Nav Hosp, New Orleans.
Benj Spratt, fifer, blank, Jan 22, 1863, vessel U S S *Ticonderoga.*
Jas Hager, landsman, blank, Jan 22, do.
Thos Daniels, landsman, variola, no date, Nav Hosp, N Y.
Robt Young, seaman, consumption, Mar 6, do.
A C Alexander, jr, ensign, blank, Feb 24, Piqua, Ohio.
Jas Lewis, landsman, pneumonia, Mar 6, Nav Hosp, Wash.
Danl N Donovan, landsman, consumption, Mar 1, Nav Hosp, Chelsea.
Robt Thompson, 2nd cl boy, diarrhoea, Feb 27, vessel U S S *Red Rover.*
J W Bathawa, seaman, typhoid fever, Feb 29, do.
Chas Anderson, q m, consumption, Nov 3, 1863, vessel U S S *Constellation.*
Peter Bense, landsman, downed, Feb 6, vessel U S S *Queen.*
Walter P Williams, seaman, chronic bronchitis, Feb 26, vessel U S S *Queen.*
John O'Connell, marine, consumption, Mar 8, Nav Hosp, Chelsea.

Died: on Mar 13, after 24 hours' illness of diptheria, Thos Sylvester, late chief messenger of the Second Aud ofc, Treas Dept, aged 65 yrs, a native of Md, & a resident of Wash City for 45 yrs. Funeral from his late residence, 602 H st, between 4th &5th sts, this Mon evening.

Died: on Mar 10, at St Paul, Minnesota, after a long sickness, of pulmonary disease, in his 29th yr, Gottleib C Grammer, formerly of Wash City, a s/o the late G C Grammer.

Died: on Feb 25, at New Brunswick, N J, Mrs Jane E Cogswell, w/o the Rev J Cogswell, D D, & d/o the late Chief Justice Kirkpatrick, of N J.

Died: on Mar 13, in Wash City, Mrs Ann Grant, aged about 70 yrs. Her funeral will take place from the residence of her son-in-law, Jas Stone, 333 5th st, on Mon evening, at 4 p m.

Orphans Crt of Wash Co, D C. Prsnl estate of Jacob Gideon, late of Wash City, dec'd.
-Geo S Gideon, Juliana Gideon, excs

Supreme Crt of D C, in Equity #83. John Paul Jones, cmplnt, vs Parker H French, Jay Cooke, Henry D Cooke, Wm G Morehead, & Harrisc Fahnestock. Subpoena to compel the appearance of Parker H French, who was not found. Meigs, clerk

Notice: To Thos Harris, formerly a clerk in the Gen P O in London, one of the chldrn of Wm Harris, late of the Paragon Hackney, Middlesex Co, dec'd, who died on or about Apr 6, 1822, & of Eliz Mary Harris, his wife, who after the death of Wm Harris mrd Chas Martin, & died Nov 18, 1862, or to the chldrn [if any] of said Thos Harris, or to his reps. The above Thos Harris is to have sailed in the packet ship *Philadelphia*, from Portsmouth, Eng, to N Y, about Dec 1836. Regarding-sum of money, entitled to under the will of his late uncle, Thos Shirley, late of Cheltenham, Gloucester Co, Eng. Apply to Edw Mortimore Archibald, the British Consul at N Y, or to Mr John Dingwall, Solicitor, 8 Token Hse Yd, London.

The U S Gov't recently confiscated the property of the following, situated at Superior, Wisc:

R M T Hunter	Saml Magoffin	W W Corcoran
Robt Ould	W W Boyce	S M Flournoy
Wm Aiken	John McQueen	

TUE MAR 15, 1864

Died: on Mar 13, Thos C Donn, after a few days illness, in his 60th yr. Funeral from his late residence, 601 H st, today.

Orphans Crt of Wash Co, D C. Case of Ada B Gaburi, admx of Leone Gaburri, M D, dec'd; settlement on Apr 9. -Z C Robbins, rg o/wills

Meeting of the ofcrs of the 2nd Pa Artl, assembled at Ft Bunker Hill, D C, Mar 9, 1864, for measures of respect to the late 1st Lt Edw Scolwell; sympathies to the parents & family of the dec'd. -Thos P Hunt, Chaplain, Thos H Mumford, 2nd Lt

Wm B Cozzens, who kept the Hotel at West Point, died there on Sunday last.

Wm B Mack, a pvt sldr in the 50th N Y vols, was on Sat last, appt'd a 3rd Ast Engr in the navy. He had made a model of the steam engine & presented it to the managers of the Pat Ofc Fair. Mr Welles thought the sldr could better serve in the navy & transferred him on board ship.

Military changes: Lt Gen Grant assigned to the command of all the armies of the U S. Maj Gen Halleck is relieved from duty as Gen-in-Chief, & assigned to special duty at Washington as Chief of Staff of the Army. Maj Gen Sherman is assigned to the command of the division of the Mississippi, lately commanded by Gen Grant, comprising the Dept of the Ohio, the Cumberland, the Tenn, & the Arkansas. Maj Gen McPherson is assigned to the command of the Dept of Tenn, recently commanded by Gen Sherman. Gen W F Smith has been nominated for Maj Gen of Vols, as a necessary preliminary to his assignment to the command of the Army of the Potomac.

Lt Col Jas M Sanderson arrived on Sat among the last batch of prisoners from Richmond. On his arrival he was notified that charges had been preferred against him by Col Knight. That while in Libby prison he disclosed to the rebel authority information of a plot to escape. He is under arrest in this city. -Chronicle

Col S C Stambaugh died at Lancaster, Pa, a few days ago, aged 65 yrs; well known & esteemed in Wash City.

WED MAR 16, 1864

Died: in Wash City, on Mar 14, of consumption, Kate, 2nd d/o Mrs Mary Van Tyne, in her 22nd year. Funeral from the residence of her mother, 420 D st, today.

Died: in Wash City, on Mar 15, of typhoid fever, Thaddeusc Morrice, s/o Mary Ann & the late David F Morrice, in his 30th yr. Funeral from his late residence on K st, between 4th & 5th, today.

Criml Crt-D C. Dennis Kenner, Cpl-9th Btln Invalid Corps, who beat & robbed John McCarthy, 69th N Y Vols, of $390 on Sun, was arrested & sentenced to 3 years in the pen.

Dennis Kenner, Cpl of the 9th btln Invalid Corps, who so shamefully beat & robbed John McCarthy, of 69th N Y Vols, of $390 on Sun, was arrested yesterday & brought before the Crmnl Crt for trial. In less than 12 hours from the time of his arrest he was tried & sentenced to 3 years in the pen.

Mr O M Harris, who was arrested some weeks ago on a charge of having disposed of Gov't property, has, after a thorough investigation, been honorably acquitted of the charge.

THU MAR 17, 1864

Mrd: on Mar 15, at McKendree Parsonage, by Rev John Thrush, Mr Geo I Cushing to Miss Fannie Williams, all of Wash City.

Died: on Mar 16, Mrs Ellen O'Donnell, aged 53 yrs. Funeral from St Peter's Chr on Fri.

Crct Crt of PG Co, Md: Crt of Equity. Bernard McCrossin & Mary Ann McCrossin, his wife, against Wm Logan. Geo W Logan & his wife, Ann Logan, jointly purchased of Thos Ferrall, late of PG Co, dec'd, *Adelphi Mills*,in PG Co; Md. Ferrall & wife deeded the land to Logan & wife in equal shares. Logan died in spring of 1846, & by his will his share went to his wife, Ann Logan for life. After her death to his nephew, Wm Logan, who about 30 years since removed to Pa, & has not been heard from since. Ann Logan died in 1861, having devised her share to Mary Ann McCrossin, in fee simple. Bernard McCrossin was appt'd her exc. –Fred'k Sasscer, clerk

Wash Corp: 1-Act for the relief of Wise & Callahan: sum of $2,723.40 to be paid them for constructing a sewer & drop on 6th st. 2-Relief of Jas Rankin: $45 refunded for a license not taken out. 3-Relief of A R Corbin: to pay Corbin or his atty G P Howell, $30, for taxes erroneously pd by him on prnsl prop for the years 1862 & 1863.

Orphans Crt of Wash Co, D C. Prsnl estate of Nicholas B Van Zandt, late of Wash, D C, dec'd. -J Mortimer Smith, John W DeKraft, adms

Zebulon Wiggin, postmstr of Stratham, N H, died on Mar 1, aged 77 yrs. He was appt'd postmstr in Feb 1822. He was probably the oldest postmstr in the U S.

FRI MAR 18, 1864

Mrd: in Wash City, at the McKendree Parsonage, by Rev John Thrush, Mr Chas T H Barrett, of Wash, to Miss Laura D Letton, of Wash City.

Mrd: on Mar 15, by Rev Fr McNally, Capt Benj F Fisher, U S Navy, to Miss Alice E Causten, y/d/o Jas H Causten, of Wash City.

Wanted: a Protestant Swiss lady desires an engagement as a teacher. Address M'lle Debotte, Newark, N J.

Senate: 1-Memorial of J N Carpenter, praying compensation for clothing stolen from him on board the U S sloop *Saratoga*, while in the port of Phil, Jan 4, 1863. 2-Cmte on the P O: bill for relief of the trustees of A G Sloo, contractor for carrying the mails between N Y, Havana, & New Orleans: which was read twice.

Brig Gen Lockwood, present Cmder of the 8th Army Corps, Middle Dept, has received official notification of the appointment of Maj Gen Lewis Wallace, of Ind, to the command of this dept.

SAT MAR 19, 1864

Died: in Wash City, on Mar 17, Mrs Sarah Crandall, aged 91 yrs. Funeral at the residence of her dght, Mrs Harrison, 52 Missouri av, Sat. Mbrs of the First Bapt Chr are invited.

Died: in Alexandria, on Mar 18, Ada Hancock LaForge, aged 19 yrs. Funeral from the residence of her father, Andrew Hancock, 416 Va av, today.

Died: in Wash City, on Mar 18, Richd J Clements, in his 33rd yr. Funeral from his late residence, M st, between 18 & 19th sts, Mon.

English papers announce the death of Sir Wm Brown, of Liverpool, & s/o Alex'r Brown, of Balt, & bro of Jas Brown, of N Y. He was a native of North Ireland, born before the emigration of his father to this country. The jr bros were, we believe, all born on this side, & of these Jas Brown, of N Y & John A Brown, of Phil, survive him. His grandson, & the grandson also on the mother's side, of Mr Jas Brown, of N Y, succeeds to the title & landed estates of the dec'd Baronet. Estate is about $35,000,000.

Mrs Bayard, w/o the Hon Jas A Bayard, late U S Sen from Dela, died last week.

Wash Corp: 1-Ptn of R R Hazard, complaining of the award of a certain contract: referred to a Special Cmte. 2-Ptn from John H Sessford, Pres of the Wash Fire Dept: referred to said cmte. 3-Cmte of Claims: adverse on ptn of Thos McCanna, for remission of a fine.

Mrs Bayard, w/o the Hon Jas A Bayard, late U S Senator from Delaware, died last week.

MON MAR 21, 1864

Deaths reported to the Navy Dept for the week ending Mar 19, 1864:
Wm Smith, landsman, sea sickness, Mar 23, 1863, vessel *Morning Light*.
Aaron Talbert, landsman, consumption, Feb 25, Hosp, New Orleans.
Geo Williams, gunner's mate, paralysis, Feb 27, steamer *Katahdin*.
Chas B Fuller, 1st cl boy, Albuminuria, Feb 29, Hosp, New Orleans.
Jas Casey, seaman, erysipelas, Mar 12, Asylum.
Jas Hardin, 1st cl boy, rubella, Mar 13, Hosp, N Y.
Jas Coulon, seaman, conc of the brain, Feb 27, steamer *Pampero*.
Martin Beekman, 2nd cl fireman, remit fever, Feb 16, vessel *DeSoto*.
Jas S Salmon, landsman, remit fever, Feb 25, do.
John Donovan, seaman, inter fever, fev 20, vessel *Choctaw*.

Jas Ryan, landsman, wound, Mar 8, Hosp, Newbern.
John Burns, Capt's mate, smallpox, Feb 12, vessel *Great Western*.
Jas Gray, mstr-at-arms, consumption, Mar 11, Hosp, Norfolk.
Noah Hodge, 1st cl boy, consumption, Feb 29, Memphis.
Henry Warner, 1st cl boy, pneumonia, Mar 1, do.
Jas Hasting, landsman, chronic diarrhoes, Mar 5, do.
Jas Winfield, capt's mate, pneumonia, Mar 6, do.
Chas E Tucker, seaman, acute bronchitis, Mar 6, do.
Geo Simpson, landsman, pneumonia, Feb 10, Onishita.
Pat Bryan, landsman, pneumonia, Dec 20, 1863, Judge Torreme.
John Woods, ord seaman, pneumonia, Mar 16, Chelsea.
Jas Harvey, qrtr gunner, meningitis, Jan 28, vessel *Mound City*.
Nelson Cayere, landsman, diarrhoea, Feb 9, do.
Jas Sullivan, seaman, typhoid fever, Feb 16, vessel *Fawn*.
Jas Frazier, landsman, smallpox, Feb 29, vessel *Benton*.
Wash Burton, capt's mate, varioloid, Mar 3, Louisville.
Benj Tillman, W R steward, smallpox, Mar 4, Nantucket.
Herbert R Pike, ord seaman, pyemia, Feb 9, Sacramento.
Patrick Ryan, landsman, chronic diarrhoea, Mar 14, Hosp, N Y.
Edw Shaw, pensioner, typhoid fever, Mar 16, Nav Asylum, Phil.

Died: on Mar 18, A H Derrick, at his residence in Wash City.

Died: on Mar 19, Lezey Jane, 2nd d/o Owen & Bedelia O'Hare, aged 3 years & 17 days. An hour later, Geo Francis O'Hare, aged 1 yr & 25 days, died. Their funeral will take place from their residence, 27 G st, this afternoon.

Died: on Mar 20, of consumption, Benj Scrivener, in his 24th yr. He leaves a wife to mourn her loss. Funeral from the McKendree Chapel, Tue.

Died: on Mar 19, of pneumonia, at the residence of his father, Saml E Coues, Dwight Coues, aged 19 yrs. Funeral svc at Chr of St Aloysius, today.

Orphans Crt of Wash Co, D C. Prsnl estate of Louisa Hunter, late of Wash City, dec'd. -Richd Wallach, adm

The 39th Ill Regt arrived in the city on Sun & marched across the Long Bridge to Va. They had with them quite a number of recruits.

TUE MAR 22, 1864
Died: in Wash City, on Mar 18, Howard McLellan, 2nd s/o Hon Geo W McLellan, 2nd Ast Postmstr Gen. He was born in Calais, Maine & was 25 years of age. He came to Wash in Apr 1861, from Augusta, Ga, & accepted the position of paymaster's clerk.

Died: in Marseilles, Mar 1, Eliz Stuyvesant, w/o Frederick S Grand D'Hauteville, of Boston, Mass, & d/o Hon Hamilton Fish, of N Y.

Died: on Mar 21, at the residence of her son-in-law, Benj T Reilly, M D, Mrs Julia M Thomson, in the 80th yr of her age, & for the last 64 years a resident of Wash. Funeral from 17th & I sts, Wed.

The U S Dist Crt at N Y last week issued a decree restoring the barque *Saxon* & her cargo, captured by the U S steamship *Vanderbilt* off the coast of Africa, to their respective British owners. The *Saxon* [Capt Sheppard] was owned by Messrs Anderson & Co of Cape Town. On Oct 30 the Federal war steamer *Vanderbilt* arrived at Pequina, & sent a boat's crew on board the *Saxon* & took possession of her. The mate, Jas Gray, was shot & killed.

N Y, Mar 21. John W Hunter, Assist Auditor-N Y custom hse, is under arrest for alleged frauds.

Md Constitutional Convention: the Democrats of Balt Co have nominated Gen Benj C Howard, C F Hale, R R Boarman, Pleasant Hunter, Wm M Isaacs, Victor Holmes, & I N Steele as candidates for the cnvntn. The Democ nominees in Kent Co are Judge E F Chambers, Geo S Hollyday, & David C Blackiston. The Union men of Kent Co have nominated John Gale, v Col Wilkins, declined. The conservatives of Talbot have nominated John Harper, Julius A Johnson, & Henry P Hopkins. -Sun

Orphans Crt of Wash Co, D C. Case of Moses Kelly, adm w a of Wm W Russell, late Paymstr U S M C, dec'd; settlement on Apr 12. -Z C Robbins, rg o/wills

On Mar 12th a negro sldr, Brown, was shot in Greensborough, Caroline Co, Md, by a young man named Massey, while in the act of shooting young Massey's father, Maj W B Massey. The negro died in a few mins. He was enlisted on Kent Island.

WED MAR 23, 1864
Grand Ball in honor of the ladies of the late fair, at the Hall in the Patent Ofc Bldg, on Mar 29, for the benefit of the families of the sldrs of D C.

Mgrs:

Hon Hannibal Hamlin, V P U S
Hon Schuyler Colfax, Sprk of Hse o/Reps
Hon Solomon Foot, of Vt, Senator

Hon Richd Wallach, Mayor of Wash
Hon Henry Addison, Mayor of Grwn

B B French	W P Dole	R W Taylor
Henry D Cooke	Jas S Grinnell	John M Brodhead
S J Bowen	Wm Whiting	John L Hayes
L E Chittenden	Fred'k W Seward	
D P Holloway	John G Nicolay	

Hons:

Edw McPherson	Wm Sprague	S C Pomeroy
John W Forney	F E Woodbridge	A Carter Wilder
Jas Dixon	Justin S Morrill	Green Clay Smith
Henry C Deming	Portus Baxter	Lot M Morrill
Hon John Conners	W T Willey	John H Rice
Cornelius Cole	Jacob B Blair	Reverdy Johnson
Augusus Frank	K V Whaley	H Winter Davis
Thos T Davis	T O Howe	Henry Wilson
Reuben E Fenton	J C Sloan	Thos D Elliot
Robt C Schenck	Ezra Wheeler	Geo S Boutwell
Jas M Ashley	N B Smithers	Z Chandler
B F Harding	Wm S Holman	John W Longyear
Wm D Kelley	John F Farnsworth	M S Wilkinson
Jas T Hale	Jas Harlan	Wm Windom
Henry B Anthony	John A Kason	J B Henderson

B Gratz Brown
Danl Clark
John P Hale
J C Ten Eyck
Theodore M Pomeroy
John F Stars
John B Steele
Gen John M Martindale
Gen M C Meigs
Col E M Greene
Col J B Fry
Gen C C Augur
Gen Henry W Benham
Surg-Wm Thompson
Surg-D W Bliss
Capt Henry L Sheetz
Col Jos Gerhardt
Wm H Tenny
John Marbury, jr
De Vere Burr
C H Nichols, M D
Benj L Jackson
A P Hoover
H I Gregory
Floor Mgrs:
Gen DeWitt C Clarke
W O Stoddard
Cmte on Invitations:
Saml P Bell
Ezra L Stevens

Wm M Shuster
Adolph Cluss
John Hitz
Job W Angus
John H Semmes
J P Bartholow
Ezra L Stevens
Ira Goodenow
Maj O R Latham
Jos J May
H C Fahnestock
A H Shepherd
M G Every
Thos Berry
Wm H Baldwin
Col John G Stephenson
Z Moses
W L Avery
Wm Whelan
Capt W T Hartz
A Coleman
C C Simpson
Henry Polkinhorn
M H Bohrer

Jas Galway
E D Gilman

D W Bliss
Chas F Stansbury

Jas R Doolittle, jr
Maj C Raymond
Capt J R Howard
J B Towers
Saml Bacon, jr
John F Ennis
John F Ellis
Wm H Phillips
Remus Riggs
Capt Montgomery
Capt Wager
Col Ward H Lamon
Selah Squires
Jos F Brown
Wm B Todd
Maj John C Cash
Geo W McClellan
A W Randall
C F McDonald
Chas F Stansbury
Maj R R Scott
Edmund F French
Edw Jordan

Nathan H Barrett
Saml P Ball

Orphans Crt of Wash Co, D C. Case of Wm H Morrison & Obadiah M Morrison, excx of Wm M Morrison, dec'd; settlement on Apr 16. -Z C Robbins, rg o/wills

Supreme Crt of D C, in Equity #180. Francis P Richards, vs Geo S S Richards, John R Richards, Chas S Wallach, Fitzhugh Coyle, Jas C McGuire & Thos J Fisher. In 1861 John Richards, late of Wash City, departed, seized of part of lot 24 in sq 491, leaving Geo S S & John R Richards, his only chldrn & heirs. Regarding-appointment of a guardian, ad litem, to take the answers of said dfndnts, Geo & John Richards, they being infant dfndnts. Chas S Wallach is a non-resident of D C. -Andrew Wylie-Justice

Portland, Me, Mar 22. Gen Neal Dow arrived here today in the noon train & was received by the city authorities & a detachment of troops from Camp Berry.

The Camel's Hair Shawl sent to the Patent Ofc Fair by A T Stewart, & drawn in the raffle by Mrs Marshall Brown, has been placed in the store of Harper & Mitchell, to be displayed for the benefit of the Protestant & Catholic Orphan Asylums.

THU MAR 24, 1864
Gen Grant, accompanied by his wife & son, & Gen Rawlins, Col Duff, Maj Rowley, & Capt Badow, his staff ofcrs, arrived in the city early yesterday & are stopping at the Willard.

Grand Ball for the benefit of the Enlistment Fund to be held at the hall of the Patent Ofc Bldg on Mar 31. Proceeds to be appropriated to aiding enlistments of Wash City.
Mgrs: Pres of the U S, V P, Spkr of Hse o/Reps, Secs of State, Treas, War, Navy, Interior, & Postmstr Gen & Atty Gen.

Army:

Gen H W Halleck	Gen Benham	Col B T Ingraham
Gen C C Augur	Capt H A Scheetz	Col E M Greene
Gen J H Martindale	Capt Benton	Col J B Fry
Gen M C Meigs	Gen G D Ramsey	

Navy

Ast Sec G F Fox	Capt H A Wise	Paymstr J S
Admr Jos Smith	Cmder Overton Carr	Cunningham
Com J B Montgomery		

Marine Corps:

Col John Harris	Maj Nicholson	Maj W B Slack

Senate: -Senators:

Grimes	Morgan	Carille
Johnson	Foot	

Hse o/Reps: Hons:

Thaddeus Stevens	N B Smithers	F P Blair
Owen Lovejoy	B W Davis	R E Fenton
Saml Hooper	John A Kasson	
R C Schenck	A C Wilder	

Ctzns:

Hon Richd Wallach	Chas Wroe	Henry Lyles
Hon Henry Addison	S J Bowen	S Y Sylvester
Wm Dixon, esq	Geo A Bohrer	E S Wisklin
Saml E Douglass	Dr S A H McKim	L A Beall
Geo Krafft	Wm Talbot	B B French
Robt Bossel	Geo A Scott	Adolph Class
Wm Bradley	Geo R Wilson	N Sargent
H N Easby	Wm Hutchinson	N Acker
S V Hurdes	Donald McCathron	C J Canfield
Henry Riley	John Holroyd	Jos Platz
J E Allen	Jas Brown	A T Richards
John T Hendlin	H McNally	J F Fugitt
L J Middleton	Thos P Morgan	Wm Hamilton
Jas F Halliday	Wm Forsyth	F Hitz
B W Reed	Geo W Riggs	C S Noyes
Saml E Culverwell	Wm Wilson	Jonas B Ellis
Zachariah Downing	Thos J Fisher	Toomas E Lloyd
W Wall	Smith Pettit	Wm Wise
John W Boteler	Andrew J Joyce	Geo Wright
Chas Kloman	Andrew Hancock, jr	John I'adley
H G Lorch	Andrew Noerr	E K Stebbins
W W Moore	M Talt	Geo P Goff
C H Utemehle	John D Hammack	John R Elvans
Jas Y Davis	Jos F Brown	Woodford Stone
W H Lamon	Thos Lewis	Gwynn Harris
Jas H English	Chas Stewart	

Exec Cmte:

Gen Peter F Bacon	A C Richards	W N Hawley
John H Semmes	S V Noyes	A R Shepherd
H C Wilson	Noble D Larner	E S Wicklin
John Seasford	Crosby S Noyes	Hudson Taylor
W W Rapley	P M Dubant	

Died: at Gtwn, on Mar 19, Mary Ellen, d/o Henry & M J King, aged 22 yrs.

FRI MAR 25, 1864
Died: on Mar 18, at Elm Point,on the Hudson river, of congestion of the brain, in his 10th yr, Frank Granger Adams, grandson of David H Burr, of Wash City.

Died: in Wash City, on Mar 24, Henry Clay Baldwin, of the firm of Baldwin Bros, s/o Almon Matilda S Baldwin, aged 35 yrs. Funeral at his late residence 467 D st, Sat.

All the rl estate of Dr M M Lewis, Wm N McVeigh, J H McVeigh, G W Davis, E W Kinchelow, H W Vandegrift, Dr Orland Fairfax, & Jas H Reid, with the prsnl property of Dr Fairfax, H W Vandegrift, & Wm N McVeigh, to be sold on Apr 9, by the U S Mrshl of the Eastern Dist of Va, under a decree under the U S Confiscation law.

Dr Franklin Bach, the oldest great grandson of Benj Franklin, died in Phil last Sat. He was born in Phil on Oct 25, 1792, the oldest s/o the oldest grandchild of Benj Franklin.

Wash Corp: 1-Ptn of Geo Savage & others, in reference to the law regulating the sale of spirituous liquors: referred to the Cmte on Police. 2-Ptn of Wm Wight & others, asking that the fish wharf be retained in its present location: referred to the Cmte on Wharves.

Henry H Sibley, of Minn, has been appt'd by the Pres to be Brig Gen on the volunteer force, to take rank from Sep 29, 1862.

The steamer *Baltimore*, actg mstr Mitchell, which left on Mon with Admr Dahlgren, who went down to Fortress Monroe, expecting to receive the body of his son, the late Col Dahlgren, arrived up yesterday with the Admiral on board, he having been again unsuccessful in his mission. Col Ould, the Confederate agent for the exchange of prisoners, sent a verbal message that the man who buried the body of Col Dahlgren could not be found in time to get it ready for transportaton, but it would be sent down as soon as possible. This gives hope to the relatives & friends that the remains will shortly be delivered to his afflicted father & family. -Star

Books & historical documents now offered to librarians, statesmen, politicians: for sale with numerous other works. –Jas L Dickens, Atty at Law, 379 L st, between Vermont & 15th st, Wash City.

SAT MAR 26, 1864
Supreme Crt of D C in Equity #181. Lloyd W Williams vs Arthur Nelson & Malvina, his wife, John Nelson & Virginia, his wife, Madison Nelson, Chas J Jenkins, John J M Sellman, et al. Regarding-decree for the sale of parts of lots 15 & 17 in sq 290 in Wash City, for payment of debts secured thereon. Arthur Nelson & Malvina Nelson his wife, & Virginia Byng, who has since mrd John Nelson, by their deed of Sep 24, 1844, conveyed to Madison Nelson, & his heirs parts of said lots. Dfndnts are non-residents of D C. -Geo P Fisher, Justice

Died: on Mar 16, after a short & painful illness, Mary E Cammack, 3rd d/o John & Mgt Cammack, aged 3 years & 8 months. Also, on Mar 24, of typhoid fever, Mgt, w/o John Cammack, aged 31 yrs. Funeral of Mrs Cammack at 493 Md av, today.

Mr Eben Meriam, Booklyn meteorologist, died at his residence on Brooklyn Hghts, on Sat last. He was born in Concord, Mass, Jun 17, 1794.

Mrs Judge Vanderbilt & her servant were both shot on Sun by an Irishman, who, it is reported, had made several threats against their lives, in consequence of the refusal of the servant to receive his addresses. Mrs Vanderbilt reached her home in Flatbush by the car which passes her hse. She was followed by the assassin, who came up with her on the threshold of her hse, where he deliberately fired 4 shots, wounding dangerously, probably fatally, both Mrs Vanderbilt & her servant. The murderer escaped. -N Y Jrnl of Commerce

Crct Crt of Montg Co, Md, in Equity. Trustees sale of the rl estate of which Jas Fling, late of said county, died seized & possessed, at his late residence in Montg Co, Md: between 17 & 18 acs. -John W Fling

Mr Eben Meriam, the celebrated Brooklyhn meterorologist, died at his residence on Brooklyn Hghts, on Sat last. He was born at Concord, Mass, Jun 17, 1794, & therefore was in his 70th yr.

MON MAR 28, 1864
Deaths reported to the Navy Dept for the week ending Mar 26, 1864:
Jas L Jordan, capt'scook, pneumonia, Feb 28, vessel U S S *Victoria.*
Edmund G Spear, landsman, variola, Mar 19, Smallpox Hosp, Phil.
John Nelson, landsman, anasaica, Mar 12, Hosp, Memphis.
Henry Denis, seaman, pneumonia, Mar 13, do.
Wm G Bendig, landsman, pneumonia, Mar 21, Hosp, N Y.
Thatcher Wyman, landsman, pneumonia, Mar 18, Hosp, Chelsea
Geo W Parks, 1st cl fireman, menengitis, Feb 23, Hosp, Norfolk.
Alex'r Lobell, landsman, consumption, Mar 15, do.
Henry Spangler, seaman, consumption, Mar 18, do.
Henry Keeling, pensioner, paralysis, Mar 21, Nav Hosp, Phil.
Wm Willis, landsman, typhoid fever, Mar 20, Hosp, Wash.
Chas Alexander, coal heaver, variola, Mar 17, Hosp, Chelsea
Peter Lewis, 1st cl boy, diarrhoea, Oct 3, 1863, vessel U S S *Clara Dolson.*
Jas M Peterson, seaman, pneumonia, Oct 25, 1863, do.
Edw Bowman, 1st cl boy, dysentery, Nov 4, 1863, do.
Watty Greely, 1st cl boy, dysenter, Nov 6, 1863, do.
Henry Keizer, 1st cl boy, bronchitis, Nov 12, 1863, do.
Geo Jackson, seaman, enteritis, Nov 14, 1863, do.
Wm Wilson, landsman, bronchitis, Dec 20, 1863, do.
Alick Boyd, landsman, rubeola, Jan 1, vessel U S S *Red Rover.*
John E Moore, landsman, rheumatism, Mar 10, vessel U S S *Wisahickon.*

Died: in Balt, Md, on Mar 27, in her 66th yr, Clementina Eliz Grierson, wid/o the late Thos Mount, of Raymond, Mississippi, & d/o the late Wm Alexander Rind, of Gtwn, D C. Funeral at Oak Hill Cemetery, Gtwn, today.

Died: on Mar 27, Mrs Ann Douglas, in her 88th yr, for more than 70 years a resident of Wash. Funeral from the residence of her son, Wm Douglas, near Benning's Bridge.

Died: on Mar 26, of typhoid fever, Wm H Reed, in his 16th yr, s/o D C & the late Cath L Reed.

Orphans Crt of Wash Co, D C. 1-Prsnl estate of Jos Bryan, late of Wash City, dec'd. -J T Cochrane, J Carter Marbury, adms c t a 2-Prsnl estate of Rezin B Elliott, late of Fairfax Co, Va, dec'd. -Milton Elliott, adm 3-Prsnl estate of Thos C Donn, dec'd. -Mary A Donn, Johny Donn, adms

Wash, D C. Boulanger's restaurant, on G st, was sold to Chas Klotz for $13,700; a lot at the corner of N J av & E st, sold to Jas Marshall, for 30 cents per ft; also a lot on A st, sold to F S Obold, for 13¾ cents per ft; also a 2 story frame hse & lot at D & 6th sts, sold to C I Brewer, for $3,300.

Hon Owen Lovejoy, mbr of Congress from 5th Ill Dist, died in Brooklyn, N Y, on Fri; attended by his wife & dght. -Evening Post [Funeral took place on Mar 27 in Plymouth Chr, Brooklyn.]

TUE MAR 29, 1864
Died: on Mar 28, of pneumonia, Mrs Emeline F Soran, aged 54 yrs, widow of the late Chas Soran. Funeral from 469 Ninth st, today.

Crct Crt of Montg Co, Md. Ratify sales made by John G England & Geo Peter, trustees, for the sale of the rl estate of John White, late of said co, dec'd. -E B Prettyman, clerk

Supreme Crt of D C, in Equity #162. Jas Edelin vs Chas A Henderson, Richd H Henderson, & Cazenove Henderson, Anna Taylor, Edw & Eliza Jones, Irene E & Chas Dupont, Jas Adams, & Richd Henderson, trustee, &c. Dfndnts except Jas Adams reside out of the District. Summons to dfndnts to appear. R J Meigs, clerk

Hse o/Reps: Mr Washburne, of Ill, announced the death of his colleague, Hon Owen Lovejoy.

The Atlanta, Ga, papers announce the arrival in that city of Mrs J Todd White, a sister of Mrs A Lincoln, who came thru the Northern lines on a flag of truce boat from Ft Monroe, bringing with her a rebel general's uniform, the buttons of which were gold pieces, amounting in all to the sum of $4,000. It is understood that she was sent thru on a flag of truce by a special pass direct from the Pres.

Official: State Dept, Mar 28, 1864. Information received from Alex'r R McKee, U S Cnsl at Panama, of the death of the following persons, viz: Wm Emmerson, residence unknown, aged about 36 yrs, seaman on board of the American steamship *Constitution*. Killed on Feb 22, 1864, by the premature explosion of a cannon. Wm Barley, a colored man from Va: found in a well on the 3rd inst, supposed to have committed suicide. Inventories of the effects left by them have also been received.

Supreme Crt of D C, in Equity #133. Mary J Hill, by her next friend, John M Varnum, vs Jos B Varnum, jr, et al. Ratify sale made & reported by the trustee. -R J Meigs

Wash Corp: 1-Ptn of Dr R C Croggon: referred to the Cmte on Ways & Means. 2-Ptn of Michl Green & others, with a bill for grading, paving, etc, alley in sq 247: passed.

WED MAR 30, 1864

Died: on Mar 29, after a lingering illness, Richd Smith, for many years cashier of the Branch Bank of the U S in Wash City, & late Cashier of the Bank of the Metropolis, in the 78th yr of his age. Funeral from his late residence, 355 H st, Thu.

Died: in Gtwn, on Mar 28, after a short illness, Blanche, d/o Wm Hunter, Chief Clerk of the Dept of State. Funeral today.

Died: on Mar 28, at Cumberland, Md, Mrs Sarah A Tucker, w/o Dr Horace Tucker, in her 24th yr. Funeral from the residence of R M A Fenwick, on H st, today.

Died: on Mar 29, of Scarlet fever, Harry Wesley Dick, aged 4 years & 7 mos, y/s/o John W & Eliza E W Dick. Funeral from his father's residence on N Y av, Thu.

Died: on Mar 29, of consumption, John Henry Ford, eldest s/o Mrs Cath Ford, aged 16 years & 11 months. Funeral from his mother's residence, G & 8th sts, today.

Died: on Mar 29, Mgt A, only child of Wm A Shedd, aged 4 yrs. Funeral at the residence of Wm P Shedd, 502 11th st, today.

Mrs Francis D Gage, who has been laboring with the S C contrabands, says that in 1862 they neither swore nor got drunk, but now they drink whiskey & swear just like white folks.

THU MAR 31, 1864

Died: in Gtwn, Mar 30, Wm Noyes, in his 76th yr. Funeral from his late residence, 85, corner of West & Green sts, today.

Obit-Gottlieb C Grammer, formerly of Wash City, & s/o the late G C Grammer, died at St Paul, Minn, on Mar 10, after a long sickness of pulmonary disease, in his 29th yr. Although he died far from his native home, he was soothed in his last hours by the assiduities of a sister's affection.

Died: on Mar 30, Maj Chas J Morrison, s/o L S & the late W H Morrison, in the 27th yr of his age. Funeral from the residence of his mother, 23 Four-&-a-half st, Fri.

The "New South," published at Hilton Head, S C, has this notice: auction sales of plantation lands in the parish of St Helena by the Direct Tax Com'rs have been closed, etc. Plantations on Port Royal Island will be leased at rate of about $2 per ac. 280 acs of the Danl Pope place, on St Helena Island, were bid off by Capt Wm J Randolph for $6,050. In one or two instances freed-men have bought the plantations on which they were formerly held as slaves, & several parties have bid ostensibly for the colored people.

Results of a Frolic. John O'Meara, while under the influence of liquor, attempted to walk on the railing of the Aqueduct bridge over Rock Creek on Tue, & fell some 50 to 60 feet. He was picked up in a horribly mangled condition & there are no hopes of his recovery.

FRI APR 1, 1864

Orphans Crt of Wash Co, D C. 1-Prsnl estate of Robt C Brent, late of Wash City, dec'd. - Eleanor Brent, admx 2-Ptn of Jas McSherry, guardian to Helen N, Mary C, & Jas C McSherry, infant heirs of Helsen McSherry, dec'd, for sale of rl est. -Wm F Purcell, sole Judge of the Orphans Crt . -Z C Robbins, rg o/wills

Carpenter in his standard History of Massachusetts, a work warmly partial to that state, says: In Jul, 1656, svr'l Quakers arrived in Mass from Barbadoes, two of whom were women. Magistrates in Boston brought the law against heresy to bear upon the intruders, & ordered their immediate arrest. After their persons had been examined for those marks which were supposed at that period to indicate such as dealt in witchcraft, no satanic signs being discovered, their trunks were rifled & books found therein ordered to be publicly burned. They were briefly imprisoned, released, & banished from the colony. A law was passed, says the same historian, in 1658, banishing the Quakers from the United Colonies of New England, & forbidding their return under pain of death. Marmaduke, Stephenson, Wm Robinson, & Mary Dyer courted the danger to which they were exposed & quietly awaited the operation of the law. In Sep, 1658, they were seized, & after trial, condemned to be hanged. The sentence was carried into effect upon Robinson & Stephenson, but Mary Dyer was reprieved upon the scaffold & again thrust from the colony. Resolute in seeking a martyr's death, she returned soon after, & was publicly executed on Boston Common. Many persons of good understanding were led to believe in the prevalence of witchcraft in the province. Among these was Cotton Mather, s/o Rev Increase Mather, for some time past the agent of Massachusetts in England, & himself a clergyman. Many victims so rapidly increased, that many of the colonists were panic stricken. The execution of Rev Buroughs, a minister of blameless life, was a terrible instance. During this period out of 28 persons capitally convicted of witchraft 19 had been hanged & one pressed to death.

Died: in Alexandria, on Mar 26, Mrs Eliz McCliesh, in her 88th yr.

SAT APR 2, 1864
Rev Dr John N Campbell died in Albany, N Y, a few days ago; formerly a Prof at the Univ of Va.

Obit: Blanche Hunter, d/o Wm Hunter, of the Dept of State, & grand-dght of Hon Wm Hunter, late Minister at the Crt of Brazil, died in Gtwn, on Mar 28, after a brief illness.

Wash Corp: 1-Communication from Jas Skidmore in relation to the fish wharf: referred to the Cmte on Fish Wharves. 2-Ptn of Johnson Simonds in relation to a wooden building erected by him in sq 690: referred to the Cmte on Police. 3-Cmte on Finance: reported back the bill for the relief of Jas Bowen: referred to the Cmte on Mkts. 4-Bill for relief of John Dunn: passed. Also, relief of B P Fletcher: passed. 5-Special cmte: referred the resolution relative to the over-charge of John Alexander, asked to be discharged from its further consideration: so ordered. 6-Bill for relief of one Whitbey: passed.

Hse o/Reps: 1-Bill reported for the relief of Julia A Ames, of Mass, whose hsbnd died from injuries received during the riot in Balt, Apr 19, 1861.

Hon Geo E Pugh has declined to stand as a State Elector on the Democratic ticket in Ohio.

P M Henry, formerly of Washington City, will please send his address to C H Barkley, Louisville, Ky.

MON APR 4, 1864
Rev John Pierpont, who will be 79 years of age on Apr 6, 1864, & in good health & in perfect vigor of his mental faculties, just completed a Digest of the Decisions & Instructions of the Treas Dept to Collectors of Customs, contained in 54 folio vols, which he has reduced to one. He began in Nov, 1861, & finished in Mar, 1864.

Deaths reported to the Navy Dept for the week ending Apr 2, 1864:
Thos Ware, 1st cl boy, drowned, Feb 29, vessel U S S *Ozark.*
Ang Monroe, seaman, killed, Mar 2, vessel U S S *Onachita.*
Jas M Green, 1st cl boy, typhoid fever, Mar 3 vessel U S S *Cricket.*
Wm Summerfield, gunner's mate, cirrhous, Mar 17, Nav Hosp, Memphis.
John Ryan, coal heaver, diarrhoea, Mar 7, vessel U S S *Pensacola.*
Michl Robery, 1st cl fireman, gastritis, Mar 8, vessel U S S *Seminole.*
Thos Hopkins, landsman, bronchitis, Mar 27, Nav Hosp, Phil.
Thos Crosby, seaman, rheumatism, Mar 24, Nav Hosp, N Y.
Clement Hall, seaman, pneumonia, do.
Chas McPherson, landsman, bronchitis, do.
Chr R Farnham, q m, drowned, Nov 20, 1863, vessel U S S *Brazitura.*
John McTully, marine, wound, Mar 19, vessel U S S *Galatin.*
Daniel P Sweeny, yeoman, wound, Mar 19, vessel U S S *Galatin.*
John Valley, landsman, wound, Mar 19, do.
Ab Reed, contraband, nostalgia, Feb 8, vessel U S S *Vermont.*
John York, ord seaman, pneumonia, Feb 25, do.
John Jones, landsman, dropsy, Mar 27, Navy Yd, Portsmouth.
Wm Robinson, landsman, contusio, Mar 16, vessel U S S *Union.*
Alfred Beach, landsman, consumption, Mar 28, Nav Asylum.
Alfred Butler, coal heaver, drowned, Mar 14, vessel U S S *Pensacola.*
Elias King, landsman, gunshot wound, Mar 14, vessel U S S *Vermont.*

M Bessamer, the inventor of the process of converting iron quickly into steel, now says he can produce a block of it, 20 tons in weight, from flinterest cast iron, in 20 mins.

TUE APR 5, 1864
Dissolution of partnership between W M Shuster & *W H Clagett, by mutual consent; the undersigned having purchased the stock & will continue as W M Shuster & Bro. -W M Shuster, H C Shuster. *Retiring from the firm-Dry Goods: Washington.

Sebastian Aman has opened the Covenient Hse 507 9th st for a restaurant: Wash.

Trenton, Apr 2-Hon Jos N Taylor, of Passaic, Spkr of the Hse of Assembly, died this morning, of congestion of the brain. He was a young man who engaged in manufactures at his home in Paterson.

A P Thompson, rebel ofcr, was killed at Paducah, struck by a shell in the breast. [No date-recent.]

Later news from Europe: The Earl of Aberdeen died on Mar 22nd. Lord Ashburton is also dead.

WED APR 6, 1864
Mrd: on Mar 30, at St John's Chr, by Rev Dr Pyne, Col J H Taylor, U S Army, to Mary Montgomery, d/o Gen M C Meigs, Q M Gen U S Army.

Died: on Apr 5, Mrs Julia Curran, relict of the late Philip Curran, of Annapolis, aged 74 yrs. Funeral from the residence of her son, Mr B B Curran, E st, Thu.

Information wanted of John Coughlin, native of parish Castlehaven, Co Cork, Ire; last heard from 5 years ago. He resided in Cherry st, N Y. Information received by his bro, Timothy Coughlin, Union st, Wash, D C.

Hon John Banks, formerly a mbr of Congress, more recently Pres Judge of Berks Co, died here on Apr 3. -Reading, Pa, Apr 4.

The nomination of Robt Beale, as Warden of the Jail of D C, was confirmed yesterday by the Senate.

THU APR 7, 1864
Died: on Apr 7, Wm Clarke Bennett, in San Francisco, Calif, in his 22nd yr. Son of Capt Richd Bennett, of ships *Richd Anderson, Fanny,* & *Euroclydon* memory, names dear to all merchants of Balt & Md. In Lone Mountain Cemetery, Calif, he rests.

Died: in Alexandria, on Apr 4, in the 42nd yr of her age, Lizzie D, w/o Henry B Clagett, & d/o the late Azarish Fuller, of Wash City.

Died: on Apr 6, Mrs Cath Slight, relict of Pringle Slight, aged 72 yrs. Funeral from her late residence 1½ st near Va av, Fri.

Died: on Apr 6, Franklin Middleton, infant s/o J B & Helen Houston. Funeral from the residence of Benj Beall, 14 La av, Thu.

Supreme Crt of D C, in Equity #80. Mary M McIntire et al vs Williams A McIntire. Ratify sale by Thos Bradley, trustee, of lot 18 in sq 285, Wash, to Wm S Thompson, for $9,029. -R J Meigs, clerk

Alanson J Prime, M D, aged 53 yrs, died on Sun last, at White Plains, West Chester Co, N Y, eldest s/o the late Rev N S Prime, & elder bro of the editors of the N Y Observer. Born in Smithtown, L I, Mar 12, 1811.

Supreme Crt of D C, in Equity #141. Alex'r Ray vs Wm A Maury, Geo A Pearre, & John Beall. Cmplnt conveyed certain premises in Gtwn to Messrs Carlisle & Maury to secure to said Pearre & Beall the debt in the deed mentioned. Debt has been pd, but no release has been executed. Maury Pearre & Beall reside outside of this Dist. -R J Meigs, clerk

FRI APR 8, 1864
Mrd: on Apr 7, by Rev Wm C Lipscomb, of the Meth Prot Chr, Mr Henry Glasspoole, of Wisc, to Mary J, y/d/o Geo H Grant, of Wash City.

Orphans Crt of Wash Co, D C. Case of Eliza B Duvall, admx of Andrew Jackson Duvall, dec'd; settlement on Apr 30. -Z C Robbins, rg o/wills

Information wanted of the relatives of Jacob Gooding, dec'd, formerly of Alexandria, Va, & a resident of Kansas & Arizona Terrs from 1856 thru 1860, & in 1861, a resident of Utah Terr. He had a sister residing in Washington City in 1860. Regarding-his pecumiary affairs-address: E R Purple, 183 Hudson st, N Y C.

Lexington, Ky, Apr 7. Mrs Lucretia Clay, w/o Henry Clay, died last night at the residence of her son, John M Clay, near Lexington, aged 83 yrs.

Henry B Cromwell, proprietor of the *Cromwell Line* of steamers, died last Sat in N Y.

Adms sale of the prsnl effects of the late Wm Aldred, dec'd; in front of our auction rms. - Green & Williams, aucts: Wash, D C

SAT APR 9, 1864
Supreme Crt of D C, in Equity #179. Meyer E Reinhard vs Septimia Barnett & John T Hallett. Bill is to procure from Septimia Barnett to the cmplnt a deed of lots 15 & 16 in sq 486. Septimia Barnett on Oct 6, 1863, constituted John T Hallett, her atty, to sell the rl or prsnl, in Wash City, which belonged to Parrott A Prindle during his lifetime, & was devised to her by his last will, dated Nov 2, 1860, probated May 11, 1861. Said lots were sold to Meyer E Reinhard. Barnett is a non resident of D C. -A B Olin, Justice; R J Meigs, clerk

Died: on Apr 6, of an affection of the brain, Ivan Ridout, eldest s/o John R & Mary E McGregor, aged 9 years & 4 days. Funeral, today, from 555 N J av, & the body deposited at Dumblane, PG Co, Md, which has been the residence & burying ground of his family for more than 200 yrs.

Judge Wm Waln Drinker, of N Y, died suddenly on Wed, while addressing the Assembly Committee on Cities at Albany. Supposed to be disease of the heart.

Mrs Quarles who concealed Col Streight & Capt Porter for 9 days, at the time of their escape from Libby Prison, has arrived in N Y with her 3 chldrn. They were all sent outside of the rebel lines & are in a destitute condition.

Senate: 1-Memorial of Garrett R Barry, a paymstr in the U S Navy, praying to be relieved from all responsibility as bondsman for paymstr John De Broe, for losses incurred due to the disaster to the U S frig *Cumberland*, accompanied by a joint resolution for the relief of said Barry. 2-Cmte on Pvt Land Claims: bill confirming the title of Jos Ford to certain lands in Rice Co, Minn: made a favorable report thereon.

MON APR 11, 1864
Senate: 1-Sec of War be directed to communicate to the Senate any information in his posession, touching the recent arrest of Capt C B Ferguson, Q M U S army, & Capt Wm Stoddard, Ast Q M of Vols, lately in charge of the Military Depot at Alexandria, Va. 2-Cmte of Claims: relief of Wm G Brown; also, relief of Darius S Cole; & for relief of Danl Wormer: all of which passed. 3-Bill for relief of Robt Wagstaff: referred to the Cmte of Claims.

Died: in Wash City, on Apr 10, Wm A Kennedy, in the 51st yr of his age. Funeral from his late residence, 535 I st. Mbrs of the Confernce of St Vincent De Paul are invited to attend his funeral on Tue at his residence, then to proceed to St Aloysius Chr, where mass will be said.

Died: of congestion of the lungs, at his late residence, near Bladensburg, Md, on Apr 10, John C Rives, in his 69th yr.

Died: in Wash City, on Apr 10, Mrs Jane Ball, aged about 70 yrs. Funeral from the residence of Mr Downs, 10th & K sts, today.

Died: in Wash City, on Apr 10, Wm A Kennedy, in the 51st yr of his age. Funeral from his late residence, 535 I st. Mbrs of the Confernce of St Vincent De Paul are invited to attend his funeral on Tue at his residence, then to proceed to St Aloysius Chr, where mass will be said.

Memphis, Apr 9. Vicksburg advices of Apr 3: rebels attacked Roche's Plantation on Fri. It had extensive cotton works & splendid bldgs, all of which were destroyed. One negro man & 4 chldrn were burned in the bldgs. The 1st Massachusetts cavalry, [colored,] 600 strong, maintained the fight with the rebels until morning, when they charged & repulsed the enemy, numbering 1,500 strong.

Phil, Apr 10. Wm D Ticknor, the eminent Boston pblshr, of the firm of Ticknor & Fields, died here suddenly this morning at the Continental Htl.

Orphans Crt of Wash Co, D C. Prsnl estate of Chas J Morrison, late of Wash City, dec'd.
-W H Morrison

Deaths reported to the Navy Dept for the week ending Apr 9, 1864:
John Gould, seaman, yel fever, Oct 9, 1863, vessel U S S *Estrella.*
Wm Talman, 1st cl fireman, yel fever, Nov 28, 1863, do.
Pat Sullivan, seaman, drowned, Mar 12, vessel U S S *Monongahela.*
Geo C Whitney, q m, blank, Mar 16, vessel U S S *Aug Dinsmore.*
Wm W Baily, landsman, pneumonia, Feb 8, vessel U S S *Princeton.*
John G Ellis, landsman, pneumonia, Feb 20, do.
Green B Jordan, landsman, variola, Feb 22, Phil.
Geo Edwards, contraband, consumption, Mar 24, Nav Hosp, Memphis.
Rich Brooks, 1st cl boy, empyemae, Apr 14, Nav Hosp, Norfolk.
Peter Mulbye, carp's mate, abscess, Mar 30, Nav Hosp, N Y.
Sidney Shepherd, landsman, pneumonia, Mar 31, do.
Edw Haines, landsman, asthma, no date, do.
Andrew Conlon, landsman, pneumonia, no date, do.
John Worms, landsman, consumption, no date, do.
Moses F Francis, landsman, pneumonia, no date, do.
Wm A Taylor, seaman, congestive fever, Mar 19, vessel U S S *Proteus.*
Jos Stanley, q m, typhus fever, Jan 1, vessel U S S *Essex.*
John Redman, q m, drowned, Jan 10, vessel U S S *Peosta.*
Jas P Williams, seaman, drowned, Feb 6, do.
John Ganning, marine, albuminnia, Apr 1, Nav Hosp, .
Henry Welsh, marine, erysipelas, Mar 28, vessel U S S *Michigan.*
Nathl H Holmes, landsman, measles, Apr 6, recg ship, *Philadelphia.*
Chrisley Miller, seaman, pleurisy, Apr 5, Nav Hosp, Norfolk.
Ervin A Salisbury, boatswain's mate, smallpox, Aug 2, vessel U S S *Petrel.*
Wm J Waggoner, 1st cl boy, congestive chills, Jan 12, do.
John W Williams, seaman, drowned, Nov 7, vessel U S S *Clara Dolson.*
Jas Moony, seaman, chronic diarrhoea, Nov 21, vessel U S S *Lexington.*

TUE APR 12, 1864
Mrd: in Balt, Md, on Mar 5, by Rev Bishop Kendrick, John B Howard to Miss Mary K Gartrell.

Died: on Apr 10, Sarah Ellen, consort of Geo W Cochran, aged 36 yrs. Funeral from the residence of her hsbnd, 497 E st, tomorrow.

Died: on Apr 11, after a short illness, Amelia Lerew, only d/o Thos & Lavinia Francis, aged 3 years & 10 days. Funeral from the residence, 356 N Y av, today.

Orphans Crt of Wash Co, D C. Ptn in the matter of Erasmus J Middleton guardian of John Albert Anderson & Wm Alexander Anderson; & Mary E Anderson, guardian to Cecilia Bertha Anderson, infant heirs of Wm Anderson, dec'd for sale of rl est. Ratify & confirm same. -Wm F Purcell, Sole Judge

The funeral of John C Rives will take place from his late residence, near Bladensburg, tomorrow.

Orphans Crt of Wash Co, D C. Prsnl estate of Henry Clay Baldwin, late of Wash City dec'd. -W H Baldwin, Edw Baldwin

Sale-on the account of the heirs of the late Guy Graham, all of sq 92 except lot 3, fronting on Connecticut av; on Apr 25. -Jas C McGuire & Co, aucts

Chancery sale [Equity #1803] in cause between Christopher Grammer & Wm B Todd, trustees of the late Gottlieb C Grammer & others, cmplnts, & Julius E Grammer & Wm H Dunkinson & others, dfndnts; lot 9 in sq 533, on C st, Wash; also lot 15 & part of lot 16 in dq 198 on L st, Wash. -Chr Grammer, Wm B Todd, trustees

WED APR 13, 1864
Died: in Wash City, on Apr 12, in the 80th yr of her age, Sallie Watson, d/o the late Josiah Watson, formerly of Alexandria, Va. Funeral from the residence of her nephew Wm H Watson, G & 19th sts, tomorrow.

The funeral of the late Wm H Thompson, today, from his late residence at Mr Massi's-461 Ninth st.

Supreme Crt of D C, in Equity #1445. John H McBlair & Augusta his wife, & John C Teneyck & Julia his wife, vs Wm Gadsby, John G McBlair, Ann S Newton & others. Above parties, Walter S Cox, trustee substituted for Chilton & Magruder, & those interested in the estate of the late John Gadsby, to appear in City Hall, Wash, D C, May 5 next. -W Redin, auditor

Supreme Crt of D C, in Equity #102. Virginia Belfils & others vs Mellaine Liomin, Jacques Belfils, Louis Meloir, Chas Zeller, Chas Liomin, Emilie Liomin & others. Hearing to determine the heirs & next of kin of dec'd Eugene Liomin; meeting on Apr 22, City Hall, Wash. -W Redin, auditor

Orphans Crt of Wash Co, D C. 1-Case of Leonidas Coyle, adm of Andrew Coyle, dec'd; settlement on May 3. -Z C Robbins, rg o/wills 2-Prsnl estate of John Douglass, late of Wash City, dec'd. -Wm Douglas

THU APR 14, 1864
Obit-Mrs Jane C Walker died on Apr 20 at the residence of Geo Dent, Chas Co, Md; d/o the late Col Ashton, of Wash City, & relict of Dudley Walker, Purser, U S Navy, in about the 56th yr of her age; communicant of the one Catholic & Apostolic Chr of the living God.

Died: at New Haven, Conn, on Apr 7, Helen Maria Gerry, d/o the late Elbridge Gerry.

Died: on Mar 9, after a lingering & painful illness, Mrs Jemima Wilson, w/o Mr Wm S Wilson, of Montg Co, Md, in her 60th yr, leaving her hsbnd & chldrn.

Orphans Crt of Montg Co, Md. Ratify sale made by Josiah Harding, exc of Ann Carroll, late of said co, dec'd. -Sam C Veris, Wm Thompson, of R. -Rob W Carter, Rg

Orphans Crt of Wash Co, D C. 1-Case of John L Kidwell, exc of Sarah Jenkins, dec'd; settlement on May 7. -Z C Robbins, rg o/wills 2-Prsnl estate of Henry W Balmain, late of Wash City, dec'd. -Ellen P Balmain, admx

Died: in Gtwn, D C, on Apr 13th, Sue, d/o Isabella & the late Thos I Davis, aged 20 yrs. Funeral today. Burial in Oak Hill Cemetery, Gtwn, D C.

Sale of nearly all of sq 992, Wash City, deed of trust from *Jos Curillinton dt'd May 13, 1854. Wm R Woodward, trustee. At the same time *Mrs Curillior, will sell lots 3 & 4 in above sq. -Jos Redfern, exc. [*Corr of Apr 15-both names changed to Cuvillier.]

FRI APR 15, 1864

Wash Corp: 1-Act for relief of H P Fletcher: sum of $70.36 refund for certain taxes erroneously pd. 2-Act for relief of A Aranson: return of $20 to Aranson, the amount of fine imposed on him for selling goods by samples. 3-Act for relief of Mr Whitby: permission granted to hold a circus or place for equestrian exhibitions upon private property by him for that purpose obtained, he paying to this corp for such privilege the sum of $60 for each week, or part thereof. 4-Act for relief of John Dunn: sum of $10 refund to Dunn, the amount of a fine imposed upon him by Justice Thompson in Feb 1863.

For sale: Elegant mansion known as the *Meade Hse*, 167 F st north. Gas & water are introduced thru-out the building, replete with all modern conveniences. The grounds contain 19,228 sq ft, tastefully laid out. –R K Scott, Atty: 425 Pa ave.

Obit-John C Rives, editor of the Congress Globe, died at his residence, near Wash, on Apr 10, in his 69th yr. He came to Washington more than 40 years ago. Burial was in Congressional Cemetery on Wed. His remains will be eventually removed to a vault at Mr Rives' country place, which dec'd was having prepared in the stone-cutting dept near the Patent Ofc, with a similar one for the remains of his late wife,

Mrshl Geo P Kane procured the release of 2 Massachusetts ofcrs: Capt F R Josselyn & Lt Remie, 11th Regt Mass Vols.

Seven negroes have been tried for the murder of Mr Neff's family near Port Hudson in Jan, & 3 of them were sentenced to be hanged.

The Rt Rev Martin John Spalding reported to have been appt'd Archbishop of Balt, is at present Bishop of the diocese of Louisville. He is a native of Ky & a learned divine of eminent ability.

SAT APR 16, 1864

Mrd: on Apr 14, by Rev Orville Dewey, Fred'k Banders McGuire & Emily Neville, d/o Mr Franck Taylor, of Wash.

Died: at his residence in PG Co, Md, on Apr 21, Thos A Cross, in the 37th yr of his age, after a short but painful illness, leaving a wife & 4 chldrn.

Supreme Crt of D C, in Chancery, #192. Wm R Riley et al, in behalf of the Mt Vernon Bldg Assoc, vs Craven Ashford, Emerella Ashford, Richd H Clarke, & A Austin Clarke. Bill for appointment of a trustee in place of Richd H Clarke & A Austin Smith, non-residents. -A B Olin, Justice; R J Meigs, clerk. Equity #191 with same cause & cmplnt followed; dfndnts are Edw M Clarke & Jane S Clarke his wife, Richd H Clarke, & A Austin Smith. Regarding lot 9 in sq 353, Wash, D C. Dfndnts are non-residents of Wash, D C. A B Olin, Justice; R J Meigs, clerk. Equity #190 with same cause & cmplnt followed: dfndnts are Jos Howard & Sarah Howard his wife, Richd H Clarke, & A Austin Smith. Regarding part of sq 903 in Wash City. -A B Olin, Justice -R J Meigs, clerk

The trial of Col Wm L Fish, formerly Military Provost Mrshl of Balt, has been concluded before the crt martial in Wash. Charged with appropriating goods for his own use; rendering false accounts to the Gov't; sending cotton or Confederate bonds to Europe. Decision will be delayed due to immense amount of testimony. -Sun

The will of the late Archbishop Hughes bequeathes to his 2 bros, Michl Hughes, of Chambersburg, Pa, & Patrick Hughes, of Lafargeville, 2 mortgaged lots in Orleans, N Y.

MON APR 18, 1864
Died: in Wash City, Apr 16, Eliz, 3rd d/o Geo W & the late Sarah E Cochran, aged 11 yrs.

The court martial of Capt H B Todd, late Provost Mrshl of Wash City, recently convened. Sentence: to be dismissed from the svc.

Criml Crt-D C. The trial of Cornelius Tuell for the murder of his wife on Feb 17, was brought to a close on Sat: verdict of guilty of murder in the first degree.

Deaths reported to the Navy Dept for the week ending Apr 16, 1864:
Jas Price, landsman, consumption, Feb 8, vessel U S S *Constitution*.
Henry Eberle, seaman, drowned, Mar 15, vessel U S S *Nyanza*.
Owen Sheridan, landsman, fracture, Mar 24, Nav Hosp, Pensacola.
Geo Smith, sgt of marines, hamoptysis, Mar 16, do.
John Clark, seaman, liver, Mar 30, Nav Hosp, Key West.
Henry Cox, ord seaman, blank, Apr 4, vessel U S S *Vermont*.
Wm Ebling, landsman, diarrhoea, Apr 5, Nav Hosp, Chelsea.
Thos McNeil, contraband, pneumonia, Apr 5, Nav Hosp, N Y.
Wm Bormeister, 2nd cl fireman, pneumonia, no date, do.
Elias Williams, landsman, variola, no date, do.
Chas Irvine, ord seaman, pneumonia, no date, do.
McNeil Rebnon, seaman, wounds, Mar 2, vessel U S S *Ft Hindman*.
Wm Downey, 2nd ast engr, remit fever, Mar 1, vessel U S S *Queen City*.
Patrick J Shea, 2nd cl fireman, remit fever, Mar 8, vessel U S S *Black Hawk*.
Daniel Budd, pensioner, inflam of liver, Mar 5, Nav Asylum.
Robt Fly, landsman, chronic diarrhoea, Mar 28, Nav Hosp, New Orleans.
Jas Fox, landsman, convulsion, Mar 9, vessel U S S *Mt Vernon*.

TUE APR 19, 1864
Died: at his residence in PG Co, Md, on Apr 11, Henry D Hatton, in his 46th yr. He leaves a wife & 5 chldrn.

Died: in Gtwn, D C, on Apr 17, Abraham Bohrer, in his 89th yr. Funeral from the residence of his dght, Mrs Marinus Willet, on High st, today.

Died: on Apr 18, after a painful illness, Mgt Florence Lichau, infant child of Philip & Eliz H Lichaw, aged 1 yr & 8 months. Funeral from their residence, 469 6th st, today. [Note: 2 spellings: Lichau/Lichaw.]

Died: suddenly, in Balt, Md, on Apr 16, Martha A Lee, widow of the late Hon Z Collins Lee, & d/o the late Thos C Jenkins. [Mrs Lee died at the residence of her brother, Thos R Jenkins, Centre st. She left her own residence, Franklin st, Sat morning to attend the funeral of one of her brother's chldrn, & as she ascended the steps in her brother's house, she fell & expired in a few minutes. She leaves 2 chldrn. -Balt, Sun]

Petersburg [Va] Express, dt'd Dalton, Apr 12. Miss Mary E Walker, surgeon of the 53rd Ohio, was captured by our pickets & brought here yesterday.

Lt Col Lemuel Towers, of the First Regt of the Dist Vols, has resigned his commission. He was among the first to enroll himself in defence of the Union & has been in active svc ever since.

WED APR 20, 1864
Mrd: on Apr 14, by Rev C C Meador, Mr Clarence M Barion, of Phil, to Miss Cath Virginia Bohlayer, of Wash.

Died: in Wash City, on Apr 19, Delphine, w/o M W Beveridge, & d/o C Cammack. Funeral from Mrs Lugenbeel's, 456 E st, today.

Died: in Wash City, on Apr 19, Wm Mitchell, infant s/o Peter & Nannie B Lammond, aged 2 months & 4 days. Funeral today.

Supreme Crt of the U S: #s 171 & 207: U S, appellants, vs Sebastian Wunez, & the U S, appellants, vs Jose Joaquin Estudillo. Appeals from the Dist Crt of the U S for the Northern Dist of Calif: opinion of the Crt, overruling the motions to vacate the stipulations dismissing these appeals.
#175: Manuel Rodrignez, appellant, vs the U S. Appeal from the Dist Crt of the U S for the Northern Dist of Calif. Opinion of Crt: affirming the decree of the said Dist Crt in this cause.
#818: Hugh B Sweeney, et al, plntfs in error, vs Hamilton Easter et al. In error to the Crct Crt of the U S for D C. Opinion of Crt, affirming the judgment of said crt, with costs.
#169: Santiago Brignardello et al, appellants, vs Matilda C Gray. Appeal from the Crct Crt of the U S for the Northern Dist of Calif. Opinion of Crt, affirming the decree of said Crt, with costs.
#178: The U S, use of Fanny B Rogers, admx, & Jas H Rogers, adm of Geo T Rogers, dec'd, plntfs in error, vs Edgar Conklin et al. In error to the Dist Crt of the U S for the Dist of Wisc. Opinion of Crt, affirming the judgment of said Crt, with costs.
#223: Matilda C Gray, appellant, vs Santiago Brignardello et al. Appeal from the Crct Crt of the U S for the Northern Dist of Calif. Opinion of Crt: reversing the decree of said Crt, with costs, & remanding the cause, with directions to award a venire facias de nova.

#130: The U S, appellants, vs Julian Workman. Appeal from the Dist Crt of the U S for the Southern Dist of Calif. Opinion of Crt: reversing the decree of the said Crt, & remanding the cause with directions to dismiss the ptn of the claimant.

#174: Ellen E White, adms of Chas White, dec'd, appellant, vs the U S. Appeal from the Dist Crt of the U S for the Northern Dist of Calif. Opinion of the Crt: affirming the decree of the said Dist Crt.

#179: Benj D Godfrey, plntf in error, vs Chas T Eames. In error to the Crct Crt of the U S for the Dist of Mass. Opinion of the Crt, reversing the judgment of the said Dist Crt, with costs, & remanding the cause with directions to award a venire facias de novo.

#130: The U S, appellants, vs Julian Workman. Appeal from the Dist Crt of the U S for the Southern Dist of Calif. Opinion of the Crt: reversing the decree of the said Dist Crt, & remanding the cause with directions to dismiss the ptn of the claimant.

#131: The U S, appellants, vs Wm Carey Jones. Appeal from the Dist Crt of the U S for the Southern Dist of Calif. Opinion of the Crt, reversing the decree of the said Dist Crt, & remanding the cause with directions to dismiss the ptn of the claimant.

#365: The U S , appellants, vs Vicente P Gomez. Appeal from the Dist Crt of the U S for the Southern Dist of Calif. Opinion of the Crt, overruling the motion to dismiss this cause.

#176: Ann R Dermott's Exc, plntf in error, vs Chas S Wallach. In error to the Crt Crt of the U S for D C. Opinion of the Crt, reversing the judgment of the said Crct Crt with costs, & remanding the cause, with directions to award a venire facias de novo.

#182: Chas Horner et al, plntfs, vs Arthur W Austin. On a certificate of division of opinion between the Judges of the U S Crct Crt for the Dist of Mass. Opinion of the Crt that almonds are subject to duty of thirty per cent ad valorem.

#184: Jos Jasigi et al, plntfs in error, vs Jas S Whitney, collector, etc. In error to the U S Crct Crt for the Dist of Mass. Opinion of the Crt, affirming the judgement of the said Crct Crt in this cause, with costs.

228: The U S, appellants, vs Manuel Laries: and

#283: The U S, appellants, vs Rufina Castro. Appeals from the U S Dist Crt for the Southern Dist of Calif. Opinion of the Crt overruling the motions to dismiss these cases.

#381: Andrea Pico et al, appellants, vs the U S. Appeal from the U S Dist Crt for the Northern Dist of Calif. On motion of Mr Coffey, Ast Atty Gen of the U S, this appeal was docketed & dismissed.

#382: The U S, appellants, vs the widow & heirs of Apolinario Miranda, dec'd. Appeal from the Northern Dist of Calif. This appeal was docketted & dismissed.

Clifton Cotton Factory for sale: prop at the head waters of St Mary's river: grist mill, tvrn, blacksmith & wheelwright shop, storehse granery, tailor & shoemaker's shop, with 8 dwlg hses attached to the property. It is situated at the head of a navigable stream, with a large & thrifty community surrounding it. Apply to T W Gough, Leonardtown, St Mary's Co, Md, or Morgan & Rhinehart, foot of G st.

News has reached the Navy Dept that the gunboat *Gallates*, Capt Guest, came near being destroyed at Cape Haytien by the bursting & ignition of a carboy of turpentine in dept adjoining the magazine. Crew exhibited the greatest heroism by standing to their posts until the magazine was submerged.

Senate: 1-Relief of Warren W Greene was taken up & passed.

THU APR 21, 1864
Died: on Apr 20, Henry Hosford, infant s/o Revere W & Mary C Gurley, aged 9 months & 22 days. Funeral at 36 Missouri av, Fri.

Trustees' sale of slaughter hse property, dwlg hses & vacant lots near the Navy Yd, Wash, belonging to the estate of the late Chas Miller; in cause wherein Geo W Miller is cmplnt & Ellen Miller et al are dfndnts, Chancery-#146. -Geo A Bohrer, E C Morgan, A Thos Bradley, trustees [Also G, H & O in sq 492; part of sq 907 on L st; also lots 2 thru 6 in sq 994 on Pa av; lot 6 is improved with a dwlg hse, being the residence of the late Chas Miller.]

Massacre at Ft Pillow. Correspondent of the St Louis Democrate, who was on board the steamer *Platte Valley*, give details of the massacre. The boat was signaled by a flatboat on the Missouri shore & took on a colored Cpl & 3 wounded men, who gave them the first account of the fight. The rebels, under Forrest, drove in the pickets on Tue: garrison of the fort consisted of about 200 of the 13th Tenn Vols & 400 negro artl, all under command of Maj Booth. Rebel army was estimated at from 2,000 to 4,000. Maj Booth, who was killed near the close of the fight, conducted the defence with great coolness, skill, & gallantly. His last signal to the boat was, "We are hard pressed, & shall be overpowered." He refused to surrender & fought to the last. Dr Fitch, surgeon of the fort, confirms the butchery of our sldrs by the rebels. Maj Bradford ran down to the river, & after he told them he had surrendered, more than 50 shots were fired at him, without hitting him.

Chicago, Apr 19. The Jrnl's ltr from Grand Ecore, 10th inst: Gen Ransom in command of the 3rd & 4th divisons of the 13th Corps, etc. Gen Ransom was in favor of advancing only in force. His wish was disregarded. While endeavoring to get the Chicago Mercantile battery off safely, Gen Ransom was severely wounded in the leg. Capt Cyrus E Dickey, his Adj, was instantly killed. Our loss was probably 2,000. Capt White is a prisoner. Lts Throop & McBride are killed.

FRI APR 22, 1864
Orphans Crt of Wash Co, D C. Ptn of Cath Venable, guardian; reported she sold all the interest & title of Geo V & Ella King, her wards, also her right & the interest & title of the adult heirs of Geo W Venable, they assenting to the same, in part of lot 4 in sq 377, to Francis McGhan for $3,148.20; ratify same. -Wm F Purcell, Judge

Mrd: in Wash City, on Apr 21, at the residence of the bride's step-father, John C Harkness, by Rev Saml M Dickson, J F Stoek, of Blue Earth C, Minn, to Sudie M Lear, of Wash, D C.

Mrd: at Gtwn, D C, Apr 20, by Rev J C Jacobia, Chaplain U S A, R J Thomas, Surg U S Army, to Miss Susan W Dixon, d/o Maj H T Dixon, of Va.

Mrd: in Brooklyn, on Apr 19, at the Strongplace Bapt Chr, by Rev E E L Taylor, Rev T Edwin Brown, Pastor of the Tabernacle Bapt Chr, to Miss Lizzie C, d/o J K Samson, of Brooklyn.

Mrd: in Wash City, on Apr 21, at Chr of the Epiphany, by Rev Chas Ball, Mr Alex'r Roberts, of Calif, to Miss Maggie Burman, y/d/o the late Henry Burman, of Upper Marlboro, PG Co, Md.

Mrd: at Trinity Chapel, N Y C, on Apr 14, Dr John M McCalla & Miss Helen Varnum, d/o the late Silas H Hill, of Wash City.

Died: in Wash City, on Apr 20, Mary A Allen, w/o A R Allen, in her 40th yr. Funeral from the
residence of her hsbnd on I st, between 6th & 7th sts, Fri.

Alexandria Gaz of Apr 19. Confiscation of property belonging to:

R L Rotchford	J B McCarty	D T Shreeve
J H Hammill, of Pr Wm	A C Landstreet	Arthur Chichester
Meade & Marye	Wm B Taylor	W H Gray
Wm Selecman	M S Partlow	Francis Mason
R T Love	I L Evans	Richd Marlow
Turner Thompson	J T Nalls	John Marlow
Geo Bailey	A T Rust	Nicholas Dawson
A D Wroe	J W Minor	Chas Dawson
John Landstreet	Geo Rust	E S Hutchison
Manydier Mason	T F Tebbs	J H McVeigh

SAT APR 23, 1864

Mrd: on Apr 21, at Trinity Chr, by Rev Osborne Ingle, Edmund H Brooke to Fanny, d/o the late John P Ingle, of Wash City.

Mrd: in Wash City, on Apr 22, by Rev Mr Ward, Mr Albert F Turner, of N J, to Miss Sarah E Bailie, of Howard Co, Md.

Died: on Apr 22, of consumption, John M Gilbert, aged 65 yrs. Funeral at the residence of his son-in-law, John B Blass, 371 13th st, Mon; interment in N Y.

Died: in Wash City, in his 76th yr, on Apr 22, Brig Gen Jos G Totten, Chief Engr U S Army. Funeral at his late residence, 203 G st, Tue. [Apr 25 paper-born on Aug 23, 1788, New Haven, Conn; 1805 grad at Military Acad; chldrn survive him.]

Died: on Apr 21, Mary Patterson, d/o John P & Henrietta Piercey Pepper, aged 1 yr & 10 months. Funeral from their residence, 475 6th st, today.

N H Miller appt'd by the Pres, to be a Justice of the Peace for Wash City & County.

Wash Corp: 1-Ptn of Chas Duke for permision to lease a certain piece of ground belonging to the Corp: referred to the Cmte on Finance. 2-Cmte on Claims to whom had been referred the ptn of Alden Richards, reported adversely on the same & asked to be discharged from further consideration: which was ordered. 3-Special cmte was referred the ptn of R R Hazard, reported the same back, asking to be discharged: which was granted.

MON APR 25, 1864

Died: in Wash City, on Apr 23, Patrick Dowling, in his 49th yr. Funeral from his late residence, 5th st, between M & N sts, today.

Deaths reported to the Navy Dept for the week ending Apr 23, 1864:
Wm Bone, 2nd cl fireman, scalded, Apr 15, vessel U S S *Chenango*.
John Heaver, coalheaver, do, do, do.
John Murphy, 1st cl fireman, do, do, do.
John Smith, seaman, do, do, do.
Nich. J Walsh, yeoman, do, do, do.
Eheo Echalaz, marine, do, do, do.
Henry Livingstone, coalheaver, so, do, do.
John White, 2nd ast engr, do, do, do.

Bernard Boyle, 1st cl fireman, do, do, do.
Arch. Flemming, coalheaver, do, do, do.
Frank P Root, 2nd ast engr, do, do, do.
Albert Murray, 2nd ast eng, do, do,do.
Mitchel Rodey, coalheaver, do, do, do.
J S Cahill, 1st ast engr, do, do, do.
Geo Wilson, seaman, do, do, do.
Jas Loyons, ships cook, do, do, do.
Martin Mitchel, landsman, do, do, do.
John M Smith, boy, do, do, do.
John Ruddy, landsman, do, do, do.
Wheeler Sherman, coxwain, do, do, do.
Jas L Macomber, yeowman, do, do, do.
Saml Randall, seaman, do, do, do.
Wm Weir, 2nd cl fireman, do, do, do.
Chas Weild, seaman, do, do, do.
Vincent Roberts, ord seaman, variola, Apr 16, Hosp, N Y.
Allen Holliday, landsman, variola, Apr 16, do.
John Butler, ord seaman, African fever, Dec 31, 1863, vessel U S S *Onward.*
Geo Bacon, pilot, variola, Mar 12, Nav Hosp, Md City.
Eber Norcross, seaman, typhoid pneumonia, Mar 8, vessel U S S *Brilliant.*
Essex Siddons, 3rd cl boy, heart disease, Mar 18, vessel U S S *Praire Bird.*
Wm Carter, contraband, pneumonia, Mar 24, vessel U S S *Tyler.*
Jas Brown, landsman, typhoid fever, Apr 3, vessel U S S *Benton*
Chas Champion, pensioner, remit fever, Apr 18, Nav Asylum.
Wm Roberts, actg mstr's mate, consumption, Apr 15, do.
Austin A Miller, coalheaver, epilepsy, Apr 17, do.
John Stratton, coalheaver, consumption, Apr 14, Nav Hosp, Chelsea.
Chas Peach, landsman, ae bronchitis, Jan 9, vessel U S S *Georgia.*
Wm Jones, seaman, dysentery, Jan 30, vessel U S S *Wyoming.*
John Fallure, marine, consumption, Apr 8, Nav Barracks, Wash.
Mich J Ryan, landsman, frac of skull, Apt 11, vessel U S S *Mercidita.*
Aremus Small, carp's mate, hemorrhage, Apr 15, Nav Hosp, Portsmouth, N H.
Timothy Riley, landsman, delirium tremens, Apr 15, Recg ship *Ohio.*
Thos Hand, landsman, diarrhoea, Apr 16, vessel U S S *Pensacola.*
Chas Williams, seaman, hemorrhage, Apr 13, do.
Chas B Wilder, actg vol Lt, gunshot wound, Apr 14, vessel U S S *Minnesota.*
Peter Anderson, landsman, pneumonia, Apr 18, Nav Hosp, N Y.
Jas P Conchony, actg vol Lt, gunshot wound, Apr 4, vessel U S S *Chillicothe.*
R H D Cooper, surgeon's steward, inflam of bowels, Apr 19, blank.

Died: in Wash City, at his residence, 472 H st, on Apr 24, Richd Burgess, in the 76th yr of his age. Funeral from the Chr of the Ascension, on Tue.

Died: in Wash City, on Apr 24, Louisa, d/o John & Norah Tretler, in the 17th yr of her age. Funeral from their residence, 457 10th st, today.

Col Wm L Fish, lately Provost Mrshl of Balt under Gen Schenck, who was tried recently by court-martial: sentenced to the Albany pen for 1 yr, without labor.

Chas Carpenter & Mathew Riley were shot on Fri, for desertion, at Ft Warren, Boston harbor.

Battles in La. 3 days fight ending in a Union victory. New Orleans Journal of Apr 16. Second day's fight-Lt Col Webb, 77th Ill, shot thru the head & instantly killed. Capt Breese, commanding 6th Missouri cavalry, severly wounded in the arm. Some of the casualties among ofcrs-killed:

Col Benedict, N Y	Col Mix, N Y	Capt Black, Iowa
Col Webb, Ill	Lt Col Newbold, Iowa	Lt Col Lindsay, Ohio

TUE APR 26, 1864

Supreme Crt of D C, in Equity #1607. Geo Bender et al vs Geo F Russell et al. Ratify sale by trustee of parts of lots 6 & 7 in sq 78, on I st, Wash, to Geo Rhinehaeart for $5,250, & part of lot 7 on I st to Jas F Gibson for $2,700. -R J Meigs, clerk

Orphans Crt of Wash Co, D C. Prsnl estate of Jacob Bigelow, late of Wash City, dec'd. -Jas N Callan, adm

Supreme Crt of D C, in Chancery. David G Day, vs John P Hilton, Otis J Preston, & Russell Stevens, adm of Levi Stowell, dec'd. In 1849 David G Day, formerly of Wash City, now of Calif, appt'd John P Hilton his agent & atty for the purpose of closing the business of said Day at Wash City. In 1850 Preston & Stowell, then residing at Wash City, were partners. On removing to Calif appt'd Hilton their agent. Levi Stowell died. Ltrs of adm of his prsnl estate were granted to Russell Stevens. The bill charges that John P Hilton has collected large sums of money, which he has refused to pay over & has converted to his own use. There is a debt owed by one Joel Downer, $996.79 with interest. [Case is one column in the paper] -A B Olin, Justice

Local-Yesterday, Lt Bondy, 15th N Y Artl, fell from the 4th story of his room at the Prescott Hse, while leaning out the window, fell to the street below, breaking his neck & killing him instantly.

Col Fish has been sentenced to be cashiered & dismissed from the svc, to pay a fine of $5,000, & confined for one year in the Albany pen.

The Meth Episc Chr in Double Creek, Queen Annes Co, Md, was fired by some incendiary on the 16th inst, & entirely destroyed.

Daring robbery by the driver of the U S Express wagon, S G Hagerty, an employ of the company at this place for the last 6 weeks. In the lot of 3 pkgs was $27,000: one addressed to Capt Rufus Ford, superintendent of the St Jos' & Omaha packet line, contained $26,000, & the other two were of smaller sums. Police are in eager pursuit. –St Louis [Mo] Herald, Apr 20

WED APR 27, 1864

Died: on Apr 25, Jane, d/o Jos L & Hannah Adamson, aged 8 yrs. Funeral at the residence on C st, near 4th st, today.

Died: on Apr 25, Miss Lizzie Wheeler, in the 24th yr of her age. Funeral from the residence of Mr G T McGlue, I st, near 18th, Wed. Services at Union Chapel, 20th st, today.

Orphans Crt of Wash Co, D C. 1-Prnsl estate of Abraham Bohrer, late of Gtwn, D C, dec'd. -G A Bohrer, exc 2-Prsnl estate of G C Grammer, late of St Louis, Mo, dec'd. -W B Todd, exc

At Port Alleghany, Pa, a few days ago, a funeral procession was passing over a bridge to bury a child of Mr Geo Moore, when the bridge gave way, &, precipitating the mourners into the water, another child belonging to Mr Moore was drowned, along with 3 of his bros' chldrn, & one or two other lives were lost.

THU APR 28, 1864

Mrd: on Apr 22, in Christ Chr, Oswego, N Y, by Rev A C Treadway, Lt Cmder John H Russell, U S N & Miss Cornelia P Treadway, d/o officiating clergyman.

Died: in Wash City, on Apr 27, Jas Allen Thom, 2nd s/o Col & Mrs Geo Thom, aged 8 years & 9 months. Funeral today.

Wash Corp: 1-Nominated by the Mayor for Com'rs of the Fire Dept-R A Bozzel, Wm E Hutchinson, P M Dubant, & John H Sessford: referred to the Cmte on the Fire Dept. 2-Cmte of Claims: bill for relief of John Williams: read 3 times & passed. 3-Ptn of J H Harleston, with a bill granting certain privileges to J H Harleston: amended, read 3 times & passed. 4-Ptn of T Swift: referred to the Cmte of Claims.

Bay horse taken by the Metropolitan Police as stolen. On Apr 28 the horse was taken from John Holland alias Johnson, [colored,] under circumstances showing the same was stolen. The owner is notified to prove the same or said horse will be sold for cash to the highest bidder, at the bazaar of
W L Wall & Co, 98 La ave, pursuant to law. –Geo R Herrick, Property clerk

Appointments confirmed by the Senate: Col S Thayer, late of the Corps of Engrs U S Army, to be Brig Gen by brevet. To be Brig Genrls of Vols:
Col H Burhan, 6th Maine Vols   Col Lewis A Grant, 5th Vt Vols
Col E M McCook, 2nd Ind Vols   Col Edw Hatch, 2nd Iowa Vols
J C Redfield to be Receiver of Pblc Moneys at Humboldt, Kansas

FRI APR 29, 1864

Mrd: on Apr 27, at the Chr of the Epiphany, by Rev Dr Chas H Hall, Gen Lucius Fairchild, of Madison Wisc, to Miss Frank Bull, d/o the late Chas M Bull, of Detroit, Mich.

Died: in Wash City, at the Navy Yd, on Apr 28, of congestion of the brain, Mr Hesekiah S Woodruff, a native of N J, in his 66th yr. Funeral from the residence of Mr G W Talburt, across from the Navy Yd, Sat.

Brd of Assessors: Wash Co: D V Burr, Geo Plant, Chas R Belt.

SAT APR 30, 1864

Mrd: on Apr 19, at Christ Chr, Nashville, Tenn, by Rev Mr Hawlow, Ast Surgeon Dallas Bache, U S Army, to Alberta P, d/o Dr D T McGavock, of Nashville.

Died: in Springfield, Mass, on Apr 27, Parris, only child of Sarah P & Maj Albert Tracy, U S Army, in the 7th yr of his age.

Died: on Apr 25, at Detroit, Mich, of consumption, Mary J Bull, eldest d/o the late Chas M Bull, of that city.

Died: on Apr 29, John Sioussa, sr, in the 83rd yr of his age, a native of Paris, France, but for the last 58 years a resident of Wash City. Funeral from his late residence, N Y av, Sat.

Died: on Apr 28, Wm Van Riswick, in his 47th yr. Funeral, Sun, from his late residence on N st so.

Senate: 1-Mr Sprague presented a memorial of T Canisius, U S Cnsl at Vienna, recommending the purchase by the U S of the invention of Dr Auer, superintendent of the imperial paper mills & printing establishment of Austria, to make paper & linen out of corn husks & leaves: referred to the Cmte on Mfgrs.

MON MAY 2, 1864

Died: in Phil, on Apr 19, Mrs Rebecca Guest, widow of the late John Guest, in the 89th yr of her age.

Died: on May 1, Elisha D Putnam, in his 69th yr. A native of N H, but for the last 12 years sojourned in the West. He was one of the surviving pensioners of the War of 1812.

Deaths reported to the Navy Dept for the week ending Apr 30, 1864:
Chas D B Andrews, landsman, compression o/brain, Apr 8, Nav Hosp, N Orleans.
Sturgis S Dator, 1st cl fireman, diarrhoea, Apr 5, do.
Philip O'Brien, 1st cl fireman, drowned, Apr 13, vessel U S S *Wave*.
Terrence O'Brien, landsman, enteritis, Apr 8, vessel U S S *Stockdale*.
Wm Laron, 1st cl fireman, diarrhoea, Ape 22, Nav Asylum.
Stephen Coomber, 1st cl boy, drowned, Apr 6, vessel U S S *Narcissus*.
Jos McCurren, landsman, drowned, Apr 6, do.
Wm Seadon, cp of marines, consumption, Apr 20, Marine Barracks.
Edw Pranesbark, 1st cl boy, chronic diarrhoea, Apr 13, Nav Hosp, Memphis.
Eugene O'Leary, ord seaman, scalded, Apr 18, vessel U S S *Chenango*.
John Riley, seaman, scalded, Apr 16, do.
Alf Yates, landsman, scalded, Apr 19, do.
Barney Cannagan, coalheaver, scalded, Apr 21, do.
Wm Hickey, ord seaman, scalded, Apr 24, do.
Peter Anderson, landsman, pneumonia, Nav Hosp, N Y.
Saml Russell, ord seaman, consumption, Apr 21, do.
Geo W Daws, landsman, pertonitis, Apr 22, do.
Richd Hopkins, seaman, pneumonia, Apr 22, do.
Augustus Kennoes, seaman, remit fever, Apr 22, Nav Hosp, Norfolk.
Andrew Brown, landsman, debility, Apr 17, do.
Stephen M Carey, actg mstr's mate, accidental shooting, Apr 22, vessel U S S *Dragoro*.
R C Canarum, coalheaver, epilepsy, Apr 17, vessel U S S *Tulip*.
John Williams, landsman, drowned, Mar 13, Navy Yd, Mare Island.
Frank Silver, seaman, scalded, Apr 25, Nav Hosp, N Y.
Patrick Fenan, 2nd cl fireman, scalded, Apr 6, vessel U S S *Wabash*.
Geo Mitchell, Capt forecastle, apoplexy, Apr 23, vessel U S S *Nipsic*.
John Wentus, ord seaman, unknown, Apr 28, vessel U S S *Nereus*.

Supreme Crt of D C, in Equity #204. Wm H & Philip I Enals, vs Mary S Ennis & Z Mitchell & Mary F, his wife. Inquire if lot 22 in sq 264, & lot 7 in sq 488 are susceptible of partition. I give notice to the parties & to R H Laskey, guardian of the minor; meet at my ofc in City Hall, Wash, May 11. -W Redin, auditor

Mr Jas Holbrook, well known special agent of the P O Dept, died at his residence in Brooklyn, Conn, on Thu, after a long illness.

Supreme Crt of D C, in Equity #162. Jas Edelin vs Chas A Henderson et al. Regarding-appoint a trustee in place of Richd H Henderson; Archibald Henderson, dec'd, on or about Oct 30, 1857; a note for $4,800 is unpd. The heirs of Archibald Henderson are: Chas A Henderson, Richd H Henderson, Cazenove Henderson, Anna Taylor, Eliza Jones w/o Edw Jones, & Charlotte Dupont, w/o I E Dupont. All of whom, as well as the said Edw Jones & Irene E Dupont, are non-residents of D C. -D K Carter, Chief Justice -R J Meigs, clerk

Sale of a portion of the library of the late Chas F Mayer, of Balt, Md; at the Auction Rms. -Jas C McGuire & Co, aucts

Lgl authorities of the Foundry Meth Episc Chr on corner of 14th & G sts, have entered into a contract to erect a more suitable structure on the present site. Contract is with Messrs Terhune & Foster, upon plans & specs prepared by Messrs Cluss & Kamberheuber, architects. More than 50 years ago, by the liberality of one man, the Foundry Chr was built. –Robt Rickets, J E Parker, on behalf of the Bldg Cmte

Ex-Govn'r Cummings, of Ga, & his wife, left Balt on Wed for Old Point, en route for the south.

Confiscation of Rebel Property: the 1,700 shares of capital stock in the Great Western R R Co, owned by Leroy M Wiley, [late of N Y, but now in the south,] & libelled by the U S Dist Atty, have been confiscated by order of Judge Betts. Wiley is an old man. He owned, it is alleged, ten million dollars worth of property, partly at the north. –N Y Post

TUE MAY 3, 1864
Mrd: on Apr 27, by Rev G G Goss, John S Dickinson, of Erie, Pa, to Ellen M, d/o Robt Clarke, of Wash City.

Obit-Cmdor Wm D Porter, U S Navy, died at N Y on Sun, after a lingering illness of 3 or 4 months. He was s/o Cmdor David Porter dec'd, & bro of Rear Adm David D Porter. Wm D Porter was appt'd a Midshipman Jan 1, 1823; Cmdor, Aug 4, 1862. Age about 50 years at the time of his death.

WED MAY 4, 1864
Mrd: on May 2, by Rev John Thrush, at the residence of the bride's mother, on L st, Mr Geo W McKee & Miss Emeline Hunt, all of Wash City.

Mrd: on Apr 24, in Columbus, Ohio, by Rev F S Hoyt, Elliott Coues, M D, U S A, of Wash City, & Miss Sallie A Richardson, of Wellsburg, West Va.

Orphans Crt of Wash Co, D C. 1-Case of Wm B Hill, adm of Ann S Hill, dec'd, settlement on May 24. -Z C Robbins, rg o/wills 2-Prsnl estate of Geo W Wheeler, late of Wash Co, dec'd. -Asbury Lloyd, Saml E Douglass, excs

Miss Sally Pollock, of Alleghany Co, Md, has been tried by a military commission at Cumberland, charged with having on sundry occasions carried ltrs to the rebels in the South. She pleaded not guilty; but was found guilty. She is to be sent to the Pa Western Pen & imprisoned for the continuance of the war.

Charged with disloyalty: Capt Geo W Russell, formerly of the Bay line of steamers, & Edw M Kerr & J J Moore, of Norfolk, were arrested & transferred to the custody of Col Woolley, provost mrshl, & paroled to report whenever wanted. -Balt Transcript

Senate: 1-Cmte on Claims: made an adverse report on the ptn of the widow of John N Craft. 2-Cmte on Naval Affairs: made a report on the application of Paymstr Belknap, U S Navy, to be relieved from all responsibility for money stolen from him in N Y, & asked to be discharged from further consideration of the subject, which was agreed to.

Headqrtrs Middle Dept: 8th Army Corps: Balt, Md, Nov 13, 1863. Having concluded to accept the place of mbr of Congress in the Hse o/Reps, to which I was elected in Oct, 1862, I hereby tender my resignation of my commission as Maj Gen of the U S Vols, to take effect Dec 5 next. –Robt C Schenck, Maj Gen [Resignation is accepted, & he is authorized to turn his command to Brig Gen Lockwood at any time. –Edwin M Stanton, Sec of War]

Wash, Jan 1, 1864. I hereby tender my resignation as Maj Gen of the U S Vols. –Frank P Blair. Accepted by the Pres of the U S. –Edwin M Stanton, Sec of War Adj Gen ofc: Jas A Hardie, Ast Adj Gen. Wash, Apr 23, 1864-Request to withdraw my resignation as Maj Gen of the U S Vols, tendered on Jan 12, 1864. –Frank F Blair [Let this be done-A Lincoln.]

Gen McPherson, having been assigned to command of dept, could not Gen Frank Blair, without difficulty or detriment to the svc, be assigned to command the corps he commanded a while last autumn? -A Lincoln
Nashville, Tenn, Mar 16, 1864. Gen Logan commands the corps referred to in your despatch. I will see Gen Sherman in a few days & consult him about the transfer, & answer. –U S Grant, Lt Gen [Gen Sherman consents to the transfer of Logan to the 17th corps, & appointment of Blair to the 15th Corps. U S Grant, Lt Gen
Gen Orders: #178: War Dept, Adj Gen Ofc, Wash, Apr 23, 1864.
1-Maj Gen F P Blair, jr, is assigned to the command of the 17th Army Corps.
2-Capt Andrew J Alexander, 3rd Regt U S Cavalry, is assigned as Ast Adj Gen of the 17th Army Corps, with the rank of Lt Col, under the 10th section of the act approved Jul 17, 1862.
By order of the Pres of the U S: E D Townsend, Ast Adj Gen

THU MAY 5, 1864

Died: in Wash City, on May 3, of consumption, Chas W Hinman, in the 35th yr of his age. Funeral from his late residence, corner 4½ & C sts, today.

Supreme Crt of D C, in Equity #174. Mary Ann Roche, cmplnt, vs Jas E Smith & Emma his wife, Alice A Roche, Mary J Roche, Sallie J Roche, Wm J Roche, & Edw B Roche, dfndnts. Subpoena is to compel the dfndnts appearance having been returned by the Marshal on Mar 23, 1864, endorsed *not found, as to Wm J Roche*. A B Olin, Justice -R J Meigs, clerk

Supreme Crt of D C, in Equity #183. Cath Scanlan vs Michl McGinnis et al. Said dfndnts, Michl McGinnis & Mary McGinnis, his wife, failed to appear. The Mrshl on Apr 8, 1864, endorsed *not found*, as to said dfndnts. - A B Olin, Justice -R J Meigs, clerk

Supreme Crt of D C, in Equity #194. Wm W, Georgiana C, & Eveline O McGill, vs Emily & Winfield S McGill & Richard Butt. Report to be given on May 13 at City Hall, Wash City, whether it will be to the advantage of the minor dfndnt, & other parties, on division of lot 14 in sq 455, Wash City. -W Redin, auditor

Supreme Crt of D C, in Equity #93. John H Francis & Martha A Francis, vs Mary E Simmons & Frances Simmons. The parties named & the trustees, Messrs Drury & Turton, to appear at City Hall, Wash, D C, on May 13, for account of the trustees & distribution of funds. -W Redin, auditor

Supreme Crt of D C, in Equity Docket 6, #1606. Chandler et al vs Chandler, Hay, et al. Ratify sale made & reported by Edw C Gantt, trustee for the sale of rl est, sales amounted to be $14, 740. -A B Olin, Justice; R J Meigs, clerk. Supreme Crt of D C, in Equity, Docket 5, #1227. John R Woods et al, vs R G Briscoe's heirs, Jas L Clarke et al. Ratify sale by trustee reported on Nov 2 & 3 last; lot 6 in sq 575 to Matthew G Emery, for $700, which he assigned to Daniel B Clarke; lot 7 in reservation C, for $651.90, & lots 3 & 4 in sq 1027, for $447.16; lots 16 & 17 in sq 1027 to Wm B Todd, for $454.33; & lots 9 & 11 in sq 1027 to Richd Barry for $195.73; & at pvt sale he sold lot 5, in sq 1027 to Matthew G Emery for $215. -R J Meigs, clerk

Orphans Crt of Wash Co, D C. Ordered that the adm of John Douglas, dec'd, sell at pblc auction the prsnl estate belonging to the dec'd. -Z C Robbins, rg o/wills [See below]

By virtue of the foregoing order: sale of the finest plants in the U S. -Wm Douglas, adm of John Douglas, dec'd.

Fire at bldg #210 Chatham st, N Y, on Monday, took the lives of Wm Henig, a German, & his wife & 3 chldrn.

FRI MAY 6, 1864
Died: at Erie, Pa, Apr 21, Letitia M, wid/o Col John Bliss, U S Army, & d/o Andrew Ellicott, dec'd.

Information from the Leg of the U S in Paris, of deaths of ctzns of the U S, lately dec'd in France: 1-Jos Haelewyck, born in N Y, died at Paris Apr 9, 1863, aged 3 yrs. 2-Mgt McCrea Rhindlander, w/o Christopher Rhindlander, born in N Y, died at Paris Jun 26, 1863, aged 38 yrs. 3-Jos Francis Guillot, gentleman, born in New Orleans, La, died at Paris Jun 30, 1863, aged 61 yrs. 4-Franklin Smith, seaman of the American ship *Naples*, died at St Dennis Aug 11,1863

Crct Crt of Montg Co, Md, Crt of Equity, wherein Geo W Riggs & others, cmplnts, & John A B Leonard & Susan H Leonard his wife, dfndnts. Sale of rl estate of Mary Ann O'Neal, dec'd, late of said county; lot #1 contains about 197 acs, with a frame dwlg hse; lot #1, 2nd part, contains about 30 acs.
Lands on which the said John A B Leonard now resides. -W Veirs Bouic, trustee

Local Item. Wm Maxwell, sldr of the 8th Pa Reserves, was arrested for the murder of E B Gilbert, a conductor on the street railway, who was shot on Feb 12 while driving his car to the depot. Maxwell was at that time on his way home in Western Pa on a furlough.

Local Item. Eliz Shorter, negress, was sent to jail on charge of stealing from the hse of Mr Wm F Pruitt, where she was a servant. $57.45 in silver & Treas notes being found on her person.

SAT MAY 7, 1864
Died: on May 5, Laura Webster, aged 4 years & 8 mos, d/o Chas E & Louisa Stanford. Funeral from the residence of Jos Downing, 8th st, between K & L, today.

Clifton Cotton Factory for sale, 380 acs, at the head waters of St Mary's river. Apply to T W Gough, Leonardtown, St Mary's Co, Md.

The death of Wm S Thayer, Cnsl Gen at Alexandria, Egypt, is announced. He is not quite 35 years old & was an 1850 grad of Harvard College.

The lynch law still holds sway in Idaho Territory. J A Salde was lately hung by an infuriated mob.

Boston Post of Thu says: Brig Gen Devens, who has just concluded a tour of military inspection thru New England, received orders yesterday to report at Fortress Monroe for duty with the Army of the Potomac, under Gen Smith.

MON MAY 9, 1864

Deaths reported to the Navy Dept for the week ending May 7, 1864:
Benj Hendrick, coalheaver, chronic diarrhoea, Apr 20, Nav Hosp, Memphis.
Jacob Kinkley, seaman, debility, Apr 21, Nav Hosp, Memphis.
Chas W Finsser, Lt Cmder, gunshot wound, Apr 19, vessel U S S *Miami*.
Levi F Hill, ord seaman, consumption, Apr 11, Nav Hosp, New Orleans.
Wm Gilchrist, contraband, bronchitis, Apr 5, vessel U S S *Memphis*.
Ch Harris, capt forecastle, pneumonia, Apr 14, do.
Wm E Remington, q m, inflam of kidneys, Nav Hosp, N Y.
Ed Murray, landsman, erysipelas, no date, do.
Jas Pindle, landsman, blank, no date, vessel U S S *Kineo*.
Jas Male, seaman, drowned, Apr 28, vessel U S S *North Carolina*.
Wm D Porter, Cmdor, blank, May 1, N Y.
Wash Sherman, surg, consumption, May 4, Phil.
Frs Tevlin, marine, consumption, Feb 14, Navy Yd, Mare Island.
Peter Johnson, seaman, pneumonia, Mar 13, do.
Michael O'Conner, landsman, drowned, Apr 23, vessel U S S *Portsmouth*.
Guliermo Sonese, landsman, disease of liver, Mar 23, do.
Nelson Jones, 1st cl boy, typhoid fever, Mar 31, Nav Hosp, Memphis.
Govr Babis, contraband, smallpox, Mar 18, do.
Chs R Robin, seaman, chronic diarrhoea, Mar 30, do.
Rt Burr, seaman, smallpox, Mar 25, do.
Jas H Yates, ord seaman, smallpox, Feb 4, do.
Merriman Chisholm, coalheaver, unknown, Mar 12, vessel U S S *Waschita*.
Moses White, 2nd cl fireman, variola, Mar 6, vessel U S S *Red Rover*.
S Schooner, cook, consumption. Feb 19, vessel U S S *Mignionette*.
Melcher Johnson, contraband, pneumonia, Mar 11, vessel U S S *Gen Lyon*
Eli Bradford, 1st cl boy, dysentery, Feb 22, vessel U S S *New Era*.
Jos Lindsey, 1st cl boy, variola, Mar 30, Donaldsonville, La.
D Barrington, 1st cl boy, typhoid fever, Apr 21, vessel U S S *Benton*
Isaac S Heal, ord seaman, pneumonia, May 1, Nav Hosp, Chelsea.
Wm Perry, q m, consumption, Mar 23, Infirmary, Balt.
Jas Montgomery, marine, pneumonia, Apr 24, vessel U S S *Massachussetts*.
Jas Clinton, coalheaver, stab, May 4, Nav Asylum, Phil.

Died: on May 3, after a protracted illness, Susan Frances, w/o Edw H Hall, of the Treas Dept.

Trustees sale of *Mt Hebron Estate*, 1,567 acs, in Howard & Balt Counties, Md; of which the late Chief Justice Thos B Dorsey died seized; near Elysville; adjoins the lands of Messrs Anthony M Johnson & Jas C McGuire & Miss Sally F Dorsey. The *Homestead*, with dwlg, is about 282 acs. -Jas Mackubin, Ellicott's Mills, trust

Supreme Crt of D C, in Equity #216. John R Murray vs Stanislaus Hamilton, Mary M Hamilton, Benj J Neale & wife, & *John A Buck & *Eleanor his wife, & others. Bill is to procure a release of part of lot 25 in reservation #10, in Wash City, from the effect of a deed of trust given by cmplnt on Aug 24, 1864, to secure to Stanislaus Murray, late of said city, dec'd, payment of $8,000, then due said S Murray as guardian of the 3 infant chldrn of Edw J Hamilton, dec'd. John C C Hamilton & Saml Hamilton have died, John C C Hamilton dying last, leaving the dfndnts, Stanislaus Hamilton & Mary M Hamilton, both minors, his only heirs-at-law. Cmplnt has pd his debt with interest & is entitled to a release. -A B Olin, Justice -R J Meigs, clerk [*Non-residents, along with Wm E Hamilton]

Died: after a protracted illness, Emila E Darden, w/o Jos Darden in her 25th yr. Funeral from the residence of her mother-in-law, Mrs Susan B Darden, 332 9th st, today. [No date-recent]

Supreme Crt of D C, in Equity #217. Jos H Skinner & Sarah A, his wife, Robt M Brown & Josephine S, his wife, & Geo L Arnold & C M, his wife, vs John L Hall. Inquire whether lot 6 & part of lot 7 in sq 876, Wash City, be to the advantage o/the cmplnts & dfndt to sell the same for purpose of division. -W Redin, auditor

Supreme Crt of D C, in Equity #135. Benj Beall & others vs Jane Boulanger & John M Jewell & others. Statement of the trustee's account in City Hall, Wash, May 31. -W Redin, auditor

Supreme Crt of D C. Bender & wife vs Russells. Statement of the trustee's account & distribution of funds, May 16, City Hall, Wash. -Walter S Cox, spec auditor

Orphans Crt of Wash Co, D C. 1-Prsnl estate of Richd Burgess, late of Wash Co, dec'd. -R W Burgess. 2-Prsnl estate of Richd Smith, late of Wash City, dec'd. -Covington Smith, excx 3-Prsnl estate of John C Rives, late of Wash City, dec'd. -Saml T Williams, Wright Rives, Franklin Rives, excs

Following nominations of Brig Gen of Vols were confirmed by the Senate on Sat:

Col Danl H Rucker	Col John W Turner
Col Robt Allen	Col Augustus V K_uts, 2nd Ohio Cavalry
Lt Col Rufus Ingalls	Col Thos K Smith, 54th Ohio Vols

Among the drafted in the 22nd ward of the city of Cincinnati on Fri last were T Buchanan Read, F B Plympton, & E Henderson, editors of the Commericial newspaper of that place.

TUE MAY 10, 1864
Mrd: on May 9, in the Parsonage of the Meth Prot Chr, 9th st, by Rev J T Ward, Mr John E Hammond to Miss Anne A Frank.

Died: on May 8, at *Green Vale*, near Washington, Philip, infant s/o Wm E & Carrie J Dougherty, of Harrisburg, Pa.

Movement on Richmond. Casualties from the battles of Thu & Fri last thus far reported to the War Dept:

Brig Gen Alexander Hays, of Pa, killed	Col Lewis, 3rd Vt, wounded
Brig Gen Jas L Wadsworth, of N Y, killed	Lt Col Foster, wounded
Brig Gen Webb, of N Y, wounded	Col Stone, Bucktail, injured by fall
Col Wilson, 43rd N Y, wounded	Col West 9th Maine, killed
Maj Fryar, wounded	Capt Bedwell, 49th N Y, casualty
Col Stone 2nd Vt, wounded	Maj Darlington, 18th Pa, casualty
Lt Col Tyler, wounded	

Cornelius Tuell, found guilty of the murder of his wife, to be hung on Jul 8th next. Peter Gooden, guilty of the murder of Geo Banks, to be hung on the same day.

WED MAY 11, 1864

Died: in Gtwn, on May 10, Mrs Cornelia Adams, w/o J W Deeble, & 2nd d/o the late Capt Horace Fuller, of Balt, Md. Funeral from the Dunbarton St Meth Episc Chr on Thur next.

Died: in Wash City, on May 10, Jessie Clay, infant d/o Virginia B & the late H C Baldwin, aged 10 months. Funeral from the residence, 467 D st, Thu.

Casualties on the James River. Fortress Monroe, May 9. On the vessel *Cmdor Jones*: paymstr Chapman, instantly killed; 3rd Ast Engr Sautell, supposed killed; Geo F Moore, pilot, died today; & 27 missing. Ensign Adams is too badly wounded to be removed. Lt S F Wade, commanding, is removed.

Orphans Crt of Wash Co, D C. 1-Case of John Little, exc of Judson Wakker, dec'd; settlement on Jun 4. -Z C Robbins, rg o/wills 2-Prsnl estate of John Crumbaugh, late of Gtwn, dec'd. -Cath V Crumbaugh, admx

Casualties in the regular army in the recent battles at Chancellorsville on Thu & Fri last: Capts Clay & Burbank, 14th U S Reg Infty, & Lt Staples, of the 11th, killed. Capt Hudson & Smedberg, & Lt Brodhead, of 14th Regt Infty, & Lts Pleasants, McIntosh, & Newby, of the 11th, Lt Swan, of the 17th, Capt Martin & Lt Simmons, of the 4th, were among the wounded.

Senate: 1-Resolution was adopted giving the use of the Hall for May 18th, for the delivery of an address on the battle of Gettysburg, by Rev John R Warder, of Pa, the proceeds to be applied to religious purposes.

Richmond Enq of May 7th says that about 1,700 Yankee prisoners have arrived at Orange Crt-Hse, & it claims that the Confederates were successful in the Fri's fight, & pushed Grant back to near Chancellorsville. The following casualties are reported: Gen Longstreet, painfully wounded in the shoulder; Brig Gen Paul Jenkins, of S C, mortally wounded; Col J Thompson Brown, of 1st Va Artl, was shot thru the head & killed outright; Col Warren, 8th Va, Cols Miller, Nance, & Garther, of S C, were killed. Gen Hattle's Alabama & Jordan's Georgia brigs suffered severely. Col Randolph, of Va, was also killed. Gen J M Jones, of Va, killed.

Thos J Beach, for many years acting editor of the Balt Sun, breathed his last in Balt on Sun last. He was a native of England & a gentleman possessing talent & education. At the time of his death he was in his 53rd yr.

Gen Sedgwick, the late Cmder of the 6th Army Corps, fell in a skirmish near Spottsylvania Crt-Hse on Monday last.

THU MAY 12, 1864

Ltr to the N Y Herald, dt'd at Piney Branch Chr, May 8: skirmish near Spottsylvania Crt-hse. Gen Robinson, early in the engagement, was shot thru the knee: limb will have to be amputated. Col Coulter now commands the division. Col Dennison, commanding the 3rd brig of the 4th div is wounded in the arm. Capt Martin is slightly wounded in the neck. His battery lost 2 killed & 7 wounded. Among the killed is Col Ryan, 140th N Y. He was formerly Ast Adj Gen of Gen Sykes, was a grad of West Point,& a young & most promising ofcr. Maj Stark of his regt, was also killed.

Orphans Crt of Wash Co, D C. 1-Case of Jane Farnham & Valentine Blanchard, adms of Robt Farnham, dec'd; settlement on Jun 4. -Z C Robbins, rg o/wills 2-Prsnl estate of Barrott A Prindle, late of Wash City, dec'd. -A Thos Bradley, adm d b n c t a

Brig Gen Horatio G White appt'd Maj Gen of Vols, to succeed Maj Gen Sedgwick as Cmder of the 6th Army Corps.

By direction of Pres Lincoln, Capt L H Ellingswood, 10th Mass vols, has been dishonorably dismissed the svc of the U S, having secured a leave of absence, on a telegram from his bro, to the effect that his father was at the point of death, which was entirely false, & for failing to return to his command after the deception had been discovered. -Star

Red River Fleet: Official Acc't of Rebel attacks upon it & the blowing up of the ship *Eastport*. Mississippi Squad, flag ship *Cricket*, off Alexandria, La, Apr 28, 1864. Ltr to Hon Gideon Welles, Sec of the Navy. Regarding: sinking of the *Eastport* caused by the explosion of a torpedo under her bottom & near her bow. Lt Cmder commanding the Eastport, S L Phelps, had done all a man could do to save her. The success of the expedition depended entirely on the sucess of the Navy in getting the transports safely to an appointed place, Springfield Landing, which would have put us in communication with the army, etc. Lt Cmder Phelps was brave & cool; Actg Mstr Geo W Rogers, of the ship *Pittsburg*, deserves great credit; Actg Mstr J S Watson defended his vessel in the most gallant manner. Zealously performed every thing required of them: Cmder R Townsend, commanding the ship *Essex*; Lt Cmder J L Phelps, ship *Eastport*; Lt Cmder Watson Smith, ship *Chillicothe*, [tempo,] Lt Cmder K R Breese, ship *Black Hawk*; Lt Cmder J P Foster, ship *Lafayette*; Lt Cmder J S Greer, ship *Benton*; Lt Cmder E K Owen, ship *Louisville*; Lt Cmder F M Ramsey, ship *Choctow*; Lt Cmder T O Selfridge, ship *Osage*; Lt Cmder Byron Wilson, ship *Ouichita*; Lt Cmder Geo M Bache, ship *Lexington*; Lt Cmder S W Terry, ship *Benefit*, [naval transport;] Act Vol Lt W R Hoel, ship *Pittsburg*; Ast Vol Lt Saml Howard, ship *Neosho*; Actg Vol Lt Geo W Browne, ship *Ozark*; Actg Vol Lt A R Langthorne, ship *Mound City*; Ast Mstr H H Garringe, ship *Cricket*; Ast Mstr J S Watson, ship *Juliet*; Act Mstr Chas Thatcher, ship *Gazelle*. -David Porter, Rear Admiral

FRI MAY 13, 1864

Died: at the Hdqrtrs of the U S M C, on May 12, Col Commandant John Harris. Funeral on Sat. He entered the Marine Corps on Apr 13, 1814 & appointed to the command of it on Jan 7, 1859. -Gideon Welles, Sec of the Navy. [Burial will be in Oak Hill Cemetery, Gtwn, D C.]

Hon Chas B Calvert, of Riverdale, Md, a Rep from that State in the last Congress, died suddenly of paralysis on May 12. Funeral at his late residence at Riverdale, May 16.

In the fight on Tue last, Gen Stevenson & Gen Rice were killed; the former was taken off by a stray shot; the latter was severly wounded in the thigh, &, an amputation being deemed necessary, he failed to rally after the operation.

The late Gen Jas S Wadsworth, who was killed in battle in Va last week, was born to a large fortune; his family home was in Genesee, N Y. His possessions were counted by townships & his tenantry by thousands.

Local: A full size plaster bust of a well know gentleman in this community, Mr Lambert Tree, Chief clerk in the City P O, was executed by Mr Thos H Dorian, a messenger in the same ofc. It is an excellent representation, & having been modeled from a photograph with out the usual sittings for such a purpose. Mr Dorian is a young man-by trade, we believe, a stone mason

Orphans Crt of Wash Co, D C. Prsnl estate of Wm Noyes, late of Wash City, dec'd. -Henry C Noyes, exc

SAT MAY 14, 1864
Died: on May 10, of aneurism, L Blanchard True, atty, formerly of Maine, but long a resident of Wash City as teacher of High Hill Seminary, & later claim agent; a grad of Bowdoin College. Remains will be taken to Maine for interment today.

Died: on May 12, of brain fever, Henry Edwin Harding, aged 23 mos, s/o Henry J & Louisa Hardy. Funeral from their residence, 22nd st, between H & I sts, today.

Supreme Crt of U S for D C. Marshal sale of the property of Wilford A Manning; sale of about 110 acs, to satisfy judgment #752 in favor of Jerusha G May. -Ward H Lamon, U S Mrshl, D C

Wash Corp: 1-Mayor nominates Leonard Simmacher as scavenger to the 2nd dist of the 4th ward, v Jacob Fisher, removed: referred to the Cmte on Police. 2-Ptn of T Reedeger was referred to the Cmte on Claims. 3-Cmte on Police: adverse on the bill granting certain privileges to J H Harleston. 4-Cmte on Mkts: to procure the opinion of the Corp Atty to the legality of the claim of Josiah Eggleston. 5-Referred to the Cmte on Financs: bill for relief of H Shultheis; & a bill for relief of John Williams. 6-Bids for laying water pipes were received from: Peter Mack, Jeremiah Costello, A Watson, Henry McArdle, Thos W Miller, Richd A Hill, & P & J P Crowley.

The battle of Tue near Spottsylvania Crt-hse. We have lost 12 Generals:

Killed:

Sedgwick	Stevenson	Rice
Wadsworth	Hays	

Wounded:

Bartlett	Robinson	Baxter
Getty	Morris	

Missing:

Seymour	Shalar

MON MAY 16, 1864
Despatch from Bermuda Hundred, dt'd May 13, reports rebel Casualties in the late battles in Va, derived from the Petersburg Register of May 12: <u>Killed-</u>

Gen Jenkins, of S C	Col Carter, Ga	Col Finney, Miss
Gen J M Jones	Col G H Forney, Ala	Gen L A Stafford, died
Col Hanse, S C	Col Avery, N C	of wounds
Col Grice	Col W W Randolph	

<u>Wounded-</u>

Col Galliard, S C	Col Shaffield, Ga	Col Lane, N C
Col Kennedy	Col Minetree	Col Sanders, N C
Col Herbert, Ala	Col Whisehead, Ga	Col Fulum, Ga
Col Houlowe	Col Board, Va	Col Miller, S C
Col Jones, N C	Col Winston, N C	

Captured-Col Davidson, N C

Estray taken by Metropolitan Police, a bay mare. -Geo F Herrick, property clerk

Deaths reported to the Navy Dept for the week ending May 14, 1864:
John P Hodge, marine, cardiac disease, Apr 24, Wash.
John Smith, seaman, pneumonia, Apr 26, vessel U S S *Portsmouth.*
D H Daniel, actg ensign, consumption, Apr 14, Nav Hosp, Pensacola.
Jackson Smith, ord seaman, cardiac disease, May 17, Recg ship North Carolina.
Vincent Lyons, ord seaman, consumption, May 3, Nav Hosp, N Y.
Henry Wilson, 1st cl boy, consumption, May 6, do.
Spencer Hughes, ord seaman, empyema, Apr 27, Nav Hosp, Memphis.
Geo Washington, contraband, contusion, Apr 30, do.
John Calligan, seaman, chronic gastritis, May 4, Nav Hosp, Norfolk.
Geo F Moore, pilot, wounds, May 8, do.
Frank Rodman, ord seaman, consumption, Apr 30, do.
Pat Turlin, *seaman, wounds, Jan 21, 1863.
Albert W Marshal, *ord seaman, wounds, Jan 22, 1863.
Jas Duffy, *landsman, remit fever, May 29, 1863.
Peter Le Provost, *seaman, remit fever, Jul 9, 1863.
Geo H Abbot, *yeoman, remit fever, Jul 31, 1863.
Timothy Baldwin, *seaman, dysentery, Sep 3, 1863.
Chs Barxter, *seaman, dysentery, Sep 23, 1863.
Chs Thomas, *gunner's mate, typhoid fever, Nov 17, 1863.
Peter Kunan, *landsman, dysentery, Nov 30, 1863.
Chs Tweedy, *ord seaman, dysentery, Dec 1883 [1883-copied as written]
Wm P O'Brien, *ord seaman, dysentery, Dec 27, 1863.
Thos Cuff, **landsman, remit fever, Oct 2, 1863.
Thos Secanb, **coalheaver, dysentery, Nov 29, 1863.
John Mullin, **landsman, dysentery, Nov 29, 1863.
Alpheus Todd, **landsman, dysentery, Dec 20, 1863.
Jas Morrison, **marine, dysentery, Jan 16.
B B Brown, **yeoman, pneumonia, Jan 18.
John Stuart, landsman, dysentery, Jan 7, vessel U S S *Anderson*; prisoner in Tex.
Geo Wilson, seaman, acute dysentery, Oct 11, vessel U S S *Cavuga*; prisoner in Texas.
De Elbert Fuller, landsman, aoynamia, May 12, Nav Hosp, Norfolk.
*Belonging to the vessel U S S *Morning Light,* & prisoners in Texas.
**Belonging to the vessel U S S *Clifton* & prisoners in Texas.

Mrd: in Wash City, on May 12, by Rev Dr Samson, Marcus B Latimer, of Va, to Miss Susie B Lowe, of Wash City.

Died: in Alexandria, Va, on May 14, of consumption, in the 23rd yr of her age, Lalla R, 2nd d/o Jas & the late Eliz Roach. Funeral from St Mary's Chr, Alexandria, Va, this evening.

Died: in Wash City, at the residence of her grandfather, Col Wm Maynadier, U S Army, 194 G st, on May 14, Lucy Ledyard, infant d/o Lt Cmder S L Phelps, U S Navy. Funeral today.

Fortress Monroe, May 12. The body of Capt Phelan, of the gunboat *Shawsheen*, was found floating in the James river yesterday, shot thru the head. At the time of the destruction of the boat he was seen to swim ashore.

Now open in Wash, a first class N Y Millinery establishment. -Miss J Stanford, #4 Mkt space, near Ninth st, Wash.

This morning brings news of the death of Col Francis Fessenden, 13 Maine Regt, while leading his brigade into the late battle on Cane river, La; second of the sons of Senator Fessenden, of Maine, who have fallen in this war. He was 27 years of age & was mrd only about a yr ago. [See May 31, 1864: page 192.]

Hartford, Conn. The embalmed body of Gen Sedgwick arrived in New Haven on its way to his native town of Cornwall, Litchfield Co, for burial.

The Register named 85 Capts & Lts killed & wounded. It says: Gen Walker, of Va, was wounded at Spottsylvania, he lost a foot. Gen Hays, of La, wounded yesterday. Gen L A Stafford, of La, died yesterday at Richmond. The Petersburg Reg of the 13th-wounded: Col T B Lamar, Fla; Col W C Holt, Ga, Col W T Hartsfield, of Ga; Col W H Willis, La, Col W C Hodge, Ga, Col E D Willet, La.

The funeral of the late Hon Chas B Calvert is appt'd to take place at 3 p m today, from his late residence at Riverdale. The friends of the family are invited to attend.

Bangor [Me] Whig says: most startling accident occurred near Camden on Fri of last week. While with a small party out after May flowers on top of that part of Megunticook Mountain near Mr Wm Barrett's pond, Miss French was caught by her dress or hoop, & carried headlong over the cliff, falling some 200 feet before striking on the rocks below. Strange as it may seem, though dreadfully bruised & many of her bones broken, she survived svr'l hours, but was entirely unconscious. Miss French was the d/o Mr Zacock French, of Lincolnville, & about 13 years of age.

Teresa Carreno will give a grand concert for the benefit of our sick & wounded in Washington from the recent battles, to be given under the sanction of Actg Surgeon Gen Barnes.

Mrs P Danse will leave America at the end of Jun to open her School in Carlsruhe Germany. Parents & guardians wishing their dghts to be under her care, are to send notice before Jun 25, either to Prof A Danse, Pittsburgh, Pa, or H Hahn, Banker, 48 Exchange Pl, N Y, where circulars may be had.

TUE MAY 17, 1864

Died: on May 16, of apoplexy, at *Green Vale* farm, near Wash, the family residence, Mrs Cecelia A Hickey, w/o Wm Hickey, in her 64th yr. On Wednesday carriages will be provided at St Aloysius Chr, to proceed to *Green Vale*, for the funeral.

Died: on May 15, at Phil, in the 33rd yr of her age, Cath, w/o A T Siousa, of Wash City. Funeral from the residence of Thos J Fisher, 420 N Y av, Wed.

Funeral of Col John Harris on Sat last, took place at the late residence of the dec'd, at the Marine Barracks. Svcs conducted by Drs Pyne & Morsell, of the Episc Chr. Pall bearers were: Cmdors Montgomery & Rodgers, of the Navy; Gens Meigs & Ramsey, of the Army; Majs Slack, Nicholson, & Cash, of the Marine Corps; Senator Foster & Rep H Winter Davis. Cortege consisted of mbrs of the Marine Corps & of the Marine Band, with the relatives & numerous friends of the dec'd. Remains were interred at Oak Hill Cemetery, Gtwn, D C.

Died: on May 16, Maggie Cameron Stitt, w/o Rev Jos B Stitt, aged 22 yrs. Funeral on Wed from the residence of Mr R Ricketts, 318 I st.

Loss of Gen ofcrs in the <u>National Army</u>:
<u>Killed-</u>

Brig Gens Wadsworth & Rice, of N Y	Hayes, of Pa
Stevenson, of Mass	

<u>Wounded-</u>

Brig Gen Torbert, of N J	Webb, of N Y
Robinson, of the Reg Army	Baxter, of Pa
Getty, of the Reg Army	W H Morris, of N Y

<u>Captured-</u>
Brig Gens:

Shaler	Crawford
Seymour	

Gens Bartlett & Owens were also slightly wounded, but as they are still at the head of their brigades in the field, they cannot be considered hors du combat.

The <u>Rebel Army</u>:
<u>Killed:</u>

Maj Gen J E B Stuart, of Va	J M Jones, of Va
Brig Gens Jenkins, of S C	L A Stafford, of La

<u>Wounded:</u>

Lt Gen Longstreet, of Va	Brig Gen Walker, of Va
Maj Gen Heth, of Va	Brig Gen Hays, of La
Maj Gen Pickett, of Va	Brig Gen Benning, of Ga
Brig Gen Pegram, of Va	

<u>Captured:</u>
Maj Gen Johnson & Brig Gen Geo H Steuart, of Md.

Brig Gen Joshua T Owens, of Pa, is not dead, as was reported; he is still on duty, having only lost a finger. Col Peter Lytle, of Phil, is said to be alive & unhurt.

For sale: splendid country seat near Balt: for particulars apply to Geo W Tinges, 3 St Paul st, Balt.

WED MAY 18, 1864

Supreme Crt of D C, in Equity #109. Peter V Hagner, Frances R Hagner, Alex'r B Hagner, Danl R Hagner, & Alex'r B Hagner & Danl R Hagner, as excs of Frances Hagner, vs Alex'r Randall, Jos H Nicholson & Eliza Ann his wife, Cleland K Nelson & Mary M his wife, Richd H Hagner, Laura S Hagner, Cora C Hagner, Kate G Hagner, Fanny Hagner, Grattan Hagner, Chas E Hagner, & Randall Hagner. Regarding-partition of the rl estate of the late Peter Hagner, of D C. Report the amount which the estate of said Frances Hagner is entitled to be reimbursed for improvement erected by her out of her own funds, upon said rl est, during her life tenancy thereof. All are to meet in City Hall, Wash, May 28, 1864. -W Redin, auditor

Mrd: on May 17, at Trinity Chr, by Rev R J Keeling, Mahlon Ashford, of D C, to Sidney Lafourcade, only d/o Jas F Bell, of Phil.

Wash Corp: 1-Ptn of John G Gardner & others: referred to the Cmte on Police. 2-Act for relief of Chas Stewart: read 3 times & passed. 3-Ptn of David L Morrison & others, to extend the sewer on 10th st, from N Y ave to M st north: passed. 4-Cmte on Police: was referred the ptn of Henry Newman in relation to a frame bldg, asked to be discharged from its further consideration.

Senate: 1-Mr Hale called up the bills granting pensions to the wid/o Maj Gen Hiram G Berry & to the wid/o Brig Gen Edw D Baker, the latter of whom was killed at the battle of Ball's Bluff: & they were passed. 2-Mr Hale called up the bill to give a pension of $50 a month to the wid/o the late Maj Gen Elijah P Whipple, killed in the battle during the present war: bill passed. 3-Ptn was presented by Mr Sumner, from Germans of N Y, praying that the word "white" may be omitted from all laws in the qualification of ctzns & voters in organizing the Territories, etc: referred to the Cmte on Terr.

Pres Lincoln has accepted the invitation to be present this Wed, at the Hall of the Hse o/Reps, to hear the Rev J R Warner's celebrated oration on the "Battle of Gettysburg."

Mrd: at St Aloysius Chr, on May 17, by Rev Fr Maguire, Geo E Falconer & Maggie R Culverwell, all of Wash City.

THU MAY 19, 1864

Mrd: in Wash City, on Apr 21, at St Aloysius Chr, by Rev Fr Maguire, Lt Alex'r J M Attridge to Miss Josephine A Joyce.

Died: on May 18, of hemorrhage, Mrs Ellenor Dougherty, in her 47th yr. Funeral from her late residence on G st, near Second, today.

Died: on May 18, Bernard, s/o John & Agnes McDermott, aged 4 months & 16 days. Funeral from their residence, 67 Missouri av, today.

Escape of prisoners from Ft McHenry on Sat: Eugene Lamar, of the Confederate army, sentenced to be hung as a spy; Wm B Compton, of Confederate army, do; Geo E Shearer, sentenced to 15 years with hard labor; L W Dorsey, awaiting trial for various charges of treason; Jas Gubbins, of Confederate army, captured near City Point. Mystery is whether they swam across the harbor or walked to town.

Senate: 1-Resolution in relation to Grumbay Goodloe was passed, allowing his re-appointment to the military academy.

Hse o/Reps: 1-Cmte on Elections: case of Jos Segar: declaring that he is not entitled to a seat as a Rep from the 1st Congressional Dist of Va. 2-Also, Lucien H Chandler is not entitled to a seat as a Representative from the 2nd Dist of Va. House adjourned.

Teresa Carreno, only 10 years of age, is almost a prodigy. Her concerts are given at Odd Fellows' Hall & she is enchanting. She is well sustained by other artists.

H N Barlow, late of Phil, offers his svcs for a few weeks in cleaning, lining, & restoring oil paintings. Orders may be left with F Lamb, Picture & Glass Frame Maker, so side of Pa ave, near 13th st.

FRI MAY 20, 1864
Wash Corp: nominated & elected Com'rs of Election for the ensuing Jun election:

Wm H Calvert	S E Thyson	E Tippett
Wm Riggles	Alex'r Admanson	Jas Richards
Lewis H Parker	Chas P Wood	Saml Miller
John W Dyer	Geo C Whiting	Henry E Marks
Geo F Kidwell	E C Eckloff	J E Cook
Robt Earl, jr	John W Clarke	John W Thompson
J P Hilton	Saml Sylvester	Saml Armistead
Geo Jillard	Chas H Anderson	Wm Beron
Francis Miller	Chas Walter	Thos H Beron
L J Middleton	Thos Galligan	Geo Mattingly
John D Thompson	John Mills	S C Magruder
Geo W Harkness	Geo M Oyster	Henry O Noyes
Jas M Towers	John V Bryan	Wm T Doniphan
Gideon W Larner	W Slater	H Wales Burroughs

Mrd: May 19th, by Rev Mr Johnson, Mr Thos E Young to Miss Emma J Otterback, all of Wash City.

Mrd: on Apr 20, in St Stephen's Chr, Harrisburg, Pa, by Rev B B Leacack, Geo D Ramsey, jr, U S Army, to Kate Bentalou, y/d/o Wm Buhler, of that city.

Wash Corp: 1-Ptn of P J McIntire, asking permision to erect a tent for recruiting purposes, in connection with a bill for his relief: referred to the Cmte on Police. 2-Ptn of Thos Mason & others for a bridge on Jackson st: referred to the Cmte on Improvements. 3-Ptn of Lewis Godfrey & others, with reference to the completion of a well & the erection of a pump: passed. 4-Ptn of the Pres of Gonzaga, with a bill to refund certain moneys to *Gonzaga College*: passed. 5-Cmte of Claims: asked to be discharged from the further consideration of the ptns of Alvin Richard: & of Nelson Wiley: which was so ordered. 6-Ptn of Patrick Donohue, with a bill granting certain powers to the Mayor: passed. 7-Bill for relief of J Redeger was referred to the Cmte of Claims. 8-Cmte on Drainage, etc: ptn from H F Barnard, with a bill for the construction of a sewer in L st, from 16th to 17th passed. 9-Certain privileges to J H Harleston: passed. 10-Cmte on Claims: adverse on the ptn of John Clark, & asked to be discharged: which was so ordered. 11-Jacob Simmacher for scavenger was unanimously confirmed. 12-Cmte on Mkts: asked to be discharged from the claim of Josiah Eggleston, said claim not being in possession of said cmte. 13-Bill for payment to Wm Thomas for superintending canal improvements: referred to the Cmte on Finances.

Mrd: on May 17, at the First Bapt Chr, on 19th st, by Rev Mr Madden, Mr G H Garison, of D C, to Miss Kate Beckby, of Alexandria, Va.

On the 22nd inst, the Hon J M Priest, V P, arrived from Sinoe in the Gov't schnr *Quail*. The following day the Pres administered the oath of ofc to the V P in the Senate chamber. [Note: this paper is dated May 20th.]

The marriage of Miss Aphia, the y/d/o his Hon Judge B R Wilson, with Mr Edw F, oldest s/o Hon E J Roye, took place in Wash City on the 27th inst. Ceremonies performed by Rev J W Roberts. We saw at the marriage the Pres & mbrs of his cabinet, mbrs of the Leg, & foreign officials. Prof Luca presided at the piano. After spending a few days at the residence of the bride's father, Mr Roye will lead his bride to his residence on Ashmun st. [Note: this paper is dated May 20th.]

On Wed Maj Gen Lew Wallace, commandant of the Middle Dept, issued an order prohibiting the further pblctn of the Evening Transcript, pblshd by Mr Wm H Nielson, in Balt, on charge of disloyalty, in publishing as a telegraphic despatch a grossly exaggerated estimate of the losses of the Army of the Potomac, & crediting the same to the Assoc Press correspondent at Wash, thereby seeking to establish reliability. [70,000 men killed, wounded, or missing, was the number used.]

Richmond Enq of the 14th inst: Gens Stuart & Fits Lee came up with the enemy at Yellow Tvrn, but being terribly outnumberd, they managed to maintain their ground, & inflict heavy loss upon the enemy. Here, in one of those desperate charges, at the head of a charging column, the chivalrous Stuart fell, mortally wounded. Our loss was severe. Col H Clay Pate & Lt Col Robt Randolph were killed. Gen Gordon was severely wounded. The funeral of Gen Stuart took place yesterday, from St James' Chr, corner of Marshall & 5th sts. Pallbearers were: Gen Bragg, Maj Gen McCown, Gen Chilton, Brig Gen Lawton, Cmdor Forrest, Capt Lee, of the Navy, & Gen Geo W Randolph, formerly Sec of War. Pres Davis sat near the front, with a look of grief upon his careworn face. Gen Ransom, commanding the Dept of Richmond, was in the church. A short svc was read by Rev Dr Peterkin. The hearse proceeded to Hollywood Cemetery, followed by a long train of carriages. No military escort accompanied the procession, but the hero was laid to his last resting place on the hillside, while the earth trembled with the roar of artillery & the noise of the deadly strife of armies-the one bent upon desecrating & devastating his native land, & the other proudly & defiantly standing in the path & invoking the blessing of Heaven upon their cause.

SAT MAY 21, 1864
Mrd: in N Y C, on May 16, at the residence of the officiating clergyman, by Rev Dr Anderson, John Skirving, of Germantown, Pa, to Miss Mary L Laimbeer, of Roxbury, Mass.

Mrd: in Raleigh, N C, on Apr 19, 1864, by Rev Dr Mason, E W Ayres, of Richmond, Va, to Sallie Peyton Sawyer, d/o Hon S T Sawyer.

Died: at his residence, *Lemington*, near Wash City, on May 20, Eleazer Lindsley, after a protracted illness. Funeral tomorrow from his late residence. Carriages will be at the hse of his son-in-law, Hudson Taylor, D & 9th sts.

Died: on May 20, of a protracted illness, Michael Shanks, a native of Gtwn, D C, but for many years a resident of Wash, in the 70th yr of his age. Funeral from his late residence, 409 F st, Sunday.

Died: on May 19, Saml H Lamborn, aged 38 yrs. Funeral from 391 E st, Sun.

Died: of typhoid fever, in Wash City, on May 20, Emma C S, w/o Capt Horatio C King, U S V, & d/o Russell Stebbins, of N Y C. Funeral at the residence of Horatio King, 510 H st, Sun; interment in N Y.

Died: on May 19, Emma, y/d/o the late Chas H James. Funeral from the residence of her mother, 409 H st, Sat.

Boston, May 19. Hawthorne, Nathaniel, author, died this morning at Plymouth, N H; stopping there in the course of a journey for his health, in the company of ex-Pres Franklin Pearce. He had been suffering with general debility for some time. He was found dead in his bed by ex-Pres Pearce.

The superintendent of the Independent Telegraph Co, Mr J Worl, & the operators arrested on Wed, in consequence of a bogus proclamation, have been promptly discharged as innocent of any connection with the fraud. -Union

MON MAY 23, 1864
Deaths reported to the Navy Dept for the week ending May 21, 1864:
John Harris, Col Commandnt, bronchitis, May 12, Marine Hdqrtrs.
Chas Ringot, actg ensign, drowned, May 7, 1864, vessel U S S *Shawsheen.*
Wm White, seaman, drowned, Mar 6, vessel U S S *Cmdor Jones.*
Nicholas J Walsh, yeoman, delirium tremens, Apr 13, 1864, Nav Hosp, N Y.
Martin Daniel, landsman, smallpox, Apr 29, 1864, Nav Hosp, Key West.
John Conway, landsman, paralysis, May 13, 1864, Nav Asylum.
John A Oliver, landsman, gunshot wound, May 5, 1864, vessel U S S *Wyalusing.*
Ralph E Lake, 1st cl fireman, gunshot wound, May 5, 1864, vessel U S S *Mattabesett.*
Wm H Demit, 1st cl boy, gunshot wound, May 5, 1864, do.
Thos Johnson 2, coal heaver, scald, May 5, 1864, vessel U S S *Sassacus.*
Wm Sutherland, 1st cl fireman, scald, May 7, 1864, do.
Jas Tillott, do,do, do, do.
John C Tabor, landsman, pneumonia, May 12, 1864, Nav Hosp, Chelsea.
Frank Roberts, seaman, apoplexy, Mar 20, 1864, vessel U S S *Osceola.*
Arnold Gregg, contraband, diarrhoea, May 8, 1864, Nav Hosp, Memphis.
Jos Slaytor, landsman, blank, May 15, 1864, Nav Hosp, Norfolk.
John Gordon, marine, consumption, May 9, 1864, Nav Hosp, N Y.
Lewis Willard, seaman, suicide, May 13, 1864, Recg ship, *New York.*
John McIrnry, landsman, drowned, Apr 7, 1864, vessel U S S *Wachusett.*
John White, pensioner, apoplexy, May 18, 1864, Nav Asylum, Phil.
Thos Lilly, landsman, drowned, Apr 12, 1864, vessel U S S *Wachusett.*
Wesley Whittington, landsman, drowned, Apr 12, 1864, do.
Edw Guy, landsman, drowned, Apr 12, 1864, do.
Edw Moses, actg mstr, inflam of liver, May 8, 1864, Portsmouth, N H.
Thos Mitchell, seaman, hemorrhage, May 17, 1864, Nav Hosp, Norfolk.
Chas A McDowell, 3rd ast engr, dysentery, May 11, 1864, vessel U S S *Ladona.*

Died: on May 21, Clifford Gordon, s/o Chas Gordon, aged 16 yrs. Funeral from the residence of his father, 265 I st, Tue.

Autobiography of the late Dr Lyman Beecher, father of Henry Ward Beecher: it is stated that his mother died of consumption 2 days after he was born. He was her only child.

Chancery sale-Supreme Crt of D C. Equity #210 & #211. Wherein Jas Mortimer Smith & Rosalie Martha his wife, cmplnts, & Eugene, Geo, Maria, Louisa Rosalie, & Nicholas B Vanzandt, minor chldrn of Geo C Vanzandt, dec'd, & Arietta L Vanzandt, minor child of Jos A Vanzandt, dec'd, heirs at law of Maria Wood Vanzandt & Nicholas B Vanzandt, dec'd, dfndnts. Lots 2 & 3 in sq 315, with framed dwlg hse; lot 4, in Davidson's subdiv. - Thos J Fisher, trustee

The Generals in Brief-Maj Gen Winfield Scott Hancock, Cmder of 2nd Corps of the Army of the Potomac, native of Montg Co, Pa, age 40 years on Feb 14 last; 1844 grad of West Point. The rebel Maj Gen Edw Johnson, captured by Hancock, in a Kentuckian, 1838 grad of West Point. Gen Steuart, not J E B Steuart, the rebel cavalryman, is Gen Geo H Steuart, a Marylander, 1848 grad of West Point. Brig Gen Robt Johnson, also captured, is a Virginian, 1850 grad of West Point. Capt Longstreet is a So Carolinian, 1842 grad of West Point. Capt A P Hill, a Virginian, 1847 grad of West Point. Capt R S Ewell, a D C man, 1840 grad of West Point.

Confirmations. Col Saml S Carroll of 8th Ohio vols, & Capt of the 10th U S Infty, to be Brig Gen of vols from May 12, 1864, for gallant & distinguished svc in the 8 days battles in the Wilderness, & at Spottsylvania Crt-Hse, Va. Wm H Waterman, of Wisc, to be super of Indian affairs for Wash Terr.

Obit-Ast Surg John R Reily, U S Army, aged 29 yrs, died at Helena, Ark, after a few hours illness; grandson of Maj Wm Reily, of the Rev army; leaves a widowed mother & a sister. He discharged his duties under every exposure: present in all of the 7 days battles before Richmond, & complimented by Gen Hancock in genr'l orders at Williamsburg in volunteering to convey an order in the heat of the engagement. He was also at Antietam, South Mountain, Fredericksburg, etc, in all of which he was attached to the regular artl, commanded by the brave Capt [now Gen] Ayers.

TUE MAY 24, 1864

Sketch of the forger of the Presidential proclamation, Jos Howard, jr, about 35 years of age. Commenced his literary career as a contributor to country newspapers; then was a correspondent of the Boston Daily Jrnl; then of the Boston Atlas & Bee. In 1852 took charge of the Leader; then the N Y Times, etc. He was with Pres Lincoln at the time of his tour from Springfield to Wash, & wrote the story in relation to Mr Lincoln's escape "in a Scotch cap & long military cloak," a statement which had not a shadow of truth in it. He also was employed by the Daily News, & at the time of his arrest was city editor of the Brooklyn Eagle.

Solomon Kohnstamm was convicted on Sat last, in the Crct Crt of the U S at N Y, of having defrauded the Gov't. A year since he was arrested, first being sent to Ft Lafayette, then transferred to the Old Capitol prison at Wash, & after being confined there some time, was released, & these proceedings commenced. On Aug 2, 1862, a check for $9,173.79, was pd to him, for the subsistence & lodging of recruits. One of these was a bill of one Louis Pfeffer, of Albany, for $1,366, this being one of the 47 indictments against him. The Gov't proved that all due Pfeffer was less than $100. -N Y Times

A car of the train on the Col & Cincinnati rd was thrown off the track at Crestline, Ohio, on Sat, killing Mr Dewitt, of the firm of Dewitt & Rounglove, of Detroit, & wounding others.

Genesee, May 21. The funeral of the late deeply lamented & gallant Gen Wadsworth is now taking place in this village. Every place of business is closed, funeral wreaths are hung upon doors, balconies, & windows, & the people fill the streets, & doorsteps, from which the long, solemn procession can be reviewed as it passes to the humble village church & to the modest rural cemetery.

WED MAY 25, 1864
Gen Alex. S Webb, wounded in the forehead during the late battles, is lying at the residence of his bro-in-law, Capt Benton, Cmdnt of the arsenal. He is a cousin of Wm B Webb, our Superintendent of Police, & a s/o J Watson Webb, Minister to Brazil. Wash, D C

Adj Gen Lorenzo Thomas has returned to Wash, in good health, from his long & arduous tour of svc in the Mississippi Dept.

The Titusville Reporter records successful strikes of oil on Oil Creek, within the past few days. The first was the Porter well on the Foster farm: flow of 200 barrels a day when first got in working order, but product has largely increased since. The other is Wheeler well on the John McClintoch farm, & at last count was flowing 200 barrels a day.

THU MAY 26, 1864
List of Gen ofcrs, etc, from the Sec of War & their status:
Reg Army:

Lt Gen Winfield Scott, retired	Brig Gen Jas W Ripley, retired
Brig Gen David E Twiggs, dismissed	Brig Gen E V Sumner, dead
Brig Gen Wm S Harney, retired	Brig Gen Jas G Totten, dead
Maj Gen John E Wool, retired	Brig Gen Andrew H Reeder, declined an
Brig Gen Robt Anderson, retired	appointment

Volunteer:

Maj Gen Cassius M Clay, resigned	Maj Gen J K F Mansfield, dead
Maj Gen Jas A Garfield, resigned	Maj Gen Wm Nelson, dead
Maj Gen Schuyler Hamilton, resigned	Maj Gen Jere L Reno, dead
Maj Gen Chas S Hamilton, resigned	Maj Gen I B Richardson, dead
Maj Gen Erasmus D Keyes, resigned	Maj Gen John F Reynolds, dead
Maj Gen Edwin D Morgan, resigned	Maj Gen E V Sumner, dead
Maj Gen Benj M Prentiss, resigned	Maj Gen John Sedgwick, dead
Maj Gen Robt C Schenck, resigned	Maj Gen Geo C Strong, dead
Maj Gen Edw D Baker, dead	Maj Gen Chas F Smith, dead
Maj Gen Hiram G Berry, dead	Maj Gen Isaac I Stevens, dead
Maj Gen John Buford, dead	Maj Gen Amiel W Whipple, dead
Maj Gen Philip Kearny, dead	Maj Gen Thos A Morris, declined
Maj Gen Ormely M Mitchell, dead	

Maj Gen Frank P Blair, resigned & resignation revoked
Maj Gen Horatio G Wright, rejected by Senate-since appt'd.
Maj Gen Wm F Smith, expired by Constitutional limitation, & re-appt'd
Maj Gen John M Schofield, expired by Constitutional limitation
Maj Gen Napoleon B Buford, expired by Constitutional limitation
Maj Gen J D Cox, expired by Constitutional limitation
Maj Gen Geo W Morrell, expired by Constitutional limitation
Maj Gen W T H Brooks, nomination withdrawn
Maj Gen John Newton, nomination withdrawn
Maj Gen Wm H French, mustered out

Maj Gen Fitz John Porter, cashiered
Brigs Gen of Vols:
Henry W Benham, appointment revoked
Thos F Meagher, resigned & resignation revoked
J J Bartlett, *expired by constitutional limitation & reappt'd*

Geo W Cullom, do	A J Hamilton, do	Henry H Sibley, do
Jos B Carr, do	Jas A Ledlie, do	John M Thayer, do
Chas T Campbello, do	Joshua T Owens, do	
Edw Ferrero, do	Gabriel R Paul, do	

Resigned:

Burns, Wm H	Harding, A C	Ross, Leonard F
Boyle, J F	Kiernan, J L	Reid, Hugh T
Buckingham, C P	King, Rufus	Shields, Jas
Beatty, John	Kane, Thos L	Strong, Wm K
Craig, Jas	McCall, Geo A	Smith, Green Clay
Crittenden, Thos T	Montgomery, Wm B	Stevenson, John D
Campbell, Wm B	Morgan, Geo W	Shackelford, Jas M
Cochran, John	Matthias, C L	Thurston, Chas M
Clement, G P	Miller, Stephen	Tyler, Danl
Denner, J W	Nagle, Jas	Taylor, Nelson
Burgee, Aharn	Orme, Wm W	Viele, E B
Dumont, Ebenezer	Phelps, John W	Van Allen, Jas H
Dodge, C C	Piatt, A S	Vinton, Francis L
Deitzler, G W	Pratt, Calvin E	Wade, Melancthon T
Farnsworth, John F	Quimby, Isaac F	
Fairchild, Lucius	Reynolds, Jos I	

Dead:

Bayard, Geo D	Keim, Wm H	Stevison, Thos G
Behlen, Henry	Kirk, E N	Sanders, Wm P
Cooper, Jas	Kirby, Edw	Taylor, Geo W
Corcoran, Michl	Lyon, Nathl	Terrill, Wm B
Champlain, T S	Lander, F W	Vincent, Strong
Chapin, Ed P	Lytle, Wm H	Wadsworth, Jas L
Farnsworth, E I	McCook, Robt L	Wallace, W H L
Hackleman, P A	Plummer, Jas B	Welsh, Thos
Hays, Alex'r	Patterson, F C	Williams, Thos
Jamison, Chas D	Rodman, Isaac P	Weed, Stephen
Jackson, J L	Rice, Jas C	York, S K
Jackson, C F	Lile, Josh W	

Declined appointments as Maj Gen:

Baker, Ed D	Haupt, Herman	Pierce, Thos L
Biddle, Chas I	Hicks, Thos H	Prime, Fred G
Brown, Harvey	Morris, Thos A	Richardson, W A
Bramlette, Thos E	Oakes, Jas	Sprague, Wm

Mustered Out:

Garrard, Theo T	Naglee, Henry M	Stone, Chas P
Morton, I St C	Porter, Andrew	Gorman, Willis A

Expired by Constitutional limit:

Busteed, Richd	Cowdin, Robt	Hovey, C E
Buchanan, R C	Gilbert, C C	Haynes, J N

Krzyanowski, W
McKinstry, Justus
Marcy, Randolph B
Naglee, Jas
Phelps, John S
Rejected by the Senate:
Cogswell, Milton
Chamers, Alex

Pee, O M
Smith, Gustavus A
Stoughton, E H
Todd, John B S
Van Vliet, Stewart

Stuart, D
Tod, J B L

Vinton, Francis L
Williams, N G
Williams, D H

Sickles, D E: re-appt'd
Lane, Jas H: cancelled
Arnold, L G: cancelled &
restored to U S A

Harkin, Jas A-revoked
Stambaugh, F S-revoked
Blenker, L-discharged

Obit-Emma, y/d/o the late Chas James, died on May 19. Six months ago disease began the work that death has completed. She was a dutiful dght & a loving sister.

Died: on May 24, John G Smith, aged 7 yrs, 7 months & 2 days, s/o John G & Christiana S Smith. Funeral at the residence of his grandfather, L O Cook, 7th & D sts, today.

Died: on May 24, Wm Edw, s/o Atwell & Frances Cowling, aged 9 months. Funeral from the residence on G st, between 13th & 14th, Thu.

Crct Crt of PG Co, Md: division of the rl estate of Geo W Hilleary, dec'd. Meeting on Jul 28 next. Wm B Hill, John Hodges, Richd S Hill, Wm D Clagett, Chas H Carter, com'rs

Supreme Crt of D C, Equity #80. Riggs & Co, & others, vs the admx, widow & heirs of the late Thos Smith. Ratify sale of: lots 19 & 64 in sq 182, for $453.60, to Algernon S Vose. Lot 63 in sq 182, for $197.28, to Henry Warren. Lot 62, same sq, for $97.28, to John O Butler. Lots 60 & 61, same sq, for $394.56, to Henry Morsell. Lots 48 thru 59, for $3,613.98, to F S Wilson.
Lot 47 in same sq, for $116.01, to Geo Jackson & Albert Noe. -R J Meigs, clerk

Hse o/Reps: 1-Cmte of Elections: reported two resolutions, declaring, first, that Wm Jayne is not, & second, that J D S Todd is, entitled to the seat as delegate from Dakotah Terr.

FRI MAY 27, 1864
Dissolution of partnership by mutual consent-between Saml Phillips & R C Brooke. Phillips will settle the busines. Wash, D C

Decree of Crct Crt of A A Co, Md; Harrietta S Chew, admx of Sam Chew, cmplnt, & Isaac Simmons & wife, & others, dfndnts. Sale of *Snowden's New Birmingham Manor*, 147+ acs, as described in a lease from Isaac Simmons & wife to Rachel Tyson, Mar 2, 1857. -Saml Snowden, 83 W Fayette st, Balt, Md. Frank H Stockett, Annapolis, Md.

Sale of carriages & harness etc, at the Carriage Repository of Thos Young, 469 Pa av, Wash.. Mr Young is retiring from the business. -W L Wall & Co, aucts

Union ofcrs captured at Durry's Bluff, arrived at Libby Prison, Richmond:

Brig Gen C A Heckman
Col Richd White
Col H H Lee

Lt Col F M Bennett
Capt Jas H Pierce
Adj R P McMannis

Lt Col W S Bartholomew
Capt J H Nutting
Capt R R Swift

Capt Elgan Kessan	Capt D Stone	Lt W G Davies
Capt R F Mills	Capt H M Phillips	Lt Justice Lyman
Capt J Belger	Adj John L Carter	Lt J M Drake
Capt J E Lewis	Lt M P Pierson	Lt J P Aedges
Capt H S McConald	Lt R Gilbert	Lt Jas H Pitt
Capt Jas Metzger	Adj John Gotchell	Lt Patrick O'Connell
Capt D W Fox	Lt H N Day	Lt H D Grant
Capt Henry Rebell	Lt J L Skinner	Lt Geo Peters
Capt H Jenkins	Lt John H Lass	

Brig Gen S Sprigg Carroll, wounded in the late battles in Va, has been removed to Wash City. He is s/o the late Wm Thos Carroll, clerk of the Sup Crt of the U S, & on maternal side, the grandson of Saml Sprigg, dec'd, a Govn'r of Md of the old school of gentlemen.

2nd Lt Jas Henry, 10th U S Infty, wounded at Spottsylvania Crt-Hse on May 12, died in Wash City yesterday from exhaustion, the result of amputation. Funeral today from Stanton Gen Hospital, Wash, D C. For 2 years he was Adj of the 37th Irish Rifles, N Y V.

SAT MAY 28, 1864
Died: on May 27, after a lingering illness, May Jane, w/o Theodore Sheckles, aged 34 yrs. Funeral from the residence of her hsbnd, 8th st, between M & N, Sun. Funeral svc at St Aloysius Chr; thence to Rock Crk Chr, [Catholic,] about 7 miles out 7th st pike.

The Pres has recently pardoned 27 of the Minnesota Indians who were concerned in the great massacre.

Supreme Crt of D C, Equity #70. Edw Owen, et al, vs Ellen Kelly, wid/o Miles Kelly, & Jas Mullquin. Ratify sale of rl estate sold by trustees, John F Ennis & Wm J Miller, viz: in sq 776-lot 3 to John E Norris for $500; lot 4 to Ellen Kelly for $570; lot 5 to Ellen Kelly for $440; lot 6 to Jas Mullquin, assignee of Timothy Downey for $410. Lot 25 in sq 625 to Ellen Kelly for $455; east part of lot 26 in sq 625 to D Quill, assignee of Ellen Kelly, for $226. -R J Meigs, clerk

Crct Crt of D C, Equity #226, wherein W Henry Farrar, Edw Thos Farrar, Jacob L Bright, & Anna Eliz, his wife, formerly Anna Eliz Farrar, & Frances Farrar by her next friend, cmplnts, & Jos F Kelley, dec'd, dfndnt; sale of all the estate of which Mary Farrar died seized; lot 26 in sq A, with improvements, 2 frame hses, Wash. -Jos F Kelley, exc of Mary Farrar, dec'd.

Supreme Crt of D C, Equity #213, wherein Martha Barnes, Jas & Thos Goodin, Geo, Robt, & Martha Owens, cmplnts, & Mary Jarboe, excx of Eliz Goodin, dec'd, dfndnt; sale of rl estate of which said Eliz had at the time of her death, part of lots 16, 17, & 18 in sq 480, Wash City, with improvements. -Mary Jarboe, excx

The 60 rebel ctzns of Fredericksburg arrested by order of the War Dept, brought here to be held as hostages for the Union wounded sldrs betrayed into the hands of the rebels by Mayor Slaughter, were taken from the Old Capitol & conveyed to Fort Delaware under guard of a detachment of the Vet Reserve Corps. -Star

194

MON MAY 30, 1864

Supreme Crt of D C, in Equity #70. Edw Owen & Ellen his wife, Jas Kahoe & Mgt his wife, & Philip Kelly, vs Ellen Kelly & Jas Mulliquen. Statement of the trustee's account at my ofc in City Hall, Wash, on Jun 21. -W Redin, auditor

Hon Joshua R Giddings, Cnsl Gen of the U S at Montreal, died suddenly at that city on Fri evening. Born at Athens Pa, Oct 6, 1795, but removed to Ohio when 10 years old; sldr in war of 1812, when but 17 years of age; in Congress for a total of 21 yrs. After the close of the war he studied law with Hon Elisha Whittlesey, & was admitted to the bar in 1820. Probable he died from an affection of the nervous system acting upon the heart.

Capt Saml Fiske, known in the literary world as *Dunn Browne*, died at Fredericksburg, Va, on Sunday, of wounds received at the battle of the Wilderness. Born in Shelbourne, Mass; 1848 graduate of Amherst. After traveling in Europe, he settled as a minister in Madison, Conn. On the breaking out of the war he obtained a Lt's commission & has since been in the field.

Died: on May 29, of inflamation of the brain, Jas Eddie, y/s/o Geo E & Eliz Kennedy, aged 2 years & 3 months. Funeral from their residence, 453 6th st, today.

Died: in Wash City, on May 28, Jas W Shields, in the 73rd yr of his age. Funeral from his late residence, 14th & I sts, Tue.

TUE MAY 31, 1864

Died: on May 29, after a long & painful illness, Mr John Granger, in his 33rd yr. Funeral from his late residence on so M st, between 10th & 11th sts, today.

Orphans Crt of Wash Co, D C. 1-Prsnl estate of John A Ellis, late of Wash Co, dec'd. -Chas M Matthews, adm 2-Prsnl estate of Matthew St Clair Clarke, late of same, dec'd. -John G Clarke, adm

Obit-Saml S Maffitt died at his residence in Elkton, on May 24, in his 46th yr; late Comptroller of Md. He was an affectionate hsbnd & father.

Died: Richd K Cralle, at Rural Retirement, Lunenburg, Va, the residence of his son-in-law, Rev Thos Ward White, on Apr 14, in the 64th yr of his age. Mr Cralle was known as the biographer of John C Calhoun, & being connected with the press of Va.

Senator Fessenden, of Maine, received a telegram from New Orleans, dated May 26, informing him that he might expect to meet his son, Gen Fessenden, in N Y on Sunday last. The report of the death of Gen Fessenden is unfounded. [See May 16, 1864: page 180.]

Detroit Free Press: explosion at Detroit at Williams' dock. The boat *Nile* had just steamed up when her boiler bursted & blew the craft into a 1,000 pieces in a moment's time. Albert W Bacon, nephew of Judge Bacon, was instantly killed. His body was thrown over Bissell's warehse, & fell on the pavement on Atwater st. Peter Sceffer, shoemaker, at work in the shop of McAfee & Fawcett, was struck by timber from the wreck & instantly killed. The steward & cook, Christopher Wayland, was blown upon the roof of a warehse, & very severely, if not fatally, injured.

Col Benedict I Heard, of St Mary's Co, Md, died on May 13, aged 74 yrs. In 1814 he participated in the battle of North Point. He was for many years a leading Whig politician, & frequently a mbr of the State Leg.

WED JUN 1, 1864
Orphans Crt of Wash Co, D C: Prsnl estate of Michael Shanks, late of Wash Co, dec'd. -Jas Adams, adm

On the person of one of the Yankees killed in the fight at Yellow Tavern was found a note-*I, John Wilheimer, 2nd N Y Cavalry, I am shot & dying*. Whoever finds me send this to Sarah Wilheimer, Brooklyn P O, N Y, my sister, & only relative in the country. -Dispatch

Furnished residence for sale or rent: hse is new, stabling for 4 horses, carriage-hse, rm for 2 carriages, coachman's rm, fine cistern, well of water, & baths, gas, & all modern conveniences. Hse is spacious: 235 Bridge st. Inquire on the premises of Mrs A E Taylor on Jun 10.

Mob Law: the printing ofcs of the Union & Jrnl, at Louisiana, Mo, were destroyed by a mob of sldrs on the May 24. Jas Monaghan, the editor of the Union, is a delegate to the Balt convention, & recently held an ofc in Wash. The editor of the Journal, A J Reed, is also a Union man, but both of them, it is stated, denounced the radicals of that state, & hence the attack on their property.

Solomon Kohnstamm, convicted of having presented false vouchers to the Gov't, was sentenced to 10 years in the State prison. [See May 24th paper.]

THU JUN 2, 1864
Obit-Mrs Anna Mills Cosby, w/o Fortunatus Cosby, died at her residence on Capitol Hill on May 31, in the 46th yr of her age, after a lingering illness. She was a d/o the late Robt Mills. Funeral from her late residence, 553 N J av, Thu.

Died: on May 31, Barnard Aloysius, only child of Wm G & Cath Gallant, aged 17 months.

The First Md Regt has been in active service for 3 years, & will be mustered out of service today. It was in all the battle of Spottsylvania Crt Hse, the mbrs having served 9 days beyond their term of enlistment. Some 300 of the men have re-enlisted as veterans, under Col Dushane, & 115 have arrived home to be mustered out. The remnant of the regt reached home under the command of Maj Schley, Capt Keughler & Reynolds, & 2nd Ast Surgeon Jos W Bagley. -Sun

Appointments by the Pres-Corps of Engrs:
Lt Col Jas K Graham to Col, Jun 1, 1863, vice Long, retired.
Lt Col Richd Delafield to Col, do, vice Thayer, retired.
Maj Danl P Woodbury to Lt Col, do, vice Graham, promoted.
Maj Jas H Simpson to Lt Col, do, vice Delafield, promoted.
1st Lt Orlando M Poe, Corps of Topog Engrs, to Capt, Mar 3, 1863.
Capt Robt S Williamson to Maj, May 7, 1863, vice Whipple, died of wounds received in battle.
Capt Quincy A Gillmore to Maj, Jun 1, 1863, vice Woodbury, promoted.
Capt Frederick E Prime to Maj, Jun 1, 1863, vice Simpson, promoted.
Capt Jas St C Morton to Maj, Jul 3, 1863, vice Meade, appt'd brig gen.
Capt Thos L Casey to Maj, Jul 3, 1863, vice Hunt, dec'd.

1st Lt Jas H Wilson to Capt, May 7, 1863, vice Williamson, promoted.
1st Lt Orville E Babcock to Capt, Jun 1, 1863, vice Gillmore, do.
1st Lt John M Wilson to Capt, Jun 1, 1863, vice Prime, do.
1st Lt Franklin Harwood to Capt, Jun 5, 1863, vice Cross, killed in action.
1st Lt John N Barlow to Capt, Jul 3, 1863, vice Morton, promoted.
1st Lt Peter C Hains to Capt, Aug 1, 1863, vice McPherson, appt'd Brig Gen.
1st Lt Francis U Farquhar to Capt, Oct 2, 1863, vice Casey, promoted.
1st Lt Arthur H Dutton to Capt, Nov 6, 1863, vice Paine, resigned.
Ordnance Dept:
Lt Col Geo D Ramsay to Col, Jun 1, 1863, vice Craig, retired.
Lt Col Wm Maynadier to Col, Jun 1, 1863, vice Symington, do.
Lt Col Wm A Thornton to Col, Sep 15, 1863, vice Ramsay, appt'd Chief clerk of ord.
Maj Robt H K Whiteley to Lt Col, Jun 1, 1863, vice Ramsay, promoted.
Maj Peter V Hagner to Lt Col, Jun 1, 1863, vice Maynadier, promoted.
Maj Robt A Wainright to Lt Col, Sep 15, 1863, vice Thornton, do.
Capt Thos J Rodman to Maj, Jun 1, 1863, vice Whiteley, do.
Capt Theodore T S Laidley to Maj, Jun 1, 1863, vice Hagner, promoted.
Capt Jas G Benton to Maj, Sep 15, 1863, vice Winright, do.
Regular Army:
1st Lt Wm H Harris to Capt, Jun 1, 1863, vice Rodman, promoted.
1s Lt Alfred Mordecai to Capt, Jun 1, 1863, vice Laidley, do.
1st Lt David H Buel to Capt, Jul 30, 1863, vice Strong, died of wounds received in battle.
1st Lt Stephen C Lyford to Capt, Sep 15, 1863, vice Benton, promoted.
2nd Lt Isaac Arnold to 1st Lt, Apr 27, 1863, vice Edson, do.
2nd Lt Wm S Beebe to 1st Lt, Jul 30, 1863, vice Buel, do.
2nd Lt Geo D Ramsay jr to 1st Lt, Sep 15, 1863, vice Lyford, do.

Marine Corps:
1st Lt Jas Forney to Capt, from Apr 23, 1864, vice Capt John C Grayson, retired.
2nd Lt Wm B Remey to 1st Lt from Feb 17, 1864, vice 1st Lt C H Bradford, dec'd.
2nd Lt Henry J Bishop to 1st Lt from Apr 1, 1864.
2nd Lt Robt L Meade to 1st Lt from Apr 2, 1864.
2nd Lt Lyman R French to 1st Lt from Apr 23, 1864.

Mrs Gov Seymour has received, thru the Bishop of Buffalo, from the Pope of Rome, $500 for the relief of the wounded U S sldrs.

FRI JUN 3, 1864
Mrd: at the residence of the bride's father, at *Kendall Green*, on Jun 1, by Rev T R Howlett, Sidney S Babcock, of N Y State, to Marion Kendall, y/d/o Hon Amos Kendall.

Mrd: in Wash City, on May 31, by Rev T Banks McFalls, at the Chr of the Assembly, Thos W B Van, of Balt, Md, & Kate Sargeant, of Wash.

Died: on Jun 1, Nellie Rosabel, infant d/o R M & Rebecca Johnson, aged 8 months. Funeral today from 34 Missouri av.

Accidental explosion of 4 monster torpedoes near Newbern, N C, on May 26, 1867. On arrival of the train at this station from Newbern, an explosion attended the removal of 4 torpedoes from the cars to the platform 40 odd sldrs & negroes were blown into eternity in an instant, & many injured. The greatest sufferer was the 132nd N Y, whose camp is adjacent to the railroad station.

Wm F Morton, of Frederick, Md, or his legal rep, to call on the undersigned, in a matter of money held in trust for him. -Walter E Gardner, Dept of Agric, Wash

Broke into the premises of the undersigned, a few days ago, two beeves, which the owner is requested to come & take away. –E J Middleton, 3 miles north of Capitol, near Fort Bunker Hill.

Maj Gen Wallace ordered the release from Ft McHenry of M J Kelly, of the firm of Messrs Kelly & Pl_t, who had been confined there about a week in company with his partner, on charge of having rebel books & photos in their store. Maj Gen Dix called upon the Gen & made a statement in regard to the case, which resulted in Mr Kelly's discharge, he giving bond in the sum of $5,000. –Balt Amer

SAT JUN 4, 1864
Lost or stolen-John R Elvan's check on Riggs & Co, dated Jun 2, 1864, for $2,696.99. -John R Elvan, 309 Pa av, Wash, D C.

N Y C-the will of Col Andrew Jackson Butler, sworn by the exec, Maj Gen Benj F Butler, at Fortress Monroe, before a Va judge; half his property is left to his bro, Gen B F Butler, one qrtr to the widow of the dec'd, who is a resident of Calif; one qrtr to be held in trust by Gen Butler till the son of dec'd shall attain his 30th yr. N Y Times

The Richmond paper states that the story of Capt David H Todd, bro of Mrs Pres Lincoln, has deserted to the enemy is fully contradicted. He is a Capt in the 21st Louisana Artillery.

MON JUN 6, 1864
Died: in Balt, Md, on Jun 5, Col Arthur H Dutton, U S Army, in his 26th yr. Funeral from St Aloysius Chr today.

Died: in Salisbury, Conn, on Jun 4, Comfort S Whittlesey, of Wash, D C.

Deaths reported to the Navy Dept for the week ending Jun 4, 1864:
Edw Kelly, 1st cl fireman, scalded, May 13, vessel U S S Sassacus.
Jos Murray, 2nd cl fireman, do, do, do.
Thos Dougherty, ord seaman, shell wound, May 23, vessel U S S Hunchback.
Wm Willet, colored 1st cl boy, typhod fever, May 17, U S Hosp, Memphis.
Wm Armstrong, coalheaver, pneumonia, May 17, do.
Wm Ball_se, contraband, consumption, May 17, do.
David H Bennett, seaman, erysipelas, May 9, vessel U S S Naid.
John Smithers, 2nd cl fireman, rheumatism, Feb 22, vessel U S S Marmora.
Arch'd Thompson, q m, pneumonia, Apr 2, vessel U S S Tyler.
John Kempton, landsman, blank, Apr 10, vessel U S S Ouchita.
John McKenne, seaman, pneumonia, Apr 10, vessel U S S Forest Rose.
Jas Brown, contraband, 1st cl boy, typhoid fever, Apr 2, vessel U S S Benton.
Daniel Harrington, landsman, typhoid fever, Apr 21, do.
Henry Johnson, contraband, coalheaver, billious fever, Apr 18, vessel U S S Gen Price.
Jos Tohuson, contraband, 1st cl boy, diarrhoea, Apr 10, vessel U S S Springfield.
Geo Cowles, seaman, typhoid fever, Apr 13, vessel U S S Black Hawk.
Wilson Wood, colored, landsman, pneumonia, Mar 29, U S Ft Hindman.
Robt Booth, contraband, 1st cl boy, diarrhoea, Sep 2, 1863, vessel U S S Petrel.
Wyatt Mason, contraband, 1st cl boy, drowned, Nov 26, 1863, do.

Richd Doyle 2nd gunner, drowned, Dec 13, 1863, do.
Lyman Green, contraband, 3rd cl boy, drowned, Jan 27, do.
Alfred Barfield, contraband, 1st cl boy, drowned, Feb 27, do.
Madison Barney, contraband, landsman, fever, Mar 13, do.
Anthony Cook, blank, consumption, Mar 29, vessel U S S *Prairie Bird*
Wm Heffley, ord seaman, killed, Apr 13, vessel U S S *Pittsburg.*
Henry Carter, contraband, ord seaman, remit fever, Apr 29, do.
Burrell Brown, contraband, coalheaver, remit fever, Apr 25, do.
Richd Croft, ord seaman, consumption, May 29, Nav Hosp, Chelsea.
Chas Williams, landsman, blank, no date, U S Hosp, N Y.
John W Bensley, blank, smallpox, May 27, Norwich, Conn.
Eri Kemp, pensioner, fistula, May 28, U S Nav Asylum, Phil.
Horace Talcott, ast paymstr, blank, May 8, Smithfield, Ky.
Jos H Brown, seaman, typhoid fever, May 8, vessel U S S *Carondalette.*
Wm Wilson, 1st cl boy, gunshot wound, May 5, vessel U S S *Mystic.*
Walter H Davis, actg mstr's mate, fall, May 27, Boston, Mass.
Henry Hayes, ord seaman, peritoniti, May 13, vessel U S S *Monongahela.*
Perkins Neafus, ord seaman, diarrhoea, May 13, vessel U S S *Octorora.*
Alva G R Mattice, landsman, drowned, May 20, vessel U S S *Tyler.*
Chas Howard, boatswain's mate, fracture, May 10, vessel U S S *Huntsville.*

Died: on Jun 4, Howard, infant s/o Zachariah & Mary J Downing, aged 4 months & 8 days.
Funeral from the residence of his grandfather, Jos Downing, 8th st, between K & L, today.

Orphans Crt of PG Co, Md, ordered that Geo H Calvert, adm of Chas B Calvert, late of PG
Co, Md, dec'd, give notice required by law. -Wm A Jarboe, rg o/wills. Said notice
followed, signed by Geo H Calvert, exc.

For sale-*Villa,* whole of sq 765: 2½ acs, Wash, D C, former property of Maj Nicholson, U S
M C; with handsome residence. -Jas C McGuire & Co, aucts

Maj Gen Carl Schurz has been placed in command of the convalescent barracks at
Nashville.

Otho S Holloway, merchant, of Flushing, Belmont Co, Ohio, had his pocket picked on Mon
in one of the sleeping cars of the Penn Central road, upwards of $2,000 in money & checks.

From the army in Va: official report: Sec Stanton to Gen Dix. War Dept, Wash, Jun 4, 1864.
Yesterday Gen Grant made an assault on the enemy's line's: captured over 300 prisoners,
mostly from Breckinridge. Another later official report, not from Gen Grant, estimates the
number of our killed & wounded at about 3,000. Ofcrs among the killed: Col Haskell, 36th
Wisc; Col Porter, 8th N Y heavy artl, & Col Morris, 66th N Y. Wounded: Gen R O Tyler,
seriously, will probably lose a foot; Col McMahon, 164th N Y; Col Byrnes, 8th Mass,
probably mortally; & Col Brooks, 53rd Pa.

Hon Thos Corwin, our Minister to Mexico, has arrived in Washington, on leave of absence,
& is stopping at the Metropolitan Hotel.

TUE JUN 7, 1864
Mrd: in Wash City, at the U S Htl, by Rev W McLain, on Jun 2, Francis Hoard to Jennis
Maurice.

Gen R O Tyler, who was wounded in the ankle on Fri whilst assaulting the enemy's line's, reached Wash City yesterday on board the steamer *Gen Howard*. His wound is quite a serious one, & feared that it will be necessary to amputate the limb. Capt W L Schezler, Lt L Kinny, & Lt C H Owens, aide on Gen Tyler's staff, who are also wounded, were brought up on the *Howard* at the same time.

Wash Corp: elected to the City Cncls:

John B Turton	Noble D Larner	B F Dyer
Jas Kelly	Jas Skirving	Donald McCathran
H C Wilson	Wm B Downing	Geo R Ruff
John A Reeves	John P Pepper	Bennett Swain
Thos H Donohue	Asbury Lloyd	Thos B Marche
J Russell Barr	Wm W Moore	Peter M Pearson
Saml W Owen	Elijah Edmonston	John G Dudley
Wm Pettibone	Chas I Caufield	W T Walker
Saml A Peugh	Wm P Ferguson	Geo Wright
Jos F Brown	Jas B Davis	John H Bird
Thos A Stevens	J B Ward	

From the army near Richmond: Official news: Sec Stanton to Gen Dix: War Dept, Wash, Jun 5. Despatch from Gen Grant's headqrtrs: enemy attacked Smith's brig, of Gibbon's div, on Jun 3: Smith's losses were inconsiderable. Our entire loss in killed, wounded, & missing during 3 days operations around Cold Harbor will not exceed, according to the Adj Gen's report, 7,500. Ofcrs lost: Col Preston, 1st Vt Cavalry, killed, & Col Benjamin, 8th N Y Cavalry, seriously wounded. Gen Stannard, serving in the 18th Corps, was severely wounded Fri.

Maj Gen Irvin McDowell, U S Vols, is, by direction of the Pres, assigned to the command of the Dept of the Pacific: headqrtrs at San Francisco, Calif. Order dated the 21st ult.

Wash Corp: 1-Act for the relief of H Shulthies: reimburse him in the amount of $16.50 for amount pd for tapping sewer in ward 4.

WED JUN 8, 1864
Mrd: at St Aloysius Chr, on Jun 7, by Rev B A Maguire, Geo A R McNeir to Emma, eldest d/o H N Henning, all of Wash, City.

Died: at Salisbury, Conn, on Jun 4, Comfort S Whittlesey, of Wash City, aged 40 yrs. Funeral from his late residence, 33 Ind av, today.

Execs' sale of the residence of the late Gen Totten, U S Army, on G st, between 18th & 19th sts, a 3 story brick hse. Inquire of Wm G Temples, 203 G st, or of Wm H Philip, 40 La av, Wash, D C.

Sale of the furn & effects, at the residence of Mrs Vincent Taylor, 227 Bridge st, Gtwn. -Thos Dowling, auct

City ordnance-Wash. Permission granted J H Harleston, 474 7th st, to extend the back porch & enclose the same as a skylight. Porch to be used as an ambrotype gallery, provided the consent of the Pres first be obtained. [See below.]

Wash Corp: 1-Act for the relief of J H Harleston: permission granted to extend the back porch to hse 474 7th st west, between E & F st. 2-Act for relief of John Williams: sum of $10.97 be refunded due to taxes erroneously pd by him on property belonging to another John Williams, in another part of the city.

Foreign: Chevalier De Hulsemann, late Austrian Minister Resident at Wash. John Geo Chevalier De Hulsemann, born at Stade, in Hanover, made his studies in Gotingen, under Heeren, Eichhorn, & Hugo; went to Vienna in 1823: then to Lisbon & to Italy. He died on Mar 8 last, at age 64 yrs, in Gorizia, in Ilyria. He leaves no immediae relations, & his property, not inconsiderable, goes to distant heirs.

Recent donation to the *Connecticut Historical Soc* is the gold scabbard naval sword presented to Admr Foote by the citizens of Brooklyn, N Y. It cost $3,000.

THU JUN 9, 1864
Mrd: on Jun 7, at the Chr of the Epiphany, by Rev Dr Hall, Henry Lovejoy to Augusta F, d/o W F Steiger, all of Wash City.

Wash Corp: 1-Resolution to thank Gen M C Meigs: for the donation of photos & drawings of the Wash Aqueduct.

Died: at Armory Sq Hosp, on Jun 8, Lt Arthur L Chase, 8th N Y Heavy Artl, s/o Dr Saml L Chase, of Lockport, N Y. He received 4 separate wounds in the fight before Richmond, on Fri last, & came up on Tue in the vessel *Lizzie Baker*. He was a nephew of Maj B B French, of Wash City, & a distant relative of Hon Sec Chase.

Official War News: Despatch from Mr Dana, at Gen Grant's headqrtrs, dated Jun 7, announced a victory by Gen Hunter over the rebels beyond Staunton, & that the rebel Gen W E Jones was killed on the battle field.

FRI JUN 10, 1864
Mrd: on Jun 8, at the E st Bapt Chr, by Rev E H Gray, Salathiel M Spaulding to Emma C Barrett, both of Wash City.

Mrd: in Wash City, on Jun 8, by Rev B H Nadal, Rev Marvin Briggs, of N Y, to Miss Emma F Fossett, of Alexandria.

Richmond papers announce the death of Col Lawrence M Keitt, formerly a Rep in Congress from S C; said to have been killed in the late fight with Wilson's Cavalry at Cold Harbor. Col Thos S Fournoy, formerly a mbr of Congress from Va, was killed in the same engagement.

The Senate has confirmed the nomination of Brig Gens Dodge & Gibbon to be Maj Gens, & Col Bailey to be Brig Gen by brevet for military svcs in enabling the Mississippi flotilla to get over the lower falls of Red river.

Hon Robt J Walker is reported to be suffering from feeble health, caused by the effects of an amateur balloon excursion taken in London in Oct last. The balloon went up very suddenly, & the rarefaction of the air affected Mr Walker severely. He has this spring gone to Egypt to recruit.

Died: in N Y C, Jun 8, Mabel, only child of Capt Horatio C & Emma C S King, age 3 months & 15 days.

SAT JUN 11, 1864

Report of the Military Commission presided over by Maj Gen Irvin McDowell, & charged with the examinaton into alleged frauds in the West Dept. Following is a summary of the report. Gen S R Curtis, in the case of the cotton of the rebel Gen Pillow, was found to have used the proceeds in supplying the contrabands, tho it was not shown specifically how all the money was applied. The whole cotton was fully accounted for, except that gold was received for it while at 17% premium, & currency pd over in its stead. 108 bales, seized from Matt Ward in Arkansas & sent to Helena, were afterward purchased at .12½, & pd to Mrs Ward. Maj H S Curtis, Maj McMinney, & Lt Guylee, of Gen Curtis' staff, it was ascertained, were interested in the purchase of 181 bales of cotton. Brig Gen Hovey was exonerated from the charge of forcibly returning 15 negroes to slavery, but was found to be connected with the traffic in cotton. Col Slack, 47th Ind, found to have traded in cotton, & to have captured silver ware from Mrs Cogswell, in Mississippi, who complained that it was not all returned. Lt Kimball, 2nd Wisc Cavalry, stole a diamond pin, which was subsequently returned. Maj Western, 24th Mo, received $560 for furnishing a guard for protecting cotton. Capt Fred S Winston, Ast Q M, was found interested in cotton in a manner not contemplated by army regulations, & of depositing the proceeds in a private banking institution instead of the U S Treas. Capt Howland, of 135 bales shipped to Chicago by one Hagan, was authorized to receive half the nett proceeds & $2,000. Others interested in cotton speculations are named: Col C C Marsh & Capt Bradley, 20th Ill; Lt Col S N Wood, 6th Missouri Cavalry, [who admitted having made $20,000;] Dr Rexsurg, 33rd Ill; Capt Jerome Bradley, Ast Q M Gen; Capt Robt Gorman, [half profits on 102 bales,] $2,500; Capt Hayden & Lt Wright, 3rd Iowa Battery; Lt Baker, 33rd Ill; Lt Flint, 10th Missouri Cavalry; & Lt Murdock, 15th Ohio Battery. Permits were shown to have been granted for cotton trading by Gens Grant, Curtis, Steele, Gorman, & Washburn, & that transportation had been furnished to some extent for pvt purposes, for which remuneration was not always received.

Mrd: on Jun 9, by Rev Mr Ward, Jas L Storer to Miss Esther Passmore, formerly of Perry Co, Ohio.

For sale-*Holly Hall*, the residence of the late Gen Sewell, near Elkton, Md, 200 acs. -Theo B Horwitz, on the premises.

Col Miller, of Oswego, heretofore reported killed in the battles of the Wilderness, is ascertained to be a prisoner & only slightly wounded.

Charlestown, W Va, Jun 2, 1864. The widow & 3 chldrn of Gen Albert Gallatin Jenkins, of the rebel army, arrived here yesterday. Gen Jenkins, wounded 3 times at the fight with Gen Crook, at Clodide Mountain, near Dublin, died at age 35 yrs. The wound which caused his death was in the arm near the shoulder; amputation was necessary & was made. He was removed to a place near Dublin, where his family joined him, & was doing well until one night the artery, which had been incautiously taken up, began to flow, causing him to bleed profusely. He owned property in Va, on the Ohio, below Kanawha, valued at $300,000. In view of the chances of its confiscation, a standing offer is made to the Gov't for it, by the parties in Cincinnati, of $200,000. The chldrn of the Gen, on reaching this place, were wretchedly clad & desititute of shoes & stockings.

Poughkeepsie, Jun 10. 14 passengers of the steamer *Berkshire* have been found. Two were recognized: Mrs Niles, of Spencertown, & Miss Niles. Total number of missing is 40.

MON JUN 13, 1864
Deaths reported to the Navy Dept for the week ending Jun 11, 1864:
Henry S Strong, yeoman, pneumonia, Mar 13, vessel U S S *Cambridge*.
Calvin Haskins, seaman, dysentery, May 13, vessel U S S *Ouichita*.
John Kirby, seaman, pneumonia, May 17, do.
Antonio Juner, contraband, ch hepatitis, May 24, Hosp, Memphis.
John Anderson, negro, landsman, consumption, May 29, do.
John Mitchell, ord seaman, consumption, May 30, do.
Jack Tayler, 3rd cl boy, chronic rheumatism, May 17, Hosp, New Orleans.
Geo Dean, boatswain mate, disease of heart, Jun 3, vessel U S S *Bermuda*.
Louis Rolls, landsman, bronchitis, no date, Hosp, N Y.
Gilbert H Moore, actg mstr's mate, gunshot wound, May 16, vessel U S S *Stockdale*.
Neals Peterson, seaman, casualty, Jun 1, vessel U S S *Josco*.
Henry Dixon, landsman, haematemesis, Jun 2, Hosp, Portsmouth, Va.
John Stratton, landsman, parotitis, Jun 3, vessel U S S *New Hampshire*.
Chas W Dawson, seaman, drowned, May 6, vessel U S S *Nymph*.
Benj G Hite, boatmate, gunshot wound, Apr 26, vessel U S S *Cricket*, Red River.
Patrick O'Donald, landsman, gunshot wound, Apr 26, do.
John Williams, ord seaman, do, do, do.
John Smith, seaman, do, do, do.
Isaac Bryant, 1st cl boy, do, do, do.
Isaac Plusher, 2nd cl boy, do, do, do.
Albert Harper, 1st cl boy, do, do, do.
Ann Johnson, laudress, do, do, do.
Martin Fisher, ord seaman, pneumonia, Jun 6, Hosp, Chelsea.
Francis McDonald, 1st cl fireman, uraemia, May 22, vessel U S S *Mackinaw*.
Thos King, ord seaman, drowned, May 6, vessel U S S *Cmdor Jones*.
Wm H Mayne, ord seaman, drowned, May 6, vessel U S S *Wm G Anderson*.
Edw E Brennard, actg vol Lt cmndng, gunshot wound, Nov 14, 1863, vessel U S S *Prairie Bird*.
Francis Dickson, coxswain, accidentally killed, Apr 28, Lisbon, Spain, vessel U S S *St Louis*.

Supreme Crt of D C: Equity #1814. Libby vs Flaherty's heirs. Ratify sale made by John E Norris & Wm F Mattingly, trustees of Wm Flagherty, dec'd. -A B Olin, Justice; R J Meigs, clerk

Actg Vol Lt W B Eaton, commanding the U S steamer *Admiral*, writing from on board that vessel, off Velasco, Texas, May 28, informs the Navy Dept of the capture of the blockade runner *Isabel*. One of the *Isabel's* screw was badly wounded, & necessary to amputate his left arm & 3 fingers of his right hand.

Cmte on Rev Pensions: names & birth places, & ages, so far as known, of the Twelve Apostles of Liberty:

Amaziah Goodwin	Summersworth, N H	105
John Goodnow	Sudbury, Mass	102
Adam Lisk	Wash Co, Pa	102
Rev Danl Waldo	Windham, Conn	101
Wm Hutchings	York, Me	103
Jas Burham	Southampton Co, Va	99

Benj Miller	Springfield, Mass	100
John Pettingill	Windham, Conn	97
Alex'r Maroney	Lake Geo, N Y	94

Saml Downing, 2nd N H Regt, no age given
Lemuel Cook & Jas Gates, no birthplace or age given

TUE JUN 14, 1864

Died: on Jun 13, Stuart, only c/o Jas J & Virginia C K Neagle, aged 17 months & 4 days. Funeral from the residence of his grandfather, J P Keller, 469 13th st, this evening.

Newark, N J, advertiser records the death in that city, on Jun 11, of Hon Jos C Hornblower, in his 88th yr; s/o Hon Josiah Hornblower, of Belleville, N J, who was born in Staffordshire, Eng, about 1730. Name is connected with the steam engine long anterior to the discoveries of Watt.

Dr Gordon Winslow, inspec of the Sanitary Commission, fell overboard from the steamer *Ripley*, coming up from the White Hse to Wash on Tue, & was drowned. He was bringing up the body of his son, Col Winslow, who was killed in one of the late fights.

Capt H S Tafft, of Wash Co, brought before me, Dan Rowland, a J P, a stray mare. Capt Tafft's ofc-167 F st, Wash, D C.

Savannah, Jun 3, 1864. Hon S R Mallory, Sec of the Navy. I have the honor to report that an expedition from my command under Lt F P Pelot, Confederate States Navy, last night carried, by boarding, the U S steamer *Water Witch*, near Ossabaw Sound, after a hard fight. Our loss is the gallant Lt Pelot, Moses Dallas, [colored pilot,] & 3 men killed, from 10 to 12 wounded. -W W Hunter, Flag Ofcr

WED JUN 15, 1864

Died: on Jun 13, Mrs Ann MacDaniel, in her 76th yr, widow of the late Ezekiel MacDaniel. Funeral from her residence, near Glenwood Cemetery, today.

Died: Jun 13th, after a lingering illness, Wm Rich. Funeral from his late residence, 296 H st, today.

Died: on Jun 14, Thaddeus, s/o John M & Mary J Sims, aged 6 months & 2 days. Funeral from their residence, 10th & N sts, today.

Orphans Crt of Wash Co, D C. Case of Moses Kelly, adm of Jos Ingle, dec'd; settlement on Jul 9. -Z C Robbins, rg o/wills

A s/o Collector Barney, of N Y, was run over by an omnibus in that city & killed.

THU JUN 16, 1864

Died: on Jun 14, after a short illness, Thos Kelly, a native of County Kerry, Ire, aged 43 yrs. Funeral from the residence of his bro-in-law, Franklin H Sage, First st, between C & D, today.

Died: at Fort Delaware., on Jun 12, Robt E Reynolds, in his 22nd yr, only child of the late Jos P & Jamima Reynolds, of Norfolk, Va.

Died: on Jun 15, Theodore Maguire, infant s/o Theodore & the late Mary Jane Sheckles, aged 7 months. Funeral from the residence of his father, 8th st, between M & N, Thu.

The property of Caleb S Hallowell, in Alexandria, Va, was sold on Jun 22. The estate of the late Stephen A Douglas will be sold today, on the premises-I st, between N J av, north K st, & First st west, Wash, D C; to be sold in various bldg lots.

Mr C F Hall, the well known Arctic explorer, who was among the Esquimaux in 1860 thru 1862, purposes to start from New London, Conn, on Jun 15, on a second expedition of discovery among the North Polar regions.

We call attention to the sale of nearly an entire sq belonging to the estate of the late Stephen A Douglas, to take place Thu on the premises, under a decree in Chancery. This val property fronts on north I st, N J ave, north K st, & 1st st west, & will be sold in good sized bldg lots.

FRI JUN 17, 1864
Mrd: on Jun 15, by Rev J T Ward, Mr Thos Brooks, of Calif, to Miss Carrie L, only d/o J L Martin, of Wash City.

Supreme Crt of D C, Equity #132. Hoover vs Hoover et al. Ratify sale of part of lot 10 in sq 119 to Caroline E Wilson for $7,950. -R J Meigs, clerk

Senate/Hse o/Reps: Act to incorporate the Home for Friendless Women & Chldrn: that Mary T Hay, Eliza M Morris, Jane F James, Eliza Wade Fitzgerald, Georgiana F Speak, Emily B Ruggles, Indiana Plant, Mary Grayham, Maria Virginia Brown, & their associates & successors, are hereby created a body corp: an institution where provision can be made by public charity for the care & relief of deserving females, & for the care of young orphan & destitute chldrn, male or female.

Memphis advices of the 13th with account of the engagement near Guntown, Miss: 2 brigades of cavalry under Gen Grierson, 2 brigs of infty, a Co of the 1st Ill Light Artl, & 2 regts of colored infty, all under command of Gen Sturgis. Ctzns report Kirby Smith in command of the enemy assisted by Forrest, Roddy, & Lee. Enemy's loss is supposed to be consideable, tho not so large as ours. Col Humphrey, 95th Ill, is reported killed. Col Warring, 4th Mo, was severely wounded. Memphis, Jun 14. Bodies of the missing infty of Gen Sturgis' expedition are coming in, our loss will probably be cut down to less than 1,000, all told. Some of the ofcrs blame Gen Sturgis, & say his management was bad.

Died: on Jun 16, Geo Morris, infant s/o Jas & Eliz M Colegate, aged 5 months.

Pres Lincoln, accompanied by Mrs Lincoln & a cmte of svr'l gentlemen, left this city yesterday on a visit to the Sanitary Fair now open at Phil. He expects to return this evening.

SAT JUN 18, 1864
Obit-Col Jas P McMahon, of the 164th N Y Vols, was killed in battle on Jun 3, in Richmond, in the 26th yr of his age.

Died: in Gtwn, D C, on Jun 16, Robt Read, in his 76th yr. Funeral from his late residence, 80 Prospect st, today.

Died: in Wash City, on Jun 17, Isaac Beers, in the 71st yr of his age. Funeral from his residence,
N C av & 3rd st, today. [I O O F notice of funeral.]

Died: at Providence, R I, on Jun 16, Isaac A Brownell, aged 45 yrs, son-in-law of Ammi B Young, of Wash City.

Died: at Paddington, on Jun 17, Maj Fitzhugh Birney, U S V, aged 22 yrs, s/o the late Jas G Birney, of Mich.

Explosion at the Washington Arsenal, near the foot of Four-&-a-half st, yesterday; missing & doubtless among the dead: Eliza Lacey, Miss Dunn, Lizzie Braccler, Bettie Brannigan, Melissa Adam, Julia McEwen & Maggie Yonson. Taken out alive & now in the hospital-Sally McElfresh, Annie Bach or Bates, & Rebecca Hull. Sarah Gunnell escaped from the building but died as she ran to her home nearby.

Maj Gen Robt Ransom, of N C, has been relieved of his command of the Dept of Richmond & appt'd to the Chief command of all the cavalry forces in the valley, v Gen Jones, who was killed in the fight about a week ago near Staunton. Gen Custis Lee is likely to be Ransom's successor in command of the forces about Richmond.

The Pres, Mrs Lincoln & their son, visited the Sanitary Fair at Phil after remaining in the Hotel until about 4 p m.

New cemetery for sldrs, near the Arlington Hse, was opened yesterday for the reception of the bodies of dec'd sldrs: grounds-200 acs, selected by Sec Stanton, & laid out under direction of Gen M C Meigs, Q M Gen. Hereafter all sldrs dying in a hospital here will be interred in this cemetery. -Star

A sldr in a hospital in Resaca, Ga, writes to a Western paper: "I see my name reported in the list of deaths at this hosp. I knew it was a lie as soon as I saw it. Hereafter when you hear of my death, write me & find out if it is so before pblshng it. Yours, convalescently, Michl Butler, Co I A7th Ohio.

MON JUN 20, 1864
Died: in Wash City, on Jun 18, Alice Ann, d/o John F & Mary E Bridget, aged 14 yrs. Funeral from their residence, 478 D st, today.

Died: in Wash City, on Jun 19, Jas A Sutton, only s/o Cath Isabella & the late Jas Sutton, aged 5 years & 2 weeks. Funeral from his mother's residence, 461 E st, today.

Died: on Jun 19, from wounds received at the battle of Cold Harbor, Lucian Lasselle, Orderly Sgt Co H, 1st Calif Regt, in his 30th yr. Funeral from his father's residence, 272 7th st, today.

Rt Rev Bishop McClosky, of Albany, has received the official announcement from Rome of his appointment to the Arch Episcopate of N Y.

Died: on Jun 18, Alexander, infant s/o Alex'r R & Mary G Shepherd, aged 6 months. Funeral from the residence of his father, 358 10th st, today.

Lord Palmerton will complete his 80th yr on the 20th of Oct next, & has been about 50 years in ofc.

Deaths reported to the Navy Dept for the week ending Jun 18, 1864.
John Majors, 1st cl boy, remit fever, Jun 3, 1864, Nav Hosp, Memphis.
Chris Olsen, seaman, remit fever, Jun 4, do.
Daniel Cherry, landsman, dysentery, Jun 11, Nav Asylum.
Geo A Baker, 3rd ast engr, congestion of brain, Jun 6, Nav Hosp, Norfolk.
Graham McLaughlin, marine, consumption, Jun 10, do.
Willis Freeman, landsman, consumption, Jun 12, do.
Jos Mahan, capt of top, drowned, Jun 9, vessel U S S Nipsic.
Chas Phares, seaman, pneumonia, Apr 3, Cincinnati.
Jas H Archibald, coalheaver, consumption, Jun 13, Nav Hosp, N Y.
S Franklin Browne, actg ast paymstr, blank, Jun 6, vessel U S S Missouri.
Benj Danils, contraband, blank, May 31, Evansville, Ind.
Morris Cummings, 1st cl boy, drowned, May 28, vessel U S S Mystic.
Javis G Farrar, mtr's mate, drowned, Jun 10, vessel U S S Dacotah.
Archibald Sims, landsman, drowned, Jun 9, vessel U S S Mackinaw.
Wm R Rigby, ord seaman, scurvy, Jun 5, vessel U S S Tacony.
Geo Maybery, 1st cl boy, heart disease, May 27, vessel U S S Chillicothe.
Geo W Craig, seaman, erysipleas, Jun 6, Mississippi Squadron.
Alfred Richardson, landsman, drowned, Jun 6, vessel U S S Delaware.
Patrick McNamara, 2nd cl boy, drowned, Jun 6, vessel U S S Minnesota.

Calamity at the Washington Arsenal on Fri-latest report on those who have died:
Susan Harris, a young girl, mbr of Wesley Chapel; Eliza Lacy; Betty Breshnahan, wife of a sldr in Gen Grant's army; Miss Collins; Miss Yonson; Eliza Adams, d/o a dealer in Centre Mkt; Miss McElfresh, who was removed to her mother's residence & died on Fri; Ellen Roach; Anna Bach, died in the hospital, Fri; Joanna Connor; Kate Horan; Miss Dunn; Julia McEwen; Mrs Tippett; Miss Murphy; Miss Lloyd; Rebecca Hull, Miss Brailor, Emma Baird; Mary Burroughs, & Ada or Willie Webster; which of the two is not certain, but that one of the sisters is dead appears beyond doubt. The remains of the victims were interred in Congressional Cemetery, yesterday. The Pres was in the long line of carriages, & also the Sec of War, Gen Ramsay, Chief of the Ordnance Bur, & other distinguished persons.

TUE JUN 21, 1864
36th Annual meeting of the Chesapeake & Ohio Canal Co, held on Jun 6, the following ofcrs chosen for the ensuing yr: Pres, Alfred Spates, of Alleghany Co

Dirs: Jos H Bradley, D C	Louis Washington, of Alleghany Co
Lawrence Brengle, Fred'k Co	A C Green, Alleghany Co
Chas Abert, Montg Co	

Lawrence A Dawson, Montg Co [in place of H Dellinger, of Wash Co.]

Headqrtrs Army of the Potomac: Jun 18. Attack made on the enemy's line yesterday by Gen Burnside was more successful than at first reported. He drove them further, taking some prisoners. Col Mix, of N Y, is reported killed; also, Col Kelly, commanding 2nd Brig of the 1st Div, 2nd Corps; Lt Col Baird, 126th N Y; Capt S O'Neill, 69th N Y; Adj McDonald, 631 N Y; & Adj Heist, 99th Pa, all killed; Lt Col McGee, 69th N Y, wounded in the face; Col Beever, commanding 4th Brig, 1st Div, 2nd Corps, wounded in the hip; & Col Crandall, 125th N Y, in the face; Col Ramsey, commanding 4th Brig, 2nd Div, hand fractured; Maj Butler, 69th N Y State militia, thigh fractured; Maj Blake, 8th N Y artl, in the head.

Mrd: on Jun 7, at St Matthew's Chr, by Rev Fr White, Henry Douglas to Annie E Chism, all of Wash.

WED JUN 22, 1864
Died: at Duddington, in Wash City, on Jun 17, after a brief illness, Maj Fitz Hugh Birney, A A G, on the staff of Maj Gen Birney. Funeral at Hampton, Western N Y, the residence of D Carroll Fitz Hugh, for interment in the family grave yard. He was 22 yrs of age & leaves his mother & wife to mourn him.

Orphans Crt of Wash Co, D C. 1-Case of Edw G Hardy, adm w a of Wm Kent Morgan, dec'd; settlement on Jul 16. -Z C Robbins, rg o/wills 2-Prsnl estate of Comfort S Whittlesey, late of Wash City, dec'd. Virginia Whittlesey, admx. 3-Prsnl estate of Susan Baltzer, late o/Wash City, dec'd. -Christopher Andrews, adm

Died: Henry K Sanger, at his residence in Detroit, age of 65 yrs. In early life he was a resident of Utica, N Y; grad of Hamilton College, at Clinton. [No date-appears recent]

Richmond papers of Jun 15-the remains of Gen Polk arrived here & were deposited in St Luke's Chr. Remains were then escorted to the Nouse train, for Augusta. Gen Polk was an 1827 grad of West Point; ordained a clergyman in 1831.

Gen Wm S Schuyler, 155th N Y, died on Monday at the Douglas Hosp, in Wash City, of a gunshot wound in the knee, received on Jun 3 in front of Richmond. He was from Saratoga, N Y.

THU JUN 23, 1864
Died: suddenly, on Jun 22, John O Harry, for 15 years Postmstr at Tennallytown, D C.

Died: in Balt, Md, on Jun 22, Forresta, the only surviving d/o the late Col Thos F W Vinson, of Rockville, Montg Co, Md, after a long & painful illness. Remains will be conveyed to Oak Hill Cemetery this day, where they will be interred. [Jun 27 paper: y/d/o the late Col Thos F W Vinson. She leaves her mother & bros.]

Died: in Wash City, on Jun 22, Beulah Stelle, infant d/o H M B & Edith McPherson, aged 9 months & 10 days. Jun 29th paper-died: on Jun 26, Wm Henry, aged 9 months & 14 days, infant s/o H M B & Edith McPherson.

Orphans Crt of Wash Co, D C. 1-Case of John H Semmes, adm of Thos Hughes, dec'd; settlement on Jul 16. 2-Case of Jacob E Lyon & Wm Q Force, adms of Chas Lyons, dec'd; settlement on Jul 16. Z C Robbins, rg o/wills

Wm H Young, a mbr of the Balt Bar, was run over this morning on Pratt st by the train from Washington & instantly killed. -Balt, Jun 22

Rev Chas Cleveland has for many years been the oldest clergyman in Boston in active svc. His 92nd birthday was celebrated in the Springfield Chapel on Sunday.

Hon Theodore H McCaleb died on Apr 29 at the *Hermitage Plantation*, Clairborne Co, Miss, in his 54th yr. -New Orleans Bee

Gen J C Robinson has so far recovered from his late amputation as to be able to ride out daily. He leaves for N Y today. [Wash, D C] He arrived at his residence in Portland, Maine, on Jun 20th.

Washington College was originally established as an academy in 1776 under the name of *Liberty Hall*.

FRI JUN 24, 1864
Mrd: at Rockville, Md, on Jun 21, by Rev Dr Boyle, Brice W Howard, of Brookeville, to Kate, 2nd d/o Wm Orendorff, of Rockville.

Died: on Jun 23, in PG Co, Md, at the residence of her son-in-law, Lucien Berry, Mrs Eliza T Berry, relict of the late Washington Berry, in the 62nd yr of her age. Burial at Rock Crk Chr, this day.

Mrs Stephan A Douglas, who arrived in Harrisburg, Pa, on Mon, on a visit to the family of Gen Cameron, received a despatch from Wash, during the day, announcing that her only bro, an ofcr in one of the D C Regts, had been mortally wounded. She immediately started on her return to Wash.

Lands on the Potomac River, PG Co, Md: for sale & furnished hse for rent: ½ a mile below Alexandria Ferry, well known as *Rozer's Ferry*: 3 tenement hses. Apply in person to J Carroll Brent, City Hall, Wash. Address Wm Henry Dangerfield, Wood Cot, near Wash City.

Died: in Wash City, Jun 23, Mrs Mary E Dyer, aged 46 yrs, widow o/the late Robt W Dyer, & d/o the late Cmdor Stephen Cassin, U S Navy. Funeral from St Patrick's Chr on Sat.

N Y Tribune of yesterday. Arrest at N Y. Mr Isaac Henderson, publisher of the Evening Post, Navy agent at this port, was arrested today by Mrshl Murray on a warrant issued by Com'r Betts, on charges embracing fraud, bribery, etc. Order issued by the Pres for his removal from ofc.

Names of Union Ofcrs at Charleston: from the Charleston Mercury of Jun 14: Yankee prisoners:

Brig Gen Seymour	Lt Col W F Bartholomew	Maj J E Clarke
Brig Gen Wessels	Lt Col J T Fellows	Maj W Crandall
Brig Gen Scammon	Lt Col C A Fairbanks	Maj J Hall
Brig Gen Shaler	Lt Col W V Stewart	Maj E W Bates
Brig Gen Hickman	Lt Col A W Taylor	Maj W T Baker
Col T G Grover	Lt Col C C Jos_n	Lt Col J Potsley
Col R Hawkins	Lt Col D Miles	Lt Col J H Burnham
Col W Harriman	Lt Col J D Mayhew	Lt Col W R Cook
Col J H Lehman	Col W C Lee	Lt Col C J Dickerson
Col O H Legrange	Col R White	Lt Col N Glenn
Maj D A Carpenter	Col H O Bol_nger	Lt Col S F Spofford
Maj H D Gant	Col H L Brown	Lt Col S B W Swift
Maj J N Johnson	Col R L Dane	Lt Col W P Lascelle
Maj O H Barnes	Col E Fardel	Lt Col W E McMickin
Lt Col E Alcott	Lt Col E G Hays	Lt Col W C Maxwell
Lt Col A F Rogers	N B Hunter	Lt Col S Merfie
Lt Col C P Baldwin	T N Higginbotham	

SAT JUN 25, 1864
Obit-Rev Wm E Wyatt, D D, died at Balt, Md, on Jun 24, in his 76th yr.

Headqrtrs Army of Potomac, Jun 22. Fighting continued: Maj Holt, 1st Mass Regt, was slightly wounded today. The 12th N Y Battery lost 4 guns by being surprised.

Hon Benj C Howard & Hon Henry May, appt'd by the recent Md Democratic State Convention as delegates to the Chicago Convention, have declined the honor.

Local ad: Seaton Munroe, Atty & Cnclr at Law: 5th st, between D & E, Wash.

MON JUN 27, 1864
Deaths reported to the Navy Dept for the week ending Jun 25, 1864:
Jas McMahon, landsman, drowned, May 29, vessel U S S *Kuhn*.
Jas Fort, seaman, heart disease, May 31, vessel U S S *Cimarron*.
Chas Rogan, landsman, blank, Jun 7, vessel U S S *Com McDonough*.
Adams Hap, landsman, diarrhoea, Jun 9, Nav Hosp, Memphis.
Ned Hunter, 1st cl boy, dysentery, Jun 11, do.
Chas Thompson, seaman, typhoid fever, Jun 12, do.
B Aberdeen, landsman, bronchitis, Jun 2, vessel U S S *Vicennes*.
Michl McDermot, fireman, remit fever, Jun 17, Nav Hosp, Portsmouth.
Pat McGiverney, coalheaver, apoplexy, May 15, vessel U S *Owasco*.
Jos Scott, landsman, drowned, Jun 2, vessel U S S *Nyanza*.
M Dennis, blank, pleuritis, Apr 26, vessel U S S *Red Rover*.
C S Wells, actg mstr's mate, diarrhoea, Apr 28, do.
Nias Hanin, 1st cl boy, pneumonia, May 3, do.
John Smith, seaman, gunshot wound, May 8, do.
Willis Craig, 2nd cl fireman, diarrhoea, May 7, do.
John Keese, ord seaman, typhoid fever, May 7, do.
Albert Coats, ord seaman, blank, May 19, do.
Chas Kalenski, seaman, gunshot wound, May 17, do.
Bateman Corsely, coalheaver, blank, May 30, do.
Wm Short, 2nd cl fireman, consumption, Jun 21, Nav Hosp, Phil.
Pat Donohoe, seaman, gunshot wound, Jun 1, vessel U S S *Exchange*.
Hy Cook, seaman, remit fever, Jun 11, vessel U S S *De Soto*.
J Vandyke, landsman, remit fever, Jun 12, do.
A Beeker, coalheaver, remit fever, Jun 15, do.
Jas E Renbey, coalheaver, remit fever, Jun 12, do.
Jas Cushing, fireman, remit fever, Jun 16, do.
Geo A Parker, A A Surg, remit fever, Jun 18, do.
Peter N Wilke, seaman, gastritis, Jun 9, vessel U S S *Iroquois*.
Michl Ready, 1st cl boy, dysentery, Jun 6, vessel U S S *Ino*.

Died: on Jun 25, after an illness of 3 weeks, Daniel Rowland, of Wash City, in his 53rd yr. He leaves a wife & 6 chldrn. Funeral from St Dominick's Chr, Mon.

Died: on Jun 25, Mgt Curne, only child of Josiah Varden & Cynthia J Grant, aged 6 months & 20 days. Funeral from residence of her grandfather, Mr Geo H Grant, 469 K st, Mon.

Died: on Jun 18, at Christiana, Dela, Alice Dorman, 2nd d/o J B C & Eliza Dundas Oldham, of Phil, aged 4 years & 6 months.

Remarkable coincidences: At Spottsylvania Crt Hse Brig Gen Henry A Walker, of A P Hill's corps, lost his foot. In D H Hills attack at Bermuda Hundred, Brig Gen Wm S Walker, was wounded in the foot & taken prisoner. Maj Gen H T Walker was shot thru the foot near Dallas, Ga, in engagement between Johnston & Sherman. The Cmder of the Stonewall brig, Gen Jas L Walker, was badly wounded in the battle of May 12, when Ed Johnston's division suffered great loss. Gen Marmaduke killed Marsh Walker, of Arkansas, in a duel. -Richmond Whip

On May 30, the Count of Paris, grandson of Louis Phillips, & heir to the Orleans title to the French throne, was mrd at Kingston-on-Thames, Eng, to his first cousin, the Princess Isabella of Orleans, d/o the Duke of Montpensier. A year ago his younger bro, the Duke of Chartres, was mrd to his first cousin, the Princess Francoise of Orleans, d/o the Prince of Joinville. These 2 young men were in this country in 1861 & 1862, serving in the U S army on the staff of Maj Gen McClellan.

The Pres has nominated Maj Jacob Zeilin, now in command of the barracks at Brooklyn, N Y, to the position of Col Commandnt of the Marine Corps, made vacant by the death of Col John Harris. Maj Zeilin has been in the svc over 30 yrs.

TUE JUN 28, 1864
Died: in Wash City, on Jun 26, in her 70th yr, Mrs Mary Moore, w/o Mr John Moore, of Wash. Funeral from her late residence, 347 F st, today.

Died: in Wash City, on Jun 27, of typhoid fever, Wm H Crowley, aged 23 yrs, s/o Patrick & Eliz A Crowley. Funeral from the residence of his father, 542 I st, today.

Tom Hyer, well-known in sporting circles, died of cardiac dropsy, suddenly, at his residence in
N Y C, on Sunday, aged 45 yrs; native of N Y State.

Died: Jos A Scoville, the N Y correspondent of the London Herald, who wrote over the signature of *Manhattan*, died on Sat last.

Undersigned will receive sealed proposals until Jun 29, for supplying the Wash Asylum with all the meat that may be required. –W G H Newman, John McDevill, Wm Slater, Com'rs of Asylum

Reports from Ga: Col Lagrange, of the 1st Wisc cavalry, commanding a brig, was captured on Jun 19.

N Y, Jun 26. The U S steam transport *Western Metropolis*, Capt Hilton, arrived yesterday from Bermuda Hundred, bringing 600 sick & wounded sldrs, among whom are Lt Col Palmer, Lt H C Lacey, Lt s B Soyles, & Capt W N Elwell. The hospital steamer *Geo Leary*, Capt Deming, from Hampton Rds, with 375 sick & wounded sldrs, also arrived yesterday.

WED JUN 29, 1864
Died: in Wash City, on Jun 28, Ulysses B, y/s/o the Rev Ulysses Ward, in his 31st yr. Funeral from the residence of his mother-in-law, Mrs Waters, 403 12th st, today.

Col Wass had been for some time quite ill, but was riding up to the front in an ambulance to reform his regt, & arrived just in time to see it gobbled up. [See below.]

Boston, Jun 27. Col Wass, of the 19th Mass Regt, who reached home today on sick leave, states that among our men in the affair on Wed was the entire brig comprising the 15th & 19th Mass, & the 42nd & 82nd N Y Regts. Barlow's & Gibbon's divisions fell back on receiving the attack of the enemy. [See above.]

Louisville, Jun 27. Col Wolford was arrested at Lebanon this morning by order of Gen Burbridge, & brought to this city tonight.

The steamer *Connecticut* arrived here yesterday from City Point,bringing up 405, including 35 ofcrs. Majority of wounded are stretcher cases. Among them:

Capt J G McBlair, aid to Gen Mott	Capt W D Morrison, 7th Md
Capt P Glynn, 69th N Y	Capt G Lovett, 107 Pa
Capt J E Steward, 3rd Delaware	Capt F A Myers, 724 Pa
Capt T Cassidy, 110 Pa	Capt D C Ketchum, 64th N Y

Confirmation by the Senate: Col Friend S Rutherford, 97th Ill vols, & Col Joshua L Chamberlain, 20th Maine vols, to be Brig Gens of vols. Danl S Dickinson, of N Y, to be Com'r on part of the U S under the treaty of Jul, 1863, for the final settlement of the claims of the Hudson's Bay & Puget's Sound Agricultural Cos.

Mr Zimmerman, of the firm of McGregor & Zimmerman, of this city, was arrested on Sun last, by the order of the Sec of War, on a charge of disloyalty.

Sgt Walsh discovered a fire at #1 Doyer, trapping the occupants, Wm Henig, a German, 23, who, with his wife Mary, 25, & their chldrn, Chas, Maria, & Wm, aged 4, 2 & 18 mos, who found it impossible to escape. In his efforts, Mr Henig fell from the 3rd floor to the pavement & was fatally injured. Mrs Henig & her 3 chldrn were burned to death. -N Y Post

Mrs Snead, w/o Col T L Snead, of St Louis, long Chief of Staff to Gen Price, recently arrived in that city from the South, having passed the Federal lines without permission from the proper authorities. For this she has been arrested & sent, for the present, to Gratiot st prison.

THU JUN 30, 1864

A Card: the undersigned, residents of Wash City, bear public testimony that we have long known Jos L Savage, a hardware merchant, doing business on Pa ave, in Wash City for the last 17 yrs. He is a native of this city, his father is among our most respectable & wealthy ctzns. His son, Jos L, also bears a high character as a ctzn & man of business. Signed:

Richd Wallach, Mayor

Wm Forsyth, City Srvyr	Hinton & Teel	Thos Donoho
Saml E Douglass, Reg	Geo H Plant	W B Todd
Sibley & Guy	Franck Taylor	King & Burchel
John Purdy	Saml Lewis	Edw C Dyer
Blanchard & Mohun	Morgan & Rhinehart	W Orme
Jos W Nairn & Bro	J L Walker	Alex R Shepherd
Wm E Spalding	Perry & Brother	Wash, Jun 29, 1864
Jas Skirving	A P Hoover	

[Note: in another column: Mr J L Savage, formerly of this city, but more recently engaged in business in N Y, has not lost the confidence of his most intimate friends & neighbors here in consequence of the late proceedings against him at N Y, in connexion with alleged official corruptions in that city.]

Died: on Jun 29, Brig Gen Jas P Taylor, Commissary Gen of Subsistence U S Army, aged 69 yrs. Funeral from his late residence, 363 H st, on Jul 1. Jul 1 paper-Brig Gen Jos P Taylor, died in Wash City on Jun 29, younger bro o/the late Maj Gen & Pres Zachary Taylor. He entered the military svc of the U S in 1813.

Orphans Crt of Wash Co, D C. Case of Asbury Lloyd, adm of J W Noell, dec'd; settlement on Jul 23. -Z C Robbins, rg o/wills

On Sat the Gov't detectives arrested, without due process of law, Dr Benj Duvall, Alfred Ray & Thos & Jas Noland, of Montg Co, Md, & confined them in the Old Capitol prison. -Union

Wm S Thruston s/o Gen C M Thruston, died suddenly, near Cumberland, on Jun 14, age 36 yrs. He had srv'd as a Capt in the reg army of the U S. Burial was on Jun 16. -Cumberland Union

The steamer *Keyport* arrived here yesterday from City Point, bringing up the army mails & the 2nd N Y Regt, 112 men, [Lt Col John Leonard commanding,] whose term of service has expired. The *Keyport* brought up the bodies of Col W W Bates, 8th N Y heavy artl; Capt S T Keene, 20th Maine; Lt Frank Hammond, 58th Mass; & Lt Jos E Colby, 32nd Maine.

A second attempt was made on Thu to launch the Monitor *Puritan*, but failed. New ways will have to be made, & it will be some 2 weeks ere another attempt to launch can be made.

Partial list of Indians captured near Petersburg: Jacke Penasenorquad, Louis Miskequat, Wm McSurraw, Michl Johnny, Jackson Wargishwebber, Adam Scohboquaheom, Peter Penrroquaquaw, Joen Nicharaw. Names taken down letter by letter as the interpreter would spell them. The provost mrshl, or commanding ofcr at Andersonville, Ga, whither the prisoners are now going, will have a sweet time in getting a list of them.

Columbian College anniversary week: exhibition on Mon at the First Bapt Chr. Speaker: Clark Mills. Gold harp, 1st prize, to Jos H France, jr; 2nd prize to Wm D Beall, jr. In 2nd class 1st prizes to both Eugene Soper & Geo Y Coffin. 3rd class the 1st prize to Howard Goodrich. Silver shields, reward for punctuality & good conduct, to above pupils & also to Geo C Schaeffer & John Kelly.

41st Annual commencement was held yesterday at the Smithsonian Instit. Salutatory by *Thos S Samson, of D C. Oration by Saml M Yeatman, D C; Geo C Samson, D C; Henry J Handy, jr; **Robt Farnham, D C; **Arthur Fendall, D C; **Albert J Wheat, D C; *J Abbott Moore, D C; *Thos J Miller, D C; *Reginald Fendall, D C. **Clarence B Young, D C. Mstr of Arts conferred on Rev H J Parks & Rev Geo V Leech. Dr of Divinity conferred on Rev Warren Randolph & Rev S G Bullfinch. [*Degree of Bachelor of Arts. **Bachelor of Philosophy]

FRI JUL 1, 1864
Mrd: on Jun 28, at St Aloysius Chr, by Rev Fr Maguire, Henry G Healy, of N Y C, to Rosalie, 2nd d/o Gen Wm Hickey, of Wash City.

Died: in Wash, on Jun 24, in his 31st yr, of congestion of the brain, Capt Degarneo Whiting, A Q M, s/o J L Whiting, M D, of Detroit, Mich.

Died on Jun 29, Louise Annette, 2nd d/o Armand & Honorine Jardine, aged 5 years & 17 days. Funeral from their residence today.

Died: on Jun 30, Mrs Maria M Watterston, wid/o the late Geo Watterston, in her 67 yr. Funeral from her late residence on Capitol Hill, Sat.

Died: on Jun 30, Sophie Matilda, infant d/o Dr Tullio S & Rebecca A Verdi, aged 37 days. Funeral from 258 G st, Sat.

Died: in Gtwn D C, on Jun 30, Eleanor Lee, only child of R L & Rebecca Cropley, aged 5 months. Funeral from 216 Bridge st, Gtwn, on Sat.

Confiscation sale in Alexandria, Va: lands, hses, etc of Geo K Witmer & Dennis R Blacklock; Wm N McVeigh & Wm H Fowle; W H Fowle, Arthur Herbert; M D Corse; David Funsten; J C Nevett; Wm Whaley; J L Pascoe & Edw Sangster; J H McLean; J H Reid; L B Taylor. Also, the stock belonging to D F Hooe; R H Dulany; W G Cazenove; Dr O Fairfax; Raymond Fairfax; Albert Fairfax. Also the hsehld furn of E S Hutchinson; Dr M M Lewis; R E Lee, & Wm N & J H McVeigh. In Fairfax Co-Arthur Herbert; Saml Cooper; R C Mason, French Forrest, G K Witmer; W S Kemper; Saml R Johnston; Wm G Cazenove; Wilmer D Corse; G H Padgett, Jos Bruin; R L Rotchford; Murray Mason. In Pr Wm Co-W Selecman; J H Hammil; J W Fairfax.

Among the wounded who arrived from City Point on the steamer *City of Albany*: Capt B F Taylor, 2nd Md; Capt B B Shuck, 48th Pa; Capt C D Carpenter, 38th Wisc; & Lt S Blandin, 58th Mass, & Lt A V Bedell, 2nd N Y Mntd Rifles.

Wash Corp: 1-Ptn of T Van Reswick & others, asking the abatement of a nuisance: referred to the Cmte on Police. Same for Wm H Upperman & 30 others. 2-Invitation from Chas Kloman, Pres of the Wash German Relief Assoc, to a grand festival on the 30th inst: accepted. 3-Resignation ltr of Jas W Spalding, Assessor of the 2nd ward: laid on the table. 4-Ptn of M Lully, asking a certain privilege: referred to the Cmte on Police. 5-Ptn of Ernestate Weber: referred to the Cmte on Finance. 6-Ptn of J L Oppenheimer: referred to the Cmte on Claims. 7-Ptn of Lewis Patten, with a bill granting him permission to erect a frame bldg. 8-Ptn of L W Pumphrey: referred to the Cmte on Police.

SAT JUL 2, 1864
Died: at Hyattsville, on Jun 30, Mary Eliz, w/o John B Wheeler, & d/o Jas D Chedal, aged 26 yrs. Funeral from her father's residence, 404 D st, today.

Bowie & DeKrafft, Genr'l Agency for Army & Navy Pay, Pensions, & all other Military Claims. Robt Bowie, late Interior Dept, & J W DeKrafft, late Chief Clerk of U S Gen Land Ofc, with experience of many years in pblc Depts in Wash. Ofc, 425 E st, opposite the P O, Wash, D C.

The Pres of the U S yesterday nominated the Hon Wm Pitt Fessenden, of Maine, as Sec of the Treas, to fill the vacancy created by the resignation of Mr Chase. It was confirmed by the Senate.

Liverpool, Jun 19. Smith O'Brien died on the 17th. It is reported in Liverpool, on authority said to be quite reliable, that the ship *Alabama* has or will leave Cherbourg today to engage the U S steamer *Keareage*.

Commencement of Columbian College [See Jun 30th]: honorary degree of A M was conferred on Rev J H Parks, of N Y, & on Dr D W Prentiss, of Wash, D C, a grad of the Philosophical Class of 1860. Degree of A M in course, was conferred on Rev Geo V Leech, of Md, a graduate of the class of 1853.

MON JUL 4, 1864

Deaths reported to the Navy Dept for the week ending Jul 2, 1864:
Tho Taylor, blank, heart disease, Jun 9, vessel U S S *Stars & Stripes*.
Jas R Young, ord seaman, injury, Jun 16, vessel U S S *Powhatan*.
Wm Hefflin, landsman, consumption, Jun 23, Nav Hosp, N Y.
Wm Wilson, coalheaver, remit fever, Jun 22, Navy Yd, Portsmouth, N H.
Phil Sampson, 1st cl boy, consumption, Jun 15, Nav Hosp, Memphis.
Jos Leonard, ofcr's steward, chronic diarrhoea, Jun 16, do.
Hy Cotton, landsman, typhoid fever, Jun 18, do.
Pat McGeugon, landsman, consumption, Jun, Naval Hosp, N Y.
Asa Young, landsman, consumption, no date, do.
Wm Jeffries, pensioner, typhoid fever, Jun 25, Nav Asylum, Phil.
Wm Burlingame, ord seaman, yel fever, no date, vessel U S S *Tioga*.
Jas McNamara, 3rd ast eng, yel fever, no date, do.
Chas S Fitch, a a paymstr, yel fever, do, do.
John Stevens, marine, yel fever, do, do.
Isael Brown, 1st cl boy, pneumonia, Jun 24, Nav Hosp, Chelsea.
Garret Fisher, 1st cl boy, remit fever, Jun 20, Navy Yd, Portsmouth, N H.
Thos Jones, seaman, diarrhoea, May 16, New Orleans.
Rd Curling, seaman, lung disease, May 18, vessel U S S *Brooklyn*.
Ch Foster, landsman, epilepsy, Jun 8, Nav Hosp, vessel *Pensacola*.
J W Hanson, landsman, pleurity, Jun 10, do.
Wm H Parker, landsman, drowned, Jun 8, vessel U S S *Kanawha*.
John Welsh, seaman, pneumonia, Jun 21, vessel U S S R R *Cuyler*.
Wm Finley, seaman, carditis, Jun 26, Nav Hosp, Norfolk.
John Gardiner, 1st cl boy, typhoid fever, May 20, vessel U S S *Argosy*.
John J Cronwell, ord seaman, gunshot wound, Jun 15, vessel U S S *Naiad*.
John J Burger, landsman, gunshot wound, Jun 17, vessel U S S *Anacostia*.
Henry Mayer, ord seaman, vomiting blood, May 2, Balt, Md.
Syd Ward, coalheaver, chronic diarrhoea, Jun 16, Nav Hosp, Memphis.

Appointments by the Pres with the consent & advice of the Senate:
Brig Gen Quincy A Gillmore, to Maj Gen of vols, Jul 10, 1863
Col Adin P Undewood, 33rd Mass Regt, to Brig Gen of vols
Col Jos B Carr, 2nd N Y Regt, to Brig Gen of vols
Lt Col John P Sanderson, 18th Infty, U S Army, to be Col
Maj Delavan D Perkins, to Ast Adj Gen
Capt Henry Clay Wood, 11th U S Infty, to Ast Adj Gen, with rank of Maj
Maj Robt E Clary, to be Deputy Q M Gen, with rank of Lt Col
Corps of Engrs: 1st Lt to Capt:
Peter G Haines   Arthur H Dutton
Francis U Farquhar   Ranald Slidell Mackenzie
Adj Gens of vols: with rank of Maj:

Capt Maxwell V L Woodhull
Capt Henry R Dalton
Lt F A Copeland, 5th Mich cavalry
1st Lt John F Lacey, 331 Iowa vols
Lt Col Wm A Nichols, to Ast Adj Gen with rank of Col
Maj Geo L Hartsuff, to Ast Adj Gen with rank of Lt Col
1st Lt Danl D Wheeler, Vt vol, to Ast Adj Gen
Lt John D Parsons, to Ast Adj Gen
Capt Seth B Moe, to Ast Adj Gen
Lt Wm T Kittredge, to Ast Adj Gen

Capt Henry A Hale, 19th Mass vol
Lt Robt E Beecher, 73rd Ohio vol
John C Tyler, of Vt
Lt Singleton Howland, 37th Indiana vol

Naval appointments:
Cmder Henry A Wise, Chief of Bureau of Ord
Cmder Albert A Smith, Chief of Bureau of Equipment & Recruiting
Jos E Nourse, Edw A Rouget, & Edw Seager, professors of math in the Navy, from May 21, 1864
Wm E Hopkins & Paul Shirley, to be Cmders in the Navy

To be paymstrs in the Navy:
Frank H Hinman, of Ohio
Robt P Lislie, of Pa

Horace P Tuttle, of Mass
Geo D F Barton, N Y
W R Winslow, Mass

W Goldsborough, Md

To Be Chaplains in the Navy:
Geo W Smith, D C

Geo D Henderson, Kansas

H B Hibben, Ind
J D Benglors, R I

Marine Corps:
To be Col Commandnt: Maj Jacob Zelfin
To be Col: Maj Wm L Shuttleworth
To be Lt Cols: Wm R Kintzing & Capt Jas H Jones
To be Majs:
Capt Thos Y Field

Capt Chas G McCawley

Capt Geo L Graham

1st Lt to Capt:
Wm H Cartter
McLane Tilton

John H Higbee
Frank Munroe

Robt W Huntington
Jos F Baker

2nd Lt to 1st Lt:
Wm Wallace
Edw C Saltmarsh

Geo C Stoddard
Chas F Williams

A Whittemore Ward
Jas B Young

Appointments to 2nd Lts:
Henry C Sloan, Wisc
Gouverneur Morris, N Y
Kent D Davis, N Y
A S Taylor, N J
Jas M T Young, Md

Wm B Murray, Iowa
Geo C Reid, Ohio
Erastus R Robinson, N Y
J Henry Denig, Ind
Edmund P Banning, N Y

Hoffman Atkinson, W Va
John A Rodgers, N Y

Civil Appointments:
Jos Holt, of Ky, to be Judge Advocate General
Wm McKee Dunn, of Ind, to be Ast Judge Adv Gen
Sidney Edgerton, of Idaho Terr, to be Govn'r of the Terr of Montana
Ammi Giddings, of Conn, to be Assoc Justice of the Supreme Crt of the Terr of Montana
Lorenzo P Williston, to be Assoc Justice of the Supr Crt of the Terr of Montana
Henry P Rorsey, of Maine, to be Sec of the Terr of Montana
Cornelius F Buck, of Minn, to be Mrshl of the U S for the Terr of Montana
Edw B Nealy, of Iowa, to be Atty of the U S for the Terr of Montana
Ira Bartlett, of Ill, to be Assoc Judge for Dakota Terr
Warren T Lockhart, of Ind, to be Register of the Land Ofc at Carson City, Nevada Terr.

Orphans Crt of Wash Co, D C. Case of Mrs Emma Gibbs, admx of John H Gibbs, dec'd; settlement on Jul 26. -Z C Robbins, rg o/wills

Mr Isaac Daniels, the late of the sldrs of the Rev, residing in N Y C, died on Jun 29, aged 109 yrs. He served under Gen Washington, & fought in the battles of Monmouth, Trenton, & White Plains. He also served in the war of 1812.

An officer recently visited the battle-field of the *Wilderness* & writes: estimated that 15,000 of our men, & as many more of rebels, lie here unburied, & as 6 weeks have passed since the battle, imagination in its wildest fancies cannot begin to paint the spectacle.

Crt of Inquiry commenced at Memphis to investigate the facts concerning the recent disaster under Gen Sturgis. Composed of the following ofcrs: Brig Gen Buckland & Brennan & Col Kapner, with Capt A Gaddis as Judge Advocate.

Boston, Jul 3-Hon Josiah Quincy died last night at his country seat in Quincy, aged 92 yrs. Aside from the infirmities of old age, he was in good health, & rode out the day before his death. Funeral in Arlington st Chr on Jul 6.

Died: on Jul 2, Dr B Johnson Hellen, in his 35th yr. Funeral St Aloysius Chr, Tue.

Died: on Jul 2, Geo McClelland, infant & last child of Geo & late Mary E McClelland, aged 6 months.

WED JUL 6, 1864
Died: in Wash City, on Jul 4, Miss Rossanna D Coons, in the 64th yr of her age. Funeral from the residence of Wm G Moore, 18 K st, today. Friends of her nephew, Mr Geo S Gideon, are invited to attend.

For sale or rent: first rate frame hse with 9 rms, with 29,000 ft of ground, with a variety of fruit trees: 575 G & 13th sts & Pa ave east. Inquire on the premises: D Carroll

For sale: large well built 3 story brick hse, with back building: 171 Second st west, between B & C sts. Apply to Chas H Lane, 424 Pa ave.

Died: on Jul 3, 1864, in her 76th yr, Mrs Mary O'Neal, relict of the late H G O'Neal, of the Fourth Auditor's Ofc.

Among the acts passed during the 38th Congress, just closed: Relief of

Julia A Ames	Land warrant to Richd Fitch, of Ohio
Lt Wm P Richner, 77 Ohio Vol Infty	Pension of Isaac Allen
Geo F Nesbitt	Est of B F Kendall
Mary Jane Skaggs	Wm Sawyer & others, of Ohio
Dr Chas M Wetherill	Maj N S Brinton, paymstr U S Army
Relict of Richd G Murphy	Wid/o C A Haun

Sarah Robinson, wid/o John L Robinson, late mrshl of Ind
Settle account of the late Capt Danl Hebard, U S Vols.
Prize money due to Cmder Abner Read, U S N, to his widow, Constance Read.

THU JUL 7, 1864
Academy of Visitation, Jul 1-Honors in the Senior Circle: [Local Item]

Miss Julia Turner, of Mo   Miss Josephine Harman, Md
Miss Agatha O'Neale, D C   Miss Florence Heldreth, Mass
Miss Maggie McCarty, Pa   Miss Nannie Pickrell, D C

Ex-Lt Gov John Tracy died at his residence in Oxford, N Y, on Jun 18, age 88 yrs.

Ex-Gov Andrew H Reeder, formerly Gov of Kansas Terr, died at his residence at Easton, Pa, after a short illness, on Jul 5.

Friends of Col Danl McCook, who was reported mortally wounded in the assault on Kenesaw Mtn, Ga, will be gratified to learn the report was erroneous. He is now in Nashville; wounded in the shoulder, not dangerously.

Wash Corp: 1-Ptn of A M Vermillion: referred to the Cmte on Claims. 2-Ptn of Thos J Galt asking certain privileges: referred to the Cmte on Wharves. 3-Communication of Jas English: moved to be taken up.

Foreign mscl: The City of *Edinburgh* is about to be created a Roman Catholic Archbishopric. Hereto the Bishops of the Holy See in Scotland have been of the grade of missionaries, or "in partibus," etc.

Fire in Louisville, Ky, on Sat, originated in one of the fine blocks of 4 story stone front hses on Main st, erected by Mr Jos Peterson, at a cost of not less than $100,000. Fire started in the hse occupied by Dr Magruder, medical purveyor, filled with all kinds of hospital stores.

Balt, Jul 6. From the movements among the enemy at Harper's Ferry today, it was supposed that Hunter's forces were pressing them in the rear. There is every reason to believe Hunter will be heard from to some purpose before long. Every precaution has been taken by Gen Wallace to guard against the surprise movement of the enemy in this direction. Last night Mrs Dixon, an estimable Union lady, & a resident of Point of Rocks, was killed whilst sitting at her door, near the post ofc, by a shot fired by a rebel from the opposite side of the Potomac.

A party from the Treasury left Gtwn on a pleasure trip to Harper's Ferry on Sat, on the canal packet *Flying Cloud*. On their return, while at dinner, the boat was fired on. Being about 50 yds from the lock, & no one to open it, we made to the side of the canal, & jumped ashore. Messrs R Davis, Knight, Cooper, & Gray tried to open the lock, but were fired on by the rebels who now had reached the tow path. We jumped for the hills, & saw the boat fired, after they had taken every thing of value. Capt Hobert was the last man seen on the boat, & fears for his safety are entertained. There were 17 men on the excursion, 11 of whom have returned: Messrs Larman & son, Valk, Read, N Davison, J Davis, C Yates, Smith, Fowl, Shaffer, & Gray. Missing: Capt Hobert, Messrs R Davis, Knight, Cooper, W Jermer, & J Ordan.

FRI JUL 8, 1864
Died: in Wash City, on Jul 6, of pulmonary consumption, Mr Geo W Beall, aged 54 yrs, a native of Md, but for many years officially connected with the Gov't in Wash. Funeral from his residence, F & 11th sts, today.

Died: in Brooklyn, N Y, Jul 7, in the 2nd yr of her age, Mary Love, d/o the late Maj Josiah Watson, U S M C.

Died: of scarlet fever, at his father's residence, in Brooklyn, N Y, on Jul 5, Chas J, s/o Chas Batchelor, aged 20 years & 2 months. Funeral from the residence of his father, today, burial in Greenwood Cemetery.

Supreme Crt of D C, in Equity #146. Geo W Miller, cmplnt, vs Ellen, Chas, Thos J, & Ellen Miller, jr, Henry C & Mary E Greenfield, Geo & Mary B Hutton, Saml & Victoria J Cross, Horatio & Cath V Browning, & Wm H, Sarah E, & Emma J Otterback, dfndnts. Statement of the trustees' account at City Hall, Jul 30; also the amount of dower of said C Miller's widow in the sales made by said trustees. -W Redin, auditor

Orphans Crt of Wash Co, D C. Case of Mgt Lyons, admx of Eliz Braiden, dec'd; settlement on Aug 2. -Z C Robbins, rg o/wills

SAT JUL 9, 1864
Local Matter-Cornelius Tuell, white, convicted of the murder of his wife, was hung yesterday. Peter Gooden, negro, convicted of the murder of Geo Banks, negro, had his execution deferred.

Maj Addison Garland, U S M C, died at the Mare Island barracks, San Francisco, Calif, on Jun 21. His appointment to the service is dated Oct, 1834.

Dr W B Shedd is curing all chronic disease, both in ladies & gentlemen, by a new method in the use of Electro-Magnetism in its various modifications, combined with the Electro-Medicated Vaper Bath. Ofc & residence at 447 8th st, between E & F sts, & #63 E Balt st, Balt, Md.

Decree of the Crct Crt of Montg Co, Md; wherein Saml P Robertson & others, cmplnts, & Alonzo A Wilkins & others, dfndnts. Sale of the farm, 60¾ acs, of the late John L Wilkins, with dwlg hse. -Geo Peter, trustee.

MON JUL 11, 1864
Deaths reported to the Navy Dept for the week ending Jul 9, 1864.
Jos A Colver, landsman, consumption, Jun 28, hosp, Chelsea.
Edwin T Irvin, landsman, drowned, Jun 12, vessel U S S *Sangus.*
Stephen Collins, 2nd cl boy, drowned, Jun 30, do.
Nat W Silloway, landsman, pneumonia, May 21, vessel U S S *Cherokee.*
Frederick H Dyer, actg mstr's mate, remit fever, Jun 11, Marine Hosp, Key West.
John Thompson, pilot, apoplexy, Jun 13, Marine Hosp, Key West.
Wm Pickens, 1st cl boy, heart disease, Jun 10, do.
Robt Wisner, actg mstr's mate, yel fever, Jun 28, do.
John Harrold, machinist, remit fever, Jun 11, do.
Wm Buck, landsman, pneumonia, Jun 8, vessel U S S *Vermont.*
Josiah Lownes, landsman, pneumonia, Jun 27, do.
Jefferson Ford, actg mstr, cholera morbus, Jun 18, Military Hosp, Beaufort, N C.
Henry Engel, seaman, typhoid fever, Jun 20, Hosp, Memphis.
Bill Peterson, blank, debility, Jun 21, do.
E Perkins, actg mstr's mate, consumption, Jun 22, do.
Bush Naylor, 1st cl boy, dropsy, Jun 23, do.
Asa O Winter, actg ast paymstr, yel fever, Jun 28, vessel U S S *Union.*
Michl Ford, machinist, yel fever, Jun 29, do.
Albert Bell, 1st cl boy, enteritis, May 14, vessel U S S *Avenger.*

Henry Doane, seaman, gastritis, May 12, vessel U S S *Peosta.*
Taylor Doyle, 1st cl boy, remit fever, Apr 3, vessel U S S *Chillicothe.*
Robt Higgins, coalheaver, gunshot wounds, Apr 26, vessel U S S *Juliet.*
Lewis Jones, landsman, gunshot wounds, Jan 27, vessel U S S *Prairie Bird.*
Silvester Pool, actg ensign, gunshot wounds, Apr 26, vessel U S S *Fort Hindman*
Dempsey Smith, 1st cl boy, asthma, Jan 26, vessel U S S *Clara Dolsen.*
Jas R Wales, mstr at arms, gunshot wounds, Apr 27, vessel U S S *Juliet.*
Willis Allen, 1st cl boy, drowned, Jan 27, vessel U S S *Key West.*
Edw Burns, landsman, drowned, Jun 28, vessel U S S *Tecumseh.*
John L Colby, seaman, chronic diarrhoea, May 19, vessel U S S *Mound City.*
Geo Davis, landsman, small pox, Mar 15, vessel U S S *Benton*
Harry Folkerth, seaman, drowned, Jun 5, vessel U S S *Peosta.*
John Lamport, landsman, congestive fever, May 18, vessel U S S *Mound City.*
John Henry, landsman, drowned, Jun 11, Pacific Squadron.
Wm A Walker, seaman, pneumonia, Jun 10, vessel U S S *Magnolia.*
Benj Ware, 1st cl boy, disease of kidneys, Jun 24, U S Naval Depot, Key West.
Francis F Mitchell, seaman, debility, Hosp, Chelsea.

Supreme Crt of D C, in Chancery, #738. Eliz Brent vs Chas E Brent. John Carroll Brent, trustee, reports sale of lots 1 & 25 in sq 420, to Wm H Easton, for $1,102; ratify same. -R J Meigs, clerk

Orphans Crt of Wash Co, D C. 1-Prsnl estate of Rosanna D Coons, late of Wash City, dec'd. -Wm G Moore, adm. 2-Prsnl estate of Mary E Dyer, late of Wash City, dec'd. -Edw C Dyer.

Lost between the Jewelry Stores of Mr Semkens & Mr Hood, 3 gold studs & a pr of sleeve buttons, [a set] on Tue. Liberal reward for their return to the Intell ofc, & thanks of the owner.

Despatch dt'd at Harrisburg on Fri says: last night Hagerstown was still burning. Gen Couch has just app'td Gen Rawley, commander of the Pittsburgh district, to the command of the troops in the Cumberland Valley.

Balt, Jul 10. An ambulance has just arrived with wounded ofcrs: Capt Adam Ekin, A A G of Gen Rickett's staff, & Capt Payne, 106th N Y; the former badly wounded, the latter severely in the hip.

Gen Wallace retreating to Balt. Wash, Jul 10: official report from Maj Gen Wallace: battle took place between the forces under his command & the rebel forces at Monocacy today, [Sat] beginning at 9 a m till 5 p m; our forces overpowered by the superior numbers of the enemy, & were forced to retreat in disorder. Col Seward, N Y heavy artl, was wounded & taken prisoner; Brig Gen Tyler was also taken prisoner. Enemy's force is at least 20,000. – Edwin M Stanton, Sec of War Note: the above is unfounded-Col Seward came out of a sick hospital at the front to lead his regt, which formed a portion of the division of the troops detached from Gen Grant's army. They arrived in Balt on Fri.

TUE JUL 12, 1864
Died: in Gtwn, D C, on Jul 10, Mrs Eliz T Harrison relict of the late Gustavus Harrison, in the 70th yr of her age. Funeral from her late residence, 26 Gay St, today.

Died: in Wash City, on Jun 11, G C Schotte, aged 71 yrs. Funeral from his late residence, B st, between First & Second, today.

Crt Martial in Cincinnati, of Capt F W Hurtt, Ast Q M of U S vols. Sentence: to be dishonorably dismissed from svc of the U S, with loss of all pay & allowances now due or to become due. -E D Townsend, Ast Adj Gen. Jun 17, 1864

Col Winslow, 5th N Y, was brought from the front early last month, suffering from a shoulder wound received in a battle at the head of his Regt near Mechanicsville, & that while en route to Alexandria, the father of the Col, drowned. His arm was amputated soon after his arrival at the Mansion Hse Hospital, Alexandria. He suffered until Jul 7, his mother with him when he died. His body was taken to N Y.

Phil, Jul 11. Two morning trains from Balt were captured by the rebels at Magnolia, about 20 miles from Balt. Maj Gen Franklin was captured. The station hse was burned. The rebels were repulsed by our gunboats at Bush & Gunpowder rivers. One of our trains was recovered.

Appointments by the Pres, with consent of the Senate: Brig Gen Alvin P Hovey & Brig Gen John G Barnard, U S vols, to be Maj Gens by brevet. Brig Gen Stephen G Burbridge, U S vols, to be Maj Gen, by brevet. Col Chas J Paine, 2nd La vols, to be Brig Gen.

A trunk belonging to Mr J W Gleason, containing $15,000 in gold & securities, was stolen on Wed last at N Y from the deck of the steamer *Ocean Queen*, in which he had just arrived from Havana.

WED JUL 13, 1864
Mrd: on Jul 12, by Rev Mr Ward, Rozalvo F Cole to Helen Coquillard, both of N Y C.

38th Congress. Public-#163. An Act to incorporate the Potomac Ferry Co. That Henry D Cooke, John B Hutchinson, H C Fahnestock, Thos Clyde, & Wm B Hatch, & their associates & successors, or a majority of them, are hereby created & constituted a body politic & corporate by the name & style of the Potomac Ferry Co.

Correct list of the casualties that occurred to the 25th N Y cavalry, commanded by Maj S W McPherson, on Mon, in the skirmishing out 7th st beyond Ft Stevens. Killed: 1st Sgt A C Starbit, Co A; Sgt Thos Richardson, Co B; Pvt Elijah Huftein, Co A. Wounded: Sgt W K May, Co A, slightly in neck; Sgt D Whitney, Co A, slightly; John Sherlock, Co A, severely; Jonathan W Byrnes, Co B, in face; John Quinn, Co B, mortally; John Tierney, Co B, body & arm; Cpl G H Evens, Co C, slightly; 1st Lt C G Tounsley, Co D, in groin; Patrick Cannon, Co D, severely in arm; 1st Sgt H M Nevins, Co E, wrist; Cpl Geo Russel, Co E, head, severely; Geo Etienne, Co F, severely in leg; J Maloney, Co K, severely in shoulder, & died this morning. In the skirmishing in front of Ft Stevens the following casualties occurred. In the 98th, 102nd, & 139th Pa regts, Geo Cump, fracture of right leg; Cpl Henry Pellser, in thigh & breast, probably mortal; Arthur Corbin, left shoulder, slight; Jacob Rimer, right leg, severe; Oliver Shay, wounded in the right hip, slight; John McCormick, in right thigh, flesh wound; Christian Brandt, thigh; Fred'k Franck, neck; Frank Wingeston, fracture right arm; Sgt Jacob Sweitzer, left; Sgt Wm Boyer, in arm; Geo Flinton, ankle; Sgt Geo Margood, Co E, 98th Pa, was killed. The 98th Pa lost, in all the operations yesterday, 14 wounded & 2 killed. The 3 regts of the 1st brigade, 2nd div, of the 6th Corps, which went into a skirmish near Silver Spring on Mon, lost 1 killed & 13 wounded.

Guardian's sale of lot 4, in sq 218, on I st, Wash, D C. -Mrs Eliza Ann Drane, guardian. -Green & Williams, aucts

Mr Wurth, proprietor of the N Y Htl, corner of 7th & E sts, left the hse on Mon to go to the market, & has not been seen since. He was been unwell for some days, but not seriously. He was a man of temperate habits. Information to his family will be gratefully received.

Geo W Bates, 2nd Regt R I vols, was beaten with a baton by a policemen, who found him prostrated near the steps of the Nat'l Htl. Judge Fisher, of the Supr Crt of D C, heard the commotion & asked what was the matter? Bates was perfectly sober & stated that he had been up 2 entire nights on duty & had fallen asleep, when he was aroused by the ofcr. Bates was released when the Judge followed him to the station hse, & represented his case to the ofcr in charge. [Jul 14 paper: the Ofcr McElfresh found a man sleeping in the street of the Nat'l Htl, & attempted to arouse him by tapping him on the shoes with his baton. The sldr, Bates, seized McElfresh violently, tearing his coat & refusing to let go. The ofcr struck him on the head to release himself. Mr Elfresh is a very small man, & the sldr was a stout built fellow.]

Rebel cavalry charged the Stone Bridge, over the Monocacy, on the Balt pike on Sat, since which time nothing has been heard of Gen Tyler or his staff ofcrs who were with him, viz: Capt Frank J D Webb, A F; Capt Pratt, 3rd P H B, & Lt Goldsborough, Actg A D C.

THU JUL 14, 1864
Died: on Jul 13, after a short & painful illness, Mrs Eliza Fales, w/o N W Fales, aged 64 yrs. Funeral from the residence of her hsbnd, H & 9th sts, today.

Skirmish on Tue, Gen McCook determined to dislodge the rebel sharpshooters, who were making themselves annoying from the Carbery place, & the hse of Mr Lay, known as the *Carbery Hse*, on Rock Creek, to the left of Ft Stevens. Our loss in this charge was about 300, in killed & wounded, including the following ofcrs: Adjt Wm B Laughlin, killed; Lt Col Visher, 43rd N Y killed; Lt Col Johnson, 49th N Y, killed; Capt Lambert, 49th N Y, killed; Maj Jones, 7th Maine, killed; Maj John W Crosby, 61st Pa, arm amputated. Maj Crosby was wounded in the *Wilderness*, & had joined his regt just in time to take part in this fight.

Partial list of the deaths in the skirmishing in front of Ft Stevens on Tue: Maj Jones, 7th Maine, thru the shoulder, dead; Maj Crosby, 61st Pa, amputation of left arm; Lt Col Johnson, 49th N Y, in breast; Lt David Lambert, 49th N Y, killed, shot thru the head; Pvt Jas Dunnegan, right arm; Sgt Campbell, 102nd Pa, leg; Lt McLaughlin, 61st Pa, killed; Col Fisher, 43rd N Y, killed; Cpl Jerome Hill, 45th N Y, shoulder; Sgt John M Blackstone, 43rd N Y, side; Sgt Chas H Davis, 43rd N Y, groin; Pvt Geo W Farrer, 43rd N Y, killed; John H Fralick, shoulder; Wm Stone, 43rd N Y, back; Wm Lagrange, 43rd N Y, arm & leg; Wm Clapper, 43rd N Y, left wrist; Wm Middlebrook, 43rd N Y, left arm; Geo Pendigham, 43rd N Y, left wrist. The following, who were wounded within a day or two in front of Washington, are at Carver Hosp: Geo O Wise, Wm Nichols, Jas H Orsten, Thos Cox, Michl Grimes, Robt Powell, Geo F Parlow, N J Welcome, Chas H Fuller, Wm Price, Wm Hazard, Paul Farnham, Eastman Dulin, Orton Cole, A F Barrenson, John Gillespie, & Frank Hill, all of 2nd Mass; Geo Gerrold, 18th Mass; Geo A Bessey, 59th Mass. The following wounded ofcrs have been taken to Mt Pleasant Hosp, viz: Col Jno F Ballier, 98th P V; Capt Davis Cossett, 122nd N Y; Lt John E Bailey, 7th Maine; Lt Wm H Comeus, 10th Mass; Lt Wm Wilson, 98th P V; Lt Geo Shuler, 98th P V; Maj John W Crosby 71st P V. Jacob Tolpell, of the 2nd D C vols, is also at this hospital wounded.

Supreme Crt of D C, in Equity #212. Earle & Co, vs Douglas Scott, Harriet Scott, Edw Williams, Jonathan H Carter. Subpoena to compel the appearance of the dfndnts, on May 7, 1864, has been returned, *not found*. Dfndnts to appear before the first Tue of Dec next. - R J Meigs, clerk

Law of the U S passed at the 1st session of the 38th Congress. The gov'ts of Russia & Great Britain have granted to Perry MacDonough Collins, of Calif, a ctzn of the U S, the right to construct & maintain a line of electric telegraph thru their respective territories, from the mouth of the Amoor river, in Asiatic Russia, by way of Behring's Strait & along the Pacific coast to northern boundary of U S.

FRI JUL 15, 1864
Farm for sale-40 acs, 3 miles north of the Capitol on Lincoln av; adjoins the farms of Wm W Corcoran, Conway Robinson, & E J Middleton. -Eliz Wood, on premises.

Orphans Crt of Wash Co, D C. Case of Richd Lay, adm e t a, of Thos Carbery, dec'd; settlement on Aug 2. -Z C Robbins, rg o/wills

Wash Corp: 1-Communication from Jacob Fleishell, suggesting additional legislation in relation to measurements now in use in the mkts of Wash City: referred to the Cmte on Police. 2-Ptn of J Prince, to erect a frame bldg against a brick: referred to the Cmte on Police.

Harford Co, Md, Jul 11, 1864-Rebels appeared at Jerusalem Mills, & requested horses from Mr David Lee. They spared the mill & proceeded to Magnolia, in time to capture the 8:40 A M train from Balt. Valuables of the employees & passengers were taken, the latter generally spared. Col Gilmor spared the station hse because it was occupied by the mother & sisters of Mr Lytle, the agent, also the tank hse, as its burning would have jeoparded the dwlg, & deprive the large number of ladies & chldrn passengers on the train of water, etc. The raiders visited the farm of Gen Cadwalader, near Magnolia, & carried off about 30 horses. None of his other property was injured.

Mr Busey, lock-keeper aout 5 miles from Gtwn, reports that no damage is done the canal at Muddy Branch, which is 20 miles above Gtwn.

The 5th Wisc Vols, & the 6th Maine, of the 1st div of the 6th Corps, were among the troops who came to the defence of Washington from Grant's army, & were encamped at Ft Stevens. Their time had expired, but they patriotically agreed to remain on duty as long as there was any danger to Wash.

SAT JUL 16, 1864
Died: in Wash City, on Jul 15, after a long illness, Mary Eliz, eldest d/o John F & Sarah A Calan. Funeral from St Patrick's Chr, Sun.

Died: on Jul 15, Albert M, s/o Albert & A J Ray, in his 6th yr. Funeral from 292 H st, today.

Thanks to the patriotism & help of the following men during the late emergency in this city:

Col N W Daniels, of La	Tyler Southall	Lt S S Balch, 6th U S C
Jas C Welling	Chas H Armes	Chas W Boteler, jr
S A Peugh	Chas W Morris	Benj B French, jr
H J Leavenworth	H A Goldsborough	Selden Hetzel
C S Noyes	Col Lem Towers	Alpheus N Brown

And the following ofcrs of the 71st N Y Vols, viz:
Lts G W Brower   Clinton Bradshaw   Q M Sgt Chas Eselle
M H Brien   Jas M Curtis
Capt John B Tanner, War Dept
-Geo C Thomas, Maj Gen Comd't Militia & Vols, Wash, Jul 14, 1864

Affairs at Petersburg, Jul 11. Col Davis, of the 39th Mass, was killed this afternoon, while sitting in his tent. The rebel battery attempted to throw shells into a large fort being erected, & one came into Col Davis' tent, rolled beneath the chair whereon he was sitting, & exploded. He received a mortal wound, of which he died within an hour. He was a tried & gallant ofcr, whose loss is much lamented.

Since the commencement of Grant's campaign, 1,000 nurses & surgeons have been sent to the army-775 of the number were ladies.

Died: on Jul 14, Anna-Costia Boyle, in the 18th yr of her age, d/o Ann Eliza & Junius J Boyle, U S Navy. Funeral from the residence of her father, Gay & Congress sts, Gtwn, today.

MON JUL 18, 1864
Died: on Jul 17, Mrs Norah Digges, the eldest d/o the late Daniel Carroll, of Duddington, in the 73rd yr of her age; at the residence of her son-in-law, Dr Jas E Morgan; relict of the late W Dudley Digges, of PG Co, Md. Funeral on Tue.

Deaths reported to the Navy Dept for the week ending Jul 16, 1864:
David Marren, landsman, yel fever, Jun 29, vessel U S S *Tioga.*
Oscar T Hill, seaman, drowned, Jun 20, vessel U S S *Naumkey.*
Jas Healey, blank, blank, Jun 24, Nav Hosp, Pensacola.
Thos Washington, 1st cl boy, typhoid fever, Jul 1, Nav Hosp, Memphis.
Jacob J Thompson, landsman, chronic diarrhoea, Jul 1, do
Chas H Gooding, coxwain, do, do, do.
Edw St Clair, seaman, chronic diarrhoea, Jul 3, do.
Richd Gillis, coalheaver, sunstroke, Jul 4, vessel U S S *Santiago de Cuba.*
John Miller, 2nd ast engr, drowned, Jul 5, vessel U S S *Robb.*
Smith Rowland, capt forecastle, pluritis, Jul 3, vessel U S S *Circassian.*
Jacob Burding, seaman, pneumonia, Jul 5, Nav Hosp, N Y.
Aaron J Kuth, landsman, gastritis, Jul 5, do.
Fred Allen, ord seaman, consumption, Jul 6, do.
John W Ellis, landsman, pneumonia, Jul 10, do.
Rhod Green, blank, heart disease, Jul 7, do.
Edw Hawkins, landsman, Jul 10, Nav Asylum.
John Dunn, coalheaver, drowned, May 8, vessel U S S *Wat-ee.*

Charleston, Jul 4, 1864. Gen S Cooper, Adj & Inspec Gen: on Jul 3 the enemy landed svr'l regts on the south side of James Island, supported by 2 monitors & several gunboats in the Stono, & after a sharp skirmish, captured 2 pieces of artl & commenced entrenching, etc. Yesterday 700 to 1,000 men, on barges, attacked Ft Johnson, & were repulsed., with a loss to the enemy of 140 prisoners, with their ofcrs & accoutrements, & 5 barges. Many were killed & wounded. Our loss was very slight. The party from North Edisto landed at White Point,soon met & driven back. So far the enemy has been repulsed with the loss of about 600 men. -Saml Jones, Maj Gen

Orphans Crt of Wash Co, D C. 1-Case of John McDermott, adm of Thos Turner, dec'd; settlement on Aug 9. 2-Case of Mrs Eliz A Byington, admx of Saml Byington, dec'd; settlement on Aug 9. -Z C Robbins, rg o/wills

Hon Jas F Simmons, formerly a Senator in Congress from R I, died at his residence in R I on Thu last, in the 69th yr of his age.

Sunday last will be remembered by our Catholic fellow-ctzns as the occasion of the farewell of their esteemed Bishop, the Rt Rev M J Spaulding, D D, prior to his entering the duites of Archbishop of Balt, as successor to the most Rev Francis Patrick Kenrick. The Cathedral of the Assumption was densely crowded, & the scene was very impressive.

Rebel account: Meridan, Jul 7. Gen Braxton Bragg: enemy evacuated Jackson yesterday. Brig Gen Adams fought them, punishing them very severely. They are now on retreat to Vicksburg. Brig Gen Gholson is severely, tho no dangerously wounded. The enemy are advancing in force from Lagrange towards Ripley. I am prepared to meet them. –G D Lee, Lt Gen

Brig Gen S A Rice died at his home in Oskaloosa, Iowa, on Thu, from the effects of wounds received & exposure in Gen Steele's expedition.

TUE JUL 19, 1864
Mrd: Jul 18, by Rev Dr Ryan, Lt Col D K Wardell to Miss Anna M Weeden, of Wash City.

Died: on Jul 18, at Providence Hospital, Jas L Cassin, aged 41 yrs. Funeral from the chapel of Mt Oak Cemetery, Gtwn, today.

Burial ground near Ft Stevens, 29 Union sldrs who were killed in the conflict of Jul 12th, graves are labelled with their names & Regts, as follows:

Wm B Laughlin 1st Lt, 61 Pa	C S Christ, battery G, 2nd Artl
A Mallott, 97 N Y	Sgt C Marguard, 98 Pa
___ Stoneman, 43 N Y	Cpl G S Gordon, 1 R I
R Castle, 43 N Y	R Kennedy, 122 N Y
G S Bavett, 43 N Y	D l Hogecom, 122 N Y
J Davidson, 43 N Y	A Ashbough, 61 Pa.
G W Farrer, 43 N Y	H McIntire, 61 Pa
A Mosier, 122 N Y	A Dowen, 77 N Y
J Bentley, 122 N Y	E Garvin, 61 Pa
A Manning, 77 N Y	F Walker, 98 Pa
J Ellis, 61 Pa	J Dolan, 2 Mass
J Pocket, 7 Maine	M De Graff, 43 N Y
H Gilbert, 49 N Y	P Bower, 61 Pa
H Chandler, 122 N Y	P Lovett, 16 Mass

W Bramhall, being compelled to go to Calif, offers for sale the best sutlership in the country, worth at least 10 Regts. Call at 519 12th st, Wash. -W Bramhall

The Pres commissioned the following as Justices of the Peace: John S Hollingshead, Geo Mattingly, Benj S Kinsey, Patrick McKenna, Jona W Baruaclo, F A Boswell, E R Sheckell, Benedict Milburn & Jas Kelley.

Col Danl McCook, [Actg Brigadier,] of the celebrated fighting McCook family of Ohio, died on Sun at Cincinnati, of wounds received at the battle of Kenesaw Mountain. He is the 4th of the McCook family who have been killed since the rebellion-the father & 3 sons-& what is most singular, all have been killed or died in the month of Jul.

Mrs Jane Pishon, [formerly exhibited as Miss Jane Campbell,] Barnum's fat woman, died at her residence at Brookfield, Conn, Jun 30, aged 24 years. Her coffin was 6 feet long, 18 inches deep, & 3 feet wide, & it took 10 men to place the body into it. She weighed 680 lbs at one time.

WED JUL 20, 1864

Trustee's sale of land in the village of *Long Old Fields*, PG Co, Md, tracts belonging to the estate of the late Wm M Bowie, dec'd, viz: 87¾ acs, adjoins the premises of Jas J Jarboe; 31 acs adjoins the lands of N M McGregor & the estate of the late Z H Beall. -Saml B Hance, trustee

Orphans Crt of Wash Co, D C. Case of John T Mitchell, adm of Evelyn M Melville, dec'd; settlement on Aug 13. -Z C Robbins, rg o/wills

Naval Intell: 1-Rear Admr D T Farragut, writing to the Navy Dept from on board his flagship *Hartford*, Jul 6, reports the destruction by fire of the blockade runner which was chased on shore near Ft Morgan, Mobile harbor, on Jul 1. 2-Admr Dahlgren, from on board his flagship *Philadelphia*, in Stono river, S C, Jul 10th, informed that on the 8th inst the U S steamer *Sonoma*, Lt Com Matthews, captured the small side-wheel steamer *Ida*, which vessel left Sapelo the night before, bound to Nassau. He also reports the capture of the rebel schnr *Pocahontas*, on Jul 7, by the U S steamers *Azalea* & *Sweet Briar*, while attempting to pass out of Charleston harbor bound to Nassau. Gen Canby, now commanding the Dept of the Gulf, is making extensive preparations for military operations against the rebels in his dept. A large force is being concentrated at Morganzia, on the Mississippi, while a rebel force is reported to be about 9 miles from there.

THU JUL 21, 1864

Passed at the 1st Session of the 38th Congress: Pblc #186. Act granting lands to aid in the construction of a railrd & telegraph line from Lake Superior to Puget's Sound, on the Pacific coast, by the northern route. Erected into a body corporate, etc, titled " Northern Pacific Railroad Co:" Maine:

John A Poore	Chas P Kimball	Anson P Morrill
Saml P Strickland	Augustine Haines	Saml J Anderson
Saml C Fessenden	Edwin R W Wiggin	Wm Sears
Mass:		
I S Withington	John Newell	John O Bresbey
Josiah Perham	Austin L Rogers	Geo Shiverick
Jas M Becket	Nathl Greene, jr	Edw Tyler
A W Banfield	Oliver Frost	Filander J Forristall
Abiel Abbott	John A Bass	Ivory H Pope
N Y:		
Geo Opdyke	Philander Reed	John C Fremont
Fairley Holmes	Geo Briggs	
John Huggins	Chauncey Vibbard	
N J:		
Ephraim Marsh	John P Jackson, jr	

Pa:
S M Felton
John Toy
O J Dickey
Conn:
T M Allyn
Moses W Wilson
N H:
Jos A Gilmore
Onslow Stearns
Minn:
Cyrus Aldrich
H M Rice
Vt:
E A Chapin
R I:
Jas Y Smith
Wm S Slater
Ill:
Seth Fuller
Wm Kellogg
U S Grant
Kansas:
J M Winchell
Calif:
Richd F Perkins
Richd Chenery
Va:
Wm F Mercer
Md:
John H B Latrobe
W Va
Greenbury Slack
Ky:
Thos E Bramlette
Ohio:
John Brough
John A Bingham
Oran Follett
Dela:
John A Duncan
Ind:
Thos A Morris
Mich
Saml L Case
Henry L Hall
Wisc:
Edw H Broadhead
Alex'r Mitchell
Oregon:
J C Ainsworth
Orlando Humason

B F Archer
G W Cass
J Elgar Thompson

Horace Whittaker
Ira Bliss

E Emerson
Fred'k Smyth

John McKusick
H C Waite

John Gregory Smith

Isaac H Southwick
Earl P Mason

Wm B Ogden
Wm G Greene
Leonard Sweat

Elsworth Cheesebrough

Saml Brannon
Geo Rowland

Jas W Brownley

W Prescott Smith

A J Boreman

Frank Shorin

John Gardner
S S L'Hommedieu
Harrison G Blake

Saml M Harrington

Jessse L Williams

David H Jerome
Thos E Gilbert

Benj Ferguson
Levi Sterling

H W Corbett
Henry Failling

John A Green

Wm E Chandler

Stephen Miller

Geo Merrill

Henry W Blodgett
Porter Sheldon

Jas S Emery

Henry Platt

Philo Chamberlin

C A Trowbridge

___ Marshal

227

Dakota Terr:		
J B S Todd	J Shaw Gregory	
M K Armstrong	J Le Berge	
Wash Terr:		
John Mullan	S D Smith	
Anson G Henry	Chas Terry	
Iowa:		
H W Starr	Wm Leighton	John L Davies
Platt Smith	B F Alien	
Nixon Denton	Reuben Noble	
Mo:		
Willard P Hall	H Gayle King	
Geo R Smith	John C Sargent	
Idaho Terr:		
Wm H Wallace		
D C:		
J H Lathrop	Henry D Cooke	H E Merrick

Died: in Wash City, on Jul 19, at the residence of her bro, Mr Wm Linkins, after a long & painful illness, Miss Harriet Linkins, in her 34th yr. Funeral from the N Y Av Chr, today.

U S Mrshl's sale, D C: land called *Mt Pleasant*, Wash Co, D C; also tract called *Pleasant Hill*; owned by the late Jesse Brown, seized & levied upon as the property of Jesse B Haw, in favor of David & Chas S English. -Ward H Lamon, U S Mrshl D C

Wash Corp: 1-Ptn from Peter Mack: referred to the Cmte on Improvements. 2-Ptn from T G Seybold, with a bill to pave the footway on sq 284: referred to the Cmte on Improvements. 3-Cmte on Improvements: reported back the ptn of P Keff & others, with a bill to grade & gravel Carroll st: passed. 4-Ptn of C H M Wood: referred to the Cmte on Claims. 5-Ptn of Saml Kirby: referred to the Cmte on Finance. 6-Ptn of Josiah Eggleston: referred to the Cmte on Mkts. 7-Ptn of Philip A Jullian & others: referred to the Cmte on Finance.

FRI JUL 22, 1864
U S Mrshl sale of confiscated property in Eastern Dist of Va:
Alexandria City-
Geo L Witmer & Dennis B Blacklock-lots 5 thru 9, Fairfax st, to F M McDonald-$120
Wm N McVeigh & Wm H Fowler-hse on Royal st, to W D Massey, for $900
Wm H Fowler-lot, s w corner of Prince & Payne sts, to D B Adams, for $30
Arthur Herbert-lots, # 2 & 10, Madison, st, to J D B Adams for $140
Montg D Corse-lot on King st, to Mr Duncan for $100
David Funsten-8 acs, Wash rd, to J D B Adams for $180
Jas C Nevitt-lot on Duke st, to J D Adams for $90
Wm Whaley-lot on Queen st, to J W Armstrong for $200
Lot on corner of Queen & Patrick st, to W D Massey, for $200
John L Pascoe & Edw Sangster-qrtr sq, Prince & West sts, to W D Massey-$200
Jas H McLean-lot, Cameron & Fayette sts, to J D Adams for $40
Jas H Reid-qrtr sq, Wolf & Alfred sts, to J D Adams for $40
Lot on corner Wilkes & Alfred sts, to Mr Duncan for $70
Lawrence B Taylor-hse on Prince st, to Mr Duncan for $90
McVeigh Hse, on Cameron st, now occupied by Mr Geo M Davis, sold for $190

Fairfax Co, Va:
Arthur Herbert-farm 60 acs, to Maj Wm Silvey, $125
Saml Cooper-farm, 20 acs, to same, $165
French Forrest-*Clermont Plantation*, 360 acs, to Dr E Bentley, $1,900
Geo K Witmer-farm, 48 acs, with new dwlg hse, to Maj W Silvey, $180
W S Kemper-*Clifton Farm*, 210 acs, to J G Verplanck, $150
Saml R Johnston-*West Grove farm*, 350 acs, to S A Reid, $1,525
W Cazenov-farm, 17½ acs, to W B Dobson, $255
Farm, 54 acs, to Thos Antisell, $500
Wilmer D Corse-farm, 117 acs, not sold.
Geo H Padgett-4 acs, to Otis Smith, $200.
Lot on Little River Turnpike, to B McNeill, $175.
In Pr Wm Co:
Wm Seleeman-*Swan Point farm*, 150 acs, to W Duncan, $300.
The *Louisiana Kentucky farm* 250 acs, to J D Adams, $75.
Hse & lot in Occoquan to John Berry, $100.
John H Hamill-hse & lot in Occoquan, to J Berry, $85.
John W Fairfax-*Freestone Point* farm, 600 acs, to W Duncan, $2,100.

Died: on Jul 20th, of scarlet fever, Florence Eliz, youngest child of Jno D & Rosannah Brandt, aged 11 months & 10 days.

Levy Crt of Wash Co, D C, to survey from Glenwood Cemetery to Middleton's gate to be made for the purpose of opening it to the width of 60 ft. By order of the Crt, N Callan, clerk Levy Crt.

Harvard College commencement Jul 20: Dr of Laws conferred on Reuben Atwater Chapman, of Mass; Wm Pitt Fessenden, of Maine; Chas Francis Adams, of Mass; Edw Laboulurge, of France. Degree of Mstr of Arts: Wm Philips Tilden, Boston; Fred'k Law Olmstead, Calif; Jas Alfred Page, Boston; Hall Train Bigelow, Cambridge; Wm Morris Hunt, Boston; Nathl Eaton, Balt. Among the grads who received the degree of B A was Robt Todd Lincoln. Edw Everett was selected to deliver a course of lectures on international law during the ensuing yr at the law school.

Orphans Crt of Wash Co, D C. Case of Andrew Goddard, exc of Jane Goldsborough, dec'd; settlement on Aug 13. -Z C Robbins, rg o/wills

SAT JUL 23, 1864
Snicker's Ferry, Va, Jul 20, 1864. Forces under Maj Gen Wright have pursued Early & Breckinridge from Wash to this place, etc. Among the casualties on the 18th, at Island ford, were Col Washburne, 116th Ohio, wounded; Col Frost, 11th Va, wounded in the bowels; Lt Col Murray, 5th N Y, heavy artl, serving as infty, missing, & known to be severely wounded. Whole loss was 300 men. The enemy's loss was 500 by their own statements.

St Jos, Mo, Jul 21. Guerillas occupied Caldwell Co. Some 500 men marched on Plattsburg, Clinton Co, when the surrender of the garrison, consisting of 2 companies of militia, was demanded in the name of the Confederate States. Capt Turner, commanding the post, refused to surrender, & told his men to escape. A fight ensued, in which Capt Turner was killed. 1,000 men under Gen Ben Loan will soon be here from Andrew Co.

Died: in Lynchburg, Va, on Jul 4, Abigail B, w/o Rev Henry W Dodge, in the 48th yr of her age; formerly of Wash City.

MON JUL 25, 1864

Mrd: on Jul 21, at the Chr of the Ascension, by Rev Dr Pinckney, Franklin Rives, s/o the late John C Rives, to Jeannie Tree, d/o Lambert Tree.

Supreme Crt of D C, in Equity #266. Wm Thompson vs the heirs at law of Patrick Leydan, dec'd. Said Leydan, of Winchester, Fred'k Co, Va, on Jun 18, 1847, was seized of part of lot 16 in sq 514 in Wash., D C; conveyed same to Agar Bassett, his heirs & assigns. Leydan died without issue. Regarding-legal title to said part of lot vested in the cmplnt in fee simple. -Geo P Fisher, Justice

Supreme Crt of D C, in Equity #139. Cornelius Kane & others vs Thos Sinon, Mgt Sinon, & others, widow & heirs of John Sinon. Statement of the account on Aug 16, at my ofc, La av. -Rich H Laskey, spec auditor

Died: on Jul 24, Cath Lillian Wade, in the 7th yr of her age. Funeral from her parents' residence, 672 M st, today.

Orphans Crt of Wash Co, D C. 1-Case of Saml E Douglass, adm of Patrick Fitzgerald, dec'd; settlement on Aug 16. -Z C Robbins, rg o/wills   2-Prsnl estate of Henry S Ward, late of Wash City, dec'd. -Conrad Finkman, exc

Deaths reported to the Navy Dept for the week ending Jul 23, 1864:
Hardy Gordon, 2nd cl fireman, drowned, May 27, vessel U S S *Gazelle.*
John H Griswold, ord seaman, varioloid, Jun 7, vessel U S S *Valparaiso.*
Henry Donson, landsman, do, do, do.
Thos White, landsman, pleurisy, Jun 18, vessel U S S *New Hampshire.*
Jas Brown, landsman, consumption, Jun 24, do.
Henry Gofferman, contraband, pleurisy, Jun 27, do.
Fred W Werchus, coalheaver, pneumonia, Jun 30, do.
Gustave Finck, qrtrmstr, acute diarrhoea, Jun 7, vessel U S S *Princess Royal.*
Josiah Beard, landsman, continued fever, Jun 15, Nav Hosp, Chelsea.
John Clark, coal heaver, disease of kidneys, Jul 15, do.
Wm Nelson, pilot, paralysis, Jun 23, vessel U S S *Rodoulph*
Franklin Mitchell, landsman, pernicious fever, Jun 23, Pacific Squadron.
Geo Stevens. landsman, pernicious fever, Jun 20, do.
Geo C Brooks, ord seaman, gunshot wound, Jun 16, vessel U S S *Wyalusing.*
John Prouse, seaman, scrofula, Jul 16, Nav Hosp, Wash.
Danl Forbes, contraband, landsman, drowned, Jun 27, vessel U S S *Port Royal*
Danl Smith, 1st cl boy, consumption, Jul 12, Nav Hosp, Portsmouth, Va.
John Thompson, 2nd cl fireman, heart disease, Jul 19, Nav Asylum
H B Joshlyn, pensioner, debility, Jul 20, do.
David Segarson, paymstr's clerk, paralysis, May 29, vessel U S S *Wyoming.*
Wm Kelly, contraband, acute dysentery, Jul 19, Nav Hosp, Chelsea.
Wm Layton, colored, landsman, typhus fever, Jul 10, vessel U S S *Jas Adger.*
Jas Kennett, landsman, drowned, Jul 15, vessel U S S *Home.*
Jas Healy, landsman, acute diarrhoea, Jun 24, Nav Hosp, Pensacola.
Thos Warmouth, landsman, yel fever, Jun 24, do.
Thos Kennedy, landsman, gunshot wound, Jul 16, vessel U S S *Mendota.*
Wm F Pottle, ord seaman, gunshot wound, Jul 10, do.
John Small, ord seaman, dysentery, Jul 3, Mltry Hosp, Hammond, Beauford, N C.

Supreme Crt of D C, in Equity #2. A Thos Bradley & Mahlon Ashford, trustees, report sales to Geo Staffen of part of lot 7 in reservation D for $2,000; part of lot 6 in same sq for $3,000; & that John Jacobs purchased parts of lots 12 & 13 in sq 543 for $1,000; ratify same. -Jones & Ashford, Solicitor for cmplnt.

TUE JUL 26, 1864
Mrd: on Jul 25, by Rev Byron Sunderland, Zach B Brooke to Deboarah C, d/o Jas Mankin, all of Wash City.

Died: on Jul 23, after a protracted illness, Hannaet, w/o Alexander Ray.

Died: in Gtwn, D C, on Jul 21, Geo Poe, aged 85 yrs.

Died: on Jul 25, Edwin Henry, s/o Jas & C H Skirving, in the 18th yr of his age. Funeral from the residence of his father, 377 E st, Wed.

Died: on Jul 25, Cornelius Lander, only child of Cornelius T & Mary A Bowen, aged 11 months & 22 days. Funeral from their residence, 560 N J av, today.

Pres Lincoln has commutted the sentence of the following, to be shot to death, to be imprisoned at hard labor during the war at Dry Tortugas, Fla: Wm T Hill, 14 Infty; Geo D Bell, 12 Infty; Geo McKnight, 14 Infty; John Wellington, 7 Pa Res Corps; Geo T Goodrich, 122 N Y, Martin Hart, 6 Pa cavalry; & Thos Congden, 65 N Y. They are now confined in the Old Capitol prison.

Orphans Crt of Wash Co, D C. 1-Case of Cleophile B Burr, admx of Henry A Burr, dec'd; settlement on Aug 13. -Z C Robbins, rg o/wills 2-Prsnl estate of Benj Johnson Hellen, late of Wash City, dec'd. -Grafton Tyler

WED JUL 27, 1864
Died: on Jul 26, Eliza J Moreland, aged 62 yrs. Funeral from the residence of Jos G Waters, 50 Third st, Gtwn, D C, today.

The late Maj Gen Jas B McPherson, who fell in the battle before Atlanta on Fri last, was a native of Sandusky, Ohio, 36 years of age; 1853 grad of West Point.

Battle at Winchester on Sunday: it was announced that Col Mulligan, [of Lexington, Mo, fame,] commanding a brig in the fight of Sun was killed. He has for the past year done much service in Western Va along the line of the Balt & Ohio Railrd. Gen Averills' forces sustained the heaviest loss, as the rebels massed a large force against them, etc.

THU JUL 28, 1864
Mrd: at the Chr of the Epiphany, on Jul 27, by Rev Dr Hall, Hollis White, of Niagara Falls, N Y, to Agnes, d/o the late Dr Jas Sykes, formerly of St Louis, Mo.

Died: on Jul 26, Patrick Kelly, a native of Catletown Co, Limerick, Ire, in the 61st yr of his age. Funeral from his late residence, F st & 15th, today.

Died: in Wash City, on Jul 26, of diptheria, Joanna Auchmutz, y/c/o Sally F & the late Capt Richd Wainwright, U S Navy, aged 3 years & 4 months.

Died: in Wash City, on Jul 27, of gastro-typhoid fever, Arabella Walton, w/o Brig Gen Francisc Barlow, commanding 1st div 2nd Corps, Army of the Potomac.

Died: on Jul 27, Wm F, infant s/o Wm B & Susana Cudlipp, aged 13 months & 7 days. Funeral from their residence, 500 K st, today.

Chancery sale of large quantity of unimproved property; Robt Coltman et al, cmplnts, & Jas Adams, exc & trustee of Chas L Coltman, dec'd, et al, dfndnts.

Crct Crt of D C, in Equity #145. Adms sale of prnsl effects of the late Mrs Louisa Hunter, dec'd, at 466 6th st. -Green & Williams, aucts

The steamer *Lizzie Baker* arrived in Wash on Tue from Point Lookout with a large quantity of hsehld furn, found in a hse about 6 miles from Fredericksburg, & belonging to Sothoron, who is in the rebel service. Also a piano with sheet music inscribed with the name of Miss Mary Sothoron. -Star

FRI JUL 29. 1864
Died: Jul 28, Thos F Anderson, in his 72nd yr. Funeral from his late residence, 461 6th st, Sat.

Died: on Jul 27, Eleanor, w/o Saml Hanson, & d/o the late Gen Mountjoy Bayly, aged 73 yrs. Funeral from the residence of Miss Rebecca Smith, 4½ st, today. [Wife & mother, & sincere friend-from obit of Jul 30]

Appt'd as agents for the District in recruiting in the Confederate states: Arthur Shepherd, Eastern Va; Geo T Finnegan, N C; Wm Finley, Miss; C E Green, for Ga & Ala; Geo H Mitchell, S C & Fla.

Maj Jos M Kennedy, 9th N Y cavalry, transmitted to his father, in this city, the following record, in his letter of Jul 23; list of our men wounded at Spottsylvania, taken to Ewell's 2nd Corps Hospital, & died there: A G Spencer, F, 5 Mich, Jun 1, right leg amputated; Sgt W Wright, F, 5 Mich, May 22, right leg amputated; J Hoch, I, 49 Pa, May 22, resection knee joint; E Alca, D, 141 Pa, Jun 3, do; Sgt E Dubois, G, 23 N Y, Jun 6, right leg amputated; Cpl G Kelly, H, 178 N Y, Jun 5, left foot amputated; J Davis, K, 164 N Y, May 26, breast; W Kimpton, C, 77th N Y, May 22, left arm amputated; Cpl H Cunningham, C, 63 Pa, Jun 8, fracture of the thigh; C E Hodge, I, 121 N Y, May 22, left breast; J Davison, I, 77 N Y, May 23, right breast; Sgt Martin Norton, G, 5 Mich, Jun 3, right groin; Cpt J Workman, G, 96 Pa, Jun 9, left leg amputated; Cpt W J Otts, L, 26 Pa, May 22, right leg amputated; Cpl Fred. Morrison, E, 69 N Y, Jun 8, side & arm; Cpl S J Hall, B, 110 Pa, May 31, shoulder; O Beckley, H, 24 Vt, Jun 4, left thigh amputated; E Clark, H, 49 Pa, Jun 4, left thigh amputated.

Commissioned J P for Wash Co, D C: Mathias V Buckey, Nicholas Callan, Henry Reever, Edgar Bates, & Asa Gladman.

G P Folsom, an additional paymstr in the U S Army, was arrested in Wash City on charge of defalcation. The amount to be about $10,000.

SAT JUL 30, 1864
Mrd: on Jul 28, by Rev John Thrush, Sgt Wm H Anderson, U S Cavalry, & Miss Emma Crawford, of Wash.

Died: suddenly, on Jul 28, Mrs Mary Maria Cassin, w/o Jos R Cassin, of Wash City, & d/o Thos B Berry, of Chas Co, Md, in her 25th yr. Funeral from her late residence, 7th & M sts, today.

Died: in Gtwn, on Jul 27, Edith, d/o Dr F & Eleanor M O'Donnoghue.

Orphans Crt of Wash Co, D C. Case of Philip Clark, exc of Thos Clark, late of Wash, D C, dec'd; settlement on Aug 23. -Z C Robbins, rg o/wills

MON AUG 1, 1864
Dept of State-Deaths of American ctzns in France, at Paris
Jul 3, 1863, at Paris, Helen Julia Beaumont, aged 22, native of N Y.
Aug 17, 1863, at Paris, David Jos Mulbury, aged 32, native of Md,
Sep 13, 1863, at Paris, Joel Rathbone, aged 57, native of N Y.
Oct 5, 1863, John Douglas Bates, aged 63, native of Boston.
Nov 23, 1863, at Paris, Maria Rose Caroline Mampy, aged 61, native of Charleston, S C, & wid/o Jean Jacques Reimoneny, of Guadaloupe.
Nov 30, 1863, at Paris, Harriet, w/o Geo Collier, & d/o Stephen Reaony & Maria Radford, his wife, aged 28, native of the U S.
Dec 30, 1863, at Nice, Geo Washington Vanderbilt, aged 25 yrs, native of N Y, Capt in the U S army.
Feb 13, 1864, at Pau, Lower Pyrenees, Sarah Bowdoin Winthrop, aged 75 yrs, native of Boston, & w/o Geo Sullivan.
Feb 22, at Pau, Lower Pyrenees, Fannie Eliza Ogden, aged 21, native of New Orleans, & w/o Wm Grayson Mann.
Feb 25, 1864, at Nice, Maria Eugenia Baremore, aged 19, native of N Y.

Deaths reported to the Navy Dept for the week ending Jul 30, 1864:
Jesse Williamson, 1st cl boy, diarrhoea, Jul 11, Nav Hosp, Memphis.
Wm Seymour, coalheaver, typhoid fever, Jul 11, do.
John Holmes, ord seaman, dysentery, Jul 12, do.
Cato Brown, blank, diarrhoea, Jul 16, do.
Chas P Tenney, actg 3rd ast engr, consumption, Jul 22, Nav Hosp, N Y.
Amos Beams, landsman, consumption, Jul 24, do.
Nelson Peterson, seaman, blank, Jul 25, do
Geo Smith, landsman, disease of brain, Jul 11, recg ship *Princeton*.
A C Burgess, sailor, variola, Jun 1, Military Hospital, New Orleans.
Wm Childers, landsman, acute diarrhoea, Jun 19, do.
Michl Fullum, seaman, typhoid fever, Jun 28, Mil Hosp, Hilton Head.
Wm Johnson, sailor, typhoid fever, Jul 22, Mil Hosp, Stanton, Wash, D C.
John J Young, landsman, drowned, Jun 20, vessel U S S *Alleghany*.
Thos Andrews, ord seaman, congestion of the lungs, Jul 23, U S recg ship *Ohio*.
Chas McDonald, coal heaver, consumption, Jul 24, do.
Jas Regan, landsman, tetanus, Jun 29, vessel U S S *Elk*.
Lambert K Sayres, yeoman, typhoid fever, Jul 1, Nav Hosp, Pensacola.
Francis L Grindle, seaman, remit fever, Jul 2, vessel U S S *Bienville*.
Wm Hawkins, seaman, gunshot wound, Jul 8, vessel U S S *Hartford*.
Edw Young, landsman, disease of heart, Jul 3, Nav Hosp, Portsmouth, Va.
Edw Downey, lansman, drowned, Jun 13, vessel U S S *Union*.
Asa C Winters, actg ast paymstr, yel fever, Jun 28, do.
John Jackson, seaman, consumption, Jun 30, do.
Wm Gowim, ord seaman, gunshot wound, Jun 27, vessel U S S *Kearsarge*.

David Wiley, pensioner, paralysis, Jul 28, Nav Asylum.
David Brown, do, do, Jul 27, do.
Walter W Ingalls, landsman, gunshot wound, Jul 6, vessel U S S *Pequot*.
Jas R Low, do, do, Jul 19, do.
Addison Garland, Maj, U S M C, disease of the heart, Jun 20, U S Navy Yd, Mare Is.
Barnard O'Connell, sgt marines, dysentery, Jun 30, do, Calif.

Died: on Jul 30, after a lingering & painful illness, Chas Lee, infant s/o Chas P & Minnie J Hunt, aged 9 months & 16 days. Funeral from their residence, 410 D st, today.

Sanduskey, Ohio, Jul 29. The funeral of Gen McPherson took place today at Clyde. Among the mourners were the mother, grandmother, 2 sisters & 2 bros.

Rev Martin John Spalding, D D, the new Archbishop of Balt, arrived in there on Sat, with his bro, Rev R J Spalding, V G, & Rev D Rensel, his sec, from Louisville, Ky.

Rev Julius E Grammar, a native of Wash, now rector of a church in Columbus, Ohio, has accepted a call to St Peter's Chr in Balt. -Cincinnati Gaz

TUE AUG 2, 1864
Died: on Jul 20, at Paris, Fauquier Co, Va, Wm E G Keen, formerly of Wash City.

Died: at Patterson Pl, Ellaville, PG Co, Md, on Jul 31, Georgie Henrietta, infant d/o John P & Henrietta Piercy Pepper, aged 7 months & 1 day. Funeral from the residence of her father, 475 6th st, today.

Adms sale of furn & hsehld effects at the residence of the late Jos Bryan, of Ala, on Pa av, Wash, D C, on Tue. -John T Cochrane, J Carter Marbury, adms, c t a.

The remains of Col Mulligan, hero of Lexington, Mo, arrived at Cumberland, Md, on Fri. He fell at Winchester on Jul 25. His wife reached Winchester a few hours after he had breathed his last. She will proceed to Chicago tomorrow with his remains.

WED AUG 3, 1864
Died: on Aug 2, Laura Clarke Rhees, w/o Wm J Rhees, after a short illness. Funeral from the residence of H H McPherson, 7th st rd, today.

Died: on Aug 1, Thos Fenelon, infant s/o Peter C & Mary L Howle, aged 7 months.

Died: at his residence, on N Y av, on Aug 2, Wm Ariss Miller, for many years a clerk in the Treas Dept. Funeral from St Matthew's Chr, tomorrow.

We understand that Jas S Mackie, who for nearly 15 years has been at the head of the Spanish-American Div of the Diplomatic Bureau of the Dept of State, has resigned his position, with intention of residing in N Y as Sec of the Consolidation Coal Mining Co.

THU AUG 4, 1864
Mrd: at Naples, Italy, Monsieur Stefano Roche to Louise, d/o the Chevalier Pascal Massone.

Family groceries: new store just completed-Geo T Smith & Co, 511 7th st, Wash.

Wounded ofcrs & sldrs who arrived in Wash City yesterday from City Point: Col J Scatlin, 109 N Y; Lt Col W D Wright, 27 Mich; Lt Col P B Stillson, 109 N Y; Lt Col B G Barney, 2 Pa heavy Artl; Capt L S Holden, 20 Mich; Capt G Jardine, 21 Ind cavalry; Capt S S Gilgore, 14 U S Infty; Capt R H Scofield, 27 Mich. Capt J H Brown & Capt H H Daniels, 2 Mich; Capt H B Barnard, 2 N Y mntd rifles; Capt J H Day, 179 N Y; Capt A C & C A Blanchard, 35 Mass; Capt J A Holman, Pa Artl.

Died: in Wash City, on Aug 3, after a brief illness, Saml S Williams, in the 42nd yr of his age. Funeral from his late residence, 271 8th st, Sat.

Died: on Aug 2, Chas Edw, s/o Wm & Sallie Bryan, aged 7 months & 10 days. Funeral from their residence, 9th & L sts, today.

Died: on Aug 3, Ida, y/c/o Wm H & Adele Clagette, aged 15 months. Funeral, today, from 130 H st.

Rev Daniel Waldo died at Syracuse on Sat last, nearly 102 years old, having been born in Sep, 1762. He was a 1796 grad of Yale College. By his death the number of Rev pensioners is reduced to eleven.

Wm H Martin, hack-driver of Wash City, tried by crt-martial for receiving money from a soldier & purchasing for him a suit of ctzn's clothes, therby aiding him to desert, was sentenced to 6 months in the pen at Albany, N Y, & fined $100.

Wm H Carter, ctzn of Md, guilty of furnishing goods & medical supplies to the enemy, acting as a spy, & breaking his oath of allegiance, is to be hung on Fri, near the Old Capitol prison. The Pres of the U S having approved the sentence. [Aug 6-Reprieved by the Pres; sentence suspended until further orders.]

SAT AUG 6, 1864
Orphans Crt of Wash Co, D C. Prsnl estate of Geo Poe, jr, late of Gtwn, D C, dec'd. - Toulmin A Poe, Walter S Cox, Neilson Poe, excs

Wholesale arrests in Frederick, Md: following persons & their families, who, it is understood, are to be sent South:

Hugh McAlaer	Valerius Ebert	G W T Harley
Alfred J Ritter	Mrs John W Heard	Miss Eveline Elder
Alex'r B Hanson	Godfrey Koontz	Dr Thos J McGill
Jas Schley	Rev Jos H Jones	Mrs R Burton
J J Sellman	Richd Holland	Chas Cole
Mrs Mary A Schleigh	Geo Potts, sr	Dr W T Wootton
A J Delashmutt	Robt Johnson	

[Aug 10-the Pres has rescinded the order issued by Gen Hunter banishing the rebel sympathizers of Frederick, Md, beyond the Union lines.]

Died: on Aug 3, Chas L, s/o John K & Christiana A F Wade, in his 15th yr.

Died: on Aug 4, Jas Carrico, in his 74th yr. Funeral from his late residence, 20th & E sts, today.

Died: on Aug 4, after a lingering illness, Ellen Louisa, aged 16 mos, only c/o Geo W & Sarah E Pulaski.

Died: on Aug 5, after a severe illness, Mrs Eliza White, consort of Enoch White. Funeral from the residence of her son-in-law, Jas S Topham, 180 4th st, today.

MON AUG 8, 1864

Died: on Aug 7, Julia J, infant d/o Wm E & Mary Cox, aged 1 yr, 5 months & 12 days. Funeral from 480 L st, today.

Death of Peter K Wagner, the oldest printer & editor in New Orleans, is announced. He was, it is stated, a bro of the editor of the old Federal Rpblcn, published in Balt in 1812.

Obit-Arabella Wharton, w/o Brig Gen F C Barlow, of U S Army, died on Jul 27.

Deaths reported to the Navy Dept for the week ending Aug 6, 1864:
John Wilson, ord seaman, gunshot wound, Jun 17, vessel U S S *Cmdor Perry.*
Jos Webb, do, do, do, do.
Thos J Gerrans, 1st cl boy, blank, Jul 24, vessel U S S *Vicksburg.*
Wm H Stickney, ord seaman, measles, Jun 15, vessel U S S *Alleghany.*
Thos Connelly, boatswain's mate, diarrhoea, Jun 19, Nav Hosp, Memphis.
David Bell, 1st cl boy, diarrhoea, Jun 21, do.
Rollen Ober, 1st cl boy, consumption, Jun 23, do.
Arregan Travillion, ord seaman, diarrhoea, Jul 24, do.
Geo Thompson, 1st cl boy, scrofula, Jul 24, do.
N N Buckingham, 2nd ast engr, yel fever, Jun 29, N Y.
Henry Blackwell, 2nd cl fireman, injuries, Jul 13, vessel U S S *Virginia.*
Wm R Carter, landsman, drowned, Jul 1, vessel U S S *Tallahatchie.*
Wm E Loper, seaman, drowned, Jul 16, vessel U S S *Kennebec.*
Henry Brown, landsman, typhoid fever, Jul 13, Nav Hosp, Wash.
Jas Augustas, cook, drowned, Jul 5, vessel U S S *Kansas.*
Robt Winsor, mstr's mate, yel fever, Jun 28, vessel U S S *Dale.*
John Branagan, landsman, yel fever, Jul 3, do.
Frank Connelly, do, do, do, do.
Jos A Denman, ensign, yel fever, Jul 4, Key West.
Oliver J Jones, 1st cl boy, yel fever, Jul 5, vessel U S S *Dale.*
John Smith, landsman, yel fever, Jul 6, do.
Hiris Riddle, ord seaman, yel fever, Jul 10, do.
Fred A Brooks, ord seaman, consumption, Jun 20, vessel U S S *Restless.*
Henry Keene, landsman, dysentery, Jun 29, vessel U S S *Nita.*
Patrick Kenney, coalheaver, yel fever, Jul 10, do.
Leonard Rose, landsman, yel fever, Jul 4, do.
Nelson H Johnson, mstr, yel fever, Jul 8, vessel *J S Chambers.*
Chris McDonough, landsman, remit fever, Jun 27, vessel U S S *Iuka.*
Toomas Winters, landsman, yel fever, Jul 5, do.
Benj Berry, 1st cl boy, variola, Jun 24, Key West.
Frederick Merrick, 1st cl boy, variola, Jun 28, do.
Gul Wind, do, do, Jun 5, do.
J B Purcell, surgeon's steward, yel fever, Jul 8, vessel U S S *Dale.*
W R Richardson, passed Ast Surgeon, yel fever, Jul 20, do.
Ed Lattimer, ord seaman, yel fever, Jul 17, vessel U S S *Nita.*
Wm Fitzgerald, 1st cl boy, yel fever, Jul 17, do.
Jos Langdon, q m, yel fever, Jul 25, do.
Wm Wilson, 2nd cl fireman, yel fever, Jul 23, vessel U S S *Iuka.*

John Hanson, landsman, yel fever, Jul 16, vessel U S S *Marigold.*
Robt Small, landsman, yel fever, Jul 18, vessel U S S *Engineer.*
Tecumseh Steece, Lt, yel fever, Jul 15, vessel U S S *San Jacinto.*
Michael Welch, seaman, stricture, Jul 15, Nav Hosp, Pensacola.
Jas Grandy, seaman, congestive fever, Jul 5, Nav Hosp, New Orleans.
Wm E Loper, seaman, drowned, Jul 16, vessel U S S *Kennebec.*
Alex McGee, landsman, dysentery, Jul 9, vessel U S S *Nyanza.*
John Gogan, coalheaver, gunshot wound, May 6, vessel U S S *Granite City.*
Stephen Tyrrell, ensign, gunshot wound, do, do.
John Petus, q m, do, do, do.
W Tydall, landsman, do, do, do.
Jas Smith, landsman, pneumonia, Aug 1, Nav Hosp, Chelsea.
Geo Johnson, landsman, smallpox, May 12, vessel U S S *Lockwood.*
Andrew Shark, landsman, debility, Jun 2, vessel U S S *Cmdor Hull.*
Jas Cretty, ord seaman, drowned, Jul 30, vessel U S S *Gettysburg.*
Jas Smith, ord seaman, variola, Jul 4, vessel U S S *Valparaiso.*
Jas Whaley, landsman, variola, Jul 7, do.
Wm B Copelin, landsman, diarrhoea, Jul 22, do.

TUE AUG 9, 1864
Died: on Aug 6, at Salisbury, Conn, Andrew S C, y/s/o Hon Andrew & Mary C Wylie, aged 16 months.

Local-fire reduced the warehse of Mr Presley W Dorsey, on 7th st, to ruins. The Gov't steam-engines under the direction of Mr Wm Dixon, Chief engr, were promptly on the spot. By the falling of a wall, Mr Silas Eggleston, an elderly ctzn was crushed to death.

Persons arrested by the military authorities in Delaware some days ago & brought to Balt; confined in Ft McHenry:

John Cochran	Geo White	Saml Danforth
Chas Ash	Fletcher Price	W L Weir
John Smalley	Isaac Grubb	Wm H Cann
Jos L Baldwin	Geo P McCrone	W W Stroup
Chas Cannon	E P Cochran	Philip Marvel
R B Cochran	R Rankin	Thos M Ogle
E B Jefferson	Jas McCrone	Delaware Davis
John Rodney	Chas A Jum	Dr Merrit
Douglas McCoy	J Frank Hazel	

WED AUG 10, 1864
Died: on Aug 9, Louis T, y/c/o John & Eliza Wilson, aged 4 yrs, 1 month & 16 days. Funeral from their residence-503 17th st, today.

THU AUG 11, 1864
Mrd: on Aug 9, at the Chr of the Ascension, by Rev Dr Pinckney, A T Leech to Miss Irene Fleury, both of Wash City.

Died: in Gtwn, D C, on Aug 10, Gideon Pearce, in his 81st yr. Funeral from his late residence, 119 Prospect st, today.

Hon John Brown Francis, for many years a leading ctzn of R I, died at his residence in R I on Tue last. He has been Govn'r & srv'd in both hses of Congress.

The *Alabama* & the *Kearsarge* Naval engagement in the British Channel, on Jun 19, 1864, from information from the wounded & paroled prisoners of the Confederate privateer *Alabama*, the ofcrs of the U S sloop of war *Kearsarge*, & ctzns of Cherbourg. Ofcrs of the Kearsarge: [Jun 19, 1864]
[Ldmn-landsman; Sm-seaman-Ord s-ordinary seaman; Stew-steward; Cxswn-coxswain; frmn-fireman; Q M-quarter master]

John A Winslow-Captain-N C
Jas S Thornton-Lt Cmder-N H
John M Browne-Surg-N H
J Adams Smith-Paymstr-Maine
Wm H Cushman-Chief Eng-Pa
Jas R Wheeler-Actg Mstr-Mass
Eben M Stoddard-Actg Mstr-Conn
David H Sumner-Actg Mstr-Maine
Wm H Badlam-2nd Ast Eng-Mass
Fred L Miller-3rd Ast Eng-Mass
Sidney L Smith-3rd Ast Eng-Mass

Henry McConnel-3rd Ast Engr-Pa
Edw E Preble-Mdshpmn-Maine
Danl B Sargent-Pymstr clerk-Maine
S E Hartwell-Capt's clerk-Mass
Frank A Grahm-Gunner-Pa
Jas C Walton-Boatswain-Pa
Wm H Yeaton-Actg Mstr's Mate-U S
Chas H Danforth-Actg Mstr's Mate-Mass
Ezra Bartlett-Actg Mstr's Mate-N H
Geo A Tittle-Surg's Steward-U S
Carson B DeWitt-Yeoman-U S

Crew of the U S steamer *Kearsarge*, Jun 19, 1864: Natives of U S:

Jason N Watrus-Mstr at arms
Chas Jones-Sm
Danl Charter-Ldmn
Edw Williams-Ofcr's Stew
Geo Williams-Ldmn
Jas Wilson-Cxswn
Wm Gowen [died]-Ord s
Jas Saunders-Q M
John W Dempsey-Q M
Wm D Chapel-Ldmn
Thos Perry-Btswn mate
John Barrow-Ord s
Wm Bond-Btswn's mate
Jas Haley-Capt of Fo'castle
Robt Strahn-Capt Top
Jas O Stone-1st cl boy
Jacob Barth-Ldmn
Jno H McCarthey-Ldmn
Jas F Hayes-Ldmn
John Hayes-Cxswn
Jas Devine-Ldmn
Geo H Russell-Armorer
Patrick McKeever-Ldmn
Nathan Ives-Ldmn
Dennis McCarty-Ldmn
John Boyle-Ord s
John C Woodberry-Ord s
Geo E Read-Sm
Jas Morey-Ord s
Benedict Drury-Sm
Wm Giles-Sm
Timothy Hurley-Ships' cook
Michl Conroy-Ord s
Levi W Nye-Sm

Jas H Lee-Sm
John E Brady-Ord s
Andrew J Rowley-Qrtr Gnr
Jas Bradley-Sm
Wm Ellis-Capt Hold
Henry Cook-Capt After guard
Chas A Read-Sm
Wm S Morgan-Sm
Joshua E Carey-Slmkr's mate
Jas Magee-Ord S
Benj S Davis-Ofcr's cook
John F Bickford-Cxswn
Wm Gurney-Sm
Wm Smith-Qm
Lla'e T Crowley-Ord s
Hugh McPherson-Gnr's mate
Taran Phillips-Ord s
Capt Winslow-long a ctzn of Mass
Joachim Pease-Sm
Benj H Blaisdell-1st cl frmn
Joel B Blaisdell-1st cl frmn
Chas Fisher-Ofcr's cook
Jas Henson-Ldmn
Wm M Smith-Ldmn
Wm Fisher-Ldmn
Geo Bailey-Ldmn
Martin Hoyt-Ldmn
Mark G Ham-Crpntr's mate
Wm H Bastien-Ldmn
Leyman P Spinney-Coal heaver
Geo E Smart-2nd cl frmn
Chas A Poole-Coal heaver
Timothy Lynch-Coal heaver
Will H Donnally-1st cl frmn

Sylvan's P Brackett-Coal heaver
John W Sanborn-Coal heaver
Adoniram Littlefield-Coal heaver
John W Young-Coal heaver
Will Wainwright-Coal heaver
Jno E Orchon-2nd cl frmn
Geo W Remick-1st cl frmn
Joel L Sanborn-1st cl frmn
Jere Young-1st cl frmn
Wm Smith-1st cl frmn
Stephen Smith-2nd cl frmn
John F Stackpole-2nd cl frmn
Wm Stanley-2nd cl frmn
Lyman H Hartford-2nd cl frmn
True W___riest-1st ck frmn
Jos Dugan-1st cl frmn
John F Dugan-Coal heaver
Jas W Sheffield-2nd cl frmn
Chas T Young-Ord sgt
Austin Quimley-Cpt-Marines
Roscoe G Dolley-Pvt-Marines
Patrick Flood-Pvt-Marines
Henry Hobson-Cpl-Marines
Jas Kerrigan-Pvt-Marines
John McAleen-Pvt-Marines
Geo A Raymond-Pvt-Marines
Jas Tucker-Pvt-Marines
Isaac Thornton-Pvt-Marines
Wm Y Evans-Nurse
Wm B Poole-Q m
From elsewhere:
Wm Aladorf-Ldmn-Holland
Jose Dabney-Ldmn-Western Islands
Benj Button-Coal heaver-Malay
Jean Bois____-Coal heaver-France
Vanburn Francois-Ldmn-Holland
Peter Ludy-Sm-Holland

F J Veannoh-Capt after-guard
Chas Hill-Ldmn
Henry Jameson-1st cl frmn
Jno G Batchelder-Pvt of Marines
John Dwyer-1st cl frmn
Thos Salmon-2nd cl frmn
Patrick O Connor-2nd cl frmn
Geo H Harrison-Ord s
Geo Andrew-Ord s
Chas Moore-Sm
Geo A Whipple-Ord s
Edw Wallace-Sm
Thos Marsh-Coal heaver
Thos Buckley-Ord s
Edw Wilt-Capt Top
Geo H Kinne-Ord s
Augustus Johnson-Sm
Jeremiah Horrigan-Sm
Wm O'Halloran-Sm
Wm Turner-Sm
Joshua Collins-Ord s
Jas McBeath-Ord s
John Pope-Coal heaver
Chas Mattison-Ord s
Geo Baker-Sm
Timothy G Canty-Sm
John Shields-Sm
Thos Aloway-Sm
Philip Weeks-Sm
Wm Barnes-Ldmn

Geo English-Sm-Eng
Jonathan Brien-Ldmn-Eng
Manual J Gallardo-2nd cl boy-Spain
John M Sonius-1st cl boy-Holland
Clement Antoine-Coal heaver-Western
Islands

Casualties from the engagement with the steamer *Alabama*, Jul 19, 1864, Cherbourg, France
John W Dempsey, Qrtr gunner, compound comminuted fracture of right arm, lower third,
& forearm. Arm amputated. Wm Gowen, Os, compound fracture of left thigh & leg.
Seriously wounded. Jas McBeath, Os, compound fracture of left leg. Severely wounded.
All these men were wounded by the same shot, a 68 pounder, which passed thru the
starboard bulwarks below main-rigging, narrowly escaping the 11 inch pivot gun. -John M
Brown Surg U S Navy [The Alabama was a barque-rigged screw propeller & the heaviest
of her rig.] The paroled prisoners, [4 ofcrs] on shore at Cherbourg evinced no hostility
whatever to their captors, but were always on the friendliest of terms with them. All alike
frequented the same hotel in the town, [curiously enough-The Eagle,] played billiards at the
same café, & bought their pipes, cigars, & tobacco from the same pretty little brunette on
the Quai du Port. Following are ofcrs & crew of the *Alabama* saved by the *Kearsage*: [The
Kearsage headed out to sea as soon as the Alabama was spotted.]
Francis L Galt-Va-Ast Surg   Jos Wilson-3rd Lt

Miles J Freeman-engr-English
Jon W Pundt-3rd ast engr
Benj L McCaskey-btswm
Wm Forrestall-Q m-English
Thos Potter-frmn-Englisg
Patrick Bradley-frmn-English
Saml Williams-frmn-Welshman
John Orrigin-frmn-Irishman
Geo Freemantle-Sm-English
Edgar Tripp-Sm-English

John Neil-Sm-English
Thos Winter-frmn-English
Martin King-Sm
Jos Pearson-Sm-English
Jas Hicks-Capt hold-English
R Parkinson-Wardrm stwd-English
John Emory-Sm-English
Thos L Parker-boy-English
Peter Hughes-Capt top-English

[All the above belonged to the *Alabama* when she first sailed from the Mersey, John Neil, John Emory, & Peter Hughes belong to the "Royal Naval Reserve."]

Wm Clark-Sm
David Leggett-Sm
Saml Henry-Sm
John Russell-Sm
Henry McCoy-Sm
John Smith-Sm
Edw Bussell-Sm
Jas Ochure-Sm
John Casen-Sm
Henry Higgin-Sm
Frank Hammond-Sm
Michl Shields-Sm
David Thurston-Sm
Geo Peasey-Sm
Henry Yates-Sm
Henry Godsen-Ord s
David Williams-Ord s
Henry Hestlake-Ord s
Thos Watson-Ord s
John Johnson-Ord s
Match Maddock-Ord s
Richd Evans-Ord s

Wm Miller-Ord s
Geo Cousey-Ord s
Thos Brandon-Ord s
Wm McKenzie-Cxswn
Jas Broderick-Cxswn
Wm Wilson-Cxswn
Edw Rawes-Mast at arms
Hy Tucker-Ofcr's cook
Wm Barnes-Qr gnr
Jacob Verbor-Sm-wounded
Wm McGiule-Cxswn
John Benson-Coalheaver
Jas McGuire-Coalheaver
Frank Currian-frmn
Peter Laperty-frmn
John Riley-frmn
Nicolas Adams-Ldmn
Jas Clemens-Yeoman
Jas Wilson-boy
Robt Wright-Capt m top-wounded
Wm McGuire-Capt f top-wounded

These men, almost without exception, are subjects of her Majesty the Queen. There were 3 others, who died in the boats, names not known.

Following reported to have been killed or drowned:

*David Herbert Llewellyn-Surg-Welshmn
Wm Robinson-Crpntr
Jas King-Mstr at arms Savannah pilot
Peter Duncan-frmn-English
Andrew Shillings-Scotchmn
Chas Puist-Coal passer-German
Fred'k Johns-Purser's stew-English

Saml Henry-Sm-English
John Roberts-Sm-Welshman
Peter Henry-Sm-Irish
Geo Appleby-Yeomn-English
A G Bartelli-Sm-Portuguese
Henry Fisher-Sm-English
-*A mistake

The above all belonged to the orginal crew of the *Alabama*. The *Deerhound* carried off, according to her own account, 41, the names of the following are known:

Raphael Semmes-Capt
John M Kell-1st Lt
Arthur Sinclair jr-2nd Lt
W H Sinclair-Mdshpmn
J S Bullock-Actg Mstr
E A Maffit-Mdshpmn

E M Anderson-Mdshpmn
M O'Brien-3rd Ast Surg
Geo T Fullam-Mstr's mate-English
Jas Evans-Mstr's mate
Max Meuluier-Mstr's mate
J Schraeder-Mstr's mate

W B Smith-Capt's clerk   J G Dent-Q m
J O Cuddy-Gunner   Jas McFadgen-frmn-English
R K Howell, Lt of Marines [This person is bro-in-law of Mr Jefferson Davis.]

Rebel rout at Moorfield, Va. Report of Gen Averill: Jul 7. I overtook the enemy under
McCausland, Johnson, Gilmor, & McNeil, about 3,000 strong: number killed & wounded of
the enemy is unknown, but large. 400 prisoners taken. Col Peter/Peters, 21st Va, rebel, was
mortally wounded. Gen Johnson was captured with his colors & 3 of his staff, but passing
undistinguished among the prisoners, effected his escape. My loss is 7 killed & 21
wounded. Maj Conger & Lt Clark, 31 Va cavalry, were killed while leading a charge. Capt
Kerr, 14th Pa cavalry, severely wounded while penetrating the enemy's lines, in a gallant
effort to capture the rebel commander. McCausland fled to the mountains. He will have
difficulty in finding his command.

Supreme Crt of D C, in Equity #277. Benj Summy vs Elisha C Hubbard & Emeline B, his
wife, John P Dickinson & Wm Little. Regarding-Appointment of a trustee in place of John
P Dickinson, absent from this district, as are all the dfndnts. Andrew Wylie, Justice -R J
Meigs, clerk

Died: on Aug 10, in her 4th yr, Frances Everette, d/o C B & Regina Hough. Funeral from
their residence, 282 9th st, today.

FRI AUG 12, 1864
Died: on Aug 11, suddenly, of chronic croup, Jesse, 2nd s/o Josiah & Maria Louisa Melvin.
Funeral from 354 O st, today.

Sarah Hollingsworth died recently in Phil, at age 110 yrs. She retained her mental faculties
to the last, although physically helpless.

Dr Reynolds, the American Cnsl, died at St Marie's, St Domingo, Jul 22.

St Louis counterfeiters arrested at St Louis & lodged in the Old Capitol: Louis Sleight; Jas
Vezey; Fred'k Biebusch; Wm Horner; Chas Hathaway, of St Louis; John Frisby & John
Brown, of Nauvoo; & the Johnston family, of Indianapolis. A dentist, D McCarthy, alias
Woods, of Indiana, acted as an agent for the concern.

Southern papers contain the news of the wounding [probably mortal,] of Capt Michl W
Cluskey, late editor of the Memphis Avalanche, & a few years since postmstr of the Hse
o/Reps. He was struck in the side by a minie bullet in one of the battles before Atlanta, &
bled profusely at the mouth. He is a s/o Mr Cluskey, the well-known engineer & architect
of this city, & tho he was born in Ga, most of his life has been spent among our people. -
Chronicle

Releases at Fred'k, Md: 1-Mr Frank Houser, telegraph operator at Monocacy Junction, who
was arrested a short time since on charge of disloyalty, has been honorably acquitted.
–Fred'k Examiner 2-Mr Jas L Norris, one of the proprietors of the Rpblcn Ctzn, who was
ordered to be sent south, returned to his home in this city on Thu last. It appears the rebels
would not receive him, &, retracing his steps to our lines, he was released by order of the
provost mrshl at Harper's Ferry. We have heard nothing of the whereabouts of Mr
Baughman & his family. –Fred'k Examiner

Brig Gen Wm Birney relieved from command of the Florida dist by Gen J P Hatch, to report to Gen Butler at Fortress Monroe.

SAT AUG 13, 1864
Mrd: at Rockburne, Wash Co, Md, on Aug 11, by Rev John Martin, Rev Osborne Ingle, of Balt, to Mollie M, d/o Anthony Addison.

Died: in Wash City, on Aug 11, Lillian Tebbs, 4th d/o D H & Martha E Tebbs, aged 2 years & 12 days. Interment in Balt, Md.

Died: in Wash City, on Aug 12, of scarlet fever, John, infant s/o Mary & Capt John O'Hagan, aged 1 year, 9 months & 12 days. Funeral from 195 N J av, today.

Wash Corp: 1-Ptn from J Gordon & B Reiss: ptn of Jas T Fry & others: both referred to the Cmte on Improvements. 2-Ptn of Mrs M A Bannerman & others: referred to a special cmte.

MON AUG 15, 1864
Deaths reported to the Navy Dept for the week ending Aug 13, 1864:
Saml Williams, pensioner, asthma, Aug 4, Naval Asylum.
Daniel Francis, negro, landsman, t b, Aug 1, Nav Hosp, N Y.
Geo M Bacon, landsman, inflam of brain, Jul 11, vessel *Admiral*.
Wm Jefferson, coxswain, dysentery, Jul 30, do.
Jas Miller, blank, drowned, Jun 16, Portsmouth.
Albert C Burgess, ord seaman, variola, Jun 1, New Orleans.
Marcus Rivers, negro, 2nd cl boy, drowned, Jul 2, vessel *Fearnot*.
Frederick Sipe, ord seaman, Asiatic cholera, Mar 25, Jamestown.
Dominic Morey, 2nd cl boy, consumption, Jun 27, Hosp Memphis.
John Reynolds, landsman, yel fever, Jul 15, Huntsville.
Richd Jones, landsman, pneumonia, Aug 3, Ohio.
Allen Chatman, negro, c m, chronic diarrhoea, Jul 25, Hosp, Memphis.
Stephen H Hill, marine, consumption, Aug 1, do.
Henry Clay, landsman, drowned, May 11, vessel *Dahlia*.
Horace Greeley, 1st cl boy, inflam of brain, May 21, vessel *Black Hawk*.
John Sharfaphy, marine, drowned, Jul 22, do.
John Brindley, 1st cl boy, chronic diarrhoea, Jul 5, New Albany, Ia.
Stephen L Harris, landsman, consumption, no date, Hosp, N Y.
Geo Flores, seaman, pneumonia, no date, do.
Jas M Cole, marine, drowned, Jul 31, vessel *Cimaroon*.
Jos Scott, ord seaman, gunshot, Apr 29, Ft Hindan.
Lafayette J Brown, paymstr, disease of bowels, Jul 24, St Paul, Minn.
John W Smith, landsman, chronic diarrhoea, Jul 23, vessel *Augusta Dinsmore*.
John Montgomery, landsman, consumption, Jul 13, do.
Humphrey Fischer, landsman, gunshot, Jul 1, vessel *Metacomet*.
Jas McKay, recruit, smallpox, Feb 1, Camp Douglas, Ill.
Goss Green, pilot, gunshot, Apr 21, Batesville, Ark.
Chas B Sherman, fireman, smallpox, Feb 25, vessel *Vidette*.
Jas C McIntyre, c h, congestive fever, Feb 21, vessel *Britannia*.
Jas H Fates, seaman, smallpox, Feb 24, vessel *Washita*.
Jas D Monroe, mstr at arms, smallpox, Feb 22, do.
Michl Flannigan, seaman, inflam of bowels, Feb 21, vessel *Sentinel*.
David Gibson, 1st cl boy, drowned, Jun 29, vessel *Forest Rose*.
Wm Kerr, seaman, blank, Jun 15, vessel *Choctaw*.

John P Hasby, landsman, consumption, May 6, vessel *Mound City*.
Albert Heil, contraband, inflam of bowels, May 14, vessel *Avenger*.
Nicodemus Reason, 1st cl boy, interm fever, Jun 16, vessel *Washita*.
Geo F Black, seaman, remit fever, Jun 17, do.
Caleb Adams, contraband, congestive fever, Jun 13, Pittsburg.
Jack Murton, alias Wm Seymour, ord seaman, Congestive fever, Jun 25, Chillicothe.
Southern Rayfield, landsman, pneumonia, Aug 6, Hosp, vessel *Chelsea*.
Bernard Casady, contraband passenger, drowned, Aug 5, vessel *Iris*.
Wm J Trott, actg mstr's mate, debauch, Aug 2, vessel *Arethusa*, at sea.
Henry G Black, c mate, typhoid fever, Jul 30, vessel U S S *Springfield*.
Jas H Algier, seaman, typhoid fever, Jul 27, vessel U S S *Black Hawk*.

Orphans Crt of Wash Co, D C. Prsnl estate of Thos Brown, late of Wash Co, dec'd. –Mary E Brown, R R Pywell, excs

TUE AUG 16, 1864
Orphans Crt of Wash Co, D C. Case of Richd H Clarke, adm of John D Hogan, dec'd; settlement on Sep 6. -Z C Robbins, rg o/wills

Killed on board the U S steamer *Hartford* in the action with the rebel *Fort Morgan* & fleet, Aug 5, 1864: David Morrow, q m; Wm Osgood, ord seaman; Thos Baine; Benj Harper, seaman; Wm Clark, boy; Chas Schaffer, seaman; Frank Stillwell, nurse; Geo Walker, landsman; John C Scott, ord seaman; Thos Wilde; Wm Smith, boy; Wm Andrews, C A G; Frank Musel; ____ Carwell; Lewis McLane, landsman; Thos Stanton; Peter Duncan; Th Baines.

Col David Chambers died at Zanesville, Ohio, Aug 8th. He was aid to Gen Lewis Cass during the war of 1812.

Capt Wm Hemstreet, 18th Missouri Infty, records in the Chattanooga Gaz the effects in the Camp Fuller Brig, near Rossville, Ga, on Jul 14, of a remarkable stroke of lightning which killed & wounded 15 sldrs. Cpl John Taylor, Co I, & Pvt John Hensel, Co I, were killed.

Fortress Monroe, Aug 13. The steamer *N Y* arrived this morning from Aiken's Landing, with 460 Federal prisoners in charge of Maj John E Mulford, Ast Agent of exchange. Among them: Lt Col Mansfield, 2nd Wisc; Maj Motley, 1st Mass Cavalry; Lt Col Foot, 121st N Y; Lt Silver, 16th Ill cavalry.

Orson C Cone, editor of the Somerset [N J] Messenger, was taken into custody on Wed & conveyed to Newark for examination on the charge of publishing articles in his journal discouraging enlistments.

WED AUG 17, 1864
Died: suddenly, on Aug 5, on board the steamer *Fulton*, Hilton Head, Mangle Mintherne Thompson, of N Y.

Orphans Crt of Wash Co, D C. 1-Case of Chas M Matthews, adm d b n c t a, of Raphael H Boarman, dec'd; settlement on Sep 6. -Z C Robbins, rg o/wills 2-Prsnl estate of S S Williams, late of Wash Co, dec'd. -Maria S Williams, admx 3-Prsnl estate of Cornelius O'Leary, late of Wash City, dec'd. -Jas O'Leary, exc 4-Case of Wm R Woodward, adm of Jos Miller, dec'd; settlement on Sep 3. Z C Robbins, rg o/wills

Died: at Columbia, Pa, on Aug 1, Chas Robt Maxwell, aged 7 years & 4 mos, s/o Surgeon C D Maxwell, U S Navy, & Miriam K Maxwell, of Wash. [Father now on duty on the Pacific coast.]

Patapsco Female Institute, Ellicott's Mills, Md. So favorably known for many years past, still continues in active operation. Rob H Archer, Principal, Ellicott's Mills P O, Md [Ad]

List of the ofcrs of the monitor *Teccumseh*, sunk at Mobile: Cmder, T A M Craven; Lt, J W Kelley; Actg Ast Surg, Henry A Danker; Actg Ast Paymstr, Geo Work; Actg Mstr, Chas F Langley; Ensigns-F H de Estamanville, G Cottrell; Engrs, Chief John Farron; 1st Asts, Chas Pennington, W L Penell; 3rd Asts, F Scott, W D Kay; Clerk to Capt, Isaiah Conley.

The Chicago people are raising a fund to purchase a handsome property for Mrs Col Mulligan, whose hsbnd was lately killed in the Shenandoah Valley.

Savannah papers chronicle the arrival of Gen Stoneman & 500 of his men as prisoners of war at Macon, & exult over it as success enough for one campaign.

THU AUG 18, 1864
Trustees sale of land near the Insane Asylum; 2 deeds from Chas J Uhlmann to me, one dated Dec 30, 1862, the other Jan 3, 1863; land in Wash Co known as *Woodstock*, & latterly as the *Kosciusko Place*; plat accompanying the deed, from Moses Kelly & Mary W Kelly, his wife, to Chas J Uhlmann. -Horace J Frost, trustee

Wash Corp: 1-Resolution relative to the decease of R T Knight, late a mbr of the Brd: passed. 2-Ptn of P J Tawney, with bill authorizing the curbstones on sq 629: passed.

Thos R Byrnes: 402 F st, near 7th: will clean, reguild, rebronze, & alter all kinds of gas fixtures, candelabras, clocks, etc, at short notice & moderate charges.

The venerable ex-Pres Day, of Yale College, entered his 92nd yr last week.

FRI AUG 19, 1864
Dissolution of partnership between Edw Owen & Saml W Owen, tailoring business, under the firm of E Owen & Son, for the last 20 yrs, by mutual consent. Saml W Owen will be at their old stand, 212 Pa av, Wash, D C.

From Atlanta, Ga: battle of Utoy Creek: near Alanta, Aug 6, 1864. The loss is near 500 men. The 100th Ohio alone lost near 150, Col Slevin, of the regt, being among the severely tho not dangerously wounded. Lt Tracy, of Gen Reily's staff, is severely wounded. Col Thirtemann, 16th dismounted Ill cavalry, was thrown from his horse & had his leg broken.

SAT AUG 20, 1864
Orphans Crt of Wash Co, D C. Case of Marvin J McClery, adm d b n of Jas McClery, dec'd; settlement on Sep 3. -Z C Robbins, rg o/wills

Died: at Long Branch, N J, on Aug 16, Clarence Jerome Gallaher, infant s/o B Frank & Eliza A Gallaher, late of Wash City, aged 8 months & 24 days. This is the 3rd affliction of this family in less than 3 yrs.

Died: on Aug 19, after a brief but severe illness, Col John H Reily, in his 67th yr. Funeral from his late residence, 405 N Y av, Sun.

The hse in which Wm Penn & his family lived in Phil was recently purchased by a ctzn & will soon be demolished. Occupied by Penn in 1700, & in this hse his son John Penn was born. It is now about 175 years old, & the last relic of the Penn family.

MON AUG 22, 1864

Deaths reported to the Navy Dept for the week ending Aug 20, 1864:
Jas A Bell, landsman, typhoid fever, Aug 13, Nav Asylum.
Wm Ball, landsman, yel fever, Jul 29, vessel *Eugenia*.
Jas Barlow, landsman, yel fever, Jul 28, vessel *Wanderer*.
Michl Murry, paymstr's steward, yel fever, Jul 29, do.
Cyrus M Campbell, ast 3rd engr, remit fever, Aug 2, vessel *Myanza*.
Jas Despaun, landsman, yel fever, Jul 27, vessel *Dale*.
Wm H Bradford, ast mstr's mate, yel fever, Jul 29, Hosp, Tampa Bay.
Richd Fitzgerald, ord seaman, yel fever, Jul 31, do.
Edw H Watkeys, ast engr, yel fever, Jul 30, do.
Jas D Shey, 2nd cl boy, drowned, Jul 25, vessel *J L Davis*.
Owen Maines, seaman, gunshot wound, Aug 5, vessel *Assipee*.
John Smith, qrtr gunner, diarrhoea, Jul 13, vessel *Otsega*.
David Morrow, qrtr gunner, gunshot wound, Aug 5, Hartford, at Mobile.
Wm Osgood, ord seaman, do, do, do.
Thos Bain, blank, gunshot wound, Aug 5, do.
Benj Harper, seaman, gunshot wound, do, do.
Wm Clark, boy, do, do, do.
Chas Schaffer, seaman, do, do, do.
Frank Sidwell, nurse, do, do, do.
Geo Walker, landsman, do, do, do.
John C Scott, ord seaman, do, do, do.
Thos Wilde, blank, gunshot wound, Aug 5, do.
Wm Smith, boy, do, do, do.
Wm Andrews, c a g, do, do, do.
Frank Munsell, blank, gunshot wound, Aug 5, do.
Louis M Lane, landsman, do, do, do.
Peter Duncan, blank, do, do, do.
Thos Baines, blank, do, do, do.
Thos Staunton, blank, do, do, do.
___ Cannel, blank, do, do, do.
Alfred James, landsman, dysentery, Aug 17, Hosp, Washington.
Jas Hackett, sgt marines, consumption, Aug 17, Marine Barracks, Brooklyn.

Died: at Dublin, Indiana, of whooping cough, on Aug 9, John Underwood Lawrence, infant s/o L Lovell & Susan L Lawrence, aged 4 months.

City Point, Aug 19. Under a flag of truce the rebels recovered the body of Gen Chambliss, slain recently within our lines. Col Osborn & Lt Col Plympton, both, I believe, of the 3rd N H, are among the wounded in the recent fights.

TUE AUG 23, 1864

Died: in Wash City, on Aug 22, of typhoid ever, Frances L, d/o G & Thomazine M Rowzee, & grand-dght of the late Saml & Mary A Lewis, in her 19th yr. Funeral from the residence of the parents, P st, between 14 & 15th sts, today.

The death of Gen Grifin Stedman, fallen before Petersburg, is one of the saddest events of the war. He was a young man of noblest qualities: born at Hartford, Conn, grad at Trinity College. His family mourns his loss. –Jour Com

Mrs Wm Key Howard, who was arrested in Balt about 4 months ago by military authority & conveyed to Washington, where she was placed in the Old Capitol prison, was, on Fri last, unconditionally released by order of the Pres. -Sun

WED AUG 24, 1864
Mrd: at the Parsonage of the Trinity Chr, Gtwn, D C, on Aug 23, by Rev Fr Jamison, Wm Alexander Oliver, U S Navy, to Miss Mary Eliza Carter, d/o John Carter, recently of Va, now of Phil.

Mrd: on Aug 23, at St Peter's Chr, by Rev Fr J B A Broirellit, Geo W Humphreys, of Balt, Md, to Eliza Jane Fletcher, of Wash.

Died: on Aug 23, Henry Coombs, c/o Chas H & Mary M Johnson, aged 1 yr, 1 month & 4 days. Funeral from the residence of Martin Johnson, 392 E st, today.

Died: near Wash, on Aug 21, of typhoid fever, Jas Cary, oldest s/o Jas & Mgt Selden, aged 17 yrs. Funeral from his grandmother's residence near Rock Crk Chr, today.

Explanation of Gen Early: burning of Chambersburg. Recently, in Md the hse of Gov Bradford was burned without my orders. I must add that I approved it, for retaliation for the burning of Gov Letcher's hse, whom I know to be a very poor man, whose family was not allowed 5 mins to remove clothing or other valuables. When in front of Washington, some of my troops were very determined to destroy the hse of Mr Francis P Blair, & had removed some of its furn, probably supposing it to belong to his son, the mbr of the Federal Cabinet. I stopped the proceedings. The hse of his son, Montgomery Blair, a mbr of the Cabinet was subjected to a different rule. In Culpeper Co, in Eastern Va, where Gen Meade held his headqrtrs, almost every hse & bldg has been burned. Recently they burned the residence of Andrew Hunter, near Charlestown, with all it contents, requiring his family to stand by & & witness the destruction. They did the same to the hse of Edmund J Lee, near Shepherdstown, & to the bldgs of Hon Alex'r R Boteler.

Harper's Ferry, Aug 21: engagement between the Army of Western Va & the rebel force in Shanandoah Valley. Gen Wilson, of Gen Torbett's Cavalry corps engagd on our right, etc. Wounded: Lt Col Geo E Chamberlain, 1st Vt; Lt Col A A Hale, 6th Vt; Maj G W Dwinell, 6th Vt; Capt B D Fabgar, 6th Vt; Lewis Redenbach, 61st Pa; Lt Chas C Money, 2nd Vt; Lt J N Price, 61st Pa; & Actg Adj John Caldwell, 61st Pa.

Died: at Dublin, Indiana, of whooping cough, on Aug 9, John Underwood Lawrence, infant s/o L Lovell & Susan L Lawrence, aged 4 months.

THU AUG 25, 1864
Col Philip Herbert, 7th Texas cavalry, died at Kington, La, on Jul 27, from effects of a wound received at the battle of Mansfield, on Apr 8, 1864. He was a former mbr of Congress from Calif. He made himself notorious in the winter of 1857 by killing one of the waiters at the Willard Htl, in Wash City.

The Mormons in London have been holding a series of meetings under the auspices of Brigham Young, jr, & Orson Pratt. They chose Young as European Pres & his father as Pres of the Mormons all over the world.

English papers announce the death of Mr Chas Wentworth Dilke, proprietor & for many years editor of the London Atheraeum. Also died, Mr Robson, the celebrated London actor; & Rev Jos Romilly, for many years Registrar of Cambridge Univ.

FRI AUG 26, 1864
Wash Corp: 1-Ptn from Thos Holmes, in reply to the ptn of Wm Bannerman: referred to a spec cmte. 2-Ptn of John L Brown: referred to the Cmte on Improvements. 3-Ptn of Geo Lea: referred to the Cmte on Finance. 4-Adverse on the nomination of Jos Williamson for police cnstble of ward 2: recommending its rejection: nomination was rejected. 5-Similar report on the case of Chas H Hurdle as police cnstbl of ward 3.

Died: in Wash City, on Aug 25, Kate, y/c/o H L & C BV Chapin, aged 6 months. Funeral from 514 L st, today.

The Pres has appt'd Gen Hancock a Brig Gen in the Regular Army.

Claims against the Mount Carbon Coal Co, incorporated by the laws of Illinois, etc, to be presented with vouchers, to Geo H Forster, Pres , Wall st, N Y C.

SAT AUG 27, 1864
Hon John Appleton died in Portland, Me, on Aug 22.

Fenton Beavers, convicted by a crt martial in Wash City, of being a spy & violating his oath of allegiance, was hung yesterday, in the yard of the Old Capitol prison. He belonged to Mosby's Cavalry.

Bids for 2,000 barrels of flour were opened at the ofc of the Commissary of Subsistence in Wash City on Thu. Among the bidders: John A Green, Wm H Edes, D L Shoemaker & Bro, G W Mears, A Ross Ray & Bro, & others. The Messrs Ray were the lowest bidders.

Richmond Dispatch of Aug 22 mentions the arrival in Richmond during Sat & Sun of 2,400 Union prisoners, who were captured on Fri during the fight for the Weldon railrd. Amongst them are
Cols: Wm R Hartshorn, 190th Pa, Infty; Jas Carle, 4th Pa reserves; G Gilbert Rey, 104th N Y.
Lt Cols: Wm a Leech, 90th Pa; Saml A Moffett, 94th N Y Infty.
Majs: Jacob M Davis, 90th Pa; E Rodgell, 149 N G; John A Wolfe, 190th Pa; Milton Weildler, 2nd Pa
Capts:

Jas A Wood	Byron Parsons	A N Richardson
Jessie Armstrong	Jos O Lord	John Hall
John B McDonald	John J Torbert	Jasper M Griggs
Carsell McClennand	Thos H Abbott	F R Kinsly
Emanuel D Roth	Ezra J Trull	U K Berkest
E J Kratzor	John Daly	Fred'k Guyer
E E Ziegler	H A Wiley	Z B Adams
Byron Porter	Jas A Gault	H B Fox
Clinton Perry	John H Chipman	L Black

A B Horton   E P Luther   S H White
F Coppas   E R Sage

Erroneous report has obtained currency regarding the recent death in England of Mr Douglass F Forrest, s/o Cmdor French Forrest, formerly of the U S Navy. A letter dated Aug 13 was received from him.

MON AUG 29, 1864

Deaths reported to the Navy Dept for the week ending Aug 27, 1864:

Geo Lacy, coxswain, asthma, Aug 18, vessel U S S *Nereus.*
Wm E Denby, landsman, drowned, no date.
Stephen E Parsons, landsman, diarrhoea, Aug 9, Nav Hosp, Memphis.
Dennis Gibbs, landsman, remit fever, Aug 10, do.
John Maroney, seaman, tetanus, Aug 15, do.
Thos J Gerrans, 1st cl boy, typhoid fever, Jul 24, vessel U S S *Vicksburg.*
Moses Stump, ord seaman, typhoid fever, Jul 8, Nav Hosp, Portsmouth, Va.
B F Bazor, seaman, congestive fever, May 13, Hosp, Evansville, Ind.
Wm Thorp, seaman, typhoid fever, May 6, do.
Jos W Palmer, seaman, bronchitis, May 13, do.
Norman Leslie, landsman, drowned, Aug 6, vessel U S S *Kenwood.*
Saml Preston, coalheaver, drowned, Jul 20, vessel U S S *Choctaw.*
Richd Harelew, ord seaman, congestion, Aug 4, vessel U S S *Ozark.*
Geo Matthews, ord seaman, gunshot, Aug 11, vessel U S S *Prairie Bird.*
Geo O Northrop, seaman, drowned, Jul 28, vessel U S S *Naiad.*
Benedict Nelson, capt foretop, inflam of brain, Aug 8, vessel U S S *Ozark.*
Thos Demuel, landsman, injuries, Aug 22, Nav Asylum.
Frank Wilson, landsman, gunshot, Aug 5, vessel U S S *Philippi.*
Wm H French, q m, gunshot, Aug 5, do.
Chas Sage, capt foretop, pneumonia, Aug 16, vessel U S S *Susquehanna.*
Wm H Hegginbotham, actg ensign, gunshot, Aug 5, vessel U S S *Hartford.*
Adolphus Pulte, seaman, gunshot, Aug 5, do.
Wm H Cook, actg mstr's mate, gunshot, Aug 5, vessel U S S *Brooklyn.*
Eli Harwood, Chief cook, gunshot, do, do.
John Ryan, landsman, do, do, do.
Chas B Seymour, seaman, do, do, do.
Thos Williams, seaman, do, do, do.
Lewis Richards, seaman, do, do, do.
Michael Murphy, marine, do, do, do.
Wm Smith, marine, do, do, do.
Richd Burke, coalheaver, do, do, do.
Anthony Dunn, 1st cl fireman, do, do, do.
Jas McDermott, landsman, do, do, do.
Andrew E Smith, coalheaver, gunshot, Aug 5, vessel U S S *Hartford.*
Francis Campbell, 2nd cl fireman, do, do, do.
Chas Stevenson, 2nd cl boy, do, do, do.
David Curtis, landsman, do, do, do.
Jas Williams, mstr at arms, gunshot, Aug 5, vessel U S S *Lackawana.*
John Troy, capt foretop, do, do, do.
Chas Anderson, ord seaman, do, do, do.
Richd Ashley, boy, do, do, do.
Frank Levay, ord seaman, gunshot, Aug 5, vessel U S S *Oneida.*

Thos Gibson, marine, do, do, do.
Albert Phillips, capt foretop, do, do, do.
John C Penson, seaman, do, do, do.
Jas Agan, 1st cl fireman, Scalded, Aug 5, do.
Emanuel Boyakin, cabin steward, gunshot, Aug 5, do.
Robt Lennox, landsman, do, do, do.
Patrick Dorris, landsman, missing, killed or drowned, Aug 5, do.
John Stewart, landsman, gunshot, Aug 5, vessel U S S *Metacomet*.
W H Davis, seaman, by splinter, Aug 5, vessel U S S *Octorora*.
Danl Godfrey, coalheaver, gunshot, Aug 5, vessel U S S *Kennebec*.
Jas Alexander, landsman, gunshot, Aug 5, vessel U S S *Hartford*.
W S Hayden, actg ensign, typhoid fever, Jul 6, vessel U S S *Penguin*.
Henry W Briggs, capt's mate, gunshot, Jul 30, vessel U S S *Potomska*.
John H Williams, landsman, remit fever, Jul 20, Infirmary, Balt.
Michl Seirey, landsman, inflam of brain, Aug 5, vessel U S S *Mt Vernon*.

Orphans Crt of Wash Co, D C. 1-Case of Louisa Kearney, excx of Jas Kearney, dec'd; settlement on Sep 17. -Z C Robbins, rg o/wills 2-Prsnl estate of Thos F Anderson, late of Wash City, dec'd. -Eliza M Anderson, excx

Gen Forrest's late daring raid upon Memphis on Aug 21. Ctzns & sldrs going ab't the streets were halted, & in many cases killed or wounded by the rebels, & wherever a negro was seen he was hotly pursued & shot down: 10 reported killed. Expedition under the command of Maj Gen Forrest in person, consisted of the following regts: 3rd Tenn cavalry, Col Barlow; 12th Tenn cavalry, Col Nealy; 14th Tenn cavalry, Col Logwood; 15th Tenn cavalry, Col Stewart; 16th Tenn cavalry, Col N Wilson; 21st Tenn cavalry, Col John Newsom; 22nd Tenn cavalry, Col Russell; 2nd Miss Cavalry, Col Bob McCullough; 18th Miss Cavalry, Col Chalmers. The rebels struck for Gen Washburn's headqrtrs, first visited by a force of ab't 200, under Col Jesse Forrest, who found it deserted. Lt Harrington, 3rd U S Artl, was in the ofc when the rebels first appeared. They made him a prisoner & placed him behind the counter with Mr Benthold, the clerk, when a bullet coming thru the window from the street pierced his head, killed him instantly. His person was immediately plundered. Pvt Alex McCowan, 8th Iowa, who was on guard, was taken prisoner. Chas Roach & Ed Boswell were on duty at fire engine hse #5: Roach was killed, Boswell escaped. Pvt M Jones, 140th Ill, guard at Gayoso Hosp, failed to surrender & was shot in the shoulder. Josiah T Roberts was shot down.

TUE AUG 30, 1864
Copy of a ltr written to Gen Grant by Lydia Slocum on the death of her grandson, Gen Jas B McPherson, who fell in battle. Followed by Gen Grant's reply. Clyde, Ohio, Aug 3, 1864. To Gen Grant-Dear Sir: I hope you will pardon me for troubling you with the perusal of these few lines from the trembling hand of the aged grandma of our beloved Gen James B McPherson, who fell in battle. When it was announced at his funeral from the public print that when Gen Grant heard of his death he went into his tent and wept like a child, my heart went out in thanks to you for the interest you manifested in him while he was with you. I have watched his progress from infancy up. In childhood he was obedient and kind; in manhood interesting, noble, and persevering, looking to the wants of others. Since he entered the war others can appreciate his worth more than I can. When it was announced to us by telegraph, that our loved one had fallen, our hearts were almost rent asunder; but when we heard that the Commander-in-Chief could weep with us too, we felt, sir, that you had been as a father to him and this whole nation is mourning his early death. I wish to inform you that his remains were conducted by a kind guard to the very parlor

where he spent a cheerful evening in 1861, with his widowed mother, two brothers, only sister, and his aged grandma, who is now trying to write. In the morning he took his leave at six o'clock, little dreaming he should fall by a ball from the enemy. His funeral services were attended in his mother's orchard, where his youthful feet had often pressed the soil to gather the falling fruit, and his remains are resting in the silent grave scarce half a mile from the place of his birth. His grave is on an eminence but a few rods from where the funeral services were attended, and near the grave of his father. The grave, no doubt, will be marked, so that passersby will often pause to drop a tear over the departed. And oh, dear friend, a few lines from you would be gratefully received by the afflicted friends. I pray that the God of Battles may be with you, and go forth with your armies till rebellion shall cease, the Union be restored, and the old flag wave over our entire land! With much respect, I remain your friend, Lydia Slocum, Aged 87 years and 4 months. Reply of Gen Grant: Headqrtrs Armies of the U S, City Point, Va, Aug 10, 1864. Mrs Lydia Slocum-My Dear Madam: Your very welcome letter of the 3d instant has reached me. I am glad to know the relatives of the lamented Major Gen McPherson are aware of the more than friendship existing between him and myself. A nation grieves at the loss of one so dear to our nation's cause. It is a selfish grief, because the nation had more to expect from him than from almost any one living. I join in the selfish grief, and add the grief of personal love for the departed. He formed for some time one of my military family. I knew him well, to know him was but to love him. It may be some consolation to you, his aged grandmother, to know that every officer and every soldier who served under your grandson felt the highest reverence for his patriotism, his zeal, his great, almost unequalled ability, his amability, and all the many virtues that can adorn a commander. Your bereavement is great, but cannot exceed mine. Yours, truly, U S Grant, Lieut Gen

Indian massacres at the west: Capt Haskell & Dr Renner, just from Beatrice & Big Sandy, bring reports from the scene of Indian trouble. Details were included in the deaths at Uhleg ranch-Theo Uhleg & Joe Uhleg were killed. At ranch owned by Mr Comstock, Harvey Butler & M C Kelly were killed. Geo Hunt shot thru the leg. Laura Roper is missing. Female bodies were scalped. At Pawnee ranch, P Burke, of Beatrice, was shot in the back of the head while riding, the ball coming out of his mouth. The Indians scalped him alive & left him. He reached the Pawnee ranch, where he died.

Rev Dr Anderson, of St Louis, has just been tried & found guilty, by a military commission, of disloyalty to the Govt.

Taken up: a white & yellow Buffalo cow. Owner will please prove property, pay charges, & take her away. –John Grinder, near the first toll gate, Bladensburg rd.

Mrd: in Wash City, on Aug 24, by Rev W McLain, Mellen Lathrop to Mattie D Clark.

Orphans Crt of Wash Co, D C. Case of Mrs Lydia A Hoover, admx of Samuel Hoover, dec'd; settlement on Sep 20. -Z C Robbins, rg o/wills

WED AUG 31, 1864
Orphans Crt of Wash Co, D C. Prsnl estate of Eliza E Moreland, late of Gtwn, D C, dec'd. -J G Waters

Bristol, E Tenn: Aug 24, 1864. Three hundred Yankee cavalry dashed into Rogersville on Aug 21 & captured the Hon J Hieskeil, C K Shields, Col Walder, Capt Clay, & 19 privates.

Gen A J Smith is reported as sweeping thru eastern Mississippi & Ala.

Richmond papers-Enquirer: Brig Gen John C C Lowder, of Ala, killed.

THU SEP 1, 1864
Died: Aug 30th, Mrs Plenope Ball, in her 69th yr, wid/o the late Dabney Ball, sr.

Jas Lydam, of Montg Co, Md, convicted of being a spy, & to be hung yesterday, has been respited until further order.

39th Mass Regt, which was stationed in Wash City doing provost duty before being sent to the army of the Potomac, suffered quite severely in the late fight on the Weldon railroad, losing some 200 men in killed, wounded, & prisoners. Casualties among the ofcrs: Lt Col Pierson, severely wounded; Lt W T Spear, killed; Lts Reed, Susseault, & Severns, wounded; Capts Fred & Willard Kingsley, Tuell, Hutchins, & Lts Baker, Hanson, Tidd, Hoses, & Chapman, missing & supposed to be prisoners. Star

$20 reward for strayed or stolen gray mule, on Aug 27. H Polkinhorn, Huntington, near Bethesda Chr, Rockville turnpike.

Rebel account of the late battle: the Weldon railroad has again brought grief. On Thu Gen A P Hill assaulted the enemy's works near Reams' Station, 12 miles from Petersburg, securing 2,000 prisoners & 9 pieces of cannon. Wounded: Gen Anderson, of Ga, & Col Chas Marshall, of Va, the latter in the arm.

THU SEP 2, 1864
Mrd: on Sep 1, by Rev Prof Shute, Mr Chas McD Brown, y/s/o Edmund F Brown, to Miss Julia F Myers, eldest d/o Mr John Myers, all of Wash City.

Died: on Sep 1, Susie K Ingle, d/o the late Jos Ingle, of Wash City. Funeral from the residence of D W Middleton, on Capitol Hill, Fri.

Military arrests on Aug 23, at the law ofc of Jos M Palmer, Frederick, Md: Meredith Davis, Jos M Palmer, Dr Chas Smith, Alfred Ritter, John A Lynch, Chas W Ross, Geo A Hanson, John Ritchie, David O Thomas & W Bantz. It was thought the meeting was held for sinister purpose, but these men were selected to represent this county in the State Convention held in Balt in June last & were there to app't a delegate to supply a vacancy. Col Jacob M Kunkel was selected to attend the Convention. The parties were released. -Frederick [Md] Examiner

I O O F notice of the funeral of Jas R Gurgerson, on Fri. -P H Sweet, grsec.

Frank Russell Reading, proprietor of the *Guide*, published in Wash City, was arrested recently for uttering treasonable language in D C; to be imprisoned in Fort Delaware for 5 yrs. -Star

SAT SEP 3, 1864
Mrd: in Wash City, on Sep 1, at the Chr of the Epiphany, by Rev Richd Channing Moore, of Wmsport, Pa, G Bedell Moore, s/o the officiating clergyman & grandson of the late Bishop Moore, of Va, to Alice S Clements, d/o Robt H Clements, of Wash.

Mrd: on Sep 1, at St Aloysius Chr, by Rev Fr Hietzleberger, Edw A Ellsworth, U S Army, to Miss Fannie Diggs, d/o Mr S J Diggs, of Wash.

Died: at the residence of his grandmother, Mrs Cecelia Spalding, in St Mary's Co, Md, on Aug 27, of congestion of the brain, Edw Dyer Spalding, in his 19th yr, 2nd s/o H C Spalding, of Wash, D C, & Mgt Ann, d/o the late Cmdor Stephen Cassin, U S N.

Orphans Crt of Wash Co, D C. Case of Mary A Smith, admx of Thos Smith, dec'd; settlement on Sep 24. -Z C Robbins, rg o/wills

MON SEP 5, 1864

Deaths reported to the Navy Dept for the week ending Sep 3, 1864:
David Mabee, 2nd cl boy, pneumonia, Jun 20, Nav Hosp, Newbern.
John M Whitney, a a surg, drowned, Aug 16, vessel U S S *Norwich*.
John Schorter, landsman, drowned, Aug 22, vessel U S S *Princeton*.
Jos H Kenney, landsman, enteritis, Jul 30, vessel U S S *New Hampshire*.
Geo A Swindle, landsman, consumption, Aug 7, do.
John McCauley, landsman, gunshot wound, Aug 5, vessel U S S *Lackawana*.
Benj F Brookings, ord seaman, diarrhoea, Jul 28, Nav Hosp, N Orleans.
Henry O Young, landsman, diarrhoea, Jul 26, do.
Jos McKenney, landsman, remit fever, Aug 3, do.
John F Stoddard, ord seaman, congestive fever, Aug 7, do.
Wm Farley, landsman, disease of heart, Jul 3, vessel U S S *Randolph*.
Wm Taylor, landsman, disease of lung, Aug 24, Nav Hosp, Chelsea.
John Gartland, coal heaver, typhoid fever, Aug 1, Nav Asylum.
Daniel Furlong, blank, drowned, Aug 19, vessel U S S *Western World*.
Dennis Brucia, landsman, drowned, Aug 13, vessel U S S *A Hugel*.

Orphans Crt of Wash Co, D C. Prsnl estate of Wm Kirkland, late of Gtwn, D C, dec'd. -Mgt A Kirkland, excx, c t a.

French Governess wants a situation in some respectable family or school. Address-Marie Beranger, c/o Cnsl Gen of Switzerland, Wash City, D C.

Mr John Savage, formerly of Wash, has left N Y for New Orleans to be editor of the New Orleans Daily Times, the new Union paper.

TUE SEP 6, 1864

Mrd: in Wash City, on Sep 2, by Rev W McLain, Jared Hoag & Mgt Ann King.

Supreme Crt of D C, # 98. Julius N Granger vs Adele Douglas et al. Ratify sales made by Thos J Fisher & Walter D Davidge, trustees. -R J Meigs, clerk

Buffalo, Sept. The propeller *Scotia* was run into by the propellar *Arctic*, at Dunkirk on Fri night. Persons drowned: Mrs Cath Dickson & child; Mrs Henrietta Haines, of Toledo; G H Hicock, cook of the *Scotia*.

Tudor Place for rent: spacious villa, well furnished, & beautifully situated on the Hghts of Gtwn, within a few mins walk of the street cars. Apply on the premises.

WED SEP 7, 1864

Mrd: on Sep 6, in the Ninth st Meth Prot Chr, by Rev J T Ward, Mr Robt C Hewett to Miss Rachel M Simpson, both of Wash City.

Died: at Sldr's Home, near Wash, on Sep 6, Mrs Mary C Dimick, w/o Col J Dimick, U S Army. Funeral at Rock Crk Chr on Thu.

Died: on Sep 5, after a painful illness, Susie, w/o Wm B Cudlipp, in the 22nd yr of her age. Funeral from the residence of her hsbnd, 500 K st, today.

Orphans Crt of Wash Co, D C. Case of Richd H Clarke, exc of Eliz Orme, dec'd; settlement on Oct 1. -Z C Robbins, rg o/wills

THU SEP 8, 1864

Died: in Wash City, on Sep 4, Lucy Ann, w/o Martin Buell, & d/o the late Wm Blanchard, in the 55th yr of her age.

Supreme Crt of D C, in Equity #129. Saml Miller's excx vs Ignatius Fries & others, heirs of John M Fries & Maria B Peters, & others, heirs of Francis Peters. Parties & trustees to meet at my ofc in City Hall, Sep 30. -W Redin, auditor

Richmond Examiner of Tue-Gen John Morgan was surprised & killed & his staff captured at Greenville, Tenn.

Gen Dix has declined the use of his name as a candidate before the Republican State Convention for Govn'r of N Y. The Convention met yesterday.

Jos B Morse, editor of the Boston Traveller, a Rpblcn sheet, has retired from that paper after a connection of 7 yrs. His convictions of duty to his country led him to the support of McClellan & Pendleton against Lincoln & Johnson, & this he could not do while editing a Republican paper.

FRI SEP 9, 1864

Died: on Aug 22, in Leesburg, Loudoun Co, Va, Mr Edwin Drish, aged 31 yrs, y/s/o Wm Drish, & hsbnd of S Indiana Powell, of Wash, D C.

Died: on Sep 5, at the residence of her father, Mr A B Waller, near Newark, Dela, Maria G Kilby, aged 31 years & 2 mos, widow of the late Isaac H Kilby, of Eastport, Maine.

Died: in Marion, Va, Georgine M, w/o Dr H J Garrett, & d/o the late W S Derrick, of Wash City.

The St Louis Republican announces the death of Ex-Gov Augustus C French, of Ill, who died at his home in Lebanon, on Sun last, of typhoid fever.

Gen John H Winder, per the Richmond Enq of Sep 3rd, says: *This ofcr, well known in this city, has been removed from command at the post of Andersonville, Ga, we learn, for incapacity & inhumanity to prisoners.*

SAT SEP 10, 1864

Trustee's sale of *Greenbury's Point Farm*, 300 acs, on the Severn river, A A Co, Md; in the cause of Jas Iglehart, cmplnt, & M C Taylor & Thos Armstrong, adms of Daniel Dall & others, dfndnts. There is a large dwlg hse. -Frank H Stockett, Annapolis, Md; Edw Israel, 34 St Paul st, Balt, Md, trustee. [Creditors of Jas Iglehart, jr, dec'd are hereby notified.]

Mrd: on Sep 6, by Rev T R Howlett, Jos C Pugh, of Brooklyn, N Y, to Miss Mary Miller, d/o Jas Miller, of Wash City.

Rl estate for sale; authority from Wm P Bryan, The *Landham Farm*, 440 acs, in Piscataway Dist, PG Co, Md; with large dwlg, but out of repair. -Fendall Marbury, Saml B Hance, agents & attys for Wm P Bryan.

MON SEP 12, 1864

Died: in Gtwn, D C, on Sep 10, Geo Thomson, in his 73rd yr, for many years Chief Clerk of the Topog Bur, & late of the Engr Dept. Funeral from his late residence, 42 First st, today.

Deaths reported to the Navy Dept for the week ending Sep 10, 1864:
Alex G Post, surg's steward, yel fever, Jul 22, vessel U S S *Huntsville*.
John Reynolds, landsman, yel fever, Jul 15, do.
Geo Gregg, seaman, remit fever, Aug 24, Nav Hosp, Memphis.
Edwin Myers, seaman, remit fever, Aug 26, do.
Eugene Boydzeth, coalheaver, drowned, Aug 29, vessel U S S R R *Cuyler*.
Wm E Burke, seaman, gunshot wound, Aug 13, vessel U S S *Agawam*.
R Battles, landsman, bronchitis, Sep 3, Nav Asylum.
Patrick M Baker, landsman, consumption, Sep 2, Nav Hosp, N Y.
Wm Leslie, ord seaman, apoplexy, Jul 8, vessel U S S *Saratoga*.
Jos Day, landsman, consumption, Sep 3, vessel U S S *Yantic*.
John W B Smith, W r cook, dysentery, Jan 16, vessel U S S *Kennebec*.
D F Blake, landsman, consumption, Jun 10, vessel U S S *Wateree*.
A Muskajean, seaman, heart disease, Jun 11, vessel U S S *Niagara*.
Mortimer McCarty, 1st cl boy, entititis, Aug 30, vessel U S S *Ohio*.
Thos Brayson, 1st cl boy, erysipelas, Aug 31, Nav Hosp, Chelsea.
Roland Smith, ord seaman, pneumonia, Aug 31, do.
M Callahan, marine, gunshot wound, Aug 3, vessel U S S *Miami*.
Alex Middleton, q m, drowned, Aug 24, vessel U S S C P *Williams*.
John Williams, ship's cpl, gunshot wound, Aug 13, vessel U S S *Agawam*.
W Wilson, ord seaman, gunshot wound, do, do.
John Dunn, coalheaver, wound, Aug 6, vessel U S S *Brooklyn*.
Geo W Stride, seaman, remit fever, Aug 11, Nav Hosp, New Orleans.
Oliver T Simpson, carpenter, yel fever, Aug 15, vessel U S S *Portsmouth*.
Geo A Wooley, ord seaman, diarrhoea, Aug 27, Nav Hosp, Pensacola.
R Deans, 1st cl fireman, consumption, Aug 25, do.
Wm Ager, coalheaver, burns, Aug 6, do.
Lewis Lord, landsman, wound, Aug 6, do.
R Prentiss, Lt, gunshot wound, Aug 6, do.
Timothy Hynes, marine, gunshot wound, Aug 6, do.
Wm Thompson, ord seaman, gunshot wound, Aug 10, do.
Saml Vanavery, coalheaver, burns, Aug 6, do.
John Peacock, 1st cl fireman, burns, Aug 6, do.
R Condon, ord seaman, typhoid fever, Aug 16, Nav Hosp, New Orleans.
John T Cole, ord seaman, remit fever, Aug 15, do.
Geo Thompson, seaman, gunshot wound, Aug 26, vessel U S S *Brooklyn*.
John Miller, seaman, gunshot wound, Aug 25, do.
Isaac Young, ord seaman, gunshot wound, Aug 25, do.
R G White, seaman, do, do, do.
Jas Moore, ship's steward, dysentery, Aug 20, vessel U S S *Sebago*.
Chas E Milliken, ord seaman, gunshot wound, Aug 25, vessel U S S *Seminole*.

P D Young, 2nd ast engr, typhoid fever, Aug 15, vessel U S S *Gen Lyon*.
Wm Thomas, 2nd cl boy, drowned, Jul 17, vessel U S S *Springfield*.
H G Black, carp's mate, typhoid fever, Jul 30, do.
T W Roberts, actg ensign, debility, Aug 17, vessel U S S *Ozark*.
R Maran, seaman, drowned, Aug 13, vessel U S S *Naiad*.
Jas Tully, Capr's mate, drowned, Jul 1, vessel *Forest Rose*.
Geo P Vance, actg ensign, internal injury, Aug 17, vessel U S S *Peosta*.
M Wilson, 1st cl boy, measles, Aug 12, Hosp, Vicksburg.
Jack Windall, 1st cl boy, drowned, Aug 13, vessel U S S *Nymph*.
Jas E Thayer, marine, gunshot wound, Jul 1, vessel U S S *Mackinaw*.
John H Stotsenburgh, actg mstr's mate, yel fever, Jul 19, vessel U S S *Honomas*.
John B Carroll, marine, dysentery, Jul 12, vessel U S S *Somerset*.
R Coleman, landsman, remit fever, Jul 23, do.
John E Blythe, marine, remit fever, Jul 15, do.
John C Dugan, seaman, remit fever, Aug 31, Nav Hosp, Memphis.
Geo Allen, 1st cl boy, chronic diarrhoea, Aug 31, do.
Monroe Street, 1st cl boy, remit fever, Sep 2, do.
Samuel Robinson, landsman, consumption, Apr 8, vessel U S S *Saratoga*.

Dr R S McKaig, of Cumberland, Md, incarcerated in the military prison at Wheeling for the past several weeks, has been released & returned home.

Sale of farm at Crownsville, Md, near Annapolis: 345 acs: where Thos Tongue now resides. Located 2 miles from Round Bay; on Annapolis & Elkridge R R; with dwlg. -M Bannon, 32 St Paul st, Balt, Md.

Hon Albert S White, Judge of the U S Dist Crt of Ind, died on Sep 4, at his residence near Stockwell, Tippecanoe Co, of congestion of the lungs.

Dr T H Bagwell & his family have been sent from their homes in Portsmouth, Va, beyond the Federal lines, not to return during the war.

TUE SEP 13, 1864
Died: on Sep 12, in the 70th yr of his age, Geo Cochran. Funeral from the residence of his son, Geo W Cochran, 497 E st, on Wed.

Obit-died, on Sep 5, at the residence of her father, Mr A B Waller, near Newark, Dela, Mrs Maria G Kilby, aged 31 yrs, widow of the late Isaac H Kilby, of Eastport, Maine.

$100 reward, 4 horses stolen from the pasture of the late Dr B Lee, dec'd. -Wm Seton Belt, adm of Dr B Lee, Upper Marlboro, Md.

Orphans Crt of Wash Co, D C. 1-Case of Edwin Tastet, adm w a, of Nicholas Tastet, dec'd; settlement on Oct 1. -Z C Robbins, rg o/wills 2-Prsnl estate of John H Reily, late of Wash City, dec'd. -Susan W Reily

Dr Dougherty & Dr Stubblefield, arrested in Cumberland, Md, some time ago by order of Gen Hunter, & sent to Wheeling, were released on Tue by order of Gen Crook.

Melville A Bronson, of Fall river, Mass, died very suddenly on Mon. He applied some pain killer to a defective tooth, & fell forward on the floor & died almost instantly.

WED SEP 14, 1864

Died: in Wash City, on Sep 13, Eliz D Fuller, w/o Hon T J D Fuller, after a protracted illness, from disease of heart. Funeral from 355 K st, today.

Died: on Sep 13, after a short illness, Sarah E, w/o Jesse J Judge, aged 24 yrs. Funeral, Wed, from 746 N J av.

Wanted-a competent teacher in a private family, with two chldrn, residing on Seneca, Montg Co, Md. Address to Chas Vinson, 86 Pa av, Wash, D C.

Qrtrmstr Gen Meigs has been promoted to Brvt Maj Gen.

Ex-Gov Bigler has been nominated for Congress in Clearfield Co, Pa.

THU SEP 15, 1864

Died: Sep 8, at the residence of his uncle, in Montg Co, Md, Edw W Cropley, in his 35th yr.

The hotel-building lately erected by Mr John H Semmes, on La av, between 6th & 7th sts, has been leased by Mr Wm Sluyter, & will be conducted on the European plan.

Orphans Crt of Wash Co, D C. Case of Jas F Halliday, exc of Martha C Byrne, dec'd; settlement on Oct 8. -Z C Robbins, rg o/wills

Mr Park Benjamin died at his residence in N Y C on Sep 12, in his 55th yr, after a brief illness. He was born in 1809 at Demerara, in British Guiana, where his father was a merchant. Grad of Trinity College, Hartford, in 1829 & removed to N Y in 1837. -Evening Post

Wash Corp: 1-Mayor nominates for Fire Com'r John W Thompson vice Wm E Hutchinson, resigned: referred to the Cmte on the Fire Dept. 2-Communication from the Mayor, enclosing a communication from Wm L Hodge: referred to the Cmte on Improvements. 3-Ptn of Geo & Jos Miles, laborers at Northern Mkt, for an increase of pay: referred to the Cmte on Mkts. 4-Ptn of Louisa Noll, for return of a fine pd by her: referred to the Cmte on Claims. 5-Ptn of Ulysses Ward & others: with a bill for paving the carriage way of K st, from 7th to 8th st west: referred to the Cmte on Improvements. 6-Ptn of Jos A Kennedy: referred to the Cmte on Claims. 7-Communication from P H Donegan, making suggestions for improvement of the Canal: referred to the Cmte on Canals. 8-Ptn of Edmund F Brown: read 3 times & passed. 9-Cmte on Police: asked to be discharged from the ptn of Jos Schaffield: which was ordered.

Mrs Richd Wilson & her dght will receive, in addition to their day Scholars, 6 young ladies as boarders. Address-Mr R Wilson, 71 Centre st, Balt, Md.

FRI SEP 16, 1864

Died: at his residence *Woodley,* on Bayou Grosse Tete, in the parish of Point Coupee, La, on Aug 31, the Hon Henry Johnson, in the 82nd yr of his age. Gov Johnson was a native of Va, but removed to Louisiana in early life.

Died: on Sep 15, John J Geiger, sr, aged 73 yrs. Funeral from his late residence, Fourth st, above Mass av, on Sep 16.

Masonic notice-tribute to our late bro John Clapham, W M of Wash Navy Lodge.

Horse stolen from the farm of Dr E W Warfield, near Matthew's post ofc, Howard Co, Md, on Sep 13. Reward-$25. -E W Warfield

Supreme Crt of D C, in Equity #95. Michl Delany & wife, vs Thos J Villard, Richd H Delany, Thos S Delany, & Jonah Delany. Dfndnts failed to appear Nov 11, 1863 & are out of D C; heirs to appear by first Tue of Dec next. -Geo P Fisher, Justice; R J Meigs, clerk.

Accident at Ft Slocum, 4 miles north of Wash, on Wed; shells thought to be empty, exploded, wounding Henry Pouquette & B F Marshall-each had a leg amputated; Dennis Hare-severely wounded in the arm; all of the 1st N H Heavy Artl.

SAT SEP 17, 1864
Rev Geo Potts, D D, Pastor of the Univ Presby Chr, N Y, died on Sep 15, in his 64th year.

The Newark Adv announces the return home of the 8th Regt of N J, whose term of service has expired. It numbers 70 men & 5 ofcrs. 100 men, recruits & re-enlisted men, were left in the field & have formed into a btln known as the 8th N J Btln, & comprising 3 companies, in command of Capt Stelle. The regt left the state in Sept, 1861, 900 strong, & has since had 500 recruits, [making 1,400,] & now has only about 175 left.

Seventh Ward Exemption Fund Assoc: mbrshp is $100: John H Semmes, appt'd Treas. The object of this assoc is to procure substitutes for those drafted & held to service if the fund is sufficient, if not, to divide the amount equally amongst them. Assoc is confined to the residents of 7th Ward. Cmte:

Thos E Lloyd, chrmn-	Dr R C Roggon	John H Bird
Wm J Murtach	Wm S Davis	John R Elvans
C C Anderson	Wm J Foster	
F A Boswell	Wm Cammack	

Gen Martindale has again tendered his resignation on account of ill health. He has come up from the army.

MON SEP 19, 1864
Died: on Sep 18, Mrs M Bowen, relict of Thos Bowen, in her 81st yr. Funeral from the residence of her son-in-law, Wm T Duvall, 379 3rd st, Tue.

On Sep 14, Brig Gen Joshua B Howell, commanding a brig in Maj Gen A H Terry's div, was accidentally killed when his horse fell on him. Age about 65 yrs.

Deaths reported to the Navy Dept for the week ending Sep 17, 1864:
Jas Cowan, 1st cl boy, yel fever, Aug 1, vessel U S S *Roebuck.*
Chas Travis, do, do, Aug 3, do.
J W McLachlan, paymstr steward, yel fever, Aug 4, do.
Rd McKeon, landsman, yel fever, Aug 14, do.
Geo S Engles, landsman, yel fever, Aug 13, do.
T W Twining, landsman, do, do, do.
Luther Nickerson, a mast cmdg, yel fev, Aug 15, vessel U S S *J S Chambers.*
Thos J McCann, pay steward, pay steward, yel fever, Aug 5, do.
Hy E Hopkinson, an ensign, yel fever, Aug 13, do.
Horace J Chase, yeoman, yel fever, Aug 10, do.
Hy McKenzie, gunner's mate, yel fever, Aug 12, do.

Jos Steffins, q m, yel fever, Aug 11, do.
Michl Gleason, capt of hold, yel fever, Aug 12, do.
Thos Hardin, seaman, yel fever, Aug 5, do.
Jas Slavin, ord seaman, yel fever, Aug 14, do.
Hiram Cripps, ord seaman, yel fever, Aug 11, do.
Jos Balkyard, landsman, yel fever, Aug 10, do.
Harvey S Simmons, landsman, yel fever, Aug 10, do.
Jos McClosky, 1st cl boy, yel fever, Aug 6, do.
Alex Watts, a m mate, yel fever, Aug 11, do.
Wm Wilkerson, landsman, yel fever, Aug 9, do.
J F Van Nert or Nett, a m mate, drowned, Aug 18, do.
John Parrish, landsman, consumption, Aug 22, Nav Hosp, Chelsea.
Rt Norce, steamer, gunshot wound, Aug 22, vessel U S S *Pembina*.
Geo R Mann, a a surg, nervous debility, Aug 20, vessel U S S *Pocahontas*.
Rd Walsh, coalheaver, drowned, Jul 25, vessel U S S *Atlanta*.
Pat Respen, coalheaver, dysentery, Jun 24, vessel U S S *Cambridge*.
Jas Benson, seaman, dysentery, Aug 30, vessel U S S *J Adams*.
John H Carroll, surg's steward, typhoid fever, Aug 25, vessel U S S *Minnesota*.
Bexton Somers, seaman, dysentery, Aug 17, do.
John Morrow, landsman, consumption, Aug 21, do.
John S Kearkey, landsman, drowned, Aug 28, vessel U S S *Manhattan*.
John H Cox, actg ensign, yel fever, Aug 31, vessel U S S *Dale*.
Geo White, seaman, injury from fall, Sep 13, vessel U S S *North Carolina*.
Jas R Hayles, landsman, dysentery, Sep 6, Nav Hosp, Norfolk.
Phil C Kennedy, capt marines, consumption, Aug 31, Ellicott's Mills.
Geo Schultz, Chief engr, yel fever, Aug 19, Key West.
Lawrence Jones, landsman, typhoid fever, Aug 18, vessel U S S *Daffodil*.
Paris Scott, landsman, caries, Aug 18, vessel U S S *Jno Adams*.
Peter Santiago, W r steward, diarrhoea, Aug 18, vessel U S S *Home*.
Geo Scott, landsman, drowned, Sep 7, vessel U S S *Tulip*.
Jas Seddons, 3rd cl boy, chronic diarrhoea, Sep 6, Nav Hosp, Memphis.
John Campbell, landsman, typhoid fever, Sep 14, Nav Hosp, Wash.
Chas Anderson, landsman, consumption, Sep 15, Nav Asylum.
Henry Baker, seaman, paralysis, Jun 13, vessel U S S *Cyane*.
Jeremiah Sills, boy, unknown, Jun 3, vessel U S S *Water Witch*.
Thos J Kinnard, landsman, dis of heart, Jul 23, vessel U S S *Wabash*.
Geo Washington, landsman, dropsy, Aug 10, do.
Robt Gibson, landsman, dis of lungs, Aug 10, do.
Wm May, landsman, dis of brain, Aug 18, do.
Frs M Swift, mstr at arms, dis of brain, Aug 20, do.
Geo Patterson, ord seaman, fracture, Aug 3, do.
Boyle Sturt, 3rd cl boy, pleurisy, Juns 15, vessel U S S *Mahaska*.
Pat Dougherty, 2nd cl fireman, typhoid fever, Jul 25, vessel U S S *South Carolina*.

Four great grandsons of Cmdor Jas Nicholson, of Rev Navy, all who bear his name, have
entered the Union army as privates. On srv'd under Rosecrans, in Western Va, where he
died; another srv'd on the Potomac & in S C-he died on Folly Island; the 3rd was in hopeless
captivity at Richmond & Camp Sumter, Ga-his fate is unknown; the 4th just entered the 5th
Pa Artl, Col Gallupe, ordered to Wash. All are natives of Fayette Co, Pa.

Orphans Crt of Wash Co, D C. 1-Case of Wm H Watson, adm of Andrew J Watson, dec'd; settlement on Oct 8. 2-Case of John L Edwards, exc of Mary E C Edwards, dec'd; settlement on Sep 8. -Z C Robbins, rg o/wills

TUE SEP 20, 1864
Obit-died at Wheeling, Va, on Jul 11 last, Jos Caldwell, aged 86 yrs.

Died: in Cumberland, Md, on Sep 15, Lucy Norville, aged 17 mos, d/o Richd H & Mary R Jones, & grand-dght of Wm Hunter, of Dept of State.

Died: on Sep 19, Mrs Julia Burgevine, aged 66 yrs. Funeral from St Patrick's Chr, F st, Tue.

Country residence for sale, *Pleasant View Seminary*, lately occupied by Miss Mary Keech as a school, at Hyattsville, Md. -Henry T Scott, 48 Broadway, N Y

Orphans Crt of Wash Co, D C. 1-Case of Sophie Vierbuchen, admx of John Vierbuchen, dec'd; settlement on Oct 4. 2-Case of Rosina Huhn, admx of Michael Huhn, dec'd; settlement on Oct 8. -Z C Robbins

The Hagerstown, Md, mail states that near Tilghmantown, in that county, on Sep 10, the 9 & 11 yr old sons of Jos Palmer were killed by the accidental discharge of a rifle. The oldest was killed instantly, the younger survived 48 hours in great pain.

Mr Frank Russell Reading, convicted by court martial for treasonable language in D C, fell back on his claim as a British subject. He has been in this country for 10 yrs, most of the time in the employ of the Gov't. Lord Lyons decided not to interpose protection. He has been sentenced to hard labor at Dry Tortugas for 5 yrs. Jas H Veatch, of Gtwn, is sent to the same place.

WED SEP 21, 1864
Mrd: on Sep 20, by Rev Dr Gray, Louis C Wilson, of Raleigh, N C, to Louisa Eliz Kent, of Alexandria, Va.

Orphans Crt of Wash Co, D C. 1-Case of Robt M Johnson, adm of Andrew Minatree, dec'd; settlement on Oct 12. -Z C Robbins, rg o/wills 2-Prsnl estate of Wm D Porter, late of N Y C, dec'd. -Jos H Bradley, jr, W H Clagett, adms. [N Y World will please copy.]

Chancery sale, Equity #181; Lloyd W Williams, cmplnt, & Arthur Nelson & others, dfndnts; parts of lot 15 & 17 in sq 290, Wash, D C. John C Kennedy, trustee -Jas C McGuire & Co, aucts

Harper's Ferry, Sep 19. Hon Edwin M Stanton, Sec of War: Sheridan moved on the enemy this morning at daylight. Soon after the movement commenced heavy & continued firing was board for 2 hours, then ceased, apparently receding, & was resumed about 9 o'clock, & has continued to this hour, 12 M, apparently in the vicinity of Bunker Hill. –John D Stevenson, Brig Gen

Richmond Enq says: rumor that Gen John H Winder had been removed from command at Andersonville, Ga, is entirely without foundation.

Mr Abraham Wakeman, postmstr at N Y, has been appt'd surveyor of that port, & to begin on Oct 1. Mr Jas Kelley appt'd postmstr in his stead.

The income of the 4 Rothschilds of Europe is est'd at nine millions a year, or a $1,000 an hour.

THU SEP 22, 1864

Died: in Wash City, on Sep 18, Harry Clark, y/c/o Edw M & Jane S Clark.

Supreme Crt of D C, in Equity #58. Wm G Deale vs Wm B Mickum, Sarah G Mickum, Henry N Lansdale, Walter Lenox. Dfndnts not found. The dfndnts to appear by 1st Tue of Dec next, otherwise the bill may be taken for confessed. -R J Meigs, clerk

Information wanted of Matilda Wetherall, colored, d/o Mrs Salie Colman, & half sister of Robt H Colman. She hailed from Red Bank, Shenandoah Co, Va. -Robt H Colman, Poughkeepsie, N Y

The undersigned have associated themselves with Geo T Smith & Co, Grocery, Wine & Liquor business, 511 7th st, Wash, D C. -Thos W Steuart, John T Foster, Geo T Smith.

Harper's Ferry, Va, Sep 20. We have just received the body of Gen David Russell, commanding a division of the 6th army corps. It will be sent to N Y. The rebels lost Gens Rhodes & Wharton. -John D Stevenson, Brig Gen

Harpers' Ferry, Sep 20. Hon Edwin M Stanton: The body of Gen Russell will be embalmed & forwarded to N Y. Gen McIntosh, with his leg amputated, has just come in, & is in good spirits.

Wash Corp: 1-Ptn of N Phelan & others with a bill to pave & curb front of sq 759: passed. 2-Ptn from Lewis Johnson, Jas A Wise, & others, in relation to widen the alley in sq 429: referred to the Cmte on Improvements. 3-Ptn from Moses Kelly, the Cashier of the Bank of Metropolis, with a bill authorizing the Collector of Taxes to correct the assessment on the stock of said Bank: referred to the Cmte on Finance. 4-Cmte on Police: reported favorably on the Mayor's nomination of Jas Cull for police magistrate of ward 6: confirmed. 5-Bill read for the relief of Emil S Frederick. 6-Cmte on Canals: communication from Geo W Frankland: to be sent to the Mayor.
Rhodes, Gen Wharton, Gen Gordon, & Gen Ramseur. -Jno D Stevenson, Brig Gen

Harper's Ferry, Sep 21: Rebel generals killed & wounded is correct: Gen Rhodes, Ramseur, Gordon, Terry, Goodwin, Bradley Johnson, & Fitz Lee. Prisoners will approximate 5,000. J D Stevenson, Brig Gen [Another paragraph below this one: Gens Rhodes, Wharton, Bradley T Johnson, Gordon, York, & Goodwin, the 2 first of whom were killed & the others badly wounded. We have captured 2,500 prisoners, 9 battle flags, representing 9 different regt organizations, & 5 pieces of artl, with caissons. Spec correspondence of the Balt American. Headqrtrs Middle Military Div, Winchester, Sep 19, 1864.] More information on the same: among the killed & wounded: Col Babcock, 75th N Y, wounded in the thigh. Col Ebright, 12th Ohio, 3rd div, 6th Corps, killed. Capt Wright, of Gen Devon's staff, killed. Capt Robenbaugh, 2nd U S Cavalry, wounded in the arm. Capt McGueaton, 2nd U S Cavalry, Aid de Camp to Gen Merritt, killed. Maj Vandenburg, 14th N J, 3rd div, 6th corps, killed. Maj Dillingham, 10th Vt, 3rd div, 6th corps, killed. Lt Col Brewer, 7th Mich Cavalry, killed. Lt Jackson, 1st Mich Cavalry, arm shot off. Lts Mathews & John Allen, 1st Michigan Cavalry, killed. The Michigan Brig, Gen Custer's command, claim the honor of killing Gen Rhodes during the fierce conflict which ensued when they charged a portion of his division.

Harper's Ferry, Sep 20. Hon E M Stanton, Sec of War: despatch from Gen Sheridan: we fought Early from daylight till between 6 & 7 p m: drove him thru Winchester, & beyond the town. We captured 2,500 to 3,000 prisoners, 5 pieces of artl, 9 battle-flags, & all the rebel wounded & dead. Their wounded in Winchester amount to some 3,000. We lost in killed, Gen David Russell, commanding a div of the 6th army corps, & wounded Gens Chapman, McIntosh & Upton. The rebels lost in killed the following Gen ofcrs: Gen Rhodes, Gen Wharton, Gen Gordon, & Gen Ramseur. –Jno D Stevenson, Brig Gen

Univ of Mich-Med Dept: located at Ann Arbor: on Oct 1 next will enter upon its 13th course of annual lectures. –S H Douglass, Dean of the Faculty

FRI SEP 23, 1864
The paper hangers of Wash agree that they will have fixed prices for their work, viz: satin paper-.35; gilt paper-.40; borders & moulding-.60:

John Alexander	Francis Willner	Kidwell & Henderson
John Markriter	L F Clark	Bishop & Alexander
L A Miners	Geo Willner	Douglas Moore
Thos Riffle	Wm Hounschild	
L J Rothrock	Kaufman & Schaffer	

In the case of Lt Edgerly, he was dismissed from the army, without trial, by Mr Lincoln's order, for distributing Democratic tickets. Are all the ofcrs & sldrs to be dismissed who do the same thing this time? Mr Lincoln will have to issue a call for a new army. [Order, Mar 13, 1863: Lt A G Edgerly, 4th N H vols, dismissed the svc of the U S for circulating copperhead tickets, & doing all in his power to promote the success of the rebel cause in his state. Sec of War-L Thomas, Adj Gen]

Supreme Crt of Wash Co, D C. 1-Equity #138. Robt F Allen & Edwin Harris & Augusta, his wife, vs Letitia Allen, Letitia B Allen, & Maria L Allen. Parties & trustees to meet on Oct 4, City Hall, Wash, D C. -W Redin, auditor 2-Equity #217. Jos H Skinner & Sarah A, his wife, Robt M Brown & Josephine S, his wife, & Geo L Arnold & C M, his wife, vs John L Hall. Parties named, the trustee, & John W Maury, guardian ad litem of John L Hall, to meet in City Hall, Wash, on Oct 3.
-W Redin, auditor 3-Equity #109. Alexander B Hagner & Daniel R Hagner, excs, vs Alexander Randall & others heirs of Peter Hagner. Parties to meet at City Hall, Wash, D C, on Oct 5; regarding-building an ofc on part of lot 15 in sq 141, & its allowance to the excs of Mrs Hagner out of the proceeds of the estate of Peter Hagner. -W Redin, auditor

Died: on Sep 22, Mary Lee, infant d/o D H & Martha E Tebbs, aged 5 months.

Lt Peel, 40th N Y, was shot thru the head while looking thru an embrasure in one of our forts. He was instantly killed. –Headqrtrs Army of Potomac, Sep 20

SAT SEP 24, 1864
Miss Lillie Bennett will give instruction in music, at her residence, 529 H st, Wash.

Mr Benj F Wilkins, Chief clerk of the stamp division of the Gen P O, was arrested on Tue last, on charge of abstracting postage stamps to his own use. Geo W Alexander, formerly a clerk in the Dept, was also arrested in same case.

Mr & Mrs Barney Williams commence an engagement on Mon next, the 26th, at Grover's theatre.

Baltic Fire Ins Co: Ofcs: 650 Broadway & 54 Wall st, N Y: cash capital-$200,000. Dirs:

Wm S Corwin	John H James	Wm Tilden
Robt Dunlap	Russell Crane	Amos C Littell
Edw C Robinson	Conrad Braker, jr	Chas G Cornell
Henry P Degraff	Nathan Clark	Wm P David
Chas Hudson	Walter W Price	Patrick Dickie
John W Sageman	Henry Silberhorn	Tristam Alien
Jas W Trask	Albert Webb	Richd F Carman
John S Martin	Jacob Fink	R M Vail
Ebenezer H Pray	John Hayward	Wm S Corwin, Pres
Pearson S Halstead	Harford B Kirk	Wm H Kipp, Sec
Thos McLelland	J H Johnson	

Rev W H Channing will preach in the Unitarian Chr tomorrow at 11 a m.

Capt Ellis, Actg Inspec Gen of Gen Torbert's division of cavalry, reached here from the front in the Valley, bringing 8 rebel battle & regimental flags captured by that division in the engagement of Mon last. 6 of the men bearing them were the actual captors: Geo Reynolds, Co I, 6th N Y cavalry; Patrick McEnmore, 6th N Y cavalry; Color Cpl Chester B Bowen, Co I, N Y dragoons; Geo E Meach, 56th N Y cavalry; Gabriel Cole, Co I 5th Mich cavalry; Andrew J Lorish, regimental commissary Sgt 1st N Y cavalry.

MON SEP 26, 1864

Orphans Crt of Wash Co, D C. Prsnl estate of Isaac Beers, late of Wash Co, dec'd.
-Isaac Beers, jr, B F Beers

Deaths reported to the Navy Dept for the week ending Sep 24, 1864:
Jas J Pendu, boy, inflam of brain, Sep 12, Nav Hosp, N Y.
Chr Hight, landsman, consumption, Sep 12, do.
Jas Harris, ord seaman, drowned, Sep 7, vessel U S S Potomska.
Peter Blaku, ord seaman, drowned, Sep 14, vessel U S S Ohio.
Fra Brier or Prier, ord seaman, fracture, Aug 24, Nav Hosp, Pensacola
Wm J Smith, marine, diarrhoea, Aug 29, do.
Geo Mensing, ord seaman, fever, Aug 25, do.
Wm Elden, seaman, wound, Aug 31, do.
Jas Finnie, landsman, disease of bowels, Sep 22, vessel U S S Gramus.
L M Reese, actg Ast Surg, rheumatic fever, Sep 1, vessel U S S Argosy.
John Dunlop, actg ast mate, wound, Jun 24, vessel U S S Naumkeag.
Chas Johnson, ord seaman, consumption, Aug 5, vessel U S S Niagara.
Jas Ellis, ord seaman, consumption, Jul 30, do.
Calvin Estis, 1st cl fireman, peritoritis, Sept 17, Nav Hosp, Norfolk.
Thos Hodge, blank, pneumonia, Sep 10, vessel U S S Volunteer.
Eben Field, landsman, typhoid fever, Aug 29, vessel U S S Roebuck.
Daniel Stone, actg mstr's mate, typhoid fever, Aug 30, vessel U S S Roebuck.
Owen Daniels, landsman, remit fever, Aug 14, vessel U S S Adelia.
John Thomas, coxswain, blank, Sep 8, vessel U S S Michigan.
Terence Devlin, marine, typhoid fever, Sep 14, vessel U S S New Ironsides.
Henry Brown, seaman, inflam of lungs, Sep 2, vessel U S S Kittatiny.
Chas Horton, 1st cl boy, dysentery, Aug 15, vessel U S S Honeysuckle.

Henry Jenkins, 1st cl boy, pneumonia, Sep 5, Key West.
Daniel Black, ord seaman, inter fever, Sep 8, Nav Hosp, Pensacola.
Ed Collins, 2nd cl fireman, burns, Aug 20, do.
Peter Pitts, landsman, wound, Aug 29, do.
Ed Riley, landsman, dis of liver, Sep 2, vessel U S S *Circassian*.
Wm Voglesong, ord seaman, drowned, Aug 13, vessel U S S *Naiad*.
Lewis Ecorn, ord seaman, dysentery, Sep 7, vessel U S S *Port Royal*.

Died: on Sep 25, Benj Williamson, of Scotland, but for the last 46 years a resident of Wash City, in his 72nd yr. Funeral from his late residence, 400 11th st, Tue.

Died: at some time unknown, during the past 6 months, Maj H C Grout, paymstr U S Army. [Corr of Sep 28-Death of Maj H C Grout was a hoax.]

Mr Harrrison H Dodd, lately arrested in Indiana for alleged disloyalty & conspiracy against the Gov't of the U S, he being, it is said, the Chief ofcr of a secret order known as the "Sons of Liberty" was arraigned before a military commision at Ind on Thu last. Cnsl protested he was not in the military or naval svc of the U S. Judge Advocate's answer to the protestate to be presented.

TUE SEP 27, 1864
Died: on Sep 26, Cath A Whelan, w/o Thos Feran, of Wash City. Remains will be removed to Phil for interment.

Died: at Rosedale, D C, Matilda Devereux, d/o Geo F & Maria D Green, aged 9 months.

Orphans Crt of Wash Co, D C. Prsnl estate of Benj Evans, late of Wash City, dec'd. -Geo W Harvey

Supreme Crt of D C. 1-Equity #215. Murray & Semmes vs Cornelius J Desmond, Thos & Mary Ratcliff & Wm & Mary Keithly. Statement of the account of Mary Desmond, dec'd; City Hall, Oct 6. -W Redin, auditor 2-Equity #180. Francis P Richards, vs Geo S S & John R Richards, Fitzhugh Coyle, & McGuire & Fisher. Parties & Lucian Peyton, guardian ad litem, to meet on Oct 7 at City Hall, Wash. -W Redin, auditor

Hon R W Wells died on Thu at the residence of his son-in-law, in Bowling Green, Ky.

Exchanged prisoners: Ft Monroe, Sept 26. The flag of truce steamer *New York* arrived here from Varina, on the James River, en route for Annapolis, with 850 Union prisoners just released from southern prisons. Among them are the following ofcrs: Brig Gen W J Bartlett, Lt J J Barclay, 11th Pa; Lt B D Hemming, 3rd Pa; Capt W H Watkins, do; Capt G Perry, 1st N Y; Lt E G Griswold, 1st Vt; Capt McDoran, 155th N Y; Capt J McKean, 5th N Y; Capt C E Chase, 1st D C Cavalry; Lt S R Sage, 144th Ohio; Lt W F Doughty, 2nd Pa; Adj A B Capron, 111th N Y; Lt J T Connally, Lt C W Ostrander, 122nd N Y; Capt A J Hough, 9th N H; Capt J M Tripple, 39th N Y; Lt Fisher, 39th N Y; Lt J H Cane, 1st Conn; Lt N D Meacham, 9th Ohio; C Hurlbut, Lt M Schmittner, 28th Ohio; Lt S Brennemann, 2nd Pa; Lt E G Abee, 36th Wisc; Lt M C Cowdery, 2nd Ohio; Lt R S Dome, 5th N H; Lt R S King, 7th Ind; Lt G K Brady, 14th U S Infty; Lt J E Shefard, 9th Maine; Capt H Lee, 14th Conn.

Died: on Sep 26, of consumption, Capt H W Martin, in his 35th yr. Funeral on Wed from his late residence, 8th & D sts.

Died: on Sep 26, after a lingering illness, of consumption, Thos P Wilson, jr, in his 23rd yr. Body to be taken to Phil from the residence of his father, Thos P Wilson, sr, 8th & D st.

WED SEP 28, 1864
Died: on Sep 26, Mrs Eliz A Foulkes, consort of the late John E Foulkes, & d/o the late Wm Lambel, in her 56th yr. Funeral from the residence of her bro-in-law, A F Kimmell, 361 C st, Thu.

Report from Chattanooga that Gen Stoneman is to be exchanged for the rebel Gen Goven, lately captured at Jonesboro.

Died: after a short but painful illness, on Sep 27, Dr John E Daly, aged 40 yrs. Funeral from his late residence, 291 B st, Thu.

Died: in Wash City, on Sep 27, after a protracted illness, Mr Cath Hodges, widow of the late Benj Hodges, of PG Co, Md, in her 78th yr. Funeral from the residence of her son, Geo W Hodges, 426 I st, Thu.

Supreme Crt of D C. 1-Equity #145. Robt Coltman, Chas T Smith & Mary F, his wife, & John W Moore & Sarah B, his wife, vs Jas Adams, Rebecca Coltman, sr & jr, & the Corp of Wash. Parties named & the guardian ad litem of the minor dfndnt, to meet at City Hall, on Oct 8, rg estate of the late Chas L Coltman. -W Redin, auditor 2-Equity #146. Geo W Miller et al, vs Ellen Miller et al.

Account of sales made by the trustees of the estate of the late Chas Miller, of the value of the dower of his widow, at City Hall, on Oct 19. -W Redin, auditor 3-Equity #1606. Jane M McCrabb vs Joshua Humphreys. Dfndnt did not appear; ordered to appear by the 1st Tue of Dec. -D K Cartter, Chief Jstc

THU SEP 29, 1864
Supreme Crt of D C, in Equity #305. Henry Crow, Thos Crow, & Sarah Harris, vs Jas, Chas, & Wm Matthews, & Edw Huist & Mary Ann his wife. Regarding-sale of late estate of Jas Redman, dec'd, for distribution among his heirs, some of the original parties have died; title is solely vested in the cmplnts & dfndnts as his heirs. Dfndnts reside out of this Dist. -R J Meigs, clerk

Wash Corp: 1-Communication from M J Wildheimer: laid on the table. 2-Ptn from W W Bien & B S Brown: referred to the Cmte on Police. 3-Ptn of C Boyle & others: referred to the Cmte on Drainage & Distribution of Water. 4-Ptn of Henry Kleiber for pay for extra svcs: referred to the Cmte on Claims.

FRI SEP 30, 1864
Wash City Orphan Asylum: Brd of Mgrs:

Mrs S P Lee	Mrs J W Maury	Mrs G S Gideon
Mrs Dr Brown	Mrs J F Harkness	Mrs E Hall
Mrs Wm M Merrick	Mrs Col Jacob Zeilin	Mrs E Green
Mrs Mullikin	Mrs Dr Washington	Mrs Dr Stone
Mrs Temple	Mrs M A Gilliss	Mrs A E Hasler
Mrs S Coleman	Mrs S P Hill	

Died: on Sep 29, Christian G Klopfer, in his 79th yr; native of Saxony, but a resident of the country for 58 yrs, the last 40 spent in Wash City. Funeral from his late residence, 521 K st, Sat. [Columbia Topographical Soc notice-Oct 7.]

Supreme Crt of D C, in Equity #146. Geo W Miller vs Ellen Miller et al. Ratify sales made by trustees. -R J Meigs, clerk

SAT OCT 1, 1864
Died: on Sep 30, Jos Warner, y/c/o John B & Mary E Wiltberger. Funeral from their residence, near Rock Crk Chr, Sat.

Three chldrn, Wm, age 2 yrs, John aged 4 yrs, & an 11 yr old, of Casper Snyder, living near Fremont st, Balt city, ate weeds growing in a lot & were poisoned. Wm & John died on Wed. The eldest is alive in precarious condition. -Sun

Died: in Calif, on Jul 29 last, Clement Cox, formerly of Gtwn, in his 34th yr.

Supreme Crt of D C, in Equity #228. Vincent M Burch vs Frederick A Burch, et al. Thos Burch, late of PG Co, Md, died in Apr, 1847, seized of rl estate in Wash Co, D C. He left as his heirs: Thos W Burch, Fred'k A Burch, Eliz Ann, w/o Rich I Jones, Olivia, w/o Saml F Clark, & Jas Albert Burch, chldrn of his first wife, & the cmplnt, Vincent M Burch, & others, who have since died intestate & without issue, chldrn by his 2nd wife, & legal title descended to said heirs, subject to the trusts of the will of said Thos Burch; that Richd I Jones has since dec'd, & his widow, Eliz Ann, mrd with Jas W Drane,. & has since dec'd, leaving as her heirs-Richd L, Ann E, Thos W, & Mary O Drane; Olivia Clark has since dec'd, leaving her son Jas E Clark, her sole heir; Jas Albert Burch has dec'd, leaving his chldrn, Mary E, Sarah F, & Adelaide Burch, his heirs. Under the will of Thos Burch, Mrs Eliz Ferrall selected for her use lot 20 in sq 517. Fred'k A Burch is a non-resident & cannot be found within the jurisdiction of this crt. -R J Meigs, clerk

The funeral of the late Cmdor Conover took place yesterday, at Christ Chr, So Amboy, N J. Bishop Odenheimer, of the N J diocese, & Rev Mr Burton, rector of the Chr, officiated. Choir was under direction of Dr Cutler. Cmdor was 73 years old at the time of his death. He had long been in the U S Navy, his last cruise was off the coast of Africa, with the squadron which returned home in 1860. -N Y Post

MON OCT 3, 1864
Deaths reported to the Navy Dept for the week ending Oct 1, 1864:
Wm H Goldsmith, seaman, remit fever, Sep 15, Nav Hosp, Memphis.
John Morrisy, ord seaman, dysentery, Sep 16, do
Jas N Reynolds, 2nd cl fireman, diarrhoea, Sep 20, vessel U S S *Ft Morgan*.
Randall Tibbetts, landsman, measles, Sep 21, Nav Hosp, Chelsea.
Chas Williams, seaman, pneumonia, Sep 19, do.
Jas Had, landsman, debility, Sep 8, Nav Asylum.
Alexander Fivey, landsman, wounds, Aug 22, Nav Hosp, Pensacola.
John W Burns, seaman, wounds, Sep 9, do.
Wm Ruffin, landsman, drowned, Aug 23, vessel U S S *Stepping Stones.*
Jas J Matthews, capt foretop, peritorilis, Sep 12, vessel U S S *St Marys*
Edw Ward, ord seaman, chronic diarrhoea, Sep 22, Nav Hosp, N Y.
J A Wilcox, landsman, consumprion, Sep 23, do.
Michael McCune, 2nd cl fireman, consumption, Sep 27, vessel U S S *Ft Morgan.*
Saml C Smith, landsman, typhoid fever, Sep 27, do.

Wm Allen, ord seaman, pneumonia, Sep 22, Nav Hosp, Chelsea.

John F E West, landsman, measles, Sep 28, do.

Edw Scattergood, 2nd ast engr, ersysipiles, Sep 20, vessel U S S *Maratuza*.

John Cosgrove, seaman, drowned, Aug 29, vessel U S S *Vicksburg*.

C Mercer, landsman, dysentery, Sep 19, vessel U S S *New Hampshire*.

Mrd: on Oct 1, by Rev B H Nadal, Mr Chas L Brown to Miss Kate E Sherwood, y/d/o Saml Sherwood, of Wash City.

Died: on Sep 22, of consumption, at the residence of Jas Williams, near Laytonsville, Montg Co, Md, Chas Stewart Holden, of N Y C, in his 33rd yr.

Hon Thos F Marshall died Sep 22, at his residence, near Versailles, Woodford Co, Ky, aged about 64 yrs.

TUE OCT 4, 1864

Died: at Ft Leavenworth, Kansas, on Sep 25, Mary E, w/o Lt Jas A Snyder, U S Army, & d/o E A Aliason, of Gtwn, D C.

Died: on Oct 2, Marion Eliz, w/o Thos H Maddox, & d/o the late Noah Fletcher. Funeral from 466 E st, today.

Died: on Oct 1, Dr Robt Mayo, in his 81st yr.

Information wanted of Mary R Ward, who resided in Wash City about 20 years ago, by her bro. Address-G W Ward, Frankfort, Ky.

Confiscation-the prop of Hugh Latham, M Y Partlow, J Lewis Evans, J T Nalls, Danl F Hooe, R R Fowle, W G Cazenove, Wm T Early, & J H McVeigh, hses & lots in this place, to be sold on Oct 22. Also C A Baldwin & Co's machinery for manufacturing shoes to be sold. -Alex Gaz

WED OCT 5, 1864

Mrd: on Oct 3, at the residence of the bride's father, by Rev J A McCauley, Mark R Woodward to Martha J Pursell, both of Wash City.

Mrd: on Sep 22, at Christ Chr, by Rev A P Stryker, Bayney Hart, of Wash, & Josephine A, y/d/o the late Maj Jos C Cockey, of Balt, Md.

Supreme Crt of D C, Equity #80. Riggs & Co & others, vs Thos Smith's heirs, widow & admx. Ratify sale by W Redin, trustee, of lots 30 thru 35 in sq 182, in Wash, to F S Wilson, for $1,427.76; and lot 36 in sq 182, to Jacob Frank, for $580.72. -Geo P Fisher, Jus S C, D C

Supreme Crt of D C. Cox & Morgan, vs Susan, Thos H, & Anne M C Walker, widow & heirs of Wm Walker. Trustees & guardian ad litem, to appear at City Hall on Oct 27. -W Redin, auditor

For rent-Franklin Hse, 8th & D sts, Wash. -P Kavanagh, 17 N High st, Balt, Md. Or-Dr Wm Gunton, Wash City, D C.

Orphans Crt of Wash Co, D C. 1-Case of Ann Moran, excx of David Moran, dec'd; settlement on Oct 25. -Z C Robbins, rg o/wills 2-Prsnl estate of Washington Berry, late of Wash Co, dec'd. -Thos W Berry, adm d b n c t a, 82 W Fayette st, Balt, Md.

The English mails bring news of the death of Capt Speke, African explorer, suddenly on Sep 15 by the accidental discharge of his own gun, while shooting near Corsham, Wilts. His age was 38 yrs.

John S Tyson, sr, mbr of the Balt bar, died at his residence, *Mt Ida*, Ellicott's Mills on Oct 3, aged 67 yrs. Soon after his return from Wash, on Sat last, he was suddenly taken ill.

THU OCT 6, 1864
Died: in Forestville, PG Co, Md, on Sep 27, Mary Eleanor, only d/o Dr H W & Lavinia T Brent, aged 16 months & 20 days.

Died: on Oct 5, Dr Geo M Dale, aged 33 yrs. Funeral from Chr of the Ascension, H st, today. Obit-A fellow ctzn of Wash; a kind hsbnd, father, & friend.

Two more battle flags captured in the Valley at Fisher's Hill, by Pvt Geo G Moore, Co D, 11 West Va Volunteers, & by Pvt John Creed, Co D, 23rd Ill.

Died: on Oct 5, Mr Thos Y Robinson, of the Q M Dept, aged 24 yrs, s/o John G Robinson. Funeral from the residence of his father, 439 7th st, Fri.

Orphans Crt of Wash Co, D C. Prsnl estate of Thos P Wilson, late of Wash Co, dec'd. -Jno D McPherson, adm

Killed in the battle of the Wilderness, May 5, Col David T Jenkins, of Vernon, Oneida Co, N Y.

The father of Col Jenkins, the late J Whipple Jenkins, died in Vernon in 1852.

J S Baldwin, late Chief Justice of the Supreme Crt of Calif, died on Sep 30th.

David F Jamison, Pres of the S C Convention, which adopted the ord of secession, died on Sep 14.

FRI OCT 7, 1864
Died: on Oct 5, Eliz A, d/o the late Maj Geo W Walker. Funeral from the residence of her mother, near Rock Creek Chr, Fri.

Tailors' Soc of Wash, viz: Jos Thompson, Christian Bode, Mr Van Doran, Edw Drew, Mr Linney, Messrs Duval & Bro, Mr Wm Stampood, & Mr Judd. -John Irving, sec

Fire in Gtwn, D C, consumed the ware hse on Water st, property of Wm H Edes. It spread rapidly to the stables of J H Ridgway; & the cooper shop of J H Ridgway was partially consumed.

SAT OCT 8, 1864
If Dr Chas H Laub is in Wash City, a friend most earnestly desires to see him. Information to be given at the ofc of the Ntl Intell.

Died: after a long & severe illness, in Wash City, on Oct 6, aged 61 years & 4 mos, Mr A G Herold, formerly of Balt, Md, but for the last 43 years a resident of Wash. Funeral from his late residence, 636 8th st. Mbrs of I O O F, Masonic Fraternity, & Navy Yard Beneficial Soc are invited.

Lt John R Meigs, of the Engr Corps, & only s/o Brvt Maj Gen Meigs, Q M Gen, was killed by bushwhackers on Monday last, while making a military survey, in the Shenandoah Valley. His body has arrived in Wash for sepulture.

Supreme Crt of D C, in Equity #73. Cath Garity, vs Bridget Garity, Mary Kelly, Jas Kelly, & Peter B Garity. Subpoena to dfndnts to appear, returned-not found. Dfndnts to appear on or before 1st Tue of Mar, 1865. -R J Meigs, clerk

Wm Kester, an errand boy, has robbed merchants in Cincinnati, Ohio, of $10,000, by unlocking post office boxes. $7,000 was recovered.

Supreme Crt of D C, in Equity #274. Jas Green, & others, vs John Magee, Hugh Magee, & Thos Magee. Subpoena to dfndnts to appear, returned-*not found*. Same to appear by 1st Tue in Mar 1865. -R J Meigs, clerk

MON OCT 10, 1864

Died: on Oct 8, in her 85th yr, Mary Ellis, wid/o Saml B Ellis. Funeral from the residence of her son, Wm M Ellis, 730 N J av, today.

Died: on Oct 9, Emma Beverley Stark, w/o Henry Stark, & d/o Capt Wm B Randolph.

Deaths reported to the Navy Dept for the week ending Oct 8, 1864:
Thos Cummingham, 3rd ast engr, yel fever, Jul 2, vessel U S S *Merrimack*.
John Heffron, landsman, yel fever, Jul 30, do.
Sam Johnson, 1st cl boy, yel fever, Sep 8, do.
Hy Peer, landsman, heart disease, Sep 12, Nav Hosp, New Orleans.
Owen Rooney, landsman, yel fever, Sep 12, do.
Chas W Snow, actg ensign, typhus fever, Sep 11, do.
Amos Vodre, seaman, apoplexy, Aug 31, vessel U S S *Carrabassett*.
Hy Picket, 2nd cl boy, meningitis, Sep 26, Nav Hosp, N Y.
Wm H Foster, gunner's mate, consumption, do.
Jos H Breckinridge, landsman, pneumonia, Oct 3, do.
John Carpenter, landsman, typhoid fever, Sep 29, do.
Wm Hardy, landsman, drowned, Sep 8, vessel U S S *Connecticut*.
W McGin, q m, heart disease, Aug 13, vessel U S S *Wateree*.
Hy Hugh, ord seaman, disease of stomach, Sep 27, vessel U S S *Mendota*.
Wm King, capt of hold, gunshot wound, Sep 17, vessel U S S *Currituck*.
Lewis Eldridge, seaman, congestion of lungs, Aug 25, vessel U S S *Susquehanna*.
John Montrose, landsman, rheumatism, Sep 29, vessel U S S *Wabash*.
Chs Sage, cpt of forecastle, pneumonia, Aug 16, vessel U S S *Susquehanna*.
John H Jones, 2nd ast engr, yel fever, Oct 2, vessel U S S *Victor*.
Jerem. Redmond, seaman, dysentery, Sep 26, Nav Hosp, Wash.
Aug R P Abott, seaman, measles, Oct 3, Nav Hosp, Chelsea.
Geo H Chalmers, marine, heart disease, Jul 13, Nav Hosp, Mare Is, Calif.
W Spalding, marine, consumption, Jul 27, do.

Orphans Crt of Wash Co, D C. Case of Eliz A De Vaugh, admx of Thos S De Vaugh, dec'd; settlement on Nov 1. -Z C Robbins, rg o/wills

Supreme Crt of D C, in Equity #271. Cammack, Harvey, & others, against, Eliza Connington, A S Dent & wife, Jos T, Virginia, Wm & Eliza Connington. Parties named & creditors of Michl Connington, dec'd, to appear at City Hall, Oct 17. -W Redin, auditor

Crt of Chancery made in a cause of Banner against England, persons claiming to be next of kin to Isaac Wood, formerly of Lincoln, in Lincoln Co, who was for many years a lunatic, & died in York, Dec, 1849; are, by their solicitors, by Nov 21, 1864, prove their claims at the Chambers of the Vice Chanc, Sir John Stuart, 12 Old Sq, Lincoln's Inn, Middlesex. -Alfred Hall, Chief Clerk. Clarke, Son, & Rawlins, 29 Coleman st, London, Plntf's solicitore. [His grandfather, Clement Wood, is believed to have settled in America, probably in Va, in or about 1748. Another Clement Wood, the first cousin of the lunatic, settled in Va in 1784. Information is required when these persons died, & connecting them with the lunatic, as to their descendants. Hinkley & Morris, Cnslrs, 43 N Chas st, Balt, Md.]

Ex-Gov Jared W Williams, of N H, died at Lancaster, N H, on Sep 29.

TUE OCT 11, 1864
Died: on Oct 9, in her 83rd yr, Mrs Ann Ball, wid/o the late Robt Ball, sr. Funeral from her late residence, near Ball's Cross Rds, Alexandria Co, Va.

Orphans Crt of Wash Co, D C. Case of Thos Sandilands, adm of Jas Reid, dec'd. Settlement on Nov 1. -Z C Robbins, rg o/wills

Ex-Gov Reuben Wood died at his residence at Rockport, Cuyahoga Co, Ohio, on Oct 8, age 73 yrs.

Clerks charged with fraud: Wm P Lowrey, Frank H Scott, & Peter Dausch, all in the q m dept, at Balt, Md. All committed to jail. -Sun

Despatch from Harrisburg, Pa, states that 5 of the alleged Columbia Co insurgents have arrived there, under guard, from Ft Warren: John McHenry, Com'r of the County; Danl McHenry, Treas; Saml Kline, John Rautz, & F Smith ctzns. To be tried by the special military commission now sitting there.

WED OCT 12, 1864
Candidates for Congress: those with an asterisk are mbrs of the present Congress-
Pennsylvania:
Democratic:

*S F Randall	*S E Ancona	A J	J L Dawson
Wm W Reilly	H M North	Glossbrenner	J H Hopkins
C Buckwalter	*M Strouse	*A H Coffroth	W J Kountz
Geo Northrup	*P Johnson	R L Johnston	*J Lasear
H P Ross	*C Dennison	Theo Wright	
B M Boyer	V E Piollett	Wm Bigler	
John C Beatty	*Wm M Miller	W L Corbett	

Rpblcn:

John M Butler	*Wm D Kelley	*J M Broomall	*Thaddeus
*C O'Neill	*M R Thayer	W H Heister	Stevens
*L Myers	Geo Bullock		H Fisher

J L Selfridge	*Jos Balley	*G W Scofield	*Thos Williams
W W Ketcham	A McClure	C V Culver	G V Lawrence
U S Mercur	A A Baker	S Fuller	
G F Miller	S Earlson	*J K Moorhead	

Orphans Crt of Wash Co, D C. 1-Case of F McNerhany, adm of Geo McNaughton, dec'd; settlement on Nov 5. 2-Case of Jas D Clary, exc of Wm S Clary, dec'd; settlement on Nov 5. -Z C Robbins, rg o/wills

Marylander's in Va who, having served 3 yrs, desire to be released from the Confederate army: mbrs of Capt Wm F Dement's battery of 2nd Md Artl, & Marylander's entitled to their discharge from military svc of the Conf states: P A A Contee, Wm H May, Geo G Combe, Marshall Forbes, & John H Shuste. The following mbrs of the same military organization were discharged upon writs of habeas corpus, sued out upon the same grounds as the above: Wm P Compton, John G Harris, Saml T Thomas, Joshua E Stinchcomb, & John C Hardy.

Died: at Balt, Md, on Oct 8, in her 79th yr, Mrs Mary C Breckinridge, relict of the late Hon J Cabell Breckinridge, of Lexington, Ky.

Lt Gen Scott has returned to N Y from West Point in feeble health.

Sldr shot. Francis Bagley, Sgt in 51st N Y vols, was arrested on Monday at Pa av & 10th st, Wash. He attempted to escape & was shot, expiring shortly. His discharge papers were found on him. -Union

THU OCT 13, 1864
Mrd: in Wash City, on Oct 6, by Rev Mr Keeling, Wright Rives, s/o the late John C Rives, to Belle Maury, d/o the late John W Maury.

Died: in Wash City, on Oct 11, after a short but painful illness, Miss Annie T Askew. Funeral from the residence of Mr Chas Lemon, sr, 495 L st, today.

Taken up by me as an astray, one bay mare: Isaac P Childs, Half st & N st, Wash.

Ctzns of Wash to meet at City Hall on Oct 14, to take measures to meet the draft in Wash City:

Richd Wallach	J Russell Barr	Asbury Lloyd
Jos F Brown	Wm W Rapley	Chas E Evans
Wm T Walker	Henry C Wilson	John G Dudley
Thos E Lloyd	Wm Pettibone	Geo Wright
Chas I Canfield	Jas Skirving	J B Ellis
John H Semmes	Chas H Utermehle	P M Dubant
Crosby S Noyes	John B Ward	Thos Berry
Jas Kelly	Bennet Swain	S W Owen
Wm W Moore	John B Turton	Thos Lewis
Geo F Gulick	Geo H Plant	John P Pepper
Wm P Ferguson	S A Peugh	Jas B Davis
Donald McCathran	John A Rheem	Elijah Edmonston
Richd Morgan	Noble D Larner	
Wm Tolbert	T A Stephens	

Joshua Bates, London banker, died in London, on Sep 24, in his 76th yr. He was a native of Mass., & at age 15 years entered the counting hse of Wm R Gray, of Boston. In 1826 he formed a house in London under the name of Bates & Baring. -N Y Commercial

Two chldrn of Mrs Mary German, aged 2 & 5 yrs, were smothered to death in Balt, Md, on Tue, from a fire they set to a bed, while the mother was out.

Addison Brown, of Gtwn, sentenced to 5 years imprisonment at Fort Delaware for giving aid & information to the enemy during the invasion of Md in Jul last.

FRI OCT 14, 1864
Mrd: at St Paul's Chr, on Oct 12, by Rev Dr Butler, Dr D Webster Prentiss to Miss Emelie A Schmidt, all of Wash City.

Mrd: at St Patrick's Chr, on Oct 13, by Rev P F McCarthy, Thos J Shea, of Halifax, N S, to Mary R, d/o P Sweeney, City P O, Wash.

Died: on Oct 13, Mary, w/o A Thos Bradley. Funeral at Oak Hill Cemetery, Sat.

Supreme Crt of D C: announcement of the death of Chief Justice Roger B Taney, age about 87 yrs. The writer remembers when his father, mother, 4 brothers & 3 sisters were around him, but for many years he has been alone.

SAT OCT 15, 1864
Mrd: on Oct 12, at McKendree Chapel, by Rev John Thrush, Chas Garnett Gordon, formerly of Gtwn, D C, late of Calif, to Miss Parthenia E, d/o Wm P McKelden, of Wash City.

Mrd: on Oct 12, at McKendree Chapel, by Rev Dr W M D Ryan, Wm Blagrove McKelden to Miss Alice M, d/o J T McIntosh, all of Wash City.

Supreme Crt of D C, in Equity #1596. F W Sellhausen vs B Schadd's excs & heirs. Account of trustee's sale; City Hall, Wash, on Oct 28. -Wm R Woodward, spec auditor

Mrs A Spier removed to 491 11th st, Wash City, & will open her choice millinery on Oct 13.

For sale-The *Lodge*, about 102 acs, in PG Co, Md, in Spalding's Dist, with commodious dwlg hse. -G M Finotti

Indianapolis, Oct 12, 1864. New mbrs of Congress elected:

Ralph Hill, U	Ebenezer Dumont, U	Schuyler Colfax, U
John H Farquhar, U	H D Washburne, U	Jos H Defrees, U
Geo W Julian, U	Godlove S Orth, U	Thos N Stillwell, U
Present mbrs:		
H W Harrington, D	Ebenezer Dumont, U	Jos K Edgerton, D
Wm S Holmes, D	Danl W Voorhees, D	Jas F McDowell, D
Geo W Julian, U	Godlove S Orth, U	
	Schuyler Colfax, U	

MON OCT 17, 1864
Died: in Wash City, on Oct 13, Sallie, y/d/o Mary Washington & Dr Warwick Evans, aged 16 months.

Deaths reported to the Navy Dept for the week ending Oct 15, 1864:
Edw Badger, landsman, typhoid pneumonia, Sep 2, vessel U S *New Hampshire.*
Albert Mortimer, ord seaman, consumption, Sep 2, do.
John Wood, seaman, debility, Oct 6, vessel U S S *Thorn.*
Lyman C Granger, actg Ast Surg, blank, no date, Pittsford, Vt.
Stephen Moore, negro, cook, typhoid fever, Sep 27, Hosp, Memphis.
Saml Gates, 2nd cl boy, consumption, Sep 28, do.
Isaac Applebury, negro, debility, Oct 1, do.
Jas Harris, ord seaman, drowned, Aug 30, vessel U S S *Potomska.*
Patrick Keiran, landsman, dysentery, Sep 30, Hosp, Beaufort, N C.
Wm Coffee, landsman, drowned, Sep 15, vessel U S S *Pentoosac.*
Ed Galligan, ord seaman, yel fever, Sep 21, vessel U S S *Roebuck.*
Sanford O Fry, paymstr's steward, typhoid fever, Sep 25, vessel U S S *Montauk.*
Jas Muir, paymstr's clerk, meningitis, Oct 9, Hosp, Norfolk.
Wm Cole, ord seaman, pentonitis, Oct 9, do.
Isaac C Smith, landsman, drowned, Aug 8, vessel U S S *Com Read.*
John C McGinnis, marine, typhoid fever, Oct 5, U S Hosp, N Y.
Michl Smith, negro, landsman, consumption, Oct 8, do.
Wm Cummins, beneficiary, asthma, Oct 11, Nav Asylum.
Andrew James, landsman, variola, Jul 7, Quarantine Hosp, Balt.
John Ready, seaman, pneumonia, Jul 27, Batl Infirmary.
Filo W Widener, landsman, yel fever, Sep 20, Hosp, Key West.
Jas Redman, landsman, yel fev, Sep 22, do.
John P Whipple, Chief engr, congestion of brain, Sep 26, do.
Jas Sutherland, landsman, typhoid fever, Sep 17, vessel U S S *Hendrick Hudson.*
John Clear, landsman, remit fever, Sep 25, vessel U S S *Canobassett.*
John Brown, landsman, drowned, Sep 29, vessel U S S *Oneida.*
Robt J Barry, seaman, gunshot, Sep 13, vessel U S S *Shenandoah.*
Henry L Dearing, actg surg, cong remit fever, Oct 2, Hosp, Pensacola.
Timothy Sullivan, marine, remit fever, Oct 2, do.
Washington Innis, landsman, inflam of bowels, Sep 22, do.
Alonzo Steinberg, landsman, dysentery, Sep 30, do.
Geo Ware Wilson, Ast Surg, yel fever, Sep 24, vessel U S S *Hetzel.*
Andrew Davis, 1st cl boy, disease of brain, Aug 28, vessel U S S *Somerset.*
Chas Haflan, seaman, pneumonia, Oct 3, vessel U S S *Restless.*
Anthony Ryan, coalheaver, remit fever, Sep 18, U S Hosp, New Orleans.
Peter Moeller, sailing mstr's mate, dysentery, Sep 13, U S Hosp, Port Royal.
Chas King, landsman, smallpox, Sep 23, U S Hosp, New Orleans.
Surim Rabershaw, ord seaman, consumption, Sep 23, do.
John K Mytinger, armorer's mate, yel fever, Sep 23, do.
Thos King, marine, consumption, Sep 25, do.
Benj Smart, landsman, pneumonia, Aug 20, vessel U S S *Ft Henry.*
Wm Wade, seaman, pneumonia, Aug 18, do.
John Wren, coalheaver, yel fever, Sep 3, vessel U S S *Adela.*

Supreme Crt of D C, in Equity #290. Saml Allsop against John B Turton, adm, & Frederick, Annie, & Mary Dillow, heirs of Wm Dillow. Parties named Wm H Ward, guardian ad litem of the minor dfndnts, & creditors of Wm Dillow, dec'd; to meet at my ofc, City Hall, Wash, on Oct 24. -W Redin, auditor

Mr Junius Brutus Booth, eldest s/o the great Booth, to appear at Ford's New Theatre tonight. For 18 years he has performed in Calif, & is comparatively unknown, as was his bro, Edwin Booth.

Died: at his residence in Wash City, on Oct 1, Dr Robt Mayo, aged 82 yrs, native of Va, but for the last 35 years a resident of Wash.

On Sat the remains of the late Roger B Taney, Chief Justice of the U S were conveyed from Wash to Frederick, Md, in a special train of 2 cars. Friends gathered at his late residence, on Indiana ave, near Third st, among whom were Pres Lincoln, Sec Seward, Atty Gen Bates, & Postmstr Gen Dinnison. Procession included Rev Fr Walter, of St Patrick's Chr, Dr Grafton Tyler, of Gtwn, one of the physicians who attended the dec'd; pallbearers, viz: Messrs J M Carlisle, W J Stone, jr, D W Middleton, clerk of Sup Crt, W M Lamon, Mrshl of D C; Conway Robinson & Mr Tyler, of Frederick; J Mason Campbell & son; Jos Taney, nephew of the dec'd, & we believe, the only male relative of the *name* living. Messrs Howard & Perrine are also relatives of the dec'd. Solemn high mass was celebrated. Burial in the cemetery of that place.

Orphans Crt of Wash Co, D C. Prsnl estate of Norah Digges, late of Wash City, dec'd. -Geo W Young, John Carroll Brent, excs

New Haven, Conn, Oct 15. R R accident today instantly killed: brakesmen, Horace Beebe & Eugene Parsons. Critically injured: Saml H Chittenden, who can hardly survive.

TUE OCT 18, 1864
Mrd: on Oct 13, at Chr of the Ascension, by Rev Dr Pinckney, Dr W J Craigen, of Wash & Rebecca D Pue, d/o Chas R Pue, of Elkridge, Howard Co, Md.

Died: on Oct 15, at N Y, Emily M, w/o Col John Lorimer Graham, & y/d/o the late Isaac Clason.

Tax Certificate lost-on lot 5 in sq 458, sold May 15, 1863, in the name of Edw DeKrafft, & bought of the advertiser. -Michael Nash

For sale-my estate on the Patuxent river, *Town Creek*, 800 acs, with dwlg hse. -Geo Forbes, Leonardtown, Md.

Orphans Crt of Wash Co, D C. Case of Nancey W Harvey, excx of Henry L Harvey, dec'd; settlement on Nov 18. -Z C Robbins, rg o/wills

Military news-we regret to announce the death, by yellow fever, of Col D B Harris, Chief Engr of Gen Beauregard's staff. Gen Beauregard reached Columbus, Ga, on Fri, & went immediately to his command.

WED OCT 19, 1864
Mrd: at the N Y Av Chr, on Oct 8, by Rev Dr Gurley, Valrous G Austin, formerly of Va, to Mrs C B Renner, d/o the late Daniel Renner, of Gtwn.

Died: on Oct 17, Miss Virginia A Church, d/o Chas B & Matilda S Church, in her 17th yr. Funeral from their residence, 11th st, between Md av & C st, today.

Died: on Oct 17, after a long & painful illness, Augustus T Sioussa, in the 32nd yr of his age. Funeral from his late residence, N Y av, between 12th & 13th sts, today.

Col J P Sanderson, Prov Mrshl Gen of the Dept of Missouri, died at St Louis on Sat.

Hon Nicholas Brewer, Judge of the 2nd Judicial Crct of Md, died at his residence in Annapolis, on Oct 15, after a protracted illness, in the 69th yr of his age.

THU OCT 20, 1864
Died: at her residence, in Gtwn, on Oct 16, after a short illness, Mrs Bettie Boyd Gibbs, w/o Dr Jas B Gibbs. [She was a wife, mother, dght, sister, & friend.]

Phil papers announce the death, at his residence in that city, of Maj Gen David B Birney, Cmder of the 10th Army Corps of the U S. He died Thu last, of malarious fever, contracted while in the discharge of his military duties.

Mrd: on Oct 19, by Rev Geo W Samson, Dr Thos C Smith to Miss Cornelia F Hazard, both of Wash City.

Wash Corp: 1-Cmte on Police: asked to be discharged from consideration of the ptn of Martin King: referred to the Cmte on Finance. 2-Nominations by the Mayor: A B Talcott for superintendent of the Police & Fire Alarm Telegraph: Thos Morrison for operator, & John H Faulkner for batteryman: held over for one week. 3-Ptn of Mrs A G Herald: referred to the Cmte on Police.

Diplomatic appointments announced: M Mercier to Madrid; M Chateau Renard to Wash; M Bennedetti to Berlin; Baron de Talleyrand to St Petersburgh; M Reculat to Frankfort, & Count Massignan to Teheran.

FRI OCT 21, 1864
New Albany [Ind] Ledger, Oct 18. The steamer *J C Swan*, on Sun, while laying at tow-head, on Cumberland river, exploded her boiler & became a total wreck. A large number of persons were killed, including: Capt J D Smith, John Elliott, & Mr Harrison, pilots; Mr Graves, mate; Mr Ferguson, a passenger. Five passengers & sldrs are missing.

Obit-Annie Teresa Askew died on Oct 11, of typhoid fever, in Wash.

Died: on Oct 20, of typhoid fever, in his 16th yr, John W Kearns, only s/o John Kearns, clerk in the 6th Auditor's ofc. Funeral from his father's residence, 506 L st, Fri.

SAT OCT 22, 1864
Died: at Augusta, Ga, on Sep 29, Henry B Middleton, s/o Robt W Middleton, of Wash City, in the 27th yr of his age. He was mtsr-at arms on board the U S mortar schnr *Dan Smith*, & was captured on Sep 8, 1863, at the storming of Ft Sumter. At the time of his death he was, with other paroled prisoners, on his return home from Andersonville, Ga.

Orphans Crt of Wash Co, D C. Case of Eliza M Clampitt, admx of Wm H Clampitt, dec'd; settlement on Nov 15. -Z C Robbins, rg o/wills

Wanted: a good gardner wanted by Conway Robinson, near Sldrs' Home.

MON OCT 24, 1864
Deaths reported to the Navy Dept for the week ending Oct 22, 1864:
Andrew J Hough, carpenter, consumption, Sep 2, Nav Hosp, Portsmouth.
Jas Wilson, q m, pneumonia, Oct 10, Nav Hosp, Norfolk.
Daniel Keurny, landsman, diarrhoea, Oct 12, do.
Alexander McCarron, landsman, drowned, Aug 23, vessel U S S *Narragansett*.
Jas Clarke, 2nd cl fireman, consumption, Aug 26, do.
Frank H Vedder, 2nd cl boy, disease of brain, Oct 7, Nav Hosp, N Y.
Jeremiah Foley, landsman, diarrhoea, Oct 14, do.
Chas Denton, seaman, palsy, Oct 6, vessel U S S *Union*.
Gus M Shaw, landsman, inflam of throat, Oct 4, do.
John S Pero, 2nd cl engr, dysentery, Oct 1, vessel U S S *Ladona*.
Silas Beatty, landsman, drowned, Sep 12, vessel U S S *Valparaiso*.
Chas C Wells, landsman, drowned, Sep 23, vessel U S S *Sonoma*.
Wm Ridley, seaman, drowned, Sep 28, vessel U S S *Acacia*.
John McGinnis, 1st cl fireman, drowned, Oct 14, vessel U S S *Vermont*.
Henry McKenley, seaman, effects of drink, Oct 6, vessel U S S *Ohio*.
Chas McGravey, musician, apoplexy, Oct 18, Marine Barracks, Brooklyn.
Jas C Crocker, mstr's mate, blank, Sep 13, W Barnstable.
Jas Bennett, landsman, measles, Oct 19 Nav Hosp, Chelsea.
John McCawley, landsman, diarrhoea, Oct 8, Nav Hosp, N Y.
Jas C Brown, seaman, disease of heart, Oct 9, do.
John Carroll, fireman, yel fever, Jul 11, vessel U S S *Tahoma*.
Chas Bell, seaman, yel fever, Jul 21, do.
Martin Peter, seaman, yel fever, Jul 23, do.
John Taylor, coalheaver, yel fever, Jul 24, do.
J J Waters, seaman, yel fever, Jul 25, do.
J R Batsford, 2nd cl engr, yel fever, Jul 25, do.
Willard E Clute, 1st cl boy, yel fever, Jul 27, do.

Brady's new Gymn for physical culture, 82, 84, 86 La av, Wash. -Abner S Brady

T Pursell & Son, dealers in China, Glass, Lamps, etc: 341 Pa av, Wash.

Farm for sale in Montg Co, Md: 160 acs of land, with dwlg hse. Also, a farm of 190 acs adjoining, with dwlg hse & stable. 25 farms in Montg Co & a number of hses & lots, in the city for sale. -F Mace, Agent for the sale of Md lands, 517 7th st.

Sale at Croom, near the premises, rl estate known as *Hackthorne Heath*, upon which Dr John T Eversfield now resides, adjoins the lands of Messrs Richd D Burroughs, C C Magruder, & Jas I Bowie; 550 acs; per decree of the Crct Crt of PG Co, Md. -Saml H Berry, Daniel Clarke, trustees

Orphans Crt of Wash Co, D C. 1-Prsnl estate of Abner C Peirce, late of Wash Co, dec'd. -Perrie Shoemaker. 2-Case of Jas Keleher, exc of Wm Bush, dec'd; settlement on Nov 15. -Z C Robbins, rg o/wills

Dr J Phillips has removed to 256 F st, Wash City.

TUE OCT 25, 1864
Numerous lots for sale in Wash; under the will of the late Edmund Reiley. [Same were listed.] -Patrick McKenna, John Carroll Brent, trustees

Mr Lincoln-a reminiscence. His only term of Congressional service was during the period when I had the honor to preside over the Hse of which he was a mbr. He helped me to the Spkr's chair by his own vote, & I really wish I could find it in my conscience to return the compliment at this moment. [Laughter] But I cannot forget a speech he made in Jul, 1848, in reference to the nomination for the Presidency of a distinguished Democrat who still lives to enjoy the respect of all who knew him. By the way, Mr Speaker, [said he,] did you know that I am a military hero? Yes, sir, [continued he] in the days of the Black Hawk war I fought, bled, & came away. Speaking of Gen Cass's career reminds me of my own. I was not at Stillman's defeat, but I was about as near it as Cass was to Hull's surrender; & like him, I saw the place soon afterward. It is quite certain that I did not break my sword, for I had none to break, but I bent a musket pretty badly on one occasion. If Cass broke his sword, the idea is, he broke it in desperation: I bent the musket by accident. If Gen Cass went in advance of me in picking berries, I guess I surpassed him in charges upon the wild onions. [Laughter] If he saw any live fighting Indians it was more than I did, but I had a good many bloody struggles with the mosquitos; &, although I never fainted from loss of blood, I can truly say I was often very hungry. Mr Speaker, if I should ever conclude to doff what ever our Democratic friends may suppose there is a black cockade Federalism about me, & hereupon they shall take me up as their candidate for the Presidency. I protestate they shall not make fun of me, as they have of Gen Cass, by attempting to write me into a military hero. [Great Laughter] -Speech of Mr Winthrop.

Died: on Oct 3, at the residence of Mr J Wilson Iglehart, A A Co, Md, Miss Priscilla Davidson, aged 74 yrs, sister of Mr John Davidson, of Gtwn.

WED OCT 26, 1864
Mrd: on Oct 25, at Wesley Chapel, by Rev B H Nadal, Wm B R Cissel to M C Riggles.

Orphans Crt of Wash Co, D C. Prsnl estate of John Casey, late of U S Army, dec'd. -Chas Riley, exc

Mr Chas L Howard, agent for the Sanderson's Minstrels, informs that owing to an accident, this troupe, from the Md Instit, Balt, will not perform until Oct 27.

Ford's Theatre: Massinger's fine play of "A New Way to Pay Old Debts," is announced for this evening, Junius Brutus Booth appearing as Sir Giles Overreach, a character in which his father had no equal. The favorite actress, Alice Gray, appears as Mgt.

On Oct 14 Col Mosby struck the Balt & Ohio R R at Duffield, destroying a U S mail train, consisting of a locomotive & 10 cars. 20 prisoners & 15 horses were captured. Among the prisoners, were 2 paymstrs, with $168,000 in Gov't funds. -R E Lee, Gen

Hernia or Rupture: P E Minor, M D, has discovered a permanent & radical cure for the above. Treatment is internal, does not interfere with business. Ofc 234 Pa ave, near 13th st.

A large McClellan meeting was lately held at New Orleans. Spkrs: J A Rozier, W R Mills, Gov Riddell, Hon G A Fellows, & Lt Jerome.

THU OCT 27, 1864
Tribute of respect-to the late Benj A Davis, by the Columbia Topog Soc, Wash. -Wm R McLain, Pres; J C Proctor, rec & cor sec.

Mrd: in Wash City, Oct 25, by Rev Mr Austin, Jas W Conner to Louisa A Divine, of Leesburg, Va.

Mrd: in Wash City, on Oct 26, by Rev Dr Wm Pinkney, Lt Kent D Davis, Marine Corps, U S Navy, & C Elise Woodruff, d/o Maj J C Woodruff, Corps of Engrs, U S Army.

Died: on Aug 30, 1864, in Weldon, N C, in the 24th yr of his age, Wm Amos, only c/o the late Dr Granville S & Emily W Farquhar.

Sale of prsnl property, at *Northampton*, the residence of Mrs V Sprigg. -Thos G Pratt, Annapolis, Md, for Mrs Sprigg.

Col Jos P Collins, 29th Ind Regt, a nephew of Dr Jas A Collins, of Chicago, has recently died in Atlanta. He is the 7th male relative of Dr Collins to be a casualty of this war.

FRI OCT 28, 1864
Martinsburg, Va, Oct 25-the guerrillas made another haul of a Brig Gen. Gen Dufie, who had been to the front, was riding down the pike from Winchester in an ambulance, with an escort of cavalry. Having made a gap between & Gen & his guards, the guerrillas dashed in & grabbed the whole ambulance party, whisking them off before the escort came up. The cavalry came in safely. Dr Hayes, the medical director at this Point,has sent to Balt 2,500 wounded men since the last battle. About 1,300 left at Winchester, & some 40 or 50 here.

Dissolution of the partnership between G W Hinton & Wm S Teel, Merchant Tailors; by mutual consent. Teel will continue the business at the old stand, 358 Pa av, Wash.

Hon Wm Hallam Tuck, of Annapolis, Md, appt'd Judge of the 2nd judicial crct; vice Judge Brewer, dec'd; a native of Upper Marlboro, PG Co, Md. –American

SAT OCT 29, 1864
Mrd: at St John's Chr, Gtwn, D C, by Rev Dr C M Butler, of Phil, on Oct 27, Thos Hyde to Fannie, d/o Chas E Rittenhouse.

Mrd: in Wash City, on Oct 27, at Trinity Chr, by Rev Wm Suddand, of Phil, Capt John R Spangler, 6th U S Cavalry, to Helen R Green, d/o J Green, M D.

Died: in Balt, Md, on Sep 7, Richd M Harrison, formerly a mbr of the Wash Bar, & an influential ctzn of Wash.

Louisville, Ky, Oct 25. On account of the capture of the Totten Hospital mail by guerillas, under a notorious woman named Sue Mundy, & the murder of the mail carrier, 4 guerillas who call themselves confederate Capts, all of whom were recently captured on the Cumberland river, were yesterday taken from the Exchange barracks here & shot in retaliation for the aforesaid murder.

Capt Braine & his associates, who were arrested at Bermuda after capturing & destroying the vessel *Roanoke*, have been liberated.

Advices from the Upper Missouri say that Gen Sully has gone into winter qrtrs at Fort Sully. The Winnebago Indians are in a starving condition.

Hon Henry G Stebbins, mbr of Congress for the 1st Congressional dist of N Y, has sent his resignation to Gov Seymour.

MON OCT 31, 1864

Deaths reported to the Navy Dept for the week ending Oct 29, 1864:

Henry Pendlebury, 1st cl boy, consumption, Sep 15, vessel U S S *Saratoga*.
Wm L Brown, landsman, consumption, Jul 9, do.
John Q A Capron, marine, typhoid fever, Oct 23, Navy Yd, Portsmouth.
John McMolkin, marine, apoplexy, Oct 31, vessel U S S *Miami*.
Henry A Wakefield, landsman, disease of kidneys, Oct 20, Nav Hosp, N Y.
John Rully, landsman, diarrhoea, Oct 24, do.
Alexander Welts, actg mstr's mate, drowned, Aug, U S steamer *Cricket*.
Edw Redding, seaman, drowned, Aug, do.
Geo Imaman, ord seaman, drowned, Aug, do.
S Ward, landsman, congestion of brain, Oct 6, Key West.
Moses Petuson, 2nd ast engr, fever, Oct 6, vessel U S S *Whitehead*.
Patk Holland, landsman, dysentery, Sep 19, vessel U S S *Blackhead*.
C H Mason, 1st ast engr, yel fever, Oct, U S S Va.
S S Glass, 2nd ast engr, do, do, do.
E C Bowman, ast paymstr, do, do, do.
Wm L Adair, 1st ast engr, yel fever, Oct, vessel U S S *Arkansas*.
Oliver Carr, 3rd ast engr, yel fever, Oct, vessel U S S *Hollyhock*.
Henry Bruce, capt aft guard, yel fever, Oct 1, Nav Hosp, New Orleans.
Henry Bruesseng, seaman, yel fever, Oct, do.
Frank Hannible, landsman, yel fever, Sep 28, do.
Patrick Hays, landsman, yel fever, Sep 30, do.
M J Marshall, seaman, yel fever, Oct 2, do.
Thos McGough, 2nd ast engr, yel fever, Sep 29, do.
B Salpaugh, 1st cl fireman, yel fever, Sep 29, do.
Wm Ticanor, seaman, yel fever, Oct 4, do.
H S Neely, landsman, cholera morbus, Sep 25, vessel U S S *Selma*..
Saml Davis, landsman, drowned, Oct 13, vessel U S S *Black Hawk*.
Theoph Giles, landsman, congestion of lungs, Oct 25, Nav Hosp, Norfolk.
Thos Hynes, seaman, consumption, Oct 6, vessel U S S *Cyane*.
C B Dorrance, actg ensign, gunshot wound, Oct 9, vessel U S S *Sebago*.
Jas M Harris, 2nd ast engr, nervous exhaustion, Oct 6, vessel U S S *Cayuga*.
Geo Mare, landsman, gunshot wound, Oct 11, vessel U S S *Pembina*.
Edgar A Miller, landsman, gunshot wound, Oct 9, vessel U S S *Sebago*.

Mrd: on Oct 25, at the residence of the bride's father, by Rev Mr Nadal, Gilbert M Woodward, of Wisc, to Ella R, d/o the late Selby Parker, of Wash.

Mrd: on Oct 27, at St John's Chr, Brooklyn, N Y, by Rev Geo F Seymour, Robt H Broom to Mary Louise, d/o R D Thompson.

Died: in Wash City, on Oct 27, Aaron Divine, in the 83rd yr of his age. He was a native of Va & was a soldier in war of 1812. His remains were deposited in Oak Hill Cemetery, at Gtwn, on Sat, in accordance with his earnest desire.

TUE NOV 1, 1864

Military arrests in Harford Co, Md, several days since; Col J Carroll Walsh, Jas H Burkhead, Geo W Billingslea, & Albert Downey, all ctzns of said county, brought to Wash City, by order of Gen Wallace.

The corner-stone of the new Catholic Chapel of the *Imaculate Conception* was laid with imposing religious ceremonies: located on 11th st. The schools which are to be opened by the priesthood will be of great benefit to the rising generations. The Rev Mr Walter, pastor of St Patrick's, officiated. Rev F E Boyle delivered the discourse.

Gov Cony, of Maine, appt'd Nathan A Farwell U S Senator to fill the unexpired term of Sec Fessenden.

Brig Gen Jas J Archer, of Md, died at the residence of Gen Jos E Anderson in Richmond, on Monday. He had been taken prisoner at Gettysburg & confined on Johnson's Island.

Peter Baumgras, Portrait Painter. Studio, 486 12th st, between E & F sts. [Late King's gallery.]

Coal & Wood of all description for sale: ofc, corner K & 14th sts west. –E H Fuller

The steamer *City of Manchester*, from Liverpool, brings news of the death of the Duke of Newcastle. He was the one who accompanied the Prince of Wales on his tour thru the U S in 1860 & was greatly esteemed for the dignity & courtesy of his manners.

WED NOV 2, 1864

Mrd: on Nov 1, at Trinity Chr, by Rev Mr Keeling, Mr John Purdy, of Wash City, to Miss Sarah Crane, of St Mary's Co, Md.

Died: in Norfolk, Va, on Oct 18, Piercy Murphy, in the 14th yr of his age, s/o Cmder P U Murphy, formerly of the U S Navy.

Died: at Wood Lawn, Montg Co, Md, on Nov 1st, Rev Daniel Motzer. Funeral at Oak Hill Cemetery, today.

Died: on Nov 1, of typhoid fever, Ella Virginia, twin d/o Benj C & Martha S Wright, aged 6 yrs, 1 month & 25 days. Funeral from the residence of her father, 521 K st, Thu.

Orphans Crt of Wash Co, D C. 1-Prnsl estate of Priscilla Cosgrove, late of Wash City, dec'd. -H Naylor, exc 2-Case of M Julia Barrett, admx of Jos A Hastings, dec'd; settlement on Nov 26. -Z C Robbins, rg o/wills

Partnership between H Browning & Jno M Keating is dissolved by mutual consent. Browning will continue the business. Washington

Handsome 1st class residence for sale: #365 K st, near 12th: mastic front, 3 stories & basement high-18 rms. Stable on the alley: stall for 3 horses, carriage rm, harness & coachman's rms, & large loft for hay, etc. For terms apply to C C Meador, 339 Pa ave, opposite Metropolitan Htl.

Indianapolis, Oct 31-R R accident 6 miles from Lafayette: 28 bodies taken from the wreck, majority were returned sldrs. Among the killed was Rev B F Winans, of the Sanitary Commission.

Dr Morsell, having resigned his parish, leaves Wash City for Balt. Pastoral connexion dissolved after 9 yrs. He carries with him the esteem & good wishes of all who knew him.

THU NOV 3, 1864

R M Hall & Co, rl estate brokers, have recently sold: hse on Mass av, owned by F L Harvey, to D R Smith, $6,200; hse on N st, owned by John Mathews, to Geo W Kellogg, for $2,400; hse on N st, owned by John Mathews, to Mrs Kate L Merriman, for $2,500; hse on Capitol Hill, 1st & B st, owned by Geo W Howell, to Dr Benj B Wilson, for $8,200.

Military execution. On Oct 29, six Confederate prisoners of war were executed, by shooting, in retaliation for the murder of Maj Jas Wilson & his 6 comrades. Executed were: Jas W Gates, 3rd Missouri cavalry, C S A; Harvey H Blackburn, Co A, Colman's Regt Arkansas cavalry, C S A; John Nichols, Co G, 2nd Missouri cavalry, C S A; Chas W Minniken, Co A, Crabtree's Arkansas cavalry, C S A, Asa V Ladd, Co A, Burbridge's Missouri Regt of cavalry, C S A; & Geo T Bunch, Co B, 3rd Missouri cavalry. Procession started from the Gratiot st prison. -St Louis Rpblcn, Oct 30th

Died: at Lexington, Ky, on Oct 27, Levi O Todd, in his 50th yr. Mt Todd was a bro of Mrs Pres Lincoln.

Mrd: in the Chr of the Epiphany, by Rev Smythe Pyne, Rector of St John's Chr, on Nov 2, Wm J Gilbert, of N Y, to Miss Laura, 2nd d/o A Sidney Tebbs, of Platte Co, Missouri.

Michl W Cluskey, formerly Postmstr of the Hse o/Reps, has recovered from the wounds he received in battle, & has been elected a member of the rebel Congress from the Memphis dist. -Union

The Duke of Newcastle: his Dukedom was created in 1756, but his Earldom was granted by Queen Elizabeth in 1572, & his barony of Clinton dt'd as far back as 1299, & was granted by Edward I. Born in 1811 he mrd the only d/o the 10th Duke of Hamilton & Brandon in 1832, but had to obtain a divorce from her in 1850. The Duke is succeeded in his titles & estates by his eldest son, the Earl of Lincoln, now in his 31st yr.

Wash Corp: 1-Ptn of Z M P King & others: referred to the Cmte on Improvements. 2-Ptns of Mrs M A Bannerman & Dr Thos Holmes: bill in relation to embalming & storing dead bodies in Wash City: bill read 3 times & passed. 3-Mayor's nomination of M Y Holly as Operator of the Fire Alarm & Police Telegraph, v John Blackie, rsgnd: nomination confirmed. 4-Act for the relief of Admiral Jos Smith: referred to the Cmte on Claims. 5-Cmte on Claims: ptn of Lt Col Jno H Oberteuffer, for damages done his carriage: laid on the table. 6-Ptn of C Hosmer & others, with a bill to lay a flag footway in 7th ward: passed. 7-Cmte on Finance: bill for relief of Rev J A Waller, asked to be discharged from its further consideration. 8-Cmte on Claims: ptn of Henry Kleiber was passed. 9-Cmte on Claims: ptn of Alicia McDonald, for her relief: passed.

Cmdor Jos B Hull has been ordered to report on Nov 10 as Cmder of the Navy Yd at Phil.

FRI NOV 4, 1864

Died: on Oct 31, Annie Roberts, w/o Capt C A Reynolds, U S Army, in the 24th yr of her age. Funeral from the residence of her father, Dr J M Roberts, 433 G st, today.

Died: on Nov 3, in PG Co, Md, aged 32, Eliz D, w/o Thos J Barclay, & d/o Israel M Jackson. Funeral today.

Supreme Crt of D C. Mary Ann Roche against Jas E Smith & Emma, his wife, & Alice A, Mary J, Sallie J, Wm J, & Edw B Roche. Regarding-sale of lots 12 & 13 in sq 286, to J P Milburn, was bona fide. -Wm Redin, auditor

Belvidere land case: decision of Justice Grier, of the U S Crct Crt, rendered on Tue. Mr Croxall, of Balt, a great grandson of Robt Morris, the great financier, claimed the whole own of *Belvidere* as entailed property. The entire tract-600acs, was conveyed by Morris in 1793 to trustees for the benefit of his dght, Mrs Croxal, [the grandmother of the present claimant,] * her heirs by her then hsbnd, Chas Croxall. The plntf claims that this was a strick entailment, & altho his own father & the chldrn of Mrs Croxall sold the property to bona fide purchasers 40 years ago, yet that he, as the eldest son in line of succession, can recover it from the present possessors. Judge Grier decides against the claims on 3 distinct grounds: 1-That the Legislature in 1818 docked the entail by a special act. 2-That Thos Croxall, the eldest s/o Mrs Croxall, & father of the claimant, gave a deed for the property in 1823, which binds both father & son. 3-That the statute of limitations, called the 30 years act, effectually barred the plntf, & confers a good title on the present possessors. It is supposed that this decision will definitely settle the case. -Newark Adv

Supreme Crt of D C, in Equity #1595. F Sellhausen, vs Mades, exc of B S Chad et al. Ratify sales made by trustee reported on Sep 20. -R J Meigs, clerk

Supreme Crt of D C. Edw R Ward against Geo S Krafft, Sarah Krafft, & Philip H, Wm R, & Geo W Ward, & others. Regarding-sale of lot 10 in sq 403 to Pierce Shoemaker, was bona fide. -W Redin, auditor

Rev Matthias Harris, Chaplain U S Army, was relieved from duty at Ft Washington, Md, on Oct 10, & assigned to duty at Ft Foote, PG Co, Md.

SAT NOV 5, 1864

Mrd: on Nov 3, at the Chr of the Epiphany, by Rev Dr Ryan, Mr Kennard Cox, of Phil, to Miss Rhoda O'Neal Williams, of Wash, D C.

Mrd: at the First Bapt Chr, on Nov 3, by Rev Dr Hill, Henry G Ayer, of N H, to Sarah E, d/o the late Jas W Shields, of Wash City.

Died: on Nov 3, in Wash City, Eliphalet T Grover, aged 35 years & 9 months. The remains of the dec'd will be conveyed from his late residence, 425 13th st, to the Balt & Ohio R R depot, on Nov 6.

Orphans Crt of Wash Co, D C. Prsnl estate of Susan K Ingle, late of Wash Co, dec'd. - Moses Kelly

Brig Gen T E Ranson, commanding the 17th Army Corps in Sheridan's army, died at Rome, Ga, on Sat last, of dysentery. He was s/o Col Ranson, of the regular army, who was killed at Chepultepec. -N Y Post

Benj Greenleaf, whose name is known to every school boy in the North, died last Sat in Bradford, Mass, aged 78. Writer of Greenleaf's Arithmetic & Algebra.

Col Cyrus Butler, deputy provost marshall, was killed in Clearfield Co, Pa, last week, while attempting to arrest a drafted man, Lounsberry, who failed to report.

MON NOV 7, 1864

Deaths reported to the Navy Dept for the week ending Nov 5, 1864:
Chas Burns, landsman, pneumonia Oct 26, Asylum.
Thos Quigley, landsman, gunshot wound, Oct 9, vessel U S S *Winona*.
Lawrence O Brigham, landsman, typhoid fever, no date, Nav Hosp, N Y.
Edw R Clark, seaman, blank, Sep 14, near Richmond.
John Judge, ord seaman, injuries, Oct 7, vessel U S S *Ft Jackson*.
Edw Ambleman, 1st cl boy, remit fever, Oct 7, vessel U S S *Arthur*.
John Gray, seaman, fracture, Oct 14, Nav Hosp, Pensacola.
Wm B Hulse, 2nd cl fireman, inflam of lungs, Oct 11, do.
Jas McCann, 1st cl fireman, lockedjaw, Oct 17, vessel U S S *Bermuda*.
Michael Shay, coal heaver, typhoid fever, Oct 17, do.
Robt Clutt, coal heaver, gunshot wound, Jun 14, vessel U S S *Somerset*.
Michael Hill, landsman, killed, Jul 14, vessel U S S *Judge Torrence*.
Harrison Clark, landsman, blank, Aug 27, vessel U S S *New National*.
Wm Dickson, 2nd cl fireman, drowned, Sep 11, vessel U S S *Wachita*.
Edw Wise, landsman, drowned, Sep 19, vessel U S S *Moose*.
Robt Ferris, landman, wound, Sep 10, vessel U S S *Marmora*.
John S Meyett, q m, dysentery, Oct 13, vessel U S S *Cricket*.
Henry Gordon, steward's cook, remit fever, Sep 29, vessel U S S *Arkansas*.
Dennis Welsh, coal heaver, yel fever, Oct 5, do.
John Prior, coal heaver, yel fever, Oct 2, do.
David O'Leary, coal heaver, yel fever, Oct 9, do.
Marshall Stone, steward, yel fever, Oct 11, do.
Wm Noble, 2nd l fireman, yel fever, Oct 12, do.
Thos S Curdon, coal heaver, yel fever, Oct 14, do.
Wm McDonald, qrtr gunner, yel fever, Oct 16, do.
John Powers, 2nd cl fireman, yel fever, Oct 18, do.
Michael Fitzpatrick, seaman, yel fever, Sep 21, vessel U S S *Westmoreland*.
Augusta Behsensen, sgt marines, disease of heart, Oct 30, recg ship *North Carolina*.
Wm H Cassidy, actg mstr's mate, dysentery, Oct 30, N Y.

Died: at Carlton Glen, near Bladensburg, Md, on Nov 6, of diptheria, Janie A Carlton, aged 20 yrs, d/o Henry L & Ann W Carlton. Funeral today.

Died: at his residence in St Louis, Mo, on Oct 27, after a lingering illness, Dr Wm Maffitt, in the 53rd yr of his age.

Died: on Nov 6, Fanny Eliz, y/d/o Mary F & Wm G Brock, aged 4 years & 1 mo. Funeral from their residence, 8th & G sts, today.

Maj Gen Marmaduke, Brig Gen Cabell, & 4 rebel colonels, captured by Gen Pleasanton at the battle of Osage, left St Louis on Thu for Johnson's Island.

Mr Bowman, connected with the Louisville Democrat ofc, met with a fatal accident on Sun. He attempted to get out of his buggy, when his fowling piece, a double-barrelled gun, was accidentally discharged, both loads taking effect in his head & causing instant death.

Potatoes just received by schnr *Francisco* from Maine, a fine cargo of Prince Albert's & Jackson white potatoes, & for sale at 11th st wharf. Apply to Capt on board, or to Geo & Thos Parker & Co. -W P Dennison, Gtwn, D C

TUE NOV 8, 1864

Mrd: Nov 3, by Rev Dr Butler, Mr Wm Dayton to Miss M E Beardsley, both of Wash City.

Mrd: Nov 3, by Rev Dr Butler, Mr Frank Taylor to Miss L V Beardsley, both of Wash City.

Military arrests in Md: Dr E W Mobberly, John Smith, John Bartholaw, Dr S Leroy Swoomstedt, W W Walker, & Elisha Swoomley, on Sat, brought to Balt on Sun & locked up to await trial; charges not made public. Dr H L Bousief, of Fred'k Co, was brought to Balt on Sun, & placed in the military prison. -Sun

Brigham Young has just finished a tour among the southern settlements of Utah. He visited 37 of them & spoke 39 times.

THU NOV 9, 1864

Stray cow came on my premises in Jun. -John B Wiltberger, near Rock Crk Chr, Wash, D C.

Mrd: Nov 4, by Rev R J Keeling, Miss Delilah Jordan to Mr Robt Allen, formerly of Richmond, Va.

Supreme Crt of D C, in Equity #322. Geo R Adams & others, ofcrs & mbrs of the Mutual Bldg & Loan Assoc, vs Richard H Clarke, A Austin Smith, Saml Gregg, Frank Darley, trustees, & heirs of the late Eliz Fenton. Regarding-appointment of a new trustee or trustees; Eliz R Fenton being, by her trustee, the said *Saml Gregg, seized of lot 4 in sq 413, Wash City, conveyed the same to said Clarke & Smith in trust to secure writing obligatory made by the said E R Fenton & Frank Darley, her trustee, in favor of said Assoc; same failed to pay their monthly payments, etc. Since the execution of said deed of trust, Eliz R Fenton has died leaving Eliz G Darley, w/o Frank Darley, Daniel V Fenton, *Matthias R Fenton, Chas B Fenton, Edw F Fenton, Tacey R Fenton, Anna H Fenton, & Jas L Fenton, & that since time the said Jas L Fenton has died, leaving Martha R Fenton, his widow, & Jas Fenton & Anna Maria Fenton, his chldrn & heirs. *Non-residents of this Dist. -R J Meigs, clerk

Accident on the Phil, Wilmington, & Balt R R on Nov 7; Albert L Smith, aged 18, of Wash, D C, killed instantly; Lt Chas E Carroll, of Vet Reserve Corps, both thighs broken & injured about the head, died an hour afterwards. Valentine Stern, injured about the head. Wounded-Jeremiah Brickley & Chas Alexander, of Wilmington, Dela; Michael Berthe, Phil; Lt A M Copeland, 81st N Y vols; Jos Bernard, of Maine, slightly; Prof Saunder, of Phil, about the head; Mrs Smalley, of Phil, bruised; Kate Thompson, Gtwn, D C, bruised; Mrs Frances, of Wash, do; Mr Jerome, scalded; Susannah Elliott & child, slightly injured.

THU NOV 10, 1864

Col Sam Medar died at Columbus, Ohio, on Nov 7. One of the oldest newspaper editors in Ohio.

Death of 6 miners on Fri of last week at the red ash colliery of Geo H Potts & Co, near Minersville, Pa: Thos Richards & David Williams, Welshmen; Jos Bearman, a German, Robt Duffy, Michl Finney, & Michl Scully, Irishmen. They had gone into the mine to clear away the rubbish & were overcome by noxious gas that filled the place.

On Oct 14 a passenger train from Balt to Wheeling was destroyed by a gang of Mosby's men, & 2 paymstrs of the U S army were robbed of more than $200,000. On Nov 2 Adj Wm B Norman arrested at the Eutaw Hse, in Balt, Md, Mrs Mary Ann Kline, her son, Dr John H Kline, & her niece, Miss Nancy O'Bannon, the first two of Loudoun Co, Va, & the latter of Duffield's Sta, Jeff Co, Va, on the charge of being connected with the outrage. $1,662 was found on the person of Dr Kline. -Balt American

Retaliatory executions-prisoners taken from prison in Lexington, Ky, & shot: Elijah Horton, of Carter Co; Thornton Laferty, of Pendleton; R W Yates, of Hunt; J L Jones, of Texas; Wm Long & R E Hunt, of Mason; Wm Tidha, of Boone; & Wm Darbra, of Pendleton.

Wash Corp: 1-Ptn from Geo Page & others, with a bill to pave & curb sq 467: passed. 2-Ptn of Admr Jos Smith: passed.

John R Shelton was arrested at the Eutaw Hse, Balt, on Fri, upon the charge of robbing the guests. He robbed Wm Knott of $80 & bank notes.

FRI NOV 11, 1864
Supreme Crt of D C: at Law #1080. John Schneider vs Louis Windholz & Henry Lekne. Plntf is to employ new cnsl to defend his interest. -B S Davis, atty

Farm for sale-M Bannon, as agent for Wm T Coggeshall; farm in PG Co, Md; 140 acs, near Beltsville, with good hse. -M Bannon, 32 St Paul st, Balt, Md.

Supreme Crt of D C, in Equity #320. Lewis M Nixdorf & others, vs Emma J Smith & others, all heirs of Henry Nixdorf, dec'd. Regarding-partition of lot 9 in sq 61 in Wash City. -W Redin, auditor

Supreme Crt of D C, in Equity #311. John F Cross, vs Thos H Green & wife, Alexander C Cross & others, all heirs of Alexander Cross, dec'd. Regarding the partition of lot 6 in sq 847 in Wash City. -W Redin, auditor

Supreme Crt of D C, in Equity #152. Libbey & son, vs Harriet Lancaster & Wm P Smith & wife, widow & heirs of Basil Lancaster. Statement of trustee's account & distribution of funds, City Hall, Wash, Nov 18. -W Redin, auditor

Sale of rl estate on or near the Wash R R: M Bannon, trustee, sold the country seat of Geo Wheeler, 50 acs, near Laurel Sta, for $190 per ac, to Wm T Steiger, Wash. Also, the market farm of F G Harman, near Hanover Switch, for $4,000. The farm of Isaac Hartman, of Balt, near Beltsville, 270 acs, for $6,000, to Mr Townsend, of Dela. Also, 87 ac farm in Green Spring Valley, formerly occupied as an Orphans Home, to B V Richardson, of same county, for $12,000. A farm on Frederick rd, 156 acs, price $6,000. A lot in Ellicott's Milles, 4 acs, $1,500, to Dr Feinour, of Balt, Md.

SAT NOV 12, 1864
Mrd: on Oct 19, at the residence of Col Wm Chapman, by Rev Wm W Hickox, Henry Wheelock Chapman to Jane H Van Vliet, all of Green Bay, Wisc.

Supreme Crt of D C, in Equity #1563. Moore et al, vs Kirk, et al. Ratify sale by E C Carrington, trustee, of parts of lots 7 & 9 in sq 437, to Mr Hamilton, for $950. -R J Meigs, clerk

Mosby captured a lot of men the other day, near Newtown, among whom was Capt Brewster, commissary of the 3rd cavalry div. After marching them to a Point near Winchester, they were obliged to draw lots to determine their fate, as 7 of them were to be hanged in retaliation for the 7 of Mosby's gang who were hanged by Gen Custer. Capt Brewster drew a blank & was destined to go to Richmond. Three were hung & others shot. The unfortunate were: Chas E Marvin, 2nd N Y cavalry; Cpl Jas Bennett, 2nd N Y cavalry; Geo H Sowle, 5th Mich cavalry; [Sowle escaped;] Sgt Dodge, 1st Vt cavalry; Frank Hooker, 5th Mich cavalry; L H Hoffnagel, 153rd N Y; & one man supposed to belong to the 4th W Va Infty or the 23rd Ohio, whose name is unknown.

MON NOV 14, 1864
Deaths reported to the Navy Dept for the week ending Nov 12, 1864:
Edw Ringgold, boatswains's mate, drowned, Oct 14, vessel U S S *John Adams.*
Frank Blake, 1st cl boy, typhoid fever, Oct 24, vessel U S S *Canandaigua.*
Andrew Anderson, coalheaver, suicide, Sep 7, vessel U S S *Narragansett.*
Bazel Brown, marine, consumption, Sep 11, Nav Hosp, Mare Island.
Henry Linden, seaman, dysentery, Oct 12, vessel U S S *St Marys.*
Michl Hasson, boy, remit fever, Oct 9, do.
Isaac Roberts, seaman, remit fever, Nov 2, Nav Hosp, Norfolk.
Frank Cassel, landsman, accident, Sep 11, vessel U S S *O H Lee.*
John H Seivers, seaman, bleeding from lungs, Nov 4, vessel U S S *Queen.*
Chas Daily, landsman, diabetes, Oct 27, Beaufort, N C.
Jack Conner, landsman, fracture, Nov 1, do.
Jas O'Neil, coal heaver, anemia, Nov 7, Nav Hosp, N Y.
John Andrews, landsman, consumption, May 29, Nav Hosp, Memphis.
Jack Windad, 1st cl boy, drowned, Aug 16, vessel U S S *Nymph.*
Moses W Moore, seaman, remit fever, Jul 14, vessel U S S *Avenger.*
Wm W Hickenbotham, landsman, measles, Apr 5, vessel U S S *Clara Dolson.*
Jas L Dawson, landsman, inter fever, Sep 14, vessel U S S *Hastings.*
John M Hensley, landsman, drowned, Apr 14, do.
Wm Wright, landsman, consumption, Jul 22, vessel U S S *Forest Rose.*
Abner Dalton, 1st cl boy, drowned, Oct 15, vessel U S S *Nymph.*
Frank Walter, ord seaman, drowned, Jul 25, vessel U S S *Pittsburg.*
Wm Pritchard, seaman, variola, Jun 20, vessel U S S *Fairy.*
S Anderson, seaman, congestive fever, Oct 12, vessel U S S *Mound City.*
Robt Hunt, landsman, congestive fever, Mar 21, do.
Rd Richard, 1st cl boy, drowned, Jul 22, vessel U S S *Ft Hindman.*
John Canty, landsman, drowned, Jul 4, vessel U S S *Lafayette.*
Geo Harrison, 1st cl boy, typhoid fever, do.
Jos Hudson, 1st cl boy, diarrhoea, Apr 12, vessel U S S *Gazelle.*
Frank Herman, seaman, remit fever, Jul 21, vessel U S S *Peri.*
Jackson Sullivan, seaman, drowned, Aug 11, do.
Sidney Osborne, qrtr gunner, wound, Apr 26, vessel U S S *Osage.*
Sabin Gebo, coalheaver, remit fever, Sep 3, do.
Wesley West, coal heaver, drowned, Oct 7, vessel U S S *Gen Lyon.*
R Beattie, landsman, drowned, Jul 15, vessel U S S *Louisiana.*

Jas Williams, seaman, drowned, Jul 12, vessel U S S *Argosy*.
Robt Payne, coal heaver, sound, May 14, vessel U S S *Ozark*.
Patrick H Sullivan, actg mstr's mate, remit fever, Aug 1, do.
Primus Lazare, landsman, pneumonia, Oct 11, vessel U S S *Wachita*.
Geo F Black, seaman, remit fever, Jun 17, do.
Wm Dickerson, seaman, remit fever, Jun 17, do.
Wm Johnson, seaman, typhoid fever, Aug 17, vessel U S S *Cricket*.
Jos Robinson, 1st cl fireman, remit fever, Sep 20, do.
Nich Hill, landsman, gunshot wound, Jul 14, vessel U S S *Judge Torrence*.
Wm Thomas, 2nd cl fireman, drowned, Jul 20, vessel U S S *Springfield*.
Wm Carter, fireman, pneumonia, Mar 24, vessel U S S *Tylor*.
Dr Hamilton, apoplexy, Sept 3, vessel U S S *Great Western*.
W H Jendish, 2nd cl fireman, drowned, Aug 30, do.
P Nickirons, landsman, drowned, Sep 10, do.
Wm Bryant, coalheaver, inter fever, May 2, vessel U S S *Neosho*.
Jas Cassidy, seaman, drowned, May 9, do.
Timothy Coleman, seaman, sound, Jun 11, do.
Chas Lower, seaman, wound, Jun 14, do.
Jas Sullivan, seaman, typhoid fever, Feb 14, vessel U S S *Fawn*.
Jas Henry, fireman, varioloid, Jun 24, do.
Thos Bennett, 1st cl pilot, wound, Jun 24, do.
Alex M Lond, landsman, casualty, Nov 8, vessel U S S *Unaditta*.
Chas Brown, seaman, disease of heart, Nov 9, Nav Asylum, Phil.
John Williams, seaman, diarrhoea, Nov 3, Beaufort, N C.
Wm A Downing, 2nd cl boy, cholera, Nov 9, vessel U S S *Wabash*.

Died: at his residence, 4th & L sts, in Wash City, on Nov 12, Patrick Wilson, in the 51st yr of his age. He was a faithful & efficient guard at the public jail. He leaves a large family. Funeral from his late residence today.

Wash, Nov 10. Gen McClellan's resignation is received by the War Dept. It will be accepted by the Pres immediately.

TUE NOV 15, 1864
Mrd: on Nov 12, by Rev Dr Gurley, Capt Gustave St Albe, of Vienna, Austria, Additional Aide-de-Camp on Maj Gen Augur's Staff, & Madame Marie A Berault, nee Anderson, of Wash City.

Died: in N Y, on Nov 12, Miss Electa Bingham, age 62 yrs. Funeral at Oak Hill Cemetery, on Wed.

Supreme Crt of D C, Equity #271. Cammack, Harvey & others, vs Eliza Connington & others. Parties & trustees & creditors of Michael Connington, dec'd, to meet at City Hall, Wash, on Dec 5. -W Redin, auditor

Rl estate for sale: deed of trust from David Barry & Eliza Barry, his wife; 300 acs in Surratt's Dist, PG Co, Md, rl estate of the said Eliza Barry, dec'd. -Fendall Marbury, Saml B Hance, trustees

Actg Ensign H B Chase, of the U S steamer *State of Georgia*, fell overboard from the vessel at N Y on Monday, & before he could be rescued was drowned.

Funeral of the late Nicholas, Count de Giorgi, late resident Austrian Minister at N Y, who died on Tue at the Clarendon Htl, took place on Fri at St Stephen's R C C, Rev Dr Cummings. The Count was born in Dalmatia, Austria, & was 55 years of age. –N Y paper

Provost Mrshl Gen: release on parole, to report when called upon by the Sec of War, the following named mbrs of St Louis Univ, drafted in St Louis, Mo: Rev John L'Esperance, Jos E Kelley, John T H Sealer, & John W O'Neill. –Jas B Fry, Prov Mrshl Gen [The above, says the Rpblcn, virtually exempts the reverend gentlemen therein named, it being understood that the Sec of War will make no call upon them for svc.]

WED NOV 16, 1864
Surrogate's Crt-Nov 14. The will of Andrew J Butler. This day set down for the admission of the will of Gen Butler's bro, in which the Gen was left sole exec. Mr J K Hackett appeared with Gen Butler. Mr C M Hall appeared for Ludwig Brauer & Fred'k W Schonfield, inhabitants of New Orleans & creditors of the estate. The Surrogate admitted the will to probate, there being no opposition on behalf of parties in interest. Mr Hackett said the estate was sworn to in the ptn as to $200,000, but he was instructed to say it was much less, but the Gen had no objection to give security in that amount. The Surrogate accordingly fixed the security in the penal sum of $400,000. The Surrogate declined to sign a certificate or admit service, attaching all the property in his hands in behalf of S & A J Smith, creditors of Gen Butler, to the amount of $150,000. Gen Butler came into the court, with cnsl, & gave bonds in the sum of $400,000, & then received letters of test. The will gives to Gen Butler & his heirs absolutely one half part of all the prnsl estate & property of the testate which at the time of his decease shall be found east of Rocky Mountains. It also gives to the Gen for the use of the testator's, son, Geo Harris Butler, $\frac{1}{4}$th of his prnsl property, situated as above, also $\frac{1}{4}$th part of all property not so situated. The son's portion is to be invested by the Gen until he[the son] arrives at the age of 30 yrs, when it is to pass absolutely to him. The balance of the estate goes to Johanna Butler, w/o the Testator. The will was executed at N Y on Sep 18, 1863. [Saml Smith & Andrew W Smith against Benj F Butler, who were pvt bankers, doing business under the firm of Saml Smith & Co, 27 Camp st, New Orleans.]

The Mobile Tribune says the valuable property belonging to Uriah P Levy, an ofcr in the Yankee navy, & known as the *Monticella Estate*, has been ordered by the Confederate States Crt to be sequestrated, & the receiver authorized to sell the same at public auction. This estate was once the residence of Thos Jefferson.

Exc's sale of prsnl estate of the late John Clapham, dec'd; on Oct 19. -Wm B Jackson, exc. – Green & Williams, aucts

Destructive fire on James River: Nov 14: all the bldgs at Rocky Landing, included Judge Bayer's residence, were destroyed by fire today/

Orphans Crt of Wash Co, D C. Case of Wm E Howard, adm w a of Yelverton P Page, dec'd; settlement on Dec 10. -Z C Robbins, rg o/wills

THU NOV 17, 1864
Mrd: in Saratoga, N Y, on Nov 15, at the residence of Chancellor Walworth, Brig Gen M D Hardin, U S Vols, to Miss Estelle Graham, grand-dght of Chancellor Walworth.

Died: on Nov 15, Leonard Selden, s/o Geo & Sarah Digges, aged 14 months & 9 days. Funeral from the residence of his grandmother, Mrs Mary Walker, this day.

Orphans Crt of Wash Co, D C. 1-Prsnl estate of Eliz A Foulke, late of Wash City, dec'd. -A F Kimmel, adm. 2-Prsnl estate of John E Foulke, late of Wash, D C, dec'd. -A F Kimmell, adm d b n.

The apparatus for projecting torpedoes under hostile vessels, which did the work for the rebel ram *Albemarle*, was invented by J L Lay, of Buffalo, N Y. Six vessels have already been constructed with this apparatus, & one is about to leave N Y for Fortress Monroe.

FRI NOV 18, 1864
From the N Y Evening Post of Wed-Gen Butler's N Y campaign. Maj Gen Butler left N Y for Wash yesterday & will go to the front. The troops which were placed under his command for special svcs sailed for the James river on Mon, their svcs, fortunately, not having been required. As no breach of the peace occurred there was no occasion to land a man in this city. The troops arrived at Ft Hamilton & Govn'rs Island on Mon preceding the election. On Tue they were placed on board of steamers, & vessels were stationed at various points opposite the Battery, & in the North & East rivers. This disposition of the military was made in order to prevent possible collisions, & to avoid the appearance of intimidation at the polls. Gen Butler yesterday issued the farewell order. Maj Gen Danl Butterfield & Brig Gen Webb were detailed in the city. Brig Gen Gordon was absent on sick leave. Provisional division was under command of Brig Gen Hawley, from the Army of the James, & the regts of the regulars from the Army of the Potomac. Headqrtrs of N Y C, Nov 15, 1864. The Commanding Gen acknowledges his obligations, altho not all in actual svc, for their prompt action in reporting for duty, & most efficiently supervising the several districts assigned them, giving valuable aid in transmitting all information necessary to secure the peace of the community & the honor of the country. Cols: M Murphy, Barney, W B Barton, Foster, J B Wilson, Banks' staff. Lt Cols: O Ferrier, Morgan, Talicoke, J M Raymond. Majs: A C Colgrant, H Gahell, T O Brien, J W Payne, Chas J Seymour, Tremaine, F E Gray, Portar. Capts: F G Burke, A W Norcross, M Dougherty, Chas T Green, W E Van Wyck, Lewis Mehrmein, Hall, Watson, D F Wright, G F Beatler, M A Stearns, F M Hendricks, C Hulten, G B Halstead, L Crosby, Banks' staff; E L Molunoux. Lts: S R Morgan, F W Roberts, F Powell, A R Landlow, H B Loomis, O Machale, Jas S King, A Van Brants, F Corvel, M J Smith, W T Simms, Hse o/Reps C Adams, Chas Herzoy, Lyons, E B Elliott, Alfred W Craven, Ralph Ellis. Thanks are given to Mr Norman Wiard, who tendered his steamer *Augusta*, for the movement of the troops. By command of Maj Gen Butler: A F Puffer, Capt & Acting Ast Adj Gen

Died: on Sep 25, near Pulaski, Tenn, Wm L Peckham, formerly of Wash. At the time of his death he & a few other Union sldrs were guarding Sulphur trestle, when they were attacked by a force of rebels. Lt Peckham was shot & died instantly.

Providence, R I. John Pitman, for 40 years Judge of the U S Dist Crt for the dist of R I, was found dead in bed on Nov 17; age 80 yrs.

Fruit trees for sale: John Saul, 396 7th st, corner of H.

John R Davis, a Friend, residing at Achusnet, Mass, & aged 98 yrs, cast his first vote on Tue last.

Released from the Old Capitol: 4 of the clerks of Messrs Johnson & Sutton, charged with selling goods to blockade runners, released on Wed, upon giving their paroles to appear as witnesses when called upon: W B Murray, John B Steir, Asbury Baker, & J S Gregory.

Mrs Florence Shehan, charged with furnishing ctzns clothing to sldrs, was arraigned yesterday before a military commission & pleaded guilty. She said her hsbnd was the sldr she furnished with clothing. She obeyed, she said, as a good wife should. He had written her to bring him some clean clothing, in which he could come home. She thought his term of svc had expired.

Thos Fletcher, of St Nicholas Restaurant, F & 15th sts, was tried on Tue at the military commission rooms on the charge of illegal recruiting. At the close of the trial he was released, having been on bail, but was afterwards re-arrested & sent to the Old Capitol.

SAT NOV 19, 1864
Died: on Nov 16, near Harper's Ferry, Chas P Leake, aged 22 yrs. Funeral from his late residence, Alexandria, Va, tomorrow.

Headqrtrs 19th Army Corps: Nov 16, 1864. In the cavalry skirmish on Sat the rebel Lt Col Thos Marshall, a grandson of Chief Justice Marshall, was killed within a mile of his residence. A light skirmish occurred yesteday near Luray between a party of Gen Powell's cavalry & a small force of rebel cavalry. Rebels were driven in the direction of Mount Jackson.

John Rantz, charged with conspiring to resist the draft in Columbia Co, Pa, has been sentenced to pay a fine of $1,000 & to be imprisoned 2 years in Ft Mifflin. Saml Kline was sentenced to 2 yrs. The trial was by military crt.

Brig Gen H Wessels assigned to duty in Wash as commissary Gen of Prisoners, v Col W Hoffman, relieved & ordered to the command of all camps & hospitals West of the Miss. Gen Wessels will have command of all prisoners east of the Mississippi. Col Hoffman has been breveted Brig Gen for meritorious svc.

MON NOV 21, 1864
Deaths reported to the Navy Dept for the week ending Nov 19, 1864:
Chas Daily, landsman, diabetes, Oct 27, vessel U S S *Maratanza.*
Edwin Hellman, 1st cl boy, typhoid fever, Nov 1, vessel U S S *Mendota.*
Andrew Manson, seaman, dysentery, Nov 7, Nav Hosp, Norfolk.
Johnson Blunt, landsman, consumption, Nov 14, do.
Wm Powers, seaman, consumption, Nov 13, do.
R S Spangler, landsman, dysentery, Nov 12, vessel U S S *Montgomery.*
Geo Franks, seaman, drowned, Nov 12, vessel U S S *Mackinaw.*
Robt M Hay, yeoman, typhoid fever, Oct 23, vessel U S S *Canabassett.*
John Harris, seaman, dysentery, Oct 28, Nav Hosp, Pensacola.
Robt Allen, landsman, yel fever, Oct 17, do.
John G Bonman, q m, yel fever, Oct 17, do.
Ira W Bragg, Ast Surg, yel fever, Oct 21, do.
John Brogan, coalheaver, yel fever, Oct 7, do.
Michael Doyle, coalheaver, yel fever, Oct 17, do.
Hudson Farrell, landsman, yel fever, Oct 5, do.
Jno McKinzee, landsman, yel fever, Oct 12, do.
Jas Reach, 2nd cl fireman, yel fever, Oct 10, do.
John C Smith, mstr-at-arms, yel fever, Oct 21, do.
Wm H Tummey, landsman, yel fever, Oct 13, do.
Thos C Yookey, paymstr's steward, yel fever, Oct 5, do.

Nicholas Dillon, actg 3rd ast engr, yel fever, Oct 24, do.
John F Coleman, landsman, acute dysentery, Oct 17, do.
Edw Well, seaman, acute dysentery, Oct 27, Nav Hosp, New Orleans.
Geo Pellsbury, ord seaman, exhaustion, Sep 25, vessel U S S *Chickasaw*.
Wm C Belcher, landsman, drowned, Oct 4, vessel U S S *Keystone State*.
Jas E Rudd, landsman, drowned, Oct 4, do.
Wm West, seaman, drowned, Oct 8, vessel U S S *Lancaster*.

Lt Gen Grant came up to Balt on Fri, with several ofcrs, & proceeded on to Burlington, N J, on a visit to his family, who are adjourning at that place.

By order of Gen Burbridge, 5 guerillas were shot to death at Henderson, Ky, last Sun, in retaliation for the murder of Union men in that region. Three of them were bros, named Horton, & 2 others named Forrest & Fry. Executed by a negro regt now stationed in that city. All were killed instantly by the first fire, all being shot thru the heart. -St Louis Union

Mrd: on Nov 10, at Gtwn, D C, by Rev Smith Pyne, Wm R Philip, of Wash, to Miss Eliza P Worthington, d/o John G Worthington, of Gtwn.

TUE NOV 22, 1864
Mrd: on Nov 15, by Rev F E Boyle, at *Avon*, the residence of the bride's father, Turner W Wilson to Aimee, eldest d/o Wm E Stubbs, both of Montg Co, Md.

Died: recently, at Richmond, Mr Edw B Robinson, printer, aged about 63 yrs. He was a resident of Washington for more than 30 years prior to the present rebellion.

Died: on Nov 20, of consumption, Jos McCarthy, in the 27th yr of his age. Funeral from his late residence, 5th & G sts, today.

Ephraim & Lydia Ann Harner, of Germany twnshp, Adams Co, Pa, lost 5 chldrn by death between Oct 28 & Nov 5, of diptheria. Their ages ranged from 3 to 14 yrs.

In the case of A J Stansbury against Wash City, in the Crct Crt, claiming $10,000 damages on account of injuries from falling into an area on 13th st, the jury gave a verdict for the city. The case goes to the Supreme Crt of D C.

The Balt Sun states that Thurlow Weed, the veteran editor of the Albany Evening Jrnl, is now in Wash, negotiating the purchase of the Nat'l Intell. The above is news to the proprietors of the Intell.

WED NOV 23, 1864
Obit-died at the residence of her nephew, Thos J Chew, in Calvert Co, Md, on Oct 15, Mrs Eliz L Young, relict of the late Josias Young, & d/o Rt Rev Dr Claggett, the first Bishop of Md. She had survived all of her bros & sisters, but left a number of their descendants to venerate her memory. -Parsonage of St Thos, Nov 1864

Supreme Crt of D C, in Equity #340: Philip May vs Francie L Smith, et al. Regarding-procure a release to Philip May of a deed of trust on lot 1, in Wash Co, D C, called *Pleasant Plains*, made by W G W White to Francis L Smith et al on Oct 5, 1854. May acquired by purchase from Jas M Carlilse, as trustee. Smith is a non-resident of D C. -R J Meigs, clerk

Walter S McFarlan, formerly a reporter in Wash City, is being admitted to the Boston bar, having recently studied law at the Howard Law School. -Local

Ex-Gov Fairbanks, of Vermont, died on Sunday at his home in St Johnsburg.

Capt McNeill, the veteran scout & partisan leader whose exploits promise to be repeated by his gallant son, died in Harrisonburg on Nov 10, of wounds received on Oct 3 last.

THU NOV 24, 1864
Died: on Nov 21, Jane Snyder, w/o M Snyder, of Wash City, in her 59th yr.

Sarah Jane Smith, of Wash Co, Ark, sentenced to be hung on Nov 25, by a military commission at St Louis, for cutting Gov't telegraph wires.

Messrs Hiram McCullough, Edwin H Webster, Chas E Phelps, Francis Thomas, & Benj G Harris were chosen at the late election in Md to represent the state in the next Congress, which will commence its session on the 1st Mon of Dec of next yr.

SAT NOV 26, 1864
Mrd: on Nov 24, at St Aloysius Chr, by Rev Fr Hitzelberger, Capt Columbus J Queen, Commissary of Subsistence U S Army, to Kate, d/o Thos L Noyes, all of Wash City.

Mrd: on Nov 22, by Rev John Thrish, at the residence of the bride's father, Mr W G Steinmetz, of Prussia, to Miss Jennie C, d/o W P McKelden, of Wash City.

Died: on Nov 12, John F Stack, native of Tralee, county of Berry, Ire, formerly of Brooklyn, for the last 6 years a resident of Wash.

Orphans Crt of Wash Co, D C. Case of John P Franklin, exc of Stephen P Franklin, dec'd: settlement on Dec 17. -Z C Robbins, rg o/wills

Mrs Joshua R Giddings died at Jefferson, Ashtabula Co, Ohio, on Nov 15.

Mrs Sarah Hutchins, w/o Thos Hutchins, recently sentenced by the Military Commission at Balt, for attempting to send a sword to the rebel Col Harry Gilmor, & of illegal correspondence with the rebel States, has been sentenced to 5 years labor in the pen & a fine of $5,000. [Nov 30-Mrs Hutchins was incarcerated in the prison at Fitchburg, Mass.]

MON NOV 28, 1864
Deaths reported to the Navy Dept for the week ending Nov 26, 1864.
Killed by explosion of boiler of the U S steamer *Tulip* Nov 11:

John Raffenburg, mstr's mate	Jas Campbell, 2nd cl fireman
John Hammond, mstr's mate	Wm H Simmerson, 2nd cl fireman
Wm H Smith, actg mstr commanding	Benj Pollock, 2nd cl fireman
Geo H Parks, 3rd ast engr	Henry Johnson, steward's cook
John Gordon, 3rd ast engr	Thos Carter, wardroom stewart
Chas Henning, pay steward	Chas Ruoff, capt's steward
Wm McCormick, surg's steward	Peter Johnson, seaman
Jas Jackson, pilot	Martin Blatzin, ord seaman
John Roberts, boatswain's mate	Patrick Quinlin, ord seaman
John Allison, 2nd cl fireman	Jas Robinson, coal heaver
John Nolan, 2nd cl fireman	Geo H Niles, coal heaver

Jas Carroll, coal heaver
John Colley, coal heaver
G W Wilson, landsman
Wm O'Connell, landsman
Jas Bracken, landsman
Rd Conover, landsman
Thos Watson, landsman
Jas Leary, landsman
Dd Preyser, landsman
Beverly Burk, landsman
Elijah Jefferson, landsman
Robt Warren, landsman
Benj Brown, landsman

Waverly Mason, landsman
Frank Green, landsman
Wm Fletcher, landsman
Chas Sterns, 1st cl boy
Battle Fitzhugh, 1st cl boy
Noah Brooks, 1st cl boy
Jas Bulger, 1st cl boy
John Diggs, 1st cl boy
Jules Tallot, 1st cl boy
Wm Lindsey, blank
Geo Ireland, boy
Jas Porter, 2nd cl fireman
Michael Holland, cook

_____ Smith, recently discharged from the vessel *Yankee*, Nov 11, U S steamer *Tulip*.
H C Chase, actg ensign, drowned, Nov 11, N Y harbor.
John Driscoll, landsman, consumption, Nov 8, vessel U S S *Ft Morgan*.
John G Everett, q m, drowned, Aug 2, vessel U S S *Avenger*.
Chas A Bliss, actg vol Lt, tarolysis, Oct 28, vessel U S S *Newbern*.
Saml Champs, seaman, bleeding from lungs, Nov 8, vessel U S S *Shamrock*.
Jacob Egr, 1st cl fireman, disease of heart, Nov 15, vessel U S S *New Ironsides*.
Henry Jackson, actg ensign, wounds, May 9, vessel U S S *New London*.
John Jacobs, capt forecastle, wounds, vessel U S S *Granite City*.
Andrew J Reynolds, landsman, yel fever, Oct 1, Nav Hosp, New Orleans.
Jas W Penson, landsman, yel fever, Oct 14, do.
Jas Throop, landsman, yel fever, Oct 15, do.
Geo Hale, seaman, yel fever, Oct 22, do.
Antonia Silva, landsman, yel fever, Oct 22, do.
John B Powers, landsman, syphilis, Oct 21, do.
Alonzo F Sawyer, coxswain, yel fever, Oct 21, do.
C F Walderman, act ensign, yel fever, Oct 22, do.
John Williams, qrtr gunner, fracture, Oct 31, Nav Hosp, Pensacola
Hanson Cover, landsman, drowned, Nov 20, vessel U S S *Com Read*.
Jas McLoughlin, boatswain's mate, wound, Nov 7, vessel U S S *Pontiac*.
Matt. Somers, 1st cl boy, wound, Nov 7, do.
L F Brown, landsman, wound, Nov 7, do.
John McDaniel, landsman, wound, Nov 7, do.
Edw Lynch, capt forecastle, wound, Nov 7, do.
Chas Nelson, ord seaman, wound, Nov 8, do.
Jas W Davis, ord seaman, inflam of brain, Nov 13, Nov Hosp, Chelsea
John Williams, qrtrmstr, wounds, Oct 24, vessel U S S *Tacony*.

Ltr from Pres Lincoln, Nov 21, 1864, to Mrs Bixby, Boston, Mass: Dear Madam: *I have been shown on the file of the War Dept a statement of the Adj Gen of Massachusetts that you are the mother of five sons who have died gloriously on the field of battle. I feel how weak and fruitless must be any word of mine which should attempt to beguile you from the grief of a loss so overwhelming; but I cannot refrain from tendering to you the consolation that may be found in the thanks of the Republic they died to save. I pray that our Heavenly Father may assuage the anguish of your bereavements, and leave only the cherished memory of the loved and lost, and the solemn pride that must be yours to have laid so costly a sacrifice upon the altar of freedom. Yours, very sincerely & respectfully. A Lincoln*

Orphans Crt of Wash Co, D C. 1-Case of Ferdinand Ehrhardt, adm of John A Thoele, dec'd; settlement on Dec 20. -Z C Robbins, rg o/wills 2-Case of Wm F Mattingly, adm w a of Hannah Ulrich, dec'd; settlement on Dec 20. -Z C Robbins, rg o/wills

Supreme Crt of D C, in Equity #284. Mary R & Sarah E Ricard, & Mgt A Queen, & Saml W Queen, vs Martha L, Joshua W, & Geo T Ricard. Statement of the trustees' account, City Hall, Wash, Nov 26. -W Redin, auditor

Crct Crt for PG Co, Md, in Equity #445. Francis J Shulze & M Alice Shulze, his wife, vs John H Strider. Regarding-appointment of a new trustee in the stead of John H Strider, who has removed to parts unknown, from Wash City, his former residence. On Jan 2, 1855, pending a treaty of marriage between them, M Alice Shulze, with consent of said Francis, conveyed to Richd O'Mullikin, her bro, prsnl estate & property, to hold as trustee for the sole use of said M Alice, property not to be subject to the control of said Francis J Shulze after their marriage. John H Strider was appt'd trustee in place of R O'Mullikin. - Frederick Sasscer, clerk

Monticello, the former residence of Thos Jefferson, in Albemarle Co, Va, was sold at auction on Thu, under the sequestrian act, for $80,500. Benj F Ficklin was the purchaser.

Personal: 1-The health of Judge Catron, of the U S Supr Crt, is said to be rapidly failing. 2-Hon John P Hale, of N H, sailed for Europe on Wed last. 3-Maj Gen D N Couch arrived at his home in Taunton, Mass, on Tue. 4-Gen Asboth has been compelled by the severity of his wounds to retire for the present from active svc in Fla & go to New Orleans for medical attendance. He is succeeded by Gen Bailey. 5-Brig Gen Sully arrived in Milwaukee on Tue, with Capt Nathl Pope, of his staff, on an official visit to Gen Pope.

TUE NOV 29, 1864

Died: on Nov 27, in her 92nd yr, Miss Eliz Washington. Funeral from the residence of her nephew, Geo A W Randall, 12th & D sts, today.

Died: on Nov 26, Mrs Ellen Dwyer, widow o/the late Thos Dwyer, aged 67 yrs. Funeral from St Peter's Chr, today.

Died: on Nov 17, at *Monticello*, PG Co, Md, Mrs Mary Morsell, w/o B K Morsell, long a resident of Wash City.

For sale-the farm on which I recently resided: 246 acs, in PG Co, Md. -Benton Tolson, Surrattsville, PG Co, Md.

Wash Corp: 1-The amount of $15 be paid to Benj Woodfield for deposit to the credit of the Corp for use of a stand in the Northern Mkt.

The executor under the will of the late Stephen A Douglas presented to the County Crt, yesterday, receipts showing he had paid to Mrs Douglas over $7,500, & to the 2 chldrn over $7,000-being proceeds from the estate, after paying all the debts. -Chicago Tribune, Nov 15

St Louis Rpblcn: Maj Gen Alfred Pleasanton appt'd to the command of the Dist of St Louis, Dept of Missouri.

Gen Thos Ewing, jr, who has been for 9 months past commander in this Dist, is assigned to the command of the Dist of Rolla. Gen McNeil is going to Warrensburg.

WED NOV 30, 1864

Died: at Little Rock, Ark, Dr G Erving Bonford, s/o the late Col Geo Bomford, U S Ordnance. [No date]

Supreme Crt of D C, in Equity #215. Murray & Semmes, vs Desmonds, adm, & heirs. Ratify sale made by Wm Y Fendall, trustee. -Andrew Wylie -Meigs, clerk

Col D H Vinton promoted to a brvt brig generalship in the regular army. He has been in the U S military svc for 43 yrs, 28 of which he has been employed in the q m dept. He has been engaged in nearly all the active military operations of our armies since the yr 1836.

N Y, Aug 1, 1864. To Cmdor John Rodgers, U S Navy: fellow ctzns present him with a svc of plate, with every highest respect & esteem: in the management of the iron clad *Weehawken* during her first perilous & stormy cruise: the capture of the rebel ram *Atlanta*, the most formidable armored vessel which our enemy has yet put afloat:

Chas Knapp, Pa	J Ericsson, N Y	Jas Gregory, N Y
Alex'r Swift, Ohio	Chas L Frost, N Y	J B & W W Cornell, N Y
Harrison Loring, Mass	Corn H Delamater, N Y	Zeno Secor, Jersey Cty-
Geo C Bestor, Ill	Geo W Quintard, N Y	N J
Geo B Stetson, Mass	Jos Colwell, N Y	

St Andrew's Soc of Wash: election of ofcrs: Wm R Smith, Pres

Fred'k McGuire, 1st V P	Alex'r Gardner, Corr Sec	J P Wilson, Treas
Jas Guild, 2nd V P	Thos W Spencer, Rec Sec	
Mgrs:		
H B Todd	Andrw Small	John Reekie
David Knox	John Rutherford	A B McFarlan

The 10th Anniv of this Soc will be celebrated at Weicker's restaurant this evening, the 30th.

THU DEC 1, 1864

Mrd: at Balt, Md, on Nov 29, by Rev Mr Dickson, Chas C Tucker, of Wash, to Mary A Evans, d/o L Cowles, of Balt.

Died: on Nov 29, Jas Davis, in his 59th yr, formerly of Alexandria, Va, but for the last 19 years a resident of Wash City. Funeral from his late residence, 385 5th st, today.

Died: on Nov 30, Mrs Ann Harbaugh, w/o the late John Randolph Harbaugh, aged 46 yrs. Funeral from 437 6th st, today.

Wash Corp: 1-Ptn of Wm Hildebrand, & also the ptn of Richd Jones: referred to the Cmte on Claims. 2-Ptn of Geo E Ward: referred to the Cmte on Finance. 3-Same for the ptn of Albert Brooks. 4-Bill for relief of Wm Thomas: laid over. 5-Bill of Chas Stewart: referred to the Cmte on Improvements. 6-Ptn of Robt Werner, for return of certain moneys: referred to the Cmte on Claims. 7-Ptn of Thos L Noyes & others in relation to foot bridges: referred to the Cmte on Improvements.

Mr Paul R Shipman, late editor of the Louisville Jrnl, recently arrested & ordered to be sent south, has been unconditionally released by Gen Burbridge. He is in Louisville. -Nashville Union

FRI DEC 2, 1864

Died: on Nov 30, Wm Dalton, a native of Yorkshire, Eng, & for the last 30 years a resident of Wash City, in his 57th yr. Funeral from his late residence, 431 F st, today.

Died: at Sandy Spr, Md, on Nov 29, Mary H Brooke, w/o Wm S Brooke, & d/o Benj & Mgt E Hallowell, in the 26th yr of her age. She left 2 little dghts, one 23 mos, & the other 3 months.

Sale of rl estate on the Wash R R: farm of 140 acs, near Beltsville, to E Larman, of Wash, for $5,700; farm of 219 acs, A A Co, Md, to Wilson Disney, for $4,200; farm of 27 acs, near the above, property of a drafted man, to Mr East, of Balt, for $500.

Resignation of ofcrs of the U S vols, to take effect Nov 30, 1864:
Maj Gen John A McClernand   Brig Gen Neal Dow.
Brig Gen Eleazer A Paine

Albany Argus: Pres Lincoln has pardoned Wm T Smithson, the Washington banker, charged with corresponding with the enemy, & Wm Yokum, superintendent of contraband depot at Cairo charged with kidnapping negroes. Each was under a 5 years sentence to the pen in that city.

Episc Chr of the Ascension, on H st, Rev Dr Pinckney-Rector: admission to church membership by confirmation: amongst those who were dedicated was the Hon Chas Mason, who was accompanied to the altar by his beautiful dght, each vowing to conform to the rites of Christian fellowship, & always obey God's law. -Union

Sentence of rebellious ctzn: Robt M Harrover, ctzn, was tried before the military commision of which Gen Doubleday is Pres. Charge: Violation of the laws of war. Harrover, a native of Va, & late resident of Wash City, D C, was enrolled in Wash City, in the spring of 1863, & thereby became liable for the draft. Harrover did proceed from within our lines into those of the so-called Confederate states, during the latter part of Jul, 1863, & went to Richmond, Va, to enlist in an unlawful band of guerrillas, known as Mosby's band, & remain there until his arrest about Oct last. He pleaded not guilty. Court found him guilty & sentenced him to be shot to death by musketry at such time & place as the Sec of War may direct. 2/3rd of the commission concurring therein. Sentence was commuted to confinement at hard labor in the pen for 10 yrs. Clinton prison, N Y, is the designated place.

SAT DEC 3, 1864

Died: in Wash City, on Dec 1, Aloysius N Clements, in his 42nd yr. Funeral from his late residence, M & 13th sts, today.

Died: on Dec 2, of membrous croup, Wm Henry, 2nd s/o Brig Gen D H Rucker, aged 6 years & 10 months. Funeral from St Matthew's Chr, Sun.

H G Fant & Richd Pettit have this day withdrawn from the firm of Rittenhouse, Fant & Co. The business hereafter will be cont'd under the name of Rittenhouse, Fowler Co. Messrs Fant & Pettit have also withdrawn from the Bank of Commerce, Gtwn, D C. [This is followed by: Persons having business with the undersigned will find him at the Banking Hse of Rittenhouse, Fowler & Co. -Hamilton G Fant.]

Two large store-rms for rent, over the store of Messrs Siousea & Ennis, 325 Pa ave, near 7th.

The late Prof Benj Silliman, senior, died at his residence in N Haven, Nov 24, aged 84 yrs. Yale loses a valued ofcr & American Science loses a devoted student. –Springfield [Mass] Republican

MON DEC 5, 1864

Obit-Julia M, w/o Col John Henry Waring, in the 52nd yr of her age, died at the residence of her dght, Mrs Richard Duckett, in PG Co, Md, on Nov 26. She was the d/o Judge Worthington, of Balt: mrd in PG Co, Md over 30 years ago: mother of a large family.

The Pblc Ledger, of Phil has been purchased by Geo W Childs, the well known book publisher. Messrs Swain & Abell, after 28 years of successful management of the paper, retire with a fortune estimated at several million dollars.

Tragedy in N Y prison: John Donovan, a discharged sldr, locked up for intoxication, seized an iron bar & struck down 2 of his companions, Jas McDonald & Wm Kenedy, both of whom died. Another man, Wm George has since died from a fractured skull. Shots were finally fired at him, one of which lodged in the shoulder of Geo Henry Hill, inflicting a serious wound.

TUE DEC 6, 1864

Died: Jas C McFarland, aged 72 yrs, in Charlestown, Kanawha Co, Va, recently. He was born in Haverill, Mass, on Oct 1, 1792. His family removed to Ohio, at Marietta, while he was quite young. In 1832 he was selected as Pres of the Bank of Va, Branch Bank at Charlestown. He was a husband, father & brother.

On Thu Mr & Mrs Chas Stratton, better known as Gen & Mrs Tom Thumb, arrived at Liverpool in Wash City from N Y. The diminutive couple were accompainied by some servants, including a nurse with the baby, which is almost as big as its father. –Liverpool paper, 12th

Southern papers report the accidental death, a few days ago, of the Hon W R W Cobb, formerly a Rep in Congress from Ala, & more recently a mbr of the Confederate Congress, from which he was expelled [he not being present] for his supposed loyalty to the U S. He is said to have been killed by the discharge of one of his own pistols, which fell to the ground from his person & inflicted a fatal wound.

WED DEC 7, 1864

Trustee's sale of lot 9 in sq 559, Wash Co, D C; deed of trust by John Holleron & Mary, his wife, dt'd Jun 4, 1864. -John E Norris, trustee

Fatal result of recklessness. At Vicksburg, Lt Dee, commissary of subsistences of the cavalry forces, was killed recently by Capt Jesup, 4th Ill cavalry. Both ofcrs were somewhat intoxicated & were playing Wm Tell. Dee placed a cup on his head & Jesup fired at it. As he pulled the trigger, Dee raised his head a little, & the ball went thru his forehead. Jesup is now under arrest.

THU DEC 8, 1864

Died: on Dec 6, after a lingering illness, Chas Edw Brent, s/o the late Col Wm Brent, in the 38th yr of his age. Funeral from St Peter's Chr, today.

Supreme Crt of D C. 1-Equity #246: Barclay, vs Douglas, et al. Ratify sale made by Will Y Fendall, trustee. -R C Meigs, clerk 2-Equity #1438: B W Kennon, vs M V Kennon & others. Ratify sale of part of *Mt Pleasant* to John H Snyder for $6,764.37. -R J Meigs, clerk

The death sentence of Miss Sarah Jane Smith, of Arkansas, age under 17 yrs, was commuted by Gen Rosecrans to imprisonment during the war.

FRI DEC 9, 1864
Died: in Boston, Mass, on Dec 6, Maria Cornelia Ritchie, d/o Hon Jas T Austin, & w/o Dr Geo H Lyman, Medical Inspec, U S Army.

Died: in N Y C, on Dec 8, of malignant ulcerated sore throat, Mary Louisa, eldest d/o Robt H & Harriet E P Gallaher, aged 10 years & 10 months. Remains will be brought to Wash, 421 15th st, for interment. Funeral from St Matthew's Chr, Sat.

For sale: Mitchell's Park Hse, adjoining Grover's Theatre: doing a business of $100 per day. Apply on the premises. –Caleb W Mitchell

Senate: 1-Ptn from Wm C Bryant, Henry W Longfellow, Horace Greeley, John A Dix, Gen U S Grant, Geo Bancroft, & others, praying the founding & support of a Nat'l Home for the totally disabled sldrs & sailors of the Army & Navy: referred to the Military Cmte.

SAT DEC 10, 1864
Mrd: on Oct 18, in Iowa City, by Rev Mr Asman, Geo W Kitchen, of Clark Co, Va, to Emma Snowden, d/o Truman Fairall, of Alleghany Co, Md.

Died: at her residence, 502 E st, on Dec 9, Mrs Eliza Coyle, relict of Andrew Coyle, sr. Funeral at the First Presby Chr on Dec 11.

Died: in Wash City, on Dec 9, Chas B, s/o L F & Mary C Clark, aged 9 yrs. Funeral from their residence, 418 H st, today.

Wash Corp: 1-Ptn of John Bligh & others for a water main: referred to the Cmte on Drain & Distribution of Water. 2-Cmte on Claims: adverse report on the ptn of C L Lockwood & Co, & asked to be discharged: which was ordered. 3-Cmte on Claims: adverse on ptn of Louisa Noll for the return of a fine paid by her, & asked to be discharged: which was ordered. 4-Communication from C D Hess & John T Ford, in relation to an increase of price in theatrical licenses. Cmte on Police asked to be discharged from their further consideration: so ordered.

Convention of Mfgrs & Dealers in Tobacco re-assembled at Cooper Institute, N Y, on Thu: Wm A Lawrence, presiding. Permanent ofcrs: Wm E Lawrence, Pres; V Ps: Jos Hall, N Y; David C McCammon, Pa; Christian Ax, Md; David Campbell, N J; F N Brown, Conn; Isaac A Brewser, Mass; W S Huntoon; R I; H Crane, Mo; Mr Schott, Ohio; Jas F Power, D C. Rec Sec-F A Schroeder, N Y. Cor Sec-Edw Burke, N Y. Treas, David A McAlpine, N Y.

MON DEC 12, 1864
Died: on Dec 9, after a long & severe illness, Jos Cross, in the 58th yr of his age. Funeral from his late residence, Va av & 2nd st, today.

Died: on Dec 10, H R Schoolcraft, aged 72 yrs. Funeral from his late residence, 256 F st, today.

Orphans Crt of Wash Co, D C. Prsnl estate of Peter A Brinsmade, late of Wash City, dec'd. -Jas G Smith, adm

Miss Mary Martin, who has kept a brdg hse on K st, near Connecticut av, for the past 6 mos, accidentally set fire to her clothes on Fri. She died 3 hours later: age about 29 yrs.

Hon Reuben E Fenton, Govn'r elect of N Y, has resigned his seat in the Hse o/Reps, to take effect on Dec 20.

TUE DEC 13, 1864
Died: in Wash City, on Dec 12, after a long & painful illness, Susan L Ennis, w/o Mr Gregory Ennis, of Wash City, in her 64th yr. Funeral from the residence of her hsbnd, 282 F st, Wed.

Supreme Crt of D C. 1-Equity #221: Sarah Ann Brown & Alfred B Foreman, vs Wm A, Jas O, Andrew, Calvin, Dolly, Almira, & Waite J Brown, heirs of John W Brown. The above & N C Stephens, trustee, to meet at City Hall, Wash, on Dec 27, for distribution. -W Redin, auditor
2-Equity #215: Murry & Semmes, vs Cornelius J Desmond, Thos & Mary Ratcliffe, & Wm & Mary Keithly. The above, creditors of Mary Desmond, & Wm Y Fendall, trustee, to meet at City Hall, Wash, on Dec 29, for distribution of funds. -W Redin, auditor
3-Equity #254: Brown vs Brown, et al. Ratify sale made by Jos H Bradley, jr, trust. -R J Meigs, clerk
4-Equity #350: Martha Deter & Frances C Robinson, vs John A & Wm Anderson. Regarding-partition of lot 16 in sq 368, Wash. E Carusi, guardian ad litem, & parties named to meet at my ofc in City Hall, Wash, on Dec 20. W Redin, clerk
5-Equity #109: Peter V Hagner, Francis R Hagner, Alex'r B Hagner, Daniel R Hagner, & Alex'r B Hagner & Danl B Hagner, excs of Frances Hagner, against Alexr Randall, Josh H Nicholson & Eliza A his wife, C K Nelson & Mary M his wife, Richd H, Laura S, Cora C, Kate G, Fanny, Grattan, Chas E & Randall Hagner. Parties named & Alexr B Hagner, trustee, to meet at City Hall, Wash, on Dec 26. -W Redin, auditor
6-Equity #246: Richd Barclay, against Adele Douglas & Robt M & Stephan A Douglas, [widow & heirs of Stephen A Douglas,] Wm H Russell, J C Burche, & Danl P Rhodes, excs of said Douglas, & others. Distribution of the purchase money of sq West of sq 623, Wash City; in City Hall, Wash, on Dec 22. –Redin
7-Equity #1563: Moore, & other creditors, against Geo E Kirk. Creditors of said Kirk, & E C Carrington, trustee, to meet on Dec 24, at my ofc in City Hall, Wash, on Dec 24, for distribution of funds. -W Redin, auditor
8-Equity #174: Mary Ann Roche against Jas E Smith & Emma his wife, & Alice A, Mary J, Sallie J, Wm J, & Edw B Roche. Parties named & A Lloyd, trustee, to meet at my ofc in City Hall, Wash, on Dec 21. -W Redin, auditor
9-Equity #254: Adelaide J Brown against Thos B, Wm V H, Geo H Harrington, & Arvin Brown. Parties named & J H Bradley, jr, trustee, to meet at my ofc in City Hall, Wash, on Dec 23, for distribution of funds. -W Redin, auditor
10-Equity #1628: Edw R Ward against Geo S Krafft, Sarah Krafft, & Philip H, Wm R, & Geo W Ward, & others. Parties named & A Lloyd, trustee, to meet at my ofc in City Hall, Wash, on Dec 28, for distribution of funds. -W Redin, auditor

Since Mr Lincoln's inauguration in 1861, there have been 5 changes in his cabinet: Mr Stanton for Mr Cameron, Mr Usher for Mr Smith, Mr Fessenden for Mr Chase, Mr Dennison for Mr Blair, & Mr Speed for Mr Bates.

Gen Meade has been made a full Maj Gen in the regular army, to date from Aug 18, 1864-to rank next to Gen Sherman.

WED DEC 14, 1864

Mrd: at St Paul's Chr, Chestertown, Md, on Dec 6, by Rev Jas Hubard, Frank C Cosby, Paymstr U S Navy, to Miss Lottie M, d/o Saml W Spencer, of Chestertown.

Died: on Dec 13, Jas W Campbell, eldest s/o Jane & the late Daniel Campbell, in the 31st yr of his age. Funeral from the residence of his mother, 414 6th st, Thu.

Supreme Crt of D C. 1-Equity-Myers et al, vs Parsons et al. Ratify sale by trustee of parts of lots 93 & 94, on High st, to Geo W Chamberlin for $1,450; & part of lot 90, to Patrick McCarty for $2,437.50. -R J Meigs, clerk. 2-Equity #52. In the matter of the estate of Julia Keep. Statement of the account of said Julia Keep on Dec 30, at my ofc in City Hall, Wash. -W Redin, auditor

On Sat, by order of the Sec of War, Louis Heilburn, Saml Heilburn, Isaac Sickles, Meyer Wallach, & Philip Wallach, merchants of this city, charged with selling goods to blockade-runners, & who had been released on parole, were recommitted to the Old Capitol.

THU DEC 15, 1864

Died: on Dec 14, Mrs Ann Lovejoy, aged 65 yrs, w/o Jno L Lovejoy, of Wash City. Funeral from the residence of her hsbnd, 409 12th st, Fri.

Wash Corp: 1-Act for relief of John T Channcey & John H Thompson: $32.60 pay to Channcey, & $19.75: being for 18 days svcs rendered as Chief & ast engr of the Vol Fire Dept, ending with the organization of the present pd Fire Dept. 2-Act for relief of Jas A Kennedy: $38.70 to Kennedy for having been erroneously assessed on part of lot 6 in sq 4_9.

Senate: 1-Cmte on Naval Affairs: resolution tendering the thanks of Congress to Capt John A Winslow, U S Navy, his ofcrs & men on board the vessel *Kearsarge*, for their successful conflict with the piratical craft *Alabama*: passed. 2-Same cmte: thanks of Congress to Lt Wm B Cushing, U S Navy, his ofcrs & men, for their gallantry in destroying the rebel iron-clad *Albemarle* on Oct 27 last: passed.

The "*Ecclesiastical Seminary of Our Lady of Angels*," at Suspension Bridge was totally destroyed by fire Mon. A student, a lad from Brooklyn, Thos Hopkins, perished in the flames. The bldg was quite a large one & valued about $20,000.

The Pres has nominated to the Senate, & that body has confirmed, David McDonald as U S Judge for the Dist of Indiana, v Hon Albert S White, dec'd.

Brig Gen Robt B Potter, commanding the 2nd div of the 9th Army Corps, has been promoted to be Maj Gen by brevet for distinguished & gallant conduct in the several actions since crossing the Rapid-Ann, to take rank from Aug 1, 1864.

FRI DEC 16, 1864

Mrd: on Dec 13, at St Aloysius Chr, by Rev Chas H Stonestreet, Dr Theodore S West, of Alexandria, Va, to Mary Vandalia, d/o John L Lancaster, of Md.

Brown stone dwlg hse for sale: on the premises is a model stable with stalls for 4 horses, coach hse, harness closets, & coachman's rm. Apply to John Ogden, 519 7th st, between Pa av & D st.

John B McKay, a returning surgeon, was arrested Wed, by Ofcr Holbrook, on the charge of abstracting from the city post ofc ltrs addressed to John B McClure. From some of these letters he ascertained that Mrs J McNaughton would obtain on Tue, thru Messrs Hall & Fletcher, claim agents, a claim of $800 against the Gov't. McKay sent a colored boy, Adams, to get the claim, but the scheme had been discovered & he was given papers of no value. Mr McKay was taken before Justice Boswell, who committed him to jail for court. - Rpblcn

Music for Balls & Parties: L Weber's Cotillon Bank. Leave order at the Music Depot, corner of 11th st & Pa ave; Gantier's Restaurant; or at Mr Weber's residence, 569 7th st, between G & I sts, N Y.

Mail Robber caught: on Sat last, John B Zimmerman was arrested at Chicago in the act of presenting one of the missing drafts from the mail bag that was robbed on Nov 1.

Military Arrests. Levin L Waters, State Senator elect for this county, & Dr Danl W Jones & Jos Brattan, Judges of the Orphans Crt for this county, were arrested by Brig Gen Lockwood & sent to Balt, via Dela R R, on Fri. -Somerset [Md] Phoenix

Gen Nelson A Miles has been brevetted Maj Gen for gallantry in the field by the request of Gen Meade. Gen Miles is perhaps the youngest general ofcr now in the army. He entered the svc as 1st Lt in the 22nd Mass. He was subsequently commissioned as Col of the 61st N Y, from which position he was promoted to Brig Gen.

SAT DEC 17, 1864
Died: on Dec 15, of scarlet fever, Geo Langdon Thom, eldest s/o Col & Mrs Geo Thom, in the 12th yr of his age. Funeral from Col Thom's residence, 19th & I sts, Sat.

Geo Parker & Sons, fine groceries, 343 & 345 Pa av. -Geo Parker, Geo T Parker, & Saml G Parker. -Wash City

Pension Ofc frauds. C A Hollenbeck, of Athens, N Y, was on Sat last sentenced to 3 years imprisonment by Judge Shipman, U S Crct Crt, N Y C, for causing to be presented to the Pension Ofc fraudulent bounty land claims.

MON DEC 19, 1864
Died: on Dec 17, at Dr Palmer's, Montg Co, Md, J B Towers, s/o the late John T & Susan B Towers, in his 27th yr. Funeral from Chr of the Ascension: leaving Dr Borrow's, E st, today.

Died: on Dec 18, Mary E Randolph. Funeral from the residence of her grandfather, 374 12th st, today.

Sale by deed of trust, by Phillip Hill, jr, & Anna V Hill, his wife, dt'd Dec 30, 1863; all right & title of the portion of the rl estate of the late Thos B Craufurd, which was allotted to Anna V Craufurd, now Anna V Hill; about 220 acs with new & commodious dwlg hse; adjoins the lands of Thos E Berry, Benj B Padget, & others; 6 miles from Wash. -Edw W Belt, Saml B Hance, trustees

Mrs Brough, w/o Henry J Brough, of Hartford, Conn, while engaged in writing a letter to her hsbnd in N J, was burned to death in a few moments by a kerosene lamp being overturned & setting her clothes on fire.

Maj Gen Auger has assumed command of the military district of Wash, thereby relieving Col Wisewell, which is considered equivalent to merging the dept of Wash & the military district into one, although no specific orders have been issued. Col Wisewell ordered to Sandusky, Ohio, to assume command of Johnson's Island.

TUE DEC 20, 1864
Died: at the residence of his father, Col R E Clary, U S Army, Memphis, Tenn, on Dec 10, R E Clary, jr, late of the U S Army, aged 28 yrs.

Died: in N Y C, on Dec 18, of diptheria, Genevieve, y/d/o Robt H & Harriet E P Gallaher, of N Y, aged 13 months & 24 days. It is but 10 days since the death of the eldest dght, Mary Louisa, & the present makes the seventh funeral from the residence of one of the grandfathers, John S Gallaher, since Jan 9, 1862. Funeral from St Matthew's Chr, this morning.

Supreme Crt of D C, in Chancery, # 98. Julius N Granger vs Adele Douglas et al. Ratify sales made by Thos J Fisher & Walter D Davidge, trust. -Meigs, clerk

Col T Ingraham, 38th Mass vols, is announced as Provost Mrshl Gen Defences north of Potomac. Lt T Ingraham, 38th Mass vols, in charge, will report for instructions to Capt Slipper, A A G, pass ofcr, at these headqrtrs. Capt Theo McGowan, A A G, will relieve Capt C M Merritt, A Q M, as judge advocate at Central Guardhse. Capt Merritt, on being relieved, will report for assignment to duty & for instructions as to the disposition of pblc property in his possesion to Col M I Ludington, Chief q m dept of Wash. Capt E M Camp, E Q M, in charge of Sldrs' Rest, will report direct to these headqrtrs.

Execution of deserters: 4 sldrs were hung as an example to the Army of the Potomac on Fri last, having been found guilty of the crime of desertion: John Thompson, 5th N H; Christopher Suhr, 7th N Y; Chas Hornwell, 7th N Y; & W Kane alias Carter. The first 3 belong to the 2nd Corps & the last to the 5th. John McNulty, another found guilty of the same crime, was pardoned. Suhr & Hornwell died in Confederate uniforms. The men deserted to the Confederates, & then returned to the Federal army, claiming to be Confederate deserters.

WED DEC 21, 1864
Information wanted of Mgt Walsh, a native of Ire, who came to Wash City 6 years ago. Will be received at 178 Second st, Wash City.

Supreme Crt of D C, Equity #293. John P Myers, Wm P Thomas, Edw Bangs & Eleanor E Bangs against Martha Parsons, Jane Buchey, Matthias V Buchey, & John Beall. Parties named & W S Cox, trustee, to meet on Jan 3, at City Hall, Wash, for distribution of funds. - Wm R Woodward, spec auditor

Hon Wm L Dayton, U S Minister to France, died at Paris on Dec 2, of apoplexy. He was born at Basking Ridge, N J, Feb 17, 1807; 1825 grad of N J College. Pvt letter gives these details-he & his son took a walk, they parted & Mr Dayton went to call on a gentleman friend at the Htl du Louvre, not finding him, he called on a lady acquaintance & it was there that he died. This is a bereavement to his family & a severe loss to his country.

THU DEC 22, 1864

Mrd: on Dec 14, by Rev R J Keeling, Mr Geo E McConnell, U S Navy, to Miss Mary L Greenfield, of Wash City.

Mrd: on Dec 14, by Rev R J Keeling, in Trinity Chr, Arnold Petrie to Miss Annie F Allen, of Wash City.

Mrd: on Dec 15, by Rev R J Keeling, Chas H Voute to Miss Minnie B Evans, of Wash City.

Died: on Dec 18, Eugene Hamilton, infant s/o John A & Eleanor Ann Busk, of Balt, Md.

Senate: 1-Ptn from Geo W Matsell & Co & Harper & Bros, praying an alteration of the law for carrying periodicals by the overland mail: referred to the Cmte on the P O & Post Rds.

The rebel Gens Marmaduke, Cabell, & Gordon passed thru Boston on Sat to Ft Wayne.

FRI DEC 23, 1864

Order of Orphans Crt of Montg Co, Md:-sale of prsnl est, on the premises, of the late B W Waters, near Brookeville, Md. -Z D Waters, Thos E Sollers, adms

Orphans Crt of Wash Co, D C. Claims against the estate of Jos Cross, late of Wash, dec'd; by Dec 17 next. -R H Laskey, exc

Naval promotions: Rear Admr David F Farrgut to Vice Admr, U S Navy from Dec 21, 1864.
Cmder Jas Findlay Schenck to Cmdor, from Jan 2, 1863.
Cmder Richd W Meade to Capt from Jul 16, 1862.
Lt Egbert Thompson to Cmder from Jul 16, 1862.
Lt Cmder Jas S Thornton, the exec ofcr of the U S steamer *Kearsarge*, to be advanced in his grade ten numbers. [See paper of Aug 11, 1864.]
Cmder Wm H Macomb to be advanced in his grade 10 numbers for distinguished conduct in the capture of the vessel *Plymouth*, [N C,] with its batteries, ord stores, etc, on Oct 31, 1864, by a portion of the naval division under his command.
To be Chief Engrs:
1st Ast Engrs Geo Severius Bright, Philip Inch, Henry Mason, Eben Hoyt, B E Cha___ing, G B N Tower, B B H Wharton, & Jas W Whitaker.

SAT DEC 24, 1864

Died: in N Y, on Dec 20, Robt W Coleman, of Cornwall, Lebanon Co, Pa.

Supreme Crt of D C, in Equity #23. Duncan C Clark, by his next friend, John P Poe, vs Jas L Clark et al. Ratify sale by John P Poe, trustee, of lot 6 in sq 253, with improvements; & part of lot 18 in said sq, to Geo H Plant, for $11, 950, -R J Meigs, clerk

Wash Corp: 1-Act for relief of Admr Jos Smith: refund for amount erroneously pd by him for tapping sewer in front of lot 5 sq 402, on Sep 29, 1864: sum of $79.

Mscl Item: Jas Street is 100 years old & the oldest man in Wisc. He was mrd lately to a young widow of 88 summers.

MON DEC 26, 1864

Maj Henry G Davidson died at Louisville, Ky, on Nov 21, in his 34th yr; s/o the late Col Wm H Davidson, of Louisville, who died a few years ago, having entered the Catholic Chr on his death bed. Maj Davidson, was born at Carmi, Ill, Nov 8, 1831. He studied law under his uncle, Hon Wm Wilson, Chief Justice of the State.

Died: in N Y, on Dec 24, Chas A May, late of the U S Army, & s/o the late Dr J F May, of Wash City, aged 46 yrs. [Dec 29 paper-Born in Wash, D C, in 1818; mrd the d/o Geo Law, & took up residence in N Y C.]

Supreme Crt of D C, in Equity #283. Eli Davis vs Mary A Turner, et al. Cmplnt is holder of a note for $301.95, made by Mary A Turner & Arthur J West, on Apr 17, 1858. Same is unpd & Turner is a non-resident of D C. -R J Meigs, clerk

Mrs Hutchins has been released by order of the Pres, & arrived at Balt yesterday. Col Wm S Fish, 1st Conn Cavalry, late provost mrshl of Balt, also released.

The farm of the late Ethan A Jones, on Wash Branch rd, was sold to Mr J T Walker for $40.20 per acs. It has 160 acs, with a large frame dwlg hse. Another tract, 125 acs, brought $40 per acre: same purchaser.

Lt Morris, U S Navy, died of pneumonia, at the Gen Hosp in Mound City, Ill, on Dec 14.

WED DEC 28, 1864

Mrd: at Gtwn, D C, on Dec 27, by Rev John Early, S J, Pres of Gtwn Coll, Mr N J L Nicodeman to Miss Fannie E Pettit, of D C.

Died: on Dec 25, Mrs Ellen Pumphrey, in her 75th yr, widow o/the late Levi Pumphrey. Funeral from 10 La av, today.

Died: in N Y, on Dec 23, Capt R A Morsell, U S R S. Funeral from Dr J R Piper's, 7th & D sts, today.

Died: on Dec 27, Ale'r Gau, mbr of the Prussian Leg. Funeral from the residence of his bro-in-law, Chas Eames, 451 14th st, Thu.

Supreme Crt of D C, in Equity. Gilbert Vanderwerken vs Robt Ould & Ctzns Bank of Rubensville. Deed of Mar 22, 1856, cmplnt conveyed to Robt Ould for lot 25 & part of lot 26 in sq 882, Wash City, & part of lot 43, of Old Gtwn, etc, have not been fully paid. Dfndnts are non-residents. -R J Meigs, clerk

The estate of the late Eben Sutton, of So Danvers, proves to be larger than was at first supposed, amounting to about four millions. The rl est, much of it in Andover & Lawrence, is estimated at one & a half millions. Leaving no chldrn, & having made no will, this large estate descends to the widow & his bro, Gen Wm Sutton. -Boston Jrnl

John M Wood, of Portland, Me, died at Boston on Sat. His disease was lung fever, & his illness had lasted only a week. He has been a mbr of the Maine State Leg: always interested in railroads. He was 51 years of age.

THU DEC 29, 1864

Died: on Dec 23, at Bolington, Loudoun Co, Va, John S Jacobs, in his 39th yr.

Died: Dec 22, at his residence in N Y C, Mr Jas W Shaw, at age 97 yrs, 10 months & 8 days.

Railroad casualty: Cleveland Leader of Dec 24: accident happened to the mail train on the Cleveland & Pittsburg rd, yesterday. Among the first taken out was Oliver H Perry, of this city, who had with him his gun & a valuable dog, being on a hunting excursion. The d/o J H Robinson is left alone & an orphan. Her father, mother, & self were on their way from their home in Michigan to make a holyday visit to friends in Pa. Her parents were torn from her.

Died: on Dec 28, Miss Nellie J Utermehle, 2nd d/o Geo W & Sarah Utermehle, in the 17th yr of her age. Funeral from their residence, 425 Mass av, today.

Col Chas A May died suddenly of disease of the heart, at the N Y Htl, on Sat last. He was born in Washington, in 1818, & appt'd 2nd Lt of the 2nd Regt of Dragoons in 1836. He resigned his commission in 1860, & having mrd the d/o Geo Law, took up his residence in N Y C, where he has since lived. For several years past he has been Superintendent of the 8th Ave R R. –Com Adv

FRI DEC 30, 1864
Mt Vernon Marble Works, E st, between 6 & 7th sts, Wash. -Wm Rutherford

Hatter & Furrier, 356 Pa av, Wash City. -Jas Y Davis.

Military, Naval, & General Agency: ofc & residence 202 I st. -Saml V Niles

Steam Book & Job Printing: 375 & 376 D st, Wash. -H Polkinhorn & Son

A suit has been instituted against the city of New Haven by the friends of Lt Hewison, who was killed by a weight falling from a political banner in Chapel st a few weeks ago. The parties claim $10,000 damages.

Gen Hood's losses in Tenn: Killed-Maj Gen Cleburne; Brig Gens Granberry, Gist, Stahl, Williams, & Adams. Wounded-Maj Gen Brown; Brig Gens Carter, Monigel, Quarles, Cockrell, & Scott. Prisoners-Maj Gen Johnston; Brig Gens Jackson, Smith, Rucker, & Gordon. The rebel Gen Quarles, who was wounded at Franklin, has been taken. [From Special Correspondent of the N Y Times.]

SAT DEC 31, 1864
Appropriations made during the 1st session of the 38th Congress:
Svcs of Warren W Green on Ft Kearney & Honey Lake wagon rd, 1857: $47.79.
Svcs of Dr Chas M Wetherill, chemist of the Agric Dept: $750.
John O'Connell, money advanced for raising troops in Md: $2,000.
Richd G Murphy, amount charged to & paid by him as agent for Sioux Indians: $1,800.
Relief of the heirs of Noah Wiswall: $100.
L F Cartee, surveys of lands in Oregon, Oct 14, 1860: $3,033.50.
John Dickson, of Ill, damages sustained, regarding 100,000 bushels of corn tendered by said Dickson, under contract: $21,000.
Legal reps of Israel C Wait, late Lt U S Navy: $1,500.
Danl Wormer, for timber & materials furnished by him in the construction of the pier at Little Sodus bay, on Lake Ontario: $1,778.36.
Daris S Cole, same as above: $2,224.00

Wm G Brown, same as above, in 1853: $99.00

Chas L Nelson, agent for improvement of the harbor of Burlington, Vt, from Jan 15, 1853 to Apr 2, 1853, at $4. per day: $303.00

Mary Kellogg, to settle the accounts of Spencer Kellogg, dec'd, as 1st Lt of Infty, from Sep 14, 1861 to Oct 28, 1861; & as 4th mstr in the navy, from Aug 1, 1862 to Sep 18, 1863, the date of the execution of said Kellogg at Richmond, Va, by rebels: indefinite.

Carlisle Doble, carrying mails between Taylor's falls, Minn, & Superior, Wisc, from Arp to Nov, 1857: indefinite.

Died: on Dec 30, John, eldest s/o Jacob Young & Mgt Scheitlin, in the 7th year of his age. Funeral from the residence of his grandmother, Mrs John Hitz, 29 so A st, today.

Died: on Dec 30, Annie Lee, aged 6 years, 8 months & 17 days, d/o Jas M & Mary R Wright. Funeral from the residence of her father, in PG Co, Md, on Sun.

Commencement of operations: Sat, Dec 24, 1864. On the vessel *Ticonderoga*, from the bursting of a 10 pounder. Killed:-seamen:

L Wietz	J Ward	Jas M Duffy
C Heile	Jas McCormick	
W Senith	Jas McMillen	

Wounded:-seamen

Edw R Bowman, leg	Jas Williams, left leg	S B Martin, hip
Chas Brown, leg	Snyder, eye	C Collins, hip
Wm Jones, arm	Jacob Hilt, hip	W H Milliken, left leg
Lt S G Vascello, wounded.		

On the vessel *Juniata*, from the bursting of a 100 pounder: Killed-Lt Pile, Marine Corps; Lt D D Wempler, blown overboard & drowned; Jas Heston, boatswain, killed. On the vessel *Yantic*, from the bursting of a 100 pounder-killed: Actg Ensign Edw Winnemore & a man unrecognised.

Obit-Emily M Graham, of N Y C, w/o John Lorimer Graham, died on Oct 15, 1864; y/d/o Mr Isaac Clason. Mrd John L Graham in 1822. She was the mother of 9 chldrn, 7 of whom survive to mourn her loss. Mrs Graham was a member of the Dutch Reformed Chr.

SUN JAN 1, 1865

Supreme Crt of D C, in Equity, # 1563. Moore & Co vs Geo E Kirk et al. Dfndnt, Murray & Semmes, J B Wilson, S S Prentice, & John Van Riswick, all claim to be creditors of said Kirk. -Geo P Fisher, Justice Supreme Crt D C

Andrew Judson Rowell, Rpblcn of Vermont, died recently of typhoid fever.

Hon Geo M Dallas died at his residence in Phil yesterday, in the 73rd yr of his age. He was an 1810 graduate of Princeton College.

Local: 1-Our friend, Capt Jas Y Davis, under the Metropolitan Htl, offers a large & varied assortment of ladies furs of excellent quality & superior finish. His stock of gentlemen's furs & carriage robes is also very extensive & attractive. 2-Our old friend Gautier is still in the zenith of his glory at 252 Pa ave, catering for the pleasure & comfort of hosts of friends. 3-Fine Havana, or who use the weed in any shape, can be gratified to their heart's content by calling upon Cochran, at either of his fine stores #s 276 & 398 Pa ave. 4-Elegant watches, jewelry, silver, etc, at Messrs M W Galt & Bro. 5-Barney Hart, [sucessor to Jost,] 181 Pa ave, above 17th st, offers a choice assortment of wines, liquors & cigars. 6-Geo T Smith & Co, 511 7th st: fine groceries. 7-Bogue & Donnelly, whole sale & retail grocs, 188 Bridge st, Gtwn. 8-Kidwell & Son, Pa ave, near 14th st: first-class drug store with a high reputation. 9-Wm E Spaulding-rl estate. 10-Rankin & Co, 101 Water st, Gtwn: wines, brandies, whiskeys, etc. 11-Riley & Bro: #36 Central Stores, Pa ave, between 7th & 8th sts: dry goods. 12-H Burns & Co, 408 Pa ave: boots & shoes.

Hon Wilham Helmick, formerly Mbr of Congress from Ohio, just resigned his position as Chief clerk in the Pension Ofc, due to the utter inadequacy of the salary. [If the Chief clerk could not support his family decently on annual income of $2,200; what must be the condition of those unfortunate clerks who, with large families, only receive $1,200?]

Brooklyn Lunacy Case, verdict for Miss Underhill. Case of Miss Caroline A Underhill against her aunt, Miss Maria C Olcott & her cousin Geo M Olcott, concluded Dec 28 with a verdict for the plntf, who was awarded by the jury .60 damages. Action brought by Miss Underhill to recover damages for false imprisonment, who having been confined in the Bloomingdale Lunatic Asylum in Jun, 1863, by her relatives, who affected to regard her as insame. After a detention of one month, she was released by the insistence of one of her bros, but was returned to it in Sep last of the same year. Miss Underhill is a by no means ill-looking lady, about 37 years of age, well educated, & possessed of considerable poetic power. She was a zealous mbr of Henry Ward Beecher's Chr.

MON JAN 2, 1865
Died: on Dec 31, Zelina M, w/o Arthur L McIntire, Wash, D C, in the 59th yr of her age. Funeral from her late residence: 457 M st, Jan 3.

Died: on Dec 30, at Toledo, Ohio, Mrs Helen M Walbridge, w/o the Rev Henry H Walbridge, & sister of Chief Justice Chase.

The funeral of the veteran actor, Jas W Wallack, in N Y, was extremely private.

Local: 1-Our friend Thompson, 419 8th st: garments for the man. 2-Steamed oysters & billiards: Rodier's, 32 & 33 Hight st, Gtwn, near the Canal. 3-Moses: extensive warerooms, 519 7th st: assortment of furn. 4-Reynolds & Co: 500 9th st: gas fixtures. 5-I Thomas Davis, wholesale dealer in salt: 83 Water st, Gtwn. 6-Polkinhorn & Son continue to execute, at their steam book & job printing establishmnet, 375 & 377 D st, near 7th. 7-Gilman's drug store: 350 Pa ave. 8-Jas C McGuire & Co: auction rms. 9-Gardner's Photographic Gallery, 11 7th st. 10-Wall, Stephens & Co, 322 Pa ave: gentlemen's & boy's fine clothing.

Chas Clark, proprietor of a monkey show on Pa ave, was arrested on Sat by Ofcr Williams, on charge of enticing sldrs to gamble after admitting them into his show. Fined: $50.71.

TUE JAN 3, 1865
Died: at Nice, France, on Dec 8, of consumption, Miss Jennie E Ross, aged 26 yrs, eldest d/o the late Jas Ross, M D, N Y C. [Richmond papers please copy.]

Died: on Jan 1, after a short but painful illness, Saml S Black, in his 48th yr. Funeral from his late residence on Union st, today.

Died: on Jan 2, Mrs Eliza S Baker, w/o the late Albert J K Baker, in the 64th yr of her age. Funeral from her late residence: 242 7th st, today.

Fire & loss of life last night in a hse on L st, between 13th & 14th sts: #428, occupied by an old colored woman named Caroline Hill, Mrs Bonce & others. #421 was partially burn-occupied by Mr Kelsey. Caroline Hill was burned to death. Her body was brought out by Mr Michl Green & some colored men, & taken to the hse of Lizzie Pendel near by. Property is owned by Wm R McLean, wood dealer. [Jan 5 paper: funeral yesterday from Mrs Warren's, colored, 15th & K sts.]

Sat night Sgt W S Hurley, 4th precinct of Metropolitan Police, was presented by the ofcrs of his command with a silver tea service costing $150. The present was well merited.

Gtwn Corp ofcrs elected: Recorder-Walter S Cox
Clerk of Corp: Wm Laird
Inspec of Flour: Mr Geo Shoemaker over Mr D McCann.
Inspec of salted provisions & gauger of liquors: Mr John C Johnson
Tax Collector: Mr Chas D Welsh
Mkt Mstr: Mr L L Clemen's, over Mr Jos Nicholson
Police Magistrate: M V Buckey
Inspec & Marker of Lumber: Mr H Wingate over Mr Wm H Simms
Weigher of Hay, straw, & fodder: Mr H Ritter, over Mr Jos Nicholson
Wood Corder & Measurer: Mr H Burrows
Trustee of the Poor: Mr M Buckey, over Mr J H Newman
Inspec of Fire Engine: Mr W H Chamberlain

Chimney Sweep: Geo W Chamberlain
Assessors: Mr W C McGee-14 votes; Mr Thos Dowling-5 votes; J C Heister-6 votes; E J Shoemaker-6 votes; Jno Marbury-7 votes; Geo W Beall-2 votes; M V Buckey 2 votes. Shoemaker & Heister were elected Assessors.
Brd of Appeals: Geo W Beall, Wm H Gody, & Dr Cragin
Srvyr: W C Smith
Water Engr: J H Newman

Judges:

Jos H Birch	S T Brown	J Nicholson
Henry Wingate	Wm L Shoemaker	J Ramsburg
Danl McCann	W C McGee	B M Burrows
E Chapman	H G Ritter	Geo L Sherwood

Water Board:

R A Shinn	C Peck

Guardians of Gtwn Schools:

Geo W Beall	John Marbury, jr	Wm C McGee
A Hyde	Dr C H Cragin	
W L Dunlop	Thos Jewell	

Messenger: Isaac Burch
Harbor Mstr: W S Sherman
Cmtes to examine & Revise enrollment lists:

Jos F Burch	Chas D Welch	H G Ritter
H Burrows	H Cray	John H Newman
J Powers	Jos Nicholson	Danl Collins
Dr Chas H Cragin	Thos Johnson	L L Clements

WED JAN 4, 1865

Orphans Crt of Wash Co, D C. 1-Case of Jos F Kelly, exc of Mary Farrar, dec'd; settlement on Jan 28. -Z C Robbins, rg o/wills. 2-Prsnl estate of Jos B Towers, late of Wash City, dec'd.
-Jno A Baker, adm

Three small hses in Bates' alley, between 6 & 7th & G & H sts, were sold to Jas Wm Plant for $2,235.

Appt'd examining surgeons by the Commission of Pensions: Dr Thos Sanborn, Newport, N H; Dr J V Cobb, of Rome, N Y, & Dr Edw E Lee, of Newburgh, N Y.

Jonah Webster, a ctzn, was arrested yesterday charged with selling ctzns' clothes to sldrs.

J J Bogue has established, at the s w corner of High & Bridge sts, an ofc where merchants most do congregate, to ascertain the price of gold & stocks, the quotations being supplied very frequently during each day & evening.

THU JAN 5, 1865

Died: in N Y C, on Jan 4, of diptheria, Harriet Adelaide, 4th d/o Robt H & Harriet E P Gallaher, aged 6 yrs, 5 months & 17 days. This is the third child of the family carried off by this disease since Dec 8 last. The funeral will be the eighth from the hse of the grand parents since Jan 9, 1862. Funeral at St Matthew's Chr, Thu.

John D Edmond & Co has on hand a large assortment of hardware, & cutlery, etc. Located at the Intelligencer Bldg.

Gtwn: Henry Kengla, butcher connected with the purchase of the Tobacco warehse for a mkt, was fined $5.44 by Justice Buckey yesterday for obstructing the mkt-mstr while removing planks which served as a passage-way from High st to the butchers' stalls in the warehse. Justice Buckey fined Jos Adams, P J Callahan, & Jos Ehrmantraut, $20 ea, last evening, for selling liquor to sldrs, & the last named $20 additional for not having a license.

Local: Crmnl Crt yesterday, Judge Fisher presiding: case of Wm Maxwell, charged with the murder of Ezekiel B Gilbert, a conductor on the street car, on Feb 12th last. Mr Comington prosecuted & Mr J B Adams for the defense. Jurors: Thos E Jacobs, Michl Green, Chas H Gibbons, Chas A Snyder, Jesse Harshman, E E O'Brien, I S Barker, Watkins Tolson, Aaron D Harmon, John W Wray, Jos Lyons, John W Burns. A G Dean principal witness.

Petersburg Express of Jan 2: A detachment of 100 of the 13th Pa cavalry, under command of a Maj McCabe, was ambushed by a party of 4 Confederate Scouts, & actually forced back from their expedition. Maj McCabe was killed. This ofcr was one of the most brutal tyrants who ever oppressed a community or abused power, & the rejoicing is general over his death.

FRI JAN 6, 1865
Died: on Jan 5, in Wash City, Mary Hughes, infant d/o A Thomas & the late Mary C Bradley. Funeral today.

Gtwn, D C: fined for retailing liquor without a license: Jas Batemen, Andrew Buckey, Cath Magan, & Alic Anderson.

In Equity, #1606. Chandler et al, vs Chandler Hay et al. Ratify sale made by Edw C Gantt, trustee. -R J Meigs, clerk

Mr Geo Nitzey has been awarded the contract for paving F st north, from 5th to 14th st, Wash City. The kind of stone to be used is that which has proved so serviceable on Balt street, in Balt.

Wm Maxwell, charged with killing Esekiel B Gilbert, the conductor of the city railroad car, in Feb last, was found guilty of manslaughter. Local Item

Cornelius Edwards & Thos R Hopkins were arrested for assaulting & abusing Miss R Cursey on 14 st, on Wed. Local Item

Maj J R O'Beirne, late of the 37th N Y, & now of the 22nd Vet Reserve Corps, has been appt'd Provost Mrshal of D C, v Capt J C Putnam, resigned.

German Relief Assoc: Ofcrs elected: Pres, John Hitz. V Ps: A Maedel, C Statz, F Muhlinghaus, E E Gangewer, A Kreitler, F Shoenecker, C Steinmetz; Gtwn. Mr H Semken, treas; E Shucking, rec sec; Dr R Rhyner, corr sec; Mr A Cohen, financial sec; Mr Selhausen, storekpr; Mr A S Chansbach, super of cmnsn in Alexandria; Mr C Ebert, librarian. Cmte: Messrs Cluss, Gangewer, Kreitler, & Schellhaus. [Jan 16 paper: Agent in Alexandria: Od Manslach. Agent at City Point: O Matz. V P-A Marvel, J Statz, J H Gangewer, H Kreitler, J Statz, J W Shoenecker, W Steinmetz. H Semken, treas. Chas Ebert, Librarian-613 N st. Others remain the same.]

309

Geo N Noble & John Fenes were arrested yesterday in a shed on N Y ave by ofcrs Rennekin & Cooney, while changing their sldr clothing for those of ctzns. They said they had arrived from Massachusetts & had not been assigned to any particular regt.

Louisville, Jan 4. Owensburg, Ky, has been taken possession of by the rebels under Maj J Walker Taylor, our forces evacuating.

SAT JAN 7, 1865

Died: in Leesburg, Loudoun Co, Va, on Nov 17, 1864, Mrs Eliz S Osburn, relict of Col Nicholas Osburn, in the 82nd yr of her age.

Police appointments-Wash: T R Holson, patrolman in 3rd precinct, vice Wm B Thomas, dec'd; Jas L Warwick, do, vice Francis Leishear, rsgn'd; C Creran, patrolman, in 7th precinct, vice T F Pendal, rsgn'd; Jas T Taylor, do, vice A T Donn, rsgn'd.

Lewis J Gray was arrested on charge of bigamy, preferred by his wife, Lavinia L Gray. She had learned of this thru Mr John H Barth, a merchant on the avenue. Case dismissed as there was no other witness. Wash, D C

Died: on Jan 4, at the U S Insane Asylum, Capt Edw C Gordon, late of Wash City, formerly of the U S Navy.

R M Hall & Co sold the splendid estate of Mrs Nannie Haw, lying on Boundary st & 7th, including 30 acs, at $30,000, to Hon Wm P Dole, Com'r of Indian Affairs, & Judge Wright, of Indiana. Also, lot on Capitol Hill, lot 4 in sq 762, at $585, to Dr Breed, from Jas Owner. Also, hse & lot on M st, Island, from A Evans, to Jos White, at $800.

Restaurant: Mr Jas Steel, corner of L & 8th st. [Local ad]

On Thu the cellar of Mr Jos Platz's restaurant, on Pa ave, was robbed of cigars & champagne. John Cole, colored man, recently in his employ & discharged, is suspected. Ofcrs Geo F Hotchkiss & Jas M Bushie searched his premises & found evidence. Goods were also found at the hse of Patrick Gibbons, [white] who alleges he bought the articles.

Senate: 1-Finance Cmte: reported back a ptn asking for the remission of duty pd on material used in the manufacture of dresses worn by the Sisters of Charity, & asked that the cmte be discharged from further consideration of the same. So ordered.

Hon Jacob M Howard, of Michigan, who has been re-elected to the Senate, is now 60 years of age. He is a native of Vermont & went to Michigan in 1832: first elected to Congress in 1840, serving 2 yrs: in 1854 chosen Atty Gen of the State, serving 6 yrs. In 1862 was elected to the U S Senate v Kinsley S Bingham, dec'd. He has been an active mbr of the Military, Judiciary, Land Claims, & Pacific R R Cmtes.

Surgeon Chas H Crane, U S Army, is performing the duties of Surgeon Gen; Dr Barnes being absent at the front.

SUN JAN 8, 1865

Gen Ranson has been relieved of the command of the Dist of Charleston, Gen Taliaferro succeeding him.

Gen G W Smith is now in Augusta.

The heaviest income tax payer in Fall River is Mr M C Durfee-$79,782.

Killed in Balt yesterday: laborers engaged in the demolition of some bldgs in Holliday st, Balt: Timothy Preston, John Sweeny, & ___Costello. Other escaped with slight injuries.

Funeral of the late Wm L Dayton, U S Minister to France, took place on Thu last from the State Hse at Trenton, N J.

The stable of Mr Edw Deeth, Fayette st, was set on fire last Fri, & entirely consumed. Efforts should immediately be made to complete the reservoir on the hill in the neighborhood.

Died: in Gtwn, on Jan 6, Maj D D Perkins, U S Army, aged 38 yrs. Funeral at his late residence: 102 West st, Gtwn, today.

Died: on Jan 7, of typhoid fever, in the 35th yr of his age, Jas Dunford, native of England, but for a number of years a resident of Wash City. For the past 3 years he was a clerk in the Metropolitan Htl. He leaves many friends who will mourn his loss. Funeral from his late residence: 353 13th st, today.

Maj Gen Edw Johnson & Brig Gen H R Jackson & Thos H Smith, of the rebel army, passed thru en route to Ft Warren.

An old actor, Louis Kramer, has just died at Geneva, Switzerland, in a singular way. He was playing King Lear, & in his excitement swallowed a portion of his artificial beard, which stuck in the windpipe & choked him.

Rev Mr Jamieson, Ast Pastor of Trinity Chr, who has for months been prostrated by illness, is convalescing & expected in a short time to be able to resume his duties.

Mr Wm S Teel has a splendid assortment of gentleman's goods, of latest styles, both for civilian & military men. Located under the Metropolitan Htl

MON JAN 9, 1865
Phil Furniture Warerooms, 508 7th st, Wash City. -W B Moses

Mrs Lincoln has decided to hold drawing-rooms every Sat for the reception of ladies & gentlemen, who may accompany them. She was presented recently with a handsome pair of horses, [to replace those burned when the White Hse stable was destroyed by fire, [by Geo S Gidson, Pres of the City Railroad.]

Balt, Jan 8. Henry M Flint, the newspaper correspondent "Druid," of N Y World, has been arrested by the military authorities on the charge of disloyalty. He is now in custody.

Phil, Dec 7, 1865. The loyal men of this city will purchase & present to the wife of Lt Gen Grant a new first-class residence among us, furnished from top to bottom. It was her New Yr's present: cost nearly $50,000: located on Chesnut st near 21st. The wid/o the dec'd Gen Birney has been presented with a hse costing $10,000 & an additional $20,000 have been invested for her benefit, thus making her & her family entirely comfortable.

Mr F M Kenney, corner of Pa ave & 14th st, surprised a robber in his hse, who made his escape, & has not yet been arrested.

Commitments to the Central Guard Hse: Chas Prall for smuggling liquor across the bridge into Alexandria. Manuel Dridson [colored] for stealing Gov't property; both held for Capt McGowan's investigation.

TUE JAN 10, 1865
The funeral of Mr Jos M Padgett, late mstr laborer of the Naval Ordnance yd, was on Jan 9; burial in Congressional Cemetery. He was an employee of Gov't for some 30 yrs.

Criml Crt-D C. Trial of Wm H Berry & Wm H Cox, for the murder of Cassim de Armand, pvt of the 12th regt Vet Res Corps, on Dec 26. Quigley, other party implicated in the murder, has not yet been arrested.

Benj F Morris, policeman, died on Monday, of consumption, after a long illness. He leaves a wife & 2 small chldrn.

Died: on Jan 6, Willie Garnett, aged 2 years & 10 mos, y/s/o Robt & Eliz Guest Israel. Funeral from their residence 526 I st, Sun.

Corr of the Enrollment List:

Robt Self, erroneous enrollment	Henry B Offutt, physical disability
John Smith, over age	J A Rolls, over age
John Woodland, furnished substitute	Manck Lansburg, alien
Edw Brownie, 2 years in svc	John H Wallis, physical disability
John T Varnell, physical disability	Reed William, alien
John B Taylor, furnished substitute	John R Zimmerman, physical disability
H Dockman, alien	Henry Eaton, physical disability
C C Bryan, furnished substitute	

Mr J R Torney sues Levi Abrams to recover possession of the premises 558 Pa ave, occupied by Abrams as a store. Six months notice to vacate was served but Abrams claims he cannot be forced to leave the premises. Alleged that Torney has sold his interest. Case postponed.

Deaths of sldrs: recorded at the ofc of Capt J M Moore, A Q M, 21st & F sts:

W B Primble, Co B, 411th Pa	Wm N Smith, Co D, 69th N Y
Thos Connor, Co F, 51st N Y	Hiram H Phipps, Co B, 20th Ind
W A Copp, Co C, 57th Pa	Mathias Walker, Co B, 148th Pa

Died: on Jan 9, Sarah E Zimmerman, in the 66th yr of her age. Funeral from the residence of her son, John R Zimmerman, E Capt st, between 2nd & 3rd, Wed.

The will of Col Colt, of Hartford, has been contested by his bro.

WED JAN 11, 1865
Brig Gen Jos D Cox has been made Maj Gen. Maj Benj F Fisher has been made Col & Chief Signal Ofcr, v Myer, whose term has expired by constitutional limitation.

Orphans' Crt-yesterday: 1-Geo F Gulick appt'd guardian of Mary E Little. 2-Danl E Croux appt'd administer of the estate of Victor Croux, dec'd.

Crmnl Crt-yesterday: 1-Mary Dano, indicted for larceny, tried, & the jury being unable to agree, were discharged. 2-W H Light, alias Wright, indicted for larceny was found guilty. 3-In the case of W J Iron, alias Reddy, indicted for the murder of Danl Lahive, on Nov 2 last, was set for today. 4-Sally Austin for keeping a hse of ill fame, a nolle pros was entered. This is her 3rd indictment for the same offence: fined $2,000.

Jas C McGuire & Co sold, yesterday, a lot on North N st, between 9th & 10th sts, to Geo C Wilson, for 31 cents per sq ft.

Henry Wingate has received the appointment of Measurer at this port, & entered upon his duties. -Gtwn

Wash Corp: 1-Ptn of A R Sparks & Co, giving them the privilege of erecting a pvt lamp in place of a Corp lamp: bill rejected.

Gtwn students meet on the occasion of the death A Shorb Mathias, which occurred on Jan 4. Mr Jas Normile called to the chair; Jas Fitzpatrick, Sec. G P Gouley, Saml Anderson, John Walter, S A Douglas, G Lockwood, E Morrison, P H Redmond-reps.

Local-the fisheries of Dr Ritchie, called *Cloud's landings*, 1 mile above the aqueduct, were rented yesterday, as follows: Landing 1-Robt Simmons, $750; 2-Wm Mankin, $680; 3-Edw Mankin, $125. Two small landings on the Va side to Wm & Jas Simmons, for $70. Prices are 5 times cost of a few years ago.

Correction of the enrollment list of Wash, viz:

Saml Bradley, over age	John Singleton, over age
Lemuel O Wright, over age	Wm Miller, alien
Jas T Offutt, pd commutation-1863	John P Flaherty, over age
Dennis Caughlin, furnished sub	Eugene Freau, over age
Wm H Wiggins, pd commutation-1863	Maurice S Pool, pd commutation
David Shey, over age	Malcolm B Gordon, pd commutation
Wm H Ward, erroneous enrollment	Patrick Harbert, alien
Jas McQueen, furnished sub	Who Goodall, pd commutation, 1863
Springfield Hammerschlag, alien	John Slater, pd commutation, 1863
Herman Schulter, alien	Wm Hazel, over age
Edw Fitzgerald, over age	John Lee, physical disability
John Colbert, over age	

Ast Sec of the Navy, Fox, has gone to Boston to attend the funeral of a dec'd relative.

Deaths of sldrs recorded at the ofc of Capt J M Moore, A Q M, Wash:

Chas Shlote, Co K, 15 N Y hvy artl	E B Robson, Co M, 7 N Y-hvy artl.
Francis L Brate, Co F, 7 N Y-hvy artl	Julius C Ortner, Co D, 59 N Y
Olif Solson, Co I, 85 N Y	

Orphans Crt of Wash Co, D C. Case of Violet A Williams, admx of Wm H Williams, dec'd; settlement on Feb 4. -Z C Robbins, rg o/wills.

THU JAN 12, 1865

Chancery sale- Equity #341, Matilda Grammer vs Todd & Probasco; part of lot 15, & lot 16, in sq 258, on 13th; with several frame hses; Wash, D C. -Wm B Todd, Henry Probasco, trustees; Jas C McGuire & Co, auctioneers

Capt Elias M Greene, founder & builder of Freedman's Village, at Arlington Hghts, has tendered his resignation, which has not as yet been accepted.

Col Isaac O Barnes, U S Pension Agent at Boston, died in that city on Jan 7. He was connected by marriage with the family of the late Judge Levi Woodbury, of N H.

Martin Johnson, an old ctzn of Wash, died on Jan 10, in the 68th yr of his age. He was a native of N J, but for the last 40 years he resided in Wash City. Some 20 odd years since he was foreman of the Globe ofc, & then for many yrs, a clerk in the 6th Auditor's ofc. He was a prompt mbr of the Lodge of I O O F, which body met last night to make arrangements for his funeral this afternoon.

Deaths of sldrs reported by Capt J M Moore, A Q M:

Patrick O'Neil, Co D, 2nd btln V R C	Daniel Healy, Co _, 29 N Y hvy artl
H J Kern, Co K, 53 Pa	John H Vanwormer, Co A, 7 N Y hvy artl
W Butler, teamster of Q M Dept	1st Lt A F F Hall, Co D, 3rd rgt V R C

Correction of the enrollment list-Washington:

Pat Lynch, phys disability	Jacob Diser, phys disability
Matthew Pepper, furnished aub, Jul, 1861	Jas Smith, phys disability
Joshua Green, phys disability	Danl Humphreys, furnished sub in Dec, 1863
John Kilpatrick, enrolled in Pa	
Wm L Davis, phys disability	Jas P Tustin, phys disability
Saml Queen, furnished sub in Jun, 1864	Selig Kohlbert, over age
Jas Henley, phys disability	Theo Tenhalft, phys disability
Gwynn Harris, furnished sub in Jun, 1863	Geo Haskey, phys disability
John Hughes, enrolled in Pa	

Dates of Secession:

Mississippi-Jan 9, 1861	Texas-Mar 4, 1861
Alabama-Jan 11, 1861	Virginia-Apr 24, 1861
Florida-Jan 11, 1861	No Carolina-May 21, 1861
Georgia-Jan 19, 1861	Tennessee-Jun 9, 1861
Lousiana-Jan 26, 1861	

Died: on Jan 11, in Washington City, of typhoid fever, in his 24th yr, Lt Kent D Davis, U S M C, s/o the late Col Saml B Davis, of Delaware.

I O O F mbrs to meet today, to attend the funeral of Grand Treas Martin Johnson. -F W Fowler, sec; P H Sweet, Gr Sec. Interment at Glenwood Cemetery. Pallbearers: W R McLean, J F Havenner, John R Wright, W E Roberts, W E Richards, Jas H Ford, J G Robinson & Chas Crawford.

Mrd: at *Locust Grove*, Chas Co, Md, on Jan 3, by Rev Robt Prout, John Guaph & Sarah Dickinson, all of Chas Co, Md.

Mrd: on Jan 5, at Sandy Point, Chas Co, Md, at the residence of the bride's father, by Rev Robt Prout, Jas W E Frazer, of Fred'k Co, to Josephine A, eldest d/o Mr Geo Waters.

Richmond Whig, Jan 5/6. 1-Gen Ransom relieved of the command of the Dist of Charleston; Gen Talliaferro succeeding him. 2-Gen Quarles, reported to be mortally wounded, will probably recover: he loses his right arm. 3-Gen L J Gartrell is slowy improving. He had 2 ribs broken by a shell at Coosswatchie. 4-The object of the Hon A R Wright, of Ga, in the north, was to procure a parole for his son, a prisoner at Camp Chase, wounded. 5-The Chattanooga [Griffin] Rebel regrets to learn that Capt Thos T Henry lost an arm in the late fight at Franklin. He was dangerously wounded in the arm & breast in the fight at Re_saca, & scarcely recovered when he went into the late battle. Capt Henry is the eldest s/o the Senator from Tenn, who had 3 sons in the army from the beginning of the war, one of which was killed at Shiloh. The third is well known aid of Gen Hood.

Com'r F W Blackford, late of the Brd of Enrollment of D C, who was tried before Gen Brigg's court martial upon the charge of conduct prejudicial to good order & military discipline, has been dismissed the svc.

Columbus [Miss] Rpblcn: Miss Bell, d/o the Hon John Bell, & Mrs & Miss Woods, of Nashville, arrived here yesterday. During the middle of Dec they went from Nashville to Columbia, waited at the latter place until Gen Hood captured it, & then came south. They left here yesterday en route for Tuscaloosa.

FRI JAN 13, 1865
Died: at Forestville, PG Co, Md, on Jan 6, of diptheria, Jas R, eldest s/o Dr H Waring & Lavinia T Brent, aged 5 years & 9 months.

Mrs Hannah Meyer Fitzroy, wid/o the late Rt Hon Henry Fitzroy, M P for Lewes, died. She was the 2nd d/o the late Baron Nathan Mayer Rothschild, M P for London city. The dec'd lady was a d/o Baron Rothschild, but he was never mbr for London. The mbr for London is Baron A N Rothschild, & is now alive.

On Wed John Burke, employe of the Q M Dept, committed suicide by cutting his throat with a razor, at the Q M Hospital, where he had been admitted-Sep 13, 1863.

Mr McGuire-auctioneer: sale on Sat: letter of Lafayette to Mr Madison: $16.50. Signature of Napoleon Bonaparte: $8.50; John Hancock signature, $6.50; Von Humboldt signature, $4.75; Andrew Jackson ltr: $6; Thos Jefferson to Lafayette ltr: $9; Thos Jefferson's address to Tammany Soc: $5.50; Touissant L'Ouverture signature: $5.50.

Appointments by the Brd of Fire Com'rs: Engrs: L B Greer, Wm A Shedd. Firemen: Geo W Harrison, J D Birch. Fred'k Foot, hostler, suspended for disobedience of orders, was reinstated.

Gen Geo E McClellan & his family are in Phil, making a farewell visit to their relatives, prior to their departure for Europe next week.

Mr J M Holloway, s/o Com'r Holloway, has been appt'd Chief Messenger of the Patent Ofc, v R W Goggin, transferred to the machine dept. Mr H formerly held this position, but resigned some months ago for the purpose of entering the army.

SAT JAN 14, 1865
Rl estate, Wash, D C. Wm Babbington bought a lot at H & 3rd sts at .40 per ft; the adjoining lot, on H st, to S Seimmons, .25 per sq ft; 2 lots on E st, between 17 & 18th sts, at .17 per sq ft, to Wm H Phillip.

Supreme Crt of D C, in Equity, #321. Horatio R Maryman vs Wm D Prout, et al. Secure a conveyance of legal title to rl estate in sq 867, Wash; from heirs of Wm Prout to cmplnt as trustee under the will of Zachariah Hazel. Hazel died before all money was pd. He devised same to said cmplnt in trust for the chldrn of himself & his wife, the d/o said Hazel. Prout also died. Wm Prout left Rachel Prout, his widow, & Wm D Prout, Danl F Prout, Mary C Prout, & Fanny R Prout, now w/o John T Vinson, his chldrn. Latter are non-residents. -R J Meigs, clerk

Died: on Jan 12, Albert J K Baker, s/o the late Albert J K & Eliza Baker, in his 25th yr. Funeral from his late residence-242 7th st, Sun.

Died: on Jan 12, of diptheria, Nellie, aged 2 years & 11 mos, d/o Geo A C & Eliza Smith. Funeral from the residence of her father, 383 9th st, Sat.

Nomination of Geo Hill, jr, for Mayor: letter dated Gtwn, D C, Jan 11, 1865: A W Eastlack, C T Edmonston, John H Numan. Ltr dt'd Jan 12: Geo Hill, jr, accepting the nomination.

Mr Jacob Young recently received the appointment of Aid to the Revenue, v Mr T J Lazenby, rsgnd.

Silver tea svc presented to Col Chas M Alexander, 2nd D C vols, by the ofcrs & men of his command. Also a large framed card written in such a manner as to make an ordinary observer believe that it is an engraved document. This work was done by John D Williams, a pvt of 2nd D C vols. In the centre of the card is a picture of Col Alexander, & at the bottom is the Latin motto: *Fidem Serra*. It is now on exhibit at H Semkens' Jewelry Store, 330 Pa ave.

The draft-Wash, D C-names stricken from the enrollment list for causes assigned:
Physical disability:

Willie Hayes	John H Blake	Lloyd Pumphrey
G W Pope	Jacob Horner	E D Clapp
John M Emory	W B Taylor	Saml Roger
John Matthews	Stephen Smith	Robt Brett
John Viedt	Francis C Griardella	

Over age:

V K Rhemhardt	Emerson Etheridge	John Cummusky
Jedediah Gittings	Jas Tobin	

Alien:

Daniel Maloney	David Raradon	Patrick Raradon
Edw Connelly	Michael Riordon	Henry Heigh

Furnished substitute:

John F Pfile, Oct 1864	Robt Downing, Jan 13, 1864
Chas Bauman	S Stinemetz, Jan 12, 1864
Thos Cissell, Jan 13, 1864	J W Rollins, Jan 12, 1864
Richd T Morsell, Aug 15, 1864	Thos B Cross, Aug 10, 1864
Saml Lee-enrolled in N Y.	
John Slater, pd commutation Sep 15, 1864	

SUN JAN 15, 1865
Died: in Wash City, Jan 14, Julia G, 2nd d/o the late Edwin S & Eliz McClery, aged 14 years & 3 months.

316

Supreme Crt of D C, in Equity. Heirs of Eliza F Fisher, dec'd, vs A Y P Garnett et al. The respondent is the Surgeon Gen of the Confederate army, Dr Garnett, late of Wash City, who several years ago executed a deed of trust or mortgage on the property on 9th st, in which he then resided, as security for a debt due Miss Fisher-$$1,900. This property was seized & on Sep 9, 1863 it was sold to Alex'r R Shepherd for $2,200. Cmplnt wants the mortgage satisfied out of the proceeds of the sale by the U S to Shepherd.

U S Dist Crt, D C. U S vs the interest of Wm T Smithson in rl est-confiscation case. Mr Smithson, well known banker of Wash City, convicted in a military crt for treasonable practices, pardoned by the Pres & now at large. His rl estate in D C was confiscated. Present proceedings is to have the decree of confiscation recinded, it not yet having been carried into effect.

Orphans Crt of D C: wills of Wm H Fanning & of Eliz Graham were fully proven & admitted to probate.

Frank Hutton, age 5 yrs, s/o Dr Hutton, was seriously injured when a large sign of Tiber's bakery, on Four-&-a-half st, fell on him yesterday.

Wm Berry & Wm H Cox, arrested on charge of killing Cassin D'Armand, on Dec 26, were released at the suggestion of the Grand Jury. Wash, D C.

The draft-Wash, D C; names stricken from the enrollment list for causes assigned:
Physical disability:

Wm Sumner	Wm Murphy	John Burgess
Albert Newman	Henry C Cooper	W S Wright
Jacob Hoffman	S M Carpenter	
Chas H Bliss	Nathaniel Berry	

Over age:

Richd Butler	Jos Ballinger	Patrick Slemon
Wm Albert	Jas N Price	

Alien:
Daniel Alworth
Erroneous enrollment:

John B Stuvenal	Benj J Hamner	Benj F Cooper
Henry C Cady	A E Newton	

W A Davis, three years svc
John C Hise [could be alien]

MON JAN 16, 1865

Supreme Crt of D C, in Equity, #181. Lloyd W Williams, vs Arthur Nelson, et al. Ratify sale by John C Kennedy, trustee, of part of lot 15 in sq 290, Wash City, to Lemuel J Middleton, for $1,659.37; & lot 17 in sq 290, to same, for $1,586.92. -R J Meigs, clerk

Supreme Crt of D C, in Equity, #363. Bridget McNamara, cmplnt, vs Patrick Hurly, dfndnt. Jerry Hurly died in Apr 1864 indebted to the cmplnt for $652. Said Hurly died intestate without chldrn. Patrick Hurly is bro of Jerry Hurly, dec'd, & the latter left no other bro or sister, or descendant. Jerry Hurly died seized of lot 13 in sq 447, Wash City. Bill prays that the said property may be decreed subject to the paymnet of the cmplnt. Patrick Hurly is a non-resident. -R J Meigs, clerk

Orphans Crt of Wash Co, D C. 1-Case of Mary Lynch, excx of Ambrose Lynch, dec'd; settlement on Feb 4. 2-Case of John Sessford & Julia Sessford, excs of John Sessford, dec'd; settlement on Feb 4. Z C Robbins, rg o/wills

Mrs Peggy Fite died a few days ago in Wilson Co, Tenn, aged 103 yrs. From Mr Thos D Fite, one of her grandsons, we learn that she was born on Apr 12, 1761; her hsbnd, Leonard Fite, was a sldr in Rev war. Mr & Mrs Fite emigrated to Tenn from N C, & settled what was called *Nash's Lick*. Mrs Fite has lived with her 3rd son, Jacob Fite, in Wilson Co, for a number of yrs, her hsbnd having died some years since in Smith Co. On Apr 12, 1861, at celebration of her 100th birthday, was her oldest, a son, aged 80 yrs, & her youngest, a dght, 59, 71 grandchldrn, 305 great grandchldrn; 71 great great grandchldrn; & 2 great great great grandchldn.

Died: in Wash City, on Jan 14, Julia Gibson, 2nd d/o the late Edwin I & Eliz McClery, & grand-dght of the late Hon Selah R Hobbie, aged 14 years & 3 months. Funeral from the Chr of the Epiphany this day.

German Sldrs Relief Assoc, 29 so A st, Wash, D C-mbrs:

John Hitz	H Semken	J H Gangewer
A Shucking	Chas Ebert	H Kreitler
O Matz	P A Selhausen	J W Shoenecker
Rud Rhyner	A Marvel	W Steinmetz
E Cohen	J Statz	Od Manslach

Died: on Jan 14, of dropsy, Jas Skirving, in the 42nd yr of his age. Funeral from his late residence 377 E st, tomorrow. [I O O F notice-Jan 17] [Jan 17-stove & tinware dealer, 11th & Pa av. He has been confined to bed since Aug.] Interred at Oak Hill Cemetery, Gtwn, D C.

Sophia Kittle has recovered $3,000 in a N Y court, from Wm Walsh, for breach of promise.

Trustee's sale of *Key's Quarter*, recently the residence of Clement D Hill; 773 acs, in Nottingham Dist, PG Co, Md; in cause in which Chas Hill, cmplant, & Clement D Hill, dfndnt. -John B Brooke, trustee

Miss Annie E Costa was robbed of her pocket-book as she occupied a berth in a sleeping car, from Phil. Wm Taylor was arrested Sunday by Ofcr Curran. -Local

TUE JAN 17, 1865
Maj Gen Godfrey Weitzel, Cmder of 25th Corps, U S Vols, mrd Miss Louise Bogen, on Jan 16, by
Rev W H Harrison. The Genrl's bro, Capt Louis Wetzel, & Capt Fitch, were bridemen. Miss Tillie Bogen, sister of the bride, & Miss Perlie Wilber, were bridemaids. Reception was at the spacious mansion of Mr Peter Bogen, father of the bride.

Mrd: on Dec 22, at St James' Chr, Richmond, Va, Robt H Maury to Bettie, d/o Saml Greenhow.

Died: on Jan 14, at the Navy School Hospital, Annapolis, Md, of typhus fever, Miss Rose M Billing, d/o Mrs Rebecca K Billing, of Wash City. Funeral from the Meth Prot Chr, 9th st, Tue.

Men released from the draft, Washington, for causes assigned: Jas Cottingham, Robt Silibey, W H H Barclay, & Jas H Dyer, physical disability. W H Harrison, accepted.

Deaths of sldrs on the 15th & 16th reported to Capt Moore's ofc:

Hiram Grant, Co G, 7 Maine vols

Andrew Nealy, Co C, 48 Pa

Hiram Demming, Co D, 3rd N Y

Luke Parshall, Co G, 189 N Y

Richd Leusen, Co C, 15 N Y hvy artl

Simeon Frick, Co C, 34 N Y btry

Travis W Singettany, rebel, Co E, 18 N C vols

Hudson Gurney, who died in England recently, was 90 years of age, & worth $10,000.

Wash, D C: drawn to fill deficiencies in the draft: Paul Bronavira, North Capt st, near railrd depot.
Geo P Cook, jr, corner Pierce & 1st sts. F M McGruder, McGruder's farm; Lewis Lyles, Brown's farm; Lewis Simms, Camp Relief; Richd Washington, near Brightwood; Henry McLinden, engine hse, Mt Pleasant Hosp; Chas Moore, Mrs McDaniel's farm

Miss Mollie McDonough, of Charlestown, Va, died in the Old Capt prison on Jan 15, of typhoid fever. She was arrested about 3 months ago on charge of aiding in the murder of Capt E M Buchanan, at Charlestown, on Sep 27 last.

WED JAN 18, 1865
Names taken from enrollment list for the draft, Wash, D C, for causes assigned:

Physical disability:

Geo A Papier	Jas Foy	
John Carson	John B Wurdeman	

Over age:

Geo E Baker	John Sullivan	Geo Lee
Patrick Hempsey	Thos Stone	Wm D Heneline
John Breck	John Connell	R E Magee
Thos Fitzgerald-2	Patrick Dulbarty	
Michl Brown	John Rover	

Under age:

Jas M Major	Chas T Wright

Alien:

Michael Fitz	Edw Dwyer
John Fitzgerald	Patrick Cronin

John H Gibson & Barney Moore, deserter from rebels
Wm Fuss, Dennis O'Connell & John B Barraut, furnished substitute
A J Soper, Wm Summaker, J G Hannah & Edw Williams, erroneous enrollment
John Super & Louis Webb, now in svc
S P Thurston & John A Rice-enrolled in Mass
Freeman N Blake, enrolled in Kansas
W A Mansfield, enrolled in Md
T Weaver & Wm McKeegan-enrolled in Pa
J B Clarke, paid commutation, Aug 1863
Cause not legible:-Frederick Holden, ___ S Cozzens, Bernard J Hanley.

Orphans Crt of Wash Co, D C. 1-Prsnl estate of Geo Thomson, late of Gtwn, D C, dec'd. - D L Shoemaker, adm. 2-Case of Jas H Lowry & Cath M Johnson, exc & excx of Anne Lowey, dec'd; settlement on Feb 11. -Z C Robbins, rg o/wills

Wm H Fry, journalist & musical composer, died at Santa Cruz, West Indies, on Dec 21, of pulmonary disease. -Phil, Jan 17

Mrd: on Jan 15, by Rev Dr Linthicum, Mr Chas H Fish to Miss Clara D Fisher, all of Savage, Howard Co, Md.

Died: at his residence in Wash City, on Jan 17, Wm J Stone, sr, in his 67th yr. Funeral from St John's, Prot Episc Chr, on Thu.

Mr Jas Robertson, formerly of N Y State, but for several years a resident of Wash City, died on Jan 13, very suddenly, at the Gov't Insane Hospital. Age about 55 yrs.

Local: New street cleaning machine of D D Foley will be exhibited today, weather permitting.

Rl estate sales, Wash: lot on K st to Jas E Turton, .65 a ft; small brick hse on First st, to S V Noyes, $2,500; lot on G st, to Michl Shaw, .14 a ft.

Mr H H Kinne, a relative of Mrs Sec Welles, clerk in the finance div of the Indian Bureau, died very suddenly yesterday, at his boarding hse, 331 F st, of congestion of the lungs. His remains were conveyed to Centre Co, Pa, where his wife & chldrn reside.

Mrs Grace Mix, sister/o Capt Elisha Peck, of the U S Navy, & mother/o Chas E Mix, Chief clerk of the Indian Bur, died on Mon of dropsy, at her residence in New Haven, Conn, at age 76.

THU JAN 19, 1865
Orphans Crt of Wash Co, D C. Case of Sarah Page, admx of Lucien Page, dec'd; settlement on Feb 11. -Z C Robbins, rg o/wills.

Wm H Edes died at his residence, Congress & Dunbarton sts, on Jan 17, in the 60th yr of his age. Funeral in the Dunbarton st Meth Episc Chr on Fri. He was a man of industry & perseverance, & the artificar of his own business.

Deaths of sldrs reported to the ofc of Capt Moore, A Q M, Wash:

Lewis Braddel, Co I, Prov Cavalry	Lake Parshall, Co G, 189 N Y
John Pough, Co K, 1 N J Cavalry	Richd Lanseer, Co C, 15 N Y hvy artl
John West, Co C, 18 Vet Res Corps	Simon Fank, Co C, 34 N Y Btry

Col Lewis Bell, who fell mortally wounded in the storming at Ft Fisher was native of N H; a half bro of Chief Justice Bell, & of the late Jas Bell, late a mbr of the U S Senate. Entered the service early in the war in the N H volunteers.

Draft-Wash, D C; names stricken from the enrollment list for causes assigned:
Erroneous enrollment:

Daniel F Wilt	J T Lane	Henry A Kirkman
Wm H Wilson	Frederick Gollinghoffer	Wm Turner
Wm McElwee	Ridout Wellington	

Physical disability:

Mathew Catarson	Philip Nephuth	Chas E Fisk
Thos J Latham	Jas Butterly	Jas T Boss
L B Seigamond	Jas Lauman	Geo Hackey

Patrick Knox   S N Hyde   Richard E Booth
Now in svc:
Chas B Brady   Wm H Hanning
Over age:
Wm Johnson   John Cudmore
Patrick McNulty   Edw Butt
Alien: John Connor
Chas Hayes, pd commutation in 1863
B C Betts & Daniel Killigran, 2 years in svc.

Com H A Wise, Chief of the Bur of Ord, & Mrs Wise, d/o the late Edw Everett, have left Wash City for Boston, to attend the funeral of the dec'd.

Confirmations by the Senate yesterday: Brig Gen Alfred H Terry to be Maj Gen by brevet. Chas H Dyer, of Ill, to be cnsl at Boulogne. Elisha E Rice, of Maine, to be cnsl at Hakodadi, Japan. Wm Taussig, Coll of Internal Rev for the 1st Dist of Missouri.

FRI JAN 20, 1865
Died: on Jan 19, Robt H Clements, in the 81st yr of his age. Native of Dumfries, Va, & for the last 36 years a resident of Wash City. Funeral from the hse of his son-in-law, J E Hilgard, 250 H st.

U S Supreme Crt-#53-Thos J Miles, appellant, vs Wm D Caldwell, appellee. Appeal from decree of Crct Crt of U S for Missouri: regarding judgment of 80 acs of land in Marion Co, Mo. Names extracted: Ezra Syles Ely; Mgt Carswell, Saml McClellan; Saml Carswell, of Phil, died in 1822 lvg 4 chldrn, youngest child, Saml Kinsey Carswell, a minor. Carswell mrd & died in 1829 leaving a widow & 1 child, Mary Ann Ely Carswell. The widow died in Aug 1830. Her infant aged 2 years & 3 months passed to the guardianship of Ely. Mrs Mgt Carswell was his mother-in-law. On Oct 2, 1843, Mary Ann Ely Carswell mrd Thos J Miles.

SAT JAN 21, 1865
Draft-Wash, correction of the enrollment list & causes assigned:
Physical disability:
Saml T Drury   Geo W Blagden   Chas M Richards
Thos J Parker   John H Barr   Geo Addison
Geo J Waite   John McCrystal
Wm A Marshall   Richd H Moore
Over age:
John W Shugert   Fred'k Bates   Richd Franklin
Timothy O'Brien   John Bush   Henry H Oliver
Harmon Burns   Patrick Griffin   Jas Joyce
Richd Bresnehan   John Banks   Chas Hadaway
Alien:
Cornelius Sullivan   Patrick O'Day
Now in svc:
John Hall   Wm Taylor
Erroneous enrollment:
John E Chessman   Wm J Cummings   Thos Shoemaker
L Scrissie   Geo W Abbott   Edmund Shaw
C F Lord   Henry A Sylvester   Frank B Benedict

Furnished subs:
Wm E Fletcher   H S Johnson   Thos H Robinson
John A Jordan   Jas Cook
2 years in svc: Chas Seyler
Pd commutation in 1863: John Selby
Under age: -John H Weeden
Deserters from rebels: D H Whisman & E W Whisman

Special ofcrs for correcting the enrolment lists:

I F Mudd	W H Hoover	Theodore Burns	R B Pumphrey
J G Robinson	M S Pool	Wm	Geo R Cook
J R Wright	J M Johnson	Nottingham	Jas R Cook
E H McKean	J E Miles	Jos Tait	R T Talbert
C T Heinicke	Wm McDermott	Jacob Dyer	Geo H Dushane
Wm O'Neal	Alex Eaton	J M Dalton	Thos Jeff Frazier
S R Sylvester	E G Dyer	W P Brown	
Wm Hussey	B F Bears	E M Boteler	
C H Anderson	J W Mead	J B Peake	
Danl Myers	J P McKenna	John Vanhorn	

Died: on Jan 20, John Henry, s/o Wm T & M C Diggs, in the 4th yr of his age. [Upper Marlborough papers please copy]

Orphans Crt of Wash Co, D C. Case of Anthony Hyde, adm of Wm Smith Hyde, dec'd; settlement on Feb 11. -Z C Robbins, rg o/wills

Funeral of the late Wm H Edes took place yesterday with burial in Oak Hill Cemetery. Pallbearers: Hon Henry Addison, Mayor of Wash City, Asa Pickerell, John Dixon, Capt Brown, Francis Wheatley, & Evan Lyons.

Deaths of sldrs reported at the ofc of Capt Moore, ast q m, Wash, D C:
John W Rogers, M, 1st Maine cavalry   Henry Place, Co K, 24th Vet Res Corps
Edw Campbell, Co A, 14th Conn   Jos Reeves, Co H, 1st N H hvy artl

U S Supreme Crt, #78 & #104. Gardner P Drury, appellant, vs Thos Foster & Hannah S Foster, his wife, appellees. Crct Crt of Minnesota in equity: regarding rl estate.

SUN JAN 22, 1865
Died: on Jan 21, Kate Burnett, infant d/o John D & Agnes McChesney. Funeral from the residence of her grandfather, Edw H Fuller, 257 Mass av, Mon. [N Y & Brooklyn papers please copy.

Died: on Jan 21, at Mrs Bannerman's, Bvt Brig Gen Chas Wheelock, U S V, in his 52nd yr.

Attack on Fort Fisher: failure of the Parrott rifled guns: Report of fleet Capt K R Breest. List of killed & wounded. North Atlantic Squad, U S flagship *Malvern*, Jan 17, 1865. [Coverage-3 cols.]
Killed in the assault:
Lt S W Preston, Flag Lt
Lt B H Porter, commanding flagship *Malvern*
Ast Surg Wm Longshaw, U S steamer *Minnesota*
Actg Ensign Robt Wiley, U S steamer *Montgomery*

Killed by explosion of magazine in Ft Fisher, Jan 16:
Actg Ast Paymstr R H Gillett, U S steamer *Gettysburg*
Actg Ensign J S Leighton, steamer *Gettysburg*
Wounded in the Assault:
Lt Cmder W N Allen, U S steamer *Tuscarora*
Lt g M Bache, U S steamer *Powhatan*
Lt R H Lamson, commanding U S steamer *Gettysburg*
Actg Vol Lt F F Baury, U S steamer *Colorado*
Ensign R D Evans, U S steamer *Powhatan*
Ensign Ira Harris, *Powhatan*
Act Eng L R Chester, U S steamer *Pontoosuc*
Act Eng Jas Bertwistle, steamer *Minnisota*
Act Ensign F A O'Connor, *Minnesota*
Actg Ensign G W Coffin, steamer *Gettysburg*
Act Ensign B Wood, U S steamer *Tristram Shandy*
Actg Master A J Louch, U S steamer *Mackinaw*
Act Mstr's Mate E K Green, steamer *Mackinaw*
Act Mstr's Mate J M Simms, steamer *Minnesota*
Act Mstr's Mate A F Aldridge, steamer *Tuscarora*
Total killed-74; wounded-213; missing-22

Orphans Crt of D C: 1-The will of the late Jas Skirving was proved & ltrs of test were issued to his widow, Caroline M Skirving; John T Given, excs. Estate bequeathed to his family. 2- Chas M Matthews received ltrs of adm on the estate of the late Chas W Bennett. 3-Jos Beasley appt'd exc of the estate of the late Ellen Pumphrey.

Local-Mr Wm Rabbit, aged 60 yrs, fell & broke his leg yesterday; attended to & then taken to his home on 8th st, between D & E sts.

Mr Wm Ellis, at the Post Ofc Restaurant, 60 Congress st, presents creature comforts at all times to cheer the inner man. This is a long established hse.

Rodier's White Hse Restaurant, 32 & 33 High st, near the canal, is almost synonymous with Gtwn. Tony can & does prepare as good a table as can be desired.

MON JAN 23, 1865
Deaths of sldrs reported at the ofc of Capt Moore, ast qrtrmstr, Wash:

Jos F Stockbridge, Co E, 1st Maine Cavalry	Robt Haller, Co D, 7th N Y Vols
Patrick Cochran, Co A, 155th N Y	Frank H Jenkins, Co L, 1st N H hvy artl
Henry C Everett, Co D, 32nd Mass	Martin Duekle, Co G 15th N Y hvy artl

Deaths in the Navy of the U S , reported to the Chief Bur of Med & Srvy, for week ending Jan 21, 1865:
John Wilson, seaman, Dec 2, U S steamer *Com McDonough*.
Adam Bigg, landsman, Dec 12, U S steamer *Pampero*.
Wm B McMichael, actg mstr's mate, Dec 15, U S sloop *Portsmouth*.
Jas Wood, seaman, Dec 27, U S sloop *Vincennes*.
Francis Rowe, capt of hold, Jan 1, 1865, U S bark *Restless*.
Wm T Wiley, landsman, Jan 5, 1865, Nav Hosp, N Y.
John Ferguson, seaman, Jan 12, 1865, Nav Hosp, Chelsea.

Saml Jackson, landsman, Jan 13, 1865, Nav Asylum.
Michael Higgins, 1st cl boy, Dec 13, U S steamer *Carrabagsett*.
Jas Robinson, colored, Jan 10, 1865, Nav Hosp, Norfolk.
Kent D Davis, 2nd lt marine corps, Jan 11, 1865, Wash City.
Thos Nelson, seaman, Jan 6, 1865, Nav Hosp, N Y.
John Barker, landsman, Jan 10, 1865, do.
Daniel S Smith, seaman, Jan 12, 1865, do.
Harvey L Ranson, actg ensign, Jan 14, 1865, Kingston.
Oscar Bailey, capt of hold, Sep 21, U S brig *Sea Foam*.
John Wildey, colored, cook, Dec 23, N Y.
Richd Lee, colored, landsman, Dec 20, U S steamer *Young Rover*.
John Haynes, colored, seaman, Dec 29, Gov't Hosp for Insane, Wash.
Chas Franklin, ord seaman, Jan 14, 1865, Nav Hosp, N Y.
Prince Martin, contraband boy, Jan 2, 1865, U S steamship *Merrimac*.
John H Carr, qrtrmstr, Jan 3, 1865, U S sloop *Macedonian*.
Chas Mervine, landsman, Jan 16, 1865, U S steamship *Powhatan*.
Basley Jones, colored, landsman, Jan 16, 1865, Nav Hosp, Chelsea.

Orphans Crt of Wash Co, D C. 1-Case of Jas L Barbour, adm of Horace Edelin, dec'd; settlement on Feb 11. -Z C Robbins, rg/o wills

John King was arrested on Sat for having in his possession a horse stolen from Mr Patrick Holmes, Capitol Hill, Wash, D C.

Died: on Jan 22, India Johnson, w/o Dr S S Turner, aged 27 yrs. Funeral from the residence of her father, Henry N Johnson, Ninth st, Tue.

Died: on Jan 2, at the Wash Asylum, Wm Lyman.

New Ad: John R Elvans & Co: 87 La ave & 308 C st, Wash, D C. Dealers in iron & steel.

TUE JAN 24, 1865
Deaths of sldrs reported at the ofc of Capt Moore, A Q M, Wash, D C:

Gustavus Simmond, Co K, 15 N Y hvy artl	Wm Vennon, Co C, 12 N Y
Saml Meckle, Co A, 4 Pa cavalry	Fenton Johnson, Co E, 10 N Y vols
Nathan Preston, Co C, 6 Pa hvy artl	Nathan Gibb, 2nd Provisional cavalry
Jas Ray, Co K, 81 Pa	

Maj Leopold Blumenburg, provost marshal of the 3rd Dist of Md [Balt], has been removed upon charges of cruelty & other misdemeanors, & Capt Harry Clayton, of the Purnell Legion, has been appt'd in his place.

The new Enrolment: in addition to the names heretofore pblshd, Messrs Wm H Hines, C J Hamilton, Jas McGlue, Fielder R Dorsett, sr, Henry Burch, W H H Barclay, Philip Hauptman, Jas Codingham, John German & Frank Holtzman, have been commissioned as enrollers, for ward #1. Messrs Frank Miller, J Rapley, C W Cunningham, Jas Fowler, C W Mitchell, Chas Williamson, L W Denham, G Powell, & Geo Bauer, for ward #2. Messrs McKean, Mudd, Robinson, Quick, Severson, Wooldridge, Hutton, Wright, & Henricks for ward #3.

Funeral of the late Brig Gen Chas Wheelock took place yesterday from 447 Pa av, Wash; remains were taken to Boonville, N Y, for interment. Silver plate on the coffin bearing the inscription: *Bvt Brig Gen Charles Wheelock, died January 21, 1865, aged 52 yrs, 1 month, and 7 days*. Among those who visited the remains was Miss Carrie Sheads, a lady to whom the dec'd gave his sword to secrete just before his capture at Gettysburg, in order that it might not fall into rebel hands.

WED JAN 25, 1865

Mrd: on Jan 19, at Metropolis View, the residence of the bride's father, near Wash City, by Rev Fr Lynch, Frank Wolfe to Maria C Magruder, eldest d/o Thos C Magruder, all of D C.

Died: on Jan 23, Mrs Anna Addison, relict of Capt Wm H Addison, U S Army. Funeral on Thu, at the residence of the family of the late Dr Watkins, 429 9th st.

Among the casualties in the 169th N Y by the explosion at Ft Fisher were: Col Alonzo Alden, commanding the brig, both legs broken, wounds considered mortal. Capt Ferguson, Lt McGregor, both killed. Lt Van Santford, wounded. Capt Chas D Merrill, badly wounded. Lt Faulkner, slightly. Of the ofcrs who came ashore from the war steamer *Gettysburg* out of curiosity, & were standing on the parapet of the fort, nearly opposite the magazine, at the time of the explosion. Actg Ensign Stowell S Leighton & Pymstr Gillette were killed & nearly buried by the falling debris. Near these lay a handsome young man, Ralph C Huse, surg of 3rd N Y regt, with one leg broken & the other paralyzed by a blow from some heavy missile.

Stricken from the draft enrollment of Wash, for causes assigned:

Under age:
Geo Rush	Lawrence O'Connor	Leon Jones

Over age:
Patrick Healin	Albert Carte	Chas Bonner
Washington Cox	Patrick Gleason	Thos Thornton

Furnished sub:
Anthony Washington	Edwin Hunt	Herbert Stuer

Physical disability:
John Goldin	F G Heilberger	Jas Thomas
John Vanderbilt	W Brown	Lewis Schmidt
Lewis W Linsaberger	Andrew Lynch	Jas Anderson

Erroneous enrollment:
Ambrose Merrill	W M Gindall	Thos G McManus
Ed Medlar	Gerald Piper	
J Glidden	Albert Middleton	

2 years in svc: Asaph Dodge

Deaths of sldrs reported to Capt Moore, A Q M, Wash:
Wm W Marsh Co I, 14th N Y hvy artl	Ernest Bundenburg, 7th N Y hvy artl
Jas P Ward, Co C, 21st Pa cavalry	Chas M Whiting, Co I, 31st Vet Res Corps
Edw Keiley, Co K, 173rd N Y	Fred'k Gardner, Co M, 24th N Y cvly

Geo Hill, jr, is about to commence the manufacture of paper, at the foot of Potomac st, Gtwn. He will give constant employment to from 20 to 25 persons

Died: on Jan 24, Mrs Charity Croggon, relict of the late Wm Newton Croggon, a native of Truro, in County of Cornwall, England, in the 67th yr of her age. Funeral from the residence of her son-in-law, C W Pettit, 398 Mass av, on Jan 26.

Gen Terry, the hero of Ft Fisher, is 37 years old, a little over 6 ft high, very slim & straight, has a large head, brown hair, blue eyes; is a cousin to Rose Terry, the magazine writer, & is unmrd.

THU JAN 26, 1865
Mrd: at St Aloysius Chr, on Jan 24, by Rev Chas H Stonestreet, Albert A Brooke to Virginia C Myers, both of Wash, D C.

Gen McClellan will sail for Europe today in the steamship *China*, with his wife & child. He leaves with some reluctance, but the health of his wife is such that their medical advisers counsel a brief residence abroad as necessary to its restoration. They will remain in England but a few days, in France hardly longer, & proceed to Rome, remaining there several weeks, thence to Dresden or south of France for the summer months, returning in the fall or early winter. –N Y World

Promotions in the 6th Auditor's Ofc: W H Colledge, of Ohio; J Porter, of Pa; & E J Evans, of N Y, from 2nd to 3rd class clerks-salary, $1,600 per annum. J K Upton, N Y; J W Baden, D C; Wm W Young, Pa; W R Hooper, Mass; D P Waters, Mass; S E Dickinson, Pa; W O Denison, Ky; & Jos Peck, D C, from 1st class to 2nd class clerks-salary, $1,400 per annum.

Uriah Forrest, of Montg Co, Md, confined in the Old Capitol prison since Aug last, was released on Tue; charged on Oct 13th last for giving aid to the enemy.

FRI JAN 27, 1865
Died: on Jan 26, after a long & painful illness, John Fletcher, in his 64th yr. Funeral from his late residence 6th & I st, Sat.

Terrance Finnegan died on Jan 26 from the effects of a gunshot wound in the leg. John McCabe asknowledged he had shot Finnegan, but not intending to kill him. Last Aug he caught Finnegan in the act of kissing his wife. The dec'd was at one time a pvt of Co E, 15th N Y engrs & honorably discharged Jun 25, 1863. He was lately employed at the arsenal as a laborer. Wash, D C

Deaths of sldrs reported at the ofc of Capt Moore, A Q M, Wash:

Reuben Brown, Co B, 4th N Y hvy artl	Henry H Stultz, Co G, 11th Pa
John Wenglein, 5th, 21st Btln V R C	Michael Johnson, Co G, 4th Pa cavalry
Daniel French, Co D, 1st Md	

Mr August Belmont, well know banker, accompanied Maj Gen Geo B McClellan on the trip to Europe.

Drawn to serve as jurors for the next term of the Crct Crt-Wash: commencing Feb 7. [All Wash City except those marked Gtwn or county-*Wash*.]

Jos Darden	Columbus Denham	John King
L Spanier	R Cohen, jr	David Shoemaker-
I S Harvey	Wm Skinner	county
Columbus Alexander	Jas V Galt	J H Caldwell
Evan Hughes	Richd Bridgett	Patrick McDevitt

SAT JAN 28, 1865

Trustee's sale of land in Calvert Co, Md: cause in which Thos B Billingsley, et al, cmplnts, & Arthur Harris, et al, dfndnts. Sale of part of the lands of Arthur Harris; 195 acs; adjoins the lands of Levin Skinner, Geo Chambers, the heirs of Jas Ross, & others, known by the names of *Taney's Right, Blind Tom's,* & *Taney's Delight;* same as described in a deed from John H Rhodes & others to John Parran. -Alexander B Hagner, Daniel R Magruder, trustees

Orphans Crt of Wash Co, D C. 1-Case of Henry E Marks, adm of Marion M Taylor, dec'd; settlement on Feb 18. 2-Case of Saml Jas Datcher, adm of Francis Datcher, dec'd; settlement on Feb 11. -Z C Robbins, rg o/wills

Died: Jas Roach, on Jan 27, after a long illness of dropsy, in the 50th yr of his age. Leaves a family of orphan chldrn, his wife & 2nd dght having but recently died. His beautiful homestead on Prospect Hill, adjoining Arlington, has had to undergo the ravages of military necessity. Ft Albany having been erected within 100 ft of his hse. A gentleman of long & favorably known to the residents of the District. Funeral from St Mary's Chr, Alexandria, tomorrow, Sunday.

Another homicide, yesterday, Wm Jones, dec'd; bro-in-law to Geo Moody; also a bro-in-law to Farquhar Daniels. Daniels shot Jones in an altercation at the former's hse. Daniels was committed to jail for court.

Deaths of sldrs reported to Capt Murray, A Q M, Wash, D C:

John Violet, Co A, 13th Pa cavalry	Edw Hennessey, Commissary Sub Dept
Jacob Buckpink, Co A, 16th Mich vols	Jacob Eranea, Co A, 7th N Y

SUN JAN 29, 1865

Deaths in the Navy for the week ending Jan 28, 1865:
Georga F Crofis, landsman, Oct 5, U S steamer *Kathaderi.*
Wm Garrison, landsman, Oct 14, U S steamer *Selma.*
Edw B Warren, 1st cl fireman, Nov 11, U S steamer *A Dinsmore.*
John Brown, ord seaman, Nov 24, U S steamer *New Hampshire.*
Wm McLacklain, qm, Dec 17, U S steamer *Nyatza.*
Chas H Mathews, landsman, Dec 19, U S steamer *Oneida.*
Wm Sallett, prisoner of war, Dec 24, Nav Hosp, St Helens, S C
Isaac Cornwell, landsman, Jan 7, U S steamer *Memphis.*
Daniel Capers, landsman, Dec 27, U S steamer *South Carolina.*
Thos McDonell, seaman, Dec 27, Milita Hosp, Hilton Head, S C.
John Griffin, landsman, Jan 19, Nav Hosp, Norfolk, Va.
Wm T Mason, coalheaver, Jan 18, U S steamer *Calypso.*
Wm Dugan, seaman, Jan 19, U S recg ship, *North Carolina.*
Geo W Banks, seaman, Feb 8, 1864, U S hosp ship *Red Rover.*
John Straw, seaman, Feb 22, do.
Emanuel Steward, 1st cl boy, Apr 11, do.
Willis Winsell, landsman, Apr 17, U S steamer *Ouachita.*
Robt Hotman, Dec 26, do.

Lafayette Kilbourn, landsman, Dec 24, do.
Wm Thorp, seaman, May 6, U S steamer *Brilliant.*
Benj F Bazor, seaman, May 13, do.
Jas W Palmer, seaman, May 13, do.
Geo C Gregory, seaman, Jul 15, U S steamer *Silver Lake.*
John McTrain, 1st cl boy, Aug 25, U S steamer *Victory.*
Jas L Abraham, landsman, Dec 27, do.
Saml J Harper, seaman, Sep 2, U S steamer *Gen Lyon.*
Jos Buckley, seaman, Sep 8, U S steamer *Kickapoo.*
Henry P Chase, landsman, Oct 2, U S steamer *Forrest Rose.*
Peter Owens, landsman, Oct 2, U S steamer *Paw-Paw.*
Willfred M Chappell, landsman, Nov 6, U S steamer *Marmora.*
Robt F Sackett, landsman, Nov 9, U S steamer *Forrest Rose.*
Herbert H Dean, landsman, Nov 21, U S steamer *Peri.*
Geo W Dockery, landsman, Nov 23, U S steamer *Springfield.*
John Thompson, seaman, Nov 23, U S gunboat *New Era.*
Fred Waters, 2nd cl fireman, Nov 26, U S steamer *Avenger.*
Edw Allen, landsman, Nov 29, U S steamer *Fair Play.*
Frank Hawkins, landsman, Jan 11, do.
Willard Brown, seaman, Dec 6, U S steamer *Gen Pillow.*
Spencer Owens, ward rm steward, Dec 6, U S steamer *Curfew.*
Herman, Meyer, ord seaman, Dec 18, U S steamer *Exchange.*
Harris Griffith, seaman, Apr 28, U S recg ship *Grampus.*
Andrew A Randall, actg mstr's mate, Jan 18, 1865, U S rev steamer *Princetown.*
Richd Rollins, yeoman, Jan 3, 1865, barge *Bounty.*
David Lynch, 2nd cl fireman, Jan 7, 1865, U S steamer *Dale.*
Robt Wiley, actg ensign, Jan 15, 1865, U S steamer *Montgomery.*
Wm Dunne, actg ensign, Dec 28, U S steamer *Mathew Vossler.*
John Hellens, landsman, Jan 1, 1865, Islington Lane Army Hosp.
Patrick Grasby, coalheaver, Jan 23, 1865, Nav Hosp, N Y.

Correction of draft enrollment, Wash, D C, for causes assigned:

Alien:

John Conner	Jacob Doduch	
Jas Maxwell	A Levole	

Detailed in Navy Yd:-J F Barnes
Enrolled in Indiana:-C E Kirkwood
Erroneously enrolled:-L J Boleter
Enrolled in N H:-Horatio Sturdrant
Enrolled in Maine:-Alonzo Weeks
Under age:-J M Shiner
Now in svc:-R B Claston

Enrolled in Mass:

Enrolled in N Y:

J B Ross	W A Wiley	W F Moffat

Furnished a sub:

Allen Kaufman	C E Wilson	Randolph Eichorne
Jos Gawler	C M Fellows	Andrew Hessler

Physical disability:

H Yost	Jas Coleman	J M A Spottswood
Chas Klarking	C B Leslie	Maurice Joyce

(Enrolled in Mass: W H Sprague / Wm E Ayres)

328

C W Walton	E M Farley	Geo W Bates
J W Rhodes	Jas Croggin	Jas P Harris
Patrick Donnelly	Wm P Thompson	Wm Fagan
John B Cooper	Robt H Cassel	Jacob Russels
C L Lammond	Albert Ludwick	
L A Elmore	Thos Martin	

Enrolled in Md:

W C Steir	Levi Meredith	R M Green

3 years in svc:

O D Thatcher	John Lloyd	Jos Reed

Pd commutation in 1863:

Geo Parker	Elder Rodgers	Harvard Granvile
C Parkinson	John M Roberts	

Over age:

David Fisher	J B Hunter	H Smith
C R Appleton	Wm Bayley	Patrick Cronin
Peter Duckhart	H Carter	Benj C Bennet

2 years in svc:

Augustus Norton	C W Morgan	Dr Riley
Wm Madney	R J Johnson	

Enrolled in Pa:

Thad Slentz	Lewis R Hampton	W Doores
Jos M Parker	Frank Alivein	

Orphans Crt-D C. 1-The will of the late Henry Rowe Schoolcraft was full proven; the w/o the dec'd, Mary Howard Schoolcraft, is excx. It is dated Mar, 1850, & leaves his property except some in Michigan & some prsnl effects, which are given to his chldrn. In this will his wife, John L Schoolcraft, of Albany, N Y, & Gen John H Howard, of S C, are named as excx. In 1856 a codicil was made, wherein the wife of the testator is made sole excx. 2-The will of Martin Johnson was proven, Martha H Johnson gave bond as excx. 3-The will of Jos Kellum Whilldin was partially proved, Mrs Mary Brown Whilldin is excx. 4-The will of the late Wm J Stone, sr, which was filed for probate, the w/o the dec'd, Mrs Eliz Jane Stone, is excx. 5-The final acc't of Mr Jos Kelly, exc of the estate of Mary Farnham, was approved & passed. 6-The Account of Jas McScherry, guardian of Helen N, Mary C, & Jas C McSherry, approved. 7-The will of Wm H Edes was partially proven. Mgt Edes & Daniel Edes are excs.

MON JAN 30, 1865

Orphans Crt of Wash Co, D C. Case of Mary Ann Davis, admx of Jos W Davis, dec'd; settlement on Feb 21. -Z C Robbins, rg o/wills

Supreme Crt of D C, in Equity, #1606. Daniel Chandler, Mary Chandler, Joshua Humphreys, & Mary Ann Humphreys, vs Wm Chandler & Cath, his wife, Walter Hay, Benj E Gantt, Walter C Gantt, Mary S W Gantt, Ann H Gantt, Edw C Gantt, Lucy Gantt, Richd Gantt, Cath S Gantt, Jane C Gantt, Mgt Riche Chandler, Mary J Chandler, Wm L Chandler, & John F Broome. Statement of trustee's account at my ofc, Wash, on Feb 6. - Walter S Cox, spec auditor

Jan 27 a deserter was executed at City Point, the name of the culprit was Newell W Root, alias Geo H Harris, 1st Conn Hvy Artl: orders issued Jan 24.

U S Supreme Crt, #94; Rachel Campbell, appellant, vs B W Reed, exc of Wm Campbell. Crct Crt of D C. Wm Campbell, by his will, made provision for his widow & several illegitimate chldrn. After paying all his legacies the fund in dispute remained in the hands of the exc undisposed of. Wm Campbell & Rachel Campbell were both colored, free slaves. Their marriage produced no chldrn. The chldrn by Wm Campbell were born when he was a slave in Va, by his first wife, she too a slave. After her death he obtained his freedom & removed to Wash & mrd the appellant.

Died: on Jan 29, inflamation of the lungs, Anna Hamilton, y/d/o Geo W & Cath J Hinton, aged 2 years, 2 months & 19 days. Funeral from their residence 493 Md av, Tue.

TUE JAN 31, 1865
In the matter of the ptn of Ann Randon, guardian to Ann V & Benedict M Hilton, orphans of John E Hilton, dec'd. Ratify sale by guardian together with her interest & title & of the adult chldrn of Benedict Random, dec'd; lot 1 in sq 75, Wash City, to Jas McGrann for $1,544.24. -Wm F Purcell, Sole Judge

Andrew Jackson Burroughs was shot & killed in the Treas bldg by a woman who gave her name as Mary Harris, of Ill; on Jan 30. Harris said she had been engaged to the dec'd for a number of years, & he had failed to fulfill his engagement. She was in great distress because of her parents. She has been committed to jail. Feb 1-dec'd mrd a Miss Amelia Boggs, of Chicago, about 18 months ago; he was bro of Dr Burroughs, President of the N W Univ at Chicago. Mary Harris' proper name is Kate, & she is also mrd, but lived unhappily with her hsbnd. They were both formerly of Burlington, Iowa, & she denied that she was engaged to Burroughs.

Deaths of sldrs reported to Capt Murray, A Q M, Wash, D C:

John W Gilbert, Co I, 1st N H hvy artl	John D Flanders, Co F, 1st N H hvy artl
Nelson A Young, Co A, 8th Pa cavalry	Henry Bucky, Co H, 1st Md
Geo A Richards, Co I, 131st Ohio	Peney Smith, Co G, 140th Ind
Stephen D Harris, Co A, 8th Pa cavalry	T Parris, Co D, 1st Dela

Correction of the enrollment lists, causes assigned; Wash, D C:

Physical disability:

Jas Page	Michl Clune	Geo H Gaddis
E Linney	Aug Bigger	Chas Cumberland
Thos D Wilson	Saml Jones	Wm H Calhoun
Thos Dudley	Geo Better	Chas Sword
L B Moses	Chas Shroth	John Delzeila
Thos Kelleher	Jas H Robinson	Edw L Sheckells
Isaac Bradley	Alex'r Polack	Albert Patterson
Edw Esputa	Henry N Sipes	
M D Speyer	Henry Cohill	

Over age:

Patrick Murray	Nicholas Speakes	John Mullen
Jos F Noyes	Edw Quirk	
Philip Hessmer	John Rich	

Furnished sub:

Jos Jackson	C H Langdon	Geo Bogus
Zach Baker	Wm D Baldwin	Geo Callaghan
J E Bell	Wm Kinner	Jas J Morgan

Erroneous enrollment:

John Nulty	Jacob Reitz	

3 years in svc:

Hugh Reagan	Michl O'Connor	Michael Fitzgerald
John Farnham	John Ryan	

Alien:

Richard Young	Jas Martin	S Cohen
John McClellan	Patrick Sullivan	

Enrolled in Pa:

John Hull	Alex'r J Swartz	Geo W Flynn

Enrolled in Md:

Edw Atkinson	John Gillett	
Lewis E Gross	Jas E Gross	

Now in svc:

Harvey Hoffer	Wm McLane	R B Claston

Enrolled in Mich: John Green
Drafted & detailed in Navy Yd: Lawrence Dilger
Enrolled in Ill: Jas C McClellan
Enrolled in Mich: John W Green
2 years in svc-Wm H Howell
3 years in svc: Martin Casey
Deserter from rebel army: J R McGregor
Enrolled in N Y: John Hungerford

Died: on Jan 30, after a short & painful illness, Mary Ann Reis, w/o Benj Reis, in the 41st yr of her age. Funeral from the residence of her hsbnd, 267 G st, today.

WED FEB 1, 1865
Harrison Barker & Simeon Denty, doing business in Alexandria, were arrested on Sat charged with selling goods to go thru the lines, & sent to the Old Capitol prison.

Died: in Richmond, Va, on Jan 20, Mrs Esabella Ritchie, relict of Thos Ritchie, in her 76th yr.

Obit: Eugene F Skinner, only bro/o Gen St John B S Skinner, died in Eugene City, on Dec 15, 1864; aged 55 yrs, 3 months & 2 days. Born in Essex Co, N Y, Sep 13, 1809; emigrated to Oregon with his family in 1846; pioneer white settler in Willametta valley. [From the Eugene City [Oregon] Review.]

The s/o Mr J J Coombs drowned in the Gtwn channel on Monday. He fell thru the ice while skating. His body has not been recovered. Local Item

Franklin Mkt: 180 Pa ave, between 17th & 18th sts. Fresh supply of marketing constantly on hand. All deliveries free of charge. –C F Schoolman

Brigs & Maj Gens, etc, awaiting orders, some off duty on account of sickness or wounds. Sickles, Ricketts, Asboth, Barlow, R O Tyler, Schimmelpfenning, Paul, Gresham, Underwood, Connor, McIntosh, Bradley, Long, Eagan, & Stannard. Brig Gens Hayes & Duffie are P O Ws. Gen Hayes is now released on parole to distribute supplies sent to our sldrs in rebel prisons. As of the 1st of Jan, 1864, in svc: 66 Maj Gens; 267 Brig Gens: of these 245 are in command, 200 of whom are Brig Gens.

Col Taylor, 2nd Md, says that on Sun last Messrs Alex'r H Stephens, V P of the Confederacy, R M T Hunter, & 2 others, requested permission to come within our lines near Ft Hill, but were refused by the picket until the return of Gen Grant, who was absent at the time.

THU FEB 2, 1865

Deaths of sldrs reported to ofc of Capt Moore, A Q M, Wash, D C:

John Magerly, Co H, 76th N Y	Jacob Young, Co E, 51st N Y vols
Robt M Feskett, Co C, 4th N Y hvy artl	Robt Redick, Co F, 1st N Y light artl

Corrections in the enrollment for causes assigned, Wash:

Aliens:

Wm Lynch	Timothy Mullen	John Sullivan
Michl Cooney	David Hyde	

Physical disability:

Jos Ashler	Robt Simons	W C O'Mears
Jos Harris	Irving S Vassal	Wm Quigley
Wm H Douglass	Wm Crown	Robt Henry
J R Kennedy	Jas Hudson	Edw Fox
Harrison Jackson	E C Eckloff	Jas Barry
H Blair	J B Crutchett	S B Wibert
Jos E Thomas	Edw O'Connor	F A Lueber
L C Oliver	Henry Walther	John Parkhurst
W T Schlosser	Michl O'Brien	

Enrolled in Vt:

Enrolled in N Y:

	John C Holmes
	Lee Leveridge

Over age:

Levi Logan	G S White	John McNamara
Jas Skinner	Louis H Waine	Omar R Whiting
Geo Smith	Nathan W Hilbron	John Welsh

Furnished sub:

Isaac W Nichols	Saml Polkinhorn
Geo E Messer	Wm C Nolan

Enrolled in Ind:

Enrolled in N Y:

Over Age:

	Wm A Lake	
	Robt Gridley	Henry A Scott
	Stephen Ferguson	

Deserter from rebels:

Jas Gilmer	Albert Hamilton
Robt Greenwood	John W Kiser

2 years in svc:

F A A Evans	Nicholas Doyle

Enrolled in N J:

Isaac Marshall

3 years in svc:

A M Shephard	Symns Stillwell	John Lerfert

Now in svc:

John Lyons

Enrolled in Pa:

Robt Woolsey	Henry J Lynn	Peter Able
Richd McLaughlin	Andrew Irons	Danl Harper
Fred Schold, dead.		

Col A Starling & Lt Col A R Weir, 35th Ky vols, dishonorable mustered out of the svc of the U S. Charge: transferring men from company to company, thereby fraudulently swelling the ranks. [Feb 3 paper: Regarding: Col A Starling. Order was published, but since has been revoked, & he has been honorably mustered out.]

Peter Connelly was appt'd guardian to the orphans of Matthew Cullen.

The large mansion belonging to the heirs of the late Chas Coltman, 14th & M sts, purchased by Justice Wiley, of the Sup Crt of this Dist, for $25,000.

Shocking case of infanticide: some 3 months since, Jas H Myers & his wife moved into a tenement on Mr Geo Wells' farm, in Ross twnshp, having been engaged as a farm hand by Mr Wells. On Sun, a boy residing in the family of Mr Wells, while passing the hse occupied by Mr Myers, heard the cries of an infant, & hastented to inform Mrs Wells. Mrs Wells went at once to the Myers' residence, & discovered Mrs Myers lying on a bed, she having just given birth to a male child. The infant was lying upon another bed in the same room, with its skull apparently crushed in, & blood gushing from its mouth. Dr Ewen was sent for, but the baby died before his arrival, having survived about 2 hours. Myers, a young man, states that he has been mrd but a few months. Mayor Morrison charged Myers with killing the child, as there were heel marks apparent on the side of the skull. –Pittsburg Evening Chron

Orphans Crt, D C. 1-Will of the late Wm J Stone was fully proved & ltrs test were issued to Mrs Eliz Jane Stone, excx. 2-Ltrs of adm, with w a, issued to Wm S Graham on the estate of Eliz Graham. 3-Peter Connelly apt'd guardian to the orphan Matthew Cullen. 4-First & final accounts of Robt G Lumpkin, exc of Thos Lumpkin, & of Hugh Murray, adm of Mary Murray: approved & passed.

FRI FEB 3, 1865
Deaths of sldrs reported at the ofc of Capt Moore, A Q M, Wash:

M J West, teamster, Q M D	Fred'k Brant, Co E, 11th Pa
Gail Wood, Co K, 26th Ky	John Kumanns, Co F, 51st N Y
John J Royal, Co K, 6th Maine btry	Herman Prescot, Co E, 1st N H hvy artl

Lemuel Beckett, hackman charge'd with robbing Mr S P Corbett of $400, near Camp Casey, was held to bail in sum of $600. -Local Item

Coroner's inquest: Martha Ann Chase, colored, was accidentally shot on Wed by her cousin Basil Chase. -Local Item

Mrd: on Feb 2, at the Chr of the Epiphany, C M Walker, Fifth Auditor of the Treas, to Miss Claire Albrecht, a ward of Chief Justice Chase.

SAT FEB 4, 1865
Sarah Reeves was arrested Feb 2, on charge of stealing a gown & breastpin from Rebecca Bowman. Same was found on her person. Reeves committed to jail. -Local

Senate has confirmed the appointment of Brig Gen Geo G Meade to be Maj-Gen of vols, from Aug 18, 1864, v Grant, appt'd Lt Gen.

John T Holohan, recruiting & substitute agent, 239 I st, Wash, D C.

SUN FEB 5, 1865

Deaths reported to Chief of the Bur of Med & Surgery, during week ending Feb 4:

Adolphus Schultz, landsman, Dec 28 schnr *M A Wood.*
Jas H Couch, coalheaver, Jan 4, Nav Hosp, N Orleans.
Jas Henry, 1st cl boy, Dec 7, do.
Christopher Davis, landsman, Jan 9, do.
John Flood, landsman, Jan 11, Nav Hosp, Pensacola.
Wm Unitt, coalheaver, Jan 13, do.
Geo Flynn, seaman, Jan 24, recg ship *Princeton.*
Jos Lewis, boatswain, Jan 23, Charlestown, Mass.
Alfred Dolvin, colored, landsman, Jan 8, Nav Hosp, St Helena Is, S C.
Wm Cephas or Seaphus, colored, landsman, Dec 27, do.
Geo Handy, do do, Jan 11, vessel U S S *New Hampshire.*
Jacob Simmons, do, do, Jan 17, do.
Fountain Beasley, do, do, Jan 13, do.
John Mulligan, ord seaman, Jan 27, Nav Hosp, Norfolk.
Benj Whitby, appr boy, Jan 27, vessel U S S *Sabine.*
Peter McIntyre, seaman, Jan 28, Nav Hosp, N Y.
John Smith, seaman, Jan 16, marine hosp, Key West.
Thos Pepper, 1st cl boyk, Dec 23, U S steamer *Jacob Bell*
Michael Mahon, coalheaver, Jan 28, Nav Hosp, Chelsea.
T R Jones, seaman, Dec 30, hosp ship *Red Rover.*
John Hess, seaman, do, do.
Jas Johnson, Jan 5, do.
Zenia W Austin, landsman, Jan 11, do.
Chas Daily, seaman, Jan 17, do.
Patrick Murray, landsman, Jan 15 U S steamer *Nereus.*
Jos Moran, coxswain, Jan 15, do.
Frederick Untiedt, seaman, Jan 15, do.
Benj F Hackney, landsman, Jan 15, U S S steamer *Pequot.*
Thos Williams, 1st cl fireman, Jan 15, U S steamer *Yantic.*
Wm Lemon, mstr-at-arms, Jan 15, do.
Jas McGrath, marine, Jan 15, U S steamer *Ft Jackson.*
Alex C Warren, coxswain, Jan 17, U S steamer *Santiago.*
Hans Anderson, Jan 17, U S steamer *Gettysburg.*
Henry Wadmouth, marine, Jan 16, U S ship *Powhatan.*
John J Hutchinson, landsman, Jan 21, U S steamer *New Ironsides.*
Frederick R Stow, actg ast paymstr, Jan 5, U S steamer *Trustram Shandy.*
Thos J Lynch, marine, Jan 16, U S ship *Tuscarora.*
Robt Garnett, seaman, Jan 28, Nav Hosp, Norfolk.
Jos Tucker, appr boy, Feb 2, U S steamer *Sabine.*
John Fountain, marine, Feb 1, Nav Asylum.

Corrections to the enrollment list, Wash, causes assigned:
Pd commutation in 1863:
Irwin P Minksell   Wm H Getzendamer
Furnished Sub:
Alexander R Edgehill   Wm H Steuart
Enrolled in N Y:
Albert E Dixon
Enrolled in Pa:

Daniel Harper
Enrolled in N J:
Wm S Wilson
Over age:
John B Morgan
Jacob Carrington
Leonard W Stewart
Wm W Taylor
Enrolled in Conn:
Saml Bingham
Aliens:
Morrity Neisser
Herman Hannuersdreay
John Humphreys
Daniel McRae
Geo Hertrich
John Mahoney
Jacob Legar
John Kelcher
John Wincher
Jacques Cleinker
Under age:
Andrew Woolbridge
Physical disability:
S C Boynton
3 years svc:
John Beaty
Deserter from rebel
army:
Bernard Silverbury
Now in svc:
Wm Morgan

Enrolled in Md:
Louis Clunk
2 years svc:
Chas Robinson

E S Browns

Matthew Myers
John Paxton
Patrick Driscoll
John Foster

Theodore Burkhert
Ignatius Stovell
Henry Cook
Frank Rest
Louis Bauer
Thos Somnerschall
Edw Enwright
Danl Herbert
Henry Lutz
Sebastian Aman

E E Forsyth

Wm Jones

Robt Staples

Henry Wells
Wm Brown
Benj Miller

Christopher Xander
John Helbig
Cornelius Halpin
Jos Lebean
Fred Zeimer
Valentine Wager
Peter Creagle
Edw Collonis
Felix Born

Louis L Brunett

Orphans' Crt, Feb 4. 1-The will of Wm H Edes, late of Gtwn, was admitted to probate, & David Edes & Mgt Edes appt'd excs. 2-The will of John Fletcher was fully proven. Jos H Fletcher is named sole exc. 3-The will of Bernard O'Reilly, partially proven in 1856, was fully proven yesterday, & admitted to probate & record.

Local rl estate sales: hse & lot on 17th st to Marcus Pearl, $4,000; hse & lot on C st to Conrad Dietch, $1,800; hse & lot on C st to John G Barthel, $1,700; hse & lot, 245 13th st, to R Simpson, $2,750; hse & lot on 9th st to John Grinder, $1,000; hses & lots-247-249-251 13th st [3] to Chr. Rupert, $2,550 each; 80 acs on Bladensburg rd to C M Alexander, $12,400; hse & lot on 4th st, to R Wilson, $2,300.

Died: on Jan 4, Lely, aged 4 years & 9 mos, oldest d/o Alfred & Ella Ray, late of Wash Co. Funeral from the residence of her parents, Highlands, Montg Co, Md, Mon.

Died: on Jan 4, of typhoid fever, Eliz, only d/o John W Reynolds, in her 10th yr. Funeral today.

MON FEB 6, 1865

Orphans Crt of Wash Co, D C. Prsnl estate of Eliz Graham, late of Wash City, dec'd. -Wm S Graham, adm.

Local Item: Edwin Forrest, tragedian, was born in Mar, 1806. At age 12 years he appeared on the stage in the Walnut-St Theatre, Phil. Edmund Kean, tragedian, died Mar 25, 1833, f/o Mr Chas Kean, also an actor.

Mrs Jean M [Davenport] Lander has a claim before Congress for money due her late hsbnd, Gen F W Lander, for svcs to the Gov't on a Western exploring party.

Feb 5, the male child of Ann Louisa Daniels was smothered to death at her home on 6th st, between Mkt & Frederick sts. Coroner Woodward was called, but deemed an inquest unnecessary. -Wash, D C

Crt of Appeals of Md. Jan Term, 1865. Annapolis, Feb 3, 1865. #4: Ann M Alther vs Jacob Wisner et al. Appeal from the Crct Crt for Balt Co, in equity. Decree affirmed with costs to the appellees. #5: Cath Alther vs Jacob Wisner et al. Ditto. #6 & #7: Jas Turner & wife et al, vs Charlotte Withers et al, & vice versa. Cross appeals from the Crct Crt for Balt Co, in equity. Argument concluded by Wm S Waters for Turner & wife. #8: Thos Whitridge et al, vs Edw Rider. Appeal from the Crct Crt for Balt Co. Argument commenced by Geo Wm Bunn for the appellants, & Wm Pinckney Whyte for the appellee. On motion of W Brener, Jas E Hignutt, of Caroline Co, Md, was admitted & qualified as an atty of this crt.

Local 1-John J Beall, one of our most enterprisng young merchants, has constantly on hand at his warehse, 87 Water st, a good supply of grain, feed, & flour. 2-Mr J Thos Davis, wholesale dealer in salt, 83 Water st. Our Gtwn merchants possess facilities for trade not attainable elsewhere. 3-Shinn's Union Bottling Depot-modest title given by our enterprising fellow-ctzn, Riley A Shinn, to his extensive business on Green & Olive sts.

Phil Furn Warehse: 508 7th st, also, 519 7th st. Wash City. -W B Moses

Yesterday Ofcr Coome arrested a man named Chas Darragh, on charge of beating Danl Murphy, on Sat night, & robbing him of $10. Murphy was so badly beaten as to be unable to appear at the hearing. Justice Giberson committed the accused to jail for a further hearing.

Local: On Sat, a sldr named W Gates, was robbed of $50 in a restaurant on the corner of 12th & H sts. Jas Pike represented himself as bar-tender, & on being tendered a $50 note by Gates, left the bar room.

Wash Corp: 1-Ptn of Michl Reardon, asking payment for damages done to his property by the overflowing of a Corp sewer: referred to the Cmte on Claims.

TUE FEB 7, 1865

Moved my grocery store to 481 9th st, Wash, D C, from 9th & D sts. -Richd J Ryon

Gen hardware & variety store, 482 Pa av, Wash, D C. -Geo Savage.

Hardware & Cutlery, 61 La av, Wash, D C. E Wheeler & Son

Hardware & Cutlery, 513 7th st, Wash, D C. John D Edmond & Co

Family groceries, 325 Pa av, Wash, D C. C Maurice Sioussa, Gregory I Ennis.

Monticello Restaurant, 13 Bridge st, Gtwn, D C. A Rodier, G W Thecker, proprietors

P O Restaurant, 50 Congress st, Wash City. Wm Ellis & D J Welles, proprietors

Wine merchant, 181 Pa av, Wash City. Barney Hart, successor to B Jost

Wholesale & Retail groceries, 1st & High sts, Gtwn. T A Carroll

Dealer in sale, 83 Water st, Gtwn, D C. -I Thos Davis

Deaths of sldrs reported to Capt Murray, A Q M, Wash, D C:

Lewis Mulling, Co B, 180th Ohio vols	John Doran, Co H, 51st N Y vols
John F Riley, Co B, 50th Ohio vols	Wm N Shaw, Co H, 95th N Y
Edw Loyd, Co F, 2nd Md vols	Cornelius L McGuire, Co A, 205th Pa.

On Friday night Geo Pritchard attempted suicide after being rejected by a widow who lives on 13th st, between G & H, Wash, D C.

Died: on Feb 5, Jas R Draine, only s/o Mary & the late Chas Draine, in his 21st yr. Funeral at the residence of his mother, 390 10th st, Wed.

Died: on Feb 6, John Christian Hitz, eldest s/o Geo W & Lucy Hitz, aged 6 yrs. Funeral from the residence of his grandmother, Mrs E Wetzel, 471 3rd st, Wed.

Geo Bealor, who keeps a confectionary store, was fined $20 for selling on Sun. Ofcrs found him engaged in selling. Local Item

Carpenter & bldr, 214 B st, Wash. -Jos A Mockbee

Held for trial: Saml Woodyard, colored, charged with robbing Geo Bell, also colored, of $60, at the hse of Jas Lawrence, some evenings since. Accused held to bail to answer the charge in court.

WED FEB 8, 1865
Crct Crt-D C. Zephaniah Jones vs John P Ingle, exc of Ann R Dermott, dec'd; in litigation for many yrs; regarding the construction of *Avenue Hse*, on Pa av, Wash City; case postponed. Miss Dermott was well-known in Wash City.

The Macon Telegraph of Dec 25 says that Lt Gen Pemberton has been assigned to active duty.

Arrival of Union prisoners from Varina. Fortress Monroe, Feb 6. Col Mulford, on the flag-of-truce steamer *N Y*, arrived with 1,100 released Union prisoners, about 40 of whom are ofcrs. Gens Carter & Pennypacker, both of whom were wounded at Ft Fisher, are still here at Chesapeake Hosp, & slowly recovering. Gen Pennypacker's wound was a severe one, & it will be some time before he fully recovers.

Correction of the draft enrollment, Washington, causes assigned:

Alien:

Roger Wall	Michl Daley	John Bauf
Daniel Sullivan	Thos Lee	Thos Murphy
Casper Herbert	Jas Sullivan	Jas Nash
Morris Mary	Patrick McAuliff	Michl Nash
Thos Dark	John Gray	Lawrence Hickey
Thos Carfield	Daniel Burk	Jas Smith
Peter White	Michl McAnny	Mathias Breen
Saml Horwitz	Andrew Burkley	Jas J Boyd
Edw P Walch	Jas Garrity	Owen Sullivan
J F Mendis	Conrad Mayer	Edw Leonard

Over age:

John Morgan	Felix McKenne	John Noonan
S Hurenkins	Lloyd Hicks	John Hurley
Thos Francis	Wm Gilbert	Wm Mattingly
John Ketzel	Isaac Clarke	John Welsh
Henry Baley	Thos H Langley	John Hill
Rody Craver	Chas Stewart	John W Cann
John Martin	John E Mills	Robt Wilson
Wm Curtain	Thos Lomas	

Physical disability:

M J McCardel	Jos H Henlein	Jas B Bryant
Jas F Gibson	L W Stevenson	John Shea
Jas Wilson	W A Caldwell	Patrick Downey
____ Durkley	Christian Price	Michl Fenton
Wm A Franklin	H L Chapin	Wm Anderson
Jas H Myers	Chas Forster	Jacob Ollsman
Thos Keithley	C H Folwell	A W Sweeney
John Woods	J N Davis	C F Edmonston
S F Gates	John Flaherty	F C Bailey
Geo B Bean	Henry G Gibbs	Patrick Maher
John B Knott	Jos Martin	Richd H Trunnell
Jas A W Clarvoe	S A H McKim	Wm Dottaran
Wm H Bailey	Benson Gates	Alex McKane
Nath'l W Lowe	Jos C Walker	Martin Flannigan
Jas M Allen	John Ober	

Drafted & detailed in Navy Yd:

W B Williamson	Wm Bellsworth

Now in svc:

Geo Dean	Martin O'Day	Gilbert H Brindee

Under age:

Albert F Pike	Wm Adams	Ward H Goosbeck

3 years svc:

Stephen D Church	Robt A Wilson
John Broderick	Andrew J McNamee

Enrolled in Md:
Thos Coon
Wm Gardner
John Getz
Benj Mason

Lawrence Fritz
Jos Waters
Wm H Server
Chas Chaney

Jas Chaney
Wm Hummerickhouse

Enrolled in N J:
Oliver W Cook

Enrolled in Maine:
Geo Carey
Jeremiah Philbrook

Lewis T Coombs
Chas H Parker

Enrolled in Conn:
Jas Gilfillen

Enrolled in Wisc:
Isaac Cheshire

Furnished sub:
Jas B Johnson
Jas H Reed

Fayman Welles
E O Sanderson

Geo Gant
Patrick White

Deserters from the rebel army:
Thos Harrison
Jas B Dawson
J Taylor

A M Garner
Chas J Oker
Geo Mills

August Noack
Jas S Southard

Enrolled in Pa:
Adam Scholer
Henry McIntire
Enrolled in N Y:
John G Jenkins
W T Bouldew

J R Jones
Warrington Somers

L M Vincent
Geo F Morey

Jas Smith

John Foster
Edgar M Carr

Enrolled in Vt:
Dennis A Goff

Lucian R Nourse

Enrolled in Mass:
Geo Mason

Enrolled in Ohio:
Rezin W Allison

Pd commutation in 1863:
W K Miller

Wm H Seward

2 years in svc:
John Ross
Herman Tecsey
Michl Mullen

Danl Shanehan
Michl Pendergast
Newell F Odton

Richd E Jordan

5th Corps in the advance: The fight at Hatcher's Run: Enemy's rifle-pits captured. The 2nd Corps moving with the 5th. Gordon's rebel troops encountered-our line repeatedly attacked. Headqrtrs Army of the Potomac, Feb 5, 1865. Our loss during the day was quite light-probably not over a 100 altogether. Col Murphy was wounded in the knee, not severely, while giving orders to his men. His assistant Adj Gen, Lt McTavish, was mortally wounded; Lt Graham, 14th Conn, wounded in the breast severely; Lt Wm Tibbitts, 19th Mass, killed; Lt Morris, 10th N J. wounded in the thigh & head; Lt A Bartlett, 14th Conn, killed. –W D McGregor

Marietta R R Accident: Cincinnati, Feb 7. Thos N Whiteson, a mbr of the Leg of this county, was among the killed in the recent accident on Marietta R R.

THU FEB 9, 1865

The 5th Corps Repulsed.: Several ofcrs wounded: attack on the 2nd Corps. Headqrtrs Army of the Potomac, Feb 6, 1865. Cavalry, under Gen Gregg, captured the train at Dinwiddie Crt Hse, while on its way to N C for supplies. Capt Arrowsmith, of Gen Gregg's staff, had his leg badly bruised by his horse falling on him. Gen Meade was on the field all day, but was not wounded, as reported. Maj Pease's horse was shot under him while he was communicating with the 5th Corps. Brvt Brig Gen Irwin Gregg, commanding a brig of cavalry, was wounded in the ankle Gen Davis was wounded severely in the shoulder. Maj Tremains, of Gen Gregg's staff, was badly wounded in the foot. Col Bankhead, of Gen Warren's staff, was wounded in the hand. Brvt Brig Gen Morrow, commanding 3rd Brig 3rd Div of 5th Corps, was wounded in the shoulder. Capt Cowdrey, assist adj gen on Gen Baxter's staff, was mortally wounded, & Col Tilden, 12th Maine, wounded in the leg. About 150 prisoners were taken, among them was Col Allen, 24th N C, formerly an ofcr in the 12th regulars.

Chancery Crt-Dfndnt is Surgeon Gen of the rebel army, Dr A Y P Garnett, age about 45 yrs, formerly of Wash City; in 1846 contracted a debt to Eliza F Seymour of $1,500-deed of trust on his property on 9th st, & then his residence. Debt never pd. Mrs Seymour died; property was confiscated [with/out reference to mortgage] & sold to Alex'r R Shepherd on Sep 9, 1862. Exec is cmplnt; case to come up shortly for a hearing.

Senate: 1-Ptn of Dorsey Edwin Wm Towson, of Gtwn, asking that his name be changed to Dorsey Edwin Wm Carter. 2-Ptn of Henry W Longfellow, asking that inferior offices in the gift of the Gov't be filled by persons honorably discharged from the U S army or Navy.

Nominations by the Pres to the Senate. To be Maj Gens, Vol force:
Brig Gen Wm B Hazen, to date from Dec 13, 1864, v McClernand, resigned;
Brig Gen Thos J Wood, v Crittenden, resigned.
To be Maj Gens by Brevet, Vol force:
Brig Gen Chas R Woods, from Nov 20, 1864
Brig Gen John M Corse, from Oct 5, 1864
Brig Gen Giles A Smith, from Sep 1, 1864
Brig Gen M D Legget, from Sep 1, 1864
Brig Gen John W Geary, from Jan 12, 1865
Brig Gen John E Smith, from Jan 12, 1865
Brig Gen A S Williams, from Jan 12, 1865
Brig Gen Judson Kilpatrick, from Jan 12, 1865
Brig Gen Absalom Baird, from Jan 12, 1865
Brig Gen Wm F Barry, from Sep 1, 1864
Brig Gen Rufus Saxton, from Sep 12, 1865

Brig Gen Adelbert Ames, from Jan 15, 1865
Brig Gen John M Brannan, from Jan 23, 1865
To be Brig Gens Vol force:
Brvt Gen N M Curtis, & Col, of 142nd N Y vols, to date from Jan 15, 1865, v W H Powell, resigned.
Col B F Potts, 32nd Ohio vols, from Jan 12, 1865, v Mahlin D Manson, resigned.
Col John M Oliver, 15th Mich vols, from Jan 12, 1865, v Thos A Rowley, resigned.
Col John G Mitchell, 113th Ohio vols, from Jan 12, 1865, v A W Ellet, resigned.
Col Jas S Robinson, 82nd Ohio vols, from Jan 12, 1865, v Jacob Ammen, resigned.
To be Brig Gens by brevet, Vol force:
Col G A Pennypacker, 97th Pa vols, from Jan 16, 1865
Col J C Abbott, 7th N H vols, from Jan 15, 1865
Brvt Col Cyrus B Comstock, U S vols, from Jan 15, 1865

The Buffalo Courier announces the death of Mr Wm F Ketchum inventor of the mower & reaper, known by his name. He resided in Buffalo more than 30 yrs.

Mrs F W Lander, formerly Miss Davenport, made her entree at Niblo's Garden on Mon in triumph before a brilliant audience. Hon C M Walker & his bride, with their bridal party, including Sen & Mrs Sprague from Wash City were present.

FRI FEB 10, 1865
Supreme Crt of D C, in Equity, #314: Eldred W Mobberly & Louisa, his wife, Ann Worthington, Wm H Johnson & Laura I, his wife, Chas E Worthington & Maria L, his wife, against Ella Johnson, Thos P Brashear, Chas H Brashear, & John R Jones & Sarah L, his wife, & others. Report if the rl estate of the late Thos Cook is susceptible of partition among his heirs & the heirs of Ann Brashear. Meeting on Mar 3, at the Crt-hse, City Hall, Wash. -W Redin, auditor

Died: on Feb 9, Hugh McWilliams, in his 24th yr. Funeral today at half past two o'clock, from the residence of his bro, 230 D st, between 3rd & 4½ sts.

Death of sldrs reported yesterday at the ofc of Capt Moore,
A Q M, U S A, 21st & F st.

Sgt Lemuel Tulerit, G, 5th Tenn	John Marbly, F, 180th Ohio
Alfred Sutton, J, 129 Ind	Thos Hevlin, C, 140th Ind
Jas D Segar, B, 103rd Ohio	Danl A Richards, B, 180th Ohio
Levi Miller, K, 12th V R C	David Shepherd, C, 140th Ind
John Tate, C, 8th Minn	Nicholas Clarke, G, Q M U S A
Jas W Basil, E, 130th Ohio	Asa L Patten, T, 174th Ohio

Last night Ofcr Spencer brought from the depot a young lad, Michl Dunn, about 13 years of age. He said he lives at 183 Eliz St, N Y C. He says he & his father came to Wash on Wed, looking after a bro, who, they had been informed, had enlisted in the army. The father met an acquaintance, a sldr, at the depot, leaving Michl, & has not yet returned. The boy expresses the belief that something has happened to his father, else he would not have been thus left alone.

Supreme Crt of D C, in Equity, #379. Sarah Ann Matilda Dove, cmplnt, vs Robt W Dove, dfndnt. Dfndnt is a resident of Va, ordinary process of law cannot be served on him. Ordered that dfndnt appear on or before May next. -R J Meigs, clerk

Sudden death: Capt Jas Melvin Gilliss, U S Navy, the accomplished Super of the Nat'l Observatory, died suddenly yesterday of a stroke of apoplexy, aged 52 yrs. He entered the Navy on Mar 1, 1827: has been but little at sea. Establishment of the Nat'l Observatory was mainly due to his efforts, & on Sep 17, 1842, he was ordered to superintend the erection of the bldg. On Nov 16, 1848, he was ordered to make astronomical observations in So America: returned in Nov, 1852. He leaves a wife & 5 chldrn, & we understand that a much loved son in the army, who has for months been imprisoned in the south, reached his home the evening before the death of his father.

SAT FEB 11, 1865
Supreme Crt of D C, in Equity, #177. Eleazer Lindsley & others vs Jos L Ingle & others. Ratify sale by John C Kennedy, trustee, of lot 2 in sq 382, Wash City, to Wm H Phillip for $38.92; lot 1 in sq 602, to Moses Kelly for $287.31; lot 2 in sq 604 to Moses Kelly, for $262.38; lots 7 & 8 in sq 613 to Wm B Todd & Wm H Philip, for $240; lot 2 in sq south of sq 667 to Wm B Todd & Wm H Philip, for $311.68. -R J Meigs, clerk

Crct Crt-D C. J C Krauth vs Corp of Washington. Krauth enlarged his frame hse. City ordnance prohibits the erection of a frame hse within 24 ft of any other hse: fined $20.

Chas Hibbs vs Wm Lipscomb; issue between a landlord & tenant. Lipscomb leased the hse at 506 Massachusetts ave of Hibbs in 1861. The latter desires to terminate the tenancy. Hibbs lately took up residence in N Y. Power of atty excuted to his son-in-law, Wilson E Brown, of Wash City.

Died: Mr John Varden, one of the oldest ctzns of D C; janitor of the nat'l museum for almost 25 yrs; died on Feb 10, after a severe illness, contracted by his efforts to preserve the property under his charge during the late fire at the Smithsonian.

Maj Gen John M Parker, assigned to the command of the Dept of Ky, vice Gen Burbridge; entered the army as a colonel of the 14 Ill Vols in May 1861. He is a native of Ky. His home is in Carlinville, Ill & a lawyer by profession.

Died: on Feb 5, at her residence in Fairfax Co, Va, Mrs Julia Terrett, aged 72 yrs.

Died: on Feb 9, Capt Jas M Gilliss, U S Navy, Super of the Nat'l Observatory, in the 55th yr of his age. Funeral from the Observatory, today.

Water rents due by Feb 15. Randolph Coyle, water reg, Wash.

Deaths of sldr reported to Capt Moore, A Q M, U S A:
John B Taylor, qrtrmstr blacksmith, under Super Riley; Andrew Williams, Co F, qrtrmstr cavalry; John Connor, Co C, qrtrmstr U S A; Edwin ____ Co G, 36th Mass; Marcus L McVay, Co D, Ohio
John W Ford, Co K, 4 N J Vols, was robbed of $32 last night at F & 10th sts, Wash; said he was subject to epileptic fits, of which he had one at Central Sta.

MON FEB 13, 1865
Dedication of Capitol Hill Presby Chr, Feb 12. Rev John Chester, s/o Rev Wm Chester, D D, came here to inspect the field. Chas E Lathrop & Robt Leitch-elders; J R Arrison, Jas T Burtchard & Jas Simpson-deacons. Carpenter work by Elwood Conner, of Burlington. Chapel is located on 4th st east, near Pa av.

List of deaths in the Navy reported for week ending Feb 11, 1865:
Jas Armstrong, 1st cl fireman, Jan 19, Nav Hosp, New Orleans.
Daniel McLean, qrtr gunner, Jan 21, do.
Chas H Hurd, actg ensign, Jan 23, do.
J H Downs, boatswain, Nov 24, vessel U S S *Iroquois.*
B F Cooper 2nd cl fireman, Jan 17, vessel U S S *Lanapee.*
Robt B Harlow, 1st cl fireman, Jan 30, Nav Hosp, Portsmouth, Va.
Thos Cruminey, seaman, Jan 31, do.
Hiram L Hankey, landsman, Jan 31, do.
Patrick McCartey, capt after guard, Jan 24, do.
John Calhoun, pvt marine, Feb 4, do.
John W Ford, seaman, Feb 5, do.
Henry Smith, ord seaman, Feb 5, do.
Elmer Lewis, landsman, Jan 21, Nav Hosp, Memphis, Tenn.
Nelson McCormick, landsman, Jan 25, do.
Thos Rogers, seaman, Jan 28, do.
Henry Williams, seaman, Jan 28, do.
John A Lewis, pilot, Dec 20, 1864, vessel U S S *Valley City.*
Daniel Croney, landsman, Jan 24, Nav Hosp, Tenn.
Thos Stevens, actg ensign, Jan 21, Nav Hosp, Port Royal, S C.
Jas Smith, colored, landsman, Feb 3, Navy Yd, Wash City.
Jas Sullivan, 2nd cl fireman, Dec 28, vessel U S S *Ft Jackson.*
Henry Sands, ord seaman, Dec 25, 1864, vessel U S S *Tacony.*
Dempsey Connor, landsman, Jan 30, vessel U S S *Young America.*
Jas Martin, boatswain's mate, Dec 21, 1864, vessel U S S *Ft Jackson.*
Jas Cotgrove, seaman, Dec 19, U S frig *Colorado,* at sea.
Thos McCormick, 2nd fireman, Dec 21, do.
Wm A Goodridge, Dec 25, 1864, vessel U S S *Colorado.*
J G Bragg, landsman, Dec 28, 1864, vessel U S frig *Colorado.*
Geo J Landon, 1st cl boy, Jan 10, do.
Robt Little, ord seaman, Jan 13, do.
Josiah Nason, seaman, Jan 19, do.
H E Lambert, landsman, Jan 19, do.
Frank Stitson, pvt marine, Jan 28, do.
Daniel Bent, landsman, Jan 4, do.
Noah Pratt, landsman, Jan 31, do.
John Curtis, seaman, Dec 22, vessel U S S *Chicopee.*
Bracley Mood, landsman, Jan 7, U S frig *Wabash.*
Randolph Van Grepen, or Ferguson, capt after guard, Jan 15, vessel U S S *Monticello.*
Jos Daniels, seaman, Jan 15, do.
Zachariah Gresher, landsman, Jan 15, do.
Shadrack Hutchinson, landsman, Jan 15, do.
John Smith, 1st cl fireman, Dec 25, vessel U S S *Mackinaw.*
David D Wemple, lt, Dec 24, U S steamer *Juniata.*
Jones Pile, 2nd lt of marines, Dec 24, do.
Henry Payne, capt of the forecastle, Dec 24, do.
Theodore Abo_, 2nd cl fireman, Dec 24, do.
Jas D Ennes, 1st cl boy, Dec 24, do.
Patrick Sullivan, landsman, Dec 10, vessel U S S *Aries.*
Jas Hogan, ord seaman, Feb 4, U S steamer *Albatross.*
Leonard Edwards, 2nd cl boy, Jan 1, U S steamer *Kensington.*
Thos Edwards, landsman, Jan 29, Nav Hosp, N Y.

John Thompson, blank, Feb 5, do.
Geo Bing, seaman, Oct 13, 1864, vessel U S S *O H Lee*.
Wm Sewell, landsman, Jan 24, U S steamer *Matthew Vasaar*.
Jas M Gillis, capt, Feb 9, Nav Observatory.
Marion Boughmer, ord seaman, Jan 26, U S steamer *Kickapoo*.
Herman, Dexter, ord seaman, Jan 28, U S steamer *Metacomet*.
Walter C R Davis, seaman, Feb 8, Norfolk, Va.
A Dean Tubbs, actg ast surg, Jan 6, Cape Haytien, Hayti.
Wm Johnson, 1st, seaman, Jan 27, U S steamer *Suwanee*.

Hdqrtrs Army of the Potomac, Feb 10. Executed today in this army for desertion: Jas L Hicks, 67 Pa vols, 3rd div of 6th corps, & Saml Clement, 32nd Maine vols. The latter was convicted of cowardice, in addition to desertion. Hugh F Riley, 11 Mass vols, was also to have been shot today for desertion, but the sentence has been suspended. Dismissed from the svc for various offences: Ast Surg Rudolph Greiss, 15 N Y hvy artl; Lt Wm F Reisinger, 200 Pa vols; Capt J M Mansfield, 186 N Y vols.

Adms sale of Law, History, Poetry, books of the late Horace Edelin. -Jas L Barbour, adm -Jas C McGuire & Co, auctioneers.

Died: on Feb 12, Ellen G, w/o John Robt Ashey, in her 35th yr. Funeral from Trinity Chr, 3rd & C sts, Tue.

Died: on Feb 12, Anna C Lepreux, w/o A Lepreux. Funeral from the residence of her hsbnd, Pa av & 12th st, Tue.

The funeral of Capt J M Gilliss took place from his late residence on Sat. Remains were deposited in a vault at Oak Hill Cemetery.

TUE FEB 14, 1865
Rl estate for sale: hses & lots. Wm E Spalding, rm #4, Intelligencer bldg, Wash.

Rl estate brokers; J F Wollard & E E Gilbert, 371 D st, Wash, D C.

Deaths of sldrs reported to Capt Moore, A Q M, U S Army: Feb 12-Jas Gillion or Gillinn, Co F, 1st U S Sharpshooters; Geo Huff, do, 180 Ohio; Jas P Hughes, Co E, 111 Ohio; Edw B Morton, Co F, 91 N Y; Matthew Skaggs, Co K, 26 Ky; John Weber, Co E, 7 N Y. Feb 13- Chas Hall, Co H, 1 N H hvy artl; Gabriel Clark, qrtrmstr's div; Athington Selby, Co E, act hosp steward; Wm M Monroe, 1st regt, 1st army corps.

Paintings & engravings; J Markriter, 486 7th st, Wash.

Senate: 1-Ptn of Mrs Mary Howard Schoolcraft, wid/o the late Indian historian, Henry D Schoolcraft, asking payment to her of the salary due him from the Gov't at the time of his death: referred to the Cmte on Claims. 2-Ptn of Andrew J Wilcox, of Balt, praying that steps be taken for the closing of the war: referred to the Military Cmte.

The Baron de Bazancourt, the official war writer & historiographer of the French Gov't, has just died suddenly. You will also see extended notices of the deaths of Proudhon, the distinguished thinker & writer, & of the famous Col Charras. -Paris Cor N Y Times

Mr Robt Lincoln, s/o the Pres, was yesterday nominated to the Senate to be an Ast Adj Gen of vols, with the rank of Capt. He is to serve upon the staff of Lt Gen Grant.

City News: 1-Common Cncl: John W Simms elected to fill the vacancy occasioned by the death of the late Jas Skirving. In the absence of the Sec, Mr W H Pope was app'td Sec pro tem. 2-Ptn of John W Clark, for the remission of a fine: referred.

Draft Assoc meeting yesterday: Mr Geo Hill, jr presiding; Mr Edw Shoemaker, actg sec. Among those present: Mr J M Stake, Mr J C Parker, & Mr John A Ross.

WED FEB 15, 1865
Rl estate in Louisiana:-the property belonging to the estate of the late Dr J P C Wedersandt, the *Harlaem Plantation*, 35 miles below the city, comprising 1,240 arpents of land, with dwlg hse; highest bid of $58,000 was rejected, not being the required amoun't.

Sale of country seat near Laurel, Howard Co, Md; belonging to the heirs of Rev Richd Waters; 87 acs with brick dwlg hse; adjoins the lands of Wm T Steiger, Geo Wheeler, & John Holland. -M Bannon, trustee, 32 St Paul st, Balt, Md.

Andrew J Donelson, adopted s/o Andrew Jackson, prominent ctzn of Tenn, took the amnesty oath & is now able to go where he pleases in that State.

Jos Lawless was shot on 14th st yesterday by Tascar Harris, a colored man, without provocation. Lawless, whose residence in on D st, between 13 & 13½ sts, is expected to recover. Harris is lodged in the station hse.

The funeral of Thos Holliday Hicks, ex-Gov & Senator from Md, will take place from his late residence-Metropolitan Htl, Wash, today. He died Feb 13, 1865, age 67 yrs. Remains will be deposited in the vault of the Congressional Cemetery, whence they be be taken to Dorchester Co, Md, for interment as soon as navigation opens. Gov't Hicks had recently sold his farm to a northern gentleman, & had signified his intention of retiring from the Senate. Feb 16-Among the mourners: T Pratt Hicks, s/o the dec'd; Mrs Woodside, step-dght of the dec'd, with her hsbnd, Bond Chaplin, private sec of the dec'd.

Deaths of sldrs reported to Capt Moore, A Q M, U S Army: Jonathan McClain, Co K, 180 Ohio; Gen W Glass, Co I, do; Theodore Chrisam, Co C, 24 Vet Res Corps; Geo Hamson, battery A, 4th U S A; Emile Fanbert, Co C, 29 Mass; Thos J Howard, Co D, 17 Vt.

Last night Michael Flamel, sldr, was run over by a car of the City Passenger railway. His wounds were dressed at Clark's drug store.

THU FEB 16, 1865
Gen Pegram, rebel ofcr who was killed at the battle of Hatcher's Run, on Feb 6, was the same, who with 1,400 men, fell into the hands of Gen McClellan, at the battle of Rich Mountain, Va, very early in the war, & was paroled. He is a native of Richmond, a grad of West Point. He was mrd in Richmond the week before his death.

Mrd: on Feb 2, by Rev Dr Finkel, R E Hymann & Mgt Ann Wolf, d/o Sophia & W Wolf, of Alexandria, Va.

Mrd: on Feb 14, at the Fourth Presby Chr, 9th st, by Rev John C Smith, the Rev Geo H Smyth, pastor of the Sixth Presby Chr of Wash City, to Josepha, y/d/o Josiah Goodrich, of Wash, D C.

Deaths of sldrs reported to Capt Moore, A Q M, U S Army:

A J Masks, Co I, 12 V R C
Geo W Baily, Co D, 174, Ohio
Jas Mitz, Co E, 931 N Y
Cpl Abraham Tope, Co B, 8 Minn
Robt C List, Co K, 183 Ohio
Geo Nickols, sgt maj, 5 U S Cavalry
John Summers, 21 U S L A

Michael Melson, Co G, 180 Ohio
Zenas Colby, Co H, 33 Mich
Wm M Legg, Co B, 180 Ohio
E J Powell, Co K, 180 Ohio
Chas Roe, musician, Co H, 103 Ohio
Wm Six, Co D, 174 Ohio

Trustee's sale of country seat near Annapolis junction; the farm & improvements belonging to the heirs of the late John Ward; 100 acs; adjs the lands of Francis Dandletts, M Fitzsimmons, & John C Thompson. -M Bannon, 32 St Paul st, Balt, Md.

W W Corcoran has donated nearly 2 acs of land in Wash City as a site for a new bldg to the Wash City Protestant Orphan Asylum.

Patrolman Geo Rennaker, of the 4th ward, who was injured by being run over by a street car on Tue, had to have his leg amputated above the knee. Wash, D C. [Geo R Rennaker died at his residence on 10th st, near M st, on Feb 16. Remains will be interred at Prospect Hill Cemetery.]

FRI FEB 17, 1865
Furnished hse for rent in Gtwn, the residence of the late David English. -Walter S Cox, 40 La av or 101 Gay st, Gtwn, D C.

Died: on Feb 16, Geo W Hitz, aged 4 years & 2 mos, only surviving s/o Geo W & Lucy Hitz. Funeral from the residence of his grandmother, Mrs Eliz Weitzel, 417 3rd st, Sat.

Died: in Oregon City, on Jan 2, 1865, Wm C Dement, in the 42nd yr of his age, native of PG Co, Md, & for many years a resident of Wash, D C. He was among the first settlers of Oregon.

John F Lusby was arrested yesterday for the outrage on little Octavie Rousseau, on Nov 24. Lusby enlisted in the 2nd Dist regt & is held to bail for hearing.

Actg Vol Lt B W Loring has been ordered to the Wash Navy Yard, to take charge of the recruiting ofc at the station.

Deaths of sldrs reported to Capt Moore, A Q M, U S Army:

Alexander Parmly, Co H, 16 Ky
Theodore M Huntingdon, Co H, 23 Mich
Edw Crawford, Co B, 174 Ohio

Aaron Overhold, Co I, 183 Ohio
Jas M Canal, teamster, under Super Riley

SAT FEB 18, 1865
Orphans Crt of Wash Co, D C.. Case of John Hitz, exc of John Hitz, dec'd; settlement on Mar 14. -Z C Robbins, rg o/wills

Information wanted of Mrs Maggie Gein. Last heard from she was boarding in Gtwn & very ill. Please address, Mrs C Gault, 335 W Lombard st, Balt, Md.

Died: suddenly, at the hse of a neighbor, on his way home, on Feb 16, Prof A G Pendleton, U S Navy, in his 46th yr. Funeral from the New Jerusalem Temple, N Capt st, on Sat.

Died: on Feb 17, Bernard Giveny, a native of County Cavan, Ire, but a resident of Wash City for the last 40 yrs, aged 76 yrs. Funeral from his late residence 363 5th st, on Sun.

Died: on Feb 17, Mr Thos H Maddox. Funeral from the residence of Mrs B P Fletcher, 446 E st, today.

Died: on Feb 17, at his residence, 505 E st, Geo T Smith, in his 33rd yr. Remains will be taken to Wilmington, Del, by train.

Capt Beall, the rebel spy, now at Ft Lafayette under sentence of death, owned a large plantation in Jefferson Co, Va. His fortune was about $1,500,000 & he is heir apparent of Lord Egelby, of England. He is only 32 years of age.

Arrest of burglars: Wm H Elrod, Jos Light, Chas Smith, Martin Walsh, Arinda Remington, & Sarah Price, alias Weaver, on charge of being concerned in the robbery of the jewelry store of Jacob Baum, 7th & G sts, Wash, a few nights since.

MON FEB 20, 1865
Deaths in the Navy for the week ending Feb 18, 1865:
F S Hayford, ord seaman, Jan 15, vessel U S S *Colorado.*
Geo H Winsor, landsman, do, do
Thos Cosgrove, ship's cpl, Jan 15, vessel U S S *Vanderbilt.*
Jas Green, boatswains's mate, do, do.
Wm Paul, marine, Jan 16, do.
Henry Brown, pensioner, Feb 11, Nav Asylum.
Wm Seaman, seaman, Jan 16, vessel U S S *Santiago de Cuba,* at sea.
Edw F Davis, landsman, Jan 21, Nav Hosp, Norfolk.
Jas Lynch, seaman, Jan 31, Nav Hosp, Memphis.
John Steiner, 1st cl boy, Feb 3, do.
Benj Roberts, landsman, Feb 5, do.
Everett Caswell, 1st cl fireman, Feb 6, Nav Hosp, Portsmouth, Va.
Jas McDonald, landsman, Feb 8, do.
John W Baker, colored, landsman, Feb 11, do.
Jas McCormick, seaman, Dec 24, vessel U S S *Ticonderoga.*
Ludwig E Wiltz, seaman, Dec 24, do.
John Hill, seaman, Dec 24, do.
Chas G Siles, ord seaman, do, do.
Jas T Ward, landsman, do, do.
Jas McMillen, landsman, do, do.
Jas T Duffy, landsman, do, do.
Wm Sinton, 2nd cl boy, Dec 21, do.
Geo L Smith, colored, landsman, Jan 28, U S gunboat *Kineo.*
John S Griscom, actg ensign, Dec 25, vessel U S S *Mackinaw.*
Martin Berne, landsman, Jan 15, vessel U S S *Wabash.*
Wm C Holt, landsman, do, do.
Alonzo Kitts, landsman, do, do.

Wm Daley, marine, Jan 17, do.
Wm Faston, ord seaman, Jan 18, do.
John H Fields, mstr-at-arms, Jan 31, vessel U S S *Aries*.
Chas Lewis, qrtrmstr, Jan 27, vessel U S S *Shockokon*.
Peter Christian, seaman, Feb 2, Nav Hosp, N Y.
Clement Antone, seaman, Feb 8, Nav Hosp, Chelsea, Mass.
Wm Kirby, marine, Feb 8, do.
Wm W Cox, cpl of marines, Feb 13, Nav Asylum.
Mathias Hansen, marine, Feb 3, Nav Hosp, N Y.
Richd Ellis, colored, ord seaman, Feb 2, vessel U S S *Britannia*.
Jas Rontongo, ord seaman, Jan 24, Nav Hosp, Pensacola.
Peter S Harris, ord seaman, Jan 30, Nav Hosp, New Orleans.
Wm Ellis, landsman, Jan 2, vessel U S S *Cyane*.
Geo Harland, ord seaman, Jan 26, vessel U S S *Lancaster*.
Wilbur F Neil, landsman, Feb 12, vessel U S S *Ronoke*.
Johnny Boy, seaman, Jan 26, vessel U S S *Isonomial*.
Saml Mackin, ord seaman, Jan 10, vessel U S S *South Carolina*.
Frank Johnson, boy, Feb 9, Nav Hosp, N Y.
Burrill Jarvis, landsman, Feb 1, vessel U S S *Cimerone*.
Thos Stevens, actg ensign, Jan 19, Nav Hosp, St Helena Island, S C.
Wm B Wilson, marine, Dec 24, do.
Philip Knepp, ord sgt of marines, Nov 30, vessel U S S *Mingoe*.
Saml S Clark, marine, Oct 21, vessel U S S *Jamestown*, Japan.
Wm Brown, seaman, Sep 22, vessel U S S *Relief*.
A S W Shelcutt, seaman, Jan 13, Tunica Bend, Miss.
Mortimer Tower, landsman, Dec 10, Genr'l Hosp, Hilton Head, S C.
Warren Boynton, ord seaman, Dec 9, vessel U S S *Saratoga*.
Asa Simmons, prisoner of war, Jan 11, vessel U S S *South Carolina*.
Chas Wilson, seaman, Jan 16, vessel U S S *Geranium*.

TUE FEB 21, 1865
Crct Crt-D C. 1-Stewart Gwynne vs Lafayette C Baker; civil action for damages sufferd by
the plntf for his imprisonment, alleged to be contrary to law, by the dfndnt. 2-Salmon B
Colby, caveator, vs Henry Xelowski, alleged legatee. Regarding the will of Jousuff Bey, a
Turk, who was brought to Wash in 1852 or 1853 by J Ross Browne. Bey died in Aug 1854,
leaving no kindred in this country, but some $19,000 in gold & other interests. Bey left
relatives in Bessarabia, of Turkey in Europe.
3-Jas Towles vs Edw Hall: action to recover between one & two thousand dollars, for the
svcs of the plntf's son, a clerk of the dfndnt. Dfndnt is a well known grocer, & Jas Towle,
jr, the s/o the plntf, his clerk, is alleged to have been, in some degree, delinquent &
inefficient in his duties; the former withheld an increase of wages, but still retained the boy.
Crt adjourned.

Funeral svcs of the late Brig Gen Winder took place on Feb 9, at Columbia S C. Body was
escorted to Trinity Chr, with burial in the cemetery.

The Hon Thos Bennett, ex-Gov of S C, died on Jan 30, at Anderson Crt Hse.

Deaths of sldrs reported to Capt Moore, A Q M, U S Army:
Feb 17-
Lewis Manger, Co K, 41st N Y   Wm W Chesly, Co F, 120th N Y
Chas A Rice, Co C, 9th V R C

Feb 18-
Jas Hayes, 27, 2nd btln, V R C
Thos McGee, sgt, Co M, 25th N Y cavalry
Jediddiah Blake, Co M, 13th Mich btry
Jos Carson, Co K, 50th Ohio
Zenas A Buttefield, Co G, 32nd Mass
Wm J Knight, Co D, 7th N J
Jas C Bull, Co F, 109th N Y
Feb 19-
John J Orr, Co C, 77th Ohio
Simon S Mead, Co I, 140th Ind
Feb 20-
Henry Kupe, Co A, 129th Ind
Flavius J Garrigus, Co K, 140th Ind
Jerrey Rooney, Co F, 3rd U S infty

David Fagin, Co G, 50th Ohio
John Johnson, Co H, 112th Ill
John Hartman, Co B, 134th Ohio
Wm L Siner, Co E, 124th Ind
Paul Anster, 47, 2nd btln V R C
Hiram Williams, 47, unassigned V R C
Davis Headley, 16th Ind btry

Wm H Schalossee, Co F, 140th Ind

J G Robinson, Co C, 46th N J
Savenu F Jones, Co D, 12th Ind

Richmond Whig, Feb 15. Gen W P Wofford is on his way to North Georgia, with orders from the War Dept to take command of that dept.

Richmond Sentinel: Feb 16. 1-Maj Venable, of Gen Wade Hampton's staff, has arrived in Va, having made his escape by leaping from the cars near Phil. 2-Lt J Taylor Wood, Confederate States Navy, promoted to the rank of Capt for meritorious svc. 3-Capt Raphael Semmes, Confederate States Navy, promoted to Admiral for meritorious svc.

WED FEB 22, 1865
For sale in A A Co, Md, rl estate of which Dr Wm Brogden died seized, *Roedown*, 598½ acs; 112 acs subject to the dower of Mrs Mary H Brogden; adjoins the lands of D McBrogden, Dr Saml Cheston, A R Clayton, Saml Jones, & Dr Jos J Duvall. -Richd J Gittings, Balt, Md - Alex'r B Hagner, trustee

Orphans Crt of Wash Co, D C. Prsnl estate of Bernard Giveny, late of Wash City, dec'd. - Bernard Hayes, exc

Died: on Feb 21, John Morgan, eldest s/o Mgt V & John T Ashford, in his 9th yr. Funeral from their residence tomorrow.

Mr Wm E Riggs, an employee in the engineer & machine dept, at the Navy Yard, Wash, was severely injured when his clothing was caught by a belt or pulley. His right leg had to be amputated & there were other injuries. He cannot possibly recover.

THU FEB 23, 1865
Criml Crt-D C; Grand Jurors:

John R Morgan	Alex'r McCormick	Jas Y Davis
P G Barry	Walter Godey	Wm Venable
A G Pumphrey	Wm P Hicks	Jas Chapman
Simon Flinn	Walter H Mazlow	Wm B Brashear
Geo Seuferle	Jas F Essex	W H Johnson
Jacob Jouvenal	Robt Campbell	J C Cross
John Patch	Henry Barron	C W Cunningham
Daniel Smith	Wm Lord	

Petit Jurors:

J W Reynolds	C C P Bond	E P Offutt

G W Stroud
Edgar H Bates
Geo Gray
Nathl Wells
Geo H Lane
Robt Ball
W H Wheatley
Geo Cassiday

John H Bird
Geo Esslerr
H C Baldwin
W E Nott
Daniel Conner
John T Scroggon
S C Wroe
T H Walker

Geo Bushnell
Daniel Myers
W V Newkirk
J Cudlip
Alfred Berdine
E Castell
Richard L Meredith

Deaths of sldrs reported to Capt Moore, A Q M, U S Army, Wash:
Feb 21-
Cineas Allen, Co D, 178th Ohio
J R Nichols, Co I, Capt, 14th Conn
Peter McCutchan, Co H, 174th Ohio
Elijah Homer, Co E, 180th Ohio
Philip Banval, Co B, 31st N J
Feb 22-
Andrew J Smith, 1st N J Ind btry
Thos J William, Co I, 180th Ohio

John Shaffer, Co B, 148th Pa
John Kane, Co G, 1st N H hvy artl
David Rudisiel, Co I, 9th V R C
Gilton Milton, teamster, Mt Pleasant Chr parish

Thaddeus Powers, Co I, 1st N H hvy artl

Died: on Feb 21, Miss Priscilla Hamilton, aged about 78 yrs, a native of Chas Co, Md, but for many years a resident of Wash City. Funeral from the residence of Mr John Sessford, 374 6th st, today.

Died: on Feb 15, at the residence of her son-in-law, Rev J S Bacon, in Warrenenton, Va, Mrs Hannah Porter, relict of the late Capt Lemuel Porter, of Boston, aged 85 yrs.

Obit-Died, on Feb 19, of apoplexy, at Camp Remount, Pleasant Valley, Md, Sgt Edgar Pitkin, 5th U S Cavalry.

For sale or lease-Metropolitan lumber, planing & sawing mill; now operated by Mr S L Partridge, Canal & 13½ sts. -Leonidas Coyle, surviving partner.

Capt C C Edelen, alias Lum Cooper, was yesterday released from the Old Capitol, on his parole to go north, & not come south of the Susquehannah river during the rebellion. He was furnished transportation to N Y.

Sailmaker Geo W Frankland has been detached from the yard, & ordered to the practice-ship Sabine, at Norfolk, Va. He has been detached from the steam frig Wabash, late flagship of the S C Blockading squad, & ordered to this yard.

Evacuation of Charleston: from the Correspondent of the N Y Herald: first sign was witnessed before daybreak this morning-18th. City & fortifications were possessed by a portion of Gen Schemmelpfennig's command from Jas & Morris Islands. Lt Col A G Bennett, 21st U S colored troops, & Col Ames, 3rd R I Artl, are said to have been the first in the city. Maj Gen Gillmore left Hilton Head, S C, in his flagboat W W Colt, for Bull's Bay. Capt H M Bragg, of his staff, in a small boat, visited Ft Sumter & placed the national colors on the parapet. Sherman, with his itinerant army, has already visited Branchville, Orangeburg, & Columbia & Lexington, & continues to prosecute vigorously his journey. He is determined to visit all the coast cities in his tour to Richmond.

Hoisting the flag on Fort Sumter: the 18th, a detachment was sent to take possession of Fort Sumter, & raise the flag which Gen Anderson hauled down nearly 4 years ago. The flagstaff of the fort had long since been shot away, & it was necessary to improvise one with the oar of a boat.

North Atlantic Squad, U S Flagship *Malvern*. Cape Fear River, Feb 19, 1865. I have the honor to report the surrender, or evacuation, of Ft Anderson. Gen Schofield advanced from Smithville with 8,000 men on the 17th. I attacked the works by water, placing the monitor *Montauk* close to the works. On the 18th, moved up closer with the monitor *Cading*, followed by the *Mackinaw, Huron*, & 12 others boats, & kept up heavy fire thru the day. In the meantime Gen Schofield was working round to get in the rear of the rebels & cut them off. The rebels did not wait, but left in the night. We lost but 3 killed & 4 wounded. –David D Porter, Rear Admiral [To Hon Gideon Welles, Sec of the Navy, Wash, D C.]

Thompson's Restaurant, 360 C st, Wash, D C. -R R Thompson, late of the Metropolitan Htl. [Local ad]

Last night Chas Knap entertained a distinguished & brillant party at his residence, on H st, in a style of magnificence rarely, if ever, seen in this city.

U S Sup Crt-Chas G Miller, plntf in error, vs Jameson C Sherry, dfndnt in error. Crct Crt of U S for Northern Dist of Ill to recover possession of lots in Ottawa city, La Salle Co, Ill. Case of W H & W Lyon against C G Miller, plntf, & Eliza Miller his wife, Wm C Richardson, & Mary Ann Williams his wife. In Apr, 1859, Miller conveyed to R S Williams, the lots in question. On Mar 15, 1850, the plntf conveyed the land to Wm H Bushnell.

FRI FEB 24, 1865
Obit-from N Y paper. Death of Gen John H Winder, native of Balt; born in Somerset Co, Md; age about 65 yrs. He was an 1820 grad of West Point.

A brilliant soiree was given at the spacious mansion of Chas Knapp on Feb 22. The cost will be $100,000. Wash, D C. [2 hses have been connected into one by tearing down walls.] Orchestra was under the leadership of Louis Weber. The street in front has been floored & carpeted.

Wm Johnson, age about 35 yrs, was found dead on First st, Wash, last night. He boarded at the hse of Peter Coyle, 2nd st, between D & Va av. Saml McManus had been with him all evening, & they had been drinking together.

From Ky: Louisville, Feb 23. Rumored invasion. The Journals special says our troops near Midway captured Col R J Breckinridge yesterday. It is reported that the rebel Col Howard Smith entered Mt Sterling under a flag of truce, & was held a prisoner by our forces there. It is believed that a rebel force may be entering Ky from that direction.

The Nashville Times of the 18th inst states that Mr A O P Nicholson, ex-editor & ex-senator, who has been confined in the military prison for some time, was released yesterday, under bonds to the amount of $10,000, to appear at the next term of the Federal Crt in this place, to answer the charge of conspiracy against the U S Gov't. Mr Nicholson refused the amnesty offered by the Pres.

Gen Steadman, at Chattanooga, has 5 rebel ctzns in custody, whom he holds as hostages, & intends to execute in retaliation for the Union non-combants murdered by Gatewood's guerillas.

Col J H Alexander, 4th U S, is now at Willard's, recovering from a severe wound he received in Mississippi with his regt.

SAT FEB 25, 1865

Chancery sale, wherein Henry Crow, Thos Crow, & Sarah Harris, cmplnts, & Jas Charles, & Wm Matthews, & Edw Hunt & Mary Ann his wife, dfndnts. Sale of lot 162 in Beatty & Hawkins Addition to Gtwn, D C, with improvements, late the estate of Jas Reman, dec'd. - M Thompson, trustee -Thos Dowling, auct

The funeral of Mr Wm E Biggs, the workman killed in the machine shop on Tue, took place on Thu, from his late residence on 11th st, to the Congressional Cemetery.

Foundry Church fair to aid in finishing the church edifice. One room is to be finished & furnished under the direction & exclusive expense of David A Gardner, who for 23 years has had charge of the juvenile class in the Sabbath school, of which he has been a mbr 36 yrs. Munificent contributions have come from Edw Owen, Wm J Sibly, B F Guy, etc. Foundry Chr was est'd in 1814, thru the labors of Rev Henry Foxhall, for many yrs, was one of the very best, & successful business men of Gtwn. He was born in 1760, near Brimingham, England; engaged extensively in the foundry business, & there his dght, Mrs *McHenry, who for many years adorned the social life of Gtwn, was born. The Irish population becoming jealous of him as an Englishman & he came to the neighborhood of Phil. When the Capital was located here he came to Gtwn, purchased a site, erected a foundry, & was for many years the contractor who supplied the Gov't all its cannon. After amassing a large fortune, he sold his foundry to the father of the rebel Senator Mason, who then moved from Analostan Island into Gtwn. Mr Foxhall was a local preacher of the Meth Episc Chr: aided in rebuilding the Meth Chapel next to the upper bridge in 1806, now used as a pblc school-hse, the Corp of Gtwn purchasing it. The old chapel was known as Foxhall's Chr. about 1814, Mr Foxhall purchased a lot on the corner of 14th & G sts West end of Wash, erected a chr edifice on it & presented the whole to the society in Gtwn, or rather conveyed the property in trust to mbrs of that church residing in this city. The Meth people of that time West of the Capitol went to Gtwn, & those east of the Capitol went to the Navy Yard to worship. Soon after bldg the church Mr Foxhall went to England, & while there the society built a parsonage on the lot adjoining the church, a 2 story frame hse. This gave Mr Foxhall some offence, as he intended to erect a fine hse to suit himself & at his own expense. The question is often asked why this is called the Foundry Chr. The fact that John Wesley & his associates, when driven from the English church, first occupied an old foundry in London as a place of worship, combined with the other fact that Mr Foxhall was the owner of a foundry doubtless suggest the name. The bldg continued to be used without much being expended upon it for some 20 yrs. About 1835 the society gave it special repairing. In 1849 it was again repaired & thoroughly remodeled. Up to this period the colored people had occupied the galleries exclusively. They became so numerous, that they built a chapel on 11th st, known as Asbury Chr. Foundry Chr was torn away last May to make place for the present structure. The old parsonage gave place in 1852 to the present handsome hse, under the pastorate of Rev Jesse T Peck, D D-an able manager of Calif. The first pastor of the Foundry Chr was Rev Thos Burch, of Irish birth; succeeded by Dr John Emery; then the good Fr Wm Ryland. The present pastor is Rev W M D Ryan, D C. Mr Foxhall, while a second time revisiting his native land, died in 1823, & is buried in his native village, near Birmingham. His only son, totally blind, preceded the father to the tomb. The remains of the dght, Mrs *McKenny, slumbers in Oak Hill Cemetery. Mr Saml McKenny, her hsbnd, & several chldrn, still survive in Gtwn. Mr Foxhall's first wife died before his first visit to England, & on his return he brought with him a second wife, who has been dead some yrs. The only surviving member of the church as originally formed being Jacob Hines, a venerable & good man, now 85 years of age-honored by all who know him. He is a mbr of a Md family of 10 sons, whose Roman-hearted father went to the enlisting depot in 1812 with 8 of the 10 sons, who bade them go & stand for their country. When this war opened, 3 of the sons still survived-Matthew, [since dec'd,] Christian & David, all well known in this city. Jacob Hines was the first name on the roll of the Foundry Chr, being appt'd leader of a class of 18 ladies, & thus commenced the church. At the time there were but 2 churches in the city, the St Patrick's & a small Presby chr. [*Dght's mrd name: first referred to as McHenry, then as McKenny.] [J M D note: just spoke with the librarian at the Gtwn Regional Library, Gtwn, D C-she said the surname is McKenny-3/18/2000.] List of the fair attendants:

Mrs Gardner	Miss Kate Waters	Miss Bates
Mrs Stinemetz	Mrs E H King	The Misses Helmick
Mrs Cluserett	Mrs Tabler	Miss Harlan
Miss Bell Shackelford	Mrs R N Bates	Miss France
Miss Annie Hirst	Mrs Kate Smith	Miss Emma Gibbs
Miss Annis Hilton	Miss Yager	Miss Olivia Cross
Miss Terrie Cammack	The Misses Fairbanks	

Michl Sweeney, a restaurant keeper, was accidentally shot on Thu by a pistol in the hands of an intoxicated man named Watson. The wound is not serious. Watson was arrested & fined $20 for carrying the weapon.

F N Blake, of the Navy Dept, appt'd by the Pres, confirmed by the Senate, U S cnsl at Erie, Upper Canada.

The Pres has recognized the appointment of a British cnsl at Buffalo, on the American side, in the person of Henry Wm Hemans, the s/o the poetess. These are new consulates, established by the 2 Govts.

Miss Harriet Lane, so well known as the presiding lady of the Exec mansion during the Admin of Mr Buchanan, is in Wash City as the guest of Madame Berghman, the w/o the Sec of Leg from Belgium.

MON FEB 27, 1865
Mrshl's sale of all right, title, claim, etc of W W Seaton in lot 11 in sq 431, in favor of Jas Adams against W W Seaton, surviving partner of Gales & Seaton. -Ward H Lamon, U S Mrshl D C

Orphans Crt of Wash Co, D C. Prsnl estate of Geo T Smith, late of Wash City, dec'd. -J C Baugner

Persons wishing substitutes can be accommodated by calling at A Johnson's, 319 E st, Wash, D C. At the lowest rates. Runners will be paid the highest price for substitutes.

Local item-Jas Smith, aged 35 yrs, was fatally stabbed by Patrick Leary last evening at 21st & K sts. Leary resides with his wife in the neighborhood & it is thought that he was in a fit of jealousy. Both were thought to be sldrs belonging to Hancock's corps.

Mrd: on Feb 23, by Rev Fr McCarty, Columbus O Alexander to Miss Sarah C Keleher, d/o Jas T Keleher, all of Wash, D C.

Died: in Wash City, on Feb 25, Clemtina A, w/o Hon Edgar K Whitake, formerly of Needham, Mass, aged 38 yrs.

Died: in N Y, on Feb 17, Geo O Marsh, aged 32 yrs, s/o Hon Geo P Marsh, Minister of the U S to Italy.

Died: at his residence in this county, Feb 5th, Dennis Duvall, jr, in his 30th yr. He was a dutiful son & bro. At time of his death he was the mainstay of his aged father & sisters. PG Co, Md, Feb 24, 1865

Obit-Haym M Salomon, ctzn of N Y C, died in that city on Feb 15, in his 80th yr. For the past forty years he had been engaged in pressing Congress for his claim for indemnification for the pecuniary losses of his patriotic father during the Rev war.

TUE FEB 28, 1865
Opening of Gonzaga Fair hall: F st: last night. Performance of Mrs Cecilia Young Kretschman was greeted with applause. The piano, one of Chickering & Son's, was furnished by John F Ellis, 306 Pa ave. The bldg was erected for the benefit of St Aloysius Chr & the extensive parochial schools connected therewith. For the past 4 years Fr Wiget has been furnishing instruction, gratuitously, to some 700 chldrn.

Robt Lyon, s/o Mr Lyon of G st mess-hse, First Ward, was killed last evening by the discharge of a musket in the hands of one of the carpenters, Holtzman. Employees had been drilling & the muskets were supposed to be all unloaded.

Richmond Sentinel, Feb 23: Regarding-John Yates Beall; shows the spirit of the young Confederate sldr who lies under sentence of death in a Northern prison. Ltr follows from Johny Beall, dt'd Ft Lafayette, Feb 14, 1865-Dear Will: Ere this reaches you, you will, most probable, have heard of my death thru the newspapers, that I was tried by a military commission & hung by the enemy; & hung, is assert, unjustly, etc. Remember me kindly to my friends. God love my mother; the girls, too.
-John Y Beall

Died: on Feb 26, Mrs Cath Bates, widow of the late Thos Bates, aged 77 yrs. Funeral from her late residence *Pomona*, near Ft Totten, on Mar 2.

Died: on Feb 27, of gastric fever, Emeline Delia, y/d/o W H & Eugenie C Fear, aged 3 years 7 months & 9 days. Funeral from 486 G st, Tue.

WED MAR 1, 1865
Orphans Crt of Wash Co, D C. Prsnl estate of Jas M Gillis, late of Wash City, dec'd.
-R S Gilliss, admx

Local: Michl Rice, a rebel deserter, was arrested yesterday by Ofcr Taylor, on charge of stealing a valise from Capt C C Meechem. Rice carried the valise to his room in the boarding hse of Mrs Kelley, near Balt depot, by whom he was suspected of having stolen it. She notified the ofcr, who arrested Rice, whilst in the act of donning the Capt's military uniform, taken from the valise.

Hospital steamer *State of Maine*, arrived in Wash City with sick & wounded sldrs from City Point. Hersey Bogart, Co C, 210th P V, died when the boat was near Wash.

<u>Nat'l Inauguaration Ball: Genr'l Supervisory Cmte:</u>

Hon B B French, Chrmn	Maj Thos H Gardner	Henry D Cooke,Treas
Hon Lewis Clephans	T B Brown	W R Irwin, Sec
Hon D P Holloway	J R Elvans	

<u>Cmte on Invitations:</u>

Hon B B French	Hon J G Nicolay	Maj Thos H Gardner
Hon J W Forney	Hon Lewis Clephans	Hon D P Holloway
Hon Edw McPherson	J R Elvans	

For Balt: P S Chappell, Col Thos Sewell, jr
For Phil: Geo Trott, Adolph Borie
For N Y: Chas Stetson, Hon Abram Wakeman
For Boston: John T Heard, Geo Keyes

<u>Cmte on Printing:</u>

John D Defrees	D C Forney	W J Murtagh

<u>Cmte on Decorations</u>

Job W Angus	Ira Goodenow	A Cluss
Saml P Bell	D W Bliss	W Beron
John S Hayes	John Alexander	Capt D G Thomas
Z D Gilman	M T Parke	

<u>Cmte of Floor Mgrs & on Music:</u>

Jas Galway, Chrmn	Geo N Morris	A T Lilsie
Dr D W Bliss, alt Chrmn	N G Sawyer	David Stewart
Henry Clay Swain	Niel Dennison	A Caldwell
C H Heustis	Geo H Plant, jr	Lewis Clements
Nathan H Barrett	C C Graham	Z D Gilman
B B French, jr	John T Parsons	Maj W M Reynolds
A L Bayer	Lyman S Sprague	John L Thompson

<u>Cmte on Refreshments:</u>

Geo H Plant	A R Shepherd	T B Brown
W A Newman	Lewis Clephane	Job W Angus

<u>Mgrs</u>

Hon Hannibal Hamlin	Hon Nath B Smithers	Hon W H Wallace
Hon Schuyler Colfax	Hon John A J Creswell	Hon G E Upton
Hon John W Forney	Hon Green Clay Smith	Lt Gen U S Grant
Hon Edw McPherson	Hon E B Washburne	Maj Gen W T Sherman
Hon John Sherman	Hon John A Kasson	Maj Gen W S Hancock
Hon Jas Dixon	Hon Amasa Cobb	Maj Gen C C Augur
Hon John Conness	Hon John R McBride	Maj Gen A Doubleday
Hon Henry Wilson	Hon A Carter Wilder	Brig Gen J B Fry
Hon Z Chandler	Hon Killiam V Whaley	Brig Gen Jos Holt
Hon M S Wilkinson	Hon H G Worthington	Brig Gen B W Brice
Hon B Gratz Brown	Hon Francisco Perea	Brig Gen E D Townsend
Hon Edwin D Morgan	Hon John F Kinney	Col J A Ekins
Hon Wm Sprague	Hon Geo E Cole	Col J A Hardee
Hon Solomon Foot	Hon Saml G Daily	Maj J B Benton
Hon E H Rollins	Hon H P Bennett	Maj Saml Brick
Hon John F Starr	Hon J B S Todd	Maj E E Paulding
Hon Wm D Kelley	Hon Chas D Preston	Maj John Hay

Vice Admr D G Farragut
Rear Admr D D Porter
Rear Admr Jos Smith
Com Henry A Wise
Com J S Montgomery
Com F B Isherwood
Capt G V Fox
Capt Overton Carr
Lt Com W N Jeffers
Lt T P Ives
Col Jacob Zeilin
Maj Wm B Slack
Hon J M Edmunds
Hon J H Barrett
Hon W P Dole
Hon Jos J Lewis
Hon R W Taylor
Hon J M Brodhead
Hon Thos L Smith
Hon B B French
Hon John Wilson
Hon S J Wilabor
Hon C M Walker
Hon E Sells
Hon F E Spinner
Hon Nathan Sargent
Hon S B Colby
Hon Hugh McCulloch
Hon Edw Jordan
Hon Wm Whiting
D R Goodloe
Geo H Plant
T B Brown
J T Clements, jr
A C Riccards
A G Ball

Wm Dixon
G E Lathrop
S P Morrill
Hon E A Rollins
Col Frank Holbrook
John Prince
J H Brown
F C Cate
Saml G Lane
A P Farden
Capt J Frazier
C S Mattoon
Hallet Kilbourne
M E N Howell
Hon Leonard J Barwell
Geo Cowle
C King
Hon G W Anderson
F N Blake
R Wallach
Henry Addison
Jos F Brown
A Lloyd
Gen Geo C Thomas
Gen R C Weightman
Jas Adams
E C Carrington
John Potts
Jas C Kennedy
Chas H Knap
Sayles J Bowen
J Lorimer Graham
Chas H Nichols
C H Fahnestock
Saml P Brown
H D Cooke

W R Irwin
DeWitt C Clarke
John H Semmes
A R Shepherd
Col J A Magruder
Hudson Taylor
Franklin Philp
Martin Buell
Geo E Baker
W S Huntington
W B Todd
Z C Robbins
R J Meigs, jr
Jos Gerhardt
H Grossmayer
J B Motley
Geo H Shelly
John Van Buskirk
Arnold Petrie
D W Bartlett
Saml Wilkeson
W B Shaw
Wm Swinton
Whitela Reid
Ben Perley Peore
U H Painter
H A Whiteley
Noah Brooks
Sydney Andrews
L A Gobright
C S Noyes
W J Murtagh
Pym'r J Scott
Cummingham

THU MAR 2, 1865

Wm Fitzgerald, 4th N Y heavy artl, fell from his saddle on 15th st, Wash., yesterday evening, & the wheel of his wagon crushed his head, producing almost instant death. He had served his country for 2½ yrs, age about 22 yrs, unmrd. His parents reside some 40 miles above N Y C, on the Harlem railroad.

Deaths of sldr reported to Capt Moore, A Q M, U S Army:
Feb 28-Jas C Hudson, Co D, 1st Army Corps   Saml Coon, Co D, 180th Ohio
Robt Swaig, Co F, 180th Ohio
Mar 1-Thos Irvin, Co A, 183rd Ohio   Eugene Callahan, Co B, 9th V R C
Henry Means, Co I, 10th V R C

Orphans Crt of Wash Co, D C. Case of John R Minor, exc of Jas M Minor, dec'd; settlement on Mar 25. -Z C Robbins, rg o/wills.

Capt Bradford, of the rebel army, s/o Gov Bradford, of Md, was released from the Old Capitol yesterday on parole, & ordered to report to his father.

Died: at N Y C on Feb 27, Anna Maria, wid/o the late Hon Robt Leroy Livingston, of Claverack, Columbia Co, N Y, in her 73rd yr. She was the sister of the late Dudley Digges, of PG Co, Md. She was a native of this part of the country, where her youth & much of her mrd life was spent. Early part of her life was passed at the family estate, *Washburton*, near Ft Wash.

Dover, Del, Mar 1. Gov Cannon, of Dela, died this morning after a short illness.

Soiree of the Young Men's Christian Assoc, on Tue evening at the City Hall. Mrs H C Butts, of Gtwn, sang, with thrilling effect, & took part in a duet with Mr Robinson, of the Navy Dept. Mr Ewer, of the 2nd Auditor's ofc, & formerly of Boston, created quite a furore with his fine tenor voice. Prof Meding, the organist of St John's Chr, presided at the pianoforte. Mr Gillette, a s/o the Rev Dr Gillett, read an essay on Hamlet. Mr Winslow also recited, with fine effect, a beautiful poem.

Miss Houck, residing on Mass ave, near 7th st, was knocked down & run over by a runaway horse & wagon at the Northern mkt yesterday. It is feared she has internal injuries. She was conveyed home by Patrolman Leach.

THU MAR 3, 1865
The property in England known as the Jennings estate, has been claimed by the American heirs, descendants of the bro & sister of the English Jennings, the former of whom settled in Va & the latter in N H. Estimated at several million pounds.

Committee for inaugural ceremonies: La Fayette S Foster, J R Doolittle, J B Henderson.

Died: on Mar 1, at Woodley, Jane, w/o R J Bowen, in her 66th yr. Funeral at the Oak Hill Cemetery, today.

Died: in Phil, on Feb 26, Mrs Susan D, w/o Geo W Camblos, formerly of resident of Wash City.

Orphans Crt of Wash Co, D C. Ptn of Francis Mohun, guardian to Anne Mohun, orphan of Michael P Mohun dec'd, for ratification of sale of rl est. -Z C Robbins, rg o/wills

Wm F Purcell is a Judge of the Orphans Crt.

Govn'r Cannon, of Dela, died at Bridgeville this morning, at 3 o'clock. His noble efforts against secession, which resulted in the salvation of his state, are fresh in the grateful memory of all loyal people.

Rodier's White Hse Restaurant, steamed oyster & billiard saloon, 32 & 33 High st, next to the Canal, Gtwn, D C. [Local Ad]

Second Inauguration of Abraham Lincoln as Pres of the U S. Mrshl's Notice: D C, Wash, Mar 2, 1865. The following named gentlemen having been appt'd by me as assist mrshls to attend on the Pres of the U S in the procession from the Exec Mansion to the Capitol, & the ceremonies, are to meet at my ofc, 410 Fst, tomorrow, at 11 a m. -Ward H Lamon

U S Marshals reported:
John S Keyes, Mass
Wm Millward, PPhil
Robt Murray, N Y
A C Sands, Ohio
R Sherman, R I
Chas Clark, Maine
C C P Baldwin, Vt

Ctzn Aids reported:
F S Cleaveland, Conn
J P Bartholow, Wash
S P Hanscom, Wash
Wm Stowe, Mass
Ex-Gov Newell, N J
Maj Gen Julius Stahl, N Y
John McManus, Pa
Franklin Johnson, Pa
Erasmus J Middleton, Wash
Jas W Clayton, Md

Chas Dickey, Mich
Earl Bill, Ohio
Col Jones, Ill
Geo W Phillipps, Wash
Robt Lamon, Wash
Wm a Mulody, Wash

Col Blake, Ind
W T Sellick, Wisc
C B Denio, Calif
Judge Delehay, Kansas
E Van Riper, N J
Edw Gregg, Pa
Dr Stephenson, Ind
Capt W W Smith, Iowa
Jas Currens, Pa
Chas Sherrell, N Y

SAT MAR 4, 1865
Inauguration of the Pres of the U S, on Mar 4, 1865: following names have been sent in to rep the states & territories:
Gen John C Caldwell, Maine
Maj Evarts W Farr, N H
Edw S Dana, Vt
Ma Chas N O Rogers, Mass
Walter C Simmons, R I
Hon Benj Noyes, Conn
Col E M Whitaker, N Y
Dr A P Fardon, N J
A S Fuller, Pa
B F M Hurley, Md
H M Slade, Ohio
Jas H Clements, Va
Prof H S Hedrick, N C
J P M Epping, S C
Harrison Reid, Fla
Capt Danl H Bingham, Ala
Gen A Alderson, Miss

E Murphy, La
Gov Wm Babb, Tenn
Col Jas W Irwin, Ky
J J Cummings, Ind
Dr J S Bangs, Ill
J H Gray, Mich
G W McKean, Mo
Maj Robt J Stevens, Calif
B N Hawes, Iowa
Maj G W Barter, Wisc
H H Brackett, Minn
Edw E Fuller, Kansas
Col R W Furnas, Neb
Stephen Gage, Nev
Hon G E Upson, Montana
Wm H Burleigh, Dakota

Deaths of sldrs reported to Capt Moore, A Q M, U S Army:
Mar 2-
Mathias Embree, Co C, 20th N Y
Kersey Bogart, Co C, 210th Pa
Wm Fitzgerald, unassigned, V R C
Mar 3-
Franklin Collins, Co K, 10th V R C
Calvin Stewart, Co C, 100th Pa

Neil McLeod, Co C, 20th Maine
Jos Hadden, unassigned, V R C
E R Harmon, rebel, Co B, 26th S C

Geo W Britton, Co F, 9th N Y hvy artl
John Roberts, Sgt, Co C, 2nd U S light artl

Military execution at the Old Capitol: Sgt Chas Sperry, Co E, 13th N Y cavalry, was shot to death at noon yesterday in the prison yard. He was convicted of unauthorized absence from duty, drunkenness, & aggravated assault. Wash, D C

MON MAR 6, 1865

Inauguaration ceremonies of Abraham Lincoln for a second term took place on Sat. Despite the mud & the lowering impact of the weather, there were thousands of spectators. At the head of the procession rode Superintendent Richards, followed by a body of 30 policemen, abreast, stretched across the ave; next Chief Marshal Goodloe & his aids; squad of 16th N Y cavalry, commanded by Capt Leary; band of 1st brig Vet Res Corps; section of the 4th U S artl, Lt K___ in command; 1st brig Vet Res Corps, commanded by Col Gile, headed by the Finley Hospital band. Corp authorities of Wash, escorted the visiting delegation of the Balt municipal gov't. Visitors arrived at 11:20 & were received by Alderman Utermehle & Cnclmn Larner. Mayor welcomed them in a short speech, to which Dr Wayson responded. After the ceremonies they again returned to the City Hall where they passed a few hours in a very social manner. Procession: the visiting Phil firemen were next in line; Mr Wm Dickson, of U S Steam Fire Brig, acting as marshal. The Good Will engine, marshaled by W J Pascue, was headed by the Liberty Cornet Bank; the Preserverance Hose was marshaled by John J Butler, of the U S Mint. "Uncle Jake" Tripler, the oldest fireman of Phil, marched with this company. Next came the Franklin Hose, marshaled by Chas Darragh; next W H Hines, foreman of #1 Union; #2-John Maddox, foreman, with steamer; #3-Jas W Lowe, foreman, with steamer; Hook & Ladder Co, John T Chauncy. The 34 ladies who were to represent the different states of the Union, & walk behind the firemen, were dispensed with, owing to the inclement weather. The East Wash Lincoln & Johnson Club, headed by Mr Collector Dixon, & marshaled by Jas C D__lin, came next in line. Interesting feature: a miniatrue moniture gotten up by Mr Wm Beron, & other workmen of the Navy Yard. Mstr Morris, of the yard detailed 4 seamen & 4 naval apprentices to man the ship, with a gun's crew, under Mr Geo Dice, from the naval ord yard, fired salutes. Next came a band marshaled by G Z Collison. Capt Tilton had command of a detachment, assisted by Lts Young, Reed, Robinson, & Sgt Maj Dunn. Next- 2nd Btln V R C-144th Co-Sgt Conway; btln 45th regt U S colored troops, from Camp Casey, Capt Brown & Lts Walton & Roberts. Hays' Brass Band-colored. Delegations of colored Odd Fellows: lodges-John F Cook, J F N Wilkinson, G W Gainer, B E Gant, & E Bell. Giesboro cavalcade, over 100 on horseback., were headed by the mounted band of the 31st U S Cavalry. At 15 mins before 12 V P Hamlin escorted the U S elect to the desk, & the Cabinet appeared, followed by the Supreme Crt of the U S. The Pres was seated in front of the Sec's table. Chief Justice Chase administered the oath to Mr Lincoln, & in a clear voice, Mr Lincoln delivered his inaugural. The procession reformed. Pres Lincoln was accompanied in his carriage by his son, Master Tad Lincoln, & Senator Foster, of Conn. Next carriage-Mrs Lincoln, with Senator Anthony, of R I; then the carriage of Robt Lincoln & next 2 foreign ministers. The sldrs were detailed by Col Ingraham..

Mstr C V Morris, of the Navy Yd, was accidentally hit when the last charge was fired from the turret, on his return from the inauguration ceremonies. Injury is painful but not serious.

An outrageous assault was perpetrated on Walter S Cox, our City Recorder, & his relative, Thos Cox, on Sat evening, by drunken roughs. John Baltzer & Jas Simmons, sentenced $10 each & held them in $1,000 bond for appearance at court.

Mrd: at Forest Chapel, PG Co, Md, Feb 23, by Rev Harvey Stanly, Jennie R, 3rd d/o the late Chas Hume, many years a clerk in the U S Treas Dept, to Hobart Duvall, of PG Co, Md.

Died: on Mar 5, after a lingering illness of many months, Mrs Eliz Cole, aged 82 yrs. Funeral from the residence of her son-in-law, Mr J D Brandt, 254 8th st, today.

Died: on Feb 26, at Elmira, N Y, Susan H, widow o/the late Hon John C Clark, & w/o Wm H Phillips, aged 65 yrs.

Crt Martial trials: Capt A J Marsh, 11th Vet Reserve Corp, resident in N Y, on trial before the genr'l crt martial of which Brig Gen H S Briggs, U S V, is Pres, & Maj H B Burnahm, Judge Adv. The Judge Adv moved a postpontment of one week in consequence of the abscense of witnesses, but the accused, whose cnsl [who is also his bro] desired to attend court at his home in Ohio, the case postponed until the 1st Mon in Apr. Lt Col Constant Luce, 17th Mich Infty vols, has also been on trial before the same crt. His case is still progressing.

TUE MAR 7, 1865
Private Acts passed at the last session of the 38th Congress: Relief of:

Geo W Murray	Henry O Brigham
Deborah Jones	Geo A Schreiner
Chas M Pott	Alex'r J Atocha
Geo Mowry	Mary Shircliff
Jacob Weber	Rebecca S Harrison
Emily A Lyon	Chapin Hall
Isaac R Diller	W H & C S Duncan
Mary Scales Accardi	Saml L Gerould
Louis Roberts	Chas A Pitcher
Solomon Wadsworth	John Hastings, coll of Pittsburgh
Almond D Fisk, dec'd-heirs	

Relief of Chas Anderson, assignee of John James, of Texas.
Relief of Wm H Jameson, a paymstr in the U S Army.
Relief of Harriet & Emily W Morris, unmrd sisters of the late Cmdor Henry W Morris.
An act to change the name of Dorsey Edwin Wm Towson, of Gtwn, D C, to that of Dorsey Edwin Wm Carter.
An act granting a pension to Rachel Mills, widow o/Peter Mills, dec'd, late a maj in the U S Army.
Relief of Jean M Lander, widow of F W Lander, dec'd.
Pension of Sophia Brooke Taylor, widow o/the late Maj Francis Taylor.
Relief of Benj Vreeland, surg in the navy of the U S.
Relief of John Hastings, collector of the port of Pittsburgh.
Pension to Ellen M Whipple, widow o/the late Amiel N Whipple, U S Army.
Relief of Mary A Baker, widow o/Brig Gen Edw D Baker.
Pension to the widow of the late Maj Gen Hiram G Berry.
Pension to Thos Bootle
Pension to Ezekiel Darling
Pension to Eliz B Seppien

Died: on Mar 2, Mary Luney, w/o Wm Luney.

Earlier inauguration ceremonies: John Adams, on Mar 4, 1787 at Phil; in ltr to Mrs Adams the next day, a solemn scene it was, indeed; & it was made more affecting to me by the presence of the Gen; me thought I heard him say, Ay, I am fairly out & you are fairly in. Thos Jefferson, on Mar 4, 1801, rode his own horse without a single guard or servant;

hitched his horse to the palisades, & entered the Senate Chamber. Mrs Madison consented to preside for a time at the White Hse, where he received his friends. Jas Madison, Mar 4, 1809, was a day of jubilee. Mrs Madison was about 20 years younger then her hsbnd, whom she mrd in 1794, when he was in his 43rd yr; she was then the widow of a lawyer of Pa named Todd, who died in less than 3 years after their marriage. Her maiden name was Polly Paine, & her father had removed from Va to Phil, & belonged to the Soc of Friends. Mar 4, 1813, Mr Madison was re-inaugurated. The White Hse was burned in Aug, 1814, by the British. Jas Monroe was inaugurated on Mon Mar 5, because the 4th was on a Sunday. He delivered his address on a platform before the Capitol, erected for the occasion. John Quincy Adams, Mar 4, 1825, was inaugurated with similar ceremonies sanctioned by Washington & Madison. Andrew Jackson. Mar 4, 1829, saddened by the recent death of his wife, declined an escort or procession, & rode on horseback to the Capitol. Martin Van Buren, Mar 4, 1837, left the White Hse in the beautiful phaeton built of the wood of the frig *Constitution*, presented to him by the ctzns of N Y C; a lovely day. Wm Henry Harrison, Mar 4, 1841, delivered his long inaugural from the platform at the east from of the Capitol. John Tyler, Apr 4, 1841, took the oath of ofc at his residence. Jas K Polk, Mar 4, 1845, a rain storm marred the inauguration; a ball that night was at Jackson Hall. Zachary Taylor, the 4th being a Sunday, the inauguration was on Mar 5, 1849; about 20,000 persons assembled in front of the Capitol. Millard Fillmore, succeeded to the ofc on Jul 9, 1850, due to the untimely death of Gen Taylor; Jul 11th, he pronouned the oath of fidelty to the Constitution of the U S. Franklin Pierce, Mar 4, 1853, one of the finest witnessed here; began to snow as the Pres left for the White Hse; that evening there was a ball. Jas Buchanan, Mar 4, 1857, a glorious spring-like day; ball in the evening. Abraham Lincoln, Mar 4, 1861; threats had been made & Gen Scott ordered a large military force. Sharp-shooters occupied the roofs of houses along Pa av. On the Pres' return to the White Hse, the doors were opened & thousands passed rapidly thru, shaking hands with the Pres. The ball was at the City Hall, adjoining a temporary ball-rm.

Deaths reported to Capt Moore, A Q M, U S A, Wash, D C:
Mar 4-

Jos Cornell, Co I, 9th N Y hvy artl
Geo W Woodworth, 44th, 2nd btln, V R C
John Davidson, Co A, 23rd Mich

Jos Shuck, Co I, 12th V R C
Jas Scudder, Co H, 146th N Y

John Coon, Co E, 180th Ohio
Isaac Shipman, Co H, 11th Pa
Chas M Branstitter, Co E, 180th Ohio

Jas R Davis, 27th Mich
Thos Scott, Co K, 1st army corps
Brig Gen Chas Wheelock
Mar 5-
Melvin Trent, Co G, 8th Tenn
unknown sldr, cavalry
Mar 6-
John Redney, Co K, 180th Ohio
Jas Howard, teamster, under
Superintendent Hardli

WED MAR 8, 1865
The remains of Sen Hicks were taken from the vault of the Congressional Cemetery, having been placed there on Feb 15, & conveyed to Balt, thence to Dorchester Co, Md on Thu, for final interment.

John Schlosser & Jas Welles were arrested yesterday for assault on John Darnes, on Water st. Each fined $10 & costs.

Crt of Appeals of Md: Annapolis, Mar 6, 1865. #26: Richd A Frazier vs Mary A J Frazier. An appeal from Crct Crt for Kent Co. Cause submitted on written arguments by Geo Vickers for the appellant & J A Wickes for the appellee.

Orphans Crt , D C. 1-The will of the late Caroline Thurston was proven & admitted to probate. 2-Ltrs of adm on the estate of Thos Neary, dec'd, were issued to John P Murphy, & he was appt'd guardian of the chldrn of the dec'd. 3-Thos Ragan & Julia V Ragan were appt'd guardians of the chldn of Daniel Ragan, dec'd. 4-Francis Genau was granted ltrs of adm on the estate of John Genau, dec'd. 5-Final account of Peter O'Donnoghue, exc of the estate of Michael McCarthy, was approved & passed.

Died: on Mar 7, Mary Francis, y/c/o Maggy A & Jas Lackey, aged 13 months. Funeral on Wed [this afternoon,] from 471 Mass ave.

THU MAR 9, 1865
U S Supreme Crt, #111, Jas W Badger, appellant, vs Erastus B Badger & others. Appeal from the Crct Crt of the U S for the Dist of Mass. Jas W Badger, with whom was joined David J Badger, complnts, against Danl B Badger & others. Bill was dismissed as to David J Badger. Danl B Badger died & a bill of reviver was filed against Erastus B Badger, his son, exc & sole heir. Jos Badger died after filing an answer, & the bill has not been revived against him. Danl B Badger, with bros & sisters, are the chldrn & heirs of Danl Badger, who died intestate in 1819, leaving a widow, Ann Badger. Danl D & Jos Badger were appt'd adms; their second account claimed a false balance of $2,456.33. The Supreme Crt has affirmed the judgment of the crt.

Died: on Mar 7, Richd Butt, in his 73rd yr; one of the commissioners of the Metropolitan Police. Funeral from his late residence, near Brightwood, 7th st rd, today.

Died: on Mar 8, Jas McGuire Merrick, aged 3 months & 16 days, s/o Richd T & Nannie Merrick. Funeral from the residence of Jas C McGuire, 445 E st, today.

Deaths of sldrs reported to Capt Moore, A Q M, U S Army:
Mar 7-
Lysander C Hinds, Co M, 2nd N Y hvy artl
Chas Scott, Co B, 32nd Mass
Philip Whalen, Co D, 58th Mass
Benj Hughes, Co E, 180th Ohio

Alex'r W Parks, Co K, 174th Ohio
Robt A Baynes, musician, Co F, 189th Ohio

Mar 8-
Alonzo Bivans, Co E, 69th N Y

The Pope is about to send the Empress Charlotte of Mexico a pure white rose composed of pearls & diamonds.

Paintings, silver-plated ware, photographic albums, fancy toilet soaps, etc. P J Bellew & Co, 510 7th st permanently established in 1860.

Mehemet Pasha, Grand Admr of the Turkish Navy, died on Jan 20th, after a brief illness, & was buried the following day with full military honors, in the family turbeh adjoining the Kilitch-Ali Pasha mosque, Tophaneh.

FRI MAR 10, 1865

Lt Col Trumbull, 1st Conn artl, has been ill of pneumonia for some days, at 422 N Y av, carefully nursed by his bro, Sec of State of Connecticut, & by his bro-in-l, Wm C Prime, of the Jrnl of Commerce. He is believed to be improving.

Died: on Mar 9, at his lodgings, 450 12th st, after a short illness, Edw Graham, clerk in the ofc of the Sec of War, in his 75th yr. Funeral today.

Trustee's sale of the 2 story frame hse on 7th st, between N & O sts, sq 417, Wash, belonging to the heirs of the last Jas Holdridge. -Wm Kilgour, trust & atty

Alexandria City election on Wed: Chas A Ware elected Mayor. Cnclmn elected: [Paper creased.]

W J Coving	Rob Portner	A Jamieson [Possibly
Chas L Neale	Jeff Ta__y	Jamieson]
Saml Baker	S N Garwood	A Moran
W D Massey	John Moore	Robt Wade
_m Arnold	Fred'k Daw	Jas L Dyson
Paul R Evans		

The Ball of the U S Steam Fire Brig was given in the hall of the Patent Ofc last night. Mr Wm Dickson, Chief engr of the steam fire brig, was mstr of ceremonies. He wore the large silver medal lately presented to him by Baxter's Fire Zouaves. For the preservation of order, Sgt Skippon & a detail of 20 men were present, but their svcs were not required.

Yesterday, the eldest child, a boy about 13 years of age, of Mr Wm E Biggs [the workman who was fatally injured at the machine shop of the yard about 2 weeks ago] was kicked by a horse in front of the livery stable of Mr E A Sanderson, on 7th st. His right temple was crushed in, & he is unconscious. He was taken to the drug store of Mr Bates. Drs Coombes & Ensign trepined the skull, with little hope of saving his life. Mr Biggs was left with 4 chldrn in needy circumstances at the time of her hsbnd's sudden death. She resides at the corner of 11th & M sts. She is entitled to commiseration of the charitable.

SAT MAR 11, 1865

Deaths of sldrs reported to Capt Moore, A Q M, U S Army:

Mar 9-

John E Wood, Co I, 10th N Y hvy artl	Thos McGee, Co F, 1st Ala, rebel deserter
Frank Bouckare, Co M, 10th Miss	

Mar 10-

Jas Pettit, Co C, 10th V R C	Clem T Johnston, cpl, Co D, 140th Ind
Frank Wright, Co A, 12th V R C	Wm H Clark, sgt, Co L, 3rd N J cavalry

Orphans Crt of Wash Co, D C. Case of Thos Hutchins, adm of Sarah V Robinson, dec'd; settlement on Apr 4. -Z C Robbins, rg o/wills

N Y, Mar 10-Maj Gen Whiting, a rebel prisoner, died at Governor's Island today.

Died: on Mar 10, Saml McElwee, sr, age 72 yrs. Funeral from his late residence, 440 6th st, tomorrow. Interment in the Congressional Cemetery. Native of Balt, Md; hsbnd & fr. He aided in the defence of Balt in 1812 & removed to Washington soon after.

Died: on Mar 10, at his residence on Hghts of Gtwn, John Harry, in the 84th year of his age; native of Hagerstown, Md, but for the last 50 years a highly esteemed resident of D C

Gens Burnside & Macey arrived in the city yesterday, & are stopping at the Willard.

MON MAR 13, 1865
Judson Mitchell an old & esteemed ctzn, died at his residence on Gay st, Gtwn, on Mar 12; aged 73 yrs. Funeral on Mon, from the Meth Episc Chr, Dunbarton st.

Died: on Mar 11, Mrs Eliz Havenner, w/o Thos Havenner, in the 70th yr of her age. Funeral from the residence, 347 C st, today.

The last draft in Wash City caught the following Met Policemen, viz: Ofcrs Holson, of Gtwn; Harris, Parker, Watts, Straub, Crook, Smith, Gordon, Shelton, Gorman, & Whitemore, of Wash. Also, S E Arnold, detailed for clerical duty at police headqrtrs. All have been on the force for some time.

Fred'k Kroeger, St Chas Restaurant, 200 & 202, corner of Pa ave & 15th st. [Local ad.]

Saml C Totten, a Gov't teamster, who left his team to take care of itself, was handed over to the military authorities, & the wagon & horses sent to the Q M Dept.

Danl Stolcup, a teacher from the neighborhood of Ball's Cross Rds, instead of teaching the young ideas how to shoot, conceived he had a right to ride on the side walk; but Justice Buckey thought otherwise, & having law & the safety of pedestrians on his side, fined Mr Stolcup $5 & costs.

TUE MAR 14, 1865
Medical graduates of Jefferson Medical College in Phil, on Friday, among them were: Jas Bacon, Geo H Hall, & Thos H Roberts, of Md; J A Bishop, of West Va, & B D De Kalb, of Va. Among the grads of the Univ of Pa on the 17th were: Lehman Cooper, Saml T Roman, Wesley M Sharp, A F Stayman, & Jos A Stayman, of Md; Albert F A King, W W Johnston, Alfred Lee, & Edmund A Zevely, of D C; Wm De C Gray, Wm R Lewis & Chas T B Moore, of Va. Mr Zevely is the s/o the Hon A N Zevely, 3rd Ast Postmstr Gen.

Deaths of sldrs reported to Capt Moore, A Q M, U S Army;
Mar 11-Unknown sldr; a ltr on his person was addressed to Jas Rohr. He drowned in canal near Fort Sumner.

Mar 11:
Wm Harris, Co K, 10th N Y hvy artl
Francis Taube, cpl, Co H, 15th N Y hvy artl
Leonard Veholeg, Co H, 25th Mich

Geo A Soule, Co D, 1 Maine cavalry
Josiah Moore, Co H, 57th Pa

Mar 12:
Geo W Benton, Co F, 14th N Y hvy artl
Henry Detmering, Co J, 8th Minn vols

Wm Cooley, Co B, 151st N Y vols
Alvin K Morrow, Co K, 107th Pa

Mar 13:
John Mannix, Co H, 4th U S infty
Alexander Hurst, Co D, 39th N Y

A B Hudson, Co C, 1st Me vols
Wm Warhurst, Co B, 120th N Y

On Sunday, Hiram Dowden, age 17 yrs, a clerk in the shoe store of C F Cummings & Co, Wash, was shot & killed by a sldr, name unknown, for cheering for Jeff Davis. The sldr has been arrested.

Official War Bulletin. Capture of Charlottesville, great destruction of property, rebel Cmdor Hollins is killed. DATE

Crct Crt-D C. U S vs Edw Stubbs, Wm E Stubbs, Geo W Riggs, et al. Action on official bond. The first named dfndnt, & principal, is dead, the suit is prosecuted against the survivor's sureties.

On Sun last the cavalry command of Col Cambrill had a severe skirmish with a large force of Mosby's guerillas between Vienna & Falls Chr. Later in the evening a party of about 30 guerillas, supposed to be of the same gang, made a dash at the residence of Mr T B Munson, taking possession of such edibles as were available, & carrying off one colored man & 6 horses. Mr Munson was absent at the time, else he would have been captured. A detachment of 80 men of the 16th N Y cavalry were captured on the road between Prospect Hell & Vienna. They were escorting a train from the former to the latter place, when a party of guerillas who had hid in a ravine sprang up in their rear, while another party confronted them. Our forces were perfectly surprised & obliged to surrender.

Despatch from R E Lee, Genr'l, Mar 10: our loss was not heavy. Lt Col J S King was killed, & Brig Gen Hume, Cols Hagan & Morrison, & Maj Davis, Ferguson, & others were wounded.

Died: at the Christian Home & Infirmary, Balt, Md, on Feb 8, Geo W Parks, aged 26 yrs, late of Wash, formerly of Michigan. Rev A W Clark, Warden of same, will be pleased to hear from the friends of the dec'd. Michigan papers please copy.

WED MAR 15, 1865
Rev Stephen L Dubuisson, formerly of Alexandria, Va, died in Aug last in Pau, France. He was a native of St Domingo & with his parents escaped the massacre of 1798.

A Wisc paper contains the account of Jos Crele, claimed to be the oldest man living. The record of his baptism in the Catholic Chr of that city shows him to be 139 years of age; first mrd in N Orleans 109 years ago; now resides near Portage City, with a dght by his 3rd wife, who is 70 years of age.

Fire, yesterday, in the hse occupied by Mrs Mary Ann Payne, on Rockville rd, near Tennallytown; loss about $1,000.

Died: on Mar 13, at the residence of her bro-in-law, Thos Blagden, at *Argyle*, near Washington, Mary Silliman, w/o Rev Geo Jones, U S Navy, & d/o Gold S Silliman, of Brooklyn, N Y. Remains will be taken to Brooklyn for interment.

Died: on Mar 12, Lilla, infant d/o John & Rachel A Gordon.

Supreme Crt of D C, in Equity, #183. Scanlin vs McGinness et al. Asbury Lloyd, trustee; ratify sale of lot 3 in sq 677, Wash City, to Jane Chrisman for $1,210. A B Olin, Justice

Wash City News: The resignation of Mrs Emily E Jordan, teacher of Secondary School #5, 3rd Dist, was received & accepted. Mr Wilson introduced a resolution authorizing Mr S J Thompson, 1st Dist Male Grammar School, to introduce Bryant & Stratton's system of book-keeping into his school: adopted. Application of Miss Mary Potter for a teachership: referred to the Cmte on Examination.

THU MAR 16, 1865

Col Hugh H Janeway, 1st N J cavalry, age 23 yrs, went into the regt at age 19 as 2nd Lt. He has grown to be a Col, & has been nominated brvt Brig Gen. He is home on furlough with his 12th wound.

Rl estate sales-Wash: Jacob Staub purchased a lot of land on High st, $29 per front ft. It belonged to Mr Thos Waters. Wm S Matthews sold a brick hse at Prospect & Mkt sts to Capt Sauger for $6,500; & the lot of land adjoining for $2,000.

Tragedy in Queen Annes Co, Md. Occurred in Wye Neck on Wed last. John B Paca, age 26, & his uncle, Alfred Jones, age 36, were killed. John B Paca, the dec'd, & his bro Edw Tilghman Paca, now in the rebel army, were heirs to *Wye Farm*-some 14,000 acs, thru their uncle, Col Wm B Paca, who is part owner & trustee of the property. The interst of Edw Tilghman Paca was confiscated & sold at pblc auction on Jan 12 last. Col Wm B Paca becoming the purchaser. Alfred Jones & his nephew, John B Paca, joint owners, remained on the place, not with-standing the sale. Altercation ensued over a fence. Henry B Paca, bro of the dec'd, was present. Col Wm B Paca & his two sons, Jas & Tilghman Chew, were arrested. -Balt Sun of Monday

Orphans Crt . 1-The will of the late John Harry was submitted to probate; estate bequeathed to his family, & his widow, Harriet Eliza Harry, as excx. 2-The will of the late Cath Bates was partially proven. 3-W S Hurley was appt'd guardian of the orphan chldrn of the late Thos Keating; Rebecca E Raymond, guardian of the orphans of Jas T Raymond, & Chas Walter, guardian of the orphans of D Remler. 4-Accounts approved & passed, viz: First acc't of Mgt McNamara, excx of the estate of Martin McNamara; sixth acc't of Chas Keenan, guardian of the orphans of R B Nally; sixth acc't of Chas Keenan, adm with will annexed of the late Lewis Sanders; 14th acc't of John P Pepper, exc of Dorcas Galvin, & 1st & final acc't of Richd Lay, exc of Thos Carbery, dec'd. 5-Ltrs of adm on the estate of Jos N Padgett were issued to Eliz Padgett; & similar ltrs were issued to Helen Hartman on the estate of Ferdinand Hartman.

Deaths of sldrs reported to Capt Moore, A Q M, U S Army:
Mar 14:
Sylvester Hagerman, Co E, 140th Ind   Wyman Pettengill, Co B, 1st N H hvy artl
Franklin Copsy, Co D, 108th Ohio   John Statlen, Co K, 6th Pa hvy artl

Mar 15:
Edw Murphy, watchman, Q M Dept   Truman Dwyer, Co D, 11th Vt

Charged with defrauding the Gov't: Chas Cook, formerly ticket agent at the Balt & Ohio railroad depot; Chas Williams, ticket agent at the Sanitary Commission rooms, & Jas Thompson, have been arrested by Gov't detectives, & committed to the Old Capitol prison, on charge of defrauding the Gov't of $30,000 by abstracting Gov't transportation tickets from the ofc, at the depot, & selling them for their own benefit.

Gtwn Affairs: Town Meeting on Tue in the Custon Hse; Jenkin Thomas, in the chr, & Wm Albert King, actg sec. Cmte: to determine who of those drafted are entitled to assistance.

Hon Henry Addison	Riley A Shinn	John Marbury, jr
Esau Pickerell	J C Heiston	Danl Brown
F Wheatley	Jas Goddard	Edw Lynch
Chas S English	Geo Hill, jr	

Louisville, Mar 15-Jerema Clark, alias Sue Munday, the noted guerilla, will be hanged this afternoon.

FRI MAR 17, 1865

Died: in Gtwn, on Mar 16th, after a short & painful illness, Mrs Virginia, w/o Jas H Ridgway, in her 26th yr, leaving her hsbnd & 4 small chldrn. Funeral from her late residence, 39 First st, Sat.

Supreme Crt of D C. Jas F J McClery, J C Gardiner & wife, J F Clements & wife, H Lank & wife, against Morven J McClery & wife, Fannie H McClery, Julia G McClery, Mary R McClery, & Eliz H McClery. Parties named & trustee to appear at City Hall, Wash, on Apr 7. -W Redin, auditor

British Parliament has been in existence 600 yrs, this year.

The mother of the Queen of Holland died at Hague on Mar 1.

SAT MAR 18, 1865

Sup Crt of D C, in Equity, #1747. McClery, et al, vs McClery, et al. Walter D Davidge & Wm F Mattingly, trustees: sale of lots in Wash. to C Cammack, jr; Wm B Todd, Frank Riley, & to Gedey & Rheems; ratify same. -R J Meigs, clerk

Deaths of sldrs reported to Capt Moore, A Q M, U S Army:
Mar 16:

Robt Phillips, Co B, 14th Conn	Frank Hart, Co I, 53rd Pa
Wm H Neroon, Co F, 14th Ind	

Mar 17:
John R Barney, Co E, 21st Vet Res Corps

Notice: Vincent M Burch against Eliz Ferrall, Thos W Burch, Fred'k A Burch, Jas W Drane, for himself, & as guardian ad litem for Richd L Jones, Ann E Drane, Thos W Drane, Mary O Drane, Sarah F Burch, & Adelaide Burch, Lamuel F Clarke, for himself, & guardian ad litem of Jas E Clarke, Mgt Burch, & Mary C Burch. Parties to appear on Mar 25, City Hall, Wash. I shall inquire & report who are entitled to the rl estate of the late Thos Burch, dec'd. -W Redin, auditor

Died: in Balt, on Mar 14, John W, only s/o Augustus P & the late Ann Skinner.

Died: on Mar 17, Agnes, y/d/o John & Kate Hitz, aged 16 months. Funeral from their residence, 6th & Pa av, Sun.

MON MAR 20, 1865

Additional appointments have been made for Maj Gen Hancock's First Army Corps:

Col, Geo W Gist	Maj Wm F Fr_hock	Capt Wm L Yeckley

1st Lts:
Wm H Brown
Matthias Reiching
2nd Lt:
W Allison Norman

Wm E Horton
John W Whitney

The hse occupied by Mr Allen Goodrich, corner of 8th & N sts, being a frame hse, was destroyed by fire, on Sat. Ofcr Drane sounded the alarm. Those occupied by Mr Geo King, Mrs Mary E Langley, Mr Addison B Gladmon, & Mr T H Thumler, were entirely burnt out. Most of the furniture saved.

Despatch from O O Howard, Maj Gen: Fayetteville, N C, Mar 11, 7:30 p m. Today we have added Fayetteville to the list of cities that have fallen into our hands. Hardee, said to have 20,000 men, withdrew across the river yesterday & last night. He is reported en route for Raleigh. The rebels skirmished in the town & fired artillery upon the hses occupied by women & chldrn. They burnt the bridge at this place & removed all the pblc stores up the railroad that they could. Gen Sherman is here well. Many men are wanting shoes & clothing, yet the army never was in better spirits.

Deaths of sldrs reported to Capt Moore, A Q M, U S Army:
Mar 18:
Saml F Grove, Co H, Independent Pa light artl
Omar Miller, Co K, 10th Vet Res Corps

Silas M Marshall, Co G, 1st Maine hvy artl

Mar 19:
Josiah W Taylor

Sgt Maj Vet Reserve Corps

Mr A T Grimes, who resides below Giesboro, found the body of a drowned man with a pair of skates on the feet. Mr J J Coombs identified the body as his son who drowned on Jan 30th.

The s/o Mr Ignatius Dyer, aged about 5 yrs, was accidentally shot & critically wounded yesterday on Bridge st. C C Fearson, Wm Garret & Wm Young, some-what intoxicated, encountered another party on the street, when Fearson, without any cause, drew a revolver & fired, hitting the boy. Fearson made his escape, but Garret & Young were taken to the police station.

Assembly's Presby Chr, Rev T B McFalls, pastor, 5th & I sts: meeting last night. Gen A B Eaton presided; choir under Mr Chamberlain; Chas Callender delivered an address. Teachers:

Miss Henning
Mrs E Ellis
G Miller
A Falconer

Miss Fanny Lord
Miss Alice Lord
Mrs Stier
Miss Fannie Hoover

J J Gilbert
Miss Chesley
Miss Cassidy

Missionary School: Mr W J Redstrake, superintendent; Saml Spearing, sec; T Frank Herbert, librarian.

Hon Geo Brown, of the Toronto Globe, it is said, sold 5,000 acs of the Bothwell est, containing oil wells, to an American Co, for the sum of $289,000. The purchasers belong to N Y.

Capt W H Crebbs was arrested last evening for riding furiously thru the street. Justice Buckey fined him $5, but he refused to pay it, saying that, tho dressed as a civilian, he belonged to the army, & was not amenable to civil process, particularly as the Dist is under martial law. He was then turned over to Col Ingraham.

Wash Corp: 1-Ptn from John W Smoot: referred to the Cmte on Police. 2-Ptn of T Edw Clark & others, with a bill to cause the footway to be paved, etc, on front of sqs 874 thru 877: referred to the Cmte on Improvements. 3-Act to authorize John L Brown to close the alley in Sq 247.

TUE MAR 21, 1865
Mrd: on Feb 28, in Trinity Chr, Nice, France, by Rt Rev the Bishop of Calif, assisted by Rev J Childus, English chaplain at Nice, Wm Ingraham Kip, jr, s/o the officiating Bishop, to Eliz Celementia, eldest d/o the Hon Wm E Kinney, late Minister of the U S to the Crt of Turin.

Orphans Crt of Wash Co, D C. Case of John T Cochrane & John Carter Marbury, adms of Jos Bryan, dec'd; settlement on Apr 11. -Z C Robbins, rg o/wills

Supreme Crt of D C, in Chancery, #402. Jas R Clayton & Virginia, his wife, vs Harriet Williamson, John B Williamson, Jos B Williamson, Chas B Williamson, *Samuel Barron & *Mary Ann his wife, Chas E F Richardson & Charlotte his wife, John W Reed & Sarah E his wife, Chas A Huntress & Eliza his wife, & James H T Barron. Bill states that Benj Williamson died, in Wash City, D C, in Sep 1861, intestate, possessed in fee simple, in Wash City, viz: lots 6, 7 & 8 in sq 342, by the heirs of John Davidson; part of lot 7 in sq 345; part of lot 2 in sq 414, & part of lot 19 in sq 516; that the said Harriet Williamson is the widow of said dec'd; & that Virginia E Clayton, John B Williamson, Jos B Williamson, Chas B Williamson, Mary Ann Barron, Charlotte Richardson, Sarah E Reed, Eliz Huntress, & Jas H T Barron, are the only heirs at law of Benj Williamson, dec'd. [*non-residents of D C] -R J Meigs, clerk

Jas C McGuire sold, at auction, yesterday, the dwlg hse on I st near 20th, to Mr Geo J Johnson, for the sum of $9,980.

Captured battle flags & name of the party who captured it:

Maj H B Compson, 8th N Y cavalry	Pvt G Ladd, 22nd N Y cavalry
Capt C C Bruton, A D C to Gen Custer,	Pvt C Anderson, 1st N Y cavalry
22nd-N Y cavalry	Pvt W Carmon, 1st N Y cavalry
Lt S Kuder, 8th N Y cavalry	Pvt P O'Brien, 1st N Y cavalry
Lt R Niven, 8th N Y cavalry	Pvt M Crowley, 22nd N Y cavalry
Sgt Jas Conklin, 8th N Y cavalry	Pvt C A Cohen, 8th N Y cavalry
Sgt R Bourey, 1st Va cavalry	Pvt John Miller, 8th N Y cavalry
Cpl H H Bickford, 8th N Y cavalry	
Cpl H Harvey, 22nd N Y cavalry	

These men were of the 3rd division, under command of Gen Cuser, & were mostly of the 2nd brig, Col Wm Wells, 1st Vt cavalry, commanding.

Wash Corp: 1-Nomination of Ebourne Bird, as Inspec of Lumber, was confirmed. 2-Act for relief of Wm Nottingham, pd $76.85 for repairs made to the Eastern Mkt hse by Nottingham. 3-Act for the relief of C H Berger: refund of $10 for license improperly issued. 4-Act to pay John H Oberteuffer for damages sustained to his property, in the evcavation of 6th st: sum of $200.

WED MAR 22, 1865

Died: at his residence, *Beall's Manor*, Montgo Co, Md, on Mar 20, Mr Thos Beall, aged 70 yrs. [Balt Sun & Clermont Co, Ohio, papers please copy.]

Died: on Mar 20, after a long illness, Leonard Storm, in his 74th yr. Funeral from his late residence, 601 I st, today.

New Orleans, Mar 13. Assassination of Gen Hindman. Reported that the rebel Gen Hindman, while en route to Mexico, was shot by some persons unknown, but they were supposed to be Confederates, between Oakham & the Rio Grande. When killed he was in advance of a train of a number of wagons & ambulances freighted with tobacco, etc.

Arrests of supposed pirates: N Y, Mar 21. Robt Green & Ernest W Pratt, found on the steamer *Corsica*, from Nassau, secreted in the capt's & purser's rooms, were arrested as rebel pirates who served on the steamer *City of Richmond*, which was sent out by the notorious Cranshaw, of London, with an armament for the pirate Olinde; both of whom were without sufficient passports, & are undergoing exam before Gen Dix.

Lizzie Saunders, a servant in the employ of Mr Barrett, was arrested yesterday on charge of having stolen a $50 treas not & gold & silver from her employer. Committed to jail to await trial. -Local Item

The Wash Instit of Reward for Orphans of Patriots was organized Sun last in a meeting in the Cncl Chamber, of City Hall. Rev Dr Samson, V P, took the chair; Mr Stitt was elected Sec pro tem: Mr M C Hurt, elected a mbr of the exec cmte, v Mr Macartney, who declined. Mbrs of the Brd of Aldermen & Brd of Common Cncl of Wash, to wit:

Rapley	Pettibone	Edmonston	Ruff
Turton	Brown	Lloyd	Talbert
Kelly	Lewis	Gulick	Swain
Wilson	Stephens	Canfield	Lloyd
Rheem	Larner	Furguson	Noyes
Plant	Simms	Davis	Wright
Barr	Pepper	Ward	Dudley
Peugh	Utermehl	Morgan	Walker
Owen	Moore	McCathran	

Mbrs are requested to solicite contributions to provide for the destitute orphans of those of the ctzns of Wash who have died, or who shall hereafter die, in the svc of the U S during the present rebellion. Resolution was adopted.

Gen Thos Meagher was suspended from command on the 10th inst, by Gen Schofield, under orders from the War Dept.

THU MAR 23, 1865

Deaths of sldrs reported to Capt Moore, A Q M, U S Army:
<u>Mar 20:</u>
Philip Butts, Co M, 198th Pa   Albert Ramsdale, unassigned, V R C
<u>Mar 21:</u>
Jas George, Co D, 11th Pa
Jacob M Yeargen, Co D, 4th N C, rebel
deserter
Geo A Carser, Co A, 164th N Y

Geo F Eastbrooks, Co H, 20th Maine   John Effinger, Co K 7 N Y
John East, Co D, 198th Pa

Mrd: on Mar 21st, by Rev S P Hill, Edwin H Trust, of Balt, to Lizzie, d/o Francis Mattingly, of Wash City.

Supreme Crt-D C. 1-Jos Hertford advs Mgt Hertford. Ptn & cross-bill for divorce. The wife filed first on charges of extreme cruelty; the hsbnd filed charging adultery. 2-Margarretta Zappone vs Americus Zappone. Ptn for divorce. Mr Z is an Italian teacher of languages, & is also a dentist & physician. The ground alledged is cruelty of treatment, etc. Alimony is prayed for.

Dispatch of Mar 20. Among the horses captured on Gen Chestnut's place, in S C, was the superb stallion presented to Pres David by the Viceroy of Egypt.

FRI MAR 24, 1865
Chancery Crt. Isabella Hurdle vs Chas Hurdle. Ptn for divorce. Adultery is charged against the hsbnd; the child is given to the mother; father to pay $40 per mo.

Criml Crt-D C. 1-Chas Darragh, indicted for robbery; full acquittal. 2-Jas Shadboldt, assault & btry; fined $75. 3-Tip Snyder, alias Celadon Snyder, indicted for keeping a hse of ill fame; convicted in his personal absence. 4-Chas H Cornwell, convicted of converting notes in the Treas. New trial argued.

The funeral of Remegius Burch, late of the Sanitary force of the Met Police, took place on Mar 23. His remains were placed in a vault in the Glenwood Cemetery.

The property of Abraham Rencher, ex-Gov & mbr of Congress from N C, has been seized by the Gov't, the owner being an armed rebel. The propery has been in possession of Mr R B Dietrich, who had a lease upon it.

Died: at his residence in Balt, Md, on Mar 23, Jos D Danels, U S N, late exec ofcr of the U S steamer *Vanderbilt*. His disease was contracted at the recent attack on Ft Fisher, being in command of the naval brigade.

Appointments by the Pres of assessors & collectors of internal revenue:
Lewis C Gunn, assessor for 1st dist of   Simeon Stansifer, coll of 3rd dist of
Calif   Indiana
Frank Soule, coll of dist of Calif   Benj F Brown, coll of 4th dist of Pa
E D Rusking, ast coll of the dist of Ark

Wanted: a convenient hse, pleasantly located in a healthy part of Wash City, containing about 8 or 10 rooms. Address Gen T J Bartholow, d/o J P Bartholomow, ofc 558 7th st, Wash.

Col Louis Schirmer's trial yesterday before the crt-martial of which Maj Burnham, U S A, is Judge Advocate. Evidence of Pvt Wm Kalt, Pvt Rudolph Huber, & Cpl Alex'r Mayer, all of the 15th N Y Heavy Artl, Col Schirmer's regt, who proved that their names on certain bounty pay-rolls, purporting to be their receipting signatures, were not genuine signatures, & that the $300 bounties were not pd to them.

Promoted: clerks in the Internal Rev Svc:

From 3rd to 4th class:

Saml M Wilcox	G W Windall	C A Mackin
J B Taylor	J C Jamson	
F A Howard	B F Stem	

From 2nd to 3rd class:

Israel Dille	T Poesche	W N Jenks
J G Kimball	C Forster	E G Upson
G B Heywood	J B Stevens	S S Sumner
D A Chambers	W O Chapin	Isaac Pugh
D A Clayton	E Tompkins, jr	R H Ball
H L Fisher	S P Doolittle	C B Young

From 1st to 3rd class:

G A Clifford	J A Cushing

From 1st to 2nd cl:

H P Denner	L B Peneling	S J Koontz
S P Lewis	F Barrere	W W Dean
E H Breckenridge	J T Noyes	Thos Cathcart
J W Stokes	E Green	
C P Freeland	J E Ray	

SAT MAR 25, 1865

Mrd: in Wash City, on Mar 16, by Rev Dr Fugitt, of Balt, F M Draney, of Warren Co, N J, to Miss Salome H Wheeler, d/o the late Thos Wheeler, of Balt.

Mrd: at 283 7th st, on Mar 23, by Rev Dr Nadad, Mr Geo B Rowell, of Waterford, Vt, to Miss M J Gartrell, of Wash City.

Died: at Phil, on Mar 18, in her 22nd yr, after a painful & protracted illness, Bettie Conrad, w/o Saml Welsh, jr, & eldest d/o the late Cmder Wm S Young, U S Navy. Her hsbnd, mother, & infant child survive her.

Criml Crt-D C. Mary Nuttrell, indictment for larceny; verdict-not guilty by reason of insanity. She will be sent to the asylum for the insane.

Rl estate sale, Wash: lot in sq 784 to Walter H Madlow, $700; part of lots 5 & 6 in sq 285 to W J Metzerott, 45 cents per ft; part of lot 10 in sq 928, with frame hse, to J C Backer, $7,010; part of lot 12 in sq 373, with frame hse, to Sam'l Ker, $2,305; part of lot 5 in sq 405, with brick hse, to Geo W Careleson, $2,575; part of lot 3 in sq 319, with frame hse, to W Danenhower, $2,285; lot 13 in sq 241, with 2 frame hses, to A B Keyes, $2,050; lots on 21st st, to Jas Tobin, 9 cents; lot adjoining to Jas Keewe, 10 cents.

Military Affairs: 1-Maj Gen John Gibbon has been assigned to the command of the 24th army corps. 2-Capt W H W Krebs, A D C, relieved from duty as Commissary of Musters of the 22nd army corps, [Gen Augur,] & Capt W A LaMotte, A G, U S V, has been appt'd in his stead. 3-A R Jewell, a detailed sldr, & Chief clerk at Gen Augur's headqrtrs, promoted to a 2nd Lieutenency on the Gen's staff. 4-Gen Sheridan is still at White Hse landing, recruiting his men. 5-Gen Meigs has gone to Beaufort, N C. 6-The rebel Col Mosby, it is said, now has 600 men under him. They are divided into 2 gangs of 300 each, & are operating in Pr Wm & Loudoun Cos, Va.

Other witnesses at the trial of Gen Louis Schirmer: Kurt Kirchbert, Gustave Koehler, Ernst Warnfried, Otto Meyer, Adolph Neuville, John Boker, & Lt John Veith. Examined on the part of the Gov't since our last notice of the trial.

Church, the artist, has just lost his only child. It was buried at Hartford Tue afternoon.

Deaths of sldrs:
Mar 23:
-A_bert E Joy, C, 120th N Y   Timothy Shaw, F, 179th N Y
Mar 21:
Chas Branch, I, 10th Vet Reserve Corps   Henry Foster, 11th Mass
Wm H Golden, D, 180th Ohio   Thos Jones, A, 1st U S A
Octavis Lucas, I, 4th U S Cavalry   John D Walton, watchman, Q M Dept
Edw S Holcomb, B, 12th Vet Reserve
Corps

MON MAR 27, 1865
Lt Wm G Stapleton, late q m, 164th N Y vols, Corcoran's Legion, died suddenly on Sat at the Greason Hse, Wash. Cause supposed to be apoplexy. He was from Buffalo, N Y, & had no relatives in this country. Wash, D C

Geo Gates, a young man, was fatally injured in the yard during the storm on Thu. He was buried yesterday from the residence of his mother, a widow, on 5th st, with several small chldrn dependent on her for support. Mr J H McCathran, who was drafted, will have a concert given for his benefit this evening. Local Item

District Vols, 1st & 2nd regts, D C Vols, have been consolidated, regt now numbers 1,200 men, & is on duty at Alexandria, Va. Promotions:
Capt Robt Clarke to Maj   2nd Lt M Dische, to 1st Lt & q m
Pvt J F Kelley, to 1st Lt & adj   1st Lt J M Smith, to Capt
2nd Lt Wm Young, D F Silks, & J L Kelley, to 1st Lts
Sgt Maj Wm H Champion, St J Callahan, Q M Sgt J H Sage, Cpl R Littleton, & Pvt A R Sewall, to 2nd Lts

Edw Ryan, lately employed on the Treas extension, was accidentally shot & killed by John Connors, a watchman at the Gov't warehse, on Mar 25. Wash, D C

Mrs Ann W Smith,aged 77 yrs, a well known ctzn who possessed a large fortune, died. [No date-appears recent.]

Pvt sale of my farm, *Woodley*, 33+ acs, with well-built dwlg; in Wash Co, D C, on Tenallytown, directly east of St Alban's Chr. -P A Bowen

Deaths of sldrs reported to Capt Moore, A Q M, U S Army:
Mar 25:
Henry Vanduzen, Co C, 44th N Y   Edw Goodwin, teamster, Q M Dept
Wm Alexander, Co G, 9th N Y heavy artl   Cpl Peter Gargan Co E, 10th N Y cavalry
Patrick Rogers, Co E, 48th Pa   Thos C Bowman, Co C, independent lght
Thompson Bills, Co D, 4th Pa cavalry   artl, Pa
Mar 26:
Nicholas Fry, Co A, 11th Pa   John Bremer, Co C, 2nd N H
John Lower, Co C, 178th Ohio

Lemuel Cullen, an employee in the Laurel factory, Md, was arrested yesterday on charge of stealing $30 from a fellow workman on Tue. He was committed to jail. Local

For rent-*Mt View*, a portion of the estate of the late John H King, dec'd; about 20 acs; one mile n w of Gtwn, D C. -W Albert King, Adams Express ofc, Gtwn, D C

Orphans Crt of Wash Co, D C. 1-Case of Louisa Korff [now Memmert,] excx of Herman G Korff, dec'd; settlement on Apr 22. 2-Case of John O'Donnell, jr, adm of Barney Donnelly, dec'd; settlement on Apr 22. -Z C Robbins, rg o/wills

Rl estate sales: lot 121 & part of lot 122, on Beall st, with 3 frame bldgs, to Mr Colin Crusor, $3,360; frame hse & lot on Monroe st to Mr Danl Gibbons, $980; another on the corner of Beall & Green sts to Mr Martin O'Donnohue, $1,700.

Died: on Mar 21, at St Geo, Dela, Lucy L Page, w/o Jery Lee Page, formerly of Salem, Mass, for many years a resident in Fairfax Co, Va, & recently of Wash, D C, aged 83 yrs.

Died: on May 26, Mrs Ann W Smith, aged 77 years & 12 days. Funeral from her late residence, 335 Pa av, Tue.

Orphans Crt . Mar 25 1-Thompson Ragan appt'd adm of the estate of Danl Ragan, dec'd. 2-The first acc't of John L Hawkins, guardian to the orphan chldrn of W A Brown, dec'd, approved & passed. 3-First acc't of N S Lincoln, adm of the estate of E D Leazer, approved & passed. 4-Second acc't of Frances Hawkins, adms of the estate of W A Brown, dec'd, approved & passed. 5-First acc't of Theodore F Stokes, adm of the estate of W R Derrons, was approved.

Criml Crt-D C. Frank Simpson indicted for keeping a place for sale of lottery tickets. He was sentenced to a moderate fine & imprisonment.

TUE MAR 28, 1865
Mr Chas G Cook, arrested on charge of being concerned in fraudulent sales of Gov't transportation tickets, has been unconditionally released from the Old Capitol prison.

Died: Mar 27, Horatio Beall, aged 44 yrs. Funeral on Wed from his late residence, 486 L st.

The mail steamer *Dictator* arrived here yesterday from City Point, bringing up captured rebel ofcrs Col F W McMasters, 17th S C; Col H A Brown, 1st N C; Col J T Moran, 23rd N C; Lt Col J G Casey, 50th Va; Lt Col W P Moseby, 21st Va; Maj T D Love, 24th N C; & Maj A W Gibbons, 45th Ga, & 103 rebel ofcrs of the rank of Capt & Lt, all of whom were captured on Sat last, at Ft Steadman. They were sent to the Old Capitol prison.

Last night 2 sldrs belonging to the 2nd D C regt, named Henry Acton & Wm Sweeney, entered a restaurant near the Marine Barracks, knocked down the barkeeper, & robbed the moneydrawer of $40. The police of the Navy Yard Precinct are after the thieves.

With regret we learn of the decease of the only child, an infant, of Mr Rosing, the much-esteemed Charge D'Affaires of the Hanseatic Rpblcs, which occurred yesterday.

Louisville journal states that Govn'r Bramlett has furnished all of his slaves with free papers.

E M Linthicum's Coal Wharf, at the foot of Mkt st, is rapidly approaching completion. Evans & Teemyer are the contractors.

WED MAR 29, 1865

Deaths of sldrs reported at the ofc of Capt Moore, A Q M, U S Army:

Mar 27:

Woodbury G Hicks, Co L, 1st N H hvy artl

Wm B Guinnip, Co J, 189th N Y

Jos A Walter, Co F, 14th N Y hvy artl

Edw Hart, Co D, 16th Mich

Mar 28:

Frank H Clark, Co E, 16th Conn

Peter Clark, Co H, 8th Minn

Danl Titus, Co M, 198th Pa

Thos M Fantlinger, Co C, 105th Pa

Franklin Brown, Co I, 180th Ohio

Martin Alley, Co F, 2nd regt, 1st army corps

Thos Martin, sent from the front to be forwarded to his friends in N Y. No one here to receive him.

Jos D Danels, late Actg Lt Cmder of the U S steamer *Vanderbilt*, died in this city yesterday, after a short illness, in his 37th yr. He entered the navy on Oct 19, 1841. At the recent capture of Ft Fisher, N C, he took a severe cold, which finally resulted in his death. He was s/o the late Cmdor Danels, of Balt. Balt Sun, Mar 24

Criml Crt-D C. 1-Danl Stundon, young Irishman aged about 22 yrs, charged with assault & battery on a near 70 yr old negress: sentenced to 3 years in the Albany, N Y, pen. 2-Mary Cady, larceny. 3-Mary Adley, receiving stolen goods. These parties are sisters-in-law. Mary Cady-convicted. Mary Adley-crt adjourned-verdict, not guilty. 4-Lafayette C Baker, terminated in a nolle prosequi.

Orphans Crt-D C. 1-The will of Cath Bates was proven & admitted to probate. Cath M & Ann Bates were granted ltrs testamentary. 2-Wm Crux was appt'd guardian to the orphans of Jas M Minor. 3-Huidah Robinson appt'd admx of Neal C Robinson, dec'd. 4-The will of John Ossinger was filed & partially proven.

Died: on Mar 28, after a long & protracted illness, Mr C G Wildman, in his 55th yr. Funeral from his late residence at 168 F st, Thu.

THU MAR 30, 1865

Rl estate sales: Wash: lot on so C st, to Jos Williams, 19 cents per foot; lot 5 in sq 725 with 2 brick hses & old frame hse; the west hse & lot purchased by John Pendegrass for $930; the east hse & lot to Mrs C Twish, for $1,000; all of the back lots purchased by A Best at 7¼ cents per foot; part of lots 25 & 27, all of lot 26, to John Bohn, for .14 per foot.

Mrd: on Mar 28, by Rev Geo Smith, Mr John Thompson to Miss Virginia Harbaugh, d/o the late J Randolph & Ann Harbaugh.

Saml Welles, the efficient constructing engineer of this yard, having been detached & ordered to the Mare Island Navy Yard, near San Francisco, Calif, introduced his successor, Mr Wm Dennison, of Boston, Mass, to the several ofcrs & master workmen of the Wash Navy yard yesterday.

Orphans Crt of Wash Co, D C. Case of Milton Elliott, adm of Rezin B Elliott, dec'd. Settlement on Apr 22. -Z C Robbins, rg o/wills

The many friends of Mr I H McCathran will be gratified to learn that the complimentary concert on last Mon at E Wash M E Chr, for his benefit, realized nearly $400. The fine quintettes, executed by Messrs Dawson, Hodgson, Ball, Tabler, & Noyes, will long be remembered at the Navy Yd. We hope that Mr Ball, who has been drafted, may have as much success with his next concert.

FRI MAR 31, 1865
Ofcrs convicted by crt-martial, have been promulgated, viz: 1-Lt Chas E Tucker, aiding a sldr to desert-2 years hard labor in the pen. 2-Capt Hugh, 10th Pa vols, drunkenness on duty & mutiny-dishonorably dismissed the svc, with loss of all pay & allowances. 3-Lt Edw Howard, 1st D C cavalry, drunkenness on duty & breach of arrest, sentenced to be cashiered.

Died: in Wash City, Mar 20, of pneumonia, Lt Col Thos S Trumbull, 1st Connecticut artl, aged 30 years.

Criml Crt-D C. 1-Ann Tracey, larceny-acquittal. 2-Fanny Dines, larceny: 3 months in prison. 3-Mgt Clagett, larceny, guilty. 4-Hugh McMann, keeping a disorderly hse, to be concluded. 5-Mary Harris, indicted for the murder of A J Burroughs, dfndnt was arraigned, & pleaded not guilty.

From the Richmond Exam, Mar 27
Damage done at Fayetteville by the Yankees:
All the arsenal bldgs burned
Fayetteville Observer ofc burned
W B Wright's residence burned
C B Mallet's residence burned
Mr Banks' residence burned
Branch Bank of the State of N C burned
Crt hse & jail burned
All the cotton factories burned
John Waddell was killed on his plantation, 4 miles east of Fayetteville
John T McLean, W T Horne, & Maj Howly were all hung, to extort from them where their valuables were hid, but were taken down uninjured.
Warehses occupied by the Rockfish Co were burned

City News: the shooting of A J Burroughs: arraignment of Miss Mary Harris, who is charged with the murder by shooting him in the Treas bldg, on Jan 30th last, was arraigned in Crmnl Crt, Judge Olin. Robt Beale, the warden; Mr Geo H Fayman, guard. Mrs Fales, with the prisoner. Judge Chas Mason, a former ctzn of Burlington, Iowa, whence the prisoner comes, & who, with other ctzns of Iowa, has taken a deep interest in the case, was present. The clerk, Mr Middleton, read the indictment. Trial set for Apr 24th. Prisoner's cnsl are Jos H Bradley, sr, W Y Fendall, of Wash City, & Hon D W Voorhees, of Indiana.

Lt Chas E Tucker, convicted of aiding a sldr in an attempt to desert, & of breach of arrest, was sentenced to be cashiered, to lose all pay & emoluments, to be forever incapacitated from holding any ofc of honor, trust, & profit in the U S, & to be confined at hard labor in a pen for 2 yrs.

Capt Hugh Alexander, 10th Pa vols, convicted of drunkenness on duty & mutiny, was sentenced to be dishonorably dismissed the svc, with loss of all pay & allowances.

SAT APR 1, 1865
John Thompson, between 16 & 17 years of age, came to Wash City, to avoid being conscripted into the rebel army. His parents reside in Hanover Co, Va.

Deaths reported to the ofc of Capt Moore, A Q M, U S A:
Mar 29:
Wm Laughlin or McLaughlin, Co D-63rd N Y
Lewis Hall, Co B, 8th N-hvy artl
Edw Bannon, Co C, 2nd Mass
Elijah Perkins, Co H, 16th K
Mar 30-31-not legible.

R Pendegrast, rebel, Co D, 43rd N C
Cpl Cornelius Nell, Co B, 1st D C cavalry
John Burke, Co C, 10th N Y

Augustus Henry Fiske, lawyer of Boston, died on Thu, aged 60. He was a Harvard grad.

Maj Gen Thomas in his official report of the operations of his army from Sep 7, 1864 to Jan 20, 1865, says: 13,180 prisoners of war were captured; 72 pieces of serviceable artillery & many battle flags were captured.

Capt Fox, Assist Sec of the Navy, left Wash City yesterday for Savannah, on business connected with his dept. He was accompanied by his wife, Mr J G Nicolay, & J M Forbes & dghts, of N Y.

MON APR 3, 1865
Mr Jacob Little, financier & broker, died at his residence in Union Sq, N Y, on Mon, after a long & painful illness. He was born in Newburyport, Mass & came to N Y about 1817. Funeral at Grace Chr.

Prof Jas Callaghan died on Mar 30th from consumption. He was born in Phil, but while an infant removed to the Southern States. Age over 60 yrs. He was a Grad at Gtwn College. - City News

Orphans Crt . 1-Geo H Gulick appt'd guardian to the orphan of the late Jas Lakens. 2-Will of the late John Fletcher admitted to probate. 3-Inventory of the prsnl estate of Jas Williams filed. 4-Ltrs of adm issued to Maria Bush, admx of Jas Bush.

Died: on May 21, after a painful & lingering illness, Mrs Ann M, w/o Daniel Hauptman, in her 71st yr. Funeral from her late residence, 512 11th st, today.

Deaths of sldrs reported to the ofc of Capt Moore, A Q M, U S Army:
Apr 1:
J H Bennett, Co G, 1st N H hvy artl
J P Castor, rebel, Co G, 25th N C
Jos Bauer, Co I, 7th N Y
Wm M Ward, Co B, 8th N Y hvy artl
Apr 2:
John B Farrel, Co B, 1st D C cavalry

Jas Foreman, rebel, Co E, 59th Ala
Martin Grey, unassigned, died at Ft Storm
Henry Workmuster, Co K, 93rd Pa

Madison L Fabes, Co C, 1st Mass hvy artl

Peter Lackey, a sldr belonging to Campbell Hospital, was robbed yesterday morning, of his pocketbook containing $30, in the bar rm of the western Htl, corner of Marble alley & Pa ave. A man named Collins was arrested. Collins was also fined $20.58 for carrying a slung-shot on him.

Thos Fox, a detective of police of Alexandria, Va, was arrested at the 7th st wharf on Sat, by the provost guard, charged with assaulting a ctzn. He was committed to the Central Guard-hse to await trial.

TUE APR 4, 1865
Died: on Apr 2, after a protracted illness, Mrs Mary M Phillips, relict of the late John Phillips, of Carlisle, Pa, in her 81st yr. Funeral at the residence of her son-in-law, John E Norris, 375 3rd st, today.

Orphans Crt of Wash Co, D C. Case of Eliza R Williams, admx of Jas Williams, dec'd; settlement on Apr 25. -Z C Robbins, rg o/wills

Bailiff's sale-in the suit of Mary J Platt, of Wash City, against Geo H Ingersoll; mscl furn. -Jos F Kelley, blf

Chancery sale of rl estate in Gtwn; cause in which E M Linthicum & Co, cmplnts, & the widow & heirs at law of Richard Jones, dfndnts; [#249;] lot 216; lots 15 thru 19 in Peter's sq, on High st, with 2 story brick hse & frame Carpenter & Wheelwright Shops. -J Carter Marbury, trustee -Thos Dowling, auct

Mr Stephen J Joyce, one of the editors of the Balt Rpblcn, charged with publishing extracts of a disloyal character, & who, after being sent south & returning, had been imprisoned in Fort Delaware 14 mos, has been released.

WED APR 5, 1865.
Mr Geo Russell was shot in an altercation on Apr 3. Arrested were Wm Shedd, Saml Dawes, Geo W Bowers, & Wm M Leaman. Russell was wounded. Wash

Col Wm De Lacey, 16 N Y vols, Corcoran's Legion, & late of the 37th N Y vols, Irish Rifles, has just passed thru Wash City on leave, having been severely wounded for the fourth time.

Edmund H Brooke, of Md, the last 3 years Chief clerk of the Pay Dept, U S A, has been made an additional paymaster, & detailed as Chief of the clerical force in the Paymaster General's Ofc.

Dissolution of the partnership of Chas W Boteler, jr, & John Q Willson, having expired by limitation. Business will be continued by Boteler.

Died: at Detroit, Mich, on Mar 31, Mrs Edmunds, w/o Hon J M Edmunds, Com'r of the General Land Ofc.

Orphans Crt –D C. 1-The will of Christopher Weber was fully proven, & admitted to probate. Ltrs test were issued to Chas Weber. 2-The inventory of the prsnl estate of Martin Johnson was returned by the exc & passed.

Deaths of sldrs reported to the ofc of Capt Moore, A Q M, U S A:

Apr 3:

Sgt Alex Everett, rebel, Co B, 56th N C

Peter Houghtaling, Co M, 15th N Y hvy artl

Geo Carr, Co B, 198th Pa

Timothy M Ervin, Co G, 11th Pa

Apr 4:

Jas Corcoran, Co G, 14th U S infty

Chas L Augusta, Co C, 1st Maine

John Robinson, teamster, Q M Dept

John Lodon, died at Armory Sq Hosp

Henry Mullin, Co H, 1st Maine

John Heck, Co K, 93rd Pa

Patrick Welch, laborer, Q M Dept

Wm D Toult, 4th Pa cavalry

John Young, Co H, 7th V R C

Alex Markle, Co A, 120th N Y

Sgt Jas T Hardy, rebel, 60th Ga

Michl Caton made a furious assault yesterday on Chas H Keller & Chas W Thecker, inflicting severe wounds on both. He was fined $10 & held in $500 bail.

THU APR 6, 1865

Died: on Apr 5, Bennie, child o/Edmund F & Mgt A French, aged 7 months. Funeral on Fri.

Died: on Apr 5, Virginia A, w/o Edw Dawson, aged 29 yrs. Funeral from her late residence, 206 6th st, Fri.

Grafton D Hanson, of Wash City, succeeds Maj Brooke as Chief clerk of the Paymstr Gen's ofc.

[See Edmund H Brooke, page 364.]

Deaths of sldrs reported to the ofc of Capt Moore, A Q M, U S A:

Apr 5:

Franklin Hadley, rebel, Co D, 28st N C

Thos Reed, Co A, 91st N Y

Geo Wise, Co E, 6th N Y

Jas Chaney, Co D, 20th Maine

Theodore Mastaff, Co A, 183rd Pa

Otto Lenge, Co H, 65th N Y

Geo J Gulick, Co B, 11th N Y

Benj Suber, 210th Pa

Ward Burdick, Co A, 179th N Y

Wm H Heller, Co K, 198th Pa

Arlington mansion: 4 years ago Robt E Lee, then a Lt Col of cavalry in the Union army, & now Cmdr-in-Chief of the rebel army, was with his family in the happy possession of that magnificent inheritance. The mansion was erected by the honored son by adoption of the Father of his country. Now it is a cemetery & nearly 5,000 sldrs have been buried there. In 1853 Mrs Custis, mother of Mrs Gen Lee, died in the Arlington mansion & was buried nearby. In 1857 Mr Custis died, & his remains were deposited by her side. Two marble columns mark the remains of Geo Wash Parke Custis & Mary Lee Fitzhugh, his wife. Mr Custis inherited this estate from his father, who was the s/o Mrs Gen Washington by a former hsbnd. His mother died in 1802, when he was about 25 years of age, & came here from Mt Vernon with his wife. This union brought 4 dghts, 3 died in infancy. Mary Custis, w/o Gen Robt E Lee is the only one surviving. Mr Custis' father, John Parke Custis, died at Eltham, Md, of camp fever in 1781, age 27. He had mrd at age 19, Eleanor Calvert age 15, of Mt Airy, Md, a descendant of the 2nd Lord Balt. At age 23 she was a widow with 4 chldrn. Gen Washington adopted the 2 younger chldrn, Eleanor Custis, 2½ years of age, & Geo Wash Parke Custis, aged 6 months. The following are the chldrn of Gen Lee: Geo Washington Custis Lee, about 33; Mary Custis Lee, about 30; Wm Henry Fitzhugh Lee, about 27. Annie Lee died at Berkeley Springs in 1863, & would have been about 25; Agnes

Lee, about 23; Robt E Lee, about 20, Mildred Lee, about 18. None of them mrd except Wm Henry Fitzhugh, whose wife, Miss Charlotte Wickham, died in 1863 at Richmond. The eldest son, Geo, graduated at the head of his class, at West Point,in 1854. Wm Henry was farming upon the White Hse estate, which belonged to the Custis inheritance, when the war opened. Robt was at military school in Va. The sons are all ofcrs in the rebellion. The 3 surviving dghts are with their mother, it is believed, has latterly been at Lynchburg. Mr Custis' mother owned the *White Hse* estate, & resided there, when she became the wife of Gen Washington. Gen Robt Edmund Lee is s/o Gen Henry Lee, of Rev memory, & known as *Light Horse Harry*, whose mother was the beautiful Miss Grimes, Gen Wash's first love. Gen Harry Lee mrd twice: by the first he had 2 chldrn, Henry, an ofcr in war of 1812, & Lucy. By his 2nd wife, Miss Carter, of Shirley, he had 5 chldrn: Anne & Mildred, & his sons Chas Carter, Robt Edmund-the General, & Sidney Smith. Gen Robt E Lee was born in 1808.

Geo Constantine Collins, mbr of the bar, died in Phil on Tue, after a long illness.

Phil, Apr 5. Hon John Sherman, Senator from Ohio, & bro of Maj Gen W T Sherman, arrived here last night from N C.

FRI APR 7, 1865

Capt Wm Madigan was killed at Gaines' Mills, Va, during the 7 days battles, in 1862. At the beginning of the war, he was President of the Boston Printer's Union.

Deaths of sldrs reported to the ofc of Capt Moore, A Q M, U S A:

Hiram Johnson, Co F, 18th V R C
Wm Zeiler, Co G, ___ rgt, 1st army corps
Augustus B Fullerton, Co A, 1st Vt hvy artl
Jos Bailey, Co G, 5th Vt
Henry Apel
Jas S Loghry, Co C, 189th N Y
Thos Mitchell, Co B, 10th N J
Irwin W Hialt, Co I, 180th Ohio

Christopher Leondermans, Co C, 4th Dela
Adam Beaty, Co F, 122nd Ohio
John Wilbart, Co H, 187th N Y
Patrick Gallancosdy, 11th Pa cavalry
John Haran, 8th Pa cavalry
Wm Constable, 1st U S cavalry
Capt Monoah S Hammer, rebel, Co E, 21st Va

Rt Rev Wm H Delancy, Bishop of the Diocese of Western, N Y, of the Prot Episc Chr, died at his residence in Geneva, N Y, on Wed last.

The Pres has made the following appointments of collectors & assessors of internal rev: W L Wilson, vice H J O'Morrison, assessor of 2nd dist of Minn.
Lewis C Gunn, vice Caled T Fay assessor of 1st dist of Calif.
Frank Soule, vice Wm Y Patch, coll of same dist.
E D Rushing, assessor, & C A Harper, colls in State of Ark.
Benj H Brown, vice John M Riley, coll of 4th dist of Pa.
Simeon Stansifer, vice J S S Hunter, coll of 3rd dist of Ind.
John C Dunlevy, vice Wm Miner, assessor of the 3rd dist of Ohio.

Rl est-Washington: J T Dobbin bght 2 lots on E Capt st, between 6 & 7th sts, for .20 per foot.

Mr Michael A Ford, S J, died at Gtwn College on Apr 6, in his 24th yr, a native of Boston, Mass.

Criml Crt-D C. 1-Lewis Watson, assault, convicted & fined $25. 2-Wm Patterson, grand larceny; guilty, motion for a new trial. 3-Richd De Lacey, disorderly hse; case is on trial. 4-Richard Delaney, disorderly hse, guilty. 5-Henry C Shoals, assault & battery; guilty. Granted a new trial. 6-Jas Heney, assault & battery, guilty. Fined $30, or in default thereof, 2 months in prison.

Died: Apr 6th, Mrs Eliz Toole, relict o/late Edw Toole, of Petersburg, Va, aged 84 yrs. Funeral from residence of Mrs Heydon, 381 Pa av, today. [Balt Sun copy]

Died: Zenus Barnum, proprietor of Barnum's Htl, this morning at his residence, Mt Vernon Pl & Cathedral st; age about 56 yrs, & leaves a wife & 2 chldrn. He was exc & adm of the estate of Andrew McLaughlin, as well as of David Barnum. -Balt American

SAT APR 8, 1865

Mrs Ewell, w/o Maj Gen Ewell, arrived in this city on Wed for the purpose of looking after her money & property. The sum of $100,000, belonging to her, has been seized by the Prov Mrshl Gen. Mrs Ewell was not molested but she was ordered to be sent South, & not to return during the war under penalty of being treated as a spy. -St Louis Rpblcn

Gen Wm H Adams, ctzn of Western N Y, died in Albany on Fri. He was one of the original builders of the Erie Canal.

John E Latham, dealer in dry goods, 137 Pa av, Wash, D C. [Local ad]

Deaths of sldrs reported to the ofc of Capt Moore, A Q M, U S A:

John Switzer, Co B, 57th Pa	Henry Gerving, Co K, 15th N Y hvy artl
John Swartz, Co B, 210th Pa	Francis Corpion, Co H, 11th Pa cavalry
Jas Critchlow, Co C, 91st Ind	Andrew Rowles, Co B, 100th Pa
Asa Bohannaw, Co F, 20th Maine	Ethan Whipple, Co B, 2nd R I
Jonas C Melvin, Co B, 321st Mass	John W Merrell, Co G, 1st N H hvy artl.
Chas B Vickery, Co D, 1st Maine	

Criml Crt-D C. 1-Wm B Weed, convicted of larceny of a coat from O W Ballard-mercy of the crt. 2-John McCabe, indicted for the murder of Timothy Finnegan in Feb last, jury was empannelled but not sworn. Jury: Michael Talty, Alfred Burdine, Lewis Wright, John T C Croggan, R L Ross, Chas P Barnard, Ed F Offutt, Jas Mankin, G T C Clark, Wm Haggerty, Chas Boyle, & Thos C Wells.

Died: at Gtwn College, on Apr 7, Rev Henry Hoban, S J. Funeral at the College on Sun.

Died: on Apr 7, Willie Alfred, s/o L F & Mary C Clark, aged 2 years & 10 months. Funeral today.

Rl estate sales, Wash: Frame hse & lot on Mass av to Dr Howard, $3,050; brick hse & lot on K st to John E Carter, $2,325; lot 18 in sq 38, L & 24th sts to Jas Chapman, .20 per foot.

Mrshl's sale of barge John Bland, to satisfy claim of Jonas Steelman for wages. -Ward H Lamon, U S Mrshl D C

MON APR 10, 1865

The grocery store of Mrs A Reamy, on N Y av, was entered by 2 colored men, who struck Mrs Reamy on the head, by which she was severely injured: money & tobacco taken. Police are diligently trying to find the thieves. -Local Item

Fire consumed both the black-smith shop of Mr Wm T Duvall, on Wash. St, & the carpenter shop of L Knowles. -Local Item

Deaths of sldrs reported to the ofc of Capt Moore, A Q M, U S A:

Simon Johnson, Co D, 140th N Y cavalry
John Falkenstan, Co E, 52nd N Y
Peter Houghtoling, Co M, 15th N Y hvy artl
Loren D Gilling, Co F, 185th N Y
Allen C Grant, 6 Mo
Jos Davidson, Co G, 1st Mich cavalry
J C Serman, rebel, Co D, 1st N C cavalry

Geo W Forster, Co L, 1st Maine cavalry
Albert M Curling, Co H, 111th N Y
Henry Albers, Co A, 32nd Mass
Edwin M Hicks, Co A, 7th Mo
Eria A Johnson, Co B, 1st Maine cavalry
Cpl Clinton D Stillman, Co I, 189th N Y
Wm E Knesskern, Co E, 2nd N Y hvy artl

____ Lamberson, Peter Campbell, Wm E Mathews, & Thos Davis, q m ambulance drivers

Mrd: in Phil, on Apr 6, by Rev Kingston Goddard, Maj Henry S Goddard, P M U S A, to Ella M, d/o Isaac S Waterman, of Phil.

Died: at Winona, Minn, on Apr 2, Mrs Mary Howlett, w/o Rev T R Howlett, pastor of the Cavalry Bapt Chr, of Wash City. Funeral svcs in Brooklyn, N Y, on Fri.

Died: at Saybook Ferry, Connecticut, on Apr 6, of consumption, Wm H Hildreth, jr, in his 26th yr.

Orphans Crt of Wash Co, D C. 1-Prsnl estate of Ann W Smith, late of Wash Co, D C, dec'd. -Jane O Mahon, excx. 2-Case of Geo E Jillard, adm of Benj F Hackett, dec'd; settlement on May 2. 3-Case of Eliza M Clampitt, adm of Wm H Clampitt; settlement on May 2. 4-Case of John H Ingle & Osborne Ingle, excs of John P Ingle, dec'd; settlement on May 2. -Z C Robbins, rg o/wills

Orphans Crt . 1-Will of the late Ann W Smith, proven, & ltrs of test granted to Mrs Jane O Mahon. The testatrix bequeaths her estate to her dghts, Mrs Mary A Gibson & Mrs Jane O Mahon. 2-Cath Bauman was granted ltrs test on estate of the late Paul Bauman, dec'd; bequeathed his estate to his wife. 3-Anna Lewis appt'd guardian to the orphan chldrn of Job P McIntosh, dec'd.

TUE APR 11, 1865

True Garland, for 25 years the stage-driver between Pittsfield & Concord, N H, died Fri at age 46.

Deaths of sldrs reported to the ofc of Capt Moore, A Q M, U S A: Apr 9:

John Abney, rebel, Co D, 45th Ga
Albert Hough, Co H, 1st Mich cavalry
Geo S Russell, Co D, 1st Maine cavalry
2nd Lt Robt B Miller, rebel, Co A, 34th Va
2nd Lt D N Patterson, Co E, 46th Va
Apr 10:
Wm Bente, Co A, 198th Pa

Geo P Farrar, Co K, 185th N Y
Marshall Leavitt, Co D, 6th Mo
Lafayette Clark, Co D, 7th Mich
Henry Wamback, Co I, 102nd Pa
Hugh Price, Co 5, 21st btln V R C

Edw Wilselm, Co F, 81st Pa

Daniel W Thompson, Co G, 1ˢᵗ N H hvy artl
Edw W Butler, Co H, 6ᵗʰ Mo
Geo P Lawrence, Co F, 4ᵗʰ N Y hvy artl
Peter Kelley, Co G, 91ˢᵗ N Y
Fred'k Mick, Co E, 15ᵗʰ N Y hvy artl
Henry E Sinnett, Co F, 122ⁿᵈ N Y
John Lynn, Co F, 37ᵗʰ Mo

John Buck, Co G, 7ᵗʰ Mo
Cpl Henry Mauren, Co K, 7ᵗʰ Md
Elphannan Stephens, Co G, 190ᵗʰ Pa
Sgt Jas D Fitz, Co G, 17ᵗʰ Pa cavalry
Danl Keizer, Co K, 99ᵗʰ Ohio
Laretis Graudy, 267ᵗʰ Pa
Patrick Gallance, Co C, 11ᵗʰ Pa cavalry

Army Directory: Sec of War: Hon Edwin M Stanton-ofc: 2ⁿᵈ floor War Dept
Assist Sec of War: Hon C A Dana-ofc: 3ʳᵈ flr War Dept
General-in-Chf: Ofc-in charge of Capt G K Leet, Assist Adj Gen, #29 Winder's Bldg, 2ⁿᵈ flr
Chief of Staff: Maj Gen H W Halleck-Ofc, corner F & 17ᵗʰ sts
Adj Gen: Brig Gen L Thomas-ofc, War Dept
Bur of Military Justice: Brig Gen Jos Holt, Judge Adv Gen-ofc, Winder's Bldg
Judges Adv: Maj L C Turner, Judge Adv, Dept of Wash, etc-ofc, 539 7ᵗʰ st
Theophilus Gaines, Maj & Judge Adv, 22ⁿᵈ Army Corps-ofc, 531 14ᵗʰ st
Solicitor of the War Dept: Hon Wm Whiting-ofc, Rm 31, War Dept
Inspec General's Dept: ofc, 537 17ᵗʰ st
Bur of the Signal Corps: Col B F Fisher, Chief Sig Ofcr_ofc, 167 F st

Q M Dept:
Brvt Maj Gen M C Meigs-ofc, Corcoran's Art Bldg, corner of Pa ave & 17ᵗʰ st
Brvt Brig Gen Chas Thomas, Assist Q M Gen
Col L B Parsons, in charge of 4ᵗʰ div Q M Gen Ofc
Col A J Perry, in charge of 2ⁿᵈ div
Col J J Danna, in charge of 6ᵗʰ div
Col B C Card, in charge of 7ᵗʰ & 9ᵗʰ divs
Col Geo D Wise, in charge of 3ʳᵈ div
Col G V Rutherford, in charge of 8ᵗʰ div
Col S L Brown, in charge of 5ᵗʰ div
Brig Gen D H Rucker, Depot Q M-ofc, corner G & 18ᵗʰ sts
Capt R Brinkerhoff, Ast Q M Vols, Post Q M-ofc, 232 G st
Capt J H Crowell, Ast Q M, in charge of Rents & Construction of bldgs
Capt Jas G Payne, Ast Q M, with Gen Rucker
Capt C H Tompkins, Ast Q M-in charge of Q M Stores, wagon transportation, etc
Capt C Baker, Ast Q M, with Capt Tompkins: Inspec of Camps, horses, & mules
Capt C S Barrett, in charge of receiving & forwarding ordnance-ofc, arsenal
Capt H B Lacey, Ast Q M, in charge of receiving & issuing Q M Stores & Payment of crews of Gov't vessels-ofc, foot of G st
Capt Danl G Thomas, Military Storekpr
Capt E M Camp, Ast Q M, in charge of receiving & messing sldrs
Capt Saml D Lauffer, Ast Q M, in charge of forage
Capt Benj Burton, Ast Q M, in charge of R R transportation
Capt E S Allen, Ast Q M in charge of River transportation
Capt J G C Lee, Ast Q M, Depot Q M, Alexandria, Va
Capt J M Moore, Chief Ast Q M-ofc, corner 21ˢᵗ & F st
Col M I Ludington, Chief Q M Dept of Wash
Capt A S Nesmith, Ast Q M, with Col Ludington
Capt T K Church, Ast Q M on staff of Gen Slough, Alexandria

Cavalry Bur:

Under command of Maj Gen Halleck, Chf-of-Staff-ofc, 302 H st

Brvt Brig Gen Jas A Ekin, in charge of purchase & inspection of horses, & Q M duties

Capt Geo T Browning, Ast Q M, in charge of Depot of Cavalry at Giesboro Point,D C

Subsistence Dept:

Brig Gen A B Eaton, Cmsry Gen-ofc, on La Fayette Sq, corner H st & Jackson Pl

Lt Col G Bell, Depot Cmsry, ofc, 223 G st

Medical Dept:

Brig Gen J K Barnes, Surg Gen-ofc, corner 15th st & Pa ave

Col Madison Mille, Med Inspec Gen U S Army

Lt Col John Wilson, Med Inspec U S Army, Inspec of the Army of the Potomac-ofc, at Rev
Dr Samson's, Columbian College, Wash, D C

Surg R O Abbott, Med Dir, Dept of Wash-ofc, 534 14th st

Surg Basil Norris, to attend ofcrs of the regular army-ofc, corner 14th & G sts

Surg Thos Antisell, to attend ofcrs of the vol army-ofc, in a frame bldg on the space
between 18th & 19th sts, so side Pa ave

Surg C Sutherland, U S A, Med Purveyor-ofc, 212 G st, near 18th

General Hospitals are under the charge of Surg R O Abbott

U S Army Medical Museum:

H st, between 14th st & N Y ave. Open daily, except Sun, from 9 a m to 4 p m.

Examing Brd for Ast Surgs of Vols:

Thos Antisell, Pres-ofc, in a frame bldg in the space between 18th & 19th sts, so side Pa ave

Pay Dept:

Brvt Brig Gen B W Brice, Pymstr Gen, in charge of the Dept-ofc, corner F & 15th sts

Maj E H Brooke, Examination of Accounts-ofc, 211 F st

Maj Hutchins, Discharge Ofc of all ofcrs

Maj Rochester, Discharge Ofc of all ofcrs

Maj Potter, Discharge ofc of regulars

Maj Taylor, Discharge Ofc of vol sldrs

Engr Dept:

Brig Gen R Delafield, Chief Engr-ofc, Winder's Bldg

Ord Dept:

Brig Gen A B Dyer, Chf-ofc, Winder's Bldg

Military Dept of Wash:

Maj Gen C C Augur, Commanding Dept & Military Govn'r Dist Col-Headqrtrs, 14th st,
near N Y ave

Brig Gen J A Haskin, Chief of Artl, Dept of Wash, ofc with Maj Gen C C Augur

Capt H W Smith, Ast Adj Gen, Discharge Ofc for Dept-ofc, 536 14th st

Col T Ingraham, Provost Mrshl Dist of Wash

Defences of Wash;

Lt Col B S Alexander, Additonal Aide-de-Camp & Maj of Engrs

Col J H Taylor, Chief of Staff to Gen Augur
Maj Gen E A Hitchcock, Com'r for Exchange of Prisoners
Brvt Brig Gen Wm Hoffman, Cmmsry Gen of Prisoners
Brvt Brig Gen D C McCallum, Super of Military R R
Brig Gen A P Howe, Inspec of Artl, U S Army
Capt J A Slipper, A D C with Gen Augur
Brig Gen J C Caldwell, Pres of Commission for Exam of Ofcrs reported for dismissal

State Agencies located in Wash:

Maine: H A Worcester	Indiana: Wm H DeMotte
Mass: Lt Col Gardiner Tufts	Ill: Newton Crawford
Ohio: Jas C Wetmore	N J: Lt Col J C Rafferty
N Y: Col Edwin R Goodrich	Wisc: W G Selleck
Pa: Col Francis Jordan	Md: Stephen W Douney
Conn: Rev Wm A Benedict	Ky: C C Pennybaker
Vt: Col Frank Holbrook	Iowa: Gen Cowle
N H: Col Larkin Mason	Minn: J F Stock
R I: Lt Col Jas T Benedict	Dela: Box 651, P O
Mich: Dr Tunnicliff	

Provost Mrshl Gen's Bur:

Provost Mrshl Gen
Brig Gen J B Fry-ofc, War Dept

Ofcrs in the Provost Mrshl Gen Ofc:
Col N L Jeffries, Ast to P M G
Capt W Owens, 5th U S cavalry

Disbursements, accounts, returns,etc, under the Enrolment Act:
Maj Geo W Burton, Ast Adj Gen of Vols, in charge
Capt Saml Dana, 17th infty, disbursing ofcr
Capt H R Rathbone, 12th U S infty, disbursing ofcr
Capt Richd Loder, 4th artl, disbursing ofcr
Capt F H Barroll, 2nd infty, disbursing ofcr

Enrollment, etc:
Capt Geo E Scott, Vet Reserver Corps, in charge

Deserters, descriptives lists, etc:
Maj T A Dodge, Vet Reserve Corps

Vet Reserve Corps:
Capt Jas McMillan, 2nd infty, A A A G

Med Ofcr:
Surg J H Baxter, U S vols

Acc'ts of disbursing ofcrs under appropriation for collecting, drilling, & organizing vols:
Maj Chauncey McKeever, Ast Adj Gen

Gen Lee has surrendered. Mon one week ago, Washington was wild with joy over the fall of Richmond, & yesterday the excitement was renewed & the joy of the people knew no boundaries, the occasion being the capitulation of the Army of Northern Va, commanded in person by Gen Robt E Lee, to Lt Gen U S Grant.

WED APR 12, 1865
St Patrick's is the oldest Catholic Chr in D C, founded about 1800. Rev Mr Plunkett was the first pastor; Rev Wm Matthews was 2nd pastor, from Jul 31, 1804 til his death on May 1, 1854. He was born of wealthy parents in Md & educated in France. The first assistant pastor was Rev Stephen Dubuisson, whom all Catholics will remember as being very active in connection with the miraculous case of Mrs Ann Mattingly.

General ofcrs who have become prisoners of Gen Grant since Apr 5:

<u>Gen</u> Robt E Lee

<u>Lt Gens</u>

R H Anderson	R S Ewell	J B Lonsgstreet

<u>Maj Gens</u>

C A Battle	Bushrod R Johnson	Geo E Pickett
Nathan G Evans	J L Kemper	Thos L Roper
Arnold J Elsey	J B Kershaw	Danl Ruggles
Chas W Field	Fitzhugh Lee	Cadmus M Wilcox
Gordon Grymes	Lunsford J Lomas	
Henry Heath	Wm Mahone	

<u>Brig Gens</u>

R H Clinton	Jos R Davis	D K McRea
A L Long	Dearing	A C Myers
Thos Anderson	De Bose	L B Northrop
Bankhead	Echols	W H Payne
Barksdale	Caesar Finnegan	Geo S Patten
Rufus Barringer	Gary	W R Peck
Seth Barton	Gorgas	Wm N Pendleton
Henry L Banning	Eppa Hunter	John A Preston
Bryant	Thos Jordan	M W Ransom
Goode Bryan	Lane	G M Sorrell
Ellison Capers	Alex R Lawton	Geo H Stuart
H Carter	G W Custis Lee	Isaac M St John
Philip Cook	Robt D Lilly	D A Weisinger
Jas Conner	A L Long	G C Wharton
Corse	John McCausland	Wm C Wickham
Cosby	McCombe	Henry A Wise
W B Cox	McGowan	

<u>Cols:</u>

W H Taylor	John W Lea	Robt Ould
F S Boss	Peter McGlashan	Thos Smith
Chas Forsyth	John S Mosby	
John S Hoffman	Mumford	

<u>Lt Cols:</u>

P G Baldwin	J L Corley	J G Casey
Murphy	A A Cole	John C Pemberton

<u>Majs-4:</u>

G T Venable	C Marshall	
G B Gerald	Henry G Payton	

Surgeon   S Guild, Med Dir.

Orphans Crt-D C. The excs of John C Rives, dec'd, ordered to sell in London, the cnsls named in the petition, & that they invest the proceeds in U S securities, as prayed. The amount is over one hundred thousand dollars in gold.

Deaths of sldrs reported to the ofc of Capt Moore, A Q M, U S A:

Jas H Wager, Co H, 125th N Y
S Jessup, rebel, Co C, 4th Ga
Cpl Jas Harris, Co L, 21st N Y mntd rifles
John Anderson, Co A, 1st Maine
Evi Martin, Co K, 10th V R C
E L Winnie, Co K, 22nd Mich
John Fay, Co M, 2nd Conn hvy artl
John Hall, Co H, 61st N Y

John Donnelly, Co B, 198th Pa
John Hall, q m teamster
Saml R Fessenden, Co D, 147th N Y
John B Ritchie, Co D, 157th Pa
Saml Brightbill, Co K, 209th Pa
Allen H Earley, rebel, Co I, 4th Ga
John Gabbot, Co C, 5th Vt

Died: on Apr 11, Louis G Bartholma, aged 2 years & 8 months. Funeral from the residence of his parents, on 3rd st, between F & G sts, Wed.

THU APR 13, 1865

Deaths of sldrs reported to the ofc of Capt Moore, A Q M, U S A:

David Fozier, Co K, 1st Maine cavalry
Robt Wells, Co G, 24th N Y cavalry
Danl Wilson, Co F, 110th Ohio
Wm Miller, Co H, 2nd vet Md vols
J R Martindale, Co I, 5th N Y
Jerome L Cartis, Co G, 2nd Mich
Jessie Davidson, Co E, 1st Mich

G Sherman, Co J, 6th N H
Myren White, Co D, 4th N Y hvy artl
Jas Freel, Co G, 69th Pa
Daniel Goff, Co D, 179th N Y
Henry Sheppard, Co G, 52nd N Y
John Walker, Co G, 1st Md
Asa A Rich, Co G, 122nd N Y

John McCabe was found guilty of the murder of Terence Finnegan. Verdict-manslaughter. Recommended the prisoner to the mercy of the crt.

Supreme Crt of D C, in Equity. Cath Scanlin against Michl McGinnis & Mary, his wife, & Oscar B Chrisman & Jane, his wife. Parties name above & trustee to appear at my ofc in City Hall, Wash, Apr 22. -W Redin, auditor

War Dept: Apr 12. Maj Gen Dix, N Y: The capture of Selma by our forces is reported by Maj Gen Geo H Thomas. The surrender of Lynchburg is also officially reported. -Edwin M Stanton, Sec of War

Wm Cullen Bryant, the veteran editor & poet, has purchased the homestead of Welcome & Cyrus Tillson, of Cummington, Mass, & will beautify & improve it for a summer residence. Mr Bryant is a native of Cummington & the inhabitants will gladly welcome him back.

Md Fire Ins Co of Balt: ofc #5, Intell Bldgs. -Nathl Pope Causin [Local ad]

FRI APR 14, 1865

Died: on Apr 13, in Berth Amboy, N J, at the residence of her son, P R Hawley, Mrs Wilhelmina D Hawley, relict of the late Wm Hawley, D D, Rector of St John's Chr, in Wash City.

Surgeon W O Baldwin, of the Brd of Enrollment of D C, has resigned to go into private practice in Washington City.

Deaths of sldrs reported to the ofc of Capt Moore, A Q M, U S A:

S N Adams, Co D, Ohio
Geo M Spencer, Co B, 2nd N Y mntd
Geo Wolf, Co G, 4th Pa cavalry
Jas Kennedy, Co H, 189th N Y
Franck Schuck, Co F, 7th N Y
Patrick Clune, Co A, 7th Wisc
Francis Hig___, 91st N Y

Saml S D Smith, Co E, 4th Pa cavalry
Wm Peterson, Co B, 189th N Y
___ Lollid, Co E, 79th N Y
Ludwig Pramer, Co C, Pa
Horace Pride, Co D, 207th Pa
Downs, Co G, 4th regt 1st army corps

Will of Josiah Quincy was admitted to probate Aug 29, 1864. It is dated Dec 30, 1862. The estate is valued, for payment of stamp duty, at $700,000. He gives his 3 dghts, Eliza Susan Quincy, Abby Phillips Quincy, & Maria Sophia Quincy, all the hsehld furniture, at his death, in his mansion houses in Boston & Quincy, & the stock in the stables thereto belonging. Also a right to hay, milk, & eggs from his farm during life. Also the occupaton of his mansion house in Quincy, with its especial appurtenances, during the life of the longest liver-to be kept in repair by the executive. Also a life estate in his house #5 Park st, as long as one lives. Also an annuity of $7,200 to be paid to those living, till all are dead; & he appoints J Ingersoll Bowditch to be the receiver of said annuity for them & their adviser, at the expense of the estate, with power to enter on any part of his estate, if payments are one month behindhand. In case of said Bowditch's refusal, he appoints Peleg W Chandler to said position; if he declines, the Judge of Probate is to appoint-said Bowditch & Chandler to give no bonds. To his son Josiah, in fee, if living-or, if dead, to his eldest surviving son, if any, in fee-if none, to Josiah's heirs then living, in fee-the remainder of his mansion house & all his other real estate in Quincy, all the furniture, etc, in the hse in Quincy usually occupied by said Josiah & in the stable thereof all his farming stock, etc, on the Quincy farm, subject to devise to the dghts; but the devisee is to pay off certain mortgages as specified. To his dght Mgt Morton Greene $5,000, & a right to select as hers such portion of the lot in Mount Auburn, where her hsbnd is buried, as she will-the residue thereof to be used to receive such of his descendants as she may desire, & no others. To his dght Anna Cabot Lowell Waterston an annuity of $1,500 & $5,000 to her hsbnd, if he survives her. There are legacies to each son & dght of Josiah Quincy, & Edmund Quincy, & to his domestics. To his sons Josiah & Edmund he leaves his library, to be shared equally, but to remain in his house in Park st during the continuance of his dghtr's life. To Josiah, the family portraits, etc. Also, 2 pews in Quincy Church, reserving seats for his unmrd dghtrs. To his son Edmund, portraits by Stuart of himself & his late wife. To his dght Eliza Susan, all political & literary writings of himself & his father, to preserve or destroy them at her discretion, & at her death to appoint to either of his male descendants. Also, his portrait; also, a life interest in Washington's gorget, remainder to the Massachusetts Historical Soc, to be placed among their most precious relics. He commands to the care of his son Josiah & heirs, my father's tomb, in Quincy, to be unopened & kept in repair for a century from his decease. Also, the family tomb in Quincy & tomb in Mount Auburn, the latter to receive besides me only my three unmarried dghts, & then be closed forever. To the care of his son Edmund the tomb in Dedham containing Edward Dowse & wife. All the residue & remainder, including lapse devises; to go to Josiah & Edmund equally. He appoints his sons Josiah & Edmund exectors. –Boston Daily Adv

Patriotic demonstrations: the General Rejoicing: city was ablaze; flags floated from the pblc bldgs, hotels, the Capitol was the great centre of attraction: the dome dazzled with countless lights.

Some of the private businesses & residences illuminated & decorated:

Banking hse of Jay Cooke & Co
Callan's Drug Store
Residence of J P Keller, on 13th st, above F
Residence of Jas O'Bryon
Rms of Hon Amos Reed, 457 13th st
Maj Scholfield
Mrs Ringgold
Mrs Bergman
Mr C B Baker, 269 I st
Gonzaga College, illuminated
Residence of Mr McKean, K & 7th st
Mr Barlow, restorer of pics
Andrew Hancock, restaurant
Gautier, restaurant
J Alexander, paper hanger
Dyer, dealer in cigars & liquors
Lewis, jeweller
Madam Dubois & Mrs Voss
Kirkwood & Williard's Htls
Grover's Theatre
Murray's htl, Pa ave
Thompson, gas fitter
J C McGuire & Co's warehse
Woodward's hardware & stoves
Sibley & Guy, hardware & stoves
Allen, Clapp & Co, rubber store
7th st:
F Deitrich & Bro, hatters
L Renner, shoes & clothing
F Sellhausen, tobacconist
J Ruyser, clothing
D Seloerberg, fancy goods
Chas Kumner, fancy goods
Harvey & Co, undertakers
W H Martin, hair dresser
R Buchly, furn & carpet
A Mendleson, Calif clothing store
Residence of Dr Scholl
Thos G Ford, leather dealer
Kroeger's Restaurant
Jno Jung, tailor
B Newman, dry goods
Louisiana ave:
M T Parker
T W Wight
T W Van Hook
W R Sturgis
E Wheeler & Son
Barbour & Semmes
Pvt residences in centre of the city:
Mayor Wallach

Blanchard & Mohun, bkstore
Schneider, bell hanger, etc
Simpson Hse
Russell's restaurant
Potentini's restaurant
John & Co bankers
Snow & McKnew, grocers
Middleton & Beall, grocers
Gen Barnett, 16 ½ st
Hudson Taylor's & Philp & Solomons'-
bkstores
Residence of Gen Hoffman, I st, between
17th & 18th sts
Residence of Maj McBlair, 21st st & Pa
ave
Maj Pelouse, 267 G st
Residence of Mr Baker, 264 g st
Residence of Mr Gordon, 265 G st
Residence of Mr Jacobs, 262 I st
Geo Kraft, bakery, 18th st & Pa ave
A S Chamberlin & Co
O'Neal's restaurant
Store of Barney H_rk
J H Bacon, grocer
Mr B Prossise, bakery, on D st

Hellmuth, baker
L Blout, fancy store
Z Borland, jeweller
H Sieners, grocer
S Emerick, clothing
A Eberly, stoves
A Craft, shoe store
Benj Cudlip, dyeing
W Schwing, Union Hse
Henry Kropp, cigars & tobacco
J E Behren's Saloon
W G Hurley, Patent Ofc Restaurant
Louis Pribram, millinery
S Goodman, shoes & clothing
Hammerschiag's confectionary

E E White, Smith & Morrison
B F Morsell, Nichols & Sherman
J T Elvans
Wall & Co
John H Semmes

Maj Nicholson

Jas Adams
Mrs Clark
W H Morrison
On F st:
Residence of Hon M G Emery
Residence of Michl Larner
Residence of Judge Usher
Residence of Cornelius Wendell
Residence of Douglas Moore
Residence of Dr J Eliot
Residence of Mr Wm W Moore, 5th & F sts
Residence of Mr Dennison, P M Gen, 16½ st

Col Thompson
J C McGuire
Bacon, Colgate

Blanchard & Mohun, bksellers, 11th & Pa ave
Residence of Hudson Taylor, 9th & D sts
Residence of Mrs Farnham, 11th & M sts
Residence of Alderman Barr's, opposite Mrs Farnham's
Hse of Capt C H Tompkins, 11th between K & Mass ave
Totine restaurant, Messrs Copeland & McMillan, proprietors
Francis Lamb, dealer in pic frames, etc

Arlington mansion, formerly the residence of Gen Robt E Lee, as viewed from Capitol Hill, presented a most brilliant & imposing appearance.

Also decorated:
Jno S Topham, saddlery
Ballanyne, bkstore
Green & Williams, aucts
Shepherd, bkseller
Bellew, fancy store
Moses, furn
Rosenthal, boots & shoes
J D Edmond, hardware
C S Whittlesey, paints, oils, etc
Zimmerman, furn
Harrover, stove dealer
Mrs Fowler, whose 3 sons are all in the army
K st:
Residence of Mr Schultz
A Siever, restaurant
M Homan
Mrs Billings
Mr Savage
Also decorated:
W D Wyvill & Co
Dr Scolley
McDermott, carriage maker
Mrs Bannerman, 447 Pa ave
Mrs Fitzgerald's brdg-hse
Mrs Cudlipps, bdg hse
W H Upperman & Co
Teal, Brown & Co, 324 Pa ave & 476 7th st
Thos E Lloyd, 7th st
Residence of Maj Wallach
Residence of Jos H Bradley
Purdy, concert saloon
Whitehurst, ambrotype gallery
Duvall & Bro, clothing store

Colley, dry goods
Gibson, restaurant
King & English, restaurants
Mr Blanchard
Dr Shedd
Greens' Htl
Herndon Htl, corner of 9th st
S P Brown, Navy agent, 9th st
Residence of Jos Hodgson, N Y ave
G Waltermade, tobacconist

Lt Col D A Murray, Ohio cavalry
Residence of Mr Wm Johnson, 8th & L sts
Residence of Mr Robt Downing
Mrs Dr E O Wren, who has been serving with her 4 sons in the army

Murray's Htl
McKnew & Co, Pa ave
Messrs Wyckoff & Dennison, store
C H Lane, store
G W Cochran, cigar store
Gross, cigar store
Walker & Co
Brown's china store
Geo & Thos Parker
Browning & Keating
Anderson & Co
Purcell, store
F Plugge, tobacconist
Galt & Bro

Kloman
Seldner
D W Mahon
P Hoover
E H & H I Gregory
M T Parker
J P Herman
Jackson & Bro
Messrs:
H Otterach
Rhodes
Sanderson
Steel
Thornton
Coombs
Jas Tucker
C W White
Capt Frank, Navy
Henry Bright
Gaddis Bros
Crane
S A H Marks
Tolson
Geo & Chas Miller
Boisseau, of the Rpblcn
Bohrer
Talberts
W E Hutchinson
Geo Wilson
Noakes, pblc gardener
O'Donnell
Krouser
Mullan
Jenkins
Thornton
F E Clark

Jesse B Wilson
L Selden & Co
T Gilman
Ofc of Capt Thomas
Residence of F P Blair
Ofc of Capt R Brinkerhoff, post mstr
Residence of Mr John Hitz, Cnsl, 6th & Pa
av

J W Casteel
Jas & J B Peake
McStiner
Langley
McDonough
Fletcher
Peter Mack
C E Lathrop, naval storekpr
J B Davis
M E Bright
F Van Reswick
Ferguson
Craig
Pugitt
Richards
Lamble
Gulick
Canfield
Mrs Whiney
Capt Wells, Q M
Mrs Carter
John Thompson, Fire Com'r
Capt Wells, Q M
Capt Baden, of the P O
Dr McKim
Dr Davis
Dr Walsh, of the School Brd

1-A large picture of Gen Jackson was displayed in the window of Montgomery Blair's residence. 2-There was a transparency representing Jeff Davis in an army wagon drawn by 6 mules, with a scaffold in the distance, & the rope hanging & the noose in readiness. The driver, mounted on the wheel mule, was represented with the following words issuing from his mouth: "Free transportation for Traitors." 3-Upon the Wash Corporation front, in gas jets, was the word "Grant;" in the centre of the bldg was the word "Union," & upon the east wing, also in gas jets, the word "Sherman."

SAT APR 15, 1865

Pres Lincoln & his wife, together with other friends, last evening visited Ford's Theatre, for the purpose of witnessing the performance of the American Cousin. The newspapers announced that Gen Grant would also be present, but that gentleman, instead, took the late train of cars for N J.

CONSPIRACY AND MURDER. THE PRESIDENT ASSASSINATED. ATTEMPT TO MURDER Mr SEWARD. THE ASSASSINS NOT ARRESTED, BUT BELIEVED TO BE

KNOWN. Tragedy of last night. Ford's Theatre. The President has been assassinated. Mr Seward's house was entered and he & his son, Hon Frederick W Seward, were stabbed. The Pres was shot in the head and some of his brain was oozing out. Maj Potter and Maj Rathbone assisted by others, carried the Pres from the Theatre, to the house of Mr Ulke. Mrs Lincoln was assisted in crossing the street by Miss Laura Keene & others. Maj Rathbone had received a wound in the arm. At five o'clock this morning the President was still alive, but was rapidly sinking. Large crowds still continue in the street, as near to the house as the line of guards allow.[This is on page 2 of the newspaper.]

The military authorities have despatched mounted patrols in every direction, in order, if possible, to arrest the assassins, while the Metropolitan Police are alike vigilant for the same purpose.

Important order: Wash, Apr 15, 1865. In view of the melanchonly events of last evening, I am directed to cause all places where liquor is sold to be closed this entire day & night. The Sgts of the several Precincts are instructed that this order is enforced. –A C Richards, Superintendent

Page 3: Wash, Apr 15, 1865, 1:30 a m. To Maj Dix, N Y: This evening, about 9:30 p m, at Ford's Theatre, the President, while sitting in his private box with Mrs Lincoln, Miss Harris, and Maj Rathbone, was shot by an assassin, who suddenly entered the box and approached behind the Pres. The assassin then leaped upon the stage, brandishing a large dagger, or knife, & made his escape in the rear of the theatre. The pistol ball entered the back of the head of the Pres and penetrated nearly thru the head. The wound is mortal. The Pres has been insensible ever since it was inflicted, and is now dying. At a cabinet meeting, at which Gen Grant was present, today, the Pres was very cheerful and hopeful, and spoke very kindly of Lee & other ofcrs of the rebel army, and the establishment of the Gov't in Va. All the mbrs of the Cabinet, except Mr Seward, are now with Mr Lincoln. I have seen Mr Seward. He & Fred'k Seward are both unconscious. –Edwin M Stanton, Sec of War

Mrd: on Apr 13, at the N Y Av Presby Chr, by Rev Dr Gurley, Mr J P Diller, of Hanover, Pa, to Miss Bell Barber, of Wash City.

Mrd: in King's Chapel, Boston, on Apr 12, Lt Cmder John H Quackenbush, U S N, & Maria L Howe, d/o Jos N Howe, of that city.

SUN APR 16, 1865
Junius Brutus Booth, bro/o J Wilkes Booth, announced to appear at Pike's Opera Hse tonight, Cincinnati, was compelled to leave the city in great haste. Cincinnati, Apr 15

The Pres breathed his last at half-past seven o'clock this morning; Capt Robt Lincoln, s/o the Pres, & the Pres' agonized family were at his bedside, along with members of the Cabinet. The remains were removed from the residence of Mr Peterson, 453 10th st, about 10 o'clock. John Wilkes Booth was the murderer of our Pres. His hat, spur, and pistol were secured at the theatre. The man who stabbed Mr Seward & his sons is John Surratt, of PG Co, Md. He is a young men with light hair and a goatee. The horse he rode was hired at Naylor's stable, on 14th st. His father is said to have been postmaster of PG Co, Md. J Wilkes Booth, alleged murderer, has been loitering around Washington for some months without occupation. He is well known as one of the best pistol shots and sword-fencers in the country. He is s/o Junius Brutus Booth, the great tragedian.

The oath of ofc was administered to the Vice Pres, Hon Andrew Johnson, this morning. Fortunately he was in Wash City in these critical times.

Edwin Booth, brother of the assassin of the Pres, has been playing an engagement at the Boston Theatre for the past 3 weeks, & took his farewell this evening. Boston, Apr 15

The embalming of the Pres was performed by Mr Harry P Cattell in the Pres' bedrm in the White Hse. The coffin was made by Harvey & Co, 7th st, assisted by Mr Frank T Sands, undertaker. The coffin had a silver plate with the inscription: *Abraham Lincoln, 16th President of the United States, Born Feb 12, 1809, died April 15, 1865.* The coffin is 6 feet 6 inches long.

The Pres' last autograph was on a card to Hon Geo Ashmun, just before starting for the theatre: *Allow Mr Ashmun and friend to come in at 9 A. M. tomorrow.* A Lincoln April 14, 1865.

Funeral obsequies of Pres Lincoln are to take place on Thu next. Dr P D Gurley, pastor of the N Y Ave Presby Chr, where the Pres & family have been accustomed to worship, is to be the officiating clergyman, as it is understood. The remains will be temporarily deposited in the vault in the Congressional Cemetery, & in due time conveyed to Springfield, Ill, for interment. The pew in the church occupied by the Presidential family has been draped in mourning, & will be vacant during the svc today.

Deaths of sldrs reported to the ofc of Capt Moore, A Q M, U S A:

Wm J Arneigh, Co H, 5th Pa	Marion Hillike, 7th V R C
Lorenzo Rowe, rebel Co F, 22nd Va	Henry Clark, Co B, 4th N J
Jacob Shoman, Co I, 68th N Y	Hay Pointer, rebel, Co A, 24th N B
John B Summeis, Co D, 210th Pa	Cpl Failin, rebel, Co L, 53rd N C
Lewis Daniels, Co B, N Y	John Camp, Co G, drummer, 8th N Y, hvy
Jacob Smith, Co H, N Y	artl
John Quilty, Co E, N Y	Sgt Miles G Sparks, Co M, 10th N J
Cpl Robt M Dennert, Co K, 39th Mass	Sgt Wm B Tibbetts, Co K, 1st Maine
Kirkoff, Co A, 57th Pa	cavalry
Sgt S Mann, rebel, Co F, 46th Va	Nelson H Atwood, Co C, 6th Vt

MON APR 17, 1865

John Wilkes Booth is the youngest son of Junius Brutus Booth, by his second wife. He was born in 1838 in Md, in the vicinity of Balt. He is unmrd.

Deaths of sldrs reported to the ofc of Capt Moore, A Q M, U S A:

Apr 15:

Cathurn Kimball, U S hosp	Geo Kaufman, Co D, 210th Pa
Herman Conrad, Co H, 15th N Y	Michl Martin, Co D, 18th Mass
Cpl Saml R Frysinger, Co B, 79th Pa	John J P Crawford, Co D, 91st N Y
H W Davis, Co K, 56th N J	Wm Brazoel, Co B, 5th N Y
Michl Delancy, Co A, 69th N Y	Benj Woodman, Co A, 63rd N Y
L L Eure, rebel, 5th N C	Patrick McDowell, rebel, Co B, 1st S C
Franklin Wilkes, Co D, 17th N Y	Rifles
Geo D Whitmore, Co F, 27th Mass	

Apr 16:

Cpl John M Mills, Co A, 57th Mass	Chas Moore, Co B, 148th Pa
Isaac Swartsfager, Co K, 148th Pa	Augustus Wolf, Co I, 35th Mass

Chas Rideout, Co C, 31st Maine
Patrick Dowling, Co K, 16th Mich
Austin Lamerlain, Cpl, 12th N Y
Ennis Barber, rebel, Co C, 46th Va
Cpl John W Backley, Co C, 59th Ala
Jos Hicks, Co I, 56th N C
Wm L Phillips, Co F, 5th Wisc

Isaac Tinner, Co I, 14th N Y H A
D B Studley, Co G, 2nd Conn hvy artl
Thos Holmes, Co I, 69th N Y
I F Graves, rebel, Co H, 45th Ga
Geo A Bucklie, Cpl, 10th Vt
Thos Urch, Co F, 211th Pa

Pres Andrew Johnson was born in Raleigh, N C, on Dec 29, 1808. He lost his father at age 4 years, At age 10 he was apprenticed to a tailor & served him 7 years.

When a pistol shot was heard in the second box of the right-hand side of the stage of Ford's Theatre, persons in the theatre imagined that it was a part of the play. Meantime, the assassin appeared on the edge of the box, crying, "Sic Semper Tyranis," & flourishing a dagger, leaped to the stage. He crossed the stage rapidly exclaiming, " Revenge," and again flourishing his dagger disappeared, saying, "I have done it." Miss Laura Keene appeared on the stage, and with great self-possession implored the audience to be silent. The President was seen to turn in his seat, & persons leaped upon the stage and clambered up to the box. His clothes were stripped from his shoulders, but no wound was at first found. He was entirely insensible. Maj Potter, paymaster of the army, & Maj Rathbone, assisted by others carried the Pres from the theatre, the blood from the death wound falling upon the floor, stairway, and sidewalks as he was borne to the house opposite, which was that of Mr Peterson. Mrs Lincoln was assisted in crossing the street with the Pres in a frantic condition, uttering heart-rending shrieks. She was assisted by Miss Laura Keene & others. Maj Rathbone received a wound in his arm, which he had intentionally covered up to prevent excitement. He then fainted. At police headqrtrs it is understood that Mr Hawk, of Laura Keene's troop, has been held to bail to testify to the identity of the suspected assassin of the Pres, whom he is said to have recognized as a person well known to him.

$10,000 reward will be pd to the party or parties arresting the murderer of the Pres, Mr Lincoln, & the assassin of the Sec of State, Mr Seward & his son.

Capt John Yates Beall who was hanged on Governor's Island, N Y, on May 24, was, on his father's side, descended from Rob Roy, whose history is well known to the readers of Sir Walter Scott's novels. On the mother's side he claimed direct descent from the border chieftain, Belted Will. [The line continues with names: Howard, Witherington, Orfeur; Lamplugh; Yates, Aglionby] When about 16 John Yates Beall came to England with his grandfather, the late Mr John Yates. On the breaking out of the civil war he took up the cause of the Confederates & srv'd under Stonewall Jackson.

Supreme Crt of D C, in Equity, #181. Lloyd W Williams vs Arthur Nelson & wife, John Nelson & wife, Madison Nelson, Chas J Jenkins, John J M Selman, & Joe N Fearson. Parties named, the trustee, & all having claims against Arthur & John Nelson & their respective wives, to meet on May 9, City Hall, Wash, D C. -W Redin, auditor

Died: on Apr 14, at her late residence in Balt, Violeita, d/o Maj Thos Lansdale, of the Md Line, & relict of the late Gov Saml Sprigg, of Md.

TUE APR 18, 1865
Died: on Apr 13, at Rockville, Md, Rachel L, d/o Maj Danl Fowler, of Hudson, N Y, & relict of the late Wm Prout, of Wash City.

Died: on Apr 16, of consumption, Saml C Davison, in his 55th yr. Funeral from the family residence, 514 Mass av, today. [Phil papers please copy]

The Mrshl of the Dist of Col is charged with the conduct of the civil procession. The Mrshl of D C has nominated the following as mrshls for the funeral procession of Pres Lincoln.

Jos H Bradley
Col Wm B Randolph
Geo W Phillips
Wm A Mulloy
Robt Lamon
Dr Noble Young
Gen E C Carrington
Col L J Middleton
Gen P F Bacon
John H Semmes
E J Middleton
A T Bradley
D R Goodloe
Wm B Webb
Col Saml E Owens
Z D Gilman
Jos h Bradley, jr
Saml J Philip
Edw Baldwin
Elias E White
Wm Y Fendall
A S H White
C W Boteler, jr
J P Bartholow
J P Klingle
A R Potts
Thos Blagden
W M McCullon
Valentine Harbaugh
Michl Conley
J W Aulick
Wm Burchell
S D Castleman
G T McGlure
Thos P Morgan
Jos Redfern
Geo W Forsyth
Wm Barclay
J H Cladwell
Edw Wroe
J Ross Ray
Horatio Easby
Owen O'Hare
Thos J Fisher
Edw C Dyer
Frank Guy

Reuben Johnson
Andrew J Joyce
Geo H Plant, jr
H A Chadwick
W S Hook
C C Sprague
Wm Guyson
Geo T Langly
Andrew Noerr
Capt John G McBlair
Geo T Raub
J Carter Marbury
A B Stanton
F J Sykes
A R Shepherd
J W Thompson
Wm E Spalding
Maj Wm Wall
Wm L Wall
Col Jos C Willard
C C Willard
John F Acker
Jas M Barker
John Carroll Brent
Geo Oyster
B B French, jr
W C Bestor
John W Baden
Jas Casparis
B F Dyer
Michl Duffey
John Grinder
K H Lambell
John Mills
John J Jolley
Peter Maack
Alfred Richards
Jas H Richards
Dr Seth J Todd
Geo A Bassett
Wm H Lenny
John Van Reswick
Jos Prather
Henry Burns
A H Clark
Wm Douglass

Edw C Klopfer
John Davis
Henry Turner
Robt Pywell
Saml Rainey
John Braxton
J W Olcott
Jas Kelleher
John C Cook
Jas W Pumphrey
J P Dennis
Wm Bright
Thos Geary
Robt Earl
Edw Cowling
John C Howard
J Matlock
Thompson Naylor
Patrick Fleming
Allen Dorsey
Chas A Murphy
J H Arnold
A F Bully
C H Brown
Geo Barbour
John E Bates
R M Coombs
S A H Marks, jr
Adam Gaddis, jr
Henry Otterback
H C Greenfield
H Browning
G H Gaddis
Lemuel L Gaddis
Geo A Bohrer
Chas Miller
Geo Miller
Michl Homiller, jr
Jas G Naylor
John O Donohoo
Wm Lord
John Lord
Chas Stewart
Geo Eslin
Wm Finley
Francis A Lutz

D B Clark	John J McCullom	Henry Dudley
Thos Galligan	Josiah Egleston	John Dudley
J F Ellis	Jos B Downing	Geo Wright
Geo Parker, jr	Robt Downing	Thos W Riley
Morris Sioussa	Jas Schriver	Saml Pumphrey
Rudolph Eickhorn	J W Boteler	R B Clark
F K Page	B L Jackson	Benj Clark
Saml Bacon, jr	John Baker	Peter Fagan
Jas Callan	Jas A Wise	Robt Johnson
Wm Bryan	Thos McGuire	Thos Walker
Jos B Bryan	R A Shinn	Otto Boswell
W B Williams	Geo Hill, jr	Chas Church
M Thyson	John Stake	Chas Cassell
Chas Kloman	Edw Hendly	Robt Graham

-Ward H Lamon, U S Mrshl, D C

Notice: The pblc will be admitted to view the remains of the late Pres this day from half past nine a m to five p m. Ofcrs will be in attendance to give directions, which must be promptly obeyed.

Several persons, since the death of our martyred Pres Lincoln, suggested that there would be a peculiar fitness in depositing his remains in the vault which was originally designed & constructed beneath the dome of the Capitol for the burial of Washington. Gen Meigs has already made such a suggestion.

WED APR 19, 1865

Supreme Crt-D C, in Equity, #177. E Lindsley & wife & others vs Jos L Ingle & others, heirs of Wm Ingle, late of Stafford Co, Va. Parties named & trustee are to appear on May 10th at my ofc, City Hall, Wash. -W Redin, auditor

Argument on Monday night between Hugh McMahon, property of Ward's Hall restaurant & Jas Keithley, bartender, over money which Mc Mahon accused Keithley of stealing, [which was found in McMahon's trunk] resulted in Keithley stabbing McMahon 5 times. Keithley is about 21 years of age & 5 feet in height, well set, with light hari & eyes, & of a rather pleasant appearance. He was committed to jail.

Died: on Apr 18, Richd Harrison, infant s/o Harrison & Fannie Burr, aged 1 yr, 1 month & 21 days. Funeral from the residence of John T Given, on 3rd st, Thu.

Mbrs of the Vestry of Christ Church, Gtwn, elected for the ensuing yr:

John Marbury	Chas M Mathews	B B Williams
Philip T Berry	Walter S Cox-Reg	John B Davidson
Evan Lyons	Grafton Tyler	

It is stated that John Wilkes Booth was to have commenced an engagement at the Louisville [Ky] Theatre, Mar 20, but he failed to fulfill it without assigning any sufficient reason, & the manager employed another actor. The cause of his delinquency is now painfully apparent.

Mr Fred'k Seward has regained full consciousness & yesterday recognized his wife. There is now strong prospect of recovery of both Mr Seward & his son.

THU APR 20, 1865

Funeral svc of the late Pres Lincoln was at the President Mansion. Among those in attendance at the funeral of Pres Lincoln were 8 survivors of the war of 1812, viz: Chapman Lee, Fielder R Dorsett, Smith Minor, Thos Foster, R M Harrison, Isaac Burch, Jos P Wolf & Capt John Moore. The civilian pall bearers were: O H Browning, Geo Ashmun, Thos Corwin, & Simon Cameron. Rev Dr Gurley, D D, of the N Y Av Presby Chr, in which the dec'd Pres had worshipped, feelingly delivered the funeral sermon.

Oak Hill Cemetery, Gtwn, is to deliver the body of little Willie Lincoln to Dr Chas Brown, to convey it to Springfield, Ill, for reinterment by the side of his fr. Three years ago when little Willie died, Drs Brown & Alexander, the embalmers, prepared his body so handsomely that the Pres had it twice disinterred to look upon it.

His crime Premeditated-John S Clark, bro-in-l of John Wilkes Booth, has furnished us by the Hon Wm Millward, U S Mrshl of the Eastern Dist of Pa, a letter written by Booth in Nov, 1864. The letter [1861] is as follows: My Dear Sir: You may use this as you think best. But as some may wish to know when, who, and why, and as I know not how to direct, I give it [in the words of your _aster]-To whom it may concern: Right or wrong, God judge me, not man. For be my motive good or bad, of one thing I am sure, the lasting condemnation of the North. I love peace more than life. Have loved the Union beyond expression. For four years have I waited, hoped, and prayed for the dark clouds to break, and for a restoration of our former sunshine. To wait longer would be a crime. All hope for peace is dead. My prayers have proved as idle as my hopes. God's will be done. I go to ___ and share the bitter end. I have ever held the South were right. The very nomination of Abraham Lincoln, four years ago, spoke plainly, war-war upon Southern rights and institutions. His election proved it, Await an overt act. Yes, till you are bound and plundered. What folly! The South was wise. Who thinks of argument of patience when the finger of his enemy presses on the trigger! In a foreign war I, too, could say, "country, right or wrong." But in a struggle such as ours, [where the brother tries to pierce the brother's heart,] for God's sake, choose the right. When a country like this spurns justice from her side, she forfeits the allegiance of every honest freeman, & should leave him, untramme'ed by any fealty soever, to act as his conscience may approve. People of the North, to hate tyranny, to love liberty and Justice, to strike at wrong & oppression was the teaching of our fathers. The study of our early history will not let me forget it, and may it never. This country was formed for the white, not for the black man. And looking upon African slavery from the same stand point held by the noble framers of our Constitution, for one, have ever considered it one of the greatest blessings [both for themselves and us] that God ever bestowed upon a favored nation. Witness heretofore our wealth and power; witness their elevation and enlightenment above their race elsewhere. I have lived among it most of my life, and have seen less harsh treatment from master to man than I have beheld in the North from father to son. Yet, Heaven knows, no one would be willing to do more for the Negro race than I, could I but see a way to still better their condition. But Lincoln's policy is only preparing the way for their total annihilation. The South are not, nor have they been fighting for the continuance of slavery. The first battle of Bull Run did away with that idea. Their causes since for ___ have been as noble & greater far than those that urged our fathers on. Even should we allow they were ___ at the beginning of this contest, cruelty and injustice have made the wrong become the right, and they stand now [before the wonder and admiration of the world] as a noble band of patriotic heroes. Herafter, reading of their deeds, Thermoopyim will be forgotten. When I aided in the capture and execution of John Brown, [who was a murderer on our Western border, and who was fairly tried and convicted, before an impartial judge and jury, of treason, and who, by the way, has since been made a god,] I was proud of my little share in the transaction, for I deemed it my duty, and that I was helping our common country, to perform an act of justice. But what was a crime in poor John Brown is now considered [by themselves] as the greatest and only virtue of the whole Republican party. Strange transmigration! Vice to become a virtue, simply because more indulged in. I thought then, as now, that the Abolitionists were the only traitors in the land, and that the entire party deserved the same fate of poor old Brown, not because they wish to abolish slavery, but on account of the means they have ever endeavored to use to effect that abolition. If Brown were living, I doubt whether he himself would set slavery against the Union. Most or many in the North do, and openly curse the Union, if the South are to return and retain a single right guaranteed to them by every tie which we once revered as sacred. The South can make no choice. It is either extermination or slavery for themselves [worse than death] to draw from. I know my choice. I have also studied hard to discover upon what grounds the right of a state to secede has been denied, when our very name, United States, & the Declaration of Independence, both provide for secession. But there is not time for words. I write in haste. I know how foolish I shall be deemed for undertaking such a step as this, where, on the one side, I have many friends & everything to make me happy, where my profession also has gained me an account of more than twenty thousand dollars a year, and where my great personal ambition in my profession has such a great field for labor. On the other hand, the South have never bestowed upon me one kind word; a place now where I have no friends, except beneath the sod; a place where I must either become a private sldr or a beggar. If _give up all of the former for the latter, besides my mother and sisters, whom I love so dearly, [although they so widely differ with me in opinion,] seems insane; but God is my judge. I love justice more than I do a country that disowns it; more than fame and wealth; more [heaven pardon me if wrong] more than a happy home. I have never been upon a battle-field; but O my countrymen! Could you all but see the reality or effects of this horrid war, as I have seen them, [in every State, save Virginia,] I know you would think like me, and would pray the Almighty to create in the Northern mind a sense of right and justice, [even should it possess no seasoning of mercy,] and that He would dry up this sea of blood between us, which is daily growning wider. Alas! Poor country. Is she to meet her threatened doom? Four years ago I would have given a thousand lives to see her remain [as I had always known her] powerful and unbroken. And even now I would hold my life as naught to see her what she was. O, my friends if the fearful scenes of the past four years had never been enacted, or if what has been but a firthful dream, from which we could now awake, with what overflowing hearts could we bless our God and pray for His continued favor. How I have loved the old flag can never now be known. A few years since and the entire world could boast of none so pure and spotless. But I have of late been seeing and hearing of the bloody deeds of which she has been made the emblem, and would shudder to think how changed she had grown. O how I have longed to see her break from the mist of blood and death that circles round her folds, spoiling her beauty and tarnishing her honor. But no, day by day has she been dragged deeper and deeper into cruelty and oppression, till now [in my eyes] her once bright red stripes look like bloody gashes on the face of Heaven. I look now upon my early admiration of her glories as a dream. My love [as things stand today] is for the South alone. Nor do I deem it a dishonoring attempting to make for her a prisoner of this man to whom she owes so much of misery. If success attends me, I go penniless to her side. They say she has found that "last ditch' which the North have so long derided, & been endeavoring to force her in, forgetting they are our brothers, and that it's impolitic to goad an enemy to madness. Should I reach her in safety and find it true, I will proudly beg permission to triumph or die in that same "ditch" by her side. *A Confederate doing duty upon his own responsibility.* J Wilkes Booth

Mr Caesar Brown was killed on Tue when thrown by the sudden movement of the train. He died yesterday. -Wash, D C

FRI APR 21, 1865
Cincinnati, Apr 20-The Nashville papers announce the death of Andrew Jackson, jr, the adopted s/o Gen Jackson.

War Dept: $50,000 reward will be pd by this Dept for the apprehension of the murderer of our late beloved Pres. $25,000 will be pd for the apprehension of G A Atzerot, somtimes called *Port Tobacco*, one of Booth's accomplices. $25,000 will be pd for the apprehension of David C Harold, other accomplice. –Edw M Stanton, Sec of War

The coffin containing the remains of little Willie Lincoln were taken from the vault, in which they have reposed since 1862, in Oak Hill Cemetery, Gtwn. Willie's remains will accompany those of his father. Geo S Koontz, Genr'l Agent of the Balt & Ohio R R, has charge of all arrangements at the depot.

Orphans Crt of Wash Co, D C. Case of Cath V Crumbaugh, admx of John Crumbaugh, dec'd; settlement on May 13. -Z C Robbins, rg o/wills

Mrd: on Apr 20, at the residence of the bride's father, by Rev Dr C H Hall, Dr Wm E Poulton to Miss Lydia E Mills, d/o Capt John Mills, of Wash City. No cards.

East room of the White Hse-Mrs Lincoln's relatives were present, viz; Dr Lyman Beecher Todd, Gen John B S Todd, C M Smith, and Mr N W Edwards, the late Pres' bro-in-law. Capt Robt Lincoln sat during the services with his face in his handkerchief, weeping quietly, and little Tad, his face red and heated, cried as if his heart would break. Mrs Lincoln was weak, worried and nervous. No blood relatives of Mr Lincoln were to be found.

Rl Est Brokers: located on the -s e corner of Pa av & 15th st, Wash. -Geo W Mitchell, Geo C B Mitchel, Thos A Mitchell. Local ad

Died: on Apr 20, of consumption, Jas Leroy, s/o Leroy H & the late Mary Berryman, in his 22nd yr. Funeral from the residence of his father, 7th st, today.

J D Reamer, merchant at Hagerstown, Md, was arrested there on Tue, & brought to Wash City, upon charge of having some knowledge of the conspiracy to murder Mr Lincoln & his cabinet. He is an Alabamian by birth & intensely disloyal.

Brick hse, 13 Potomac st, Wash, formerly occupied by the late Offord Boucher, has been sold at auction for $2,750, to Arthur Cooper. Richd H Darnes bought a lot on Prospect st, between Potomac & Mkt sts, for $29.50 per front ft.

Deaths of sldrs reported to the ofc of Capt Moore, A Q M, U S A:

Edwin Osborn, Co D, 9th N Y	John Redwick, Co K, 126th Ohio
John Brady, Co B, 9th N Y	Elias Martatt, Co F, 5th Wisc
Saml Mayes, Co F, 155th Pa	Cpl David Smily, Co H, 69th N Y
John Stewart, Co D, 77th N Y	Fred'k Livinhagan, Co B, 95th N Y
2nd Lt Wm Mehan, Co C, 188th N Y	Jas E Rodgers, Co B, 97th N Y
Cpl Jesse F Wade, Co G, 170th N Y hvy art	Thos Roley, Co K, 210th Pa
	Wm Rumsey, rebel, Co H, 6th Va

Jas A Goit, Co H, 95th N Y
Sgt Benj S McCallis, Co A, 66th N Y
Robt Duckett, teamster, Q M Dept
Isaac Meil, rebel, 16th Missouri infty

Simeon Keisler, Co E, 9th N Y heavy artl
Wm Kenney, Co M, 100th Pa
Liba B Washburn, Co D, 100th N Y
cavalry

John Sykes, a colored man, died in the 4th Ward Station hse on Apr 20, of disease of the heart.

SAT APR 22, 1865

Abraham Lincoln, was born Feb 12, 1809, in Hardin Co, Ky. He died age 56 years 2 months & 3 days. At age 8 years his father moved to Spencer Co, Indiana. His mother died when he was age 10 yrs. His father mrd a second time to a Miss Sally Johnson, who was an excellent mother.

Supreme Crt of D C, in Equity, #317. Lewis Grammer & others vs Todd, Dunkinson, & others. Wm B Todd, trustee, reported that he sold to Baldesarre Moranghi, lot A in sq 731 for $1,300; to Geo Barren, lot B in same division, for $1,130; to Henry Schaefer, parts of lots 12 & 13 in sq 407, for $4,000; to J C Walker, lot 9 in sq 297, for $942.50; to John L Pfau, 48 acs of land, for $2,400; to Saml Norment, lot 2 in reservation C, for $1,116.50. Ratify same.

Orphans Crt of Wash Co, D C. Case of John Gordon, adm of Ann Maitland, dec'd; settlement on May 6. -Z C Robbins, rg o/wills

Orphans Crt of Wash Co, D C. Case of Wm H Baldwin & Edw Baldwin, excs of Henry Clay Baldwin, dec'd; settlement on May 13. -Z C Robbins, rg o/wills

Mr John Cox, East Balt, furnished the hearse for conveying the remains of Pres Lincoln.

Hon Jas Speed, the Atty Gen, has taken possession of his hse, 284 H st. The hse was lately occupied by Col Seymour, engr of the Wash aqueduct. Mr Speed's wife & family will join him by May 1.

Geo B Love committed suicide by cutting his jugular vein with a penknife, in the guard-room of Fort Thayer, on Wed. Two conflicting discharge papers from the U S army were found on his person. He had the appearance of a man of genteel birth & education.

MON APR 24, 1865

Supreme Crt of D C, in Equity, #350. Martha Detro et al, vs John Albert Anderson et al. Thos J Fisher, trustee, sold to Geo B Wilson, lot 16 in sq 368, Wash City, for $741. Ratify same. -R J Meigs, clerk

Supreme Crt of D C, in Equity, #332. Eliz A DeVaughan vs Thos H DeVaughan, Eliz S DeVaughan, infant heirs at law of Thos S DeVaughan, dec'd.

Ratify sale by Thos J Fisher, trustee, of part of lot 14 in sq 62 to Chas J DeVaughan, for $2,350. -R J Meigs, clerk

Orphans Crt of Wash Co, D C. 1-Case of Harriet LeCompte, admx of Harriet C Nesbit, dec'd; settlement on May 16. R C Robbins, rg o/wills. 2-Prsnl estate of Judson Mitchell, late of Wash Co, dec'd. -J T Mitchell, exc

Mr Trueman Dorsey, formerly of Marlboro, Md, who has resided for some time past at Wilmington, N C, embarked with his family for Balt on the ill-fated steamer *Gen Lyon*, which was lost at sea on Mar 31, by burning at sea. The entire family consisting of hsbnd, wife & 7 small chldrn, perished. They leave relatives & friends in Balt city & lower counties of Md. The mother of Mr Dorsey, of Balt, is at present with her dght, at the residence of Capt A A Semmes, U S N, bro/o Jno H Semmes, of Wash City, in Germantown, Pa, awaiting the arrival of her son & his family, when she received this terrible intelligence.

Orphans Crt-D C. 1-Will of Judson Mitchell, dec'd, partially proven, ltrs test were granted to John J Mitchell. 2-Inventories of the prsnl estate of Richd Butt, dec'd, & the estate of Patrick Lamer were entered & filed. 3-First & final account of Louisa Korff, admx of Herman G Korff, dec'd, approved & passed. 4-Account of Eliza Warder, excx of the estate of Jas Warder, dec'd, approved & passed.

Died: at Andersonville, Ga, on Aug 13, Thornley F Everett, of Md. At the time of his death he was a prisoner of war. [Alexandria & Balt papers please copy.]

TUE APR 25, 1865
Supreme Crt-D C. Mgt Hertford vs Jos Hertford: ptn for divorce; extreme cruelty on the part of the hsbnd. He responded in a cross bill. Decree in favor of the petioner: divorce a mensa et thoro. Alimony of $50 per mo, & she is to have custody of the minor chldrn. He has to pay the costs of suit.

Deaths of sldrs reported at the ofc of Capt Moore, A Q M, U S A:
Apr 24:

Aba W Strong, battery H, Indep Pa Artl
Thos Sheridan, Co C, 198th Pa
Geo W Nathard, Co G, 2nd Ohio Cavalry
Wm Parmer, Co F, 10th V R C
Henry Hilton, Co B, 19th Mass
Willard O Bennett, Co H, 185th N Y
Cassius C Star, Co K, 6th Ohio Cavalry
Edwin H Flag, Co E, 7th Wisc
Jas T Richards, Co E, 189th N Y
Saml McMurran, rebel, Co A, 17th Va Infty

John S Hagans, Wm Werley, [rebel,] Danwith Artl
Michl Marly, Co F, 8th N Y hvy artl
Jos E Clough, Co B, 11th Mass
Jos H Watts, Co A, 110th Pa
Henry M Harrison, Co E, 6th Mich Cavalry
Edw J Williams, Co A, 16th N Y Cavalry
John E Hinner, Co C, 67th Pa

Died: on Apr 24, in his 23rd yr, Wm J Wise, eldest s/o Jas A & Harriet A Wise. Funeral from their residence, 429 7th st, Wed.

Died: on Apr 22, at his residence near Binghamton, N Y, from an affection of the heart, Cmdor Wm W McKean, U S N, in the 64th yr of his age.

Fair at Gonzaga Hall: opened last night: tables displaying everything imaginable in the line of fancy articles, confectioneries, etc:

Mrs Geo T Finegan
Mrs Shiel
Mrs Halloran
Mrs Thomas
Mrs Kearon
Miss Queen

Mrs Mohue
Mrs Dunbar
Mrs Roach
Miss Mary Scanlon
Mrs Mary Elliott
Mrs Jos J May

Miss Carusi
Mrs Davis
Mrs Coyle
Mrs J Simms
Misses O'Donnoghue
Mrs Woodward

Miss O'Donnell	Mrs Kennedy	Miss Alice Herbert
Miss Kennedy	Miss Whelan	Mrs Harvey
Miss Mary Coleman	Mrs Cutts	Mrs Lizzie Goddard
Miss King	Mrs S A Douglas	Mrs Sylvester

WED APR 26, 1865

Died: on Apr 25, of consumption, Jas E Williams, in the 27th yr of his age. Funeral from the residence of his parents, on 8th st, between M & N sts, Thu.

Supreme Crt of D C, in Equity, #31. Pickrell vs Grant & others. Ratify sale of premises in said bill by trustee, to John G Carter, for sum of $2,325. -R J Meigs, clerk

Harvey Ford, an old man in New Haven, very depressed by the news of Pres Lincoln's decease, dropped dead in the evening.

Gen Washburton has tendered his resignation to Gen Thomas, to take effect May 1. His reason is that the war is virtually over.

New Social Temple was instituted last evening & has been named the Martha Washington.

Mrs D P Hinckling, Sister Presiding	Mrs Westerfield, Sister Recorder
Jas E Darrell, Bro Presiding	Mrs W W Ashdown, Sister Treas
Danl P Hinckling, Bro Past	Joy J Edson, Bro Financial Rec
Mrs Edson, Sister Past	Geo A Mark, Bro Usher
Miss Freeman, Sister Vice	Miss Edson, Sister Usher
Edw H Pearson, Bro Vice	Mrs Laura Langley, Sister Guardian
Chas Westerfield, Bro Recorder	Benj F Moffett, Bro Sentinel

THU APR 27, 1865

Capt Geo B Halsted, Assist Adj Gen, yesterday presented to the Sec of War twelve colors captured from the enemy by the 5th Army Corps, while under Gen Sheridan's command, at the battle of Five Forks, Va, Apr 1, 1865. Names of the captors:

Capt A E Fernald, 20th Maine vols.

Capt J W Scott, Co D, 157th Pa vols. The Flag captured belonged to the 16th S C vols, & taken by him from the hands of the color bearer on the line in the engagement of the Five Forks.

1st Lt Jacob Koogle, Co G, 7th Md vol inf.

Pvt David Edwards, Co H, 146th N Y vols, of Watervile, Oneida Co, N Y

Pvt Geo J Shopp, Co E, 191st Pa vols, of Wayne Co, Pa.

Pvt Jos Stewart, Co G, 1st Md veteran vols, of Phil, Pa. Flag was a fine new garrison flag of large dimensions.

Sgt Hiran A Delavin, Co I, 14th Pa vols: flag of the 11th Va infty.

Pvt C N Gardner, Co E, 32_ Mass vols, 1st btln sharpshooters, of So Scituate, Plymouth Co, Mass

Cpt Augustus Kauss, Co H, 15th N Y heavy artl, of N Y C

Pvt Adebert Everson, Co D, 185th N Y vols

Sgt Robt F Shipley, Co A, 140th N Y, of Wayne Co, N Y

1st Sgt Thos J Murphy, Co B, 146 N Y vols, of N Y C

Died: in Wash City, on Apr 26, Samuel Hanson, in his 79th yr. Funeral from the residence of Miss Rebecca Smith, Pa av, today.

Died: on 28th instant, after a painful illness, Mrs Ellen Allen, consort of John Allen. Carriages from her late residence on 8th st & Pa, to Providence Hosp, to convey remains to Mt Olivet.

Crct Crt, D C. John Wiley & Emily F his wife, vs Marshal Brown & Jesse B Haw. Third trial, past jury not able to agree. Dfndnt surviving, Marshal Brown & Tillotson P Brown were sons of the original proprietor of Brown's Htl, Wash City. A generation ago when the circumstances accurred-Tillotson P Brown, at age 19 yrs, while at school in Alexandria, made the acquaintance in Wash City, of Eliz Phillips, d/o a Md farmer. The social station & character of Eliz was objectionable to Tillotson's family. Eliz & Tillotson became the parents of a dght & Tillotson treated her as such. This dght is the present Mrs Wiley, plntf in the suit. Brown watched over & educated her, & even elegant maintenance of the mother, is a reputed fact to our ctzns for 20 years back. This young lady mrd Mr John Wiley, of Balt, some years ago. As Mr Brown was approaching the end of his life, he was mrd, by Rev B A Maguire, a Catholic priest, to Eliz Phillips, the mother of Emily F Wiley. In Dec 1861, Brown died intestate. The widow qualified as admx, settled the estate, & a large balance is on hand.

Died: on Apr 13, in Nashville, Tenn, A G W Barton, Hospital Steward, U S A, aged 55 yrs. Entered the svc as a pvt in Co A, 2nd Pa Reserve, in May, 1861; severely wounded at the battle of Antietam, Sep 17, 1862, & incapacitated for active duty. Entered the svc again in Mar, 1863, as hospital steward in the Reg army. Born & reared in the Valley of Wyoming.

Orphans Crt of Wash Co, D C. Case of Wm G Ridgely, adm of Stephen Gough, dec'd; settlement on May 20. -Z C Robbins, rg o/wills

Gen Patterson, of Phil, & Gen Abercrombie, U S army, have recently bought farms in Talbot Co, Md

FRI APR 28, 1865
Rl est-Thos O'Beirne bought a 3 story brick hse on 4th st, between N & O sts, Wash, for $1,300.

Yesterday morning the assassin of Pres Lincoln, John Wilkes Booth, was captured. The body of Booth was brought to Wash City on the tugboat *Idea*, Capt Wilson, and was in charge of Lt Dougherty & a squad of the 16th N Y cavalry. Col E J Conger & Lt L B Baker were ordered to proceed to arrest Booth & Herrold. They were found at Garrett's farm, near Port Royal, on the Rappahannock. Mr Garrett denied knowledge of any strangers being in the vicinity. His son, John M Garrett, however, in-formed Lt Baker that 2 men were secreted in the barn. A parley occurred for about an hour and a half. Sgt Boston Cotbett left the ranks without orders, & placing the muzzle of his pistol thru a crack of the barn, fired, & shot Booth thru the neck. He died at 22 mins past seven o'clock, the same hour & minute at which the Pres died. Both Herrold, who was taken alive, and Booth's body are in Wash City.

Mrd: on Apr 27, at the First Congretional Methodist Chr, by Rev Geo W Samson, D D, Mr Israel Deming to Miss Linda Compton, all of Va. No cards.

Mrd: on Apr 27, at the Chr of the Epiphany, by Rev Dr Hall, Mr John B Stouvenel, of N Y, to Mary Ives, d/o the late Presley B Jewell, of Phil. No cards issued. [Phil & N Y C papers please copy.]

Died: on Apr 27, Geo B, eldest s/o C F E & Charlotte E Richardson, aged 10 years & 6 months. Funeral from their residence, 473 L st, Fri.

Obit: Mrs Violetta Lansdale Sprigg died on Apr 14, at her late residence on Saratoga st, Balt, Md, relict of the late Gov Sam'l Sprigg, of Northampton, in this county, in her 77th yrs. Dr Nathl Smith, of Balt, attended her. Burial rights were said by Rev Dr Mahan, of St Paul's, Balt, & repeated by Rev Dr Pyne, recently of St John's, Wash, as her remains were committed to the Carroll vault, in the Gtwn Cemetery. It is the purpose of the family to remove the remains of the late Gov Sprigg from Queen Anne's Chr yard in PG Co, Md.

Geo M Selden, who died at Troy lately, left $26,000 to fund the Selden Institute for educating & maintaining female nurses.

SAT APR 29, 1865
Died: Richd S Coxe, on Apr 28, one of the father's of the Washington bar, at his residence in Washington City, aged 73 yrs. Funeral from his late residence on Sun.

Sketch of Booth: the elder Booth, of Hebrew descent, drank to excess, left his wife in England with a flower girl & settled on a farm near Balt; brought up many chldrn, while his first possessed went down to a drunken & broken hearted death. He himself wandered westward & died on the way. His widow, Mrs Rosalle Booth, lived discreetly & frugal with her 6 chldrn, viz: Junius Brutus, Edwin Forrest, John Wilkes, Jos, & the girls. Mrs B now resides with her dght in 19th st, N Y. John S Clarke dwells in princely style in Phil, with the dght whom he mrd. Edwin Booth dwells also on 19th st. Junius B Booth kept in the West. Jos Booth tried the stage & failed. He is now in California. A son of Booth by his first wife became a first class lawyer in Boston & never recognized the rest of the family. John Wilkes Booth, the 3rd son, was shot dead on Wed for murder. On the morning of the murder Booth breakfasted with Miss Carrie Bean, d/o a merchant, & a respectable young lady, at the National Hotel.

Attys & Solicitors of Claims; 214 Pa av, Wash. -Chas Mygatt, Geo S Thompson, of Ill, & Isaac Hackett. [Local ad]

C S Bundy, Atty a Law & Solicitor of claims. 247 F st, Wash, D C. [Local ad]

Cnslrs at Law; 12 A st, Wash. -Thos Ewing, of Ohio; Britton A Hill, of St Louis, & O H Browning, of Ill. [Local ad]

MON MAY 1, 1865
Orphans Crt of Wash Co, D C. Case of Maria Dickens, excx of Asbury Dickens, dec'd; settlement on May 22. -Z C Robbins, rg o/wills

Mrd: at St Aloysius Chr, by Rev Mr Stonestreet, on Apr 27, Mr Edgar S Brooke to Miss Emma S Barnaclo, d/o Jonathan W Barnaclo, all of Wash City.

Noble J Thomas, a former well known resident of Wash, but who has been in the rebel army since the outbreak of the rebellion, was arrested in Wash City, on Fri. Among the charges was that he had acted as a spy & informer, & he pointed out Union men from this city to the rebel authorities in Alexandria. The same were imprisoned & punished. Mr W H Harrison & Mr Geo Hilton, residents of the 6th ward, were sworn. Thomas was committed to jail for a further hearing.

City News-John Day, a pvt of Co F, 6 Mich cavalry, was shot on Sat by Pvt Geo A Hyatt, Co B, 18th Regt V R C, & died. Hyatt had Day under arrest & he had attempted to escape. Hyatt was fully justified in shooting the dec'd.

The dying murderer: a mattress was brought down, on which they placed Booth & propped his head & gave him water & brandy. The women of the hsehold were joined by another son, who had been found in one of the corn cribs, watching the horses to see that Booth & Herrold did not steal them. Booth muttered, "Tell mother I died for my country. I thought I did the best." Baker repeated this, saying at the same time, "Booth, did I repeat it correctly." Booth nodded his head. He bled very little, although shot quite thru, beneath, and behind the ears, his collar being severed on both sides. His hands were paralyzed and when he saw his hands said: "Useless, Useless." These were the last words he uttered. His body was sewed up in a saddle blanket. This was his shroud; too like a sldr's. Herrold had been tied to a tree, but now was released for the march. Booth's only arms were his carbine, knife, & 2 revolvers.

TUE MAY 2, 1865
Died: on May 1, after a long & painful illness, Rezin Orme, aged 77 yrs. Funeral from his late residence, 120 C st, Wed.

Orphans Crt of Wash Co, D C. Case of Nannie Haw, admx of Jesse B Haw, dec'd; settlement on May 23. -Z C Robbins, rg o/wills

Cincinnati Gaz-Cairo, Apr 28. Account of disaster from the Memphis Bulletin. The steamer *Sultana*, Capt Mason, arrived from New Orleans, Apr 26, with about 2,200 people on board, 1,964 were exchanged prisoners from Vicksburg. Explosion of her boilers occurred & hundreds of people were blown in the air. Capt Geo Clayton survived; the bible of a family named Spikes, of Assumption Parish, La, was found, names recorded were Saml D Spike & Eleitha Spike, mrd Oct 31, 1837-it was learned that the father, mother, 3 dghts & 2 bros, & a niece were lost. Wm Rawberry survived; the body of Wm Cradles, Co I, 1st Va cavalry, from Wheeling, Va, was found, he had taken the precaution to label himself. L Brooke of the 2nd Mich cavalry survived, also Lt J N Seffer, 175 Ohio. [May 5th paper-Mrs S W Hardin, jr, recently mrd, was lost. Her hsbnd was of the firm of Cushman, Hardin & Co, Chicago. Mr Hardin was unsuccessful in finding his wife. He was formerly Adj of the 53rd Ill infty.]

The Bros Lansburg's dry goods establishment has become a fashionable resort, & this day will exhibit Merchandes de Modes of Paris. [Local ad]

The burner of the U S steamer *St Paul* was hung. The Navy Dept yesterday received a despatch from Actg Rear Admr S P Lee, commanding Mississippi Squadron, with a report of Actg Mstr Fitzpatrick, commanding the U S steamer *Siren*, dt'd Apr 22, respecting an expedition sent by Brig Gen Osborne to Brownsville, Tenn, of 3 cols. They returned on the 22nd, having captured 10 ofcrs & 12 men. In a skirmish, on that day, Gen Selby's adj was killed. One of the men captured is the fellow that has been passing for Luxton, for the burner of the U S steamer *St Paul*. Gen Osborne hung him from a cottonwood tree. His proper name is Wilcox, & he has a father living in Tenn.

Wash, D C, Apr 1, 1865. The undersigned has sold out his lumber yard to Nathl B Fugitt, with whom all persons indebted to me are earnestly requested to make immediate settlement, in order to facilitate the closing up of the affairs of the old concern. -Jos Fugitt, Lumber Dealer, 6th st west, near Pa ave.

Memphis Bulletin's account of the disaster. The steamer *Sultana*, Capt Mason, arrived from New Orleans, last night, the 26th, with about 2,200 people on board, 1,964 of whom were exchanged Federal prisoners from Vicksburg, the balance being refugees & reg passengers, proceeding towards St Louis. She left the coal pile about 1 o'clock this morning, had made some 8 or 10 miles, when an explosion of one of her boilers occurred. The boat took fire & in a short time she was burned to the water, & now lies on a sandy beach near Fogleman's Landing. People were blown in the air: some were borne by the current as far down as the levee at this city, & this was the first sign the ofcrs of the boats in port received of the terrible disaster. *Sultana* ofcrs: Mstr J C Mason: 1st clerk, W J Gamble; 2nd clerk, Wm Stratton; pilots, Geo Cayton & Henry Ingraham; engrs, Nathan Wintenger & Clemens West; mate, Wm Roeberry; steward, Henry Cross. Geo Cayton & Wm Rawberry were the only ofcrs known to be saved, except Clemens, who is almost dead. The body of Wm Credles, Co I, 1st Va cavalry, from Wheeling, Va, was found. Following named persons drifted down & were saved at Fort Pickering:

Lt J N Seffer, 175th Ohio
Sgt Lew Milts, 10th Ind cavalry
Sgt Wm M Duke, 42nd Ohio
L Brooke, 2nd Mich cavalry
Cmsry Sgt Zacharis, 7th Mich
Cpl Peacock, 9th Ind cavalry
W H Chance, 9th infty
E Spencer, 8th Mich cavalry
R Talkiton, Ind cavalry
M Daly, 18th infty
J Parker, 95th infty
J R Delander, 3rd Ind cavalry
P M Brown, 6th Ky cavalry
H Van Fleet, 14th Ohio
M Reynolds, 89th Ind
H P Hunt, 36th Ind
M J Gray, 6th Tenn cavalry
O L Shelton, 6th Tenn cavalry
J Benson, 40th Ind
J Kitting, 2nd Mich
A Diphre, _ Ohio
E Matthias, 64th Ohio
J Thatcher, 46th Ohio
J Haley, 102nd Ohio
B Falshoman, 9th Ind cavalry
D Hites, 102nd Ohio
J W Jackson, 5th Ky cavalry
H B Wallace, 124th Ohio
G H Hodger, 9th Ohio cavalry
G Deericher, 13th Mich
3rd Tenn cavalry:

L Cook, 28th Ohio
F Carr, 7th Ohio cavalry
John Devis, 9th Ind
S E Whiter, 55th OHio
W McMurry, 4th Tenn cavalry
J Wescott McClothiers, Ohio cavalry
R T Hall, 2nd Ky cavalry
J W Dunsmore, 1st Mich engrs
J Moore, 175th Ohio
C Post, 175th Ohio
J Newland, 4th Ohio cavalry
J Welch, deck hand
G M Sheppard, 10th Ind & his fr the Ind agent
Capt J Walker Elliot, 44th colored
Lt J F Elliott, Co C, 125th Ind
Lt Suvain, 9th Ind cavalry
Lt W F Livas, Co A, 10th Ind cavalry
Lt Burnett, 12th Ky
Lt Dickinson, 2nd Mich cavalry
Lt McCard, 97th Ohio
Lt Larkin
Lt Squire, 101st Ohio
Capt Taggart, 101st Ohio
Lt Earle, 1st Mich engrs
Lt Davis 71st Ohio
Maj Carlin, 71st Ohio
Capt Foster, 58th Ohio
Capt Hake, 115th Ohio

C M Eldridge
J Baker
B Hamilton
N R Russell
M Jordan
M Thomas

J M Dougherty
Levi Heckner
M Thomas
J M Dougherty
J Milsape
S Weese

J Kanlse
J Deeker
J Pryor
F Wood
J B Lackey
M Ramsey

WED MAY 3, 1865

Orphans Crt of Wash Co, D C. Case of Wm R Woodward, adm of Terrence Leonard, dec'd; settlement on May 23. -Z C Robbins, rg o/wills

Orphans Crt of Wash Co, D C. Prsnl estate of Lafayette J Brown, late of Wash City, dec'd. -Julia Brown, excx

Hon Benj G Harris, rep in Congress from the 5th Dist of Md; arraigned for trial before a Gen Crt Martial at 467 14th st. Wash, composed of the following ofcrs: Maj Gen J G Foster, Maj Gen John G Parke, Maj Gen O B Wilcox, Brvt Brig Gen G H Sharp, Brig Gen J A Haskin, Brig Gen Wm Gamble, Col Chas Albright, 202nd Pa vols; Lt Col O F Babcock, Aide-de-camp, Capt U S engrs; Maj W W Winthrop, Judge Advocate, who were present. The following ofcrs were detailed, but were not present: Maj Gen A A Humphreys & Brvt Maj Gen John A Rawlins. Charge: Violation of the 56th article of war. Specifications first. In this, that Benj G Harris, a ctzn of Md, & a mbr of the U S Congress, did relieve with money, to wit: the sum of two dollars, the pblc enemy, to wit: Sgt Richd Chapman & Pvt Wm Read, of Co K, 32nd regt: Virginia infantry, sldrs of the army of the so-called Confederate States of America, then in rebellion against & at war with the U S, he, said Harris, then & there well knowing said Chapman & Read to be sldrs of said army, & treating & offering to relieve them as such, & at the same time advising & inciting them to continue in said army & to make war against the U S, & emphatically declaring his sympathy with the enemy & his opposition to the Govt of the U S & its efforts to suppress the rebellion. This at or near Leoanrdtown, St Mary's Co, Md, on or about the 26th day of Apr, 1865. Specifications second. In this, that Benj G Harris, did knowing harbor & protect the pblc enemy, to wit: Sgt Richd Chapman & Pvt Wm Read, etc, by procuring them to be lodged & fed in a private house, & furnishing them with money therefore, he, the said Harris, knowing them to be sldrs of said army, & treating & offering to give them money as such, & at the time advising & inciting them to continue in said army, etc, & emphatically declaring his sympathy with the enemy & his oppositin to the U S Gov't in its efforts to suppress the rebellion. This at or near Leonardtown, St Mary's Co, Md, on or about Apr 26, 1865. Chapman & Read were examined & cross-examined yesterday before the court. The trial will continue today.

Rl estate sale of a 2 story frame hse on M st, between 12 & 13th sts, to Mgt Brown, for $1,225. Thos Powers bought a lot of ground on N st between 11 & 12th, Wash.

Thos J Crawford, of White Mountain fame, died at Lancaster, N H, on Apr 23, of dropsy.

Mrs Betsy P Eastman, of Salisbury, N H, completed her 103rd yr last Sun.

Obit: Mrs Isabella F Croghan, w/o Dr P A Croghan, died on Apr 28, of consumption. She was a kind friend, a fond sister & a devoted wife.

THU MAY 4, 1865

The hse on 10th st, opposite Ford's Theatre, owned by a German family by the name of Peterson, had rented the room where the Pres died to Wm Clark. He has slept in the bed since the Pres' death, as usual. Gustavus Clark, formerly of Boston, was one of those who assisted in taking the Pres over to the hse.

Sgt Boston Corbett, 16 N Y cavalry, who shot Booth, belongs in N Y C. He was born in England about 33 years ago & is by trade a hat-finisher.

Balt, May 3. Two ctzns of Calvert Co, Md, were brought to this city yesterday, viz: D Nathan W Browne & Wm Cochran, & 3 other men, on charge of having been concerned in the recent assassination of U S sldrs for some time past stationed in the above county. Cochran was pd $150 for killing the first sldr. Lt O'Bryan, superintendent of the Gov't farms in the lower counties, was shot, but escaped. His horse was killed.

Local-Hugh Strider, age 12 yrs, & Wm Curran, age 10 yrs, were committed to jail for stealing $22 from the store of Mr Jas Whitmore.

Died: at Carver Hosp, in Wash City, on May 2, Jas H Maxwell, 10th Regt Maine vols, aged 21 yrs.

Died: at the Naval Acad, Newport, R I, on Apr 28, of typhoid fever, Midshipman J Horace Eaton, eldest s/o Maj J H Eaton, Pay Dept U S A, aged 16 years & 7 months.

Died: on May 3, Marian H, c/o Capt Thos & Mgt Stackpole, aged 2 yrs.

Criml Crt-D C. Chas H Cornwell, convicted of abstracting pblc records; released from jail on security of $6,000. Appeal taken to the Supreme Crt.

City ordinances-Wash: 1-Relief of Wm Ready, $50, for falling into creek on H st. The Corp not having proper protection at the bridge crossing. 2-Refund of $75 to Wm H Franklin, for license which he failed to get by not having the required number of signers.

FRI MAY 5, 1865
Orphans Crt of Wash Co, D C. Case of Jas A French, adm of Ann French, dec'd; settlement on May 2. -Z C Robbins, rg o/wills

Gtwn College-Mr Jos King, S J, died after a brief illness on May 4. Native of Wash & in his 28th yr.

Jos N Fearson bought a 2 story brick hse & small frame bldg on Bridge st, between Potomac & Mkt, for $1,760. Wash, D C.

Paperhanger & Upholsterer-Francis Willner, 125 Pa ave, between 19th 20th sts, Wash, D C. [Local ad]

Mrs Hoge, a passenger on the steamer *Sultana*, was found dead, but holding fast to the limb of a tree that had dropped to the water.

The Tenn Senate has offered a reward of $5,000 for the capture of the late Govn'r Harris, of that state, one of the worst traitors of Jeff Davis' diabolical gang.

SAT MAY 6, 1865
Gtwn, D C. Sale of farm near Gtwn, & tavern on Rockville Turnpike; farm-33 acs, belonging to Jas Britt, dec'd. Farm adjoins the farms of Lewis C Kengla & Henry Kengla. On the same day we will sell two 2 ac lots of which Mary Britt died seized & possessed, on the road leading to Hamilton Loughborough's farm, now occupied by Benj Riley; formerly part of H W Blount's farm. -Hugh Caperton, Fred W Jones, trustees. Thos Dowling, auct

Mr Pliny Miles, well known as an advocate of cheap postal facilities in America, died at Malta, on Apr 6, attended by several American residents.

John R Ridgly, of Balt, was fined $20 for attempting to sell goods without a license. Local News

Died: suddenly, in N Y, May 2, Thos J White, 2nd s/o W G W White, of Wash, D C, in his 35th year.

Died: in Wash City, on May 3, Robt Ludwell, infant s/o Perry A & Sallie J Fitzhugh, aged 10 months.

Jefferson Davis is today a fugitive from justice; born in Ky in Jun 31, 1808, the illegitimate s/o Jas Davis, a noted horse-trader, of Hopkinsville, Ky; settled with Jefferson when he was very young in Vicksburg, Miss. Jefferson entered West Point at 16 years & was an 1828 grad, near the foot of his class. In 1832 he offended Gen Zach Taylor by running away with & marrying his dght.

Beverly Tucker, of Va, is described as a drunken vagabond, in consequence of being the nephew of John Mason, of Va. He was born in 1827 in Winchester Va.

Clement Claiborne Clay, one of the accomplices of the assassin of Pres Lincoln, was born in Madison Co, Ala, in 1819; s/o Clement Comer Clay, formerly Gov of Ala, & who still lives in Huntsville, Ala. The son mrd in early life, Miss Virginia Carolin Tunstall, of Va.

MON MAY 8, 1865
To the ctzns of D C: many loyal ctzns are of the opinion that the former residents of the Dist, who have participated in the rebellion, should not be permitted to return or remain within its vicinity, & that those who have approved of their treasonable acts & desire future association with them should be regarded as partakers of their guilt. Pblc meeting will be held May 9 in front of the City Hall. Ctzns of D C, who have willingly endeavored to destroy the Gov't can have no home in the Captial of the nation. Patriotism, as well as our own safety & peace, call for the proposed action.

J F Brown	G W Bushee	Asbury Lloyd	W P Ferguson
N Sargent	N D Larner	Geo H Plant	Jno G Dudley
J A Graham	C I Canfield	C S Noyes	J E F Holmead
W H Baldwin	J W Simms	J H Johnson, j p	Jonas B Ellis
Z C Robbins	C W White	Z Richards	H Wingate
W H Campbell	Wm Slater	A M Gangawer	W E Hutchinson
Devere Burr	M McNelly	Z D Gilman	Wm T Ford
P M Pearson	J Burbank	R B Clark	Chas Baker
Philip &	W H Parker	John H Semmes	S H Sherman
Solomons	B F Gettinger	Benj F Clark	D W Mc_ann
M Semken	J N Ford	A G Alden	Wm H Tenny
G W Goodall	Jas H Ford	Hudson Taylor	J A Magruder
John F Hilton	Wm A Cook	H Semken	J E Maddox
J F Page	A J Raddcliffe	Benj F French	J W Jayne
John R Elvans	Co	J W Angus	A P Thayer
Geo R Wilson	A M Scott	Geo Boyden	J H Gray
Levi Beardsley	M Mobley	A R Shepherd	A Chester
Chas King	Newton	J E Heriel	Riley A Shinn
J W Thompson	Crawford	H D Cooke	Chas S English

Wm H Godey	J L Henshaw	C Hosmer	R H Graham
H G Ritter	J Venable	Saml P Bell	J E Kendall
Wm M Davis	A F Bulley	T E Lloyd	S J Bowen
Fielder R	E A Adams	S A H McKim	Henry Janney
Dorsett	John H Peake	Wm Dixon	John Wilson
T Edw Clark	W S Huntington	Lewis Clephane	
W_If G	Jas H Peake	F A Boswell	
Newman	F A Willet	M T Parker	
Augustus Edson	John Trimble, jr	E Wheeler	

It notes that there were many others.

Robt Chamberlin & Malcolm Jones were arrested Sat, for setting fire to the stable of Mrs Doughty, on 3rd st, between High & Mkt. They were held in $300 each for trial. Wash, D C

Died: on May 6, Washington Dorothy, in his 40th yr. Funeral at 355 N Y ave, today.

Died: on May 7, Grace M, aged 2 months & 2 weeks, c/o John & Agnes McDermott. Funeral from 67 Missouri av, today.

Died: in Wash City, on Apr 18, of typhoid fever, E Ryneal, aged 40 yrs. Remains interred in Green Hill Cemetery, Martinsburg, West Va.

Navy Yd, Wash. Sonny Carr, age 7 yrs, s/o Cmder Carr, was rescued from drowning yesterday. Willie Jefferies, age 8 yrs, s/o Cmder Jefferies drowned.

Suicide-on May 7, August Meyer went to his room at Mr Kummer's, 414 7th st, & severed his left hand. He was a wholsale Tobacconist & his store was at 327 Pa av, Wash, D C. He was about 45 years of age & unmrd. [May 9th paper-August Meyer committed suicide on Sunday by jumping from a 3rd story window. Remains were interred yesterday in Glenwood Cemetery.]

Maj Gen Halleck has established, in Richmond, a Bur of Pblc Archives, & appt'd Col R D Cutts, aide-de-camp, "Archive Keeper."

Russia: The Czarowitch died at Nice on Sun. The Czar, Princess Dagmar, & the Queen of Denmark were with him.

Gtwn affairs: 1-Mr Stake presented the memorial of Cruit & Son, asking permission to enclose part of Montgomery st: referred to the Cmte on Sts. 2-Mr Craig offer a resolution to place a hydrant on Montg st, near Olive, in conformity with the ptn of several ctzns.

TUE MAY 9, 1865

Obit-died on Mar 17, Washington Carvallo, aged 26 yrs, s/o his Excel Manuel Carvallo, late Chilian Minister at Wash for many yrs, & now Chilian Minister to Belgium, residing at Brussels, & grandson of Jas H Causten, our aged & respected fellow ctzn.

Died: on May 7, 1865, at the Navy Yd, Wash, accidentally drowned endeavoring to save a younger playmate, Willie N, only s/o Cmder Wm N & Lucy Le G Jeffers, aged 7 years & 6 months. Interment in Phil.

Died: at the residence of Mrs H A Wheeler, Prospect st, Gtwn, on May 8, Miss Eliz Oram, authoress, late of N Y C. Funeral on Wed.

Orphans Crt of Wash Co, D C. 1-Case of Maria Shanahan, admx of Dennis Shanahan, dec'd; settlement on May 30. 2-Ptn of Maria Shanahan, guardian; reports she has sold all the interest & title of Sarah Shanahan, her ward, & also all the interest of Maria Shanahan, widow of Dennis Shanahan, dec'd; in lot 14 in sq 559 to H Dempsy, north half for $760; south half to M Consadine for $750; ratify & confirm same. -Z C Robbins, rg o/wills

One half of the *Hermitage*, 1,000 acs in all-is property of the state of Tenn, according to a card from Thos J Donelson, twin bro of Andrew Jackson, jr, dec'd.

French historian, Michelet, after describing the assassination of Henry IV, by Ravaillac, says, "that the terrible instability of the monarchical gov't at once becomes manifest on the death of Henry IV."

Dear Friend: lose no time in consulting Dr Darby, Wash, D C: 499 7th st. It will be cheaper, finally, than trifling with quacks & swindling imposters.

Wade Hampton recently ran his sword thru a wounded Union sldr, & it is said his fears of being tried for murder had something to do with his refusal to surrender.

A number of leading ctzns of N Y, among whom are Moses Taylor, Augustus Belmont, Thurlow Weed, Marshall O Roberts, & others, have made up the handsome purse of $1,000 for the brave sldr, Robinson, who, while acting as nurse, saved Sec Seward's life. The money has been received by Mr Seward, & will be presnted to Mr Robinson, who is recovering from his injuries slowly, at Douglas Hospital.

Marylanders in Richmond: Col Geo P Kane left there 2 weeks before the evacuation, & nobody seems to know or care whither he has gone. Gen Geo H Steuart, the former Cmder of the First Light Div of Md vols: presumed he surrendered with Johnston's army. Maj Griswold, of Md, was Provost Mrshl of Richmond for a time, got into trouble, & was sent to take command of the prison at Salisbury. John A Bowen, who was in the Balt Custom Hse under the Buchanan dynasty, held an office under Griswold, & followed him to Columbia, where he became sutler to the prison. Gen Brad Johnson failed as a military cmder, & was removed from the command of the Md brigade & put in charge of the prison at Salisbury. Other Marylanders in Richmond: Thos W Hall & Wm H Quincey.

WED MAY 10, 1865
Cnsl selected for arraignment of conspirators: David E Herold-Mr Fred Stone, Mr Jos H Bradley, & J M Carlisle. Lewis Payne-Mr Mason Campbell. Mrs M E Surratt-Hon Reverdy Johnson & Mr Wm W Kirby. Saml A Mudd, Mr Robt Jas Brent, of Balt. The other prisoners, viz: Saml B Arnold, Michael O'Laughlin, Geo A Atzerott, & Edw Spangler, did not name cnsl.

The assassination: more arrests. The Wash correspondent of the N Y Herald: arrest at the hse of Gen Danl Ruggles, C N A. Expedition under Col L C Baker; detachment of cavalry under command of Lt Pete McNaughton, of Co H, 16th N Y, left in the steamer *Monitor*, Capt S W Morton, arrived at Walnut Tree Landing shortly after sundown. He went to the residence of Gen Ruggles, distant about 9 miles, & captured Lt M B Ruggles, of Mosby's guerillas. Lt A R Bainbridge who had stopped at the hse of his friend, Lt Ruggles, was also placed under guard.

Albert Pike is said to be living in seclusion at his home in the Indian Nation.

Decors, a famous Winnebago chief, died recently at Lincoln, Wisc, aged 133.

The prisoners, David E Herold, Lewis Payne, Saml B Arnold, Michl O'Laughlin, Geo A Atzerott, Saml A Mudd, & Mrs M E Surratt, on being brought before the Military Commission yesterday were asked whom they desired to select for their counsel, when they named the following gentlemen:
Herold-Mr Fred Stone, Mr Jos H Bradley, & Mr J M Carlisle
Payne-Mr Mason Campbell
Mrs Surratt-Hon Reverdy Johnson & Mr Wm W Kirby
Saml A Mudd-Mr Robt Jas Brent, of Balt.
The other prisoners did not name counsel.

New Haven, May 8: A C Eggleston, a merchant of Guilford, was shot while standing in the doorway of his store, by a young man named Andrew Knowles, also a resident of Guilford. Eggleston cannot live. A sister-in-law of Mr Eggleston had received the attention of young Knowles, a matter which caused a difficulty between the parties. Knowles fled on horseback to Saybrook, on the Conn river, & is supposed took passage on the night boat for N Y from Hartford to Lynne, after midnight.

THU MAY 11, 1865
Supreme Crt of D C, in Equity, #314. Mary E, Emily M, & John G Elliott, against Mary A Elliott, widow, & Cecilia Ann & Chas Elliott, heirs of Wm P Elliott. Parties named & trustee to appear at my ofc in City Hall, Wash, on May 24. -W Redin, auditor

Josiah Hackett & Thos Hayes were arrested yesterday for fighting in the streets, & fined by Justice Buckey. -Local Item

Died: on May 10, Boydanna, infant d/o F A & Mary Lutz. Funeral from their residence, 404 C st, today.

Died: on May 9, Jos B Hall, in his 76th yr. Another of the defenders of 1812 is gone. Funeral from his late residence, 374 12th st, Thu.

The funeral of the late Francis Bloodgood will take place today, Thu, at the chapel in the Oak Hill Cemetery, Gtwn, D C.

The 2 Garretts, in whose father's barn, at Port Royal, Booth & Herold were found, were released today on parole. They will be witnesses in the trial of the assassins.

FRI MAY 12, 1865
Died: on May 11, Saml Sherwood, aged 65 yrs, an old & respected ctzn of Wash; mbr of the Meth Chr; defender of 1812; long a resident of Wash City; an old typo. Funeral from the residence of the family, 429 6th st, Sat. [N Y & Balt papers copy.]

Notice-The Rev Henry Renton, A M, Keise, in county of Roxburg, Scotland, Wm Renton, silk mercer, Princess st, Edinburgh, & others, trustees of the late Wm Renton, merchant, Edinburg; seeking Thos Laidlaw Renton, his son, who emigrated to the U S & has not been heard of since 1813, in which yr it is alleged he left New Orleans for Texas. If alive, or if dead, his lawful issue, if any, to appear therein & claim the fund for his or their interest. -Andrew Grierson, W S, agent for the Trustees of the late Mr Renton, Edinburgh, Fiftsenth st, Union Sq.

Mrd: at First Bapt Chr, 13th st, on May 10, by Rev A D Gillette, Lt J T H Hall, of Brooklyn, N Y, to Julia A, d/o J C Lewis, of Hopeton, D C. No cards.

Rl estate sale-Wash. Jos B Bryan purchased a 3 story brick hse on Pa ave, together with a brick hse on Canal st, for $20,500. Moses Kelley bought a lot on 2nd st, between U & V sts, for 2½ cents per sq foot.

Lt Col N T Colby, 19th Regt Vet Reserve Corps, has been appt'd military superintendent of the Old Capitol & Carroll prisons.

Gen Ingalls, Chief Q M of the Army of the Potomac, is to establish his headqrtrs in Wash City, the effects of his ofc having arrived here this morning from City Point.

Dr Tumblety, alias Blackburn, chief of the rebel dept for the importation of yellow fever, has been brought to this city, & is lodged in the Old Capitol prison. He is just as vain, gaudy, dirty, & disgusting as ever. He wears the same stunning clothes, & it is widely suspected that by collusion with others, he procured his own arrest on this singular allegation, in order to add a little to his already disreputable notoriety.

Mrs Lincoln has nearly recovered & leaves for Chicago one week from today.

Galveston papers of late announce that Maj Gen Wharton, of the rebel army, has been shot by a Col Baylor, of the same svc. This is Gen John A Wharton, of Brazona Co, Texas. Wharton entered rebel svc in 1861, as a Capt in Terry's regt of Texas rangers, & as such fought at Mumfordsville, Ky, on the occasion of Terry's death. He was promoted rapidly & at Shiloh commanded the regt as Col. He was promoted Brig Gen on that date, & a year or so subsequently, Nov 10, 1863, was promoted to Maj Gen. He engaged in all of Wheeler's campaigns.

The hardware store of John D Edmond & Co, 513 7th st, is certainly one of the most attractive of its kind in Wash City.

First Sgt Wm Houtz, having been lately promoted to 2nd Lt, was last evening presented with an elegant sword & sash by the mbrs of Co K, 150th Pa vols, [Bucktails.] Presentation was made by T W Chandler on behalf of the compnay. The Keystone band played several popular airs.

SAT MAY 13, 1865
Crim'l Crt-D C. Jas H Turner, guilty of larceny, 3 years in Albany pen.

Mrshl's sale of confiscated prop: lot of ground in Nottingham Dist, PG Co, Md, *Keys Qrtr*, 773 acs, belonging to Clement D Hill, of said county. Hill having been an ofcr in the rebel army. Purchased by Chas C Hill, of PG Co, Md, for $2,500.

City News-case of Mrs Bessie Perrine, of Balt, charged with giving aid & comfort to the enemy. Witnesses: Mr A C Perry & Mr Clarke Fisher, Ast Engr, U S N. Testified: Emily Meyer, employed as a nurse by Mrs P to look after her child. Mrs Harper, who left Balt in company with Mrs Perrine.

Thos A Olive, convicted of manslaughter, in having killed Danl Lightfoot, colored, & sentenced to 4 years in the pen, has been pardoned by Pres Johnson.

413

The remains of Pres Lincoln were to be placed in the city vault in Oak Ridge Cemetery. Mrs Lincoln felt that Oak Ridge Cemetery, a retired & beautiful grove in the environs of Springfield, would be in better accord with her hsbnd's rpblcn tastes than the centre of a noisy city.

Sec Fred'k Seward is recovering steadily & rapidly. His wounds do not pain him now, & the gashes upon his face & throat have healed. He has worn the ingenious steel frame by which his jaw is kept in place now for about a week, [because his jaw was broken,] & he & is getting used to it somewhat.

Hon Jas Harlan returned to Wash City yesterday, from a short visit to Iowa, & took lodgings at the Nat'l.

Gen F P Blair has arrived in Wash City & is adjourning at the residence of his father.

MON MAY 15, 1865

The Conspiracy. Assassination of Lincoln. Coverage of the first day's pblc proceedings-9 cols, with questions & answers. Trial of the accused-first day's pblc proceedings: sworn, John Lee, a witness for the prosecution, of the military police force of Wash City; Louis J Welchmann, do, boarder at Mrs Surratt's, 541 between 6th & 7th sts, Wash, he accompanied Mrs Surratt, a mbr of the Catholic Chr, to svcs regularly, he too being Catholic. John M Lloyd, wit for the prosecution. R Jones, do. Mrs Emma Offutt, sister-in-law to John M Lloyd, was in hearing distance, in the yard, when Lloyd had a conversation with Mrs Surratt on the evening of the night the Pres was assassinated. Mr Lloyd resides at Mrs Surratt's tavern, Surrattsville.

Orphans Crt, May 12, 1865: 1-The inventory of the prsnl estate of the late Jas Hurdle was entered & filed; & the first account of Ann Hurdle, excx of the est, was approved & passed. 2-The will of Adelaide Brown, dec'd, was partially proven. 3-The account of Artemosia Bean, guardian of the orphans of Benj Bean, dec'd, was approved & passed.

A model of B Tyson's improvd Bee Hive is now on display at the Seed & Hardware store of J P Bartholomow, 558 7th st.

Wanted-Land Scrip-Holders of the above scrip, to be located in the state of Va, can find a purchaser by addressing or calling on Jon W Hasbrouck: 179 N Y ave, btw 3rd & 4th sts.

Keystone Malleable & Gray Iron Works-Stanley G Flagg, mfgr of every description for gas, steam & water. Ofc & wareroom: 218 N 3rd st, Phil, Pa. Works, 1,109 North Front st, below Girard ave.

TUE MAY 16, 1865

Assassination of Lincoln. Trial of the accused-Fri. Henry Van Steinacker, a witness for the prosecution, had been for several years in the military svc of the so-called Confederate States. Mrs Mary Hudspeth, do, resides in Harlem, N Y. Wm E Wheeler, do, resides in Chicopee, Mass. G W Bunker, do, with the Ntl Htl, Wash City, for nearly 5 years as a clerk. John Deveney, do, living in Wash but home is Phil, at least his father lives there. Lt Gen Ulysses S Grant, do. Sam'l Knapp Chester, do, actor. [Monday] Mary Van Tine, do, resides at 420 D st, Wash. Billy Williams, colored, wit for the prosecution. Bernard J Early, do. Sam'l Streett, do. Lyman S Sprague, do, clerk at Kirkwood Hse, Wash. David Stanton, wit for the prosecution. David C Reed, do.

Mrd: on May 10, at the Fort St Presby Chr, in Detroit, Mich, by Rev Dr Eldridge, Capt J P Ward, of Detroit, & Adelia English, of Wash, D C.

Died: on May 13, Edw Chapman, in the 62nd yr of his age. Funeral from his late residence, Congress & Dunbarton sts, Gtwn, today.

Orphans Crt of Wash Co, D C. Case of Mrs Maria E Howard, excx of Dr Hamilton P Howard, dec'd; settlement on Jun 5. -Z C Robbins, rg o/wills.

Crct Crt, D C: May 15, 1865. Emily F Wiley vs the excs of Tillotson P Brown, dec'd. Messrs Davidge & Bradley, yesterday, argued the case. Mr Bradley had not concluded when the crt adjourned.

Capt Thos Stackpole: Ship Broker: Rm 3, 2nd flr, Intell Bldg. Wash, D C [Local ad.]

WED MAY 17, 1865
Orphans Crt of Wash Co, D C. Prsnl estate of Patrick O'Brien, late of Wash City, dec'd. -Hanora O'Brien, admx

Assassination of Lincoln. Trial of the accused-Monday. Brooke Stabler, witness for the prosecution, resident of Wash City. Peter Taltavull, do, keeps the restaurant next to Ford's Theatre, the Star Saloon. Sgt Jos M Dye, do. John E Buckingham, do, resides in Wash, night doorkeeper at Ford's Theatre. Jas P Ferguson, do, resides in Wash City, in the restaurant business, 452 10th st. Wm Withers, jr, do, belongs to the orchestra at Ford's Theatre. Capt Theodore McGowan, do. Maj Henry R Rathbone, do. Joe Simms, colored, do, resides in Wash, works at Ford Theatre. John Miles, colored, do, works at Ford Theatre. John F Sleickmann, do. [Tue] Jos Borrough, do, used to work for Ford Theatre. Mrs Mary Jane Anderson, do, resides between E & F & 9th & 10th sts, Wash. Mrs Mary Ann Turner, do, resides in the rear of Ford's Theatre. Wm A Browning, do, pvt sec to the Pres. Maj Kilburn Knox, do. John C Hatter, do, employed at the War Dept. Dr Robt King Stone, do, family physician of the late Pres. Polk Gardner, do. Sgt Silas T Cobb, do, on duty at the Navy Yd bridge. Will T Kent, do. Lt Alexander Lovett, do.

Hughes, Isacks, & Denver: Attys & Cnslrs at Law: corner Dela ave & north A st, Wash, D C. [Local ad.]

Albert A Wilson, dealer in all kinds of Boots & Shoes: 131 Pa ave, near 19th st. [Local ad.]

THU MAY 18, 1865
Exc's sale of lots 13 & 14 in sq 165, Wash, being the vacant lots on the corner of I st & Conn av. -Wm G Temple, U S N, exc of Gen Totten's est. Inquire of Mr Jas Eveleth, Engineer Dept U S A, in Winder's Bldg.

Assassination of Lincoln. Trial of the accused-Tue: Joshua Lloyd, a witness called by the prosecution. Col H H Wells, witness called for the prosecution. Wm Williams, do. Simon Gavacan, do. Mrs Emma Offutt, do. Willie S Jett, do. Sgt Boston Corbett, do.

Geo D Prentice, of the Louisville Jrnl, is lying very sick at the St Cloud Htl, Nashville. Clarence D Prentice, his son, lately a rebel ofcr, has taken the oath of allegiance to the Federal Gov't.

Supreme Crt of D C. 1-Toulmin A Poe, Florence Poe, & Genevieve Poe, vs Eliz Poe & Fernando Poe. All to report to my ofc, City Hall, Wash, on May 27; rg the partition of part of sq 59- & 836. 2-Jos Libbey & others vs Sarah Brown, Augustus Brown, & others, widow, adm, & heirs of Wm Brown, dec'd. Parties named & creditors to meet at City Hall, Wash, May 26. -W Redin, aud

Died: at Hammanassett, Dela Co, Pa, on May 13, age 71 yrs, Mary Montgomery Meigs, w/o Dr Chas D Meigs, of Phil, & mother of Gen M C Meigs, Qrtrmstr Gen, U S Army.

Died: at the residence of Mr Thos Peter, Montg Co, Md, May 15, Sarah Agnes Peter, d/o Sarah Norfleet & Maj Geo Peter, aged 37 yrs. [Dght & sister.]

Assassination of Lincoln. Trial of the accused-Tue: Lt Alexander Lovett, witness for the prosecution; & Joshua Lloyd, witness called by the prosecution. [Wed] Wm Williams, Simon Gavacan, Mrs Emma Offutt, & Willie S Jett, witnesses for the prosecution.

FRI MAY 19, 1865
Assassination of Lincoln. Trial of the accused-Wed: John Fletcher, witness called for the prosecution. John Greenawalt, do. John F Coyle, do. Hezekiah Metz, do, resides in Clarksburg dist, Montg Co, Md. Sgt Z W Gemmill, witness called for the prosecution. Thos L Gardiner, do. Thu-Louis J Weichmann, recalled for the prosecution. A R Reeve, resides in Brooklyn, L I, N Y, witness called for the prosecution. John Greenawalt-recalled. Wm Clendenin, wit for the prosec. Jas L McPhail, do. Lt W R Keim, do. Washington Briscoe, do. John Potts, do. Nathan Rice, do. Joshua T Owen, do. W H Ryder, do, resides at Chicago, Ill.

SAT MAY 20, 1865
Orphans Crt of D C. 1-Final account of Cath V Crumbaugh, admx of the estate of John Crumbaugh, dec'd, approved & passed. 2-Final account of John H Russell, adm of the estate of Patrick Larner, dec'd, passed. 3-Ann Delaney appt'd guardian of the orphans of Caleb Delaney, dec'd. 4-Ptn of Henry May, guardian to the chldrn of Jos L & Mary F Reynolds, of Mississippi, ordered that the funds in his hands be transmitted to the proper guardian of the domicil & persons of said wards; & that Mr May be discharged from all accountability for the same.

Supreme Crt of D C, in Equity, #442. Zeph English, cmplnt, vs Alice Riggs, Jas W Bacon, Romulus R Bacon, John P Bacon, Albert Bacon, Alice H Bacon, Jas P Erskine & Amelia his wife, Robt Colegate & Mary E his wife, Saml G Battle & Henrietta his wife, Chas H Graff & Illinois his wife, & Geo H Baker & Julia M his wife, heirs-at-law of the late Romulus Riggs, Cornelius Stribling & others, dfndnts. Lot 148, in Beall's addition to Gtwn, was sold & intended to be conveyed by Elisha Riggs & Jas W Bacon, as excs of said Romulus Riggs, both dec'd, to John E Carter; but the deed by said Elisha Riggs is defective; bill is to cure such defect. Dfndnts & C Stribling are non-residents of this Dist. -R J Meigs, clerk

Cairo, May 18. The Memphis Argus has information that the rebel Gen Forrest was killed at Parkville, Ala, on the 13th, by 4 of his own men, to avenge the death of 6 of their comrades ordered to be shot by Forrest the day before, for exulting over the news of Johnston's surrender, which Forrest did not believe.

Sale of Old Capitol & grounds; decrees of Crct & Supr Crt of D C; #164 & #1066 in equity; Jas Adams & others, cmplnts & J D Banson, Ingle, & others, dfndnts; lots 14 thru 19 sq 728, Wash City. -Jas Adams, Jno H Ingle, W Redin, trustees

Assassination of Lincoln. Trial of the accused-Thu: A B Olin, witness for the prosecution. Isaac Jaquette, do. Wm Eaton, do, went to Booth's room under authority of the War Dept. Lt Wm H Terry, do, attached to the ofc of the Provost Mrshl of Wash. Wm McPhail, do, regarding letter of confession of Saml Arnold. Jas L McPhail, recalled, regarding letter of Saml Arnold. Littleton P D Newman, witness for the prosecution. Eaton G Horner, do, he & Voltaire Russell arrested Saml Arnold at Fortress Monroe on Apr 17. Maj Henry R Rathbone, recalled. Joe Simms, do. John J Toffey, do. Daniel J Thomas, witness called for the prosecution, lives a mile & a qrtr from Dr Mudd's & acquaintance of same, bro of Dr John C Thomas, of Woodville. Edw C Stewart, do, telegraph operator at the Metropolitan Hotel, Wash City. Fri-Chas H Rosch, do. Wm Eaton, recalled. Wm Wallace, do, arrested O'Laughlin at his bro-in-law's hse 57 Exeter st, Balt. Jas J Gifford, do, builder of Ford's Theatre.

MON MAY 22, 1865
Died: near St Albans, Wash Co, D C, on May 20, Elenor Virginia, relict of the late Enos R Childs, in her 62nd yr. Funeral from St Albans Chr on Mon.

Died: on May 20, after 12 months painful illness, Martha Ann, w/o Nicholas Phelan. Funeral from St Peter's Chr, Mon.

Assassination of Lincoln. Trial of the accused-Sat: Mrs Martha Murray, witness called for the prosecution, her hsbnd keeps the Herndon Hse. Wm H Bel, colored, do, living in the hse of Sec of State, Seward, working at the door. Sgt Geo F Robinson, do, nurse at Mr Seward's. Maj A H Seward, do, s/o Hon Wm H Seward, Sec of State. R C Morgan, do, in svc of the War Dept, under orders to be at Mrs Surratt's hse, 541 H st. Maj H W Smith, do, identified Mary E Surratt who raised the veil, which had covered her face. Surg Gen Jos K Barnes, do, called to Seward's hse after he was wounded. Thos Price, do, found a coat with blood on it in the vicinity of Fort Bunker Hill & Fort Saratoga. Chas H Rosch, recalled, present when Payne was searched. Spencer M Clark, witness called for the prosecution, regarding-Booth's boots. Edw Jordan, do, do. Stephen Marsh, do, do. Wm H Bell, recalled. Sgt Geo F Robinson, do. Jacob Ritterspaugh, witness for the prosecution, boarded in Mrs Scott's hse & Edw Spangler also roomed there. Capt Wm M Wermerskirch, witness for the prosecution. Lt John W Dempsey, do. Louis J Weichmann, recalled. Col H H Wells, do. Mrs Eleanor Bloyce, colored, witness called for the prosecution, resident at Bryantown. Mrs Becky Briscoe, colored, do, lives at Mr John McPherson's near Bryantown, d/o last witness. Sat-Hon C A Dana, witness for the prosecution, Ast Sec of War; Maj T T Eckert, recalled. Surg Jos K Barnes, recalled. Frank Bloyce, colored, witness called for the prosecution, lives in Chas Co, Md. Robt Nelson, colored, witness called for the prosecution, from Va but lives in Wash. John Wilson, witness for the prosecution. Jos B Stewart, do, at Ford's Theatre on night of the assassination. Robt Anson Campbell, resident of Montreal, Canada, first teller with the Ontario Bank.

TUE MAY 23, 1865
Elected commissioners in Wash:

Ward 1-

John Harrison	Phil Hampton	U D Hilton
Saml Duvall	Geo F Kidwell	Lewis H Parker

Ward 2-

Z Richards	John P Hilton	Thos C Wilson
J Miller	Lewis Clephane	John W Earp

Ward 3-

Jas M Towers	A R Shepherd	Chas P Wannall
Saml Tyson	Geo E Whiting	Jas Mankin

Ward 4-

John W Clark	Wm H Hoover	Thos Galligan
Jos P Stanley	Chas Walter	Peter F Bacon

Ward 5-

John Mills	Stephen Wales	J H Richards
G M Oyster	Wm Slater	E T Tippett

Ward 6-

Wm Houke	S M Briggs	Thos P Waite
Geo Hunt	Saml R Turner	Josiah L Venable

Ward 7-

Geo Mattingly	G W Hinton	Jos Pearson
S C Magruder	R H Graham	C C Anderson

Assassination of Lincoln. Trial of the accused-Mon. Miss Honora Fitzpatrick, witness called for the prosecution, resident of Wash. Capt Edw P Doherty, do, 16 N Y cavalry that captured Herold & Booth. Wm E Clever, do, keeps a livery stable on 6th st, Wash. Mrshl Jas L McPhail, recalled. Jos Borroughs, recalled. Dr T S Verdi, witness for the prosecution, physician. Jas L Maddox, do, employed at Ford's Theatre last winter & rented the stable for Booth for his horse. Maj T J Eckert, recalled. Fred'k H Hall, witness for the prosecution, regarding letter written by Lt W Alston-reared in Ala, s/o Wm J Alston. Lt Reuben Bartley, witness called for the prosecution, in Signal Corps svc since 1863, in svc since 1862, prisoner in Richmond from Mar 3 to Jul 16, 1864, Libby Prison-imprisoned until Dec 10, 1864. Lt Col R B Treat, witness for the prosecution, Chief Commissary of the Army of the Ohio.

WED MAY 24, 1865

Jeff Davis' family sent south, Fort Monroe, Va, May 22. Mrs Davis & her 4 chldrn, her bro & sister, & the w/o Clement C Clay, on board the steamer *Clyde*.

Mrs Lincoln, with her 2 sons & a few friends, left for Chicago on Mon which is to be her residence for the present.

Telegraph announces the death of Hon Jeremiah Clemens, of Ala. He was born at Huntsville, Ala, in 1814. Died of congestion of the lungs at his native place, Huntsville.

Died: on May 22, Francis Dodge, jr, in his 29th yr. Funeral from the family residence, 156 Congress st, Gtwn, today. May 25-The cortege proceeded to Oak Hill Cemetery, Gtwn.

Cairo, May 21. Natchez dates of the 15th inst, say that Gen Farrar has just returned from an expedition to Harrisburgh, La, where he captured the entire rebel garrison.

THU MAY 25, 1865

Died: on May 23, in the 70th yr of her age, Mrs Ann Turton, w/o Ferdinand Turton, a native of Pentrich, Derbyshire, Eng, but for the last 5 years a resident of Wash. Funeral from the residence of her son, John B Turton, 123 H st, Thu.

Died: on May 22, of typhoid fever, Fred'k Filius, in his 54th yrs. Funeral at his late residence on 8th st, near Boundary, Thu.

Among the captured rebels confined in Northern forts: Sen R M T Hunter, Va; Lt Gen R S Ewell, Va; Brig Gen Seth Barton, Va; Brig Gen Corse, Va; Col Harry Gilmer, Md.

The following named general ofcrs have resigned their commissions in the vol svc:
Maj Gen A E Burnside   Maj Gen Franz Sigel   Brig Gen Raum
Maj Gen Carl Schurz   Brig Gen A L Lee

FRI MAY 26, 1865
Mrd: on May 23, at the residence of L F Clark, by Rev Mr McCarty, Gregory I Ennis to Clara Cissell, all of Wash City.

Mrd: on May 16, at Bloomsburg, Pa, by Rev D J Waller, Rev S M Andrews, D D, of Doylestown, to Miss Harriet M Waller, of Wilkesbarre, Pa.

Died: on May 25, of cholera infantum, Ellen Boteler, infant d/o John Q & Ellen Willson. Funeral from their residence: 317 K st, today.

Meeting yesterday of 4th ward voters in the Aldermen's Chambers, City Hall: all who were opposed to the ward ticket nominated last week were invited. Dr T G Clayton presided, & Dr John Clark was appt'd sec. Chas H Utermehle was nominated for Alderman, & Messrs M G Emory, Nicholas Acker, & D McLaughlin, for Common Cncl. Mr Saml Wise was nominated for assessor.

Assassination of Lincoln. Trial of the accused-Thu: Voltaire Randall, witness for the prosecution, he had arrested Arnold; Salome Marsh, do, in military svc in 1861 as Lt in 5th Md Vol Infty & srv'd until Aug 31, 1864, was p o w in Libby Prison, Richmond, from Jun 15, 1863, til Mar 21, 1864. Fred'k Memment, do, p o w at Winchester, Va, on Jun 15, 1863 & exchanged on May 1, 1864. Benj Sweerer, do, colored Sgt, 9th Md regt, captured on Oct 18, 1863. Wm Ball, do, enlisted in military svc in Apr, 1862, captured May 17, 1864, confined at Andersonville, Ga, p o w for 11 months & 23 days. Erastus W Rose, do, clerk at Libby Prison. John Latouche, do, 1st lt, Co B, 25th Va btln, Confederate. Geo R Magee, do; John Caldwell, do, reside in Gtwn. Mary Simms, do, slave of Dr Sam'l A Mudd. Elzee Eglen, do, Dr Sam'l A Mudd was his boss. Sylvester Eglen, do, lived with Dr Sam'l Mudd's father.

SAT MAY 27, 1865
Sale of *Howard Grove,* on South river, A A Co, Md; 383 acs. Cause wherein Louisa Howard, cmplnt, & Mgt L Howard & Thos C B Howard, dfndnts. Frank H Stockett, trustee, Annapolis, Md.

Assassination of Lincoln. Trial of the accused-Thu: Melvina Washington, witness for the prosecution, slave of Dr Saml A Mudd. Milo Simms, do, do. Wm Marshall, witness for the prosecution, bred & born a slave of Mr Willie Jameston. Rachel Spencer, do, slave of Dr Sam'l Mudd. Rev B F Wiget, witness called for the accused, Mrs Mary F Surratt, the Pres of Gonzaga College, F st. Rev Francis E Boyle, do, Catholic priest at St Peter's Chr, Wash. Rev Chas H Stonestreet, do, pastor of St Aloysius Chr, Wash. Mrs Eliza Holahan, do, boarded with Mrs Surratt. Miss Honora Fitzpatrick, recalled. Geo H Calvert, do, resides near Bladensburg. B F Gwyne, do, resides in PG Co, Md. Geo Cottingham, do, Spec ofcr. Bernard J Early, recalled as witness for Michl O'Laughlin, left Balt with same. Edw Murphy, do, resides in Balt. Danl Loughran, do, resides in Wash City. Geo Grillet, do, resides in Wash. Henry E Purdy, do, superintendent of Rullman's Htl, Wash. John H Fuller, do, resides in Wash. Thos Cottingham, recalled for the accused, Mary E Surratt.

Dismissed the svc: Lt J H Vanderelice, 14th U S infty, has been dismissed the svc of the U S, & disqualified from holding any ofc of any honor or trust in the U S Gov't, for receiving bribes. Lt R C Horrigan, 50th Mass vols, dismissed for presenting a false account to a paymaster & receiving money thereon, dismissed the svc with forfeit of all pay & allowances.

The Union Light Guard, Lt Jamieson, which acted as a bodyguard to the late Pres Lincoln, will set in the same capacity for Pres Johnson.

Mr John T Ford, proprietor of the Ford's Theatre, was yesterday unconditionally released from the Old Capitol Prison, where he has been confined since his return from Richmond, a few days after the assassination of Pres Lincoln.

Yesterday the Grand Jury of D C presented to the Crmnl Crt true bills on indictments charging Jeff Davis & John C Breckinridge with high treason.

MON MAY 29, 1865

Mrd: in Albany, May 25, at the residence of the bride's father, by Rev Mr Bridgman, T Ewing Miller, to Miss Amanda J Harris, d/o Hon Ira Harris.

Died: in Balt, on May 26, Thos T H, s/o John S & Mary Garland, & grandson of John H Houston, of Wash City, aged 4 yrs.

Orphans Crt of Wash Co, D C. Prsnl estate of Richd S Coxe, late of Wash City, dec'd. -J M Carlisle, Jos H Bradley, excs

Criml Crt-D C. 1-Benj Carroll, alias Bryan Carroll, guilty of larceny, 2 months in jail. 2-Isabella Johnson, guilty of assault & battery with intent to kill, 2 months in jail.

Assassination of Lincoln. Trial of the accused-Fri. Witnesses for Mary E Surratt: B F Gwynn, recalled. Rev Peter Lanihan, Catholic priest who resides near Beantown, Chas Co, Md. Rev N D Young, Catholic priest, St Dominick's Chr, 6th st, Wash. Geo H Calvert, recalled. Wm L Hoyle, resides 58 Missouri av, Wash. Witnesses for Michl O'Laughlin: P H Maulsby, resides in Balt, Md, bro-in-law to O'Laughlin. Lewis W Chamberlayne, witness for the prosecution, resides in Richmond, Va; Henry Finegas, do, resides in Boston, Mass. Chas Dawson, do. Chas Sweenay, do, home is N Y State. Jas Young, do, p o w in Andersonville, Ga & Charleston & Florence, S C. John S Young, do, resides in N Y. John Nothey, witness for accused, Surratt, resides in PG Co, Md. Dr John C Thomas, witness for accused, Dr Saml A Mudd, resides in Woodville, PG Co, Md. Sam'l McAllister, do, clerk at the Pa Hse, Wash City. Jeremiah T Mudd, do, resides in Chas Co, Md. Francis Lucas, do, lives in Chas Co, Md, near Bryantown. John C Thompson, do, resides in Chas Co, Md. Sat: Geo F Edmunds, witness for the prosecution, resides at Burlington, Vt. Col Wm R Nevins, do, resides in N Y. Betty Washington, witness for accused, Saml A Mudd, was a slave for Mudd. Jeremiah F Mudd, recalled. B F Gwynn, recalled, bro of Andrew & Geo Gwynn.

Orphans Crt of Wash Co, D C. 1-Account of Harriot M Sullivan & John B Blakey, excs of the estate of John T Sullivan, dec'd, approved & passed. 2-Inventory of late Richd S Coxe, dec'd, approved & filed. 3-Account of Bushrod W Reed, exc of estate of Wm Campbell, dec'd, passed. 4-Rl estate of the minors of Caleb Delaney, dec'd, entered & filed. 5-Account of Jas Auld, exc of estate of Alex'r Morrison, dec'd, passed. 6-Account of Reuben

C Johnson, adm of the estate of Philip C Johnson, dec'd, passed. 7-Account of Louisa R Joy, admx of Amelia McDaniel, dec'd, passed. 8-Account of Maria Dickins, excx of Asbury Dickins, dec'd, passed. 9-Will of Mrs Louisa Hunter, relict of Gen Hunter, dec'd, ctzn of Wash years ago, made in 1852, codicil in 1858. Bulk of property to her adopted dght, Mrs Marian Young, & her niece, Mrs Emily Featherston Haugh. Will offered for probate in Richmond in Nov 1864.

Supreme Crt of D C. Saml R James, native of Wales, & sldr of the Union army, honorably discharged, now naturalized ctzn of U S.

TUE MAY 30, 1865
Assassination of Lincoln. Trial of the accused-Sat. Jeremiah Dyer, witness called for the accused, Saml A Mudd, lives in Balt, born & raised in Chas Co, Md. Frank Washington, do, lived at Dr Mudd's, belonged to Lydia Ann Dyer before the emancipation. Baptist Washington, do, worked for a while at Dr Mudd's. Albin J Brooke, do, lives at Calvert College, near New Windsor, Md. Geo Booz, do, lives with Mr Henry L Mudd, next to Bryantown. Mrs Mary Jane Simms, do, resided at Dr S A Mudd's & sometimes at her sisters. Augustus S Howell, witness for the accused, Mary E Surratt, resident of Md.

Orphans Crt of Wash Co, D C. Case of Sam'l T Williams, Wright Rives & Franklin Rives, excs of John C Rives, dec'd; settlement on Jun 20. -Z C Robbins, rg o/wills

Trustees of Wm T Smithson have appt'd Wm Hurley, our Atty or Agent to close the trust. -John S Edwards, Chas Wilson, trustees

We will adjust your ordnance & Q M returns. –J Loewenthal & Co, 207 Pa ave, Wash, D C.

Wash Corp: 1-Cmte on Police: reported back a bill for the relief of Michl Reardon: passed. 2-Ptn of W D Cramprey: referred to the 2nd ward delegation. 3-Cmte on Canals: reported back the communication of Messrs Cluss & Kammerheuber, with a resolution providing for the printing of their report: passed.

Actg Rear Admr H K Thatcher, commanding the West Gulf Squad, reports to the Navy Dept, under date of U S flagship *Stockade*, off city of Mobile, May 18, 1865, that Admr Frank Buchanan, senior ofcr of the late rebel Navy, arrived at that place on the 17th inst & surrendered himself.

WED MAY 31, 1865
Assassination of Lincoln. Trial of the accused-Sat. Augustus S Howell, witness for the accused, Mary E Surratt. Eli D Edmonds, U S N, witness for the accused, David E Herold. Mon: Thos Davis, witness for Sam'l A Mudd, lives at Dr S Mudd's. Geo D Mudd, do, practitioner of med in Bryantown, Chas Co, Md, his father & my father were first cousins. Col Martin Burke, U S A, witness for the prosecution, had charge of Robt C Kennedy, who was hanged at N Y in Mar last. Godfrey Jos Hyams, do, resides now in Detroit, Mich, prior in Toronto, Canada. W L Wall, do, merchant & auction of Wash City. A Brenner, do, clerk for Mr Wall, Wash. Thos L Gardiner, recalled.

Criml Crt-D C. 1-Eliz Brown acquitted for the murder, by choking, of Cath Kane. 2-Chas Cornwell, embezzling-$2,000 fine.

Orphans Crt of Wash Co, D C. 1-Case of Morven J McClery, adm of Christiana McClery, adm; settlement on Jun 24. -Z C Robbins. 2-Prsnl estate of Leonard Storm, late of Wash City, dec'd. -J W Barnaclo, adm

Yesterday, Chas H Cornwell, late a clerk in the Redemption Bur of the Treas Dept, & charged with abstracting bonds, etc, placed in his hands for destruction, was sentenced in the Crmnl Crt. The crime was perpetrated 2 years ago. He was for a long time confined in the Old Capitol Prison, & then transferred to the jail of the Dist. Owing to the fact of his long imprisonment; to the fact he had returned to the Gov't the amount he alleged he had embezzled, & to the fact this was his first offence, the Crt sentenced him to pay a fine of $2,000, & stand committed until the sentence should be complied with. The Judge spoke of how his crime how affected his aged mother, his wife & dght.

Orphans Crt of Wash Co, D C. 1-Will of Adelaide Bowman, dec'd, proven, exc ltrs granted to Danl Atkins. 2-Account of M Julia Barrett, admx of Jos A Hastings, dec'd, passed. 3-Account of Eliza M Clampitt, admx of Wm H Clampitt, dec'd passed. 4-Account of Chas M Mathews, adm d b n c t a of Raphael H Boarman, dec'd, passed. 5-Final account of Harriet Le Conte, admx of Harriet C Nisbit, dec'd, passed. 6-Final account of Wm G Ridgely, adm of Stephen Gough, dec'd, approved & passed. -Barnaclo, adm

THU JUN 1, 1865
Nashville, May 31. Hon Justice Catron, Assoc Justice of the Supreme Crt of the U S, died in this city last night.

Hon Justice Catron, Assoc Justice of the Sup Crt of the U S, died in Nashville, May 30.

Assassination of Lincoln. Trial of the accused-Monday. John H Downing, witness for the accused, Saml A Mudd, lives near Mt Pleasant, Chas Co, Md. Henry L Mudd, jr, do, lives about 3 miles from Bryantown. John F Hardy, do, lives in Bryantown, Chas Co, Md. Dr J H Blanford, do, lives in PG Co, Md. Robt F Martin, do, he knew Henry L Mudd & his bro, Dr Sam'l A Mudd; J H Montgomery, do. Tue: Lewis F Bates, witness for the prosecution, resides in Charlotte, N C. Robt F Martin, recalled. Jeremiah Dyer, do. John C Courtney, witness for the prosecution, resides in Charlotte, N C. Marcellus Gardiner, witness for the accused, Sam'l A Mudd, saw Dr Mudd at Rives' Chr on the Sun after the assassination. Jacob Ritterspaugh, recalled. Joshua S Naylor, witness for the accused, Sam'l A Mudd, resided in PG Co, Md. Wm A Mudd, do, lives a little over a mile from Dr Mudd. Francis S Walsh, witness for accused, David E Herold, resides on 8th st, Wash City. Jas Nokes, do, resident of the Navy Yd since 1827. Wm H Keilotz, do, has lived next door to Mr Herold for 13 yrs.

Maj Gens Couch, Washburne, & McMillan have resigned their commissions; also, Brig Gens Lee, Starkweather, Sullivan, Weber, Meagher, Nicholson, & Averill.

Festivities at *Silver Spring*. Francis P Blair, sr, invites, thru his son, Maj Gen Blair, to all the general ofcrs of the 17th Army Corps to a banquet to be given tomorrow afternoon at Silver Spring. It is understood that the Gen will announce his determination to tender his resignation & return to civil life in Missouri.

SAT JUN 3, 1865
John B Wiltberger, near Fort Totten, brought before me a stray mare. -C H Wiltberger, J P.

Criml Crt-D C. 1-Wm Sullivan guilty of assault, fined $10. 2-Otis Stafford guilty of assault & battery, fined $10. 3-Betsey Johnson not guilty of larceny. 4-Mary Murray guilty of assault & battery: 3 months in jail. 5-Wm J Gordon, alias Wm H Allen, guilty of larceny: fined $15. 6-Alonzo H Besson & John Lynch on trial for assault & battery with intent to kill.

Died: on Jun 1, Violet, infant d/o John B & Violet Abell. Funeral at the residence on Va av, between 6 & 7th sts, today.

Died: on May 29, at Alexandria, Va, in the 2nd yr of her age, Edith Arnold, only c/o John W & Ceceila Jeffries.

Gtwn affairs-rl estate sales: lot of ground on Mkt st, between 3rd & 4th sts, to R Marcy, for $1,400. Two 2 story brick hses , #s 1 & 4 on Fourth st, to former to A Yates, for $310, & the latter to Thos Evans, for $400. Frame hse on 2nd st, between Warren & Lingan sts, to Timothy Sullivan, for $1,050.

Died: on Jun 1, of consumption, Rebecca E Thomas, aged 29 years & 1 mo, w/o Johnson P Thomas, & d/o John & Mary A Miles.

Assassination of Lincoln. Trial of the accused, Wed. H Clay Ford, witness for the accused, Edw Spangler, treas of Ford's Theatre; Wm Withers, jr, recalled. Jas R Ford, witness for Edw Spangler, manager of Ford's Theatre. J L Debonay, do, playing *responsible utility* in the theatre. Jas J Gifford, do, ushers were to inform him if the locks on private boxes needed repair. Dr Sam'l A H McKim, witness for the accused, David E Herold, resides in Wash. Thu-Chas A Boigi, witness for Edw Spangler, he & Spangler boarded at the same place. John Goenther, do, boarded in same hse as Spangler. Thos J Raybold, do, has not lived permanently in Wash.

SAT JUN 3, 1865
Assassination of Lincoln. Trial of the accused, Tue: Emma Herold, witness for the accused, David E Herold, sister of same. Edw Johnson, witness for the accused, Mary E Surratt, p o w, captured at Nashville, about Dec 15, & now confined at Fort Warren, Boston harbor. Mrs Mary Jenkins, witness for David E Herold, regarding rent receipt. Mrs Eliz Potts, do, regarding receipt. H K Douglass, witness for Mrs Mary E Surratt, was maj & adj gen in Confederate svc. J Z Jenkins, do, resides in PG Co, Md. Jos T Nott, do, do. Oscar Heinrichs, do, engr ofcr in svc of Confederate States. Anna E Surratt, do, arrested on Apr 17, sister of John H Surratt. Jas F Leaman, witness for the accused Geo A Atzerodt. Saml McAllister, recalled. Washington Briscoe, do. Jas Kelleher, do, one of the proprietors of the livery stable at 8th & E sts. Saml Smith, do, stable boy at Mr Kelleher's. Saml McAllister, recalled. Jane Herold, do, sister of David E Herold. Wed-Hartman Richter, do, cousin of Atzerodt & lives in Montg Co, Md. Wm S Arnold, do, bro of Sam'l Arnold & resides in Hookstown, Balt Co, Md. Frank Arnold, bro of Sam'l Arnold & now lives in Balt Co. Jacob Smith, witness for the accused Saml Arnold, lives in Hookstown, Balt Co, Md. John T Ford, witness for Edw Spangler, resides in Balt city. C D Hess, do, manager of Grover's Theatre, Wash. Henry M James, do, at Ford's Theatre on night of the assassination. J P Ferguson, recalled. F H Dooley, witness for the accused Geo A Atzerodt, an apothecary at 7th & La av, Wash. Henry L Mudd, jr, recalled. Dr Chas W Davis, witness for the accused David E Herold, resides near the Navy Yd, Wash.

MON JUN 5, 1865

Gen Crt-Martial, Wash, D C, May, 1865: Benj G Harris, ctzn, guilty; to be forever disqualified from holding any ofc or place of honor, trust, or profit under the U S, & to be imprisoned for 3 years in the Pen at Albany, N Y.

Assassination of Lincoln. Trial of the accused-Fri. Thos J Raybold, cont'd; Henry E Merrick, witness called for the accused, Edw Spangler, clerk at Ntl Htl. Wm R Smith, do, superintendent of the Botanical Grdn. Jas Lamb, do, employed at Ford's Theatre. Jacob Ritterspaugh, do. Louis J Carland, do. Jas Lamb, do. G W Bunker, recalled, clerk at Ntl Htl. Chas B Hall, witness for the accused Saml Arnold, clerk at Mr Wharton's, Fortress Monroe. Geo Craig, do, do. Mathew J Pope, witness for the accused, Geo A Atzerodt, lives at the Navy Yd & keeps a stable. Jas Lusby, witness for the accused, Mrs Mary E Surratt, resides in PG Co, Md. Mgt Branson, witness for the accused Lewis Payne, lives at 16 No Eutaw st, Balt, Md. Mgt Kaighn, do, svt at the boarding hse of Mrs Branson.

Died: on Jun 3, in her 86th yr, Mrs Mary M Dufief. Funeral from her late residence, 381 12th st; thence to St Patrick's Chr; then to Gtwn & deposited in the family vault of Mr Richd Pettit.

Mrd: in Trinity Chr, San Francisco, Apr 29, by Rev Dr Wyatt, W S Edwards, Ast U S Coast Survey, to Lucy W, y/d/o the late J Watts Beebee, of N Y.

TUE JUN 6, 1865

Having removed to my Farm, I offer my rl estate in Loudoun Co, Va, for sale. -Edwin C Brown, Middleburg, Va

Mrd: at the First Presby Chr, by Rev Mr Graves, on May 31, Jos C Wiswall, of the Dept of Agric, to Miss Florence E Carter, d/o R W Carter, of Wash City.

Mrd: on Jun 4, by Rev Fr McNelly, Geo Moore, of Phil, to Susie C Carrico, grand-dght of the late Jas Carrico, of Wash.

Died: suddenly at the residence of his father in Fairfax Co, Va, Emile, s/o John & Lydia K Waggaman, in his 8th yr. Funeral from residence of Dr Saml C Smoot, 128 Pa av, Tue.

Trial for the accused-Fri. Richd Montgomery, witness for the prosecution, ctzn of N Y. Sat-Jas B Merritt, do, native of N Y or Canada. Sandford Conover, do, resident of Montreal, Canada since Oct last, resided in Balt, & in Richmond as clerk of the Confederate War Dept. Conover recalled on Monday.

Died: on Jan 4, Clara V, d/o F A & Mary Lutz, in her 4th yr. Funeral from their residence, 404 C st, today.

Died: on Jun 5, Hester Maria, infant c/o Francis & Annie E Lamb, aged 11 months. Funeral from their residence, 14th st, near T st, today.

WED JUN 7, 1865

Supreme Crt of D C, in Equity, #422. Robt, Wm, Jas, Eliz, & Jane Britt, Benj Riley & Mary A, his wife, & M Buchman & Martha, his wife, vs Richd & Emily Britt. Parties named & trustees, Caperton & Jones, to appear at my ofc in Gtwn on Jun 28. -W Redin, auditor

Assassination of Lincoln. Trial of the accused-Fri. Dr Chas H Nichols, witness for the accused Lewis Payne, superintendent of the Gov't Hosp for the insane. Chas Dawson, recalled. Jos T Nott, recalled, no particular home since the death of his wife 8 years ago. Thos J Raybold, witness for the prosecution, resides near Surrattsville, PG Co, Md. A V Roby, do, resides near Surrattsville, PG Co, Md. Sat-Leonard J Farwell, witness for the accused Geo A Atzerodt. John B Hubbard, witness for the accused Lewis Payne, in charge of the prisoner, at times. Col W H H McCall, do, in charge of the prisoner, at times. Dr Jos H Blanford, recalled. Lt John W Dempsey, recalled. Jas O'Brien, witness for the accused Edw Spangler, clerk in the Q M Gen ofc. Susan Stewart, witness for the accused Saml A Mudd, lives at Mr John Murray's, near Bryantown. Primus Johnson, do, [colored.] Chas Bloyce, do, colored, lives at Mr Adam's near Woodville. Marcus P Norton, witness for the prosecution, resides in Troy, N Y. Leonard S Roby, witness for the accused, Saml A Mudd, lives in Chas Co, Md. John R Giles, witness for the accused Michl O'Laughlin, resides at 456 Pa av, Wash. David C Reid, recalled. Jos S Sessford, witness for the accused, Edw Spangler, ticket seller at Ford's Theatre. Anna Ward, witness for the accused Mary E Surratt, resides at the female school in 10th st, Wash.

Orphans Crt of Wash Co, D C. Case of Jas A French, adm of Ann Tench, dec'd; settlement on Jul 1. -Z C Robbins, rg o/wills

Supreme Crt of D C, in Equity, #836. Bird & other creditors of Zachariah Hazel, vs Horatio R Merryman, adm, & John H, Richd A, Almira E, & Zachariah A Merryman, devisees of said Zachariah Hazel. Creditors of Zachariah Hazel to meet at my ofc on Jun 29, City Hall, Wash. -W Redin, auditor

It is said that the Pres has determined to issue, in a day or two, an amnesty proclamation pardoning all rebel ofcrs below the rank of Maj.

THU JUN 8, 1865
Result of the election-Wash Corp:

Collector, Wm Dixon	Srvyr, Wm Forsyth

Reg: Saml E Douglass

Aldermen:

Saml W Owen, v Geo H Plant, defeated	Saml Cross, v Richd Morgan, declined
Thos Lewis, v N D Larner, defeated	Thos E Lloyd, present incumbant

W B Magruder, v W W Rapley, declined a re-election

Cnclmen:

Jas H Hazel	Elijah Edmonston
John Tynan	C H Anderson
John A Rheem	W W Moore
Saml A Peugh	Wm Talbert
H Clay Stewart	John E Herrill
Andrew J Joice	Carey W White
A G Hall	John G Dudley
John W Simms	Geo Wright
Washington B Williams	W T Walker

Assessors:

Geo W Harkness	Thos W Burch

Died: at Wrentham, Mass, suddenly, Jun 6, John Thos H Chever, aged 22 yrs, s/o B H Chever, fomerly of Wash City. He was formerly attached to Gen Casey's staff & was a young man of fine qualities & promise.

Assassination of Lincoln. Trial of the accused-Mon. Wm A Evans, witness for the prosecution, resides in PG Co, Md. John L Thompson, do, resides in Md. Dorley B Roby, do, born in Chas Co & raised in PG Co, Md. Wm A Evans, recalled. Fannie Mudd, witness for the accused Saml A Mudd, sister of the accused.

FRI JUN 9, 1865

Orphans Crt of Wash Co, D C. Case of Richard Wallach, adm of Louisa Hunter, dec'd; settlement on Jul 1. -Z C Robbins, rg o/wills

Mrd: on Jun 6, by the Rector of Trinity Parish, Miss Matilda A Barry, of N Y, to Gustave S Waldheim, of Sweden.

Mrd: in Montg Co, Md, on Jun 8, by Rev Wm Pinkney, Zachariah Berry, of PG Co, Md, to Miss Mary B Canby, of Montg Co.

Assassination of Lincoln. Trial of the accused, Mon. Mrs Emily Mudd, witness for the accused Saml A Mudd, resides in Chas Co at the prisoner's father's, Mr Henry L Mudd. Jas Ferguson, witness for the prosecution. John H Barr, witness for the accused Geo A Atzerodt. Betty Washington, recalled, living at Dr S A Mudd's hse since the week after Christmas. Chas Duell, witness for the prosecution, lives in Wash. Wm P Wood, witness for the accused Mary E Surratt, superintendent of the Old Capitol Prison. John Acton, witness for the accused, Saml A Mudd, lives on the road to Bryantown. Mason L McPherson, do, lives near Bryantown. John McPherson, do, lives near Bryantown. John T Langley, do, lives near Bryantown. Benj W Gardiner, do, saw the prisoner at church on Sunday. Peter Trotter, do, lives near Bryantown. John F Davis, do, lives in PG Co, Md. Thos Davis, recalled. Frank Washington, recalled. Tue-D W Middleton, do, clerk of the Supreme Crt of U S. Daniel J Thomas, witness for the prosecution. Lemuel L Orme, witness for the accused Saml A Mudd, has known the prisoner since he was about 13 or 14 years old. Henry L Mudd, jr, recalled. John F Davis, recalled; Dr J H Blanford, recalled. Dr Chas Allen, do, resides in Wash City. Henry A Clark, do. Eaton J Horner, recalled.

Robt T Lincoln, s/o the late Pres, has sent to the Sanitary Fair the original M S of his father's message to Congress approving the bill for the abolition of slavery in D C. It is dated Apr 16, 1862.

The rebel Gen Saml Jones, Cmdor Hunter, & Capt Lewis, who have been paroled, reached Fortress Monroe on Tue.

SAT JUN 10, 1865

Assassination of Lincoln. Trial of the accused-Wed. Geo Booz, recalled. Richd Edw Skinner, witness for the accused Saml A Mudd, resides in Chas Co, Md, has been a svt of Mrs Thomas, m/o Daniel J Thomas. John W Wharton, witness for the accused Saml Arnold, lives in Balt city, business is outside Fortress Monroe. John Ryan, witness for the prosecution. Frank Stith, do. Jas F Young, do, works in the War Dept. Minnie Pole, witness for the accused Saml Arnold, lives in Balt city. P T Ransford, witness for the prosecution, clerk in War Dept. John T Holohan, do, has resided in Wash all his life.

MON JUN 12, 1865

Mrs L H Sigourney, poetess, died at Hartford, Conn, Jun 11, age 76 yrs. Born in Norwich, Conn on Sep 1, 1791. Her maiden name was Huntley.

Supreme Crt of D C. 1-In Equity, #389. Geo W Adams, vs Cath, John Q, & Kate Adams. Parties to appear at my ofc in City Hall, Wash, on Jun 21. 2-In Equity, #421. Wm H Marle, David P Marle, Wm J Ogden & wife, vs Cath E, Frances R, & Frances De Sales Marle. Parties to appear at my ofc in City Hall, Wash, on Jun 20. -W Redin, auditor

Assassination of Lincoln. Trial of the accused-Wed. Witnesses: Jas A McDevitt, witness for the prosecution, ofcr who arrested Weichmann. J Z Jenkins, recalled. Andrew Kallenback, witness for the prosecution, resides near Surrattsville, PG Co, Md. Jas J Jarboe, witness for the accused Saml A Mudd, resides in PG Co, Md, & his bro, Wm, who has a son about 18 years of age also resides in PG Co, [Jas is sometimes called Judson which is his middle name.] Dr J H Blanford, recalled. Anna E Surratt, recalled. Jas A McDevitt, recalled. Thu-John C Holland, witness for the accused Saml A Mudd, provost mrshl of the 5th Congressional Dist of Md, ofc at Ellicott's Mills, Howard Co, Md. Alexander Browner, witness for the accused Geo A Atzerodt, lives in Fort Tobacco, Md. John H Baden, do, lives in Anacostia dist, PG Co, Md. Francis R Farrell, witness for the prosecution, lives near Bryantown, Chas Co, Md. Louis P Harkins, do. Edw Frazier, do, resides in St Louis, Missouri for the last 9 or 10 yrs. Marcus P Norton, do, saw the eldest d/o Hon John P Hale in the company of Booth at the Ntl Htl before Mar 3. Henry Burden, witness for the accused Geo A Atzerodt, lives in Troy, N Y. Eli J Watson, witness for the accused Saml A Mudd, lives in PG Co, Md, near Horse Head.

Orphans Crt of Wash Co, D C. Prsnl estate of John A Sison, late of Wash City, dec'd. -Wm F Mattingly

Died: in Wash City, on Jun 5, at the residence of her aunt, Mrs Spalding, Miss Mary Amelia Cleary, aged 19 yrs, eldest d/o Mr Nicholas Cleary, formerly of Wash City.

TUE JUN 13, 1865
Orphans Crt-D C. 1-Will of Frederick T Wilson, dec'd, partially proven, Wm M Wilson, sole exc. 2-Ltrs of adm on estate of John Ryan, dec'd, issued to Jas Ryan. 3-Final account of John R Minor, exc of the estate of Jas R Minor, dec'd, approved & passed.

Crct Crt-D C. 1-Alexander C Klaucke, of Hamburgh, aged 27, was naturalized; as were also John Laubscher, of Bavaria, & Chas P Hesse. Hesse & Klaucke were sldrs.

Equity Crt-Jun 12: Cossley vs Cossley. Decree of divorce.

Orphans Crt of Wash Co, D C. 1-Case of John T Cassell, adm of John A Cassell, dec'd; settlement on Jun 27. 2-Case of Jas Adams, adm of Michl Shanks, dec'd; settlement on Jun 27. -Z C Robbins, rg o/wills

Died: on Jun 11, Mrs Eliza Gartland, relict of the late John Gartland, of Phil, aged 60 yrs. Funeral from St Peter's Cath Chr, Tue.

Died: at New Castle, Dela, on Jun 8, Frances Eliza, only c/o Lt Col John M & Augusta B Wilson, aged 10 months & 9 days.

Died: on Jun 12, after a brief illness, Geo Humphreys, infant s/o Edw A & Sarah N Gallaher, of Wash City, & grandson of John S Gallaher, aged 1 yr, 9 mos, & 5 days. Funeral from St Patrick's Chr, today.

Assassination of Lincoln. Trial of the accused-Fri. A B Olin, recalled, resided in Troy, N Y for 20 years prior to coming to Wash City about 2 years ago. Mary Mudd, witness for the accused Saml A Mudd, sister of Saml A Mudd; John Waters, do, lives in Chas Co, Md; Polk Deakins, do, lives near Gallant Green, Chas Co, Md. John T Turner, do, lives in PG Co, Md. Jos Waters, do, lives at Gallant Green, Chas Co, Md. Frank Ward, do, lives at Horse Head, PG Co, Md. Danl W Hawkins, do, lives near Bryantown, Chas Co, Md. Honorah Fitzpatrick, recalled. Jane Herold, do, lives on 8th st, Wash City. Mrs Mary E Nelson, do, sister of David E Herold. Wm J Watson, do, lives in PG Co, Md. John T Ford, recalled. Jas E Russell, witness for the prosecution, lives in Springfield, Mass. Wm L Crane, do, agent of Adams' Express Co in N Y. Daniel H Wilcox, do, resides in Augusta, Ga. Jules Soule, do, resides at present in N Y. Maj T T Eckert, recalled. Wm Wheeler, witness for the prosecution, came to Wash on Apr 15, from Lansingburg, near Troy, was resident of Vt. Silas H Hodges, do, Examiner-in-Chief in the Patent Ofc, formerly resided for 20 odd years in Rutland, Vt. Chas A Dana, recalled. Benj W Gardiner, recalled. Geo D Mudd, recalled. Sat-Daniel E Monroe, witness for the accused Saml A Mudd, lives in Chas Co, Md, below Beantown. L A Gobright, do, journalist. J L Ripple, witness for the prosecution, 1st Lt in the svc & was a p o w at Andersonville for 6 months. Rev Chas H Stonestreet, witness for the accused Saml A Mudd, was Pres of Fred'k College, Md, in 1850, then to Gtwn College in 1851. Henry G Edson, witness for the prosecution, atty.

The Funeral of D Whelan will take place at St Aloysius Chr tomorrow.

WED JUN 14, 1865
Supreme Crt of D C. 1-Equity #447: J R Keene & wife, J C Howard & wife, E H Smith & wife, D F Robinson & wife & Mary E Conrad, vs Arther L Keene & John Keene. Question if *Friendship*, in this county, about 10 acs, & bldgs thereon, are susceptible of partition among the heirs of Godfrey Conradt. -W Redin, auditor 2-Equity #350: Martha Deter & Frances C Robinson, vs John A & Wm Anderson. T J Fisher, trustee, parties name, & creditors of Eleanor Deter, dec'd, to meet at my ofc in City Hall, Wash, on Jun 22. -W Redin, auditor

Mrd: on Jun 13, at the Chr of the Ascension, by Rev Wm Pinkney, Edw T Fletcher to Miss Marion Sebastian, all of Wash.

Died: at the Gov't Hosp for the insane, on Jun 12, after a brief illness, in the 29th yr of her age, Mrs Ellen G Nichols, w/o Dr C H Nichols, & eldest d/o the late John W Maury, of Wash City. Funeral at Trinity Chr, today.

The d/o Chas Cotesworth Pinckney, aged 70 yrs, is receiving rations at Charleston. 15,000 people like her draw their supplies of rice from Uncle Sam.

Assassination of Lincoln. Trial of the accused, Mon. Mrs Lucy Ann Grant, witness for the accused Lewis Payne, lives in Warrenton, Va. Jas B Henderson, recalled. Richd Sweeny for the accused Mary E Surratt, acquainted with J Z Jenkins-bro o/Mrs Surratt. Richd Montgomery, recalled. Jacob Shavor, witness for the prosecution, lives in Troy. Willis Hamiston, witness for the prosecution. Horatio King, do, resides in Wash City. Wm H Rohrer, do. Tue-Dr Jas C Hall, witness for the accused Lewis Payne, examined the prisoner; John T Hoxton, witness for the accused Mary E Surratt, resides in PG Co, Md. Rachel Semus, colored, witness for the accused Mary E Surratt, has lived at Mrs Surratt's for 6 yrs. John M Lloyd, recalled. Wm W Hoxton, do, resides in PG Co, Md. Henry Hawkins, colored, do, formerly a slave of Mrs Surratt.

THU JUN 15, 1865
Orphans Crt-D C. 1-Final account of Jas G Smith, guardian of Laura A Stillings, passed. 2-John H Semmes, adm of the prsnl estate of Rose M Harte. 3-Mr W M Wilson adm of the estate of F T Wilson, dec'd.

Died: on Jun 13, Mrs John D Kurtz. Funeral from the residence of her hsbnd, Maj John D Kurtz, 10 8th st, Gtwn Hghts, today.

Died: at New Orleans, on Jun 2, after a brief illness, Dr Ambrose L White, of N Y C, in his 62nd yr. Dr White was a native of this Dist, & a resident of Wash in early life, where he leaves many relatives & friends.

Mrd: at the Chr of the Epiphany, on Jun 13, by Rev Chas H Hall, Dr I V D Middleton, U S Army, to Maggie H, d/o the late Wm M Thompson, of Balt, Md.

Assassination of Lincoln. Trial of the accused-Tue. Mrs Emma Offutt, recalled. T T Eckert, do. John V Piles, witness for the accused Mary E Surratt, resides in PG Co, Md. Richd Montgomery, recalled. J L Debonay, recalled. Andrew Kallenback, do. Surg Gen J K Barnes, do. Wed-Ast Surg Geo L Porter, witness for the prosecution, examined the prisoner Payne. Dr Jas C Hall, recalled. Dr Basil Norris, witness for the prosecution, examined the prisoner Payne.

FRI JUN 16, 1865
Sale of land in T B, PG Co, Md, of which Cornelius G Wildman, lately died, possessed: 230 acs with dwlg hse. Other tract, on Indian Head Rd, called *Cold Snowy Friday*: 92 acs. -Edw W Belt, trustee

Boston, Jun 15. On Tue, at Saugus, Maine, Geo, aged 16 yrs, s/o Gavin Holiday, shot & mortally wounded his father, then took his own life.

Died: at the residence of his father, corner of Beall & Montgomery sts, Gtwn, D C, Wm Preston Bohrer, in his 28th yr.

Raleigh, N C: Govn'r Holden took possession of the ofc in the Capitol yesterday, heretofore used as the Exec Dept, & entered regularly on the discharge of his arduous duties.

Women make a raid on snuff. A number of women & well-grown chldrn made a raid upon Messrs Jas M Venable & Co's snuff factory, yesterday, & a considerable quantity of the "Carolina Bello" carried off. The quantity stolen has not been exactly ascertained. – Petersburg Express

Hon Thos Connoly, M P for Donegel, Ireland, has tendered to Gen Lee a home for himself & family in any part of Great Britain he may select. The generous offer has been declined.

SAT JUN 17, 1865
Lt Gen Winfield Scott completed his 79th birthday on Tue last.

Mrd: at Dunbarton st Meth Episc Chr, on Jun 8, by Rev N J B Morgan, Mr Saml Stinemetz, of Wash, D C, to Miss Mary E, d/o Mr Lewis Payne, of Gtwn, D C.

Died: on Jun 16, at her uncle's, W Gibson, near Bladensburg, PG Co, Md, Rachael E White, w/o Jas L White, in the 23rd yr of her age. Funeral today.

Died: on Jun 16, at Colebrook, PG Co, Md, Jas L Addison, 3rd s/o the late John Addison, in his 65th yr. Funeral from his late residence today.

The property of John Slidell, in New Orleans, was sold a few days ago, under the confiscation act, at very low figures.

Assassination of Lincoln. Trial of the accused, Fri. Robt Purdy, witness for the prosecution, resides in Marshall Co, W Va. Danl S Eastwood, do, lives in Montreal, Canada. Abram Russell, do, is a city judge of N Y C.

MON JUN 19, 1865
Orphans Crt of Wash Co, D C. Prsnl estate of Rose M Harts, late of Wash City, dec'd. -John H Semmes, adm

Hon David Culver died at his residence in Lyme, N H, on Jun 14.

Sale of farm belonging to Mrs John H King, on Bridge rd, 21 acs, purchased by Daniel M Lightfoot, of Tennallytown, for $5,350. *White Haven*, or the *Garrity estate*, on Bridge rd, 11 acs, purchased by Mr J L Carbery, for $2,425.

Orphans Crt-D C. 1-Final account of Robt Britt, adm of Jas Britt, dec'd, passed. 2-Will of Edw Chapman, dec'd, partially proven. 3-Final acc't of Wm G Temple, exc of John G Totten, dec'd, passed. 4-Eliz H McCleery, guardian of the minor chldrn of Edwin J McCleery, dec'd, authorized to invest the money of her wards to the best advantage. 5-Robt Britt gave bond-$5,000, as guardian of the orphans of Jas Britt, dec'd. 6-Cassandra V Johnston gave bail in sum of $2,400, as guardian of the orphans of Jas A Johnston, dec'd. 7-Will of Surg Wm Whelan was partially proven, Mrs Adeline Whelan, sole legatee, excx.

Died: on Dec 31, 1864, in Balt City, Geo A Porter, in his 54th yr. Ottoman Cnsl for Balt & Wash.

Died: after a lingering illness, Katie J, 2nd d/o Jos T & Mgt Ann Mitchell, aged 10 years & 11 months. Funeral from her father's residence on 6th st, between Pa av & D st, Mon.

John G Nicolay, Cnsl de Paris, & late pvt sec to Mr Lincoln, & Miss Bates, of Pittsfield, Pike Co, Ill, were mrd last week, in Ill.

TUE JUN 20, 1865
Orphans Crt of Wash Co, D C. Prsnl estate of Ephraim B Rodbird, late of Wash City, dec'd. -Mary W Rodbird, admx

Assassination of Lincoln. Trial of the accused, Mon. Arguments of Cnsl for defence, Mr Johnson's argument. Defence of Herold.

Died: on Jun 17, Mary Stewart Jordan, sister of R S Jones. Funeral at the Fourth Presby Chr, 9th st, today.
Wash City News. Yesterday Hon David S Gooding, the newly appt'd Marshal, was fully qualified, & gave bond in the sum of $20,000 for the faithful performance of his duty.

Yesterday, Henry C Burnett, formerly a mbr of the Hse o/Reps of the U S from Ky, & latterly a mbr of the rebel Senate from Ky; & John P Murray, a mbr of the late rebel Congress from Tenn, made application at Col Ingraham's ofc to have the oath of allegiance to the U S administered to them. The oaths were administered.

Henry W Johnson, of Canandaigua, N Y, with his wife & 4 dghts, & Danl Walker, of Carbondale, Pa, embarked for Liberia on the 3rd inst in the bark *Thos Page*. Mr Johnson, who is a free negro, was admitted to practice law in the Supreme Crt of the State at Rochester, N Y, about a year since, & has chosen Liberia as his future home. By his own efforts, in spite of the hindrances of poverty & race, he has educated himself & family, acquired a responsible knowledge of the law, & made himself one of the finest speakers in the state.

WED JUN 21, 1865
Died: in Brooklyn, N Y, on Jun 18, Gertrude, infant d/o Dr J W H & Maria L Lovejoy, of Wash City.

Died: at the Parsonage of the East Wash M E Chr, on Jun 20, Rev Henry N Sipes, pastor of said church. Funeral from there on Fri.

Died: on Jun 20, after a short illness, in his 69th yr, Alexander C Kidwell. Funeral from his late residence on N st, Wed.

Assassination of Lincoln. Trial of the accused, Mon. Defence of O'Laughlin & Arnold. Tue, defence of Spangler.

THU JUN 22, 1865
Edmund Ruffin committed suicide by shooting himself. [Virginia affairs]

Mrs Frances Adelaide Seward, w/o the Hon Sec of State, died on Jun 21, age 59 yrs, at her residence in Wash City, surrounded by all her family mbrs, except her son Frederick. Her remains were taken to Auburn, N Y, the late home of the dec'd. [She was the d/o the late Judge H Miller, of Auburn & she leaves 3 sons & 1 dght.]

Mrd: on Jun 19, at Castleton, Vt, by Rev J W Diller, of St Luke's Chr, Brooklyn, Eugene E Ellery to Sarah M, d/o Capt Frank Ellery, U S N.

Mrd: on Jun 20, at Copal Parish Chr, Richmond Co, Va, by Rev Andrew Fisher, Dr D R Hagner, of Wash City, & Sarah Howard, eldest d/o the late Col Jas M Smith, of Northumberland Co, Va.

Assassination of Lincoln. Trial of the accused-Wed: defence of Payne; & statement by Atzerodt.

FRI JUN 23, 1865
Mrd: in Pittsfield, Ill, on Jun 15, by Rev Mr Burnham, Mr John G Nicolay, late of Wash, D C, to Miss Theresa Bates, of Pittsfield.

Mrd: on Jun 22, by Rev Chas H Hall, at the Chr of the Epiphany, Harry C Whiting to Sallie M Evegeth, both of Wash City.

Died: in Claremont, N H, on Jun 17, of maladies contracted in the recent war, Dr Jeffrey Thornton Adams, aged 33, late an acting surgeon in the navy, & only surviving s/o Jos T Adams, of the Treas Dept.

Died: on Jun 22, after a lingering illness, Mary Jane, w/o Capt Chas E Mitchell, aged 41 yrs. Funeral from her late residence, 7th st, between D & E sts, Sun.

Died: in Raleigh, N C, on Jun 19, of disease contracted during the late civil war, Henry Clay Settle, aged 22 yrs, a native of Gtwn, D C.

Died: on Jun 20, at the residence of Z C Gilman, in Wash City, Mary Emma, infant d/o Dr Chas E & Mary Goddard, U S A.

Lt Col Robt Boyd & Capt B F McGraw, of the 2nd D C vols, who were dismissed the svc some time ago, have been fully restored, to their rank, with full pay.

Assassination of Lincoln. Trial of the accused-Wed. Defence of Geo A Atzerodt. Defence of Mrs Surratt.

SAT JUN 24, 1865
Rear Admr Saml F Dupont, U S N, died at Phil; nearly 50 years of svc.

Judge Wm Wilkins died on Jun 23, at his residence, *Homewood Sta*, age 86 yrs. -Pittsburgh, Jun 23.

Orphans Crt of Wash Co, D C. Case of Virginia Whittlesey, admx of Comfort S Whittlesey, dec'd; settlement on Jul 14. -Z C Robbins, rg o/wills

Assassination of Lincoln. Trial of the accused-Fri. Geo B Hutchinson, witness for the prosecution, native of Eng, enlisted in the military svc of the U S from Jun 12 to Nov 12, 1864; defence of Arnold; Mr Ewing's argument on the law in the case of Dr Saml A Mudd.

Philip, aged about 9 yrs, s/o Mr Minrekine, baker, on Va av, drowned near Blagden's wharf, Wash.

Criml Crt-D C. 1-Christopher C Fearson & Wm Garrett: Fearson guilty of assault & battery which resulted in wounding a little s/o Mr Ignatius Dyer, of Gtwn; sentenced to 10 days in jail & fined $50. Nolle pros in the case of Garrett.

Mrd: in Chr of the Ascension, on Jun 22, by Rev Wm Pinckney, Saml H Bacon to Jennie R Langston, d/o the late Wm R Langston, of Balt.
[See Jun 26, 1865.]

Died: on Jun 22, Chas Somes, y/c/o John & Frances L Ober, aged 21 months & 28 days. Funeral from 483 L st, Sun.

MON JUN 26, 1865
Supreme Crt of D C, in Equity, #451. Chas O'Neal, Thos O'Neal, J Hollingsworth & wife, J C Harkness & wife, E M Spedden & wife, J N Davis & wife, & Eliza J O'Neal, vs Horatio Gates O'Neal & Robt M Beale, guardian ad litem, heirs of Horatio G O'Neal, Godfrey Koontz, Calvin Page & Geo Hoskins or Hopkins. Statement of division of rl estate on Jul 1, City Hall. -W Redin, auditor

Assassination of Lincoln. Trial of the accused. Coverage of the defence of Dr Mudd may be found in the paper, dated Jun 26, 1865.

Orphans Crt-D C. 1-Sophia Koch gave bail, $800, as guardian of the chldrn of Chas J Koch, dec'd. 2-J Carter Marbury exc of Edw Chapman, dec'd, gave bond, $50,000, his sureties being Chas M Mathews & Geo S Gideon. 3-Account of Ellen Jacobs, guardian of the orphans of B E West, dec'd, approved. 4-Inventory of the prsnl estate of Frederick T Wilson, dec'd, filed. 5-Final account of Morven J McCleery, adm of Christiana McCleery, dec'd, approved. 6-Inventory of the prsnl estate of Saml Warner, dec'd, filed. 7-Ptn of Geo S Morse, for letters of adm on estate of Calvin O Morse, dec'd, filed. 8-John R Minor gave bail, $3,000, as guardian of the chldrn of Jas M Minor, dec'd.

Orphans Crt of Wash Co, D C. 1-Case of John L Edwards, adm c t a of Sarah C Crawford, dec'd; settlement Jul 18. -Z C Robbins, rg o/wills. 2-Prsnl estate of Edw Chapman, late of Gtwn, D C, dec'd. -J Carter Marbury, exc

Died: on Jun 25, Geo Augustine, infant s/o John H & Mary F Mattingly, aged 3 months & 10 days.

Died: on Jun 25, Frances Almeda Gesner, infant dght & only c/o Brower & Frances A Gesner. [N Y papers please copy]

Died: on Jun 23, Chas Smith, infant c/o Cmdor Chas & Mary H Wilkes.

Died: at Bush Hill, Va, on Jun 24, Helen Pelham, infant d/o the Rev Pelham & Helen M Williams. Funeral at Oak Hill Cemetery Chapel on Mon.

Mrd: in Wash City, on Jun 24, by Rev Fr Hitzelberger, Mr John M Richards, of Norwich, Chenaugo Co, N Y, to Miss Sarah M, y/d/o the late Andrew R Locke, of Wash, D C.

Mrd: on Jun 22, at the Chr of the Ascension, by Rev Wm Pinkney, Saml H Bacon to Jennie R Sangston, d/o the late Wm R Sangston, of Balt. [See Jun 25, 1865.]

Wash, D C. Mgt Martin was murdered by her hsbnd, John Martin, by violent assault, in a house on L st near 6th st. She died on Jun 24.

TUE JUN 27, 1865
Mrd: on Jun 25, at the residence of the bride's father, by Rev Chas H Stonestreet, S J, Saml Bootes, of Gtwn, D C, to Mary Bonner, d/o Thos M Blount, of Wash City.

Died: on Jun 24, Sarah E Schneider, w/o C A Schneider, in her 34th yr, leaving a disconsolate family by her sudden death. Funeral from her late residence, 181 K st, today.

Died: at Tudor Place, Gtwn, D C, Jun 26, Mary Alexander, 2nd d/o M D L & Martha R Simpson. Funeral this evening.

Wash Corp: 1-Ptn of W W Bean & others, & of Henry Fladung & others: referred to the Cmte on Improvements. 2-Ptn of Geo Peacock: referred to the Cmte on Police. 3-Ptn of Amos Kendall: referred to the Cmte on Improvements. 4-Cmte on Finance, reported back the Mayor's communication enclosing a proposition from L Gaddis to purchase certain lots belonging to the Corp, asking to be discharged: which was so ordered. 5-Cmte on Claims:

relief of John Wallach & Lewis Eisenger: passed. 6-Cmte on Drainage: relief of Patrick Brennan: passed.

Auburn, N Y, Jun 24. Obsequies of Mrs Wm H Seward this afternoon drew together from far & near a large concourse of sympathizing friends. Govn'r Seward, borne down with sorrow, followed the remains into the church & then to the cemetery. The pall-bearers were: Govn'r E T Troop, Lt Govn'r Geo W Patterson, R M Blatchford, Thurlow Weed, Jas G Seymour, Geo McGreer, Christopher Morgan, Hollis White, David Wright, B F Hall, & Abijah Fitch. The Reverend Clergy, Mr Brainard, with Baron Stoecki, the Russian Minister, Maj Gen Hancock, Maj Gen Butterfield, & Brig Gen Mitchell followed the casket.
Mourners: Mr Seward sustaining & himself sustained by Mrs Worden, [the sister of Mrs Seward,] & his dght, followed by his son, Gen W H Seward & wife; his bros, Polyodre & Geo W Seward; his nephew, the Rev Augustus Seward; Mrs Clarence A Seward, the Hon Mr Pomeroy, Mr & Mrs Chesbro, Mrs Morgan, Miss Homer, Mrs Weed, Mrs F Whittlesey, & a number of others. The Sec was attended by Dr Norris, of the U S Army. Also, Jas Kelley, Judge Peabody, Jas F Freeborn, Jas C Derby, of N Y; Geo Dawson & Danl Milligan, of Albany; Michl McQuade, of Utica; W S Updike, Saml P Allen, & Fred'k Whittlesey, of Rochester; Col E B Morgan, & W H Bogart, of Aurora, & Spencer Benedict, of Washington. In the family group of mourners were the domestics, Nicholas & Harriet Bogart, colored, who have been servants for more than 30 yrs. [Service of the Episcopal Chr was read.]

Sir John Richardson, the Polar voyager & friend of Sir John Franklin, died recently in England of apoplexy, aged 78 yrs.

Wash Corp: 1-Ptn of W W Bean & others, & of Henry Fladung & others: referred to the Cmte on Improvements. 2-Ptn of Geo Peacock: referred to the Cmte on Police. 3-Ptn of Amos Kendall: referred to the Cmte on Improvements. 4-Cmte on Finance, reported back the Mayor's communication enclosing a proposition from L Gaddis to purchase certain lots belonging to the Corp, asking to be discharged: which was so ordered. 5-Cmte on Claims: relief of John Wallach & Lewis Eisenger: passed. 6-Cmte on Drainage: relief of Patrick Brennan: passed.

WED JUN 28, 1865
Assassination of Lincoln. Trial of the accused, Tue. Argument of Mr Bingham; Nathan Anser, witness for the Gov't, resident of N Y. John Catlin, do, resides in Selma, Ala, printer. J B Merritt, recalled.

Orphans Crt-D C. 1-Eugene Chapin filed a bond, $1,600, as guardian of orphans of Henry Queen, dec'd. 2-Virginia E Daniel gave bond of $500 as guardian of the orphans of Wm S Daniel, dec'd. 3-Final account of Jos Killian, adm of the estate of Leander Shaumberger, approved. 4-Fred'k D Culver gave bond of $5,000 as adm of the estate of Willie K Calvert, dec'd. 5-Accounts of Mary A Greene, guardian of the orphans of Danl Gold, dec'd, approved. 6-Distribution of prsnl estate of Michl Shanks, dec'd, presented by Jas Adams, adm, approved. 7-Johanna Cross gave bond of $800 as guardian of the orphan child of Jos Cross, dec'd.

Died: on Jun 27, after a lingering illness of 12 mos, Mary T Burr, relict of the late Richd R Burr, in her 64th yr. Funeral from her late residence, 3rd & F, Thu.

Died: at Bush Hill, Va, Helen Pelham & Agnes Pelham, infant dghts of the Rev Pelham & Helen M Williams.

Col Browning, the Pres' private secretary, who has been quite unwell for a week past, has gone to his father's residence, in Md, to recruit his health. -Star

Quebec Fire, Jun 22, 1865: the attic of the hse occupied by Mr Jas Tucker, tailor, at the upper end of Diamond Harbor, was discovered to be on fire. By the time the police reached the ground & the feed-mains were turned on, the fire had spread to adjoining hses. The hse on the opposite side of the street caught fire: the Christian Bros School hse & Chapel were saved. The Mayor, Lord Alex'r Russell, ordered out two companies of the Rifle Brig & & 7th F___ & the Royal Artl. Furniture & belongings were strewn for several 100 yds down the street. 130 hses burnt.

Hon Edw Hubbard, of Va, is here making an application for pardon under the proclamation of the Pres, his property exceeding the $20,000 limit of the amnesty. -Star

The Judgeship made vacant by the death of Justice Catron lies between Mr Horace Maynard & Judge Darrell, of La.

Mr Conway, of Kansas notoriety, is in Wash as bearer of applications for pardon from twenty five rebel merchants of Richmond.

Henry J Foote, ex-rebel Senator from Tenn, has applied for pardon under Pres Johnson's amnesty proclamation. Foote is at present sojourning in Montreal.

THU JUN 29, 1865
Died: on Jun 28, Lewis Eugene, infant c/o L F & Mary C Clark, aged 10 months. Funeral today.

Mrd: on Jun 27, at Rock Crk Chr, D C, by Rev J A Buck, Wilmot Knowles to Sarah E Sheckell.

Criml Crt-D C. 1-Mary E & Harriet Berry: Harriet pleaded guilty-1 yr in prison. Mary was acquitted. 2-Philip Smith guilty of keeping a bawdy hse: 6 months in jail. 3-Adeline Harrison, guilty of larceny: 1 yr in the pen. 4-Mary J Thomas, guilty of larceny: 1 yr in the pen. 5-Ann Tracey, alias Ann Wright, guilty of keeping bawdy hse: 6 months in jail. 6-Arthur Dolan, guilty of larceny: 2 years in the Albany pen. 7-Wm Brown, guilty of larceny: 2 days in jail. 8-Patrick Brennan, not guilty of assault & battery.

Among the applications for pardon received yesterday by the Pres were those of ex-Govn'r Vance, of
N C, & John A Gilmer.

The Richmond newspaper states that the rebel guerilla leader Mosby has been paroled, & is now residing at his home in Charlottesville, Va.

Capt Geo A Burnett, of Pres' Body Guard, has, by order of the crt-martial, been dismissed the svc, with loss of all pay & allowance. He was charged with appropriating forage belonging to the U S to private use. 1st Lt Jamieson has commanded the guard since the arrest of Capt Bennett.

During the month of June the Clerk of the Crt, Mr R J Meigs, has issued 153 marriage licenses, 23 of them were to colored couples.

Yesterday thieves robbed the residence of Justice N H Miller, on F st, & robbed a secretary of $1,200 in greenbacks. While Mrs Miller was showing a room that was for rent to one of the parties, the other two affected the robbery.

FRI JUN 30, 1865

Chas McDonald, s/o Col Augus McDonald, of Hampshire, charged with being concerned in some late assaults upon Union ctzns in Loudoun & Fauquier Cos, was pursued, shot, & killed in Middleburg, last week, by a party of cavalry sent in pursuit of him.

David Hill, age 10 yrs, was injured when a pile of lumber near the warehse of Adams Express Co, gave way & fell upon him. His life is despaired of. Wash, D C

Mrd: on Jun 26, at Grace Chr, Balt, Md, by Rev John H Hobart, Fred'k L Trayser to Laura M Hoffman, both of Balt.

Mrd: on Jun 29, at the Parsonage in Wash City, by Rev P D Gurley, John C Hopper, of N Y C, to Miss Sarah D, d/o the late Rev D Van Ohuda, of Albany, N Y.

Died: at Piney Point,Md, on Jun 26, Annie E, infant d/o Jas F & Sallie C Moore. Funeral Fri.

Died: on Jun 28, Mrs Maria A Queen, relict of the late Chas J Queen, in her 68th yr. Funeral from her late residence, 289 7th st, then to St Patrick's Chr.

Died: on Jun 29, Jonathan Balton, in the 59th yr of his age. Funeral from his late residence, 156 Four-&-a-half st, Fri.

Died: on Jun 29, of dyptheria, Theodore Howard, s/o Edw & Isabella J Myers, aged 4 years & 4 months. Funeral from their residence, 33 Second st, Gtwn, Fri.

Crmnl Crt, D C: before Judge Wylie: Edw C Carrington, D A, prosecuting. Thu, Jun 29, 1865. 1-U S vs Wm Rogers: larceny: dfndnt pleads guilty & was sentenced to an imprisonment of 1 yr in the Albany pen. 2-U S vs Jas Keithley: murder: prisoner is indicted for killing Hugh McMahon, some months ago. McMahon was proprietor of a restaurant, corner of 2nd st & Pa ave, & the prisoner was in his employ as a barkeeper. A difficulty occurred between them, & it is charged that Keithley stabbed the dec'd with a stiletto, the death resulting from the stabbing.

Phil, Jun 29: Wm B N Cozens, who is charged before a military commission in this city with defrauding the Gov't in contracts for tents, was today arrested by orders from Wash.

SAT JULY 1, 1865

Orphans Crt of Wash Co, D C. Ptn of Susannah Polton, guardian to orphans of Chas A Polton, dec'd; sale of lot 21 in sq 499 in Wash City, to Chas Allen for $1,830; ratify same. - Wm F Purcell, Judge

Criminal Crt, D C. Naturalization papers were granted to John Lynch, a sldr, Julius Lowenthal, a minor, & Carl Hartel, a sldr.

Sales of rl estate in D C: lease of *Crystal Springs*, with 10 years to run, to Geo T Finnegan for $4,700. Part of lot 9 in sq 568, to Thos Hume for $3,255. Lot 23 in sq 37, to Geo S Parker, at .21 per ft. Lots 3 & 5 in sq 87, to Anthony Bell, for .05¾ cents per foot. 4 story brick hse on lot on E st, between 2nd & 3rd sts, to Henry Dudley, for $7,500. Square of ground, 6th & H sts, to Philip Maack, for $8,000.

The trial of Mary Harris for the murder of A J Burroughs in Jan last, will be commenced in the Crmnl Crt on Mon. Cnsl for Miss Harris: Messrs Jos H Bradley, sr, Hon D W Voorhees, Judge Mason, Judge ____, & W Y Fendall.

MON JUL 3, 1865

Phil, Pa. Jul 2-Jos B Fry, well known composer of the opera, Lenore, died yesterday.

Wash City-on Sat, while Thos Lewis was superintending the work on a building he is erecting on D st, some lumber gave way & he was crushed on the hand when a large headstone being raised fell on him. He is resting at his home at 9th & O sts.

Orphans Crt of Wash Co, D C. 1-Account of Francis S Walsh, guardian of John Hall, & first account of the same, guardian to Josephine, Cornelia, & John Hall, orphans of John Hall, dec'd, passed. 2-Inventory of prnsl estate of Michael G Stapleton, dec'd, filed. 3-Account of Bernard Geier & Johanna E Ruppert, guardians to Chas & Louisa Thomas, orphans of Chas Thomas, dec'd, passed. 4-Final account of Maria E Howard, excx of the estate of Dr Hamilton P Howard, dec'd, passed. 5-Distribution of prsnl estate of Dr H P Howard, dec'd, filed. 6-Prsnl estate of Rachel Dant, dec'd, filed. 7-Account of Ann Crown, excx of Jeremiah Crown, dec'd, passed. 8-Michael Thompson appt'd guardian to orphans of Woodford Stone, dec'd. 9-Copy of the codicil to the will of Cath K Gaither, dec'd, received from the clerk of the Crct Crt of Berkeley Co, W Va, recorded in this court.

Mrd: on Jul 2, by Rev Mr Purington, Albert T Lawrence, of Salem, N J, to Miss Mary E Pierce, of Balt, Md.

Mrd: on Jun 29, at St Anne's Chr, Annapolis, Md, by Rev Cleland K Nelson, John Reade Magruder & Emily Erving, d/o Col Jos H Nicholson.

Died: on Jul 1, at the residence of F McNerlany, near the Navy Yd in Wash City, Edw M Tyler, aged 5 years & 10 mos, s/o W W & Mary L Tyler, formerly of Richmond, Va. [Richmond papers please copy]

Died: on Jul 1, near Wash, D C, Cath S, infant child of Clement & Marian Young.

Died: on Jul 1, Mary Thompson, only dght & y/c/o R Oliver & Hannah M Polkinhorn, in the 2nd yr of her age.

Died: on Jul 2, Edw Pearce, of Gtwn, D C, after a lingering illness. [Kent Co, Md papers, please copy]

Died: at Salisbury prison, N C, on Jan 28 last, W P Venable, s/o the last Geo W & Cath Venable, of Wash City, in the 32nd yr of his age.

Died: on Jul 2, after a long & painful illness, Walter Sewall, in his 63rd yr. Funeral from his late residence, 355 8th st, on Mon.

16th Commencement of the Med Dept of Gtwn College was held at Gonzaga Hall on Jul 1; degree of Dr of Med conferred on: Sam'l S Bond-Pa; Thos Byrnes-Pa; Chas T Brown-Conn; Geo H Caldwell-Mass; Jos A Eastman-N Y; Geo E Fuller-Mass; Jos Tabor Johnson-Mass;

John S Miller-N Y; Geo J Norcross-N H; A Eliot Paine-Mass; Jas T Sothoron-Md; Chas W Stockman-Maine; John C Watkins-Mass; Edw H Ware-Maine; John K Walsh, D C.

Orphans Crt of Wash Co, D C. Case of John S Williams, exc of Cath Gaither, dec'd, settlement on Jul 25. -Z C Robbins, rg o/wills

TUE JUL 4, 1865
Jos Reese Fry died at his residence in Phil, on Jul 1, after a long illness; s/o the late Wm Fry, publisher; & a bro of the lamented Wm H Fry, of literary, musical, & other accomplishments. The death of his bro occurred last yr.

Mrs Sarah Spaulding & her little dght, Annie, were killed by lightning in Petersburg, Va, a day or two since.

Mrd: on Jul 2, by Rev Geo V Leech, Abram F Barker, of Newport, R I, to Fanny Rushmond, of Alexandria, Va.

Corp of Gtwn: meeting on Fri: Alderman Geo W Beal, presiding. Mr Wm C Magee, chrmn of the School Brd, sends invitation to the Corp to attend the school exam. 2-Ptns received from Francis Gross, Lewis Kengle, & other butchers, praying that country people may not be interfered with if they desire to sell produce in the mkt: referred to the Cmte on the Mkt. 3-Ptn of Jos Dyer, for the removal of a wooden bldg near his premises: referred to the Cmte on grievances. 4-Ptn of Wm H Ritter to leave the old mrkt standing was agreed to.

Died: in Phil, on Jun 28, Julius E Hilgard, infant s/o Chas F & Ellen R Stansbury, late of Wash City. Funeral from Ryland Chapel on Jul 5.

Died: in Wash City, on Jun 30, at the residence of Maj J C Cash, John Farr Leslie, in the 8th yr of his age, s/o the late Jas M Leslie, of Phil.

City Item: yesterday we stepped into the Boston Mkt, kept by the prince of caterers, Mr Chas Mallard, on Pa ave, between 17th & 18th sts. Abundance of good things were exhibited for sale.

Maj Gen Geo Crook has been relieved from command of his cavalry corps & ordered to report to the Adj Gen, by letter, from his place of residence.

Maj Gen John Pope, with Gen Smith & Col Morgan of his staff, is in Wash City. Gen Pope is here by orders. Regarding: Consultation will be concerning the condition & necessities of his military division.

THU JUL 6, 1865
Orphans Crt of Wash Co, D C. Case of Chas M Matthews, adm of John A Ellis, dec'd, settlement on Jul 2. -Z C Robbins, rg o/wills

Mitchell & Sons, rl estate brokers. Pa Av & 15th st, Wash, D C. Geo W Mitchell, G E Mitchell, Thos A Mitchell. [Local ad]

Local Item. Youthful pick pockets: John Anderson, aged 14; Thos Crosley, aged 16, Jos McLaughlin, aged 14, Frank Foster, aged 19, arrested on charge of picking the pocket of a sldr in the Centre Mkt Hse.

Geo Hite, Cpl of Co K, 4th regt of Gen Hancock's corps, committed suicide yesterday by shooting himself with his musket, near South Carolina ave, Wash City. He enlisted in Wooster, Ohio, where he leaves his wife & a young child.

Died: Jas A Wise, of typhoid fever, at his residence on 5th st, in the 47th yr of his age. Funeral from his late residence, 4_9 7th st, on Fri.

Died: on Jul 5, at the Gov't Hosp for the Insane, Bela N Stevens, A M, M D, the First Assist Physician of same. Funeral at Trinity Chr, 3rd & C sts, today. Remains will be taken to N H for interment.

City News. Lewis Payne, David E Herold, Geo A Atzerodt, & Mary E Surratt, convicted of conspiring with John Wilkes Booth & others for the murder of the late President of the U S & mbrs of his cabinet, were told they will pay the penalty of their terrible crime. The scaffold erected last night will hold all of the condemned. All to be executed at the same time. Jul 8-Alzerodt was visited by his mother & his wife. Herold's sisters, 7 in number, bid him farewell. Mrs Surratt's dght stayed with her until 12 o'clock.

Died: at Barnsville, Md, on Jul 3, Wm Ezra Linwood, in his 7th yr, only child of Dr G W & H E Bowlan.

Died: on Jul 4, near Rockville, Montg Co, Md, Wm R Riley, infant s/o Wm R & E K Riley.

Died: Mr Jas Dundas, ctzn of Phil, on Jul 4, at age 77 yrs. He was a native of Alexandria, Va, but long a resident of Phil, where he was much esteemed & respected.

FRI JUL 7, 1865
Today Lewis Payne, David E Herold, Geo A Atzerodt, & Mary E Surratt, convicted of conspiring with John Wilkes Booth & others for the murder of the late Pres of the U S & mbrs of his Cabinet, will pay the penalty of their terrible crimes. Orders for executions were directed to Maj Gen W S Hancock, & yesterday, with Gen Hartrauft, visited the cells of the condemned prisoners & communicated to them the fact that they were to suffer the extreme penalty of the law. Payne received the information with stolid indifference. Atzerodt: his feelings overcame him, & requested a clergyman should be sent to him, but named no one. Herold was taken completely by surprise, & a look of solemnity at once overspread his countenence. He had thought all along that his punishement would be a long term of imprisonment. He expressed a desire to see his sisters, & his wishes will be gratified. His sisters have seen him very frequently since the trials began. Mrs Surratt did not appear to be much moved at first, but a moment's thought revealed to her the position in which she stood, & she pleaded earnestly for more time to prepare for eternity, & asked that Fr Walter & Fr Wiget should be called to give her spiritual advice. She looks pale & thin. The scaffold was erected last night in the enclosure adjoining the penitentiary bldg, & inside of the wall, which is 25 feet high. All condemned will be executed at the same time: the ropes will be the best manilla: the coffins, burial clothes, etc, are being prepared in the Arsenal. The 27th Michigan vols, on duty at the Penitentiary, will act as guards. No one will be admitted except such as have passes signed by Gen Hancock.

Brig Gen D H Rucker, Chief Q M of the Depot of Wash, has been promoted to the rank of brvt Maj Gen U S vols. This is a deserved compliment to a faithful & energetic public ofcr.

Memphis Argus says the city was startled by the report that Col John R McClanahan, one of the editors of the Memphis Appeal, had been killed by falling from a window of the Yazoo Hse.

The grave of Pres Lincoln's mother is located in Spencer Co, Ind, near the village of Gentryville, embowered amid the majestic forest trees of the country. There is neither headstone nor monument to denote the sacred spot, and the place where the remains lie buried is an unfrequented locality. A short time before his death Mr Lincoln wrote a letter, expressing his intention to visit the grave this summer, and cause a suitable monumnet to be erected. He expressed the regret that the business cares of life had so so long compelled him to postpone this duty.

Yesterday Justice Thompson committed the following boys to jail for court, viz: John Anderson, aged 14: Thos Crosby, aged 16; Jos McLaughlin, aged 14; & Frank Foster, aged 19. They were a portion of the gang of juvenile thieves who prowl about the Smithsonian grounds & mkt hse & steal anything they can lay their hands on. At present, they robbed a sldr named Goe Haslip, of his watch, while he was asleep in the mkt. They cut Haslip's pocket out & took his watch, discharge papers & a small amount of money. They also robbed Saml Patterson, a sldr, of money & papers, by picking his pocket. McLaughlin has just been released from jail, where he had been confined on charge of stealing a piece of merino from Mr May's store.

SAT JUL 8, 1865
Wheeling, Va, Jul 7. Last night, Capt John List was killed, & Maj McPhail, Chief Paymstr of this dept, was wounded by the provost guard firing on escaped prisoners.

Harrisburg, Jul 7. Gov Curtin has signed the death warrants of David Gregory & Wm Hopkins, for murder. They will be executed Aug 11, in Phil, Pa.

Mrd: on Jul 6, by Rev Wm Pinkney, at the residence of the bride's father, Maj Carle A Woodruff, U S A, & Emma, d/o Chas E Upperman, of Wash City.

Mrd: on Jul 5, at the Assembly Chr, by Rev T B McFalls, Mr Frank Herbert to Fannie, d/o Wm Lord, all of Wash City. No cards.

Abraham Day, a revolutionary patriot, 100+ years of age, has died at Cornish, Mass. [The paper was creased & the additional years over 100 were unreadable.]

Mrs Livingstone, the aged mother of Dr Livingstone, African traveller, died in Scotland on Jun 18.

Madame Kosauth, the w/o the famous Hungarian leader, had died at Genoa, after a 10 years illness.

Sterling Price, the rebel Missouri general, will probably go to Mexico-not to fight, but to engage in silver mining with his bro-in-law, Dabney Garth, of Brooklyn, N Y, & others, who are extensively interested, by recent purchase, in valuable silver mines in that country.

MON JUL 10, 1865
Died: in Wash City, on Jul 8, Annie Mason Baldwin, in her 8th yr, d/o Virginia B & the late H Clay Baldwin. Funeral from the residence of Wm W Moore today.

Died: on Jul 8, Lilly, y/d/o Franklin & Virginia Etchison, aged 7 months & 2 days. Funeral from Mrs Choate's, 471 6th st, today.

More on the assassination of the Pres. Geo Andrew Alzerodt was born in the kingdom of Prussia in 1836, came to this country with his parents in 1844 & arrived in Balt, Md, a year later. They moved to Westmoreland Co, Va, where his father was a blacksmith. Alzerodt was apprentence to the coachmaking business & in 1856 he went to Wash, D C, & worked for Mr Young, & Mr McDermott, well known coachmakers. In 1857 he joined his bro at Port Tobacco for 4 yrs.

Supreme Crt of D C, Equity #419. Rose B Gray & Laura H Stettinius against Wm B Todd & Alexander R Shepherd, trustees. Ratify sale to Jos B Bryan of part of lot 6 in subdivision of lot 1 in sq 460, for $20,050; & to Moses Kelley of lot 10 sq 611, for $239 73; & to P Riley of part of lot 14 in sq 532 for $400, be confirmed. -R J Meigs, clerk

Supreme Crt of D C, Equity #420. Marie Dubois vs Francois Dubois, her husband, claiming a divorce a mensa et thoro on the ground of the wilful desertion & abandonment of her by him. -Wm F Mattingly, Solicitor for ptner.

Miss Sylvia Ann Howland, the wealthiest lady in New Bedford, died on Sunday at the age of 59. She was worth between 1 & 2 million dollars. For many years she was a mbr of the firm of Isaac Howland, jr, & Co.

Miss Clara Barton, d/o Judge Barton, of Worcester, Mass, has published a list of missing sldrs & left Wash City for the purpose of enclosing the area of ground at Andersonville where so many Federal prisoners perished from want & exposure. She has obtained 17,000 head-boards for the purpose.

Wash Corp: 1-Ptn of John Ward, praying remuneration: referred to the Cmte on Claims. 2-Ptn of Lemuel Gregg, concerning a certain improvement: referred to the Cmte on Improvements. 3-Ptn of Thos W Riley for relief: referred to the Cmte on Claims.

Reduced Organization of the Army of the Potomac:
First Div, from 6th Corps: Brvt Maj Gen G W Getty, commanding div
1st Brig: Brig Gen T Seymour commanding
2nd Brig, Brvt Maj Gen Frank Wheaton commanding
2nd Div, from 2nd Corps: Brvt Maj Gen Gershom Mott, commanding div
1st Brig, Brig Gen R De Trobriand commanding
3rd Brig, Brvt Maj Gen G N Macy commanding
2nd Brig, Gen B R Pierce commanding.
3rd Div, from 6th Corps-Brvt Gen R _ Ayres, commanding div
1st Brig, Brig Gen J L Chamberlain commanding
3rd Brig, Brig Gen Jos Hayes commanding
2nd Brig, Brig Gen Henry Bas__ commanding

Ford's Theatre opens tonight with *Octoroon*, in which many of the mbrs of the company already recognized as favorites here will appear.

Actg Rear Admr S P Lee has reduced the Mississippi Squad to the peace basis: flagship *Tempest*, the transport *Gen Lyon*, towboats *Samson* & *Brown*, & tug *Thistle*. 1st Div of the squad placed under command of Lt Cmder E Y McCauley. 2nd Div, Lt T T Cornwell. 3rd

Div, Lt Cmder T P Foster. The vessels *Gen Bragg, Gen Price, & Little Rebel*, all captured vessels, are to be retained on blockade duty at the mouth of the Red river.

Yesterday 5 chldrn of Mr Gray, a feed merchant, doing business on Mass ave, were sitting in the carriage, when the horse attached thereto ran off at a furious rate, & the carriage overturned. All the chldrn were thrown out & more or less injured-one of them, it is feared, fatally.

Rl estate sale of valuable prop: Mr Jas S Hallowell will offer at pblc sale on Jul 20th, his property on North Fairfax st, Alexandria, Va.

TUE JUL 11, 1865
Cemeteries of Wash. Congressional Burial Ground formerly known as The Washington Parish Burial Ground, was projected in 1807; by emigrants to the Federal city; Henry Ingle, Geo Blagden, Griffith Coombe, Saml N Smallwood, Dr Fred'k May, Peter Miller, J F Frost, & Cmdor Thos Tingy, et al. The cemetery was placed under the direction of Christ Church, Washington parish. First person buried there was Hon Uriah Tracy who died in Wash City on Jul 19, 1807. Hon Jas Jones, of Ga, died here on Jan 11, 1801; Hon Jas Jackson, Brig Gen in Rev war, died on Mar 14, 1806; Hon Levi Casey, of S C, died Feb 3, 1807-these three having died prior to 1807 were re-interred in Congressional Cemetery from a grave yard beyond the city limits. Also buried: Hon J P Henderson, Senator from Texas, died in Wash City on Jun 4, 1858; Senator Bowden, of Va, died of smallpox, in 1862. Monuments honor Geo Clinton & Elbridge Gerry, who both died in Wash City while Vice Pres of the U S. Clinton died in 1812 at age 73 & his chldrn raised a monument to his honor. Others-Gerry died suddenly on Nov 22, 1814; Wm Wirt, mbr of the bar, died at his home in Balt in 1834. Maj Gen Jacob Brown died in 1824; Maj Gen Alex'r Macomb, his successor, in 1841, Cmders-in Chief of the American army. Others noted are Alice Mary Parker, died Dec 23, 1861, in the 13th yr of her age; John Walker Maury, died May 17, 1861, aged 2 years & 2 mos; Ann M, w/o Francis Mohun. A memorial was placed over the grave of the w/o Jas Casparis. *Our Brother*-here lies the remains of Geo A Gardiner, convicted in Wash City some dozen years since, as the author of the Mexican mine fraud, who took a deadly potion from his vest pocket & fell dead upon the prison floor after the second trial. Memorial was erected by a bro & sister. John Bayne, then residing at the Navy Yd, was convinced of his guilt, & the only juryman averse to acquittal. The cemetery has been enlarged several times & will soon be 35 acres..

Supreme Crt of D C. Duncan C Clarke vs Anne I Clarke, widow, & Jas L, Julia L, Thos J, Ann J, & Chars W Clarke, heirs of Michael M Clarke. The above, & John P Poe, trustee, to appear at City Hall, Wash, on Jul 31. -W Redin, auditor

Supreme Crt of D C. Henry B Graham vs John & Wm S Graham, & Jas Henning & wife. Final distribution on Jul 29 of Guy Graham, dec'd. -W Redin

Died: on Jul 10, Arthur Grayson, infant s/o Wm M & Harriet Galt, aged 16 months. Funeral from 345 12th st, Tue.

Died: on Jul 9, Miss Anne Wright. Funeral on Jul 11, at the residence of her bro-in-law, Maj J D Kurtz, 10 8th st, Gtwn Hghts.

Wanted to puchase, a dwlg hse on Pa av. -Nathan Boates, Wilmington, Dela.

Died: in Gtwn, on Jul 10, Mrs Mary Shaaff Stevenson, relict of the late Hon Andrew Stevenson, of Va, in her 58th yr. Funeral from her late residence on First st, on Tue. [Richmond & Savannah papers, please copy.]

WED JUL 12, 1865
Presidential appointments of postmasters:

Thos Ireland, Annapolis, Md
John Schleigh, Hagerstown, Md
Wm D Massey, Alexandria, Va
Alexander Sharpe, Richmond, Va
Jas M Boreman, Parkersburg, W Va
Geo Lander, Fayetteville, N C
Wm Ebom, Wash, N C
Robt Peysert, Bethlehem, Pa
Massachusetts:
Geo M Osgood, Cambridge
Wm H De Costa, Charlestown
Newell Sherman, Waltham
Geo W Weston, Plymouth
John G Palfrey, Boston
Adam Hunt, Milford
John M Earle, Worcester
Maine-
Chas T Greenleaf, Bath
Jas M Deering, Saco
Jason Weeks, Bangor
Illinois-
David A Cooke, Mendota
Jas T Corry, Waukegan
Presco Wright, Springfield
Indiana-
Jas H McNeely, Evansville
Jas H Fetter, Peru
N Y-
Harmon Bennett, Norwich
Saml H Welles, Penn Yan
Conn-Edw A Brown, Danbury
Theodore J Dasham, Stanford
Ky-
Jas Howard, Mt Sterling
Others:
Vt-Jas G French, Montpelier
N H:-Chas O Eastman, Claremont
Ohio-Seth Marshall, Painesville
Nebraska Terr-Geo R Smith, Amaha City

Mrs Ann Jane Pritchard, Minersville, Pa
Geo W Patton, Altoona, Pa
Mrs Mgt Sillyman, Pottsville, Pa
Wm C Wiley, Wash., Pa
Geo Zinn, Carlisle, Pa
Jas Bingham, Hollidaysburg, Pa
Daniel Price, Newark, N J
E G Randall, Portland, Oregon

J L Skinner, Amherst
Edwin B Smith, Westfield
Sam'l Raymond, Andover
Edwin P Hill, Haverhill
Geo S Merrill, Lawrence
Cyrus W Chapman, New Bedford
Henry Chickering, Pittsfield

Jas A Bickcell, Augusta
Benj G Dennison, Brunswick

John D Strand, Jacksonville
Saml S Parker, Kankakee

Achilles Williams, Richmond

Harry H Starkweather, Norwich
Wallis Bull, West Meriden
Robt C Noramore, Derby
Arthur B Caleb, Middletown

Jas M Moore, Columbus

Calif-Thos J McCormick, Marysville
Minnesota-Cornelius F Brick, Winona
Kansas-Daniel R Anthony, Leavenworth City

Mrd: on Jul 8, by Rev Fr Walter, Mr S A Wilkins to Miss Martha Bradley, of Wash City.

Died: on Jul 11, after a long & painful illness, Miss Josephine Thompson. Funeral today from the residence of her bro-in-law, B T Reilly, 501 7th st.

Died: in Wash City, on Jul 9, at the residence of her son, Capt B F Sands, U S N, Mrs Rebecca Sands, in the 81st yr of her age. Balt papers please copy.

Applications for pardon, up to Jul 8, were grads of West Point, or formerly attached to the U S army: none have been pardoned yet:

From Va:

Jos R R Anderson	Edw Johnson	G A Thompson
L L Fauntleroy	G W Lay	T G Williams
Wm Gilham	Richd B Lee	G E Pickett
J L Goode	L L Lowman	
Frank Huger	A L M Rust	

Others:

N C: T H Hoomes
Tenn: R _ Fain Marshal

Tenn: T Polk
Alabama: J L White

Md: E Boyd
Texas: T L Roped

No state given:

J M Barton	Geo Deas	A B Montgomery
Wm N R Beal	J W Frazer	S P Moore
W L Cabell	A M Haskill	E B D Riley
Chas C Campbell	S Marmaduke	Chas G Rogers

Following applicants for a pardon were educated at the U S Naval School, or formerly attached to the U S Navy: none pardoned yet:

From Va:

Wm Burnett	J S Henderson	C B Poindexter
John M Brooke	R W Hunter	Wm Sharp
Geo W City	T Alphonso Jackson	W B Sinclair
F Chatard	C W Jordon	Wm L Smith
A M DeBree	C H Kennedy	A S Taylor
John DeBree	S S Lee	E C Thornberry
R J Freeman	Chas H Leady	John K Tucker
_ B Fairfax	H H Lewis	H B Tyler
French Forrest	R P Loyall	W E Wisham
Jas F Harrison	Geo Minor	
W D Harrison	Hugh N Page	

Alabama-3:

A L Bradford

C F Tabs

Joel S Kennard

Florida-2:

W W J Keely

John R Mitchell

Md-2:

Chas H McBlair
Tenn-1: Geo A Howard
La-1: W W Hunter

J Ernest Meicer
Ga-1: Chas J Graves
N Y-1: W H Parker

No state given-2:

John H Parker

J W Cooke

Ex-Govn'r John Letcher, of Va, has been released from the Old Capitol prison by direction of Pres Johnson, upon the condition that he go immediately to his home in Va, & give his parole to remain there subject to the order of the Pres.

THU JUL 13, 1865

Wigwam for sale, situated at 339 G st, Wash City. -J K Rogers & Co

Orphans Crt of Wash Co, D C. Prsnl estate of Wm Ford, late of Wash City, dec'd. -Lucinda A Ford, Admx, w a

Supreme Crt of D C. Ratify sale of part of lot 3 in sq 784 to A Schwartz for $732; & part of lot 8 in sq 758 to Wm H Harrington for $652 02. -R J Meigs, clerk

Present to the captor of the assassins Booth & Herold. Pair of Colt's pistols on exhibition at Messrs Galt & Bros, jewellers, inscribed: *Presented to Captain E P Doherty, 16th N Y cavalry, the captor of the assassins Booth and Herold. By the officers of the regiment.* [Rosewood & maple, studded with mother of pearl]

Mrd: on Jul 12, by Rev Dr Samson, Aquilla R Allen, of Wash City, to Annie E Johnstone, of Petersburg, Va. [Petersburg & Norfolk papers please copy.]

Died: on Jul 12, Maria Louisa, y/d/o Geo F & G L M Raub. Funeral from the residence of her parents, C & 15th st, Thu.

Died: at Wash City, D C, on Jul 11, Nannie W, w/o Maj E W Dennis.

FRI JUL 14, 1865
Orphans Crt of Wash Co, D C. Case of Maria Uhlmann, admx of Chas J Uhlmann, dec'd; settlement on Aug 8. -Z C Robbins, rg o/wills

Another child brutally ravished in Mass: Boston, Jul 13. Alice Burns, who attended a picnic in Weston yesterday, was seduced away from her young companions & brutally ravished by 3 ruffians, aged 17 to 21 yrs, named Richd C Bains, Robt Lambert, & John McGuerny. The have been arrested. Alice was found by her friends in a perfectly insensible state. She still remains in a very critical condition.

M Bannon, trustee, sold a few days ago a farm of 361 acs on South river, A A Co, Md, to J S Hall, Bangor, Maine, for $6,500; also a farm of 100 acs at St Jas, Howard Co, to M Vaughan, of Balt, for $2,300.

Presidential appointments of postmasters:
Geo Hill jr, Gtwn, D C
Jas T Pritchard, Lynchburg, Va
Warren W Whig, Norfolk, Va
David Emery, New Castle, Pa
Peter Heck, Uniontown, Pa
Wm M Briner, Reading, Pa
Jonathan Jessop, York, Pa
Ephraim S Jackson, Providence, R I
Edw Perrin, Pawtucket, R I
Thos Coggeshall, Newport, R I
Daniel J Clark, Manchester, N H
Geo A Benedict, Cleveland, Ohio
Jesse B Webb, Salem, Ohio
Geo Rowland, Sacramento city, Calif
F J Jackson, Appleton, Wisc
Danl Bassett, Minneapolis, Minn
Thos M Hogan, Columbus, Ga

Richd Price, well known business man for nearly half a century, of Phil, died at his residence on Arch st, on Jul 8, after an illness of some months. -Phil Ledger

SAT JUL 15, 1865
Supreme Crt of D C, in Equity, #273. Garity vs Garity. Ratify sale by R P Jackson, trustee for Patrick Garity, dec'd. -R J Meigs, clerk

Died: at Leonardtown, St Mary's Co, Md, on Jul 7, of bilious fever, Mrs Sarah A Heard, relict of Jas M Heard, aged about 35 yrs.

Died: on Jul 14, Otho Boswell jr, in his 33rd yr. Funeral from 7th st Presby Chr Sunday.

A passenger on the steamer *Cuba*, which sailed from N Y on Jul 12, for Europe, was our young townsman, Mr R Ross Perry. He is probably the youngest person who ever received the degree of A M from Gtwn College at its annual commencement held on Jul 3.

Brig Gen W T Bartlett, commanding the 1st div, 9th corps, has, at his own request, been relieved of the command, & ordered to report, from his home, to the Adj Gen.

MON JUL 17, 1865
St Peter's Sunday School: [Catholic] Capitol Hill: Jul 17: Medals to:

Jas Boudran	Maggie Howell	Annie Conway
John Moss	Sarah Luxon	Jas Boudan
Alice Smith	Mary Kilfoil	Maggie Howell
Sarah Greenwell	Va Waters	
Augusta Meade	Cora Hutchinson	

Mrd: on Jul 11, at the residence of Conway Robinson, in D C, by Rev Jas A Buck, Mr John Milledge, jr, of Augusta, Ga, to Miss Fanny Conway Robinson, of Va, d/o the late Edwin Robinson.

Wash Corp: 1-Ptn of Francis F Cook: referred to the Cmte on Claims. 2-Ptn of Wm Bagnam for a certain privilege: referred to the Cmte on Police. 3-Ptn of John McCallum & others, asking that curbstones be set on sqs 786 & 816: referred to the Cmte on Improvements. 4-Ptn of E L Stevens & others for a brick side-pavement south side of Md ave: referred to the Cmte on Improvements.

B F Rittenhouse promoted from a 4th class to the Chief clerkship of the Register's Ofc, Treas Dept.

Mr Chas Jas Jeffries, the author of "Jeannette & Jeannot," a popular song a dozen years ago, died recently in London.

Pres Lincoln's funeral cost Washington $25,000.

TUE JUL 18, 1865
Orphans Crt of Wash Co, D C. 1-Case of Wm G Moore, exc of Rosanna D Coons, dec'd; settlement on Aug 8. -Z C Robbins, rg o/wills 2-Prsnl estate of Mary M Dufief, late of Wash City, D C, dec'd. -Saml Fowler, adm

Died: on Jul 17, aged 7 months & 17 days, Fannie Naomi, infant d/o John W & Eliza K Dick. Funeral from their residence, 206 N Y av, tomorrow.

Female physicians in Phil: 23 students have just graduatd from the Female Med College of Pa, which institution is now in the 16th yr of its existence. The Phil N American says there are some 6 or 8 female physicians in that city whose daily practice is equal to that of the average of male physicians. One of them keeps 3 horses in constant use.

Died: in Lowell, Jul 9, Jos Manahan, until recently & for many years a clerk of the U S Treas Dept, Wash, aged 68 yrs.

WED JUL 19, 1865

Orphans Crt of Wash Co, D C. 1-Distribution of the net proceeds of the estate of Comfort S Whittlesey, dec'd, amounting to $13,616.22 approved. 2-Resignation of F Golden, an excs of the estate of Cath Golden, was accepted, & Robt A Golden appt'd in his place. 3-Distribution of the estates of J J Fink, dec'd, $359.71, & Sarah C Crawford, dec'd, $3,174.55, both approved. 4-Eliz J Folsom was appt'd guardian of Maria E Folsom. The will of Cath Golden, & that of Christy Robinson, were admited to record.

Orphans Crt of Wash Co, D C. 1-Case of Sophia Ridgely, admx of Wm G Ridgely, dec'd; settlement on Aug 12. 2-Case of Conrad Finkmann, exc of Henry S Ward, dec'd; settlement on Aug 12. 3-Case of Eliza Jane O'Neal, admx of Horatio G O'Neal, dec'd; settlement on Aug 8. -Z C Robbins, rg o/wills

Died: on Jul 7, in his 54th yr, at Chester, Morris Co, N J, E M Topping, formerly Prof of Languages at Princeton College, but for the last 18 years a resident of Balt.

Madame Eliza B Jumel, widow of Aaron Burr, died on Sunday last, at Washington Hghts, N Y, aged over 90 yrs. She was mrd in early life to M Jumel, who died leaving her with one child. Her property is probably left to her grandchldrn, the chldrn of her dght. -N Y Post, 17th [See Jul 21st paper.]

Cairo, Jul 15. Maj Putnam, of Gen Canby's staff, has arrived here, on his way to Wash, with the flags surrendered by Gen Dick Taylor.

Ltr from a prominent Union Man, recently from Texas, now a resident of Missouri, settles a disputed question: Sam Houston is dead. The Union men of Texas lament his loss. He died of a broken heart. The secessionists hung upon his trail from the day he was deposed. The newspapers of Texas endeavored to convince the world that the old hero of San Jacinto had changed his opinions, but he died as he lived, loving the Union, & not convinced as they would will.

THU JUL 20, 1865

Verdict in the case of Miss Mary Harris, who was charged with the murder of Adoniram J Burroughs, was concluded yesterday. Verdict: not guilty.

Crct Crt of PG Co, Md, Crt of Equity, #474. Jas Woods vs Nabley Woods. Decree to divorce the cmplnt from the dfndnt. The cmplnt is a resident of PG Co, Md, & has resided in said county for 5 yrs; intermrd during 1855 with the dfndnt. On or about Jul 10 of same year, his wife for over 3 years uninterrupted. -Fred'k Sasscer, clerk-PG Co, Md

Died: on Jul 18, at Providence Hosp, Jared A Ford, formerly of Hagerstown, Md, in his 28th yr. The dec'd was formerly an attache of this ofc. A wide circle of friends lament his early death. Funeral at St Peter's Chr, Capitol Hill, Thu.

Died: on Jul 19, Eliza A Tyler, d/o J B & Caroline Greenwell, aged 22 yrs. She leaves 3 chldrn to mourn her loss. Funeral from the residence of her father, 167 F st, Thu.

Died: at the residence of Mrs Richard Smith, on Jul 19, Mrs Mary E Allen, in her 76th yr. Funeral from St Matthew's Chr, Thu.

Gtwn Affairs. The John Gibson, Capt Kelley, of the Atlantic Steamship Co's line, sailed from Snow's Wharf yesterday, & the following is her list of passengers:

Mr & Mrs Arny & family	Miss J Adams	Dr Worcester
Mrs McKay & lady	Mrs McLane	C H Gates
Miss Forrest	J W Clarke	Jas Hanly
Miss Sprague	H H McPherson	W H Haight
Mr R A Shinn	Mr F A Miller	
	W H Swords	

Of Gtwn College

Rev B Sestini, S J	H Early, S J	Rev Mr Hubert, S J
P F Finnegan, S J	Jos A Nolan, S J	

FRI JUL 21, 1865

Died: Edwin Harriman, on Jul 20 at Providence Hosp, Wash City, in his 56th yr, after an illness of 6 mos; native of Haverhill, Mass. Funeral from the hospital on Fri.

Died: on Jul 20, Rose, y/d/o Wm E & Maria P Spalding, aged 5 months & 20 days. Funeral from the residence of Wm E Spalding, 15th st, today.

Boston, Jul 20. The w/o Gen Ewell proceeded to Fort Warren yesterday, with an order from Pres Johnson for the release of her hsbnd. On taking the oath of allegiance he was liberated, & both left for the south last evening.

Duties confided to the following ofcrs:

At Portsmouth, N H, Paymstr C J Emery	At San Francisco, Cal, Paymstr E C Doran
At Boston, Msss, Paymstr R H Clark	
At Balt, Md, Paymstr E T Dunn	

Our ctzns will be surprised to learn that Mr A S Clark, formerly of Missouri, who has been in Wash City of late yrs, & connected with reputable gentlemen in the prosecuting of claims against the Gov't, has suddenly left the city just as facts are made known that he has been guilty of forging the names of Capt Van Camp & Mr Mehan, clerk of the Capitol, whereby he raised some hundreds of dollars in money. Other persons are sufferers as endorsers, etc. Mr Riggs & Lewis Johnson & Co are losers by forgeries. He left the city early yesterday morning.

Miss Mary Harris, acquitted for the murder of Mr A J Burroughs, in the Crmnl Crt on Wed, left the city yesterday for Balt, & after a short sojourn there she will leave for the west.

Madame Eliza B Jumel died yesterday at her residence on Washington Hghts. Her decease was not unexpected; age & feebleness had done their work, & dissolution had been imminent for a long time. She was mrd in early life to M Jumel, a French gentleman, who died leaving her with one child. Later her singular marriage with Aaron Burr brought her into pblc notice. They were mrd about the yr 1832, but the alliance was soon followed by separation. Since that time she has lived at her residence on Washington Hghts. She resumed the name of her previous husband many years since. She owned a considerable tract of rl estate on this island. Her property is probably left to her grandchldrn, the chldrn of her dght. -N Y Post, 17th [See Jul 19th paper.]

Morristown, N J, Jul 18. Peter Cu_uel, recently convicted of the murder of his wife, has been sentenced to be executed on Nov 24. Application for a new trial has been heard.

SAT JUL 22, 1865

Died: Rt Rev Alonzo Potter, in San Fran, on Jul 4; 6 days before his 65th yr. He was born in Dutchess Co, N Y, & bro/o Bishop Potter of N Y diocese. Three of his sons, Gen Robt R Potter, Howard Potter, Clarkson A Potter, are in professional & commercial life in N Y C.

Died: Geo Shoemaker, age 73 yrs, at the residence of his son-in-law, Coates Walton, in Phil on Jul 20. For the past 46 years Mr Shoemaker was an inspector of flour for the port of Gtwn, D C. Funeral from his late residence, 141 West st, Gtwn, D C, on Jul 22. To proceed to Oak Hill Cemetery.

Mt Vernon: originally one-half of 5,000 acs assigned to Washington's great-grandfather, who in conjunction with Nicholas Spencer patented it from Lord Culpeper in 1670. In division of his estate the father of Washington assigned this tract of his estate to his elder bro Lawrence. Lawrence died in 1752 leaving his wife the d/o Sir Wm Fairfax, of Belvoir, & 1 child-a dght, who died w/out issue. The estate fell to Geo Washington. In 1759 Geo mrd Mrs Martha [nee Dandridge] Custis, mother of 2 chldrn. Geo & Martha were both 27 years of age at their marriage. In his will Washington divided the estate into 3 parts: mansion with 4,000 acs left to his nephew Bushrod Washington, an Assoc Justice of the U S Sup Crt. At the death of Mrs Washington, in 1801, Judge Washington became the proprietor of Mt Vernon-til his death in 1829. He being mrd to Anne, d/o Col Thos Blackburn. Having no issue, the estate was left to his nephew, John A Washington, from whom the Ladies Mt Vernon Assoc purchased the mansion, tomb & 200 acs for $200,00. Woodlawn estate was given to Maj Lawrence Lewis, a nephew, whose wife was Nelly Custis, grand-child of Mrs Washington & adopted d/o Gen Washington. Maj Lewis erected Woodlawn in 1805 at a cost of $24,000. Maj Lewis, s/o Betty Washington Lewis, sister of Geo Washington, died at Arlington in 1841 & his wife died in 1852. The remains of both, with those of a dght, the w/o Chas M Conrad, Fillmore's War Sec, being deposited in the Mt Vernon vault. Woodlawn estate was sold by his only son Lorenzo Lewis, to a colony of Quakers from N J. The mansion now belongs to John Mason who came there from N H in 1850. Lorenzo Lewis died some years ago in Clark Co, & the other dght, the w/o Mr Butler, is living in Mississippi. John A Washington went to Fauquier Co with his family in 1860 to a farm called Wareland. His wife died soon after. He fell as colonel of a rebel regt in 1861, leaving 7 chldrn. These chldrn inherited some 1,000 acs near Mt Vernon mansion. In 1831 a new vault was erected & the remains transferred. The tomb of Washington was held sacred on both sides during the scourge of the rebellion.

Postmstrs appt'd: Chas Williams-Fredericksburg, Spottsylvania Co, Va.
Henry Massie-Charlottesville, Albemarle Co, Va.
Thos G Simms vice Thos C Howard-Atlanta, Fulton Co, Ga.
Pleasant M Compton-Milledgeville, Baldwin Co, Ga.
J H R Washington-Macon, Bibb Co, Ga.
Henry Burham vice W J Windham-Huntsville, Madison Co, Ala.
W J Bibb vice Thos Welsh-Montgomery, Montg Co, Ala.
Joshua Jones-Trenton, N J [re-appt'd]
John T Jenkins-New Brunswick, N J [do]
D R Lathrop-Montrose, Pa, [do]
Jas R Magie vice Jos E Wyne-Macomb, McDonough Co, Ill.
Gordon Farmer vice Peter M Reynolds-Hoboken, N J.

Died: at Montrese, Montg Co, Md, on Jul 21, Georgia Murphey, infant d/o Geo W & Virginia Harrison, aged 1 yr & 8 months. Funeral from the residence of her grandfather, Thos Smith, 8 Water st, Alexandria, Jul 22.

MON JUL 24, 1865

Orphans Crt of Wash Co, D C. Case of Lt Col Lorenzo Sitgreaves, adm w a of Gen Thos Jessup, dec'd; settlement on Aug 15. -Z C Robbins, rg o/wills

Died: on Jul 21, Jas H, infant s/o Jas H & Virginia D McKenney, aged 9 months & 14 days.

Died: at his residence on Jul 22, Hamilton Loughborough, in the 59th yr of his age. Funeral from Trinity Chr, Gtwn, Tue.

Died: at Pulaski, Oswego Co, N Y, on Jul 22, of bilious fever, Eliza, w/o J T Stevens, aged 31 yrs.

Died: on Jul 23, Ellen Young, aged 46 yrs. Funeral from the residence of her son-in-law, Geo W Dant, 549 Md av, on Mon.

The funeral of the late Patrick McKenna, an old & respected ctzn of the 5th ward, took place yesterday from his late residence on Pa av; then to St Peter's Chr, Wash City, & then to Mt Olivet Cemetery.

Orphans Crt-D C. 1-Account of Richard P Jackson, guardian to Mary J, Ann M, & Ellen R Jones, orphans of Thos S Jones, dec'd, approved & passed.
2-Ratify sale of rl estate of orphans of John Brereton, dec'd, by Eliza A Drane, their guardian by Aug 15 next.
3-Account of Mary A Donn & Johny Donn, adms of the estate of Thos C Donn, dec'd, approved & passed.
4-Ptn of Emily Featherston Haugh for appointment of Richd Wallach as adm w a of Louisa Hunter, dec'd, was filed.
5-The last will of Saml Lusby, dec'd, was filed for probate.
6-Maj Franz Passagger, Co L, 1st N Y Cavalry, granted letters of adm on prnsl estate of Capt R G Pendergrast, of same regt, & filed a bond with Hans Frederick Huge & Geo Dille as sureties.
7-Final account of Jas A French, adm of the estate of Ann Tench, dec'd, passed.
8-The last will of Christy Robison, dec'd, partially proven.
9-Last will of Susannah Stewart, dec'd, filed; Mr John W Clark, exc.
10-Eliz J Felson, guardian of Maria E Felson, dec's, gave a additonal bond.
11-Robt W Fenwick gave bond of $5,000 as guardian of Katie Ball, orphan of Wm N Ball, dec'd.
12-Will of Wm G McKinstry dec'd, was further proven.
13-John H McChesney gave addition bond as guardian to Emily P & Saml S Richardson, orphans of John H Richardson, dec'd. He being authorized to sale of rl estate of said ward.
14-Thos Phillips was appt'd adm of the estate of Dabney Ball, dec'd, d b n c t a.
15-Report of Mary A Mothershead, guardian of John M Laskey, to ratify sale of rl estate of said orphan.
16-Account of Mgt E Eckloff, admx with will annexed of the estate of Emma A C Goddard, dec'd, was approved & passed.
17-Firsr account of Moses Kelley, guardian of Mary P Ingle, as guardian of Jos L Ingle, approved & passed.

TUE JUL 25, 1865

Supreme Crt of D C, #246. Richard D Barclay vs Daniel P Rhodes, exc, & Adele Douglas & Robt M & Stephen A Douglas, widow & heirs of Stephen Douglas & others. Statement of the account of Stephen A Douglas on Aug 15. -W Redin, auditor, City Hall, Wash

Supreme Crt of D C, Equity, #344. Eldred W Mobberly & wife, Ann Worthington, Wm H Johnson & wife, Chas E Worthington & wife, against, Ella Johnson, Thos P Brashear, Chas H Brashear, & John R Jones & others. Regarding-sale of property to advantage of the minor dfndnt, & all parties interested. -W Redin, auditor

Supreme Crt of D C, Equity, #471. Mordecai Yarnall & Eliza J, his wife, vs Maria S, Susan S, & Christopher Johnston, Hugh McBirney & Isabella his wife, Henry M & Maria S Johnston, jr, Geo S Inglis, John A Inglis, Geo McNeale & Susan his wife, & John F Johnston, [heirs of Robt N Johnston,] Benj D Dallam & Jane J, his wife, Robt D Muir, Saml C Hepburn, & John D Powell & Annie L, his wife, & others, heirs of Eliz S Hepburn. Cmplnt, M Yarnell, purchased of the said heirs of Eliz S Hepburn, ground in Gtwn on West st, with the dwlg hse, late the residence of Eliz S Hepburn, for $5,000; legal title is vested in the named heirs of said Robt N Johnson. Bill is to appoint a new trustee & conveyance of said premises. Dfndnts are non-residents of D C. -R J Meigs, clerk

Died: at his residence near Beltsville, Md, on Jul 23, Henry Stark, native of N H, but for many years a resident of Wash & vicinity.

Died: in Phil, at the residence of her hsbnd, 768 So Wash Sq, on Jul 20, in her 40th yr, Mary B, w/o Hon John Ross, principal chief of the Cherokee Indians. Interment is to be in the Wilmington & Brandywine Cemetery.

Local Item-Edw Maher was charged with swindling N H Miller of $597, & held for crt.

Mrd: on Jul 7, Miss Evelina de Rothschild, 2nd d/o Baron Lionel de Rothschild, to her cousin Ferdinand, in the Baron's new mansion at Hyde Park Crnr, London.

WED JUL 26, 1865

Orphans Crt of Wash Co, D C. Case of R W Burgess, adm of Richard Burgess, dec'd; settlement on Aug 19. -Z C Robbins, rg o/wills

Supreme Crt of D C. Geo D Abbott vs Chas Wierman et al. Ratify sale of lot 11 in sq 222 with improvements, Wash City, to Gen Geo D Ramsay, for $15,600. -R J Meigs, clerk

Died: in Balt, Md, on Jul 12, John G Proud, ctzn of Balt; born in New Bedford, Mass, on Nov 26, 1776. He moved to Balt in 1801; in 1804 he mrd Miss Eliza Sophia Coale, d/o Dr Saml S Coale. Resided in Elkridge, in what is now Howard Co, for about 20 yrs, returning in 1835 to Balt.

Orphans Crt-D C. 1-Thos Phillips adm of prsnl estate of Dabney Ball, dec'd; J Russell Barr & Thos Hume his sureties. 2-Will of late Otho Boswell was proven & Edwin V B Boswell gave bond as adm; sureties are R C Croggon & Marriott Boswel. 3-Richd Wallach adm of estate of Louisa Hunter, dec'd; Thos Berry & Marshall Brown his sureties. 4-8th account of John Little, guardian of Julia Little was passed. 5-Will of Christy Robison was proven & Rachel Campbell admx. 6-Will of Mrs Mary Stevenson was proven & Cath J Magruder gave bond as admx; sureties are Simon B Bissell & Eliza M Stevenson.

Orphans Crt of Wash Co, D C. Ptn of Mary A Mothershead, guardian of John M Laskey, infant child of John T Laskey, dec'd; ratify sale of lot 3 in sq 87 in Wash City. -Wm F Purcell, Judge -Z C Robbins, rg o/wills

Equity Crt. Maria Susie Volkman vs Henry Volkman. Decree of divorce; respondent retains custody of their child Matilda, & is ordered to pay the petitioner $25 per month, & pay costs of suit.

Died: on Jul 24, Fannie Kyle, d/o Robt C & Fannie K Fox, aged 5 months & 12 days. Funeral on Wed at the residence of Hon Amos Kendall; Kendall Green.

Died: on Jul 25, at the Institute for the Deaf & Dumb, Edw LeBaron, infant s/o Edw R & Jane M Gallaudet. Remains will be taken to Connecticut this evening.

Gtwn affair-the obsequies of the late Hamilton Loughborough took place in Trinity Chr on Jul 25. His remains were conveyed to the graveyard within the College grounds. He was a grad of Va Univ & an eminent lawyer.

THU JUL 27, 1865
Pres appt'd Wm J Murtagh Com'r of the Met Police for D C, vice Richard S Butt, dec'd.

Hon D S Gooding, U S Mrshl for D C, left for a visit to his home at Greenfield, Ind. He will return in Sept.

Mrd: on Jul 8, by Rev B H Nadal, Asbury Lloyd to Bettie H Stone, both of Wash City.

Aaron Burr & the late Madame Jumel. Burr was perhaps the most accomplished gentleman of his day, as well as the intellectual peer of any of the illustrious characters with whom he contended in rivalry. In fact, his genius was beyond them all; its magnetism will forever warm everything connected with him. Madame Jumel, who died at 90 odd yrs, in N Y, was a Miss Capet, & is said to have been born in the cabin of a French frig in the yr 1769. It is also recorded that her mother died immediately after her birth, when her charge was confided to the captain of the vessel, who handed over the little bundle to an elderly lady in Newport, R I. She advanced to a pretty girl. Jumel died in his 70th yr.

Equity Crt: Jul 26, 1865: 1-Estate of John P West, dec'd. Decree confirming the Orphans' Crt decree. 2-Hahn vs Hahn. Order of ratification & reference to auditor. 3-Davis vs Turner. Decree appointing W Y Fendall trustee to sell.

Sale of 2 story brick dwlg on B st, between N J & 1st st, to R H Ball, for $3,150. The vacant lot that adjoins the property was sold to W H Heustis for fifty-three cents per sq ft. Sale of lot 3 in sq 368, on M st, between 9th & 10th sts, with a 3 story brick dwlg, to Geo Varnell, for $6,325. Sale of part of lot 1 in sq 286, on 13th, between I & N Y ave, with 2 story & attic brick dwlg, to W L Walter, for $4,000.

FRI JUL 28, 1865
Sup Crt of D C, Equity Docket 7, #424. Hahn & Hahn vs Sauter et al. Ratify sale by Chas H Utermehle, trustee, of rl estate of John Santer, dec'd. -R J Meigs, clerk

Died: on Jul 27, of bilious dysentery, Rich'd, eldest s/o Richard & Amelia A Davis, in his 6th yr. Funeral from the residence of C W Claxton, 60 High st, Gtwn, Fri.

Died: Gen Jos G Swift, late of the U S army, at Geneva, N Y, on Sun last, in the 82nd yr of his age.

Sentences by Naval Crt-Martials: Navy Dept, Jul 17, 1865. Genr'l Order #61.

1-Jos Demartine, o s U S steamer *Silver Cloud*, tried Apr 11, 1865, found guilty of desertion & sentenced to be confined at hard labor in any pen the Sec of the Navy may direct, for 10 years; at the expiration of that time to be dishonoraby discharged from the naval svcs, & to lose all pay & emoluments then due. Sentence approved & prisoner sent to state prison at Joliet, Ill.

2-John R Bowen, cabin steward, U S steamer *Tyler*, tried Apr 3, 1865, found guilty of desertion & sentenced to be confined at hard labor in the Ill Pen at Joliet, Ill, for 2 yrs; to lose all pay & emoluments then due, & to be dishonorably discharged the naval svc.

3-Richd Molker, o s, U S steamer *St Clair*, tried Apr 21, 1865, found guilty of desertion & sentenced to forfeit all pay & emoluments now due him, or that may become due him, & be confined in the pen at Joliet, Ill, for 1 year at hard labor, & then to be dishonorably discharged from the Navy.

4-Carl Becker, o s, U S steamer *St Clair*, tried Apr 21, 1865, guilty of desertion: sentenced to be imprisoned at hard labor for 2 years at the pen at Joliet, Ill. Dishonorable discharge & loss of all pay & emoluments.

5-Fred'k Gre_ber, o s, U S steamer *St Clair*: same as above-#4.

6-John Brennan, seaman, U S steamer *Naumkerg*: tried Apr 23, 1865, guilty of desertion in time of war: sentenced to 2 years in any Navy yard the Sec of Navy may select, at hard labor, & to wear a chain with ball attached weighing 12 lbs, & to be dishonorably discharged, with loss of 1 year's pay. Case is considered as coming within the terms of the proclamation, inasmuch as the prisoner was arrested at the Naval Rendezvous, where he claims to have been waiting to deliver himself up. Sentence was set aside.

7-Newton Walters, coalheaver, U S steamer *St Clair*, tried Apr 21, 1865, guilty of desertion & to be imprisoned 1 year in the pen, & loss of all pay & emoluments now due. The accused being a mere boy of 16 years & almost imbecile, is considered unfit for naval svc. The sentence was remitted, & Walters was discharged.

8-Austin Ensign, seaman, U S steamer *Benton*, tried Apr 11, 1865, found guilty of absence without leave, drunkeness, & assaulting his ofcr: sentence-to be confined at hard labor for 5 years, & to forfeit all pay, etc. Accused was unanimously recommended to clemency by the mbrs of the crt, who represent that he has been for 4 years in the svc, having been correct & obedient hitherto; that this was his first offence, & that drunkenness was the real cause of all these acts. The sentence has been entirely remitted, & the accused returned to duty.

9-Franklin Lukemire, landsman, U S steamer *Mound City*, tried Apr 14, 1865, guilty of desertion, & sentenced to 10 years in the Ill State Pen, at Joliet, Ill: to forfeit all pay & emoluments now due, or may become due, except 2 months pay as landsman, to be pd him at the expiration of his incarceration. 5 years imprisonment was remitted by Actg Rear Admr Lee.

10-Jas Simmons, seaman, tried May 2, 1865, guilty of using seditious language & evincing disloyatly, in that he expressed satisfaction, both in words & conduct, when the assassination of Pres Lincoln was announced in his hearing, & was sentenced to be imprisoned for 2 years in such prison or place of confinement as the Sec of the Navy may designate: to forfeit all pay now due, or which may become due to him during his term of enlistment; to be dishonorably discharged from the Navy, & never again to be permitted to serve under the Gov't of the U S. Sentence approved. –Gideon Wells, Sec of the Navy

SAT JUL 29, 1865

Orphans Crt of Wash Co, D C. Case of Thos P Morgan, adm of Sarah Smith, dec'd; settlement on Aug 19. -Z C Robbins, rg o/wills

Died: Rev Fitch W Taylor, the oldest chaplain in our navy, & schoolmate of Wm Wirt, died in Brooklyn on Mon.

Died: at her residence in Madison, Conn, on Jul 23, Cath W Hand, widow of the late Jos W Hand, of Wash, D C, aged 64 yrs.

Died: at the residence of her son-in-law, J E Reeside, Mrs Mary Mc Mullan, in her 82nd yr. Funeral on Sat.

Died: on Jul 27, at the residence of A E Smoot, Chas Fenelon Smoot, aged 10 yrs. Funeral at the Congressional Burial Ground today.

John B Gough, the temperance lecturer, reports an income of $9,000 a yr.

Abraham Lincoln & Jefferson Davis were born in the same Congressional dist of Ky, & within the same 12 months.

Wash City News. 1-A H Vermillion, a bar-tender, was arrested by Ofcr Harbin, for assaulting him while in the discharge of his duty, & was held to bail for crt by Justice Handy. 2-Michl Roy, a sldr belonging to an Ohio regt, was cut over the head & badly wounded yesterday by a party of roughs. Ofcr Ourand conveyed him to Douglas Hosp, where his wounds were dressed, & then conveyed him to Providence Hospital, where he will be attended until his wounds are healed.

Gtwn Affairs: the steamer *E C Knight*, Capt J J Mason, of the Atlantic Steamship line, reached Snow's wharf last evening, having on board as passengers Messrs Morris S R Robertson & lady, E Edmonston & Theo Walmsley.

The steamer *Balt*, of N Y & Wash line, sailed from her wharf, foot of High st, yesterday, with the following passengers:

C H Parsons	H W Murray	Mstr Hicks
Dr Shearer	Mr Osborne	John Williams
R G Alcott & son	T Reswick & son	Thos Smith
Mrs Jas F Essex & son	Mr Smith & 4 ladies	
John Graham	Mr Kahn	

MON JUL 31, 1865

Died: in Wash City, on Jul 29, Sarah Frances, only d/o Jos K & Lucy A Potts, in her 18th yr. Funeral from her parents residence, 312 9th st, on Jul 31.

Orphans Crt-D C. 1-Will of Wm T T Mason, dec'd, filed. Nicholas Carroll Mason, exc. 2-Will of Ellen Griffin, dec'd, filed: Dennis Griffin, exc. 3-Addition inventory of the prsnl estate of Wm H Starr, dec'd, entered & filed. 4-Will of Henry Stark, dec'd, proven. Mrs H R Pickett, Jane R Codwise, & Bettie R Calvert declined to act as excxs; same granted to Mrs Mary Meade Turner, who gave bond of $4,000. Her sureties were Wm B Randolph, Jane R Codwise, & Cornelia P Randolph.

Died: on Jul 29, after a long & painful illness, Mary C Pomeroy, w/o Geo B Pomeroy. Funeral from the residence of her son-in-law, M Holtzman, on L st, between 23rd & 24th, on Mon. [Balt papers please copy]

TUE AUG 1, 1865
Co-partnership notice-Mr Thos Russell has associated with me in my business; importer of wines, liquors, cigars. Edw C Dyer, 256 Pa Av, Wash, D C

Died: on Jul 9, at the residence of his son, in Wash City, Thos Dyer, formerly of Saco, Maine, age 82 yrs. Maine papers please copy.

During the first 3 weeks after the assassination, Mrs Wm Henry Seward was constantly, day & night, at the bedside either of her hsbnd or that of Frederick, & those exertions have since hastened the death of a lady equally distinguished for the excellent qualities of her head & her heart. No less noble was the conduct of their dght, Miss Fanny, an untiring attendant upon her suffering relatives. On account of the shattered jawbone, the physicians asked Mr Seward not to speak, but it was difficult to get him to comply.

Fortress Monroe, Jul 30. The steamer C W Thomas, Capt Doane, arrived this morning from Richmond with Col Wm L James, Q M of this district, among her passengers.

Another effort will be made tomorrow to raise the old frig Congress, sunk off Newport News.

Wm J Pickerson, a sldr, is now confined at Fortress Monroe, sentenced to 6 months imprisonment & forfeiture of $10 per mo, for calling his superior ofcr an unmitigated puppy. As he has passed thru 20 battles, with honor, his townsmen are petitioning for his release.

WED AUG 2, 1865
Equity Docket #7. Leomin vs Leomin: ratify sales made by Chas H Utermeehle, trustee, of the rl estate of Eugene Leomin, dec'd. Am't of sales to be $7,815. -Andrew Wylie, [at chambers] R J Meigs, clerk

Supreme Crt of D C, in Equity, #466. Wm H Morrison & Jas R D Morrison vs Andrew V D Mills & Emma T Mills his wife, & Chas P Culver & Louisa E Culver his wife. Bill is to obtain a partition of the rl estate of Chas J Morrison, dec'd, late of Wash Co, D C, who died intestate in 1864. Cmplnts & dfndnts, Emma T Mills & Louisa E Culver, are his only heirs at law. Dfndnts are non-residents of D C. -By order of the crt.

Orphans Crt of Wash Co, D C. Prsnl estate of Henry Stark, late of PG Co, Md, dec'd. -Mary M Turner, excx

Friday was the 87th birthday of Rear Adm Chas Stewart, who was born in Phil, Jul 28, 1778. He is still active & hearty.

Died: on Jul 31, Lemuel D Williams, aged 34 yrs. Funeral on Wed, from his late residence, First st east. Capt Williams died at his residence on Capitol Hill, of congestion of the brain, leaving a widow & 6 chldrn. He was a mbr of the Wash Light Infty.

Gtwn, D C. Henry M Sweeny appt'd successor to Geo Shoemaker, dec'd. We congratulate the stockholders & directors of the Farmers & Mechanics Bank.

Died: on Aug 1, at the residence of John H McCutchen, Hyattsville, PG Co, Md, Harrie Burnett, infant son of Jas W & Maggie Twyman, aged 7 months & 23 days. Funeral from the residence of J C Gibson, 355 7th st, today. [Richmond, Va, & Paducah, Ky, papers please copy.]

Hartford, Aug 1. The murder of Mrs Benj Starkweather, aged 46 yrs, & her 14 yr old dght, were discovered chopped to death in bed at the village of Oakland, in Manchester. A son named Albert, aged 24 yrs, was suspected & arrested.

Aug 4. Oakland, Ct, near Hartford: Mrs Starkweather, sister-in-law of Nathan Starkweather, of this city, & her dght, Harriet Ella, killed with an axe.

Orphans Crt , D C. 1-Final acc't of Sam'l Pumphrey, adm of Wm Downs, dec'd, approved & passed. 2-Chas H Poor & Wm A Poor gave bond as excs of the estate of Charlotte Poor, dec'd. Bondsmen are John F Webb & Wm B Webb. 3-Will of Geo W Mitchell, dec'd, proven, & Eleanor Mitchell, excx. Sureties are Rebecca Mitchell & Martha Goldsmith.

The monument to the memory of the late John McDonogh, of Balt, was dedicated on Mon at Greenmount Cemetery, in Balt City, with an eloquent address delivered by J H B Latrobe.

Rubin Callan, of Yarmouth, N S, drowned in the river on Mon evening; one of the crew of the schnr *Nelly Brown*, Capt D Higgins, which had just arrived off the foot of Washington st, with a cargo of ice from Boston, Mass, & was about to bathe, when he slipped from the edge of the vessel. His head reached the surface soon after; but he seemed to be powerless to rise again. His body has not been removed. [Local Item. Aug 3 newspaper. The body of Reuben Killam was discovered yesterday. John Bird, cook of said schnr, shoved him overboard, which caused him to be drowned.]

Toledo, Jul 31. A young man named Fred Heilkamp was murdered here, & robbed of a small amount of money & a gold watch, early yesterday. No arrests have been made.

Local Item-Thos Dowling sold Conrad's Tavern, in Tenallytown, & over 10 acs of land to Capt Thos Stackpole for $9,075. The hotel has been a tavern stand for half a century past.

City News. The trial of Foster Daniels, indicted for the murder of his bro-in-law, last winter, has been set for Thu in the Criml Crt.

THU AUG 3, 1865
Died: on Aug 2, of typhoid fever, in the 18th yr of his age, Z Taylor King, s/o Martin & the late Angela R King. Funeral on Sat at the residence of his father then to St Peter's Chr. He was a teacher at St Peter's Sunday School. Balt & Norfolk papers please copy.

Trinity Chr in N Y is reputed to be a very wealthy corporation. It owns property valued at 20 millions of dollars, which is located in the very heart of the city. Most of this property was rented to John Jacob Astor, on a 99 years lease. This lease expires next year. There are 336 lots, & it is a curious fact that Wm B Astor has only had to pay seventy-five cents on each of these lots, while the rent he receives for them amounts to from five hundred to two thousand five hundred dollars each.

The steamer *Florida* was employed by the Gov't to convey the conspirators, Dr Mudd, Arnold Spangler, & O'Laughlin, to the place designated as thieir abode until they shall have expiated their great crime of being concerned in the death of Pres Lincoln.

Brd of Met Police Com'rs: meeting yesterday: Mr Wm J Murtagh appeared as a Com'r v Jos F Brown, & Dr C H Nichols v Richd S Butt. Com'rs from Wash: Geo S Gideon, Sayles J Bowen, & W J Murtagh; from Gtwn, Mr W H Tenney, & from the county, Dr C H Nichols. Mr Gideon is Pres of the Brd, & Mr T A Lazenby, of Gtwn, sec. Chas Walter was elected Police Magistrate, v Gilbert L Giberson. The resignation of A E Spencer, patrolman, was received. John T Cronin, late sgt of the 7th precinct, was dismissed from the police force. Wm R Tennant, Wm D Williams, & Fenton D Paxson were appt'd patrolmen.

Died: on Jul 19, in Bergen, N J, at the residence of his aunt, Mrs Richard Gip, John Howard, y/s/o John W & Annie M Compton, of Wash, D C, aged 10 yrs, 2 months & 16 days.

FRI AUG 4, 1865
Sup Crt of D C, Equity, #306. Floriah Leomin & others, vs Mellaine Leomin, Jos A Blair, Henry B McElfresh, & others. Distribution between widow & heirs of Eugene Leomin, City Hall, on Aug 26. -W Redin, auditor

Died: on Aug 2, Mary A Sessford, w/o Geo A Sessford, in the 34th yr of her age. Funeral from her late residence, 499 7th st, today.

Brig Gen O O Howard, late Maj Gen in the vol forces, breveted Maj Gen in the reg army, to date from May 30th, for gallant & meritorious svc. Maj Gen Augur has received a brvt promotion to Brig Gen in the reg army. His Chief of Staff Lt Col J A Taylor, of 6th cavalry, is brvt'd Col in the reg svc.

Havana press despatch: Mr C S Shanahan, correspondent of the N Y Herald, who arrived in the country only a few weeks since, died at the Iturbide Hotel, in Mexico, on Jul 15.

Edw C Carrington, U S Atty for the district of Col, was yesterday reappointed to that position, his first term being about to expire.

Patrick Fay, arrested & held to bail to answer the charge of robbing August Hoffman, was re-arrested on a bench warrant, the grand jury having indicted him for the robbbery. Hoffman is a sldr, & in order to have the attendance of the cmplnt & witnesses, a speedy trial became necessary.

SAT AUG 5, 1865
Ads: 1-Nathl B Fugitt, Lumber Dealer, 6th st, Wash, D C.
2-C B Church & Co, Lumber of all kinds, Md av & 11th st, D C.
3-John O Evans & Co, Woods, Lumber, Four & a half st, D C.
4-First Natl Bank of Wash, H D Cooke, Jay, of Cooke & Co, Pres.
Wm S Huntington, Cashier, 15th st, D C.
5-H W Hamilton, Sash, Doors, Blinds, etc, 562 7th st, D C.
6-Carpenter bldr & contractor, John B Williamson, K st, D C.
7-Henry Simons, Natl Wagon & Coach Works, 525 N Mkt st, Phil.
8-John McDermott & Bros, Coach Mkrs, 455 Pa av, D C.
9-T T Fowler & Co, Ice, 10th st wharf, D C
10-T Pursell & Son, China Glass, Earthenware, etc, 341 Pa av, D C.
11-C Witty, Carriages, 456 Broadway, N Y.

12-Plumber, Steam & Gasfitter, Jas B Simpson, 344 C st, D C.
13-Dr B Gesner has removed to 433 11th st, D C.
14-Waverly Hse-rms by day or week, 451 8th st, S G Langley, proprietor, D C.
15-Melville Hse, 22nd & G sts, John T O'Brien, prop, D C.
16-U S Hotel, Pa av, D C, M H Bean & Co, proprietor, D C.
17-City Restaurant, Pa av & 14th st, P Murphy, D C.
18-Met Htl, Pa av, A H Potts, proprietor, D C.
19-Blacksmiths & Wheelwrights Hardware, 87 La av, John R Elvans & Co, D C.
20-Hardware, J P Bartholow, 558 7th st, D C.
21-Hardware, John D Edmond & Co, 513 7th st, D C.
22-Booksellers & Stationers, 9th & D sts, John P Brophy & John T Burch, D C.
23-Merchant Tailor, S W Owen, successor to E Owen & son, 212 Pa av, D C.
24-Hse painter & Glazier, C T Bowen, 53 La av, D C.

All persons are warned against crediting my wife, Mary O'Sullivan, as I will not be responsible for any debts incurred by her unless upon written orders given by myself. - Robt O'Sullivan

Mrd: at Roxbury, on Jul 27, by Rev Dr Putnam, Gustavus B Maynadier, of Wash, D C, to Mary R, d/o the Hon John S Steeper, of Rosbury, Mass.

Died: in Wash City, on Aug 4, Miss Mary N *Folmer, d/o the late Geo & Mary *Fulmer. Funeral from the Fitzgerald Hse, Pa ave, Sunday. [*2 splgs]

Funeral of the late Maj Robt K Scott will take place at the Chr of the Epiphany, 13th & G sts, this morning. Local Item

Local rl estate sales: Leomin prop, hse & lot to Henry Keller for $2,000; 3 story brick hse & lot to Michl Sheahan for $2,225; frame hse & lot to Jos McIntosh for $1,005; frame hse, 72 Washington st to Jesse Reeder for $635; frame hse 70, same st, to Harry McCoy for $650; frame hse on N J av to John Hall for $675; also to same, frame hse for $625. Properties are in sq 529, 518 & 57.

Brvt Maj John T Clements, C S, has been mustered out of the U S svc & appt'd Pension Agent for North Missouri. He will leave next week.

MON AUG 7, 1865
Thos A McLaughlin offers his svcs as a rl estate agent: dwlg, 263 F st, D C.

Orphans Crt-D C. 1-Acc't of Cath V Booth, guardian of Jas C & John F A Crampton, approved. 2-Appraisement of rl estate of the orphans of David Moran, dec'd, filed. 3-Acc't of Martha E Page, guardian of the persons & ests of Rezin A, Julia F, & Eliz E Page, orphans of Yelverton P Page, dec'd, passed. 4-Will of Geo W Mitchell admitted to probate. 5-Final acc't of Barbara L Hume, admx of estate of Lucia R Berry, dec'd, passed. 6-Mr J W Clark remounced his appointment as exc of the estate of Susannah Stewart, dec'd. 7-Will of Patrick McKenna was filed; dec'd's widow & A P McKenna are excx. 8-Julius L Rider appt'd adm of estate of Heremiah M Huxley, dec'd. 9-Prsnl estate of Louisa Hunter, dec'd, approved & passed. 10-Inventory of prsnl estate of Hugh McMahon, dec'd, approved & passed. 11-Wm E Morcoe appt'd guardian of Mary V, Wm E, D Walker, & Florence Howard, heirs of Martha E Howard, dec'd. He gave bond of $2,000 with S E Douglass & E M Drew as sureties. 12-Delia Wyebel was appt'd admx of estate of Julius Wyebel, dec'd.

Mrd: on Jul 21, Adm J A Dahlgren, age 55 yrs, to Mrs Madeline Vinton Goddard, d/o the late Hon Sam'l F Vinton, of Ohio, by Dr Cummings, of St Stephen's Chr. The bride must be about 28 or 30 years of age. This is the Admiral's 2nd venture on the ocean of matrimony. -N Y World

Died: at her residence in Edenton, N C, on May 6, Mrs Louisa A Sawyer, widow of the late Dr Sawyer. She was a loving mother & sister.

We announce that Mrs Stover, the Pres' dght, & 3 chldrn; Col Robt Johnson, s/o the Pres; & his son-in-law, Senator Patterson, of Tenn, arrived in Wash City on Sat.

Miss Nelly Morgan, d/o Thos P Morgan, was crowned Queen of Love & Beauty by the Knight of the First Honor. -Local News

Died: Maj Frank North, in Wash City, age 27 yrs, on Sat evening of typhoid fever, at the Nat'l Htl. He was Additional Paymastr U S A & attended by his young & fond sister.

Lemuel Norton, alias Wm Stevens, was arrested on Sat on charge of forgery. -Local Item

Police Matters, Wash, D C. W Veman arrested for larceny of $27 from a sldr named Wm Frost; money was recovered. 2-John Thomas, John Simpson, John Carroll, & John Anderson, all small boys, arrested for attempting to rob a man. 3-John H Dixon, chg'd with larceny of a watch from Charity Soloman: committed to jail for crt.

TUE AUG 8, 1865

The funeral of Capt Percival Drayton was held yesterday in Oak Hill Cemetery. The coffin was furnished by Mr L Williams. The plate bore the inscription: *Capt P Drayton, U S N/Chief of Bur of Navigation. Died Aug 4, 1865, aged 54 yrs.* The handles, of which there were six, were of solid silver, & of a most beautiful design, representing, in relief, the American eagle, the national flag, & an anchor, & surmounted by stars of the same metal. An exquisite cross of white flowers intermingled with sprigs of green, made by Mrs Porter, w/o Cmdor Porter, was placed upon the coffin, which was draped with the American flag. Marine Corps, commanded by Maj Graham, & Capt Munore, Lts Collins, Nokes, Williams, Young, Reed, Goodrell, Watson, & Sgt Maj Dunn, escorted by the Marine Band were in attendance. The pallbearers were Admr Porter, Cmdor Harwood, Paymstr Bridge, Chief Engr Isherwood, Chief of Construction Lenthall, Cmder A Smith, Capt M F Smith, Capt R Taylor, Maj Gen Augur, Brig Gens Ramsey, Hardie, & Nichols. The Chief mourners were Mrs Hoyt, Alex'r Hamilton, & J H Brooks, [Capt Drayton's messenger.] Capt Drayton entered the Naval svc as a midshipman on Dec 1, 1827, was ordered to the frig *Hudson*. In 1831 he was sent to the Naval School at N Y, & a year later was ordered to join the Mediterranean squad. Promoted to Lt in 1838, ordered to command the schnr *Enterprise*. In 1842, joined the sloop of war *Yorktown*,: in 1840 ordered to the ship *Columbus*, of the East India squad: in 1850, attached to the steamer *Mississippi*: 2 years after transferred to the ship *Independence*, etc. He commanded the ship *Pocahontas* in the attack upon the forts at Port Royal, S C, etc. He was a tall commanding figure, his features expressing much determination & mental strength.

Hon Robt J Walker has purchased the mansion of Mr Barreds, on H st, which was built by Mr Fowler, of Alexandria. The price was $37,000, of which $12,000 is to be paid down.

WED AUG 9, 1865

Orphans Crt-D C. 1-Mrs Eliz Brown, admx of estate of Tillottson P Brown, dec'd, filed a ptn for a rule upon Mrshl Brown to show why he had not answered a former demand. Citation was issued. 2-Report of the sales of the prsnl estate of Chas J Uhlmann, dec'd, filed. 3-Will of Mary N Fulmer was filed. 4-Wm L Freeman gave bond as guardian of Amelia Lacey; sureties are Chas Syphax & Wm S Wilson. 5-Acc't of Mary A Greene, guardian of Wm J & Sidney K Gold, passed. 6-Distribution of prsnl estate of Rosanna D Cooms, dec'd, returned by W G Moore, exc, approved & passed. 7-Sarah Parrish gave bond as guardian of Albert J Parrish; sureties are Robt W Goggin & Jennis A Parrish. 8-Acc't of Geo Seaton & Geo Bryant, excs of estate of Geo Bryant, dec'd, passed. 9-Will of Dolly Ann Williams was proven & admitted to probate; Jas Johnson received letters test; sureties are Chas Walter & John T Donaldson.

Died: on Aug 4, Josephine, d/o Wm S & V M Parke, aged 5 years & 8 months. Funeral from the residence of her father on First st, between L & M, today.

Died: at the residence of Mr Richard Hill, in PG Co, Md, Miss Kitty Smith, in her 73rd yr. Remains will be brought to St Dominicks' Chr for a solemn mass today.

Died: in Gtwn, D C, on Aug 8, Geo W Longden, in his 65th yr. Funeral from his late residence, 100 Fayette st, on Aug 10, svcs at Trinity Chr.

Some heartless villain yesterday robbed John Permillion, a blind man, of $650, at his residence known as *Brickyard Hill*, High St. The sufferer's chldrn were asleep & Mr Permillion & his wife were in the market following their vocation. On their return to breakfast, she saw the broken money-box near their dwlg, rifled of its contents.

Died: on Aug 7, Jas Tucker, in his 81st yr, over 40 years a resident of Wash. Funeral today. Mr Tucker was born in England & came to this country at an early age.

THU AUG 10, 1865

Reward-$300: escaped on Aug 3 while en route to the Albany Pen:
1-Horatio M Malony, hails from Phil, age about 30 or 35 yrs, 5' 7".
2-Jas T Rodgers, from N H, age about 23 yrs, 5' 8".
3-Jos McCoy, alias Ladrue, has look of a thief, 5' 9".
4-Chas H McVeigh, from Wash, age about 18 yrs, 5' 7".
-Robt Beale, warden U S jail, Wash, D C.

Sup Crt of D C, Equity, #112. 1-Ptn of Eliz Byington, admx of Saml Byington, dec'd, & guardian to the infant chldrn of dec'd. Ratify sales made by T Edw Clark, trustee, in amount of $5,115.38.
-R J Meigs, clerk 2-Equity #448. Wm Loring vs Eliz Loring. Dfndnt not found & not a resident of
D C. Aug 7, 1865. -R J Meigs, clerk

The Ames family, at Easton, Mass, shovel manufacturers, report incomes of: Oakes Ames-$231,475; Olives Ames-$200,153; & their 3 sons, $30,000 ea; Horation Ames, another bro of the family is a maker of wrought-iron cannon at Windsor Lock, Conn.

Died: at Newport, R I, on Aug 3, Donaldson Courtright Lowry, born at Erie, Pa, Feb 26, 1859, aged 6 years 5 mos, & 11 days, eldest s/o Lt Cmder R B Lowry, U S N, & Lizzie Courtright Lowry.

FRI AUG 11, 1865

Criml Crt-Judge Wylie, Aug 10, Edw C Carrington, D A. U S vs John F Lusby, accused of rape & murder on a little girl name Octavia Rousseau, causing her death. Accused has acknowledged his guilt, per witnesses.

For rent-my farm: *Glymont*, 840 acs; on the Potomac river, in the free state of Md, about 25 miles from Wash City. -Leonard Marbury, on the premises.

For sale-4 acs of rl estate adj Mrs Naylor's. Fendall Marbury, T B P O, PG Co, Md.

Miss Lillie Bennett will give instruction in music at her residence at 529 H st, Wash.

Mrs Thompson, w/o John Thompson, Knox Co, Tenn, recently presented her liege with triplets. The young Thompsons are doing well.

Died: in Oakland, Jul 16, T D Mitchell, formerly of Wash, D C, in his 25th yr.

Died: in Wash City, on Aug 9, Alida Ernestine, infant d/o Z M P & Henrietta L King, aged 2 yrs. Funeral on Fri from the residence of her father, corner of Vermont av & 15th st.

In Memoriam: of Percival Drayton, U S Navy, native of S C, bro of Gen Drayton. He lived & died a Christian gentleman. W M G

SAT AUG 12, 1865

New ad-attys at law: Thos H Ford, of Ohio; L G Hine, of Mich; 254 G st, Wash.

New ad-Jos Radcliffe & Son, Gen Com Merchants, 272 Camden st, Balt, Md.

New Dry-Goods store, just opened by John S Yates; 9th st above D, Wash, D C.

Desirous of closing up the business of the estate of Jas Skirving; sale of stoves, grates, & ranges. -Caroline H Skirving; John T Given, excs, 267 Pa av, Wash.

Mrd: on Aug 8, by Rev Wm B Edwards, Rev Geo M Berry, of the Balt Conference, to Miss Emma Myers, d/o the late Chas Myers, of Gtwn, D C.

Died: on Aug 10, Jas, only c/o Jas M & Mary J Dalton, aged 11 months & 25 days. Funeral from the residence of his father, Pa av, between 8th & 9th sts, Sat.

Death of a Patrolman-Randall Colbourne, of the Metropolitan Police, died on Aug 11 at his residence in Gtwn; after a long illness. He was an original appointee to the force.

Wash Corp: 1-Ptn of Jas E Morgan & others: referred to the Cmte on Drainage, etc. 2-Ptn of J A Hopkins: referred to the Cmte on Improvements. 3-Ptn of Edw Kubel & Jacob Roth: referred to the Cmte on Improvements. 4-Account of Dr B Geaner was presented: formerly referred to the Cmte on Claims. Cmte discharged from its further consideration. 5-Cmte on Pblc Schools, reported back the communication of O Corvin, about establishing swimming schools in Wash City, asked to be discharged: which was so ordered. 6-Ptn of Edw Foster: referred to the Cmte on Drainage, etc. 7-Ltr from J S Williams, a Com'r of the Northern Mkt, asking the passage of a law to prevent hogs from roaming at large in the mkts: referred to the Cmte on Mkts. 8-Ptn of W C Johnson & others, asking grading & paving of 2nd st, between E Capt & A sts: referred to the Cmte on Improvements.

Desirous of closing up the business of the estate of Jas Skirving; sale of stoves, grates, & ranges. -Caroline H Skirving; John T Given, excs, 267 Pa av, Wash.

MON AUG 14, 1865

For sale or rent-my farm, 487½ acs, opposite Aquia Crk. -Saml W Adams, Nanjemoy, Chas Co, Md.

Orphans Crt-D C. 1-Ptn of A C Cassell, guardian to chldrn of J A Cassell, dec'd, was filed. 2-Will of Patrick McKenna fully proven, Mary M McKenna & Andrew P McKenna excx. 3-Inventory of estate of Henry W Gray, dec'd, was filed. Final acc't of Martha E Gray, admx, was approved & passed. 4-Delia Weibel gave bond as admx of estate of Julius Weibel, dec'd; sureties are John Ardeezer & Caspar Barnhard. 5-Inventory of prsnl estate of Dolly Ann Williams, dec'd, was filed. 6-Distribution of estate of John A Ellis, dec'd, was approved & passed. 7-Distribution of estate of Wm W Turner, dec'd, was approved & passed. 8-Mary E Morsell gave bond as guardian of Jas B & Chas A Wimer, orphan chldrn of Jas Wimer, of Jacksonville, Fla; sureties are John W Morsell, R T Morsell, & Edw M Drew. 9-Final acc't of Mrs Mary A Turner, admx of estate of Wm Turner, dec'd, was approved & passed.

Trustee's sale of *Retreat*, late the property of Wm Ferguson, dec'd, some 400 acs; also *Meadow*, 40 to 50 acs. -John W Mitchell, trustee

Orphans Crt of Wash Co, D C. Prsnl estate of Henry Lehne, late of Wash, D C, dec'd. -B Lehne, excx

The Guatemalayan Minister assassinated: recently in Leon on the person of Don Enrique Palacois, by a person named Rivas. The Minister was shot in his own residence at a late hour of the night. We see no cause assigned in the pblc journal for the assassination.

The bronze statue of Lt Meigs, s/o Qrtrmstr Gen Meigs, is completed at the studio of Mr Fisk Mills, 459 Pa av; designed to deck the tomb of the departed in Oak Hill Cemetery, Gtwn, D C. Lt Meigs was killed by a guerilla on Oct 3 last, while honorably discharging his duties in the Shenandoah Valley as chief engineer on Sheridan's'staff. The head & face is pronounced an excellent likeness of the dec'd, & was moulded entirely from a photograph. Fisk Mills, the artist, is s/o Mr Clark Mills, the noted sculptor.

Sup Crt of D C, in Chancery, #1822. Francis Wheatley vs Jas A Johnson et al. Ratify sale by David A Burr, trustee. -R J Meigs, clerk

Pardons by the Pres were today granted to John Leifer, of Murfreesboro, Tenn, & Henry T Elliott, of Tenn.

Died: on Aug 13, after a long & painful illness, Mary, only d/o Thos & Sarah F Donoho. Funeral from their residence at 366 D st, this afternoon.

TUE AUG 15, 1865

Appointments by the Pres: 1-Assessors of Internal Rev-Thos K Carroll for the First district of Md; Wm M Gray for the 4th district of Ga. 2-U S Mrshl: Wm G Dickson, for the district of Ga. 3-Warden of the Jail: Thos B Brown to be Warden of the jail of D C, vice Beale, removed. 4-U S Cnsl: Augustus Canfield, to be U S Cnsl at Zou Chou, China. 5-Appraiser of Merchandise: Hooper C Hicks, for the port of Balt. 6-Collector of Customs: Robt W Chadwick, for the district of Ocracoke, N C. [Mr Thos B Brown filed his bond in the sum of $5,000 for the faithful performance of his duty. His sureties are Dr Jos Borrows & A C Richards.]

Died: on Aug 13, Grace, w/o Alfred Richards, in her 39th yr. Funeral from her late residence at 765 N J av, Tue.

Died: in Balt, on Aug 12, Georgianna V, w/o Thos Poultney, jr, & d/o the late Col John McClellan, U S A.

Police matters: 1-Dennis O'Lowrey, alias Cunningham, was arrested by Ofcr Frazier as a suspicious character. He was locked up for a few hours. 2-Geo W Allen was committed to the Workhse for 90 days. 3-John Simpson, Thos Lynch, & Wm Linskey, all boys, were committed to jail on charge of robbing John W Scott of $60. Ofcr S W Taylor effected the arrest. 4-John R Williams arrested by Ofcr Garner for the larceny of a lot of clothing from Saml Wright: committed to jail for crt by Justice Walter.

Gtwn Affairs: the steamer *John Gibson*, Capt Kelly, arrived at Snow's wharf last evening, from N Y. Among her passengers were J D Parkinson & wife, Miss C Parkinson, & Miss M Parkinson.

Orphans Crt of Wash Co, D C. Case of Wm H Clagett & Jos H Bradley, Jr, admx w a of Wm D Porter, dec'd; settlement on Sep 23. -Z C Robbins, rg o/wills

WED AUG 16, 1865
Inquest on Monday at Oak Hill Cemetery over the remains of the late Mr John T Meem, who died suddenly last Thu & was buried on Sat. He had piles & Dr J H Thompson, of Wash, treated him. Mrs Meems, widow of the dec'd, discovered his condition on Thu morning. Mr J G Meem, his bro, called the Dr on Thu when he was in a critical condition. Symptoms of an overdose of opium. Investigation postponed. [There were more details including: the one ounce of opiuum to be administered in an enema every 4 hours, in a 2 oz syringe, prescribed by Dr Thompson Meem also inhaled chloroform while being examined by Dr Thompson about 3 p m. Opium in an enema has generally less than ½ the affect of that taken in the mouth, etc.]

St Louis, Aug 11. Gen Hancock & family have arrived on a visit to his mother-in-law, Mrs Russell.

Public sale of land near Collington P O upon which John G Mitchell recently resided, 200 acs; dwlg hse, barn, stable ect, all built since 1857. -Danl Clarke, atty-at -law, Upper Marlboro, Md.

Homicide on the canal on Mon; Simon C Myers was struck in the face with a stone by Capt John Barger, of the boat *Mollie*, & was knocked overboard & drowned. Parties all belong near Four Locks, Wash Co, Md. The *Mollie* ran into the vessel *Maude*, Capt Shook, in trying to pass her, as both were bound West for Cumberland, when the altercation ensued. Local News

Died: suddenly, at New Castle, Dela, on Aug 12, Dr Jas Couper. Funeral on Thu.

Orphans Crt-D C. 1-Acc't of Mrs Eliza Anne Drane, guardian of the heirs of John Brereton, dec'd, approved & passed. 2-Acc't of Anthony Bowen, exc of estate of Richard Brooks, dec'd, approved & passed. 3-Acc't of Alice E Caustin, guardian of the chldrn of Mary Caustin, approved & passed. 4-Final acc't of Sophia Ridgley, admx of the estate of Wm G Ridgley, dec'd, approved & passed. 5-Sale of the rl estate of the orphans of John Brereton, dec'd, finally ratified.

City News-trial of Capt Henry Wertz was postponed; charge-violation of the laws of war; charged with maliciously designing to impair & injure the health & destroy the lives of prisoners of war in his custody. Capt Wertz was born in Switzerland, removed to this country in early life & settled in La; possessed a large plantation near New Orleans & a number of slaves; espoused the Confederate cause.

Wm Edmonston, a huckster, was arrested on complaint of Mrs Mary Wisbecker, who charged he ran off with her dght, the wife of a sldr, when he had a wife living. Mr Edmonston soon became tired of his 2nd love & returned to Wash City leaving her behind.

Presidential Appointments made yesterday:
Thos C Theaker, of Ohio,, to be Com'r of Patents, Aug 15.
B Franklin Martin to be Collector of Internal Rev, 7th district of Ohio.
Jesse Wheeler to be Assessor of Internal Rev, 2nd district of N C.
John Hudson to be Assessor of Internal Rev, 1st district of Va.
Francis A Fuller to be Srvyr of Customs, district of Wilmington, N C.
Saml A Pancoast to be Direct Tax Com'r, district of Ga.

Hon E A Rollins, the indefatigable Assist Com'r of Internal Rev, leaves the exhausting duties of his post today on a month's relaxation & recuperation among the Mountains of his N H Home.

Maj Gen Banks intends to reside permanently in New Orleans, where he will practice law.

THU AUG 17, 1865
Ad: Springwood Select Home-School, for young ladies; located near Leesburg, Loudoun Co, Va. Principals-Mr & Mrs G Washington Ball.

Gtwn Affairs: tournament, composed wholly of Gtwn youth, came off last evening on Analostan Isl: view of the excellence of the equestrians & the closeness of the contest. Named young gentleman entered the lists:

Saml E Wheatley	H A Eliason	H B Davis	Jas Dickson
A C Pickrell	Rosia W Welch	Edw K Legg	
W W Wheeler	Suthon B	Geo B Chew	
	Cropley	Wm L Eliason	

Chief Mrshl-Mr B W Downman
Knight of Herald: Morris Cropley

Judges

Robt P Dodge	Miss Laub	I Thos Davis
Edw Hall	Harry C Noyes	E D Hartley
Miss Brooke	Geo Magruder	E B Barrett

The Hon John Smith, Judge of the Crct Crt of Allegany Co, Md, died suddenly near Cumberland on Mon last while riding on horseback. Disease of the heart attributed to his death. Balt American

Jas Dorsey, workman at the Capt bldg, was killed there yesterday when struck by falling timbers. He was a widower, having buried his wife about 6 weeks ago. He leaves no chldrn.

Brig Gen Pennybacker, who was severely wounded at Fort Fisher, was today removed from the Chesapeake Hospital to Norfolk. The bldg used by the Hospital was, before the war, a female college, & it is now being cleared out previous to being turned over to its original owners.

FRI AUG 18, 1865
Saml Caswell, of Barnstead, N H, is 106 years of age, & has never drank intoxicating liquors nor used tobacco in his life. His wife is age 96 years & living.

Mrs Maria Thornton, widow of the celebrated Dr Wm F Thornton, died on Wed, in Wash City, at age 100 yrs. She was d/o the unfortunate Dr Dr Dodd of London, who was executed for forgery in 1777. Her mother emigrated to Phil under the name of Brodeau, soon after her hsbnd's death, bringing her dght with her. The marriage of Dr Thornton & Mrs Maria Thornton was childless.
[See pg 456: Aug 22, 1865.]

Homicide on Wed near L st; Miss Mary A Good, a relative of Miss Eliza Ward, on a visit from Balt, was shot while walking near 2nd st. She died yesterday afternoon. The young ladies were going to visit Mrs Coleman, an aunt of the young ladies. Mrs Mary Good, mother of the dec'd, testified that her dght was her only support. It was said that a man had escaped from the guard-hse & that the sldr was ordered to shoot at him by his commanding ofcr. The sldr was Henry Raymond, a pvt of Co B, 16th N Y heavy artl.

City Affairs: Yesterday Bridget Conlan appeared before Justice Walter & charged one Mary Fitzgerald with profanity, & obtained a warrant for her arrest. The warrant was placed in the hands of Roundsman Kelley, who proceeded to execute it, & was surprised to find in his prisoner a woman 86 years of age. Justice Walter dismissed the case. These parties hailed from that locality in the 4th ward known as English Hill, a certain class of the inhabitants of which give the police more trouble & annoyances than all the rest of that ward taken together. The neighborhood is infested with low groggeries, where the vilest mixtures & poisons are sold under the name of whiskey, gin, etc.

Died: at St Louis, on Jul 26, Mary Virginia, w/o Dr Jas H Peabody, of Wash City.

SAT AUG 19, 1865
Amnesty pardons were granted by the Pres to L L Stevenson & Michl G Harman, of Staunton, Va. New applicant was rebel Genrl J A Smith, of Tenn.

Died: in Savannah, Ga, on Aug 11, Frank Gillespie, aged 10 mos, only s/o D A & Josephine E O Byrne, & grandson of the late Bennett Clements, of Gtwn.

Died: on Aug 17, Mrs Caroline Campbell, late w/o Rev Wm W Campbell, of Wash City. Funeral at her late residence at 539 11th st, on Sat.

Died: on Aug 16, Mrs Anna Maria Thornton, wid/o Dr Wm Thornton, in her 90th yr. Funeral from her late residence at 303 G st, this morning.

Died: on Aug 18, at the residence of her son-in-law, Z D Gilman, Mrs Mary H Barr, wid/o the late Robt M Barr, of Pa.

Died: of consumption, on Aug 14, in her 20th yr, at the residence of her uncle, G W L Kidwell, in Wash City, Miss Mary G, d/o S R Dawson & Mary [Kidwell] Dawson, dec'd.

Jury held an inquest over the remains of Miss Mary Good, who was shot Wed, near Camp Barry: jury composed of:

Thos A Burns	Isaac Aspinwall	John T Ward
Jos A Minnick	Oscar K Harris	Jos Daniels
Jas H Alexander	John Hargesheimer	Sewell R Mansfield
Henry C Knoop	Saml T Cooley	Chas W Reams

Mr Jos Chatham was with the ladies when the shooting occurred. Henry Raymond, the sentry who fired the shot, testified he was on duty at the post; was called on by the cpl to take 2 prisoners to the guard hse. Lt told witness to load his carbine; one of the prisoners attempted to escape & ran off. Witness was told to fire at the man & thus compel him to halt. He called out 7 times to the man to halt, & then fired, but aimed above the prisoners head, as he did not wish to kill him. The witness did not see the ladies pass by, & when he fired it was so dark he could not see 2 rods before him. Lt Chas H Farnsworth testified that he was on patrol duty on the day of the shooting. Capt Julius Windsbecker testified that he knew Lt Farnsworth since 1863: that he was an orderly man, never had seen him intoxicated. John Mulloy testified that he saw a man running around the corner: saw the guard fire: did not see the ladies at the time. A J Duval testified that he saw the guard when he fired: did not see the ladies: only one shot was fired: thought the sentry pointed the gun at the prisoner. A M Sprague was called to explain the location: Dr Jos M Homeston examined the wound with Dr Taylor. Farnsworh would not have ordered the gun to be fired if he knew the ladies were about. Wm Grandall testified he was about 12 feet from the ladies when the shot was fired. Killing was accidental: dec'd died on Aug 17. Yesterday the corpse was placed in a coffin & conveyed to Balt, where it will be interred.

The steamer E C Knight, Capt Morris, arrived at Snow's wharf last evening. Passengers-

W T Walker	Oliver Johnson	Wm Buckingham
Chas E Walker	Jacob Schoyer	Capt Seymour & lady
J Snyder & lady	Geo Schoyer	

MON AUG 21, 1865

Supreme Crt of D C, in Equity, #498. Jas Adams vs Albert Noyes, Mary E Mackall, John C McCabe, Maria V McCabe, Emily Poitiux, Eugene Poitiux, Henry C Noyes, Mary C Fitzpatrick, Cecelia Fitzpatrick, Joanna Bright, Geo Bright, Stanislaus Hamilton, Mary M Hamilton, Rosa Young, John R Young, Williamana Fitzpatrick, Anna Fitzpatrick, & Jas N Fitzpatrick. Bill to app't a new trustee in place of Wm Noyes, late of Wash City, dec'd. John C Fitzpatrick, late of Wash City, dec'd, was indebted on or about Mar 21, 1848, to Thornton F Hickey. Hickey transferred the note to Jas Adams. Large portion of note remains unpaid. Wm Noyes has died leaving 5 chldrn, to wit: Albert Noyes, Mary E Mackall, Maria V McCabe, w/o John C McCabe, *Emily Poitiux, w/o *Eugene Poitiux, & Henry C Noyes; the said John C Fitzpatrick died about 3 or 4 years ago, intestate, leaving *Mary C Fitzpatrick, an infant child of a dec'd son, *Cecelia Fitzpatrick, Joanna Bright, w/o Geo Bright, Stanislaus Hamilton & Mary M Hamilton, chldrn of dec'd dght *Rosa Young, w/o *John R Young, Williamana Fitzpatrick, Anna Fitzpatrick & Jas Fitzpatrick. *Non-residents of this dist. -R J Meigs, clerk

Orphans Crt of Wash Co, D C. 1-Case of Jas O'Leary, exc of Cornelius O'Leary, dec'd; settlement on Sep 12. 2-Case of Susan W Reily, excx of John H Reily, dec'd; settlement on Sep 12, 1865. -Z C Robbins, reg of wills

Orphans Crt of Wash Co, D C. Prsnl estate of Geo Shoemaker, late of Gtwn, dec'd. -Ed Shoemaker, Geo Shoemaker, jr, adms

Gtwn affairs: Lectures on reminiscences of Gtwn by Rev Dr Thos B Balch, a lineal descendant, on his mother's side, of Col Geo Beall, who, on Sep 19, 1751, set up his tent in the woods on the grounds now occupied by the seminary of Miss English; to be held during the winter.

Died: on Aug 19, after a lingering illness, Maj Geo Bender, in his 80th yr. Funeral on Monday afternoon.

Orphans Crt-D C. 1-Ltrs of adm to Eliz Meem on estate of John T Meem; to Ed & Geo Shoemaker on estate of Geo Shoemaker, dec'd; to Jas H Clarke on estate of John E Dunscome. 2-Inventory on prsnl estate of Otho Boswell, dec'd; 2nd acc't of Alice E Causten, guardian to Mary Carvallo Causten; final acc't of Jessie McDermott, admx of Wm McDermott, approved & passed. 3-Will of the late Ellen Griffin, bequeathing her property to her relatives, was partially proven.

Died: in Petersburg, Va, on Aug 18, after a lingering illness, Mrs Mary Slade, w/o Dr Jos N Schoolfield, & d/o the late David English, of Gtwn, D C.

TUE AUG 22, 1865
New paint,oil & lamp store, 398 D st, Wash City. -Geo Ryneal, jr. [ad]

The late Mrs Anna M Thornton. A grave mistake [as her friends's see it] was made in stating that she was a d/o the late Dr Dodd. Mrs Thornton at age 16 years mrd in 1791 the late Dr Wm Thornton. In 1796 he, with his wife & her mother, removed to Wash & resided there until their respective deaths. [See pg 455: Aug 18, 1865.]

Mrd: on Aug 5, at the residence of the bride's father in St Mary's Co, Md, by Rev Fr DeWolfe, Wm A Ward, of Wash City, to Miss Amelia R, eldest d/o John L Lancaster.

Died: at Atlantic City, on Aug 21, Reed, infant s/o Dr P J Horwitz, U S Navy. Funeral from 241 I st, today.

Sup Crt of D C, in Equity, #471. Mordecai Yarnall & Eliz J, his wife, vs Maria S, Susan S, & Christopher Johnston, Hugh McBirney & Isabella, his wife, Henry M & Maria S Johnston, jr, Geo S Inglis, John A Inglis, Geo McNeale, & Susan his wife, John F Johnston, [heirs of Robt N Johnston,] Benj R Dallam, & Jane J, his wife, Robt D Muir, Saml C Hepburn, & John D Powell, & Annie L, his wife, & others, heirs of Eliz S Hepburn. Cmplnt purchased of heirs of Eliz S Hepburn, ground in Gtwn, with dwlg hse, late the residence of Eliz S Hepburn, for $5,000; legal title is vested in heirs of Robt N Johnston; bill is to appoint a new trustee, & conveyance from all dfndnts of said premises to said cmplnt; dfndnts are non-residents of this District. -R J Meigs, clerk

Local-suicide. Powell Hess, a German, aged 56 yrs, committed suicide by shooting himself with a six-barrelled Colt's revolver, at his residence at 562 G st; from testimony of his wife. Mr John Hess is a bro of the dec'd. He leaves no chldrn.

Dr Pritchard, who poisoned his wife & mother-in-law, was executed at Glasgow on Jul 28, in the presence of an immense crowd.

WED AUG 23, 1865

For sale or rent, my property in Wash, formerly my residence, 14th & Mass ave, Wash City. -Chas Hill, Upper Marlboro, PG Co, Md

Orphans Crt of Wash Co, D C. 1-Prsnl estate of Anna M Thornton, late of Wash Co, dec'd. 2-Case of Wm Y Fendall, adm of Mary Y Dundas, dec'd; settlement on Sep 16. 3-Case of *Grafton Tyler, exc of Benj Johnson Hellen, dec'd; settlement on Sep 31. -Z C Robbins rg o/wills. [*Dr could preceed Tyler's name: print is incomplete]

Died: Nicholas H Green, Crct Crt clerk for A A Co, Md, at his residence in Annapolis, Md on Sat. He was grandson of Nicholas Harwood, clerk of the convention that framed the constitution of the Md in 1776 & 77; cont'd as such until 1810, when his son-in-law, Wm S Green succeeded him-until 1845. The dec'd Nicholas H Green, was the s/o Wm S Green & succeeded by Col Jos H Nicholson. Mr Green leaves a wife & several chldrn. -Balt Sun

Thos C Connolly was yesterday commissioned by the Pres a justice of the peace for Wash Co, D C.

Police matters: 1-Maria Simms arrested for stealing a breastpin from Florence Wilson-held her to bail for crt. 2-Louisa Hays arrested for selling liquor without a license-fined $21.77. 3-Chas Ranes, about 50 years old, arrested for rape upon Nancy Clarke-held to bail for crt. 4-John Reed arrested for stealing $17 from Jas E Bensley-committed to jail to answer. 5-Elias Rothschild arrested for larceny of pocketbook, property of C Broodigan. A Rothschild, father of Elias, accomplice: both held to bail.

Orphans Crt-D C. 1-Acc't of Wm H Langley, exc of estate of John Hayne, dec'd, passed. 2-Ptn of Mgt Foley, guardian of John & Martin Foley, file for sale of rl estate belonging to the wards. 3-Acc't of Martha E Gray, admx of estate of Henry W Gray, dec'd, passed. 4-Will of Mrs Anna Maria Thornton fully proven; letters of exc granted to J Bayard H Smith, of Balt. Sureties: B Ogle Taylor & John A Smith. 5-Inventory of prsnl estate of Saml Webster, dec'd, returned by Creach St Clark, adm, filed. 6-Hilary M Smith qualiflied as adm of estate of Wm A Graham, dec'd. Sureties: Amelia V Graham & Wm H Pettitt. 7-Bridget Kelley admx of estate of Jas F Kelley, dec'd. Sureties: John Gibson & Geo Gibson. 8-Alfred C Cassell, guardian of Wash. J F & Wm M Cassell, gave bond of $6,000 with Geo T Cassell & Martha V Cassell as sureties. 9-Stanton Coleman qualified as guardian of Moses Jones by giving bond of $300. Aaron Lee & Henry Coleman as sureties.

Died: at St Paul, Minn, on Aug 11, Anna, eldest c/o Capt Robt L Eastman, U S army, & of M Angela Eastman, aged 2 yrs, 10 months & 28 days.

Partnership to practice law is D C is this day dissolved. -Francis Thomas; S W Downey

THU AUG 24, 1865

Geo A Clifford, age about 38 yrs, yesterday either fell from the window in the upper story of the Nat'l Htl, or threw himself. His young son was asleep in the room at the time. He was a clerk in the Internal Rev Bur from Ill. He leaves a wife & 5 chldrn.

Died: at Phil, on Aug 21, John Meredith Read, infant s/o Dr P J Horwitz, U S Navy, aged 6 months & 25 days.

J W Sherman, age 63 yrs, our Cnsl at Pr Edward Island, died on Aug 11, of congested lungs. His father was Cmder of the vessel *Walk-in-the-Water*, on Lake Erie, about 1820, while his bro commanded a beautiful steamer on Lake Champlain.

Gtwn Affairs: the steamer *John Gibson*, Capt Jas R Kelly, arrived at Snow's wharf from N Y, yesterday, with the following passengers:

M Cloggitt	Miss Lancaster	S Snedeker & wife
H E Sanford	F Burlingame	W H H Browne & wife
T Harper	H B Gates & wife	

FRI AUG 25, 1865

Trial of Henry Wirz. Witness account by Dr John C Bates a resident of Ga, detailed to Andersonville on Sep 19, 1864 & left on Mar 26. Account includes a letter written by Wirz, dated Andersonville, Ga, May 7, 1865. States he is a native of Switzerland, & was before the war a ctzn of Louisiana, & by profession a physician. The letter continues: I was very seriously wounded at the battle of Seven Pines, near Richmond, Va, & have nearly lost the use of my right arm. Unfit for field duty, I was ordered to report to Brvt Maj Gen John H Winder, in charge of Federal prisoners of war, who ordered me to take charge of a prison in Tuscaloosa, Ala. My health failing me, I applied for a furlough & went to Europe, from whence I returned in Feb, 1865. I was then ordered to report to the commandant of the military prison at Andersonville, Ga, who assigned me to the command of the interior of the prison. The duties I had to perform were arduous & unpleasant, & I am satisfied that no man can or will justly blame me for things that happened here & which were beyond my power to control. I do not think that I ought to be held responsible for the shortness of rations, for the overcrowded state of the prison, [which was of itself a prolific source of fearful mortality,] for the inadequate supplies of clothing, want of shelter, etc, etc. Still I now bear the odium, and men who were prisoners have seem disposed to wreak their vengeance upon me for what they have suffered. I, who was only the medium, or, I may better say, the tool in the hands of my superiors. This is my condition. I am a man with a family. I lost all my property when the Federal army besieged Vicksburg. I have no money at present to go to any place, &, even if I had, I know of no place where I can go. My life is in danger, & I most respectfully ask of you help & relief. If you will be so generous as to give me some sort of a safe conduct, or what I should greatly prefer, a guard to protect myself & family against violence, I should be thankful to you; & you may rest assured that your protection will not be given to one who is unworthy of it. My intention is to return with my family to Europe as soon as I can make the arrangements. In the meantime, I have the honor, General, to remain. Very Respectfuly, your obedient servant, Hy Wirz, Captain C F A. This letter was sent to Maj Gen J H Wilson, U S A, commanding, Macon, Ga.

Cemeteries of Wash: Glenwood Cemetery was incorporated by an act of Congress on Jul 27, 1854, original incorporators were Chas B Calvert, Geo Parker, Wm B Todd, Jas C McGuire, Wm A Bradley, Chas A Wallach, Abner Miller, Wm Banks, Jos B Close, Wm Phelps, Wm S Humphreys, & Randolph S Evans. Laid out by Capt Geo de la Roche, 90 acs, dedicated on Aug 2, 1854; Mr G Clendenin, super-intendent. Inscriptions include: 1-Wm M Morrison & his son, Maj C J Morrison, both of whom died in 1862. 2-Memory of Geo Humes & his wife Priscilla Duvall. 3-On the gate is Chas W Utermohle. 4-Eliza M, w/o Jos S Wilson. 5-Lot of Robt Farnham with *To my husband*, one-*Our Lilly*, another simply *Alice*. 6-Enclosure of Mrs Tillotson Brown: *Jessie, Georgie, Cassie, Johnnie*, a dght & 3 grandchldrn, is noticeable. 7-Obelisk in memory of *Rev Levin J Gillis*, 1st pastor of

Ascension Chr, who was mrd in the mansion hse now occupied by the superintendent of the cemetery, to the d/o Dr Bradley, the proprietor, from whom these grounds were purchased. 8-Pedestal inscribed *Mary & Nettie, little dghts of B L & L E Nevins*. 9-Shaft in memory of E C Compton; 10-Headstone to *Ella, beloved wife of Jas W White*. 11-Memory of Philip C Johnson & wife. 12-Memory of wife & little child of Robt J Lackey, now D A of Southern district of Missouri. 13-Enclosure of Geo W Calvert with *Little Jessie*. 14-Enclosure of Chas M Keys to memory of a wife & dght. 15-Enclosure of Wm Poulton. 16-Memory of Rev J R Carpenter, chaplain of 1st regt of D C vols. 17-Shaft of Thos Bates. 18-Enclosure of Jas Handley. 19-Lot of Ezekiel McDaniel. 20-Lot of Geo W Cochrane. 21-Memory of Benj C Grenup, killed on May 6, 1865, by the wheel of an engine carriage, mbr of the Columbia Engine Co, while in the discharge of his duty.
[Mount Auburn Cemetery, 100 acs, was founded in Boston, in 1831. Greenwood, 360 acs, in N Y C, in 1842. Laurel Hill Cemetery, 55 acs, is in Phil.]

Supreme Crt of D C, in Equity. John F Cross vs Julia R Cross & others. Ratify sale of rl estate to Wm S Young for $147.14. -Andrew Wylie -R J Meigs, clerk

Mrd: on Aug 8, at St John's Chr, by Rev Belham Williams, Lizzie, d/o the late Dr Chr S Frailey, of Wash City, to Rev Henry R Pyne, of Clinton, N Y.

Mrd: on Aug 15, at Thermopylae, Rappahonnock Co, Va, the residence of the bride's father, by Rev Fr Towle, Jas L Carbery, of Gtwn, D C, to Miss Eliza Ann, d/o the late Dr Mark Reid.

The President yesterday granted pardons to the following: C H Slocombe, of Louisiana & Henry Taylor, of Va.

SAT AUG 26. 1865
Boston, Aug 24. Trial of Antoine Van Weimer, Geo W Northredge, Patrick Shay, & John Dolan, charged with rape committed on Aug 13, were all found guilty & sentenced to life in the State Prison.

Trial of Henry Wirz. Witness' accounts: Dr John C Bates had resided in Louis-ville, Jefferson Co, Ga; forced to enter the rebel army in Jun 1864. Dr A W Barrows was captured at Plymouth & reached Andersonville in May 1864 & placed in the hospital until Oct 9, 1864, when he escaped & made his way to Pensacola & joined the Union forces.

The late Gen Jos G Swift died recently at his residence at Geneva, N Y. He was the first cadet appt'd to the Military Academy at West Point: appt'd in 1802. He died at age 85 yrs.

For sale: farm on which I reside: 296½ acs near Upr Marlboro, Md; & dwlg hse. -John Hodges, jr

Mrs Jane Seymour, age 65 yrs, was shot & killed at the residence of her son-in-law in Memphis, on Monday night, by person unknown.

Supreme Crt of D C, Equity #274. Eliz Green vs Magee & others. Ratify sale reported by R P Jackson, of rl estate of Hugh Magee, dec'd, to the amount of $4,242.64. -R J Meigs, clerk

Pres granted pardon to: Jas D Coleman, Caroline Co, Va; H J Randolph, Albemarle Co, Va; T J Randolph, do; Benj F Drew, of Va; Milton P Jarnagan & Jos S Claghorn, of Savannah, Ga.

Died: on Aug 24, of typhoid fever, Julia Sessford, d/o the late John Sessford, of Wash City. Funeral from the residence of Saml Kelly, 17th & C sts, Sat.

MON AUG 28, 1865

Trial of Henry Wirz. Witness' accounts: Dr A W Barrows was from Amherst, Mass, resided there 10 years & was med student before the war, joined his regt at Little Wash., N C, captured May 20, 1864. Robt M Kellogg was examined.

Died: Mrs Rosalind A Hovey, w/o Gen Alvin P Hovey, at the St Nicholas Htl, in N Y, on Thu; d/o the late Caleb B Smith; mrd to Gen Hovey a short time since.

Crct Crt of PG Co, Md-Eleanor L Lee & W Seton Belt, adms of Benj Lee, & others, vs Mary L Contee, Danl Clark, adms d b n of John Contee & others. Sale of in PG Co, Md, of which the late John Contee died seized, at his residence called *Pleasant Prospect*, 575 acs, with lge brick mansion, adj the land of Col Oden Bowie, Chas C Hill, Miss Duckett, & others. -Thos G Pratt, Danl Clarke, trust.

Sale of land, in PG Co, Md, which the late John F Jones died seized, being the same rl estate conveyed from John F Jones to Danl C Digges & John C Mullikin, on Apr 1, 1856, called *Maiden's Dowry* & a tract called *Gray Eagle*. Thereto attached & in the same county, in Centreville, about 13 acs conveyed to John F Jones by Wm W Fowler, improved by a tavern, stable & small hse. -Daniel Clarke, trustee

N Y Evening Post-Edw B Ketchum, of the firm of Morris Ketchum, Son & Co, whose forgeries of gold certificates have hade him so notorious, was arrested on Friday, between 5th & 6th aves, near his lodgings.

Maj John P Heiss, a native of Nicaragua, & many years a resident of Wash City, died in N Y on Aug 22nd

Died: on Aug 29, Josias Allen Green, aged 31 yrs. Funeral from the residence of his father, Ammon Green, 323 North B st, today.

Died: on Aug 26, Miss Eliz C Bolton, aged 73 yrs, sister of the late Cmdor Bolton, U S N. Friends of Cmdor & Mrs Chas Wilkes are invited to attend the funeral on Tue.

Died: in Balt, on Aug 25, Cornelia B, infant d/o J B H & Henrietta Smith, aged 18 months.

Died: at the residence of her parents in Montg Co, Md, near Gtwn, D C, on Aug 18, Eleanor Kearley Miller, eldest d/o E P & Rebecca W Miller, aged 17 years & 6 months.

TUE AUG 29, 1865

Orphans Crt of Wash Co, D C. Case of Andrew Noerr, adm of John C Roemmele, dec'd; settlement on Sep 19. -Z C Robbins, rg o/wills

Wm Earnshaw, Chaplain U S Army & Superintendent of the Sldrs' Ntl Cemetery at Stone river, gives notice that he shall disinter all the bodies of that & other battle-fields, for purpose of burying them in the beautiful grounds now being prepared. If friends are determined to remove any of the remains to their homes, they should inform him of the fact, giving the name, rank, co, regt, brig, & div to which the dec'd was attached. Forwarding will be as directed.

New Ad-Fine Groceries, Richard J Ryon, 481 Ninth st, Wash, D C.

U S Patent ofc-Ptn of Hiram W Hayden, of Waterbury, Conn, for extension of patent dt'd Dec 16 1851: inprovement in *machinery for making kettles* etc. -T C Theaker, Com of Patents

For sale or rent-*Smith's Point farm*, 487½ acs, Chas Co, Md. Apply to Saml W Adams, Nanjemoy, Chas Co, Md.

Re-issue of land warrants: 1-160 acs to Eliz Benson, widow of Giles Benson, granted Jun 14, 1858. 2-160 acs to Pedro Jose Jolona, granted Mar 27, 1862.
3-120 acs to Mary, widow of Robt Douthill, granted Sep 4 1856. -Jos H Barrett, commissioner.

Died: on Aug 25, in Alexandria, Va, Mrs Eliza Morgan, in her 72nd yr.

Died: at Fort Leavenworth, Kan, on Aug 19, Abby Jane, w/o Dr W E Waters, U S Army, & d/o Wm A Evans.

Obsequies of the late Brig Gen Marcellus M Crocker took place Aug 28. Remains were conveyed from the Willard Htl to the B & O R R depot, to be taken to his home in Des Moines, Iowa. His stricken wife who arrived in Washington too late to see her husband alive, accompaines the remains in the mournful journey.

Amnesty pardons were granted by the Pres yesterday to: John P Branch, Thos Branch, Jas R Branch, Geo W Boding, E Fontaine, Chas A Rose, Wm Allen, John Kevan & Wm Kevan. All Virginians.

Trial of Henry Wirz. Witnesses' accounts: Robt H Kellogg, enlisted Aug 11, 1862, mustered out Jun 1, 1865, captured Apr 20, 1864 & taken to Andersonville, then to Charleston & Florence. Thos C Alcoke, 72nd Ohio infty, captured at Wolf river, Miss, sent to Andersonville in 1864, resides at Cincinnati, Ohio, born & raised there, enlisted in 1861. Saml D Brown entered the U S svc in Oct 1861, mustered out Jun 1865, captured at Plymouth, N C & reached Andersonville on May 4, 1864. Jacob D Brown was a sldr from Jan 1862 until Jun 1865, prison from May 31, 1864 until Sep 9.

WED AUG 30, 1865
Burlington, Vt, Aug 28. Mrs Ephraim Griswold, a wealthy old lady who resides in Williston, Vt, was found murdered in her barn this morning. Her hsbnd was absent from home at the time. Perpetrator of the deed is yet unknown.

Mrd:Aug 29, by Rev Dr Ryan, Benj Reiss to Adeline H, d/o the late Lt Wm Lowe, U S N.

Died: on Aug 27, in Yonkers, N Y, after a painful illness, Sarah C, w/o Ira Goodnow, Doorkeper of the Hse of Reps, U S, aged 50 yrs. Mrs Goodnow was born & reared in this community.

Died: on Aug 29, Beth Lester, 2nd d/o Jas F & Marion Walker, aged 2 yrs. She will be buried from the residence, 456 D st, today.

Died: on Aug 29, after a long & painful illness, Mgt Scott, wid/o Capt West Scott. It may be truly said of her that she died a child in Jesus. Her funeral will take place from the residence of her father, Hon Wm F Purcell, 3rd & F sts, Thu.

Died: Adj Jas M Kelley, 2nd D C vols, in Alexandria, Va, on Sunday. He was buried at the sldr's cemetery with honors of war.

Case of estate of the late Andrew J Butler, bro o/Gen Butler, exc, came up in Surrogate's crt on Mon. Property in this state is valued at $72,000. -N Y Herald

Trial of Henry Wirz. Witness' acounts: Dr G G Roy was on duty at Andersonville & assigned there on Sep 1864; Dr Isaiah H White was Chief surg. Surg B A Vanderkief, a surgeon in the U S svc, was at present on duty in Balt; was at Annapolis from May 1863 until May 1865 & directed the treatment of Union prisoners from Andersonville. He was educated in Holland & a regular med grad. Martin T Hogan was a sldr of the 1st Ind cavalry & prisoner 4 times during the war; taken to Andersonville on Aug 6, 1864. Jos B Keyser of the 120th N Y vols was captured in James City Co, Va, on Oct 10, 1863, confined at Richmond then to Andersonville in Feb 1864.

THU AUG 31, 1865

The 258th anniversary of the landing of the first English colony on the coast of N Eng [A D 1607} was observed at Popham. Hon Chas T Gilmore, of Brunswick, pres of the day, & Hon J N Patterson, of Hanover, orator. -Bath, Me, Aug 29

Ingleside Academy for young ladies, near Catonsville, 20th session will commence. Mrs Jas Gibson, principal, Catonsville, Balt Co, Md.

For sale-*Franklin*, 425 acs, in PG Co, Md, with dwlg hse. S B Boarman, Bank of Wash.

Trial of Henry Wirz. Witness' accounts: Alexander W Persons, in Confederate svc for 4 yrs, on duty at Andersonville from Feb 1864 until Jun 1, 1864, reporting to Gen John H Winder. Benj F Clark was in the rebel medical purveyor's dept in Richmond & on duty in N C. Jas Van Valkenburg resided near Macon, Ga, & has been at Andersonville. Boston Corbett was a prisoner in Jul or Aug 1864. Dr F G Castlen was stationed at Andersonville from May to Sep 1864, had been surgeon of the 3rd Ga reserve regt. Andrew J Spring of the 16th Connecticut vols arrived in Andersonville in May, 1861.

Young Ladies Seminary, Gtwn, D C. -Mrs H A Wheeler, principal.

Brookeville Acad, Montg Co, Md. -J Dunlin Parkinson, A B, principal.

Sale of val rl estate in New Castle Do, Dela: family mansion & farm called *Eden Park*, 185 acs.
-Florencio J Verier, trustee, 615 Walnut st, Phil, or Thos F Bayard, Wilmington, Dela.

Ad-O'Hare & Noonan, plumbers, steam & gasfitters. 402 D st, Wash, D C. -Owen O'Hare, Tim V Noonan

FRI SEP 1, 1865

Mrd: Miss Mary A Sheridan, a sister of Maj Gen Sheridan, & Capt Wilson, of the Cumberland Army, recently at Somerset, Perry Co, Ohio.

Removals in the City P O due to the reduction of mail on account of the disbanding of the army:

R F Allen	Jas Clephane, sr	Robt Nevitt	Geo W Swain
Chas McD	Fred'k Cook	Delano Piper	R B Thomas
Brown	Augustus Edson	Thos Rich	Rudulph Worch
Henry Busey	John T Hunter	A B Scrivener	

Died: Aug 31, Miss Louisa G McCalla, d/o John M McCalla. Funeral: Fri at 9-Indiana ave.

Died: on Aug 29, in Montg Co, Md, after a brief illness, Blanche Birch, y/c/o Wm H & Sophia Birch, aged 9 years, 11 months & 29 days.

Sale of bldg lots at D & 2nd sts, Wash, at public auction. Ptn of Jas McSherry, guardian of Helen N, Mary C, & Jas C McSherry, minor heirs ofThos Carbery, dec'd. -Jas McSherry, guardian.

SAT SEP 2, 1865
For sale-4 farms opposite *Mt Vernon*. Take the steamer *Columbia* at Washington or Alexandria & land at my residence, *Marshall Hall*. Communicate by letter-Thos Marshall, Pamunkey, Chas Co, Md.

Commissioners' sale of rl est, Wash, D C: division of rl estate of Benj Bean, dec'd. -Wm Dixon, Wm Nottingham, W P Ferguson, Geo R Ruff, Wm A Fletcher

Farm of 100 acs for sale in Montg Co, Md, with well built cottage. -Geo N Beale, Sligo P O, Montg Co, Md, or at his residence adjoining the above farm.

Local-jury returned a verdict that John T Meem came to his death from causes unknown to them.

Fifty-three years ago the obit of Pres Johnson's father [Jan 10, 1812] appeared in the Raleigh [N C] Star: died in this city on Sat last, Jacob Johnson; followed by an account of Thos Henderson of how Jacob Johnson saved him from drowning. In the same paper is the death notice of the mother of Wm Gaston.

Trial of Henry Wirz. Witness' accounts: Mr Nazareth Allen, of the 3rd Ga Reserves, on duty at Andersonville, reported when his age was called, between 45 & 50. J F Heath sworn, had been a capt in the Confederate svc & in part of 1864 was at Andersonville. Wm Dillard sworn, in Confederate svc & at Andersonville from May 20 last to Sept. Judge Daniel Hall of Ga, residing 10 miles from Andersonville, visited the vicinity of the prison in Dec 1864.

Wash Corp: 1-E V Boswell confirmed for Apothecary to the poor of the 7th ward, in place of Otho Boswell, dec'd. 2-W C Hall, mgr of the U S Telegraph Co, asked permission to run 2 wires over the roof of the City Hall: same was referred to a special cmte-Messrs Noyes, A Lloyd, & Owen. 3-Ptn of J Bleigh & others, with a bill for setting curbstones & paving the carriageway in 12th st west: referred to the Cmte on Improvements. 4-Ptns of Cath Smith & W McCauley, for remittance of certain fines: referred to the Cmte on Claims. 5-Ptn of Hugh McGinnis, with a bill for his relief: referred to the Cmte on Claims. 6-Ptn of John Doherty & Michl Duffy & others: adverse report by the Cmte on Claims: cmte asked to be discharged, which was so ordered. 7-Ptn of Mrs M A Lathrop: same as above-#6.

474

Boston, Sep 1. Last night at So Dedham, Mrs Marston, w/o Dr Carlos Marston, shot & killed the Dr & her 10 yr old dght, Cora, & then killed herself. Dr M was about age 40 years & came from N H, having resided in So Dedham about 3 months.

Trustees' sale of rl estate at the residence of the late John Contee: *Arthur's Sealed Enlarged*, or *Webb's*, 230 acs; & *Woodland*, about 400 acs. Richd B B Chew, Daniel Clarke, trustees

MON SEP 4, 1865
Northernway, N H, Sep 1. Miss Fanny McGregor, of Boston, d/o Jas McGregor, Pres of the State Bank of Boston, was accidentally killed at a pistol firing range by Mr Henry C Mayer, this morning.

For sale-my farm in Pamunkey Neck, Chas Co, Md, about 382 acs, where I reside. -H R V Cawood.

Ad-John R Offutt, hse & sign painters, upholstering & varnishing. 398 9th st. Wash, D C

Died: Wm Douglas, on Dec 2nd , at his residence, 591 H st, of typhoid fever, in his 51st yr. Funeral from his residence this afternoon, Sep 4.

Died: on Sep 2, at White Sulphur Springs, Dub Gap, Pa, after a lingering illness, Susan Robertson, 2nd d/o John H & Eliza W Semmes, aged 11 years, 5 months & 1 day. Funeral from their residence on Md av on Tue.

Died: on Sep 3, Mary E, d/o the late Jas Watson. Funeral from the residence of her bro, W H Watson, G & 19th sts, today.

Died: on Sep 2, after a short illness, Col Jasper M Jackson, late of Md, in his 83rd yr. Funeral from the residence of B L Jackson, 333 Pa av, Thu.

Trial of Henry Wirz. Witness' accounts: O S Belcher, 16 Ill cavalry, prisoner from Mar 8 to Sep 8, 1864. Jas H Davidson, 4th Iowa cavalry, captured in 1863 & taken to Belle Isle until Feb 1864, then to Andersonville in Mar. Capt J H Wright, formerly a capt, was sworn. Jas H Fanning, formerly Lt Col of the 1st Ga Reserves, which was stationed at Andersonville, was called. Thos Hall, mbr of the U S Marine Corps, was sworn. He was a prisoner at Columbia & Charleston, S C, & last at Andersonville, Ga; taken there in Mar 1864. Assist Surg Wm Balser, U S V, was on duty at Hiton Head & detailed at Jacksonville, Fla, where he treated the diseases of the prisoners who came from Andersonville. Jas Clancey, 38th N Y vols, taken to Andersonville a prisoner in Jun 1864 until Nov. Oliver B Fairbanks, Co E, 9th N Y cavalry, captured in Oct 1863, taken to Libby prison then to Andersonville in Feb 1864. He knew Wirz to kick his [witness's] stepfather; who died a month after he was kicked. He told him not to tell his wife, Fairbank's mother, the awful condition he was compelled to die in. Note was written Camp Sumter, Andersonville, Ga, Aug 21, 1864, signed Richard Fairclough.

Pres has remitted the death sentence in cases of Pvts H S Humphrey, Co C, 5 M V; Robt Brown, Wm Walters & Thos Manley, 15th unattached company, Mass, heavy artl, convicted of desertion, & commutes the sentence to 5 years imprisonment at hard labor from Aug 1, 1864.

TUE SEP 5, 1865

Cmdor John Collins, long of the U S navy, died on Sat at No Conway, N H, where he was visiting. He was born in 1795.

Ptn to Pres Johnson signed by over 400 residents of Holly Springs, Marshall Co, Mississippi, Aug 1 1865; solicit Exec clemency for Jefferson Davis, now confined in Fortress Monroe. Signed: Mrs W S Featherston, Mrs A C McEwen, Mrs Martha Robinson, Miss E C Polk, Misses Alice Morgan & Mary Morgan, & 410 others.

John B Brewster, Co E, 31st Mass, shot himself in the heart with a Colt revolver at Mobile on Aug 23. -Alabama

Capt R A Winder, s/o Gen John H Winder, of rebel prison notoriety, is confined in the old Capitol prison.

Suicide-Chas Vease, 4th U S artl, on Sun last, at No 1 Barracks, Sldrs Rest.

Death from accidental shooting-on Sat last, Capt J D Morrison, Co E, 194 O V I, from Senecaville, Ohio; while in a scuffle. He leaves a wife & child. -Local

Died: on Sep 3, of typhoid fever, John Watson Shaw, aged 19 years & 2 mos, eldest s/o John Brien & Isabella Shaw. Funeral at the First Presby Chr on Tue.

The Grand Jury of Md on Thu returned indictments for treason against Bradley T Johnson, Geo Freaner, John G Howard, Thos Fitzhugh, & Henry G Gilmor, the guerilla.

WED SEP 6, 1865

Orphans Crt of Wash Co, D C. Case of Covington Smith, exc of Richd Smith, dec'd. -Z C Robbins, rg o/wills

A military commission has been organized at Vicksburg for the trial of H P Reeves, charged with being a guerilla, violation of the laws of war, & the robbing & murder of Col Mellow, an old resident of Vicksburg.

Sudden death on Mon at the Kirkwood Hse, Wash , D C. Thos Irwin Hughes, #s 4 & 6 Pine sts, N Y, came to his death from causes unknown. His bro Jas Hughes, arrived here to see the remains.

Mrd: on Sep 5, by Rev John McNally, Mr S Henriques to Miss Rebecca Scott, d/o the late Maj W B Scott, both of Wash City.

Died: on Sep 5, Lawrence M Morton. Funeral from the residence of his mother, 117 West st, Gtwn, D C, on Wed.

Alex'r Dudley, President of the York River railrd, has had his pardon restored to him by Pres Johnson.

The Pres on Sat had yesterday granted pardons to the following named persons, under the provisions of the amnesty proclamation.

T W Edwards, Va	J Ingersoll, Ala	R G Morris, Va
Thos Leslie, Va	J H Bunley, Va	R F Morris, Va
Sanderson Thrift, Va	Jonathan Bliss, Ala	P McCormick, Va

J L Menshaw, Ga
H W Barksdale, Va
W G Young, Va
Alex Tinsley, Va
S G Tinsley, Va
Thos Tinsley, Va
L O Washington, Va
T B Bethea, Ala
John Willis, Miss
M Jones, Miss
Benj C Yancey, Ga
W D McNioh, Tenn
A H Chalkely, Va
J B Davis, Va
J D Hammersley, Va
O W Purcell, Va
John G Shotts, Va
J W Taylor, Va
G F Watson, Va
Maclary Wickham, Va
P T Sayre, Ala
John Wooster, N C
M M Davis, Va
J C McCabe, Va

Oscar G Paroley, N C
Henry Savage, N C
Robt Payne, Va
N M Tregerant, Miss
J H Hansbuerger, Va
Saml Miller, Va
J C Eskridge, Va
Wm Gibboney, Va
Robt Gibboney, Va
G C Kent, Va
H McGavock, Va
Stephen McGovock, Va
H Newberg, Va
C C Tate, Va
G P Duncan, La
John A Liggat, Va
M H Effinger, Va
David Forrer, Va
G H Christman, Va
Moses Yerkel, Va
J D Williamson, Va
John Cowen, Va
W G Thompson, Va
S A Coffman, Va

Thornton Thomas, Va
J B Strayer, Va
W M Gilbert, Va
Isaac Paul, Va
A H Newman, Va
H H Beck, Va
T K Miller, Va
John B Johnson, Tenn
V K Gleverson, Tenn
John B Palmer, N C
David Armstrong, Va
M J Moyerhoeffer, Va
Thos Moore, Va
J W Lee, Va
E G Kemper, Va
J W Herring, Va
John O Harris, Va
Edw Coles, Va
E J Armis, Va
A P Estridge, Va
A J Mathews, Va
Wm Martin, Va

Trial of Henry Wirz. Witness' accounts: J Nelson Clark was sworn, prisoner at Andersonville May 28, 1864. Vincent Halleck, 72nd N Y vols was taken to Andersonville on May 1 or 2 1864. Edw L Kellogg, 20th N Y cavalry was taken to Andersonville about Mar 1, 1864. Same for Jos R Achuff, of the 24th Ohio, who was a prisoner in Mar & thence to Charleston in Aug; tells of a man named Hicks of the 75th Ill who died; also of Geo White of Germantown, Pa, who wrote a message to his mother, before he died. Dan'l W Bussinger, 10th Pa Reserve, prisoner in Jun 1864, fed 3 sick men from his own allowance, i e; Hugh Lynch, Wm Kyger, & Wm Waterhouse, of the 3rd Pa cavalry; all eventually died. Horatio B Furrill, 72nd Ohio, prisoner Jun 19, 1864, was sworn. Robt Myrtle, Co B, 97th Pa, was at Andersonville May 16, 1864. Frank Maddox, 35th U S colored troops, prisoner from Apr 1864 until Feb

THU SEP 7, 1865
Trial of Henry Wirz. Witness' accounts: Jos Adler, 2nd Massachusetts Cavalry was sworn: prisoner at Andersonville from Mar to Sep 1864. Wm H Jennings, 8th U S colored troops, was prisoner from Feb 1864 until Feb 1865. Thos N Way was sworn & was a prisoner from Feb to Sep 1864. Same for C H Stearns, 1st U S sharpshooters, who was a prisoner in Jul 1864. Same for Alexander Kimmell, 7th Ohio cavalry, prisoner from Feb 27 until Sep 25, 1864. Wm Willis Scott, 6th W V cavalry, prisoner in Aug 1864. L S Pond, 2nd N Y heavy artl, prisoner on Jun 28, 1864. Rufus Munday, 25th Ohio, was a prisoner from & after Feb 3, 1865. Abner A Kelley, 40th Ohio, prisoner from May to Nov 1864. Sidney Smith, 14th Conn, prisoner from May until Sep 9, 1864. Godfelds Brunner, 14th Conn, prisoner from Feb until Sep 1864. Thos H Howe, 102nd N Y, prisoner on & after Jul 29, 1864.

Died: on Sep 5, Robt Lee, s/o Thos J & Mary A Galt, aged 2 years & 6 months. Funeral from the residence of his parents, 10 La av, Thu.

Sudden death at the Ntl Htl last night; Lt S B Walworth, age about 30 yrs, of congestion of the brain. Papers on his person indicate he was of the 15th N Y cavalry.

Orphans Crt of Wash Co, D C. Case of Mary Cover, admx w a of Henry Cover, dec'd; settlement on Sep 30th. -Z C Robbins, rg o/wills

The obsequies of the late Lawrence Mortimer Morton took place yesterday from the famly residence: 115 West st. Burial in Oak Hill Cemetery, Gtwn, D C. He leaves his mother & 4 sisters to mourn his departure.

Died: in Gtwn, D C, on Sep 2, in the 65th yr of her age, Mrs C A Miller, w/o Hezekiah Miller. [Balt papers please copy.]

FRI SEP 8, 1865

Chas W Schuermann, recently returned from Calif, will give music instructions at his residence: 402 16th st, Wash, D C

Sup Crt of D C. Cath Garity & others vs Bridget Garity & others. Distribution on Sep 19 of the fund of Patrick Garity. W Redin, auditor

Sup Crt-D C, Equity #301. Robt B Clarke vs Maria Clarke & others, Distribution of the fund of Wm M Clarke. -W Redin, auditor

Died: on Sep 6, Mrs Eliza Davey, native of Devonshire, Eng, in her 69th yr. Funeral from the residence of her son, Henry Davey, 8th & L sts, Fri.

Died: at Eckington, near Wash, D C, on Sep 7, Edw N Mann, of Raleigh, N C, in his 23rd yr. Funeral on Sat. [Va & N C papers please copy]

Died: on Sep 7, of diptheria, Albert, infant s/o Jos J & Alice L Coombs, aged 3 years & 2 days. Funeral from their residence, 249 I st, Fri.

Phil, Sep 7. Reading, Sep 7: Brig Gen Schimmelpfennig died this morning at Wernersville, near this city. Burial on Sat.

Richard M Hall, formerly of Indiana, but for the last 5 years a resident of Wash, has been appt'd Rg of Deed for D C, vice Dr N C Towle.

Enterprising.-Messrs Geo W Riggs & Geo H Plant have purchased of Mr Joshua Pearce the sq of ground bounded by 14 & 15th sts & Q & R sts, containing about 157 sq ft, at 20 cents per ft.

Trial of Henry Wirz. Witness' accounts: John W Case, 47th N Y, prisoner at Andersonville from Aug 20 until Sep 17. Edmund Richardson resided in Albany, Ga & had been to Andersonville several times. Chas J Williams, 1st NJ cavalry, prisoner on & after Mar 12, 1864.

Sup Crt-D C, equity #343. Thos P White vs Wm T Robb et al. Ratify sale by trustee, Asbury Lloyd, of lot 1 in sq 952 to Thos P White for $825. Geo P Fisher

Orphans Crt of Wash Co, D C. Case of Maria S Williams, admx of Saml S Williams, dec'd; settlement on Sep 23. -Z C Robbins, rg o/wills

SAT SEP 9, 1865
New Ad-Stone Works. -Nicholas Acker, N J av & E st. Wash, D C.

Fine dwlg for sale, 2 story & attic brick; lot is 75 x 50, fronting on 21st st; at present occupied by Gen D H Rucker. -Jas C McGuire & Co, auctioneers

Sale of the interest of the orphan chldrn of John A Cassell, dec'd, property in Wash, D C. - Alfred C Cassell, guardian. Green & William auctioneers

Trial of Henry Wirz. Witness' accounts: Lt Prescott Tracey was sworn, captured in Jun 1864 & taken to Andersonville. Wm Krouse, 7th Pa Reserves was a prisoner from May until Sep 1864. Capt C M Selph was sworn, was on duty in the ofc of the Adj & Inspec Gen at Richmond. He knew the hand-writing of Howell Cobb; letter of Cobb dt'd Macon, Ga, May 5, 1864 followed. Capt J H Wright testified that he had been in the Confederate svc & knew the hand-writing of Maj Turner & Capt Wirz. Another report came from Dr Isaiah White, Chief Surg at Andersonville.

Richard B Winder, now confined in the Old Capitol, is not a s/o Gen John H Winder.

Mrs Wirz, the w/o the prisoner, is now here, & one day this week attended the court where her hsbnd is being tried. She is about 40 to 45 years of age. She came from the Plains of Dura, near Andersonville, where Wirz's family resided, having come from Tuscaloosa.

Mrd: on May 1, by Rev T B McFalls, Mr Franklin M Jones, of Phil, to Miss Marchia Ann Burns, of Wash, D C.

MON SEP 11, 1865
Spotswood Augustine Washington died at his residence at Middleport, Ill, on Aug 24, aged 54 yrs. His father was Bushrod Washington, jr, s/o Col Wm Augustine Washington, who was bro of Bushrod Washington, sr, judge of the U S Sup Crt. The latter was the s/o Lawrence Washington, bro of Geo Washington. His oldest son, Bushrod D Washington, receives the private & official seal of Washington.

Died: Sep 10, Creighton Armbrustes, infant s/o Creighton M & Mary S Wheeler. Funeral-Sep 11.

3rd Infty-this regt is the oldest in the U S svc, & is now stationed at the Arsenal in Wash City, under the command of Maj Archer, with Lt Helm as adj. Its history would form an interesting volume, embracing events of the Mexican war & an almost complete record of the Army of the Potomac.

Mr Jas G Holland, ast paymstr U S navy, arrived in Wash City to settle his accounts. He is a native Washington. For the past 2 years he has been connected with the U S schnr *Geo Mangham.*

Trial of Henry Wirz. Witness' accounts: Col D T Chandler was sworn. He had been in the svc of the Confederate Gov't. John E Marshall, 42nd N Y vols was prisoner at Andersonville. Wm N Peebles was on duty at same in 1864. W W Crandall, 4th Iowa, was at the prison in 1864. Louis Van Buren, 2nd N Y cavalry, was a prisoner from & after Jun 7, 1864.

Boston, Sep 8. Ex-Gov John Page died this morning at Haverhill, N H.

TUE SEP 12, 1865
Trustee's sale-deed of trust from Jas Fitzgerald, late of Wash City, dec'd, dt'd Feb 18, 1851; lot 8 in reservation 10, with improvements, Wash City. -Henry Naylor, trustee -Green & Williams, auctioneers

Sup Crt of D C, Equity #317. Louis Grammer, Julius E Grammer, Matilda Grammer, & Alice Grammer, vs Wm B Todd & Wm H Dunkinson & wife. Statement of account of G C Grammer, Jr, dec'd, on Sep 22. -Wm R Woodward, Spec Auditor

Sup Crt of D C, Equity #305. Henry Crow, Thos Crow, & Sarah Harris vs Jas Matthews, Chas Matthews, Wm Matthews, & Edw Hunt & wife. Statement of the trustee's acc't on Sep 23. -Wm R Woodward, Spec Auditor

Crct Crt of Montg Co, Md-Crt of Equity. Sale of rl estate of Saml Shreeve, dec'd; at his late residence on the pblc rd from Wash City to Spencerville: lot 1 of 67+. acs; lot 2 of 148+ acs; lot 3 of 94+ acs; lot 4 of 113+ acs; 426 acs as before stated, on the rd from Wash, near the farms of Dr Wash. Duvall, Francis Valdenar, Lloyd Green & Fawcett's Factory. -W Veirs Bouic, trustee in Rockville, Md; Mr Culver on the premises; Mr Jas H Shreeve, in Wash City.

Died: on Sep 11, Dr John M Roberts, aged 50 years & 3 months. Funeral from his late residence, 433 G st, Wed.

Died: on Sep 11, of diptheria, *Gracie, d/o Thos & *Eliz Jewell, in the 9th yr of her age. Funeral from the Meth Prot Chr, on Wed. [Sep 13 changes: *Grace d/o Thos & *Ann Eliza Jewell. Funeral from Meth Prot Chr, Congress St, Gtwn.]

Trial of Henry Wirz. Witness' accounts: Maj Gen J H Wilson was sworn. He was a capt of engineers & maj gen of vols. He had examined the Andersonville prison. Lt Col Geo Welling, 4th Ky cavalry, was sworn & testified. Patrick Bradley, 7th Mass, was a prisoner from & after Apr 1864. John Fisher, 8th U S colored infty, was bucked & gagged & whipped at Andersonville. Henry C Lull, 146th N Y, was a prisoner at Andersonville.

WED SEP 13, 1865
Orphans Crt of Wash Co, D C. Case of Eliza M Anderson, excx of Thos F Anderson, dec'd; settlement on Oct 7. -Z C Robbins, rg o/wills

Yesterday, the street car conducted by Wm McCauley, ran over the 5 yr old d/o Mr John King, who lives on 8th st. She died about 3 hours after the accident. Her father is an ensign in the navy & attached to the yard in Wash City.

Trial of Henry Wirz. Witness' accounts: Jas Ormond, of Atlanta, Ga, was adj at Andersonville under Wirz. Jas Armstrong, of Macon, Ga, was also an important witness. Maj Proctor, of Mammoth Cave, Ky, was commissary at Andersonville when Armstrong was absent, sick. Lt Gamble, of Tallahassee, Fla, was in command of the battery. Felix De La Baum, 39th N Y vols, was a prisoner from Jul 1864 until Apr 1865. Rev Wm W Hamilton, pastor of a Cath Chr in Macon, Ga, was sworn. He visited the prison in May 1864. Chas E Tibbles, 4th Iowa vols, was a prisoner from Mar until Sep 1864. John H Goldsmith, 14th Ill, was a prisoner from Oct 11, 1864 until Mar 18, 1865. Jasper Culver, 1st Wisc, was a prisoner from & after Mar 16, 1864.

Died: in Wash City, after a protracted illness, Grafton Powell, in his 62nd yr. Funeral from the residence of his son-in-law, John C Shafer, 110 14th st, Thu.

Wash City News-trustees of Pblc School. Application of Miss S A H Witherow for a teacher was referred. The resignation of Miss Sabra P Abell, teacher of #2 second Dist, was accepted. New mbrs, Messrs C H Utermehle & Cassell, would occupy the same postitions on the cmtes as had been filled by their predecessors, Messrs O C Wight & Jas B Elis. Mr Tustin presented to the Brd a copy of Rev Dr Carter's Elements of Genr'l History: referred to the Cmte on Text-bks.

Orphans Crt of D C. Sale of unimproved rl estate on north G st, Wash City: ptn of guardian of the infant chldrn of Henry A Felson, dec'd. -Eliz J Felson, guardian

Mustered Out: the 31st Mass heavy artl, which has been garrisoning Fts Slocum, Stevens, Sumner, Lincoln, Reno, & Totten. Number about 1,200 men. The Col of the regt, W S Abert, a native of our city, needs no farewell. A West Pointer, holding high positions under McClellan & Banks, his military record is one Washington may be proud of. The majs of the regt are Geo S Wooster, L B Whiton, & J N Richardson, one of the heroes of the N C fights, twice wounded. Fort Slocum was placed in his charge. Ast Adj Geo P Richardson, a Gettysburg hero, bro to the Maj, leaves with the 3rd. Capt E J Russell, who commands at Fort Stevens, & Lt E G W Cartwright, who had charge of Fort Totten, together with Capt A W Brigham, commander at Fort Lincoln, leave us also. These forts will be dismantled during the fall.

Mrd: Sep 5th, at Christ Chr, by Rev Mr Olds, J Faulkner Cook, recently of the Black Horse Cavalry, to Lucy C, d/o Wm Van Metre Henry, of Warren Co, Va.

Capt J B Jones, 19th U S infty, arrived here today from Augusta, Ga, via N Y, bringing with him about 1,100 lbs of gold & silver bullion, with a small amount of coin, with the aggregate value of perhaps $200,000. This wealth was recovered by the Treas agent, & is said to be part of the spoil captured from Jeff Davis. Capt Jones has delivered the money to the U S Treasurer.

Surgeon Reyburn, of Freemen's Bureau, who was ordered by Gen Howard to inspect the condition of the colored people living on "*the Island*" in Wash City, reported that about 4,000 to 5,000 reside in that section: large majority crowded in small board huts from 10 to 12 feet sq. These shanties accommodate from 2 to 6 persons, & are rented by the rapacious owners at the rate of from $3 to $5 per mo. A great amount of distress was not found among them. Owing to the unfavorable nature of the location, which is exposed to missmatic influence from the Potomac, a large amount of sickness & mortality was found to exist. There is almost entire absence of proper drainage, & the lack of personal cleanliness on the part of the colored people. -Wash Cor of Boston Jrnl

At the Med Soc of the D C meeting held Sep 12, the death of Dr John M Roberts was announced.

THU SEP 14, 1865
For sale-farm of 100 acs in Montg Co, Md. Also a tract of 93 acs near the above.
-Mrs S G K Hunter, near Rockville, Md.

Nicholas Ratto, an Italian boy, aged 11 yrs, left his mother in Wash City, some 14 months since, & attached himself in some capacity to the 22nd Pa cavalry regt, en route for Harper's Ferry. His mother is in great solicitude to learn whether he is living. Information may be addressed to the undersigned, who will pay $50 for restoration of the lad, or $25 for info. - Jos C G Kennedy, 380 H st, Wash, D C.

Dr John C Bates has been appt'd Direct Tax Com'r for the state of Ga. Dr Bates was a Union man, and [to use his own expression] "he entered the Confederate service to keep out of it"-that is, he volunteered as a surgeon in order to avoid being forced into the trenches. He did all in his power to alleviate the sufferings of the prisoners at Andersonville. He is a particular favorite of the returned prisoners.

All of the D C vols have been mustered out. The 1st & 2nd district regts, [consolidated,] Col Graham commanding, were mustered out & pd off on Tue. Regts numberd 700 men. The flags & official records of the regts were at once turned in to the War Dept. The following ofcrs of the 1st district regt have been in the svc since 1861, viz: Lt Col Boyd, who enlisted as a Capt, & Capt M P Fisher; Capt John Y Donn & Capt B F Magraw, all of whom went in as Lts in 1861, when the war first broke out.

Rl estate sale: W L Wall & Co, aucts, sold, on the premises, the following lots, etc, by order of Asbury Lloyd, atty for the heirs: lots 5 in sq 768, purchased by W Nottingham, for 16 cents per ft; lots 6 & 7 to Rudolph Frederick, at 7¼ & 7¾ cents per ft; lot 8 to J B Davis at 7¾ cents; lot 9 to A Lopez, at 12 cents; lot 2 in sq 795 to J F Vanhorn, at 10½ per ft; hse & lot in sq 795 to Mrs Bean for $1,450; hse & lot in sq 791 to Eliza Smith for $425; lot 11 in sq 945 to D Jones, at .24 per ft; lot 10 in sq 945 to same, at 16¼ cents per ft; lot 9 same sq, to T E Clarke, at 18¾ cents per ft; lot 8 same sq to T F Fox at 13¼ cents per ft; lot 12, same sq, to D Jones, at 23+ cents per ft; hse & lot 14, same sq, to T F Fox, for $580. Messrs J C McGuire & Co, sold lot corner of Md ave & 4½ st, to Wm P Wood, for $5,000; lot at the s w corner of 9th & I sts, to S D Marlow, for $3 per sq ft; lot on north side of K, near 10th st west, to M R Coombs, for 78 cents per sq ft.

Orphans Crt of Wash Co, D C. Prsnl estate of Mgt Lyons, late of Wash, D C, dec'd. -Emma Derrick, admx

Police matters-D C: Saml Lankfort arrested for being intoxicated was locked up for 6 hours. Mary Hawkins was arrested in the First ward & fined for the same. Jas Burke & Winchester Faulkes, in Gtwn; Ann Clark, S J Kinsey, Jas Maloney, Ellen Foley, John W Jones, Edw Bowers, Cath Cunningham, Jas McAllister, Philip Burns, John Payne, Thos Steel, Henry Tye, Henry King, of the 4th ward; Geo Colson, Geo Jones, Patrick Duffey, B B Davis, & Jas Hagan, in the 3rd ward; F P Wyville, Thos Greenhatch, & Fred Garry, in the 2nd ward; Mgt Martin & Pat Maroney, in the 7th ward, were arrested for intoxication, & fined or dismissed by the several justices. Jesse Fowler was arrested for threats of violence against Caroline Fowler & was sent to jail. Wm Collins was arrested for selling liquor on Sun & fined $20.90 by Justice Boswell. Saml McManus was charged with assault upon Thos Green & gave security before Justice Boswell for his appearance at crt to answer. Chas Kaufman, Jos Straus, Seldner & Co, H Rosenberg, M Ring & Co, Leopold Rosenan, Danl Samweis, Wm H Slater, Weizenfeld & Co, L A Levy, E Kaufman, J H Leper, J L Upp_uhoimer, Wm Wolff, O'Meara & Crawford, & M J Young, clothing dealers on the ave, were arrested for occupying a space more than 2 feet from the bldg line for the display of their goods. They were all taken before Justice Walter, who imposed a fine of $5 on each one

Gtwn: meeting of the Directors of the Oak Hill Cemetery last evening. Among other business transacted, Mr Jas W Deeble was elected secretary & treasurer for the ensuing yr.

FRI SEP 15, 1865

Crct Crt of D C, Oct 26, 1859, in the cause of Augusta McBlair & others vs Wm Gadsby & others. Equity #1415-sale of bldg lots in Wash. -Walter S Cox, Tru

Orphans Crt of Wash Co, D C: sale of rl est; Ptn of Agatha C Lynch, guardian of Ambrose S Lynch. -Agatha C Lynch, Guardian

Orphans Crt of Wash Co, D C. Prsnl estate of Mary Stevenson, late of Gtwn, D C, dec'd. -Walter S Cox, adm, w a.

Died: on Sep 10, at Ashburton, near Balt, at the residence of John S Gittings, Mrs Anne Eliza Ritchie Cross, w/o Wm B B Cross, of Wash City & d/o the late Thos Ritchie, of Richmond, Va.

Died: at her father's residence, Mr John Logsdon, in Balt Co, on Sep 14, of consumption, Maria, w/o Geo W Downey, aged 27 years & 7 months. Funeral from the residence of her uncle, Mr P Thyson, 293 7th st, on Fri.

Died: in Wash City, on Sep 13, in her 70th yr, Mrs Mary Smith, wid/o the late Dr Philip Smith. Funeral from the residence of her son, Mr F McNerhany, 460 I st, Fri; svcs at St Peter's Chr.

On Wed in Equity Crt a decree in the case of John B Carlin against Lardis F Hubbel & Helen M Hubbel, his wife, Jos F Brown, W O Riddle, & Susan Hartman. Carlin & his wife, the present Mrs Hubbel, were domiciled here & had 2 chldrn. Mr Carlin left the city about 1861. Mrs Carlin later removed to Livingston Co, Mich, with her 2 chldrn. There she obtained a divorce on ground of alledged desertion. She remrd & had custody of the chldrn. The rl estate in Wash City was in question in regard to the proceeds of same.

Mrd: at Emanuel Chr, Balt, on Aug 17, by Rev Dr Schenek, Capt J Gales Ramsey, 2nd artl, to Miss Annie R Morris, d/o Gen W W Morris, U S Army.

Wash, D C, Police Com'rs dismissed: Det Michl L Barry; Patrolman Elijah Action-general inefficiency. Patrolman Geo C Harris-neglect of duty. Patrolman Jas H Bell-intoxication. Patrolman W W Hurdle & Patrolman W B Williams-dismissed. Complaint against W W Hudson was dismissed. R T Taylor was fined $5, & same amount to be pd the owner of the dog he shot. Sgt H C Hepburn, to be reduced in rank.

Police matters-D C: 1-Jas Monahan, Wm Stone, John H Zerman, John Shack & Ellen O'Leary, all arrested for selling spirits w/o license. 2-Emily Trovett, charged with stealing $500 from her sister, Anna Trovett; also with stealing a silk dress, the property of Josephine Wolf. Emily held for further hearing. 3-Patrick Ryan, Martin O'Hare, Wm Flanigan, arrested for selling liquor w/o a license.
4-Albert Vermillion arrested for disorderly conduct & assault & battery at Steele's restaurant, on the Navy Yd.

Mrd: on Sep 14, at Wesley Chapel, by Rev Dr Nadal, Miss Sue J McKelden, of Wash City, to M W Beveridge. [Corr of Sep 18: Mr W Beverilge to Sue J, d/o J C McKelden, all of Wash City. Leesburg papers please copy.]

Account of death by accident at Fort Washington: Albert Eyring was killed while making percussion powder on Aug 14, 1845; a yr later Adam Alburger while doing same. Jan 30, 1863, shell exploded killing Henry Berckman, Chas Wright, John Money & Henry Sheets. On Aug 15, 1863, Wm Johnson was killed by explosion of small-arm cartridges. On Nov 5, Owen McNavy & J McCarty, killed by explosion of a box of ammunition in the Penitentiary. Jos Miller was killed by a shell on Apr 11, 1864. On Jun 17, 1864, the great explosion took the lives of 21 girls, to whose memory has been erected a beautiful monument in Congressional Cemetery. One of the characters at the Arsenal is Sgt Thos Vickers & his wife. He was born in Shardlow, Eng, Aug 22, 1788. He has been there since Nov, 1836.

SAT SEP 16, 1865

Ex-Gov Wm Medill died on Sep 2, at his residence in Lancaster, Ohio. He was a native of N J & came to Ohio in 1829.

Sup Crt of D C, Equity #497. Geo W Harvey vs Wm M Brown et al. Bill is to procure a decree for the sale of certain rl estate of dfndnt, Ellen J Brown; proceeds to the payment of a debt of the dfndnts due to cmplnt. Wm M & Ellen J Brown are non-residents of D C. -R J Meigs, clerk

Mrd: on Sep 12, in Immanuel Chr, New Castle, Dela, by the rector, Rev Richd Whittingham, Geo B Balch, Cmder U S Navy, & Miss Mary Ellen Booth, d/o Hon Jas Booth, dec'd, late Chief Justice of Dela.

Mrd: on Sep 14, at St Aloysius Chr, by Rev B F Wiget, John H Byrnes to Miss Sarah F Tyler, both of Wash City.

Gtwn Affairs: Geo Hepburn & Jeremiah Hebron, both colored, were arrested yesterday for the robbery of quite a number of horses in Laurel, Elk Ridge, Halltown, & other places in Howard Co, Md, & committed to jail for a further hearing by Justice Buckey. It would be well for persons who have recently had horses stolen from them to call on Sgt Essex.

Gtwn-burglaries: Hses of Messrs Wm H Mathews & Lewis Berry, on West, next to Wash st, & Miss Kate Barnard, corner of Congress & West sts. A burglar also entered the rm of Mr Ratcliffe, took his coat & pants.

MON SEP 18, 1865

The monument by Messrs Flannery & Bro to Col J P Garesche has been completed. Lt Col Julius P Garesche was killed in 1862 leading a cavalry charge at the battle of Murfreesboro, Tenn; remains were brought to Wash City & interred in Mt Olivet Cemetery at his own request. He was born in 1821 & died on Dec 31, 1862.

Ltr from the son of the late Wm Smith O'Brien, on the death of his father, received by Dr Thos Antisell; dt'd Cahirmoyle, Newcastle, West Ireland, Jun 4, 1865. He expresses his sincere gratitude for the feelings conveyed on the death of his fr. Signed-Edw Wm O'Brien

Wash City news-reps of the trades indicated:
Painters-Donald McCathran, L Frost, E Collins, S Parker, John Handson, Jos Murphy, E Edwards, John Harris, A W Drury, R Bremer.
Carpenters-Jas Dunnington, John Lovelace, Henry C Keirl

Col Typo Soc-J C C Whaley, C B Hough, A J Cavis, C I Canfield, H L Davidson, Wm R McLean
Bk binders-John A Landvoight, Jos Marringly, W Bishop, H McIntyre
Ord Gun-carriage mkrs-R T Tulbaft, W P Brown
Pattern mkrs-Geo Brown, J & J B Larkin, Jos Taylor
Ship joiners-J L Hayghe, Jos Martin, Robt Martin
Iron Founders-Darius Darton, Plumber Lucas, Daniel Davis, John Carpenter, Thos Brown.
Saile mkrs-Edw F Casey, Chas Lear, John M Farnandis
Boil mkrs-Ira Crosson, Geo Thompson, Netemiah Robey
Coach mkrs-Patrick Cochran, Thos McWilliams, Jas J Mitchell
Tin & Sheet iron workers-Peter J Collison, Thos J Simmon & ____ Small.
Currency Bur, Treas Dept-J Q Long
Harness mkr-E L Rollins
Plasters-Chas Landers, Robt Muler
Granite cutters-John Collins, W C Clark, Jas Cassidy
Machinists & Blacksmiths-Richd Edmonds, Jos R Waltemeyer, John Eveley
Ship Carpenters-Wm McDermott, Edw Burt, John Boyd
Cabinet mkrs-J B Brashears, F Johnson, J Loan
Laborer's Dept-Wm Coleman

Died: on Sep 17, after a brief but painful illness, Mrs Sarah Edelin Black. Funeral from her residence, 600 Mass av, Tue.

Died: on Sep 16, in Gtwn, Jas Rowland Gibbs, in his 18th yr. Funeral from the residence of his father, Dr J B Gibbs, 101 West st, Mon. Burial at Oak Hill Cemetery.

Orphans Crt-D C. 1-Acc't of Job E Crampton, adm of Wm B Crampton was approved. 2-Wm B Hill gave bond of $20,000 as exc of Cath Smith. 3-Wm B Hill & Robt G Chew gave bond of $5,000 as excs of Mary E Allen. 4-Will of Henry McPherson was fully proven. 5-Chas Wilson appt'd guardian to the orphan of Saml M Leepo. 6-Acc't of Josiah Simpson, guardian to orphans of Hanson Barnes was approved & passed.

Orphans Crt of Wash Co, D C. 1-Prsnl estate of Cath Smith, late of Wash City, dec'd. -Wm B Hill, exc. 2-Prsnl estate of Mary E Allen, late of Wash City, dec'd. -Wm B Hill, R S Chew, excs. 3-Prsnl estate of Wm C Carr, late of the Co of Wash, D C, dec'd. -J Carter Marbury, adm

TUE SEP 19, 1865
Evidence against Mrs Martha Grinder, the American Lucretia Borgis, who was determined to destroy the entire family of her hsbnd, having killed 2 of his brothers; who are believed to have been poisoned-Saml, the elder about 25 years of age, died Ded 4, 1864; Jeremiah, aged about 21, died Nov 15, 1864. In one corner of the burying-lot is a child of Mrs Grinder, about 1 month old, which died last May. The homestead of the Grinder family is in Westmoreland Co, Va. The body of Saml Grinder was examined & found to have been poisoned, the first victim in the family. Charlotte Grinder, a sister of Saml, was at the hse when he died but was too sick & obliged to go home. About 5 years ago, after removing from Louisville, Ky, Martha & her hsbnd visited the homestead, remaining for about 2 months.

Mrs Wiley & her mother, Mrs Brown, residence on 5th st, adj Rev Dr Nadal's Chr; it is alleged that religious svcs at the chapel are interrupted by the barking of 5 dogs kept by

Mrs Wiley in her coach hse & yard. A warrant was issued upon the information of Mr C W Boteler, sr.

Equity Crt, Sep 18: Mary Myers vs Peter Myers, decree of divorce, with right to the petioner to receive her share of certain estate, free from the control of her hsbnd. They resided near 3rd st & Va av, where Mrs M kept a small store prior to & since her marriage. Cmplnt proved the respondent guilty of abandonment, cruelty, adultery, ill-treatment, & lesser vices.

WED SEP 20, 1865

Trustee's sale of farm in Chas Co, Md; deed of trust from Thos D Stone & wife, dt'd Sep 5, 1865; *Queechy*, 285 acs, late the property of Thos D Stone. -F Stone, trustee; Chas M Matthews, atty at law, 8th & Mkt Space, Wash City.

Exc's sale of valuable quarry, between Aqueduct & Little Falls Bridge; excs of the last will & testament of the late Wm Easby. -Agnes M Easby, Horatio N Easby, John W Easby, excs; Jas C McGuire & Co, auctioneers.

Partnership formed in wholesale & retail family grocery; 345 Pa av, Wash, under the style of Jos B Bryan & Bryan. -Jos B Bryan, C C Bryan

Orphans Crt-D C. 1-Will of Jas Tucker, dec'd, admitted to probate: letters test were issued to Jenifer C Tucker & Wm Thomas. 2-Will of Jerome Reedeger was fully proven: letters test granted to Caroline Reedeger. 3-Michl Thompson granted letters of adm on estate of Geo Murrey, dec'd. 4-Eliz H Smith granted letters of adm on estate of C De Witt Smith, dec'd. 5-Acc't of Andrew Noerr, adm of estate of John C Roemmele & Wm H Roemmele, dec'd, was approved & passed. 6-Acc't of excs of Chas Miller, dec'd, approved & passed. 7-Inventory of the estate of Patrick McKenna, dec'd, was entered & filed.

Trustee's sale *Poplar Hill*, residence of John Ford; farm lies in Chas Co, Md; 800 acs with a fine old mansion hse. -F Stone, trustee; Chas M Matthews, atty at law.

Died: on Sep 18, Mr Saml Kelly, of the 6th Auditor's ofc, in his 48th yr. Funeral from his late residence, 605 17th st, Wed.

Died: on Sep 19, after a brief but painful illness, Mary E Burch, eldest d/o Mgt & Albert Burch, dec'd, aged 24 yrs. Funeral from her late residence, 106 4½ st, Wed.

Trial of Henry Wirz. Witness' accounts: R G R Kean was in the Confederate svc, & afterwards Chief of the Bureau of War at Richmond. Watler T Davenport, a resident of Americus, Ga was sworn. Capt Noyes was sworn; was on duty at Macon Ga, from Apr 20 until May 20. Capt Jas M Moore, A Q M, U S A, from Jul 26 to Aug 16, was engaged in marking the graves of the Union sldrs who died at Andersonville; 12,912 graves were marked, 12,397 with names & 451 unknown; 64 were in the small-pox cemetery. John N Younker, 3rd U S infty, was a prisoner from Jan until Sep 1865. Jas P Stone, 2nd Vt vols, prisoner & in the stockade for 2 months. Geo Conway, 2nd N Y artl, prisoner, was sworn. D S Auckerd, 11th Pa cavalry, sworn; had been a prisoner. Maj Archibad Boyle, maj of the 25th U S colored infty, captured in Feb 1864, taken to Andersonville in Mar. Wm Bull, Co A, Means's Loudoun [Union] rangers, was a prisoner. Jas H Burns, 10th Conn, put in the stockade for attempting to escape, had seen men shot while at Andersonville.

R M T Hunter, who was paroled at Fort Pulaski a few days ago, was in Wash. yesterday, on his way to his home in Va.

THU SEP 21, 1865
Monument erected in Balt, Md, to the memory of the late Thos Wildey, the father & founder of Odd Fellowship in the U S. He was born in London on Jan 15, 1783, & came to this country in 1817, founded Wash Lodge, #1 in Balt, in 1819; died Oct 19, 1861.

Died: on Sep 18, Arvin, y/s/o the late Dr W V H Brown, aged 4 years & 9 months.

Trial of Henry Wirz. Witness' accounts: Mr Ambrose Spencer, of Americus, Ga, where he has resided for many yrs, frequently visited Andersonville Prison. Dr B J Head, who resided at Americus, was on duty at Andersonville from Jul to Aug 1864. Saml M Riker, 8th N J, was a prisoner on & after Jul 10, 1864. Geo C Smith, 4th U S Cavalry, prisoner from Apr to Sep 1864. Benj B Dykes was sworn; he has been railroad agent at Andersonville since 1861. Ambrose Henshaw, 4th U S Cavalry, prisoner from Apr until Jul 1864. Thos Walsh, 74 N Y, was at Andersonville from Feb until Oct 1864.

Rl estate sales: by Green & Williams, aucts: a 2 story frame dwlg & lot 31, subdiv of sq 431, on 7th st, between D & E sts south, to Jos Anthony for $2,500; small brick hse on parts of lots 8 & 9 in sq 411, 9th st, between D & E south, to John Darley, for $750; the drug store, corner of 3rd & Pa ave, was sold by virtue of a deed of trust yesterday, & bought by J E Jones for $6,000.

Died: on Sep 20, Nancy Polke, w/o H Lassell, formerly of Logansport, Indiana.

SAT SEP 23, 1865
Jas W Duncan, age about 25 yrs, the ex-rebel qrtrmstr & keeper of the cook-hse at Andersonville, has been committed to the Old Capitol prison by order by Gen Auger. He is a baker by trade & his present residence is in Norfolk, Va; understood he is a native of Balt, Md.

Dr G G Roy, late a surgeon at Andersonville, has prepared a full history of the prison; it will contain the names of all the Union dead, together with the numbers of their graves & their location in the cemetery.

Police-D C. 1-Geo W Ballenger, dismissed for intoxication. 2-Danl W Hopkins, reprimanded for conduct unbecoming an ofcr. 3-J W Coomes & Jas F Taylor, dismissed for same. 4-Geo W McElfresh & Richd T Taylor resigned. 5-Wm T Burdette appt'd patrolman vice Geo W Ballenger. 6-Chas W Thompson, patrolman, vice Geo W McElfresh, rsgnd. 7-John Quilter, patrolman, vice R T Taylor, rsgnd.

Trial of Henry Wirz. Witness' accounts: Dr T S Hopkins was sworn; resided in Ga; inspected Andersonville on Jul 28, 1864. Hugh B Harrold, of Americus, Ga, furnished supplies for 3 yrs. Dr B L D Rice, sworn, on duty from Aug 1864 until Mar 1865. Capt Wilson French, 17 Conn vols, prisoner in Feb 1865. J R Griffin, had been Col of the 8th Ga cavalry, was employed in trying to improve the graveyard. Sgt J E Alden, 4th Vt, prisoner on & after Jul 12, 1864. Robt Tait, 53rd Pa, prisoner from Feb until Sep 1864. Saml Andrews, 17th Ill, prisoner from Apr to Sep 1864. Wm B Francis, 17th Ohio, prisoner from Aug 20 to Sep 17, 1864. J A Kane, of btln of Calif cavalry, prisoner on & after Mar 10, 1864. Geo W Gray, 7th Ill, prisoner from Jun until Nov 1864.

Died: on Sep 21, Jos H Myers, aged 38 yrs. Funeral from the residence on 3rd st, Sun.

Rl estate sales: by J C McGuire & Co, aucts: 2 hses, 9th st between K & L, in Doughty's Row, one, #316 to W A Henderson for $4,600; one, #344, to Michl Green, $4,300. Lot corner N Y ave & 9th, to Mary Ann Scheckles, for $1.36 sq ft. By Green & Williams, aucts: lot 5, in sq 477, on 6th, between Q & R sts north, to H W Thies, for 25 cents per ft. Two 2 story frame hses on F st south, between 3rd & 4½ sts, to Pompey Jackson, for $870. Lot 3 in sq 213, on Vt ave, between N & O sts north, to Chas Smith, for [possible 17 cents per sq ft-*print is incomplete.*]

MON SEP 25, 1865
Deaths of missionaries: in Turkey-Rev Edw Dodd of cholera, & Rev Homer B Morgan of typhus fever. Boston, Sep 22

Dept of the Interest,U S Patent Ofc. Ptn of Rebecca C Wheeler, admx of the estate of Thos B Wheeler, dec'd, of Albany, N Y: extension of patent granted Dec 1851; improvement in *Grain Sieves.* Thos C Theaker, Commissioner of Patents.

Orphans Crt of Wash Co, D C. 1-Prsnl estate of Wm C Carr, late of Wash Co, D C, dec'd. - J Carter Marbury, adm 2-Prsnl estate of Cath Smith, late of Wash City, D C, dec'd. -Wm B Hill, exc

Brief notice on the death of Capt Lee Rosenthal, Hungarian by birth, & only 42 years of age at the time of his death, of congestive chill & buried at sea.

Mrs Betsy Moore, widow of the poet, died on Sep 4 at age 66 yrs. She died at Sloperton Cottage, Eng, long the residence of the author. They mrd in 1811.

Trial of Henry Wirz. Witness' accounts: Sgt G W Gray was recalled. Capt J H Wright, ofcr of the 55th Ga, qrtrmstr at Andersonvile from Feb 1864 until Feb 1865. Lewis Dyer, 12th U S colored infty, prisoner from Jul, 1864 until Feb 2, 1865.

The funeral of Jos H Myers, long employed in the Navy Yd, was held yesterday; burial in Congressional Cemetery.

TUE SEP 26, 1865
Obit-Cmdor John Collins Long, U S N, died suddenly at North Conway, on Sep 2, while on an excursion to the White Mountains. He was born in Portsmouth, N H, in 1795, joined the navy in 1811.

Orphans Crt of Wash Co, D C. Case of Wm B Todd, exc of G C Grammer, dec'd; settlement on Oct 17. -Z C Robbins, rg o/wills

John Frederick Encke, astromoner, died in Berlin lately. He was born in Hamburg in 1791.

Persons with claims against the estate of J M Miller are to present same by Oct 8. -Mgt Miller, admx

Henry S Foote, John Bell, & Neil S Brown, are all residing in Nashville. Brown has returned to the practice of law; Bell is in feeble health, & keeps very quiet; Foote is as active & bustling as ever, & says that he shall hereafter eschew politics & devote himself to the law.

Gtwn Affairs: another tournament came off at Analostan Isl last evening: given by the proprietors of the island, Messrs Rodier & Mulliner. Names of the contestants:

John Yeabower	D J Wells	D E Kraft
R E Fugitt	D Cameran	John B Davis
John Bowers	B F Riley	Jos Kuntz

The judges were Col Wm Drew, W H Paxson of Loudoun Co, W Lunsford of Warrenton, J T Towers, jr, of Wash, & Maj E Sturmfels. Mr J Merritt acted as mrshl. Miss Clara Donaldson was crowned Queen of Love & Beauty; Miss Carrie Edwards, of Balt, 1st Maid of Honor; Miss Ida Rodier, 2nd Maid of Honor, & Miss Emma Williams, 3rd Maid of Honor.

WED SEP 27, 1865

Orphans Crt of Wash Co, D C. 1-Case of Mary H Murray, surviving admx of Stanislaus Murray, dec'd; settlement Oct 21. -Z C Robbins, rg o/wills

2-Prsnl estate of Grafton Powell, late of Wash City, D C, dec'd. -J Tyler Powell, Mary A V Shafer, excs

Deed of trust from W H Parker & wife, dt'd Jan 13, 1858, by direction of the excs of the late David English, whose debt is secured thereby; sale of lot 4 in sq 168 Wash City. -W Redin, trustee -Green & Wms, auctioneers

Died: on Sep 18, Mrs Cath McJilton, in the 77th yr of her age.

Trial of Henry Wirz. Witness' accounts: Dr M M Marsh, stationed at Beaufort, S C. J B Jones was sworn, had been a clerk in the rebel War Dept since the beginning of the rebellion. Philip Cashmeyer was a detective ofcr under Gen Winder. Dr E A Fluellen was sworn; had been in the Confederate svc as Surg Gen to Gen Bragg. Rev Peter Whalen was sworn, was at Andersonville from Jun until Oct 1861. Jas H Fannin, late Col of the 1st Ga Reserves, was sworn & examined.

Death of a Catholic Bishop: news received of the death of the Rt Rev Bishop Smith, of Dubuque.

Mustered out: Maj A A Slipper, late of Gen Augur's staff.

Assoc of Painters: meeting held last evening: ofcrs of the society are C H Crown, Pres; G W Parker, V P; J V Murphy, Sec.

Rl estate sale: by J C McGuire & Co, aucts. A frame hse & lot on east side of 6th st, between N & O sts north, to Dr Seth J Todd for $1,510. A frame hse & lot on Md ave, near 1st st west, to Jos E Gedney for $2,860. Lot B, in subdiv of 629, on N J ave, near D st, to Patrick J Torney for 46 cents per sq ft. Lot N, in same subdiv, to J H Crossman for 36 cents per ft. S Norment sold that well known groc stand, 20 x 80 ft, on corner of 7th & K sts north, south of Northern Mkt, to Messrs B M Embrey & Co for $14,000.

THU SEP 28, 1865

Brig Gen Revere, formerly of the 10th Md Btry, & latterly in command of the 107th U S colored troops, stationed at Morehead City, died there a few days since. His body will be sent to his family in Michigan. Balt, Sep 26

Died: on Jun 21, at Point Lookout, in the 21st yr of his age, Saml A Ashford, y/s/o Craven & Emerella Ashford.

Trial of Henry Wirz. Witness' account: Lt John F Heath, late of the 3rd Ga reserves, was at Andersonville in 1864.

FRI SEP 29, 1865
Wm Belts & Louis Englehart, ctzns, sentenced to be imprisoned at hard labor for 6 mos, have been discharged from imprisonment at the Old Capitol Prison, Wash, D C, upon taking the oath of allegiance. Christian Lohman, ctzn, also will be discharged from the Old Capitol Prison, upon taking the oath of allegiance.

Taunton, Mass, Sep 27. The Hon Wm Bayles, formerly a mbr of Congress, died in this city this morning, aged 89 yrs.

Va P O reopened & postmstr:
Edge Hill, King Geo Co, Va-Miss Emma C Jones, postmistress vice J C Jones.
Webster, Taylor Co, W Va-S M Heironimus, vice John W Bartless, rsgn'd.
Faney Hill, Rockbridge C, Va-J P Lackey, vice John Poague
Forestville, Shenandoah Co, Va-Saml R Hockman, vice Wm Whistler
Moore's Store, Shenandoah Co, Va, John Showalter, vice C S Wander

Sup Crt of D C, Equity #145. Robt Coltman, Chas T Smith & Mary F, his wife, & John W Moore & Sarah B, his wife, vs Jas Adams, Rebecca Coltman, sr & jr, & the Corp of Wash. Parties named to attend at my ofc in the City Hall, Wash D C, on Oct 17. -W Redin, auditor

Sup Crt of D C, Equity #492. Magdaline Pfeifer, plntf, against John Pfeifer, dfndnt. Ptn for a divorce. Dfndnt is a non-resident of D C. -R J Meigs, clerk

Suicide: Hon John L Harvey, lawyer in Dubuque, Iowa, age about 35 yrs, while on the Great Western R R in a sleeping car. He leaves a family in Dubuque & his mother.

Mrd: on Sep 28, at the residence of the bride's father, by Rev Dr John C Smith, Mr Saml E Culverwell to Miss Mary Johnson, all of Wash City.

Mrd: in Gtwn, D C, on Sep 28, by Rev Dr Edwards, Brvt Lt Col D Frank Hamlink, of Rochester, N Y, to Miss Nellie, d/o S A Lazenby, of Gtwn.

Died: on Sep 28, after a long illness, Mrs Julia Wheeler Ryon, w/o Richd Ryon, aged 38 yrs. Funeral from the residence, 399 E st, today.

Died: at the residence of his son in Phil, on Sep 27, Arthur J Stansbury, formerly of Wash City, in the 84th yr of his age.

Died: in Gtwn, D C, on Sep 28, Marinus Willett, in his 78th yr; born at Fishkill, Dutchess Co, N Y. Funeral from his late residence, 168 High st, Fri.

Trial of Henry Wirz. Witness' accounts: Lt Col Persons & Dr Fluellen recalled.

SAT SEP 30, 1865

The R C C Bishop of Iowa, Bishop Timothy Smythe, died last Sun, at age 55. He was born in Co Clare, Ire, in 1810 & became a priest at age 34 yrs.

Orphans Crt of Wash Co, D C. Case of Mary E Brown & Robt R Pywell, excx of Thos Brown, dec'd; settlement on Oct 21. -Z C Robbins, rg o/wills

At the Academy of the Visitation, on Sun last, Miss Ella Bass, d/o Madame Bass, now Madame Bertinatti, w/o the Italian Ambassador, was admitted into the Catholic Chr. Local Item

Chas T Watson & J L Rodgers, who were convicted of larceny at the last term of the Crmnl Crt, & sentenced to an imprisonment of one year each, have been unconditionally pardoned by the Pres.

Rl estate sales: by J C McGuire & Co, aucts. Hse & lot on the Island, between 3rd & 4½ sts, & C & D sts, to Mrs Mary Iverton for $800. Vacant lots adjoining the same to Thos McWilliams for 27 cents per sq ft.

On Thu Mr Thos Dowling, auct, sold on a 3 story brick hse, on Bridge st, opposite Jefferson, to Mr Jos F Burch for $6,000.

Confiscation in residence-proceedings discont'd. The following, mostly ctzns of Alexandria, have succeeded in getting orders of dismissal:

E B While	John H Barnes	Matthew	W H Benton
R L Rotchford	Saml Barnes	Harrison	Dr W B Cochran
Danl G Shrieve	Lewis D Means	John M Orr	R W Leith
Robt Drance	J W Saffer	A H Rodgers	B P Noland
A Broadwater	Benj Saffer	H O Claggett	E R Oxley
Wm	R H Ish	W B Lynch	C A Baldwin
Clendenning	W B Day	A L Chichester	Bennett Hough
A Best	John Powell	B H Caldwell	Jas Kilgore
Benj Johnston	W Whiteley	A R Mott	Jas Smith
F C Weedon	W F Lee	S J Raney	W R Millan
L B Montpenson	Wesley Makeley	R M Newman	B H Cockerell
T Montpenson	J L Smith	S L Barnes	A McClean
R Brawner	C B Ball	J G Allison	John Thompson
F J Cannon	C B Tebbs	Oscar Braden	Shalto Stewart
Peyton Johnson	G W Beall	I M Orr	W W Ball
C A Baldwin	A R Mott	Saml Cumbaker	L D Means
W D Corse	T W Edwards	John W Renize	W D Ball
H W Thomas	Sanderson	J F Tebbs	J M Kilgore
P D C Lee	Thrift	Jas Ingar	W D Nutt
G W Lee	J H Simpson	J R White	Saml Cooper
W W Thornton	Henson	J A King	John Pywell
R H Cocke	Simpson	R G Chinn	Dr Orlando
J R Pugh	Wm Ayne	W G Farr	Fairfax
M Ball	R G Bouse	J Erver	
J C Kincheloe	G T Rust	John W Fairfax	

MON OCT 2, 1865

Miss B B Conover, teacher of music, 184 2nd st, Wash, D C. –Local Ad

Providence, Oct 1. Rev Dr Francis Wayland, Pres of Brown Univ for over 28 yrs, died last Sat of a paralytic stroke. He was 69 years of age.

Sudden death of Geo Ailer, age 68 years & 10 mos, esteemed ctzn; while walking with his wife last evening. He complained of feeling full about the breast & Mrs Ailer went in pursuit of a carriage. When she returned she found him lifeless. He was taken to his residence, 512 H st. Funeral on Tue.

Died: on Oct 1, of apoplexy, Mary Ann Stephens, aged 75 yrs. Funeral from the residence of her son, T A Stephens, 462 12th st, this morning. Requiem Mass at St Patrick's Chr. [Balt & Frederick, Md, papers, please copy.]

Mr Andrew Hepburn, property of the Fulton Mkt in Wash City, has been appt'd purveyor for Gen Sheridan's army in Texas & has departed to that State.

Trial of Henry Wirz. Witness' accounts: Capt J H Wright was recalled. Judge Hall of Ga was recalled. W D Hammack of the 53rd Ga, was sworn & testified.

TUE OCT 3, 1865
Sup Crt of D C holding a district Crt of the U S for the said Dist. Notice is given, that on Jun 6, 1862, the rebel war steamers *Gen'l Thompson, Genr'l Lovell*, & the war steamer *Gen'l Beauregard* were destroyed at the battle of Memphis by vessels of the U S belonging to the Mississippi Squadron, under the command of Rear Adm C H Davis; on Sep 7, 1865. The same were libelled in this crt. Said cause will stand for trial on Oct 1, City Hall, Wash, D C. -R J Meigs, clerk

Orphans Crt of D C. 1-Will of Peter McDonough, bequeathing his estate to his wife, was filed. 2-Will of Saml F McKenney, of Gtwn, admitted to probate & letters of test were issued to Chas H Cragin. 3-Case of Caroline Reedeger, excx of Jerome Reedeger, counter security was given. 4-Ltr of adm issued to Elwood Champlin on estate of Jos Sanders; to Timothy Rogers on estate of Charty McCoy; to Fred'k Seitz on estate of Adam Smith. 5-Eliza R Rhodes appt'd guardian to the orphans of Edw Rhodes. 6-Acc't of Walter Scott, exc of Chas M Williams, & of Susan W Riely, excx of John H Riely, were approved & passed.

Mrs Susan Longworth, w/o Nicholas Longworth, died at Cincinnati on Sep 29.

Govn'r Bradford has refused to sign E Louis Lowe's application for pardon.

Sup Crt of D C, Equity #518. Isabella Johnston vs Jas D, Hamilton R, Ben Wm, & Gabriel F Johnston, Geo R & Laura S Clayton, Gabrietta J Tilden & others. Bill states that the infant dfndnts are seized of part of sq 828 in Wash City, & the above dfndnts would be the heirs-at-law of said dfndnts in the event of their death, & their interest would be promoted by sale of said rl est. -R J Meigs, clerk.

Trial of Henry Wirz. Witness' accounts: W D Hammack was recalled. Vincentia Bardo was sworn; had been a sldr in the U S army & taken to Andersonville in Jun, 1864. Fred'k Gazzetti was sworn, had been a mbr of the 43rd N Y vols, Italian by birth; was sent to the prison on Mar 28, 1864.

The Annapolis Naval Academy is now completely re-established. Operations resumed yesterday, under the official superintendence of Rear Admr David P Porter, with an adequate & learned corps of professors, naval & civil. Chief Engr W W Wood is the first occupant.

St Louis, Sep 29. Order from Atty Gen Speed to the D A of Missouri: the property of Mrs Gen Ewell, estimated to be worth $60,000, has been delivered over to her agents. The property had been libelled for confiscation & the plea of amnesty & pardon made in her favor had been overruled by the crt. This order from the Exec, however, summarily terminates the case, to the great gratification of the lady's friends.

Danville, Va: on Oct 1 the tobacco factory of Keen & Walker was destroyed by fire: loss at $50,000, on which there was an insurance of $30,000.

City News: 1-Landlord & tenant case before J W Barnaclo: Chas W Schuerman vs Chas E Livingston. Plntf let the premises to the dfndnt, who sub-let the same to Ferdianand C Cate, who is & has been for some time past in possession of the premises. Schuerman wants the premises back: Livingston is beyond reach: case may go to the Supreme Crt.

Mr David R Smith has conducted the Woodbine Hse for the 3 months past & has had the mechaincs fitting it up in first-class style: carpenter work was done by Brisby & Metcher: paperhanging was done by Kidwell & Henderson: painting done by Mr S S Watts, & plumbing & gas fitting by Mr Simpson. Grand re-opening was held last night.

WED OCT 4, 1865
Orphans Crt of Wash Co, D C. Case of Jas Fitzpatrick, exc of Dominick Conroy, dec'd: settlement on Oct 29. -Z C Robbins, rg o/wills

Mrd: on Sep 28, by Rev B F Morris, at the church of the Rev Dr Sunderland, Jas A Ashley, of Minn, to Ann Scrivener, of Wash City. No cards.

Mrd: on Oct 1, by the Rector of Trinity Parish, Mr Eugene Sanderson to Miss Mgt Burk, both of Wash City.

Mrd on Oct 3, by the Rector of Trinity Parish, Dr Geo M Dove, Dr S J Todd to Miss Georgie Dove, both of Wash City.

Mrd: on Oct 3, at the 13th Bapt Chr, by Rev T Edwin Brown, of Brooklyn, G Julian Pratt, of Charlottesville, Va, to Mary E, d/o Eleazer Brown, of Wash City. [Balt, Md, Norfolk, Richmond, & Charlottesville, Va, paper please copy.]

Died: on Oct 3, in her 88th yr, Annie Bailor, colored, an old family svnt of Geo A W Randall. Funeral on Oct 4, from the corner of 12th & D sts.

Trial of Henry Wirz. Witness' accounts: Jos Thuringer, of 19th regt V R C, prisoner at Tuscaloosa, Ala Dec 1861 until Mar 1862. Antonio Mononi was sworn, spoke English so badly that the Crt could not understand him.

Rl estate sale by J C McGuire & Co, aucts: lot on 13th st, near Pa ave, to Geo C S Mitchell for .95 per sq ft; lot on Va ave, near 4½ st, to Edw Sheehey for .25 per sq ft.

THU OCT 5, 1865

Equity Crt, Oct 3, 1865. Divorce case-Clara Young vs Ezekiel Young. Clara Lewis, maiden name, mrd the dfndnt in Wash City in 1858; lived together but a very short time when he deserted her. He has ever since, & is still living in adultery with a woman of ill fame called Duck Hall, who, for some time, kept a hse of ill-fame in Wash City. Divorce was granted & maiden name restored.

Notice-application has been made to the Mayor of Wash for a deed to be issued to the heirs of Jas Birth for lot 17 in reservation 11; by virtue of a bond of conveyance from the Com'rs of Low Grounds, executed about Apr 3, 1826, to John P Van Ness, who cnvyed same to Jas Birth. -Wm W Birth, one of the heirs; C H Wiltberger, Sec

Card of thanks to the public from Thos Potentini, prior to his departure for Europe. His Ladies' & Gentleman's Restaurant will now be conducted by his nephew, Mr A Frank Potentini. -Thos Potentini, 279 Pa av, Wash, D C.

Mrd: at the Chr of the Epiphany, on Oct 3, by Rev Chas H Hall, Lt Cmder H L Howison, U S Navy, to Hannah, d/o L J Middleton, of Wash City. No cards.

Died: on Oct 4, Geo Dippell, aged 4 years & 1 month, s/o W H & Maria C Ritter.

Obit-Miss Eliza Mary P, eldest d/o Col Richd & Cath Dunbar, aged 19 yrs, died at the Ntl Htl in Wash City, yesterday. For 2 years she was a mbr of the institute of the Sacred Heart of Chicago, & for 3 years of that of Notre Dame in Indiana, whither her body will be conveyed for burial.

Trial of Henry Wirz. Witness' accounts: A Moesner, Co G 16th Conn, prisoner at Andersonville from May 1864 until May 1865. Geo W Fechnor, had been in the Union army; captured in Sep 1862 & taken to Knoxsville, Tenn; escaped, & re-captured arriving at Andersonville on Jun 1, 1864.

Ofc of Harden Express, Wash, D C, Sep 12, 1865. Following unclaimed pkgs, etc, with others without remarks, if not called for within 30 days, will be sold at pblc auction. -E S Smith, agent

C Arts	T O Brunel	A S Briggs
H A Allen	D Barker	G W Brown
Capt W I Alexander	Jon J L Black	Col Brass
I Allen	G L Becker	B Bryant
Gen Averill	E W Beatty	W Beahr
F Albion	G L Becker	Stephen Bridge
W C Armor	J Brotsman	Capt J G Barkely
J E Allison	A Benjamin	Lt S Beatty
Mrs W H Allyn	Lt F E Brodhead	M Beatty
R J Atkinson	J S Brotxman	Sgt M Bridges
Capt F A Armstrong	J Brotxman	E Burke
D Andrews	G H Blineberry-[1 val]	E Beall
W S Andrews-[a chest]	W Busch	J W Baker
J H Andrews	H K Bernard	D Burk
M T Armstrong	G C Brown	E Baron
A Allen-[a tub]	M D Burrows	Lt J Bougton
J C Albertson	M E Broughton	Briggs & Spencer
R S Barlow-[carpet bag]	F Bushee	J J Blair

Thos Bleecker
J M Burch-[1 keg]
H Bacon
H G Babcock-[1 tk]
L Bix
W L Black
Mrs G C Bancroft-[1 bbl]
W Barrett
F Brown
B M Boardman
S Brooks
A Brown
P P Berguvine
T S Binkard
J E Boyer
R Cook
R V Cake
I Cornell-[1 coffin]
S H Cooper
J C Connell
Congrove
W R Crumb-[1 leather collar]
L G Close
M Corcoran
J B Chestnut
S M Cowan
J Carly
H S Couperneil
T Coady
Jas Cummings
D I Coburn
F W Chase
T Cummings
W E Craig
E E Clark
J S Cornue
H B Cole
E Croak
H H Clough
B F Carnagy
J H Cushman
L Center
B W Coleman
W Cagger
G H Clark
Capt J O Carr
Hon C Cole
A J Crabb
J G Chandler
Lt T C Case
E Crogan

L B Crocker
F Chapman-[1 val]
Gonzaga Coolege
A A Coriels
J Coleman
F B Clifton-[1 knapsack]
J H Cole
P Chapman
C A Crandall
W H Coleman
L H Darling
Hon A L Diren
F L Darling
F Davison
C S Drake
Capt R Davidson
Jas Daly
T H Dodge
C Dunkel
Lt L Dean
Dunbar, Sherrel, & Co
J W Diltz
A Dexter
J Dumbors
D Eats-[1 carpet-bag]
Thos Eagan
J H Ewart
J P Eldridge
J Engard
H Edniger
F Emory
W L Eldridge-[C O D pkg]
F Edgerton-[1 bandbox]
J Edmons
J W Eastman-[2 cots]
Eastmead or Davis
E Elmendorf
C Eagan
F Flynn
C Foulkrod
W F Fasnas
A C Finch-[1 keg]
M Fitzmorns
C H Foot
L G Fox-[1 tin box]
J C Fackenthal
Dr J M Fowle
D Folger
B F Field
Mr Ford-[C O D pkg]
P Fredericks-[1 tin can]

G Fenner
J Floyd & Co-[1 tub]
M L Fay-[2 tubs]
J Felheimer
P Fisher
Rev A Fox, jr-[1 tub]
E J Frey
L S Foster
B D Grahan-[1 trk]
L J Goodrich
S E Goodyear-[2 kgs-C O D]
Capt M J Green
O L Gunn
Lt C Gage
M S Gilbert & Co
O F Gruner
Mrs M Gapsen
C Grosonier
C Gallagher
D Gastings
D Granmer
N Geodale
E J Greene
W K Gaines
Capt G R Graham
Col G L Graham
G W Gregory
K Granger
R Greenfield
W Gilford
G W Glass
J Hayter
J Hart
G P Hart
J Hildreth
L Hoffman
Brig Gen Herron
Prof J Henry
C O D Harden Ex Co
Jas Hess
G P Holt
A W Hughes
H House
C Huggin
E A Hoyt
D W Hoffa
Capt G G Hutchinson
L F Hyne
Capt I W Haskill
B B Hotchkiss
A Houghton

495

C B Hinsdale
J Hays
J Heliker
M Herb
S A Harris
Mr Hill
E W Holman
N S Hutchins
C H Hawkes
Lt S Healy
H Holdman
C B Hinsdale
E Hemenway
Maj H Higinbotham
G W Hagbon
D N Hunter
M Hinckle
M Henstreet
Geo Jackson-[1 trk]
T James
H Jones
A W Johnson
N Hewett
Jno Jones
Mary Jones
P L Joslyn
W Justin
S Jacoby
J Jones
T R Jones
M Johns
J Johnson
Thos Jones
W W Inman
Mrs H S Kennedy-[1 bd bx-C O D]
J Kennedy
E Kendall
J F Kennedy
J Knecht
C H Knine
P M Keller
F E King
J B Kelm
S Knecht
F S Knapp
J Kelley-[1 box-C O D]
H Karl-1 chest
J Kirchin
L Kaukapot, jr
Mrs A M Knott
J E Louis-1 chest

J H Lyons
S C Loridge
E Ladd
R E Lamphier-1 bur case
R W Lampman
J Leahy
C A Lanigan
H C Leslie
G C Latham
H T Lee
H B Lowe
Mrs I Lester
Mrs H M Lum
L Luber
W C Long
E E Lomorey
P D Mickoes
P A Mash
J Morgan
J McGill
J E Morgan
D Mitchell-1 carp bg
E Milstead, Port Tobacco
J Martin
W McKender
C Murphy
E Maxfield
J B McPeck
J McRoy
Dr S Marsh
H Morrison
F Marquard
Miss L Maby
W _ Morrison
Col R B Marcy
Rev S W Madden
C O Moore
N Munch
M Mayer
C Mason
W H Moody
P Meyers
A Merrill
C L Moore
J M Mead
G McCormick
Lt E McKnight
G McClure
H McGraw-[1 tub]
L Milhus
Sergt Martin
Geo Miller

J F Morgan
A Miller
E M Norton
J W Norscom
J Nixon-1 trk
Maj J M Norral
N Y Hosp
A O'Halloran-1 chest
N H Ormsby
E Orndall
L G Olmstead
Hon A B Olin
J Opp
A Overhouser
Miss V Parrish
Ed Putnam
C J Parmenter
L Phelps
J Pittman
A Prevost
Chas Parker
S Percivill
Jos Platz
J Phineas
G H Penfield
E M Power
D A Patch
H D Pennoyer
G H Park
G Patrick
A W Parks
H P Perry
T Peets
C T Pearce-1 chest
A Percy
R D Petil
Mrs V Parker
J P Parker-1 burial case
B F Pike
Partridge
H Pease
G W Perkins
L W Pinkham
M Quincer
Q M General-1 bale
W Rows
G A Randell
H Rosbrock
C H Ramsdell
C Roby
C F Randall
F Rowley

E Root
T C Reeves
H Rapp
W W Ryan
G W Ramsey
P E Ruggles
C Robinson
J Russell
Mr Reiter
C Raskopht
T E Reynolds
A J Searle
C Shelby
G Soffman
Lt H Sample
Dr J H Stearns
J H Smith
Shillington's Bk Store
B F Steadman-1 trk
F Stack
T Z Smith
Dr J L Stewart
J Steinwick
C Stevens
S Spencer
Geo Sinclair
J Stiller-1 casting
T W Stockton-1 coupling
Geo Sinclair
J Stiler
T W Stockton
J Schoneter
Capt M B Samson
J V Schad
Miss C W Semmess
John Shoemaker
J Siegler
Brig Gen T A Smyth
A H Shrers
Geo Short
W H Stabler
W Seay
G P Smith

E Smith
E A Sillyman
H Stabler
J Sutton
G V Scoby
C Shatluck
C Stevens
C Schader
D B Sanford
D T Smith
J Stackhouse
A Stine
M H Stephens
Miss M J Snyder-1 trk
H Stisburg-1 trk
J H Seymour-1 trk
J W Smith
T A Spencer
C C Skinner
G W Stevens-1 keg
E C Sleeper-1 keg
Sergt C E Spencer
F Statler
C Snyder
H Clay Stier
E H Sullivan
Miss M Thomas
H A Thomas
J P Tobert
Rev J R V Thomas
Clara Temple
C B Tisworth
Capt A S Taylor-1 val
G C Tompkins
T Turner
J Thomas
A W Taylor
C W Tolles
R Tuttle
W B Todd
T Tasco
C Talleon
B H Tripp

J N True
J B Tilton
J J Trombore
W E Vanantwerp-1 trunk
Maj A R Venable
Capt G M Van Buren
E A Van Wie-1 tin can
T Veran
Lt R V Wicks
J Wetherston
S Wengel
H D Warren
T Walpert
J L Webster
H Weller
A A White
J Williams
C J Wilkins
Fred Wekler
Dr C Wagner
F Walker
A Williams
Capt S W Walden
E C Wiley-1 tin can
Mrs Williams-1 sword
W B Wilson
Mr Williams
C Wallpert
J Whitman
J Whittaker
J H Wright
A B Whiting
J Wyatt
A Wechsler
C Wade
J Wright
G Whitlaw
Lt E Yerkes
J H Young
H F Yates
J Zuber

Military Freight:

H Sprague, sharpshooters
T F Looker, 8th U S infty
B Williamson, Camp Casey
J F Hoffman, Camp Taylor
Peter Coyle, Fort Foote
C P Chase, Camp Barry
W Hayman, 2nd div cavalry corps
T Skanks, U S C T

T P Pyman, 1st Mass cavalry
G N Brainer, 213th Pa vols
M A Osgood, 14th Maine
Miss V Hart, 2nd A C Hosp
C Kitchings, 16th Regt
C E Griffith, Headqrtrs 3rd A C
P Lawson, 43rd U S C T
L Shaw, jr, 7th U S C T

FRI OCT 6, 1865

Sup Crt, D C. 1-Geo D Abbott vs Chas Wierman et al. Statement of trustee's acc't into debts due Chas Wierman, which are liens upon the property sold by the trustee. -W Redin, auditor. 2-Frances M Dowling vs Mary G Dowling. Statement of trustee's acc't; sale of part of lot 20 in sq 254, sold to B F Isherwood. Creditors of Wm Dowling to exhibit same. - W Redin, auditor

Trial of Henry Wirz. Witness account: Geo W Fechnor was cross-examined; born in Lancaster, Ohio, removed to Cincinnati at any early age, & in 1853 he went into the coach mkg business. He was exchanged in Mar last under the name of Chas W Ross. [His account consists of 2 columns]

Rl est: sales by J C McGuire & Co, aucts: sold last evening the lot on s e corner of 12th & M sts, to Wm Ballantyne, at $1.20 per ft; & to the same purchaser, the adjoining lot, facing M st, at .86 per ft.

Died: Mr Geo A Meem, at his residence on Mt Wash, above Rockville, in Montg Co, Md, on Oct 1; native of Gtwn; & in the 71st yr of his age. He dwelt on the farm for the past 7 yrs. He was a kind, affectionate hsbnd & father. Mr Meem was a mbr of Capt John I Stule's company in the war of 1812 & served his country with distinction.

Police-D C. Rsgn'd: Sgt H Hepburn & T T Hurdle. Appt'd patrolman: John H Martin vice Wm T Burdett, ineligible. Michl O'Callahan, Timothy Brosman, F A A Evans, & John H

Hall. Dismissed for sleeping on their beats: Wm R Tennant, Thos Bradley, Fred'k Garner. Josiah Essex was also dismissed.

Appropriations made during the 2nd session of the 38th Congress:
1-A gold medal to Cornelius Vanerbilt, approv'd Jan 28, 1864-$3,000.
2-Relief of Geo Mowry for conveying 2 prisoners from Somerset Jail, Pa, to Pittsburg, in 1841, by order of the U S deputy mrshl-$72.12
3-To Jacob Weber for money advanced by him to pay Scott Allen, A Hyatt, Henry Olden, A W Cook, Lewis Saindollar, & Jas Garland, teamsters for the 4th regt of Ohio vol infty, Aug 1 1861 to Jul 1, 1862-$913.33
4-To Isaac R Diller for expenses for extra clerk-hire in his ofc & for destitute American ctzns-Aug 1857 & Sep 29, 1861-$3,000
5-To Louis Roberts for money he advanced to replace certain Indian indemnity goods, accidentally destroyed by fire in Nov 1855-am't not given.
6-To Henry A Brigham, amount of his check in Nov 7, 1863-$2,000.
7-To Lemuel Cook, enlisted at Hatfield, Mass, is now about 98 years of age, & resides in Clarendon, Orleans Co, N Y-$300.
8-To Saml Downing, enlisted in Carroll Co, N H, now about 98 years of age, & lives in Edinburg, Saratoga Co, N Y-$300.
9-To Wm Hutchings, enlisted at New Castle, Maine, [then Mass,]now 100 years old, & resides in Penobscot, Hancock Co, Mane-$300.
10-Alexander Moroney, enlisted at Lake Geo, N Y, as a drummer-boy, in now about 94 years old, resides in Yates, Orleans Co, N Y-$300.
11-To Jas Barham, substitute for a drafted man in So Hampton Co, Va, lives in Missouri & is in his one hundred & first yr-$300.
12-Relief of Chapin Hall for using his lumber at Louisville, Ky, by Gen McCook's div, in Sep 1862-$2,500.
13-Relief of Chas A Pitcher, for damages sustained by infringement of a patent on a machine for making brooms, 1859 to 1862-$5,000.
14-Relief of W H & C A Duncan for goods furnished Capt Walker's company, Kansas militia, in 1856-$200.80
15-To Saml L Gerould, service as clerk to genr'l crt-martial from Sep 21, 1863 to Dec 24, 1864-$179.20
16-To Jean M Lander, wid/of F W Lander, dec'd, for expenses incurred by him regarding the railroad from Puget's sound to the Mississippi river, in 1854-$4,750.
17-Relief of Mrs Lucy A Rice, late of Richmond, Va, for her courage in saving Col Streight & his party, & enabling them to escape from the rebels-$1,500.

SAT OCT 7, 1865
Died: on Oct 5, at Gtwn, D C, Miss Cecilia Cath, d/o the late Chas & Rebecca Koones, of Alexandria, Va, in her 23rd yr. Funeral from the residence of Mr John T Mitchell, 22 First st, Gtwn, today.

Trial of Henry Wirz. Witness' accounts: Augustus Kleich, 8th Pa cavalry; taken to Andersonville in Mar 1864, captured in 1863. Martin S Harris, 5th N Y vols, captured in Jul, 1864, taken to Andersonville on the 29th. Fred'k Roth, 2nd N Y cavalry, was captured at New Balt in Oct 1863, & after remaining some time at Belle Isle, was taken to Andersonville arriving Mar 20, 1864-until Sep 9. Miss Mary Ransom was sworn; she resided near Andersonville & was there at intervals from Jan until Mar 1865; she was there to relieve the Union prisoners. Rev G P Duncan, mbr of the Meth Chr, & belonged to the Tenn Conference; preached to the prisoners in Aug, 1864 & in Feb 1865.

Mscl item: It is reported that Ralph Waldo Emerson lost his entire property by the Concord Bank robbery, except his homestead.

Gtwn Affairs: 1-The bill of Mr Jas F Essex, for the livery charges of the horse belonging to the city, was referred to the Cmte on Claims. 2-Ptn of Chas Wise to be released from a fine imposed by the trial justice was referred to the Cmte on Grievanses.

In the Alexandria crts the tedium of green-bag proceedings is relieved by an occasional sprightly turn. Recently Cath Evitt was on trial for seizing Bridget O'Gormon by the hair. Cnsl for the defence moved the Crt to instruct the jury that if the dfndnt's hsbnd was, at the time, present, she was to be considered as under his coercion, on well-known principles of law, citing Blackstone, Wharton, etc. The Presiding Justice. The difficulty in this case is, that in Blackstone's time women were controlled by their hsbnds, but in these times women control their hsbnds, & such an instruction in these days would be very dangerous. [Laughter.] The instruction was refused.

MON OCT 9, 1865

For sale-200 acs of land in PG Co, Md. -John E Berry, Forestville, PG Co, Md

U S Patent Ofc. Ptn of Wendel Boltman, Balt, Md; extension of patent dated Jan 6, 1852; improvement of *Construction of Bridges*. -T C Theaker, Com'r of patents

Crct Crt of Chas Co, Md. Ptn of Peter Wood, Sr, insolvent debtor. Sale of about 500 acs in Chas Co, with dwlg hse. -Jos C Thomas, trustee

Sup Crt of D C. Vincent M Burch vs Eliz Ferrall, Thos W Burch, Fred'k A Burch, Jas W Drane for himself, & as guardian ad litem for Richd L Jones, Anne E Drane, Thos W Drane, Mary O Drane, Sarah F Burch, & Adelaide Burch, Lemuel F Clarke for himself & guardian ad litem of Jas E Clarke, Mgt Burch, & Mary E Burch. Oct 30th, at the Crt Hse, distribution of the fund from the sales made by trustee; & claims of any creditors of the late Thos Burch, must be filed. -W Redin, auditor

Trial of Henry Wirz. Witness' accounts: Dr Jos Jones was called for the prosecution. He is now a professor of chemistry in Augusta, Ga. Capt Saml Gilmore, 39th Ill, & Provost Mrshl at Norfolk, Va, testified.

TUE OCT 10, 1865

Details of Dr Mudd's attempted escape-a correspondent of the N Y Tribune, writing from the Dry Tortugas under date of Sep 25, professed the details of the attempted escape of Dr Mudd. Dr Mudd got on the steamer *Scott* at the wharf, taking advantage of the confusion of moving stores, baggage, etc, & favored by one of the crew name Kelly, concealed himself in the coal-bunkers. Mudd had gone below & had not come up again was noticed; a squad went below to search. Lt Tappan ran his sabre under an old box & a cry from Dr Mudd disclosed him in his concealment. His mortification is described as extreme. He was ironed & lodged in a dungeon.

Mrd: on Oct 3, by Rev Dr Pinkney, Frank M Ballinger, of Iowa, to Florence M Fatio, eldest d/o the late Capt Louis C F Fatio.

Died: on Oct 9, Cranstoun Laurie, infant s/o Col Jas M & Isabel C Miller, of Wash City.

Died: on Oct 8, at the residence of his aunt, in 15th st, after a brief illness, Lutz Archer, in his 4th yr. Funeral will be private. [N Y Herald & Balt Sun, please copy]

Died: in N Y C, on Oct 1, of inflammation of the brain, Moreau Lemoine Willis, formerly of Wash, D C, in his 20th yr.

Died: in Wash, D C, on Oct 9, John F Handlen, formerly of Louisville, Ky.

Died: on Oct 9, Arthur Birch, infant s/o Crawford & Josephine McLeran. Funeral at St Aloysius Chr this afternoon.

Obit: Died at his residence, Needwood, Fred'k Co, Md, on Sep 3, Saml L Gouverneur, aged about 66 yrs. Mr G was the son-in-law & exc of Pres Monroe, & for several years his pvt sec. He practiced law in N Y C, of which he was a native. Some 12 years ago he mrd Miss Lee, of Md, a grand-dght of Gov Lee, of that State.

Sup Crt of D C, Equity #502. Zephaniah Jones, cmplnt, vs Horace Stringfellow, E R Lippet, Jos Pachard, Wm Pendleton, Clement Butler, Smith Pyne, J W French, Henry H Bean, Saml Ridout, David Saunders, John Saunders, Henry May, Cath F Thompson, Robt Jones, Peter R Hawley, Eliz Hawley, Wm B Hill & Cath B Hill, his wife, Geo W Tubman & Mary E Wilmer, excs of M D Tubman, dec'd, John R Neirnsee, J C Neilson, John Garlington, Richd Simpson, Maria Anderson, Robt James, Dade Hooe, Mary Hooe, & Lucy Daniel. Subpoena issued to compel the appearance of the above named dfndnts returned by the Mrshl on Aug 31, 1865, endorsed not found. The heirs at law of the late Ann R Demott, other than above mentioned, are unknown. -Geo Fisher, Justice S C D C. -R J Meigs, clerk

Orphans Crt-D C. 1-Will of the late Louisa T Mc Calla, bequeathing her estate to her relatives & friends, & nominating her fr, John M McCalla, sr, & bro, J M McCalla, jr, was filed, & admitted to probate. 2-The will of the late Mary Eleanor Watson, bequeathing per property to her sister, Eliz D Watson, was filed. 3-The will of the late Michl Shea was filed; bequeathing all his estate to A Thos Bradley in trust for the sole & separate use of his wife Mary Shea. A protest against the will was presented by the bro of the dec'd on the ground that the dec'd was speechless at the time of making it; proceeding postponed until Oct 17. 4-Final account of W A Ross, adm of Mary Miller; of W Y Fendall, adm w a of Mary Y Dundas; of Conrad Finkman, exc of Henry S Ward; of Eliza M Anderson, excx of Thos F Anderson, were approved & passed.

John T Griffith was arrested for stealing the horse belonging to the estate of Mountjoy Case, of Poolesville, Md, who died there only last Thu. The thief's real name proved to be Amon R Miles. Mr Case's son stated that the horse belonged to his father.

Rev Dr Gurley & his lady, celebrated their silver anniversary last evening: mrd Oct 7, 1840. Mr & Mrs W W Danenhower also celebrated their 25th anniv at their residence on N Y av, Wash, D C. -Local Item

Funeral of Gen Horace T Sanders will take place from the residence of L B Miller, 452 Third st. -Local Item

Freder'k Orini was arrested on Sep 24th on charge of murdering an old man named John Haley, on Long Bridge. Haley was last seen alive with Orini, but Justice Walter did not deem the evidence sufficient to hold the accused.

WED OCT 11, 1865

Orphans Crt of Wash Co, D C. Prsnl estate of Geo Ailer, late of Wash Co, dec'd. -Sophie A Ailer, admx

Mrd: on Oct 10, at Chr of the Epiphany, by Rev Chas H Hall, Wm H Coles, jr, of N Y C, to Adelaide Hopkinson, d/o Edw B Stelle, of Wash City.

Frank P Barton, Co G 214th Pa, accidentally shot & killed Frank Congdon, a comrade, age about 19 yrs, whose friends reside in Phil. -Local Item

The Pres pardoned Mgt Weirmer, convicted last June of assault & battery with intent to kill, sentenced to 2 years in the Albany Pen.

Orphans Crt-D C. 1-Inventory of prsnl estate of John C Rives, dec'd, was filed. 2-Account of Mary Jones, excx of estate of Richd Jones, dec'd, approved & passed. 3-Will of Mary Eleanor Watson, dec'd, proved & admitted to probate. 4-Account of Cath Reynolds, guardian of minor chldrn of Jos Reynolds, dec'd was approved; as was her first account as guardian of John F Reynolds, now of age. 5-Account of Wm A Whittlesey, guardian of Oliver Whittlesey, approved & passed. 6-Peter Donnelly qualified as adm of estate of Mathew Collins, dec'd, by giving bond of $400; sureties are Patrick Barns & Jas Barnard. 7-Sophia A Ailer qualified as admx of estate of Geo Ailer, dec'd, giving bond of $6,000; also bond of $3,000 as guardian of Eleanor Ailer. 8-Jas McSherry gave bond of $14,000 as guardian of the minor heirs of Helen M McSherry, dec'd; sureties are Jos F Kelley & Wm D Dunkinson.

For sale-part of a tract of land belonging to & on which Mr S B Scaggs resides, about 2 miles from the Capitol, across Benning's Bridge; lots 1 & 2-ab't 30 acs; lot 3-22 acs; lot 4-20 acs; lot 5-10 acs with dwlg hse. -Green & Wms, auctioneers

THU OCT 12, 1865

Orphans Crt of Wash Co, D C. Prsnl estate of Geo F Huguely, late of Wash City, dec'd. -Sarah Huguely, admx

For sale-farm on which I now reside; 605 acs more or less, with dwlg hse; one mile within the stage rd from Wash to Upper Marlboro, Md. Thos Talbert, [of E]

Died: in Wash City, on Oct 11, Jacob Kleiber, in his 83rd yr. Funeral from his residence in City Hall this afternoon. He was born in Pa & came to Wash City over 60 years ago with his father, who once carried on a bakery. His son, Harry Kleiber, survives.

Died: in Gtwn, D C, on Oct 11, Henry W Ducachet, jr, M D, surgeon in charge of the garrison of Wash. Funeral, today, from 121 Wash st, Gtwn, interment in Phil.

Exec Ofc-Released on parole: John A Campbell, of Ala; John H Reagan, of Texas; Alexander H Stephens, of Ga; Geo A Trenholm, of S C, & Chas Clark, of Miss, lately engaged in rebellion against the U S Gov't. -Andrew Johnson, Pres

Mr Felix De La Baume, the great grandson of Gen Lafayette, who served over 3 years in the U S army during this war, was appt'd a clerkship in the Dept of the Interior. He was wounded severely in front of Petersburg & a p o w for 10 months at Andersonville, Ga.

Jas Arthur Whitlow, desperate burglar, was captured in a hse on Buzzard Point,as a fugitive from justice, yesterday. -Local Item

FRI OCT 13, 1865
Sup Crt of D C: cause of Jas F Wollard vs Melissa D Wollard et al, Equity #511. Sale of lot 20 & part of lot 21 in sq 455, with improvements, containing 7 frame tenements. -J M Varnum, trustee

Mrd: on Oct 12, at the Chr of the Epiphany, by Rev Dr Hall, Mr Gilbert Gordon, of N Y, to Pauline, y/d/o Col M Jordan, of Va. No cards [Richmond & Norfolk, Va, papers please copy.]

Mrd: on Oct 12, at the Chr of the Epiphany, by Rev Dr Hall, Capt Jas Gilliss, U S A, to Julia, eldest d/o C K Stellwagen, all of Wash City, No cards [Phil papers please copy.]

Mgt Jas Haggerty was arrested yesterday on the charge of practising a confidence game on certain colored people residing in Wash City.

Wm Baldwin, ctzn, who made his escape from the Old Capitol prison, but was re-captured after 6 weeks, was arrested for stealing Gov't horses. He was sentenced to 3 years imprisonment in the State Prison at Concord & a fine of $100.

Trial of Henry Wirz. Witness' accounts: Col F G Rufin was sworn; resides near Richmond, Va, & during the last 2 years was Lt Col in the Subsistence Dept of the Confederate States. Robt S Kellogg was recalled for the defense. Maj S B French testified he resided in Richmond, Va, for the past 2 yrs. Dr G G Roy recalled for the defence. J W Armstrong, jr, of Macon, Ga, was a Capt in the Confederate svc. Maj Geo M Proctor was on duty at Andersonville from Aug until Nov, 1864.

Sale of Rl est: C W Boteler, jr, auct, sold, yesterday, lot 5 in sq 158, fronting on north N st, near corner of 17th st 16 cents per ft, purchased by Richd H Lee.

Boston: Oct 11. Jas S Eaton, Princ of the Eng dept of Phillips Acad, at Andover, the well known author & teacher, died on Tue. Jas A Dix, principal editor of the Boston Daily Jrnl for a number of yrs, died this noon of consumption, after an illness of several months.

SAT OCT 14, 1865
Edwin Ward Moore died in N Y C recently, of apoplexy, in his 55th yr. He was a native of Alexandria, Va

Petersburg, Oct 13. The Rev Robt Castleman, a well known mbr of the Prot Episc Chr, was brutally murdered near Gaston, N C, on Wed night last. He was returning alone from a visit to a neighbor. The perpatrator of the crime have not been identified. The dec'd was widely known & much beloved in Va.

Sup Crt of D C, Equity #433. Ellen E, E Augusta, & Edw A Parker, vs Chas, Carrie, & Geo W Parker, heirs of Amasa R Parker. The above named, the trustee, & Saml North, guardian ad litem, are to appear at my ofc on Nov 3. -W Redin, auditor

John Maack was arrested for assault & battery on his father. The prisoner is 20 years of age, stout built, & about half drunk when arrested. -Local Item

Jas Monroe, 6th Pres of the U S, died in N Y C, at the residence of his son-in-law, Mr Saml L Gouverneur. He was buried in N Y & in 1858 his remains were removed to Richmond, & on Jul 5, 1858, they were re-interred in Hollywood Cemetery, near the city. A monument was erected over the spot by the state of Va. -Balt American

Mrd: at Chester, Pa, on Oct 12, by Rev Wm T Eva, of Phil, assisted by Rev A W Sproull, Miss Kate L, d/o Thos Reaney, of Chester, to Saml F Savage, of Wash.

Died: on Oct 13, Mrs Mary C Fenwick, aged 55 yrs. Funeral from her late residence at Locust Grove, near Wash City, on Sun.

Trial of Henry Wirz. Witness's accounts: Benj F Dilley, 54th Pa regt; was a prisoner at Andersonville from Mar 1864 until Mar 1865. F W Ille, 2nd Dela, sworn: prisoner from Jun 1864 until Sep 1864.

MON OCT 16, 1865
Orphans Crt of Wash Co, D C. Prsnl estate of Marinus Willett, late of Gtwn, D C, dec'd. - Sarah Willett, adms c t a.

Harrisburg, Oct 15. Nine persons killed when 4 cars were thrown off the track between here & Lancaster yesterday. Instantly killed were: Mrs Barr, w/o the Surveyor Gen of Pa; Col Wm Butler, a whiskey inspec, & wife, of Phil; Sarah Willett, W H Butler, Mrs Getta, & 3 families unknown.

Died: on Oct 15, Ann Eliz, 2nd d/o Robt W & Ann E Middleton, of Wash City. Funeral from their residence, 342 9th st, Tue.

Died: on Oct 14, of typhoid fever, Mrs Anna Maria Hopkins, w/o the late Philip Hopkins, a native of Annapolis, Md, but for many years a resident of Wash City, aged 49 yrs, leaving 4 affectionate chldrn to mourn her loss. Funeral from her late residence, 573 H st, on Mon.

Mrs Stover, d/o the Pres, was in Bristol on Sat week. Her hsbnd, Col Danl Stover, 4th Tenn infty, died in Nashville in 1863, & Mrs S visits her native state at the present time to have his remains removed from Nashville to Carter Co. Nashville Banner

Wash City news: last night an alarm of fire sounded & a small bldg, 356 7th st was on fire: occupied by Mr Chrisman, a turner; by Mr Dunn, an upholsterer & repairer of furn. A portion of the bldg was occupied as a lager beer saloon, & it is said the fire orignated in that part. Bldg & all its contents were totally destroyed. Mr Geo L Sheriff was the owner of the property. The bldgs adjoining were somewhat injured & were occupied by Mrs H Kandler, milliner, & Mr Shiprest, as a stamping depot. Mr Geo W Utermehle is the owner of the land on which the bldgs known as Falconer's Row are situated, but Mr Elisha Falconer is the proprietor of the bldgs. The large brick bldg on the so side, occupied by Mr Kauffman as a clothing store, & owned by Mr Harrison Taylor, was somethat injured. There was a large amount of furniture for repair in the shops of Messrs Chrisman & Dunn.

Trial of Henry Wirz. Witness account: Edw W Boats was called for the defence: was mbr of the 42nd N Y vols, captured in Oct 1863 & taken to Belle Idle, & then to Andersonville in Feb 1864 until Aug 1864.

TUE OCT 17, 1865

Sup Crt of D C. Eliz Green, Jas Green, Ellen Frasier, John Frasier, Mary A Murphy, Dennis Magee, vs Hugh, Thos, John, & John Magee, minor, Jas Green, guardian ad litem. Parties named & trustee of Hugh Magee, sr, dec'd, to appear on Nov 3, at the Crt Hse. -W Redin, auditor

Sup Crt of D C. Bird et al vs Maryman et al. Ratify sale of lot 3 in sq 728 to A Schwartz, for $732. -A B Olin, Justice; R J Meigs, clerk

Mrd: in Balt, on Oct 10, by the Most Rev Archbishop, Thos T Turner, of St Louis, Mo, to Miss Harriet S Brown, of Nashville, Tenn, d/o Mrs Genr'l Ewell.

Died: on Oct 15, Jonathan O Paulding, in his 31st yr. Funeral from 402 13th st, Tue. Mbrs of the Masonic Frat; clerks of the Pay Dept, are invited.

Died: on Oct 16, Andrew, y/s/o Alex'r & Mary Humes, of Wash City. Funeral from their residence, 5th & H sts, this evening.

Orphans Crt-D C. 1-Will of Michl Griffith, dec'd, proven & admitted to probate. 2-Mrs Cath R French qualified as admx of the estate of Brvt Lt Col Frank S French, dec'd. 3-Final acc't of Jas O'Leary, exc of the estate of Cornelius O'Leary, dec'd, was proven & passed..

Gen Howard, Super of the Bur of Freedmen, Refugees, & Abandoned Lands, having notified landholders of St Mary's Co, Md, that if they do not provide on their own estate for their former slaves now become unfit for labor, their plantations shall be seized by the Gov't & cultivated for the benefit of the aforesaid negroes. [This order has evoked considerable discussion in the papers thru out the country.]

Mr Thos Dowling, auct, sold at his salesrms in Bridge st, last evening, $5,000 of the Farmers' & Mechanics' Bank stock to Mr Wm H Tenney, at 67; $2,400 Corp of Gtwn stock, to Mr E B Barrett, at 99; & $880 of the same to Mr Wm H Tenney, at 99½.

WED OCT 18, 1865

Sup Crt of D C. 1-Equity #376. A Carothers et al vs David S Holland et al. Parties & trustee of Edw Holland, dec'd, to appear on Nov 6. -W Redin, aud
2-Equity #408. John F Sharratts et al vs Wm Brereton et al. Parties & trustee of the late Saml Brereton, dec'd, to appear Nov 7. W Redin, auditor
3-Equity #146. Geo W Miller vs Ellen Miller et al. Statement of trustee's acc't on Nov 8. -W Redin, auditor
4-Equity #534. In regard to the estate of R F Nixon & his wife Sarah A Nixon. Notice to the parties in the above cause, & the guardian ad litem, com'rs appt'd Oct 21, to divide the said estate. -A Lloyd, atty for com'rs

Died: on Oct 17, John R Spalding, in his 38th yr. Funeral from his late residence on 20th st, near G, on Wed.

Appointments & promotions in the 6th Auditor's Ofc: Adolphus Liebschutz, of Poland, appt'd 1st class clerk, v J W Nightingale, rsgn'd. Gurden Perkins, of Ill, promoted to 2nd class clerk, v Saml Kelly, dec'd. J Edmund Sheppard, of N J, promoted to 2nd class clerk, v David Bassett, promoted. J S Moffatt, of Wisc, promoted to 2nd class clerk, v P A Fitzhugh, dec'd. David Bassett, of D C, promoted to 3rd class clerk, v S S Bean, rsgn'd. Frederick Augustus Holden, promoted to 3rd class clerk, v J C Hopper, rsgn'd.

The property of John M Orr, formerly Mayor of Leesburg, Va, has been restored to his possession by the Freedmen's Bureau.

Orphans Crt-D C. 1-Wm C Jeffries qualified as adm of estate of David F Jeffries, dec'd, giving bond of $350; sureties are E H Willard & A Spicht. 2-Mary F E Purcell appt'd guardian of the orphan son of Lt West Scott, dec'd, & gave bond of $400. W F Purcell, M Thompson, & J E Williams are sureties. 3-Estate of Sarah Smith, dec'd. Adm, Thos P Morgan, appt'd in 1860 when the estate was indebted to French Forrest for about $1,100, & that he had paid various amounts to Forrest's order. Petitioner craves leave to pay claims to parties to whom Forrest was indebted. Prayer of petitioner was granted. 4-Sale of rl estate of the minor chldrn of Hannah Barnes, by adm, was ratified. 5-Will of Louisa G McCalla was proven, John M McCalla, jr, exc, giving bond of $200. 6-Will of Michl Griffeth was proven & admitted to probate; Michl Cooney, exc; sureties-Jas Stone & John Maloney. 7-Account of Elias A Eliasson, guardian of Eliz R Rhodes, & first account of the same as guardian of Ellen Rhodes, approved & passed. 8-E C Morgan qualified as adm of the estate of Wm Walker, dec'd, gave bond of $1,500; Chas Walter & W Y Fendall are sureties. 9-Will of Ursula A Mirrick was filed. 10-Account of the sales of the prsnl estate of Dolly Ann Williams, dec'd, as returned by the adm was entered & filed.

Badge of the Medical Staff of the Army: Wash , D C, Jul 15, 1865: Brvt Maj Gen J K Barnes, Surg Gen, U S A. Meeting on Jul 1, 1865, in Wash City, adopted a badge to be worn as a testimony of honorable professional svc rendered during the war, to mbrs of the corps on the rost of your ofc who have unblemished record. Very respectfully yours:

John Wilson, Med Insp, U S A
D W Bliss, Surg, U S V
N R Mosely, Surg, U S V
T R Crosby, Surg, U S V
J C McKee, Surg, U S A

W Lindsey, Ast Surg, U S A
J J Woodward, Surg, U S A
Wm M Notson, Surg, U S A
Geo A Otis, Surg, U S V

City Items: 1-Mr Barney Hart, dealer in Wines & Liquors, 181 Pa ave.
2-John S Yates, 505 9th st, above D, lively business in the Dry Goods line.
3-A well conducted hotel: P Emerich, proprietor of the European Htl, corner of Pa ave & 11th st.
4-Messrs Wall, Stephens & Co, at their Merchant Tailoring Establishment, 321 Pa ave, between 9th & 10th sts, unusually large stock of cloths, cassimerees, & vestings.
5-Messrs L Feldner & Co, have at their Fashionable Clothing Establishment, Wash Bldg, 344 Pa ave, corner of 7th st, an elegant assortment of men's & youth's clothing & furnishing goods.

WED OCT 19, 1865
Sup Crt of D C, Equity # 385. J Harry Thompson vs Rutherford & others. Settlement of account on Nov 10; parties interested & creditors of the late Tillotson P Brown & of Eliz Brown must file their claims. -W Redin, auditor

Died: after a brief illness, on Oct 17, Mrs Maria E Wroe, relict of the late Capt Saml Wroe, of Wash, D C, aged 66 yrs. Funeral from her residence on Mass av & 3rd sts, this afternoon.

Died: in Wash City, on Oct 18, Mrs Virginia H Baldwin, w/o the late Henry Clay Baldwin, aged * yrs. [*Could be 34 or 24 yrs.] Funeral from the residence of her father, Wm W Moore, on Fri.

Capt B Chambers has opened at 531 7ᵗʰ st, just above Pa ave, an elegant Shooting Gallery. He is known as a proficient, both as a marksman & teacher of this manly art. Charges are moderate as in any northern city.

Crt of Appeals of Md: Oct term, 1865. On motion of O Miller, E C Gant was admitted as an atty of this crt.

FRI OCT 20, 1865
Trial of Henry Wirz. Witness' accounts: Capt C M Selph was recalled. Saml F Hunt was sworn.

Local Item-Mr John O Howard purchased a tavern & farm, 10 acs, at Tennallytown, Wash, on Tue, for $7,000.

Died: in Fairfax Co, Va, on Oct 16, in his 66ᵗʰ yr, Alfred Lee, s/o Chas Lee, Atty Gen of the U S under admin of Wash & John Adams.

Mrd: on Oct 12, by Rev Keeling, Thos Adams to Mrs Eliza R Brodhead, both of Wash City.

Mrd: on Oct 17, at *Mill Seat*, the residence of the bride's father, by Rev Mr Harris, E D Hartley, of Gtwn, D C, to Mary Lyons, of Wash Co, D C.

Large sale of Gov't bldgs at Annapolis, Md: pblc auction under direction of Capt John Power, A Q M, at Camp Parole, Nov 7ᵗʰ, continuing until the completion of the sale. –M I Ludington, Col & Chief Q M, Dept of Wash.

Rl estate sale: lot 8 in subdiv of sq 124, on N Y ave & E st, near 20ᵗʰ, to John Statz, at 10½ cents per ft; lot 22 in same sq, sold entire, to F Stewart for $275.

Hon John V Lawrence, of Wash Co, mbr of Congress elect from the 24ᵗʰ district of Pa, died at his residence on Oct 13ᵗʰ after a short but severe illness.

Reported that the estate of Confederate Gen Gideon J Pillow, in Arkansas, some 6,000 acs, which has been held as abandoned property for some time past, has been restored to its original owner.

Mr Thos Dowling, auct, sold at Tennallytown, on Tue, a tvrn & farm of about 10 acs to Mr John O Howard for $7,000.

Capt Geo W Dutton, 10ᵗʰ Vet Reserve Corps, has been appt'd superintendent of the Old Capitol Prison, vice Capt Weest, relieved. Few prisoners in the Old Capitol now, the most prominent being Capt Wirz, Gen Briscoe, Duncan, [the Andersonville q m,] & Capt R B Winder.

The remains of Lewis Stengel, a pvt of Capt Bourne's Co, 2ⁿᵈ btln V R C, was found in the Eastern Branch, near Benning's Bridge. Coroner's inquest: he was first murdered by some person or persons unknown, & that his body was then thrown into the stream.

SAT OCT 21, 1865
U S Patent Ofc. Ptn of Alfred Platt, of Waterbury, Conn, for extension of patent dt'd Jan 13, 1852, improvement in *Buckwheat Fans*. -T C Theaker, Com'r

Pension Ofc. Re-issue of land warrants: 160 acs to Thanxful, wid/o Wm Smith, granted Aug 27, 1856. 160 acs to Sarah, wid/o Jas Ray, granted Jul 24, 1858. 160 acs to Ozias Spalding, granted Mar 21, 1861. 160 acs to Eliz Benson, wid/o Giles Benson, granted Jun 14, 1858. [Oct 23 paper.] 160 acs to Louisa, wid/o Geo Latimer, granted Jun 19, 1856. -Jos H Barrett, Com'r.

Loss of the steamer *Atlanta*: only 5 lives were saved. The bark *W E Anderson*, from Mobile, arrived this morning with David Drexler, a passenger, 2 firemen, a seaman, & a cook of the steamship *Atlanta*, who were picked up at sea on a piece of the wreck. Drexler reports that the ship left New Orleans on Oct 7, & sprang a leak on the 14th, & on the 15th, a heavy gale, when 200 miles south of Sandy Hook, at 5 in the afternoon, she broke in 3 pieces, leaving him & the 4 others on a piece from which they were rescued after floating nearly 2 days. The *Atlanta* had 17 passengers & a crew of 35. The passenger list included

Miss Wolfe	H V Maloney	Robt Callie
O Livingston	W F Lansery	Chas Smith D Myers &
Capt M R Wilson	D Dexter	lady

Mrd: on Oct 19, in Rock Crk Chr, near Wash, D C, by Rev Jas A Buck, Bvt Lt Col Oscar A Mack, U S A, to Kate, d/o Col Justin Dimick, U S A.

Died: at his residence in Madison, Conn, of chronic diarrhoea, contracted in the military svc, Chauncey M Hand, late of the N Y Bar, age 37 yrs.

Died: in Wash City, on Oct 20, Chas B H Matlock, in his 34th yr. Funeral from the residence of his father, Simeon Matlock, 414 8th st, Sun.

Died: on Oct 19, in her 50th yr, Mrs Sarah Frances Berryman, wid/o the late Capt O H Berryman,
U S Navy. Funeral from her late residence at 306 Dela av, today.

Trial of Henry Wirz. Concluding argument of Col Chipman, judge advocate.

MON OCT 23, 1865
Harriet Wilkes, alias Haughton, was found dead in a closet of her hse, 22 13½ st, yesterday. She had mrd a man named Haughton a few years ago. 3 years ago she came here with Levi L Farewell, from whom she parted for alleged cruelty. Farewell is believed to be the murderer.

Died: on Oct 17, near Warrenton, N C, his home, after a short illness, Col Thos M Crossan, a native of Pittsburg, Pa. For many years he was a distinguished ofcr of the U S navy.

At the meeting of the mechanics & workingmen, held at the City Hall on Sat, the following new delegates appeared & were received: Harnessmakers: E L Rowland, Asa McCracken, David Harney; Wash Lab: D L Johnson, G L Lawrence; Ordnance Laborers: Wm H Oberly & John Umberly.
Cmte, etc: Donald McCathran-chrmn
Cmte on mottoes:

Canfield	Clark	Haighe

Cmte on spkrs:

Mc Williams		
McCathran	Saunders	J Q Larman

Cmte on rte of procession:

McLean	Landvoit	Woltemeyer

Cmte on music:

Boyd	Porter
Dice	Larkins

Gas & fixtures:

Bradbury	Simmons
Frost	Bradley

Trial of Henry Wirz. Conclusion of the argument; physical condition of the accused.

TUE OCT 24, 1865
Orphans Crt of Wash Co, D C. Application of Agatha C Lynch, guardian for the sale of the rl estate of Ambrose S Lynch. Ratify sale of lot 25 in sq 728, to W P O'Connor, for $790. - Wm F Purcell, Z C Robbins, rg o/wills

Local police items: 1-Addison Albert committed a violent assault on John Bateman yesterday, fracturing his nose. He was sent to jail for court. 2-Geo Thecker, for selling liquor on the Sabbath, was fined $20. 3-Wm Smith, for swindling, or grand larceny of a mule & wagon valued at $100, from Fanny Link, was sent to jail.

Mrd: on Oct 23, by Rev Edmund C Bittinger, U S N, E G Osborn, U S N, to Miss Ella M Numan, of Phil.

Mrd: on Oct 19, by Rev Edmund C Bittinger, U S N, Dr W F Hutchinson, U S N, to Miss Emma C Fisher, of Phil.

Died: at Corning, N Y, on Oct 20, after a brief illness, Jas B Leach, in his 47th yr. Mr Leach was a native of N H; resided for many years in Calif; the last 6 years he lived in D C. He mrd near Gtwn, where he leaves a widow & 2 chldrn to mourn his loss. Funeral at the Chapel at Oak Hill Cemetery on Wed.

Died: on Oct 22, Mrs Roseana Chambers, w/o Wm Chambers. Funeral from her late residence on 10th st, between O & P sts, today.

Died: in Wash City, on Oct 23, Horatio Nelson, infant s/o Horatio N & Eliz B Easby, aged 2 months & 23 days. Funeral from their residence, F & 29th sts, Tue.

Orphans Crt of Wash Co, D C. 1-Will of Miss Eliz Bolton was admitted to probate; Mrs Mary Wilkes is excx. 2-Will of Johanna Grant was admitted to probate; Mr Christopher O'Hare is exc. 3-Final acc't of the excs of Geo Poe, dec'd, was passed. 4-Will of Mrs Eleanor Lang, of Gtwn, partially proven.

WED OCT 25, 1865
Rl estate sales: Lot 14 sq 453, on H st, between 6th & 7th sts, to J W Barker, $1.05 per ft. Lots 10 & 11, Reservation 11, on 3rd st, between B & C sts north, to Eliz Parrott, 90 cents per ft. Lot 19 in sq 37, on 23rd st, between L & M sts north, to Martin O'Conner, 20 cents per ft. A farm north of Bladensburg tollgate, subdivided by J B Bartruff into lots: lot 1, 7 acs, at $362 per ac, to V Hess; lot 2, 6 acs, to Wm Furmage, $100 per ac; Lot 3, 18 acs 5 perches, to Jas Miller, $340 per ac; lot 4, 14 acs 8 perches, to B Geier, $135 per ac; lot 5, 6 acs, to D Curtin, $201 per ac; lot 6, 6 acs, to Elcount, $172 per ac; lot 7, 6 acs 2 rods, $275 per ac, to same. Part of lot 16 sq 688, on so A st, near the Capitol, to J & F Hitz, $1.02 per ft. Lot G, subdiv

of sq 211, R I ave, between 14th & 15th sts, to John Morse, 28 cents per ft. Lot 6, subdiv of sq 193, on 17th st, between L & M, 27 feet front by 198 feet deep, to Mgt Foley, 16 cents per ft. Also: parts of lots 9 & 10 & lots 8 & 11, in sq 284, on K st, between 12th & 13th sts, [Franklin Row,] $1.25 per ft, to J W Nairn.

Mrd: on Oct 23, at the Parsonage of St Matthew's Chr, by Rev Fr McNulty, Mr Isaac Hess, Jr, of Balt, Md, to Miss Mary Ann Miller, of Wash City.

Mrd: at Green Bay, Wisc, Oct 9, 1865, by Rev Louis P Techiffely, Mr John D *Laws to Miss Mary Davidson, d/o Lt Col Wm Chapman, U S army. [Corr of Oct 2: Laws should be Lawe.]

Mrd: at Saratoga Springs, on Oct 19, at the residence of the bride's father, by Rev E Rowland, Mr C S W Meehan, of Wash, D C, to Miss Mary Benedict, d/o Hon Jas M Marvin, of Saratoga Springs.

From the London Evening Star we have information of the marriage on Sep 30, in London, of his Excel Baron Otto von Grunewaldt, of Revel Russia, to Miss Julia Marie Rossiter, of Chicago, sr-in-law of Hon N B Judd, late U S Minister to Prussia.

Farms near the Navy Yd bridge at auction: 120 acs being the farm formerly belonging to the late Zachariah Walker. Also Nonsuch, 660 acs with dwlg hse. Mr Theodore Mosher resides on the premises, Marlboro rd, near the Navy Yd.

Orphans Crt of Wash Co, D C.
1-Case of Matilda Capron, admx w a of Susan Eaton, dec'd; settlement on Nov 18. -Z C Robbins, rg o/wills
2-Prsnl estate of Johanna Grant, late o/Wash City, dec'd. -Christopher S O'Hare, exc
3-Prsnl estate of Chas B H Matlock, late of Wash City, dec'd. -Simeon Matlock
4-Acc'ts of Elias A Eliason, guardian of the orphan chldrn of E P Rhodes, dec'd, approved & passed.
5-Saml L Phillips qualified as adm of the estate of Ellen Warren, dec'd, giving bond of $1,000: sureties Geo W & Geo R Phillips.
6-Will of Edw Pearce, dec'd, partially proven. John W Pearce, bro of the dec'd, is name exc.
7-Simeon Matlock qualified as adm of the estate of Chas B H Matlock, dec'd, giving bon of $4,000; sureties J H Matlock & Saml M Herbert.
8-Will of Johanna Grant, dec'd, fully prove, & Christopher O'Hare, exc, giving bond of $2,000; sureties are Philip Kraft & Geo C Prienkert.
9-Final acc't of John Goddard, adm of the estate of Ann Maitland, dec'd, approved & passed.
10-Second acc't of Wm H & O H Morrison, excs of the estate of Wm M Morrison, dec'd, as far as the same related to Louisa Culver, was appv'd & passed.
11-Cath Garrety was appt'd guardian to the orphan child of Patrick Garrety, dec'd, gave bond of $1,000: sureties are Peter O'Donoghue & Thos A Newman.
12-Marcelina Jordan appt'd guardian of the orphan chldrn of Fleming Jordan, dec'd; gave bond of $1,000; sureties are Wm W Jennings & Eli Jackson.
13-Final acc't of Mary H Murray, excx of estate of Stanislaus Murray, dec'd, was approved & passed.

Crct Crt jurors' names drawn to serve beginning on Nov 7:

Wash City:

Wm H Carrico	Ephraim Wheeler	Robt Israel
Richd Roberts	Bernard Hayes	Wm P Howell
W M Ellis	Jas Holroyd	Lewis Hopkins
Alex'r Forrest	Alex'r Rutherford	
John Rodgers	Francis Miller	

Gtwn:

Robt L McPherson	Benj Darby	John M Stake
Peter Berry	Bladen Forrest	

Wash County:

R S T Cissell	Hilary Smith	F G Rohr
Conway Robinson	John Wilberger	
P J Buskey	J M Golden	

THU OCT 26, 1865

Died: on Oct 25, Matilda Seabury, w/o Almon Baldwin, aged 72 yrs. Funeral from the family residence, 451 D st, today. [Littlefield & New London papers please copy]

Died: at the residence of Rev Thos Love, near Newark, Dela, Rev Starling M Galt, in his 29th yr. Remains will be conveyed to Oak Hill Cemetery from the residence of his bro, Wm M Galt, 345 12th St, today.

Sup Crt of D C, Equity #524. Riley A Shinn vs John Cook. Injunction against Cook, proprietor of the Green Spring Brewery, to restrain him from using bottles of Shinn, marked with his name.
-Riley A Shinn, Union Bottling Depot, 57 Greene st, Gtwn, D C

Died: on Oct 25, of typhoid fever, Chas Hubbard, oldest s/o Frank B, Jr, & Matilda C Lord, in his 16th yr. Funeral from their residence, 433 G st, Thu.

New Catholic Chr proposed to be erected on the corner of 25th st & Pa ave: cost to erect the edifice is about $30,000. Meeting on Sun: Rev C I Waite presided, & Mr N Callan, jr, was actg sec. Adresses were made by the chrmn, Dr Newman, & N Callan, sr. Over $5,000 was subscribed during the evening towards the church.

Land sale-Mr Tos Talbert, [of E] sold his farm near Centreville, in this co, on Fri last, for $1600. It contained 605 acs & was purchased by Mr Niles, of Wash. -Marlboro Gazette. [Md.]

Yesterday Mr Wm H Pettitt, of Wisc, was run over by a colored boy, Amos Hamer, aged 15 yrs, who was riding a horse at a furious rate. Mr Pettitt died that evening, age about 55 yrs. He leaves a wife & family in Wisc.

FRI OCT 27, 1865

Sale of the hse & furn of the late Edw Everett took place in Boston on Oct 18.

New ad-Groceries, 9th & D sts, Wash City. - John Keyworth

Hatter & Furrier-334 Pa av, Wash City. -B H Stinemetz

511

Last night Mr L H Walker, a clerk in the Commissary Gen ofc, was instantly killed by falling from a spiral staircase inside the Avenue House; from the 4th to the 2nd floor. The dec'd is from Boston, Mass. Local Item

Mrd: at St Aloysius Chr, on Oct 17, By Rev B F Wiget, Theo Sheckels to Lizzie A Goddard, all of Wash City.

Died: on Oct 26, Mrs Cassander Ward, wid/o the late Geo Ward, in her 87th yr. Funeral from her late residence on 25th st, near Md av, on Fri.

Died: on Oct 25, Theodore Patrick, aged 7 months & 8 days, s/o Francis & Mgt McNerhany.

Col Ludington, Chief Qrtrmstr Dept of Wash, is having the remains of the Union sldrs buried south of the Potomac in 1861, exhumed & interred in the Ntl Cem, Arl.

Suicide-Local. Virginia Gray expired yesterday from a too free use of opium & laudanum.

The d/o Chas Cotesworth Pinckney, aged 70, is receiving rations at Charleston. There are 15,000 persons in the city who, like her, are drawing their daily supplies of rice from the Federal authorities.

The Eclipse was much enjoyed in N Y, & the papers praise its punctuality.

Rl estate sales: lot 7, Davis subdiv of lot 4 sq south of sq 1019, to H Polkinhorn, 7 cents a ft. Lot 7 sq 951, corner of I & 9th sts east, to Manuel Gordon, 16¼ cents per ft. Warehse fronting on Water, between 10th & 11th sts west, to Sheriff & Harvey for $8,500. One-half sq 391, between 8th & 9th sts, near the river, to T M Harvey, $3,500. Brick dwlg & lot 2 sq 315, on H st north, between 11th & 12th. Lot 4, in Davidson's subdiv of sq 168, to L B Parker, for $1 52. [Note: the last amount-*appears* to be $1.52.]

SAT OCT 28, 1865

New ad-John P Slough, law ofc, 258 F st, Wash, D C.

Died: in Gtwn, on Oct 27, Daniel Brown, aged 40 yrs. Funeral from his late residence, 2nd & Fayette sts, Sun.

Emerson Etheridge acquitted of the charges preferred against him before the Military Commission at Columbus, Ky, is now at his home in Dresden, Tenn.

Levi L Farwell accused of killing Hattie Wilkes on Sun last; at her hse on 13th st, Wash, committed suicide in his cell in N Y. Hattie's watch was on his person.

Col Ulric Dahlgren, who was killed near Richmond, on Mar 4, 1864, is expected here today & will lie in state in the Council Chamber, City Hall, Wash, D C.

Sale at the Surratt Hse, on H st, yesterday. Nearly all the articles went at low rates-& there was but little competition.

Mr Danl Brown, resident of Wash City, on Wed last, fell from a wagon laden with lumber & expired from his injuries. He leaves a widow & family of young chldrn.

Pvts Horace G Leesor, Harvey Gehr, H D Hurst, & Philip McKinn, all of Co I, 185th Pa vols, confined for some time at Fort Whipple, under charge of mutiny, released yesterday & sent to their regts.

Convicted at the present term of the Criminal Crt, viz: 1-Patrick Kelly, assault & battery with intent to kill-6 yrs. 2-Jas Williams, alias Stephen Dorsey, same offense-3 yrs. 3-John Davis alias Geo Davis, Jas Smith, Lawson Davis, Wm Martin, Jas Kennedy, Geo Smith, Jas Poe, larceny-3 years ea. 4-Jenny Slater, larceny-2 yrs. 5-Otto Baltsher, Alfred Lomas, Fred'k Milled, larceny-1 yr ea. All heading to Albany Pen. 6-Arthur Whitlow, sentenced to 3 yrs, remains here to be tried on other indictments.

Request for a National Thanksgiving: Rev B F Morris, of Cincinnati, Ohio, letter: Wash, D C, Oct 2, 1865. To Andrew Johnson, Pres of the U S. letter is from the Cmte of the First Congregational Church & Soc of Wash, regarding Thanksgiving, & signed by:

B E Morris, chrmn	C H Buxton	H A Brewster
Wm Russell	E L Stevens	C H Bliss
E W Robinson	G H Williamson	Aug H Raymond
Wm Wheeler	W R Hooper	L Deane
W S Bailey	C S Mattoon	A L Landly
S P Giddings	Dr H Barber	J B Johnson

Boston, Oct 27. Jos E Worcester, L L D, the author of Worcester's Dictionary, died at his residence in Cambridge today, aged 81 yrs.

MON OCT 30, 1865
Edw Pelouze, a clerk in the Brooklyn p o, was lately detected in the act of opening a letter. Other robberies of the mail in that city, had long perplexed the mail officials. He was taken into custody.

Died: in Gtwn, D C, on Oct 28, Mrs Susan K Williams, relict of the late Jeremiah Williams, in her 85th yr. Funeral from her late residence, 106 or 116 Dumbarton st, Mon.

Phil, Oct 29. J Barclay Harding, recently appt'd Coll of Internal Rev in the 1st district of Pa, to suceed his dec'd fr, Josper Harding, died suddenly this afternoon of congestion of the brain. He was publisher of the Evening Telegraph newspaper, & was an active supporter of Pres Johnson's administration.

Orphans Crt-D C.
1-Louisa K Leach appt'd admx of prsnl estate of Jas B Leach, dec'd, giving bond of $60,000: sureties are Ann Green, Mgt C Barber & John B Meers.
2-Final acc't of will of Maria B Williams, admx of estate of S S Williams, dec'd, approved & passed.
3-Alida A Hughton, eldest sister of Hattie Wilkes, dec'd, renounced all right to adm on the estate of her sister. Wm A Boss was appt'd adm & gave bond of $1,000: sureties are Jas Bligh & Simon Flynn.
4-Will of Edw Pearce was proven & admitted to probate & record.
5-Fourth acc't of Wm B Kibby, exc of estate of John B Kibby, dec'd, passed.
6-Will of Jane Ward, dec'd, proven; her son, John Ward, is named exc.
7-Bal & distribution of the prsnl estate of Henry W Gray, dec'd, was passed.
8-Acc't of Richd W Burgess, adm of estate of Richd Burgess, dec'd, passed.
9-Final acc't of Jas Fitzpatrick, exc of estate of Dominick Conroy, dec'd, passed.

The arrest & suicide of Levi L Farwell & his letter to his bro Chas in Wash City: "Give my effects to Charley, my bro in Wash. I am going to meet Hattie." It appeared that after eating his supper the prisoner had broken the tin plate in half, & with the rough edge severed the arteries of his right arm & bled to death.

Fatal accident on Sat while workmen were digging in the sewer in Judiciary Sq, reached 15 feet when the earth caved in from both sides, & 2 laborers, Chas Coleman & Edw Jefferson, [colored,] were buried beneath the earth. Jefferson was dug out before life was extinct. When Coleman was reached, he was found dead. His wife was present, & it was truly heart rending to hear her cries & lamentations. The body of Coleman was conveyed to his home, corner of 4th & N sts.

Sup Crt, D C, Equity #343. White vs Robb, Mantz, Dulin & White. Parties & trustee to meet at my ofc in City Hall on Nov 7. -W Redin, auditor

On Sat last Mr Bernard Bryan, a well known restaurant keeper on 8th st east, near the Navy Yd, fell on the crossing at 8th & I sts & broke his leg.

TUE OCT 31, 1865
Sale of dismantaled forts: ground occupied by the forts surrounding Wash to be turned over to the owners as soon as all the bldgs attached to the forts are sold. The first sale commenced yesterday at Battery Parrott.

Sixty-fifth anniversary of the Nat'l Intelligencer. Mr Saml Harrison Smith, in 1800, purchased of Jos Gales, sr, who was about to establish the Raleigh Register, in Raleigh, N C, the Independent Gaz & the Univ Gaz-two papers which Mr Gales had been pblshng in Phil-came with them to this city, & commenced the tri-weekly Intelligencer, the Gaz being used as the weekly, & this arrangement continued 13 yrs. In 1813 the Intelligencer was issued as a daily & weekly, & the Univ Gaz was discontinued. In 1809 Jos Gales, jr, came from Raleigh, a young man, & became joint conductor & proprietor, with Mr Smith, of the establishment. Two years subsequently, Mr Smith retired & moved into the country, & the paper was conducted solely by Jos Gales, jr, till Oct, 1812, when his bro-in-law, Mr W W Seaton, from Raleigh, became a partner, & the paper continued under the management & proprietorship of Gales & Seaton til Jul, 1862, when the partnership was broken by the death of the senior partner. After the death of Mr Gales the paper was conducted by Mr Seaton til Jan 1, 1865, when it was purchased by the present proprietors, Snow, Coyle & Co.

Orphans Crt of Wash Co, D C. Case of Valentine Harbaugh, exc of Jos Harbaugh, dec'd; settlement on Nov 21. -Z C Robbins, rg o/wills

The remains of Col Ulric Dahlgren were brought to the City Hall yesterday from the Congressional Cemetery. Funeral of the late Col Ulric Dahlgren will take place today in the First Presby Chr; friends of the dec'd & of his father, Rear Adm Dahlgren, are invited. [Nov 1-A bro of the dec'd, & both father & son took seats in the pew with the dght & sister.]

WED NOV 1, 1865
Orphans Crt of Wash Co, D C. 1-Case of Mary Ann Wright, admx of Edw Wright, dec'd; settlement on Nov 25. 2-Case of P W Dorsey, exc of Susan Worthington, dec'd; settlement on Nov 25. -Z C Robbins, rg o/wills 3-Prsnl estate of Thos McGuire, late of Wash City, dec'd. -Richd G Polley

Impression prevails that Gen Grant has purchased the residence of the late Senator Douglas. This is not the case. He purchased the one in the same row erected by Gen John C Breckinridge. The hse built & occupied by Senator Douglas is the corner one of the row, & is unsold.

Lord Palmerston, who has been repeatedly Prime Minister, has dec'd at age 81 yrs. Viscount Henry Temple Palmerston was the eldest s/o Viscount Palmerston, & his education finished at the Cambridge Univ.

N Y, Oct 31. S Osborn, naval reporter, has received a letter from Capt C F Hall, the Arctic explorer, dated at Repulse Bay, Aug 20, 1865, & is 8 months later than the letter published a few months ago. Capt Hall is in excellent health & spirits & is confident in succeeding in his mission. He hopes to find some of the surviving mbrs of Sir John Franklin's party.

TUE NOV 2, 1865
Died: on Oct 31, Lucy W McCormick, of croup, aged 14 mos, d/o Alex & Eliz McCormick. Funeral from the residence of her father, today.

The Pres' dght, Mrs Patterson, & the Pres' son, Andrew Johnson, jr, with Judge Patterson, Mrs Sec Harlan & son, Rev Dr Cummings of Chicago & son, & 2 sons of Wm Prescott Smith, mstr of transportation of the B & O R R, arrived here in a special car this morning, in charge of Wm J Walker, passenger agent of the B & O R R. They will be stopping at the St Nicholas Htl, & will leave for Burlington, Vt, tomorrow. N Y Express, 31st.

Orphans Crt-D C. 1-John T Ward qualified as exc of estate of Jane Ward, dec'd, giving bond of $2,000; sureties are W H Butler & Wm F Kinsley. 2-Richd G Polley qualified as exc of the estate of Thos McGuire, dec'd; [Bernard McGuire having renounced his right;] & gave bail of $1,000; sureties are Wm E Paten, Geo Courtney, & Chas G Polley. Richd G Polley also gave bond of $2,000 as guardian of the chldrn of Thos McGuire, dec'd. 3-Harriet Burris qualified as admx of the estate of John R Burris, dec'd, gave bond of $500; sureties, Cornelius Lent & Benoni S Lent. 4-Inventory of prsnl estate of Johanna Grant, dec'd, was filed; also the inventory of the prsnl estate of Harriet Wilkes, dec'd, & that of Edw Wright, dec'd. 5-Seventh acc't of Mary B Dayton, guardian to Wm B, Anna T, Eliz C, & A Ogden Dayton, was approved & passed.

Died: at Bellevue, D C, Oct 23, Mary, eldest d/o John B & Marie W Davidson, aged 7 years & 6 months.

FRI NOV 3, 1865
Died: on Nov 2, Richd Jos Ryon, of diphtheria, aged 2 years & 9½ mos, y/s/o Richd J Ryon. Funeral from his father's residence, 399 E st, Fri.

The deplorable catastrophe on the North River, the explosion of the steamer St John, involved the following from the N Y World. Yesterday the remains of Capt Lyons & his bride were consigned to the earth amid all the honors which human affection & public sympathy can bestow. At St Luke's Chr, the recent scene of their nuptial vows, the tragic end of the young couple created an intense desire amongst thousands to witness the ceremonies. The mother of Capt Lyons, & the father & bros of the bride were present at the church during the sad rites. Rev Mr Atwell officiated: remains were deposited in Greenwood Cemetery.

Died: on Nov 2, Mrs Mary E V Leib, w/o A R Leib, & y/d/o Clement Woodward, aged 21 years, 11 months & 19 days. Funeral from 483 11th st, on Sun.

Orphans Crt of Wash Co, D C. Case of Sally Carroll, excx of Wm Thos Carroll, dec'd; settlement on Nov 25. -Z C Robbins, rg o/wills

Laborers & Servants, Farm hands, Grooms, Hse Servants: male & female, can be procured by application at the Genr'l Business & Intel Ofc for Refugees & Freedman, corner of 14th & E sts,Wash, D C, under charge of Capt W F Sprugin.

Brady & Co: Nat'l Photography Gallery: 352 Pa ave, Wash, D C. -M B Brady & Jas F Gibson

Yesterday fire broke out in one of the wooden tenements on 8th st, near F, occupied by J C Johnson, hair-dresser: damage was slight. Chief Eng Sessford notified the occupants to change the pipe so as to pass directly into the flue, otherwise they would be liable to fire.

Messrs Hall, Kilbourn & Co, being journalists in that they pblsh a Rl Est Gaz, we feel that it should be said that Mr Kilbourn, who has connected himself with Mr R M Hall in the rl estate business, was the late able Chief Clerk of the Interior Dept, which position he resigned a while since. Mr C H Kirkindall, late paymstr in the Navy, is a mbr of the firm.

Rl estate sold on Mon: hse & lot at corner of 29th & I sts, fronting on I st, to Geo W Emerson for $5,300; also, brick hse adjoining, same size lot, to Geo W Emerson for $4,800; also, lot 9 on 20th st, to G J Johnson at 35 cents per ft; also, 2 lots at corner of 23rd st & Pa ave, fronting the Circle, being lots 1 & 20 in sq 38, containing about 5,336 sq ft, was bought by M Donohoe for 90 cents per ft.

Mr Meigs, Clerk of the Crt, during the month of Oct issued 166 marriage licenses, of which number 39 were to colored couples.

The celebrated comedian Mr John E Owens, was among the passengers who arrived at N Y on Tue in the steamer *City of Boston*, from Liverpool, invigorated by his 4 months sojourn in London.

Sales of Gov't bldgs in the dismantled forts around Washington commenced on Oct 30, at Fort Martin Scott, near Chain Bridge. The last sale occurred at Fort Bennett, south of the Potomac, near the Aqueduct Bridge, on Nov 14. Sales at Fort Martin Scott were: 1 barrack to Chas Barnes, $45; 1 ofcrs' qrtrs to John Payne sr, $21: 1 guard hse to Jos Payne, jr, $9. Battery Vermont: 1 barrack to S Queen, $32; 1 ofcrs' qrtrs to John Holland, $20; 1 log platform to S Queen, $2.50; 1 log hse frame to J Falney, $2.50; the above bldgs, in both forts were small & of poor structures. Fort Simmons, Oct 27. Ofcrs qrtrs' to J E Chappell, $36; 1 do to L D Burrows, $32, another for $39; 1 do to S F Burrows, $36, another for $36; ofc to Herman Walter, $26; 1 stone hse to L D Burrows, $214; stable to L D Burrows, $19; 1 do to L D Burrows, $16; 3 mess-hses to W H Farquhar, $62, $69, $77; 1 do to Chas Jenkins, $81; 4 barracks to W H Farquhar, $122, $195, $183, $172; ofcrs' qrtrs to S F Burrows, $50; 1 do to Chas Jenkins, $57; 1 do to J E Chappell, $56; 1 do to Chas Jenkins, $65; bunks, tables, benches, settees, to various parties amounting in the aggregate to $102.15. Fort Mansfield: 5 ofcrs' qrtrs to Saml Shoemaker, $25, $11, $50, $11, & $42. These bldgs all in a row on the purchaser's farm, are suitable for the negroes' qrtrs which he employs. 2 barracks to W H Farquhar, $125, $110; 1 mess-hse to do, $85; 1 do to Saml Shoemaker, $80; 1 surgeon's ofc to Saml Shoemaker, $9; 1 dispensary to Jesse Shoemaker, $61; laundry to Mrs Baker, $25; post hospital to W H Farquhar, $207; dispensary, [log,] to Mrs Barren, $16; wash-hse to Herman Walter, $11; stable to Jesse Shoemaker, $6; ice hse to same, $6.50; stable to Louis Shoemaker, $55; mscl stuff went for $24.

Fort Bayard: ofcrs' qrtrs to T J Buckey, $40.50; 1 do to W H Farquhar, $35.84; 1 barrack to A Eld, $87; 1 qrtrs to E Berry, $21.50; 1 do to Jas Carroll, $6; 1 do to L Poole, $7; 1 mess-hse to Louis Shoemaker, $23; 1 commissary store-hse to same, $13; stable to Perry Sherwood, $7; do to Danl Shoemaker, $5; mscl sum-$23.25. Fort Gaines: 1 ofcrs' qrtrs to B F Riley, $7; 1 do to L Poole, $14; 1 do to B Loughbborough, $20; barrack to Jos Weaver, $149.75; mess-hse to same, $78; guard hse to

S F Riley, $6; stable to Jas Weaver, $10.50; stable to J W Davis, $1. Fort Karney: 4 ofcrs' qrtrs to John McGee, $85, $39, $88, $20; 2 qrtrs, $4.50; 1 barrack to H M Smith, $1.40; do to S Queen, $1.58; 2 mess-hses to Jos R Bradley, $70, $76; 3 ofcrs' qrtrs to John McGee, $51, $32, $.0-*as written;* stable to J E Cutters, $22.25; do to John McGee, $22.50; 1 qrtrs to same, $6.50; mscl sum, $41.25. Fort De Russy: 1 barrack to Jas Barnes, $71; do to A White, $92; mess-hse to Abraham Hyman, $16; 3 mess-hses , 2 log & 1 lumber, to B T Swarts, $11, $10, & $50; 1 ofcrs' qrtrs-log to S Queen, $10.50; mscl sum, $35. Battery Smead: 1 ofcrs qrtrs to B T Swarts, $50; barrack do, $108; mess hse do, $65. Many of the qrtrs were for servants, composed of logs. The bldgs, to a large extent, are purchased by the individuals on whose land they stand, & the property all sold quite low.

SAT NOV 4, 1865

Died: on Nov 1, Josephine C, consort of Jas Wormley, jr, & d/o Wm & Josephine Slade, aged 18 years & 11 months. Funeral on Sat from her late residence, 308 I st.

Vincent Wallace, the composer is dead. He was born in Waterford, Ireland, in 1815, & his father was a military band mstr. At 15 years of age he could play on every instrument in the orchestra. His first opera was "Maritana". In 1849 he was afflicted with blindness. He went to Brazil, & thence to N Y, residing there for several yrs. Returning to Eng, he composed 2 very beautiful operas, "Lurline" & "The Amber Witch". It is said that he has left an important posthumous work in a opera entitled "Estrella".

Purchasers of Gov't bldgs sold in the dismantling of forts under the supervision of Maj Jas Gleason, continued yesterday, as follows: Fort Bunker Hill: this fort was located on land of H Queen, who had est'd the bldgs at about $800. several of his neighbors giving it as their opinion that they would not bring more than that sum at auction, Mr Queen declined taking the bldgs as satisfaction for damages. They brought $2,054 yesterday, as follows: ofc to W F Johnson, $52; ofcr's qrtrs to Jas Owens, $33; 1 do to R S Patterson, $43; guard-hse to P McGarvey, $70; horse-shed to G W Taylor, $62; blacksmith shop to H Queen, $55; stable, 30 feet wide by 200 feet long, to E Lacey, $75; store-hse to H Queen, $120; qrtrs to Job B Miner, $47; store-hse to Dr W M Tucker, $100; ofcrs' qrtrs to H Queen, $70; ordnance sgt's qrtrs to H Queen, $25; ofcrs' qrtrs to H Queen, $40; 1 do to J A Buck, $46; 1 do to S Lawrence, $26; post ofc to H Queen, $31; ofcr's qrtrs to same, $32; do to L Shaw, $47; 1 do to J A Buck, $49; 1 do to Jas Caborn, $15; guard hse to G W Talbert, $50; prison, to M H Miller, $43; barrack to Lewis Smith, $133; do to G W Talbert, $206; do to R S Patterson, $200; log stable to Bates & Bro, $20; ofcrs' qrtrs to Wm B Arnold, $21; stable to Bates & Bro, $35; qrtrs to M Wagner, $31; stable to Chas Hitmuher, $29; ofcr's qrtrs to Jas Osborn, $31; stable to J A Buck, $41; qrtrs, M Levy, $7; fence inclosing qrtrs, John B Miller, $12. Fort Slemmer: ofcrs' qrtrs to Geo Mathiot, $50; ofcrs'qrtrs to H L Carlton, $168; stable to J A Buck, $15; mess-hse to E Lacey, $88; kitchen, do, $16; qrtrs to H Queen, $20; barracks to E Lacey, $136; mscl to Jas Owens, $350. Fort Bunker Hill is located about a mile east of the Soldiers' Home. Fort Slemmer in same neighborhood.

MON NOV 6, 1865

New ad-Fine groceries, Steuart & Thomas, 511 7th st, Wash, D C. -Thos W Steurat, Wm H Thomas.

Sup Crt of D C. On Feb 9, the interest of Malvina Frye in all her money, gold, silver, & other prsnl property in the hands or which may come into the custody of John D Clark, was seized by the Mrshl of the U S for D C, & the same is libelled & prosecuted in this crt; trial at City Hall, Wash, on 3rd Mon of Nov. -R J Meigs, clerk

Sup Crt of D C. The right, title, interest & estate of John Doyle in lot 16 in sq 199 in Wash City, was seized by the Mrshl of the U S for said Dist. -R J Meigs, clerk

Orphans Crt of Wash Co, D C. 1-Prsnl estate of Virginia B Baldwin, late of Wash City, dec'd. -Wm G Moore, exc. 2-Prsnl estate of Alexander Hamilton Derrick, late of Wash City, dec'd. -Emma Derrick

Died: on Nov 5, Thos Mutter Blount, aged 63 yrs, formerly of Edenton, N C, but a resident of Wash City for many yrs. The judges & the bar, also his friends, are invited to attend his funeral on Tue from his late residence, 370 9th st.

Ad-Orange Hse-Lynchburg, Va. -Houston Rucker, proprietor

Died: on Nov 4, Bertha Lee, infant d/o Chas A & Eliz Sears, aged 10 months. Funeral from their residence, 381 11th st, Mon.

Orphans Crt-D C. 1-Will of the late Jas R Young was partially proven; the dec'd directs the erection of a monument over the remains of his parents, & divides his estate among various family connections; directs the Crt to app't an exc who shall not be a relative or connection of his family. 2-Final acc't of Dr Grafton Tyler, exc of Dr B Johnson Hellen, passed. 3-Ltrs of test on estate of Virginia B Baldwin were issued to Wm G Moore. Danl McFarlan appt'd guardian to the orphans of Henry C Baldwin.
4-Will of the late Susan K Williams was filed for probate.

Gov't sale of dismantled <u>Fort Wayne</u>: ofcrs' qrtrs to F M Magruder for $67; 1 do to P W Dorsey, for $100; 1 mess hse to Isaac Snowden, for $37; 1 do to Geo Corldensir_th, $37; barrack to Geo Mathiot, $170; 1 do to H Schenier, $180; 1 ofcrs' qrtrs to Rich Holland, $20. Owing to Mrs McDaniels having accepted the bldgs south of the Queen's Chapel rd as full indemnity for the damages to her premises which that portion of Fort Wayne was located, that section of bldg was withdrawn from the sale, leaving the guard hse to C L Heahly, for $27; store hse, do, $40; & ofcr's qrtrs, to J W McClellan, for $76.

Died: on Nov 4, Bertha Lee, infant d/o Chas A & Eliz Sears, aged 10 months. Funeral from their residence, 381 11th st, Mon.

Died: on Nov 5, in his 6th yr, Allen Strain, only c/o J H & C N Strain, & grandson of J H *H-net-n, of Wash City. Funeral from their residence, 127 F st, Mon. [*very light]

The steamer *Clipper* was destroyed by fire on the 29th ult, 70 miles above Mobile. She was run into the bank & sunk, & by the exertions of the ofcrs all the passengers were saved, while the following ofcrs were lost: Capt M English, L E Baron, steward, 2nd clerk, Walter Wheltoke, & Edw Harwell, pilot; also, the 2nd mate, one cabin-boy & several deck-hands, names unknown. The steamer was owned in Mobile.

Sup Crt of D C. The right, title, interest & estate of Wm J Bromwell in & to lot 9 in sq 3, Wash City, was seized by the Mrshl of the U S for said Dist. -R J Meigs, clerk

Rl estate sales: Green & Williams, aucts: lot 2 in sq 318, & a one story brick hse on H between 11th & 12th sts, went to Jos R Nairn for $3,425. Part of lot 11, sq 686 on C st, between Delaware ave & 1st st east, to Thos Thornley for 43 cents per ft. A brick hse & lot corner of north C & 2nd st east, to W M Tennison for $5,700. Brick hse & lot corner 7th & M sts north, to Jos R Cassin for $7,500. Lot 21 in sq 181, corner 17th & Mass ave, to Mich Green for 19½ cents per ft. Lot 31 in sq 181, to G W Durity, for 14½ cents per ft. Brick hse & lot corner of Va ave & C st south, to J H D Richards, $5,250. Lot 2 in sq 577, C st south, between 2nd & 3rd, to Geo Dearwin, for 20 cents per ft. 30 acs of land, formerly owned by J B Kibbey, to L A Tarleton for $10,500. A 2 story brick hse, 4 rms, 11 feet 3 inches front, lot 95 feet deep, 14th st, between H & I north, to T A McGlaughlin, for $2,335. Another adjoining, same size, to Jas Ginnaty, for $250. Lot 6 sq 752, 4th st, between N & O sts, to Thos O'Beirne, for 25 cents per ft.

TUE NOV 7, 1865
Orphans Crt of Wash Co, D C. Case of Walter S Coxe, Neilson Poe, & Toulmin Poe, excs of Geo Poe, Jr, dec'd; settlement on Nov 28. -Z C Robbins, rg o/wills

Sale of property in Gtwn on which I now reside; hse has 12 rms, the lot is 60 by 120. -Thos Mackall, jr -Thos Dowling, auctioneer

An accident occurred about a mile West of Ramapo, on the N Y & Erie R R on Fri night, resulting in the death of Rev Romeyn, pastor of the Meth Episc Chr at Sloatsburg, N Y

Rev Henry Ward Beecher, besides satisfying himself while in Washington, by personal scrutiny, that the Pres is "all right," procured a brevet Lt Colonelcy for his son, Lt Beecher, & a pardon for Judge Grey, of Texas, in whom he is largely interested. Springfield Rpblcn

Mr Danl E Stipes, who has been in charge of the telegraph ofc at the depot for some time past, has been relieved & ordered to the charge of the ofc at Sandy Hook. Mr J F Morrison, lately in charge of the ofc at Fred'k Junction, takes charge of the ofc in the city.

WED NOV 8, 1865
Local Memoir of the visitation of the cholera of 1832. First made its appearance among some English troops at Hindostan, in 1781. In Aug, 1817, it suddenly appeared at the City of Jessore, 61 miles north of Calcutta, in an epidemic form. In Sep, 1818, it broke out in Calcutta, etc. This fearful scourge first made its appearance in America on Jun 6, 1832: the brig *Carricks* sailed from Dublin, where the malady was raging, in Apr of that yr, with 175 emigrants bound for Quebec, where they arrived Jun 3, having lost 42 of their number, from cholera, which broke out on board soon after sailing from Dublin. The survivors were permitted to land on George Isle. Jun 10 it appeared in Montreal, & Jun 21, in N Y. Broke out in Phil, & Albany: in Aug in Boston, Balt, Wash, & in Oct spread from Cincinnati to New Orleans, etc. Break out in Washington: Mr Amos Kendall resided at the time on 12th, between G & F sts, & Postmstr Barry on 11th st due east from Mr Kendall. Dr J C Hall, then a young man was called to the case of Mr Kendall with Dr Causin, & saw the other at Mr Barry's. No doubt as to the nature of the cases: cholera. Sep 5: Mrs France, w/o John France, & Mrs Bell, w/o John B Bell, were among the victims of yesterday. Mr W J Stone tenders the use of his large bldg, corner of D & 11th sts, for a hospital, & the Central Hosp was forthwith removed from 10th st, near E. This bldg on 10th st, known as the Kirk Hse,

had been abandoned by the Medical College. On Sep 3 Dr J Borrows was appt'd an attendant physician of Central Hospital. Sep 10 report: died from the disease: Mrs Mary Harper, w/o Andrew Harper; Jos Mullikin, Benj Jarboe, the s/o Thos Burch, Mrs Este, wid/o J S Este; Mrs Cammack, widow; Mrs Halsey. Names added the next day: Saml Marcy, of Fairfax Co, Va; Timothy Crowley, boot & shoemaker; Hugh Tierney, merchant tailor; Mary Eliz, d/o John Sargeant, bookbinder. Sept 13: Female Relief Soc originated-Mrs Henrietta Elsey, president; Mrs Harriet McComb, sec; Francis Clark, treas. Sep 15: died in the last 24 hours: Miss Burch, d/o Thos Burch; Evans, ship carpenter; Edw Cross, Miss Hodson, d/o Mr Hodson, carpenter; Widow Mgt Downes, Miss Hanna, Capitol Hill. Sep 29: cmte appt'd to ascertain the number of cases of cholera which have occurred in this city. The cmte, whose report, if made, is not to be found, with regret it is said, were as follows: Messrs Kuhn & Barclay, Drs Causin & Kirkwood, Dr Sewall & Mr Bender, Dr Young & Mr W J McCormick, Messrs J Carberry & G Coombs, Messrs Clark & Friend. On Sep 2, when the epidemic was raging, the following came forward & gave their personal assistance in the hospitals till they were no longer needed, viz: Messrs P Mauro, John McLelland, John Gardiner, Wm Patterson, Geo S Gideon, J W Shields, Edw Ingle, Chas McCormick, A Denhan, & W H Campbell, the latter being attacked by the disease, but not fatally. Sep 12 the following volunteered their svcs: Messrs Clagett, Force, Wyer, W Kirkwood, Jos Heskell, J McCauley, A McCormick, L C B Bootes, G Stevenson, J E Waring, F H Kennedy, T Hardesty, Chas Hunt, W Burnes, A Watkins, D H Haskell, G D S Vail, D Boyd, E Kavanaugh, E S Childs, & Jacob Janney. Dr Sims, who died Sep 15, 63 years of age, was one of the oldest & most eminent practitioners of Wash City. Benj Lincoln Lear, a lawyer of character, fell from an attack induced by his taking a dose of calo___ & jalap on his own. Cmdor Rodgers had a severe attack, but not fatal. The old Almshse burial ground, where most of the victims were deposited, was sold some 20 years since by the city authorities, & the remains of many were at that time transferred elsewhere. The ashes of very many, however, still mingle with the dust of that locality, on 7th st, above M, which is now covered with hses. The following physicians, now of Wash City, were in practice in this city at the time of the pestilence: Drs Jones, Magruder, Hall, Borrows, Thos Miller, Noble, Young, Lindsley & Davis.

Dr Jos Emerson Worcester died a few days since at his residence in Cambridge, Mass, at age 81 yrs; born in Bedford, N H, Aug 24, 1784, & at age 6 years went with his parents to Hallis, N H, the family residence since 1750, at which time Rev Francis Worcester, his great-grandfather, was settled in ministry there.

Died: Judge W D Meek, of Ala, recently at Columbus, Miss.

Died: E W Newton, who for nearly 30 years published the Kanawha Rpblcn at Charleston, Kanawha Co, Va, recently at an advanced age.

Sup Crt of D C, Equity #400. Jos B Steward vs Fras Mohun et al. On Jun 7, 1859, Jos F Lewis conveyed lot 19 & part of lot 20 in sq 28, in Wash, to Jas Maguire in trust to secure a certain debt in said deed set forth to Violetta Williams; debt unpd, Maguire proceeded to sell same to Richd O'Dowd for $1,325, but O'Dowd declined said purchase, cmplnt agreed to take his place & made payment of $2,200. He agreed with Hester L Stevens that she might take the property & cmplnt would pay the deferred installments. Stevens died insolvent leaving these chldrn, viz: Emily Stevens, w/o Oscar A Stevens, Kate Billings, w/o John S Billings, Lucy C Stevens, & Frank C Stevens, & the latter resides out of D C. [Others named: Thos J Fisher & W J Stone.] -A B Olin, Justice

Capt Wirz was read his death sentence in the Old Capitol prison on Mon, by Gen Augur.

Died: Robt Crupper, at his residence in this city yesterday, another of our old citizens. He had been in the flour trade, & afterwards in the hardware business. At the period of his death he was connected with the Custom hse of this port. -Alexandria Commonwealth

About 100 ladies, clerks in the Interior Dept, are affected by the order that all the rooms in the Patent Ofc bldg are required for other purposes, & their svcs will be discontinued from about Nov 30th. A considerable number are employed in writing for the Dept outside, whose connection with it will remain unchanged.

Sup Crt of D C in Equity #344. Mobberly & others vs Breshear & others. Ratify sale of rl estate of Ann Breshear, sole devisee of the late Thos Cook. -R J Meigs, clerk

Judge W D Meek, of Ala, a poet, politician, & noted chess player, died recently at Columbus, Miss. Sone 20 years ago he was a resident of Wash City, & had a position in the Solicitor of the Treas. Among other poems from his pen was one with the caption of "Come to the Sunny South,:

Mr Morris Ketchum's residence & stable was sold by auction. On Mon the pvt residence & other property of Mr Morris Ketchum, of N Y, was sold at auction by order of the assignees. The pvt residence at the corner of 5th ave & 38th st was sold to Mr Isaac C Kendall for $101,000. The stable & dwlg hse #51 Forty-first st was purchased by the same person for $4,250. After wards that part of the right & titles to another bldg conveyed in trust by Mr Ketchum to E B Lent & Philo C Calhoun was sold to Mr Chas Bell for $3,555.

THU NOV 9, 1865
Keystone Farm for sale, 249 acs, in PG Co, Md. Wm S Simpson, on the premises; Thos McCullugh, Bridge st, West of 35th, West Phil.

Died: on Nov 8, Mrs Mary Dougal, in the 79th yr of her age. Funeral from the residence of W H Dougal, Gtwn Hghts.

Sup Crt, D C, in Equity. John E F Carlin vs Helen M Carlin, Jos F Brown, & others. Bill praying avoidance of a certain decree of divorce, & other relief. Some 4 or 5 years ago Carlin, the cmplnt, with one of the respondents, his wife, Mrs Carlin, were, with their 2 chldrn, residing in Wash City, he keeping grocery store & owning rl est. He went away & never returned until last summer; his wife divorced him & mrd Hubble & went to Michigan.

Capt Francis De Witt, of Ware, formerly Sec of the State of Mass, & late Commissary of Subsistence, U S A, is undergoing trial by crt-martial at Raleigh, N C, on a charge of defrauding the Gov't of a hundred thousand dollars. Hon Chas R Train, of Framingham, is defending him.

A bill was introduced in the Tenn Senate on Tue, authorizing the Gov't to sell & convey the *Hermitage* property belonging to the state of Tenn, except the 2 acs enclosing the grave of Gen Jackson, provided that the estate shall be divided into lots & sold at public auction to the highest bidder. Payment to be made in bonds of the state, & on the payment of the purchase money the Govn'r is authorized to give the purchaser a good deed in the name of the state of Tenn.

An attempt was made to poison Susie Young, who resided at 275 D st, between 13 & 13½ sts. A discharged sldr, John Wing, who was visiting the hse, gave a negro boy, Frank Williams, money to buy laudanum at the drugstore. Wing poured it in a glass & mixing it with whiskey, it is alleged, gave it to Susie to drink. Dr Phillips was called in & administered the necessary remedies, but up to a late hour last night the unfortunate girl was in a dangerous condition. The accused, 2 other sldrs, & a woman named Hattie Young, were arrested & confined in the 2nd Ward Station.

Col Jas J Dana, of the Q M Dept U S army, has received 3 brevets, Maj, Lt Col, & Col, for faithful & meritorious conduct during the war.

Gov't sale of dismantled forts: Fort Meigs: R N Darrell, ofcrs' qrtrs, $84; Thos R Brooks, barrack, $140; qrtrs, do, $61; store-hse, A T Hand, $190; Wm Ruter, barrack, $160; mess-hse, Jas Trimble, $105; guard-hse, D A Walerston, $61. Fort Davis: ofcrs' qrtrs, C A Krause, $34; mess-hse, N M McGregor, $50; barrack, J A Roby, $100; guard-hse & qrtrs, $72, Henry Naylor. Fort Wagner: mess-hse & ofcr's qrtrs, P V Vernon, $147; barrack, Thos Solomon, $104. Fort Ricketts: barracks, $58; mess-hse, $39; guard-hse, $46; ofcrs' qrtrs, Geo B Hensor, $29; do, J H Smith, $33. Fort Snyder: ofcrs' qrtrs, Zadoc Williams, $43; do, do, $76; guard hse, $68; barrack, $166; mess hse, $100; barrack, H Rothe, $97; Fort G eble: J A Middleton, ofcrs' qrtrs, $136; guard-hse, $54; mess-hse, $34; Henry Hatton, barrack, $211. The foregoing forts are all located east of the Eastern Branch. The following are south of the Potomac, near Alexandria: Fort Williams: guard hse, $38; ofcrs' qrtrs, $33; do, $17; do, $50; barrack, $87; mess-hse, $91; sinks, $19, to Josiah Willard; ofcrs' qrtrs, Geo Studds, $100; barrack, Jerry Regan, $145; do, $144. Oliver Pulman; mess-hse, B Hendrickson, $58; do, Chas Bailinger, $114.50; ofcrs' qrtrs, W Henderson, $136. Fort Williams: ofcrs' qrtrs, John Studd, $32; do, R F Roberts, $33; do, Mrs Crump, $38; do, H Rothe, $38; guard hse, John Studds, $31; barrack, Isaac Snowden, $100; do, H Rothe, $97; mess-hse, Mrs Crump, $81; do, Geo Studds, $63.

Murder of H B Grove in Balt, on last Sunday week: John Clare arrested on suspicion of being the murderer. Clare was formerly a clerk in his bros' store, in this city.

FRI NOV 10, 1865
On Wed, in Balt, J F Donohue, who keeps a country store at Bell's Ferry, Harford Co, was killed when he stepped upon the forward platform of car 43, of the Madison ave line, & whilst it was passing on Eutaw st, near Franklin, he fell, & the wheels passed over his head, cutting the head & skull dreadfully, & bespattering the track with some of the brains. He got upon the car, & placing one foot upon the dash-board soon lost his balance & was thrown directly in front of the forward axle. He was 33 years of age, & leaves a wife & 4 chldrn, & was formerly a mbr of the Balt police force.

New London, Conn. Jonathan A Harris was granted a divorce against Mrs Jane M Harris. He get a complete divorce & custody of all the chldrn, she gets no alimony. By the law of Connecticut both can marry if they choose.

Orphans Crt of Wash Co, D C. Case of Rachel T Meehan, excx of John S Meehan, dec'd; settlement on Nov 25. -Z C Robbins, rg o/wills

Mrd: at Meake's Pk, the residence of the bride's father, on Nov 6, by Rev Robt Prout, Rich H Sorrel to Mary A Pulling, all of Chas Co, Md.

Died: on Nov 9, Granville Turner, 2nd child & oldest s/o Bishop & Sarah E Cooper, aged 2 years, 5 mos & 24 days. Balt Sun & Portland, Me, papers please copy.

Sup Crt of D C, Equity #555. Fred'k S Kern, trustee, & the heirs-at-law of Wm Miles, vs Edw Van Ness, et al. Suit is to procure a release from the heirs of the late Rich'd Smith of the title to part of lot 10 in sq 428, Wash City. The late John P Van Ness sold the same to Patrick Leydane in 1843; Leydane sold to the late Wm Miles, who died intestate. Van Ness died intestate in 1846, & his heirs conveyed all rl estate to the late Richd Smith. Smith died leaving as his heirs-at-law his dghts, *Eliz R Chew, w/o *Robt S Chew, Cath B Hill, w/o Wm B Hill, & *Louisa B Smith. The only parties who would now have an interest descended from the said John P Van Ness, are *Wm H Philip, Madalina Van Ness, Louis J D'Auby, Christina D'Auby, Edw Van Ness, Chas W Van Ness, Henry D Loney, Anna Mc Loney, Nath'l H Hutton, Meta Hutton, Eugene Van Ness, Wm P Van Ness, W Irving Van Ness, Anna M Van Ness, & Gertrude Van Ness. *Non-residents of D C. -R J Meigs, clerk

The watch of Mr B H Grove, the photographer, who was brutally murdered in Balt on Oct 29, was recognized at a pawnbroker's in Wash City. It fully connects John Clare, now in jail in Balt, with the murder.

Equity Crt, Nov 9. Martha Mackall vs Brooke Mackall. Application for divorce. The cmplnt has right to all the property which she has or can claim as her prop, she shall not marry during the lifetime of the respondent. The cmplnt shall have possession of the dwlg & guardianship of the minor chldrn.

Property belonging to the following persons, in the possession of the Gov't, has been turned over to them: of Loudoun Co, Va

Wm B Lynch	R G Bowie	John Aldridge
Matthew Harrison	A M Clark	John M Orr
Geo T Rust	Isaiah T White	Robt Beverly, trustee
E V Waite	David T S__me	for-Mary Chichester
Henry O Clagget	Oscar S Brader	
T M C Payson	Mrs Dangerfield	

Mrs S G Smith, Alexandria, Va	Lewis D Means, Fairfax Co, Va
Misses Irwin, Alexandria, Va	W D Corse, Fairfax Co, Va
Miss Adeline V Somer, Falls Chr, Va	Mrs Eliz Sothoron, St Mary's, Md
Mrs Priscilla J Muse, Fairfax Co, Va	T W Gough, St Mary's, Md

The *Nutt farm*, & it is believed some other property, has been turned over to Govn'r Peirpoint, Judge Underwood, & Dr Downey, who purchased it at a tax sale in 1862.

The case of Henry Wirz: the scaffold has been erected & every preparation has been made for the execution. Wirz's arm has broken out again & a new sore is running. He is suffering intensely from it. He still, however, insists upon his innocence, & says he can meet death fearlessly.

Sale of bldgs in the dismantled forts: Fort Reynolds: ofcrs' qrtrs, $20; do, $15; ofc, $5; messhse, $111; barracks, $110; post ofc, $20; storehse, $5-all to Chase & Chittenden. Fort Scott: 3 qrtrs, each $6; one do, $4; bakery, $19; sink, $1-all to Geo Reneril. One qrtrs, $17, to J C Clark. Fort Scott is on the road to Alexandria, about midway between the Long Bridge & Alexandria, & Fort Reynolds is on the road from Alexandria to Bailey's Cross Rds.

Anthony Schoder, clerk in the U S Treas Dept, has been arrested in Battle Creek, Mich, charged with the larceny of $30,000 in five-twenty bonds, the issue of 1864.

SAT NOV 11, 1865

Horrible murder near Fred'k Md on Sat. Bowers, a negro boy about 17, murdered a white boy, Danl P Myers, aged 10 yrs. Mr Myers had sent them out to the field with some cattle, & told them to bring in some horses.

Expecting to be absent from Va for some time, I offer the farm on which I reside known as *Springfield*, in Albemarle Co, Va, for sale; 1,140 acs. -Bolling W Haxall, Gordonsville, Nov 7, 1865.

Account of the execution, yesterday, of Henry Wirz, in the yard of the Old Capitol Prison. Spiritual advisers, Frs Boyle & Wiget, were in attendance. Prisoner brought forth to the gallows: Maj Russell, Provost Mrshl walked in front, followed by Wirz, between Frs Boyle & Wiget, then came Capt G R Walbridge, commander of the prison. The last sacrament was administered as he sat on a small stool, in the rear of the drop. Charges read: prisoner was found guilty of the second charge, namely: murder in violation of the laws & customs of war; guilty of having caused the death of 3 prisoners of war in his custody: sldrs of the U S: one on or about May 15, 1864, another about Jul 11, 1864, & another about Sep 1, 1864. Maj Russell asked him if he had anything to say: "No sir, only that I am innocent, & will die like a man, my hopes being in the future. I go before my God, the Almighty God, & he will judge between me & you." To Capt Walbridge he said, "Well, Capt, good bye; I thank you & the other ofcrs of the prison, for I have been well treated." In one minute after the drop fell, the criminal was left hanging in the air: the shoulders shrugged a little, & the limbs were drawn up several times, but in about 4 mins the body ceased to swing, & was apparently lifeless: body allowed to hang 15 mins. Exam revealed the neck had been broken. Wirz had requested Lt Havens to take locks of his hair, in letters, to his wife & chldrn. It is not known if he left a message to his relatives in Europe. Books he had in his room were to be sent to his chldrn; others to Mr Schade, his counsel. He left a journal, kept since he has been in prison, & a number of letters.

U S Patent ofc. Ptn of Louisa R Ketchum, excx of the estate of Wm F Ketchum, dec'd, of Buffalo, N Y; extension of patent granted Feb 10, 1852; improvement in *Grain Harvesters*. -T C Theaker, Com'r of Patents

Crct Crt of Montg Co, Md, wherein Martha R Shaw, Wm E Shaw, & others, cmplnts, & Helen L Shaw, Benj F Shaw, Mary E Shaw, & Eliza R Shaw, dfndnts. Sale of all the rl estate of Elbert Shaw, dec'd; the home farm on the rd from Burnt Mills to Colesville, 200 acs; adjs the farms of Dr Wash Duvall, Mr E L Parker & Mrs Henry McCeney. Other farm of 175 acs, is about 4 miles from Brookeville & Wash turnpike rd. -W Veirs Bouic, trustee; Mr Wm E Shaw, residing on the premises.

Died: at Rosedale, D C, on Nov 9, Lucy A Quesenberry, d/o Eliz & the late N Quesenberry, of King Geo Co, Va, in her 16th yr. Funeral from Rosedale today.

Died: suddenly, near Bladensburg, on Nov 10, Lt Fred'k Kauffelt Harris. His remains will be taken to York, Pa, for interment. York, Chambersburg, & Carlisle papers, please copy.

Col Wm Christie, a veteran of the war of 1812, died lately in Texas.

New Drug Store, corner of C st & 3rd st. Jos Walsh, jr, Wash City.

Died: Judge Collamer, Senator in Congress from Vt: born in Troy, N Y, in 1792: but in chldhood removed with his father's family to Burlington. Grad of Vermont Univ in 1810.

Pres Johnson received word of the death of his only bro, Wm Johnson, by an accidental gunshot wound. The dec'd held the ofc of collector of the port of Velasco, Texas. He was about 65 years of age. He was born in N C, & left with his younger bro, Andrew, for Tenn, where they both settled.

MON NOV 13, 1865

At the request of Messrs F A & T Hoppe, who intend removing to Richmond, we offer for sale *Woodlawn*, 443¾ acs, with brick dwlg, about 4 miles from Charlottesville, Va. -Benson & Bro, aucts

Died: on Nov 12, Lucie, only d/o Col C D & Anna E Pennebaker, aged 9 years & 15 days. Funeral from the family residence, 516 M st, Tue.

Sup Crt of D C, Equity #559. John Purdy vs Isaac D Surratt et al. Bill to obtain sale of part of lot 20 in sq 451, Wash City. In substance John H Surratt, now dec'd, was indebted to the cmplnt, & after his death his son, John H Surratt, et al, gave deed of trust on said lot; the heirs at law of said decedent are *Isaac D Surratt, Annie E Surratt, & *John H Surratt, the younger. *Do not reside in D C. -Andrew Wylie, Justice; W Y Fendall, solicitor for cmplnt.

Shooting of Maj Henry T Dixon, at Alexandria, Va. Dixon of Warrenton, paymstr in the U S army was shot by Dr Thos C Maddox on Fri; the rencontre had its origin in 1857, when Dixon shot Maddox at Warrenton. Maj Dixon received shots in the right side, inflicting severe & it is believed, mortal wounds. He was able to give a statement. Dr Maddox received a shot which grazed his knee, carrying off a portion of his pantaloons. [Nov 14-Maj Dixon died this morning from the effects of the wounds he received. He had resided for many years in Fauquier Co, Va.

Died: Col A H Bowman, U S Eng Corps, at his residence in Wilkesbarre, Pa, Nov 11.

Death of an artist-Mr D C Johnston, at Dorchester, Mass, on Wed, in his 67th yr.

The spot selected in Westminster Abbey as the last resting place of the late Lord Palmerston, Premier, is in the north transept, where lie buried Castlereagh, Wilberforce, the Cannings, Chas Jas Fox, the Earl of Chatham & his brilliant son, & other worthies of England's history. The grave is close to the hideous monument of Lord Chatham at the great north door, entering from St Mgt's Church-yard, & on one side of the grave lies the body of Fox, & on the other those of the two Wm Pitts.

TUE NOV 14, 1865

For sale-110 acs of land on Benning's bridge rd, about 2 miiles east of the Capitol, with small dwlg hsw. -Mrs Mary Manning, on the premises.

Mrd: in Wash City, on Nov 2, by Rev J F Ware, C Dodd McFarland, of Balt, & Emily W, y/d/o the late Prentiss Chubb, of Richmond, Va.

Orphans Crt of Wash Co, D C. Prsnl estate of Hamilton Loughborough, late of Wash City, dec'd. -A H Loughborough, exc

Last night a sldr, Michl Ealiger, 12ᵗʰ Vet Res Corps, was killed at a private hse on 11ᵗʰ st, Wash, by falling down the steps & breaking his neck.

Criml Crt-Nov 11. 1-Michl O'Beirne pleaded guilty of larceny-6 months in jail. 2-Mary Cath Effert, alias Cordelia Williams, pleaded guilty to 2 indictments of larceny-1 yr in pen in each case.

Valuable land in Alleghany Co, Md, for sale, on Nov 28 next: [Fractions are not legible.]

Lochiel-5,980 acs
Common Sense-1,979 acs
Residue of *Rights of Man*-3,351 acs
Residue of *Park*-1,607 acs
Riverside-342 acs
Addition to *Paradise*-1,472 acs
Residue of *Paradise*-587 acs
Residue of *Chance*-possibly 658 acs
Oakland Farm, including *Mount Oakland*-481 acs

Residue of *Royal Chalotte*-1,362 acs
Rsrvy of all the *Chance*-1,174 acs
Rsrvy on *Kindness*-1,847 acs
Stony Ridge-388 acs
Part of the *Promised Land Surveyed*-85 acs
Milk & Honey-2,756 acs
White Oak Point-286 acs

Herrington Manor-2,367 acs [Part whereof will be reserved by the owner.]
Six Soldiers' Lots: 2,611 thru 2,614, 1,110 & 1,703, each containing 50 acs
An individed moiety of 7,873 acs being the residue of *Republic*-3,936 acs
Undivided moiety of a track of 2,998 acs composed of a part of the *Pink of Alleghany*, & of two parts of the *Rights of Man*, said moiety being-1,499 acs
Undivided ¼ part of 2,868 acs, the residue of the *Pink of Alleghany*, said fourth part being-717 acs
Undivided moiety of *Seven Soldiers'* Lots each containing 50 acs, being lots 3,882 thru 3,886, 2,018 & 2,819, said moiety being 175 acs
Undivided fourth part of lots 1,756 & 2,922, & undivided fourth being 25 acs
Titles are indisputable, & every parcel will be sold free from any incumbrances. *Lochiel* lies on the Great Savage river, the upper part not far from Frostburg, & but a few miles south of Pa. *Common Sense, The Rights of Man*, & the *Park*, are all heavily timbered & are in the same region, not far from Grantsville. *Riverside, Add to Paradise, Chance*, & the *Royal Charlotte*, lie near the Va turnpike: *Riverside* lies directly on the Potomac river, & *Add to Paradise* touches it. The *Royal Charlotte* extends to the Va line, about 6 miles southerly of Oakland. Resurvey on all the *Chances* also extends to the Va line. *Resurvey on Kindness*: Balt & Ohio R R run right thru it. *Milk & Honey & Herrington Manor*: estates adjoin & lie a few miles northerly from Oakland. *Stony Ridge* is rough, but valuable for its timber & coal. *White Oak Point* is well timbered. *Oakland Farm* is divided into 2 parts by the B & O R R. – Thos S Alexander, Geo H Williams, Wm A Fisher, Trustees. F W Bennett & Co, auctioneers [My chief object in creating the trust, was to place the property in such condition that it might be sold free of all incumbrances whatever. –Wm Schley]

Gen Geo B McClellan is expected to return to the country in the steamer *Persia*, due at N Y on Tue or Wed of this week.

WED NOV 15, 1865

Crct Crt of PG Co Md. Sale at the residence of Zachariah B Beall, dec'd, all the residue of the rl estate of said dec'd: the first known as the *Sprigg & Ferguson Farm*, 400 acs; *Eaton Farm* about 400 acs; the *Homestead*, 265 acs. The last will be sold subject to the widow's dower. Mr Jas L Brashear resides on the premises. -C C Magruder, Edw W Belt, trustees

Phil, Nov 14. Washington L Lane, editor of the Ledger, died this morning. He began with the paper as a reporter 28 years ago.

Orphans Crt of Wash Co, D C. Prsnl estate of Powell Hess, late of Wash Co, dec'd. -Rachel Hess

Pension ofc-application for re-issue of land warrants lost or destroyed: 1-160 acs to Matilda, wid/o Edmund Downey, granted Oct 6, 1857. 2-120 acs to Mary, wid/o Jacob Probasco, granted Nov 12, 1855. 3-160 acs to Louisa, wid/o Geo Latimer, granted Jun 19, 1856.

Mrd: on Nov 13, by Rev Dr Finckel, Mr Philip Pote to Miss Mgt A O'Bryan. Phil & Port Tobacco papers, please copy.

Brilliant wedding yesterday, at St Matthew's Chr; Miss Lillie A Vivans mrd Mr Lawrence J O'Toole. Bridesmaids & groomsmen were: Miss Emma Holt & Mr J L Fitzpatrick, of Balt, Miss Alice Keller, of N Y, & Mr John A Baker, Miss Kate McIntyre & J B Nalle, Miss C F Cox & Mrs Claude McIntyre. Ceremonies performed by Rev Dr O'Toole, of N Y, bro of the groom. The party proceeded to the residence of Jos Redford, a bro-in-law of the bride, where entertainment awaited.

Sales at the dismantled forts: _Fort Runyon_: barrack $53, 2 ofcrs qrtrs $43, hospital $17, to F A Salter; mess hse $69, qrtrs $17.10, to B F Shreve. _Fort Haggerty_ ofcrs' qrtrs $32, meat hse $45, to John M May; barracks $100 to J W Phillips. _Fort Corcoran_, Nov 13: stable $255, chapel $146, J W Hoover; stable $200, qrtrs $18, P McLaughlin; stable $65, store hse $16, Chas Kirby; store hse $36, N Fibre; stable $91, S Hall; orderlies' qrtrs $18, G Vanierberg; stable hse $19, do $13, do $39; qrtrs $16, do $16, Miles Gibbon; qrtrs $15, D M Bull; storehse $53, J Massey; qrtrs $38 R A Phillips; ofcrs' qrtrs $1_5, do $59, horse-shed $18, ofcrs' qrtrs $110, R S Wharton; guard hse $10.50, ice-hse $21, P M May__guar_; hse $31, Robt Cunningham; barrack $_1 C C Fearson; qrtrs $34, G B Ives; qrtrs $38, Jas E Burch; qrtrs S Levy, $7; fence $12, J B Miller; qrtrs $26, J T Buren; barrack $136, Saml Shreve; barrack, $145, Patrick Sullivan; ofcrs' qrtrs $56, C Costello; mess-hse, $56, do, $45, John Naylor; qrtrmstr's ofc $21, qrtrs $27, do, $31, shed $21, do, $9, R S Wharton; 2 wings $46, A Pierce; stable $37. C C Fearson; 2 log hses $28, Michl Long; mscl $58. It will be remembered that _Fort Corcoran_ was the first earthwork of any considerable character which was erected in the defence of Washington. It was built in the intense heat of Jun & Jul, 1861, by the 69th N Y, under command of Col Corocran, who were among the first Union troops thrown across the Potomac, & before whom the rebel bands that had been hovering around Arlington disappeared. It will be seen that the entire mass of bldgs connected with the fort sold for $2,240 in the aggregate.

Orphans Crt-D C.
1-Nancy McFee gave bond of $500 as guardian to orphans of John McFee.
2-Eliz M deZeyk gave bond of $10,000 as guardian to orphans of Oliver Whittlesey.
3-Sarah H Huguely gave bond of $1,000 as guardian to orphans of Geo F Huguely.
4-Ltrs of adm were issued to John Lang as adm of Eleanor R Lang. He gave bond of $24,000. The will of Eleanor R Lang was fully proved & admitted to probate.
5-Ltrs of adm were issued to Matilda C Roberts as admx of John M Roberts. She gives bond of $24,000.
6-Johanna Brown gave bond of $5,000 as guardian to the orphans of Daniel Brown.

Messrs Downman & Green, rl estate brokers, sold on Sat the residence of Mr Wm Shields, corner of 12th & K sts, to the Austrian Minister for $20,000.

THU NOV 16, 1865
Reward-$100. For thief & mare stolen Nov 8. -Brandt Kincheloe, near the Plains, Fauquier Co, Va.

Sup Crt-D C, Equity # 405. M A Stone & others vs. M E Flaherty & others.

Ratify sale made to W S Jones & reported by R R Crawford, trustee, of rl estate of Michl Stone, dec'd. -R F Meigs, clerk

Orphans Crt of Wash Co, D C. 1-Case of Geo W Harvey, adm of Benj Evans, dec'd; settlement on Dec 9. -Z C Robbins, rg o/wills 2-Prsnl estate of Eleanor R Lang, late of Gtwn, D C, dec'd. -John Lang, adm

M A Carter, of Carter's Wharf, has sold his farm on the Potomac, *Delview Cottage*, 1,202 acs, to P W Scrimger, of Balt, for $18,000.

Mrd: at Wesley Chapel, Wash, on Nov 2, by Rev Dr Nadal, R W Tate, of Annapolis, Md, to Mary B, d/o C H Lane, of Wash.

Obit-died in Wash City, at the residence of her parents, on Nov 12, Lucie Bealle Pennebaker, only d/o Col C D & Anna E Pennebaker, late of Louisville, KY, aged 9 years & 14 days. [Louisville papers please copy]

Died: on Nov 10, at Mobile, Gen Duff Green, of Ala.

Yesterday Lafayette C Baker was charged with grand larceny & arrest & imprisonment without warrant. He is the celebrated Chief of the Detective Corps of the War Dept & holds the rank of Brig Gen of Vols in the military svc. Local News

The Hon Jesse Lazear, late mbr of Congress from the Greene Dist, Pa, has purchased one of the finest estates near Wash City, & is about to remove upon it.

FRI NOV 17, 1865
The N Y Tribune of Wed gives the particulars of the suicide of Hon Preston King, whose home was at Ogdensburgh, St Lawrence Co, N Y. His companion on his journey from his home to N Y C was the hsbnd of his adopted dght, a young man named Bridges. Mr King was a bachelor & lived at the Astor Hse. Mr King left there on Sun evening & got on the ferry & soon after it left the pier, he threw himself from the aft part of the vessel into the river.

Mrd: 1st Lt Chas F Williams, U S M C, on Nov 15, to Miss Rosie B Fague, d/o Solomon Fague, of Wash City, at the McKendree Chapel, Wash.

Levy Crt Wash Co, D C. For widening the Lincoln av & Bunker Hill rds, this crt is condemning part of the property of the late Mrs Ann McDaniels & Washington Berry. - Nicholas Callan, clerk

Sup Crt of D C, Equity #511. Jas F Wollard vs Melissa D Wollard et al. Ratify sale by trustee of lot 20 in sq 455 to Jas F Wollard, cmplnt, for $4,522.55, & part of lot 21 in sq 455 to same for $1,666.39. -A B Olin, Justice

The Pres has appt'd Hon Chauncey M Depew, of N Y, Minister to Japan.

Mary Stemson, a white woman, was arrested yesterday by Ofcr Leach of the 3rd ward, charged with arson in setting fire to the store of Mr Coleman, on Thu morning. She is a German woman, & was at one time in the employ of Mr Ruphert, who resided near Mr Coleman. Justice Thompson deemed the evidence sufficient to warrant him in committing her to jail for Crt.

Brd of Metropolitan Police: Roundsman Jas W Gassford was appt'd sgt of the 10th Police Precinct, v Hepburn, resigned. Mr Gessford has been acting sgt since the resignation of Mr Hepburn, which occurred some time ago. Patrolman B F Barker, of the 10th Precinct, was appt'd roundsman, v Gessford, promoted. David Summers appt'd patrolman of 10th Precinct, v Barker, promoted. Patrick Doyle appt'd patrolman of the same precinct, v Terrence Walsh, dismissed for conduct unbecoming an ofcr & for beating a prisoner. Saml Shaeffer appt'd a patrolman of 7th Precinct, v Sargent G Groves, dismissed.

Yesterday a street car was demolished & 2 persons injured: collision between the train from Lynchburg & a city passenger railroad car: Mr G J Riddell was conductor, & Mr Chas Hall, driver-was making its first trip from Gtwn to the Navy Yd, & while crossing the track of the Orange & Alexandria railrd, near the West gate of the Capitol, the collission occurred. Mrs Marian G Hatton, who was in the car, on her way to take the early train for Phil, received severe internal injuries. Dr Hammond sent for Dr Dove, who conveyed Mrs Hatton to the Clarendon Htl. Mr Riddell was conveyed to his residence, 544 N J ave. Chas Hall said he did not see the train until the horses attached to his car were on the track. He then put whip to them & endeavored to get across, but the rear car of the train struck his car before it was across the track. He says some 8 or 10 cars were between his car & the engine. Mr Riddell has an excellent reputation. His leg sustained a compound fracture, & it may be necessary to amputate, but there are strong hopes of saving it.

SAT NOV 18, 1865
Mr Henry L Gordon, late proprietor of the coaches at Willard's Htl, Wash, D C, was killed by a railroad accident at Newark. He had $1,500 in his possession when he left N Y, but the money was stolen after the accident occurred. [Holderness, N H, Nov 20. The Funeral took place yesterday, with Masonic honors.] [Nov 27. Wm H Smith, of Mulberry st, Newark, was arrested in that city for stealing the packet of money.]

San Francisco, Oct 14. A few days age, nearly 2 months after he was lost, the body of Brig Gen Wright, who went down with the steamer *Bro Jonathan*, was found in Bay Flat cave, Mendocino Co. The body of the Gen's wife was found a few days before. They will be buried at Lone Mountain.

Sup Crt, D C, Equity #405. Mary A Stone & others against Ellen Stone, Wm M Flaherty, & others. Statement of trustee's acc't of the late Mich'l Stone, Dec 8, City Hall, Wash. -W Redin, auditor.

Farm for sale on which I reside, called *The Mansion*, about 600 acs, Chas Co, Md. -Wm H Gray, Nanjemoy, Md.

Farm for sale, on which I reside, 66¾ acs, with 2 story dwlg hse, in PG Co, Md. -Jas H Marlow, T B P O, PG Co, Md.

R R collision near the Capitol on Nov 16 caused some injuries; the following certificates speak for themselves: 1-I Thos E Hammond, do hereby certify that I am superintendent of the warehse dept of the Adams Express Co, where I have been employed for the past 2 yrs, & I know the bell was ringing . While looking in that direction the city passenger car crossed the track of the steam cars & I then heard a crash. Certificates of Geo Kraft & of Stephen Egan, both employed at the photographic gallery on Pa av & First st, for the past 2 yrs; also of Geo M Palmer, grocer at 548 Pa av, followed.

Montreal, Nov 17. L A Pare, the murderer of Stanislaus Barreau, was executed this morning.

Information gratis for those who wish to secure homes in East Tenn. -M McTeer, Clerk Crct Crt, Maryville, Blount Co, Tenn.

Mrd: on Oct 26, at Trinity Chr, Gtwn, by Rev Fr Charlier, John E McKay, U S N, to Helen V May, d/o the late Thos O N May, of Gtwn, D C.

$500 reward for the recovery of the body of the Hon Preston King.

We learned yesterday that Dr S C Maddox, who shot Maj Dixon, in Alexandria, a few days ago, has been acquitted; the testimony of a minister & of other persons satisfying the Crt, it is alleged, that the dec'd had followed the accused about for several days, & that Maddox was thereby placed in fear.

Troops going home: on Nov 1 there were 4 companies 4th U S Artl, a btln of the 213th Pa infty, & 2 full regts colored troops, under Gen Harkins, garrisoning the forts in the defences of Wash. Under Gen F T Dent, as a "Garrison of Washington," there were in this city the 7th, 9th, 10th, 12th, 14th, 18th, & 24th regts Vet Reserve Corps; 195th & 214th regts Pa Vols; & the 8th U S Vet, to which the 6th U S Vet were added. The 213th Pa Vols were at Annapolis, & the 195th Ohio Vols at Alexandria. The 214th Pa Vols, commanded by Gen D B McKibben, has relieved the 213th, the latter being now at the Sldrs' Rest, & to be discharged the svc & paid today.

Died: in Wash City, on Nov 17, Mary Ella Burr, y/d/o C C Burr, of the Navy Dept. Funeral in Wesley Chapel on Sun.

MON NOV 20, 1865
Farm in A A Co, Md, for sale, 171+ acs. Mr Noah W Donaldson is on the premises. -A B Hagner is atty for the owners.

Orphans Crt of Wash Co, D C. Case of Walter S Cox, exc of Eliza Lucas, dec'd; settlement on Dec 12. -Z C Robbins, rg o/wills

Coroner's inquest into the death of Henry L Gordon, of Wash City, by the late railroad disaster near Newark, N J, resulted in the verdict of manslaughter against the switchman, Edw O'Brien.

Died: on Nov 19, after a lingering illness, John B Semmes, in his 39th yr. Funeral from his late residence, 392 C st, Tue.

Rl estate sales by Green & Williams, auctioneers. Lot 12 in sq 79, 22nd st west, between G & H north, to John McDermott, for 21½ cents per ft. Frame hse & lot on 15th st west, from north of R I ave; lot 30 in sq 195 to Francis A Taverse, for $1,100. Lots 8 thru 10 in sq 236, on 14th st west, between V & W north, to Wm Bladen, for 27 cents per ft. Lot 28 in sq 236, fronting on the alley, with a frame bldg, to T J Sewell, for $531. Part of lot 16 in sq 411, on 9th st west, between D & E south, to Hugh Cameron, for 25 cents per ft. Part of lot 12 in sq 547, with a 2 story frame-hse, on 4½ st, between E & F south, to Geo Waiting, for $1,405. Part of Mrs Mary Walker's farm, [located near Rock Creek Chr,] about 20 acs, with improvements, to Christopher O'Hare, for $16,000. Lot 7 in subdiv of sq 214 on 15th st, between L & M north, to Jos Washington, for 33 cents per ft. This lot is 173 feet 6 ins in depth. Lot 11 in sq 397, on 8th st, between P & O north, to F Methorn, at 31 cents per ft. Two story frame-hse & lot on 2nd st west, between Mass ave & H st north, to J W O'Connor, for $1,510. Two-story frame-hse & lot on 8th st west, between S & T north, to Thos Lalley, for $235.

Died: in Corinto, Nicaragua, Central America, on Sep 13 last, Mrs Amelia Caroline, w/o Dr Chas H Van Patten, aged 45 years & 2 months.

Orphans Crt-D C. 1-Inventory of prsnl estate of Geo Ailer was filed. 2-Acc't of Jas Corbett, guardian to the orphans of John Sheehan, was passed. 3-Inventory of prsnl estate of Mary Y Dundas was returned by Wm Y Fendall, adm. 4-Inventory of prsnl estate of John W Voris was filed. 5-Ltrs of adm issued to Christopher Ingle, exc of Mary C Ingle. 6-Ltrs of adm issued to Mgt A Campbell on estate of Robt G Campbell. 7-Ltrs of adm issued to John C Riley on estate of Augustine N Y Howle.

Ceremonies on laying the crnr-stone of St Dominic's Church yesterday were conducted by Rev Fr N D Young, who is now some 75 years of age. The new chr is located on the corner of 6th & E sts south, [Island] was very large & imposing. The present church [the old chr,] of St Dominic was commenced in 1853, when there were not more than half a dozen Catholic families in that section of the city. The pastors who have successively presided there from the beginning are Frs Geo A Wilson, S A Clarkson, N R Young, C D Bamling, & J A Bokel, the present incumbent. The original hse & land cost some $16,000.

Ex-Pres Pierce is suffering from a dangerous illness.

TUE NOV 21, 1865
Obit-died yesterday of typhoid fever, at St Ann's Infant Asylum in Wash City, Sr Antonine, age 34 yrs. Funeral on Wed from St Matthew's Chr. The dec'd joined the Sisters of Charity at Emmetsburg, Md, in 1849.

Official: Dept of State, Nov 17, 1865. Cnsl of the U S at Bremen report the death, Sept last, at sea,
 of Henrich Ch [Von] Scheele, late from Wash City. The legal reps of the dec'd can obtain further information by addressing this dept.

Col Geo W Keener, 150th Ill vols, will stand dismissed the svc of the U S, unless, within 15 days from Nov 20, he appears before the Military Commission in session in Wash City, of which Brig Gen John C Caldwell, U S vols, is Pres, & makes satisfactory defence to the charge of absence without leave. –E D Townsend, Ast Adj Gen

Died: at the residence of Dr E Brewer, Gtwn, D C, on Nov 19, Alice Nelson, y/d/o G T & H E Getty, in the 3rd yr of her age. [Richmond, Lynchburg, & Staunton papers please copy.]

Pension Ofc, Jul 25, 1865. Application made for the re-issue of Land Warrants described therein, which are alleged to have been lost or destroyed, notice given that at the date following the description of each warrant, a new certificate or warrant of like tenor will be issued, if no valid objection should then appear. 1-Dup certificate dt'd Oct 22, 1855, giving the right to locate Bounty Land Warrant 23,535 for 160 acs, issued in the name of Benajah Sweet, father & heir at law of Danl H Sweet, dec'd, & granted Jan 22, 1820. Feb 10, 1866. 2-#73,360 for 160 acs, issued in the name of Matilda, wid/o Edmund Downey, granted Oct 6, 1857. Feb 3, 1866. 3-#30,775, for 12_ acs, issued in the name of Mary wid/o Jacob Probasco, granted Nov 12, 1835. Jan 29, 1866. 4-#30,755 for 160 acs, issued in the name of Louisa, wid/o Geo Latimer, granted Jun 18, 1856. Jan 13, 1866. 5-#36,53_, for 160 acs, issued in the name of Thankful, wid/o Wm Smith, granted Aug 27, 1856. Jan 13, 1866. 6-#81,715, for 160 acs, issued in the name of Sarah, wid/o Jas Ray, & was granted Jul 24, 1858. Dec 23, 1865. 7-#97,429, for 160 acs, issued in the name of Ozias Spalding, granted Mar 21, 1861. Nov 25, 1865. –Jos H Barrett, Com'r

U S Patent Ofc. Ptn of Martha A Dodge, admx of estate of Geo H Dodge, dec'd, of Bedford, Mass; ext of patent dt'd Jan 27, 1852; improvement in the *Ring Spinner*. -T C Theaker, Com'r of Patents.

Last night the store of Mr Edw Scanlon, corner of 3rd & K sts, was entered by burglars, & a lot of goods stolen.

WED NOV 22, 1865
Notice. Evaline A Taylor, wid/o Jos P Taylor, dec'd, & John Mc L Taylor, Jos H Taylor & Mary Taylor his wife, Sarah Rebecca Jones, Henry F Clark & Arabell Clark his wife, Albert G Lawrence & Evaline Lawrence his wife, Zachary Taylor & Wm Taylor, heirs of Jos P Taylor, dec'd, are notified that Chas Munroe, adm with will w a of estate of Jos P Taylor, dec'd, filed his petition in Probate Crt, in Hamilton Co, Ohio, alleging that prsnl estate of said dec'd is insufficient to pay his debts, etc. Said dec'd died seized of rl estate in Cincinnati, Ohio. Prayer is for sale of said premises, free of dower. -Chas Munroe, adm

Orphans Crt of Wash Co, D C. Ptn of Alfred C Cassell, guardian to orphans of John A Cassell, dec'd; ratify sale of rl est, corner of Va av & 7th st, to John H D Richards for $2,400. -Wm F Purcell, Judge

Robt Tyler, of Phil, s/o ex-Pres Tyler, who went south to join the rebellion, has been pardoned by the Pres.

Orphans Crt, D C. 1-Inventory of prsnl estate of John M Roberts was returned by the admx. 2-Ltr of adm issued to Emma Derrick on estate of A H Derrick, giving bond of $8,000. 3-Ltrs of adm issued to David Ramsay, adm of Alan Ramsay. 4-Will of Geo Barton was partially proven. 5-Will of Saml Lusby was partially proven & admitted to probate. 6-Will of Malinda Freeman was fully proven & admitted to probate.

Lt Col W P Gould, Additional Paymstr U S A, stationed on duty in Wash City since Jun, 1864, left yesterday under orders for San Francisco, Calif.

Mrd: at the Chr of the Ascension, on Nov 21, by Rev Dr Pinckney, J McH Hollingsworth to Virginia, d/o the late Wm S Nicholls, all of Gtwn.

Mrd: in Grace Chr, Balt, on Nov 21, by Rev John H Hobart, John A Barber, of Gtwn, D C to Miss Fannie R Brockenbrough, d/o John Brockenbrough, of Westmoreland Co, Va.

Died: on Nov 21, after a long & painful illness, Mrs Jane, consort of Thos Johnson, in her 31st yr. Funeral from her late residence at 21st & R sts, Thu.

Killed in battle, near Appomattox Crt Hse, Va, Apr 9, 1865, Wm C Price, Co E, 1st regt Md cavalry, oldest s/o W F Price, late of Wash, D C. He was interred at Hollywood Cemetery on Nov 12.

New ad-Dr Carl Oscarvallo, late of Douglas Hosp, has moved his ofc to F st, between 14th & 15th st.

Thos McManus was indicted for assault on Ofcr J F Parker, of Metropolitan Police, Mon. Jas Graham & Cornelius Edwards were taken into custody for being concerned in the riot & assault on Mc Manus. Local Item

The first regular census of Great Britain was taken in 1801, & has since been taken every 10 years.

Sale of Rl estate: Thos Dowling, auct, sold, on Thu last, a two-story frame & brick bldg on West st, between Montg & Mill sts, to Martin Donnoghue, for $2,000. Also, 4 small frame hses to Mr John Paxton, for $2,600.

THU NOV 23, 1865
Sup Crt-D C. 1-Cause wherein Cath Hill, cmplnt, & Henry Hill & others, dfndnts. Sale of lot 28 in sq 486 & part of lot 1 in sq 450. -A Thos Bradley, trustee; Jas C McGuire & Co, aucts. 2-Cause between J W Thompson & others, cmplnts, & Mgt F Lindsay & others, dfndnts; sale of lot 1 in sq 248, with 3 story brick dwlg. -C Ingle, trustee -C W Boteler, auct

Died: at the Convent of the Visitation, Wash, on Nov 22, Sister Mary Emanuel Stubbs, in the 40th yr of her age. She entered the Convenant, in Gtwn, in 1847. She was one of the founders of the Visitation in this city in 1830. [Spectator & Balt Catholic Mirror please copy]

Isaac Herzberg & Son's annual fall sale at 7th & D sts, Wash City; pawnbrokers.

The 61st anniversary of the founding of the N Y Historical Soc was celebrated Tue. The President, Mr Fred'k DePeyster, delivered an address.

FRI NOV 24, 1865
Pension Ofc. Re-issue of land warrant lost or destroyed: 160 acs in the name of Benaiah Sweet, father & heir of Daniel H Sweet, dec'd, granted Jan 22, 1820.

Mrd: at the Chr of the Epiphany, on Nov 23, by Rev Dr Hall, Mr W W Burdette, of Wash City, to Miss Susie E Helmick, d/o Hon Wm Helmick, of Ohio.

Mrd: on Nov 7, by Rev Dr Pinckney, Harrie Hibben, of Cincinnati, Ohio, to Miss Louise Nicholls, d/o Mr Isaac S Nicholls, of Nashville, Tenn.

Mrd: on Nov 23, at the Chr of the Epiphany, by Rev Dr Hall, Jos N Whitney, of Portland, Maine, to Mrs C S Burroughs, d/o Maj S B_innall, formerly of Watertown, N Y. No cards. Watertown papers please copy.

Despatch from Concord, N H: of Sat last, says Gen Pierce still continues dangerously sick with chronic diarrhea, tending to ulceration. Drs Morrill, of Concord, & Kimball, of Lowell, attend him.

Wash Corp: 1-Act for the relief of Sophia Peterson: sum of $50 be pd to her for a tavern license which was never obtained.

SAT NOV 25, 1865
Chancery sale-Sup Crt of D C. Lucy M Johns et al, cmplnts, & Mary Darrell et al, dfndnts. Part of lot 6 in sq 369 with brick hse. Property is on L st & the residence of the late Wm S Darrell, dec'd. -E E White, trustee

Sale of city property, belonging to the estate of the late Gen Lawson. Sup Crt of D C, Chancery #495, Barrand et al against Ransone et al. Hotel on 13th & E sts; dwlg hse on Pa av; hses & lots on G st, one called the *Wirt Hse*; hse & lot on F st; bldg lots on M st. -W Y Fendall, trustee; Jas C McGuire & Co, auctioneers

Died: on Nov 23, Annie M, d/o Rev S D & H Finckle, in her 26th yr. Funeral from her father's church, 20th & G sts, Sat.

Sale of the rl estate being the residence of the late Washington Berry, called *Metropolis View*, at the terminus of Lincoln av, opposite Glenwood Cemetery. Mr T C Magruder resides on the premises; 40 lots-from 5 to 31 acs each. -John A Middleton, Thos W Berry, trusts; W D Davidge, atty, Chas W Boteler, Jr, auctioneer

Mrd: on Nov 21, by Rev Fr Charlier, of Trinity Chr, at the residence of Capt Geo Curtis, Beall st, Gtwn, D C, Jas E Williams, atty-at-law & mbr of Wash bar, to Mrs Augusta Smith, nee Palmer, of Frederick City, Md.

Died: on Nov 24, Peter Cazenave Howle, aged 42 yrs. Funeral on Mon from St Matthew's Church.

N Y, Nov 24. The Charleston Courier of the 15th inst, reports an accident at Hope station, on the Greenville railroad, 21 miles from Columiba. One of the hacks which conveyed passengers across a break in the road was precipitated down a gulley 13 ft, in the darkness of the night, into a creek. Killed were Vice-Pres John VanWinkle,of Charleston; Mrs Anna Bedow, an English lady; Rev Dr Cohen, Prof in the Theological Seminary at Columiba, & a servant girl of Mr VanWinkle.

Died: on Nov 23, Mrs Rebecca Winn, wid/o the late T Winn, U S N. Funeral on Sat from the First Presby Chr.

MON NOV 27, 1865
Info desired of residence of the widow of Gen Jas McIntosh, C S A, who fell at Peach Ridge. The undersigned has his watch, entrusted to him a year ago by a friend, to be delivered to the widow. -Albert Pike, Memphis, Tenn

Sup Crt of D C. Danl Hagnar & wife, Wm T Brockenborough & wife, Jas Smith & Willoughby N Smith, against Agnes M Smith. Parties named, heirs of the late Jas M Smith, & to W B Webb, guardian ad litem of said Agnes, to meet at City Hall, Wash, on Dec 6. -W Redin, auditor

Died: on Nov 13, in N C, Wm W Morrison, formerly a clerk in the Navy Dept in Wash City, & latterly a major in the Confederate svc. Stonewall Jackson & Gen A P Hill were his brothers-in-law.

Reward-$2,000. For conviction of parties & recovery of safe & contents stolen from the store 392 Pa av on Mon. -F A Lutz Local Item

San Francisco, Nov 22. Genr'l Prince De Russey, of the corps of engrs, died today, aged 75 years.

Sale of Gov't property in the dismantled forts were resumed on Sat. Fort Mahan-1 barrack, $55, to J J Jouvenal; 1 barrack, $145, to Mrs M M Manning; 1 mess hse, $65, to Robt Johnson; 1 ofcrs' qrtrs, $25, to A Elliott; do, $51, to Mrs M M Manning; 1 ofcrs' qrtrs, $26, to Wm Coleman; 1 mess-hse, $33, to Mrs M M Manning; 1 guard-hse, $32, to W B Lacy; 1 stable, $9, to Wm Coleman; 1 orderly-sgts' qrtrs, $10, to Mrs M M Manning. Fort Mahan is located on the land of Dr Manning, about a mile east of Benning's bridge, over the Eastern Branch. The fort, material, etc, were purchased by Mr M M Manning for $31. The bldgs at Fort Baker have been turned over to S E Fletcher, Ann A C Naylor & Susan M Naylor, owners of the land, as indemnity for damage & occupancy.

Hon Thaddeus Stevens, who had, with his family, been some days at the Nat'l, has taken up his winter qrtrs at his old residence, 279 D st south, Capitol Hill.

Official. War Dept, Adj Gen Ofc, Wash, Nov 24, 1865. Special orders #164. 1-All persons claiming reward for the apprehension of John Wilkes Booth, Lewis Payne, G A Atzerodt, & David E Herold, & Jefferson Davis, or either of them, are notified to file their claims & their proofs with the Adj Gen, for final adjudication by the special commission appointed to award & determine upon the validity of such claims, before the first day of Jan next, after which time no claims will be received. 2-The rewards offered for the arrest of Jacob Thompson, Beverly Tucker, Geo N Sanders, Wm G Cleary, & John H Surratt are revoked. By order of the Pres of the U S: E D Townsend, Ast Adj Gen

TUE NOV 28, 1865
Crct Crt for PG Co, Md, Crt of Equity. Paulina A Berry & others, cmplnts, & Alonzo Berry & Rachel W Berry, excs of John E Berry, sr, & others, dfndnts.

Sale on the premises, at the residence of the late John E Berry, sr, *Independence,* 500 acs, more or less, PG Co, Md, adjoins lands of the late Albert B Berry, John E Berry, Jr, & others; with frame dwlg . -Alonzo Berry, Danl Clarke, trustees

Sale of land in PG Co, Md, of which the late Humphrey Beckett died seised & possessed, 350 acs, adjs the lands of John B Magruder, Richd G Cross, & others, with dwlg hse. Mr Geo W Duvall, [of Geo] residing near the land. -C C Magruder, jr, trustee, Upper Marlboro, Md

New ad-Fine groceries, 256 Pa av, Wash, D C. -Edw C Dyer; Thos Russell

Nashville, Nov 27. Frank Gurley, the murderer of Geo R McCook, reached here from Huntsville last night; where the prisoner will be executed on Fri next. [Nov 29-Sentence respited by Brig Gen Whipple.]

To All Persons Claiming Property Abroad. The undersigned has recently received from England a collection of next-of-kin & heirs at law ads relative to natives of Gr Britain & Ireland who are supposed to have come to America, copies of which he will furnish for a reasonable compensation. The following persons, their next of kin or heirs-at-law are particularly wanted, viz:

Clement Wood	Peter Fowkes	Henry Stewart
Jas Brooks	Wm Gillison	Alexander Woods
J W Bindenburg	John Hyde	Matthew Foot
Jane Morris	Robt London	Chas Jones
Henry Postte	Chas Jackson	Wm Robinson
Montague Browne	Maria Lapine	Wm Parkinson Bough
Richd Collins	Thos Miller	Thos Wilden
Josiah Davis	Jas Morgan	Eliza Ann Peacock
Saml Ducket	Thos Morris	Wm Webb
Dr Jas Duncan	Jane Perkins	Francis Follett
Capt E N Ennis	Wm Shepard	

Chas John Cozens Johnston
Wm Innis, b in Scotland in 1711

Also wanted, Thos Davis or Daviss, s/o Mary Davis, whose maiden name was Alden; last heard of in some of the cotton mills of Massachusetts; & Chas Dermer, a German, came to America in 1857 or 58.

Liberal reward for descendants of Henry Willoughly, who died in Va in 1685. Also, the sons & dghts of Thos Hurst, living in Pa, wanted. The above named persons will learn something to their advantage. -H O Smith, Monkton, Vt

Died: on Nov 26, of consumption, Mrs Harriet Farrel Webb. Funeral from 391 N Y av, Tue.

Died: on Nov 27, of diptheria, Mary Louisa, d/o Saml & Mary Ellen Barnard, aged 15 months. Funeral on Tue from High st, between 4th & 5th sts, Gtwn, D C.

Green's Restaurant, corner of 8th & E sts, Wash City. Wm Klein, C Eber, proprietors.

Sale of Pblc bldgs, etc: Fort Lyon-1 blacksmith shop, $10.25, to W J Murphy; 1 barrack, $85, to Jerry Regan; 1 ofcrs' qrtrs, $23, to John Broders; 1 ofcrs qrtrs, $100, to Hamesley & Spinks; 1 barrack, $92, to C Wessell; 1 barrack, $105, to Geo Finline; 1 barrack, $150, to Thos W Shaw; furn, $7, to Thos W Shaw; 1 mess-hse, $72, to Wm Welch; furniture, $12.50, to Stephen Bates; 1 sutler's store, $52, to Geo Taylor; 1 stable, $80, to P Ballenger. Fort Farnsworth: 1 sutler's store, $38, to P Ballenger; ofcrs' qrtrs, do, $40; do, do, $36; do, do, $37; 1 barrack, $85, to Jerry Regan; furn, $6, to J Pullman; 1 mess-hse, $64, to Thos Dewey; furn, $5, do; 1 cook-hse, $18, to A G Childe; 1 guard hse, $18, to G Spinks. Fort Lyon is located on Mount Eagle, s w from Alexandria, & is on land owned by P Ballenger, U S Barker, Peter Pullman, & Mrs Harrison. Fort Farnsworth is located on Mount Eagle, 2 miles from Alexandria, & forms part of the southern line of defence. Is is situated on land owned by C H Johnson, formerly of N J.

WED NOV 29, 1865

Buffalo Commercial Advertiser, Nov 24. Henry Henry, a sldr stationed at Fort Porter, was murdered on Sep 24 by Michl Kierchner. Michl's sweetheart, Eliz Weaver, wept bitterly at his recent execution.

Sale of lots in D C, belonging to the minor heirs of Thos Hollidge, in sq 511, on O st. -Isaac Talks, guardian.

Mrd: on Nov 25, at St Paul's Chr, Calvert Co, Md, by Rev Walter Mitchell, Robt Bolling & Nannie Webster.

Died: at Edenton, N C, on Nov 11, Cleveland Sawyer, s/o the late Dr Sawyer, of Edenton, N C.

Eleven hundred dollars has been paid to Mrs Washington, wid/o Lewis Washington, a rebel ofcr, in compensation for household property seized & sold during the war.

Sec of War has ordered the release from confinement of Geo A Harfod, late Lt Col of the 124th U S colored troops, who was sentenced by a genr'l crt-martial, to be cashiered, & confined at hard labor for 3 yrs, plus 10 yrs, unless he refund to the Gov't $2,247, of which $633, is in notes; & now imprisoned in the Ky Pen, at Frankfort, Ky. Also remitted: the unexpired portion of the sentence in the following cases, viz: John W W McCue, a guerilla, sentenced to hard labor for life: now undergoing execution of sentence at Clinton Prison, N Y. Robt G Sheppard, ctzn, to be confined at hard labor at the Dry Tortugas, for 3 yrs. John Winston, ctzn, to be imprisoned for 5 years at hard labor, with ball & chain attached; & Saml S Winston, ctzn, sentenced by the same military commission to be confined at hard labor for 10 yrs. Latter 2 are now in the Jefferson City pen, Mo.

Sale of property belonging to the Q M Dept, Nov 28, 1865. Fort Weed: ofcrs' qrtrs, $42, to P Ballinger; do, do, $10; do, do, $50; do, do, $16; do, Chas Studds, $47; do, R W Smith, $37; wood-hse, P Ballinger, $11; mess-hse, Saml Pullman, $80; guard-hse, $17, Victor Struder; barrack, $87, P Ballinger; furn in do, do, $15; ofcrs' qrtrs, $31, Saml Pullman. Fort O'Rourke: guard-hse, $16, Victor Struder; barrack, $94, Oliver Pullman; mess-hse, $72, Geo Taylor; ofcrs' qrtrs, $47, Chas Studds; sutler's shop, $11, Saml Pullman; ofcrs' qrtrs, $54, G A Simpson; store-hse, $81, Bodfish, Mills & Co; carpenter's shop, $14, Henry Johnson; hospital, do, $210; do, Thos W Shaw, $137; hosp storehse, $44, H Studds; sinks, do, $5; do, J Pullman, $2.50; furn, $8.75, J Regan; furn, $4, J Pullman; outbldgs, $11, H Johnson.

Drowned: Capt E Richter, master of the canal-boat *Ironsides*, accidentally on Mon in, one of the 6 locks, about 13 miles from Gtwn.

THU NOV 30, 1865

For sale: *Tudor Hall* in St Mary's Co, Md, 880 acs lying in & about Leonardtown, the county seat. -H G S Key, Leonardtown, Md

Dr T C Madison, a nephew of Pres Madison, who had been a surgeon in the U S army, & held the 2nd place in the medical staff of the Confederate army, & was recently pardoned, died suddenly in his seat in the cars between St Louis & Jeff City, Mo, recently.

Mrd: on Nov 28, by Rev Dr Gillette, Geo T Parker to Amanda D Sanderson, both of Wash City.

A tight-rope walker from Nashville, named T N Huntley, under 20 years of age, lost his life at Wilmington, N C, on the 24th inst, while in the act of performing.

Capt S C Elliot, long known at Norfolk as a ship-master, & later as agent for the N Y & Norfolk steamers, & during the war as a highly efficient ofcr in the Confederate svc, died at Norfolk a few days ago. The papers of that city speak with warmth & tenderness of the dec'd.

Died: on Nov 28, of typhoid fever, Gustavus Waters, in his 66th yr. Funeral from the Chr of the Ascension on Fri.

Martha Grinder, the poisoner, convicted at Pittsburg. of incredible fiendishness, has been sentenced to be hanged. She protested her innocence. The Judge exhorted her to indulge no hope this side of the grave.

The ctzns of N Y have nearly completed the arrangements to pay off a mortgage of $30,000 on the house recently purchased by Gen Grant in Washington: a gift to the General.

Sec of War: mustering out of surgeons:
Surg John Trenor, Bvt Lt Col U S vols: serving in the Dept of Ga.
Surg Alex'r T Watson, do: serving in the Dept of the East.
Surg Burkhilt Cloak, do: serving in the Dept of Ky.
Surg Chas O'Leary, do: serving the the Dept of the East.
Ast Surg Edw K Hogan, Brvt Maj U S vols.
Ast Surg O P Sweet, do.
Ast Surg S S Jessup, Brvt Capt U S vols.
Ast Surg J P Dowling, do: now serving in the Dept of Mississippi.
Ast Surg J A White, do: serving do.
Ast Surg Jos W Hayward, Brvt Maj U S vols: serving in the Dept of Va, & Ast Surg W A Gordon, Brvt Maj U S vols: now serving in the Dept of Ky.

Lt John Clingman, 50th Ohio vols, dismissed the svc, with loss of all pay & allowances, & sentenced to be imprisoned for one yr in the State Prison at Concord, N H. His crime was making a false & fraudulent claim against the Gov't & procuring the forging of signatures upon a pay-roll for the purpose of obtaining the payment of the claims.

Sale of property in the dismantled forts: Fort Wortt: 3 miles beyond Alexandria-despensary, $40; 4 ofcr's qrtrs, at $54, $53, $35, & $32; 2 barracks at $100 & $126, brick; 2 mess-hses, $45 & $96; stable, $21; walk $14; & lumber, $10.75-all the foregoing to Maj Wm Silner. 1 barrack at $68 to Geo Aula; mess-hse $85 to Mrs S Murray; brick, $11 to Henry Bontz. The Gov't bldgs at Camp Barry, some 15 in number, were also sold yesterday at prices varying from $100 to $250. A portion of the Treas workshop, near the Pres' hse, was sold for $300.

Rl estate sales: On Tue, a lot of ground on E st, near 10th, to Geo F Sharper, at 14 cents per sq ft.
Sold on Tue: a brick hse & lot on Bridge st, between Jefferson & Washington sts, to F Koester for $4,450.

Crmnl Crt-Wash: In the case of Wm Carroll, convicted of larceny, a new trial was granted. Same for John Butler, also convicted of larceny.

FRI DEC 1, 1865

Richmond, Nov 30. The Hon Littleton Tazewell, Commonwealth Atty, died this morning after a brief illness.

Report of the deaths of sldrs: The U S Burial Bureau, under the charge of Brvt Maj J H Moore, make the following report of deaths & burials: The number of white sldrs that have died in Wash, D C, from Aug 1, 1861, to Nov 29, 1865, is 15,412, & the number of colored sldrs is 6,328. The whole number that have died at Andersonville, Ga, including sldrs, sailors, employes, & ctzns, is 12,918. The number of sldrs buried at Spottsylvania C H & the Wilderness is 1,500; at Nashville, Tenn, 32,000; & at Richmond, Va, 60,000. Of the sldrs buried in & around Wash 4,220 are from N Y, 86 from Ill, 219 from Indiana, 782 from Mich, 510 from Ohio, & 200 from Conn. The number of these that died from the effect of wounds is 3,806, & 2,464 are reported to have died of typhoid fever. There are 11,285 men buried near Washington whose names & regts are unknown. The employes of Maj Moore's Bureau are now engaged in exhuming the bodies of our dead at the average rate of 20 per day.

Mr J A Van Amburgh, circus manager, died in Phil on Wed last, in his 59th yr.

Died: in Gtwn, Nov 27, in her 76th yr, Miss Mary Ann Clark, d/o Dr David Clark, formerly of PG Co, Md. [Marlborough papers please copy.]

Died: on Nov 30, Jacob Smull, in his 81st yr; for the last 40 years a resident of Wash City. Funeral from his late residence on L st, Navy Yd, Sat.

Died: in Gtwn, D C, on Nov 30, Mgt, w/o Henry R De La Reintrie. Funeral in Balt, Md, on Sat.

The Pres yesterday signed the pardon warrant of J W Bennett, of S C.

Maj John A Haddock, 12th Vet Reserve Corps, & Actg Ast Provost Mrshl Genr'l of the Western Div of N Y, has been sentenced by the Crt Martial before whom he was tried, at Elmira, N Y, "to be cashiered, & utterly disabled to have or hold any ofc or employment in the svc of the U S; that he pay a fine of $10,000 to the U S, & be imprisoned at such place as the proper authority may designate until the said fine be pd-the perod of said imprisonment not, however, to exceed 5 yrs."

Navy Yard: suspension of work. The Dept has obolished the ofc of Mstr Laborer, which position was creditably filled for a number of years by the late Jos M Padgett, & latterly by Mr C W White. Mr White was notified yesterday that his svcs were no longer needed. Boatswain Geo Smith is expected to act as foreman of laborers. The Pres did not desire such an expensive compliment as that of a vessel being kept ostensibly for his prospective use, the U S steamer *Hornet*, formerly the blockade-runner *Lady Sterling*, which has latterly been designated as the Pres' yacht, has been ordered to N Y, where she will be sold.

St Andrew's Society 11th annual festival at Aman's Restaurant. Soc organized at the residence of Capt Steuart, & each festival has been characteristic of the social customs of Scotchmen, of whom the society is chiefly composed. The ofcrs are W B Smith, Pres; Fred B McGuire, V P; T W Spence, Treas; David Knox, Rec Sec; Alex' Gardner, Cor Sec; John Guild & John Reckie, Mgrs.

A destitute blind man, Geo W Mathews, was yesterday found near the depot. He said he was raised in Jeff Co, Pa, & became blind in consequence of exposure in driving Gov't teams, & he sought admission to a hospital in Phil, where he had formerly resided, & was not only refused, but arrested, &, by order of the Mayor of that city, placed on a train for Washington-the Mayor paying his fare. Mayor Wallach sent him to the Almshse for the present. If his statements are true he should be returned to Phil with a bill of charges. We protest against Washington's being made a *cul-de-sac* for the criminals & paupers of other cities.

Canal boats arrived:
American Co: canal boats: *C Dubois, Jas Dayton, Andrew Main*
C C & I Co: canal boats: *Sprigg Lynn, Bettie, J F McCulloh, G W Birdrail, L R Fechtig.*
Central Co: canal boats: *Kate Karns, Jos F Hitch, Pearl, J E Russell, Forest Rose.*
New Hope Co: canal boats: *L M Mayer, Westfield, Middletown, Keystone.*
H & Balt Co: canal boats: *A G Green, Borden, Lady of the Lake, Mary W Wright*
Cleared:
Richd Bendin, Patrick Mills, mstr; *A Lincoln,* Augustus Weihle; *Sallie Billmyer,* John Crown; *Josiah Witt,* D Brainley; *Josephus,* C F Wenner; *Ellen,* Jacob Korde; *Maude,* Danl McCoy; *Alex'r Ray,* Wm Bradshears; *H Delafield,* do; *Mary & Anna,* E S Williams; *J P Roman,* Danl Winsow; *A C Green,* J A Comder; *Jennie Lynn,* John Lindquist; *Geo A Pearore,* Andy Snyder; *Robt Stewart,* Jacob Miller; *Potomac,* J E Rhodes.

Sales at the dismantled forts cont'd: sale yesterday at <u>Fort Ward</u>, near Alexandria: ofcrs qrtrs, $13, A Martin; ofcrs' qrtrs, $12, John Studds; 2 ofcr's qrtrs, $14, $16, H Studds; ofcrs' qrtrs, $40, John Wren; ofcrs' qrtrs, $33, Maj Wm Silvey; ofcrs' qrtrs, $36, Geo Cribling; 2 barracks, D S Gordon; each $73; barrack, O Howard, $76; mess-hse, D B McMahon, $95; additions to mess-hse, D S Gordon, $37; brick walk, H Studds, $15; furn, $7, D S Gordon; furn, $15, Chas Studds; brick walk, Henry Bontz, $22; brick walk, Chas Studds, $11; 2 sgts' qrtrs, each $16, H Studds; orderly sgts' qrtrs, John Studds, $26; stable, $13, Carey Goings.

Providence, Nov 30. News received of the death of Thos Boyton Ayres, of this city, a Lt Cmder in the navy. He died at Havre after his marriage with the dght of our Minister at Austria.

Sale of Western Gunboats: Cairo, Nov 29: sold with the plating partially removed, at Mound City today:

Indianola, $3,000	*Caroudelet,* $3,600
Tuscumbia, $3,300	*Benton,* $3,000
Missouri, $2,100	*Mound City,* $3,700
Avenger, $5,000	*Louisville,* $4,600
Vindicator, $5,000	*Essex,* $4,000
Pittsburgh, $3,100	*Chillicothe,* $3,000
Czark, $3,000	

Newburyport, Nov 30. Jacob Merrill, a returned sldr, was murdered & robbed of $500 last night.

SAT DEC 2, 1865
The tolls on the Chesapeake & Ohio Canal for the month ending Nov 30 amounted to $50,000. $14,029.56 of this amount was collected at the collector's ofc in Gtwn.

Ad-Plumbers, steam & gasfitters, 402 D st, Wash, O'Hare & Noonan. -Owen O'Hare & Tim V Noonan

Capt Jas W Moore, ass't qrtrmstr, who has charge of the burial of the dec'd sldrs in this Dist, has selected a spot on the old Ball's Bluff battle ground, where will be interred the remains of those who fell on that memorable field.

Died: after a long & painful illness, on Dec 1, Mr Anthony La Truitte, oldest s/o the late John P La Truitte, of Wash City. Funeral from his late residence on 5th st, thence to St Aloysius Chr on Sat. [Alexandria papers please copy]

Auction sale of the prsnl effects of the late Mary Caroline Fenwick, dec'd. Sale of furn, stack corn, horses, cow, carriage, etc, at her late residence 2 miles from Washington, on the new road to Bladensburg, near Kendel Green. -Mary E Smith, excx

Sales at the dismantled forts: cont'd yesterday at Fort Richardson: log barrack, $16, to Frank Keyser; 2 ofcrs' qrtrs, $21 ea, to Pitkin & Co; frame qrtrs, $5 to D S Bordon; log qrtrs, $8 to Jas Markham; frame qrtrs, $3, to D S Gordon; do, $2, to same; mess-hse & oven, $35, to Wm Knight; barrack, $53, to Jas Markland; do, $85, to Bodfish, Mills & Co; dispensary, $6, to D S Gordon; sgts' qrtrs, $10, to same; barrackk, $72, to M W Miller; sutlers' shop, $17, to M W Miller; qrtrs, $2, to M Brogden; do, $6, to Pitkin & Co; qrtrs, $3, D S Gordon; 2 small bldgs, $4, to Jas Markham; barrack, $46, to Pitkin & Co; blacksmith shop, $14; stable, $30, to D S Gordon; stable, $21, to M Miller; do, $46, to N P Corbett; orderly sgts' qrtrs, $31, J W Brown.

The will of the late Madame Jumel, wid/o Aaron Burr, has been offered for probate. It was made in 1863 when she was 90 years old. The will is contested by Mr Nelson Chase & others, who allege that they are the heirs-at-law of the estate.

St Ann's Infant Asylum was established in 1815 by the special munificense & long continued toil & care of Mrs Van Ness. It now contains about 80 little orphan girls & boys ages from 3 to 11. A new building was needed & Mr Corcoran tendered a spacious & elegant lot on 14th & S sts. Corner stone was laid, &, under a contract for the sum of $24,000, Mr J C Naylor will, within a few days, have covered in the structure, which completes his contract. The building is 101 feet on 14th st & 106 feet on S st. It is 3 stories high above the basement, with a central tower rising one story above the main bldg. It is Italian style of architecture, finished with brownstone coigns & base, 7 iron window-heads, & cannot, when entirely completed, have cost less than $50,000. Wash, D C

Meeting of the Oldest Inhabitants of ctzns of D C, held on Nov 30: J S Williams called to the chair; John F Callan appt'd sec. Association calls for any person not less than 50 years of age, who has resided in the District of Columbia for 40 yrs, may become a mbr by subscribing to the constitution & paying annually the sum of $1. Cmte appt'd: Jas Clephane, Geo Savage, & J F Callan, to prepare a constitution for the association.

Miss M J Platt, just returned from N Y with assortment of winter opera & reception bonnets; show rms at 246 Pa av, Wash City.

MON DEC 4, 1865
Sup Crt of D C, Equity #541. The Columbian College of D C against Zeph English, exc of John Withers, dec'd. Statement of the account of John Withers, dec'd, on Dec 15, at City Hall, Wash. -W Redin, auditor

On Nov 19 the hse of Col Wm H Phillips, corner of Gay & Green sts, Gtwn, was robbed of a gold watch valued at $400, $130 in Treas notes, two $2.50 gold pieces, & a number of wearing apparel. About a week ago a negro, Wm Delaney, was arrested in Phil by Detective Wm H Taggart, of that city, as a suspicious character, & upon searching him the watch was found upon his person. The police here were advised, & Detectives Kelly & Bigley were assigned to the case. The accused was sent to jail for court by Superintendent Richards, in default of $2,000 bail.

Ads-hotels & restaurants:
1-Bright's Restaurant, 233 & 233 G st, between 17th & 18th sts, Wash, City.
2-Metropolitan Htl, Pa ave, Wash City. –A R Potts, proprietor
3-U S Htl, Pa ave, near the Capitol, Wash City. –M H Bean & Co, proprietors
4-Seaton Hse, La ave, between 6th & 7th sts, Wash City. –Gilbert & Brodhead, proprietors
5-Markham's Htl, on European Plan, 212 Pa ave, adjoining Willard's Htl. –Thos P Jacks, proprietor
6-Waverly Hse, 451 8th st, Wash, D C. –S G Langley, proprietor
7-Green's Restaurant, corner 8th & E sts, Wash City. –Wm Klein & C Eber, proprietors
8-Exchange Hotel, Richmond, Va. –J L Carrington & Co, proprietors
9-Ballard Hse, Richmond, Va. –M D Maine & Co, proprietors
10-Monumental Htl, 9th & Grace sts, Richmond, Va. –D T Norris & Co, proprietors
11-Jurratt's Htl, Petersburg, Va. –Platt & Simmons, proprietors
12-Orange Hse, Lynchburg, Va. –Houston Rucker, proprietor
13-Spotswood Htl: corner 8th & Main sts, Richmond, Va. –Corkery & Millward, proprietors
14-Ebbitt Hse, corner of 14th & F sts, Wash, D C. –C C Willard, proprietor [For many years proprietor of the Hygeia Htl, Old Point,Comfort, Va.]

Died: on Dec 2, Mrs Rebecca W Conrad, w/o Chas E Conrad, & only d/o Moses T & Virginia S Parker. Funeral on Tue from her father's residence, Maine av & 6th st.

Homicide-yesterday. An affray between Jos Demeyers & John Hughes, who both lived in the same hse, at 7th & O sts, occurred, resulting in the death of Demeyers.

Yesterday Ofcr Campbell, of the 4th ward, arrested John Burns, who appeared to be suspicious due to his seeing the ofcr & rapidly proceeding away from him, with a bag full of items. Burns was sent to jail for a hearing.

Sale of Gov't bldgs, on Sat last. Brvt Maj Jas Gleason, A Q M, made the following sales: Fort Tillinghast, Alexandria Co, Va. Mr C Alexander purchased all the bldgs at this fort, as follows: 1 ofcrs' qrtrs, $39; 1 do, $57; 1 mess-hse, $25; 1 do, $18; 1 barrack, $107; 1 stable, $16. One barrack & 1 mess-hse & kitchen were reserved for the use of the Bur of R, F, & A L, by order of the Sec of War. Fort Craig, Alexandria Co, Va. Mr S Brown purchased 5 ofcrs' qrtrs at $16, $16, $18, $20, & $21; & 1 stable at $1.50. Mr V P Corbett, 1 barrack, $70; 2 mess-hses at $30 & $11. Mr Nicholson, 1 barrack, $62.50. Engr Dept: after these sales there was a sale of property belonging to the Engr Dept, among which was a large lot of valuable lumber, which was knocked off to Bodfish Mills & Co for $725. The condition of all the prop, both of the Q M & Engr Depts, was rather poor, & the bldgs not having been occupied for some time were becoming rather dilapidated. Today Maj Gleason will see the lumber & bldgs at Fort Morton & Fort C F Smith, located in the vicinity of Gtwn.

The Pres on Sat issued orders for the muster-out of Hospital Chaplains Henry Hill & John Woart.

Wash Corp: 1-Ptn of E E White & others concerning sewers: referred to the Cmte on Drainage, etc. 2-Ptn of E E Anderson & others, with a bill to grade & pave the alley in sq 539: referred to the Cmte on Improvements. 3-Ptn of Chas E Barnes for relief: referred to the Cmte on Claims. 4-Cmte on Police reported adversely on the ptn of Wm Bagnam, asking to be discharged, which was so ordered. 5-Cmte on Health: confirmed for mbrs of the Brd of Health: L J Gaddis, Seth A Elliot & Peter F Broom. 6-Bill for relief of Wm D Crampsy: referred to the Cmte on Claims. 7-Ptn of Jas Murray, asking the remission of a fine: referred to the Cmte on Claims. 8-Cmte on Police: referred the ptn of Jas McLaughlin, reported bill [C C 199] granting certain privileges to Jas McLaughlin: passed. 9-Cmte on Claims reported the bill for the relief of Saml Gregg: passed. Same cmte: referred the bill for the relief of Henry Ewalt & Bro: bill rejected. 10-Cmte on Claims: bill for relief of Mgt Kurtz: to be laid on the table.

Mr Louis Schade, late cnsl for Henry Wirz, has received affidavits from Mrs Wirz denying the assertion of Detctive Baker that she attempted to poison her hsbnd while on a visit to him at the Old Capitol Prison.

Affray in Wash City, yesterday, between Jos Demeyers & John Hughes, resulted in the death of Demeyers. Testimony was received from John F Quigley, Philip Loefler, Frank Wemmer, John O'Neal & others. Both men lived in the same hse at 7th & O sts. Demeyer & his wife lived in an upper room. Quarrel of long standing existed between the two men. Demeyer fell Hughes to the ground, & while striking Hughes, Hughes stabbed Demeyer twice. Demeyer rose & moved but a few steps when he fell & expired almost immediately. Demeyer was formerly a sldr belonging to a Pa regt. Hughes is a plasterer by trade, & about 55 years of age. Hughes intended turning himself in: he was arrested by County Ofcr King & turned over to Sgt Skippon, of the 6th Precinct.

U S Patent Ofc. Ptn of Henry G Bulkley, of Kalamazoo, Mich, for extension of patent dt'd Mar 2, 1852; improvement in *drying grain*. -T C Theaker, com'r

Dedication of the N Y Presby Chr yesterday. Lot on N st was purchased, between 10th & 11th sts, & Mr L Downing was contracted to build them a neat, comfortable hse, 40 x 66 ft, with 70 pews, which, when fully finished, & the lot enclosed, will have cost, including the lot, [71 x 120 ft,] about $10,000. Personal exertions of Dr Gurley, & considerable assistance was procured in N Y C. There is yet a small debt to be pd. Since Jul last Rev L R Fox has been employed by the N Y Ave Chr people as a minister at this mission. Invocation by Rev Mr Taylor, Bridge St Chr, Gtwn; Rev L R Fox, Rev S P Tustin, D D, benediction by Dr P D Gurley, D D

TUE DEC 5, 1865
Died: on Nov 30, at the U S Hosp at Brooklyn naval sta [a palace among hospitals, by the way,] an old sailor, Wm Conway, having served over 40 years as an enlisted sailor. Funeral from the hospital at 3 p m. -N Y Herald

Two chldrn, named Meades-9 yrs, & Norton-3 yrs, were killed by the falling of a sandbank, on Sat evening on the outskirts of Balt.

The Burnet Hse, in Cincinnati, was recently sold by A B Coleman, formerly of the Astor Hse, to S N Pike, a wealthy manufacturer of liquors, for $300,000. Said to be the largest rl estate transaction ever taking place in that city.

Information wanted.-Some time about Nov 1, 1864, Stephen P Drake, formerly editor of the *Ironton Clipper*, was in charge of a mail from Winchester to Martinsburg, & was captured by Col Mosby's Cavalry. It is supposed he was killed by Mosby's men. He leaves a wife & chldrn, who are living under a very painful suspense. Will not some of Mosby's men respond to this & let his friends know where & how he died & where he is buried? -Saml P Drake

Sale of *Warwick Spring*, 120 acs, with brick hse, near Alexandria. -Dr W F Lippitt, Charlestown, Jefferson Co, Va.

Sup Crt of D C, Equity # 317. Louis Grammer & others vs Todd, Dunkinson, & others. Ratify sale by Wm B Todd, trustee, of parts of lots 12 & 13 in sq 407 to Geo E Kennedy for $3,250; & part of lot 12 in sq 533 to John Purdy for $4,093.45; & lot 6 & lot G in sq 164 to Julius E Grammer for $4,348.40.

Mrd: on Nov 28, by Rev Wesley Boteler, at the East Meth Episc Chr, Mr Edw Boteler, of Wash City, to Miss Susie Prather, of A A Co, Md. The church was crowded with the youth & beauty of East Washington.

The funeral obsequies of Mr Jas Hutchins, a fireman of Gtwn, took place on Sun. A large concourse of ctzns moved from his residence on Bridge st to the Presby Cemetery.

Died: on Dec 4, Mrs Mary Pritchard, in her 76th yr. Funeral from the residence of her son-in-law, Mr A W Denham, on 19th st, between E & F sts.

Died: on Dec 4, after a lingering illness of several mos, Abraham Cook, in his 45th yr. Funeral from his late residence at 318 3rd st, Wed.

Orphans Crt-D C. 1-Will of Eliza Reaves, dec'd, proven & admitted to probate; Wm Y Robinson, exc, giving bond of $400; sureties are Mr Wm H Barbour & Henry E Marks. 2-Will of Mary Caroline Fenwick, dec'd, fully proven & admitted to probate & record; Mary Ellen Smith qualified as excx by giving bond of $50,000, with John A Smith, Benj Fenwick, Maria M Fenwick, Sarah C Fenwick as sureties. 3-Will of Jas R Wood, admitted to probate, Wm Paul Brown, exc, gave bond of $400, with Geo Brown & Jas B Peake, as sureties. 4-Judith E Hurley qualified as admx of the estate of Wm R Hurley, dec'd, & gave bond of $6,000, with Return J Meigs & Jno E Norris as sureties. 5-Jane Tyler appt'd guardian of Sarah W & Jas W Tyler, orphans of Albert Tyler, dec'd, & gave bond of $1,000, Thos S Scrivener & Benj Chambers are sureties. 6-Acc't of Mary E Stewart, guardian to the orphans of Geo W Stewart, dec'd; acc't of Presley W Dorsey, exc of Susan Worthington, dec'd; of Rachel T Meehan, excx of John S Meehan, dec'd; of Sally Carroll, excx of Wm Thos Carroll, dec'd, & account of Gwynn Harris, guardian to the orphans of Peter Jones, dec'd, were passed. 7-Will of Wm Hughes, dec'd, filed & fully proven. 8-Thos K Wilson qualified as adm of the estate of Geo W Wilson, gave bond of $3,000; Geo B Smith & Timothy McCarthy are sureties. 9-Final acc't of Wm B Jackson, exc of John Clapham, dec'd; final account of exc of Geo Poe, Jr, dec'd; final account of Geo W Bushee, exc of the estate of Jas Goodell, dec'd, were approved & passed. 10-The rg o/wills reported the first acc't of Elias A Eliason, guardian to Ardella V Rhodes, orphan of Edw P Rhodes, dec'd. The register also filed affidavits on the above case, & containing an endorsement rejecting a voucher. C Ingle, atty for Mr Eliason, filed exceptions to the report of the register; case cont'd until Dec 2.

Com'r Cooley, of the Indian Bur, received information from Albert Pike that the manuscript copies of the various treaties made by the so-called Confederate Gov't were stolen from him near Richmond, Va.
Reply: War Dept, Nov 27, 1865. Maj Gen Terry, commanding at Richmond, has been directed to use diligent efforts to recover the manuscript treaties. –Thos T Eckert, Actg Ast Sec of War. [To Hon Jas Harlan, Sec of the Interior.

Some of Gen Robt E Lee's military friends presented him with a piano, an elegant instrument, Louis XIV style, 7 octaves, extra richly carved case, round corners, name board is richly inlaid with mother of pearl, with the name of the maker & the words, "Presented to Robt E Lee." Richmond Enq

Reported Yellow Fever case on the ship *Stonewall*. The funeral of the late Isaac B Fort, s/o Rev W S Fort, was held at his father's residence yesterday. Mr Fort was a 3rd Ast Engineer in the Navy, & had arrived here in the *Stonewall*, from which ship he was removed on Fri, being then very sick with a fever, which was accompanied by symptoms pronounced by the medical ofcrs on board to be yellow fever, & died on Sat morning. There are none of the crew now sick.

The famed physician Dr Lambelle, in Paris, has become insane.

Sales of public property belonging to the Q M Dept, Dec 4, 1865: Fort Morton-ofcrs' qrtrs, A price, $100; barrack, J Nicholson, $70; do, A Price, $83; 2 mess-hses, $87.50, to A Price; qrtrs, $29. Fort C F Smith: mess-house, R A Philips, $52.50; log stable, S Goroun, $11; guard hse, Thos Jewell, $30; barrack, S Ball, $41; do, G N Smith, $49; mess house, Thos Jewell, $71; kitchen, Chas W Payne, $15.50; do, A Price, $15; ofcrs' qrtrs, R H Phillips, $32; do, Chas Dobson, $15; do, Chas W Payne, $29; do, B F Bunyon, $25; do, Thos Jewell, $27; do, Thos Jewell, $27; do, C C Fearson, $41; do, Thos Jewell, $40. Engineer property sold Dec 4, 1865: Fort Morton-Abattis, A Price, $54. Fort Strong-Abattis, A Price, $65. Fort C F Smith-Abattis, $62; stockade, $43; bombproof & magazzine, $400; flag-staff, $6; implement room, $25.

Rl estate sale: sold yesterday a hse & lot on Pa ave, between 17th & 18th sts, to Chas Demonet, for $12,000.

WED DEC 6, 1865
Died: at the residence of her mother, Mrs Gov Geo B Porter, Lancaster, Pa, Mrs Sarah L Porter, w/o Oliver Phelps, Jr, of Canandaigua, N Y, in her 39th yr.

Obit-died in Balt, Md, on Dec 1, Henry M Morfit, aged about 70 yrs, after an illness of many months. He was born at Norfolk, Va, where he was educated for the bar; removed to Missouri & thence to Wash City; in 1861 took up his residence in Balt. He was a devoted hsbnd & tender father.

Personal: Capt E E Camp, A Q M, U S A, who has been connected with the Q M's Dept in Wash City during the war, has been made Brvt Lt Col in the Reg army. Hon John D Stiles, of Pa, & Brig Gen Peavey, of Mass, are at the Seaton Hse. Hon Francis Thomas, Md; Gen E M McCook, U S A; Gen John Ely, of Pa; Gen J W Brown, of Balt, Hon J S Barbour, of Va, are at the Nat'l. Hon R J Walker; Messrs Mark J Stewart, J H Kenneway, R G Howe, R G Arbuthnot, & R Ragwell, of England; Gen Thos T Mumford, of Va, Hon Geo B Senter, of Ohio; Gen E Shriver, of Md; Hon W Byres, of Ark; & Harry F Swayne, of Ohio, are at Willard's.

Rl estate sale: sold yesterday lot of ground on R I ave, between 15th & 15th sts, to Dennis Dunn at 20 cents per sq ft.

THU DEC 7, 1865

Orphans Crt of Wash Co, D C. Case of Sophia C Snyder, admx of John M Snyder, dec'd; settlement on Dec 30. -Z C Robbins, rg o/wills

Sup Crt of D C, in Equity-#344. Edw W Mobberly & Louisa his wife, Ann Worthington, Wm H Johnson & Laura J his wife, Chas E Worthington & Maria L his wife, against Ella Johnson, Thos P Brashear, Chas H Brashear, & John R Jones & Sarah L his wife, & others. Statement of the acc't of Thos Cook, dec'd, on Dec 28, City Hall, Wash City. -Wm Redin, auditor

Sup Crt of D C. Riggs & others against the adms, heirs, & widow of Thos Smith. Ratify sale by W Redin, trustee, to Jas H Hazell, lots 20 & 21 in sq 182 for $870.26; to Wm Douglass, lots 22 & 23 for $693.75; to Joshua Anderson, lots 24 & 25 for $589.27; to E C Weaver, of lot 26, for $312.75; to Alexander Duhay, lots 27, 28, & 29, for $835.81. -By order of the Crt.

Sup Crt of D C, Equity #487. Fredericka Roemele & others vs Jos Roemele & others. Com'rs report of the ptn of rl estate of John C Roemele & of Wm H Roemele having been returned & filed. -R J Meigs, clerk

Sup Crt of D C, Equity # 536. Thos B Scott, Ellen R Scott, Ann H Scott, Mary E C Scott, Mary A Decamp Scott, F B Suitt, Judson S Suitt, Tyler Suitt, & J S Suitt, cmplnts, vs Alfred Claggett, Eliz Claggett, Ellen Claggett, & all other heirs-at-law of Eliz C Scott & Martha E C Scott, dec'd, & B S Baily, adm, dfndnts. Suit is to procure a decree for the sale of rl estate in Wash, D C; Eliz & Martha E C Scott died seized of same; the rl estate descended to the cmplnts & dfndnts, as heirs-at-law of same. Dfndnts, except B S Baily, adm, reside out of D C. -R J Meigs, clerk -Wm J Miller, Solicitor for cmplnts

Mrd: on Dec 5, at Warrenton, Va, by Rev John W Pugh, Mr J Thos Petty, of Front Royal, Va, formerly of Wash, & Miss Mattie A Deshields, of Warrenton.

Mrd: on Dec 4, by Rev P D Gurley, at the residence of the bride's father, J W Brown, Mr J R H Popham, of Culpeper Co, Va, to Miss Kate P Brown, of Wash City.

FRI DEC 8, 1865

Ad: Doors-Sash-Blinds, 562 7th st, Wash. -H W Hamilton

Land for sale-504 acs with frame dwlg; also my stock of farming utensils, provender, oats, etc. -Jas T Blakistone, Leonardtown, St Mary's Co, Md.

Phil, Dec 7. Patrick Finnegan was recently killed by the late boiler-explosion at the Penn Treaty Rolling Mills.

SAT DEC 9, 1865

Farm for sale in Amherst Co, Va, called *Clear Spring*, 345 acs with brick dwlg. -Edw McCormick, or Geo W Bradfield, Berryville, Clarke Co, Va.

Died: on Dec 7, Maj Wm H Gordon, 8th regt U S infty. Funeral from St John's Chr, on Sat.

Died: on Dec 3, at *Locust Grove*, near Ellicott's Mills, Rebecca S, relict of the late Marius Gilliam, of Petersburg, Va. [Petersburg papers please copy.]

Oak Hill Cemetery made an addition of some 6 acs, paying Mr Chas Dodge $8,000 for the addition. The proprietors have been offered $2,000 a year for 10 yrs, by Mr Fred'k C Crowley, for quarrying stone from the land thus purchased.

Appointments in the U S Treas Ofc. Gen Spinner has promoted C E Twombly, Ast Paying Teller, to be Chief Paying Teller of the U S Treas. P A Murden succeeds Mr Twombly as Assistant.

Pres Johnson has sent to the Senate for confirmation the name of N B Browne, to be Ast Treas at Phil, v McIntyre, resigned.

Col H B N Boynton, lately commanding the 135th Ohio volunteers, has been breveted a Brig Gen of volunteers.

Murder was perpetrated at Burlington, Racine Co, Wisc, on Sunday. The victims are 3 chldrn, a niece, son, & d/o Anthony Cook, aged respectively 13, 9, & 3 yrs. The parents were at church when the deed was accomplished. A man named Frahm has been arrested. The evidence is very strong against him. It is supposed Frahm murdered them to secure the sum of $2,000 which he knew Cook had, but which the latter took with him. The chldrn were apparently killed with an axe.

The marriage ceremonies of Lt Fred W Bailey, of 17th U S Infty, & Miss Fanny Yorke Atlee, at the Chr of the Epiphany in this city, on Thanksgiving afternoon, was performed by Dr Hall, the pastor of the church. The bridegroom is the s/o the late Dr Bailey, whose name is held in honor in this city. The bride is the only d/o S Yorke Atlee, of this city. The bridesmaids were Miss Fanny Bailey, sister of the bride, & Miss Mary Byington, d/o the late Col Saml Byington, of this city. The former was waited upon by Lt O M Mitchell, s/o the late lamented Gen O M Mitchel, & the latter by Lt S C Plummer, s/o the late lamented Gen Jos B Plummer, & both of them classmates at West Point of the bridegroom & like him in military costume, & now bro ofcrs in the same regt, of which Gen Heitzelman is the col. The bridal party was accompanied to the altar by Miss Julia Wadsworth, escorted by a youthful bro of the bride. Mrs Bailey, the m/o the bride, participated in the occasion. Among the congratulations to the happy pair, we notice Chief Justice Chase & his dght.

The Pres yesterday granted about a 100 pardons, the majority of which were Texans. Brig Gen DeWitt, of Tenn, was one of them.

Rl estate sale on Tue: part of lot 3 in sq 368, N st, between 9th & 10th sts, with improvements, consisting of a brick & frame dwlg hse, for $9,175, to S T J Morsell, the purchaser.

MON DEC 11, 1865
Danl L Gibbons, of Boston, Treas agent at Mobile, committed suicide on Dec 2, by cutting his throat.

Mrd: on Dec 5, by Rev Fr McCarthy, J V N Huyck, of N Y, to Mary M, y/d/o the late Edw Dyer, of Wash City. No cards.

Died: on Dec 9, John Powell, aged 1 yr, 11 mos, & 9 days, y/c/o John C & Mary A V Shafer. Funeral from their residence at 510 14th st, Mon.

Ad-Paperhanger & upholsterer, 464 9th st, Wash, D C. -Geo Willner

Brig Gen J H Martindale has been brevetted Maj Gen for meritorious & distinguished svcs during the war. Capt J J Hoff, Commissary of Subsistence, & at present Super of Freedmen's Affairs in Alexandria, has been brevetted Major for meritorious svcs during the war.

TUE DEC 12, 1865
Mr J R Foley, dealer in china ware etc, 316 F st, Wash, D C.

Obit-died at the Chateau de Claireau, Dept de Loiret, France, on Nov 11, of pleurisy, in her 37th yr, Katharine Macleod, w/o M Alphonse de Bourboulon, formerly Sec of the French Leg at Wash, & more recently the Minister of that Gov't in China.

Robt Jarboe visited the Monumental Hse, on 11th st, recently, & after imbibing too freely, he was relieved of his pocket-book & $100. Geo H Warren, property of the Monumental hse, & a woman named Emma Clark, were arrested as parties to the drugging of Jarboe, & Chas Smithson, Warren's barkeeper, has since given himself up, & all 3 have been held to bail. Jarboe had been put in a hack, driven out of town on Bladensburg rd, & placed upon the ground, the hack returning to the city without him.

Mr S M Glenn, who was reported to have disappeared a day or two since, has finally turned up in Norfolk.

WED DEC 13, 1865
If Henry New, of Marlborough, Wilts, Eng, who emigrated to London, C W, in 1856, & was in N Y in 1859, & in Wash in 1863, will communicate with his bro, Thos New, of Marlborough, information of great importance will be addressed to him.

U S Mrshl's sale of Chas A McEvoy's interest in Patent 13824, & reissue #800, railroad indicator, under confiscation. -D S Gooding, U S Mrshl D C

Mrd: on Dec 12, at St John's Chr, by Rev Dr Lewis, Mr Wm S Teel & Miss Belle Sioussa, eldest d/o Chas Sioussa..

Assessors of Wash:

Thos Donohue	Thos W Burch
Geo W	B F Dyer
Harkness	Chas E Nelson
Wm B Downing	John H Bird

Crmnl Crt, before Judge Fisher. The case of Lusby. Cnsl for John F Lusby, indicted for a heinous offence against Octavie Roseau, called up the case & said the facts were substantialy the same as in the murder case, in which there was an acquittal; & that the trial of that indictment had disposed of the indictment in this case. The D A took the same view, & stated that the Gov't had been at great expense in the matter of the trial, & he would not therefore prosecute any further. A *nolle prosequi* was entered.

Newark Adv states that Maj Gen Kilpatrick will sail for Chili, to which country he has been appt'd Minister, on the 21st inst.

A large congregation assembled at St John's Chr yesterday to witness the nuptials of Mr Wm S Teel & Miss Sioussa. The Rev Dr Lewis officiated.

THU DEC 14, 1865
Enterprising dry-goods firm; Messrs Lansburg & Bro, 515 7th st & 375 7th st, Wash City.

Ad-Attys & Cnslrs-at-Law, La av near 5th st, Wash. -Robt J Brent, of Balt, Md, & Richd T Merrick, of Chicago, Ill.

Mrd: on Dec 11, at Trinity Chr, by Rev Mr Keeling, Brvt Maj Wm Sinclair, of U S army, to Daisie, d/o Wm J McDonald, of Wash City.

Died: after a lingering illness, on Dec 12, Mrs Eliz E Davison, consort of Jos Davison, of Wash City, in her 43rd yr. Mrs Davison was a native of Nottinghamshire, England, where she resided during her minority & a few years after her marriage. She has resided in Washington City for several years. Her remains will be conveyed to the vault in Oak Hill Cemetery on Mon.

Died: on Dec 12, Frank Reynolds Ellis, s/o John F & Mary Ann Ellis, aged 7 years & 8 days. Funeral on Thu from their residence at 430 6th st.

Died: on Dec 13, of congestion of the brain, Jas J Dickens. Funeral from his late residence on L st, on Fri.

The cheapest place to buy prime roll-butter is at Lauckton & Sinsabaugh's cheap grocery store, 533 9th st, opposite Centre Mkt.

FRI DEC 15, 1865
Died: Signor Rovere, buffo-basso of Maretzek's opera troupe, in N Y, on Wed, of disease of the throat.

Trustee's sale of residence in Wash City; in a cause between J W Thompson & others, cmplnts, & Mgt F Lindsay & others, dfndnts. Sale of lot 1 in sq 248, fronting on K st, with 3 story brown front brick dwlg. -C Ingle, trustee -C W Boteler, auct

Rl estate sales: lot 2 in sq 631 to Dr J H Thompson, at 10 cents. Lot 4 in sq 637, to Richd Barry, at
1 5/8 cents. Lot 2 in sq 693 to Richd Barry, at 1 7/8th cents. Lots 7 thru 13 in sq 733, to Dr J H Thompson, at 2 7/8th cents. Lots 18 thru 21 in sq 733 to Dr J H Thompson, at 5½ cents. [These amounts usually refer to "per sq ft.']

SAT DEC 16, 1865
Thos Dowling, auctioneer, sold at auction the following property, in Gtwn, yesterday: 2 old frame hses on Beale st, between Wash & Green sts, to John T Essex, for $930. Small frame hse & lot on Poplar st, to Dennis Sullivan, for $400. Lot adjoining above, to D Gibbon, for $220. Small hse & lot adjoining, to Collin Cruser, for $450. Lot adjoining, to Thornton Yates, for $125.

Rev Thos Balch, a native of Gtwn, delivered his 3rd lecture on reminiscences of Gtwn. His father was Rev Stephen Balch, a grad of Princeton in 1774, who settled in Gtwn. He spoke of mbrs of the early population of Gtwn, known as bachelors; among them John Oakley, who lived in a very yellow hse on a hill; Capt Morton who was captivated by the belle of *Duck Lane*; Parson Allen who came to Gtwn in 1785 & was educated at Glasgow; Capt Thos Brooke Beall who died in 1820, in Cherry alley. Connected from time to time with different Gtwn papers were: Wm A Ryan, Jonathan Finley, Saml Anderson, W P Balch, Wm A Ryan, 2nd, O'Sullivan, Hewes, & Williamson. Old lawyers: Judge Morsell, still living in Calvert Co at great age of at least 90 yrs. Philip Barton Key, born in 1765, was mbr of Congress from Md from 1807 to 1813 & died in Gtwn in 1815; his nephew Francis S Key, was author of the Star Spangled Banner, died in 1843 at age 63 yrs. Also mentioned were Thompson Mason, Geo French, Alfred Balch, & Chas Evans, lawyers of the olden time.

Amos McFarland, engineer on the O & A R R, was fatally injured when he thought he saw an obstruction on the track & jumped off. His body was sent to relations in Westchester, Pa. The obstruction proved to be a hawk.

Died: on Dec 15, at St Vincent's Orphan Asylum, Sister Lucy Ignatius Gwynn, the Superior of the Institution. Funeral from St Patrick's Chr on Mon. [Dec 22 obit: Sister was in her 65th yr; born near Martinsburg, Va, in 1800. In 1823 she came to Gtwn to visit her sister who mrd a Catholic gentleman of that city. This was her first witness of Catholic worship. Her sisters, Mrs Jeffries & Miss Eliz Gwynne, & her bro, Walter Gwynne, late Maj Gen in the Confederate army, & all of Richmond, Va, were present in her final hours. Her Catholic sister died some years since in Gtwn. Funeral was at St Patrick's Chr on Mon; interment in Mt Olivet cemetery.

Died: on Dec 11, at Fort McHenry, Bvt Brig Gen Wm W Morris, U S Army, in his 64th yr. - Balt American

Died: on Dec 14, Mrs Mgt Pratner, aged 73 yrs, w/o Thos Talbert. Funeral from the residence near Uniontown, in Wash Co, on Sun.

Harewood, now the only military hospital in this District, contains between 300 & 400 patients, some of them serious cases. Four companies of the 2nd btln V R C, under Capt D J Durning, are on duty at Harewood.

MON DEC 18, 1865
Police Reports: 1-John Harrington, Michl Shea, John McCauley, Jos Elms, & John Sullivan, boys of from 12 to 14 years of age, were arrested on Fri by Ofcrs Sheerwood & Prall, charged with stealing Gov't sash from the qrtrs on the Aqueduct bridge, & brought before Squire Buckey. The boys were discharged on account of their youth & testified they sold the sash to Columbus C Fearson, a restaurant keeper, opposite the bridge. Fearson was arrested on Sat by Ofcr Sheerwood & held under bail for crt in the sum of $500. 2-John A Lynch, Alfred Snowden, & Martha Dodson were arrested on Fri night for disorderly conduct, & fined $5.50 ea. 3-Saml Harod [colored] was arrested for disorderly conduct & beating his wife's sister, & was fined $10.50. 4-Stephen Bates was arrested on Fri for disorderly conduct & carrying concealed weapons, & was fined $5,50 for disorderly conduct, & $20.50 for carrying concealed weapons.

Notice-the subscriber has obtained letters of adm on the prsnl estate of John B Semmes, late of Wash City, dec'd. -John H Semmes, adm

Died: in Africa, Dr Heinrich Barth, the celebrated African explorer; born in Hamburg in 1821.

Died: on Dec 16, Eleanor May, y/c/o Edmonia & the late John B Semmes, aged 13 months & 25 days. Funeral from the residence of her mother, 392 C st, on Mon.

Providence, Dec 16. Hon Philip Allen, formerly Gov of this State, died here at his residence this morning.

Wash Corp: Ptn of Patrick McHugh was referred to the Cmte on Claims. 2-Resolution of Henry C Kleiber as messenger of the Brd of Alderman for the remainder of the 63rd Cncl: read & adopted. 3-Ptn of E L Dawson: referred to the Cmte on Police. 4-Ptn of N Zange for remission of a fine: referrd to the Cmte on Claims. Ptn of Geo W Taylor: referred to the Cmte on Claims.

Fearful tragedy in Mississippi. Eight or 10 years since Jas Thompson left Brownsville, Mississippi & is supposed to have entered the army of Peru. He recently returned home, & has been organizing a company for Brazil, obtaining deeds of his father's property, & converting it into money. His father has been trying to stay these proceedings, but quite secretly. The family consisted of his step-mother, 3 half-sisters, a half bro, & a full bro, Jos, suspected of being an accomplice in a terrible tragedy. On Sun recently, Jas entered the hse with a shot-gun & killed Mgt, & the mother was then shot dead. His bro, Clay, was shot & killed instantly. Jemima was fatally shot, & Emma, the youngest, was fearfully mangled. Jas then met his father & fired twice, but without effect. He was seized & with difficulty was carried thru the incensed crowd to jail.

TUE DEC 19, 1865
Despatch to the Chicago Tribune conveys that Col Wm A Barstow, 3rd Wisc cavalry, & formerly Govn'r of that state, died at Leavenworth, on the 13th inst, of chronic diarrhoea, contracted while in the svc. He was about 60 years of age, & for a time on Gen Fremont's staff.

New Boot, Shoe & Hat store-Messrs J T McGlue, jr, & Co, just opened at 16 Pa av, Wash.

A Pretty Fancy Store-Mr H J McLaughlin, 353 7th st, Wash, D C; fancy millinery goods, laces, trimmings, hosiery.

Christmas Presents-Mr John E Prigg, 438 Pa av, Wash, D C; any article for $1.00.

Mrs R E Lee has sold her farm, near Warrenton, to Dr Drewry, of Richmond, at $40 per ac. It contains about 800 acs mkg the entire price about $32,000.

Explosion yesterday at the Arsenal bldg, Wash, D C, has killed 9 men & wounded 3. Killed were:

Jeremiah	Marshal	Michl	Thos Fealey
Mahoney	Whiteley	McDermott	Peter McGarry
Patrick Reardon	Jas Moran	John Meahan	
		Martin Coyle	
Wounded:			
Jas Lawler	Jas Crane	Chas Lynn	

Mrd: on Dec 12, in Hampshire Co, W Va, by Rev Dr Foote, David G Armstrong to Miss Hannah Gibson, d/o David Gibson, both of Hampshire.

Mrd: on Dec 16, by Rev R J Keeling, Littleton Morgan Mills to Miss Laura E Peyton; also at the same time, Henry D Gunther, jr, to Miss Laura Curtis, all of Fredericksburg, Va.

Mrd: on Dec 16, by Rev R J Keeling, Thos Wm Lion, of Va, to Miss Somerville Williams, of Fauquier.

WED DEC 20, 1865
Orphans Crt of Wash Co, D C. Ptn of Isaac Talks, guardian to the infants of Thos Hollidge; ratify sale of rl estate reported-lots 29 thru 34 in sq 511, Wash, D C. -Wm F Purcell, Judge of Orphans Crt -Z C Rollins, rg o/wills

Mrd: Dec 18th, by Rev W W Campbell, Mr Wm W Bailey to Miss Julia E Vernon, all of Wash City.

Died: Dec 19th, Miss Emily A Pearce, of Gtwn, D C. Funeral from 117 Prospect st, on Wed.

Died: on Dec 19, Sallie Rebecca, d/o Wm N & E H Rowe, in her 7th yr. Funeral from the residence of her grandfather, Thos Havenner, 347 C st, Wed.

THU DEC 21, 1865
Important rl estate sale: to take place today at the auction rms of C W Boteler, jr, of the large & valuable homestead of the late Washington Berry, called "*Metropolis View*," containing 376 acs, with valuable improvements: located on the old Bladensburg & Rock Creek roads. The property has been subdivided into 40 lots, averaging from 5 to 35 acs each.

Providence, R I, Dec 20. Saml Ames, for 10 years Chief Justice of the R I Supreme Crt, died suddenly this afternoon of apoplexy. He resigned last month on account of ill health.

Sup Crt of D C, Equity #326. Geo A Wills & others against Mary Wills, Chas Schneck & others. Statement of the acc't of the late John Wills on Jan 3, City Hall, Wash, D C. -W Redin, auditor

The funeral of the late Hon Thos Corwin took place on Dec 20, from the residence of Jas C Wetmore, Ohio State agent, on F st, Wash City. Relatives of the dec'd present: his dght, son-in-law, & bro-in-law, his nephew & niece, Mr & Mrs Ross. Interment will be in Lebanon, Ohio.

Died: Dec 20th, Mary Ann Forteney, w/o E W Forteney. Funeral from her late residence on I st, Fri.

Died: on Dec 19, in her 59th yr, Mrs Caroline Spencer, w/o Geo D Spencer. Funeral from her late residence at 387 6th st, Thu.

Died: on Dec 20, of dropsy, Valentine Blanchard, in his 51st yr. He leaves a widow & 5 chldrn to mourn his loss. Funeral from his late residence on G st, Dec 22.

Mrs Martha Page, d/o Gen B M Prentiss, committed suicide yesterday by jumping into a cistern at her father's residence at Elm & 5th sts. -Quincy [Ill] Herald, Dec 13

Senate: 1-Ptn of Dr Cheever, Parker, Pillsbury, & others, for equality before the law in the Southern States: referred to the Spec Cmte of Fifteen. 2-The Hse bill for the payment to Mrs Lincoln of $25,000: was passed.

Peaceful avocations of Ex-Generals. Burnside has gone into the railroad business at Reno & Pithole. Carl Schurz is a Washington correspondent. Sigel has become editor of a Balt paper. Franklin is superintending the Colt's armory at Hartford. W H Smith, the famous cavalry leader, has gone into the retail grocery trade at Chicago. Partick has returned to the plough; Ferrero leading the art of dancing, & Percy Wyndham is again a fencing mstr. As for the late rebel Generals, Buckner, of Ky, is now assoc editor of a New Orleans paper; Gardiner, of Port Hudson memory, is a local reporter; while the Gen who drove off Franklin & his 15,000 men at Sabine is a barkeeper at Houston. Gen G F Anderson opened a butcher's stall at Atlanta, but has become an auctioneer at Augusta. Gen B M Thomas, a West Point grad, is a clerk on a steamer plying between Mobile & Montgomery. Forrest & Wheeeler, the 2 most prominent cavalry leaders after the death of Stuart, are employed, the former running a saw mill in Tenn, & the latter doing a commission business at Augusta. Gen Lee may be seen every day at Lexington, Va, quietly walking to his duties at the college, or taking an evening ride on his famous iron grey. He has been boarding at the hotel, but his house is now being fitted in suitable style for the reception of his family. Ex-Gov Letcher may also be seen daily on the streets there, quietly smoking his pipe, & talking with his old friends & neighbors. -Exchange

FRI DEC 22, 1865
Mr Richd S Spofford, of the Atty Gen Dept, was mrd on Dec 21, at Newbury-port, Mass, to Miss Harriet Prescott, the well known authoress.

Mrd: on Dec 14, at Church Hill, So Garden, Albemarle Co, Va, the residence of the bride's grandfather, Mr B P Suddarth, by Rev Geo C Vanderslice, Mr John H Hobgood, of Tunica, La, & Miss Jennie, d/o the late John Toole, artist, of Charlottesville, Va.

Mrd: on Dec 20, at Wesley Chapel, by Rev Dr B H Nadal, Mr Wheaton H Race, of Binghamton,
N Y, to Miss Maria C Wollard, of Wash City.

Copy of the obituary of Sister Lucy Ignatius Gwynn, Superior of St Vincent's Orphan Asylum, Wash, on the 15th inst, in her 65th yr: may be found in the Dec 22nd paper.

Mr Jas R Crew, a distinguished ctzn of Atlanta, Ga, & a candidate for Mayor, was recently murdered by some unknown person. The city cncl has offered a reward of $1,000 for the apprehension of the murderer.

Maj Ben Perley Poore, compiler of the Congressional Director for the first session of the 39th Congress, has our thanks for a copy. We find it of much value for reference. [Ben is not an abrev.]

Columbus [Ohio] Jrnl, of Dec 18, says that Mr John S Rarey, of Groveport, was on Sat attacked with paralysis: the left side is implicated. At last accounts he was slightly improving in his condition, although still unable to communicate intelligibly.

Long Branch, N J, Dec 21. The schnr *Eveline Hickey*, Capt Fisher, of Phil, bound to Pawtucket, R I, with a cargo of coal, went ashore at Long Branch, & has gone to pieces. The Capt, his wife, & 2 men were lost. Two of the crew were saved.

SAT DEC 23, 1865

U S Patent Ofc. Ptn of Lewis Lewis,of Vicksburg, Miss, for extension of patent dt'd Mar 2, 1852; improvement in *Cotton Presses*. -T C Theaker, Com'r of Pats

Sup Crt of D C, in Equity. John Hazel & Zachariah Hazel vs Richd Prout, Wm D Prout, Mary C Prout, Danl F Prout, John T Vinson & Fannie R Vinson his wife. Z Hazel, dec'd, purchased lots 12 thru 18 in sq 867 from Wm Prout for $100, of which $10 was pd. Hazel died before completing the payments, after devising lot 13 to cmplnts. Prout died leaving Rachel Prout, his widow, & said Wm D Prout, Mary C Prout, David F Prout, & Fannie R Vinson, his chldrn & heirs. Heirs are non-residents. Pray for trustee to be appt'd. -R J Meigs, clerk

Mrd: on Dec 21, by Rev L D Herron, Mr John S Petty, of Columbus, Ohio, formerly of Lancaster Co, Pa, & Miss Sallie A, d/o Geo R Hunt, of Long Green Valley, Balt Co, Md.

Died: on Dec 23, after a long & painful illness, Harriet, w/o Jas Y Davis. Funeral from her late residence at 412 6th st, Sun.

Albert Wise, Micky Cooley, Martin Welsh, & Wm Smith, were arrested yesterday on suspicion of having been engaged in the robbery of the paymstr at the First Ntl Bank, all being well known to the police. -Local Item

The return of Edwin Booth to the stage will take place on Jan 3rd, at the Winter Garden, N Y, where he will play Hamlet.

Savannah, Dec 22. The trial of Gen H W Mercer, charged with murder in shooting 7 U S prisoners at Savannah last Dec, has been temporarily suspended. The authorities are awaiting orders from Washington.

The remains of Pres Lincoln were removed yesterday from their receptacle vault at Oakridge Cemetery, Springfield, to the new vault erected near the site of the proposed monument. The remains of Lincoln's chldrn were placed in the same vault. Robt Lincoln & the Dirs of the Nat'l Monument Assoc were present at the removal.

N Y, Dec 22. In the case of the Union Bank against Ketchum & Sons today, the Supreme Crt rendered a verdict against the latter in the sum of $256,000.

Gtwn [D C] Cncl: Resolution in favor of Jesse Lipscomb, remitting a fine imposed by Justice Buckey: passed. 2-Resolution authorizing a flag footway across Fred'k st: passed.

The store of Messrs Geo W Beall & Bro, corner of Canal & Bridge sts, was broken into on Thu & robbed of a considerable amount: estimated at $500.

Raleigh, Dec 23. The mail train on the N C rd ran off near Concord on Fri, killing J A White, express messenger, & Mr Oats, the baggage mstr. Other particulars are not known.

MON DEC 25, 1865

For sale-the dower of the estate of the late John W Brown, called *White House*, 213 acs 1 mile from Beltsville, Md. -Sarah A Brown, Beltsville, Md

Wash Corp: 1-Ptn of Mrs E Dillon: referred to the Cmte on Claims. 2-Act for the relief of John Wunderlich: read 3 times & passed. Brd adjourned.

U S Patent Ofc. Ptn of Nicholas Taliaferro, of Augusta, Ky, & Wm D Cummings, of Maysville, Ky; extension of patent dated Mar 20, 1852; improvement in *Smoothing-Irons*. -T C Theaker, com'r of patents

Died: on Dec 24, Mrs Eliza Cassin, consort of the late Jos Cassin, U S navy, aged 77 yrs. Funeral from the residence of Mrs H H Boone, 541 H st, Tue.

The Sec of War has conferred the brevetship of Brig Gen upon our esteemed fellow-ctzn, Maj Morris S Miller, Q M, U S A, for faithful & meritorious svcs. Maj Miller graduated in 1834, & has been connected with the Q M Dept for the last 20 yrs.

R Semmes, late Cmder of the rebel cruiser *Alabama*, was announced some days since: charge-violating the usages of war. Specification: About Jun 19, 1864, off the entrance of the port of Cherbourg, France, the said Raphael Semmes being then in command of the rebel steamer *Alabama*, & an engagement having taken place between the steamer & the U S steamer *Kearsarge*, ordered or permitted a white flag to be hoisted on board the rebel steamer, & took the opportunity of the cassation thereby caused in the engagement, & of the trust reposed in him, to make his escape from the said rebel steamer, for the purpose of avoiding the actual surrender of his person as a prisoner of war, & the responsibilites thereby incurred, & did subsequently, without having been exchanged as a prisoner, engaged in hostilities against the U S; -Gideon Welles, Sec of the Navy.

We are pleased to learn that Col J J Dana, Col A J Perry, & Col B C Card, have been brevetted Brig Gens in the regular army for faithful & meritorious svcs during the war.

Val collection of oil paintings was sold by auction in N Y on Wed: bidding was spirited. *The Musical Soiree*, by Oswald Edrmann: $1,200. *Au Revoir*, by Carl Becker: $1,000. *Thisbe*, by Carl Bewer: $700. *Love's Secretary*, by C Hubner: $580.

Prolonged litigation in the Crct Crt, on Sat, Judge Olin presiding: case of Emily F Wiley, vs Marshal Brown & others, was brought to a determination by a verdict in favor of Mrs Wiley. The parties being among our best known citizens, & the amount of property involved being very considerable.

At Trinity Chr last evening, the 66 burners did not give sufficient light to enable one to see distinctly across the room, & it was with great difficulty that Dr Keeling could see to read his notes. It is time the gas company should thoroughly examine the cause of the deficiency of light, & remedy the defects.

WED DEC 27, 1865

Sup Crt of D C, Equity # 54. Richd Lay, exc of Thos Carbery, against Jos C Ives & Cora, his wife, Edw O'Connor, & Thos J Fisher. Statement of trustee's account on Jan 17 at City Hall, Wash, D C. -W S Cox, Spec Auditor

Orphans Crt of Wash Co, D C. Case of Harriet Williamson, admx of Benj Williamson, dec'd; settlement on Jan 13. -Z C Robbins, rg o/wills

Mrd: on Dec 21, at the Reformed Dutch Chr, 23rd st, N Y C, by Rev Dr Ganse, G M Van Buren, of Wash, D C, to Gertrude B Van Buren, of the former place.

Died: on Dec 25, Henry Garner, colored, for nearly 20 years the sexton of Trinity [P E] Chr in Wash City. Funeral today.

The main portion of the old frig *Merrimac*, with her propellar, weighing 10 tons, & 30 tons of composition, have been raised by D A Underwood & Co & taken to the Portsmouth Navy Yard.

On Sun Mr Francis Smith, a provision merchant at Wmsburgh, L I, was robbed & shot at his residence, 246 south First st. He had brought from his store the previous evening the sum of $1,220, which fact was no doubt known to the robber. Mr Smith was lying in a very precarious condition at last accounts. One ball entered near the backbone, another taking effect in the pelvis.

Wash City News: Navy Yd. The U S steamer *De Soto* comes here for some slight repairs, & is expected to leave again, on Sat next, for Havana & the West Indies. Accurate list of her ofcrs:

Capt, Wm M Walker, commanding	Lts Geo W Sumner, John J Read
Lt Cmder & Exec Ofcr, John A Howell	Actg Mstr, J J Brice
Actg Ensigns, Orlando S Roberts, Paul Armandt, Fred J Locks, A J Kane	
Paymstr, Geo Cochran	Past Ast Surg, B H Kidder
Actg Chief Engr, Geo F Hebard	
Actg 1st Ast Engrs Theo D Coffee	
Actg 2nd Ast Engrs, W J Garrington & Chas C Koehl	
Actg 3rd Ast Engrs, Christopher McCormick & A D Renshaw	
Btswn, Chas Miller	Capt's Clerk, Chas J Pibbetts
Gunner, Jos Venable	Paymstr's Clerk, Geo H Lewis
Mate, R G Lawman	

Riot in Alexandria on Christmas day, by a party of drunken negroes, who broke the door of Mr Mankins' hse on corner of Patrick & Cameron sts. Mr Mankins fired at the party, killing one & wounding another. The disturbance spread, & several negroes are reported killed. The military was orderd out by the Mayor to quell the disturbance.

THU DEC 28, 1865

Brig Gen Champion Vaughan, formerly of Kansas, attempted to commit suicide by swallowing poison on Sat in St Louis. His life was saved by the prompt administration of an antidote. Gen Vaughan is the son of John C Vaughan, & served on the staff of Gen Curtis & Gen Blunt during the war.

Died: Capt Clement L West, at his residence on H st, Dec 26, in his 34th yr. Funeral from his late residence at 237 H st, Fri. He has been for a number of years connected with the architect's ofc, Capitol Extension. During the war he was appointed an ast q m, with the rank of Capt, which he resigned, & was appointed genr'l superintendent & disbursing clerk of the work on the Capitol Extension. His many friends will regret to learn of his death.

Affairs at Ellicott's Mills: copied from the Howard Co Record. Meeting by the employees of the Union, Gray's Granite, & Thistle factories, on Thur night, to present a ptn to the employers of said factories, asking the adoption of the ten hour system. Meeting organized by calling Abel Mitchell to the chair, & appointing C Herman sec. On motion of Mr C Webb, the following cmte, composed of 2 from each factory, were appointed to draft resolutions in favor of the 10 hour system, signed by the overseers, & present them to their respective employers:

Thos Webb	J Walters	C Webb	J Kirkwood
C Herman	W H Keyes	D Wilson	
B Burgee	G Curtis	A Mitchell	

1st Lt Terence Riley, 4th U S Artl, one of the ofcrs crt-martialed recently for occasioning the disturbance at Rush Barracks, on the 18th ult, has been dismissed the svc, the crt having found him guilty of the violation of the 9th article of war, conduct to the prejudice of good order & military discipline, & mutinous conduct. Maj Gen Augur, commanding the Dept, has approved the findings & sentence, & he therefore stands dismissed.

Drowned: a young man named Barnes, aged about 20 yrs, fell from the Market-st Bridge into the Canal on Christmas day, & was drowned.

N Y, Dec 27. Today Patrick McLaughlin & his family, consisting of his wife & 3 chldrn & niece, were poisoned by drinking a large dose of laudanum placed in the coffee used at breakfast. Mr McLaughlin & one dght came near losing their lives; the former is still in a precarious state.

Wash City: 1-Act for relief of Saml Gregg: sum of $223.20 to be pd for his work & labor rendered & money expended on 9th st west, between F & H sts south, as per contract with this Corp.

FRI DEC 29, 1965
Mrd: on Dec 28, at the residence of the bride's father, by Rev P D Gurley, Mr Henry C Shuster to Miss Helen M, d/o E H Fuller, all of Wash City.

President's Reception on New Years Day: reception of citizens will commence at 12 o'clock, at which hour the gates of the enclosure will be opened, & will terminate at 2 p m. Ladies will be received. Carriages will approach the exec Mansion by the east gate & leave by the West gate.

Bshp Rosecrans was shot at & slightly wounded, on Sat last, as he left the Cathedral to go to his home at the Catholic Seminary, near Sodamsville. He was accosted by 2 men who demanded his money. He made no reply but hastened his pace to a run, when he was fired at, the ball taking effect in the leg, just above the knee. Even this did not stop the Bishop, who succeeded in making good his escape. No clue as to who the perpetrators were. - Cincinnati Gaz, 25th.

Gtwn Cncl: resolution in favor of certain persons: authorizing payment to John Kaiser-$80 for repairs of pumps: to John Hess-$80.20 for removing dead horses; to Jos Libby-$74.48 for material for repair of Chain Bridge; to Robt Williams-$49.76, bal due him for repairing second alley from Congress to High st; to Bazil Burrows-$3 for repairing pavement in New Mkt; as per bills rendered.

Died: Dec 26, at West Phil, Harriet Butler, d/o the late Rev David Butler, D D, of Troy, N Y.

SAT DEC 30, 1865

Died: Richd Moring, late Maj of the 69th N Y regt, at Post Hosp last night. -Richmond, Dec 29

Jas Duncan Graham, a bro-in-l of Maj Gen Meade, & Col U S Engineers, stationed at Boston, died suddenly in this city of disease of the heart last evening. -Boston, Dec 20

Mr Jas Shepherd, who had his arm badly shattered on Christmas day by the bursting of a gun, has died of his injuries. He leaves a widow & 4 chldrn. -Local Item

Died: on Dec 28, after a long & painful illness, Jas A Fletcher, eldest s/o the late John Fletcher, in his 34th yr. Funeral from his residence on 10th st, Sat.

Died: at Flower Hill, on Dec 16, at the residence of her son, Edwin M Muncaster, near Rockville, Montg Co, Md, Mrs Harriet Muncaster, in her 83rd yr.

The Brd of Met Police Com'rs have dismissed Ofcr G W Hurdle, of the 3rd Precinct, for intoxication & gambling. T J Stele, of the 10th Precinct, was fined & ordered to be reprimanded by the Superintendant, for violation of the rules. Jas E Arnold, 8th Precinct, fined for neglect of duty. The charges against patrolmen Rossiter & Bresnaham, 5th Precinct, & Ofcr J W Davis, 8th Precinct, were dismissed.

Rev Louis R Fox to be installed Pastor of the North Presby Chr, tomorrow at 3 o'clock. Rev Dr Gurley is to preside. Rev John Chester & Rev A A E Taylor will participate.

Raphael Semmes, late commander of the Confederate vessel *Alabama*, which was sent to the bottom of the sea in an engagement with the U S steamer *Kearsage*, arrived in this city Thu night in custody of Lt L P French & Sgts Cassidy & Jones of the Marine Corps. He was arrested by Lt French on the 15th inst at his residence at Spring Hill, near Mobile, & was at the time sitting in his parlor perusing a newspaper. When informed of the object of his visit, Semmes expressed much surprise, claimed his arrest was in violation of his parole which had been freely given & accepted. Semmes' dghts were very bitter in their denunciations of the arrest. Lt French gave Semmes 12 to 15 hours to prepare for his departure. He was then taken to Mobile & placed on the steamer *Louisa* for New Orleans, whence he was brought on the steamer *Costa Rica* for N Y, arriving at the latter city on Wed. He was placed under guard in a room temporarily fitted up near the Dispensary bldg in the Navy Yd, but it is expected that he will today be removed to more commodious qrtrs adoining the Chapel. This room has been heretofore used for crt-martial purposes.

The Queen of England has a special private fortune of a qrtr of a million pounds left her by a Mr Neeld. We hope she will speedily give it to people about her who need it more & will know better than a Queen what to do with it.

Bozzel, 173
Braccler, 206
Bracken, 292
Brackett, 239, 358
Bradbury, 509
Braddel, 320
Braden, 44, 491
Brader, 10, 523
Bradfield, 546
Bradford, 64, 80, 169, 178, 197, 245, 246, 357, 444, 492
Bradley, 13, 17, 30, 40, 48, 52, 68, 76, 79, 83, 97, 101, 120, 121, 154, 161, 169, 181, 202, 207, 231, 238, 240, 259, 271, 298, 309, 313, 330, 331, 376, 390, 395, 411, 412, 415, 420, 437, 443, 463, 469, 470, 480, 499, 501, 509, 517, 533
Bradshaw, 224
Bradshears, 540
Brady, 7, 19, 43, 97, 238, 263, 275, 321, 399, 516
Brafford, 90
Bragan, 498
Bragg, 24, 50, 66, 79, 125, 188, 225, 289, 343, 350, 489
Braiden, 219
Brailor, 207
Brainard, 434
Braine, 277
Brainer, 497
Brainley, 540
Braker, 262
Bramhall, 225
Bramlett, 374
Bramlette, 20, 99, 192, 227
Branagan, 236
Branan, 109
Branch, 102, 373, 472
Brandon, 240
Brandt, 221, 229, 360
Brannan, 48, 341
Brannigan, 206
Brannin, 45, 53
Brannon, 69, 108, 227
Branson, 424

Branstitter, 361
Brant, 333
Brashear, 341, 349, 451, 526, 546
Brashears, 485
Brashers, 75
Brass, 494, 498
Brate, 313
Brattan, 300
Brauer, 287
Brauner, 68
Brawner, 145, 491
Braxton, 395
Brayson, 254
Brazoel, 393
Breck, 39, 319
Breckenridge, 130, 372
Breckinridge, 67, 93, 229, 268, 270, 351, 420, 515
Breed, 310
Breen, 338
Breese, 172, 181
Breest, 322
Bremer, 373, 484
Brener, 336
Brengle, 207
Brennan, 217, 434, 435, 453
Brennard, 90, 203
Brennemann, 263
Brennen, 27
Brenner, 421
Brent, 2, 32, 63, 107, 110, 158, 209, 220, 267, 273, 275, 296, 315, 395, 411, 412, 549
Brereton, 18, 78, 450, 464, 505
Bresbey, 226
Breshear, 521
Breshnahan, 207
Breslyn, 78
Bresnaham, 558
Bresnehan, 321
Brest, 69
Brett, 316
Brewer, 15, 157, 260, 274, 277, 532
Brewis, 17, 84
Brewser, 297
Brewster, 47, 285, 476, 513

Brice, 14, 355, 384, 556
Brick, 355, 443
Brickley, 283
Brickyard Hill, 460
Bridge, 494
Bridgers, 89
Bridges, 494, 528
Bridget, 10, 206
Bridgett, 326
Bridgette, 2
Bridgman, 420
Brien, 88, 224, 239, 288
Brier, 262
brig Bainbridge, 32
brig Carricks, 519
brig Sea Foam, 324
Brigg, 315
Briggs, 111, 137, 201, 226, 249, 360, 418, 494
Brigham, 29, 111, 282, 360, 481, 499
Bright, 34, 194, 302, 391, 395, 466, 542
Brightbill, 387
Brignardello, 167
Brindee, 338
Brindley, 242
Briner, 445
Bringler, 79
Brinkerhoff, 383, 391
Brinn, 27
Brinsmade, 298
Brinton, 70, 217
Brisby, 493
Briscoe, 88, 177, 416, 417, 423, 507
Britan, 63, 138
British Parliament, 367
Britt, 408, 424, 430
Brittan, 108, 137
Britton, 358
Broadhead, 101, 227
Broadwater, 491
Brocchus, 78, 119
Brock, 137, 138, 282
Brockenborough, 535
Brockenbrough, 533
Brockett, 137
Brodeau, 465
Broderick, 240, 338
Broders, 536

Gidson, 311
Giesboro, 359
Giesborough Manor, 8
Gifford, 16, 30, 417, 423
Gilbert, 132, 134, 140, 170,
    177, 192, 194, 225, 227,
    280, 309, 330, 338, 344,
    368, 477, 495, 542
Gilchrist, 178
Gildersleeve, 2
Gile, 359
Giles, 238, 278, 425
Gilfillen, 339
Gilford, 108, 495
Gilgore, 235
Gilham, 444
Gillespie, 222
Gillett, 323, 331, 357
Gillette, 13, 325, 357, 413,
    537
Gilliam, 547
Gilling, 382
Gillinn, 344
Gillion, 344
Gillis, 101, 224, 344, 354,
    469
Gillison, 536
Gilliss, 264, 342, 503
Gillmore, 196, 197, 215,
    350
Gilman, 52, 145, 153, 307,
    355, 391, 395, 409, 432,
    466
Gilmer, 89, 332, 419, 435
Gilmor, 223, 241, 291, 476
Gilmore, 227, 473, 500
Gilpin, 46, 146
Gindall, 325
Ginnaty, 519
Ginuaty, 72
Gip, 457
Girare, 94
Gist, 304, 367
Gittings, 29, 316, 349, 483
Given, 323, 461, 462
Giveny, 347, 349
Gladding, 124
Gladman, 72, 232
Gladmon, 80, 368
Glasgow, 124
Glass, 89, 278, 345, 495

Glassett, 62
Glasspoole, 161
Gleason, 128, 221, 258,
    325, 517, 542
Glen Allen, 51
Glenn, 63, 77, 209, 548
Glenwood Cemetery, 143,
    204, 229, 314, 371, 410,
    469, 534
Gleson, 139
Gleverson, 477
Glidden, 325
Glossbrenner, 269
Glymont, 461
Glynn, 212
Gobright, 356, 428
Goddard, 1, 55, 141, 229,
    367, 382, 402, 432, 450,
    459, 510, 512
Goddess of Freedom, 91
Godding, 13
Godey, 125, 349, 410
Godfrey, 65, 168, 187, 249
Godsen, 240
Gody, 308
Goenther, 423
Goff, 154, 339, 387
Gofferman, 230
Gogan, 237
Goggin, 315, 460
Goheen, 140
Gohlson, 15
Goings, 540
Goit, 400
Gold, 434, 460
Golden, 29, 43, 373, 447,
    511
Goldin, 325
Goldsborough, 76, 78, 101,
    216, 222, 223, 229
Goldsmith, 108, 265, 456,
    480
Gollinghoffer, 320
Gomez, 168
Gonzaga College, 36, 187
Good, 465, 466
Good_ow, 106
Goodall, 313, 409
Goode, 444
Goodell, 544
Gooden, 137, 180, 219

Goodenow, 153, 355
Goodin, 194
Gooding, 161, 224, 430,
    452, 548
Goodloe, 13, 186, 356,
    359, 395
Goodman, 389
Goodnough, 71
Goodnow, 144, 203, 472
Goodrell, 459
Goodrich, 213, 231, 346,
    368, 385, 495
Goodridge, 343
Goodwin, 63, 144, 203,
    260, 373
Goodyear, 495
Goosbeck, 338
Gord, 133
Gordon, 13, 37, 68, 93,
    188, 189, 225, 230, 242,
    260, 261, 271, 282, 288,
    291, 302, 304, 310, 313,
    340, 364, 365, 389, 400,
    423, 503, 512, 529, 530,
    538, 540, 541, 546
Gorgas, 386
Gorman, 192, 202, 364
Goroun, 545
Goss, 126, 175
Goszler, 8, 46, 127
Gotchell, 194
Gough, 5, 94, 168, 178,
    403, 422, 454, 523
Gould, 145, 163, 532
Gouley, 313
Gouverneur, 501, 504
Goven, 264
Gowen, 238, 239
Gowim, 233
Grace, 69
Graff, 416
Grafton, 518
Graham, 2, 8, 14, 20, 61,
    77, 83, 99, 119, 128,
    164, 196, 216, 273, 287,
    305, 317, 333, 336, 340,
    355, 356, 363, 396, 409,
    410, 418, 442, 454, 459,
    468, 482, 495, 533, 558
Grahan, 495
Grahm, 238

Haywood, 18
Hazard, 150, 170, 222, 274
Hazel, 121, 237, 313, 425, 554
Hazell, 546
Hazen, 340
Hazzard, 44, 71
Head, 6, 487
Headley, 349
Heahly, 518
Heal, 178
Healey, 224
Healin, 325
Healy, 95, 213, 230, 314, 496
Heap, 84
Heard, 196, 235, 355, 446
Hearn, 25, 60
Heath, 386, 474, 490
Heaton, 47
Heaver, 170
Hebard, 217, 556
Hebart, 9
Hebron, 484
Heca, 80
Heck, 379, 445
Heckman, 193
Heckner, 406
Hedrick, 358
Hee, 99
Heenan, 85
Heffley, 199
Hefflin, 215
Heffner, 32
Heffron, 268
Hegginbotham, 248
Heigh, 316
Heik, 78
Heil, 243
Heilberger, 325
Heilburn, 299
Heile, 305
Heilkamp, 456
Heinicke, 322
Heinrichs, 423
Heintzelman, 62, 114
Heironimus, 490
Heiss, 471
Heist, 207
Heister, 269, 308
Heiston, 367

Heitzelman, 547
Helbig, 335
Heldreth, 218
Heliker, 496
Hellen, 217, 231, 468, 518
Hellens, 328
Heller, 379
Hellman, 289
Hellmuth, 389
Helm, 49, 51, 479
Helmick, 306, 353, 533
Helmuth, 47
Hemans, 353
Hemenway, 496
Hemming, 263
Hempsey, 319
Hemstreet, 243
Hemsworth, 65
Henckler, 26
Henderson, 61, 94, 152, 157, 175, 179, 209, 216, 261, 357, 428, 442, 444, 474, 488, 493, 522
Hendlin, 154
Hendly, 396
Hendrick, 178
Hendricks, 94, 137, 288
Hendrickson, 522
Heneline, 319
Heney, 381
Henig, 177, 212
Henkle, 123
Henlein, 338
Henley, 314
Hennan, 77
Hennel, 498
Hennessey, 327
Henning, 200, 291, 368, 442
Henricks, 324
Henriques, 476
Henry, 27, 133, 194, 220, 228, 240, 286, 315, 332, 334, 481, 495, 537
Henry IV, 411
Hensel, 243
Henshaw, 410, 487
Hensley, 285
Henson, 238
Hensor, 522
Henstreet, 496

Hepburn, 121, 451, 467, 483, 484, 492, 498, 529
Herald, 274
Herb, 496
Herbert, 183, 214, 228, 229, 246, 335, 338, 368, 402, 440, 510
Hercus, 9
Heriel, 409
Herman, 22, 285, 391, 557
Hermitage, 411, 521
Hermitage Plantation, 208
Herndon, 390
Herne, 59
Hernsworth, 60
Herold, 268, 411, 412, 418, 421, 422, 423, 428, 430, 439, 445, 535
Heron, 100
Herran, 2
Herrick, 173, 183
Herrill, 425
Herring, 477
Herrington Manor, 526
Herrod, 77
Herrold, 403, 405
Herron, 495, 554
Hertford, 371, 401
Hertrich, 335
Hervey, 57
Herzberg, 533
Herzoy, 288
Heskell, 520
Hess, 121, 297, 334, 423, 467, 495, 509, 510, 527, 557
Hesse, 427
Hessler, 328
Hessmer, 330
Hestlake, 240
Heston, 305
Heth, 64, 185
Hetzel, 223
Heustis, 355, 452
Hevlin, 341
Hewes, 550
Hewett, 252, 496
Hewison, 304
Hewitt, 45
Heydon, 381
Heywood, 372

Ossinger, 375
Osterhaus, 10, 23
Ostrander, 263
Otis, 506
Otterach, 391
Otterback, 63, 187, 219, 395
Otts, 232
Ould, 1, 88, 96, 103, 148, 155, 303, 386
Ourand, 454
Overhold, 346
Overhouser, 496
Overreach, 276
Owen, 64, 96, 104, 139, 181, 194, 195, 200, 244, 270, 352, 370, 416, 425, 458, 474
Owens, 65, 66, 75, 87, 131, 185, 192, 194, 200, 328, 385, 395, 516, 517
Owner, 310
Oxen Hill Manor, 41
Oxford, 110
Oxley, 491
Oyster, 187, 395, 418

P

Paca, 366
Pachard, 501
packet *Flying Cloud*, 218
Padget, 300
Padgett, 1, 84, 214, 229, 312, 366, 539
Page, 25, 51, 91, 229, 284, 287, 320, 330, 374, 396, 409, 432, 444, 458, 480, 552
Paine, 21, 70, 73, 121, 197, 221, 295, 361, 438
Paint Hill, 52
Painter, 356
Palacois, 462
Palfrey, 443
Palmer, 48, 79, 97, 119, 123, 211, 248, 251, 259, 300, 328, 477, 530, 534
Palmerston, 515, 525
Palmerton, 207
Palxer, 39
Pancoast, 464

Papier, 319
Paradise, 526
Pare, 530
Parish, 46
Park, 496, 526
Parke, 18, 30, 355, 379, 407, 460
Parker, 15, 47, 48, 49, 55, 66, 76, 86, 101, 103, 106, 116, 118, 135, 136, 175, 187, 210, 215, 240, 278, 283, 300, 321, 329, 339, 342, 345, 364, 389, 390, 391, 396, 406, 409, 410, 417, 436, 442, 443, 444, 469, 484, 489, 496, 503, 512, 524, 533, 537, 542, 553
Parkhurst, 332
Parkinson, 240, 329, 463, 473
Parkison, 139, 140
Parks, 156, 213, 215, 291, 362, 365, 496
Parlow, 222
Parmenter, 496
Parmer, 401
Parmly, 346
Paroley, 477
Parran, 327
Parris, 330
Parrish, 258, 460, 496
Parrott, 75, 509
Parry, 105
Parshall, 319, 320
Parsons, 57, 78, 216, 247, 248, 273, 299, 301, 355, 383, 454
Partick, 553
Partlow, 170, 266
Partridge, 111, 350, 496
Pascoe, 214, 228
Pascue, 359
Pasha, 362
Passagger, 450
Passmore, 202
Patch, 114, 349, 380, 496
Pate, 188
Pateman, 498
Paten, 515
Paterson, 46

Patrick, 496
Patten, 41, 72, 214, 341, 386, 531
Patterson, 19, 103, 130, 170, 192, 258, 330, 381, 382, 403, 434, 440, 459, 473, 515, 517, 520
Patton, 13, 52, 443
Paul, 2, 5, 35, 41, 47, 65, 192, 331, 347, 477
Paulding, 112, 146, 355, 505
Paxson, 457, 489
Paxton, 90, 120, 335, 533
Payne, 118, 120, 144, 220, 286, 288, 343, 365, 383, 386, 411, 412, 417, 424, 425, 428, 429, 431, 439, 477, 482, 516, 535, 545
Payson, 523
Payton, 386
Pe_ton, 31
Peabody, 35, 434, 465
Peach, 17, 171
Peacock, 254, 406, 433, 434, 536
Peake, 51, 322, 391, 410, 544
Pearce, 133, 189, 237, 437, 478, 496, 510, 513, 552
Pearl, 335
Pearre, 161
Pearson, 200, 240, 402, 409, 418
Pease, 238, 340, 496
Peasey, 240
Peavey, 545
Peck, 34, 53, 60, 308, 320, 326, 352, 386
Peckersgill, 107
Peckham, 288
Pee, 193
Peebles, 479
Peel, 261
Peer, 268
Peerce, 71
Peet, 87
Peets, 496
Pegram, 16, 24, 185, 345
Peirce, 4, 275
Peirpoint, 523

Prossise, 389
Proud, 451
Proudhon, 344
Prouse, 230
Prout, 30, 37, 314, 316, 394, 522, 554
Provost, 111, 183
Prowell, 49
Pruitt, 177
Pryor, 406
Pue, 273
Puffer, 288
Pugh, 159, 254, 372, 491, 546
Pugitt, 391
Puist, 240
Pulaski, 235
Pulling, 522
Pullman, 536, 537
Pulman, 522
Pulte, 248
Pumphrey, 214, 303, 316, 322, 323, 349, 395, 396, 456
Pundt, 240
Purcell, 18, 55, 108, 120, 158, 164, 236, 330, 357, 390, 436, 452, 473, 477, 506, 509
Purdy, 212, 279, 390, 419, 430, 525, 544
Purington, 103, 437
Purnell, 34
Purple, 161
Pursell, 266, 275, 457
Putnam, 19, 89, 107, 174, 309, 447, 458, 496
Putnan, 15
Pyman, 497
Pyne, 56, 160, 185, 280, 290, 404, 470, 501
Pywell, 243, 395, 491

Q

Qiunee, 120
Quackenbush, 392
Quantril, 33
Quantrill, 50
Quarles, 45, 162, 304, 315
Quartptlacht, 15
Queechy, 486

Queen, 72, 74, 81, 116, 120, 291, 293, 314, 401, 434, 436, 516, 517
Queen Elizabeth, 280
Queen of Denmark, 410
Queen of England, 558
Queen of Holland, 367
Quesenberry, 524
Quick, 324
Quigley, 19, 96, 282, 312, 332, 543
Quill, 194
Quilter, 487
Quilty, 393
Quimby, 192
Quimley, 239
Quincer, 496
Quincey, 411
Quincy, 217, 388
Quinlin, 291
Quinn, 221
Quintard, 294
Quirk, 330

R

Rabb, 36
Rabbit, 23, 323
Rabbitt, 75
Rabershaw, 272
Race, 553
Radcliffe, 461
Raddcliffe, 409
Radford, 233
Raffenburg, 291
Rafferty, 385
Ragan, 63, 362, 374
Raglan, 35
Ragwell, 545
Raines, 14
Rainey, 16, 395
Rains, 498
Rainy, 2
ram *Albemarle*, 288
ram *Atlanta*, 294
Ramsay, 5, 9, 33, 89, 94, 132, 135, 197, 207, 451, 532
Ramsburg, 144, 308
Ramsdale, 370
Ramsdell, 496
Ramseur, 260, 261

Ramsey, 21, 37, 154, 181, 185, 187, 207, 406, 459, 483, 497
Randall, 61, 75, 87, 153, 171, 269, 293, 298, 328, 419, 443, 493, 496
Randell, 496
Randolph, 137, 158, 180, 183, 188, 213, 268, 300, 395, 454, 470
Randon, 330
Ranelagh, 115
Ranes, 468
Rancy, 491
Rankin, 130, 149, 237, 306
Ransford, 426
Ransom, 19, 169, 188, 206, 315, 386, 499
Ranson, 281, 310, 324
Ransone, 534
Rantz, 289
Rapine, 98
Rapley, 51, 114, 155, 270, 324, 370, 425
Rapp, 497
Raradon, 316
Rarey, 553
Raskopht, 497
Ratcliff, 263
Ratcliffe, 298, 484
Rathbone, 233, 385, 392, 394, 415, 417
Ratto, 482
Raub, 20, 395, 445
Raul, 89
Raulsin, 143
Raum, 49, 73, 419
Rautz, 269
Ravaillac, 411
Rawberry, 405, 406
Rawes, 240
Rawley, 220
Rawlings, 32, 43
Rawlins, 153, 269, 407
Rawstorne, 43
Ray, 86, 88, 96, 120, 161, 213, 223, 231, 247, 324, 335, 372, 395, 508, 532
Raybold, 423, 424, 425
Rayfield, 243

Rontongo, 348
Rony, 90
Rooney, 268, 349
Root, 63, 81, 146, 171,
  329, 497
Roped, 444
Roper, 250, 386
Rorsey, 216
Rosbrock, 496
Rosch, 417
Rose, 79, 83, 99, 126, 236,
  419, 472
Roseau, 548
Rosecrans, 2, 24, 32, 48,
  50, 97, 258, 297, 557
Rosefield, 8
Roseland, 55
Rosenan, 482
Rosenberg, 482
Rosenbrush, 121
Rosenthal, 390, 488
Rosing, 374
Ross, 72, 139, 192, 251,
  269, 307, 327, 328, 339,
  345, 381, 451, 498, 501,
  552
Rossiter, 510, 558
Rotchford, 170, 214, 491
Roth, 247, 461, 499
Rothe, 522
Rothrock, 261
Rothschild, 315, 451, 468
Rothschilds, 260
Rouget, 216
Rounglove, 190
Rourke, 56
Rousseau, 346, 461
Rover, 319
Rovere, 549
Rowan, 31, 62, 70, 111
Rowe, 323, 393, 552
Rowell, 306, 372
Rowland, 16, 96, 204, 210,
  224, 227, 445, 508, 510
Rowles, 381
Rowley, 153, 238, 341, 496
Rows, 496
Rowzee, 245
Roy, 394, 454, 473, 487,
  503
Royal, 333

Royal Chalotte, 526
Royal Charlotte, 526
Roye, 188
Rozer's Ferry, 209
Rozier, 276
Rucker, 67, 179, 295, 304,
  383, 439, 479, 518, 542
Rudd, 290
Ruddy, 171
Rudisiel, 350
Ruff, 96, 200, 370, 474
Ruffin, 64, 66, 265, 431
Rufin, 503
Ruggles, 111, 205, 386,
  411, 497
Rullman, 419
Rully, 278
Rummel, 73
Rumsey, 399
Runnels, 115
runner *Isabel*, 203
Ruoff, 291
Rupert, 335
Ruphert, 529
Ruppert, 437
Rush, 27, 79, 325
Rushing, 380
Rushmond, 438
Rusking, 371
Russel, 127, 221
Russell, 48, 60, 99, 102,
  104, 116, 134, 172, 173,
  174, 176, 238, 240, 249,
  260, 261, 298, 378, 382,
  389, 406, 416, 417, 428,
  430, 435, 455, 463, 481,
  497, 513, 524, 535
Russell,, 152
Russells, 179
Russels, 329
Russey, 535
Rust, 10, 170, 444, 491,
  523
Ruter, 522
Ruth, 498
Rutherford, 41, 145, 212,
  294, 304, 383, 506, 511
Rutledge, 99, 125
Rutton, 19
Ruyser, 389

Ryan, 1, 69, 88, 110, 140,
  151, 160, 171, 181, 225,
  248, 271, 272, 281, 331,
  352, 373, 426, 427, 472,
  483, 497, 550
Ryder, 79, 416
Ryland, 352
Ryneal, 410, 467
Rynex, 112
Ryon, 336, 472, 490, 515

S

Sabin, 285
Sackett, 328
Sacred Heart of Chicago,
  494
Saffer, 491
Sage, 204, 248, 263, 268,
  373
Sageman, 262
Saindollar, 499
Salde, 178
Salisbury, 47, 137, 163
Sallett, 327
Salmon, 150, 239
Salomon, 354
Salpaugh, 278
Salter, 527
Saltmarsh, 216
Sample, 497
Sampson, 215
Samson, 169, 184, 213,
  274, 370, 384, 403, 445,
  497
Samweis, 482
Sanborn, 239, 308
Sanders, 24, 75, 85, 183,
  192, 366, 492, 501, 535
Sanderson, 33, 63, 148,
  215, 274, 276, 339, 363,
  391, 493, 537
Sandilands, 269
Sands, 103, 343, 358, 393,
  444
Sandy Point, 114
Sanford, 469, 497
Sanger, 208
Sangster, 17, 84, 132, 214,
  228
Sangston, 433
Sanne, 37

Wadmouth, 334
Wadsworth, 20, 180, 182, 185, 191, 192, 360, 547
Wager, 153, 335, 387
Waggaman, 424
Waggoner, 163
Wagner, 22, 236, 497, 517
Wagstaff, 162
Wahl, 72
Wailes, 69, 70
Waine, 332
Wainright, 197
Wainwright, 231, 239
Wait, 304
Waite, 227, 321, 418, 511, 523
Waiting, 531
Wakefield, 278
Wakeman, 259, 355
Wakker, 180
Walbridge, 307, 524
Walch, 338
Walden, 32, 497
Walder, 250
Walderman, 292
Waldheim, 426
Waldo, 144, 203, 235
Walerston, 522
Wales, 79, 95, 220, 418
Walk, 26
Walker, 33, 46, 54, 61, 62, 85, 88, 89, 93, 98, 114, 125, 133, 164, 167, 184, 185, 200, 201, 211, 212, 220, 225, 243, 245, 266, 267, 270, 283, 287, 303, 312, 333, 338, 341, 350, 356, 370, 387, 390, 396, 400, 406, 425, 431, 458, 459, 466, 472, 493, 497, 499, 506, 510, 512, 515, 531, 545, 556
Wall, 71, 154, 173, 193, 307, 338, 389, 395, 421, 482, 506
Wallace, 54, 110, 111, 150, 188, 192, 198, 216, 218, 220, 228, 239, 279, 355, 406, 417, 517
Wallach, 66, 76, 101, 114, 151, 152, 153, 154, 168,

212, 270, 299, 356, 389, 390, 426, 434, 450, 451, 469, 540
Wallack, 125, 307
Waller, 253, 255, 280, 419
Wallis, 312
Wallpert, 497
Walmpole, 36
Walmsley, 454
Walpert, 497
Walsh, 4, 25, 51, 68, 116, 170, 189, 212, 258, 279, 301, 318, 347, 391, 422, 437, 438, 487, 524, 529
Waltemeyer, 485
Walter, 31, 32, 101, 125, 187, 273, 279, 285, 313, 366, 375, 418, 439, 443, 452, 457, 460, 463, 465, 482, 501, 516, 517
Waltermade, 390
Walters, 45, 453, 475, 557
Walthall, 50
Waltham, 49
Walther, 332
Walton, 232, 238, 329, 359, 373, 449
Walworth, 287, 478
Wamback, 382
Wander, 490
Wannall, 418
Wannell, 72
Waples, 119
Ward, 10, 37, 51, 72, 86, 111, 121, 170, 179, 200, 202, 205, 211, 215, 216, 221, 230, 252, 256, 265, 266, 270, 272, 278, 281, 294, 298, 305, 313, 325, 346, 347, 370, 377, 415, 425, 428, 441, 447, 465, 466, 467, 501, 512, 513, 515
Wardell, 225
Warder, 123, 180, 401
Wardon, 39
Ware, 11, 143, 160, 220, 363, 438, 525
Wareland, 449
Warfield, 117, 257
Wargishwebber, 213

Warhurst, 364
Waring, 6, 17, 28, 128, 134, 137, 296, 315, 520
Warmouth, 230
Warner, 68, 151, 186, 433
Warnfried, 373
Warren, 2, 36, 79, 142, 180, 193, 292, 327, 334, 340, 497, 510, 548
Warrener, 128
Warring, 205
Warwick, 310
Warwick Spring, 544
Washburn, 141, 202, 249, 400
Washburne, 106, 116, 157, 229, 271, 355, 422
Washburton, 357, 402
Washington, 7, 17, 87, 93, 96, 111, 141, 183, 207, 217, 224, 258, 264, 271, 293, 319, 325, 379, 388, 396, 402, 419, 420, 421, 426, 449, 477, 479, 531, 537
Washington College, 209
Wass, 211, 212
Wasson, 133
Waterhouse, 477
Waterman, 190, 382
Waters, 9, 72, 73, 104, 107, 114, 138, 211, 231, 250, 275, 300, 302, 314, 326, 328, 336, 339, 345, 353, 366, 428, 446, 472, 538
Waterston, 388
Watkeys, 245
Watkins, 3, 25, 87, 134, 263, 325, 438, 520
Watrus, 238
Watson, 54, 56, 72, 82, 120, 124, 127, 131, 133, 164, 181, 182, 218, 240, 259, 288, 292, 353, 381, 427, 428, 459, 475, 477, 491, 501, 502, 538
Watt, 204
Watterson, 76
Watterston, 83, 86, 214
Wattles, 132

LaVergne, TN USA
11 January 2010
169671LV00004B/38/P